Distances and journey times

The mileage chart shows distances in miles between two towns along AA-recommended routes. Using motorways and other main roads this is normally the fastest route, though not necessarily the shortest.

The journey times, shown in hours and minutes, are average off-peak driving times along AA-recommended routes. These times should be used as a guide only and do not allow for unforeseen traffic delays, rest breaks or fuel stops.

For example, the 378 miles (608 km) journey between Glasgow and Norwich should take approximately 7 hours 28 minutes.

Journey times

Distances in miles (one mile equals 1.6093 km)

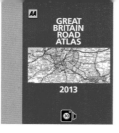

Atlas contents

Scale 1:200,000 or 3.16 miles to 1 inch

Map pages and distance times	inside front cover
Route planning	**2–20**
Route planner	2–7
Traffic signs	8–9
Channel hopping	10–11
Ferries to Ireland and the Isle of Man	12–13
Caravan and camping sites in Britain	14–17
Road safety cameras	18–19
Map pages	20
Road map symbols	**1**
Road maps	**2–173**
Britain 1:200,000 scale	2–169
Some islands are shown at slightly smaller scales.	
Ireland 1:1,000,000 scale	170–173
Motorways	**174–179**
Restricted junctions	174–177
M25 London Orbital	178
M6 Toll Motorway	179
Street map symbols	**180**

Towns, ports and airports	181–231
Town plans	182–228
Major airports	229–231
Channel Tunnel terminals	27
Central London	**232–247**
Central London street map	232–241
Central London index	242–247
District maps	**248–259**
London	248–251
Birmingham	252–253
Glasgow	254–255
Manchester	256–257
Newcastle	258–259
Index to place names	**260–308**
County, administrative area map	260
Place name index	261–308
Map pages and distance times	**inside back cover**

27th edition June 2012

© AA Media Limited 2012

Original edition printed 1986.

Cartography:
All cartography in this atlas edited, designed and produced by the Mapping Services Department of AA Publishing (A04859).

This atlas contains Ordnance Survey data © Crown copyright and database right 2012 and Royal Mail data © Royal Mail copyright and database right 2012.

 Land & Property Services. This atlas is based upon Crown Copyright and is reproduced with the permission of Land and Property Services under delegated authority from the Controller of Her Majesty's Stationery Office, © Crown copyright and database rights 2012, Licence number 100,363. Permit No. 110082.

 Ordnance Survey Ireland Ireland's National Mapping Agency © Ordnance Survey Ireland/Government of Ireland. Permit No. MP000611.

Publisher's Notes:
Published by AA Publishing (a trading name of AA Media Limited, whose registered office is Fanum House, Basing View, Basingstoke, Hampshire RG21 4EA, UK. Registered number 06112600).

All rights reserved. No part of this publication may be reproduced, stored in a retrieval system, or transmitted in any form or by any means – electronic, mechanical, photocopying, recording or otherwise – unless the permission of the publisher has been given beforehand.

ISBN: 978 0 7495 7351 5 (leather bound hardback)
ISBN: 978 0 7495 7350 8 (standard hardback)

A CIP catalogue record for this book is available from The British Library.

Disclaimer:
The contents of this atlas are believed to be correct at the time of the latest revision, it will not contain any subsequent amended, new or temporary information including diversions and traffic control or enforcement systems. The publishers cannot be held responsible or liable for any loss or damage occasioned to any person acting or refraining from action as a result of any use or reliance on material in this atlas, nor for any errors, omissions or changes in such material. This does not affect your statutory rights.

The publishers would welcome information to correct any errors or omissions and to keep this atlas up to date. Please write to the Atlas Editor, AA Publishing, The Automobile Association, Fanum House, Basing View, Basingstoke, Hampshire RG21 4EA, UK. E-mail: roadatlasfeedback@theaa.com

Acknowledgements:
AA Publishing would like to thank the following for their assistance in producing this atlas:

RoadPilot Information on fixed speed camera locations provided by and © 2012 RoadPilot® Driving Technology. Crematoria data provided by the Cremation Society of Great Britain. Cadw, English Heritage, Forestry Commission, Historic Scotland, Johnsons, National Trust and National Trust for Scotland, RSPB, The Wildlife Trust, Scottish Natural Heritage, Natural England, The Countryside Council for Wales (road maps).

Road signs are © Crown Copyright 2012. Reproduced under the terms of the Open Government Licence.

Transport for London (Central London Map), Nexus (Newcastle district map).

Printer:
Printed in China by Leo Paper Group on 115gsm paper.

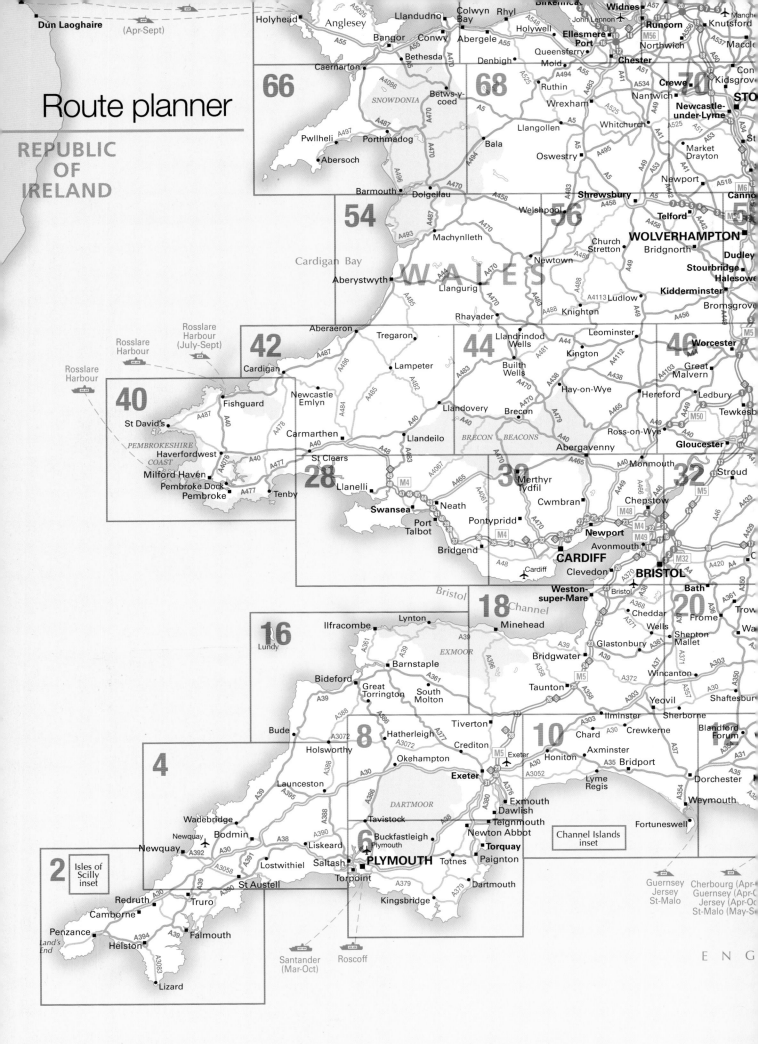

Route planner

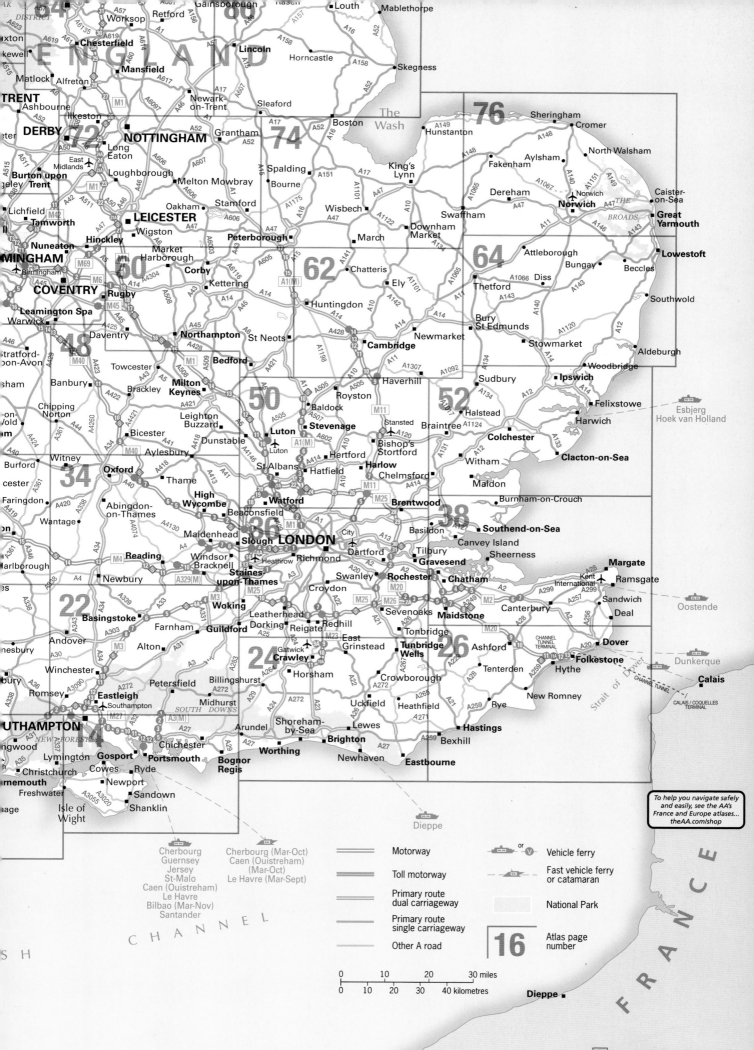

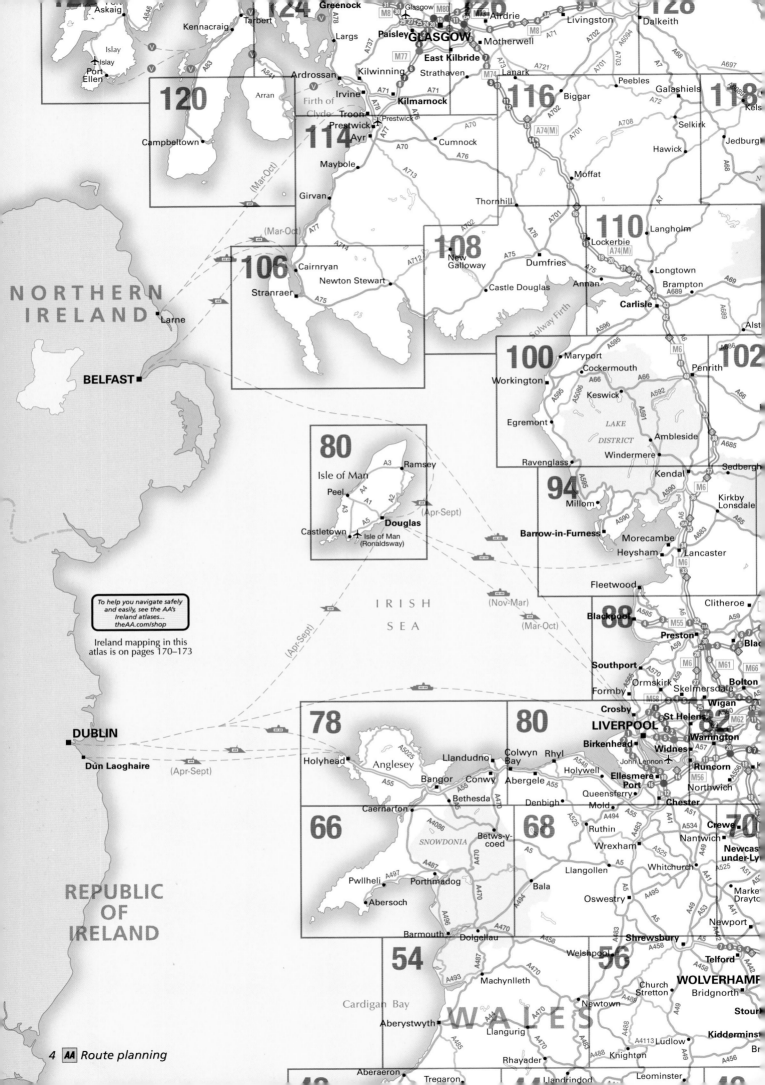

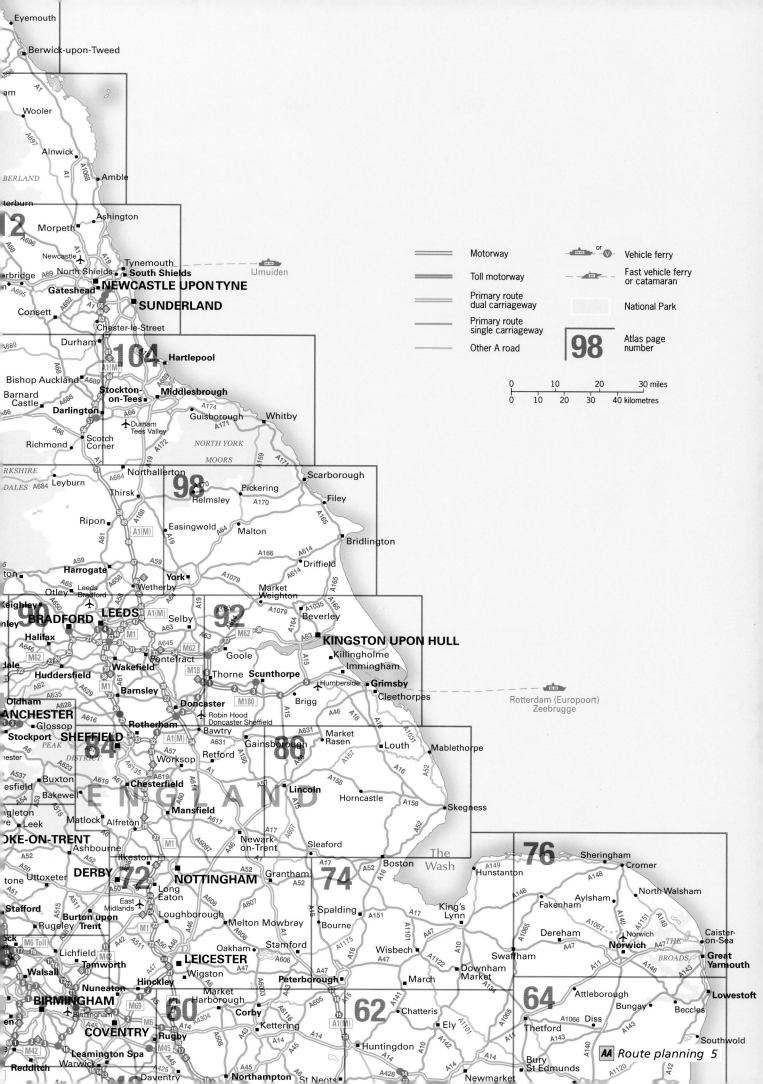

Legend

Motorway	Vehicle ferry
Toll motorway	Fast vehicle ferry or catamaran
Primary route dual carriageway	National Park
Primary route single carriageway	
Other A road	**98** Atlas page number

0 10 20 30 miles
0 10 20 30 40 kilometres

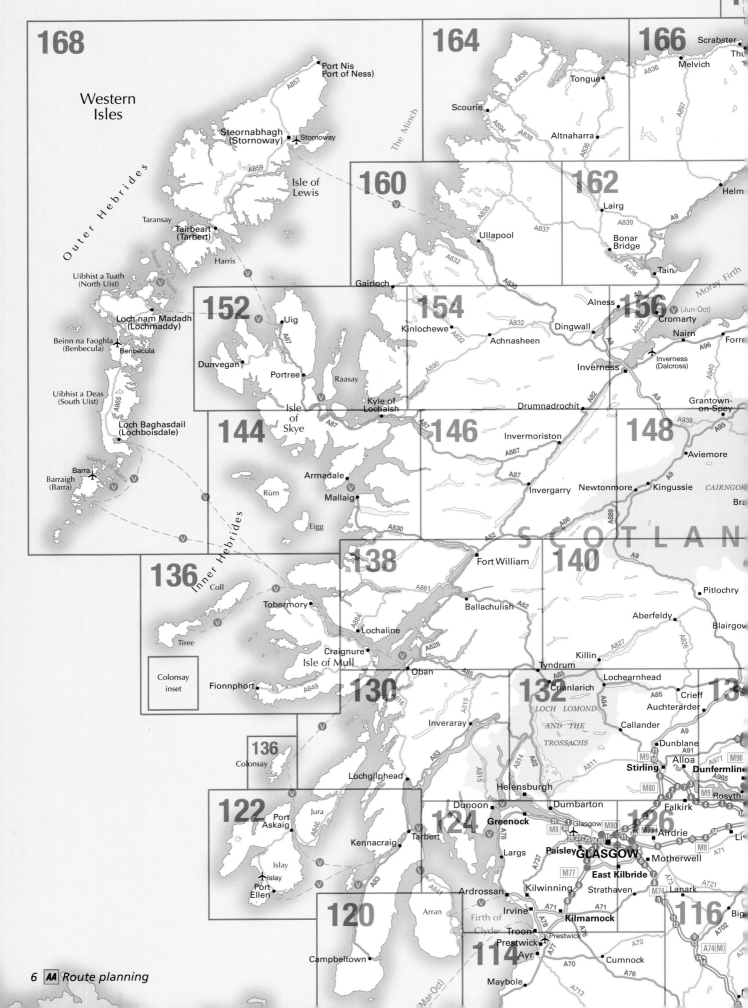

168

Western Isles

Outer Hebrides

Port Nis
Port of Ness)

A857

Steornabhagh
(Stornoway) ✈ Stornoway

A859

Isle of
Lewis

The Minch

164

A838 Tongue Melvich
Scourie A894
A838 A838 Altnaharra
A836 A836

166
Scrabster
Thu
Melvich
A836
A887

160

Ullapool
A835
A832
Gairloch

162
Lairg A839 Helm
A837
Bonar
Bridge A836
Tain

A9

Moray Firth

Taransay
Tairbeart
(Tarbert)
Harris

Sound of Harris

Uibhist a Tuath
(North Uist)
Loch nam Madadh
(Lochmaddy)

Beinn na Faoghla
(Benbecula) ✈ Benbecula

Uibhist a Deas
(South Uist)

A865

Loch Baghasdail
(Lochboisdale)

Barra
Sound of Barra
Barraigh
(Barra) ✈

152
Uig
A87
Dunvegan
Portree
Raasay
Isle
of
Skye A87
Kyle of
Lochalsh

154
Kinlochewe A832
Achnasheen
A832
A890
Dingwall

Alness
Cromarty
Nairn

156
A832 V (Jun-Oct)
Cromarty
Nairn A96 Forre
✈ Inverness
(Dalcross) A940
Inverness

Drumnadrochit A82

Grantown-
on-Spey
A938 A95

144

Armadale
Rùm
Mallaig

Eigg

146
Invermoriston
A887
A87
Invergarry

148
Newtonmore Kingussie
A9 CAIRNGOR
Aviemore
Bra

Inner Hebrides

136
Coll
Tobermory
Tiree

Colonsay
inset

A830

S C O T L A N
A89
A86
A9

138
A861
Lochaline
A884
Craignure
Isle of Mull
Fionnphort A849

Fort William

Ballachulish A82

A828
Oban A85

140

A9
Pitlochry
Aberfeldy
Blairgow
A827
Killin
Tyndrum

130
Inveraray
A83
A816

A85
Crianlarich A84
LOCH LOMOND
AND THE
TROSSACHS
A811
A82

132
Lochearnhead
Crieff
Auchterarder
Callander

13

Helensburgh
Dunoon
A815

Dunblane
A91
Alloa A977 M90
Stirling M9
Dunfermlin
A985
M80 Rosyth
Falkirk M9

136
Colonsay

Lochgilphead

122
Port
Askaig
Jura
A846
Kennacraig

124
Dumbarton
Greenock M80
Dunoon
Largs A737
Glasgow M80
M8
Paisley GLASGOW
Airdrie
M73 M8 Li
Motherwell A71

126
Falkirk
Rosyth

A78
M77
East Kilbride
Strathaven
Lanark
A721
M74

Islay ✈ Islay
Port
Ellen
A83

Tarbert

Ardrossan
Kilwinning
Irvine A71
Kilmarnock
Troon A77 Prestwick
Prestwick

120
Arran
Firth of
Clyde

114
Ayr A70 Cumnock
A70 A76
Maybole A713

A70
A74(M)

116
Big

Campbeltown

Stromness
Kirkwall
Lerwick
Kirkwall
ORKNEY
Islands
St Margaret's
Hope

Shetland Islands
are on page 169

John o' Groats

Wick
Wick

158

Cullen
Banff
Fraserburgh
Keith
Turriff
Peterhead
Aberlour
Huntly
Ellon
Oldmeldrum
Lerwick

150

Inverurie
Aberdeen
Aberdeen

Ballater
Banchory
Stonehaven

2

Brechin
Montrose
Forfar
Arbroath
ar Angus
Carnoustie
Dundee
Newport-on-Tay
St Andrews
Cupar
Glenrothes
Kirkcaldy
Firth of Forth

Dunbar
EDINBURGH
128
Dalkeith
Eyemouth
Berwick-upon-Tweed
Peebles
Galashiels
118
Coldstream
Kelso
Wooler
Selkirk
Hawick
Jedburgh
Alnwick
Amble
NORTHUMBERLAND

NORTH
SEA

FERRY INFORMATION

Hebrides and west coast Scotland
calmac.co.uk — 0800 066 5000
skyeferry.co.uk — 01599 522 756
western-ferries.co.uk — 01369 704 452

Orkney and Shetland
northlinkferries.co.uk — 0845 6000 449
pentlandferries.co.uk — 01856 831 226
orkneyferries.co.uk — 01856 872 044
shetland.gov.uk/ferries — 01595 693 535

Isle of Man
steam-packet.com — 08722 992 992

Ireland
irishferries.com — 08717 300 400
poferries.com — 08716 642 020
stenaline.co.uk — 08447 70 70 70

North Sea (Scandinavia and Benelux)
dfdsseaways.co.uk — 08715 229 955
poferries.com — 08716 642 020
stenaline.co.uk — 08447 70 70 70

Isle of Wight
wightlink.co.uk — 0871 376 1000
redfunnel.co.uk — 0844 844 9988

Channel Islands
condorferries.co.uk — 0845 609 1024

Channel hopping (France and Belgium)
brittany-ferries.co.uk — 0871 244 0744
condorferries.co.uk — 0845 609 1024
eurotunnel.com — 08443 35 35 35
ldlines.co.uk — 0844 576 8836
dfdsseaways.co.uk — 08715 229 955
poferries.com — 08716 642 020
transeuropaferries.com — 01843 595 522
transmancheferries.co.uk — 0844 576 8836

Northern Spain
brittany-ferries.co.uk — 0871 244 0744
poferries.com — 08716 642 020

EMERGENCY DIVERSION ROUTES

In an emergency it may be necessary to close a section of motorway or other main road to traffic, so a temporary sign may advise drivers to follow a diversion route. To help drivers navigate the route, black symbols on yellow patches may be permanently displayed on existing direction signs, including motorway signs. Symbols may also be used on separate signs with yellow backgrounds.

For further information see www.highways.gov.uk

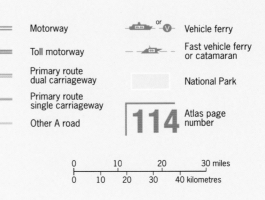

Motorway

Toll motorway

Primary route
dual carriageway

Primary route
single carriageway

Other A road

or V Vehicle ferry

Fast vehicle ferry
or catamaran

National Park

114 Atlas page
number

0   10   20   30 miles
0 10 20 30 40 kilometres

Traffic signs

Signs giving orders

Signs with red circles are mostly prohibitive.
Plates below signs qualify their message.

Entry to 20mph zone

End of 20mph zone

Maximum speed

National speed limit applies

School crossing patrol

Stop and give way

Give way to traffic on major road

Manually operated temporary STOP and GO signs

GO — Manually operated temporary STOP and GO signs

No entry for vehicular traffic

No vehicles except bicycles being pushed

No cycling

No motor vehicles

No buses (over 8 passenger seats)

No overtaking

No towed caravans

No vehicles carrying explosives

No vehicle or combination of vehicles over length shown

No vehicles over height shown

No vehicles over width shown

Give priority to vehicles from opposite direction

No right turn

No left turn

No U-turns

No goods vehicles over maximum gross weight shown (in tonnes) except for loading and unloading

WEAK BRIDGE 18T mgw
No vehicles over maximum gross weight shown (in tonnes)

Permit holders only
Parking restricted to permit holders

RED ROUTE No stopping at any time except buses
No stopping during period indicated except for buses

URBAN CLEARWAY Monday to Friday am 8.00-9.30 pm 4.30-6.30
No stopping during times shown except for as long as necessary to set down or pick up passengers

No waiting

No stopping (Clearway)

Signs with blue circles but no red border mostly give positive instruction.

Ahead only

Turn left ahead (right if symbol reversed)

Turn left (right if symbol reversed)

Keep left (right if symbol reversed)

Vehicles may pass either side to reach same destination

Mini-roundabout (roundabout circulation – give way to vehicles from the immediate right)

Route to be used by pedal cycles only

Segregated pedal cycle and pedestrian route

Minimum speed

End of minimum speed

Buses and cycles only

Trams only

Pedestrian crossing point over tramway

One-way traffic (note: compare circular 'Ahead only' sign)

With-flow bus and cycle lane

Contraflow bus lane

With-flow pedal cycle lane

Warning signs

Mostly triangular

STOP 100 yds
Distance to 'STOP' line ahead

Dual carriageway ends

Road narrows on right (left if symbol reversed)

Road narrows on both sides

GIVE WAY 50 yds
Distance to 'Give Way' line ahead

Crossroads

Junction on bend ahead

T-junction with priority over vehicles from the right

Staggered junction

Traffic merging from left ahead

The priority through route is indicated by the broader line.

Double bend first to left (symbol may be reversed)

Bend to right (or left if symbol reversed)

Roundabout

Uneven road

REDUCE SPEED NOW
Plate below some signs

Two-way traffic crosses one-way road

Two-way traffic straight ahead

Opening or swing bridge ahead

Low-flying aircraft or sudden aircraft noise

Falling or fallen rocks

Traffic signals not in use

Traffic signals

Slippery road

Steep hill downwards

Steep hill upwards

Gradients may be shown as a ratio i.e. 20% = 1:5

Tunnel ahead

Trams crossing ahead

Level crossing with barrier or gate ahead

Level crossing without barrier or gate ahead

Level crossing without barrier

Patrol

School crossing patrol ahead (some signs have amber lights which flash when crossings are in use)

Frail (or blind or disabled if shown) pedestrians likely to cross road ahead

No footway for 400 yds

Pedestrians in road ahead

Zebra crossing

Safe height 16'-6"

Overhead electric cable; plate indicates maximum height of vehicles which can pass safely

14'-6" 4.4 m

Available width of headroom indicated

Sharp deviation of route to left (or right if chevrons reversed)

STOP when lights show

Light signals ahead at level crossing, airfield or bridge

Red STOP
Green Clear
IF NO LIGHT - PHONE CROSSING OPERATOR

Miniature warning lights at level crossings

Cattle

Wild animals

Wild horses or ponies

Accompanied horses or ponies

Cycle route ahead

Ice

Risk of ice

Queues likely

Traffic queues likely ahead

Humps for ½ mile

Distance over which road humps extend

Hidden dip

Other danger; plate indicates nature of danger

Soft verges for 2 miles

Soft verges

Side winds

Hump bridge

Ford

Worded warning sign

Quayside or river bank

Risk of grounding

Direction signs

Mostly rectangular

Signs on motorways – blue backgrounds

At a junction leading directly into a motorway (junction number may be shown on a black background)

On approaches to junctions (junction number on black background)

M1 The NORTH Sheffield 32 Leeds 59

Route confirmatory sign after junction

Downward pointing arrows mean 'Get in lane'
The left-hand lane leads to a different destination from the other lanes.

The panel with the inclined arrow indicates the destinations which can be reached by leaving the motorway at the next junction

Signs on primary routes - green backgrounds

On approaches to junctions

At the junction

A46 The SOUTH Nottingham 17 Leicester 32 (M1 South) 35

Route confirmatory sign after junction

On approaches to junctions

Swansea Abertawe A483

On approach to a junction in Wales (bilingual)

Blue panels indicate that the motorway starts at the junction ahead.
Motorways shown in brackets can also be reached along the route indicated.
White panels indicate local or non-primary routes leading from the junction ahead.
Brown panels show the route to tourist attractions.
The name of the junction may be shown at the top of the sign.
The aircraft symbol indicates the route to an airport.
A symbol may be included to warn of a hazard or restriction along that route.

Signs on non-primary and local routes - black borders

On approaches to junctions

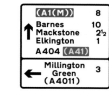
(A1(M)) 8
Barnes 10
Mackstone 2½
Elkington 1
A404 (A41)
Millington Green 3
(A4011)

Market Walborough B486

At the junction

Direction to toilets with access for the disabled

Green panels indicate that the primary route starts at the junction ahead.
Route numbers on a blue background show the direction to a motorway.
Route numbers on a green background show the direction to a primary route.

Emergency diversion routes

   ◆

In an emergency it may be necessary to close a section of motorway or other main road to traffic, so a temporary sign may advise drivers to follow a diversion route. To help drivers navigate the route, black symbols on yellow patches may be permanently displayed on existing direction signs, including motorway signs. Symbols may also be used on separate signs with yellow backgrounds.

For further information see www.highways.gov.uk

Note: Although this road atlas shows many of the signs commonly in use, a comprehensive explanation of the signing system is given in the AA's handbook *Know Your Road Signs*, which is on sale at theaa.com/shop and booksellers. The booklet also illustrates and explains the vast majority of signs the road user is likely to encounter. The signs illustrated in this road atlas are not all drawn to the same scale. In Wales, bilingual versions of some signs are used including Welsh and English versions of place names. Some older designs of signs may still be seen on the roads.

Channel Hopping

For business or pleasure, hopping on a ferry across to France, Belgium or the Channel Islands has never been easier.

The vehicle ferry routes shown on this map give you all the options, together with detailed port plans to help you navigate to and from the ferry terminals. Simply choose your preferred route, not forgetting the fast sailings; then check the colour-coded table for ferry operators, crossing times and contact details.

Bon voyage!

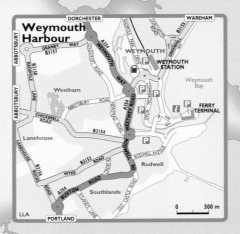

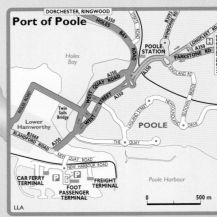

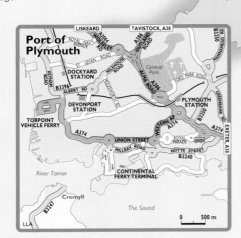

Fast ferry

Conventional ferry

ENGLISH CHANNEL FERRY CROSSINGS AND OPERATORS

To	From	Journey Time	Operator	Telephone	Website
Caen (Ouistreham)	Portsmouth	6 - 7 hrs	Brittany Ferries	0871 244 0744	brittany-ferries.co.uk
Caen (Ouistreham)	Portsmouth	3 hrs 45 mins (Mar-Oct)	Brittany Ferries	0871 244 0744	brittany-ferries.co.uk
Calais (Coquelles)	Folkestone	35 mins	Eurotunnel	08443 35 35 35	eurotunnel.com
Calais	Dover	1 hr 30 mins	P&O Ferries	0871 664 2020	poferries.com
Cherbourg	Poole	2 hrs 30 mins (April-Oct)	Brittany Ferries	0871 244 0744	brittany-ferries.co.uk
Cherbourg	Portsmouth	3 hrs (Mar-Oct)	Brittany Ferries	0871 244 0744	brittany-ferries.co.uk
Cherbourg	Portsmouth	4 hrs 30 mins(day) 8 hrs(o/night)	Brittany Ferries	0871 244 0744	brittany-ferries.co.uk
Cherbourg	Portsmouth	5 hrs 30 mins (May-Sept)	Condor	0845 609 1024	condorferries.co.uk
Dieppe	Newhaven	4 hrs	Transmanche Ferries	0844 576 8836	transmancheferries.co.uk
Dunkerque	Dover	2 hrs	DFDS Seaways	0871 522 9955	dfdsseaways.co.uk
Guernsey	Poole	2 hrs 30 mins (April-Oct)	Condor	0845 609 1024	condorferries.co.uk
Guernsey	Portsmouth	7 hrs	Condor	0845 609 1024	condorferries.co.uk
Guernsey	Weymouth	2 hrs 10 mins	Condor	0845 609 1024	condorferries.co.uk
Jersey	Poole	3 hrs (April-Oct)	Condor	0845 609 1024	condorferries.co.uk
Jersey	Portsmouth	10 hrs 30 mins	Condor	0845 609 1024	condorferries.co.uk
Jersey	Weymouth	3 hrs 25 mins	Condor	0845 609 1024	condorferries.co.uk
Le Havre	Portsmouth	5 hrs 30 mins - 8 hrs	LD Lines	0844 576 8836	ldlines.co.uk
Le Havre	Portsmouth	3 hrs 15 mins (Mar-Sept)	LD Lines	0844 576 8836	ldlines.co.uk
Oostende	Ramsgate	4 hrs - 4 hrs 30 mins	Transeuropa	01843 595 522	transeuropaferries.com
Roscoff	Plymouth	6 - 8 hrs	Brittany Ferries	0871 244 0744	brittany-ferries.co.uk
St-Malo	Poole	4 hrs 35 mins (May-Sept)	Condor	0845 609 1024	condorferries.co.uk
St-Malo	Portsmouth	9 - 10 hrs 45 mins	Brittany Ferries	0871 244 0744	brittany-ferries.co.uk
St-Malo	Weymouth	5 hrs 15 mins	Condor	0845 609 1024	condorferries.co.uk

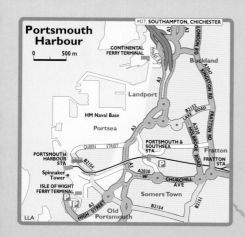

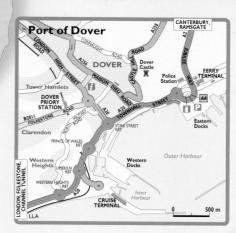

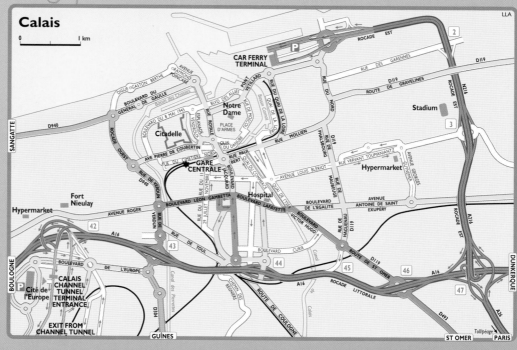

Ferries to Ireland and the Isle of Man

With so many sea crossings to Ireland and the Isle of Man this map will help you make the right choice.

The vehicle ferry routes shown on this map give you all the options, together with detailed port plans to help you navigate to and from the ferry terminals. Simply choose your preferred route, not forgetting the fast sailings; then check the colour-coded table for ferry operators, crossing times and contact details.

Fast ferry   Conventional ferry

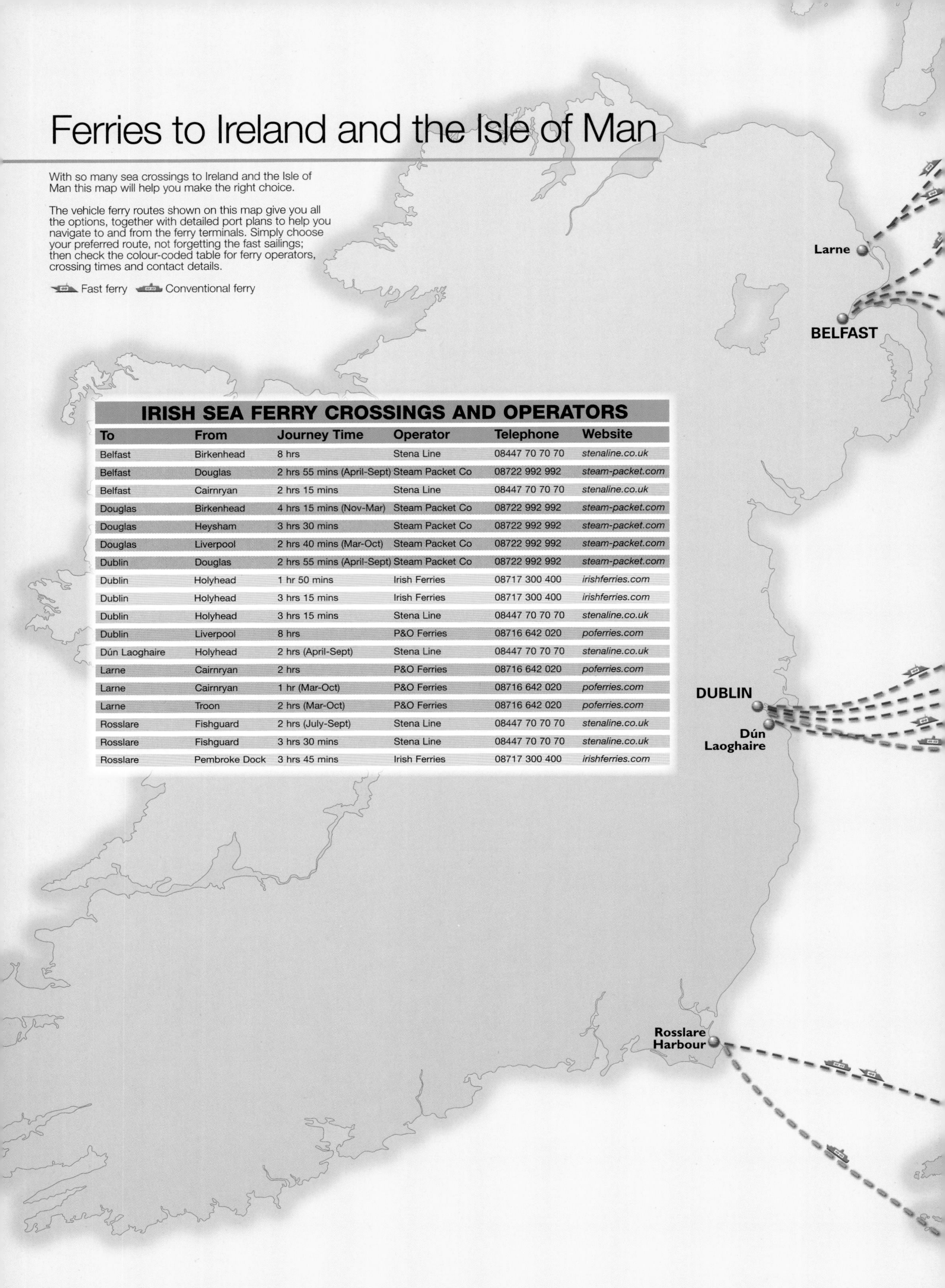

Larne

BELFAST

IRISH SEA FERRY CROSSINGS AND OPERATORS

To	From	Journey Time	Operator	Telephone	Website
Belfast	Birkenhead	8 hrs	Stena Line	08447 70 70 70	stenaline.co.uk
Belfast	Douglas	2 hrs 55 mins (April-Sept)	Steam Packet Co	08722 992 992	steam-packet.com
Belfast	Cairnryan	2 hrs 15 mins	Stena Line	08447 70 70 70	stenaline.co.uk
Douglas	Birkenhead	4 hrs 15 mins (Nov-Mar)	Steam Packet Co	08722 992 992	steam-packet.com
Douglas	Heysham	3 hrs 30 mins	Steam Packet Co	08722 992 992	steam-packet.com
Douglas	Liverpool	2 hrs 40 mins (Mar-Oct)	Steam Packet Co	08722 992 992	steam-packet.com
Dublin	Douglas	2 hrs 55 mins (April-Sept)	Steam Packet Co	08722 992 992	steam-packet.com
Dublin	Holyhead	1 hr 50 mins	Irish Ferries	08717 300 400	irishferries.com
Dublin	Holyhead	3 hrs 15 mins	Irish Ferries	08717 300 400	irishferries.com
Dublin	Holyhead	3 hrs 15 mins	Stena Line	08447 70 70 70	stenaline.co.uk
Dublin	Liverpool	8 hrs	P&O Ferries	08716 642 020	poferries.com
Dún Laoghaire	Holyhead	2 hrs (April-Sept)	Stena Line	08447 70 70 70	stenaline.co.uk
Larne	Cairnryan	2 hrs	P&O Ferries	08716 642 020	poferries.com
Larne	Cairnryan	1 hr (Mar-Oct)	P&O Ferries	08716 642 020	poferries.com
Larne	Troon	2 hrs (Mar-Oct)	P&O Ferries	08716 642 020	poferries.com
Rosslare	Fishguard	2 hrs (July-Sept)	Stena Line	08447 70 70 70	stenaline.co.uk
Rosslare	Fishguard	3 hrs 30 mins	Stena Line	08447 70 70 70	stenaline.co.uk
Rosslare	Pembroke Dock	3 hrs 45 mins	Irish Ferries	08717 300 400	irishferries.com

DUBLIN

Dún Laoghaire

Rosslare Harbour

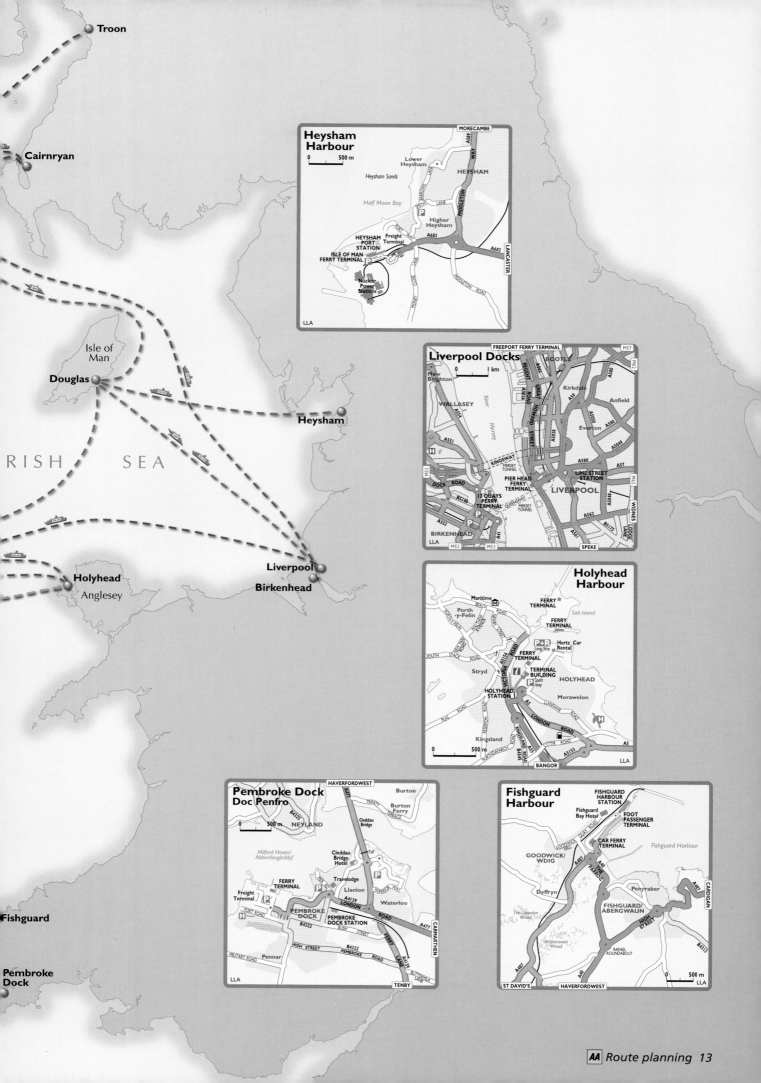

Heysham Harbour

MORECAMBE
0   500 m

Lower Heysham
Heysham Sands
HEYSHAM
Half Moon Bay
Higher Heysham
P
HEYSHAM PORT STATION
Freight Terminal
ISLE OF MAN FERRY TERMINAL
P
Nuclear Power Stations
A683
A683
LANCASTER
MIDDLETON ROAD
SOUTH BARROWS
LANE
MIDDLETON
PORT WAY
HORSE CLOSE LANE
LLA

Liverpool Docks

FREEPORT FERRY TERMINAL
M57
0   1 km
New Brighton
BOOTLE
M62
WALLASEY
River Mersey
Kirkdale
A551
Anfield
A565
A59
A5080
A580
A57
A567
Everton
A5049
H
A5053
KINGSWAY
MERSEY TUNNEL
A580
A57
M53
PIER HEAD FERRY TERMINAL
LIME STREET STATION
M62
DOCK ROAD
12 QUAYS FERRY TERMINAL
P
LIVERPOOL
WIDNES
B5146
QUEENSWAY
MERSEY TUNNEL
A562
B5175
LODGE LANE
BIRKENHEAD
A41
A561
M53
M53
LLA
SPEKE

Holyhead Harbour

Maritime
M
FERRY TERMINAL
Salt Island
Porth-y-Felin
BEACH
FERRY TERMINAL
PORTH-Y-FELIN
WYNNE
PRINCE STREET
P+R Long Stay
Hertz Car Rental
Stryd
A5154
FERRY TERMINAL
SOUTH STACK ROAD
VICTORIA ROAD
i
TERMINAL BUILDING
Short Stay
HOLYHEAD
PLAS ROAD
PRICE ROAD
NEBO ROAD
P
HOLYHEAD STATION
Morawelon
A5
LLANFAWR ROAD
LONDON ROAD
A5
Kingsland
PORTHDAFARCH ROAD
KINGSLAND ROAD
B4545
CYTTIR ROAD
B4545
H
A55
BANGOR
A5153
A5
LLA
0   500 m

Pembroke Dock
Doc Penfro

HAVERFORDWEST
A477
0   500 m
NEYLAND
B4325
Burton
TRINITY
Burton Ferry
TERRACE
Cleddau Bridge
Milford Haven/
Abberdaugleddyf
Cleddau Bridge Hotel
Toll
P
FERRY TERMINAL
Travelodge
Llanion
NEW RD
WARRIOR WAY
Freight Terminal
P
PEMBROKE DOCK
LONDON ROAD
A4139
Waterloo
H
PEMBROKE DOCK STATION
A477
CARMARTHEN
FORT ROAD
B4322
BUSH STREET
Pennar
High Street
B4322
PEMBROKE ROAD
FERRY LANE
A4139
MILITARY ROAD
BUTTERMILK LANE
LLA
TENBY

Fishguard Harbour

FISHGUARD HARBOUR STATION
Fishguard Bay Hotel
FOOT PASSENGER TERMINAL
GOODWICK HILL
QUAY ROAD
CAR FERRY TERMINAL
GOODWICK/ WDIG
A487
Fishguard Harbour
Dyffryn
A40
PARROG
Penyraber
A487
Tre-Llewelyn Wood
FISHGUARD/ ABERGWAUN
HIGH STREET
CARDIGAN
A487
Manorowen Wood
RAFAEL ROUNDABOUT
A40
B4313
ST DAVID'S
A487
HAVERFORDWEST
A40
0   500 m
LLA

Troon
Cairnryan
Isle of Man
Douglas
Heysham
IRISH SEA
Liverpool
Birkenhead
Holyhead
Anglesey
Fishguard
Pembroke Dock

Caravan and camping sites in Britain

These pages list the top 300 AA-inspected Caravan and Camping (C & C) sites in the Pennant rating scheme. Five Pennant Premier sites are shown in **green**, Four Pennant sites are shown in **blue**.

Listings include addresses, telephone numbers and websites together with page and grid references to locate the sites in the atlas. The total number of touring pitches is also included for each site, together with the type of pitch available. The following abbreviations are used: C = Caravan CV = Campervan T = Tent

To find out more about the AA's Pennant rating scheme and other rated caravan and camping sites not included on these pages please visit *theAA.com*

ENGLAND

Abbey Farm Caravan Park
Dark Lane, Ormskirk
L40 5TX
Tel: 01695 572686 **88 E9**
abbeyfarmcaravanpark.co.uk
Total Pitches: 56 (C, CV & T)

Alders Caravan Park
Home Farm, Alne, York
YO61 1RY
Tel: 01347 838722 **97 R7**
alderscaravanpark.co.uk
Total Pitches: 87 (C, CV & T)

Alpine Grove Touring Park
Forton, Chard
TA20 4HD
Tel: 01460 63479 **10 G3**
alpinegrovetouringpark.com
Total Pitches: 40 (C, CV & T)

Andrewshayes Caravan Park
Dalwood, Axminster
EX13 7DY
Tel: 01404 831225 **10 E5**
andrewshayes.co.uk
Total Pitches: 150 (C, CV & T)

Appuldurcombe Gardens Holiday Park
Appuldurcombe Road, Wroxall,
Isle of Wight
PO38 3EP
Tel: 01983 852597 **14 F10**
appuldurcombegardens.co.uk
Total Pitches: 100 (C, CV & T)

Ayr Holiday Park
St Ives, Cornwall
TR26 1EJ
Tel: 01736 795855 **2 E5**
ayrholidaypark.co.uk
Total Pitches: 40 (C, CV & T)

Back of Beyond Touring Park
234 Ringwood Rd,
St Leonards, Dorset
BH24 2SB
Tel: 01202 876968 **13 J4**
backofbeyondtouringpark.co.uk
Total Pitches: 80 (C, CV & T)

Bagwell Farm Touring Park
Knights in the Bottom,
Chickerell, Weymouth
DT3 4EA
Tel: 01305 782575 **11 N8**
bagwellfarm.co.uk
Total Pitches: 320 (C, CV & T)

Bardsea Leisure Park
Priory Road, Ulverston
LA12 9QE
Tel: 01229 584712 **94 F5**
bardsealeisure.co.uk
Total Pitches: 83 (C & CV)

Barn Farm Campsite
Barn Farm, Birchover,
Matlock
DE4 2BL
Tel: 01629 650245 **84 B8**
barnfarmcamping.com
Total Pitches: 25 (C, CV & T)

Barnstones C & C Site
Great Bourton, Banbury
OX17 1QU
Tel: 01295 750289 **48 E6**
Total Pitches: 49 (C, CV & T)

Beaconsfield Farm Caravan Park
Battlefield, Shrewsbury
SY4 4AA
Tel: 01939 210370 **69 P11**
beaconsfield-farm.co.uk
Total Pitches: 60 (C & CV)

Bellingham C & C Club Site
Brown Rigg,
Bellingham
NE48 2JY
Tel: 01434 220175 **112 B4**
campingandcaravanningclub.co.uk/bellingham
Total Pitches: 64 (C, CV & T)

Bingham Grange Touring & Camping Park
Melplash, Bridport
DT6 3TT
Tel: 01308 488234 **11 K5**
binghamgrange.co.uk
Total Pitches: 150 (C, CV & T)

Bo Peep Farm Caravan Park
Bo Peep Farm, Aynho Road,
Adderbury, Banbury
OX17 3NP
Tel: 01295 810605 **48 E8**
bo-peep.co.uk
Total Pitches: 104 (C, CV & T)

Briarfields Motel & Touring Park
Gloucester Road,
Cheltenham
GL51 0SX
Tel: 01242 235324 **46 H10**
briarfields.net
Total Pitches: 72 (C, CV & T)

Broadhembury C & C Park
Steeds Lane, Kingsnorth,
Ashford
TN26 1NQ
Tel: 01233 620859 **26 H4**
broadhembury.co.uk
Total Pitches: 110 (C, CV & T)

Brokerswood Country Park
Brokerswood, Westbury
BA13 4EH
Tel: 01373 822238 **20 F4**
brokerswoodcountrypark.co.uk
Total Pitches: 69 (C, CV & T)

Budemeadows Touring Park
Widemouth Bay, Bude
EX23 0NA
Tel: 01288 361646 **16 C11**
budemeadows.com
Total Pitches: 145 (C, CV & T)

Burrowhayes Farm C & C Site
West Luccombe, Porlock,
Minehead
TA24 8HT
Tel: 01643 862463 **18 B5**
burrowhayes.co.uk
Total Pitches: 120 (C, CV & T)

Burton Constable Holiday Park & Arboretum
Old Lodges, Sproatley, Hull
HU11 4LN
Tel: 01964 562508 **93 L3**
burtonconstable.co.uk
Total Pitches: 140 (C, CV & T)

Calloose C & C Park
Leedstown, Hayle
TR27 5ET
Tel: 01736 850431 **2 F7**
calloose.co.uk
Total Pitches: 109 (C, CV & T)

Camping Caradon Touring Park
Trelawne, Looe
PL13 2NA
Tel: 01503 272388 **5 L11**
campingcaradon.co.uk
Total Pitches: 85 (C, CV & T)

Carlton Meres Country Park
Rendham Road, Carlton,
Saxmundham
IP17 2QP
Tel: 01728 603344 **65 M8**
carlton-meres.co.uk
Total Pitches: 96 (C & CV)

Carlyon Bay C & C Park
Bethesda, Cypress Avenue,
Carlyon Bay
PL25 3RE
Tel: 01726 812735 **3 R3**
carlyonbay.net
Total Pitches: 180 (C, CV & T)

Carnevas Holiday Park & Farm Cottages
Carnevas Farm, St Merryn
PL28 8PN
Tel: 01841 520230 **4 D7**
carnevasholidaypark.co.uk
Total Pitches: 195 (C, CV & T)

Carnon Downs C & C Park
Carnon Downs, Truro
TR3 6JJ
Tel: 01872 862283 **3 L5**
carnon-downs-caravanpark.co.uk
Total Pitches: 150 (C, CV & T)

Carvynick Country Club
Summercourt, Newquay
TR8 5AF
Tel: 01872 510716 **4 D10**
carvynick.co.uk
Total Pitches: 47 (CV)

Castlerigg Hall C & C Park
Castlerigg Hall, Keswick
CA12 4TE
Tel: 017687 74499 **101 J6**
castlerigg.co.uk
Total Pitches: 48 (C, CV & T)

Cheddar Bridge Touring Park
Draycott Rd, Cheddar
BS27 3RJ
Tel: 01934 743048 **19 N4**
cheddarbridge.co.uk
Total Pitches: 45 (C, CV & T)

Cheddar C & C Club Site
Townsend, Priddy, Wells
BA5 3BP
Tel: 01749 870241 **19 P4**
campingandcaravanningclub.co.uk/cheddar
Total Pitches: 90 (C, CV & T)

Chiverton Park
East Hill, Blackwater
TR4 8HS
Tel: 01872 560667 **3 J4**
chivertonpark.co.uk
Total Pitches: 12 (C, CV & T)

Church Farm C & C Park
The Bungalow, Church Farm,
High Street, Sixpenny Handley,
Salisbury
SP5 5ND
Tel: 01725 552563 **21 J11**
churchfarmcandcpark.co.uk
Total Pitches: 35 (C, CV & T)

Claylands Caravan Park
Cabus, Garstang
PR3 1AJ
Tel: 01524 791242 **95 K11**
claylands.com
Total Pitches: 30 (C, CV & T)

Clippesby Hall
Hall Lane, Clippesby,
Great Yarmouth
NR29 3BL
Tel: 01493 367800 **77 N9**
clippesby.com
Total Pitches: 120 (C, CV & T)

Cofton Country Holidays
Starcross, Dawlish
EX6 8RP
Tel: 01626 890111 **9 N8**
coftonholidays.co.uk
Total Pitches: 450 (C, CV & T)

Colchester Holiday Park
Cymbeline Way, Lexden,
Colchester
CO3 4AG
Tel: 01206 545551 **52 G6**
colchestercamping.co.uk
Total Pitches: 168 (C, CV & T)

Constable Burton Hall Caravan Park
Constable Burton,
Leyburn
DL8 5LJ
Tel: 01677 450428 **97 J2**
cbcaravanpark.co.uk
Total Pitches: 120 (C & CV)

Coombe Touring Park
Race Plain,
Netherhampton,
Salisbury
SP2 8PN
Tel: 01722 328451 **21 L9**
coombecaravanpark.co.uk
Total Pitches: 50 (C, CV & T)

Corfe Castle C & C Club Site
Bucknowle, Wareham
BH20 5PQ
Tel: 01929 480280 **12 F8**
campingandcaravanningclub.co.uk/corfecastle
Total Pitches: 80 (C, CV & T)

Cornish Farm Touring Park
Shoreditch, Taunton
TA3 7BS
Tel: 01823 327746 **18 H10**
cornishfarm.com
Total Pitches: 50 (C, CV & T)

Cosawes Park
Perranarworthal, Truro
TR3 7QS
Tel: 01872 863724 **3 K6**
cosawestouringandcamping.com
Total Pitches: 40 (C, CV & T)

Cote Ghyll C & C Park
Osmotherley,
Northallerton
DL6 3AH
Tel: 01609 883425 **104 E11**
coteghyll.com
Total Pitches: 77 (C, CV & T)

Cotswold View Touring Park
Enstone Road,
Charlbury
OX7 3JH
Tel: 01608 810314 **48 C10**
cotswoldview.co.uk
Total Pitches: 125 (C, CV & T)

Dell Touring Park
Beyton Road, Thurston,
Bury St Edmunds
IP31 3RB
Tel: 01359 270121 **64 C9**
thedellcaravanpark.co.uk
Total Pitches: 60 (C, CV & T)

Diamond Farm C & C Park
Islip Road, Bletchingdon
OX5 3DR
Tel: 01869 350909 **48 F11**
diamondpark.co.uk
Total Pitches: 37 (C, CV & T)

Dibles Park
Dibles Road, Warsash,
Southampton
SO31 9SA
Tel: 01489 575232 **14 F5**
diblespark.co.uk
Total Pitches: 14 (C, CV & T)

Dolbeare Park C & C
St Ive Road, Landrake,
Saltash
PL12 5AF
Tel: 01752 851332 **5 P9**
dolbeare.co.uk
Total Pitches: 60 (C, CV & T)

Dornafield
Dornafield Farm, Two Mile Oak,
Newton Abbot
TQ12 6DD
Tel: 01803 812732 **7 L5**
dornafield.com
Total Pitches: 135 (C, CV & T)

East Fleet Farm Touring Park
Chickerell, Weymouth
DT3 4DW
Tel: 01305 785768 **11 N9**
eastfleet.co.uk
Total Pitches: 400 (C, CV & T)

Eden Valley Holiday Park
Lanlivery, Nr Lostwithiel
PL30 5BU
Tel: 01208 872277 **4 H10**
edenvalleyholidaypark.co.uk
Total Pitches: 56 (C, CV & T)

Eskdale C & C Club Site
Boot, Holmrook
CA19 1TH
Tel: 019467 23253 **100 G10**
campingandcaravanningclub.co.uk/eskdale
Total Pitches: 80 (CV & T)

Exe Valley Caravan Site
Mill House, Bridgetown,
Dulverton
TA22 9JR
Tel: 01643 851432 **18 B8**
exevalleycamping.co.uk
Total Pitches: 50 (C, CV & T)

Fallbarrow Park
Rayrigg Road, Windermere
LA23 3DL
Tel: 015394 44422 **101 M11**
slholidays.co.uk
Total Pitches: 32 (C & CV)

Fernwood Caravan Park
Lyneal, Ellesmere
SY12 0QF
Tel: 01948 710221 **69 N8**
fernwoodpark.co.uk
Total Pitches: 60 (C & CV)

Fields End Water Caravan Park & Fishery
Benwick Road, Doddington,
March
PE15 0TY
Tel: 01354 740199 **62 E2**
fieldsendcaravans.co.uk
Total Pitches: 52 (C, CV & T)

Fishpool Farm Caravan Park
Fishpool Road, Delamere,
Northwich
CW8 2HP
Tel: 01606 883970 **82 C11**
fishpoolfarmcaravanpark.co.uk
Total Pitches: 50 (C, CV & T)

Flusco Wood
Flusco, Penrith
CA11 0JB
Tel: 017684 80020 **101 N5**
fluscowood.co.uk
Total Pitches: 53 (C & CV)

Forest Glade Holiday Park
Kentisbeare,
Cullompton
EX15 2DT
Tel: 01404 841381 **10 C3**
forest-glade.co.uk
Total Pitches: 80 (C, CV & T)

Globe Vale Holiday Park
Radnor, Redruth
TR16 4BH
Tel: 01209 891183 **3 J5**
globevale.co.uk
Total Pitches: 138 (C, CV & T)

Golden Cap Holiday Park
Seatown, Chideock,
Bridport
DT6 6JX
Tel: 01308 422139 **11 J6**
wdlh.co.uk
Total Pitches: 108 (C, CV & T)

Golden Square Touring Caravan Park
Oswaldkirk, Helmsley
YO62 5YQ
Tel: 01439 788269 **98 C5**
goldensquarecaravanpark.com
Total Pitches: 129 (C, CV & T)

Golden Valley C & C Park
Coach Road, Ripley
DE55 4ES
Tel: 01773 513881 **84 F10**
goldenvalleycaravanpark.co.uk
Total Pitches: 45 (C, CV & T)

Goosewood Caravan Park
Sutton-on-the-Forest, York
YO61 1ET
Tel: 01347 810829 **98 B8**
flowerofmay.com
Total Pitches: 100 (C & CV)

Greenacres Touring Park
Haywards Lane, Chelston,
Wellington
TA21 9PH
Tel: 01823 652844 **18 G10**
greenacres-wellington.co.uk
Total Pitches: 40 (C & CV)

Greenhill Leisure Park
Greenhill Farm, Station Road,
Bletchingdon, Oxford
OX5 3BQ
Tel: 01869 351600 **48 E11**
greenhill-leisure-park.co.uk
Total Pitches: 92 (C, CV & T)

Grouse Hill Caravan Park
Flask Bungalow Farm,
Fylingdales,
Robin Hood's Bay
YO22 4QH
Tel: 01947 880543 **105 P10**
grousehill.co.uk
Total Pitches: 175 (C, CV & T)

Gunvenna Caravan Park
St Minver,
Wadebridge
PL27 6QN
Tel: 01208 862405 **4 F6**
gunvenna.co.uk
Total Pitches: 75 (C, CV & T)

Gwithian Farm Campsite
Gwithian Farm, Gwithian, Hayle
TR27 5BX
Tel: 01736 753127 **2 F5**
gwithianfarm.co.uk
Total Pitches: 87 (C, CV & T)

Harbury Fields
Harbury Fields Farm, Harbury,
Nr Leamington Spa
CV33 9JN
Tel: 01926 612457 **48 C2**
harburyfields.co.uk
Total Pitches: 32 (C & CV)

Hawthorn Farm Caravan Park
Station Road, Martin Mill,
Dover
CT15 5LA
Tel: 01304 852658   **27 P2**
keatfarm.co.uk
Total Pitches: 147 (C, CV & T)

Heathfield Farm Camping
Heathfield Road, Freshwater,
Isle of Wight
PO40 9SH
Tel: 01983 407822   **13 P7**
heathfieldcamping.co.uk
Total Pitches: 60 (C, CV & T)

Heathland Beach Caravan Park
London Road,
Kessingland
NR33 7PJ
Tel: 01502 740337   **65 Q4**
heathlandbeach.co.uk
Total Pitches: 63 (C, CV & T)

Hele Valley Holiday Park
Hele Bay, Ilfracombe,
North Devon
EX34 9RD
Tel: 01271 862460   **17 J2**
helevalley.co.uk
Total Pitches: 50 (C, CV & T)

Heron's Mead
Fishing Lake & Touring Park
Marsh Lane, Orby, Skegness
PE24 5JA
Tel: 01754 811340   **87 P7**
heronsmeadtouringpark.co.uk
Total Pitches: 21 (C, CV & T)

Hidden Valley Park
West Down, Braunton,
Ilfracombe
EX34 8NU
Tel: 01271 813837   **17 J3**
hiddenvalleypark.com
Total Pitches: 115 (C, CV & T)

Highfield Farm Touring Park
Long Road, Comberton,
Cambridge
CB23 7DG
Tel: 01223 262308   **62 E9**
highfieldfarmtouringpark.co.uk
Total Pitches: 120 (C, CV & T)

Highlands End Holiday Park
Eype, Bridport, Dorset
DT6 6AR
Tel: 01308 422139   **11 K6**
wdlh.co.uk
Total Pitches: 195 (C, CV & T)

Hill Cottage Farm C & C Park
Sandleheath Road, Alderholt,
Fordingbridge
SP6 3EG
Tel: 01425 650513   **13 K2**
*hillcottagefarmcampingand
caravanpark.co.uk*
Total Pitches: 35 (C, CV & T)

Hill Farm Caravan Park
Branches Lane,
Sherfield English,
Romsey
SO51 6FH
Tel: 01794 340402   **21 Q10**
hillfarmpark.com
Total Pitches: 70 (C, CV & T)

Hill of Oaks & Blakeholme
Windermere
LA12 8NR
Tel: 015395 31578   **94 H3**
hillofoaks.co.uk
Total Pitches: 43 (C & CV)

Hillside Caravan Park
Canvas Farm,
Moor Road, Thirsk
YO7 4BR
Tel: 01845 537349   **97 P3**
hillsidecaravanpark.co.uk
Total Pitches: 35 (C & CV)

Hollins Farm C & C
Far Arnside, Carnforth
LA5 0SL
Tel: 01524 701508   **95 J5**
holgates.co.uk
Total Pitches: 12 (C, CV & T)

Homing Park
Church Lane, Seasalter,
Whitstable
CT5 4BU
Tel: 01227 771777   **39 J9**
homingpark.co.uk
Total Pitches: 43 (C, CV & T)

Honeybridge Park
Honeybridge Lane, Dial Post,
Horsham
RH13 8NX
Tel: 01403 710923   **24 E7**
honeybridgepark.co.uk
Total Pitches: 130 (C, CV & T)

Hurley Riverside Park
Park Office, Hurley,
Nr Maidenhead
SL6 5NE
Tel: 01628 824493   **35 M8**
hurleyriversidepark.co.uk
Total Pitches: 200 (C, CV & T)

Hutton-le-Hole Caravan Park
Westfield Lodge,
Hutton-le-Hole
YO62 6UG
Tel: 01751 417261   **98 E3**
westfieldlodge.co.uk
Total Pitches: 42 (C, CV & T)

Hylton Caravan Park
Eden Street, Silloth
CA7 4AY
Tel: 016973 31707   **109 P10**
stanwix.com
Total Pitches: 90 (C, CV & T)

Isle of Avalon
Touring Caravan Park
Godney Road, Glastonbury
BA6 9AF
Tel: 01458 833618   **19 N7**
Total Pitches: 120 (C, CV & T)

Jacobs Mount Caravan Park
Jacobs Mount, Stepney Road,
Scarborough
YO12 5NL
Tel: 01723 361178   **99 L3**
jacobsmount.com
Total Pitches: 156 (C, CV & T)

Jasmine Caravan Park
Cross Lane, Snainton,
Scarborough
YO13 9BE
Tel: 01723 859240   **99 J4**
jasminepark.co.uk
Total Pitches: 94 (C, CV & T)

Juliot's Well Holiday Park
Camelford, North Cornwall
PL32 9RF
Tel: 01840 213302   **4 H5**
juliotswell.com
Total Pitches: 39 (C, CV & T)

Kenneggy Cove Holiday Park
Higher Kenneggy,
Rosudgeon,
Penzance
TR20 9AU
Tel: 01736 763453   **2 F8**
kenneggycove.co.uk
Total Pitches: 45 (C, CV & T)

Kennford International
Caravan Park
Kennford, Exeter
EX6 7YN
Tel: 01392 833046   **9 M7**
kennfordinternational.co.uk
Total Pitches: 96 (C, CV & T)

King's Lynn Caravan &
Camping Park
New Road, North Runcton,
King's Lynn
PE33 0RA
Tel: 01553 840004   **75 M7**
kl-cc.co.uk
Total Pitches: 150 (C, CV & T)

Kloofs Caravan Park
Sandhurst Lane, Bexhill
TN39 4RG
Tel: 01424 842839   **26 B10**
kloofs.com
Total Pitches: 50 (C, CV & T)

Kneps Farm Holiday Park
River Road, Stanah,
Thornton-Cleveleys,
Blackpool
FY5 5LR
Tel: 01253 823632   **88 D2**
knepsfarm.co.uk
Total Pitches: 60 (C & CV)

Knight Stainforth Hall
Caravan & Campsite
Stainforth, Settle
BD24 0DP
Tel: 01729 822200   **96 B7**
knightstainforth.co.uk
Total Pitches: 100 (C, CV & T)

Ladycross Plantation
Caravan Park
Egton, Whitby
YO21 1UA
Tel: 01947 895502   **105 M9**
ladycrossplantation.co.uk
Total Pitches: 130 (C, CV & T)

Lamb Cottage Caravan Park
Dalefords Lane, Whitegate,
Northwich
CW8 2BN
Tel: 01606 882302   **82 D11**
lambcottage.co.uk
Total Pitches: 45 (C & CV)

Langstone Manor C & C Park
Moortown,
Tavistock
PL19 9JZ
Tel: 01822 613371   **6 E4**
langstone-manor.co.uk
Total Pitches: 40 (C, CV & T)

Larches Caravan Park
Mealsgate, Wigton
CA7 1LQ
Tel: 016973 71379   **100 H2**
Total Pitches: 73 (C, CV & T)

Lebberston Touring Park
Filey Road, Lebberston,
Scarborough
YO11 3PE
Tel: 01723 585723   **99 M4**
lebberstontouring.co.uk
Total Pitches: 125 (C & CV)

Lee Valley Campsite
Sewardstone Road, Chingford,
London
E4 7RA
Tel: 020 8529 5689   **51 J11**
Total Pitches: 100 (C, CV & T)

Lemonford Caravan Park
Bickington (near Ashburton),
Newton Abbot
TQ12 6JR
Tel: 01626 821242   **7 K4**
lemonford.co.uk
Total Pitches: 82 (C, CV & T)

Lickpenny Caravan Site
Lickpenny Lane, Tansley, Matlock
DE4 5GF
Tel: 01629 583040   **84 D9**
lickpennycaravanpark.co.uk
Total Pitches: 80 (C & CV)

Lime Tree Park
Dukes Drive, Buxton
SK17 9RP
Tel: 01298 22988   **83 N10**
limetreeparkbuxton.co.uk
Total Pitches: 106 (C, CV & T)

Lincoln Farm Park Oxfordshire
High Street, Standlake
OX29 7RH
Tel: 01865 300239   **34 C4**
lincolnfarmpark.co.uk
Total Pitches: 90 (C, CV & T)

Little Cotton Caravan Park
Little Cotton, Dartmouth
TQ6 0LB
Tel: 01803 832558   **7 M8**
littlecotton.co.uk
Total Pitches: 95 (C, CV & T)

Little Lakeland Caravan Park
Wortwell, Harleston
IP20 0EL
Tel: 01986 788646   **65 K4**
littlelakeland.co.uk
Total Pitches: 38 (C, CV & T)

Little Trevarrack Holiday Park
Laity Lane,
Carbis Bay, St Ives
TR26 3HW
Tel: 01736 797580   **2 E6**
littletrevarrack.co.uk
Total Pitches: 200 (C, CV & T)

Long Acre Caravan Park
Station Road, Old Leake, Boston
PE22 9RF
Tel: 01205 871555   **87 L10**
longacres-caravanpark.co.uk
Total Pitches: 40 (C, CV & T)

Lowther Holiday Park
Eamont Bridge, Penrith
CA10 2JB
Tel: 01768 863631   **101 P5**
lowther-holidaypark.co.uk
Total Pitches: 180 (C, CV & T)

Lytton Lawn Touring Park
Lymore Lane,
Milford on Sea
SO41 0TX
Tel: 01590 648331   **13 N6**
shorefield.co.uk
Total Pitches: 136 (C, CV & T)

Manor Wood
Country Caravan Park
Manor Wood, Coddington,
Chester
CH3 9EN
Tel: 01829 782990   **69 N3**
cheshire-caravan-sites.co.uk
Total Pitches: 45 (C, CV & T)

Maustin Caravan Park
Kearby with Netherby,
Netherby
LS22 4DA
Tel: 0113 288 6234   **97 M11**
maustin.co.uk
Total Pitches: 25 (C, CV & T)

Mayfield Touring Park
Cheltenham Road, Cirencester
GL7 7BH
Tel: 01285 831301   **33 K3**
mayfieldpark.co.uk
Total Pitches: 72 (C, CV & T)

Meadowbank Holidays
Stour Way, Christchurch
BH23 2PQ
Tel: 01202 483597   **13 K6**
meadowbank-holidays.co.uk
Total Pitches: 41 (C & CV)

Merley Court
Merley, Wimborne Minster
BH21 3AA
Tel: 01590 648331   **12 H5**
shorefield.co.uk
Total Pitches: 160 (C, CV & T)

Middlewood Farm
Holiday Park
Middlewood Lane, Fylingthorpe,
Robin Hood's Bay, Whitby
YO22 4UF
Tel: 01947 880414   **105 P10**
middlewoodfarm.com
Total Pitches: 100 (C, CV & T)

Minnows Touring Park
Holbrook Lane, Sampford Peverell
EX16 7EN
Tel: 01884 821770   **18 D11**
ukparks.co.uk/minnows
Total Pitches: 59 (C, CV & T)

Moon & Sixpence
Newbourn Road, Waldringfield,
Woodbridge
IP12 4PP
Tel: 01473 736650   **53 N2**
moonandsixpence.eu
Total Pitches: 65 (C, CV & T)

Moss Wood Caravan Park
Crimbles Lane, Cockerham
LA2 0ES
Tel: 01524 791041   **95 K11**
mosswood.co.uk
Total Pitches: 25 (C, CV & T)

Naburn Lock Caravan Park
Naburn
YO19 4RU
Tel: 01904 728697   **98 C11**
naburnlock.co.uk
Total Pitches: 100 (C, CV & T)

Newberry Valley Park
Woodlands,
Combe Martin
EX34 0AT
Tel: 01271 882334   **17 K2**
newberryvalleypark.co.uk
Total Pitches: 120 (C, CV & T)

New House Caravan Park
Kirkby Lonsdale
LA6 2HR
Tel: 015242 71590   **95 N5**
Total Pitches: 50 (C & CV)

Newlands C & C Park
Charmouth, Bridport
DT6 6RB
Tel: 01297 560259   **10 H6**
newlandsholidays.co.uk
Total Pitches: 240 (C, CV & T)

Newperran Holiday Park
Rejerrah, Newquay
TR8 5QJ
Tel: 01872 572407   **3 K3**
newperran.co.uk
Total Pitches: 357 (C, CV & T)

Newton Mill Holiday Park
Newton Road, Bath
BA2 9JF
Tel: 0844 272 9503   **20 D2**
newtonmillpark.co.uk
Total Pitches: 106 (C, CV & T)

Northam Farm
Caravan & Touring Park
Brean, Burnham-on-Sea
TA8 2SE
Tel: 01278 751244   **19 K3**
northamfarm.co.uk
Total Pitches: 350 (C, CV & T)

North Morte Farm C & C Park
North Morte Road, Mortehoe,
Woolacombe, N Devon
EX34 7EG
Tel: 01271 870381   **16 H2**
northmortefarm.co.uk
Total Pitches: 180 (C, CV & T)

Oakdown
Country Holiday Park
Gatedown Lane,
Sidmouth
EX10 0PT
Tel: 01297 680387   **10 D6**
oakdown.co.uk
Total Pitches: 150 (C, CV & T)

Oathill Farm
Touring & Camping Site
Oathill,
Crewkerne
TA18 8PZ
Tel: 01460 30234   **11 J3**
oathillfarmleisure.co.uk
Total Pitches: 13 (C, CV & T)

Old Barn Touring Park
Cheverton Farm,
Newport Road, Sandown
PO36 9PJ
Tel: 01983 866414   **14 G10**
oldbarntouring.co.uk
Total Pitches: 60 (C, CV & T)

Old Hall Caravan Park
Capernwray,
Carnforth
LA6 1AD
Tel: 01524 733276   **95 L6**
oldhallcaravanpark.co.uk
Total Pitches: 38 (C & CV)

Orchard Farm Holiday Village
Stonegate, Hunmanby
YO14 0PU
Tel: 01723 891582   **99 N5**
orchardfarmholidayvillage.co.uk
Total Pitches: 91 (C, CV & T)

Orchard Park
Frampton Lane,
Hubbert's Bridge, Boston
PE20 3QU
Tel: 01205 290328   **74 E2**
orchardpark.co.uk
Total Pitches: 87 (C, CV & T)

Ord House Country Park
East Ord, Berwick-upon-Tweed
TD15 2NS
Tel: 01289 305288   **129 P9**
ordhouse.co.uk
Total Pitches: 79 (C, CV & T)

Otterington Park
Station Farm,
South Otterington,
Northallerton
DL7 9JB
Tel: 01609 780656   **97 N3**
otteringtonpark.com
Total Pitches: 62 (C & CV)

Oxon Hall Touring Park
Welshpool Road,
Shrewsbury
SY3 5FB
Tel: 01743 340868   **56 H2**
morris-leisure.co.uk
Total Pitches: 105 (C, CV & T)

Padstow Touring Park
Padstow
PL28 8LE
Tel: 01841 532061   **4 E7**
padstowtouringpark.co.uk
Total Pitches: 150 (C, CV & T)

Park Cliffe
Camping & Caravan Estate
Birks Road, Tower Wood,
Windermere
LA23 3PG
Tel: 01539 531344   **94 H2**
parkcliffe.co.uk
Total Pitches: 60 (C, CV & T)

Parkers Farm Holiday Park
Higher Mead Farm,
Ashburton, Devon
TQ13 7LJ
Tel: 01364 654869   **7 K4**
parkersfarmholidays.co.uk
Total Pitches: 100 (C, CV & T)

Pear Tree Holiday Park
Organford Road, Holton Heath,
Organford, Poole
BH16 6LA
Tel: 0844 272 9504   **12 F6**
peartreepark.co.uk
Total Pitches: 154 (C, CV & T)

Penrose Holiday Park
Goonhavern, Truro
TR4 9QF
Tel: 01872 573185   **3 K3**
penroseholidaypark.com
Total Pitches: 110 (C, CV & T)

Polmanter Touring Park
Halsetown,
St Ives
TR26 3LX
Tel: 01736 795640   **2 E6**
polmanter.com
Total Pitches: 270 (C, CV & T)

Porlock Caravan Park
Porlock,
Minehead
TA24 8ND
Tel: 01643 862269   **18 A5**
porlockcaravanpark.co.uk
Total Pitches: 40 (C, CV & T)

Portesham Dairy Farm Campsite
Portesham, Weymouth
DT3 4HG
Tel: 01305 871297 **11 N7**
porteshamdairyfarm.co.uk
Total Pitches: 90 (C, CV & T)

Porth Beach Tourist Park
Porth, Newquay
TR7 3NH
Tel: 01637 876531 **4 C9**
porthbeach.co.uk
Total Pitches: 200 (C, CV & T)

Porthtowan Tourist Park
Mile Hill, Porthtowan, Truro
TR4 8TY
Tel: 01209 890256 **2 H4**
porthtowantouristpark.co.uk
Total Pitches: 80 (C, CV & T)

Quantock Orchard Caravan Park
Flaxpool, Crowcombe, Taunton
TA4 4AW
Tel: 01984 618618 **18 F7**
quantock-orchard.co.uk
Total Pitches: 69 (C, CV & T)

Ranch Caravan Park
Station Road, Honeybourne, Evesham
WR11 7PR
Tel: 01386 830744 **47 M6**
ranch.co.uk
Total Pitches: 120 (C & CV)

Ripley Caravan Park
Knaresborough Road, Ripley, Harrogate
HG3 3AU
Tel: 01423 770050 **97 L8**
ripleycaravanpark.com
Total Pitches: 100 (C, CV & T)

River Dart Country Park
Holne Park, Ashburton
TQ13 7NP
Tel: 01364 652511 **7 J5**
riverdart.co.uk
Total Pitches: 170 (C, CV & T)

Riverside C & C Park
Marsh Lane, North Molton Road, South Molton
EX36 3HQ
Tel: 01769 579269 **17 N6**
exmoorriverside.co.uk
Total Pitches: 42 (C, CV & T)

Riverside Caravan Park
High Bentham, Lancaster
LA2 7FJ
Tel: 015242 61272 **95 P7**
riversidecaravanpark.co.uk
Total Pitches: 61 (C & CV)

Riverside Caravan Park
Leigham Manor Drive, Marsh Mills, Plymouth
PL6 8LL
Tel: 01752 344122 **6 E7**
riversidecaravanpark.com
Total Pitches: 259 (C, CV & T)

Riverside Holidays
21 Compass Point, Ensign Way, Hamble
SO31 4RA
Tel: 023 8045 3220 **14 E5**
riversideholidays.co.uk
Total Pitches: 77 (C, CV & T)

Riverside Meadows Country Caravan Park
Ure Bank Top, Ripon
HG4 1JD
Tel: 01765 602964 **97 M6**
flowerofmay.com
Total Pitches: 80 (C, CV & T)

River Valley Holiday Park
London Apprentice, St Austell
PL26 7AP
Tel: 01726 73533 **3 Q3**
rivervalleyholidaypark.co.uk
Total Pitches: 45 (C, CV & T)

Rosedale C & C Park
Rosedale Abbey, Pickering
YO18 8SA
Tel: 01751 417272 **105 K11**
flowerofmay.com
Total Pitches: 100 (C, CV & T)

Rose Farm Touring & Camping Park
Stepshort, Belton, Nr Great Yarmouth
NR31 9JS
Tel: 01493 780896 **77 P11**
rosefarmtouringpark.co.uk
Total Pitches: 145 (C, CV & T)

Ross Park
Park Hill Farm, Ipplepen, Newton Abbot
TQ12 5TT
Tel: 01803 812983 **7 L5**
rossparkcaravanpark.co.uk
Total Pitches: 110 (C, CV & T)

Rudding Holiday Park
Follifoot, Harrogate
HG3 1JH
Tel: 01423 871350 **97 M10**
ruddingpark.co.uk
caravans-camping
Total Pitches: 109 (C, CV & T)

Rutland C & C
Park Lane, Greetham, Oakham
LE15 7FN
Tel: 01572 813520 **73 N8**
rutlandcaravanandcamping.co.uk
Total Pitches: 130 (C, CV & T)

Seaview International Holiday Park
Boswinger, Mevagissey
PL26 6LL
Tel: 01726 843425 **3 P5**
seaviewinternational.com
Total Pitches: 201 (C, CV & T)

Severn Gorge Park
Bridgnorth Road, Tweedale, Telford
TF7 4JB
Tel: 01952 684789 **57 N3**
severngorgepark.co.uk
Total Pitches: 10 (C & CV)

Shamba Holidays
230 Ringwood Road, St Leonards, Ringwood
BH24 2SB
Tel: 01202 873302 **13 K4**
shambaholidays.co.uk
Total Pitches: 150 (C, CV & T)

Shrubbery Touring Park
Rousdon, Lyme Regis
DT7 3XW
Tel: 01297 442227 **10 F6**
shrubberypark.co.uk
Total Pitches: 120 (C, CV & T)

Silverbow Park
Perranwell, Goonhavern
TR4 9NX
Tel: 01872 572347 **3 K3**
chycor.co.uk/parks/silverbow
Total Pitches: 100 (C, CV & T)

Silverdale Caravan Park
Middlebarrow Plain, Cove Road, Silverdale, Nr Carnforth
LA5 0SH
Tel: 01524 701508 **95 K5**
holgates.co.uk
Total Pitches: 80 (C, CV & T)

Skelwith Fold Caravan Park
Ambleside, Cumbria
LA22 0HX
Tel: 015394 32277 **101 L10**
skelwith.com
Total Pitches: 150 (C & CV)

Somers Wood Caravan Park
Somers Road, Meriden
CV7 7PL
Tel: 01676 522978 **59 K8**
somerswood.co.uk
Total Pitches: 48 (C & CV)

Southfork Caravan Park
Parrett Works, Martock
TA12 6AE
Tel: 01935 825661 **19 M11**
southforkcaravans.co.uk
Total Pitches: 27 (C, CV & T)

South Lytchett Manor C & C Park
Dorchester Road, Lytchett Minster, Poole
BH16 6JB
Tel: 01202 622577 **12 G6**
southlytchettmanor.co.uk
Total Pitches: 150 (C, CV & T)

Springfield Holiday Park
Tedburn St Mary, Exeter
EX6 6EW
Tel: 01647 24242 **9 K6**
springfieldholidaypark.co.uk
Total Pitches: 48 (C, CV & T)

Stanmore Hall Touring Park
Stourbridge Road, Bridgnorth
WV15 6DT
Tel: 01746 761761 **57 N6**
morris-leisure.co.uk
Total Pitches: 131 (C, CV & T)

St Helens Caravan Park
Wykeham, Scarborough
YO13 9QD
Tel: 01723 862771 **99 K4**
sthelenscaravanpark.co.uk
Total Pitches: 250 (C, CV & T)

Stowford Farm Meadows
Berry Down, Combe Martin
EX34 0PW
Tel: 01271 882476 **17 K3**
stowford.co.uk
Total Pitches: 700 (C, CV & T)

Stroud Hill Park
Fen Road, Pidley
PE28 3DE
Tel: 01487 741333 **62 D5**
stroudhillpark.co.uk
Total Pitches: 60 (C, CV & T)

Sumners Ponds Fishery & Campsite
Chapel Road, Barns Green, Horsham
RH13 0PR
Tel: 01403 732539 **24 D5**
sumnersponds.co.uk
Total Pitches: 85 (C, CV & T)

Sun Haven Valley Holiday Park
Mawgan Porth, Newquay
TR8 4BQ
Tel: 01637 860373 **4 D8**
sunhavenvalley.com
Total Pitches: 109 (C, CV & T)

Sun Valley Holiday Park
Pentewan Road, St Austell
PL26 6DJ
Tel: 01726 843266 **3 Q4**
sunvalleyholidays.co.uk
Total Pitches: 29 (C, CV & T)

Swiss Farm Touring & Camping
Marlow Road, Henley-on-Thames
RG9 2HY
Tel: 01491 573419 **35 L8**
swissfarmcamping.co.uk
Total Pitches: 140 (C, CV & T)

Tanner Farm Touring Caravan & Camping Park
Tanner Farm, Goudhurst Road, Marden
TN12 9ND
Tel: 01622 832399 **26 B3**
tannerfarmpark.co.uk
Total Pitches: 100 (C, CV & T)

Tattershall Lakes Country Park
Sleaford Road, Tattershall
LN4 4RL
Tel: 01526 348800 **86 H9**
tattershall-lakes.com
Total Pitches: 186 (C, CV & T)

Teversal C & C Club Site
Silverhill Lane, Teversal
NG17 3JJ
Tel: 01623 551838 **84 G8**
campingandcaravanningclub.co.uk/teversal
Total Pitches: 126 (C, CV & T)

The Inside Park
Down House Estate, Blandford Forum
DT11 9AD
Tel: 01258 453719 **12 E4**
theinsidepark.co.uk
Total Pitches: 125 (C, CV & T)

The Old Brick Kilns
Little Barney Lane, Barney, Fakenham
NR21 0NL
Tel: 01328 878305 **76 E5**
old-brick-kilns.co.uk
Total Pitches: 65 (C, CV & T)

The Old Oaks Touring Park
Wick Farm, Wick, Glastonbury
BA6 8JS
Tel: 01458 831437 **19 P7**
theoldoaks.co.uk
Total Pitches: 100 (C, CV & T)

The Orchards Holiday Caravan Park
Main Road, Newbridge, Yarmouth, Isle of Wight
PO41 0TS
Tel: 01983 531331 **14 D9**
orchards-holiday-park.co.uk
Total Pitches: 171 (C, CV & T)

The Quiet Site
Ullswater, Watermillock
CA11 0LS
Tel: 07768 727016 **101 M6**
thequietsite.co.uk
Total Pitches: 100 (C, CV & T)

Tollgate Farm C & C Park
Budnick Hill, Perranporth
TR6 0AD
Tel: 01872 572130 **3 K3**
tollgatefarm.co.uk
Total Pitches: 102 (C, CV & T)

Townsend Touring Park
Townsend Farm, Pembridge, Leominster
HR6 9HB
Tel: 01544 388527 **45 M3**
townsendfarm.co.uk
Total Pitches: 60 (C, CV & T)

Treloy Touring Park
Newquay
TR8 4JN
Tel: 01637 872063 **4 D9**
treloy.co.uk
Total Pitches: 223 (C, CV & T)

Trencreek Holiday Park
Hillcrest, Higher Trencreek, Newquay
TR8 4NS
Tel: 01637 874210 **4 C9**
trencreekholidaypark.co.uk
Total Pitches: 194 (C, CV & T)

Trethem Mill Touring Park
St Just-in-Roseland, Nr St Mawes, Truro
TR2 5JF
Tel: 01872 580504 **3 M6**
trethem.com
Total Pitches: 84 (C, CV & T)

Trevalgan Touring Park
Trevalgan, St Ives
TR26 3BJ
Tel: 01736 792048 **2 D5**
trevalgantouringpark.co.uk
Total Pitches: 120 (C, CV & T)

Trevarth Holiday Park
Blackwater, Truro
TR4 8HR
Tel: 01872 560266 **3 J4**
trevarth.co.uk
Total Pitches: 30 (C, CV & T)

Trevella Tourist Park
Crantock, Newquay
TR8 5EW
Tel: 01637 830308 **4 C10**
trevella.co.uk
Total Pitches: 313 (C, CV & T)

Troutbeck C & C Club Site
Hutton Moor End, Troutbeck, Penrith
CA11 0SX
Tel: 017687 79149 **101 L5**
campingandcaravanningclub.co.uk/troutbeck
Total Pitches: 54 (C, CV & T)

Truro C & C Park
Truro
TR4 8QN
Tel: 01872 560274 **3 K4**
trurocaravanandcampingpark.co.uk
Total Pitches: 51 (C, CV & T)

Tudor C & C
Shepherds Patch, Slimbridge, Gloucester
GL2 7BP
Tel: 01453 890483 **32 D4**
tudorcaravanpark.com
Total Pitches: 75 (C, CV & T)

Two Mills Touring Park
Yarmouth Road, North Walsham
NR28 9NA
Tel: 01692 405829 **77 K6**
twomills.co.uk
Total Pitches: 81 (C, CV & T)

Ulwell Cottage Caravan Park
Ulwell Cottage, Ulwell, Swanage
BH19 3DG
Tel: 01929 422823 **12 H8**
ulwellcottagepark.co.uk
Total Pitches: 77 (C, CV & T)

Vale of Pickering Caravan Park
Carr House Farm, Allerston, Pickering
YO18 7PQ
Tel: 01723 859280 **98 H4**
valeofpickering.co.uk
Total Pitches: 120 (C, CV & T)

Warcombe Farm C & C Park
Station Road, Mortehoe
EX34 7EJ
Tel: 01271 870690 **16 H2**
warcombefarm.co.uk
Total Pitches: 250 (C, CV & T)

Wareham Forest Tourist Park
North Trigon, Wareham
BH20 7NZ
Tel: 01929 551393 **12 E6**
warehamforest.co.uk
Total Pitches: 200 (C, CV & T)

Waren Caravan Park
Waren Mill, Bamburgh
NE70 7EE
Tel: 01668 214366 **119 M4**
meadowhead.co.uk
Total Pitches: 150 (C, CV & T)

Watergate Bay Touring Park
Watergate Bay, Tregurrian
TR8 4AD
Tel: 01637 860387 **4 C9**
watergatebaytouring.co.uk
Total Pitches: 171 (C, CV & T)

Waterrow Touring Park
Wiveliscombe, Taunton
TA4 2AZ
Tel: 01984 623464 **18 E9**
waterrowpark.co.uk
Total Pitches: 45 (C, CV & T)

Wayfarers C & C Park
Relubbus Lane, St Hilary, Penzance
TR20 9EF
Tel: 01736 763326 **2 F7**
wayfarerspark.co.uk
Total Pitches: 39 (C, CV & T)

Wells Holiday Park
Haybridge, Wells
BA5 1AJ
Tel: 01749 676869 **19 P5**
wellsholidaypark.co.uk
Total Pitches: 72 (C, CV & T)

Westwood Caravan Park
Old Felixstowe Road, Bucklesham, Ipswich
IP10 0BN
Tel: 01473 659637 **53 N3**
westwoodcaravanpark.co.uk
Total Pitches: 100 (C, CV & T)

Whitefield Forest Touring Park
Brading Road, Ryde, Isle of Wight
PO33 1QL
Tel: 01983 617069 **14 H9**
whitefieldforest.co.uk
Total Pitches: 80 (C, CV & T)

Whitemead Caravan Park
East Burton Road, Wool
BH20 6HG
Tel: 01929 462241 **12 D7**
whitemeadcaravanpark.co.uk
Total Pitches: 95 (C, CV & T)

Whitsand Bay Lodge & Touring Park
Millbrook, Torpoint
PL10 1JZ
Tel: 01752 822597 **5 Q11**
whitsandbayholidays.co.uk
Total Pitches: 49 (C, CV & T)

Widdicombe Farm Touring Park
Marldon, Paignton
TQ3 1ST
Tel: 01803 558325 **7 M6**
widdicombefarm.co.uk
Total Pitches: 180 (C, CV & T)

Widemouth Fields C & C Park
Park Farm, Poundstock, Bude
EX23 0NA
Tel: 01288 361351 **16 C11**
widemouthbaytouring.co.uk
Total Pitches: 156 (C, CV & T)

Widend Touring Park
Berry Pomeroy Road, Marldon, Paignton
TQ3 1RT
Tel: 01803 550116 **7 M6**
Total Pitches: 207 (C, CV & T)

Wild Rose Park
Ormside, Appleby-in-Westmorland
CA16 6EJ
Tel: 017683 51077 **102 C7**
wildrose.co.uk
Total Pitches: 226 (C, CV & T)

Wilksworth Farm Caravan Park
Cranborne Road, Wimborne Minster
BH21 4HW
Tel: 01202 885467 **12 H4**
wilksworthfarmcaravanpark.co.uk
Total Pitches: 85 (C, CV & T)

Wolds Way Caravan and Camping
West Farm, West Knapton, Malton
YO17 8JE
Tel: 01944 728463 **98 H6**
rydalesbest.co.uk
Total Pitches: 70 (C, CV & T)

Wooda Farm Holiday Park
Poughill, Bude
EX23 9HJ
Tel: 01288 352069   **16 C10**
wooda.co.uk
Total Pitches: 200 (C, CV & T)

Woodclose Caravan Park
High Casterton,
Kirkby Lonsdale
LA6 2SE
Tel: 01524 271597   **95 N5**
woodclosepark.com
Total Pitches: 29 (C, CV & T)

Wood Farm C & C Park
Axminster Road,
Charmouth
DT6 6BT
Tel: 01297 560697   **10 H6**
woodfarm.co.uk
Total Pitches: 216 (C, CV & T)

Woodhall Country Park
Stixwold Road, Woodhall Spa
LN10 6UJ
Tel: 01526 353710   **86 G8**
woodhallcountrypark.co.uk
Total Pitches: 80 (C, CV & T)

Woodlands Grove C & C Park
Blackawton, Dartmouth
TQ9 7DQ
Tel: 01803 712598   **7 L8**
woodlands-caravanpark.com
Total Pitches: 350 (C, CV & T)

**Woodland Springs
Adult Touring Park**
Venton, Drewsteignton
EX6 6PG
Tel: 01647 231695   **8 G6**
woodlandsprings.co.uk
Total Pitches: 81 (C, CV & T)

Woodovis Park
Gulworthy, Tavistock
PL19 8NY
Tel: 01822 832968   **6 C4**
woodovis.com
Total Pitches: 50 (C, CV & T)

**Woolsbridge Manor Farm
Caravan Park**
Three Legged Cross,
Wimborne
BH21 6RA
Tel: 01202 826369   **13 K4**
*woolsbridgemanorcaravanpark.
co.uk*
Total Pitches: 60 (C, CV & T)

**Yeatheridge Farm
Caravan Park**
East Worlington, Crediton
EX17 4TN
Tel: 01884 860330   **9 J2**
yeatheridge.co.uk
Total Pitches: 85 (C, CV & T)

**Zeacombe House
Caravan Park**
Blackerton Cross,
East Anstey, Tiverton
EX16 9JU
Tel: 01398 341279   **17 R7**
zeacombeadultretreat.co.uk
Total Pitches: 50 (C, CV & T)

SCOTLAND

Aird Donald Caravan Park
London Road, Stranraer
DG9 8RN
Tel: 01776 702025   **106 E5**
aird-donald.co.uk
Total Pitches: 100 (C, CV & T)

Anwoth Caravan Site
Gatehouse of Fleet,
Castle Douglas
DG7 2JU
Tel: 01557 814333   **108 C9**
auchenlarie.co.uk
Total Pitches: 28 (C, CV & T)

Beecraigs C & C Site
Beecraigs Country Park,
The Park Centre, Linlithgow
EH49 6PL
Tel: 01506 844516   **127 J3**
beecraigs.com
Total Pitches: 36 (C, CV & T)

Blair Castle Caravan Park
Blair Atholl, Pitlochry
PH18 5SR
Tel: 01796 481263   **141 L4**
blaircastlecaravanpark.co.uk
Total Pitches: 241 (C, CV & T)

Brighouse Bay Holiday Park
Brighouse Bay, Borgue
DG6 4TS
Tel: 01557 870267   **108 D11**
gillespie-leisure.co.uk
Total Pitches: 190 (C, CV & T)

Cairnsmill Holiday Park
Largo Road,
St Andrews
KY16 8NN
Tel: 01334 473604   **135 M5**
Total Pitches: 62 (C, CV & T)

Castle Cary Holiday Park
Creetown,
Newton Stewart
DG8 7DQ
Tel: 01671 820264   **107 N6**
castlecary-caravans.com
Total Pitches: 50 (C, CV & T)

**Craigtoun Meadows
Holiday Park**
Mount Melville,
St Andrews
KY16 8PQ
Tel: 01334 475959   **135 M4**
craigtounmeadows.co.uk
Total Pitches: 57 (C, CV & T)

Crossburn Caravan Park
Edinburgh Road,
Peebles
EH45 8ED
Tel: 01721 720501   **117 J2**
crossburncaravans.co.uk
Total Pitches: 45 (C, CV & T)

Drum Mohr Caravan Park
Levenhall, Musselburgh
EH21 8JS
Tel: 0131 665 6867   **128 B5**
drummohr.org
Total Pitches: 120 (C, CV & T)

East Bowstrips Caravan Park
St Cyrus, Nr Montrose
DD10 0DE
Tel: 01674 850328   **143 N4**
*caravancampingsites.co.uk/
aberdeenshire/eastbowstrips.htm*
Total Pitches: 32 (C, CV & T)

Gart Caravan Park
The Gart, Callander
FK17 8LE
Tel: 01877 330002   **133 J6**
theholidaypark.co.uk
Total Pitches: 128 (C & CV)

Glenearly Caravan Park
Dalbeattie
DG5 4NE
Tel: 01556 611393   **108 H8**
glenearlycaravanpark.co.uk
Total Pitches: 39 (C, CV & T)

Glen Nevis C & C Park
Glen Nevis, Fort William
PH33 6SX
Tel: 01397 702191   **139 L3**
glen-nevis.co.uk
Total Pitches: 380 (C, CV & T)

Hoddom Castle Caravan Park
Hoddom, Lockerbie
DG11 1AS
Tel: 01576 300251   **110 C6**
hoddomcastle.co.uk
Total Pitches: 200 (C, CV & T)

Huntly Castle Caravan Park
The Meadow, Huntly
AB54 4UJ
Tel: 01466 794999   **158 D9**
huntlycastle.co.uk
Total Pitches: 90 (C, CV & T)

Invercoe C & C Park
Glencoe, Ballachulish
PH49 4HP
Tel: 01855 811210   **139 K6**
invercoe.co.uk
Total Pitches: 60 (C, CV & T)

Linnhe Lochside Holidays
Corpach, Fort William
PH33 7NL
Tel: 01397 772376   **139 K2**
linnhe-lochside-holidays.co.uk
Total Pitches: 85 (C, CV & T)

Lomond Woods Holiday Park
Old Luss Road, Balloch,
Loch Lomond
G83 8QP
Tel: 01389 755000   **132 D11**
holiday-parks.co.uk
Total Pitches: 100 (C & CV)

Machrihanish Caravan Park
East Trodigal, Machrihanish,
Mull of Kintyre
PA28 6PT
Tel: 01586 810366   **120 B7**
campkintyre.co.uk
Total Pitches: 90 (C, CV & T)

Milton of Fonab Caravan Site
Bridge Road, Pitlochry
PH16 5NA
Tel: 01796 472882   **141 M6**
fonab.co.uk
Total Pitches: 154 (C, CV & T)

River Tilt Caravan Park
Blair Atholl,
Pitlochry
PH18 5TE
Tel: 01796 481467   **141 L4**
rivertilt.co.uk
Total Pitches: 30 (C, CV & T)

Riverview Caravan Park
Marine Drive,
Monifieth
DD5 4NN
Tel: 01382 535471   **143 J11**
riverview.co.uk
Total Pitches: 49 (C & CV)

Sands of Luce Holiday Park
Sands of Luce,
Sandhead,
Stranraer
DG9 9JN
Tel: 01776 830456   **106 F7**
sandsofluceholidaypark.co.uk
Total Pitches: 120 (C, CV & T)

Seaward Caravan Park
Dhoon Bay,
Kirkudbright
DG6 4TJ
Tel: 01557 870267   **108 E11**
gillespie-leisure.co.uk
Total Pitches: 26 (C, CV & T)

Shieling Holidays
Craignure,
Isle of Mull
PA65 6AY
Tel: 01680 812496   **138 C10**
shielingholidays.co.uk
Total Pitches: 90 (C, CV & T)

Silver Sands Leisure Park
Covesea, West Beach,
Lossiemouth
IV31 6SP
Tel: 01343 813262   **157 N3**
silver-sands.co.uk
Total Pitches: 140 (C, CV & T)

Skye C & C Club Site
Loch Greshornish, Borve,
Arnisort, Edinbane,
Isle of Skye
IV51 9PS
Tel: 01470 582230   **152 E7**
*campingandcaravanningclub.co.uk/
skye*
Total Pitches: 105 (C, CV & T)

Springwood Caravan Park
Kelso
TD5 8LS
Tel: 01573 224596   **118 D4**
springwood.biz
Total Pitches: 20 (C & CV)

Thurston Manor Leisure Park
Innerwick, Dunbar
EH42 1SA
Tel: 01368 840643   **129 J5**
thurstonmanor.co.uk
Total Pitches: 120 (C, CV & T)

Trossachs Holiday Park
Aberfoyle
FK8 3SA
Tel: 01877 382614   **132 G8**
trossachsholidays.co.uk
Total Pitches: 66 (C, CV & T)

Witches Craig C & C Park
Blairlogie, Stirling
FK9 5PX
Tel: 01786 474947   **133 N8**
witchescraig.co.uk
Total Pitches: 60 (C, CV & T)

WALES

Anchorage Caravan Park
Bronllys, Brecon
LD3 0LD
Tel: 01874 711246   **44 G7**
anchoragecp.co.uk
Total Pitches: 110 (C, CV & T)

Barcdy Touring C & C Park
Talsarnau
LL47 6YG
Tel: 01766 770736   **67 L7**
barcdy.co.uk
Total Pitches: 80 (C, CV & T)

Beach View Caravan Park
Bwlchtocyn,
Abersoch
LL53 7BT
Tel: 01758 712956   **66 E9**
Total Pitches: 47 (C, CV & T)

Bodnant Caravan Park
Nebo Road, Llanrwst,
Conwy Valley
LL26 0SD
Tel: 01492 640248   **67 Q2**
bodnant-caravan-park.co.uk
Total Pitches: 54 (C, CV & T)

**Bron Derw
Touring Caravan Park**
Llanrwst
LL26 0YT
Tel: 01492 640494   **67 P2**
bronderw-wales.co.uk
Total Pitches: 43 (C & CV)

Bron-Y-Wendon Caravan Park
Wern Road, Llanddulas,
Colwyn Bay
LL22 8HG
Tel: 01492 512903   **80 C9**
northwales-holidays.co.uk
Total Pitches: 130 (C & CV)

Bryn Gloch C & C Park
Betws Garmon,
Caernarfon
LL54 7YY
Tel: 01286 650216   **67 J3**
campwales.co.uk
Total Pitches: 160 (C, CV & T)

**Caerfai Bay
Caravan & Tent Park**
Caerfai Bay, St David's,
Haverfordwest
SA62 6QT
Tel: 01437 720274   **40 E6**
caerfaibay.co.uk
Total Pitches: 106 (C, CV & T)

Cenarth Falls Holiday Park
Cenarth,
Newcastle Emlyn
SA38 9JS
Tel: 01239 710345   **41 Q2**
cenarth-holipark.co.uk
Total Pitches: 30 (C, CV & T)

**Deucoch
Touring & Camping Park**
Sarn Bach, Abersoch
LL53 7LD
Tel: 01758 713293   **66 E9**
deucoch.com
Total Pitches: 70 (C, CV & T)

Dinlle Caravan Park
Dinas Dinlle, Caernarfon
LL54 5TW
Tel: 01286 830324   **66 G3**
thornleyleisure.co.uk
Total Pitches: 175 (C, CV & T)

Eisteddfa
Eisteddfa Lodge,
Pentrefelin,
Criccieth
LL52 0PT
Tel: 01766 522696   **67 J7**
eisteddfapark.co.uk
Total Pitches: 100 (C, CV & T)

Erwlon C & C Park
Brecon Road,
Llandovery
SA20 0RD
Tel: 01550 721021   **43 Q8**
erwlon.co.uk
Total Pitches: 75 (C, CV & T)

**Hendre Mynach
Touring C & C Park**
Llanaber Road, Barmouth
LL42 1YR
Tel: 01341 280262   **67 L11**
hendremynach.co.uk
Total Pitches: 240 (C, CV & T)

Home Farm Caravan Park
Marian-Glas,
Isle of Anglesey
LL73 8PH
Tel: 01248 410614   **78 H8**
homefarm-anglesey.co.uk
Total Pitches: 98 (C, CV & T)

Hunters Hamlet Caravan Park
Sirior Goch Farm,
Betws-yn-Rhos, Abergele
LL22 8PL
Tel: 01745 832237   **80 C10**
huntershamlet.co.uk
Total Pitches: 23 (C & CV)

Islawrffordd Caravan Park
Tal-y-bont, Barmouth
LL43 2AQ
Tel: 01341 247269   **67 K10**
islawrffordd.co.uk
Total Pitches: 105 (C, CV & T)

Llys Derwen C & C Site
Ffordd Bryngwyn, Llanrug,
Caernarfon
LL55 4RD
Tel: 01286 673322   **67 J2**
llysderwen.co.uk
Total Pitches: 20 (C, CV & T)

Pencelli Castle C & C Park
Pencelli, Brecon
LD3 7LX
Tel: 01874 665451   **44 F10**
pencelli-castle.com
Total Pitches: 80 (C, CV & T)

Penisar Mynydd Caravan Park
Caerwys Road, Rhuallt, St Asaph
LL17 0TY
Tel: 01745 582227   **80 F9**
penisarmynydd.co.uk
Total Pitches: 75 (C, CV & T)

Pen-y-Bont Touring Park
Llangynog Road, Bala
LL23 7PH
Tel: 01678 520549   **68 B8**
penybont-bala.co.uk
Total Pitches: 95 (C, CV & T)

Plas Farm Caravan Park
Betws-yn-Rhos, Abergele
LL22 8AU
Tel: 01492 680254   **80 B10**
plasfarmcaravanpark.co.uk
Total Pitches: 40 (C, CV & T)

Pont Kemys C & C Park
Chainbridge, Abergavenny
NP7 9DS
Tel: 01873 880688   **31 K3**
pontkemys.com
Total Pitches: 65 (C, CV & T)

Riverside Camping
Seiont Nurseries, Pont Rug,
Caernarfon
LL55 2BB
Tel: 01286 678781   **67 J2**
riversidecamping.co.uk
Total Pitches: 60 (C, CV & T)

River View Touring Park
The Dingle, Llanedi, Pontarddulais
SA4 0FH
Tel: 01269 844876   **28 G3**
riverviewtouringpark.com
Total Pitches: 60 (C, CV & T)

The Plassey Leisure Park
The Plassey, Eyton, Wrexham
LL13 0SP
Tel: 01978 780277   **69 L5**
plassey.com
Total Pitches: 90 (C, CV & T)

Trawsdir Touring C & C Park
Llanaber, Barmouth
LL42 1RR
Tel: 01341 280999   **67 K11**
barmouthholidays.co.uk
Total Pitches: 70 (C, CV & T)

Trefalun Park
Devonshire Drive,
St Florence, Tenby
SA70 8RD
Tel: 01646 651514   **41 L10**
trefalunpark.co.uk
Total Pitches: 90 (C, CV & T)

Tyddyn Isaf Caravan Park
Lligwy Bay, Dulas, Isle of Anglesey
LL70 9PQ
Tel: 01248 410203   **78 H7**
tyddynisaf.co.uk
Total Pitches: 30 (C, CV & T)

Tyn Cornel C & C Park
Frongoch, Bala
LL23 7NU
Tel: 01678 520759   **68 A6**
tyncornel.co.uk
Total Pitches: 67 (C, CV & T)

Well Park C & C Site
Tenby
SA70 8TL
Tel: 01834 842179   **41 M10**
wellparkcaravans.co.uk
Total Pitches: 100 (C, CV & T)

**Ynysymaengwyn
Caravan Park**
Tywyn
LL36 9RY
Tel: 01654 710684   **54 E4**
ynysy.co.uk
Total Pitches: 80 (C, CV & T)

CHANNEL ISLANDS

Beuvelande Camp Site
Beuvelande, St Martin, Jersey
JE3 6EZ
Tel: 01534 853575   **11 c1**
campingjersey.com
Total Pitches: 150 (T)

Fauxquets Valley Campsite
Castel, Guernsey
GY5 7QL
Tel: 01481 236951   **10 b2**
fauxquets.co.uk
Total Pitches: 120 (T)

Rozel Camping Park
Summerville Farm,
St Martin, Jersey
JE3 6AX
Tel: 01534 855200   **11 c1**
rozelcamping.co.uk
Total Pitches: 100 (C, CV & T)

Road safety cameras

First, the advice you would expect from the AA - we advise drivers to always follow the signed speed limits – breaking the speed limit is illegal and can cost lives.

Both the AA and the Government believe that safety cameras ('speed cameras') should be operated within a transparent system. By providing information relating to road safety and speed hotspots, the AA believes that the driver is better placed to be aware of speed limits and can ensure adherence to them, thus making the roads safer for all users.

Most fixed cameras are installed at accident 'black spots' where four or more fatal or serious road collisions have occurred over the previous three years. It is the policy of both the police and the Department for Transport to make the location of cameras as well known as possible. By showing camera locations in this atlas the AA is identifying the places where extra care should be taken while driving. Speeding is illegal and dangerous and you MUST keep within the speed limit at all times.

Gatso™   Truvelo™   SPECS™   Traffipax™

There are currently more than 4,000 fixed cameras in Britain and the road mapping in this atlas identifies their on-the-road locations.

 This symbol is used on the mapping to identify **individual** camera locations - with speed limits (mph)

 This symbol is used on the mapping to identify **multiple** cameras on the same stretch of road - with speed limits (mph)

 This symbol is used on the mapping to highlight SPECS™ camera systems which calculate your **average speed** along a stretch of road between two or more sets of cameras - with speed limits (mph)

Mobile cameras are also deployed at other sites where speed is perceived to be a problem and mobile enforcement often takes place at the fixed camera sites shown on the maps in this atlas. Additionally, regular police enforcement can take place   on any road.

Speed Limits

Types of vehicle	Built up areas* MPH (km/h)	Single carriageways MPH (km/h)	Dual carriageways MPH (km/h)	Motorways MPH (km/h)
Cars & motorcycles (including car derived vans up to 2 tonnes maximum laden weight)	30 (48)	60 (96)	70 (112)	70 (112)
Cars towing caravans or trailers (including car derived vans and motorcycles)	30 (48)	50 (80)	60 (96)	60 (96)
Buses, coaches and minibuses (not exceeding 12 metres (39 feet) in overall length)	30 (48)	50 (80)	60 (96)	70 (112)
Goods vehicles (not exceeding 7.5 tonnes maximum laden weight)	30 (48)	50 (80)	60 (96)	70† (112)
Goods vehicles (exceeding 7.5 tonnes maximum laden weight)	30 (48)	40 (64)	50 (80)	60 (96)

* The 30mph (48km/h) limit usually applies to all traffic on all roads with street lighting unless signs show otherwise.
† 60mph (96km/h) if articulated or towing a trailer.

Read this before you use the atlas

Safety cameras and speed limits

The fixed camera symbols on the mapping show the maximum speed in mph that applies to that particular stretch of road and above which the camera is set to activate. The actual road speed limit however will vary for different vehicle types and you must ensure that you drive within the speed limit for your particular class of vehicle at all times.

The chart above details the speed limits applying to the different classes. Don't forget that mobile enforcement can take account of vehicle class at any designated site.

Camera locations

1 The camera locations were correct at the time of finalising the information to go to press.

2 Camera locations are approximate due to limitations in the scale of the road mapping used in this atlas.

3 In towns and urban areas camera locations are shown only on roads that appear on the road maps in this atlas.

4 Where two or more cameras appear close together, a special symbol is used to indicate multiple cameras on the same stretch of road.

5 Our symbols do not indicate the direction in which cameras point.

6 On the mapping we symbolise more than 4,000 fixed camera locations. Mobile laser device locations, roadwork cameras and 'fixed red light' cameras cannot be shown.

Be alert to accident black spots even before seeing the cameras

The AA brings you a Smart Phone app that provides 'real-time' updates of safety camera locations

The AA Safety Camera app brings the latest safety camera location system to your Smart Phone. It improves road safety by alerting you to the location of fixed and mobile camera sites and accident black spots.

The AA Safety Camera app ensures that you will always have the very latest data of fixed and mobile sites on your Smart Phone without having to connect it to your computer. Updates are made available automatically.

Powered by *RoadPilot*®

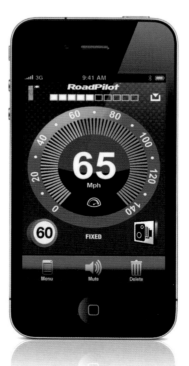

Visual Countdown
To camera location

Your Speed
The speed you are travelling when approaching a camera. Dial turns red as an additional visual alert

Camera Types Located
Includes fixed cameras (Gatso, Specs etc.) and mobile cameras

Speed Limit at Camera

Smart Phone Apps

Map pages

Road map symbols

Motoring information

M4 Motorway with number	**BATH** Primary route destination	5 Distance in miles between symbols	50 Speed camera site (fixed location) with speed limit in mph
Toll T4 Toll motorway with toll station	A1123 Other A road single/dual carriageway	or V Vehicle ferry	40 Section of road with two or more fixed speed cameras, with speed limit in mph
11 Motorway junction with and without number	B2070 B road single/dual carriageway	Fast vehicle ferry or catamaran	60 60 Average speed (SPECS™) camera system with speed limit in mph
3 Restricted motorway junctions	Minor road more than 4 metres wide, less than 4 metres wide	Railway line, in tunnel	V Fixed speed camera site with variable speed limit
S Fleet Motorway service area	Roundabout	Railway station and level crossing	P+R Park and Ride (at least 6 days per week)
Motorway and junction under construction	Interchange/junction	Tourist railway	City, town, village or other built-up area
A3 Primary route single/dual carriageway	Narrow primary/other A/B road with passing places (Scotland)	Airport, heliport	628 637 Lecht Summit Height in metres, mountain pass
1 Primary route junction with and without number	Road under construction/approved	F International freight terminal	Sandy beach
3 Restricted primary route junctions	Road tunnel	H H 24-hour Accident & Emergency hospital, other hospital	National boundary
S Primary route service area	Toll Road toll, steep gradient (arrows point downhill)	C Crematorium	County, administrative boundary

Touring information
To avoid disappointment, check opening times before visiting.

Scenic Route	Garden	National trail	Air show venue
Tourist Information Centre	Arboretum	Viewpoint	Ski slope (natural, artificial)
Tourist Information Centre (seasonal)	Vineyard	Hill-fort	National Trust property
Visitor or heritage centre	Country park	Roman antiquity	National Trust for Scotland property
Picnic site	Agricultural showground	Prehistoric monument	English Heritage site
Caravan site (AA inspected)	Theme park	Battle site with year 1066	Historic Scotland site
Camping site (AA inspected)	Farm or animal centre	Steam railway centre	Cadw (Welsh heritage) site
Caravan & camping site (AA inspected)	Zoological or wildlife collection	Cave	Other place of interest
Abbey, cathedral or priory	Bird collection	Windmill, monument	Boxed symbols indicate attractions within urban areas
Ruined abbey, cathedral or priory	Aquarium	Golf course	World Heritage Site (UNESCO)
Castle	RSPB site	County cricket ground	National Park
Historic house or building	National Nature Reserve (England, Scotland, Wales)	Rugby Union national stadium	National Scenic Area (Scotland)
Museum or art gallery	Local nature reserve	International athletics stadium	Forest Park
Industrial interest	Wildlife Trust reserve	Horse racing, show jumping	Heritage coast
Aqueduct or viaduct	Forest drive	Motor-racing circuit	Major shopping centre

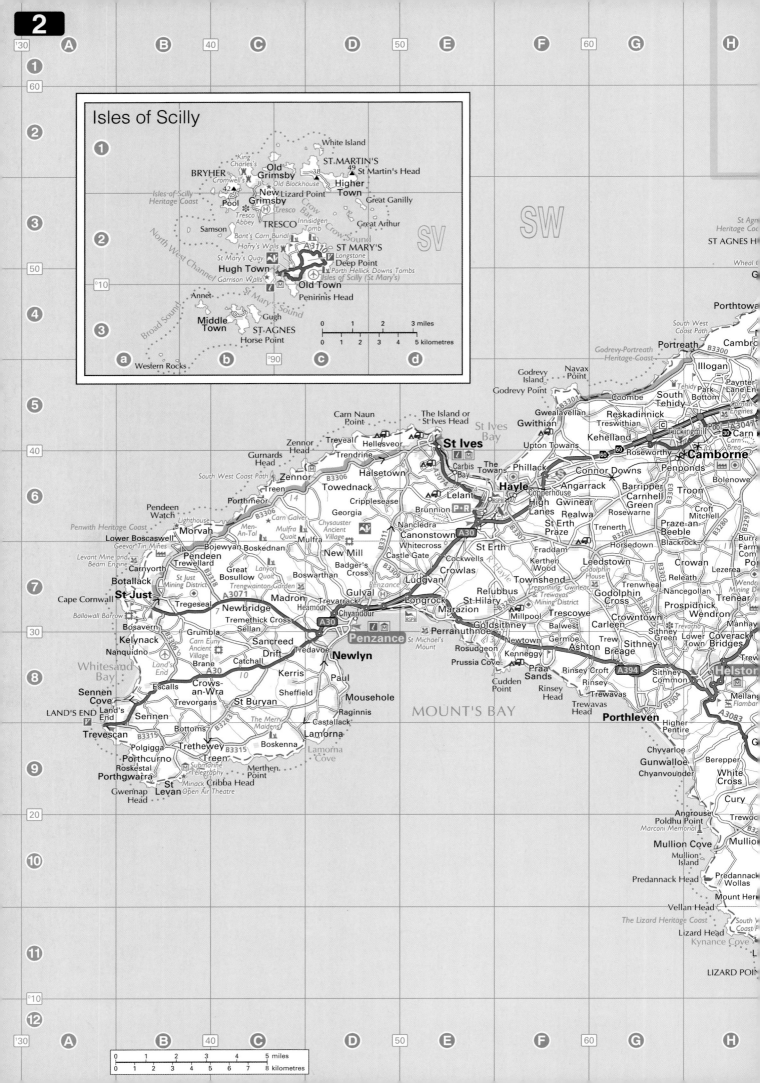

2

Isles of Scilly

White Island
ST.MARTIN'S
King Charles's
BRYHER
Old Grimsby
St Martin's Head
Old Blockhouse
Cromwell's
Higher Town
Isles-of-Scilly Heritage Coast
New Grimsby
Lizard Point
Pool
Great Ganilly
Samson
TRESCO
Tresco Abbey
Innisidgen Tomb
Great Arthur
Crow Sound
SV
Bant's Carn Burial
Harry's Walls
St Mary's Quay
ST MARY'S
Hugh Town
Longstone
Deep Point
Porth Hellick Downs Tombs
Garrison Walls
Old Town
Isles of Scilly (St Mary's)
Annet
Peninnis Head
St Mary's Sound
Broad Sound
Middle Town
Gugh
ST.AGNES
Horse Point

North West Channel
Crow Bar

| 0 | 1 | 2 | 3 miles |
| 0 | 1 | 2 | 3 | 4 | 5 kilometres |

Western Rocks

SW

St Agnes Heritage Coast
ST AGNES H
Wheal C
G

Carn Naun Point
The Island or St Ives Head
St Ives Bay
Porthtowa
South West Coast Path
Portreath
Cambr
Illogan
B3300
Paynter
Godrevy-Portreath Heritage-Coast
Godrevy Point
Navax Point
Godrevy Island
Tehidy
Park Bottom
Lane En
Coombe
South Tehidy
Cornish Engines
Tuckingmill
Carn
Gwealavellan
Reskadinnick
Treswithian
Carn
Brea
30
Camborne
Treveal
Hellesveor
St Ives
Gwithian
Upton Towans
Roseworthy
60
Penponds
Zennor Head
Trendrine
Carbis Bay
The Towans
Phillack
Connor Downs
Bolenowe
Gurnards Head
Halsetown
Copperhouse
Angarrack
Barripper
Troon
South West Coast Path
Zennor
Towednack
Lelant
Hayle
High Gwinear
Carnhell Green
Croft Mitchell
Penwith Heritage Coast
Treen
Cripplesease
Brunnion
Lanes
Realwa
Roseworne
Praze-an-Beeble
B3280
Porthmeor
Georgia
P+R
St Erth
Prize
Trenerth
Blackrock
Burra
Pendeen Watch
Carn Galver
Chysauster Ancient Village
Nancledra
Canonstown
A30
St Erth
Fraddam
Horsedown
Farm Com
Po
Lighthouse
Men-An-Tol
Mulfra Quoit
Whitecross
Cockwells
Kerthen Wood
Leedstown
Lezerea
Morvah
Boskednan
New Mill
Castle Gate
Crowlas
Townshend
Crowan
Trenwheal
Po
Lower Boscaswell
Bojewyan
Mulfra
Badger's Cross
Ludgvan
Relubbus
Godolphin House
Godolphin Cross
Prospidnick
Wendro
Geevor Tin Mines
Pendeen
Great Bosullow
Boswarthan
Penzance
St Hilary
Tregoning, Gwinear & Trewavas Mining District
Reletah
Trenear
Levant Mine and Beam Engine
Trewellard
Lanyon Quoit
Gulval
Longrock
Marazion
Millpool
Trescowe
Crowntown
Carleen
Nancegollan
Wendr
Carnyorth
St Just Mining District
Trengwainton Garden
Trevarrack
Balwest
Manhay
St Just
Madron
Heamoor
Chyandour
RSPB
Perranuthnoe
Newtown
Germoe
Trew
Sithney Green
Lower Coverack Town Bridges
Cape Cornwall
Tregeseal
Newbridge
A30
Goldsithney
Ashton
Breage
Trevano
Trew
Ballowall Barrow
Tremethick Cross
St Michael's Mount
Rosudgeon
Kenneggy
Sithney Common
Helstor
Bosavern
Grumbla
Sellan
Penzance
Newlyn
Prussia Cove
A394
Kelynack
Carn Euny Ancient Village
Sancreed
Drift
Tredavoe
Cudden Point
Praa Sands
Rinsey Croft
Rinsey
Sithney
Mellan
Nanquidno
Brane
A30
Catchall
Kerris
Paul
Rosudgeon
Rinsey Head
Trewavas
B3083
Whitesand Bay
Land's End
Crows-an-Wra
St Buryan
Sheffield
Mousehole
Trewavas Head
Porthleven
Higher Pentire
Escalls
Trevorgans
MOUNT'S BAY
Sennen Cove
Bottoms
The Merry Maidens
Raginnis
Chyvarloe
LAND'S END
Land's End
Sennen
Boskenna
Castallack
Lamorna
Gunwalloe
Trevescan
B3315
Trethewey
Treen
Boskenna
Lamorna Cove
Chyanvounder
Polgigga
Porthcurno
Merthen Point
White Cross
Roskestal
Submarine Telegraph
Cury
Porthgwarra
St Levan
Minack Open Air Theatre
Cribba Head
Angrouse
Poldhu Point
Trewoo
Gwennap Head
Marconi Memorial
Mullion Cove
Mullio
Mullion Island
Predannack Head
Predannack Wollas
Mount Her
Vellan Head
The Lizard Heritage Coast
South W Coast P
Lizard Head
Kynance Cove
LIZARD POIN
L

| 0 | 1 | 2 | 3 | 4 | 5 miles |
| 0 | 1 | 2 | 3 | 4 | 5 | 6 | 7 | 8 kilometres |

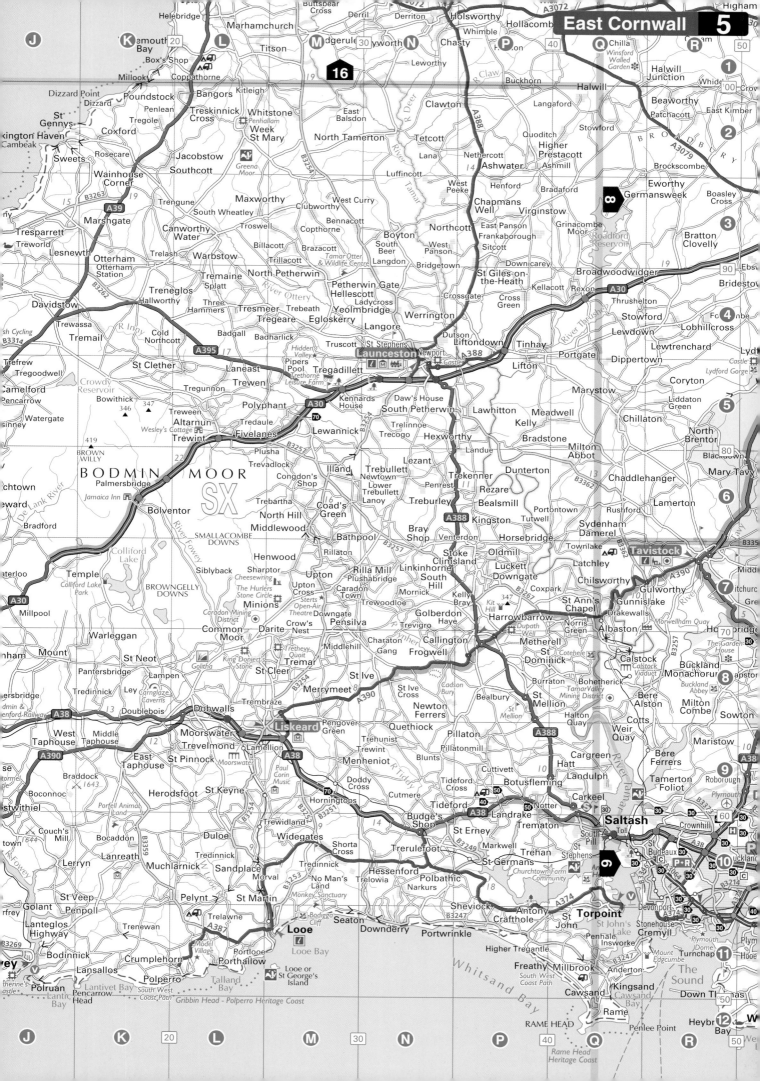

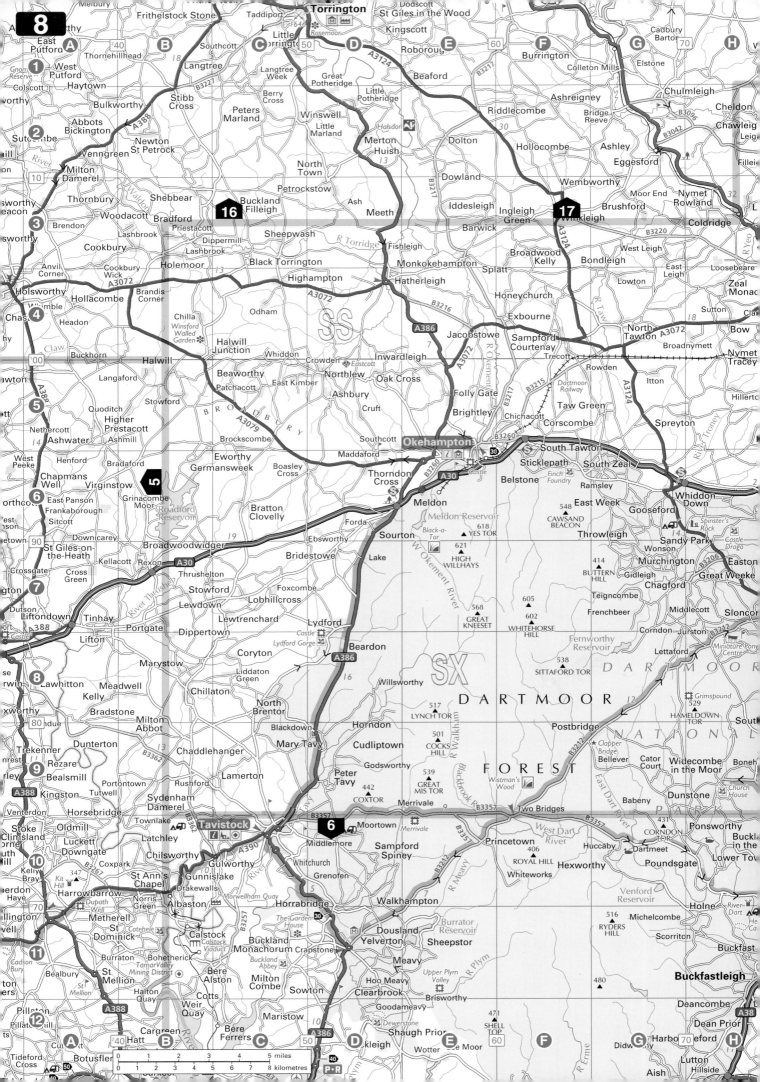

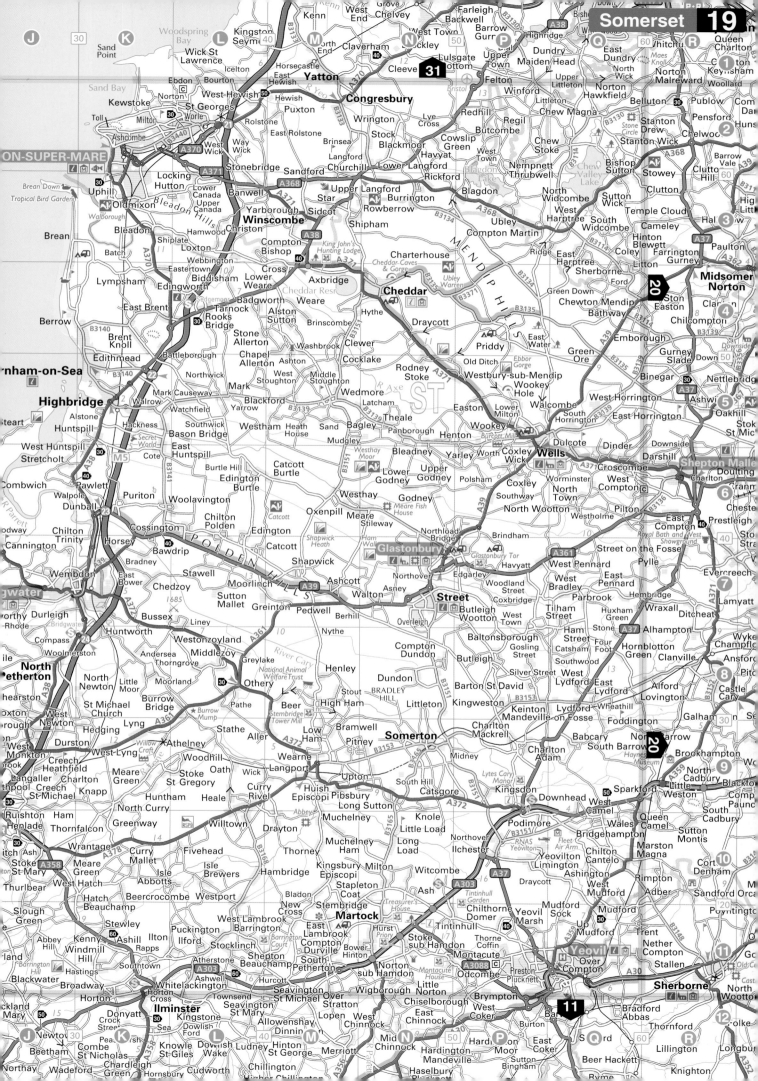

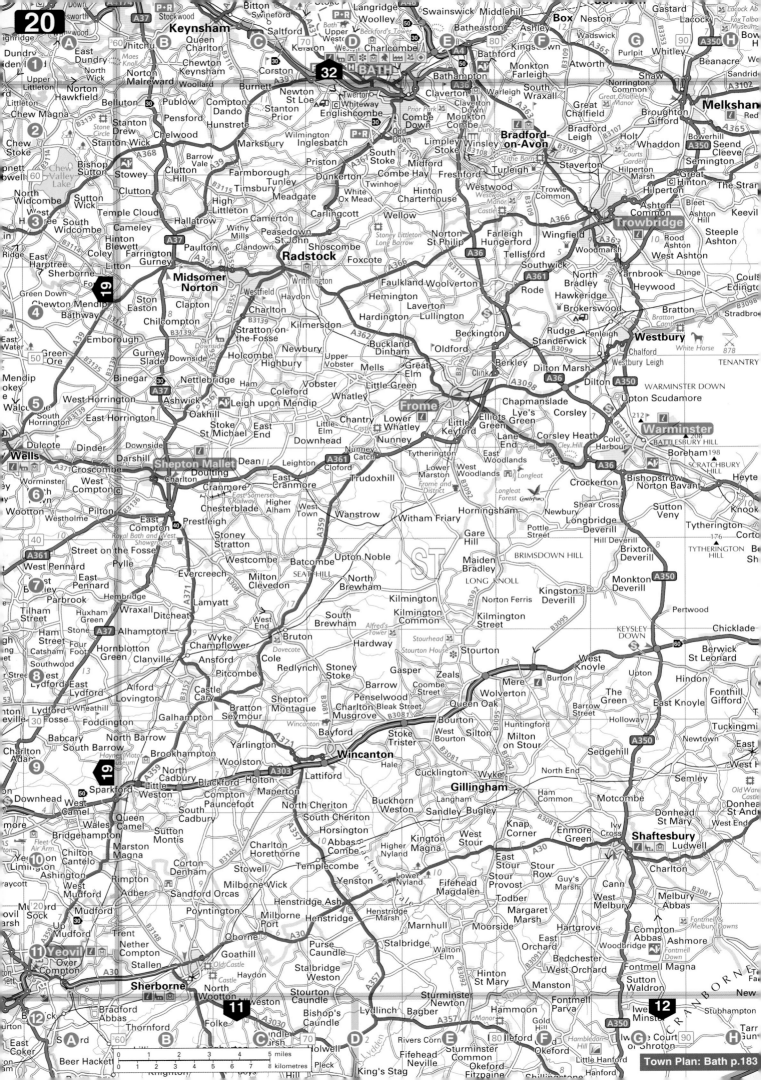

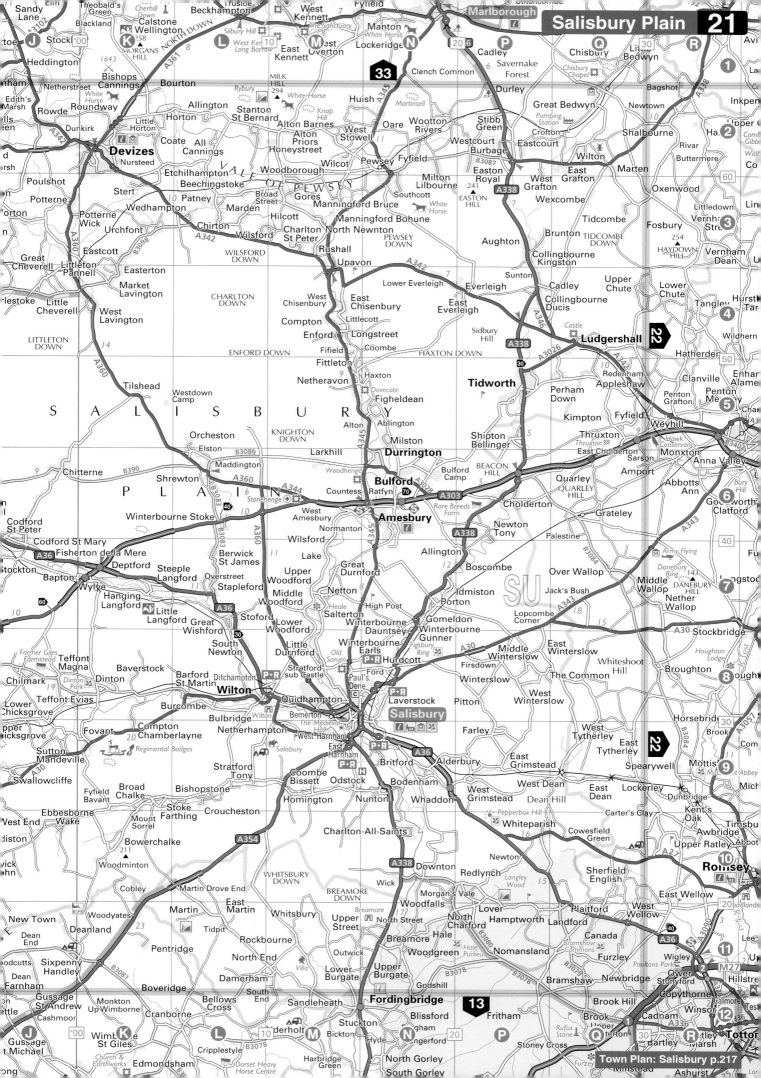

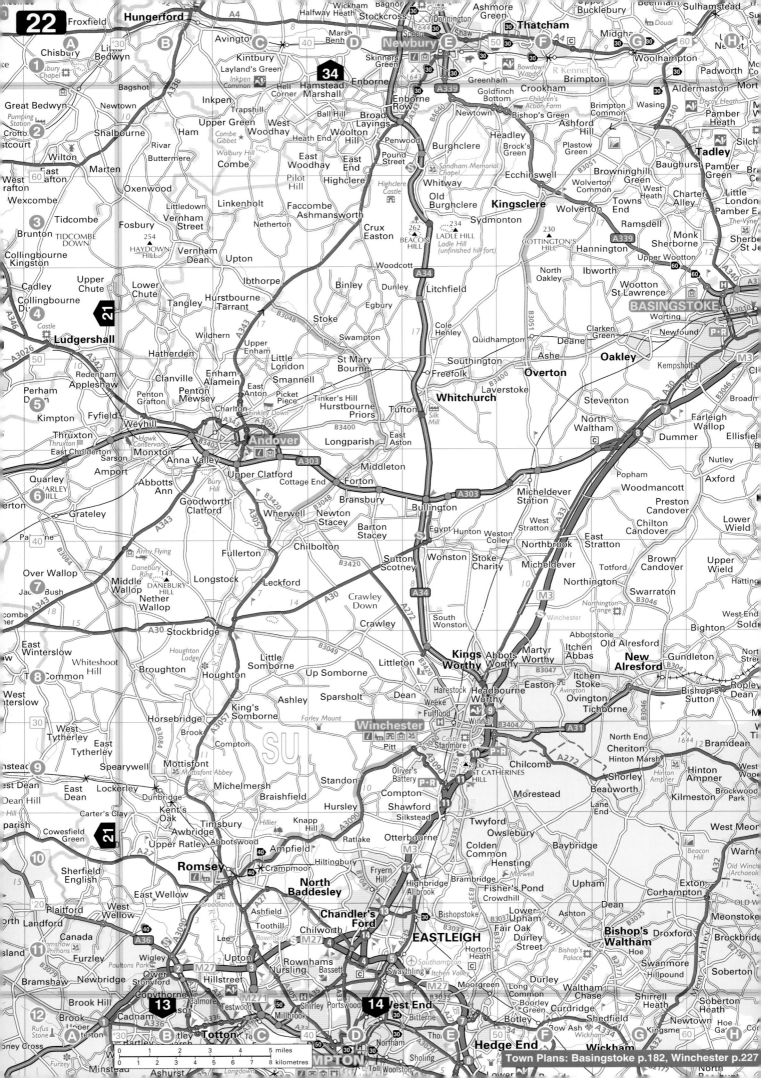

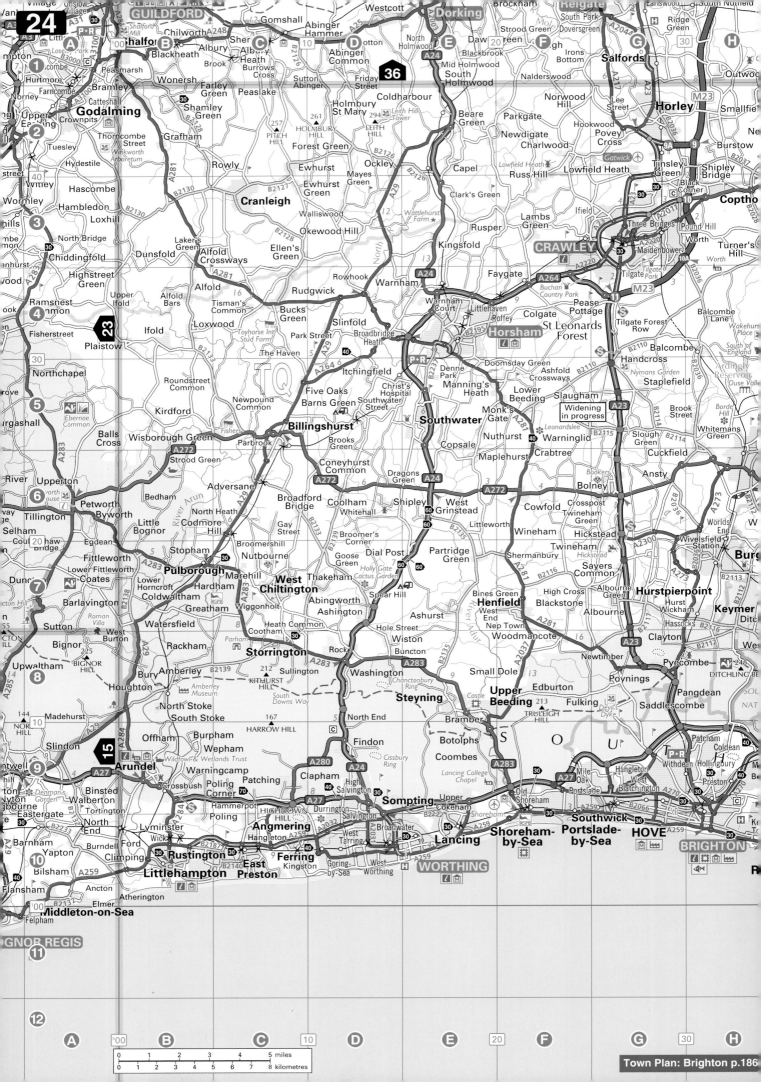

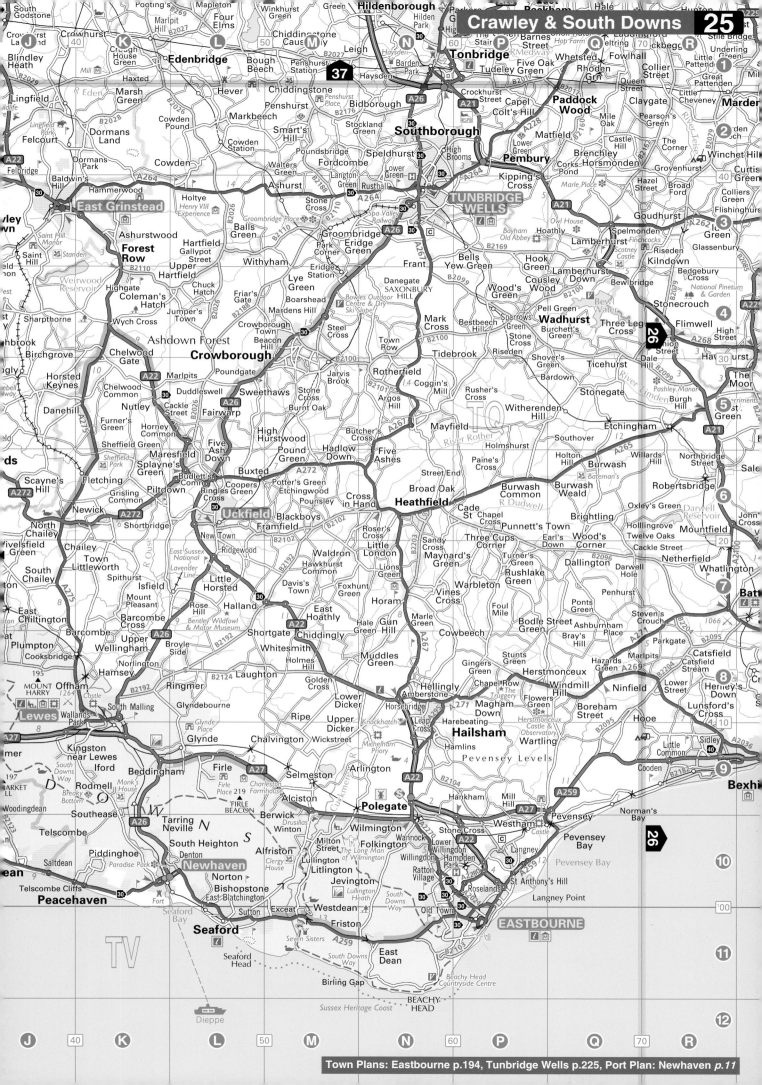

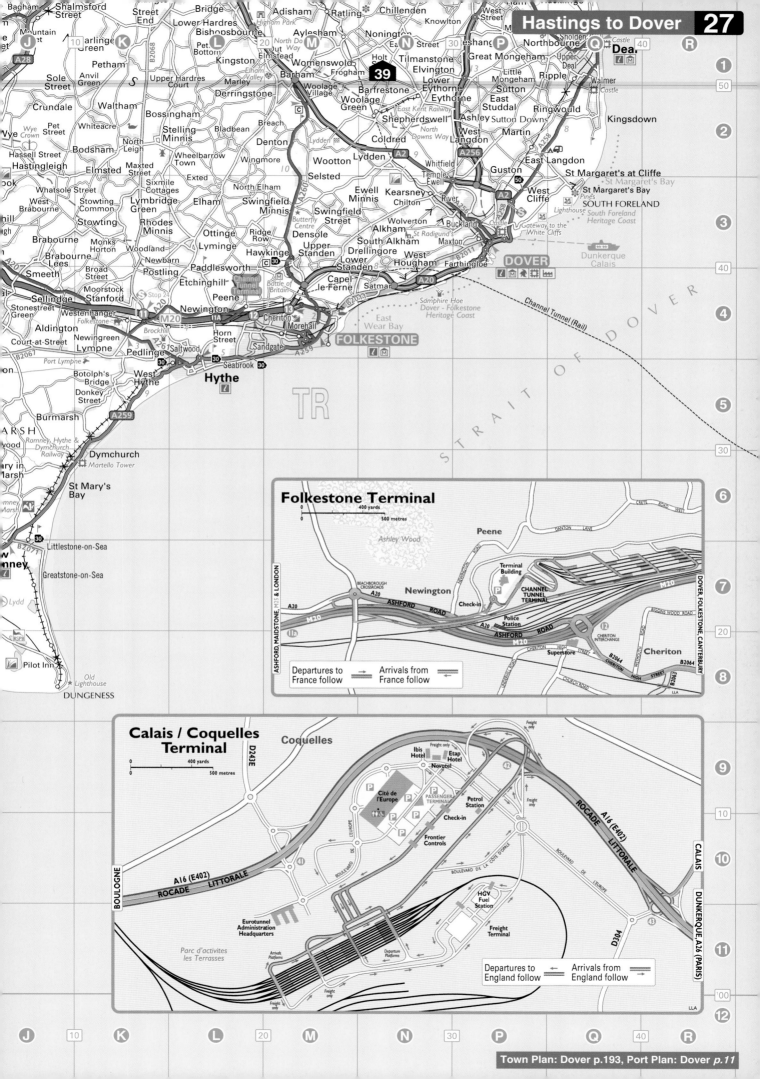

Folkestone Terminal

Departures to France follow →
Arrivals from France follow ←

Calais / Coquelles Terminal

Departures to England follow ←
Arrivals from England follow →

Town Plan: Dover p.193, Port Plan: Dover p.11

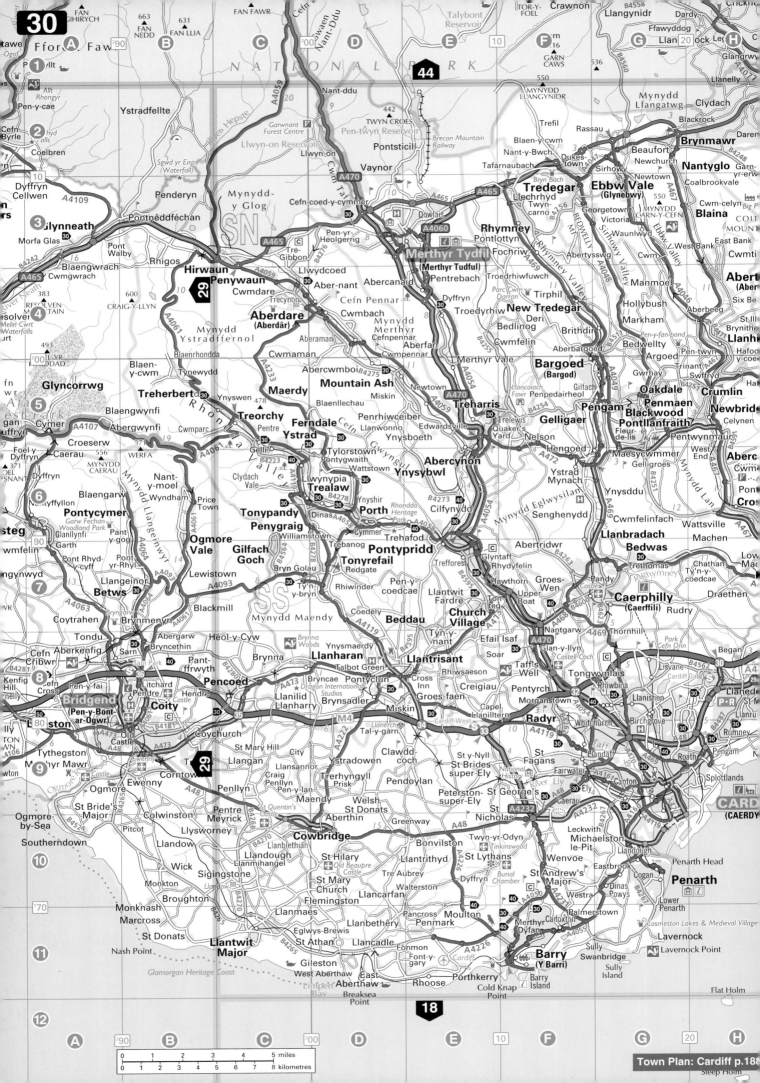

Margate

0   200 m

The Bay
Nayland Rock
Boating Lake
Lighthouse
Pier
Turner Contemporary
Lifeboat Station
Winter Gardens
Casino
FORT CRESCENT
B2051
FORT HILL
Police Station
Medical Centre
War Memorial
Tudor House
ZION PLACE
B2055
Clock Tower
Premier Inn
LONDON, CANTERBURY
A28
MARINE TERRACE
MARGATE STATION
Mag & Co Court
CAB & Old Town Hall
College Square
Bowling Alley
Kingdom Hall
Salvation Army
Theatre Royal
Holy Trinity & St John's School
Royal School for Deaf Children
BELGRAVE ROAD
EATON ROAD
Dreamland Amusement Park (closed)
All Saints Industrial Estate
Tivoli Industrial Estate
HIGH ST
QUEENS AVE
ST PETER'S ROAD
B2055
BROADSTAIRS
A255
Hartsdown Leisure Centre
Hartsdown Park
Margate FC
B2052
HARTSDOWN RD
RAMSGATE RD
A354
B2052
COLLEGE RD
RAMSGATE

Ramsgate

BROADSTAIRS
HERESON ROAD
B2054
Granville
Bandstand
Royal Victoria Pavilion (under repair)
Maritime
Royal Harbour
Marina
Lifeboat Station
MARGATE RD
CHATHAM ST
Chatham House School
St George's
Kingdom Hall
Salvation Army
Sports Centre
Priory School
Police Sta
Fire Sta
Clarendon House School
Jobcentre Plus
The Old Priory School
St Augustine's Abbey
Christchurch School
St Augustine's School
LD Lines & Transeuropa Ferries
0   200 m
LONDON, (M2), CANTERBURY
Ramsgate

TR

MARGATE
Foreness Point
Westgate on Sea
Westbrook
Cliftonville
Northdown
Kingsgate
NORTH FORELAND
Lighthouse
Reading Street
St Peter's
Broadstairs
Westwood
Dumpton
Hereson
Ramsgate
Minnis Bay
Reculver Towers
Herne Bay
Hampton
Beltinge
Reculver
Hillborough
Potten Street
Brooks End
Birchington
Garlinge
Salmestone Grange
ISLE OF THANET
Lydden
Haine
Manston
RAF Manston
Kent International
St Lawrence
Pegwell
Viking Ship 'Hugin'
St Augustine's Cross
Pegwell Bay
Whitstable
Whitstable Bay
Tankerton
Swalecliffe
Greenhill
Eddington
Broomfield
Herne
Highstead
Maypole
St Nicholas at Wade
Sarre
Acol
Monkton
Way
Durlock
Hoo
Cliffsend
A299
A28
A253
A299
A256
Chestfield
South Street
Bullockstone
Herne Common
Hoath
Upstreet
Chislet
West Stourmouth
Gore Street
Plucks Gutter
Minster
Oostende
Seasalter
Yorkletts
Highstreet
Dargate
Denstroude
Hernhill
Staplestreet
Blean
Dunkirk
Honey Hill
Tyler Hill
Upper Harbledown
Rough Common
Sturry
Westbere
Fordwich
Littlebourne
Broad Oak
Hicks Forstal
Calcott
Hersden
Grove
Preston Street
Elmstone
East Stourmouth
Westmarsh
Paramour Street
Goldstone
Richborough Roman Fort
Prince's
Sandwich Bay
Wildwood Wealden Forest Park
Druidstone
Stodmarsh
Wickhambreaux
Ickham
Preston
Cop Street
Hoaden
Weddington
Cooper Street
Great Stonar
Sandwich
Royal St George's
A2050
A290
Canterbury
Harbledown
Thanington
Chartham Hatch
Bekesbourne Hill
Seaton
Durlock
Guilton
Wingham
Marshborough
Stone Cross
Woodnesborough
Worth
Toll
Ash
A257
A2050
A28
Old Wives Lees
Chartham
Nackington
Bridge
Patrixbourne
Bramling
Twitham
Staple
Barnsole
Statenborough
Goodnestone
Heronden
Eastry
Ham
Hacklinge
Finglesham
The Downs
Castle
Deal
A2
Shalmsford Street
Street End
Lower Hardres
Bishopsbourne
Adisham
Bekesbourne
Higham Park
Chillenden
Knowlton
Nonington
West Street
Marley
Sholden
Northbourne
Upper Deal
Mountain Street
Garlinge Green
Petham
Anvil Green
Kingston
Womenswold
Holt St
Betteshanger
Great Mongeham
Sutton
Ripple
Walmer Castle
Sole Street
Upper Hardres Court
Barham
Derringstone
Aylesham
Easole Street
Tilmanstone
Elvington
Little Mongeham
East Studdal
Ringwould
Crundale
Waltham
Pett Bottom
Elmstead
Frogham
Woolage Village
Woolage Green
Barfrestone
Shepherdswell
Eythorne
East Eythorne
Lower Eythorne
Ashley
East Langdon
Kingsdown
Hastingleigh
Bossingham
Stelling Minnis
Denton
Coldred
West Langdon
Martin
B2068
A28
A260
B2046
B2065
A256
A258
A2
27
Wye
Crundale
Pet Street
Whiteacre
Ladbean
Wootton
Lyminge
North Downs Way
Whitfield
East Langdon
Hassell Street
Bodsham
North Leigh
Stelling Minnis
Wheelbarrow Town
Wingmore
Lydden
Maxted

Town Plan: Canterbury p.188

A ′60 **B** 70 **C** **D** **E** 80 **F** **G** 90 **H**

1

Rosslare Harbour (July-Sept)
Rosslare Harbour

2

STRUMBLE HEAD

40
Pen Brush
Pwll Deri

3
Pembrokeshire
Coast Path
Trefasser
Good
Manorowen
St Nicholas
Panteg

Ynys
Daullyn
Granston
Jordan
Carreg Sampson
Abercastle

4
Porthgain
Trefin
Llangloffan
Mathry
16
A487
Castle
Morris
Abereiddy
Llanrhian
Square &
Compass
B4331
Berea
Llangloffan
Fen
Letterst
30
Croes-goch
Tretio
Treffynnon
B4330
Treglemais
Cerbyd
Llandeloy

5
ST DAVID'S HEAD
Treleddyd-fawr
Carnhedryn
Caer
Farchell
River Solva
Tancredston
Pont-yr-hafod
Rhodiad-
y-brenin
Whitesand
Bay
B4583
Middle Mill
Treffgarne
Owen
Hayscastle
Hayscas
Cross
Bishop's
Palace
Whitchurch
St David's
Nine
Wells
Solva
A487
Tr

6
RAMSEY
ISLAND
Ramsey Sound
RSPB
Newgale
Pen-y-cwn
Roch
178
DUDWELL
MT
Lewest
St David's Peninsula
Heritage Coast
16
Roch Gate
Wolfsdale
PEMBROKESHIRE
COAST
NATIONAL PARK
Simpson
Cross
A487
Keeston
Can
20
Rickets Head
Nolton Haven
Nolton
Pelcomb Cross
Pelcom
Pelcomb
Bridge

7
St Brides Bay
Heritage Coast
Lambston
St Brides Bay
Druidston
Sutton
Portfield
Gate
B4341
Haroldston
West
Broadway
B4327
Dreen
Hill
Broad Haven

8
Pembrokeshire
Coast Path
Little Haven
Walton
West
Solbury
4
Talbenny
14
Tiers
Cross
10
St Brides
Walwyn's
Castle
Hasguard
Thornton
3

9
SKOMER
ISLAND
Wooltack Point
Marloes
B4327
Sandy
Haven
Herbrandston
Steynton
St Ishmael's
Honeyborc
Waterst
Broad Sound
Hubberston
Hakin
Llanstad
Marloes and Dale Heritage Coast
Dale
Great Castle
Head
Milford Haven
(Aberdaugleddau)
Pen
D
SKOKHOLM
ISLAND
Westdale
Bay
Dale
Point
Milford Haven
Angle
Angle
Bay
Pwllcrochan
(Doc
Rhoscrowther

10
St Anns Head
B4320
Castlemartin Brook
B43
′00
Rosslare Harbour
Freshwater
West
B4319
10

11
SR
Castlemartin
Warren
Linney Head
Merr
PEMBROKESHIRE C
NATIONAL PA

12
Pembrokeshire
Coast Path

A ′60 **B** 70 **C** **D** **E** 80 **F** **G** 90 **H**

0 1 2 3 4 5 miles
0 1 2 3 4 5 6 7 8 kilometres

Port Plan: Pembroke Dock *p.13*

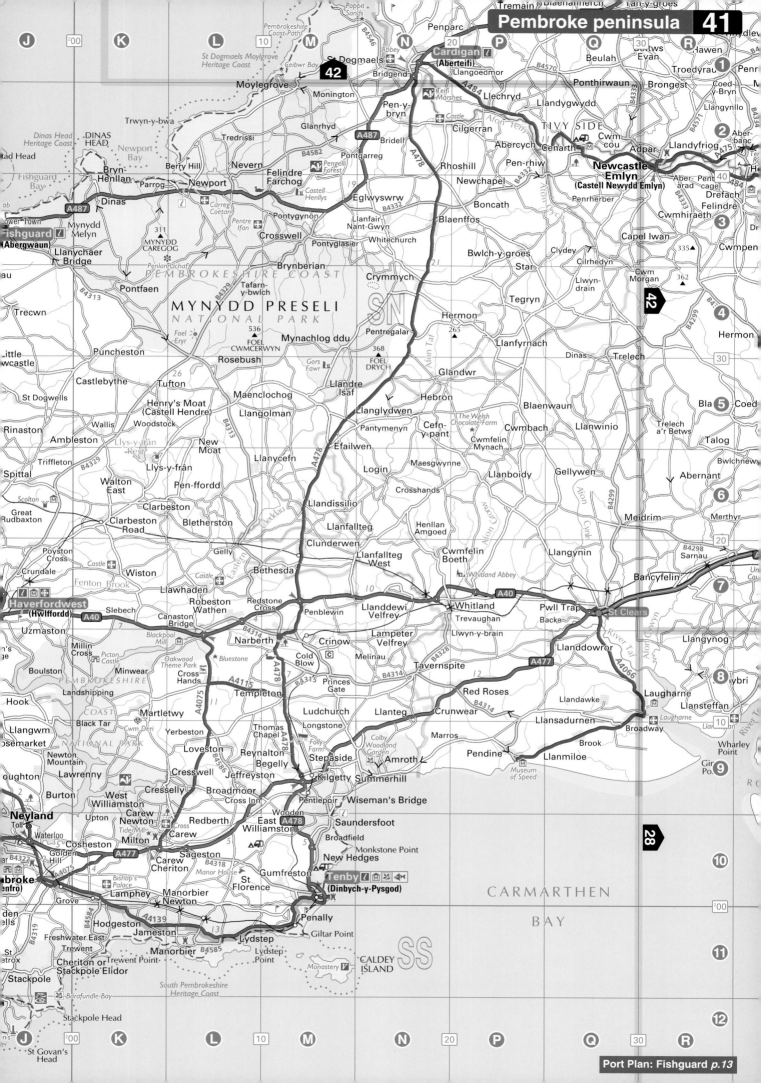

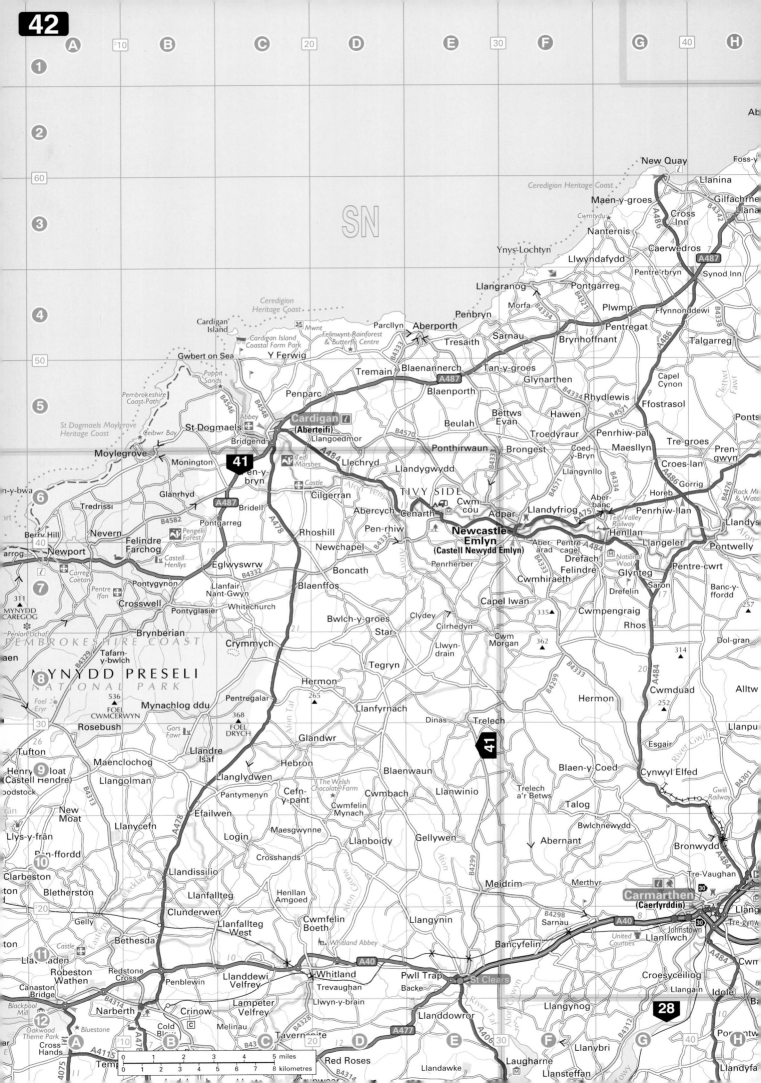

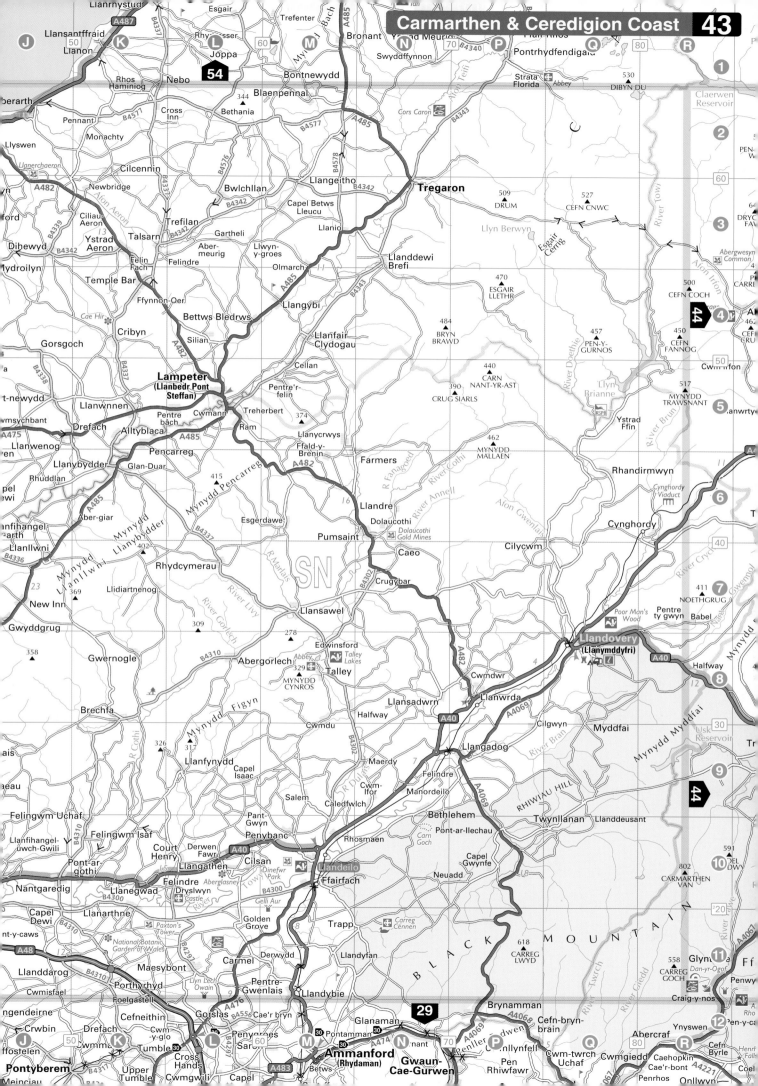

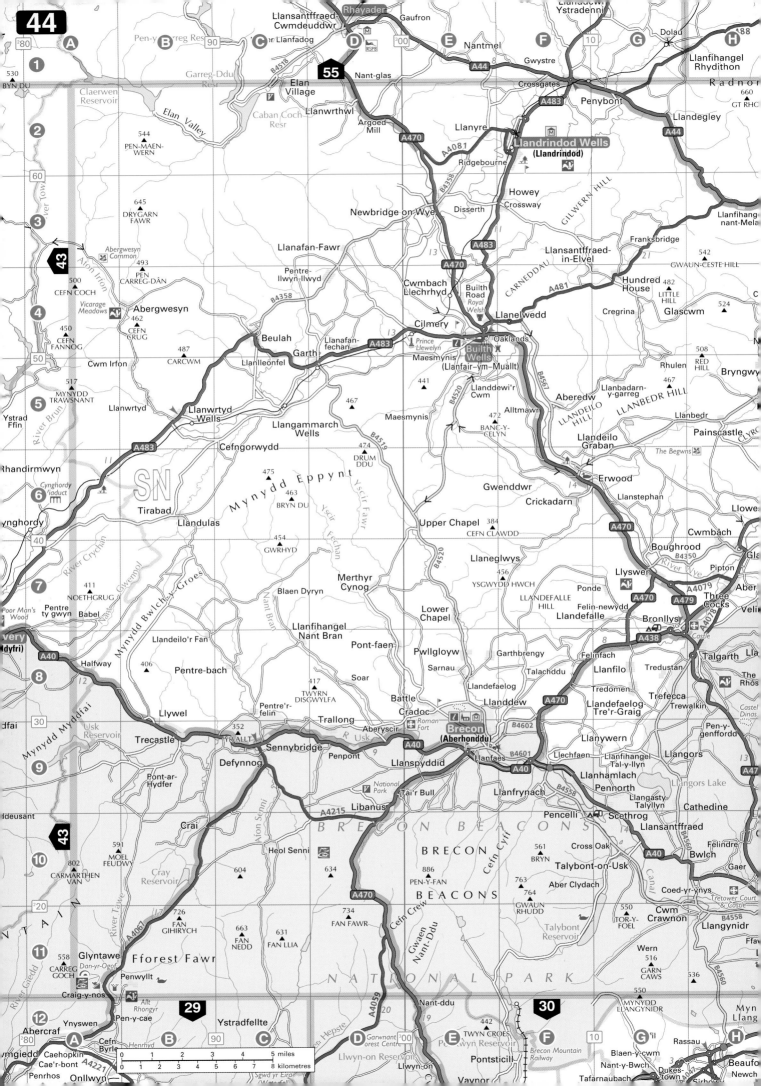

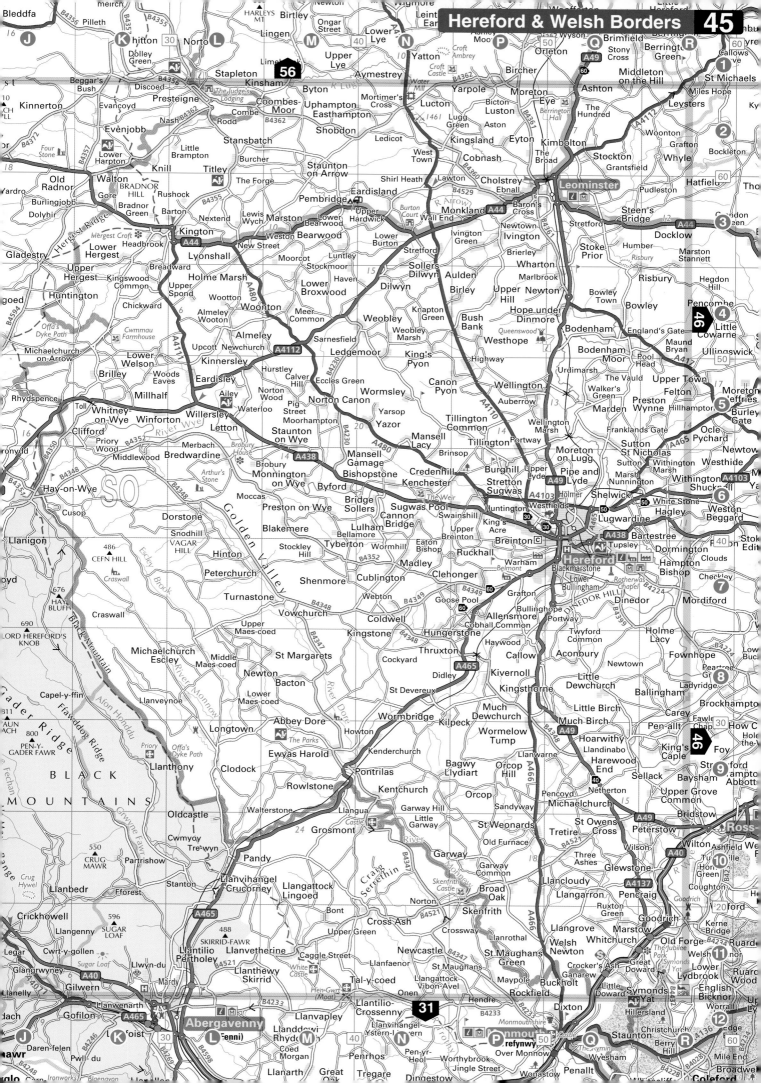

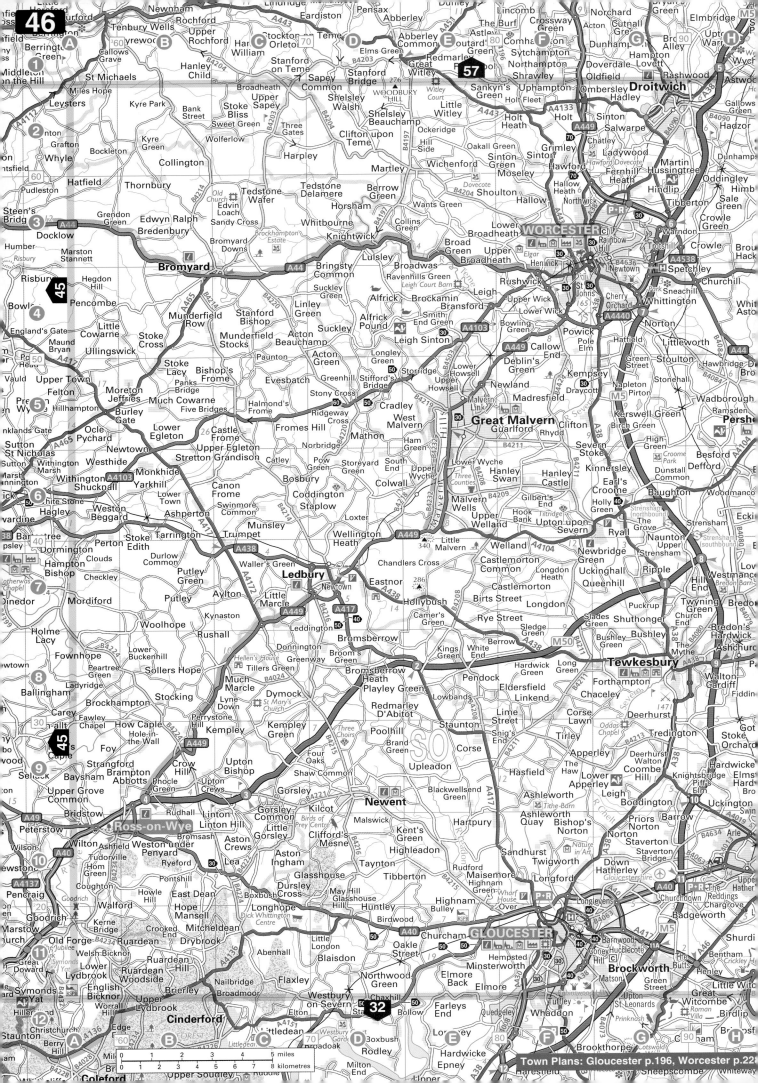

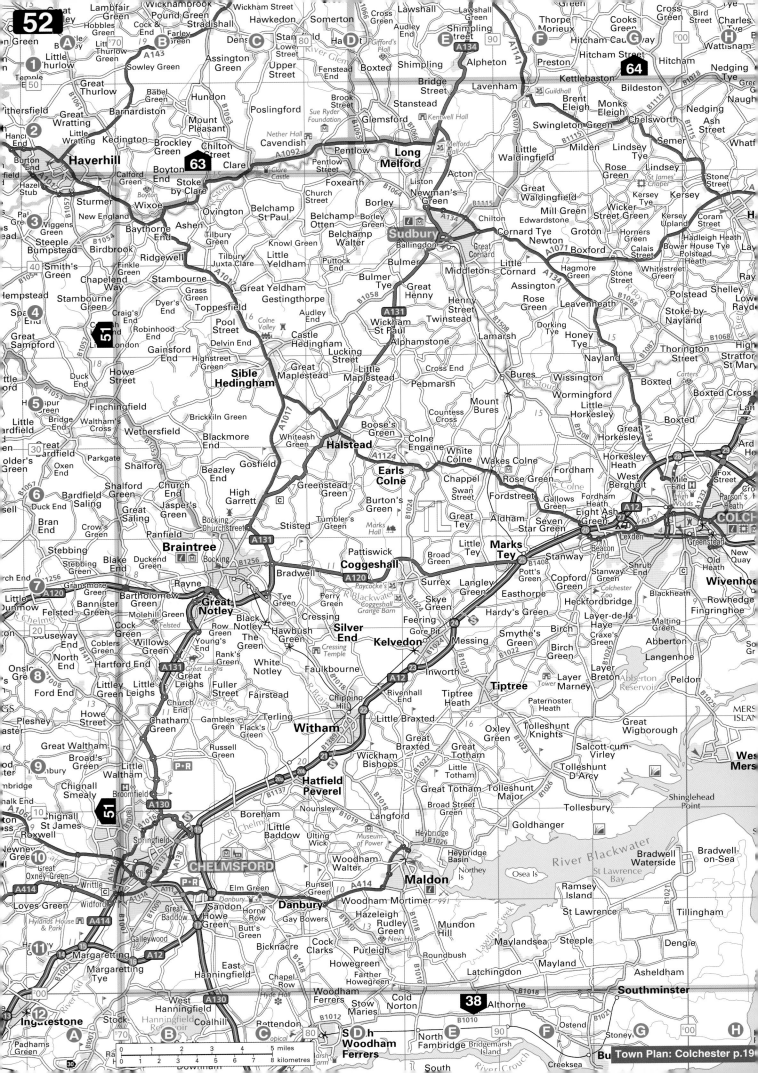

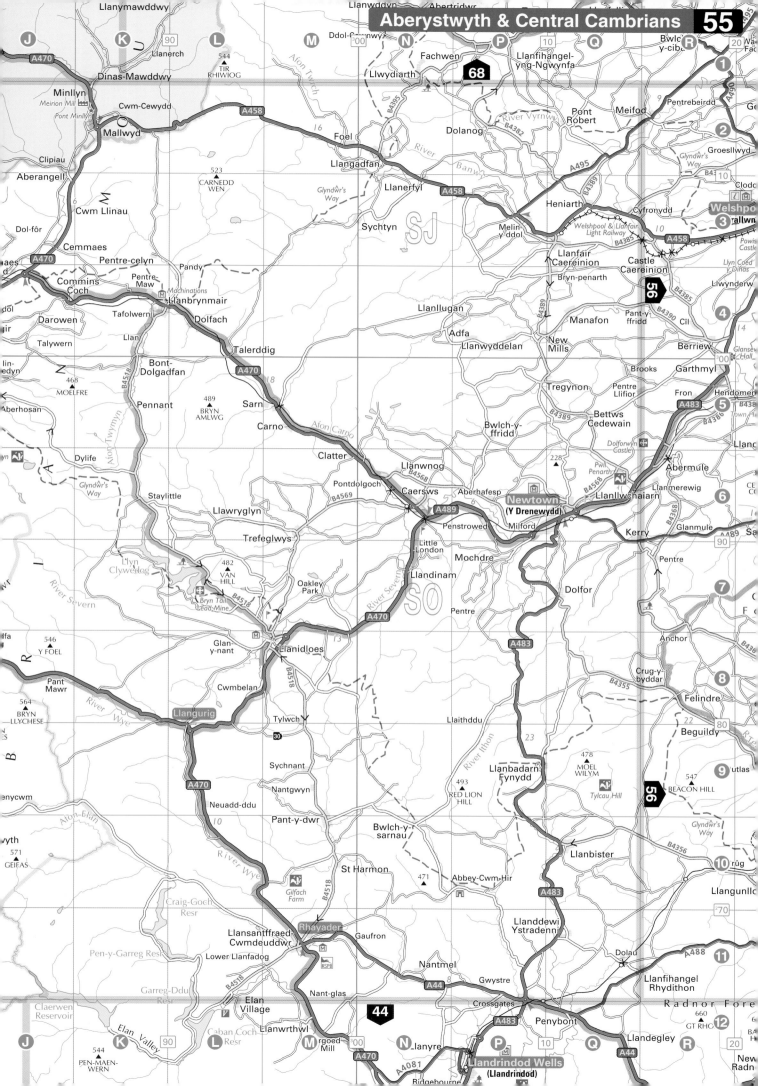

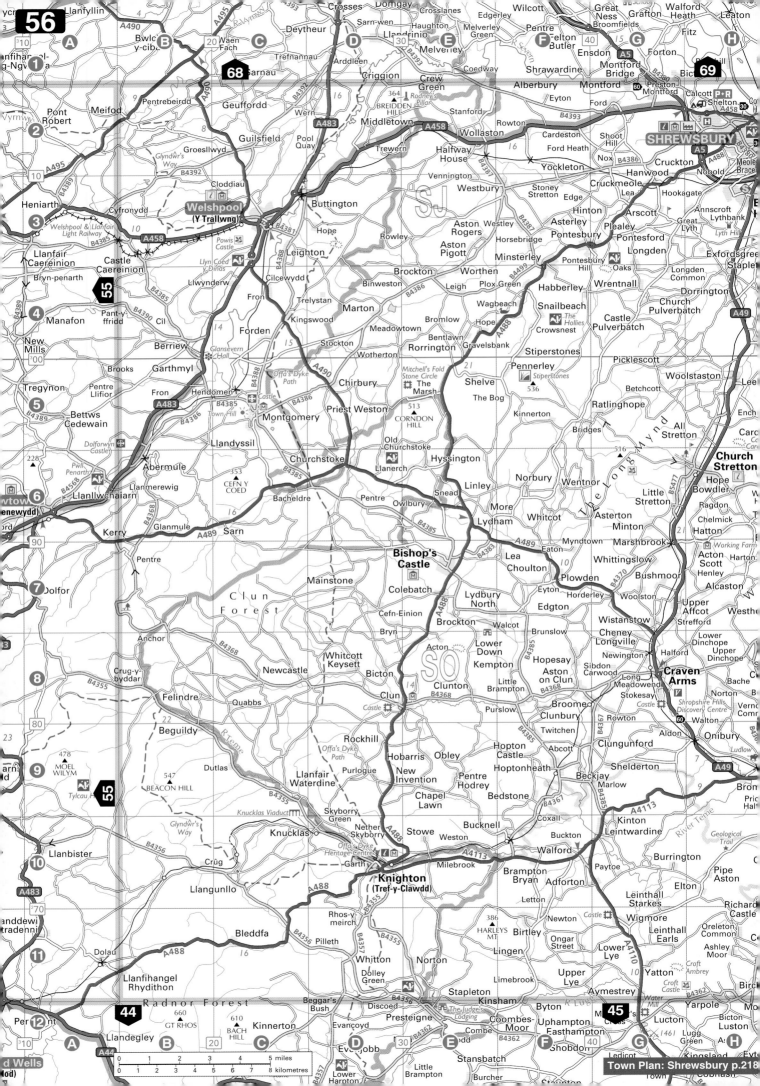

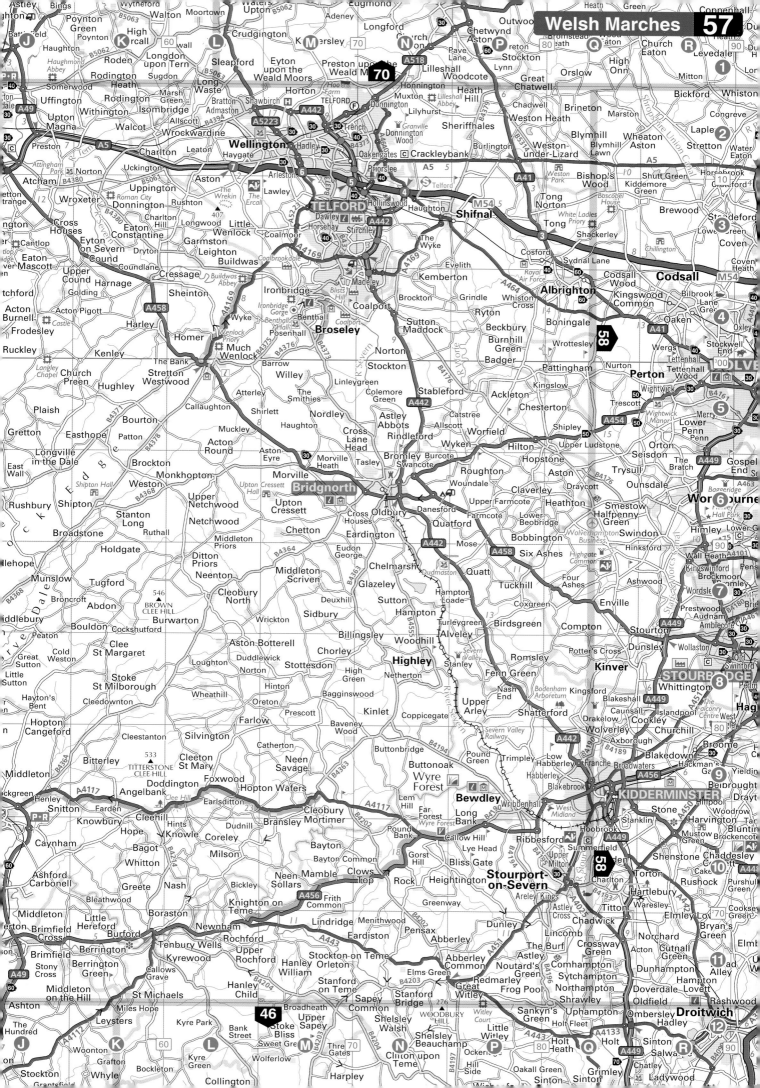

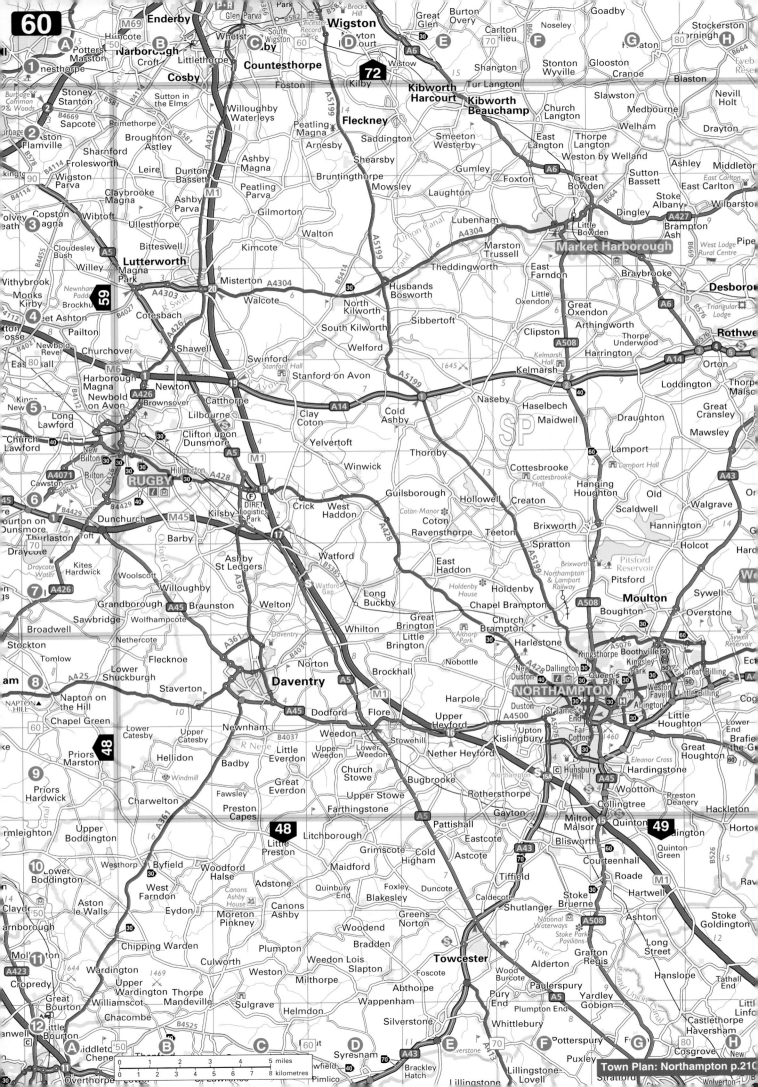

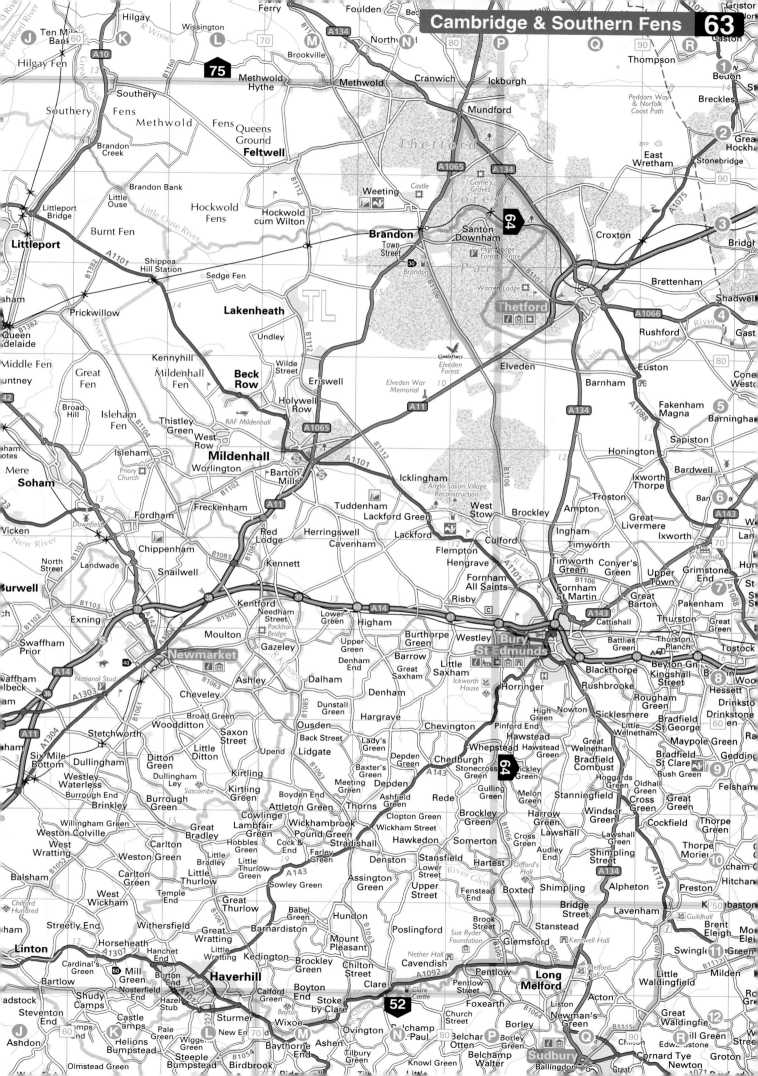

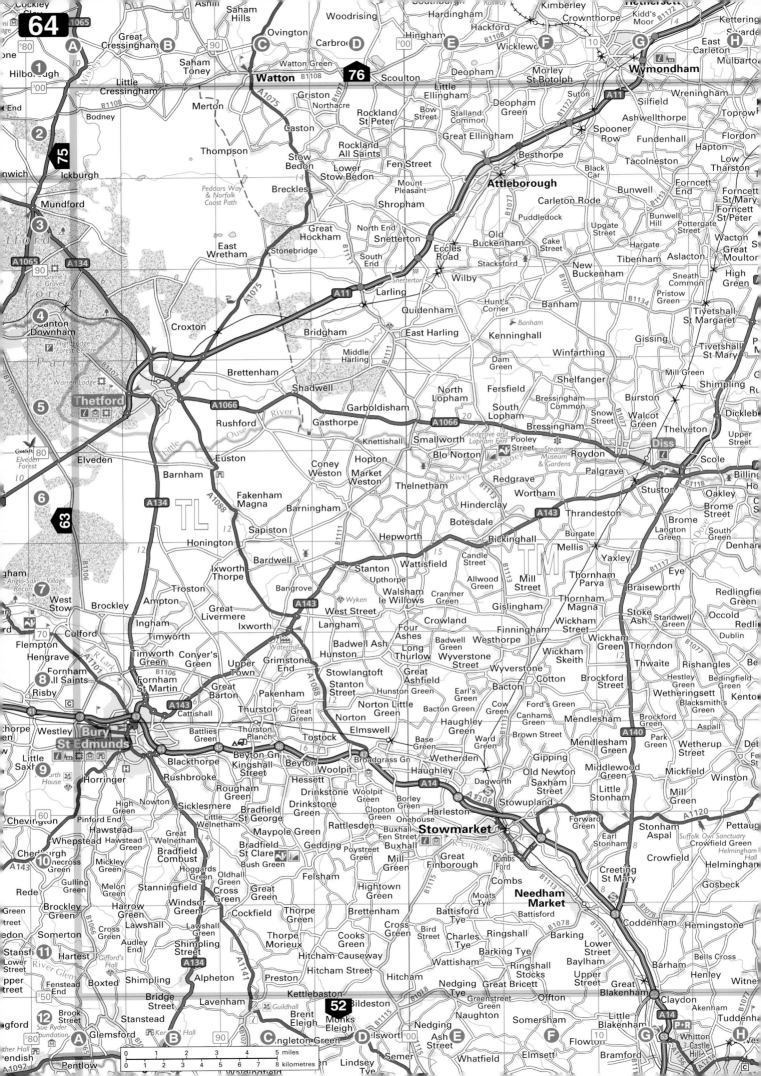

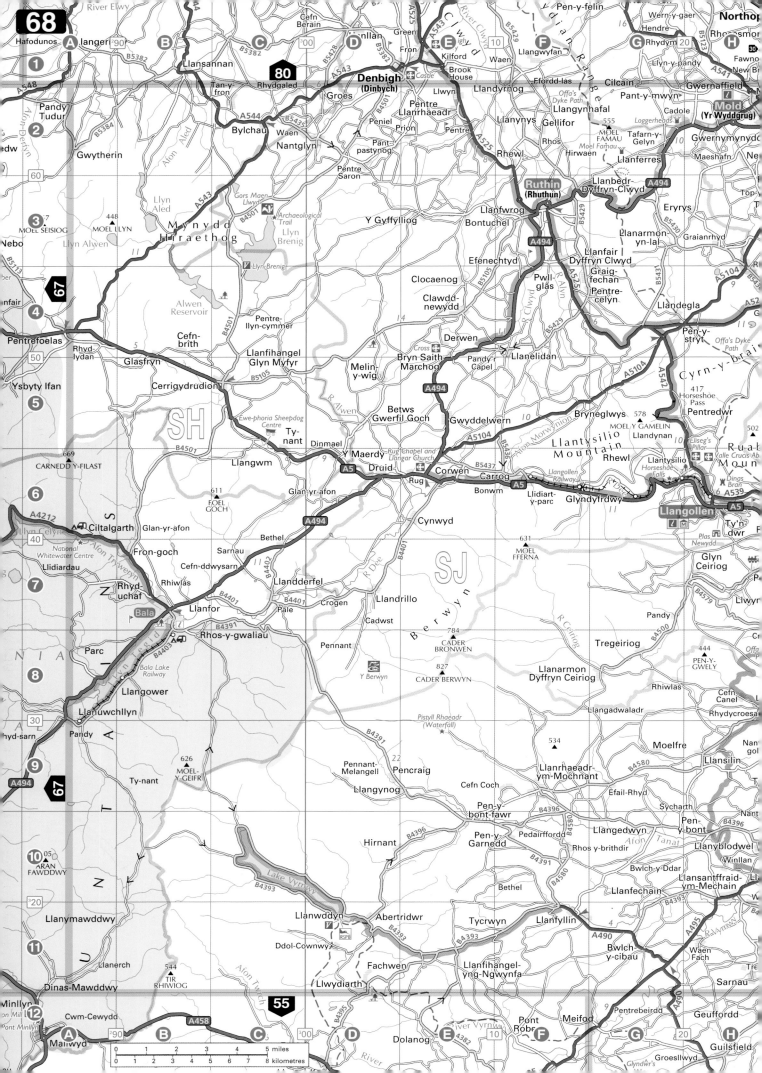

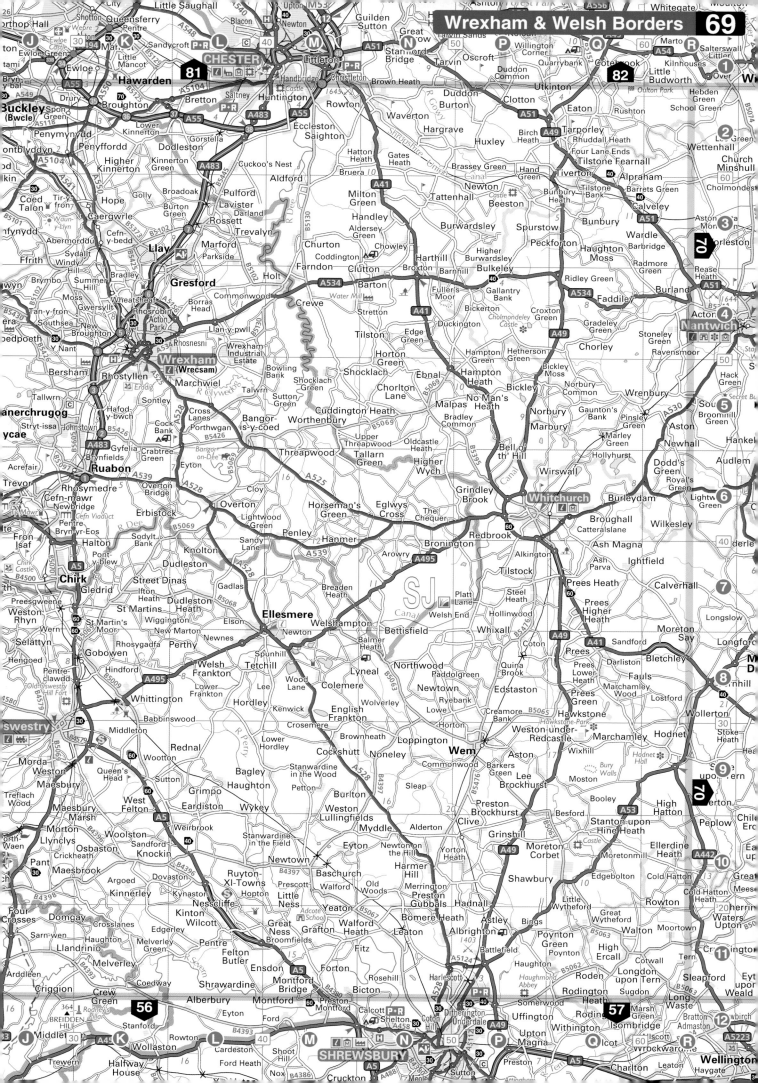

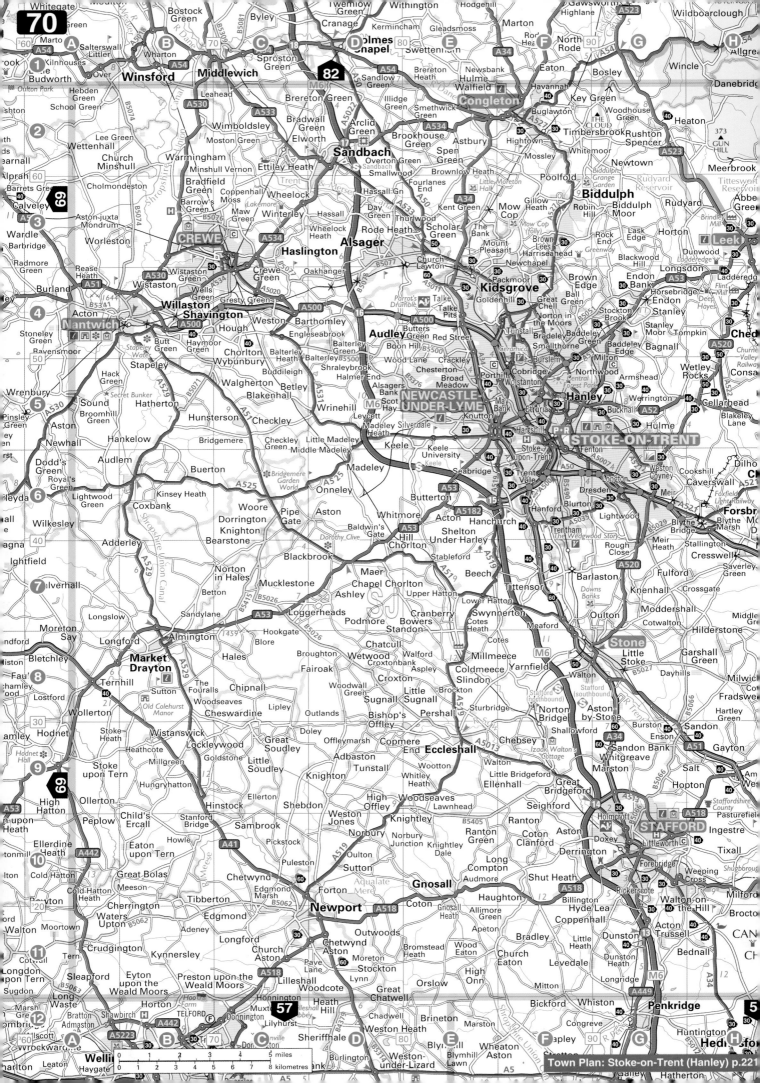

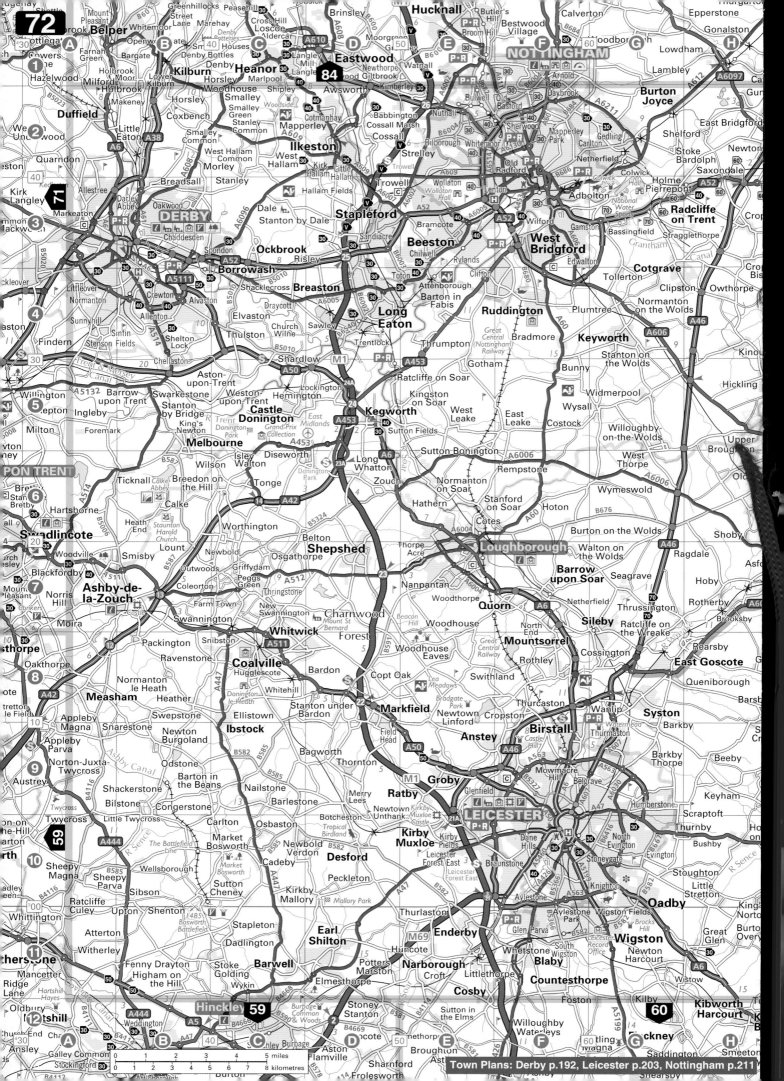

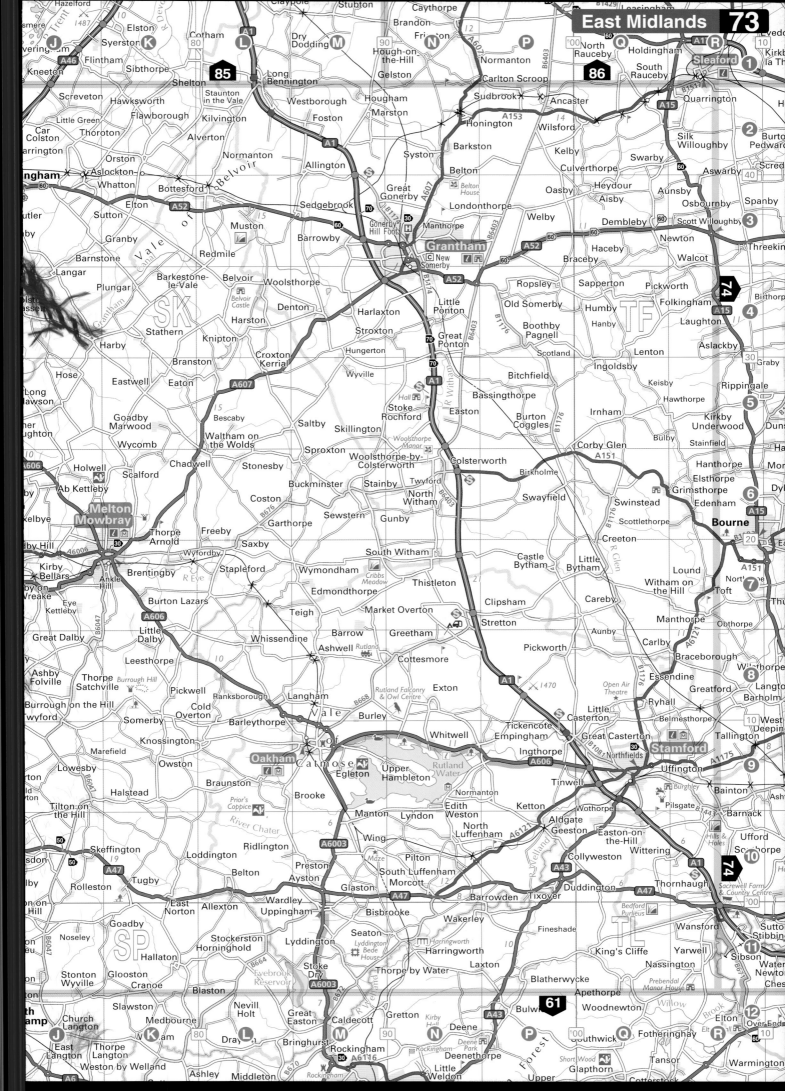

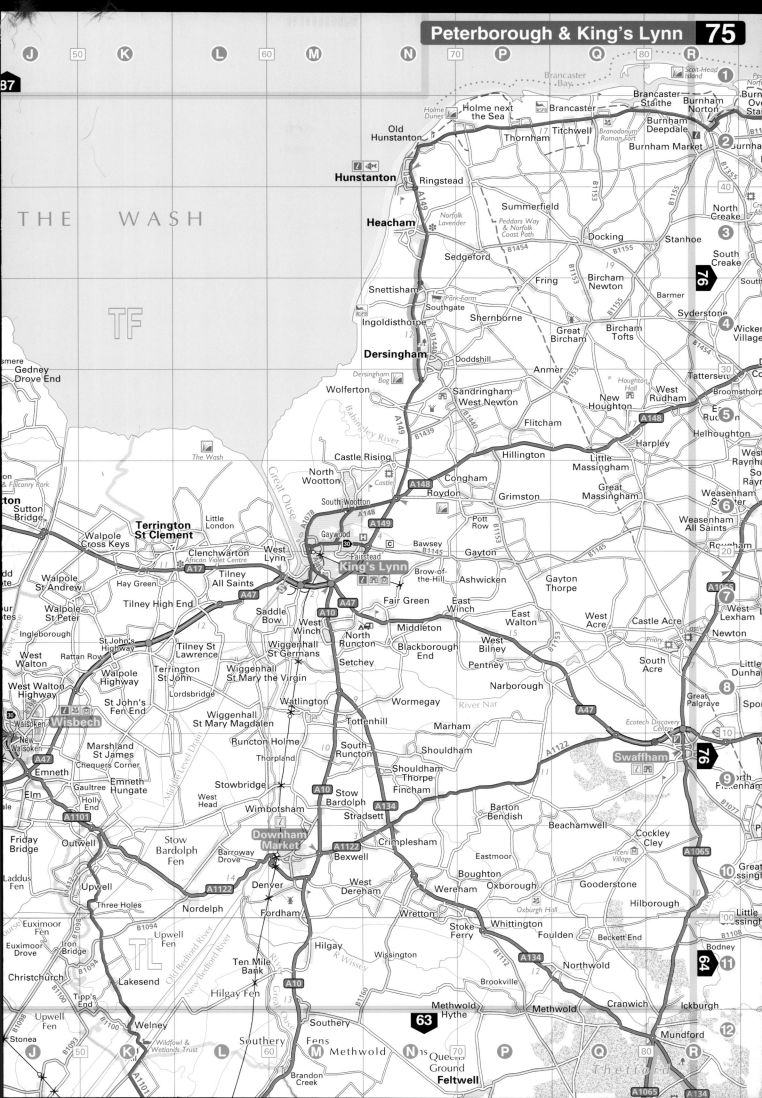

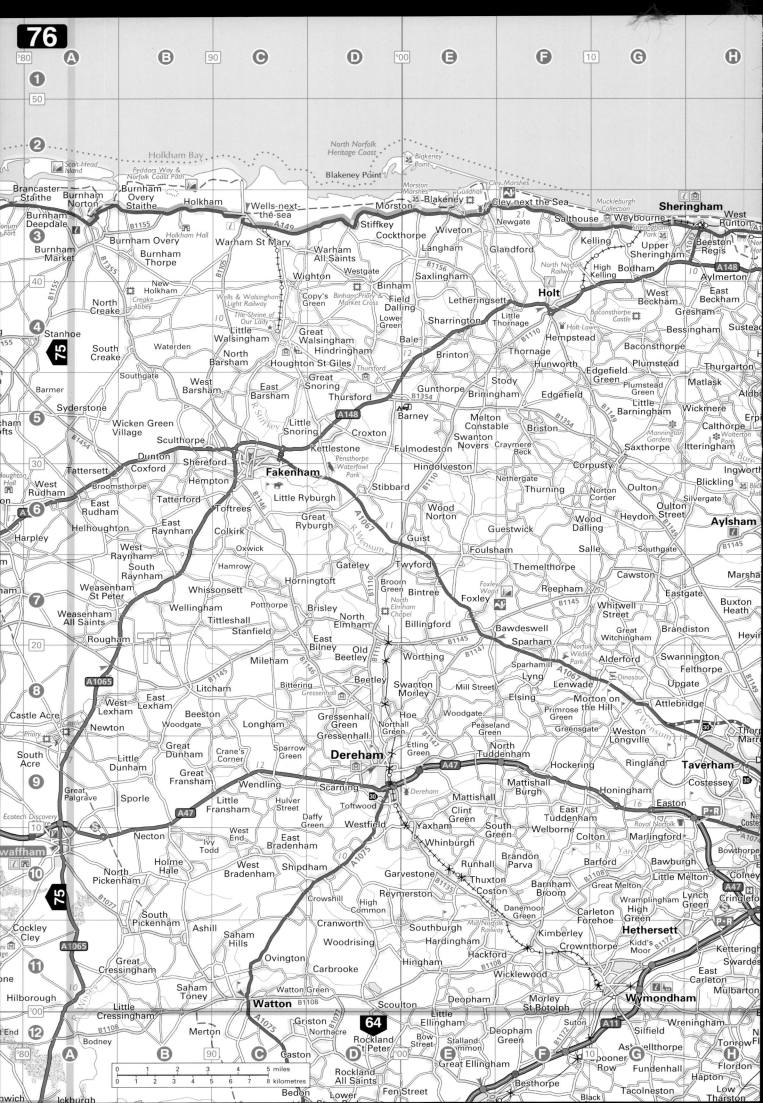

Llandudno

0   200 m

Great Orme Tramway
The Grand Hotel
TABOR HILL
OLD ROAD
PLAS ROAD
TY-COCH ROAD
HILL TERRACE
PARADE
Victoria Station
CHURCH WALKS
CWLACH
ST COURT ST
ST DAVID'S
LLEWELYN
AVENUE
NORTH
TUDNO ST
War Memorial
SOUTH PARADE
Llandudno Bay

GLODDAETH AVENUE
MOSTYN STREET
The Promenade
WHISTON PASSAGE
CLEMENT AVENUE
NEW STREET
GEORGE ST
SOMERSET ST
Town Hall
St John's
A546
BODAFON STREET
THE PARADE

DEGANWY
A546
CLONMEL STREET
CLIFTON ROAD
JAMES STREET
CLARENCE ST
Our Lady Star of the Sea
Victoria P
Holy Trinity
TRINITY SQUARE
CHARLTON STREET
Medical Centre
Adelphi
MOSTYN BROADWAY
A546
Venue Cymru
St Paul's
B5115

Conwy Archive Service
CAROLINE ROAD
ST DAVID'S PLACE
Mostyn Gallery
CONWAY ROAD
Parc Llandudno Retail Park
MOSTYN BROADWAY
Mostyn Champneys Retail Park
MOSTYN AVE

ST ANDREW'S AVENUE
LLANDUDNO STATION
VAUGHAN STREET
CYLCH TUDUR
Fire & Ambulance Station
Bowling Alley
CLARENCE CRESCENT
HASC
CAE CLYD

Ysgol Tudno
TRINITY
AVENUE
JUBILEE STREET
Police Station
GARAGE STREET
ARGYLL ROAD
Magistrates' Court
CHARLTON ROAD
CAE CLYD
CLYD
CAE CLYD DRIVE

ERYL AVENUE
KING'S AVENUE
BUILDER STREET
NORMAN ROAD
HOWARD ROAD
Superstore
FFORDD PENRHYN
CONWAY ROAD
B5115
Ysgol Craig Y Don

Ysgol Ffordd Dyffryn
DINAS ROAD
DYFFRYN ROAD
HOWBRAY ROAD
KING'S ROAD
DULYN ROAD
Coach P
COUNCIL STREET WEST
WERN WYLAN
FFORDD GWYNEDD
FFORDD DEWI
CWM
FFORDD TUDNO
FFORDD DWYFOR
CWM PLACE
MAELON
GWYDIR ROAD
CAE MAELON
A470 CONWAY ROAD
KINGSWAY
LON
CLYMLL
IDDEL ROAD
DRYC

Ysgol Morfa Rhianedd
Llandudno FC
Ysgol John Bright
BETWS-Y-COED

SH

Seawatch Centre
Moelfre
-anallgo
-arian-glas
Benllech
Red Wharf Bay
Red Wharf Bay
Puffin Island
Penmon Priory, Cross & Dovecote
Black Point
Caim
Toll
Penmon
Conwy Bay
GREAT ORMES HEAD
Great Orme Heritage Coast
Little Ormes Head
Penrhyn Bay
B5115

Glan-yr-afon
Llanddona
Llangoed
B5109
Llandudno
Llanrhos
Penrhynside
Rhôs-on-Sea
Colwyn Bay
(Bae Colwyn)
B5383
Llysfaen

Pentraeth
Llanfaes
Gaol & Courthouse
Beaumaris Castle
Dwygyfylchi
Deganwy
Conwy Bay
Tywyn
Pydew
Llandrillo-yn-Rhos
Mochdre
Colwyn
A55

A5025
B5109
Beaumaris
Penmaenmawr
Conwy
Conwy Castle
RSPB
Llandudno Junction
Llanelian-yn-Rhôs
Bryn-y-Maen
A548

inhir
Llansadwrn
Llandegfan
Capelulo
Henryd
Llansanffraid Glan Conwy
B5113
Dolwen

Menai Bridge
(Porthaethwy)
Anglesey Column
Bangor
Penrhyn
C
Llanfairfechan
A55
Penmaenan
SNOWDONIA
610
TAL-Y-FAN
Rowen
Ty'n-y-Groes
B5106
A470
Graig
Eglwysbach
River Elwy

air P G
Britannia Bridge
Penrhos
garneddn
Plas Newydd
H
A4087
A55
Nant-y-pandy
Garizim
Gorddinog
Abergwyngregyn
Caerhun
Tal-y-Cafn
Pentre'r Felin
Betws
Ta

Capel-y-graig
Waen-wen
A55
Llandygai
Tal-y-bont
Aber Waterfall
NATIONAL
Llanbedr-y-Cennin
Tal-y-Bont
Dolgarrog
Bodnant
Tal-y-Cafn
80
Dawn
Trofarth

inheli
Green Wood Forest Park
B4547
Glasinfryn
Rhyd-y-groes
580
MOEL WINION
Afon Anafon
757
Y DROSGL
942
FOEL-FRAS
Afon Dulyn
Hafodunos
Llang
Ll

Bethel
Llanddeiniolen
Seion
Pentir
Rachub
Bethesda
Gerlan
PARK
Pont Dolgarrog
Maenan
Llanddoget
River Elwy
B538

Saron
Penisarwaun
Rhiwlas
Waen-pentir
Mynydd Llandygai
Ogwen Bank
Afon Caseg
Llyn Eigiau
Vale of Conwy
Pandy Tudur
B538

Llanrug
Rhiwen
Deiniolen
1062
CARNEDD LLEWELYN
Trefriw Woollen Mill
Gwydir Castle
Pentre-tafarn-y-fedw
Gwytherin

-ont-rug
Clwt-y-bont
60
Gallt-y-foel
1044
CARNEDD DAFYDD
67
Llyn Cowlyd
Llanrhychwyn
Llanrwst
B5113

Llanberis Lake Railway
923
Dinorwic
ELIDIR FAWR
442
Pont Pen-
Llyn Ogwen
Afon Crafn
Tre-
Melin
A5
A5

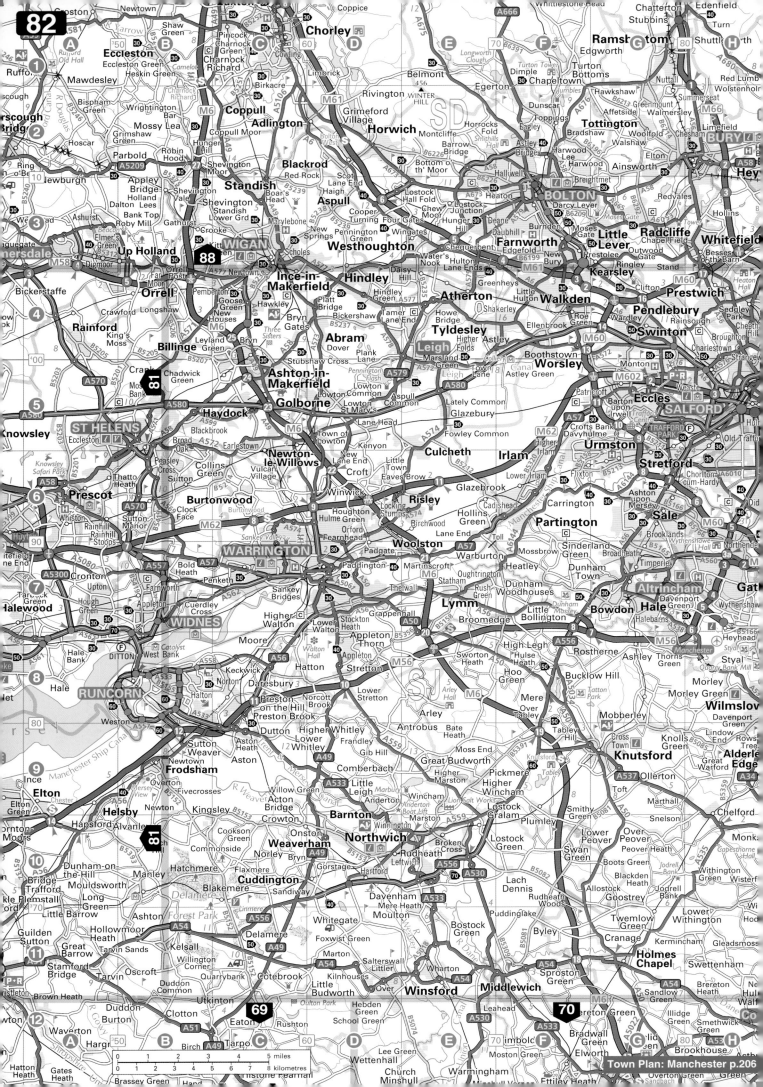

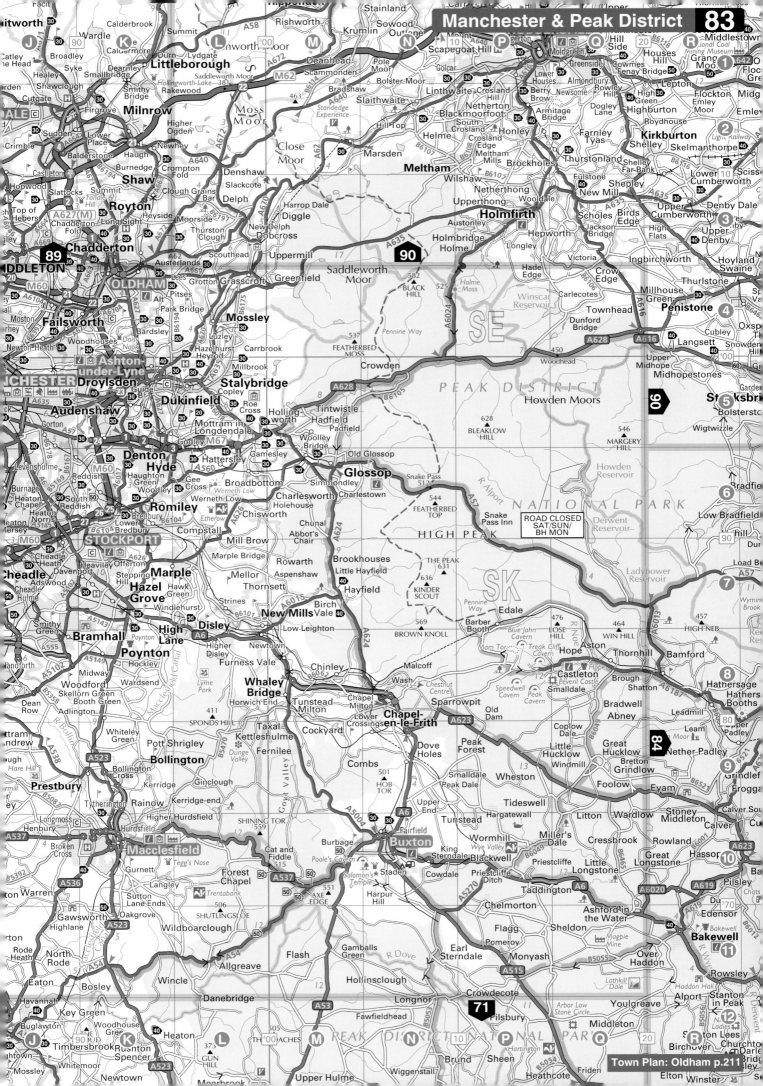

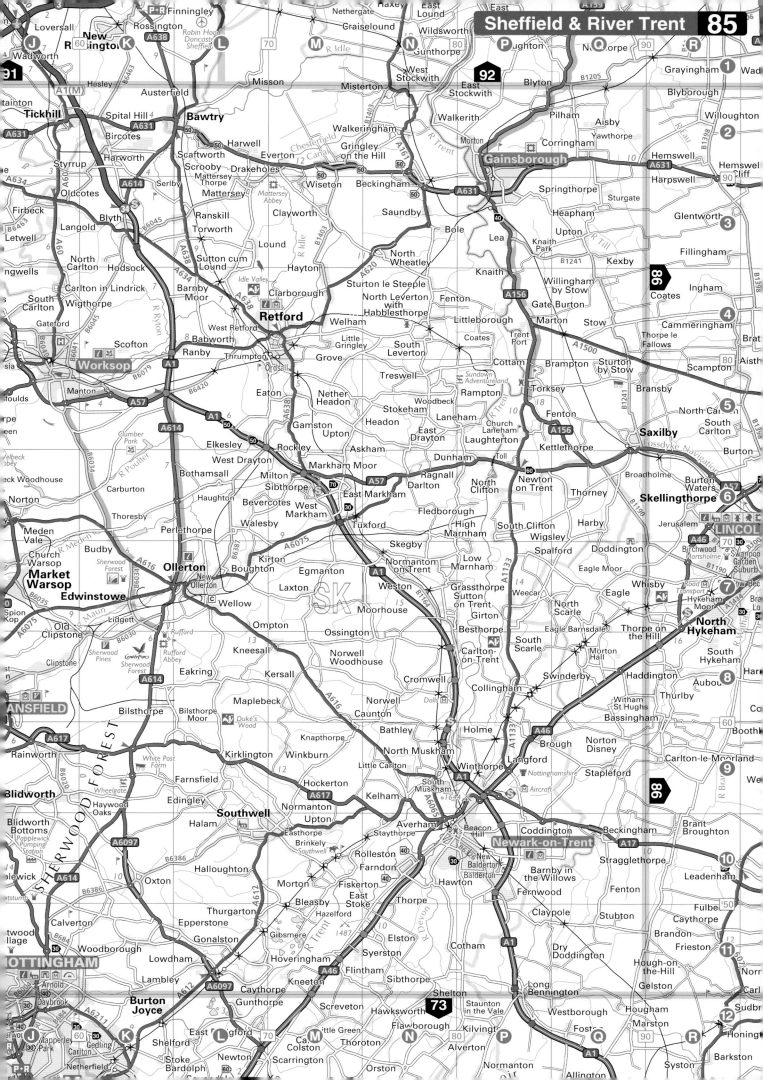

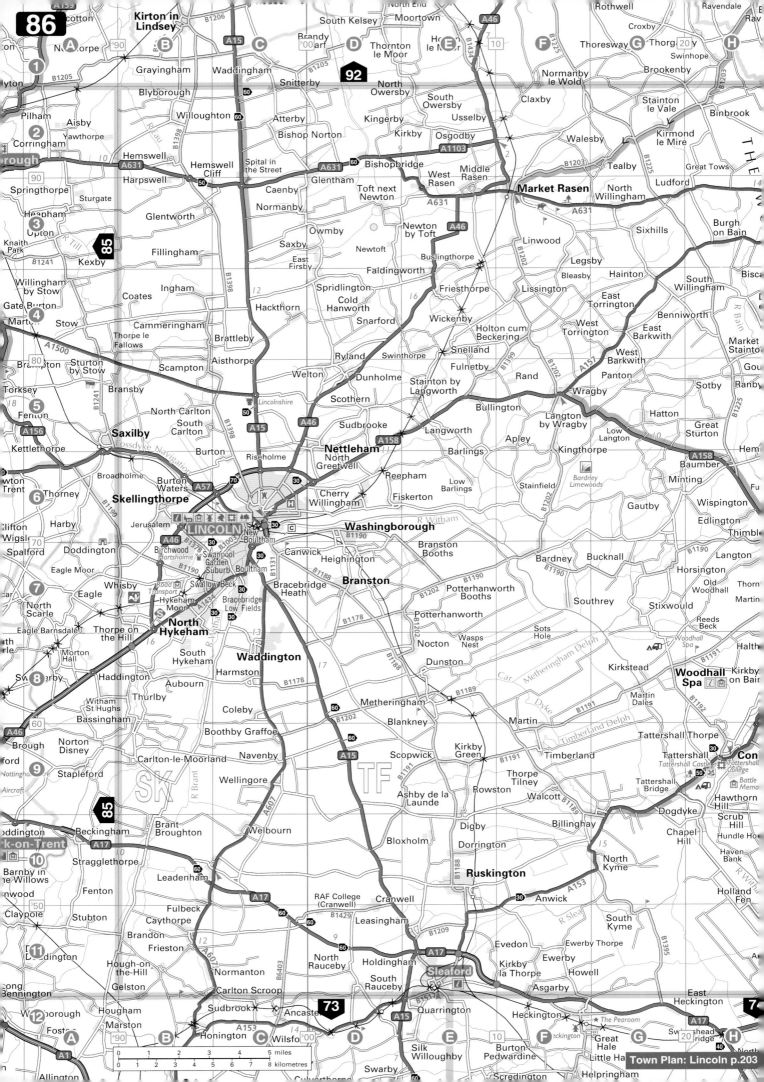

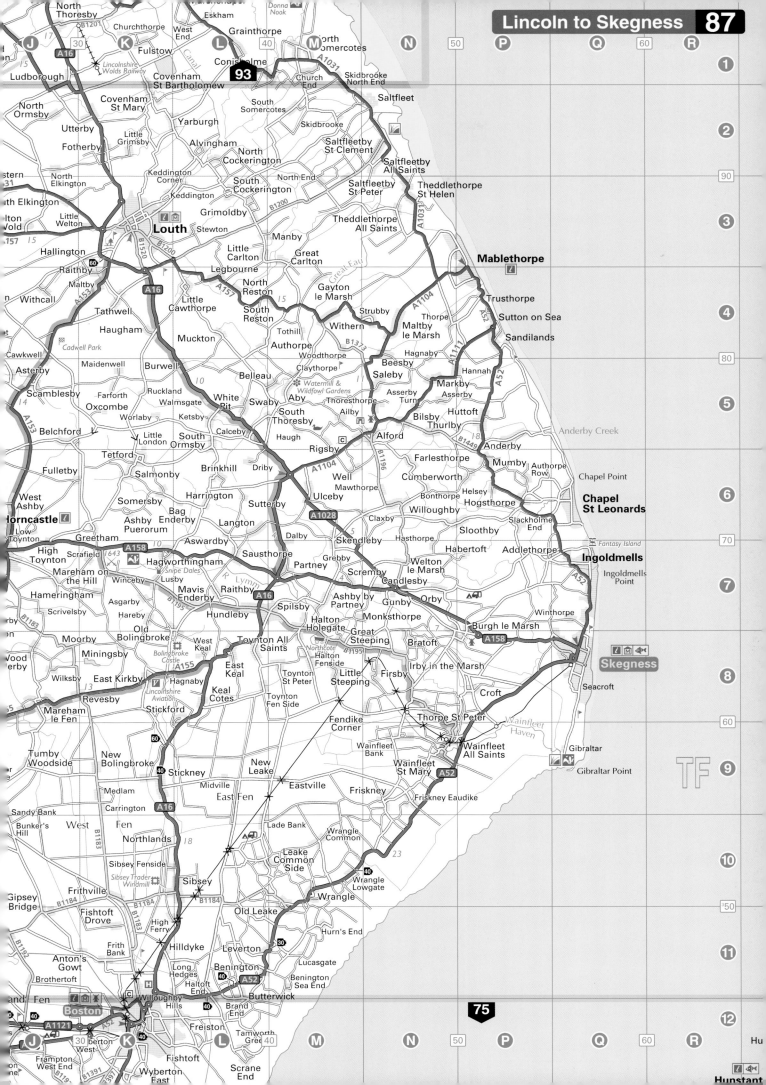

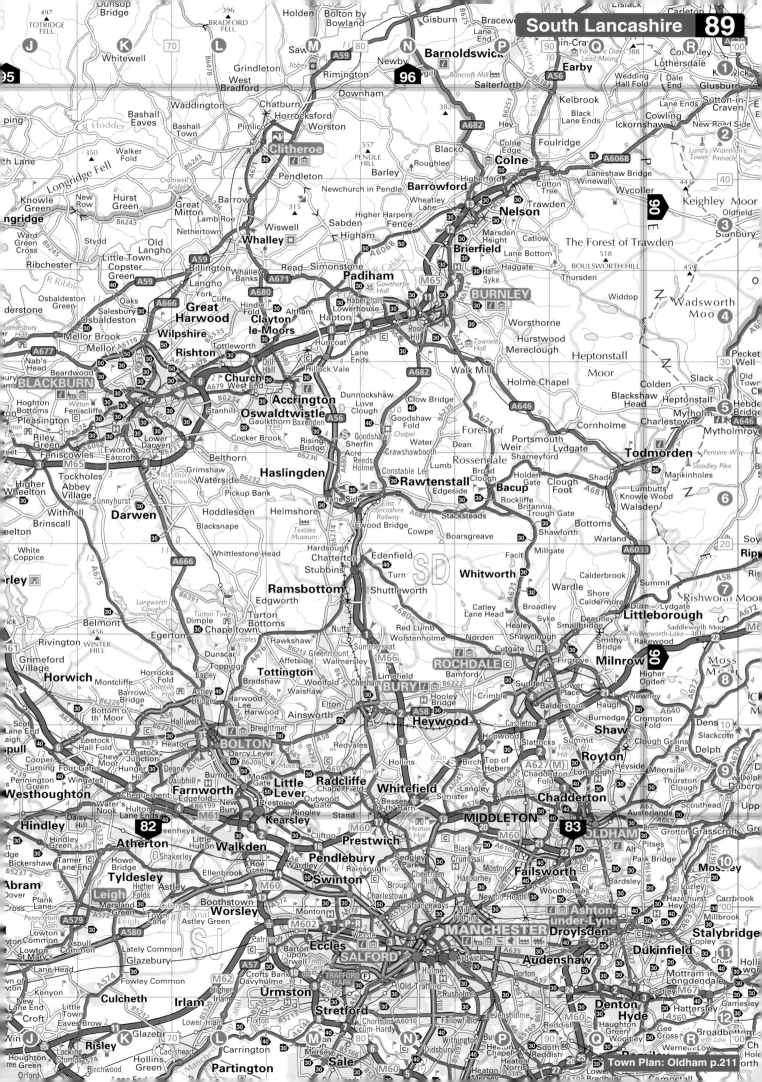

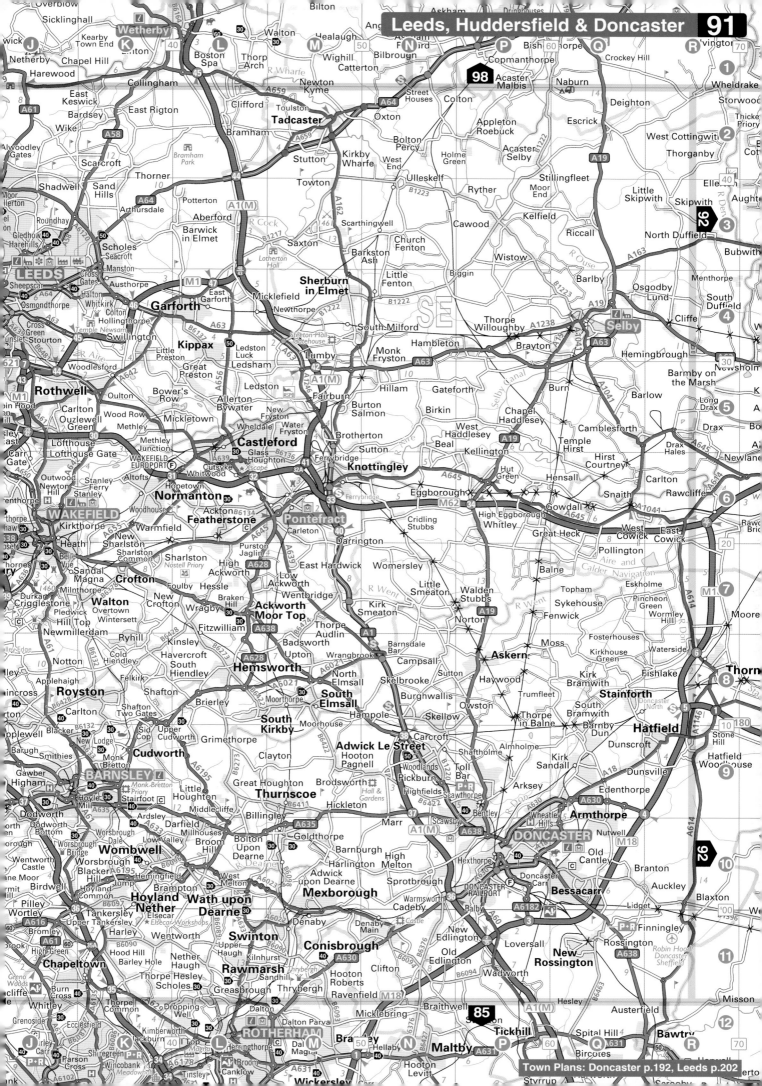

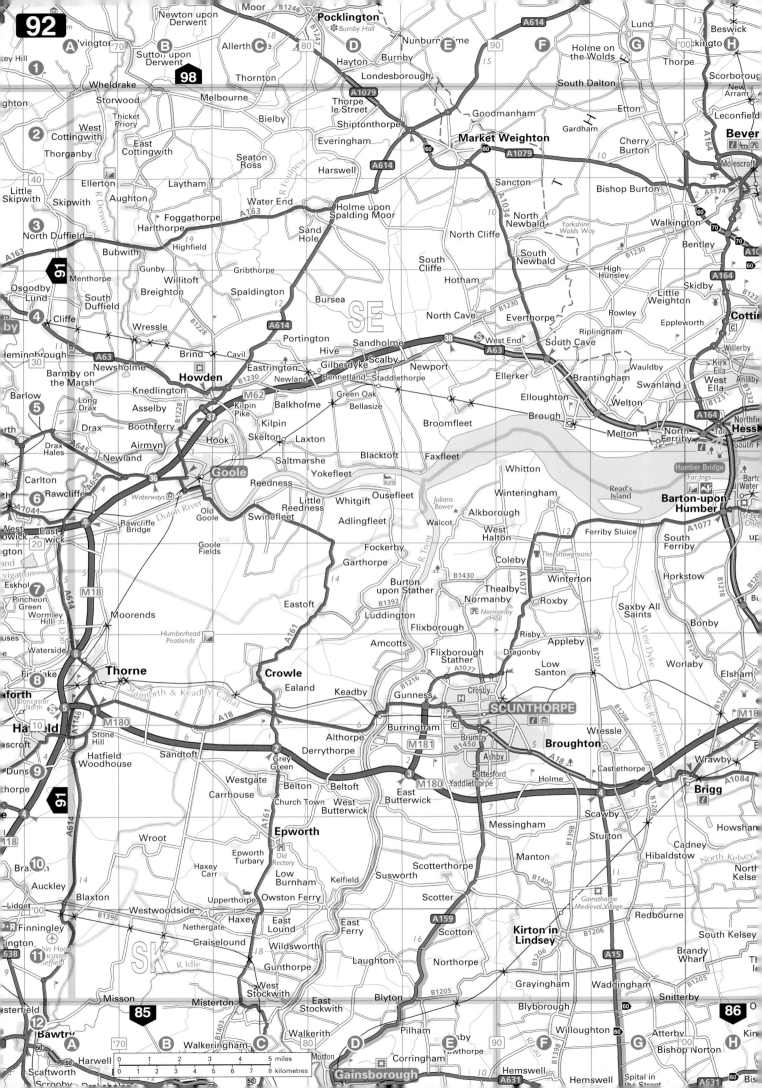

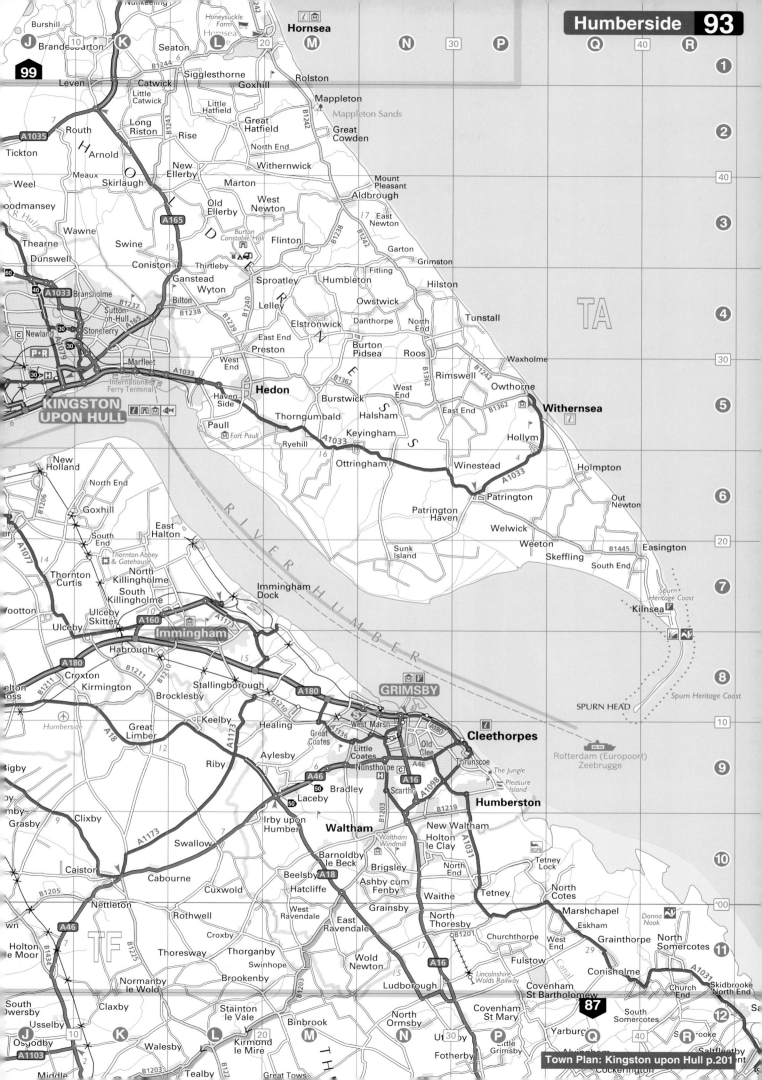

Town Plan: Kingston upon Hull p.201

99

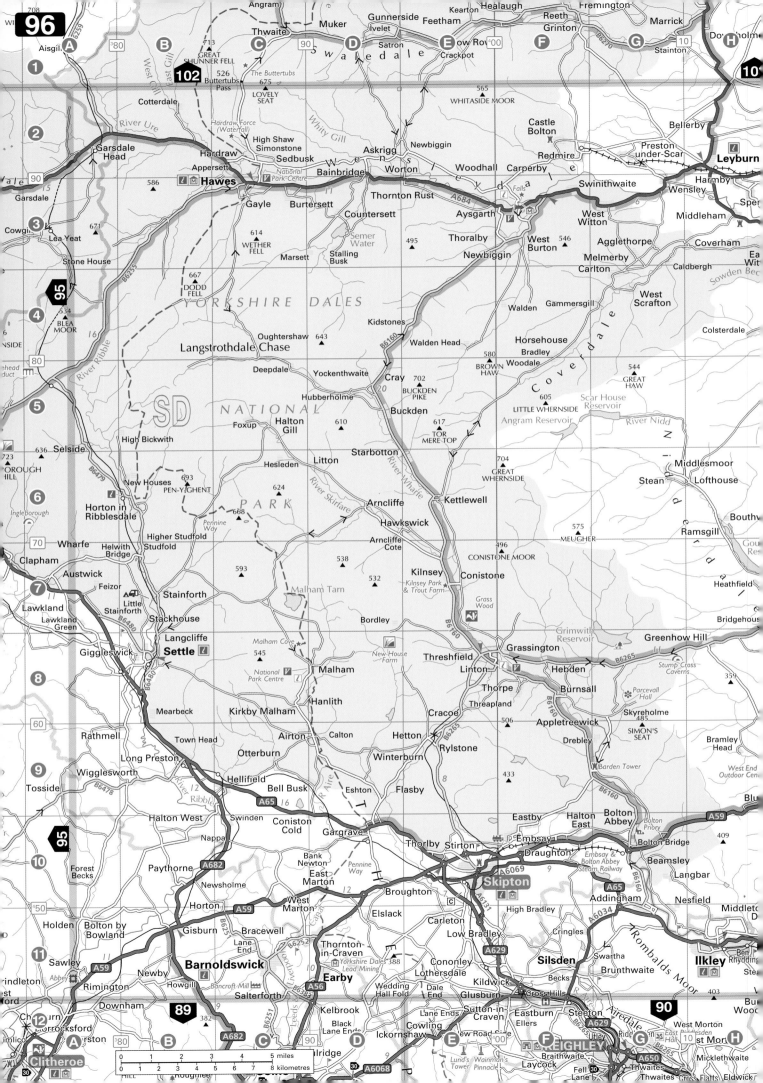

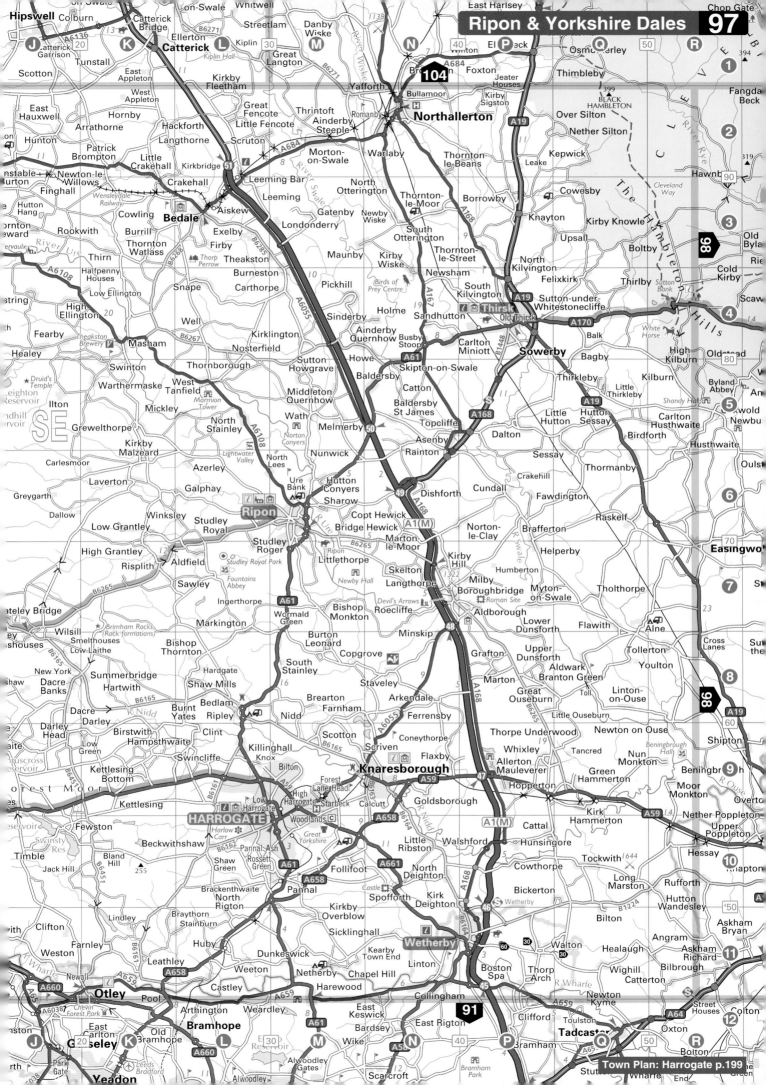

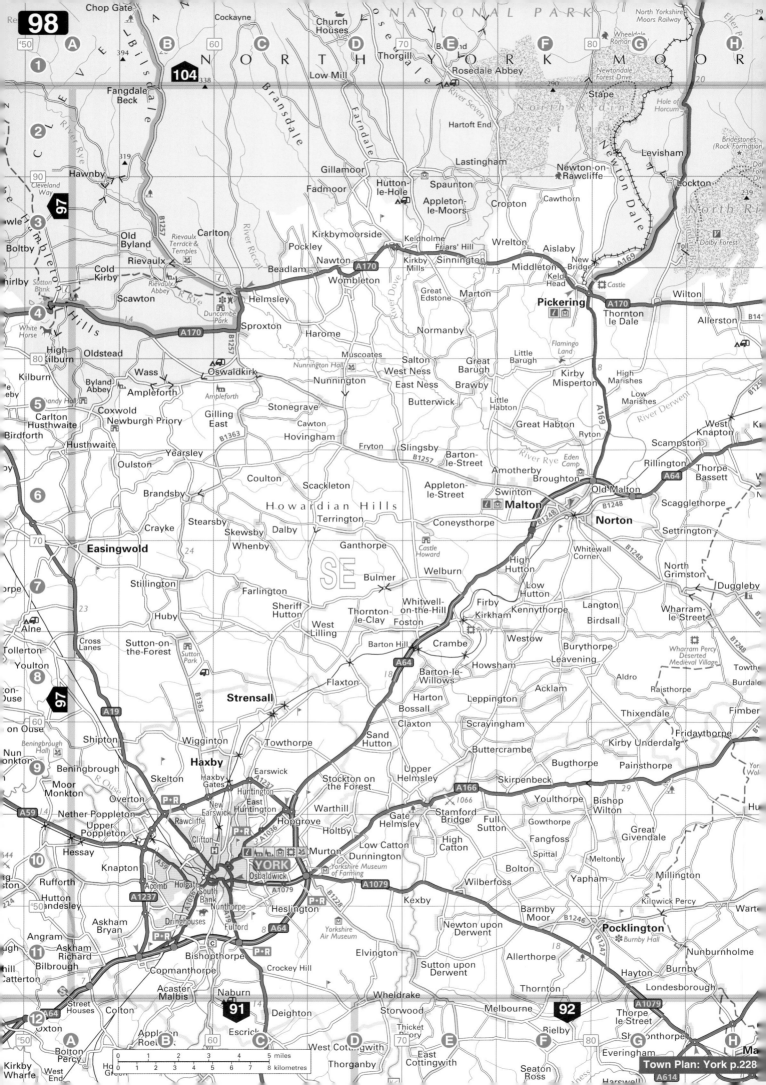

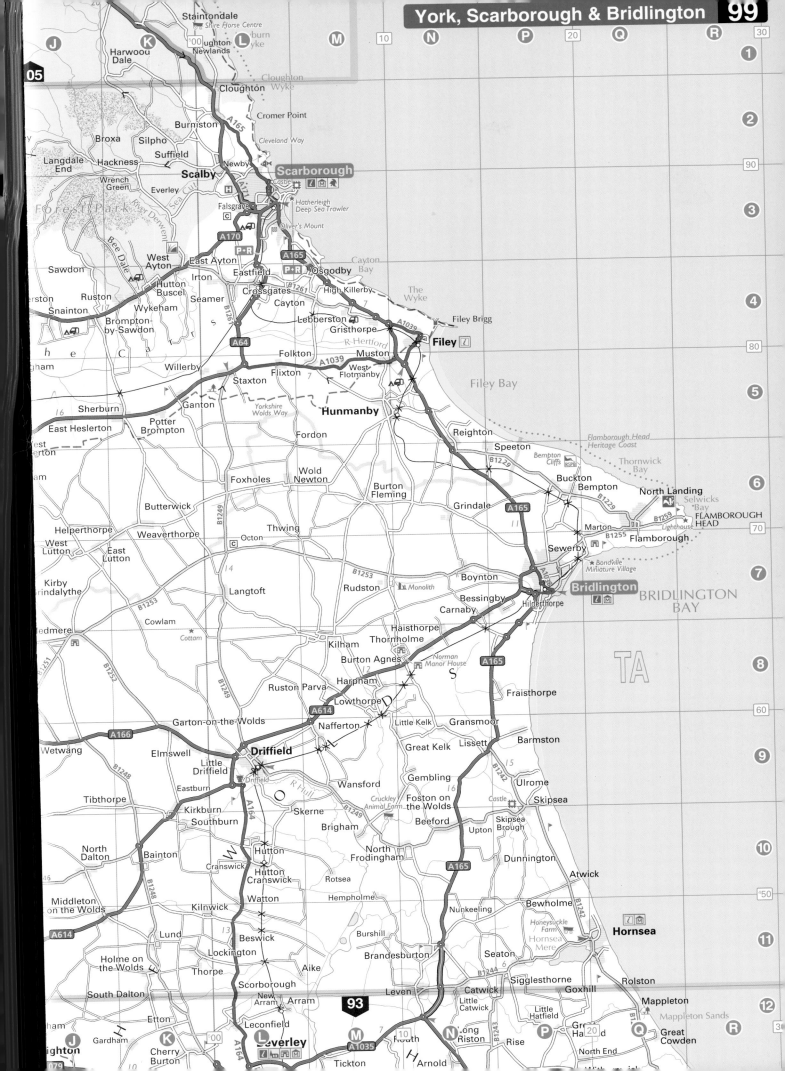

J   K   L   M   N   P   Q   R

05

Staintondale
Shire Horse Centre
Staughton Newlands
Cloughton Wyke
Cloughton
Cromer Point
Burniston
Cleveland Way
Broxa   Silpho
Suffield
Scalby
Newby
Langdale End   Hackness
Wrench Green
Everley
Forest Park
River Derwent
Sawdon
Scarborough
Castle
Hatherleigh Deep Sea Trawler
Falsgrave
Oliver's Mount
West Ayton
East Ayton
Eastfield
Osgodby
Cayton Bay
Irton
Ruston   Seamer
Hutton Buscel
Crossgates
High Killerby
The Wyke
Wykeham
Cayton
Brompton-by-Sawdon
Lebberston
Gristhorpe
Filey Brigg
Willerby
Folkton   Muston
Filey
R-Hertford
Flixton   West Flotmanby
Sherburn   Ganton   Staxton
Hunmanby
Filey Bay
East Heslerton
Potter Brompton
Yorkshire Wolds Way
Reighton
Speeton
Flamborough Head Heritage Coast
Fordon
Bempton Cliffs
Thornwick Bay
Foxholes   Wold Newton
Butterwick   Burton Fleming
Buckton   Bempton
North Landing
Helperthorpe   Weaverthorpe
Thwing
Grindale
Selwicks Bay
FLAMBOROUGH HEAD
West Lutton   East Lutton
Octon
Marton   Flamborough
Lighthouse
Kirby Grindalythe
Langtoft
Rudston   Monolith
Boynton
Sewerby
Bondville Miniature Village
Cowlam
Cottam
Bessingby
Hilderthorpe
Bridlington
BRIDLINGTON BAY
Kilham
Thornholme   Haisthorpe
Carnaby
Burton Agnes   Norman Manor House
TA
Ruston Parva
Harpham
Lowthorpe
Gransmoor
Garton-on-the-Wolds
Nafferton   Little Kelk
Great Kelk   Lissett
Barmston
Wetwang   Elmswell
Driffield
Gembling   Ulrome
Tibthorpe   Little Driffield
Eastburn
Wansford
Castle   Skipsea
Kirkburn   Southburn
R Hull
Skerne
Cruckley Animal Farm
Foston on the Wolds
Skipsea Brough
North Dalton   Bainton
Hutton
Brigham
Beeford   Upton
Dunnington
Atwick
Cranswick
Hutton Cranswick
North Frodingham
Middleton on the Wolds
Kilnwick   Watton
Rotsea
Hempholme
Bewholme
Hornsea
Lund
Beswick
Burshill
Seaton
Honeysuckle Farm
Holme on the Wolds
Lockington   Aike
Brandesburton
Hornsea Mere
Thorpe
South Dalton
Scorborough
Leven   Catwick
Sigglesthorne   Goxhill
Rolston
93
New Arram   Arram
Little Catwick
Mappleton
Mappleton Sands
Leconfield
Little Hatfield
North End
Great Cowden
J   K   L   **Beverley**   M   N   P   Q   R
Gardham
Cherry Burton
Tickton   Arnold
Leighton
Long Riston
Rise

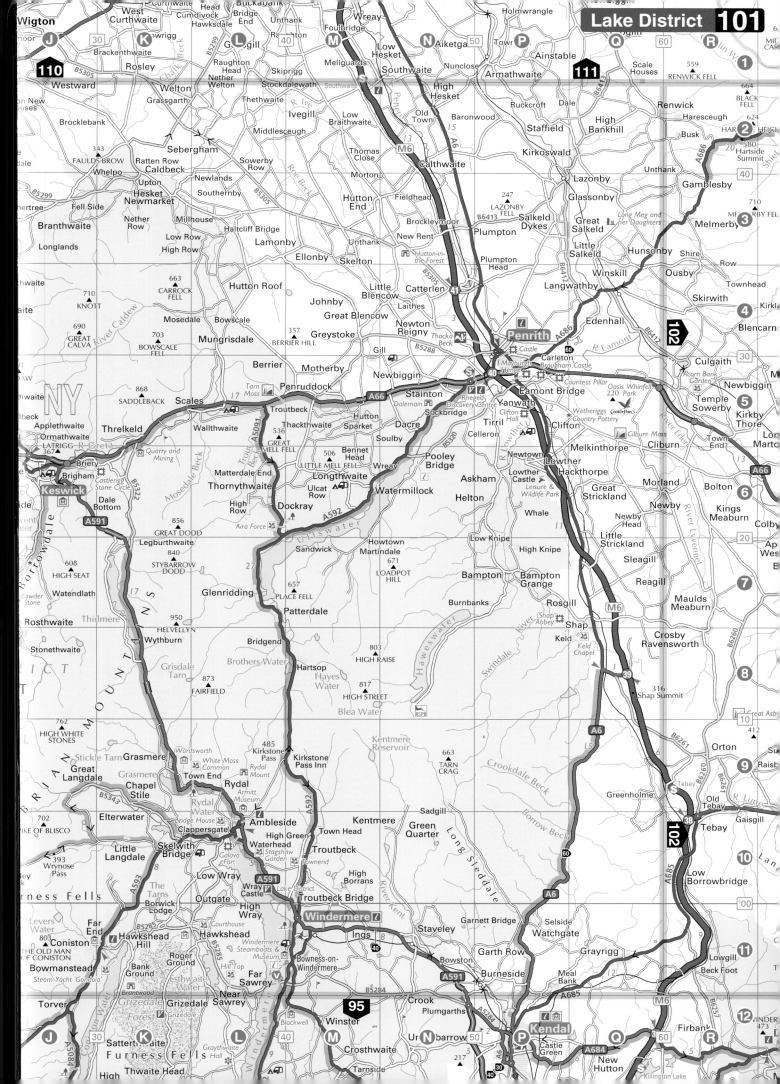

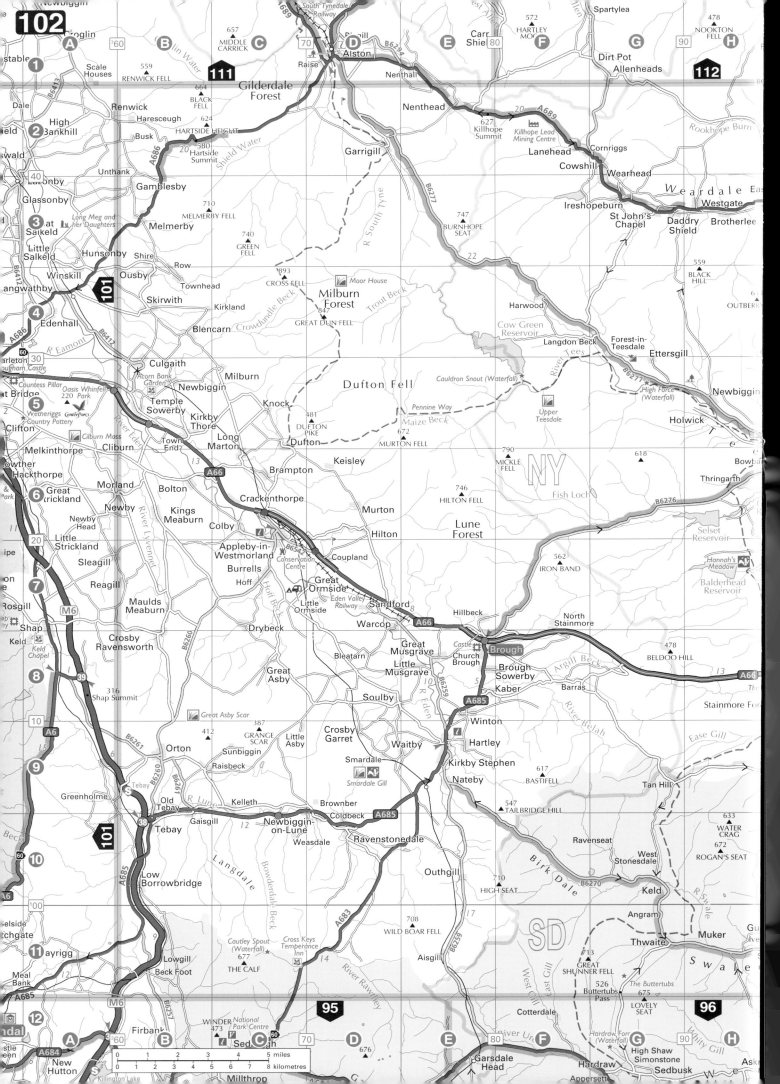

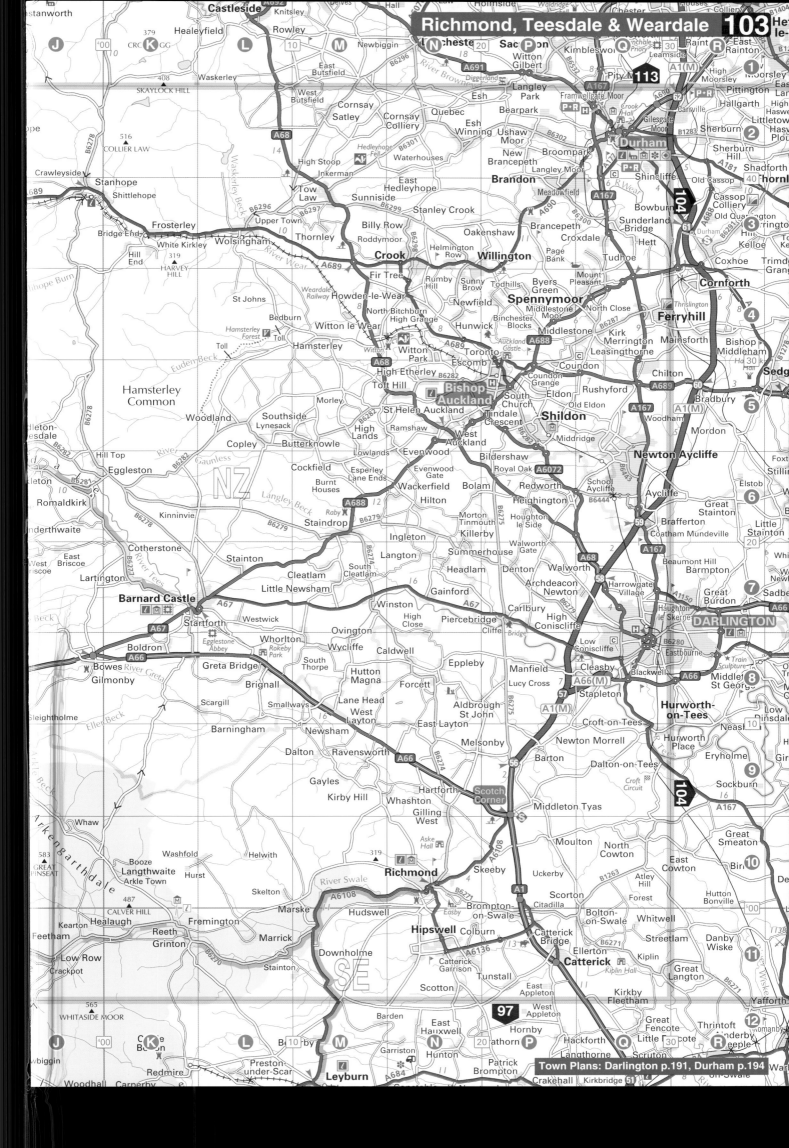

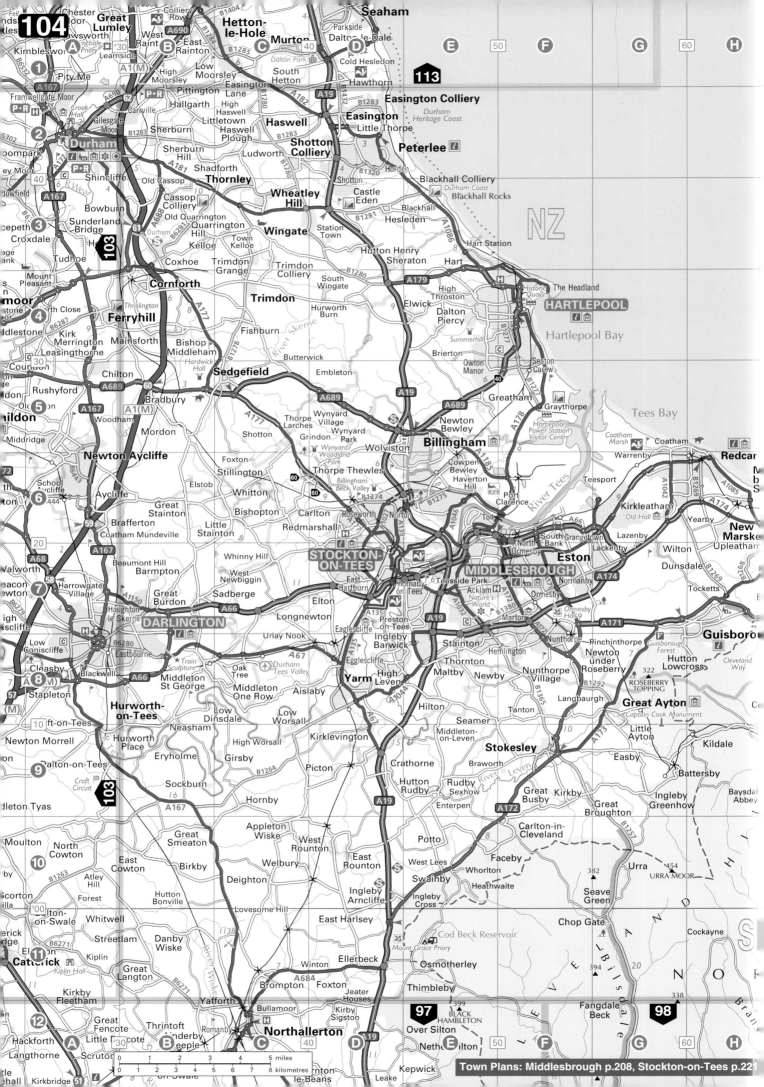

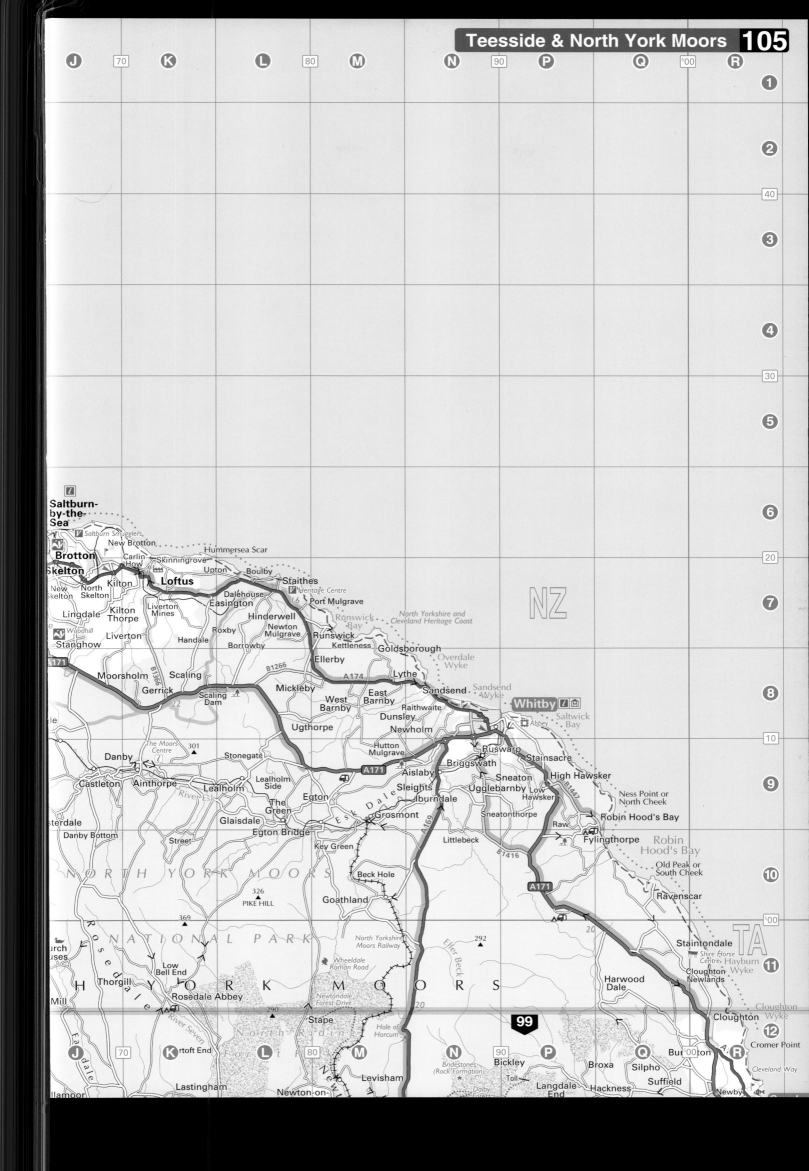

J 70 K L 80 M N 90 P Q '00 R

1
2
40
3
30
4
5
6
20
7
NZ
8
10
9
10
'500
TA
11
99
12

Saltburn-by-the-Sea

New Brotton
Saltburn Smugglers
Brotton
Carlin How
Skinningrove
Hummersea Scar
Skelton
Kilton
Loftus
Upton
Boulby
New Skelton
North Skelton
Staithes
Heritage Centre
Lingdale
Kilton Thorpe
Liverton Mines
Dalehouse
Easington
Port Mulgrave
Woodhill
Handale
Roxby
Hinderwell
Newton Mulgrave
Runswick Bay
Liverton
Borrowby
Runswick
Kettleness
Goldsborough
North Yorkshire and Cleveland Heritage Coast
Stanghow
Overdale Wyke
A171
Moorsholm
Scaling
B1266
Ellerby
Lythe
Sandsend
Sandsend Wyke
Gerrick
Scaling Dam
Mickleby
A174
22
West Barnby
East Barnby
Raithwaite
Whitby
Saltwick Bay
Ugthorpe
Dunsley
Newholm
Abbey
The Moors Centre
301
Stonegate
Hutton Mulgrave
Ruswarp
Stainsacre
Danby
Aislaby
Briggswath
Castleton
Ainthorpe
Lealholm
Lealholm Side
River Esk
Sleights
Sneaton
High Hawsker
Low Hawsker
Grosmont
Ugglebarnby
Iburndale
Ness Point or North Cheek
The Green
Egton
Esk Dale
Sneatonthorpe
Robin Hood's Bay
Glaisdale
Egton Bridge
Littlebeck
Raw
Fylingthorpe
Danby Bottom
Street
Key Green
B1416
Robin Hood's Bay
NORTH YORK MOORS
Beck Hole
Old Peak or South Cheek
326
PIKE HILL
Goathland
A171
Ravenscar
369
NATIONAL PARK
North Yorkshire Moors Railway
292
Staintondale
Church uses
Rosedale
Wheeldale Roman Road
Harwood Dale
Shire Horse Centre
Hayburn Wyke
Low Bell End
Eller Beck
Cloughton Newlands
HYORK MOORS
Thorgill
Newtondale Forest Drive
Cloughton
290
River Seven
Cloughton Wyke
Rosedale Abbey
Stape
Hole of Horcum
99
Cromer Point
Bickley
Broxa
Silpho
Cleveland Way
Bridestones (Rock Formation)
Toll
Suffield
Hartoft End
Langdale End
Hackness
Lastingham
Levisham
Newton-on-
Newby
illamoor
Dalby Forest

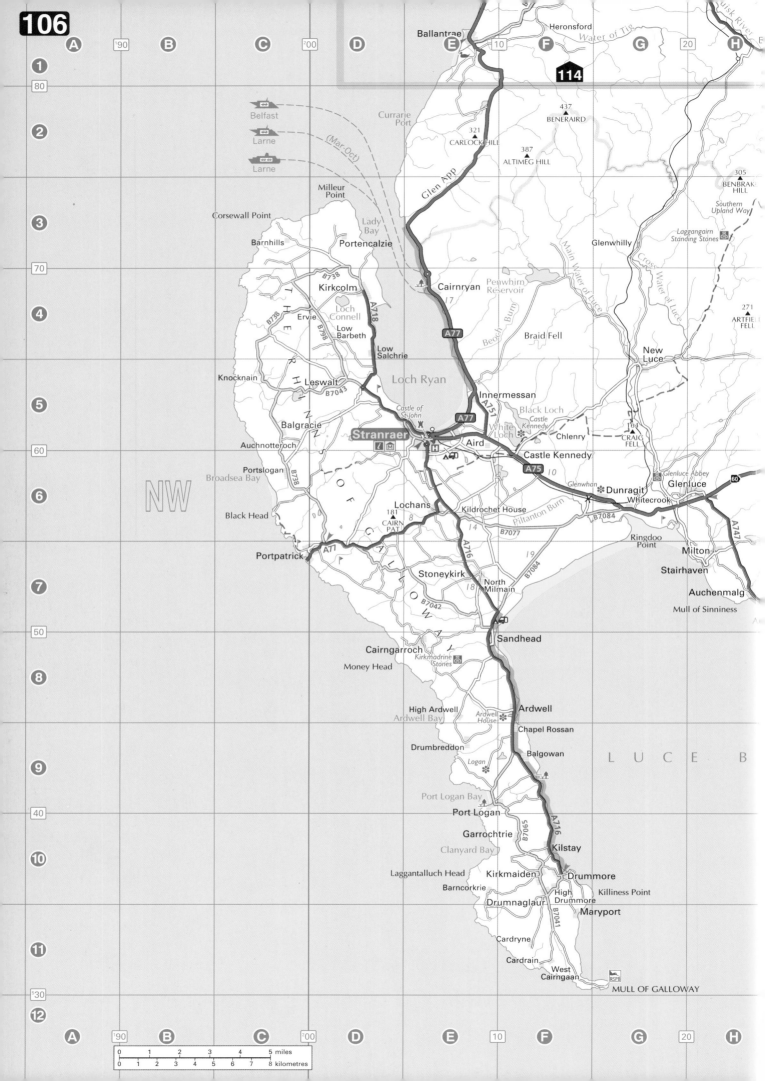

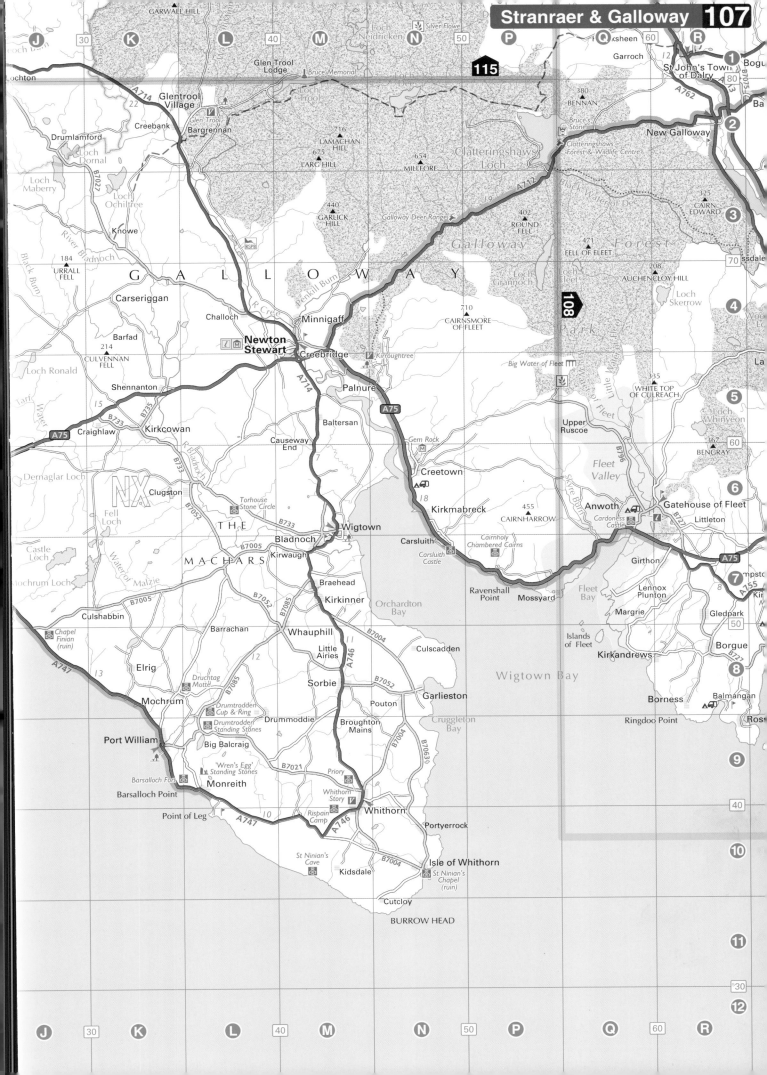

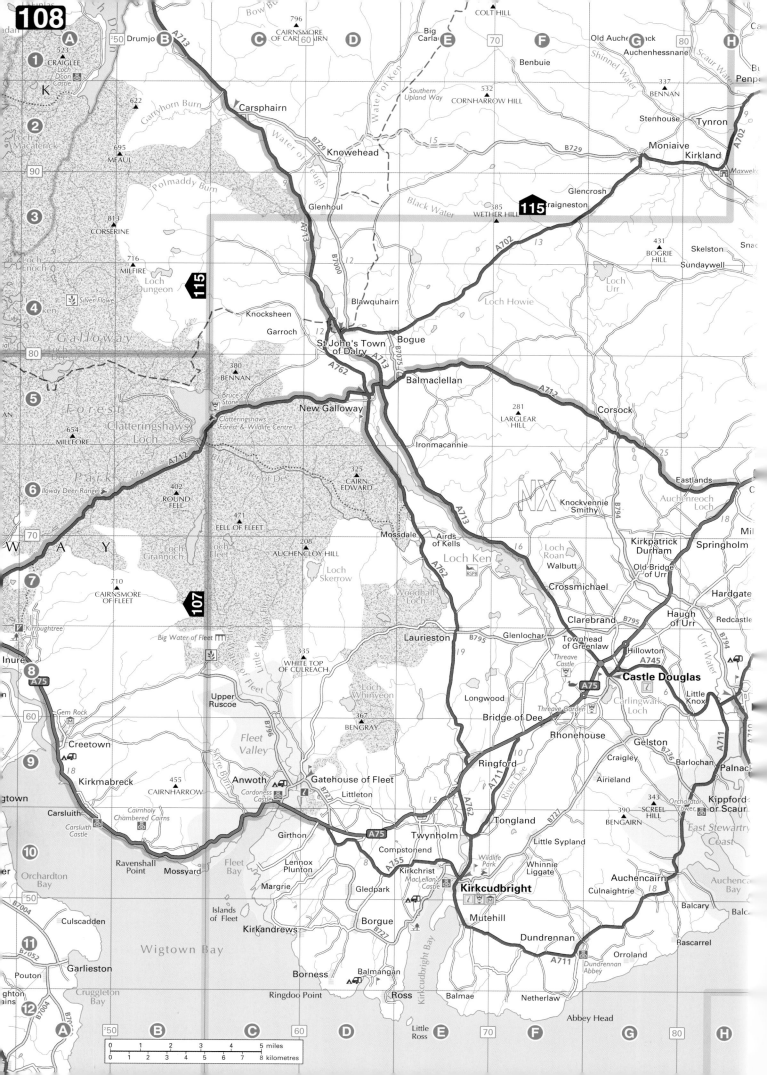

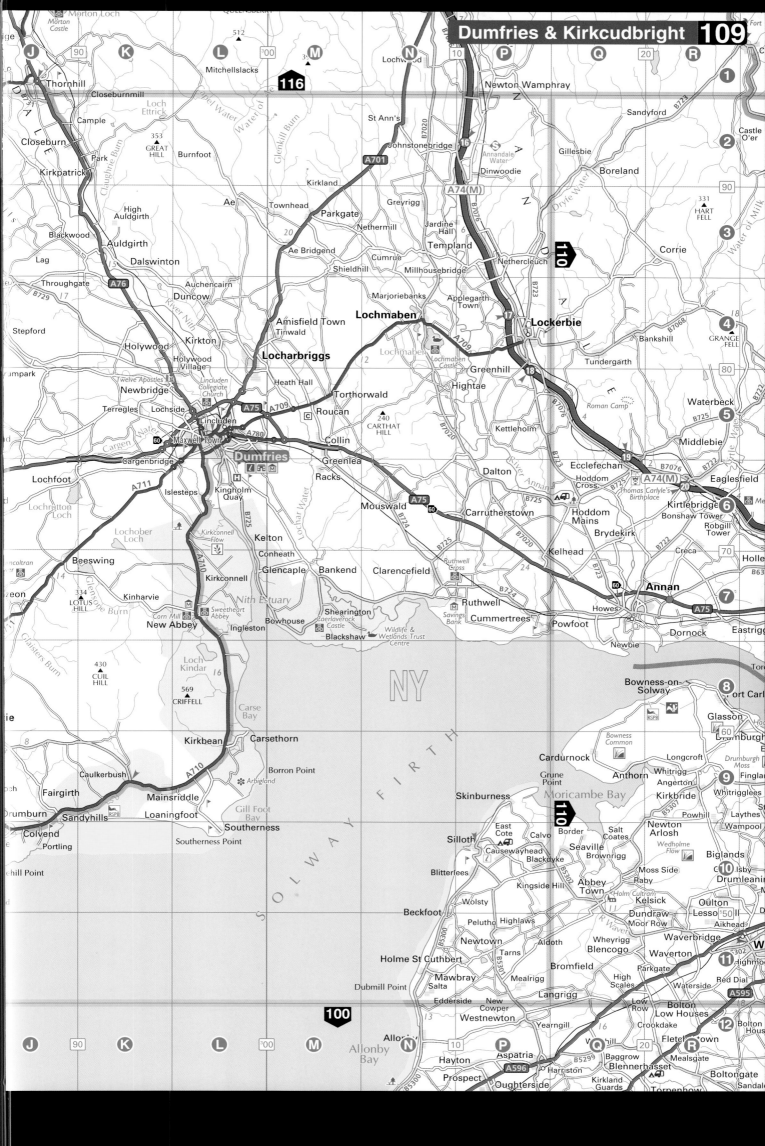

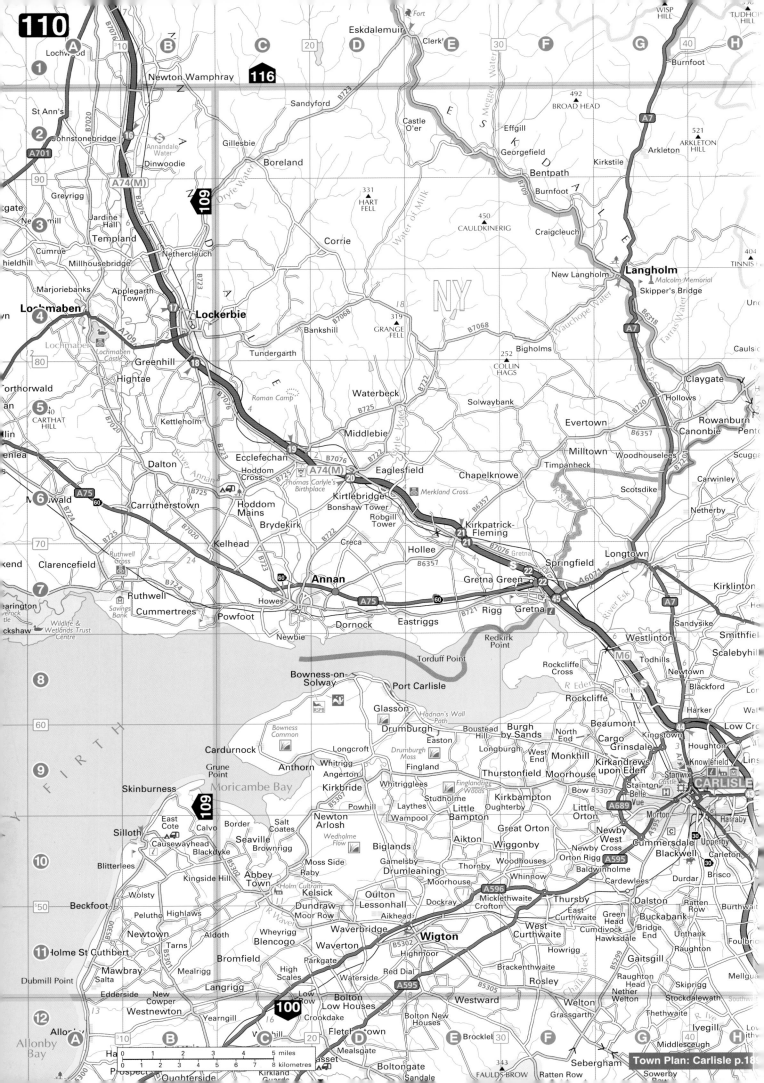

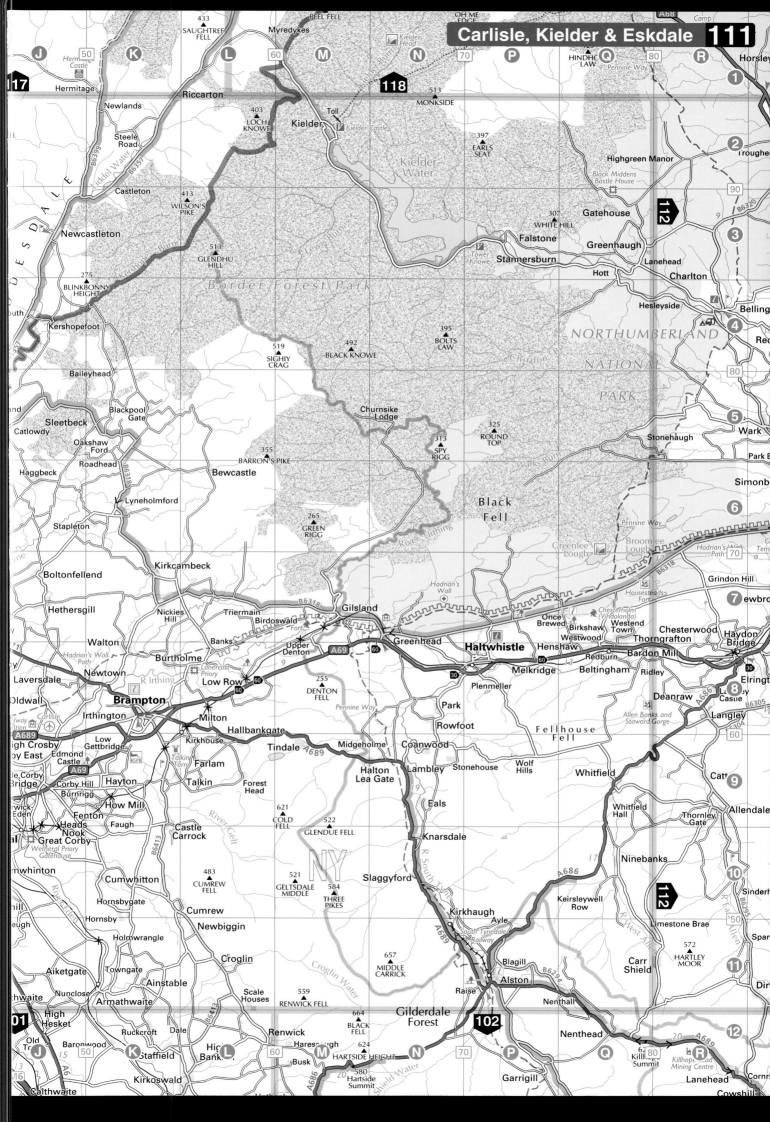

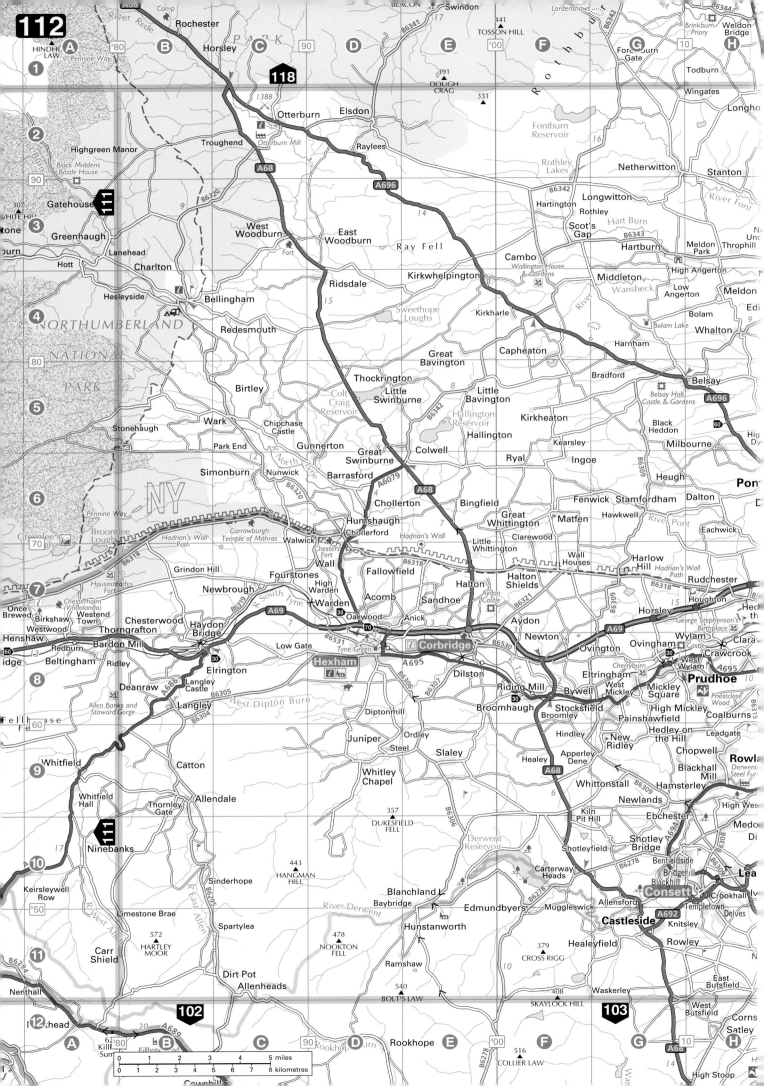

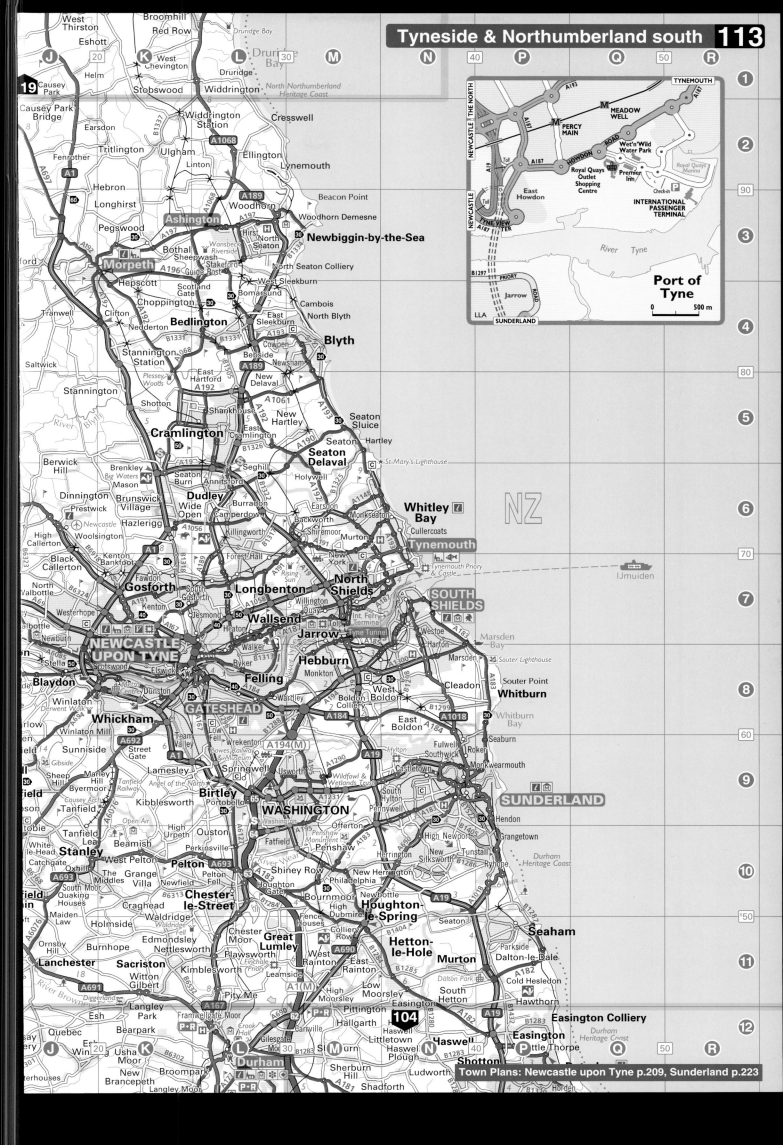

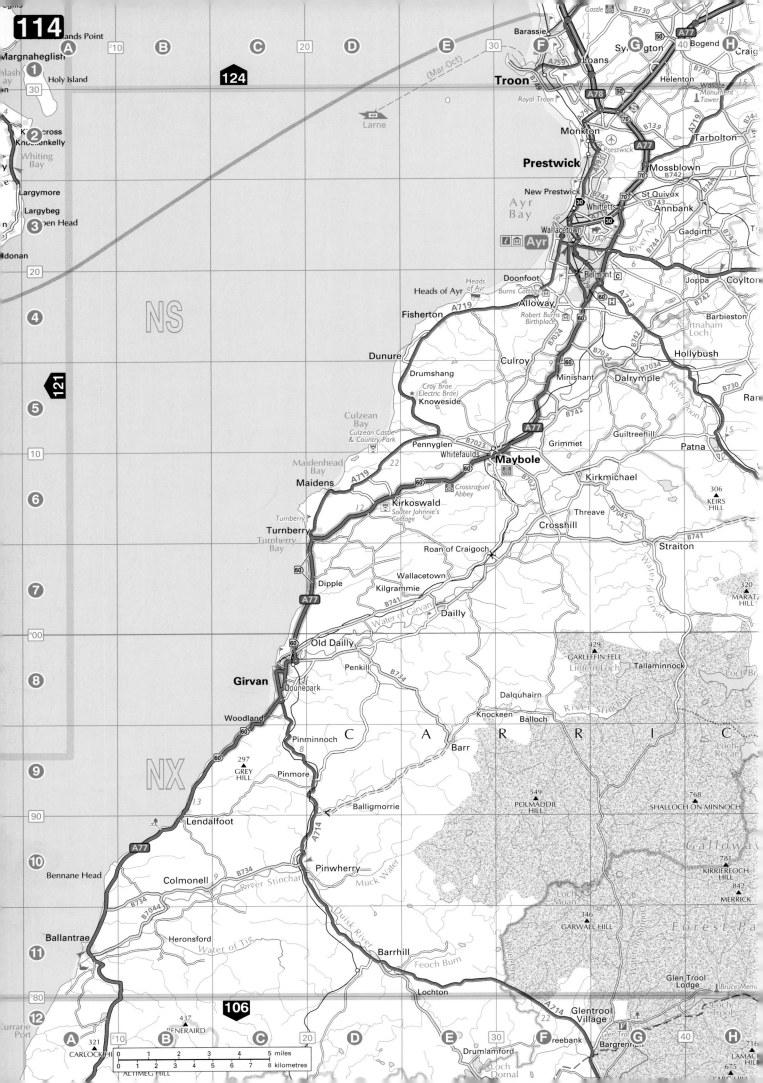

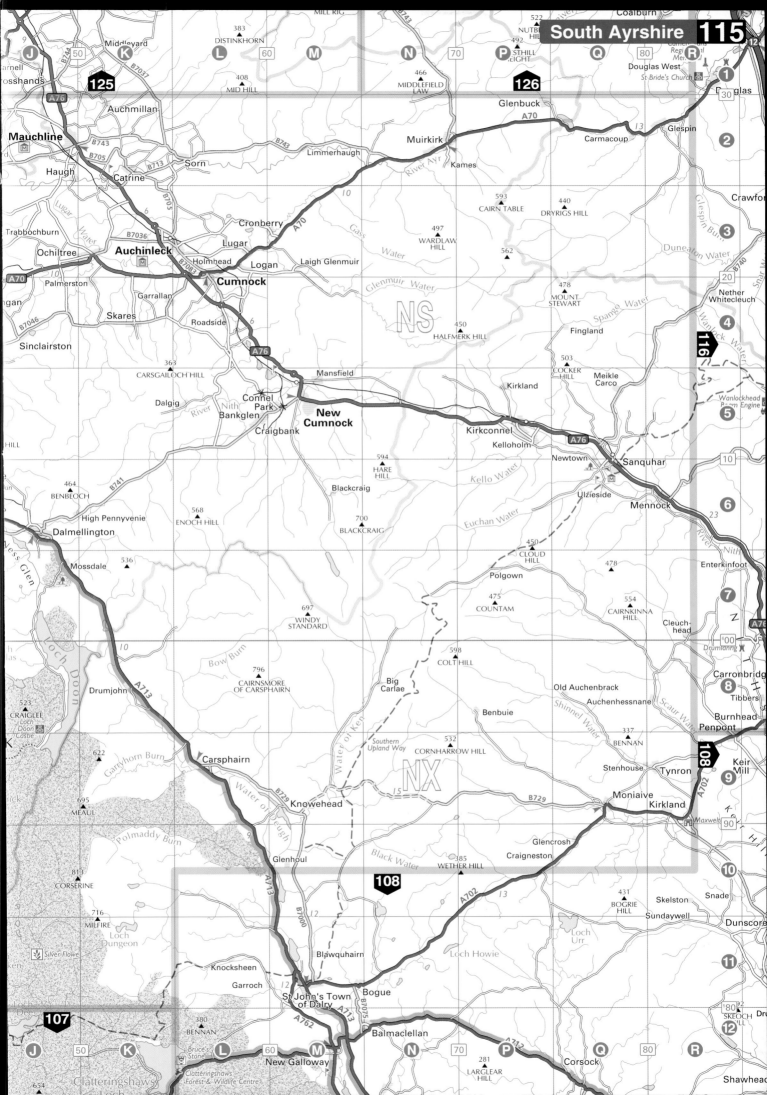

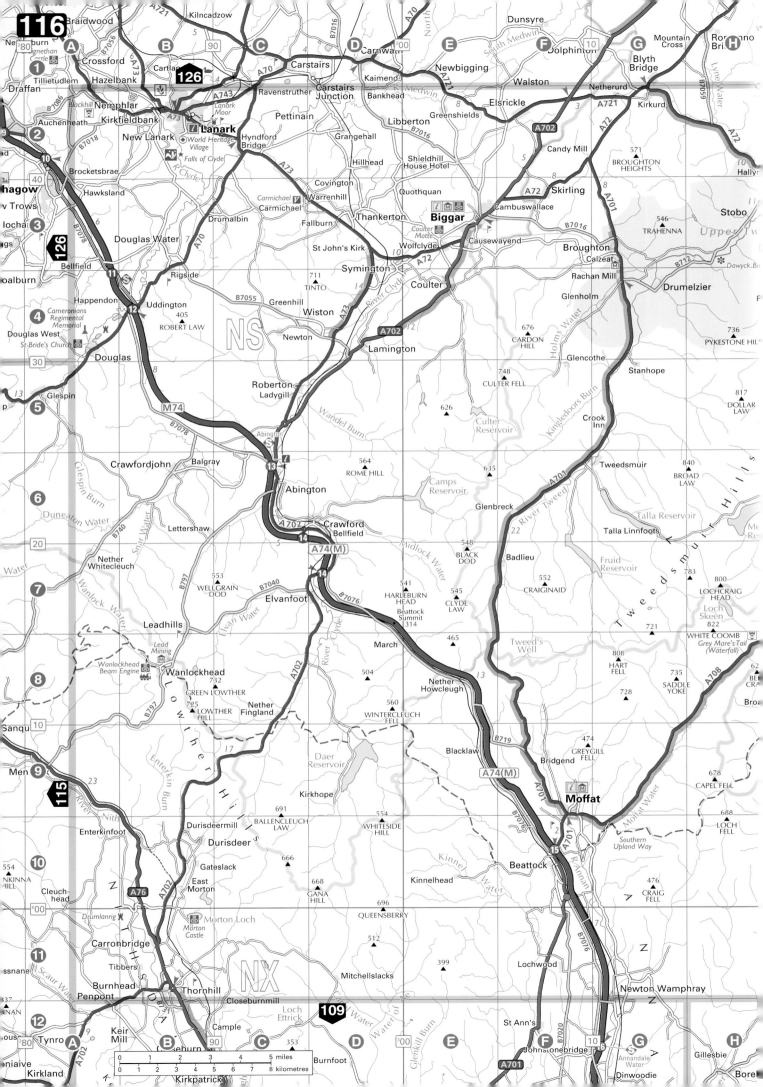

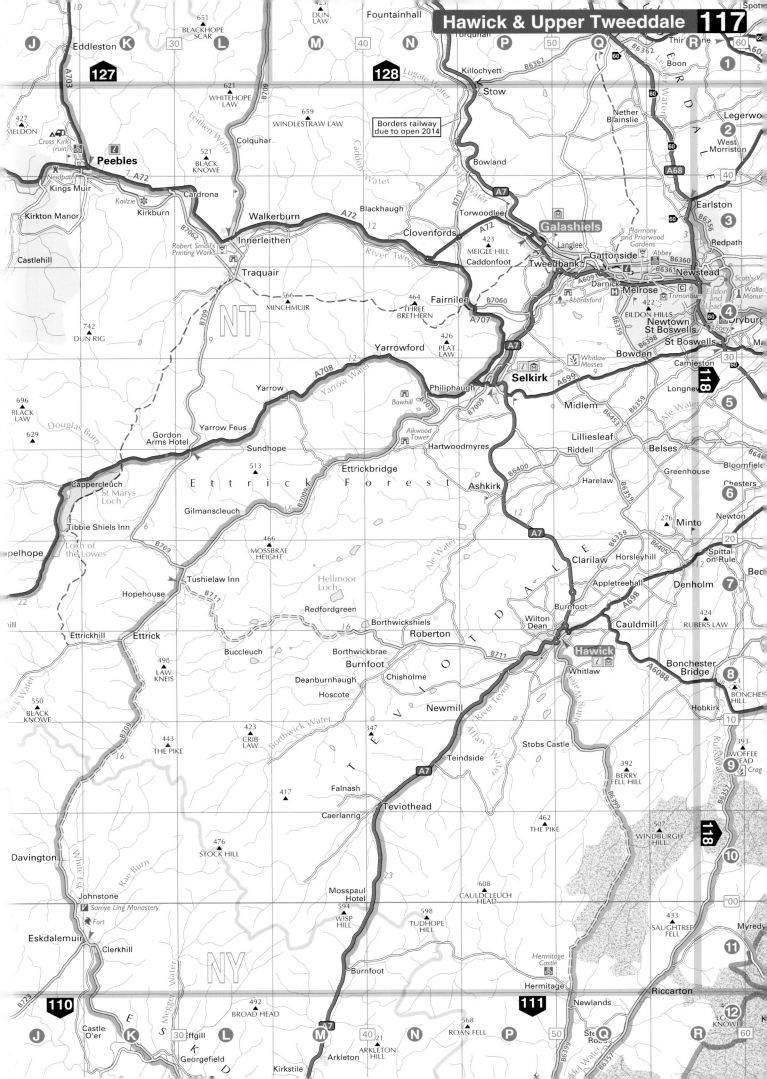

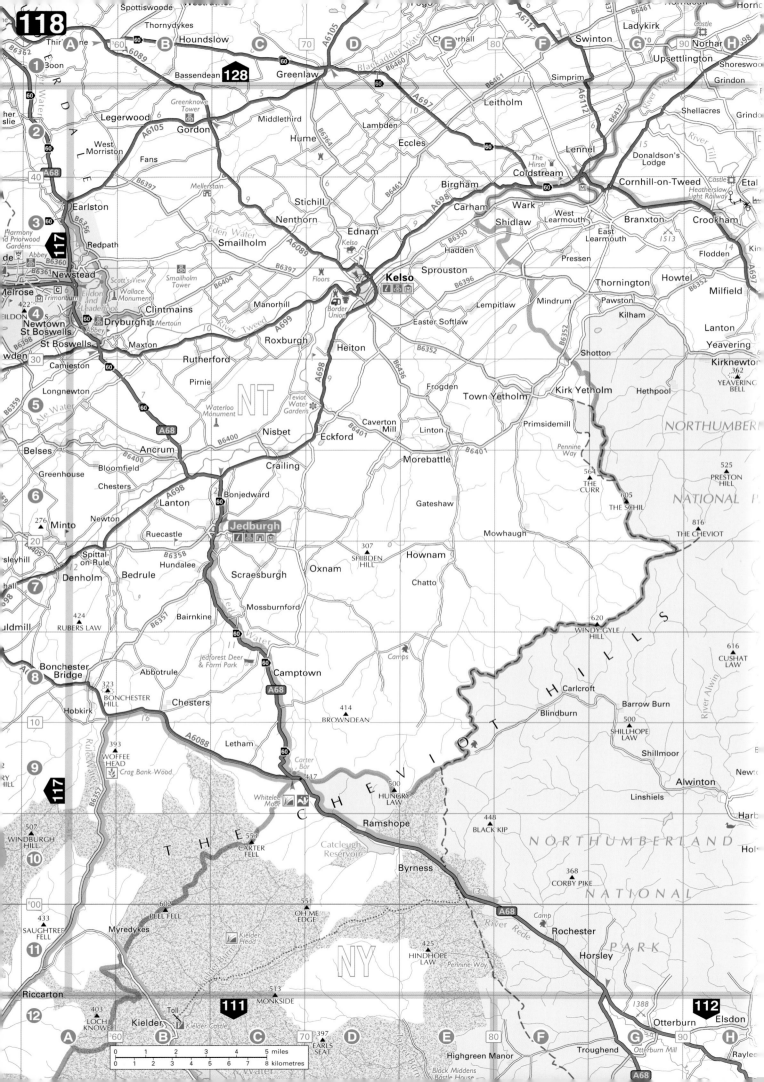

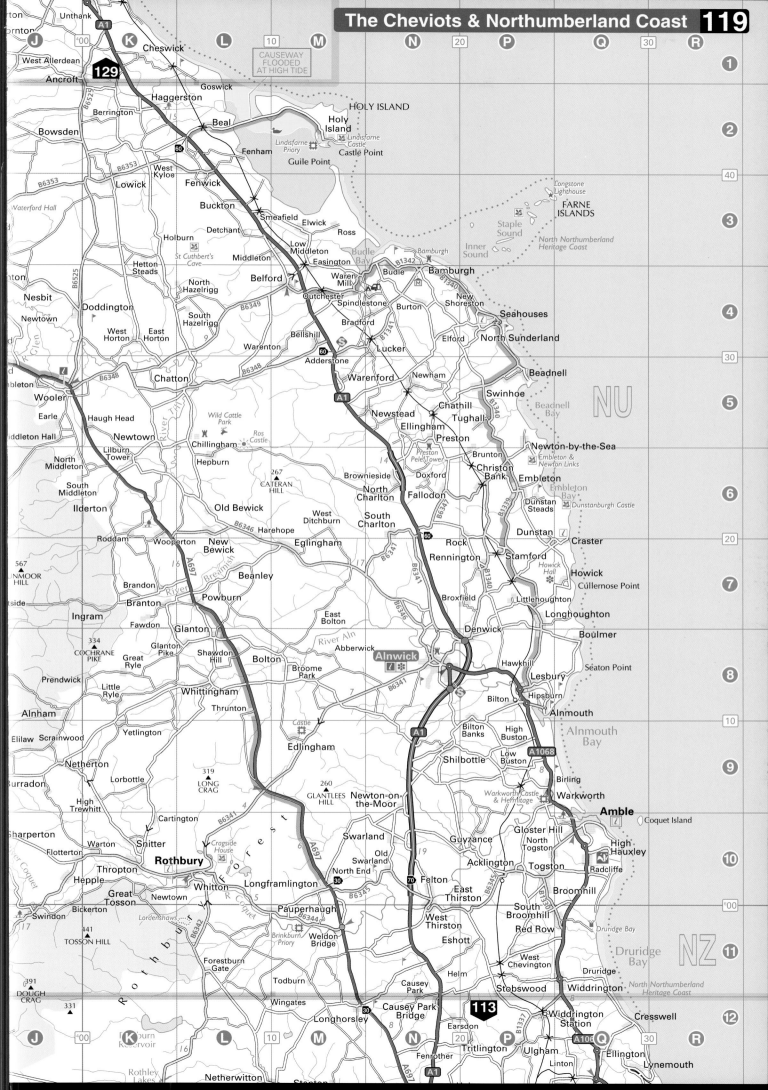

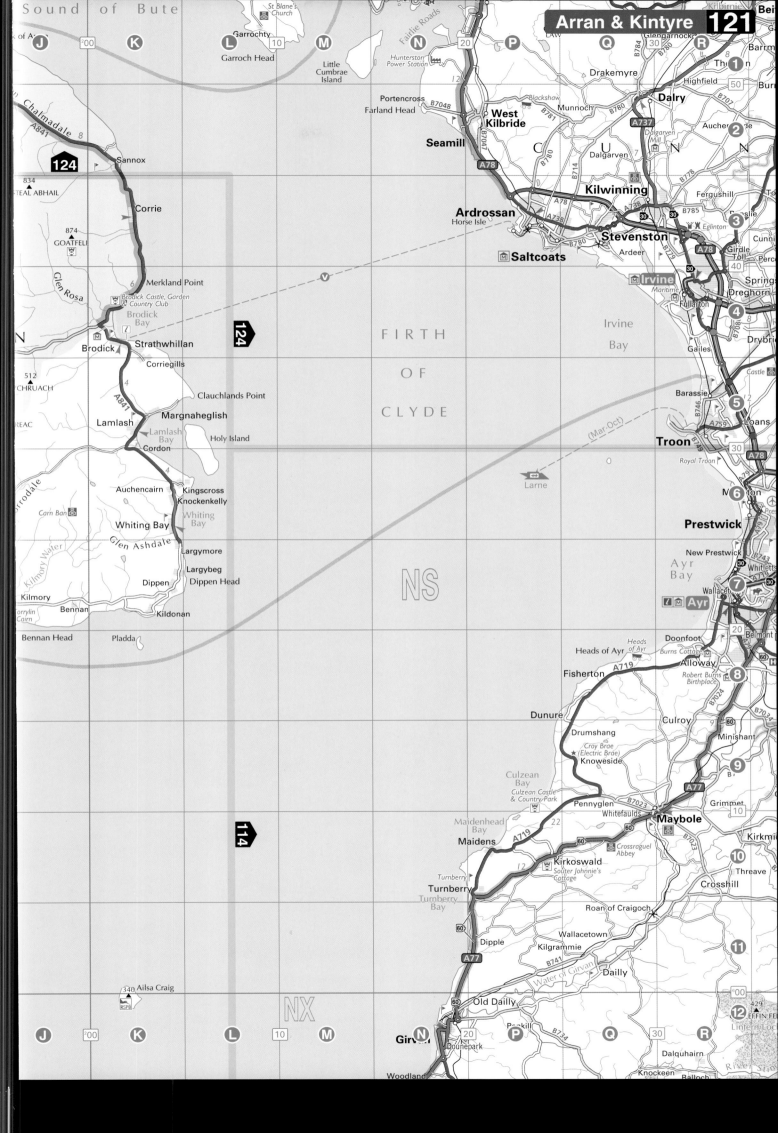

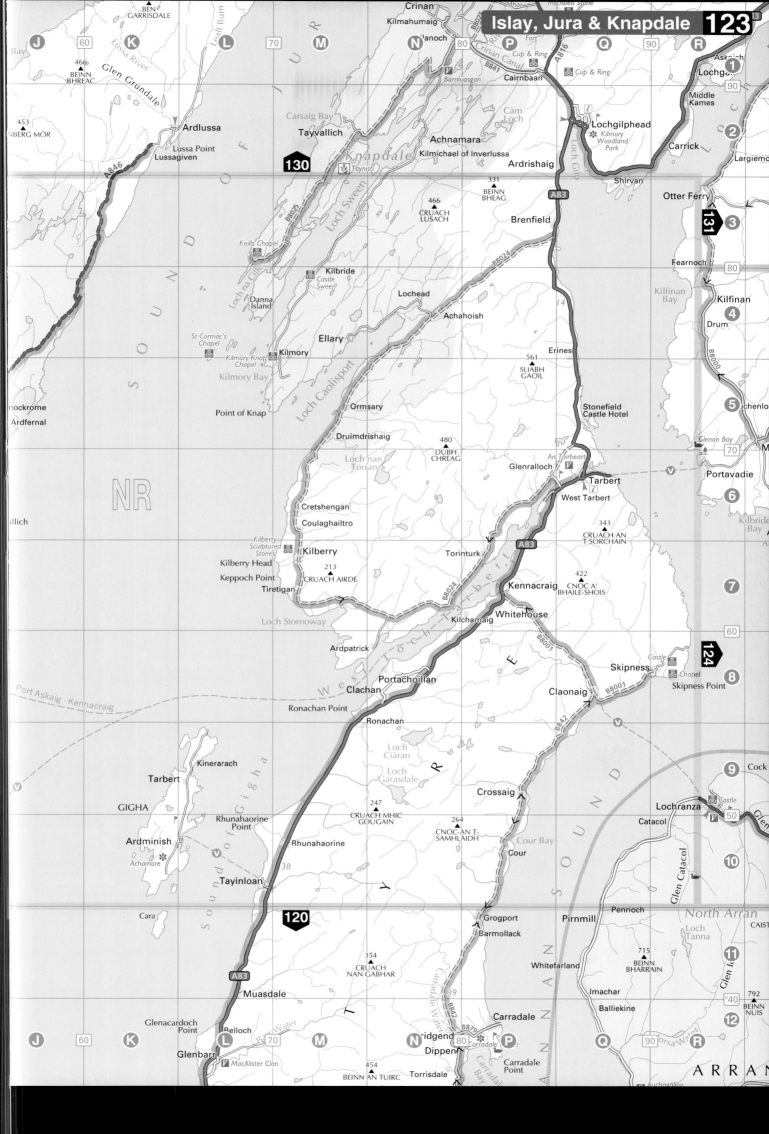

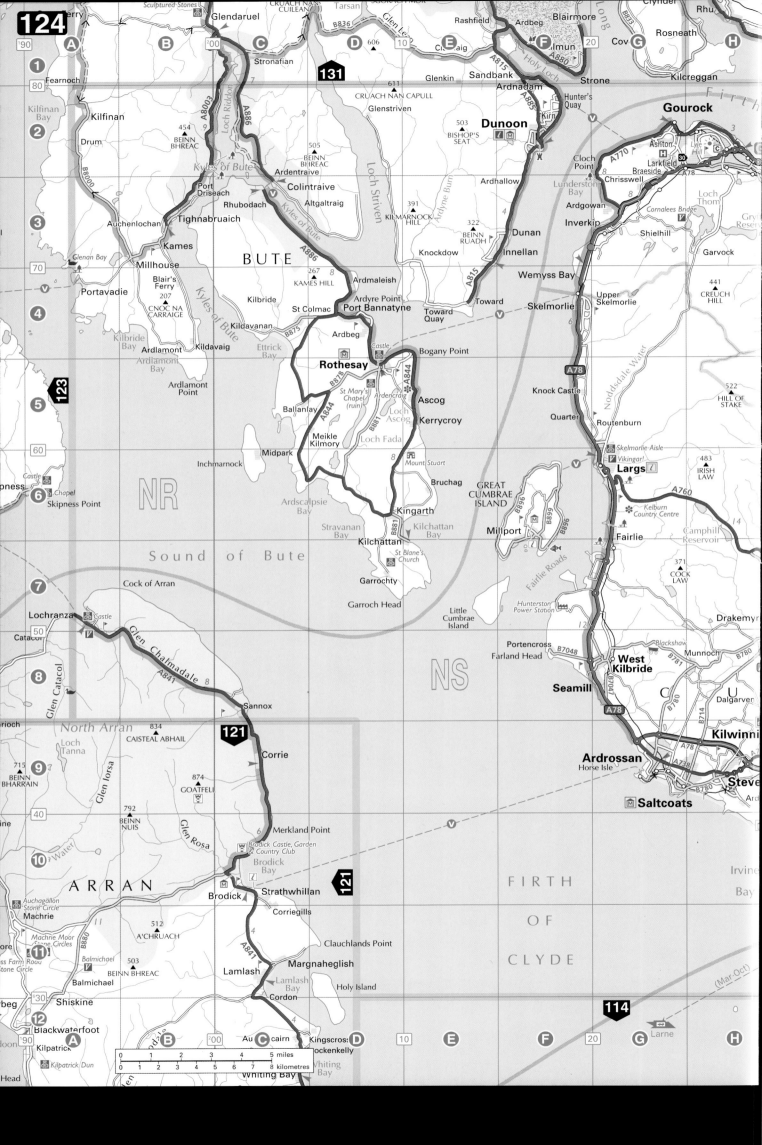

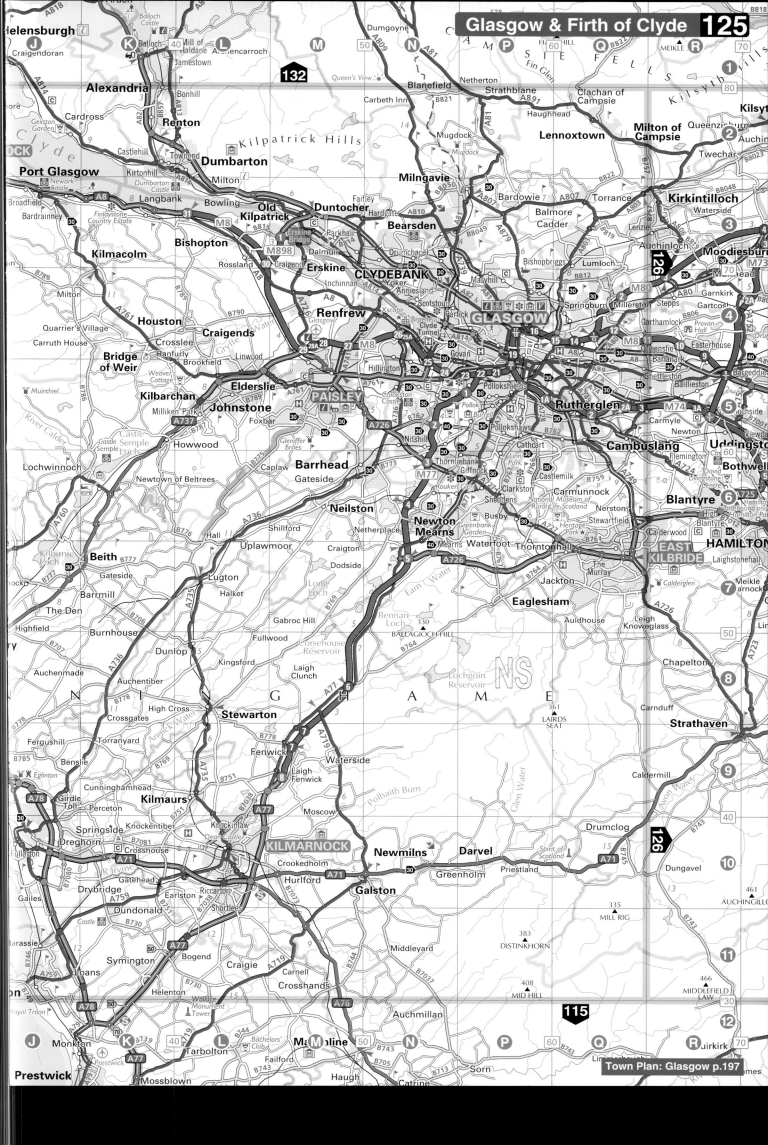

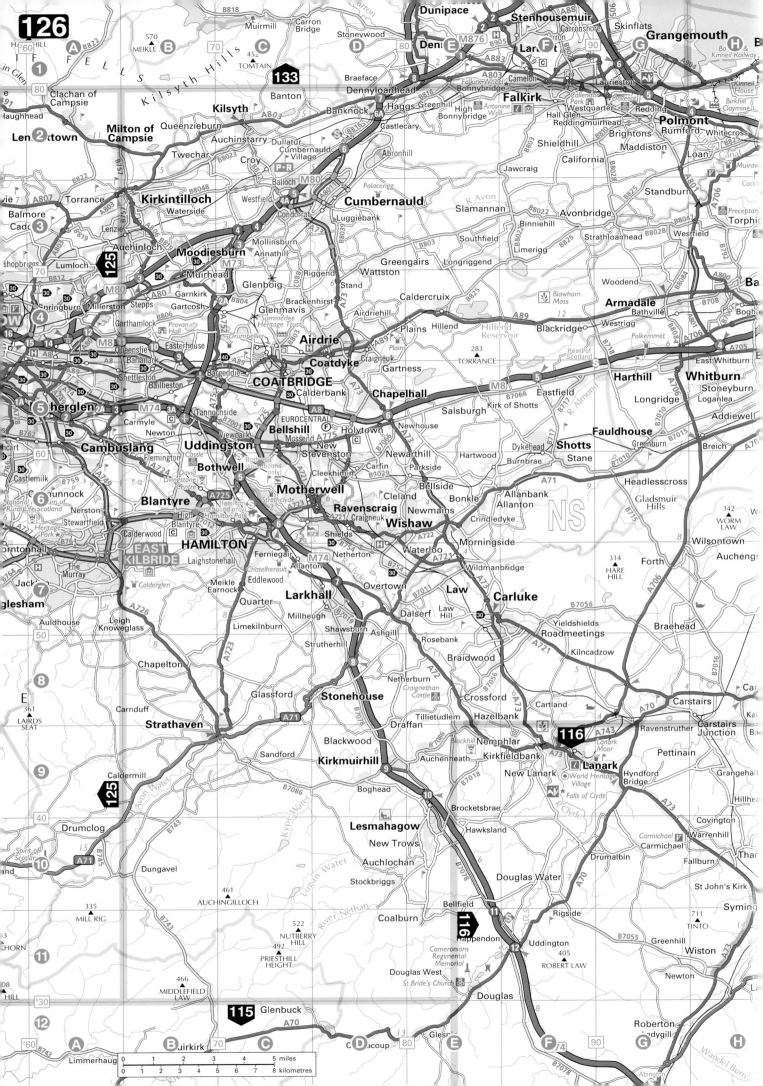

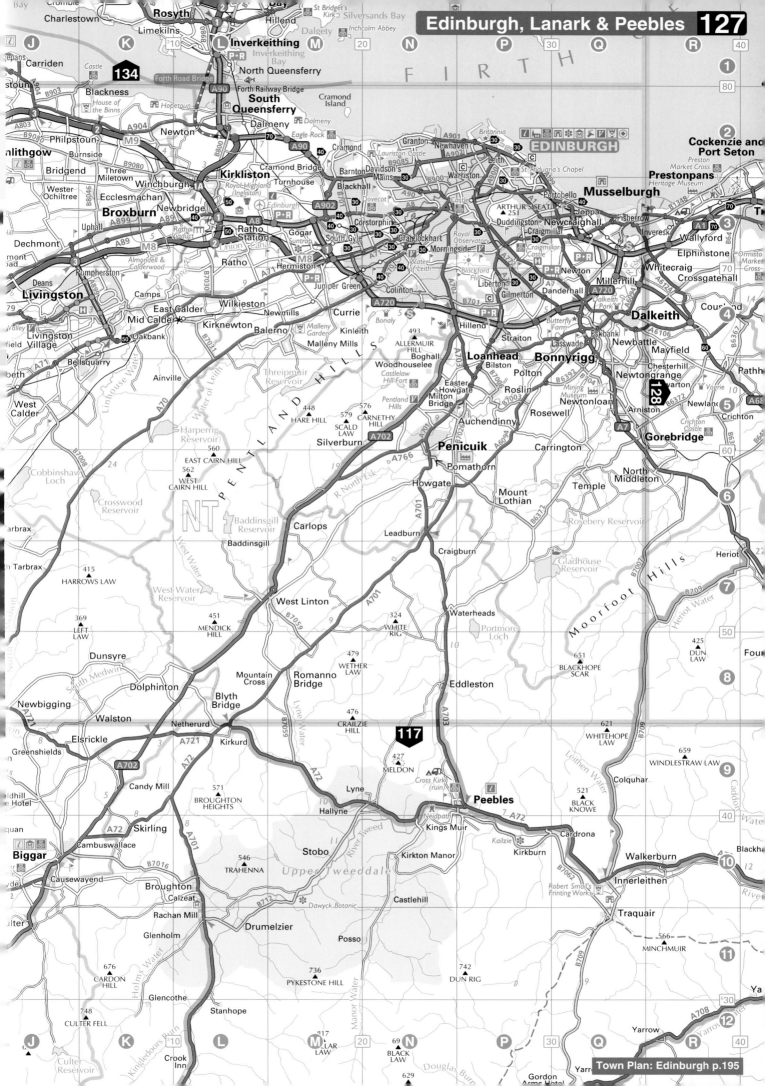

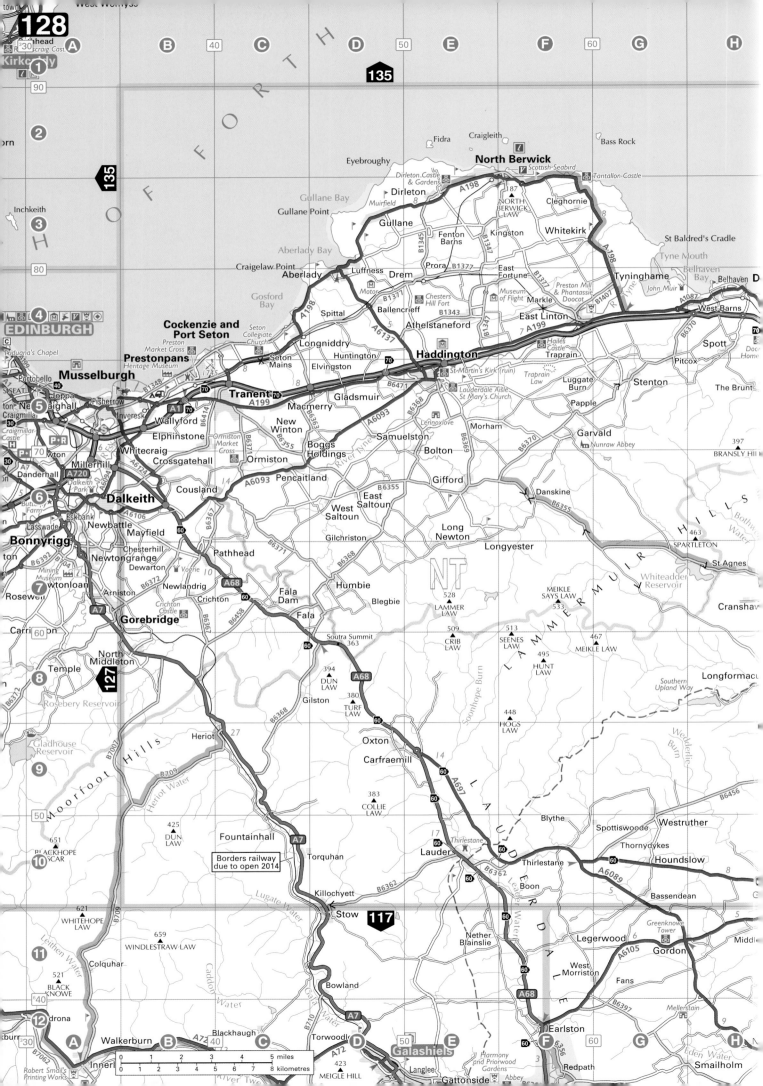

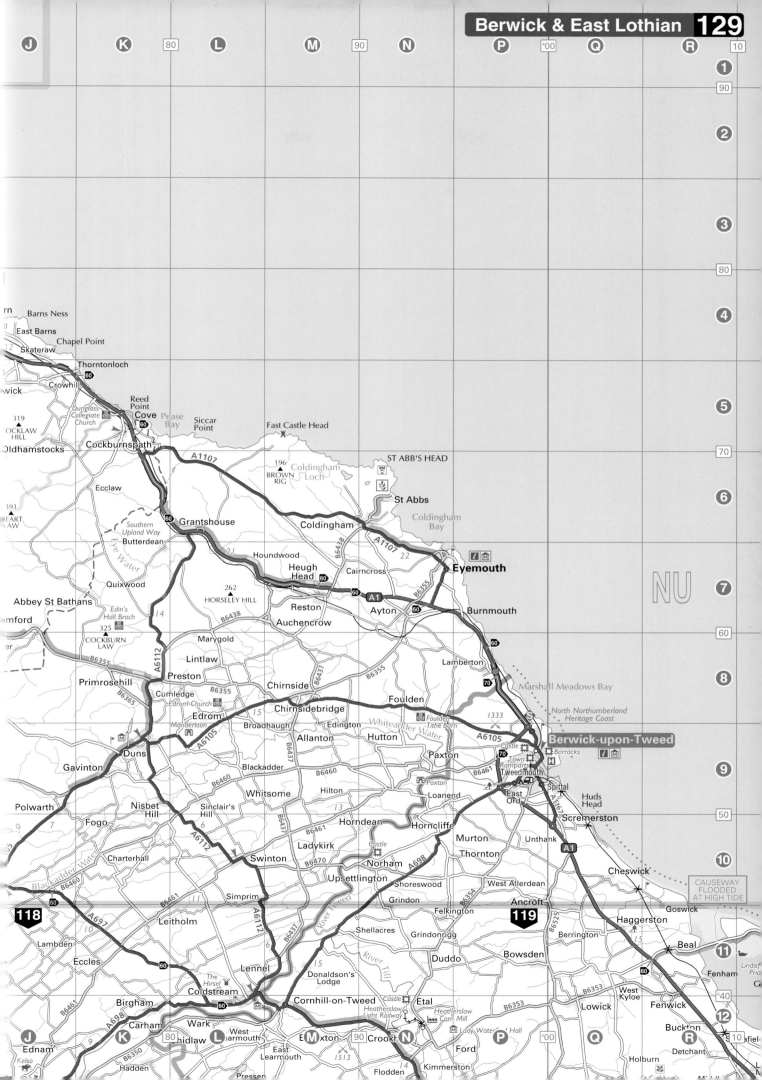

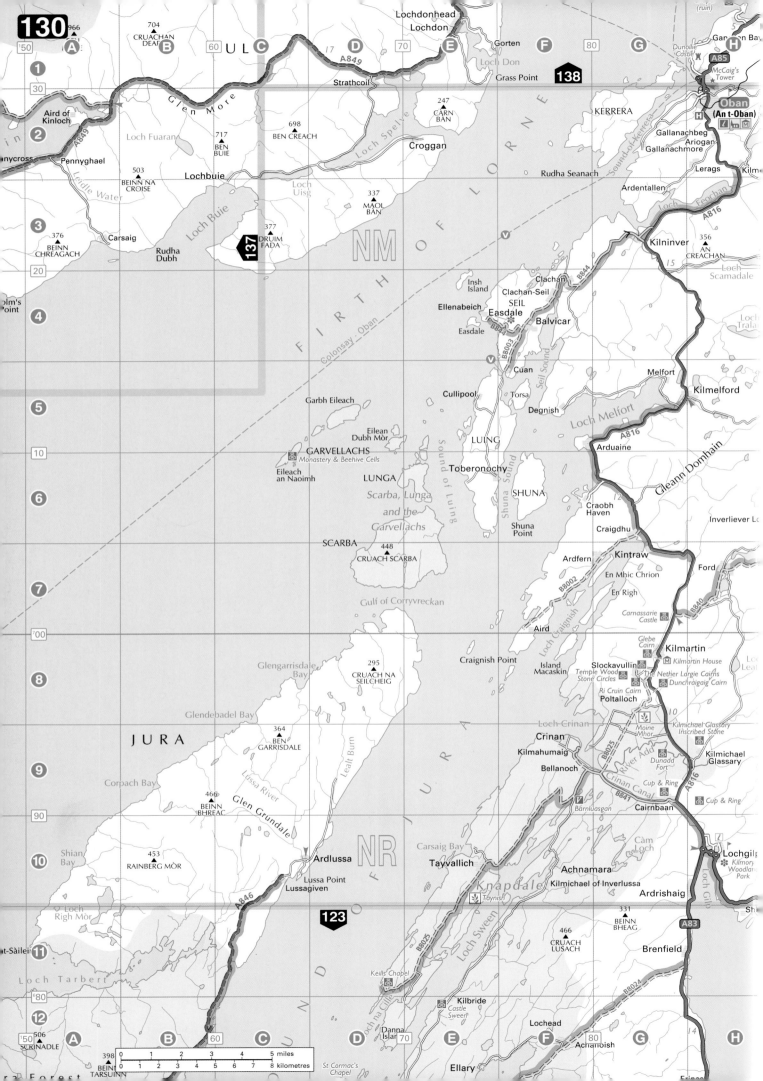

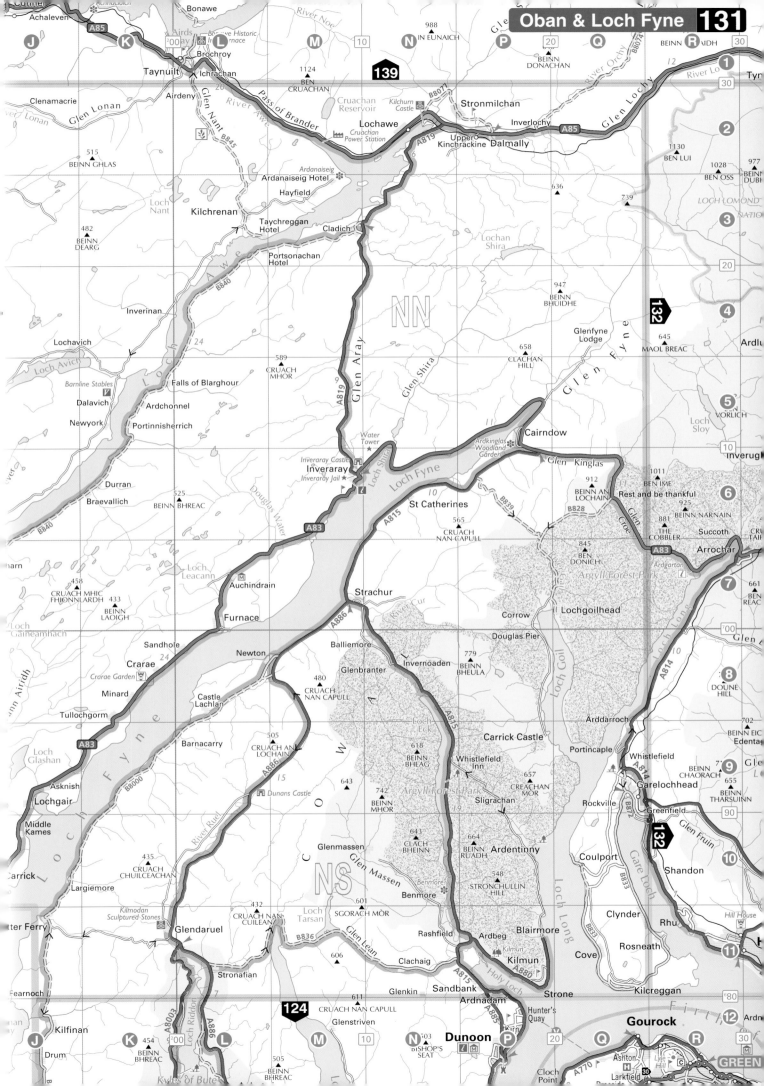

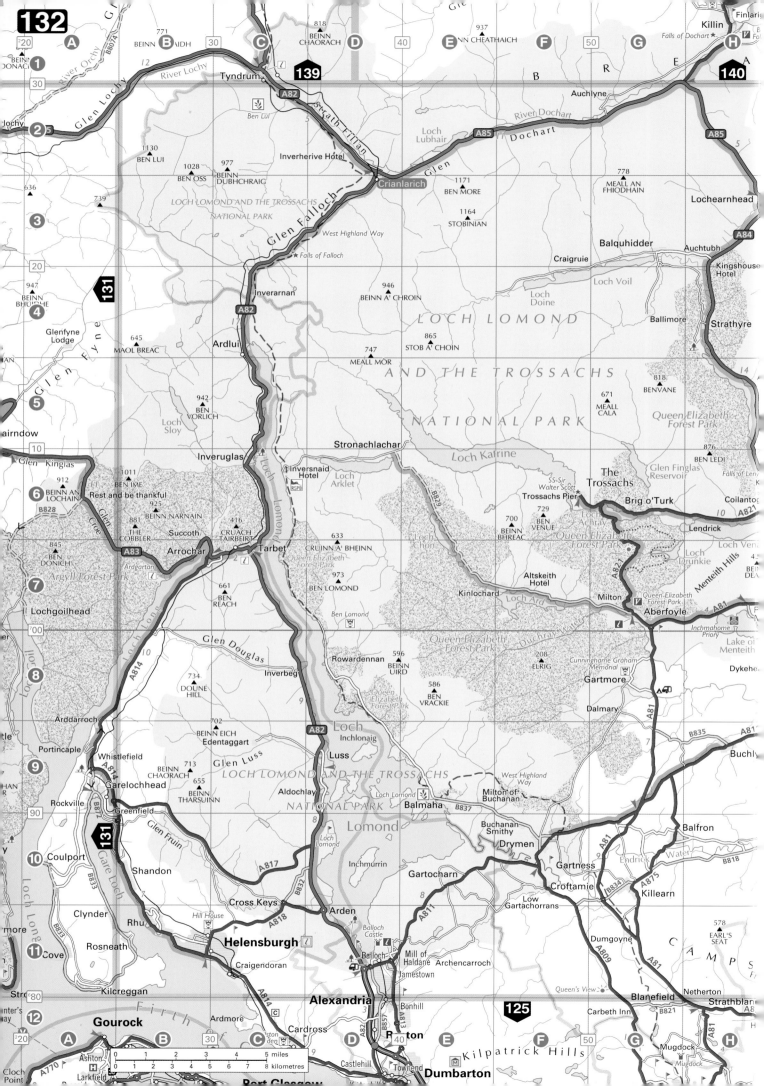

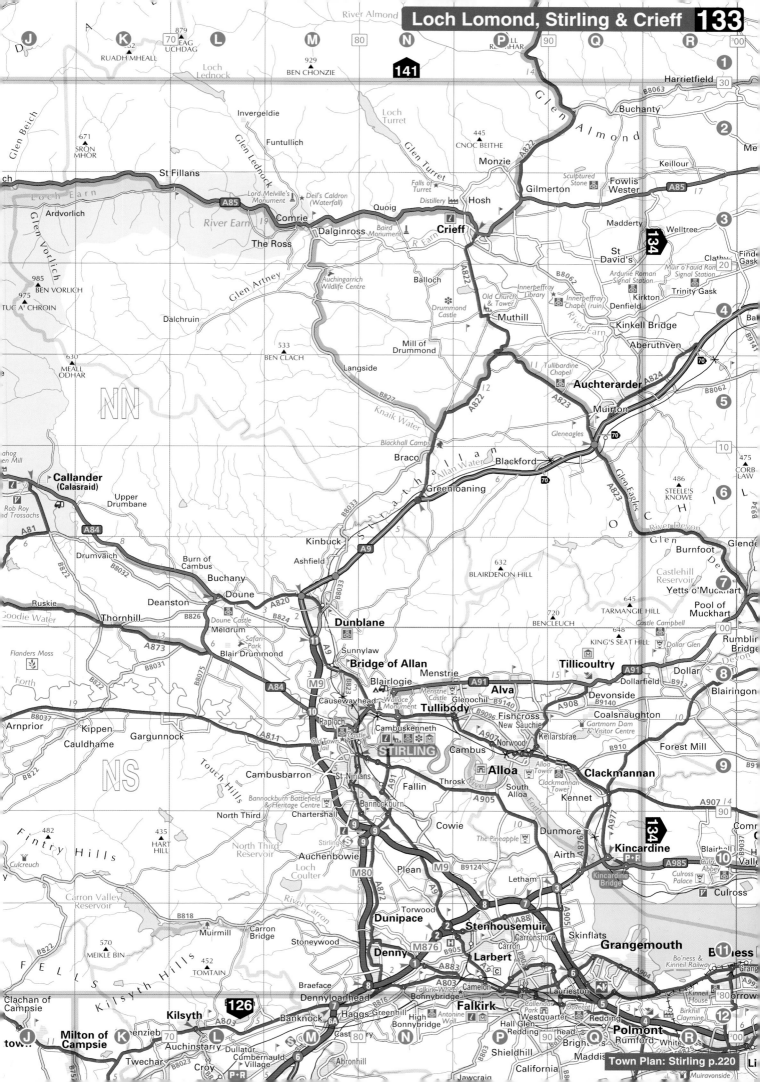

NL

COLL

Eilean Mòr
Rudha Mòr
Rudha Sgor-in
Bousd
Sorisda
Cliad Bay
B8072
Arnabost
Grishipoll
Clabhach
B8071
Hogh Bay
Ballyhaugh
Arinagour
Loch Cliad
Totronald
Acha
B8070
Coll
Feall Bay
Arileod
Uig
Eilean Ornsay
RSPB
Calgary Point
Crossapol Bay
Rudha Fàsachd
Gunna
Loch Breachacha

Caoles
Rudha Dubh
B8069
Ruaig
Rudha Port Bhiosd
Clachan Mor
Balephetrish Bay
B8068
Haugh Bay
Loch Bhasapoll
Ballevullin
Cornoigmore
Kenovay
Gott Bay
Tiree
B8068
Kilkenneth
Moss
Heylipoll
Scarinish
Middleton
B8065
Crossapoll
TIREE
Barrapoll
B8065
Balemartine
Hynish Bay
B8067
Mannel
Rinn Thorbhais
Hynish
Loch a' Phuill
Balephuil Bay

TRESHNISH ISLES

Lunga

Fla

Bac Mòr or Dutchmans
Bac Beag

Colonsay

NM

Eilean Dubh
Balnahard
Rudh' a' Geodha
Kiloran Bay
COLONSAY
Kiloran
Kilchattan
B8087
Colonsay-Oban
Scalasaig
B8086
NR
Machrins
Colonsay
Garvard
B8085
Colonsay-Port Askaig
Oronsay
Rudha Bàn
Dubh Eilean
ORONSAY
Eilean Ghurdmail

IONA
Iona Abbey & Nunnery
Baile Mòr
MacLean's Cross

Soa Island
Erraid

0   1   2   3 miles
0   1   2   3   4   5 kilometres

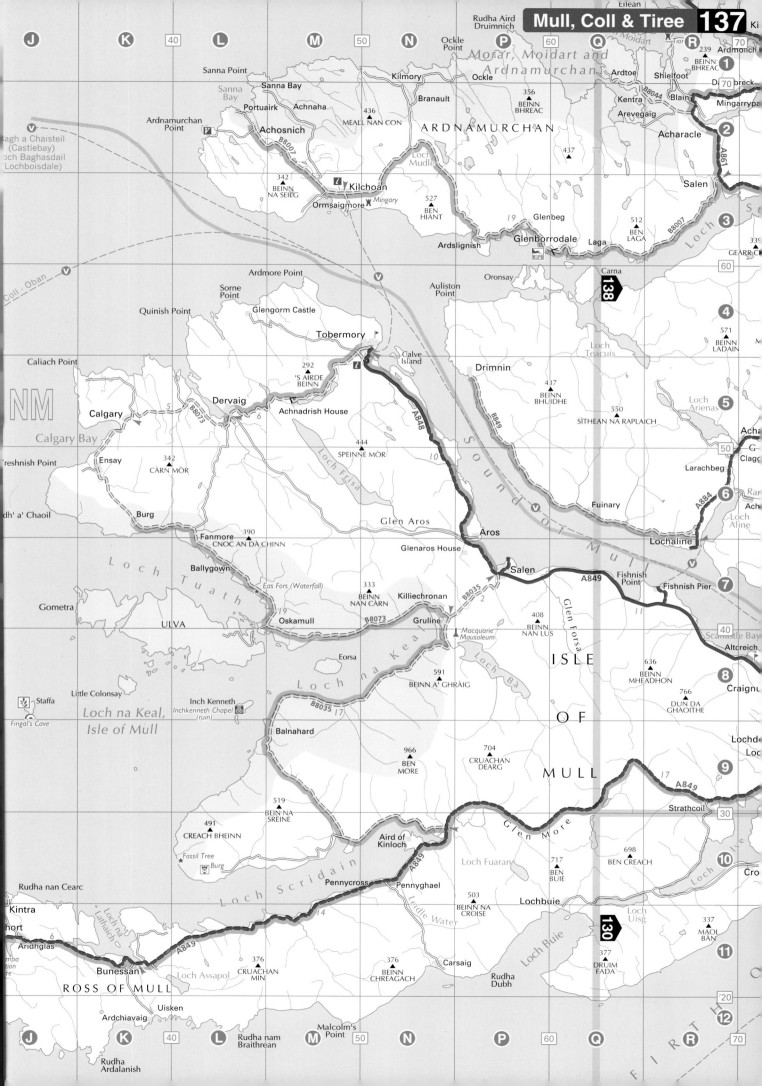

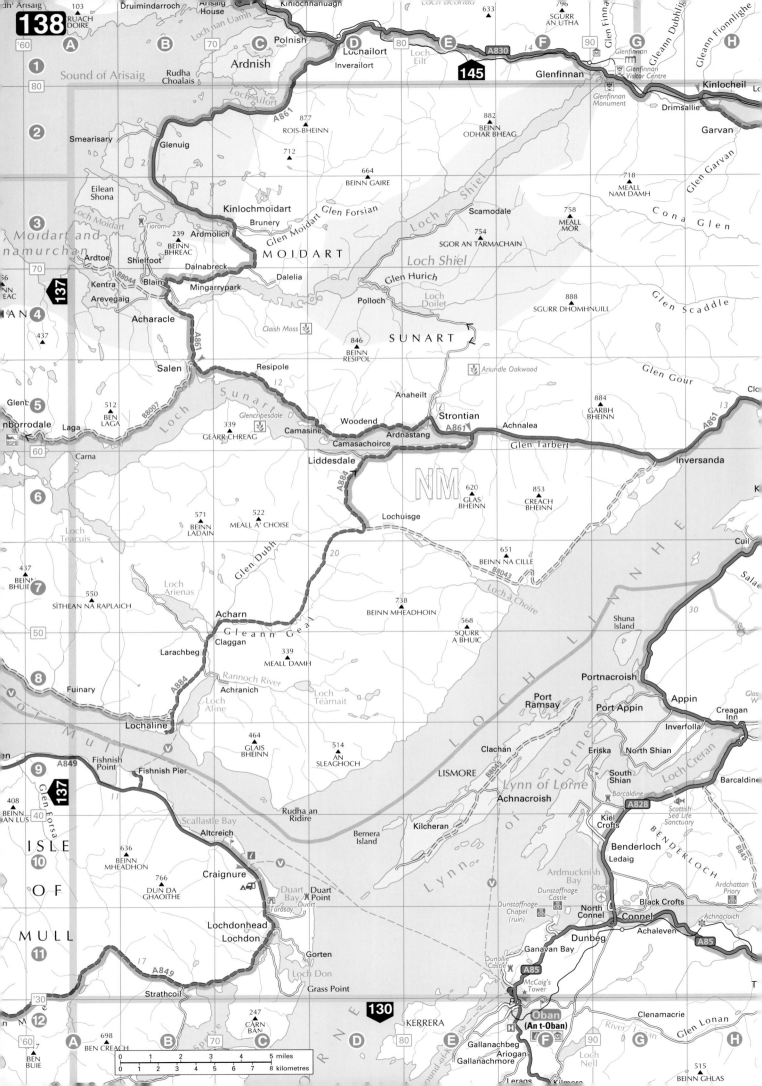

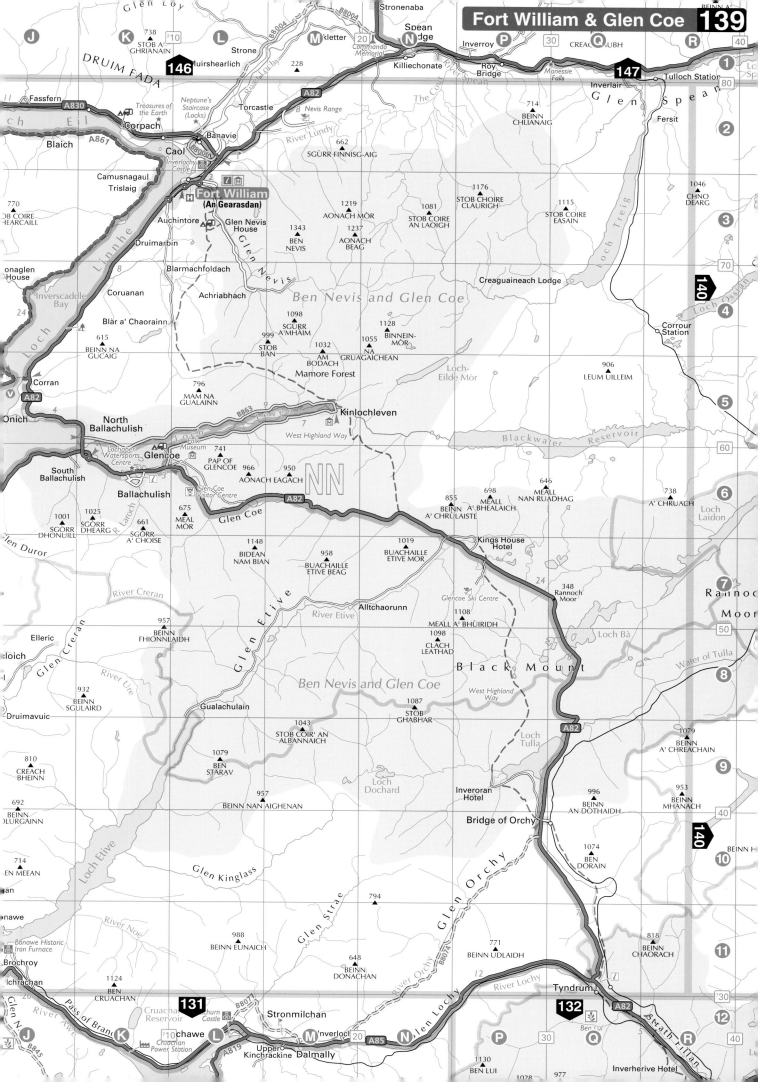

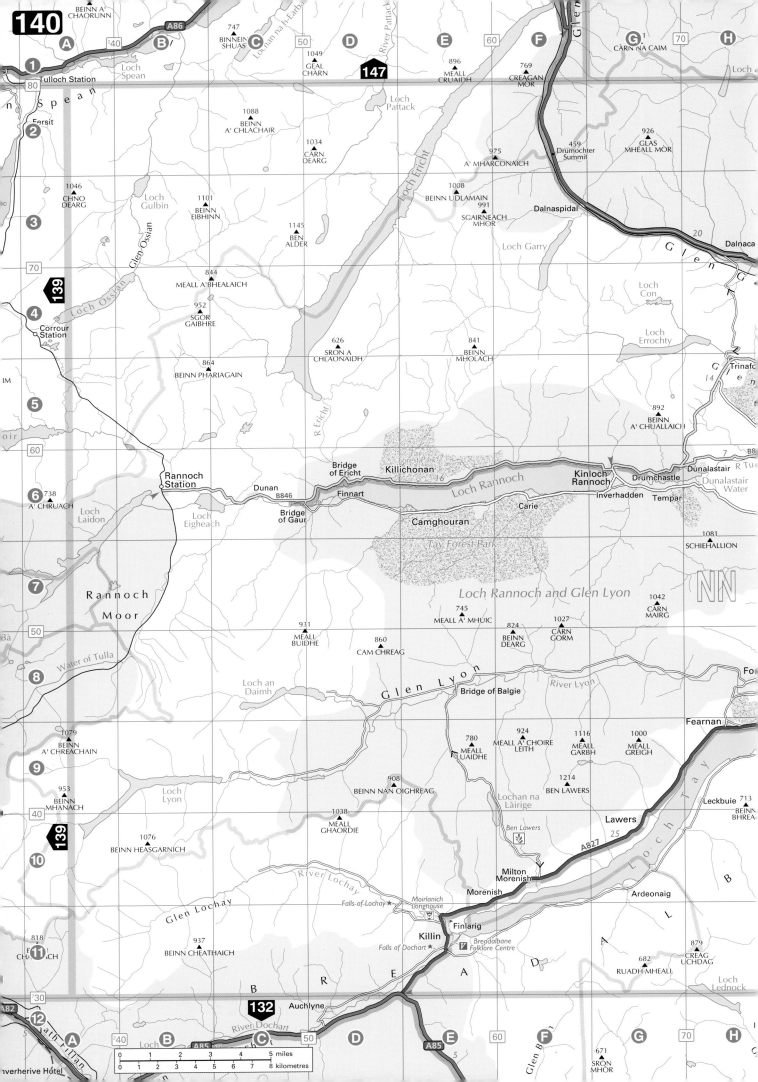

A · 240 · B A86 · C · 50 · D · E · 60 · F · G¹ · 70 · H

1

BEINN A'
CHAORUNN

240

Tulloch Station

80

Loch Spean

BINNEIN
SHUAS

Lochan na h-Earba

747

50

1049
GEAL
CHARN

147

River Pattack

896
MEALL
CRUAIDH

769
CREAGAN
MOR

GLEN

CARN NA CAIM

Loch

Spean

2

Fersit

1088
BEINN
A' CHLACHAIR

1034
CARN
DEARG

Loch
Pattack

975
A' MHARCONAICH

459
Drumochter
Summit

926
GLAS
MHEALL MOR

3

1046
CHNO
DEARG

Loch
Gulbin

1101
BEINN
EIBHINN

1145
BEN
ALDER

1008
BEINN UDLAMAIN

991
SGAIRNEACH
MHOR

Dalnaspidal

Loch Garry

20

GLEN G

Dalnaca

70

139

Glen Ossian

Loch Ossian

844
MEALL A'BHEALAICH

952
SGOR
GAIBHRE

Loch
Con

Loch
Errochty

GLEN

Trinafc

14

4

Corrour
Station

864
BEINN PHARIAGAIN

626
SRON A
CHLAONAIDH

841
BEINN
MHOLACH

892
BEINN
A' CHUALLAICH

Trinafc

5

oir

60

70

892
BEINN
A' CHUALLAICH

7

B8

6

738
A' CHRUACH

Rannoch
Station

Loch
Laidon

Loch
Eigheach

Dunan

B846

Finnart

Bridge
of Ericht

Killichonan

16

Loch Rannoch

Carie

Kinloch
Rannoch

Inverhadden

Drumchastle

Tempar

Dunalastair

R Tu

Dunalastair
Water

7

Bridge
of Gaur

Camghouran

Tay
Forest Park

Tay Forest Park

1081
SCHIEHALLION

NN

Rannoch

Moor

Loch Rannoch and Glen Lyon

745
MEALL A' MHUIC

1042
CARN
MAIRG

931
MEALL
BUIDHE

824
BEINN
DEARG

1027
CARN
GORM

8

Water of Tulla

Loch an
Daimh

CAM CHREAG

860

GLEN LYON

Bridge of Balgie

River Lyon

Fo

Bà

50

Fearnan

9

1079
BEINN
A' CHREACHAIN

Loch
Lyon

780
MEALL
LUAIDHE

924
MEALL A' CHOIRE
LEITH

1116
MEALL
GARBH

1000
MEALL
GREIGH

1214
BEN LAWERS

Lawers

Leckbuie 713

BEINN
BHREA

40

953
BEINN
MHANACH

139

1076
BEINN HEASGARNICH

1038
MEALL
GHAORDIE

908
BEINN NAN OIGHREAG

Lochan na
Làirige

Ben Lawers

25

A827

Loch Tay

10

River Lochay

Glen Lochay

Falls of Lochay ★

Moirlanich
Longhouse

Milton
Morenish

Morenish

Ardeonaig

11

818
E
CHA...ICH

937
BEINN CHEATHAICH

Falls of Dochart ★

Killin

Finlarig

Breadalbane
Folklore Centre

879
CREAG
UCHDAG

682
RUADH MHEALL

Loch
Lednock

30

A82

132

Auchlyne

River Dochart

A85

50

D

A85

E

60

F

Glen B

G

70

H

671
SRON
MHOR

5

12

A

240

B

A85

C

D

E

A85

G

70

H

nverherive Hotel

0 1 2 3 4 5 miles
0 1 2 3 4 5 6 7 8 kilometres

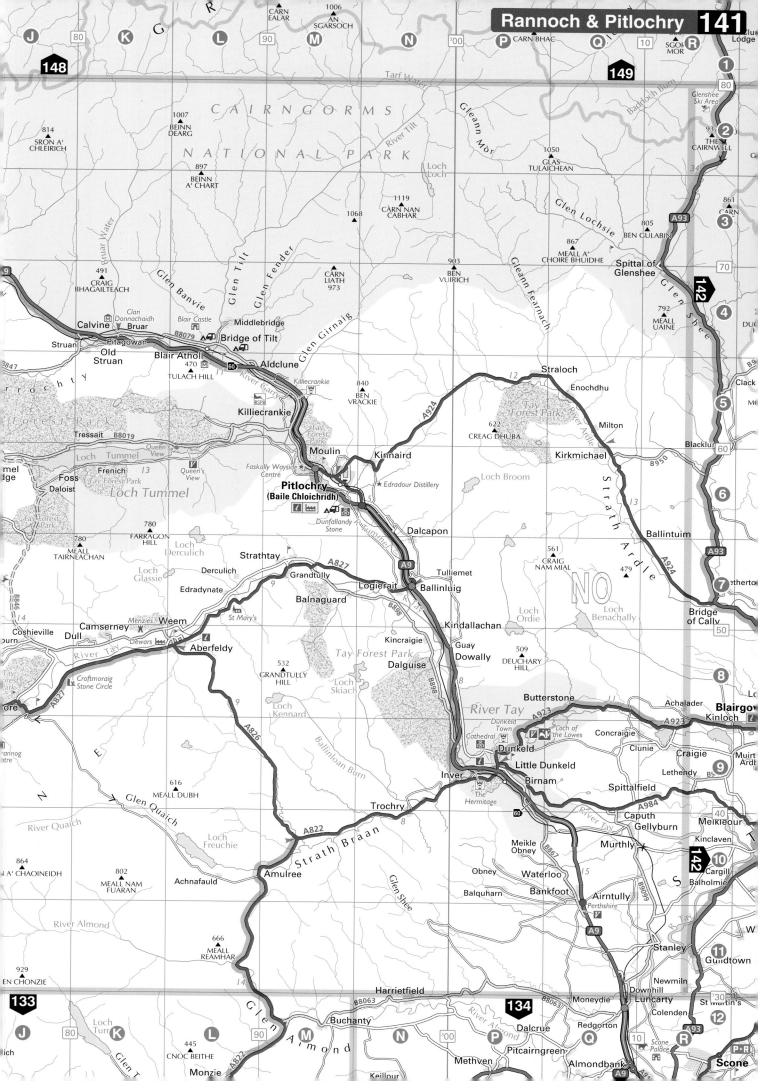

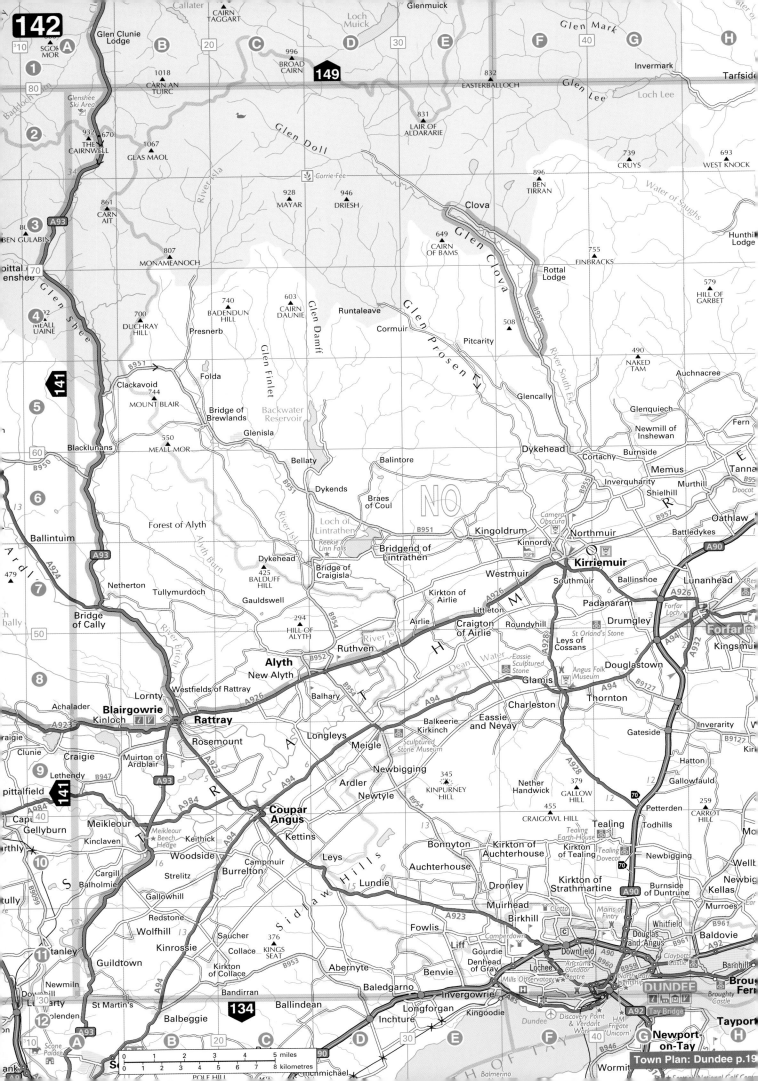

Rudha nan Clach

Fiskavaig

B8009

Fernilea

Drync

S K Y E

444
BEN LEE

conser

369
ARNAVAL

Carbost

Merkadale

A863

A40

Glen Drynoch

Sligachan

773
GLAMAIG

A87

152   Talisker
Bay

Talisker

Glen Eynort

369
BEINN BHREAC

447
BEINN
BHREAC

Grula

965
SGURR NAN GILLEAN

Loch Eynort

974
SGURR
A' GHEADAIDH

The Cuillin Hills

434
AN CRUACHIN

Glenbrittle House

Cuillin Hills

927
BLAVEN

Bualintur

1009
SGURR
ALASDAIR

Loch
Coruisk

Loch na
Crèitheac

Kirl

894
GARS
BHEINN

225
CEANN NA BEINNE

Rudh' an Dùnain

Soay Sound

139
BEINN
BHREAC

Loch
Scavaig

BI
MEA

3

Elg

Mol-chlach

SOAY

Rudh'
Aonghais

Str

C U I L L I N

NG

Rudha
Shamhnan Insir

210
CÀRN A' GHAILL

CANNA

A'Chill

Canna
Harbour

Garrisdale Point

Sanday

Sound of Canna

S O U N D

Sound of Canna

302
MULLACH
MÒR

Rudha na Roinne

'00

A Bhrideanach

570
ORVAL

Kinloch

Loch
Scresort

8   Oigh-sgeir

RÙM

810
ASKIVAL

763
SGÙRR NAN
GILLEAN

90

The Small Isles

Rudha nam
Meirleach

Sound of Rum

Bay of
Laig

Cleadale

299
AN
CRUACHAN

Rudha an Fhasaidh

Laig

EIGG

Kildonnan

393
AN SGÙRR

Sandavore

Sound of Eigg

Eilean
nan Each

MUCK

Eilean
Chathastail

'80

Port Mor

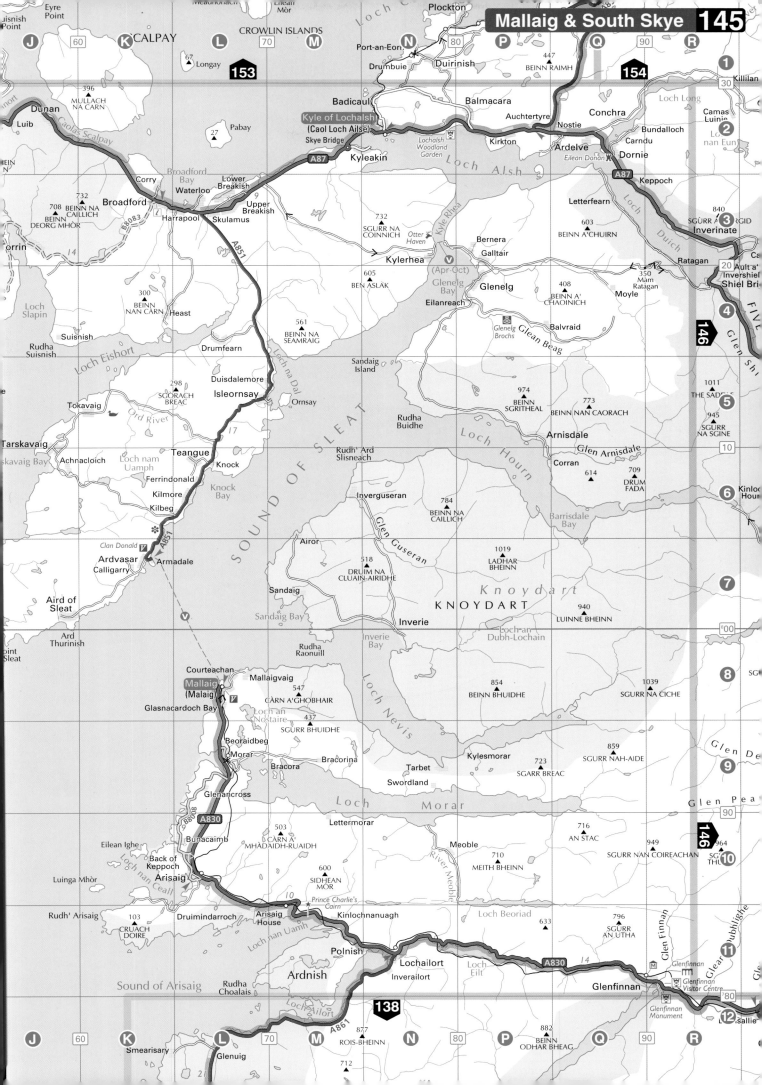

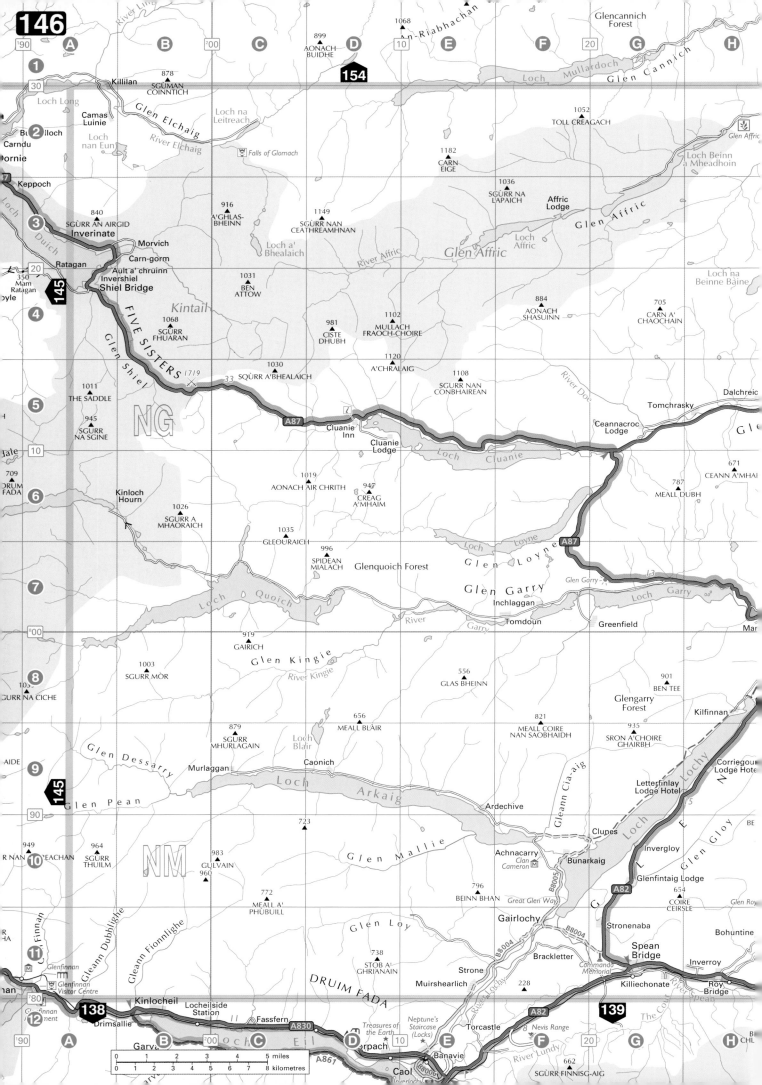

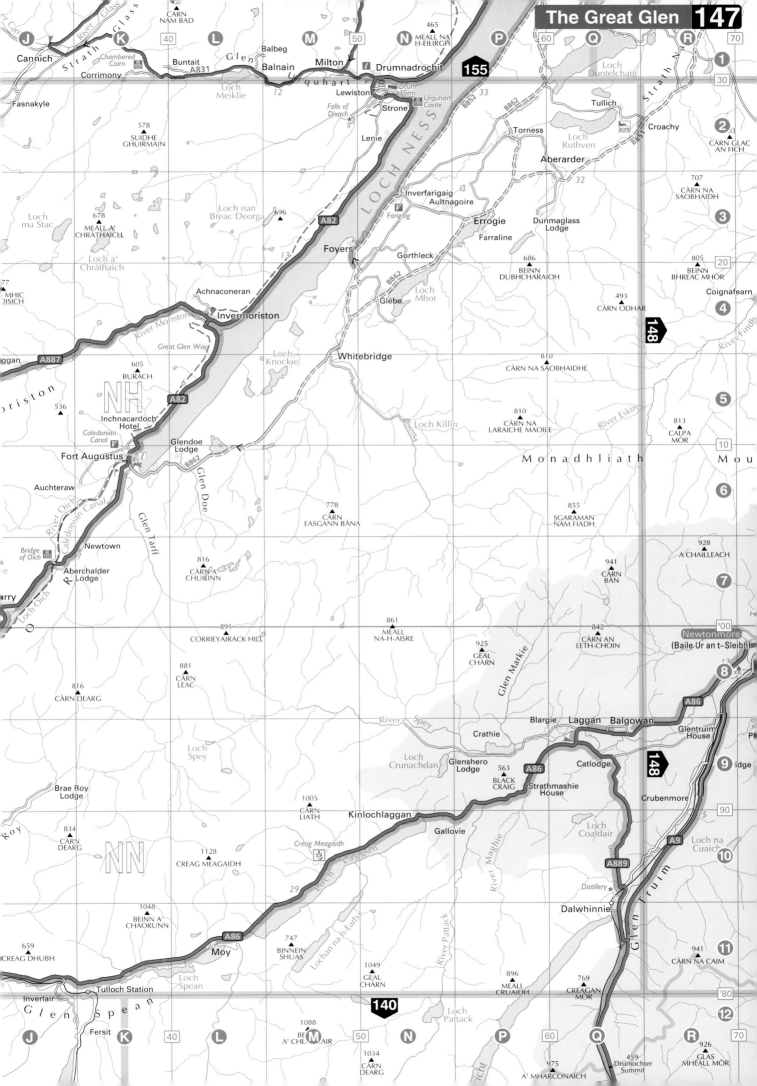

J **K** 40 **L** **M** 50 **N** **P** 60 **Q** **R** 70

Cannich
Strath Glass
River Glass
CÀRN NAM BAD
Glen
Balbeg
Milton
Drumnadrochit
155
465
MEALL NA H-EILIRGH

1

30

Chambered Cairn
Buntait
Balnain
Lewiston
Drum Farm
Loch Duntelchaig

Corrimony
A831
12
Urquhart Castle
B852 33

Fasnakyle
Loch Meiklie
Strone
Falls of Divach
B862
Torness
Tullich
Croachy

2

578
SUIDHE GHUIRMAIN
Lenie
Loch Ness
Loch Ruthven
Aberarder
B851

CÀRN GLAC AN FICH

678
MEALL A' CHRÀTHAICH
Loch nan Breac Deorga
696
Inverfarigaig
Aultnagoire
Errogie
Dunmaglass Lodge

707
CÀRN NA SAOBHAIDH

3

Loch ma Stac
Farigaig
Farraline
805
BEINN BHREAC MHÒR

Loch a' Chràthaich
Foyers
Gorthleck
686
BEINN DUBHCHARAIOH
Coignafearn
20

MHIC DISICH
Achnaconeran
Glebe
Loch Mhor
493
CÀRN ODHAR

4

River Moriston
Invermoriston
810
CÀRN NA SAOBHAIDHE

5

Great Glen Way
Loch Knockie
Whitebridge
River Eskin

A887
BURACH
605
NH
Loch Killin
810
CÀRN NA LARAICHE MAOILE
813
CALPA MÒR
10

536
A82
Inchnacardoch Hotel
Monadhliath
Mou

Caledonian Canal
Glendoe Lodge
B862

6

Fort Augustus
Glen Doe
778
CÀRN EASGANN BÀNA
855
SGARAMAN NAM FIADH

Auchteraw
Glen Tarff
A' CHAILLEACH
928

Newtown
816
CÀRN A' CHUILINN
941
CÀRN BAN

7

Bridge of Oich
Aberchalder Lodge
891
CORRIEYAIRACK HILL
861
MEALL NA-H-AISRE
842
CÀRN AN LETH-CHOIN
Newtonmore
(Baile Ùr an t-Sleibh)
00

arry
Loch Oich
925
GEAL CHÀRN

8

881
CÀRN LEAC
Glen Markie
A86

816
CÀRN DEARG
River Spey
Blargie
Laggan
Balgowan
Glentruim House

9

Loch Spey
Crathie
Catlodge
148
idge

834
CÀRN DEARG
NN
Glenshero Lodge
563
BLACK CRAIG
Strathmashie House
Crubenmore

90

Brae Roy Lodge
1005
CÀRN LIATH
Kinlochlaggan
A86
Loch Coaldair
A9
Loch na Cuaich

659
CREAG DHUBH
1128
CREAG MEAGAIDH
Creag Meagaidh
Gallovie
River Maghie
A889

10

1048
BEINN A' CHAORUNN
Loch Laggan
29
Distillery
Dalwhinnie
Glen Truim

747
BINNEIN SHUAS
941
CÀRN NA CAIM

11

Moy
A86
Lochan na h-Earba
River Pattack
769
CREAGAN MÒR

Tulloch Station
Loch Spean
1049
GEAL CHÀRN
896
MEALL CRUAIDH

Inverlair
Fersit
140
1034
CÀRN DEARG
975
A' MHARCONAICH
459
Drumochter Summit

12

Glen Spean
1088
BE A' CHL MAIR

926
GLAS MHEALL MÒR

J **K** 40 **L** **M** 50 **N** **P** 60 **Q** **R** 70

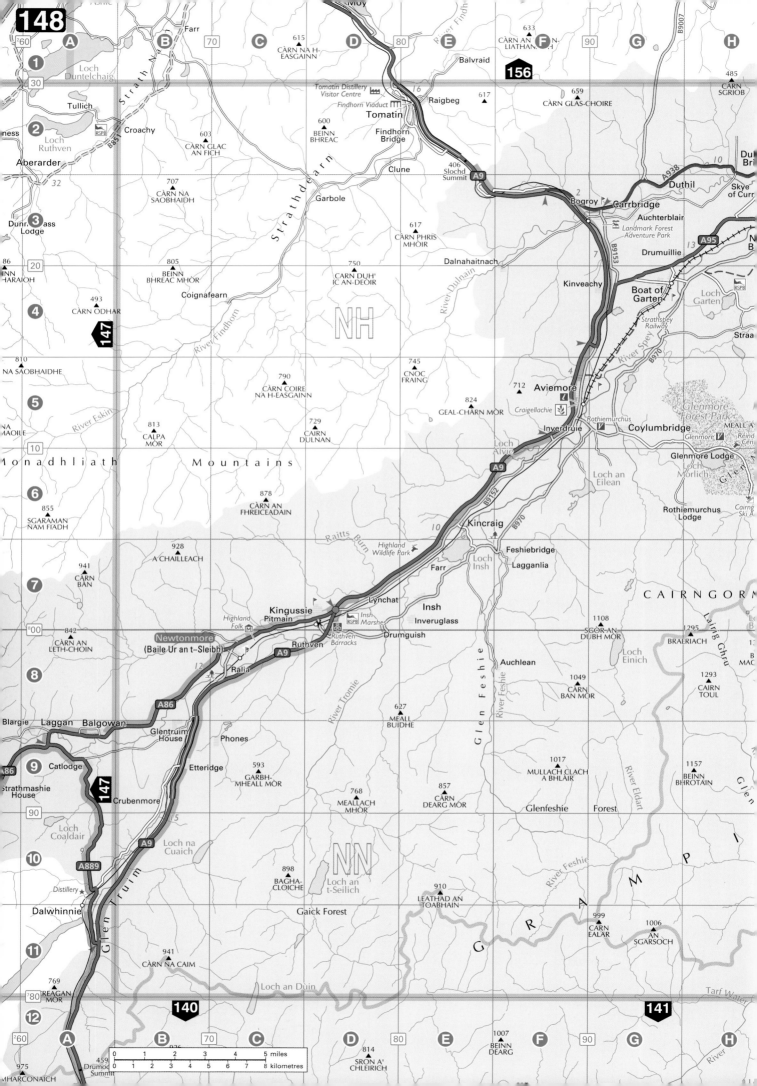

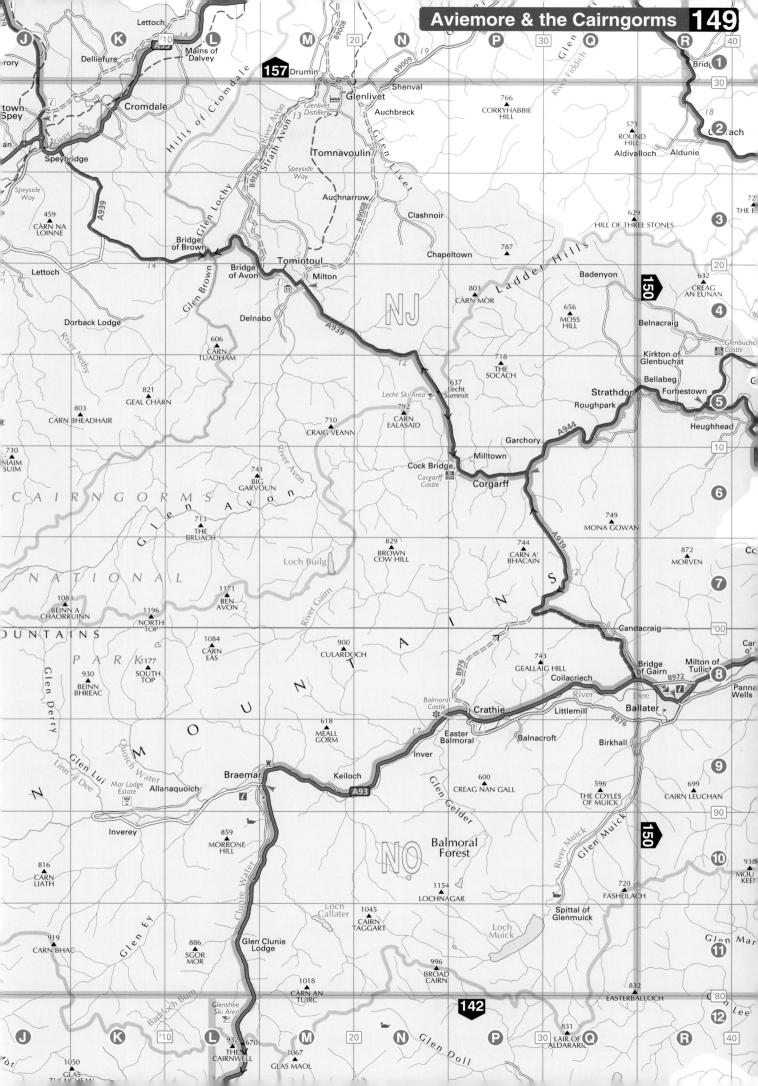

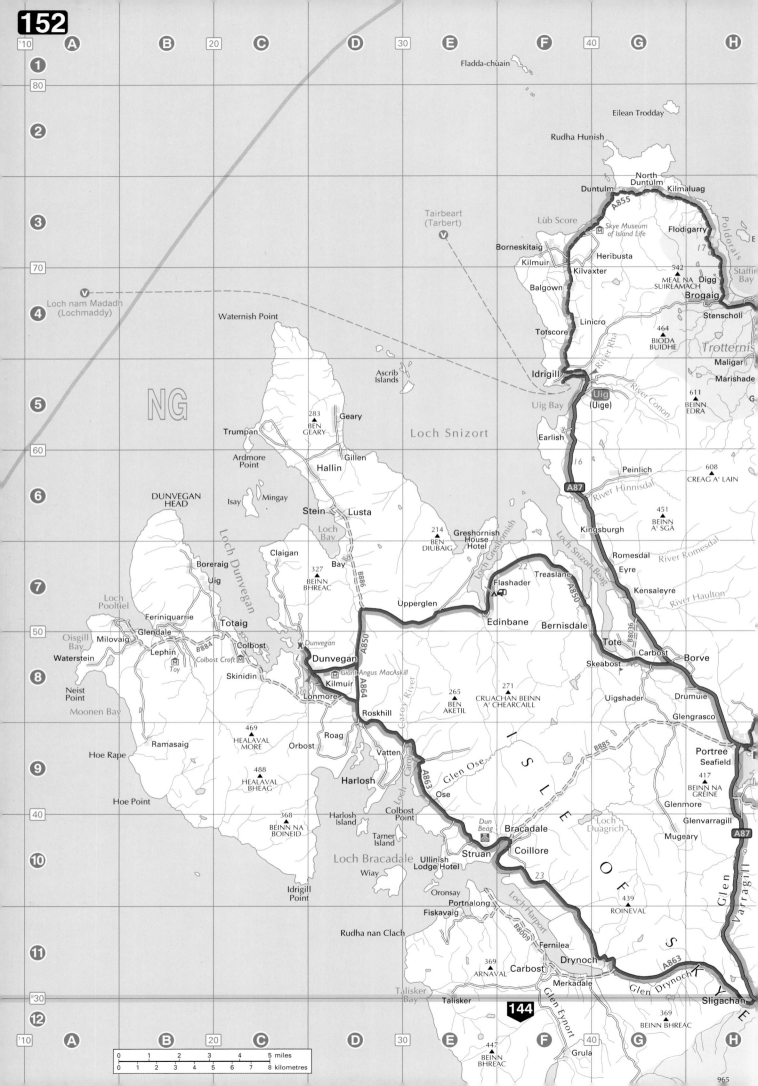

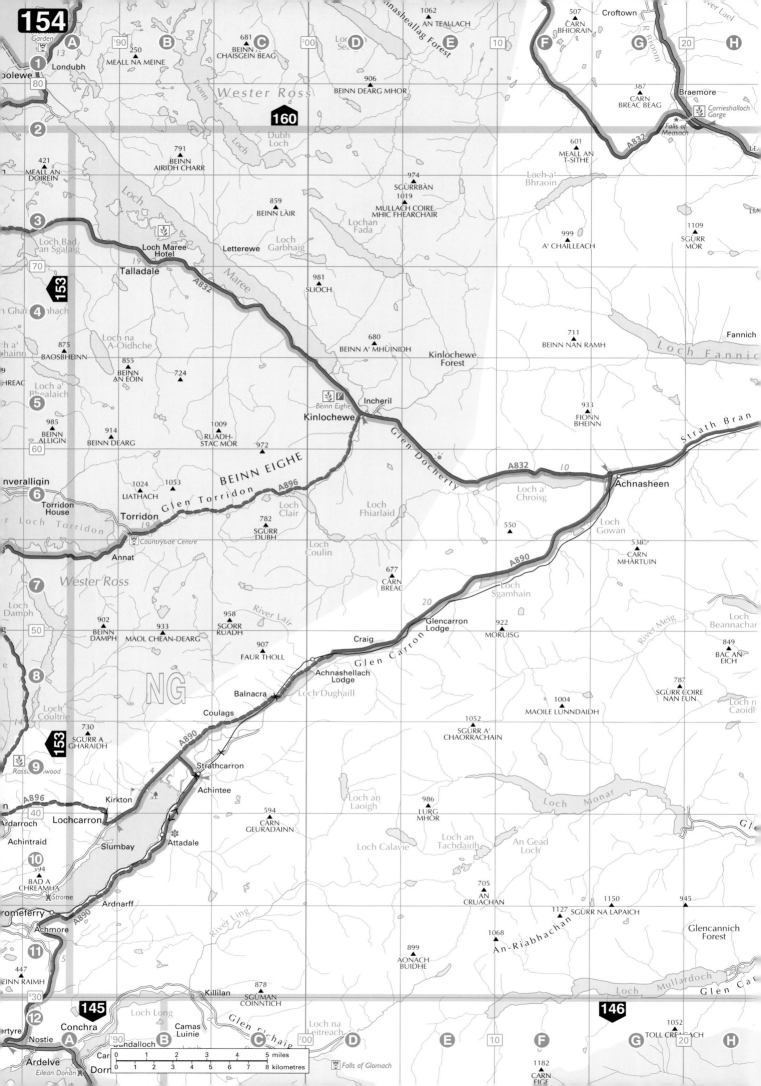

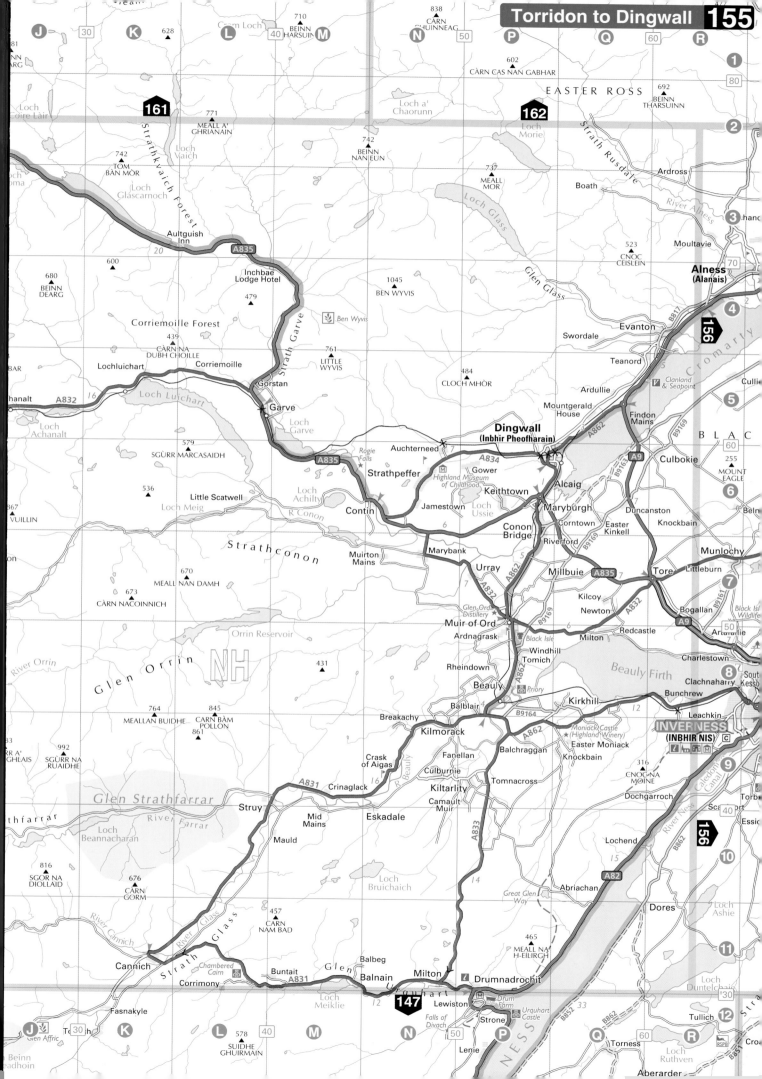

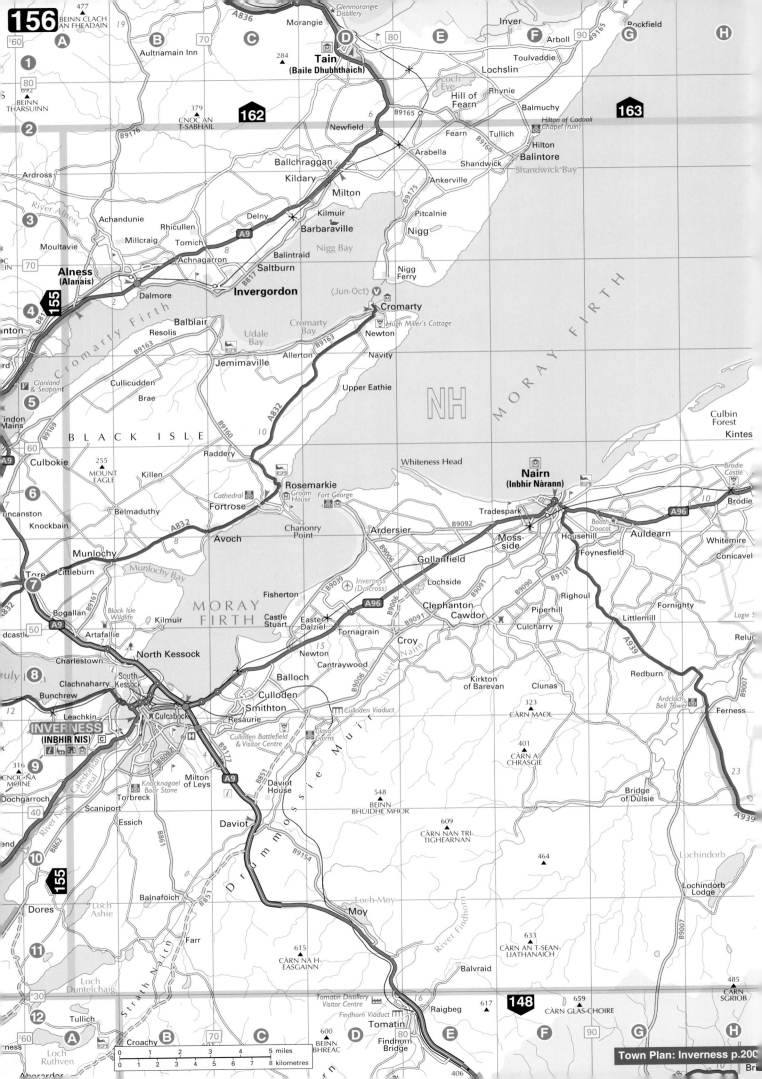

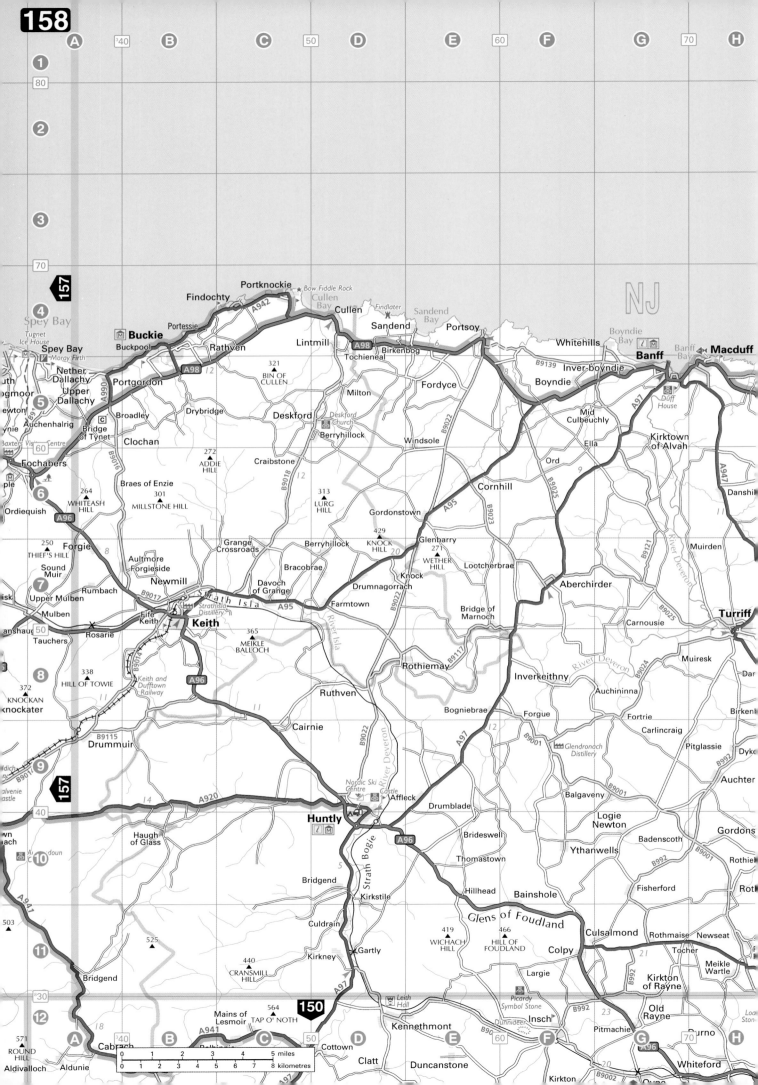

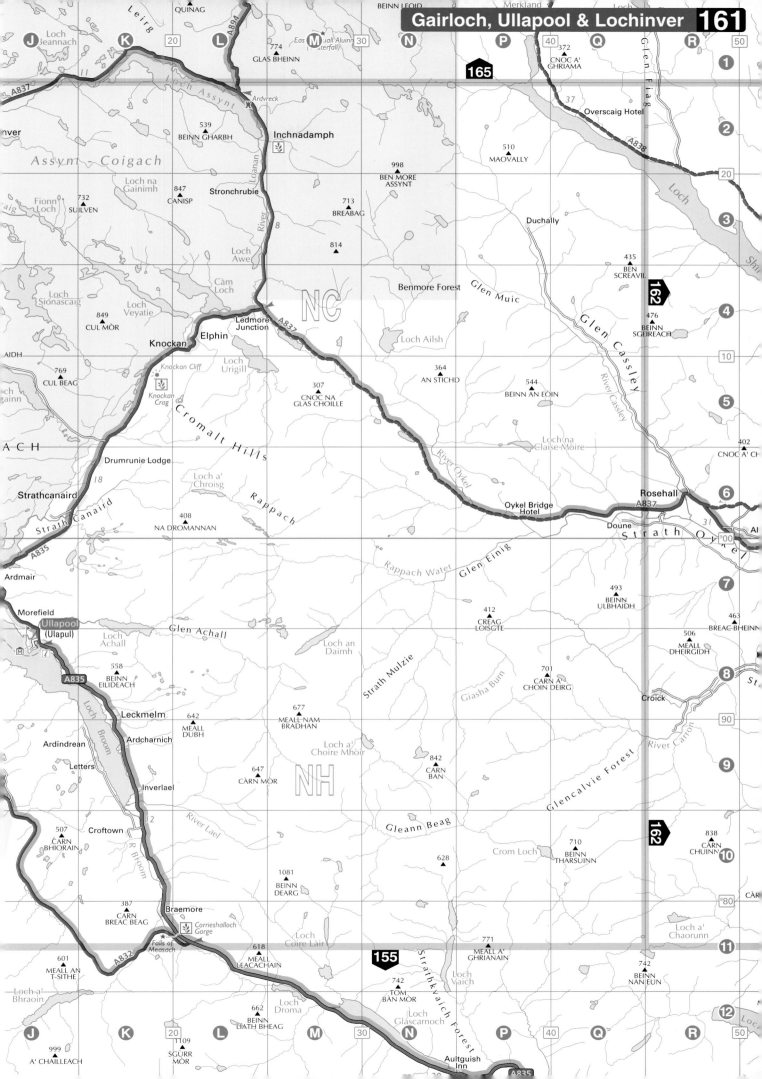

J K 20 L A894 M N P 40 Q R 50

Leirg

QUINAG
BEINN LEOID
Merkland
Glen Fiag

1

774
GLAS BHEINN
Eas M Muall Aluinn 30
(Waterfall)

372
CNOC A'
GHRIAMA

165

Loch Jeannach

A837
Loch Assynt
Ardreck
Inchnadamph

Overscaig Hotel

37

A838

2

Assynt - Coigach

539
BEINN GHARBH

510
MAOVALLY

20

Loch na Gainimh

998
BEN MORE
ASSYNT

Duchally

Loch Shin

3

Fionn Loch

732
SUILVEN

847
CANISP

Stronchrubie

River

713
BREABAG

435
BEN
SCREAVIL

Càm Loch

814

Benmore Forest

Glen Muic

476
BEINN
SGEIREACH

162

4

Loch Sionascaig

849
CUL MÒR

Loch Veyatie

Loch Awe

Loch Ailsh

10

Knockan

Elphin

Ledmore
Junction

A837

364
AN STICHD

Glen Cassley

River Cassley

5

769
CUL BEAG

Knockan Cliff

Loch Urigill

307
CNOC NA
GLAS CHOILLE

544
BEINN AN EÒIN

Loch na
Claise-Mòire

402
CNOC A' CH

Knockan
Crag

Cromalt Hills

River Oykel

6

Drumrunie Lodge

18

Loch a'
Chroisg

Rappach

Strathcanaird

Strath Canaird

408
NA DROMANNAN

Oykel Bridge
Hotel

Rosehall
A837

Doune

31

Strath Oykel

Al

A835

Ardmair

Rappach Water

Glen Einig

7

Morefield

493
BEINN
ULBHAIDH

463
BREAC-BHEINN

Ullapool
(Ulapul)

Glen Achall

Loch Achall

Loch an
Daimh

412
CREAG
LOISGTE

506
MEALL
DHEIRGIDH

8

558
BEINN
EILIDEACH

Strath Mulzie

Giasha Burn

701
CARN A'
CHOIN DEIRG

Croick

90

Leckmelm

642
MEALL
DUBH

677
MEALL-NAM-
BRADHAN

River Carron

Ardcharnich

Loch a'
Choire Mhòir

842
CARN
BAN

9

Ardindrean

Letters

647
CÀRN MÒR

NH

Glencalvie Forest

Inverlael

Gleann Beag

838
CÀRN
CHUINN

162

10

507
CARN
BHIORAIN

Croftown

River Lael

628

Crom Loch

710
BEINN
THARSUINN

R Broom

1081
BEINN
DEARG

80

387
CARN
BREAC BEAG

Braemore

Corrieshalloch
Gorge

Loch
Coire Làir

771
MEALL A'
GHRIANAIN

Loch a'
Chaorunn

11

601
MEALL AN
T-SITHE

Falls of
Measach

A832

618
MEALL
LEACACHAIN

155

Strathvaich Forest

Loch
Vaich

742
BEINN
NAN EUN

Loch-a'
Bhraoin

Loch
Droma

742
TOM
BÀN MOR

999
A' CHAILLEACH

1109
SGÙRR
MÒR

662
BEINN
LIATH BHEAG

Loch
Glascarnoch

12

Loch

J K 20 L 20 M 30 N 30 P 40 Q R 50

Aultguish
Inn

A835

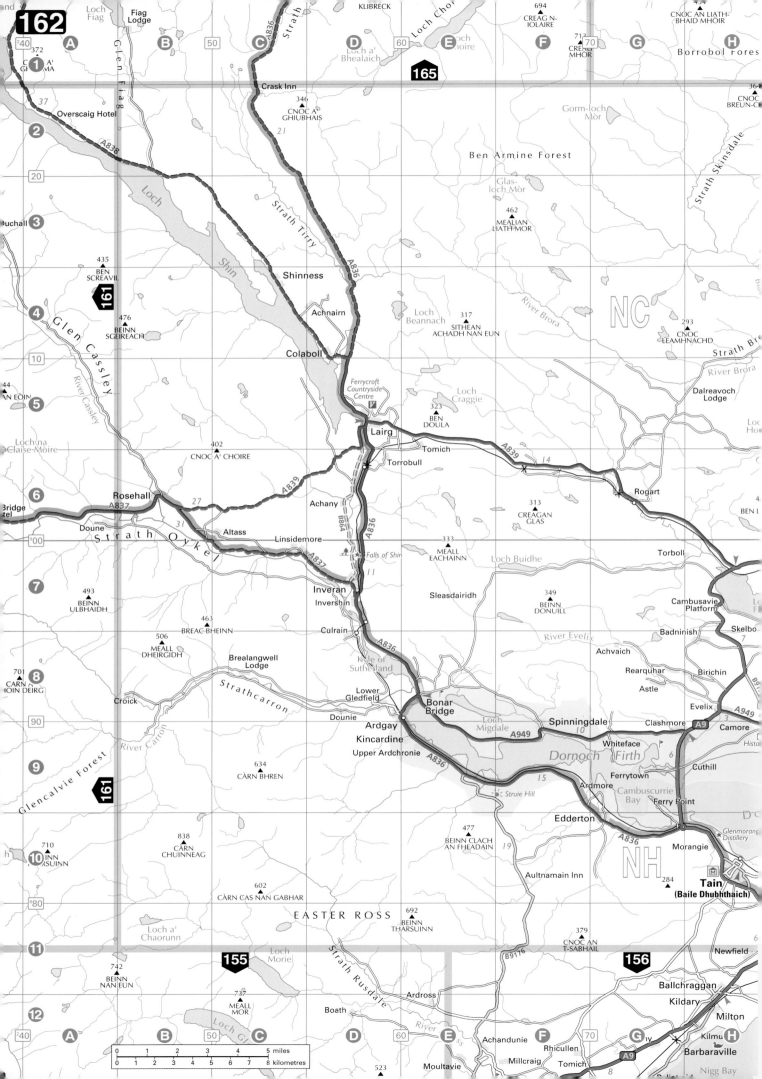

J K L M N P Q R

NA YEARNA

202

CNOC DAIL-
CHAIRN

Strath Free

90 Suisgill Ln

518

CNOC AN
EIREANNAICH

'00

705

MORVEN

626

SCARABEN

10

nscraigs

1

6

Loch
Ascaig

Langwell Forest

167

20

Borgue

388

CREAG NAM FIADH

*Learable Hill
Cairns, Stone Row
& Stone Circles*

Kildonan Lodge

Newport

Langwell
House

Berriedale

2

337

NOC NA H-
NSE MOIRE

Kildonan 416

BEINN
DUBHAIN

A897

Torrish

River Helmsdale

401

CNOC NA
MAOILE

A9

A9

20

20

3

421

CNOC NAN CRÙBAG MÒR

624

BEINN
DHORAIN

591

BEINN NA
MÈILICH

West
Helmsdale

Gartymore

Portgower

404

CREAG
THORARAIDH

Timespan

Navidale House Hotel

East Helmsdale

Helmsdale

Ord of Caithness

ND

4

nacoil
odge

Glen Loth

21

539

COL-
BHEINN

Lothmore

Lothbeg

10

5

Loch
Brora

Dalchalm

6

378

CAGAR
FEOSAIG

Backies

Carn Liath

A9

A9

Doll

Brora

6

383

HRAGGIE
Rhives

Dunrobin Castle

Golspie

'00

7

reet

rpenny

Embo

bo Street

8

noch

90

Firth

Tarbat Ness

9

Innis Mhor

Brucefield

Wilkhaven

Portmahomack

NJ

10

Inver

Rockfield

B9165

Arboll

Toulvaddie

Lochslin

'80

Loch
Eye

Rhynie

Hill of
Fearn

Balmuchy

*Hilton of Cadboll
Chapel (ruin)*

11

Fearn

Tullich

Hilton

B9166

rabella

Balintore

Shandwick

Shandwick Bay

Ankerville

itca

12

J K L M N P Q R

90 '00 10 20

B9040

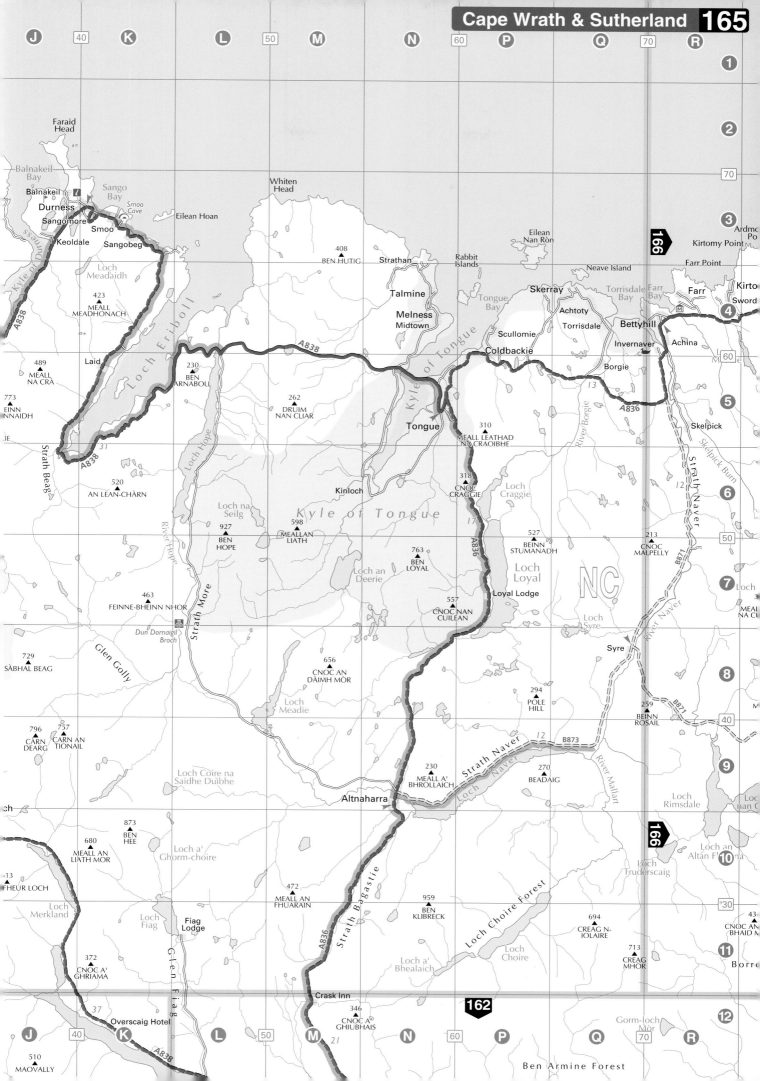

J · 40 · K · 50 · L · M · 60 · N · P · 70 · Q · R
1 · 2 · 70 · 3

166

Faraid
Head

Balnakeil
Bay
Balnakeil
Durness
Sango Bay
Smoo Cave
Sangomore
Smoo
Keoldale
Sangobeg

Eilean Hoan

Whiten
Head

408
BEN HUTIG
Strathan

Eilean
Nan Ròn
Rabbit
Islands
Neave Island

Kirtomy Point
Farr Point

Ardmo
Po
Kirto

Loch
Meadaidh

Talmine

Melness
Midtown

Skerray
Achtoty
Torrisdale Bay
Farr Bay
Farr
Sword

Torrisdale
Bettyhill
Achina
Kirto

423
MEALL
MEADHONACH

Loch Eriboll

Scullomie

Coldbackie
Invernaver
Borgie

A838

Kyle of Tongue
Tongue Bay

489
MEALL
NA CRÀ

Laid

230
BEN
ARNABOLL

262
DRUIM
NAN CLIAR

A838

Tongue
310
MEALL LEATHAD
NA CRAOIBHE

River Borgie
A836
13

Skelpick
Strath Naver
Skelpick Burn
12

773
EINN
NNAIDH

Strath Beag

A838
31

Loch Hope

Kinloch

318
CNOC
CRAGGIE

Loch
Craggie

520
AN LEAN-CHÀRN

Kyle of Tongue
17
A836

527
BEINN
STUMANADH

213
CNOC
MALPELLY

B871

Loch na
Seilg

927
BEN
HOPE

598
MEALLAN
LIATH

763
BEN
LOYAL

Loch
Loyal

NC

River Hope

Strath More

Loch an
Deerie

557
CNOC NAN
CUILEAN

Loyal Lodge

Loch
Syre
Loch

MEAL
NA CU

463
FEINNE-BHEINN NHOR

Dun Dornaigil Broch

Glen Golly

656
CNOC AN
DÀIMH MÒR

Syre
River Naver
B871
40

259
BEINN
ROSAIL

M

729
SÀBHAL BEAG

Loch
Meadie

294
POLE
HILL

796
CARN
DEARG

757
CARN AN
TIONAIL

Loch Coire na
Saidhe Duibhe

230
MEALL A'
BHROLLAICH

Strath Naver
12
B873

Loch Mallart

270
BEADAIG

Loch
Rimsdale
Loc
nan

FHEUR LOCH
13

Altnaharra

Loch Naver

166

873
BEN
HEE

680
MEALL AN
LIATH MOR

Loch a'
Ghorm-choire

472
MEALL AN
FHUARAIN

Strath Bagastie

959
BEN
KLIBRECK

Loch Choire Forest

Loch an
Altan F na

Loch
Truderscaig

30

Loch
Merkland

Loch
Fiag
Fiag
Lodge

Loch a'
Bhealaich

Loch
Choire

694
CREAG N-
IOLAIRE

43
CNOC AN
BHAID M

372
CNOC A'
GHRIAMA

Glen Fiag
A836

713
CREAG
MHOR

Borro

Crask Inn

162

Overscaig Hotel
37
A838
K · 40

346
CNOC A'
GHIUBHAIS
21

Gorm-loch
Mòr

510
MAOVALLY

Ben Armine Forest

J · K · 40 · L · 50 · M · 60 · N · P · 70 · Q · R
4 · 5 · 6 · 7 · 8 · 9 · 10 · 11 · 12

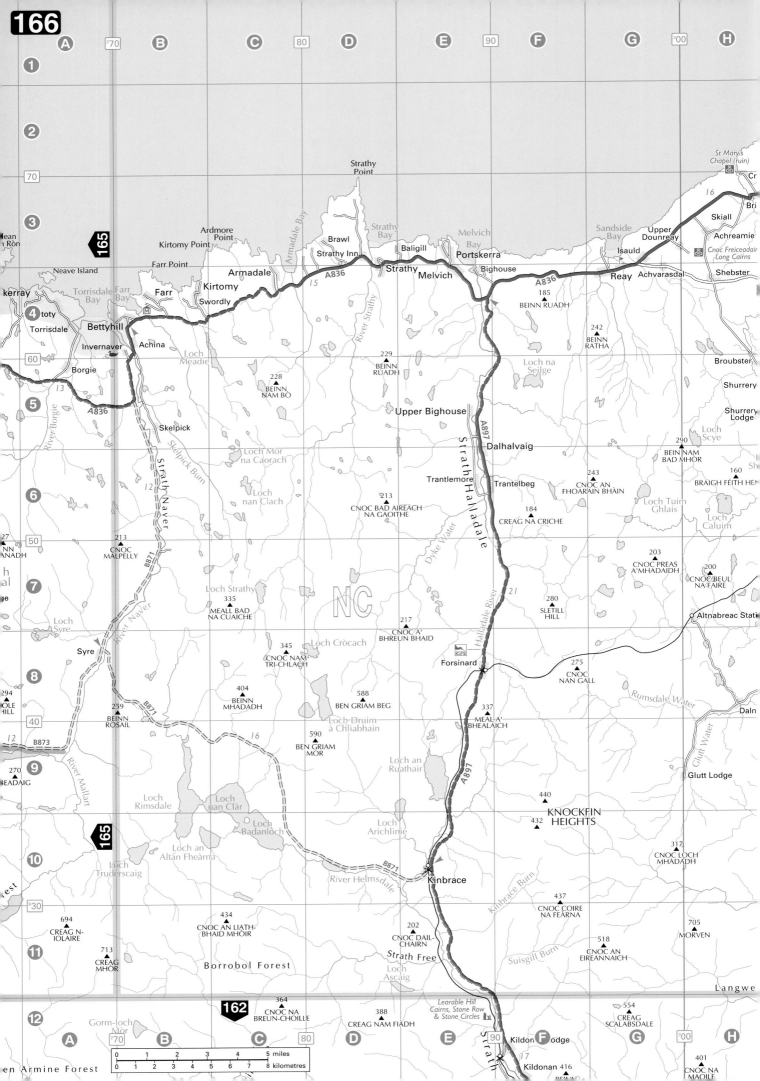

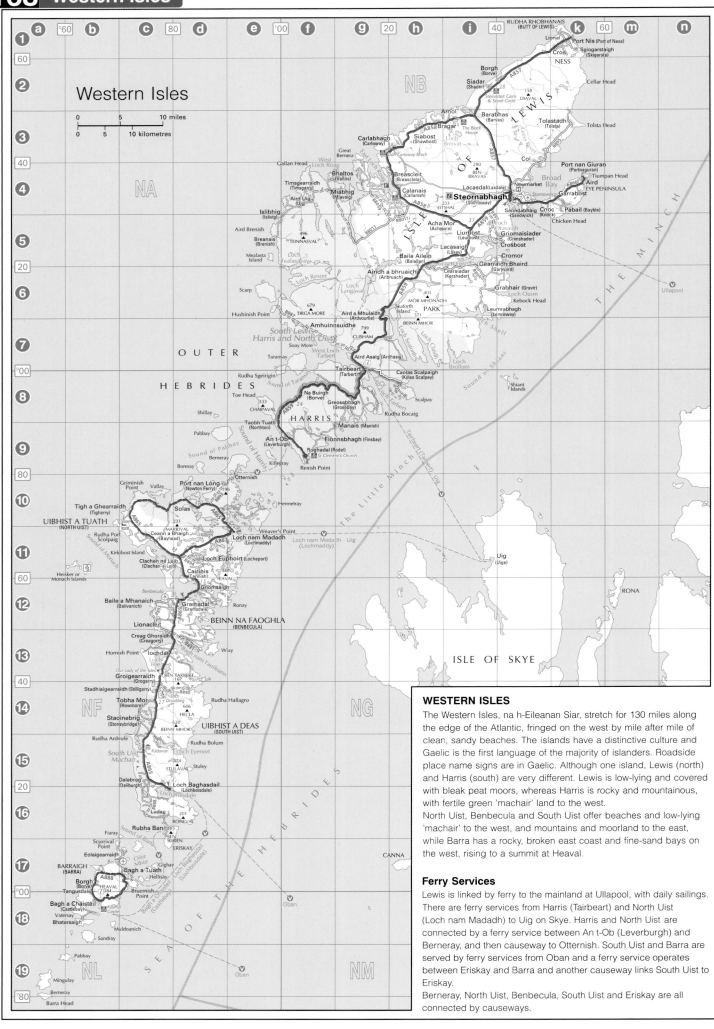

Western Isles

WESTERN ISLES

The Western Isles, na h-Eileanan Siar, stretch for 130 miles along the edge of the Atlantic, fringed on the west by mile after mile of clean, sandy beaches. The islands have a distinctive culture and Gaelic is the first language of the majority of islanders. Roadside place name signs are in Gaelic. Although one island, Lewis (north) and Harris (south) are very different. Lewis is low-lying and covered with bleak peat moors, whereas Harris is rocky and mountainous, with fertile green 'machair' land to the west.

North Uist, Benbecula and South Uist offer beaches and low-lying 'machair' to the west, and mountains and moorland to the east, while Barra has a rocky, broken east coast and fine-sand bays on the west, rising to a summit at Heaval.

Ferry Services

Lewis is linked by ferry to the mainland at Ullapool, with daily sailings. There are ferry services from Harris (Tairbeart) and North Uist (Loch nam Madadh) to Uig on Skye. Harris and North Uist are connected by a ferry service between An t-Ob (Leverburgh) and Berneray, and then causeway to Otternish. South Uist and Barra are served by ferry services from Oban and a ferry service operates between Eriskay and Barra and another causeway links South Uist to Eriskay.

Berneray, North Uist, Benbecula, South Uist and Eriskay are all connected by causeways.

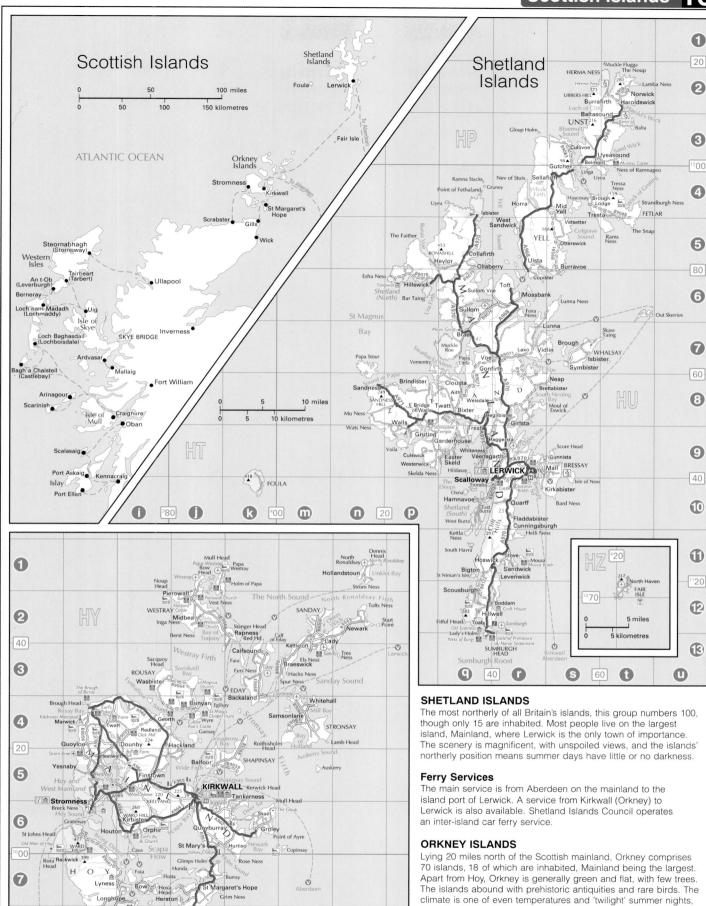

SHETLAND ISLANDS

The most northerly of all Britain's islands, this group numbers 100, though only 15 are inhabited. Most people live on the largest island, Mainland, where Lerwick is the only town of importance. The scenery is magnificent, with unspoiled views, and the islands' northerly position means summer days have little or no darkness.

Ferry Services

The main service is from Aberdeen on the mainland to the island port of Lerwick. A service from Kirkwall (Orkney) to Lerwick is also available. Shetland Islands Council operates an inter-island car ferry service.

ORKNEY ISLANDS

Lying 20 miles north of the Scottish mainland, Orkney comprises 70 islands, 18 of which are inhabited, Mainland being the largest. Apart from Hoy, Orkney is generally green and flat, with few trees. The islands abound with prehistoric antiquities and rare birds. The climate is one of even temperatures and 'twilight' summer nights, but with violent winds at times.

Ferry Services

The main service is from Scrabster on the Caithness coast to Stromness and there is a further service from Gills (Caithness) to St Margaret's Hope on South Ronaldsay. A service from Aberdeen to Kirkwall provides a link to Shetland at Lerwick. Inter-island car ferry services are also operated (advance reservations recommended).

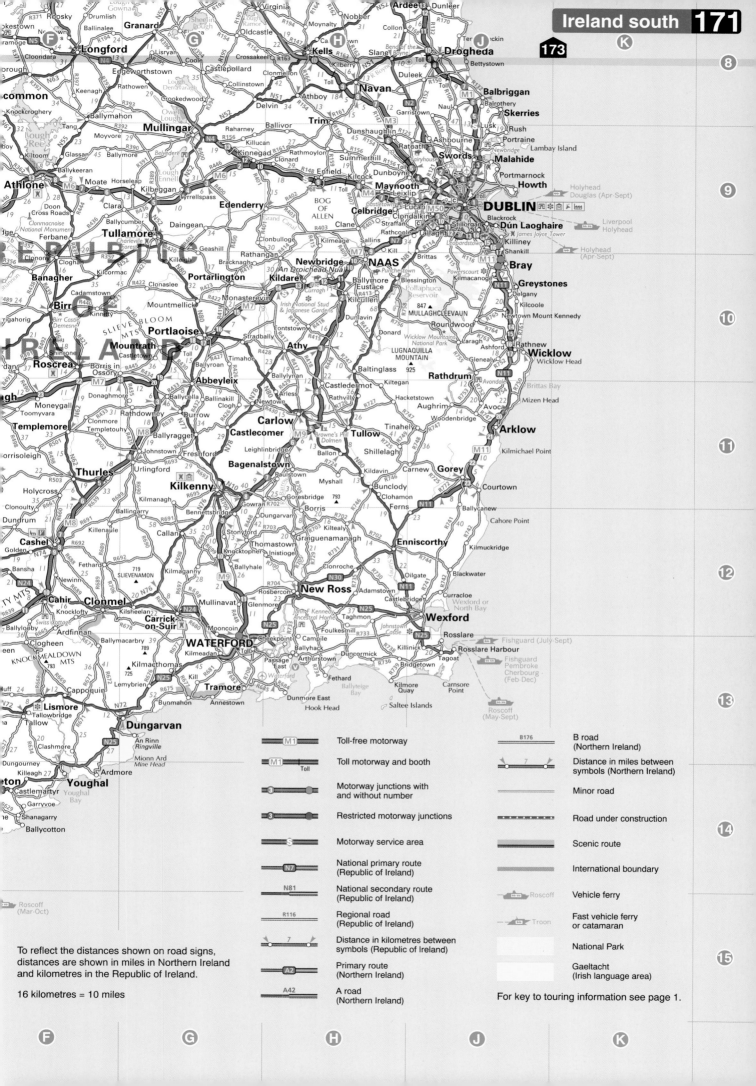

173

Legend

M1	Toll-free motorway
M1 Toll	Toll motorway and booth
3	Motorway junctions with and without number
3	Restricted motorway junctions
S	Motorway service area
N7	National primary route (Republic of Ireland)
N81	National secondary route (Republic of Ireland)
R116	Regional road (Republic of Ireland)
7	Distance in kilometres between symbols (Republic of Ireland)
A2	Primary route (Northern Ireland)
A42	A road (Northern Ireland)
B176	B road (Northern Ireland)
7	Distance in miles between symbols (Northern Ireland)
	Minor road
	Road under construction
	Scenic route
	International boundary
Roscoff	Vehicle ferry
Troon	Fast vehicle ferry or catamaran
	National Park
	Gaeltacht (Irish language area)

To reflect the distances shown on road signs, distances are shown in miles in Northern Ireland and kilometres in the Republic of Ireland.

16 kilometres = 10 miles

For key to touring information see page 1.

Ireland index

C12 Abbeydorney
D12 Abbeyfeale
G11 Abbeyleix
H12 Adamstown
D12 Adare
C14 Adrigole
H4 Aghadowey
E9 Ahascragh
J4 Ahoghill
B15 Allihies
B13 Anascaul
E4 An Bun Beag
E5 An Charraig
E4 An Clochán Liath
B14 An Coireán
B13 An Daingean
C9 An Fhairche
J7 Annalong
G13 Annestown
G13 An Rinn
D9 An Spidéal
J5 Antrim
D12 Ardagh
E5 Ardara
H8 Ardee
C12 Ardfert
F12 Ardfinnan
K6 Ardglass
B14 Ardgroom
F14 Ardmore
J11 Arklow
H11 Arless
H6 Armagh
J3 Armoy
H13 Arthurstown
G7 Arvagh
J9 Ashbourne
J10 Ashford
D12 Askeaton
H8 Athboy
D12 Athea
E9 Athenry
E8 Athleague
F9 Athlone
H10 Athy
G6 Augher
H6 Aughnacloy
J11 Aughrim
J11 Avoca

H11 Bagenalstown
D14 Baile Mhic Íre
H7 Bailieborough
J8 Balbriggan
D8 Balla
E7 Ballaghaderreen
D7 Ballina
E11 Ballina
E7 Ballinafad
G7 Ballinagh
G11 Ballinakill
F8 Ballinalee
G6 Ballinamallard
F7 Ballinamore
D14 Ballinascarty
E9 Ballinasloe
D8 Ballindine
D14 Ballineen
D12 Ballingarry
G12 Ballingarry
D14 Ballingeary
E14 Ballinhassig
E8 Ballinlough
D8 Ballinrobe
E15 Ballinspittle
E8 Ballintober
F5 Ballintra
H9 Ballivor
H11 Ballon
E9 Ballybaun
H7 Ballybay
F5 Ballybofey
C12 Ballybunion
J11 Ballycanew
K5 Ballycarry
J3 Ballycastle
C6 Ballycastle
J5 Ballyclare
G11 Ballycolla
B9 Ballyconneely
G7 Ballyconnell
F14 Ballycotton
F9 Ballycumber
C15 Ballydehob
D13 Ballydesmond
C12 Ballyduff
F13 Ballyduff
E7 Ballyfarnan
J4 Ballygalley
E9 Ballygar
E6 Ballygawley
H6 Ballygawley
K5 Ballygowan
H13 Ballyhack
G7 Ballyhaise
G12 Ballyhale
E8 Ballyhaunis
D8 Ballyhean
C12 Ballyheige
G8 Ballyjamesduff
F9 Ballykeeran
E12 Ballylanders
C14 Ballylickey
G3 Ballyliffin
C12 Ballylongford
F12 Ballylooby
H10 Ballylynan
F13 Ballymacarbry
F8 Ballymahon
D14 Ballymakeery
J4 Ballymena
H4 Ballymoney
F9 Ballymore
H10 Ballymore Eustace
E7 Ballymote
J6 Ballynahinch
J5 Ballynure

F13 Ballyporeen
G11 Ballyragget
G10 Ballyroan
H5 Ballyronan
E6 Ballysadare
F5 Ballyshannon
D10 Ballyvaughan
K5 Ballywalter
J8 Balrothery
C15 Baltimore
H10 Baltinglass
F10 Banagher
E14 Bandon
K5 Bangor
C7 Bangor Erris
F12 Bansha
D13 Banteer
C14 Bantry
D9 Barna
B6 Béal an Mhuirthead
D14 Béal Átha an Ghaorthaidh
D9 Bearna
C13 Beaufort
J5 Belcoo
E14 Belgooly
H4 Bellaghy
F6 Belleek
B6 Belmullet
G7 Belturbet
H6 Benburb
G12 Bennettsbridge
G5 Beragh
J8 Bettystown
F10 Birr
F6 Blacklion
J9 Blackrock
J12 Blackwater
E14 Blarney
H10 Blessington
D13 Boherbue
H12 Borris
F8 Borris in Ossory
F10 Borrisokane
F11 Borrisoleigh
E7 Boyle
G10 Bracknagh
J10 Bray
H13 Bridgetown
J9 Brittas
E11 Broadford
D12 Broadford
J4 Broughshane
E12 Bruff
E12 Bruree
E4 Bunbeg
H11 Bunclody
G3 Buncrana
E6 Bundoran
G13 Bunmahon
C6 Bun na hAbhna
C6 Bunnahowen
D7 Bunnyconnellan
D11 Bunratty
E13 Burnfort
H3 Bushmills
E13 Buttevant

F10 Cadamstown
E12 Caherconlish
B14 Caherdaniel
B14 Cahersiveen
F12 Cahir
H6 Caledon
G12 Callan
E9 Caltra
B13 Camp
H13 Campile
F12 Cappagh White
E11 Cappamore
F13 Cappoquin
H8 Carlanstown
J7 Carlingford
H11 Carlow
C9 Carna
G3 Carndonagh
J11 Carnew
J4 Carnlough
E7 Carracastle
F3 Carraig Airt
E5 Carrick
F3 Carrickart
K5 Carrickfergus
H7 Carrickmacross
G5 Carrickmore or Termon Rock
F7 Carrick-on-Shannon
G12 Carrick-on-Suir
F10 Carrigahorig
E14 Carrigaline
F7 Carrigallen
D14 Carriganimmy
G4 Carrigans
E14 Carrigtohill
J5 Carryduff
C9 Cashel
F12 Cashel
D8 Castlebar
J7 Castlebellingham
H7 Castleblayney
J12 Castlebridge
G11 Castlecomer
E11 Castleconnell
G5 Castlederg
H11 Castledermot
B13 Castlegregory
C13 Castleisland
C13 Castlemaine
F14 Castlemartyr
E8 Castleplunket
G8 Castlepollard
E8 Castlerea
H3 Castlerock
H6 Castleshane
G10 Castletown

B15 Castletownbere
E13 Castletownroche
D15 Castletownshend
J6 Castlewellan
B14 Cathair Dónall
C12 Causeway
G7 Cavan
H9 Celbridge
D7 Charlestown
E12 Charleville
H13 Cheekpoint
E5 Cill Charthaigh
C9 Cill Chiaráin
G5 Clady
H9 Clane
G9 Clara
D11 Clarecastle
D8 Claremorris
D10 Clarinbridge
F13 Clashmore
G4 Claudy
B9 Clifden
E6 Cliffony
G11 Clogh
F10 Cloghan
F13 Clogheen
G6 Clogher
H11 Clohamon
G10 Clonakilty
H9 Clonard
G10 Clonaslee
C9 Clonbur
J9 Clondalkin
G7 Clones
E11 Clonlara
G3 Clonmany
F12 Clonmel
H8 Clonmellon
F11 Clonmore
F10 Clonony
F12 Clonoulty
H12 Clonroche
H6 Clontibret
F8 Cloondara
K6 Clough
F10 Cloughjordan
F14 Cloyne
H5 Coagh
H5 Coalisland
E14 Cobh
H3 Coleraine
G8 Collinstown
H8 Collon
E6 Collooney
K5 Comber
D9 Cong
F13 Conna
H5 Cookstown
G8 Coole
C11 Cooraclare
G7 Cootehill
E14 Cork
C9 Cornamona
C9 Corr na Móna
D10 Corrofin
E15 Courtmacsherry
J11 Courtown
J6 Craigavon
E10 Craughwell
K5 Crawfordsburn
E8 Creegs
F4 Creeslough
D12 Croagh
E4 Croithlí
E4 Crolly
G8 Crookedwood
C15 Crookhaven
D14 Crookstown
E12 Croom
H8 Crossakeel
E14 Cross Barry
E14 Crosshaven
H7 Crossmaglen
D7 Crossmolina

J5 Crumlin
D10 Crusheen
G3 Culdaff
J4 Cullybackey
J12 Curracloe
F9 Curraghboy
E7 Curry
J4 Cushendall
J3 Cushendun
H9 Daingean
J10 Delgany
G8 Delvin
G4 Derry
F6 Derrygonnelly
G6 Derrylin
H3 Dervock
B13 Dingle
J5 Doagh
K5 Donaghadee
H10 Donaghmore
H10 Donard
F5 Donegal
E13 Doneraile
C10 Doolin
E12 Doon
C11 Doonbeg
F9 Doon Cross Roads
E14 Douglas
K6 Downpatrick
F6 Dowra
H5 Draperstown
D15 Drimoleague
E14 Dripsey
J8 Drogheda
D12 Dromahair
J6 Dromcolliher
G5 Dromore
D6 Dromore West
E6 Drumcliff
H8 Drumcondra
F7 Drumkeeran
F8 Drumlish
F8 Drumod
G5 Drumquin
F7 Drumshanbo
F7 Drumsna
C12 Duagh
J9 Dublin
J8 Duleek
J9 Dunboyne
H13 Duncormick
J7 Dundalk
E14 Dunderrow
K5 Dundonald
K6 Dundrum
F12 Dundrum
F3 Dunfanaghy
H5 Dungannon
G12 Dungarvan
G13 Dungarvan
H4 Dungiven
E4 Dunglow
F14 Dungourney
E5 Dunkineely
J9 Dún Laoghaire
H10 Dunlavin
J8 Dunleer
J4 Dunloy
D14 Dunmanway
E8 Dunmore
H13 Dunmore East
J5 Dunmurry
H9 Dunshaughlin
G11 Durrow
F11 Durrus
C15 Durrus
E9 Dysart
D6 Easky
H9 Edenderry
G8 Edgeworthstown
G4 Eglinton
F8 Elphin
H6 Emyvale

H9 Enfield
D11 Ennis
H12 Enniscorthy
D14 Enniskean
F6 Enniskillen
D10 Ennistymon
F10 Eyrecourt
G4 Fahan
C13 Farranfore
E10 Feakle
F7 Fenagh
F9 Ferbane
E13 Fermoy
J12 Ferns
F12 Fethard
H13 Fethard
G8 Finnea
G6 Fintona
G6 Fivemiletown
H10 Fontstown
H12 Foulkesmill
D7 Foxford
D11 Foynes
D13 Freemount
E8 Frenchpark
G11 Freshford
E8 Fuerty
E12 Galbally
D9 Galway
F6 Garrison
J8 Garristown
F14 Garryvoe
H4 Garvagh
G10 Geashill
J6 Gilford
D15 Glandore
E14 Glanmire
E13 Glanworth
H6 Glaslough
F9 Glassan
E5 Gleann Cholm Cille
J4 Glenarm
J5 Glenavy
B13 Glenbeigh
E5 Glencolumbkille
J10 Glenealy
C14 Glengarriff
H12 Glenmore
E8 Glennamaddy
E5 Glenties
D12 Glin
C9 Glinsce
C9 Glinsk
F12 Golden
C15 Goleen
H11 Goresbridge
J11 Gorey
D10 Gort
G5 Gortin
H11 Gowran
H12 Graiguenamanagh
G8 Granard
E6 Grange
J7 Greenore
K5 Greyabbey
J10 Greystones
H4 Gulladuff
H11 Hacketstown
D9 Headford
E12 Herbertstown
J6 Hillsborough
J6 Hilltown
F11 Holycross
K5 Holywood
G9 Horseleap
E12 Hospital
J9 Howth
B13 Inch
D14 Inchigeelagh
E14 Inishannon

D6 Inishcrone
H12 Inistioge
F6 Irvinestown
G11 Johnstown
C10 Lahinch
F8 Lanesborough
J10 Laragh
K4 Larne
C14 Lauragh
F10 Laurencetown
D15 Leap
C8 Leenane
H11 Leighlinbridge
F7 Leitrim
H9 Leixlip
G13 Lemybrien
B8 Letterfrack
F4 Letterkenny
G4 Lifford
H4 Limavady
E11 Limerick
G6 Lisbellaw
J5 Lisburn
C10 Liscannor
D13 Liscarroll
D10 Lisdoonvarna
F13 Lismore
G6 Lisnaskea
G8 Lisryan
C12 Listowel
D12 Loghill
G4 Londonderry
F8 Longford
J6 Loughbrickland
H6 Loughgall
E8 Loughglinn

E10 Loughrea
C8 Louisburgh
J9 Lucan
J6 Lurgan
J9 Lusk
F3 Machair Loiscthe
D14 Macroom
J6 Maghera
H4 Maghera
H5 Magherafelt
G6 Maguiresbridge
J9 Malahide
E5 Málainn Mhóir
G3 Malin
E5 Malin More
E13 Mallow
F6 Manorhamilton
H6 Markethill
J4 Martinstown
H9 Maynooth
J5 Mazetown
H6 Middletown
F14 Middleton
F4 Milford
D13 Millstreet
C13 Milltown
C11 Milltown Malbay
E13 Mitchelstown
F9 Moate
F7 Mohill
H6 Monaghan
G10 Monasterevin
F11 Moneygall
H5 Moneymore
E9 Monivea

0   10   20 miles
0   10   20   30 kilometres

G13	Mooncoin	H10	Newbridge	J7	Omeath	C9	Recess	C13	Scartaglin	H5	Stewartstown	E7	Tobercurry
J4	Moorfields	J6	Newcastle	E12	Oola	B8	Renvyle	J6	Scarva	J9	Stillorgan	H4	Tobermore
E9	Mountbellew	D12	Newcastle West	D9	Oranmore	E14	Ringaskiddy	C15	Schull	G12	Stonyford	F11	Toomyvara
	Bridge	F12	Newinn	D9	Oughterard	G13	Ringville	F8	Scramoge	G4	Strabane	C15	Toormore
F5	Mountcharles	D13	Newmarket	E14	Ovens	H7	Rockcorry	G5	Seskinore	G10	Stradbally	C13	Tralee
G10	Mountmellick	D11	Newmarket-on-	E11	Pallas Green New	F8	Roosky	F14	Shanagarry	H9	Stradone	G13	Tramore
G10	Mountrath		Fergus	B14	Parknasilla	H12	Rosbercon	D12	Shanagolden	H9	Straffan	H8	Trim
E10	Mountshannon	C7	Newport	D8	Partry	F8	Roscommon	J9	Shankill	E6	Strandhill	D9	Tuam
G3	Moville	E11	Newport	H13	Passage East	F10	Roscrea	D11	Shannon	K6	Strangford	E11	Tuamgraney
H6	Moy	H12	New Ross	E14	Passage West	F3	Rosepenna	D11	Shannonbridge	F5	Stranorlar	D11	Tulla
H8	Moynalty	J6	Newry	E12	Patrickswell	D15	Ross Carbery	H7	Shercock	F8	Strokestown	G9	Tullamore
F9	Moyvore	J5	Newtownabbey	H11	Paulstown	E6	Rosses Point	H11	Shillelagh	H9	Summerhill	H11	Tullow
C13	Muckross	K5	Newtownards	F5	Pettigo	J13	Rosslare	F10	Shinrone	F6	Swanlinbar	E8	Tulsk
G4	Muff	G7	Newtownbutler	G5	Plumbridge	J13	Rosslare Harbour	D9	Shrule	H4	Swatragh	D7	Turlough
E6	Mullaghmore	F8	Newton Forbes	H5	Pomeroy	G6	Rosslea	E11	Silvermines	F6	Swinford	G9	Tyrrellspass
G12	Mullinavat	H6	Newtownhamilton	H6	Portadown	F5	Rossnowlagh	G5	Sion Mills	D7	Swords		
G9	Mullingar	J10	Newtown Mount	K6	Portaferry	J7	Rostrevor	D11	Sixmilebridge	J9		G11	Urlingford
C7	Mulrany		Kennedy	G10	Portarlington	B9	Roundstone	J8	Skerries				
H11	Myshall	G5	Newtownstewart	K6	Portavogie	J10	Roundwood	D15	Skibbereen	H12	Taghmon	G8	Virginia
		H8	Nobber	H3	Portballintrae	J9	Rush	H8	Slane	J13	Tagoat		
H10	Naas			H4	Portglenone			E6	Sligo	C14	Tahilla	J7	Warrenpoint
J8	Naul	E11	Ogonnelloe	G10	Portlaoise	K6	Saintfield	G6	Smithborough	J9	Tallaght	G13	Waterford
H8	Navan	H12	Oilgate	J6	Portmarnock	G4	St Johnston	B14	Sneem	F13	Tallow	E13	Watergrasshill
D8	Neale	G8	Oldcastle	E4	Portnoo	H9	Sallins	C11	Spanish Point	F13	Tallowbridge	B14	Waterville
E11	Nenagh	G5	Omagh	J9	Portraine	D9	Salthill	D9	Spiddal	J6	Tandragee	C8	Westport
G7	Newbliss			E11	Portroe	E11	Scarriff	C9	Sraith Salach	F9	Tang	J12	Wexford
				H3	Portrush					C12	Tarbert	E14	Whitegate
				H3	Portstewart					F11	Templemore	K5	Whitehead
				E10	Portumna					F11	Templetouhy	J10	Wicklow
				C13	Poulgorm Bridge					J8	Termonfeckin	J11	Woodenbridge
				J6	Poyntz Pass					G12	Thomastown	E10	Woodford
										F11	Thurles		
										D15	Timoleague	F14	Youghal
										J11	Tinahely		
										F12	Tipperary		

Restricted junctions

Motorway and Primary Route junctions which have access or exit restrictions are shown on the map pages thus: ▣3 ▣56

Northbound
Access only from A1 (northbound)

Southbound
Exit only to A1 (southbound)

Northbound
Access only from A41 (northbound)

Southbound
Exit only to A41 (southbound)

Northbound
Access only from M25 (no link from A405)

Southbound
Exit only to M25 (no link from A405)

Northbound
Access only from A414

Southbound
Exit only to A414

Northbound
Exit only to M45

Southbound
Access only from M45

Northbound
Exit only to M6 (northbound)

Southbound
Access only from M6

Northbound
Exit only, no access

Southbound
Access only, no exit

Northbound
Access only from A42

Southbound
No restriction

Northbound
No exit, access only

Southbound
Exit only, no access

Northbound
Exit only, no access

Southbound
Access only, no exit

Northbound
Exit only to M621

Southbound
Access only from M621

Northbound
Exit only to A1(M) (northbound)

Southbound
Access only from A1(M) (southbound)

Westbound
No exit to A2 (eastbound)

Eastbound
No access from A2 (westbound)

Northeastbound
Access only from A303, no exit

Southwestbound
Exit only to A303, no access

Northbound
Exit only, no access

Southbound
Access only, no exit

Northeastbound
Access from M27 only. No exit

Southwestbound
No access to M27 (westbound)

Westbound
Access only from A4 (westbound)

Eastbound
Exit only to A4 (eastbound)

Westbound
No exit to A4 (westbound)

Eastbound
No restriction

Westbound
Exit only to M48

Eastbound
Access only from M48

Westbound
Access only from M48

Eastbound
Exit only to M48

Westbound
Exit only, no access

Eastbound
Access only, no exit

Westbound
Exit only, no access

Eastbound
Access only, no exit

Westbound
Exit only to A48(M)

Eastbound
Access only from A48(M)

Westbound
Exit only, no access

Eastbound
No restriction

Westbound
Access only, no exit

Eastbound
No access or exit

Northeastbound
Access only, no exit

Southwestbound
Exit only, no access

Northeastbound
Access only from A417 (westbound)

Southwestbound
Exit only to A417 (eastbound)

Northeastbound
No access, exit only

Southwestbound
No exit, access only

Northeastbound
Exit only to M49

Southwestbound
Access only from M49

Northeastbound
No restriction

Southwestbound
Access only from A30 (westbound)

See M6 Toll Motorway map on page 17

Northbound
Exit only to M6 Toll

Southbound
Access only from M6 Toll

Northbound
Access only from M42 (southbound)

Southbound
Exit only to M42

Northbound
Exit only, no access

Southbound
Access only, no exit

Northbound
Exit only to M54

Southbound
Access only from M54

Northbound
Access only from M6 To

Southbound
Exit only to M6 Toll

Northbound
No restriction

Southbound
Access only from M56 (eastbound)

Northbound
Access only, no exit

Southbound
No restriction

Northbound
Access only, no exit

Southbound
Exit only, no access

Northbound
Exit only, no access

Southbound
Access only, no exit

Northbound
No direct access, use adjacent slip road to jct 29A

Southbound
No direct exit, use adjacent slip road from jct 29A

Northbound
Acces only, no exit

Southbound
Exit only, no access

Northbound
Access only from M61

Southbound
Exit only to M61

Northbound
Exit only, no access

Southbound
Access only, no exit

Northbound
Exit only, no access

Southbound
Access only, no exit

M8 Edinburgh - Bishopton

See Glasgow District map on pages 254-255

M9 Edinburgh - Dunblane

Northwestbound
Exit only to M9 spur

Southeastbound
Access only from M9 spur

Northwestbound
Access only, no exit

Southeastbound
Exit only, no access

Northwestbound
Exit only, no access

Southeastbound
Access only, no exit

Northwestbound
Access only, no exit

Southeastbound
Exit only to A905

Northwestbound
Exit only to M876 (southwestbound)

Southeastbound
Access only from M876 (northeastbound)

M11 London - Cambridge

Northbound
Access only from A406 (eastbound)

Southbound
Exit only to A406

Northbound
Exit only, no access

Southbound
Access only, no exit

Northbound
Exit only to A11

Southbound
Access only from A11

Northbound
Exit only, no access

Southbound
Access only, no exit

Northbound
Exit only, no access

Southbound
Access only, no exit

M20 Swanley - Folkestone

Northwestbound
Staggered junction; follow signs - access only

Southeastbound
Staggered junction; follow signs - exit only

Northwestbound
Exit only to M26 (westbound)

Southeastbound
Access only from M26 (eastbound)

Northwestbound
Access only from A20

Southeastbound
For access follow signs - exit only to A20

Northwestbound
No restriction

Southeastbound
For exit follow signs

Northwestbound
Access only, no exit

Southeastbound
Exit only, no access

M23 Hooley - Crawley

Northbound
Exit only to A23 (northbound)

Southbound
Access only from A23 (southbound)

Northbound
Access only, no exit

Southbound
Exit only, no access

M25 London Orbital Motorway

See M25 London Orbital Motorway map on page 178

M26 Sevenoaks - Wrotham

Westbound
Exit only to clockwise M25 (westbound)

Eastbound
Access only from anti-clockwise M25 (eastbound)

Westbound
Access only from M20 (northwestbound)

Eastbound
Exit only to M20 (southeastbound)

M27 Cadnam - Portsmouth

Westbound
Staggered junction; follow signs - access only from M3 (southbound). Exit only to M3 (northbound)

Eastbound
Staggered junction; follow signs - access only from M3 (southbound). Exit only to M3 (northbound)

Westbound
Exit only, no access

Eastbound
Access only, no exit

Westbound
Staggered junction; follow signs - exit only to M275 (southbound)

Eastbound
Staggered junction; follow signs - access only from M275 (northbound)

M40 London - Birmingham

Northwestbound
Exit only, no access

Southeastbound
Access only, no exit

Northwestbound
Exit only, no access

Southeastbound
Access only, no exit

Northwestbound
Exit only to M40/A40

Southeastbound
Access only from M40/A40

Northwestbound
Exit only, no access

Southeastbound
Access only, no exit

Northwestbound
Access only, no exit

Southeastbound
Exit only, no access

Northwestbound
Access only, no exit

Southeastbound
Exit only, no access

M42 Bromsgrove - Measham

See Birmingham District map on pages 252-253

M45 Coventry - M1

Westbound
Access only from A45 (northbound)

Eastbound
Exit only, no access

Westbound
Access only from M1 (northbound)

Eastbound
Exit only to M1 (southbound)

M53 Mersey Tunnel - Chester

Northbound
Access only from M56 (westbound). Exit only to M56 (eastbound)

Southbound
Access only from M56 (westbound). Exit only to M56 (eastbound)

M54 Telford

Westbound
Access only from M6 (northbound)

Eastbound
Exit only to M6 (southbound)

M56 North Cheshire

For junctions 1,2,3,4 & 7 see Manchester District map on pages 256-257

Westbound
Access only, no exit

Eastbound
No access or exit

Westbound
Exit only to M53

Eastbound
Access only from M53

M57 Liverpool Outer Ring Road

Northwestbound
Access only, no exit

Southeastbound
Exit only, no access

Northwestbound
Access only from A580 (westbound)

Southeastbound
Exit only, no access

M58 Liverpool - Wigan

Westbound
Exit only, no access

Eastbound
Access only, no exit

M60 Manchester Orbital

See Manchester District map on pages 256-257

M61 Manchester - Preston

Northwestbound
No access or exit

Southeastbound
Exit only, no access

Northwestbound
Exit only to M6 (northbound)

Southeastbound
Access only from M6 (southbound)

M62 Liverpool - Kingston upon Hull

Westbound
Access only, no exit

Eastbound
Exit only, no access

Westbound
No access to A1(M) (southbound)

Eastbound
No restriction

M65 Preston - Colne

Northeastbound
Exit only, no access

Southwestbound
Access only, no exit

Northeastbound
Access only, no exit

Southwestbound
Exit only, no access

M66 Bury

Northbound
Exit only to A56 (northbound)

Southbound
Access only from A56 (southbound)

Northbound
Exit only, no access

Southbound
Access only, no exit

M67 Hyde Bypass

Westbound
Access only, no exit

Eastbound
Exit only, no access

Westbound
Exit only, no access

Eastbound
Access only, no exit

Westbound
Exit only, no access

Eastbound
No restriction

M69 Coventry - Leicester

Northbound
Access only, no exit

Southbound
Exit only, no access

M73 East of Glasgow

Northbound
No access from or exit to A89. No access from M8 (eastbound)

Southbound
No access from or exit to A89. No exit to M8 (westbound)

M74 and A74(M) Glasgow - Gretna

Northbound
Exit only, no access

Southbound
Access only, no exit

Northbound
Access only, no exit

Southbound
Exit only, no access

Northbound
Access only, no exit

Southbound
Exit only, no access

Northbound
Access only, no exit

Southbound
Exit only, no access

Northbound
No access or exit

Southbound
Exit only, no access

Northbound
No restriction

Southbound
Access only, no exit

Northbound
Access only, no exit

Southbound
Exit only, no access

Northbound
Exit only, no access

Southbound
Access only, no exit

Northbound
Exit only, no access

Southbound
Access only, no exit

M77 South of Glasgow

Northbound
No exit to M8 (westbound)

Southbound
No access from M8 (eastbound)

Northbound
Access only, no exit

Southbound
Exit only, no access

Northbound
Access only, no exit

Southbound
Exit only, no access

Northbound
Access only, no exit

Southbound
No restriction

M80 Glasgow - Stirling

Northbound
Exit only, no access

Southbound
Access only, no exit

Northbound
Access only, no exit

Southbound
Exit only, no access

Northbound
Exit only to M876 (northeastbound)

Southbound
Access only from M876 (southwestbound)

M90 Forth Road Bridge - Perth

Northbound
Exit only to A92 (eastbound)

Southbound
Access only from A92 (westbound)

Northbound
Access only, no exit

Southbound
Exit only, no access

Northbound
Exit only, no access

Southbound
Access only, no exit

Northbound
No access from A912
No exit to A912 (southbound)

Southbound
No access from A912 (northbound).
No exit to A912

M180 Doncaster - Grimsby

Westbound
Access only, no exit

Eastbound
Exit only, no access

M606 Bradford Spur

Northbound
Exit only, no access

Southbound
No restriction

M621 Leeds - M1

Clockwise
Access only, no exit

Anticlockwise
Exit only, no access

Clockwise
No exit or access

Anticlockwise
No restriction

Clockwise
Access only, no exit

Anticlockwise
Exit only, no access

Clockwise
Exit only, no access

Anticlockwise
Access only, no exit

Westbound
Access only, no exit

Eastbound
Exit only, no access

Northeastbound
Access only, no exit

Southwestbound
Exit only, no access

No access. Exit only to A194(M) & A1 (northbound)

Southbound
No exit. Access only from A194(M) & A1 (southbound)

Clockwise
Exit only to M1 (southbound)

Anticlockwise
Access only from M1 (northbound)

Westbound
Exit only to A11

Access only from A11

Northeastbound
No restriction

Southwestbound
Access only, no exit

M876 Bonnybridge - Kincardine Bridge

A3(M) Horndean - Havant

Northeastbound
Access only from M80 (northbound)

Southwestbound
Exit only to M80 (southbound)

Northbound
Access only from A3

Southbound
Exit only to A3

Northeastbound
Exit only, no access

Southwestbound
Access only, no exit

Westbound
Access only from A11

Eastbound
Exit only to A11

Northeastbound
Exit only to M9 (eastbound)

Southwestbound
Access only from M9 (westbound)

Northbound
Exit only, no access

Southbound
Access only, no exit

A48(M) Cardiff Spur

Westbound
Access only from A11

Eastbound
Exit only to A11

Northeastbound
Access only, no exit

Southwestbound
Access only, no exit

A1(M) South Mimms - Baldock

Westbound
Access only from M4 (westbound)

Eastbound
Exit only to M4 (eastbound)

Westbound
Exit only, no access

Eastbound
Access only, no exit

Northbound
Exit only, no access

Southbound
Access only, no exit

Westbound
Exit only to A48 (westbound)

Eastbound
Access only from A48 (eastbound)

Northeastbound
Access only, no exit

Southwestbound
Exit only, no access

Westbound
Access only, no exit

Eastbound
Exit only, no access

A66(M) Darlington Spur

Northbound
No restriction

Southbound
Exit only, no access

With A120
Northeastbound
Exit only, no access

Southwestbound
Access only, no exit

A55 Holyhead - Chester

Westbound
Exit only to A1(M) (southbound)

Eastbound
Access only from A1(M) (northbound)

Westbound
Exit only, no access

Eastbound
Access only, no exit

Northbound
Access only, no exit

Southbound
No access or exit

A194(M) Newcastle upon Tyne

Northeastbound
Access only, no exit

Southwestbound
Exit only, no access

Westbound
Access only, no exit

Eastbound
Exit only, no access

A1(M) East of Leeds

Northbound
Access only from A1(M) (northbound)

Southbound
Exit only to A1(M) (southbound)

Northeastbound
Exit only (for Stratford St Mary and Dedham)

Southwestbound
Access only

Northbound
No access to M62 (eastbound)

Southbound
No restriction

A12 M25 - Ipswich

A14 M1 Felixstowe

Northeastbound
Access only, no exit

Southwestbound
No restriction

Westbound
Access only, no exit

Eastbound
No access or exit.

Northbound
Access only from M1 (northbound)

Southbound
Exit only to M1 (southbound)

Northeastbound
Exit only, no access

Southwestbound
Access only, no exit

Westbound
Exit only to M6 & M1 (northbound)

Eastbound
Access only from M6 & M1 (southbound)

Westbound
Exit only, no access

Eastbound
No access or exit

A1(M) Scotch Corner - Newcastle upon Tyne

Westbound
Exit only, no access

Eastbound
Access only, no exit

Westbound
Exit only, no access

Eastbound
Access only, no exit

Northbound
Exit only to A66(M) (eastbound)

Southbound
Access only from A66(M) (westbound)

Northeastbound
Exit only, no access

Southwestbound
Access only, no exit

Westbound
Access only from A1307

Eastbound
Exit only to A1307

Westbound
Exit only to A5104

Eastbound
Access only from A5104

M25 London Orbital motorway

Refer also to atlas pages 36–37 and 50–51

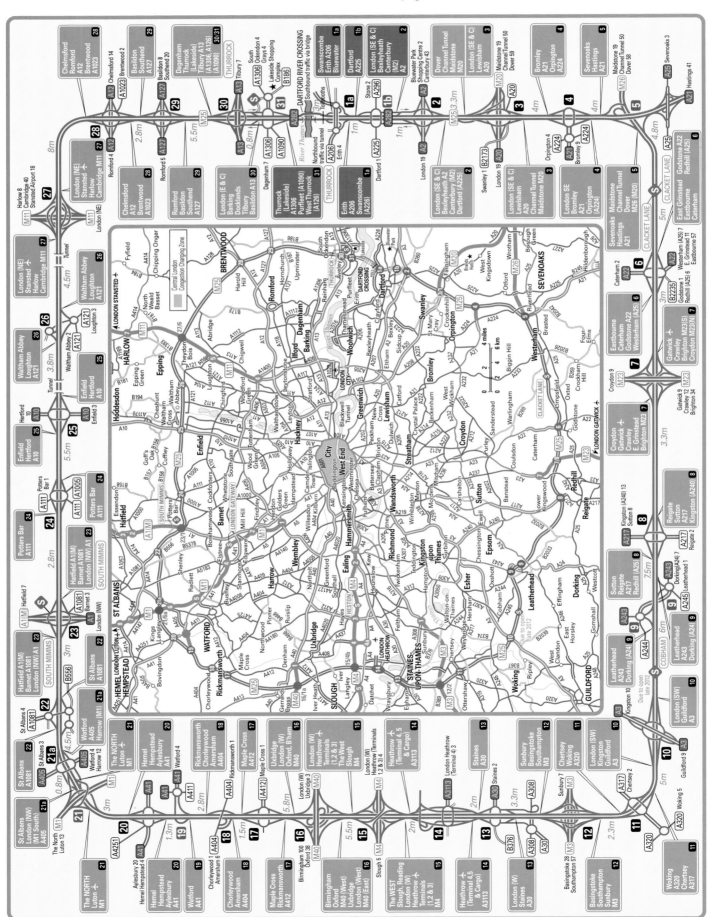

M6 Toll motorway

Refer also to atlas pages 58–59

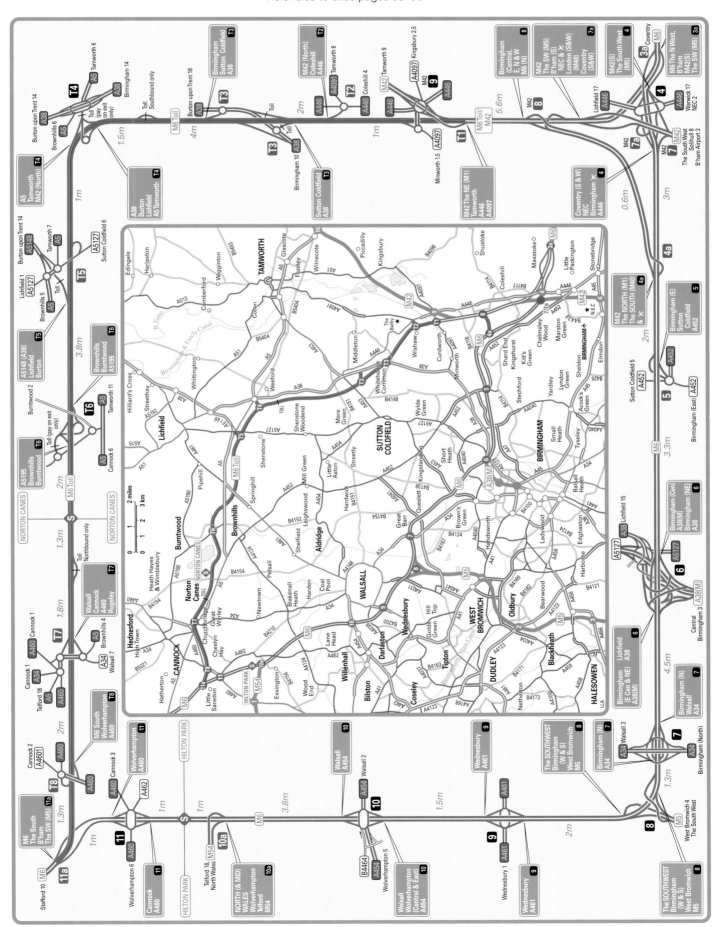

Street map symbols

Town, port and airport plans

	Motorway and junction		One-way, gated/ closed road		Railway station	**P**	Car park
	Primary road single/dual carriageway		Restricted access road	o	Light rapid transit system station		Park and Ride (at least 6 days per week)
	A road single/ dual carriageway		Pedestrian area		Level crossing		Bus/coach station
	B road single/ dual carriageway		Footpath		Tramway	**H**	Hospital
	Local road single/ dual carriageway		Road under construction		Ferry route	**H**	24-hour Accident & Emergency hospital
	Other road single/ dual carriageway, minor road		Road tunnel		Airport, heliport		Petrol station, 24 hour Major suppliers only
	Building of interest		Museum		Railair terminal		City wall
	Ruined building		Castle		Theatre or performing arts centre		Escarpment
	Tourist Information Centre		Castle mound		Cinema		Cliff lift
	Visitor or heritage centre	•	Monument, statue		Abbey, chapel, church		River/canal, lake
	World Heritage Site (UNESCO)		Post Office		Synagogue		Lock, weir
	English Heritage site		Public library		Mosque		Park/sports ground
	Historic Scotland site		Shopping centre		Golf Course		Cemetery
	Cadw (Welsh heritage) site		Shopmobility		Racecourse		Woodland
	National Trust site		Viewpoint		Nature reserve		Built-up area
	National Trust Scotland site		Toilet, with facilities for the less able		Aquarium		Beach

Central London street map (see pages 232 - 241)

30	Speed camera site (fixed location) with speed limit in mph		London Underground station		Docklands Light Railway (DLR) station
40	Section of road with two or more fixed camera sites; speed limit in mph		London Overground station		Central London Congestion Charging Zone
50→ ←50	Average speed (SPECS™) camera system with speed limit in mph		Rail interchange		

Royal Parks (opening and closing times for traffic)

Green Park	Open 5am-midnight. Constitution Hill: closed Sundays
Hyde Park	Open 5am-midnight
Regent's Park	Open 5am-dusk. Most park roads closed midnight-7am
St James's Park	Open 5am-midnight. The Mall: closed Sundays

Traffic regulations in the City of London include security checkpoints and restrict the number of entry and exit points.

Note: Oxford Street is closed to through-traffic (except buses & taxis) 7am-7pm Monday-Saturday.

Central London Congestion Charging Zone

The daily charge for driving or parking a vehicle on public roads in the Congestion Charging Zone (CCZ), during operating hours, is £10 per vehicle per day in advance or on the day of travel. Alternatively you can pay £9 by registering with CC Auto Pay, an automated payment system. Drivers can also pay the next charging day after travelling in the zone but this will cost £12. Payment permits entry, travel within and exit from the CCZ by the vehicle as often as required on that day.

The CCZ operates between 7am and 6pm, Mon–Fri only. There is no charge at weekends, public holidays or betwen 25th Dec and 1st Jan inclusive.

For up to date information on the CCZ, exemptions, discounts or ways to pay, telephone 0845 900 1234, visit www.cclondon.com or write to Congestion Charging, P.O. Box 4782, Worthing BN11 9PS. Textphone users can call 020 7649 9123.

Page 182	....	Aberdeen
182	....	Basingstoke
182	....	Bath
184	....	Birmingham
183	....	Blackpool
185	....	Bournemouth
185	....	Bradford
186	....	Brighton
186	....	Bristol
187	....	Cambridge
188	....	Canterbury
188	....	Cardiff
189	....	Carlisle
189	....	Cheltenham
190	....	Chester
190	....	Colchester
191	....	Coventry
191	....	Darlington
192	....	Derby
192	....	Doncaster
193	....	Dover
193	....	Dundee
194	....	Durham
194	....	Eastbourne
195	....	Edinburgh
196	....	Exeter
197	....	Glasgow
196	....	Gloucester

Page 198	....	Great Yarmouth
198	....	Guildford
199	....	Harrogate
199	....	Huddersfield
200	....	Inverness
200	....	Ipswich
201	....	Kingston upon Hull
201	....	Lancaster
202	....	Leeds
203	....	Leicester
203	....	Lincoln
204	....	Liverpool
79	....	Llandudno
232–241	...	LONDON
205	....	Luton
205	....	Maidstone
206	....	Manchester
39	....	Margate
208	....	Middlesbrough
207	....	Milton Keynes
209	....	Newcastle upon Tyne
208	....	Newport
4	....	Newquay
210	....	Northampton
210	....	Norwich
211	....	Nottingham
211	....	Oldham
212	....	Oxford

Page 213	....	Perth
213	....	Peterborough
214	....	Plymouth
216	....	Poole
215	....	Portsmouth
216	....	Preston
39	....	Ramsgate
217	....	Reading
217	....	Salisbury
218	....	Sheffield
218	....	Shrewsbury
219	....	Southampton
220	....	Southend-on-Sea
220	....	Stirling
221	....	Stockton-on-Tees
221	....	Stoke-on-Trent (Hanley)
222	....	Stratford-upon-Avon
223	....	Sunderland
222	....	Swansea
224	....	Swindon
224	....	Taunton
225	....	Torquay
225	....	Tunbridge Wells
226	....	Warwick
226	....	Watford
227	....	Winchester
227	....	Wolverhampton
228	....	Worcester
228	....	York

Central London

🚢 Ferry Ports

Page 151	....	Aberdeen Harbour
11	....	Calais
11	....	Dover, Port of
13	....	Fishguard Harbour
53	....	Harwich International Port
13	....	Heysham Harbour
13	....	Holyhead Harbour
13	....	Liverpool Docks
11	....	Newhaven Harbour
13	....	Pembroke Dock
10	....	Plymouth, Port of
10	....	Poole, Port of
113	....	Port of Tyne
11	....	Portsmouth Harbour
10	....	Weymouth Harbour

✈ Airports

229	....	London Heathrow
229	....	London Gatwick
229	....	London Stansted
229	....	London Luton
230	....	London City
230	....	Birmingham International
230	....	Manchester
230	....	East Midlands
231	....	Leeds Bradford International
231	....	Aberdeen
231	....	Edinburgh
231	....	Glasgow

⛉ Channel Tunnel

27	....	Folkestone Terminal
27	....	Calais / Coquelles Terminal

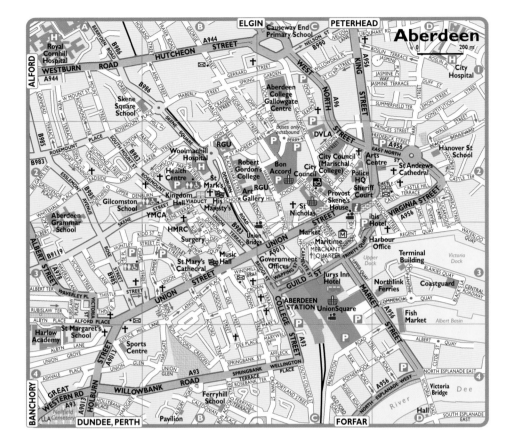

Aberdeen

Aberdeen is found on atlas page **151 N6**

C4	Affleck Street	B1	Maberly Street
A3	Albert Street	D2	Marischal Street
B4	Albury Road	C3	Market Street
A3	Alford Place	C1	Nelson Street
B1	Ann Street	C4	Palmerston Road
D2	Beach Boulevard	D1	Park Street
A2	Belgrave Terrace	C4	Portland Street
A1	Berryden Road	C4	Poynernook Road
B2	Blackfriars Street	D3	Regent Quay
D3	Blaikies Quay	A2	Richmond Street
B4	Bon Accord Crescent	A3	Rose Place
B3	Bon Accord Street	A3	Rose Street
C3	Bridge Street	A2	Rosemount Place
B4	Caledonian Place	A2	Rosemount Viaduct
C3	Carmelite Street	B2	St Andrew Street
A3	Chapel Street	C1	St Clair Street
B1	Charlotte Street	C2	School Hill
C3	College Street	B2	Skene Square
D1	Constitution Street	A3	Skene Street
B3	Crimon Place	B2	Skene Terrace
B3	Crown Street	C4	South College Street
B3	Dee Street	D4	South Esplanade East
B2	Denburn Road	A2	South Mount Street
B3	Diamond Street	B2	Spa Street
D2	East North Street	B4	Springbank Street
A2	Esslemont Avenue	B4	Springbank Terrace
C1	Gallowgate	B3	Summer Street
B1	George Street	D1	Summerfield Terrace
B2	Gilcomston Park	A3	Thistle Lane
B3	Golden Square	A3	Thistle Place
B3	Gordon Street	A3	Thistle Street
A4	Great Western Road	C3	Trinity Quay
C3	Guild Street	B3	Union Bridge
C3	Hadden Street	A4	Union Grove
D2	Hanover Street	B3	Union Street
B4	Hardgate	B2	Union Terrace
C2	Harriet Street	A2	Upper Denburn
A4	Holburn Street	D4	Victoria Road
A3	Huntley Street	A3	Victoria Street
B1	Hutcheon Street	A1	View Terrace
D1	Jasmine Terrace	D2	Virginia Street
B2	John Street	C3	Wapping Street
A4	Justice Mill Lane	A3	Waverley Place
C1	King Street	C4	Wellington Place
B3	Langstane Place	C1	West North Street
A2	Leadside Road	A1	Westburn Road
A1	Loanhead Terrace	A2	Whitehall Place
C1	Loch Street	A4	Willowbank Road

Basingstoke

Basingstoke is found on atlas page **22 H4**

C1	Alencon Link	C3	London Street
D2	Allnutt Avenue	A2	Lower Brook Street
C1	Basing View	D3	Lytton Road
C4	Beaconsfield Road	B3	Market Place
A4	Bounty Rise	C3	May Place
A4	Bounty Road	C4	Montague Place
A3	Bramblys Close	A2	Mortimer Lane
A3	Bramblys Drive	B3	New Road
A3	Budd's Close	C2	New Road
C4	Castle Road	B3	New Street
B1	Chapel Hill	C1	Old Reading Road
C2	Chequers Road	A3	Penrith Road
A4	Chester Place	A2	Rayleigh Road
B2	Churchill Way	C3	Red Lion Lane
D1	Churchill Way East	A2	Rochford Road
A2	Churchill Way West	C2	St Mary's Court
B2	Church Square	A3	Sarum Hill
B2	Church Street	C2	Seal Road
B3	Church Street	A2	Solby's Road
C4	Cliddesden Road	A2	Southend Road
C1	Clifton Terrace	B4	Southern Road
A4	Cordale Road	A3	Stukeley Road
B4	Council Road	B4	Sylvia Close
D3	Crossborough Gardens	B2	Timberlake Road
D3	Crossborough Hill	B3	Victoria Street
B3	Cross Street	A1	Victory Roundabout
A4	Devonshire Place	B1	Vyne Road
D2	Eastfield Avenue	A3	Winchcombe Road
D2	Eastrop Lane	A4	Winchester Road
C1	Eastrop Roundabout	B3	Winchester Street
D2	Eastrop Way	A1	Winterthur Way
A2	Essex Road	A3	Worting Road
B4	Fairfields Road	C3	Wote Street
C2	Festival Way		
A2	Flaxfield Court		
A3	Flaxfield Road		
B3	Flaxfield Road		
A4	Frances Road		
A4	Frescade Crescent		
C2	Goat Lane		
C4	Hackwood Road		
A4	Hamelyn Road		
A4	Hardy Lane		
A4	Hawkfield Lane		
C3	Haymarket Yard		
B3	Joices Yard		
B4	Jubilee Road		
D3	London Road		

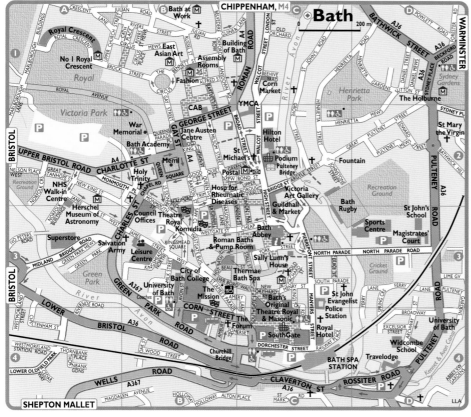

Bath

Bath is found on atlas page **20 D2**

D4	Archway Street	A3	Lower Bristol Road
C2	Argyle Street	A4	Lower Oldfield Park
B3	Avon Street	C3	Manvers Street
B1	Bartlett Street	A3	Midland Bridge Road
B2	Barton Street	B3	Milk Street
D1	Bathwick Street	B2	Milsom Street
B2	Beauford Square	A2	Monmouth Place
B3	Beau Street	B2	Monmouth Street
D1	Beckford Road	B2	New Bond Street
B1	Bennett Street	A2	New King Street
C2	Bridge Street	C3	New Orchard Street
C2	Broad Street	A3	Norfolk Buildings
D4	Broadway	C3	North Parade
A1	Brock Street	D3	North Parade Road
B2	Chapel Road	B2	Old King Street
A3	Charles Street	B1	Oxford Row
A2	Charlotte Street	C3	Pierrepont Street
C3	Cheap Street	B2	Princes Street
A4	Cheltenham Street	D2	Pulteney Road
B1	Circus Mews	B2	Queen Square
C4	Claverton Street	B2	Queen Street
B4	Corn Street	C4	Railway Place
D1	Daniel Street	B1	Rivers Street
C4	Dorchester Street	C1	Roman Road
D2	Edward Street	C4	Rossiter Road
B1	Gay Street	A1	Royal Avenue
B2	George Street	A1	Royal Crescent
C2	Great Pulteney Street	B3	St James's Parade
A2	Great Stanhope Street	C1	St John's Road
A3	Green Park Road	B3	Saw Close
B2	Green Street	C4	Southgate Street
C2	Grove Street	C3	South Parade
B1	Guinea Lane	C3	Stall Street
D1	Henrietta Gardens	D1	Sutton Street
C2	Henrietta Mews	D1	Sydney Place
C1	Henrietta Road	B1	The Circus
C2	Henrietta Street	A4	Thornbank Place
C3	Henry Street	B2	Union Street
C2	High Street	C2	Upper Borough Walls
B3	Hot Bath Street	A2	Upper Bristol Road
B3	James Street West	A1	Upper Church Street
B2	John Street	C2	Walcot Street
B1	Julian Road	A4	Wells Road
B3	Kingsmead North	B3	Westgate Buildings
C3	Kingston Road	B3	Westgate Street
B1	Lansdown Road	A4	Westmoreland Station
C1	London Street		Road
B3	Lower Borough Walls	C3	York Street

Blackpool

Blackpool is found on atlas page **88 C3**

B1	Abingdon Street	B3	Hornby Road
B3	Adelaide Street	D3	Hornby Road
B3	Albert Road	B3	Hull Road
C3	Albert Road	C4	Kay Street
C2	Alfred Street	C4	Kent Road
D4	Ashton Road	C2	King Street
B2	Bank Hey Street	C1	Larkhill Street
B1	Banks Street	D2	Leamington Road
C4	Belmont Avenue	D2	Leicester Road
D3	Bennett Avenue	C2	Leopold Grove
C4	Bethesda Road	D2	Lincoln Road
B2	Birley Street	C3	Livingstone Road
D4	Blenheim Avenue	B1	Lord Street
B4	Bonny Street	C4	Louise Street
C1	Buchanan Street	C1	Milbourne Street
C1	Butler Street	B3	New Bonny Street
D1	Caunce Street	C4	Palatine Road
C2	Cedar Square	D3	Palatine Road
C4	Central Drive	D2	Park Road
B4	Chapel Street	D4	Park Road
C1	Charles Street	D2	Peter Street
C3	Charnley Road	B4	Pier Street
B2	Cheapside	B1	Princess Parade
B2	Church Street	B1	Promenade
C2	Church Street	B1	Queen Street
D2	Church Street	D2	Raikes Parade
B2	Clifton Street	C3	Reads Avenue
D4	Clinton Avenue	D3	Reads Avenue
C2	Cookson Street	C2	Regent Road
B4	Coop Street	C4	Ribble Road
C3	Coronation Street	D3	Ripon Road
B2	Corporation Street	B4	Seasiders Way
B4	Dale Street	C1	Seed Street
B2	Deansgate	D1	Selbourne Road
B1	Dickson Road	C2	South King Street
C2	Edward Street	B1	Springfield Road
D1	Elizabeth Street	C3	Stanley Road
C1	Fisher Street	C1	Swainson Street
B4	Foxhall Road	B2	Talbot Road
D4	Freckleton Street	C1	Talbot Road
B1	General Street	C2	Topping Street
D1	George Street	B2	Tower Street
D1	Gorton Street	B3	Vance Road
D2	Granville Road	B2	Victoria Street
C1	Grosvenor Street	D1	Victory Road
D4	Harrison Road	B2	West Street
C4	Havelock Street	D4	Woolman Road
C1	High Street	B4	York Street

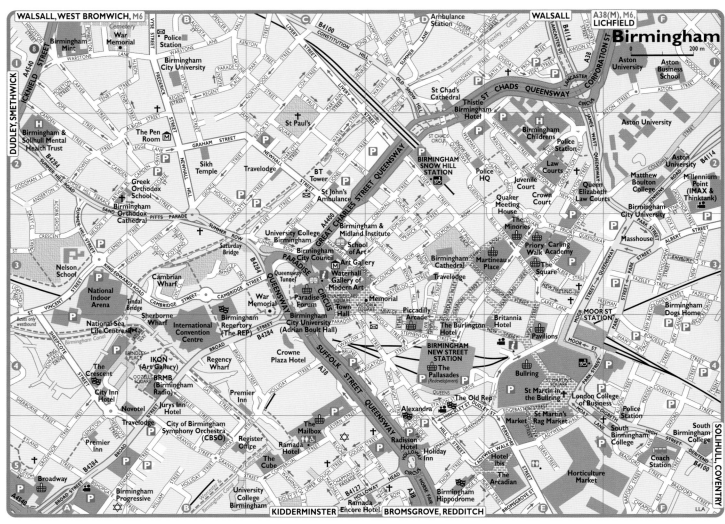

Birmingham

Birmingham is found on atlas page **58 G7**

A2	Acorn Grove
E3	Albert Street
F3	Albert Street
B2	Albion Street
F4	Allison Street
A2	Anderton Street
A2	Arthur Place
FI	Aston Street
B4	Atlas Way
F3	Banbury Street
F5	Barford Street
F3	Bartholomew Street
D3	Barwick Street
EI	Bath Row
D4	Beak Street
F4	Benacre Drive
D3	Bennetts Hill
B4	Berkley Street
A5	Bishopgate Street
C5	Blucher Street
CI	Bond Street
F4	Bordesley Street
D5	Bow Street
F5	Bradford Street
B4	Bridge Street
B3	Brindley Drive
B4	Brindley Place
A5	Broad Street
E5	Bromsgrove Street
C2	Brook Street
C4	Brunel Street
E3	Bull Street
B3	Cambridge Street
B2	Camden Drive
A2	Camden Street
D3	Cannon Street

BI	Caroline Street
E3	Carrs Lane
AI	Carver Street
C3	Chamberlain Square
C5	Chapmans Passage
B3	Charlotte Street
F5	Cheapside
D3	Cherry Street
D2	Church Street
B3	Civic Close
A3	Clement Street
DI	Cleveland Street
F2	Coleshill Street
E2	Colmore Circus Queensway
D3	Colmore Row
C5	Commercial Street
CI	Constitution Hill
D3	Cornwall Street
EI	Corporation Street
E3	Corporation Street
F4	Coventry Street
CI	Cox Street
E3	Dale End
A3	Daley Close
E2	Dalton Street
E5	Dean Street
E4	Digbeth
D4	Dudley Street
C3	Eden Place
E4	Edgbaston Street
D3	Edmund Street
B3	Edward Street
D5	Ellis Street
A5	Essington Street
D4	Ethel Street

F2	Etna Street
D5	Exeter Street
F3	Fazeley Street
C3	Fleet Street
F3	Fox Street
BI	Frederick Street
E3	Freeman Street
B4	Gas Street
B2	George Street
E5	Gloucester Street
A2	Goddman Street
C5	Gough Street
B2	Graham Street
B5	Granville Street
C3	Great Charles Street Queensway
F2	Grosvenor Street
A5	Grosvenor Street West
BI	Hall Street
DI	Hampton Street
B3	Helena Street
CI	Henrietta Street
E4	High Street
F5	High Street Deritend
C4	Hill Street
D4	Hinckley Street
AI	Hingeston Street
B2	Holland Street
B5	Holliday Street
D5	Holloway Circus
C5	Holloway Head
FI	Holt Street
D5	Horse Fair
DI	Hospital Street
E5	Hurst Street
AI	Icknield Street
D5	Inge Street
B2	James Street
E2	James Watt Queensway
F2	Jennens Road
D4	John Bright Street

BI	Kenyon Street
A4	King Edward's Drive
A3	King Edwards Road
D5	Ladywell Walk
EI	Lancaster Circus
EI	Lancaster Street
EI	Lawson Street
B2	Legge Lane
A3	Lighthouse Avenue
C3	Lionel Street
CI	Livery Street
B3	Louisa Street
EI	Loveday Street
DI	Lower Loveday Street
D4	Lower Temple Street
C2	Ludgate Hill
C3	Margaret Street
C5	Marshall Street
E3	Martineau Way
CI	Mary Ann Street
CI	Mary Street
F4	Meriden Street
F5	Mill Lane
E4	Moat Lane
E4	Moor Street
E4	Moor Street Queensway
AI	Moreton Street
C4	Navigation Street
A3	Needless Alley
A3	Nelson Street
F4	New Bartholomew Street
F4	New Canal Street
B2	Newhall Hill
C3	Newhall Street
E3	New Meeting Street
D3	New Street
E2	Newton Street
CI	Northwood Street
DI	Old Snow Hill
E3	Old Square
B4	Oozells Square

F5	Oxford Street
C3	Paradise Circus Queensway
C4	Paradise Street
E4	Park Street
AI	Pemberton Street
E5	Pershore Street
D4	Pinfold Street
AI	Pope Street
A2	Powell Street
EI	Price Street
EI	Princip Street
D4	Printing House Street
D4	Queens Drive
C3	Queensway Tunnel
F5	Rea Street
BI	Regent Parade
BI	Regent Place
BI	Regent Street
C5	Ridley Street
A5	Ruston Street
A5	Ryland Street
EI	St Chads Queensway
D5	St Jude's Pass
A3	St Marks Crescent
E4	St Martin's Square
CI	St Paul's Square
D3	St Philip's Place
A3	St Vincent Street
A2	Sand Pitts Parade
B3	Saturday Bridge
C3	Scotland Street
C5	Severn Street
DI	Shadwell Street
F4	Shaw's Passage
A4	Sheepcote Street
A4	Sherborne Street
B2	Sloane Street
D5	Smallbrook Queensway
D2	Snow Hill Queensway
BI	Spencer Street

EI	Staniforth Street
D5	Station Street
E2	Steelhouse Lane
D4	Stephenson Street
C4	Suffolk Street Queensway
A2	Summer Hill Road
A2	Summer Hill Street
A2	Summer Hill Terrace
DI	Summer Lane
B3	Summer Row
C4	Swallow Street
D3	Temple Row
D3	Temple Row West
D3	Temple Street
AI	Tenby Street
AI	Tenby Street North
A5	Tennant Street
E3	The Priory Queensway
D5	Thorp Street
B3	Tindal Bridge
F4	Trent Street
E3	Union Street
C5	Upper Gough Street
EI	Vesey Street
C3	Victoria Square
BI	Vittoria Street
BI	Vyse Street
AI	Warstone Lane
C5	Washington Street
D3	Waterloo Street
C2	Water Street
D2	Weaman Street
E2	Whittall Street
B5	William Street
FI	Woodcock Street

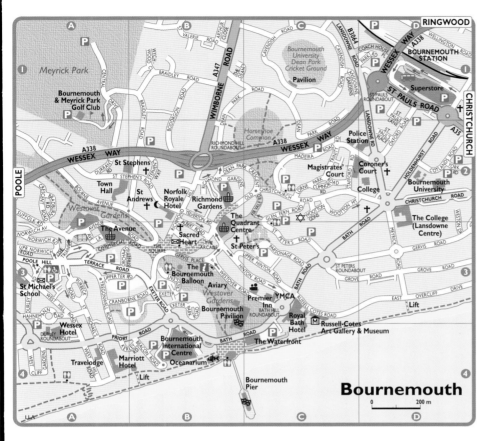

Bournemouth

Bournemouth is found on atlas page **13 J6**

B3	Albert Road
B1	Arthur Close
A3	Avenue Lane
A3	Avenue Road
B4	Bath Road
B4	Beacon Road
B2	Bodorgon Road
A2	Bourne Avenue
A2	Bradburne Road
B1	Braidley Road
C1	Cavendish Road
A1	Central Drive
D2	Christchurch Road
D1	Coach House Place
A3	Commercial Road
D2	Cotlands Road
A3	Cranborne Road
A2	Crescent Road
C2	Cumnor Road
B2	Dean Park Crescent
B2	Dean Park Road
A3	Durley Road
A2	Durrant Road
D3	East Overcliff Drive
B3	Exeter Crescent
B3	Exeter Park Road
B3	Exeter Road
C2	Fir Vale Road
B3	Gervis Place
D3	Gervis Road
C2	Glen Fern Road
C3	Grove Road
A3	Hahnemann Road
B3	Hinton Road
D2	Holdenhurst Road
A4	Kerley Road
C1	Lansdowne Gardens
C1	Lansdowne Road
C2	Lorne Park Road
C2	Madeira Road
D3	Meyrick Road
A3	Norwich Avenue
A3	Norwich Road
C2	Old Christchurch Road
A3	Orchard Street
D2	Oxford Road
D1	Park Road
C3	Parsonage Road

A3	Poole Hill
A4	Priory Road
A3	Purbeck Road
B2	Richmond Gardens
B3	Richmond Hill
C3	Russell Cotes Road
A3	St Michael's Road
D1	St Pauls Lane
D2	St Paul's Place
D1	St Pauls Road
C3	St Peter's Road
A2	St Stephen's Road
B1	St Valerie Road
C2	Stafford Road
B2	Stephen's Way
A2	Suffolk Road
A3	Terrace Road
B3	The Arcade
B1	The Deans
B3	The Square
A3	The Triangle
A3	Tregonwell Road
C2	Trinity Road
C3	Upper Hinton Road
A3	Upper Norwich Road
A3	Upper Terrace Road
D1	Wellington Road
A2	Wessex Way
A3	West Hill Road
D2	Weston Drive
B3	Westover Road
B1	Wimborne Road
C2	Wootton Gardens
C2	Wootton Mount
B1	Wychwood Close
B2	Yelverton Road
D2	York Road

Bradford

Bradford is found on atlas page **90 F4**

B3	Aldermanbury
B2	Bank Street
D2	Barkerend Road
B2	Barry Street
C4	Bolling Road
C2	Bolton Road
C3	Bridge Street
C3	Broadway
D2	Burnett Street
C1	Canal Road
A3	Carlton Street
B3	Centenary Square
C4	Chandos Street
B3	Channing Way
D3	Chapel Street
B2	Cheapside
A4	Chester Street
C2	Church Bank
A4	Claremont
C4	Croft Street
A1	Darfield Street
B2	Darley Street
A2	Drewton Road
D4	Dryden Street
B2	Duke Street
D3	East Parade
A4	Edmund Street
C4	Edward Street
A1	Eldon Place
D3	Filey Street
C3	George Street
B2	Godwin Street
A2	Grattan Road
A4	Great Horton Road
A4	Green Terrace
A1	Hallfield Road
B4	Hall Ings
B1	Hamm Strasse
C1	Holdsworth Street
A1	Houghton Place
A4	Howard Street
B3	Hustlergate
A1	Infirmary Street
B2	John Street
A4	Lansdowne Place
D3	Leeds Road
A4	Little Horton
B4	Little Horton Lane

A2	Longcroft Link
C2	Lower Kirkgate
A1	Lumb Lane
B4	Manchester Road
A1	Manningham Lane
B1	Manor Row
B3	Market Street
B1	Midland Road
A4	Morley Street
B4	Nelson Street
C1	North Brook Street
B2	Northgate
B1	North Parade
C2	North Street
D1	North Wing
D1	Otley Road
A2	Paradise Street
D2	Peckover Street
B2	Piccadilly
C2	Pine Street
B3	Princes Way
A3	Randall Well Street
A2	Rawson Road
B2	Rawson Square
A2	Rebecca Street
A4	Sawrey Place
B4	Senior Way
C1	Shipley Airedale Road
C2	Stott Hill
A2	Sunbridge Road
B3	Sunbridge Street
A3	Tetley Street
A3	Thornton Road
B1	Trafalgar Street
B3	Tyrell Street
D2	Upper Park Gate
B2	Upper Piccadilly
C1	Valley Road
C3	Vicar Lane
D4	Wakefield Road
D1	Wapping Road
A2	Water Lane
C2	Wellington Street
A2	Westgate
C1	Wharf Street
A1	White Abbey Road
A2	Wigan Street
A4	Wilton Street

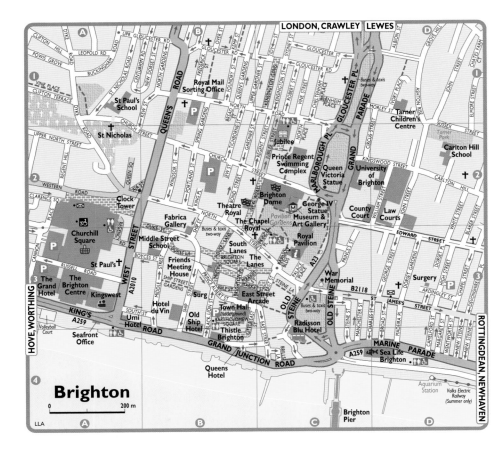

Brighton

Brighton is found on atlas page **24 H10**

D3	Ardingley Street	D4	Madeira Place
D1	Ashton Rise	C4	Manchester Street
B3	Bartholomew Square	D4	Margaret Street
B3	Black Lion Street	D4	Marine Parade
D3	Blaker Street	B3	Market Street
B2	Bond Street	C2	Marlborough Place
A3	Boyces Street	B3	Meeting House Lane
B3	Brighton Place	B3	Middle Street
D4	Broad Street	D1	Morley Street
A1	Buckingham Road	B1	New Dorset Street
D4	Camelford Street	B2	New Road
A3	Cannon Place	D4	New Steine
D2	Carlton Hill	B3	Nile Street
A1	Centurion Road	B1	North Gardens
D3	Chapel Street	C2	North Place
C4	Charles Street	B1	North Road
C1	Cheltenham Place	B2	North Street
A1	Church Road	C3	Old Steine
B2	Church Street	B2	Portland Street
C2	Circus Street	A1	Powis Grove
A1	Clifton Hill	B3	Prince Albert Street
A1	Clifton Terrace	C3	Prince's Street
D3	Devonshire Place	B1	Queen's Gardens
B3	Dukes Lane	A2	Queen Square
B2	Duke Street	B2	Queen's Road
C3	East Street	A2	Regency Road
C2	Edward Street	A2	Regent Hill
D1	Elmore Street	C2	Regent Street
B1	Foundry Street	C1	Robert Street
B1	Frederick Street	D3	St James's Street
B2	Gardner Street	A1	St Nicholas Road
D3	George Street	B3	Ship Street Gardens
C1	Gloucester Place	B1	Spring Gardens
B1	Gloucester Road	C4	Steine Street
C1	Gloucester Street	D2	Sussex Street
B4	Grand Junction Road	C1	Sydney Street
C2	Grand Parade	B2	Tichborne Street
D3	High Street	C1	Tidy Street
D1	Ivory Place	B1	Upper Gardner Street
D2	John Street	A1	Upper Gloucester Road
C2	Jubilee Street	A2	Upper North Street
C1	Kensington Gardens	C1	Vine Street
C1	Kensington Street	D4	Wentworth Street
B1	Kew Street	A2	Western Road
A3	King's Road	A3	West Street
C2	Kingswood Street	D3	White Street
A1	Leopold Road	D2	William Street
B4	Little East Street	B2	Windsor Street

Bristol

Bristol is found on atlas page **31 Q10**

A3	Anchor Road	C2	Passage Street
D3	Avon Street	C1	Pembroke Street
B2	Baldwin Street	C1	Penn Street
D4	Bath Bridge	B3	Pero's Bridge
C1	Bond Street	A2	Perry Road
D2	Bond Street	C2	Philadelphia Street
C1	Broadmead	C4	Portwall Lane
D2	Broad Plain	C4	Prewett Street
B3	Broad Quay	B3	Prince Street
B2	Broad Street	B3	Queen Charlotte Street
C2	Broad Weir	B3	Queen Square
A3	Canons Way	C4	Redcliffe Hill
C3	Canynge Street	B4	Redcliffe Parade West
C2	Castle Street	C4	Redcliffe Way
A3	College Green	C4	Redcliff Mead Lane
B2	Colston Avenue	C3	Redcliff Street
B2	Colston Street	A1	Royal Fort Road
B4	Commercial Road	B2	Rupert Street
B2	Corn Street	B3	St Augustine's Parade
C3	Counterslip	A3	St George's Road
A4	Cumberland Road	D1	St Matthias Park
A3	Deanery Road	A1	St Michael's Hill
A3	Denmark Street	B2	St Stephen's Street
A3	Explore Lane	C3	St Thomas Street
C2	Fairfax Street	B2	Small Street
C3	Ferry Street	C4	Somerset Street
D3	Friary	A1	Southwell Street
A2	Frogmore Street	A1	Tankards Close
A3	Great George Street	B3	Telephone Avenue
D1	Great George Street	C3	Temple Back
B4	Guinea Street	D3	Temple Back East
C1	Haymarket	D4	Temple Gate
A2	Hill Street	C3	Temple Street
B1	Horfield Road	D3	Temple Way
D1	Houlton Street	B4	The Grove
D2	Jacob Street	C1	The Horsefair
B3	King Street	C2	The Pithay
B2	Lewins Mead	D2	Tower Hill
A2	Lodge Street	A2	Trenchard Street
D2	Lower Castle Street	A1	Tyndall Avenue
A2	Lower Church Lane	C1	Union Street
B1	Lower Maudlin Street	B1	Upper Maudlin Street
B1	Marlborough Hill	C2	Victoria Street
B1	Marlborough Street	B4	Wapping Road
B3	Marsh Street	B4	Welsh Back
C2	Newgate	B1	Whitson Street
D2	Old Market Street	C2	Wine Street
A2	Park Street	A1	Woodland Road

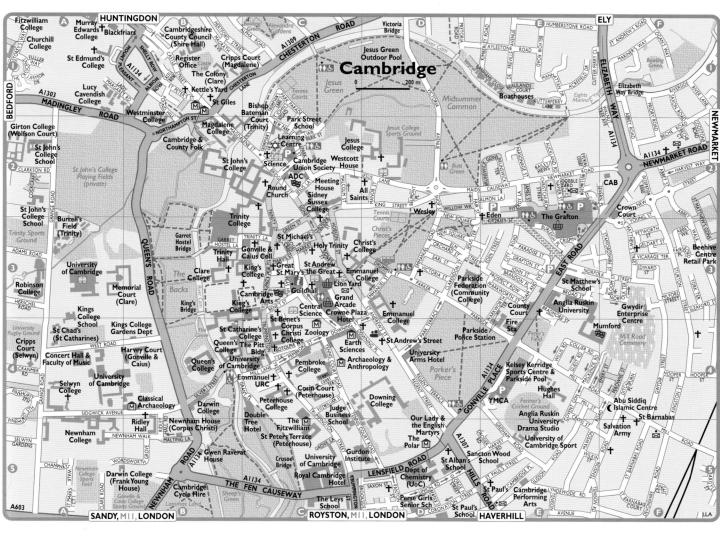

Cambridge

Cambridge is found on atlas page **62 G9**

F1	Abbey Road	E4	Collier Road	F2	Godstone Road	E5	Mawson Road	F5	St Barnabas Road
F2	Abbey Street	D5	Coronation Street	D4	Gonville Place	F3	Milford Street	C3	St Mary's Street
F3	Abbey Walk	E4	Covent Garden	E3	Grafton Street	C4	Mill Lane	F2	St Matthew's Gardens
E1	Acrefield Drive	E4	Crispin Place	A3	Grange Road	E4	Mill Road	F3	St Matthew's Street
E3	Adam and Eve Street	B5	Crusoe Bridge	A4	Grange Road	E4	Mill Street	E5	St Paul's Street
B1	Albion Row	E1	Cutler Ferry Close	B4	Grant Place	E4	Mortimer Road	B1	St Peter's Street
C1	Alpha Road	E1	Cutterferry Lane	C3	Green Street	B1	Mount Pleasant	E2	Salmon Lane
E2	Auckland Road	E1	De Freville Avenue	E5	Gresham Road	E2	Napier Street	F1	Saxon Road
E1	Aylestone Road	F5	Devonshire Road	E4	Guest Road	E2	Newmarket Road	D5	Saxon Street
E2	Bailey Mews	F4	Ditchburn Place	F4	Gwydir Street	B5	Newnham Road	F2	Severn Place
D1	Banhams Close	C4	Downing Place	F2	Harvest Way	A5	Newnham Walk	B1	Shelly Row
E1	Beaulands Court	C4	Downing Street	E5	Harvey Road	C2	New Park Street	D2	Shop Street
F2	Beche Road	D5	Drosier Road	B1	Hertford Street	D3	New Square	A4	Sidgwick Avenue
D2	Belmont Place	D3	Drummer Street	D5	Hills Road	F2	New Street	C2	Sidney Street
E1	Belvoir Road	D3	Earl Street	C3	Hobson Street	E3	Norfolk Street	B4	Silver Street
C3	Bene't Street	E3	East Road	E1	Humberstone Road	F3	Norfolk Terrace	F3	Staffordshire Street
D5	Bentick Street	E3	Eden Street	E2	James Street	B2	Northampton Street	F3	Sturton Street
F3	Bloom Street	E3	Eden Street Back	C2	Jesus Lane	F2	Occupation Road	C3	Sussex Street
E3	Bradmore Street	F3	Edward Street	D3	Jesus Terrace	D3	Orchard Street	E5	Tenison Avenue
E3	Brandon Place	F1	Elizabeth Way	E3	John Street	D5	Panton Street	E5	Tenison Road
C2	Bridge Street	D3	Elm Street	E1	Kimberley Road	E3	Paradise Street	C4	Tennis Court Road
E3	Broad Street	F4	Emery Street	B3	King's Bridge	D3	Parker Street	C4	Tennis Court Terrace
D5	Brookside	D3	Emmanuel Road	F4	King's Parade	C1	Park Parade	B5	The Fen Causeway
E2	Brunswick Gardens	D3	Emmanuel Street	E4	Kingston Street	D3	Parkside	C2	Thompson's Lane
E3	Brunswick Terrace	E2	Evening Court	D2	King Street	C2	Park Street	C3	Trinity Lane
E3	Burleigh Place	F3	Fairsford Place	A1	Lady Margaret Road	D4	Park Terrace	C2	Trinity Street
E5	Cambridge Place	D2	Fair Street	D5	Lensfield Road	E2	Parsonage Street	C4	Trumpington Street
B1	Castle Row	E2	Fitzroy Lane	F1	Logan's Way	C4	Peas Hill	D5	Union Road
B1	Castle Street	E3	Fitzroy Street	C2	Lwr Park Street	C4	Pembroke Street	F3	Vicarage Terrace
A5	Champneys Walk	C4	Fitzwilliam Street	E5	Lyndewode Road	F4	Perowne Street	D1	Victoria Avenue
B1	Chesterton Lane	B3	Garret Hostel Bridge	E4	Mackenzie Road	F3	Petworth Street	D1	Victoria Bridge
C1	Chesterton Road	B3	Garret Hostel Lane	A1	Madingley Road	B1	Pound Hill	D3	Victoria Street
E2	Christchurch Street	F3	Geldart Street	B2	Magdalene Street	F1	Priory Road	E3	Warkworth Street
D3	City Road	D5	George IV Street	B1	Magrath Avenue	E3	Prospect Row	E4	Warkworth Terrace
D3	Clarendon Street	E5	Glisson Road	D2	Maids Causeway	B3	Queen's Road	E2	Wellington Street
E2	Cobble Yard			C2	Malcolm Street	D4	Regent Street	A4	West Road
				B5	Malting Lane	D4	Regent Terrace	E5	Wilkin Street
				E1	Manhattan Drive	F1	River Lane	E4	Willis Road
				D2	Manor Street	F1	Riverside	D2	Willow Walk
				F1	Mariner's Way	F1	St Andrew's Road	A5	Wordsworth Grove
				C3	Market Street	D3	St Andrew's Street	F3	Young Street

University Colleges

C3	Christ's College
A3	Clare College
B1	Clare College
B3	Clare College
C4	Corpus Christi College
B4	Darwin College
D4	Downing College
C3	Emmanuel College
D3	Emmanuel College
A1	Fitzwilliam College
A2	Girton College (Wolfson Court)
B3	Gonville & Caius College
B4	Gonville & Caius College
C2	Jesus College
B3	King's College
A1	Lucy Cavendish College
B2	Magdalene College
A1	Murray Edwards College
A5	Newnham College
C4	Pembroke College
C4	Peterhouse College
B4	Queen's College
A3	Robinson College
B4	St Catherine's College
A1	St Edmund's College
B2	St John's College
A4	Selwyn College
C2	Sidney Sussex College
B3	Trinity College
B1	Westminster College

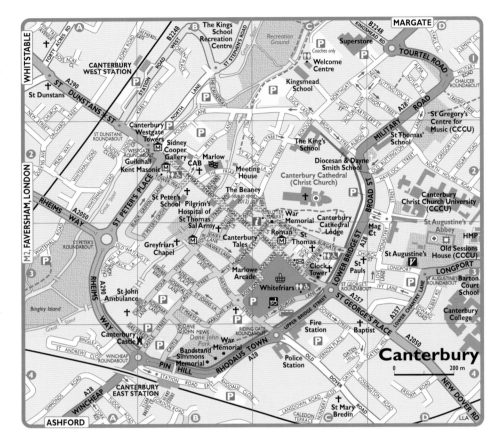

Canterbury

Canterbury is found on atlas page **39 K10**

B3	Adelaide Place	D1	Notley Street
D3	Albert Road	C4	Nunnery Fields
C2	Albion Place	C4	Oaten Hill
D1	Alma Street	C4	Old Dover Road
C1	Artillery Street	D2	Old Ruttington Lane
B3	Beercart Lane	A2	Orchard Street
B2	Best Lane	C2	Palace Street
A3	Black Griffin Lane	C3	Parade
C2	Borough	B4	Pin Hill
D2	Broad Street	B2	Pound Lane
C3	Burgate	A2	Queens Avenue
C2	Butter Market	A3	Rheims Way
C3	Canterbury Lane	B4	Rhodaus Town
B4	Castle Row	B3	Rose Lane
B3	Castle Street	B3	Rosemary Lane
C4	Cossington Road	B2	St Alphege Lane
C3	Dover Street	A1	St Dunstans Street
C1	Duck Lane	B3	St Edmunds Road
D2	Edgar Road	C3	St George's Lane
D3	Edward Road	C3	St George's Place
D4	Ersham Road	C3	St George's Street
A4	Gas Street	D2	St Gregory's Road
B4	Gordon Road	B3	St Johns Lane
B2	Guildhall Street	B3	St Margaret's Street
D2	Havelock Street	B3	St Marys Street
B3	Hawks Lane	B3	St Peter's Grove
B2	High Street	B2	St Peter's Lane
B3	Hospital Lane	A3	St Peter's Place
C3	Ivy Lane	B2	St Peters Street
B3	Jewry Lane	B4	Station Road East
C2	King Street	A1	Station Road West
B1	King's Lane	B3	Stour Street
C4	Lansdown Road	D1	Sturry Road
A2	Linden Grove	C2	Sun Street
D3	Longport	B1	The Causeway
D3	Love Lane	B2	The Friars
C3	Lower Bridge Street	D1	Tourtel Road
D4	Lower Chantry Lane	B2	Tower Way
B3	Marlowe Avenue	A4	Tudor Road
A2	Mead Way	D1	Union Street
C3	Mercery Lane	C4	Upper Bridge Street
D2	Military Road	C4	Vernon Place
B1	Mill Lane	C1	Victoria Row
D3	Monastery Street	B3	Watling Street
D4	New Dover Road	A2	Whitehall Gardens
D1	New Ruttington Lane	A2	Whitehall Road
B1	North Lane	A4	Wincheap
C1	Northgate	A4	York Road

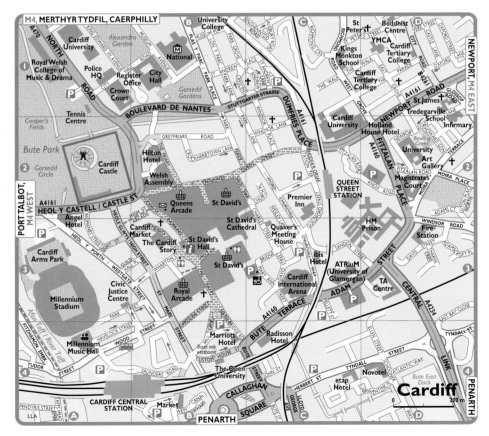

Cardiff

Cardiff is found on atlas page **30 G9**

D3	Adam Street	B1	Museum Avenue
D2	Adams Court	B1	Museum Place
D3	Adamscroft Place	D2	Newport Road Lane
D4	Atlantic Way	D2	North Luton Place
B2	Boulevard De Nantes	A1	North Road
C3	Bridge Street	D1	Oxford Lane
D4	Brigantine Place	D1	Oxford Street
C4	Bute Street	B1	Park Grove
C3	Bute Terrace	B1	Park Lane
B4	Callaghan Square	B1	Park Place
B3	Caroline Street	A3	Park Street
D1	Castle Lane	C3	Pellett Street
A2	Castle Street	A4	Pendyris Street
D3	Central Link	A3	Quay Street
B2	Charles Street	B2	Queen Street
C2	Churchill Way	C1	Richmond Crescent
A1	City Hall Road	C1	Richmond Road
D1	City Road	B1	St Andrew's Crescent
B2	Crockherbtown Lane	C1	St Andrew's Lane
B4	Custom House Street	B1	St Andrew's Place
C3	David Street	B2	St John Street
D3	Davis Street	B3	St Mary Street
D4	Ellen Street	C1	St Peter's Street
C2	Fford Churchill	C1	Salisbury Road
D2	Fitzalan Place	C3	Sandon Street
D2	Fitzalan Road	B4	Saunders Road
A4	Fitzhamon Embankment	D4	Schooner Way
D1	Glossop Road	C1	Senghennydd Road
B2	Greyfriars Road	B1	Stuttgarter Strasse
C3	Guildford Street	B2	The Friary
A3	Guildhall Place	B3	The Hayes
A4	Havelock Street	D1	The Parade
A4	Hayes Bridge Road	C1	The Walk
B2	Heol Siarl	B3	Trinity Street
C4	Herbert Street	A4	Tudor Street
B3	High Street	D4	Tyndall Street
B2	High Street Arcade	D1	Vere Street
B3	Hills Street	C2	Wesley Lane
A1	King Edward VII Avenue	B4	West Canal Wharf
D2	Knox Road	C1	West Grove
C4	Lloyd George Avenue	A3	Westgate Street
C3	Mary Ann Street	B3	Wharton Street
B4	Mill Lane	C2	Windsor Lane
D2	Moira Place	C1	Windsor Place
D2	Moira Terrace	D3	Windsor Road
		A4	Womanby Street
		A4	Wood Street
		B3	Working Street

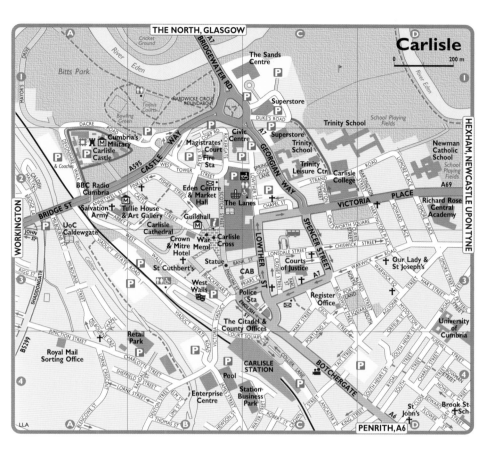

Carlisle

Carlisle is found on atlas page 110 G9

A2	Abbey Street	D2	Howard Place
D3	Aglionby Street	D4	Howe Street
A2	Annetwell Street	B4	James Street
B3	Bank Street	A3	John Street
B3	Blackfriars Street	A4	Junction Street
A4	Blencowe Street	C4	King Street
C4	Botchergate	C4	Lancaster Street
A2	Bridge Lane	B4	Lime Street
A2	Bridge Street	D2	Lismore Place
B1	Bridgewater Road	D3	Lismore Street
D3	Broad Street	C3	Lonsdale Street
C3	Brunswick Street	A4	Lorne Crescent
A2	Caldew Maltings	A4	Lorne Street
B2	Castle Street	C2	Lowther Street
B2	Castle Way	C3	Mary Street
C3	Cecil Street	A1	Mayor's Drive
A3	Chapel Place	A3	Milbourne Crescent
C2	Chapel Street	A3	Milbourne Street
D4	Charles Street	D3	Myddleton Street
A4	Charlotte Street	D3	North Alfred Street
C2	Chatsworth Square	D3	Orfeur Street
C3	Chiswick Street	D3	Petteril Street
D4	Close Street	B2	Peter Street
C4	Collier Lane	C4	Portland Place
C2	Compton Street	C3	Port-Land Place
B2	Corp Road	B4	Randall Street
B4	Court Square	B2	Rickergate
C3	Crosby Street	A3	Rigg Street
C4	Crown Street	C4	Robert Street
C3	Currie Street	D4	Rydal Street
A1	Dacre Road	B2	Scotch Street
B4	Denton Street	A3	Shaddongate
A2	Devonshire Walk	A4	Sheffield Street
C1	Duke's Road	D3	South Alfred Street
D4	Edward Street	D4	South Henry Street
B4	Elm Street	C2	Spencer Street
B3	English Street	C2	Spring Gardens Lane
B2	Finkle Street	C2	Strand Road
B2	Fisher Street	C4	Tait Street
D4	Flower Street	B4	Thomas Street
C3	Friars Court	A3	Viaduct Estate Road
D4	Fusehill Street	C2	Victoria Place
C2	Georgian Way	B4	Victoria Viaduct
D4	Grey Street	D3	Warwick Road
D2	Hartington Place	D3	Warwick Square
D2	Hartington Street	C4	Water Street
D3	Hart Street	B2	West Tower Street
B4	Hewson Street	B3	West Walls

Cheltenham

Cheltenham is found on atlas page 46 H10

C2	Albion Street	B4	Montpellier Parade
D2	All Saints' Road	B4	Montpellier Spa Road
B1	Ambrose Street	A4	Montpellier Street
D4	Argyll Road	A4	Montpellier Terrace
A4	Back Montpellier Terrace	A4	Montpellier Walk
B4	Bath Road	A1	New Street
C3	Bath Street	B2	North Street
B1	Baynham Way	D4	Old Bath Road
A3	Bayshill Road	B3	Oriel Road
A3	Bayshill Villas Lane	A3	Parabola Lane
B1	Bennington Street	A3	Parabola Road
C3	Berkeley Street	A1	Park Street
A1	Burton Street	D1	Pittville Circus
D3	Carlton Street	D1	Pittville Circus Road
B2	Church Street	B2	Pittville Street
B2	Clarence Parade	C1	Portland Street
C1	Clarence Road	C1	Prestbury Road
B2	Clarence Street	D3	Priory Street
C4	College Road	B3	Promenade
B2	Crescent Terrace	A3	Queens Parade
A1	Devonshire Street	B2	Regent Street
D3	Duke Street	B3	Rodney Road
B1	Dunalley Street	B2	Royal Well
C1	Evesham Road	A2	Royal Well Lane
C2	Fairview Road	D2	St Anne's Road
D2	Fairview Street	D2	St Anne's Terrace
A3	Fauconberg Road	B2	St George's Place
D1	Glenfall Street	A2	St George's Road
C3	Grosvenor Street	B1	St George's Street
A1	Grove Street	A2	St James' Square
B1	Henrietta Street	C3	St James Street
D3	Hewlett Road	C2	St Johns Avenue
A1	High Street	B1	St Margaret's Road
C2	High Street	B1	St Paul's Street South
B3	Imperial Lane	C3	Sandford Street
B3	Imperial Square	D1	Selkirk Street
A2	Jessop Avenue	C3	Sherborne Street
D4	Keynsham Road	A1	Station Street
A1	King Street	B4	Suffolk Parade
A1	Knapp Road	B1	Swindon Road
A4	Lansdown Road	D3	Sydenham Villas Road
D2	Leighton Road	B4	Trafalgar Street
C3	London Road	D2	Union Street
D1	Malden Road	C3	Wellington Street
A1	Market Street	C2	Winchcombe Street
A1	Milsom Street	D2	Winstonian Road
B1	Monson Avenue	C3	Witcombe Place
B4	Montpellier Grove	D1	York Street

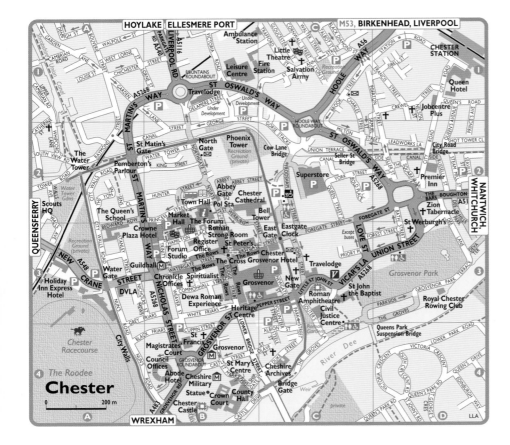

Chester

Chester is found on atlas page **81 N11**

C4	Albion Street	B3	Nicholas Street
D2	Bath Street	B2	Northgate Street
C1	Black Diamond Street	A3	Nun's Road
D2	Boughton	B1	Parkgate Road
A1	Bouverie Street	C3	Park Street
B3	Bridge Street	C3	Pepper Street
C1	Brook Street	B2	Princess Street
C2	Canal Side	C3	Priory Place
B4	Castle Street	C4	Queen's Park Road
C1	Charles Street	D1	Queen's Road
A1	Chichester Street	C2	Queen Street
D2	City Road	A2	Raymond Street
A2	City Walls Road	D2	Russell Street
B3	Commonhall Street	C1	St Anne Street
C1	Cornwall Street	D4	St John's Road
D1	Crewel Street	C3	St John Street
B4	Cuppin Street	A2	St Martin's Way
D2	Dee Hills Park	B4	St Mary's Hill
D2	Dee Lane	C4	St Olave Street
B1	Delamere Street	B1	St Oswald's Way
C4	Duke Street	B2	St Werburgh Street
B3	Eastgate Street	C2	Samuel Street
C1	Egerton Street	D2	Seller Street
C2	Foregate Street	B4	Shipgate Street
C3	Forest Street	C3	Souter's Lane
D1	Francis Street	A2	South View Road
C2	Frodsham Street	A3	Stanley Street
A1	Garden Lane	D1	Station Road
B2	George Street	D2	Steam Mill Street
C1	Gloucester Street	C4	Steele Street
C2	Gorse Stacks	C1	Talbot Street
D3	Grosvenor Park Terrace	A2	Tower Road
B4	Grosvenor Road	C1	Trafford Street
B4	Grosvenor Street	B3	Trinity Street
B3	Hamilton Place	D3	Union Street
C1	Hoole Way	C2	Union Terrace
B2	Hunter Street	A1	Upper Cambrian Road
B2	King Street	C3	Vicar's Lane
D2	Leadworks Lane	D4	Victoria Crescent
C3	Little St John Street	B1	Victoria Road
B1	Liverpool Road	C3	Volunteer Street
A1	Lorne Street	A1	Walpole Street
C3	Love Street	C1	Walter Street
B4	Lower Bridge Street	B3	Watergate Street
D4	Lower Park Road	B2	Water Tower Street
C2	Milton Street	B3	Weaver Street
A3	New Crane Street	B3	White Friars
C3	Newgate Street	C2	York Street

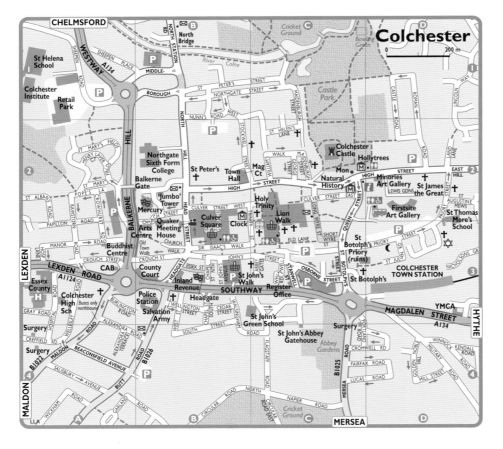

Colchester

Colchester is found on atlas page **52 G6**

C3	Abbey Gates	B1	Middleborough
A3	Alexandra Road	D4	Military Road
A4	Alexandra Terrace	D4	Mill Street
A3	Balkerne Hill	C4	Napier Road
A4	Beaconsfield Avenue	D3	Nicholsons Green
A3	Burlington Road	B1	North Bridge
A4	Butt Road	B1	Northgate Street
D1	Castle Road	B1	North Hill
B3	Cedar Street	B1	North Station Road
B3	Chapel Street North	B1	Nunn's Road
B3	Chapel Street South	C3	Osborne Street
B3	Church Street	A3	Papillon Road
B3	Church Walk	A2	Pope's Lane
C4	Circular Road East	C4	Portland Road
B4	Circular Road North	D3	Priory Street
A4	Creffield Road	C3	Queen Street
C4	Cromwell Road	A2	Rawstorn Road
A3	Crouch Street	D1	Roman Road
B3	Crouch Street	A2	St Alban's Road
A2	Crowhurst Road	D2	St Augustine Mews
C2	Culver Street East	C3	St Botolph's Street
B2	Culver Street West	C2	St Helen's Lane
D2	East Hill	B3	St John's Avenue
B3	Essex Street	B3	St John's Street
C4	Fairfax Road	D3	St Julian Road
C4	Flagstaff Road	A2	St Mary's Fields
A4	Garland Road	B1	St Peter's Street
C2	George Street	A4	Salisbury Avenue
D4	Golden Noble Hill	A1	Sheepen Place
A3	Gray Road	A1	Sheepen Road
B3	Headgate	C3	Short Wyre Street
B2	Head Street	B3	Sir Isaac's Walk
A2	Henry Laver Court	B4	South Street
B2	High Street	B3	Southway
A4	Hospital Road	C3	Stanwell Street
A3	Hospital Lane	B3	Trinity Street
D4	Kendall Road	B3	Walsingham Road
D2	Land Lane	A4	Wellesley Road
D2	Lewis Gardens	B3	Wellington Street
A3	Lexden Road	B1	West Stockwell Street
D1	Lincoln Way	B4	West Street
C2	Long Wyre Street	A1	Westway
C4	Lucas Road	C3	Whitewell Road
D3	Magdalen Street	A4	Wickham Road
C1	Maidenburgh Street	C2	William's Walk
A4	Maldon Road	D4	Winnock Road
A3	Manor Road		
C4	Mersea Road		

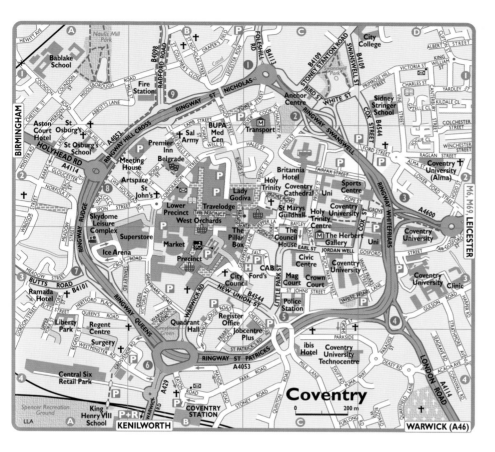

Coventry

Coventry is found on atlas page **59 M9**

A1	Abbotts Lane	A1	Mill Street
D4	Acacia Avenue	C3	Much Park Street
D2	Alma Street	B3	New Union Street
A2	Barras Lane	A2	Norfolk Street
C2	Bayley Lane	D4	Paradise Street
C1	Bird Street	B4	Park Road
B1	Bishop Street	C4	Parkside
B2	Broadgate	D1	Primrose Hill Street
B2	Burge Street	C2	Priory Row
A3	Butts Road	C2	Priory Street
A3	Butts Street	C4	Puma Way
D1	Canterbury Street	D4	Quaryfield Lane
A2	Chester Street	A3	Queen's Road
C3	Cheylesmore	B3	Queen Victoria Road
D4	Cornwall Road	C4	Quinton Road
B2	Corporation Street	B1	Radford Road
A1	Coundon Road	D2	Raglan Street
D1	Cox Street	A4	Regent Street
D2	Cox Street	A2	Ringway Hill Cross
A3	Croft Road	A3	Ringway Queens
C3	Earl Street	A3	Ringway Rudge
B4	Eaton Road	B1	Ringway St Nicholas
C2	Fairfax Street	B4	Ringway St Patricks
C1	Foleshill Road	C1	Ringway Swanswell
A2	Gloucester Street	D2	Ringway Whitefriars
D3	Gosford Street	C3	St Johns Street
B3	Greyfriars Lane	B1	St Nicholas Street
B3	Greyfriars Road	C3	Salt Lane
A4	Grosvenor Road	D4	Seagrave Road
D3	Gulson Road	A2	Spon Street
C2	Hales Street	A3	Stanley Road
A3	Hertford Place	B4	Stoney Road
C3	High Street	C1	Stoney Stanton Road
B2	Hill Street	D3	Strathmore Avenue
A2	Holyhead Road	C1	Swanswell Street
C3	Jordan Well	B1	Tower Street
B2	Lamb Street	C2	Trinity Street
B1	Leicester Row	B2	Upper Hill Street
C3	Little Park Street	A4	Upper Wells Street
D4	London Road	D1	Victoria Street
D2	Lower Ford Street	D1	Vine Street
A2	Lower Holyhead Road	B3	Warwick Road
B4	Manor House Road	B4	Warwick Road
B4	Manor Road	A4	Westminster Road
A3	Meadow Street	D3	White Friars Street
A1	Meriden Street	C1	White Street
A1	Middleborough Road	A3	Windsor Street
C4	Mile Lane	D1	Yardley Street

Darlington

Darlington is found on atlas page **103 Q8**

A3	Abbey Road	C2	Northgate
B1	Barningham Street	B2	North Lodge Terrace
B1	Bartlett Street	B4	Northumberland Street
B3	Beaumont Street	A4	Oakdene Avenue
C4	Bedford Street	A2	Outram Street
A4	Beechwood Avenue	D3	Parkgate
B3	Blackwellgate	D4	Park Lane
B3	Bondgate	C4	Park Place
D3	Borough Road	B1	Pendower Street
C3	Brunswick Street	D4	Pensbury Street
D4	Brunton Street	B4	Polam Lane
C4	Chestnut Street	A3	Portland Place
A4	Cleveland Terrace	B3	Powlett Street
C4	Clifton Road	C3	Priestgate
B2	Commercial Street	B3	Raby Terrace
A4	Coniscliffe Road	C2	Russell Street
B1	Corporation Road	B2	St Augustine's Way
C2	Crown Street	C2	St Cuthbert's Way
B1	Dodds Street	C4	St Cuthbert's Way
A3	Duke Street	D4	St James Place
B1	Easson Road	A1	Salisbury Terrace
D1	East Mount Road	B3	Salt Yard
B3	East Raby Street	A4	Scarth Street
C3	East Street	B3	Skinnergate
A2	Elms Road	B4	South Arden Street
C4	Feethams	A4	Southend Avenue
A3	Fife Road	A2	Stanhope Road North
B2	Four Riggs	A3	Stanhope Road South
C2	Freemans Place	C3	Stonebridge
B2	Gladstone Street	B2	Sun Street
B4	Grange Road	C4	Swan Street
A1	Greenbank Road	A3	Swinburne Road
B2	Greenbank Road	A2	Trinity Road
D3	Green Street	B3	Tubwell Row
C4	Hargreave Terrace	A3	Uplands Road
D2	Haughton Road	A4	Valley Street North
C1	High Northgate	A2	Vane Terrace
B3	High Row	C4	Victoria Embankment
A1	Hollyhurst Road	B4	Victoria Road
B3	Houndgate	C4	Victoria Road
D3	Jack Way Steeple	A2	West Crescent
C1	John Street	A3	West Powlett Street
B2	Kendrew Street	B3	West Row
B1	Kingston Street	B4	West Street
A4	Langholm Crescent	B4	Woodland Road
A3	Larchfield Street	A2	Yarm Road
A2	Maude Street	D3	
D4	Neasham Road		

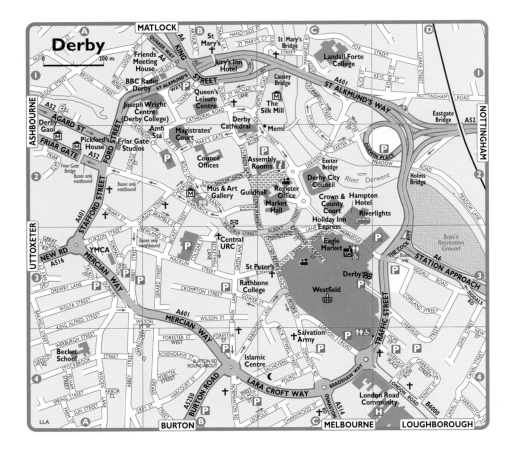

Derby

Derby is found on atlas page **72 B3**

A4 Abbey Street	A4 King Alfred Street
A1 Agard Street	B1 King Street
C3 Albert Street	B4 Lara Croft Way
B4 Babington Lane	B4 Leopold Street
C4 Back Sitwell Street	D4 Liversage Row
B3 Becket Street	D3 Liversage Street
B2 Bold Lane	A1 Lodge Lane
C4 Bradshaw Way	C3 London Road
B2 Bramble Street	B3 Macklin Street
A1 Bridge Street	C1 Mansfield Road
A1 Brook Street	D2 Meadow Lane
B4 Burton Road	D2 Meadow Road
D4 Canal Street	B3 Mercian Way
D4 Carrington Street	C3 Morledge
B1 Cathedral Road	A3 Newland Street
A2 Cavendish Court	A3 New Road
B1 Chapel Street	D4 New Street
D1 Clarke Street	D1 Nottingham Road
D3 Copeland Street	C4 Osmaston Road
B2 Corn Market	C1 Phoenix Street
B3 Crompton Street	B1 Queen Street
A2 Curzon Street	D1 Robert Street
A3 Curzon Street	B4 Rosengrave Street
C2 Darwin Place	C4 Sacheverel Street
C2 Derwent Street	B2 Sadler Gate
A3 Drewry Lane	C1 St Alkmund's Way
C1 Duke Street	B1 St Helen's Street
A3 Dunkirk	B2 St Mary's Gate
C3 East Street	C3 St Peter's Street
C3 Exchange Street	D3 Siddals Road
C2 Exeter Place	C1 Sowter Road
C2 Exeter Street	A4 Spring Street
A2 Ford Street	A3 Stafford Street
B4 Forester Street West	D3 Station Approach
A3 Forman Street	A4 Stockbrook Street
C1 Fox Street	B2 Strand
A2 Friary Street	C1 Stuart Street
B1 Full Street	A4 Sun Street
B3 Gerard Street	D3 The Cock Pitt
B3 Gower Street	C3 Thorntree Lane
B3 Green Lane	D4 Traffic Street
A4 Grey Street	D4 Trinity Street
B1 Handyside Street	B2 Victoria Street
B4 Harcourt Street	B2 Wardwick
B2 Iron Gate	A4 Werburgh Street
D4 John Street	C4 Wilmot Street
B2 Jury Street	A3 Wolfa Street
D1 Keys Street	A4 Woods Lane

Doncaster

Doncaster is found on atlas page **91 P10**

D3 Alderson Drive	B1 Montague Street
B3 Apley Road	B4 Nelson Street
A4 Balby Road Bridge	B1 Nether Hall Road
B3 Beechfield Road	A1 North Bridge Road
C1 Broxholme Lane	C4 North Street
C4 Carr House Road	D1 Osborne Road
B4 Carr Lane	C4 Palmer Street
C4 Chequer Avenue	B2 Park Road
C3 Chequer Road	B2 Park Terrace
C4 Childers Street	B2 Prince's Street
B1 Christ Church Road	A2 Priory Place
A1 Church View	B4 Prospect Place
B1 Church Way	C1 Queen's Road
C4 Clark Avenue	C4 Rainton Road
A4 Cleveland Street	C3 Ravensworth Road
B3 College Road	C1 Rectory Gardens
C4 Cooper Street	C2 Regent Square
B2 Coopers Terrace	D3 Roman Road
B1 Copley Road	C1 Royal Avenue
B3 Cunningham Road	B4 St James Street
D3 Danum Road	C1 St Mary's Road
B1 Dockin Hill Road	A2 St Sepulchre Gate
A2 Duke Street	A3 St Sepulchre Gate West
B2 East Laith Gate	C1 St Vincent Avenue
C3 Elmfield Road	C1 St Vincent Road
A4 Exchange Street	B2 Scot Lane
D3 Firbeck Road	B2 Silver Street
B2 Frances Street	B3 Somerset Road
B2 Georges Gate	C2 South Parade
C2 Glyn Avenue	C4 South Street
A4 Green Dyke Lane	A2 Spring Gardens
A1 Grey Friars' Road	A4 Stirling Street
C2 Hall Cross Hill	C4 Stockil Road
B2 Hall Gate	D4 Theobald Avenue
D4 Hamilton Road	C1 Thorne Road
B1 Hannington Street	C2 Thorne Road
A2 High Street	C2 Town Fields
C1 Highfield Road	D1 Town Moor Avenue
B4 Jarratt Street	A2 Trafford Way
C1 King's Road	C1 Vaughan Avenue
C2 Lawn Avenue	B3 Waterdale
C2 Lawn Road	D3 Welbeck Road
D4 Lime Tree Avenue	A2 West Laith Gate
D3 Manor Drive	A3 West Street
A2 Market Place	C3 Whitburn Road
B1 Market Road	B4 White Way
B1 Milbanke Street	D1 Windsor Road
B4 Milton Walk	B2 Wood Street

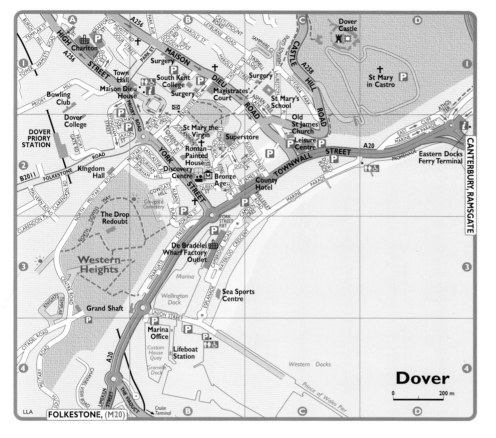

Dover

Dover is found on atlas page **27 P3**

B3	Adrian Street
B2	Albany Place
C1	Ashen Tree Lane
D1	Athol Terrace
B2	Biggin Street
A1	Burgh Hill
B3	Cambridge Road
C2	Camden Crescent
B2	Cannon Street
C1	Castle Hill Road
B1	Castlemount Road
B2	Castle Street
A3	Centre Road
A4	Channel View Road
B2	Church Street
A4	Citadel Road
A3	Clarendon Place
A2	Clarendon Road
B2	Cowgate Hill
A1	Crafford Street
B2	Dolphin Lane
C2	Douro Place
A1	Dour Street
B2	Durham Close
B2	Durham Hill
D2	East Cliff
A2	Effingham Street
B3	Esplanade
A2	Folkestone Road
B1	Godwyne Close
B1	Godwyne Road
B1	Harold Street
B1	Harold Street
C1	Heritage Gardens
A1	Hewitt Road
A1	High Street
B2	King Street
A3	Knights Templar
B2	Lancaster Road
C1	Laureston Place
B1	Leyburne Road
A4	Limekiln Street
B1	Maison Dieu Road
A2	Malvern Road
C2	Marine Parade
D2	Marine Parade
B2	Military Road
B2	Mill Lane
B2	New Street
A2	Norman Street
A3	North Downs Way
A3	North Military Road
B1	Park Avenue
B1	Park Street
B2	Pencester Road
A1	Peter Street
A2	Priory Gate Road
A1	Priory Hill
A1	Priory Road
B2	Priory Street
D2	Promenade
B2	Queen's Gate
B2	Queen Street
B2	Russell Street
B2	St James Street
C1	Samphire Close
A2	Saxon Street
B3	Snargate Street
A4	South Military Road
B2	Stembrook
C1	Taswell Close
B1	Taswell Street
A1	Templar Street
A4	The Viaduct
A1	Tower Hamlets Road
C2	Townwall Street
B3	Union Street
C1	Victoria Park
B3	Waterloo Crescent
C2	Wellesley Road
A1	Wood Street
B2	York Street
B3	York Street Roundabout

Dundee

Dundee is found on atlas page **142 G11**

B2	Albert Square
B2	Bank Street
A1	Barrack Road
B2	Barrack Road
B2	Bell Street
D1	Blackscroft
A1	Blinshall Street
A2	Blinshall Street
C1	Bonnybank Road
A2	Brown Street
C2	Candle Lane
C2	Castle Street
C2	Chapel Street
C3	City Square
C2	Commercial Street
D1	Constable Street
A1	Constitution Crescent
A1	Constitution Road
B2	Constitution Road
A2	Court House Square
C1	Cowgate
D1	Cowgate
C3	Crighton Street
D1	Dens Road
C3	Dock Street
A2	Douglas Street
B1	Dudhope Street
C3	Earl Grey Place
D2	East Dock Street
D1	East Whale Lane
B2	Euclid Crescent
B2	Euclid Street
C1	Forebank Road
B2	Forester Street
D1	Foundry Lane
C2	Gellatly Street
B4	Greenmarket
A2	Guthrie Street
A3	Hawkhill
C3	High Street
B1	Hilltown
B1	Hilltown Terrace
A3	Hunter Street
A1	Infirmary Brae
B2	Johnston Street
C1	King Street
C1	Kirk Lane
A1	Laburn Street
C1	Ladywell Avenue
B1	Laurel Bank
A1	Lochee Road
D1	Marketgait
C1	Marketgait East
D2	McDonald Street
B2	Meadowside
A2	Miln Street
C2	Murraygate
A4	Nethergate
B2	Nicoll Street
B2	North Lindsay Street
B1	North Marketgait
C1	North Victoria Road
A3	Old Hawkhill
B2	Panmure Street
A3	Park Place
A4	Perth Road
D1	Princes Street
B1	Prospect Place
C1	Queen Street
B2	Rattray Street
B2	Reform Street
B4	Riverside Drive
A4	Roseangle
C1	St Andrews Street
A1	Scrimgeour Place
A4	Seabraes Lane
C2	Seagate
A2	Session Street
C3	Shore Terrace
C3	South Marketgait
B3	South Tay Street
C3	South Victoria Dock Road
B2	South Ward Road
C1	Sugarhouse Wynd
D3	Tay Road Bridge
C2	Trades Lane
B3	Union Street
B1	Union Terrace
B2	Ward Road
D1	Weavers Yard
A2	West Bell Street
A2	West Marketgait
A3	West Port
D2	West Victoria Dock Road
C3	Whitehall Place
C3	Whitehall Street

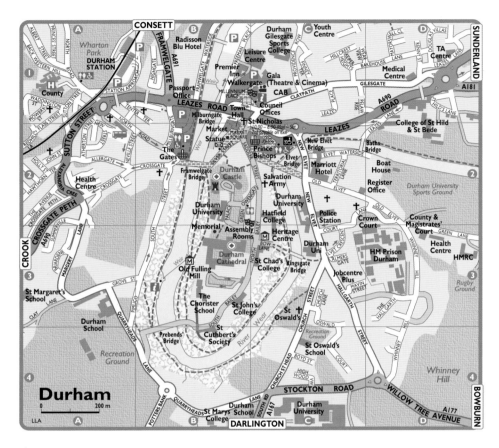

Durham

Durham

Durham is found on atlas page **103 Q2**

A1	Albert Street	D1	Mayorswell Close
A2	Alexandria Crescent	B1	Milburngate Bridge
A2	Allergate	B2	Millburngate
A2	Atherton Street	B1	Millennium Place
A1	Back Western Hill	A1	Mowbray Street
C1	Bakehouse Lane	A2	Neville Street
C2	Baths Bridge	C2	New Elvet
C3	Bow Lane	C2	New Elvet Bridge
C4	Boyd Street	A2	New Street
A3	Briardene	C3	North Bailey
C3	Church Lane	A1	North Road
C4	Church Street	C2	Old Elvet
C4	Church Street Head	C3	Oswald Court
A3	Clay Lane	B2	Owengate
C1	Claypath	B2	Palace Green
C3	Court Lane	C3	Palmers Gate
A2	Crossgate	C1	Pelaw Rise
A3	Crossgate Peth	A3	Pimlico
D1	Douglas Villas	B4	Potters Bank
C2	Elvet Bridge	B4	Prebends' Bridge
C3	Elvet Crescent	A1	Princes' Street
C2	Elvet Waterside	C1	Providence Row
C1	Finney Terrace	A3	Quarryheads Lane
A2	Flass Street	A2	Redhills Lane
B1	Framwelgate	D1	Renny Street
B2	Framwelgate Bridge	B2	Saddler Street
B1	Framwelgate Waterside	D1	St Hild's Lane
B1	Freeman Place	B2	Silver Street
C1	Gilesgate	B3	South Bailey
D3	Green Lane	C4	South Road
A3	Grove Street	B3	South Street
C3	Hallgarth Street	A1	Station Approach
A2	Hawthorn Terrace	C4	Stockton Road
B1	Highgate	A3	Summerville
C4	High Road View	A2	Sutton Street
C2	High Street	A1	Tenter Terrace
C1	Hillcrest	C2	Territorial Lane
A2	Holly Street	A2	The Avenue
A2	John Street	D3	The Hall Garth
C1	Keiper Heights	A1	Waddington Street
C3	Kingsgate Bridge	C1	Wear View
D1	Leazes Lane	D3	Whinney Hill
D2	Leazes Lane	D4	Willow Tree Avenue
C1	Leazes Place		
B1	Leazes Road		
A3	Margery Lane		
B2	Market Square		
C3	Mavin Street		

Eastbourne

Eastbourne is found on atlas page **25 P11**

A2	Arlington Road	D1	Langney Road
B2	Ashford Road	C2	Langney Road
C1	Ashford Road	B4	Lascelles Terrace
B1	Ashford Square	D1	Latimer Road
A1	Avenue Lane	B1	Leaf Road
C1	Belmore Road	B2	Lismore Road
A4	Blackwater Road	C1	Longstone Road
B3	Bolton Road	B3	Lushington Road
C1	Bourne Street	D2	Marine Parade
B3	Burlington Place	D1	Marine Road
C3	Burlington Road	B2	Mark Lane
A3	Camden Road	A3	Meads Road
B1	Carew Road	C1	Melbourne Road
A4	Carlisle Road	A2	Old Orchard Road
B4	Carlisle Road	A4	Old Wish Road
C1	Cavendish Avenue	C2	Pevensey Road
C1	Cavendish Place	C3	Promenade
C2	Ceylon Place	D2	Queen's Gardens
B3	Chiswick Place	A2	Saffrons Road
B3	College Road	A1	St Anne's Road
D2	Colonnade Gardens	D1	St Aubyn's Road
B1	Commercial Road	B1	St Leonard's Road
B4	Compton Street	D1	Seaside
C3	Compton Street	C2	Seaside Road
B3	Cornfield Lane	A2	Southfields Road
B2	Cornfield Road	A3	South Street
B3	Cornfield Terrace	B3	South Street
B3	Devonshire Place	B3	Spencer Road
C1	Dursley Road	B2	Station Street
C3	Elms Road	B2	Susan's Road
A1	Enys Road	B2	Sutton Road
A1	Eversfield Road	C1	Sydney Road
A3	Furness Road	B2	Terminus Road
B2	Gildredge Road	C3	Terminus Road
C3	Grand Parade	A1	The Avenue
A3	Grange Road	C2	Tideswell Road
A3	Grassington Road	C3	Trinity Place
A3	Grove Road	B3	Trinity Trees
B3	Hardwick Road	B1	Upper Avenue
A1	Hartfield Lane	A1	Upperton Gardens
A1	Hartfield Road	A1	Upperton Lane
C3	Hartington Place	A1	Upperton Road
C4	Howard Square	A3	West Street
B2	Hyde Gardens	A2	West Terrace
A2	Hyde Road	D1	Willowfield Road
A2	Ivy Terrace	B4	Wilmington Square
A4	Jevington Gardens	B3	Wish Road
B2	Junction Road	A3	York Road

Eastbourne

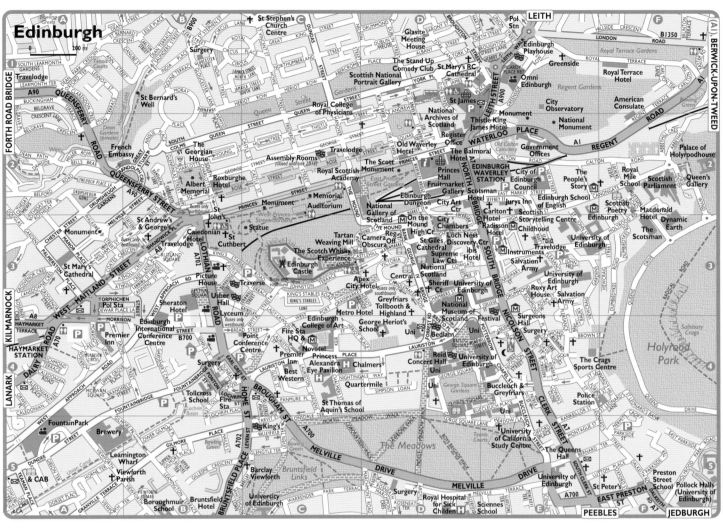

Edinburgh

Edinburgh is found on atlas page **127 P3**

F2	Abbeyhill	B2	Charlotte Square	D3	George IV Bridge	C4	Keir Street	E4	Nicolson Square	B1	St Stephen Street
C1	Abercromby Place	A3	Chester Street Gardens	D4	George Square	B1	Kerr Street	E4	Nicolson Street	C1	St Vincent Street
E3	Adam Street	B1	Circus Lane	D5	George Square Lane	B3	King's Stables Road	C4	Nightingale Way	B1	Saunders Street
D1	Albany Street	B1	Circus Place	B2	George Street	C3	King's Stables Road	D2	North Bridge	E5	Sciennes
A1	Ann Street	A1	Clarendon Crescent	C2	George Street	C3	Lady Lawson Street	C2	North Castle Street	B4	Semple Street
D5	Argyle Place	E4	Clerk Street	E5	Gifford Place	A3	Lansdowne Crescent	C5	North Meadow Walk	B3	Shandwick Place
A3	Atholl Crescent Lane	D2	Cockburn Street	B5	Gillespie Crescent	C4	Lauriston Gardens	D1	North St Andrew Street	D4	Simpson Loan
D3	Bank Street	C5	Coronation Walk	A5	Gilmore Park	C4	Lauriston Place	D1	North St David Street	E3	South Bridge
A2	Belford Road	D3	Cowgate	B5	Gilmore Place	C4	Lauriston Street	C1	Northumberland Street	B2	South Charlotte Street
A2	Belgrave Crescent	E4	Cowan's Close	E4	Gilmour Street	D3	Lawnmarket	F5	Oxford Street	E5	South Clerk Street
E5	Bernard Terrace	A1	Dean Park Crescent	B2	Glenfinlas Street	B5	Leamington Terrace	A3	Palmerston Place	A1	South Learmonth Gardens
D5	Boys Brigade Walk	A1	Dean Street	B1	Gloucester Lane	E1	Leith Street	C4	Panmure Place	D2	South St Andrew Street
A4	Brandfield Street	A3	Dewar Place Lane	A5	Granville Terrace	E1	Leith Walk	E3	Pleasance	D2	South St David Street
B4	Bread Street	B1	Doune Terrace	C1	Great King Street	A1	Lennox Street	B4	Ponton Street	C4	Spittal Street
D4	Bristo Place	A3	Douglas Gardens	B2	Great Stuart Street	C5	Leven Place	E4	Potterrow	B3	Stafford Street
C4	Brougham Street	B1	Drummond Place	C3	Greenmarket	B4	Lochrin Place	C2	Princes Street	C5	Tarvit Street
D1	Broughton Street	D1	Dublin Street	E1	Greenside Row	B4	Lochrin Street	F3	Queens Drive	C2	The Mound
E1	Broughton Street Lane	F3	Dumbiedykes Road	B3	Grindlay Street	E1	London Road	A1	Queensferry Road	C2	Thistle Street
F1	Brunton Terrace	B4	Dunbar Street	A3	Grosvenor Street	B3	Lothian Road	A2	Queensferry Street	A3	Torphichen Street
B5	Bruntsfield Place	C1	Dundas Street	A4	Grove Street	B5	Lower Gilmore Place	B2	Queen Street	E1	Union Street
D4	Buccleuch Place	A5	Dundee Street	E4	Haddon's Court	E5	Lutton Place	F3	Radical Road	B5	Upper Gilmore Place
E4	Buccleuch Street	E2	Earl Grey Street	C2	Hanover Street	A2	Lynedoch Place Lane	C3	Ramsay Lane	D3	Victoria Street
A4	Caledonian Place	F1	Easter Road	A4	Haymarket Terrace	A3	Manor Place	B2	Randolph Crescent	E4	Viewcraig Gardens
A4	Caledonian Road	E2	East Market Street	C1	Heriot Row	D5	Marchmont Crescent	B2	Randolph Lane	F3	Viewcraig Street
A4	Caledonian Street	F5	East Parkside	F5	Hermits Croft	D5	Marchmont Road	E5	Rankeillor Street	A5	Viewforth
E2	Calton Road	F5	East Preston Street	D3	High Street	D2	Market Street	E2	Regent Road	A3	Walker Street
D3	Candlemaker Row	D1	Elder Street	E3	High Street	E5	Meadow Lane	E3	Richmond Place	C5	Warrender Park Terrace
B3	Canning Street	D4	Forrest Road	F5	Holyrood Park Road	C5	Melville Drive	B2	Rose Street	D2	Waterloo Place
E2	Canongate	D1	Forth Street	E3	Holyrood Road	A3	Melville Street	D5	Rosneath Place	D2	Waverley Bridge
F1	Carlton Terrace	A4	Fountainbridge	C4	Home Street	D5	Melville Terrace	A3	Rothesay Place	A5	West Approach Road
C3	Castle Hill	C2	Frederick Street	B2	Hope Street	D5	Middle Meadow Walk	B1	Royal Circus	A3	West Maitland Street
C2	Castle Street	B4	Gardener's Crescent	F2	Horse Wynd	D5	Millerfield Place	E1	Royal Terrace	E4	West Nicolson Street
B3	Castle Terrace			E4	Howden Street	A2	Miller Row	D1	St Andrew Square	C4	West Port
C4	Chalmers Street			C1	Howe Street	E5	Moncrieff Terrace	A1	St Bernard's Crescent	E4	West Richmond Street
D3	Chambers Street			B1	India Place	E5	Montague Street	B2	St Colme Street	B4	West Toll Cross
E4	Chapel Street			B1	India Street	B1	Moray Place	D1	St James Place	A3	William Street
				B1	Jamaica Street South Lane	A4	Morrison Link	F4	St Leonard's Bank	A5	Yeaman Place
				D5	Jawbone Walk	A4	Morrison Street	E4	St Leonard's Hill	D1	York Lane
				C3	Johnston Terrace	C1	Mound Place	E4	St Leonard's Lane	D1	York Lane
						C1	Nelson Street	E4	St Leonard's Street	D1	York Place
						E2	New Street	E4	St Patrick Street	B2	Young Street

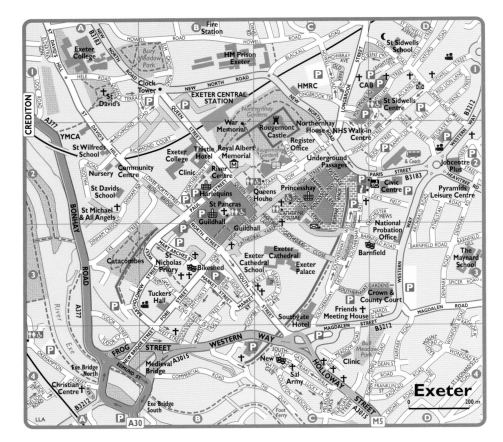

Exeter

Exeter is found on atlas page **9 M6**

D1	Acland Rd
D3	Archibald Road
D3	Athelstan Road
C2	Bailey Street
C2	Bampfylde Lane
D2	Bampfylde Street
D3	Barnfield Road
B3	Bartholomew Street West
C3	Bear Street
C2	Bedford Street
D2	Belgrave Road
C1	Blackall Road
A2	Bonhay Road
D2	Bude Street
C4	Bull Meadow Road
C2	Castle Street
C3	Cathedral Close
B3	Cathedral Yard
D4	Cedars Road
D1	Cheeke Street
C3	Chichester Mews
B4	Commercial Road
B3	Coombe Street
C3	Deanery Place
D4	Dean Street
D3	Denmark Road
A3	Dinham Crescent
A2	Dinham Road
D2	Dix's Field
C2	Eastgate
A4	Edmund Street
B1	Elm Grove Road
A3	Exe Street
D4	Fairpark Road
B3	Fore Street
D4	Franklin Street
B3	Friernhay Street
A4	Frog Street
B3	George Street
B3	Guinea Street
A2	Haldon Road
D2	Heavitree Road
A1	Hele Road
C2	High Street
C4	Holloway Street
B1	Howell Road
B2	Iron Bridge
B3	King Street
D1	King William Street
C1	Longbrook Street
B2	Lower North Street
D3	Magdalen Road
C4	Magdalen Street
B3	Market Street
C2	Martins Lane
B3	Mary Arches Street
C2	Musgrave Row
A4	New Bridge Street
A1	New North Road
B2	Northernhay Street
B3	North Street
C1	Old Park Road
D1	Oxford Road
C3	Palace Gate
D2	Paris Street
B2	Paul Street
B4	Preston Street
C2	Princesshay
C1	Queens Crescent
A1	Queen's Terrace
B1	Queen Street
D4	Radford Road
D1	Red Lion Lane
B2	Richmond Court
A2	Richmond Road
C4	Roberts Road
C2	Roman Walk
A1	St David's Hill
C2	Sidwell Street
D1	Sidwell Street
B3	Smythen Street
C3	Southernhay East
C3	Southernhay Gardens
C3	Southernhay West
B3	South Street
D3	Spicer Road
D1	Summerland Street
D4	Temple Road
A4	Tudor Court
A3	Tudor Street
D1	Verney Street
D1	Wells Street
B4	Western Way
B4	West Street
D4	Wonford Road
D1	York Road

Gloucester

Gloucester is found on atlas page **46 F11**

D4	Albert Street
B4	Albion Street
D4	All Saints' Road
C2	Alvin Street
B2	Archdeacon Street
C4	Archibald Street
C4	Arthur Street
B3	Barbican Road
B3	Barrack Square
D4	Barton Street
C3	Bedford Street
C4	Belgrave Road
B3	Berkeley Street
C2	Black Dog Way
D4	Blenheim Road
B4	Brunswick Road
B4	Brunswick Square
D3	Bruton Way
B3	Bull Lane
A2	Castle Meads Way
C3	Clarence Street
B2	Clare Street
B3	Commercial Road
C4	Cromwell Street
C1	Deans Walk
C3	Eastgate Street
B1	Gouda Way
D2	Great Western Road
B3	Greyfriars
C3	Hampden Way
C2	Hare Lane
D2	Heathville Road
D1	Henry Road
D2	Henry Street
A4	High Orchard Street
D1	Honyatt Road
C4	King Barton Street
C1	Kingsholm Road
C3	King's Square
B3	Ladybellegate Street
A4	Llanthony Road
D2	London Road
B3	Longsmith Street
C3	Market Parade
A4	Merchants' Road
B1	Mercia Road
D3	Metz Way
D4	Millbrook Street
B4	Montpellier
D4	Napier Street
C3	Nettleton Road
B3	New Inn Lane
C3	New Inn Lane
B4	Norfolk Street
C3	Northgate Street
B4	Old Tram Road
A1	Over Causeway
D1	Oxford Road
D2	Oxford Street
C4	Park Road
C2	Park Street
B3	Parliament Street
C4	Pembroke Street
B2	Pitt Street
B1	Priory Road
B2	Quay Street
A2	Royal Oak Road
C3	Russell Street
C2	St Aldate Street
C1	St Catherine Street
B3	St John's Lane
C1	St Mark Street
B2	St Mary's Square
B2	St Mary's Street
C4	St Michael's Square
B1	St Oswald's Road
C1	Sebert Street
A3	Severn Road
D2	Sherborne Street
D4	Sinope Street
B3	Southgate Street
B4	Spa Road
C3	Station Road
C1	Swan Road
C1	Sweetbriar Street
B3	The Cross
C3	The Oxbode
A2	The Quay
C1	Union Street
B2	Upper Quay Street
D4	Vauxhall Road
C4	Wellington Street
A2	Westgate Street
D4	Widden Street
C2	Worcester Parade
C2	Worcester Street

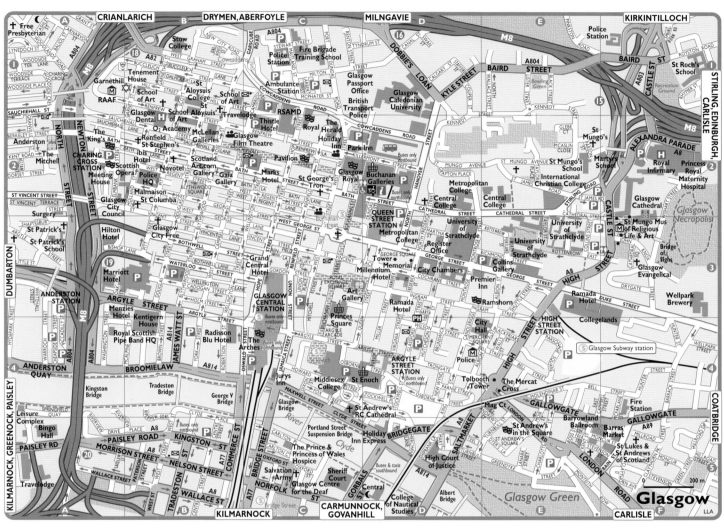

Glasgow

Glasgow is found on atlas page **125 P4**

D5	Albert Bridge	D4	Candleriggs	B1	Garnethill Street	E1	Lister Street
D4	Albion Street	C5	Carlton Place	B2	Garnet Street	E4	London Road
E3	Albion Street	A1	Carnarvon Street	C1	Garscube Road	C1	Maitland Street
F2	Alexandra Parade	F1	Castle Street	D3	Garth Street	D3	Martha Street
A4	Anderston Quay	F2	Castle Street	D3	George Square	D5	Mart Street
C4	Argyle Arcade	F3	Cathedral Square	E3	George Street	C4	Maxwell Street
A3	Argyle Street	D2	Cathedral Street	B4	George V Bridge	B4	McAlpine Street
F4	Armour Street	B5	Centre Street	C5	Glasgow Bridge	E2	McAslin Close
A1	Ashley Street	F5	Chalmer Street	D4	Glassford Street	F4	McFarlane Street
F5	Bain Street	A1	Charing Cross	E2	Glebe Court	C1	McPhater Street
E1	Baird Street	E5	Charlotte Street	C5	Gorbals Street	D5	Merchant Lane
A1	Baliol Street	A4	Cheapside Street	C3	Gordon Street	D4	Miller Street
F4	Barrack Street	F5	Claythorn Avenue	D2	Grafton Place	F5	Millroad Drive
B2	Bath Lane	F5	Claythorn Park	A2	Granville Street	F5	Millroad Street
A2	Bath Street	B4	Clyde Place	E5	Greendyke Street	C1	Milton Street
E4	Bell Street	C4	Clyde Street	F5	Green Street	C4	Mitchell Street
E4	Berkeley Street	E3	Cochrane Street	D3	Hanover Street	E5	Moir Street
E4	Blackfriars Street	E3	Collins Street	E4	High Street	E4	Molendinar Street
E1	Black Street	B5	Commerce Street	B1	Hill Street	E5	Moncur Street
B2	Blythswood Square	C1	Couper Street	B3	Holland Street	E5	Monteith Row
B3	Blythswood Street	C1	Cowcaddens Road	C3	Holm Street	D3	Montrose Street
B3	Bothwell Lane	B1	Dalhousie Lane	C3	Hope Street	A5	Morrison Street
B3	Bothwell Street	C4	Dixon Street	C4	Howard Street	B5	Nelson Street
D5	Bridgegate	D1	Dobbie's Loan	F4	Hunter Street	B1	New City Road
F3	Bridge of Sighs	A2	Dorset Street	D4	Hutcheson Street	A2	Newton Street
C5	Bridge Street	B3	Douglas Street	A4	Hydepark Street	D4	New Wynd
B4	Broomielaw	C3	Drury Street	D3	Ingram Street	C5	Norfolk Street
B4	Brown Street	F3	Drygate	C4	Jamaica Street	D3	North Frederick Street
D4	Brunswick Street	F3	Duke Street	B4	James Watt Street	D3	North Hanover Street
B1	Buccleuch Lane	D3	Dundas Street	F3	John Knox Street	E3	North Portland Street
B1	Buccleuch Street	D4	Dunlop Street	D2	Kennedy Street	A2	North Street
C4	Buchanan Street	E5	Dyer's Lane	E1	Kennedy Street	E1	North Wallace Street
B3	Cadogan Street	E4	East Campbell Street	A2	Kent Road	C4	Osborne Street
D1	Calgary Street	A2	Elmbank Street	E5	Kent Street	C4	Oswald Street
C1	Cambridge Street	C4	Fox Street	A5	Kingston Bridge	C5	Oxford Street
D1	Canal Street	E4	Gallowgate	B5	Kingston Street	D4	Parnie Street
				D4	King Street	E4	Parsonage Square
				D1	Kyle Street	A2	Parson Street
				E5	Lanark Street	B5	Paterson Street
				C1	Larbert Street	E1	Pinkston Road

B2	Pitt Street	D5	Steel Street
C1	Port Dundas Road	F5	Stevenson Street
C5	Portland Street Suspension	C1	Stewart Street
	Bridge	E2	Stirling Road
C4	Queen Street	D4	Stockwell Place
C3	Renfield Lane	D4	Stockwell Street
C3	Renfield Street	E5	Suffolk Street
C2	Renfrew Lane	F4	Sydney Street
B1	Renfrew Street	E2	Taylor Place
C1	Renton Street	E2	Taylor Street
F1	Rhymer Street	B4	Tradeston Bridge
E3	Richmond Street	B5	Tradeston Street
A4	Riverview Drive	D4	Trongate
B4	Robertson Street	D5	Turnbull Street
B2	Rose Street	C1	Tyndrum Street
E5	Ross Street	C3	Union Street
E3	Rottenrow	D4	Virginia Street
E3	Rottenrow East	A5	Wallace Street
C3	Royal Exchange Square	E4	Walls Street
F1	Royston Road	A4	Warroch Street
F1	Royston Square	A4	Washington Street
E5	St Andrew's Square	B3	Waterloo Street
E4	St Andrew's Street	B3	Wellington Lane
E2	St James Road	B3	Wellington Street
D2	St Mungo Avenue	F4	Wellpark Street
B3	St Vincent Lane	B3	West Campbell Street
C3	St Vincent Place	B2	West George Lane
A2	St Vincent Street	B2	West George Street
A2	St Vincent Terrace	B1	West Graham Street
D5	Saltmarket	C3	West Nile Street
A2	Sauchiehall Lane	C2	West Regent Lane
B2	Sauchiehall Street	B2	West Regent Street
B1	Scott Street	B5	West Street
A3	Shaftesbury Street	D4	Wilson Street
D5	Shipbank Lane	F3	Wishart Street
E3	Shuttle Street	A1	Woodlands Road
D3	South Frederick Street	A1	Woodside Crescent
F1	Springburn Road	A1	Woodside Terrace
A4	Springfield Quay	A1	Woodside Terrace Lane
D1	Stafford Street	B4	York Street

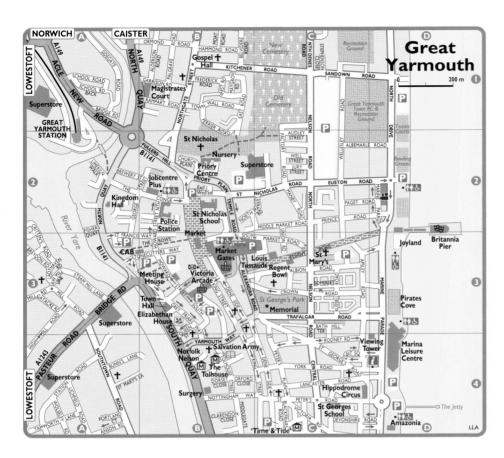

Great Yarmouth

Great Yarmouth is found on atlas page **77 Q10**

A1	Acle New Road	C1	North Denes Road
C2	Albemarle Road	D1	North Drive
C3	Albion Road	C2	North Market Road
B1	Alderson Road	A2	North Quay
B3	Alexandra Road	B1	Northgate Street
A4	Anson Road	B4	Nottingham Way
C3	Apsley Road	B1	Ormond Road
B1	Belvidere Road	C2	Paget Road
C4	Blackfriars Road	B1	Palgrave Road
A2	Brewery Street	A4	Pasteur Road
A3	Breydon Road	C2	Prince's Road
A1	Bridge Road	B2	Priory Plain
A3	Bridge Road	B4	Queen Street
A4	Bunn's Lane	B1	Rampart Road
B2	Church Plain	C3	Regent Road
A3	Critten's Road	C4	Rodney Road
C3	Crown Road	C3	Russell Road
B3	Dene Side	A3	St Francis Way
C4	Devonshire Road	C4	St George's Road
B1	East Road	B2	St Nicholas Road
C2	Euston Road	C4	St Peter's Plain
C2	Factory Road	C4	St Peter's Road
B1	Ferrier Road	C1	Sandown Road
A2	Fishers Quay	A3	Saw Mill Lane
B1	Frederick Road	A1	School Road
B2	Fullers Hill	A1	School Road Back
B1	Garrison Road	A1	Sidegate Road
A3	Gatacre Road	C3	South Market Road
A2	George Street	B3	South Quay
B3	Grey Friars Way	A4	Southtown Road
B1	Hammond Road	A4	Station Road
A3	High Mill Road	A3	Steam Mill Lane
B2	Howard Street North	C1	Stephenson Close
B3	Howard Street South	B3	Stonecutters Way
B3	King Street	A4	Tamworth Lane
B1	Kitchener Road	B2	Temple Road
A3	Ladyhaven Road	A2	The Conge
C4	Lancaster Road	B3	The Rows
A4	Lichfield Road	B4	Tolhouse Street
A2	Limekiln Walk	B1	Town Wall Road
C2	Manby Road	C3	Trafalgar Road
D3	Marine Parade	C3	Union Road
B1	Maygrove Road	C4	Victoria Road
C2	Middle Market Road	C2	Wellesley Road
B4	Middlegate	B1	West Road
B1	Moat Road	A4	Wolseley Road
C3	Nelson Road Central	B4	Yarmouth Way
C1	Nelson Road North	C4	York Road

Guildford

Guildford is found on atlas page **23 Q5**

C4	Abbot Road	B4	Millmead Terrace
B3	Angel Gate	A4	Mount Pleasant
B1	Artillery Road	D1	Nightingale Road
C1	Artillery Terrace	B3	North Street
A2	Bedford Road	C1	Onslow Road
A3	Bridge Street	B3	Onslow Street
C3	Bright Hill	C3	Oxford Road
D3	Brodie Road	C2	Pannells Court
B4	Bury Fields	B3	Park Street
B4	Bury Street	D3	Pewley Bank
C4	Castle Hill	D4	Pewley Fort Inner Court
C3	Castle Street	C3	Pewley Hill
B3	Chapel Street	D3	Pewley Way
C2	Chertsey Street	B3	Phoenix Court
D2	Cheseldon Road	B4	Porridge Pot Alley
B1	Church Road	A4	Portsmouth Road
B2	College Road	D4	Poyle Road
B2	Commercial Road	B3	Quarry Street
D2	Dene Road	C2	Sandfield Terrace
D2	Denmark Road	D3	Semaphore Road
B1	Drummond Road	C3	South Hill
C1	Eagle Road	C1	Springfield Road
D2	Epsom Road	D1	Station Approach
C1	Falcon Road	C1	Stoke Fields
C4	Fort Road	C1	Stoke Road
D1	Foxenden Road	B3	Swan Lane
A3	Friary Bridge	C3	Sydenham Road
B3	Friary Street	A3	Testard Road
B1	George Road	C2	The Bars
A2	Guildford Park Road	A4	The Mount
D3	Harvey Road	B3	The Shambles
C2	Haydon Place	C3	Tunsgate
D4	High Pewley	A3	Upperton Road
B3	High Street	D1	Victoria Road
C2	Jeffries Passage	A1	Walnut Tree Close
D2	Jenner Road	C2	Ward Street
B2	Laundry Road	C4	Warwicks Bench
B2	Leapale Lane	B1	Wharf Road
B2	Leapale Road	A3	Wherwell Road
B1	Leas Road	B1	William Road
D2	London Road	A3	Wodeland Avenue
A4	Mareschal Road	B1	Woodbridge Road
C3	Market Street	B1	York Road
C2	Martyr Road		
A1	Mary Road		
B3	Millbrook		
B3	Mill Lane		
B3	Millmead		

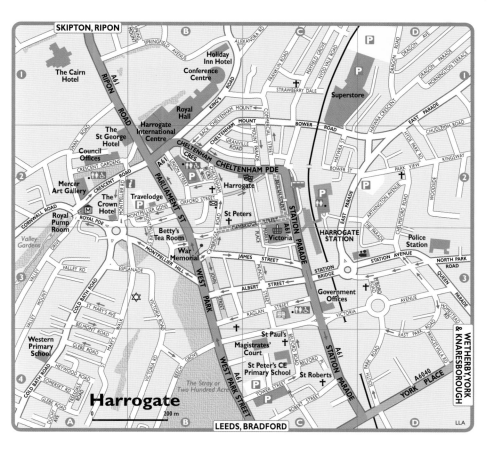

Harrogate

Harrogate is found on atlas page **97 M10**

C3	Albert Street	B2	Montpellier Street
B1	Alexandra Road	D1	Mornington Terrace
D2	Arthington Avenue	C2	Mount Parade
B2	Back Cheltenham Mount	D3	North Park Road
B4	Beech Grove	C1	Nydd Vale Road
C4	Belford Place	B2	Oxford Street
C4	Belford Road	D2	Park View
A3	Belmont Road	B2	Parliament Street
C2	Beulah Street	C3	Princes Street
C1	Bower Road	D4	Princes Villa Road
C2	Bower Street	D3	Queen Parade
B3	Cambridge Road	C3	Raglan Street
C2	Cambridge Street	A1	Ripon Road
D3	Chelmsford Road	C4	Robert Street
B2	Cheltenham Crescent	A2	Royal Parade
B2	Cheltenham Mount	A3	St Mary's Avenue
B2	Cheltenham Parade	A4	St Mary's Walk
D2	Chudleigh Road	A4	Somerset Road
A3	Cold Bath Road	D4	South Park Road
C1	Commercial Street	B1	Springfield Avenue
A2	Cornwall Road	B1	Spring Mount
A2	Crescent Gardens	D3	Station Avenue
A2	Crescent Road	C3	Station Bridge
D1	Dragon Avenue	C2	Station Parade
D1	Dragon Parade	C1	Strawberry Dale
D1	Dragon Road	A2	Swan Road
A4	Duchy Avenue	D2	The Parade
C2	East Parade	C4	Tower Street
D4	East Park Road	A4	Treesdale Road
A3	Esplanade	B2	Union Street
C1	Franklin Road	A3	Valley Drive
A4	Glebe Road	A3	Valley Mount
B2	Granville Road	A3	Valley Road
C2	Haywra Street	C3	Victoria Avenue
A4	Heywood Road	B3	Victoria Road
D3	Homestead Road	B3	West Park
D2	Hyde Park Road	B4	West Park Street
D2	Hywra Crescent	D2	Woodside
B3	James Street	D4	York Place
B3	John Street		
B1	King's Road		
D2	Kingsway		
C3	Market Place		
D3	Marlborough Road		
C1	Mayfield Grove		
B2	Montpellier Gardens		
B3	Montpellier Hill		
A2	Montpellier Road		

Huddersfield

Huddersfield is found on atlas page **90 E7**

B4	Albion Street	A2	New North Road
C4	Alfred Street	B4	New Street
C1	Back Union Street	C1	Northgate
A4	Bankfield Road	C2	Northumberland Street
B1	Bath Street	D2	Old Leeds Road
A1	Belmont Street	B3	Old South Street
C2	Brook Street	B4	Outcote Bank
C2	Byram Street	C1	Oxford Street
B1	Cambridge Road	A2	Park Avenue
D4	Carforth Street	A2	Park Drive South
B1	Castlegate	C4	Peel Street
B3	Chancery Lane	C2	Pine Street
B4	Chapel Hill	A2	Portland Street
B4	Chapel Street	B4	Princess Street
C2	Church Street	A4	Prospect Street
B1	Clare Hill	D2	Quay Street
B1	Claremont Street	C3	Queen Street
B3	Cloth Hall Street	C4	Queen Street South
C3	Cross Church Street	C4	Queensgate
B3	Dundas Lane	B2	Railway Street
A2	Elizabeth Queen Gardens	B3	Ramsden Street
A1	Elmwood Avenue	B1	Rook Street
D4	Firth Street	D2	St Andrew's Road
A2	Fitzwilliam Street	B2	St George's Square
B2	Fitzwilliam Street	B1	St John's Road
D1	Gasworks Street	C2	St Peter's Street
C1	Great Northern Street	C2	Southgate
A3	Greenhead Road	A4	Spring Grove Street
B3	Half Moon Street	A3	Spring Street
B3	High Street	A3	Springwood Avenue
A1	Highfields Road	D1	Stadium Way
B2	John William Street	B2	Station Street
C3	King Street	A2	Trinity Street
D4	King's Mill Lane	D2	Turnbridge Road
C3	Kirkgate	C1	Union Street
C2	Leeds Road	A3	Upper George Street
D3	Lincoln Street	B3	Upperhead Row
C2	Lord Street	B2	Viaduct Street
C1	Lower Fitzwilliam Street	C3	Victoria Lane
A3	Lynton Avenue	D3	Wakefield Road
A4	Manchester Road	A3	Water Street
C3	Market Place	D2	Watergate
B3	Market Street	A2	Waverley Road
A3	Merton Street	A2	Wentworth Street
B4	Milford Street	B3	Westgate
A1	Mountjoy Road	C1	William Street
B2	New North Parade	C2	Wood Street
A1	New North Road	C3	Zetland Street

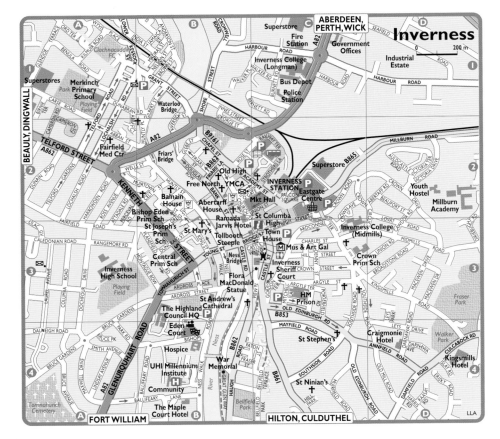

Inverness

Inverness is found on atlas page **156 B8**

D2	Abertaff Road	A1	Glendoe Terrace
B2	Academy Street	A4	Glenurquhart Road
B1	Anderson Street	C3	Gordon Terrace
D4	Annfield Road	B1	Grant Street
C3	Ardconnel Terrace	B4	Great Glen Way
B3	Ardross Street	C1	Harbour Road
C3	Argyle Street	D4	Harris Road
C3	Argyle Terrace	A2	Harrowden Road
A4	Ballifeary Lane	B4	Haugh Road
B4	Ballifeary Road	C3	High Street
B2	Bank Street	C4	Hill Park
C4	Bellfield Terrace	C3	Hill Street
A1	Benula Road	B2	Huntly Street
B1	Bernett Road	B1	Innes Street
A1	Birnie Terrace	D4	Islay Road
B4	Bishops Road	A2	Kenneth Street
B3	Bridge Street	B3	King Street
D3	Broadstone Road	D3	Kingsmills Road
A4	Bruce Avenue	A3	Laurel Avenue
A4	Bruce Gardens	A4	Lindsay Avenue
A4	Bruce Park	A2	Lochalsh Road
C1	Burnett Road	D3	Lovat Road
A3	Caledonian Road	A1	Lower Kessock Street
A2	Cameron Road	A4	Maxwell Drive
A2	Cameron Square	C4	Mayfield Road
A1	Carse Road	D3	Midmills Road
B3	Castle Road	D2	Millburn Road
C3	Castle Street	C3	Mitchell's Lane
B2	Chapel Street	C4	Muirfield Road
C3	Charles Street	C3	Old Edinburgh Road
A3	Columba Road	A4	Park Road
C2	Crown Circus	B3	Planefield Road
D2	Crown Drive	C3	Porterfield Road
C2	Crown Road	D4	Raasay Road
C3	Crown Street	A3	Rangemore Road
D4	Culcabock Road	A2	Ross Avenue
A4	Dalneigh Road	D1	Seafield Road
D4	Damfield Road	B1	Shore Street
D4	Darnaway Road	A4	Smith Avenue
C3	Denny Street	C3	Southside Place
A3	Dochfour Drive	C4	Southside Road
A1	Dunabran Road	A2	Telford Gardens
A2	Dunain Road	A2	Telford Road
B3	Duncraig Street	A2	Telford Street
D4	Erisky Road	B3	Tomnahurich Street
A3	Fairfield Road	D3	Union Road
C2	Falcon Square	C1	Walker Road
B2	Friars' Lane	B3	Young Street

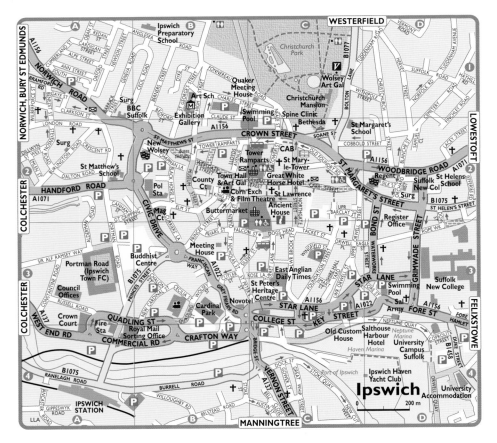

Ipswich

Ipswich is found on atlas page **53 L3**

A3	Alderman Road	A2	London Road
B1	Anglesea Road	C3	Lower Brook Street
A1	Barrack Street	C3	Lower Orwell Street
B4	Belstead Road	B2	Museum Street
B1	Berners Street	C1	Neale Street
B2	Black Horse Lane	D3	Neptune Quay
D2	Blanche Street	B3	New Cardinal Street
C1	Bolton Lane	A1	Newson Street
D3	Bond Street	C2	Northgate Street
A1	Bramford Road	A1	Norwich Road
C4	Bridge Street	C2	Old Foundry Road
A2	Burlington Road	D2	Orchard Street
B4	Burrell Road	A1	Orford Street
A1	Cardigan Street	C3	Orwell Place
C2	Carr Street	D4	Orwell Quay
B3	Cavern Street	A3	Portman Road
B1	Cecil Road	B3	Princes Street
D1	Cemetery Road	A3	Princes Street
B1	Charles Street	A3	Quadling Street
D1	Christchurch Street	B3	Quadling Street
B2	Civic Drive	B3	Queen Street
A1	Clarkson Street	A4	Ranelagh Road
C2	Cobbold Street	A1	Redan Street
C3	College Street	A3	Russell Road
A4	Commercial Road	B1	St George's Street
A3	Constantine Road	D2	St Helen's Street
B4	Crafton Way	C2	St Margaret's Street
B2	Crown Street	B2	St Matthews Street
A1	Cumberland Street	B3	St Nicholas Street
A2	Dalton Road	B3	St Peter's Street
C4	Dock Street	B3	Silent Street
D4	Duke Street	B3	Sir Alf Ramsey Way
C3	Eagle Street	C2	Soane Street
B2	Elm Street	A1	South Street
B3	Falcon Street	C3	Star Lane
B1	Fonnereau Road	C4	Stoke Quay
C3	Foundation Street	D1	Suffolk Road
B3	Franciscan Way	C3	Tacket Street
A1	Geneva Road	B3	Tower Ramparts
A2	Great Gripping Street	D1	Tuddenham Avenue
C4	Great Whip Street	C4	Turret Lane
B3	Grey Friars Road	C3	Upper Orwell Street
D3	Grimwade Street	C4	Vernon Street
A2	Handford Road	A3	West End Road
D1	Hervey Street	B2	Westgate Street
B1	High Street	B4	Willoughby Road
C3	Key Street	B3	Wolsey Street
B2	King Street	D2	Woodbridge Road

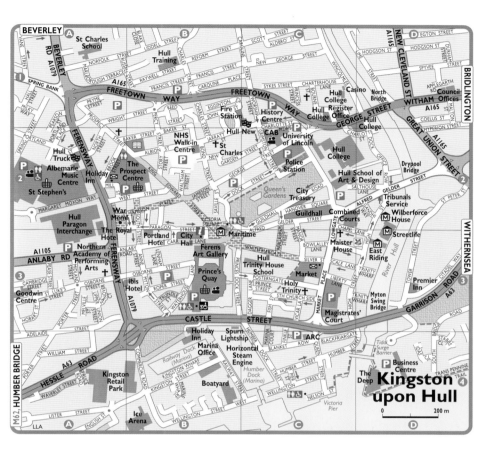

Kingston upon Hull

Kingston upon Hull is found on atlas page **93 J5**

A4	Adelaide Street	C3	Market Place
B2	Albion Street	A2	Mill Street
C2	Alfred Gelder Street	B3	Myton Street
A3	Anlaby Road	D1	New Cleveland Street
B2	Baker Street	B2	New Garden Street
A1	Beverley Road	C1	New George Street
C4	Blackfriargate	A1	Norfolk Street
C4	Blanket Row	B3	Osborne Street
B2	Bond Street	A3	Osborne Street
A2	Brook Street	B2	Paragon Street
B1	Caroline Street	A3	Pease Street
B3	Carr Lane	B1	Percy Street
B3	Castle Street	A3	Porter Street
C2	Chapel Lane	A2	Portland Place
B1	Charles Street	A2	Portland Street
C1	Charterhouse Lane	C3	Postergate
D3	Citadel Way	B3	Princes Dock Street
B4	Commercial Road	A1	Prospect Street
C3	Dagger Lane	C4	Queen Street
D2	Dock Office Row	B4	Railway Street
B2	Dock Street	B1	Raywell Street
D1	Durham Street	B1	Reform Street
B1	Egginton Street	A1	Russell Street
A2	Ferensway	A3	St Luke's Street
A1	Freetown Way	D2	St Peter Street
D2	Gandhi Way	B2	Saville Street
D3	Garrison Road	C3	Scale Lane
B2	George Street	C1	Scott Street
D1	George Street	C3	Silver Street
D1	Great Union Street	D4	South Bridge Road
C2	Grimston Street	C3	South Church Side
C2	Guildhall Road	B2	South Street
C2	Hanover Square	A1	Spring Bank
A4	Hessle Road	D1	Spyvee Street
C3	High Street	C1	Sykes Street
D1	Hodgson Street	D3	Tower Street
C4	Humber Dock Street	A3	Upper Union Street
C4	Humber Street	B2	Victoria Square
D1	Hyperion Street	B3	Waterhouse Lane
B2	Jameson Street	C4	Wellington Street
B2	Jarratt Street	B4	Wellington Street West
B2	King Edward Street	A2	West Street
B4	Kingston Street	C3	Whitefriargate
B1	Liddell Street	A4	William Street
C1	Lime Street	C1	Wincolmlee
A4	Lister Street	D1	Witham
C3	Lowgate	C1	Worship Street
A2	Margaret Moxon Way	A1	Wright Street

Lancaster

Lancaster is found on atlas page **95 K8**

D4	Aberdeen Road	A3	Lincoln Road
B4	Aldcliffe Road	B4	Lindow Street
C2	Alfred Street	C2	Lodge Street
D1	Ambleside Road	A2	Long Marsh Lane
D4	Balmoral Road	B1	Lune Street
D3	Bath Street	B3	Market Street
A3	Blades Street	A3	Meeting House Lane
D3	Bond Street	B3	Middle Street
D2	Borrowdale Road	D3	Moor Gate
C3	Brewery Lane	C3	Moor Lane
B2	Bridge Lane	B1	Morecambe Road
C3	Brock Street	C3	Nelson Street
D2	Bulk Road	C2	North Road
C3	Bulk Street	C1	Owen Road
B2	Cable Street	D3	Park Road
B3	Castle Hill	C2	Parliament Street
A3	Castle Park	D2	Patterdale Road
C2	Caton Road	B4	Penny Street
C3	Cheapside	B4	Portland Street
B3	China Street	D4	Primrose Road
B2	Church Street	D4	Prospect Street
B3	Common Garden Street	C4	Quarry Road
D4	Dale Street	B4	Queen Street
B3	Dallas Road	B4	Regent Street
D2	Dalton Road	D1	Ridge Lane
C3	Dalton Square	D1	Ridge Street
B2	Damside Street	C3	Robert Street
C1	Derby Road	C2	Rosemary Lane
C2	De Vitre Street	A1	St George's Quay
D4	Dumbarton Road	C2	St Leonard's Gate
D3	East Road	C4	St Peter's Road
C3	Edward Street	A3	Sibsey Street
A3	Fairfield Road	C4	South Road
B3	Fenton Street	A3	Station Road
C3	Gage Street	D4	Stirling Road
D2	Garnet Street	C3	Sulyard Street
C3	George Street	B3	Sun Street
D3	Grasmere Road	C4	Thurnham Street
C3	Great John Street	D2	Troutbeck Road
D4	Gregson Road	D3	Ulleswater Road
B1	Greyhound Bridge Road	A3	West Road
B4	High Street	A3	Westbourne Road
A3	Kelsey Street	A3	Wheatfield Street
D2	Kentmere Road	D3	Williamson Road
B3	King Street	A3	Wingate-Saul Road
C1	Kingsway	D2	Wolseley Street
B3	Kirkes Road	D3	Woodville Street
D1	Langdale Road	D3	Wyresdale Road

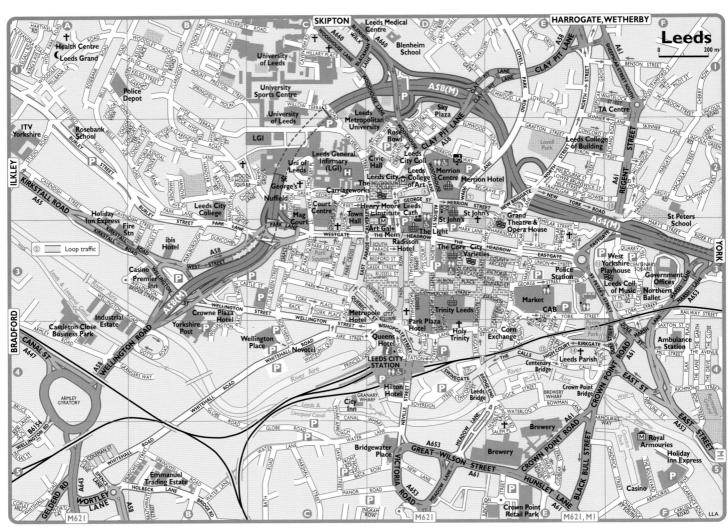

Leeds

Leeds is found on atlas page **90 H4**

B3	Abbey Street	C2	Calverley Street	D4	Duncan Street	E3	Kirkgate	E2	North Street
C4	Aire Street	A4	Canal Street	B3	Duncombe Street	A2	Kirkstall Road	C3	Oxford Place
D3	Albion Place	C4	Canal Wharf	E3	Dyer Street	E3	Lady Lane	C3	Oxford Row
D2	Albion Street	D1	Carlton Carr	E3	Eastgate	D3	Lands Lane	C3	Park Cross Street
A1	Alexandra Road	D1	Carlton Hill	C3	East Parade	C2	Leighton Street	B2	Park Lane
A4	Armley Gyratory	D1	Carlton Rise	F4	East Street	F2	Leyland Road	C3	Park Place
A4	Armley Road	B3	Castle Street	E1	Elmwood Lane	B1	Lifton Place	D3	Park Row
F5	Armouries Drive	C1	Cavendish Road	D2	Elmwood Road	F2	Lincoln Green Road	C3	Park Square East
E4	Armouries Way	A2	Cavendish Street	F4	Flax Place	B3	Lisbon Street	C3	Park Square North
B2	Back Hyde Terrace	F3	Centenary Square	A5	Gelderd Road	C3	Little Queen Street	C3	Park Square West
C5	Back Row	E3	Central Road	E3	George Street	E1	Lovell Park Hill	C3	Park Street
C5	Bath Road	F5	Chadwick Street	B4	Globe Road	E1	Lovell Park Road	F1	Pilot Street
D3	Bedford Street	F1	Cherry Row	B4	Gotts Road	D3	Lower Basinghall Street	D2	Portland Crescent
D2	Belgrave Street	B2	Chorley Lane	E2	Gower Street	E2	Lower Brunswick Street	D2	Portland Way
A1	Belle Vue Road	B2	Claremont	E2	Grafton Street	B1	Lyddon Terrace	C4	Princes Square
C2	Belmont Grove	F5	Clarence Road	A4	Grangers Way	F2	Mabgate	F3	Quarry Hill
F1	Benson Street	B1	Clarendon Road	C2	Great George Street	F2	Macaulay Street	C3	Quebec Street
B3	Bingley Street	D2	Clay Pit Lane	D5	Great Wilson Street	C5	Manor Road	D2	Queen Square
D4	Bishopgate Street	B1	Cloberry Street	D3	Greek Street	D3	Mark Lane	D2	Queen Square Court
E5	Black Bull Street	D3	Commercial Street	B2	Hanover Avenue	B3	Marlborough Street	C3	Queen Street
C1	Blackman Lane	E2	Concord Street	B2	Hanover Lane	C5	Marshall Street	F3	Railway Street
C1	Blenheim Walk	B2	Consort Street	B2	Hanover Square	F4	Marsh Lane	F2	Regent Street
D4	Boar Lane	A1	Consort View	E3	Harewood Street	E4	Maude Street	F4	Richmond Street
E4	Bowman Lane	E3	County Arcade	E4	Harper Street	D5	Meadow Lane	F3	Rider Street
F4	Bow Street	B1	Cromer Terrace	E3	Harrison Street	E2	Melbourne Street	A1	Rosebank Road
B2	Brandon Road	F2	Cromwell Street	A1	Hartwell Road	D2	Merrion Street	F3	St Cecilia Street
D4	Bridge End	B1	Cross Kelso Road	E4	High Court	D2	Merrion Way	A1	St John's Road
B5	Bridge Road	F1	Cross Stamford Street	B5	Holbeck Lane	A1	Millbank Lane	F3	St Mary's Street
E2	Bridge Street	E5	Crown Point Road	F2	Hope Road	D2	Millennium Square	F3	St Paul's Street
E3	Bridge Street	E4	Crown Street	E4	Hunslet Lane	F4	Mill Street	E3	St Peter's Street
D4	Briggate	E5	Cudbear Street	E5	Hunslet Road	F2	Millwright Street	E5	Salem Place
A2	Burley Street	C5	David Street	A1	Hyde Park Road	B1	Mount Preston Street	F4	Saxton Street
D3	Butts Court	E4	Dock Street	B2	Hyde Street	F4	Mushroom Street	E1	Sheepscar Grove
E2	Byron Street	F4	Duke Street	B1	Hyde Terrace	F4	Neptune Street	F1	Sheepscar Street South
E4	Call Lane	F4	Duke Street	D3	Infirmary Street	D4	Neville Street	E1	Skinner Lane
				D5	Junction Street	D5	New Lane	D3	South Parade
				B1	Kelso Road	D4	New Station Street	D4	Sovereign Street
				B2	Kendal Lane	E2	New York Road	A5	Spence Lane
				E3	King Edward Street	E3	New York Street	B1	Springfield Mount
				A1	King's Avenue	C4	Northern Street	B5	Springwell Road
				C3	King Street				

B5	Springwell Street
A2	Studio Road
D4	Swinegate
E3	Templar Street
F4	The Avenue
F5	The Boulevard
E4	The Calls
D3	The Headrow
C2	Thoresby Place
E2	Trafalgar Street
E3	Union Street
D3	Upper Basinghall Street
E3	Vicar Lane
D5	Victoria Road
B2	Victoria Street
B2	Victoria Terrace
D2	Wade Lane
B5	Water Lane
E4	Waterloo Street
B3	Wellington Bridge Street
A3	Wellington Road
A4	Wellington Road
A5	Wellington Road
B3	Wellington Street
A1	Westfield Road
C3	Westgate
B3	West Street
C4	Wharf Approach
E4	Wharf Street
C4	Whitehall Quay
A5	Whitehall Road
A5	Whitehall Road
F1	Whitelock Street
C1	Willow Terrace Road
C1	Woodhouse Lane
B2	Woodhouse Square
A1	Woodsley Road
A5	Wortley Lane
A5	Wortley Lane
C3	York Place
F3	York Street

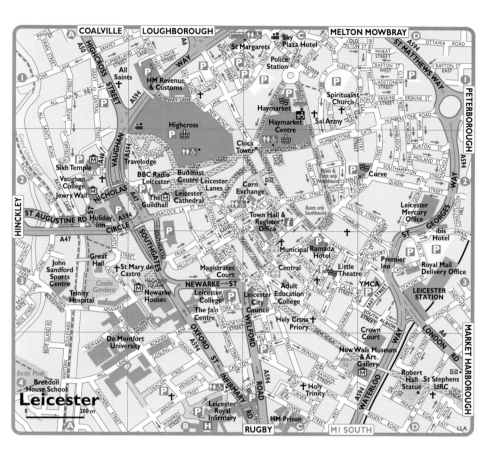

Leicester

Leicester is found on atlas page **72 F10**

C3	Albion Street	B4	Infirmary Road
A1	All Saints Road	B4	Jarrom Street
A2	Bath Lane	A1	Jarvis Street
C1	Bedford Street	C3	King Street
C1	Belgrave Gate	C1	Lee Street
C3	Belvoir Street	D3	London Road
C3	Bishop Street	B3	Lower Brown Street
B4	Bonners Lane	B3	Magazine Square
C3	Bowling Green Street	B1	Mansfield Street
B1	Burgess Street	B2	Market Place South
D2	Burton Street	C3	Market Street
C3	Calais Hill	A4	Mill Lane
D3	Campbell Street	D1	Morledge Street
B2	Cank Street	B3	Newarke Street
A3	Castle Street	C3	New Walk
C1	Charles Street	B3	Oxford Street
C3	Chatham Street	B2	Peacock Lane
C2	Cheapside	B3	Pocklington Walk
B1	Church Gate	D4	Princess Road East
D1	Clyde Street	C4	Princess Road West
C2	Colton Street	D2	Queen Street
D3	Conduit Street	C4	Regent Road
D1	Crafton Street West	D4	Regent Street
B4	Deacon Street	A2	Richard III Road
D4	De Montfort Street	C2	Rutland Street
C3	Dover Street	A2	St Augustine Road
C3	Duke Street	D2	St George Street
A3	Duns Lane	D2	St Georges Way
B1	East Bond Street Lane	C1	St James Street
D1	Erskine Street	D1	St Matthews Way
C1	Fleet Street	A2	St Nicholas Circle
B3	Friar Lane	A1	Sanvey Gate
C2	Gallowtree Gate	A1	Soar Lane
A3	Gateway Street	D3	South Albion Street
C2	Granby Street	D2	Southampton Street
A4	Grasmere Street	B3	Southgates
B1	Gravel Street	D3	Station Street
A1	Great Central Street	A3	The Newarke
B2	Greyfriars	C4	Tower Street
C2	Halford Street	A2	Vaughan Way
C2	Haymarket	D4	Waterloo Way
A1	Highcross Street	C3	Welford Road
B2	Highcross Street	A2	Welles Street
B2	High Street	C3	Wellington Street
C1	Hill Street	A4	Western Boulevard
B3	Horsefair Street	C4	West Street
C2	Humberstone Gate	D1	Wharf Street South
D1	Humberstone Road	C2	Yeoman Street

Lincoln

Lincoln is found on atlas page **86 C6**

B2	Alexandra Terrace	B2	Motherby Lane
D2	Arboretum Avenue	A2	Nelson Street
D3	Bagholme Road	B3	Newland
C1	Bailgate	A2	Newland Street West
C3	Bank Street	C4	Norman Street
B3	Beaumont Fee	C1	Northgate
A1	Belle Vue Terrace	B3	Orchard Street
A3	Brayford Way	C4	Oxford Street
B4	Brayford Wharf East	B3	Park Street
A3	Brayford Wharf North	C4	Pelham Street
C3	Broadgate	D2	Pottergate
B1	Burton Road	A1	Queen's Crescent
A2	Carholme Road	A1	Richmond Road
A1	Carline Road	A4	Rope Walk
C2	Cathedral Street	D3	Rosemary Lane
B1	Chapel Lane	A2	Rudgard Lane
A2	Charles Street West	D3	St Hugh Street
D2	Cheviot Street	B4	St Mark Street
C3	City Square	C2	St Martin's Street
C3	Clasketgate	B4	St Mary's Street
B4	Cornhill	C3	St Rumbold's Street
D3	Croft Street	C3	Saltergate
C2	Danesgate	C3	Silver Street
A3	Depot Street	C4	Sincil Street
B2	Drury Lane	B2	Spring Hill
C1	East Bight	C2	Steep Hill
C1	Eastgate	C3	Swan Street
C3	Free School Lane	B4	Tentercroft Street
C3	Friars Lane	A2	The Avenue
C2	Grantham Street	C3	Thorngate
D1	Greetwellgate	A4	Triton Road
A2	Gresham Street	B1	Union Road
B3	Guildhall Street	C3	Unity Square
A1	Hampton Street	B2	Victoria Street
B3	High Street	B2	Victoria Terrace
B3	Hungate	D2	Vine Street
D3	John Street	C3	Waterside North
D1	Langworthgate	C3	Waterside South
C2	Lindum Road	B1	Westgate
D2	Lindum Terrace	A2	West Parade
B3	Lucy Tower Street	A2	Whitehall Grove
A1	May Crescent	B3	Wigford Way
C4	Melville Street	D1	Winnow Sty Lane
C2	Michaelgate	D3	Winn Street
C2	Minster Yard	D2	Wragby Road
B3	Mint Lane	A1	Yarborough Road
B3	Mint Street	A1	York Avenue
D3	Monks Road		
D3	Montague Street		

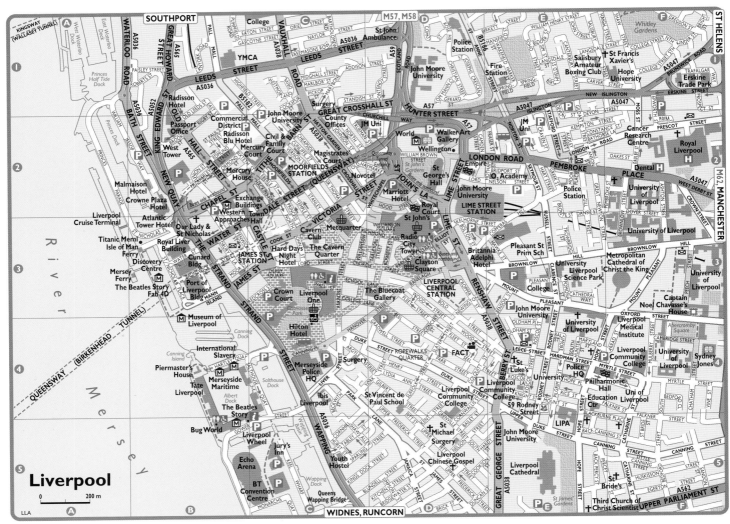

Liverpool

Liverpool is found on atlas page **81 L6**

C1	Addison Street	B2	Chapel Street	F1	Erskine Street	C5	Keel Wharf	B2	Ormond Street	E2	Seymour Street
E2	Anson Street	F4	Chatham Street	E4	Falkner Street	E2	Kempston Street	F4	Oxford Street	F1	Shaw Street
C4	Argyle Street	C2	Cheapside	B2	Fazakerley Street	D5	Kent Street	B1	Paisley Street	C2	Sir Thomas Street
F4	Arrad Street	D1	Christian Street	B3	Fenwick Street	F1	Kinder Street	B1	Pall Mall	D3	Skelhorne Street
F2	Ashton Street	D2	Churchill Way	D3	Fleet Street	B2	King Edward Street	C3	Paradise Street	D4	Slater Street
E2	Audley Street	C3	Church Street	D1	Fontenoy Street	A1	Kingsway (Wallasey Tunnel)	D3	Parker Street	E1	Soho Street
E5	Back Canning Street	E3	Clarence Street	E2	Fraser Street	D5	Kitchen Street	C4	Park Lane	C5	Sparling Street
E4	Baltimore Street	C1	Cockspur Street	B1	Gascoyne Street	E4	Knight Street	D3	Parr Street	E1	Springfield
B2	Bath Street	C3	College Lane	D1	Gerard Street	E1	Langsdale Street	F3	Peech Street	E2	Stafford Street
C4	Beckwith Street	F1	College Street North	D4	Gilbert Street	E4	Leece Street	E2	Pembroke Place	C2	Stanley Street
F5	Bedford Street South	F1	College Street South	E2	Gildart Street	B1	Leeds Street	F2	Pembroke Street	B3	Strand Street
E3	Benson Street	D4	Colquitt Street	E2	Gill Street	D2	Lime Street	E5	Percey Street	D4	Suffolk Street
E4	Berry Street	E2	Constance Street	B5	Gower Street	C4	Liver Street	E4	Pilgrim Street	C5	Tabley Street
E1	Bidder Street	C3	Cook Street	D4	Gradwell Street	D2	London Road	E3	Pleasant Street	D3	Tarleton Street
D1	Birkett Street	E3	Copperas Hill	C1	Great Crosshall Street	E2	London Road	E3	Pomona Street	C2	Temple Street
B2	Bixteth Street	C5	Cornhill	E5	Great George Street	D2	Lord Nelson Street	F2	Prescot Street	B3	The Strand
E5	Blackburne Place	D5	Cornwallis Street	B1	Great Howard Street	C3	Lord Street	A2	Princes Parade	C2	Tithe Barn Street
C5	Blundell Street	E2	Craven Street	E2	Great Newton Street	D4	Lydia Ann Street			F1	Trafalgar Way
D3	Bold Street	D3	Cropper Street	F1	Gregson Street	B3	Mann Island	D3	Ranelagh Street	E3	Trowbridge Street
D3	Bosnett Street	C2	Crosshall Street	D5	Grenville Street South	E1	Mansfield Street	C3	Redcross Street	C2	Trueman Street
D5	Bridgewater Street	F2	Crown Street	C2	Hackins Hey	C1	Marybone	D3	Renshaw Street	E5	Upper Duke Street
E2	Bridport Street	C2	Dale Street (Queensway)	C4	Hanover Street	E4	Maryland Street	C3	Richmond Lane	D4	Upper Frederick Street
B2	Brook Street	E3	Dansie Street	E4	Hardman Street	C1	Midghall Street	B2	Rigby Street	F5	Upper Parliament Street
E3	Brownlow Hill	F2	Daulby Street	E1	Harker Street	C2	Moorfields	E4	Rodney Street	D5	Upper Pitt Street
F3	Brownlow Street	C3	Derby Square	B4	Hartley Quay	B3	Moor Street	E4	Roscoe Street	C1	Vauxhall Road
F1	Brunswick Road	E2	Devon Street	E2	Hart Street	F1	Moss Street	D1	Rose Hill	C2	Vernon Street
B3	Brunswick Street	F3	Dover Street	C2	Hatton Garden	E3	Mount Pleasant	E3	Russell Street	C3	Victoria Street
F4	Cambridge Street	B3	Drury Lane	E3	Hawke Street	E4	Mount Street	D1	St Anne Street	E1	Wakefield Street
D2	Camden Street	D4	Duke Street	D4	Henry Street	F4	Mulberry Street	D5	St James Street	C3	Wall Street
C4	Canning Place	B1	East Street	B1	Highfield Street	C1	Myrtle Street	D2	St John's Lane	C5	Wapping
E5	Canning Street	B1	Eaton Street	D2	Hood Street	C1	Naylor Street	D1	St Josephs Crescent	A1	Waterloo Road
E1	Canterbury Street	C2	Eberle Street	E5	Hope Place	D2	Nelson Street	B3	St Nicholas Place	B3	Water Street
E1	Carver Street	B2	Edmund Street	E5	Hope Street	D4	Newington	B2	St Paul's Street	F2	West Derby Street
C3	Castle Street	F5	Egerton Street	E2	Hotham Street	E1	New Islington	E1	Salisbury Street	C1	Westmorland Drive
F5	Catharine Street	D3	Elliot Street	D1	Hunter Street	B2	New Quay	C4	Salthouse Quay	D2	Whitechapel
E3	Cathedral Way	F1	Epworth Street	F5	Huskisson Street	C3	North John Street	F5	Sandon Street	E1	William Henry Street
				D5	Islington	B2	Norton Street	C3	School Lane	A2	William Jessop Way
				B3	Jamaica Street	E4	Oldham Street	D1	Scotland Road	C3	Williamson Square
				C2	James Street	C2	Old Haymarket	D4	Seel Street	D3	Williamson Street
				C2	Johnson Street	B1	Old Leeds Street			D3	Wood Street
										C4	York Street

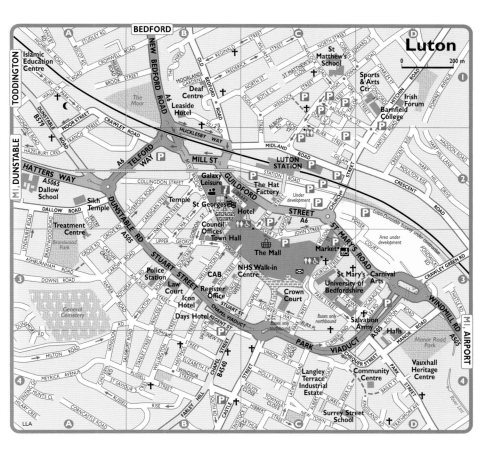

Luton

Luton is found on atlas page **50 C6**

B3	Adelaide Street	C4	Hibbert Street
C4	Albert Road	A1	Highbury Road
B2	Alma Street	C1	High Town Road
C4	Arthur Street	D1	Hitchin Road
A3	Ashburnham Road	C4	Holly Street
A1	Biscot Road	B2	Hucklesby Way
A3	Brantwood Road	B3	Inkerman Street
C1	Brunswick Street	C3	John Street
C2	Burr Street	B3	King Street
A1	Bury Park Road	C4	Latimer Road
B3	Buxton Road	B2	Liverpool Road
A3	Cardiff Road	D4	Manor Road
B2	Cardigan Street	A4	Meyrick Avenue
B4	Castle Street	C2	Midland Road
B4	Chapel Street	B2	Mill Street
B3	Chapel Viaduct	A4	Milton Road
D1	Charles Street	A1	Moor Street
C4	Chequer Street	A3	Napier Road
A4	Chiltern Road	B1	New Bedford Road
C2	Church Street	C4	New Town Street
C3	Church Street	B1	Old Bedford Road
C1	Cobden Street	C3	Park Street
B2	Collingdon Street	C3	Park Street West
D1	Concorde Street	C4	Park Viaduct
D3	Crawley Green Road	B3	Princess Street
A1	Crawley Road	B3	Regent Street
D2	Crescent Road	B1	Reginald Street
A1	Cromwell Road	A3	Rothesay Road
C4	Cumberland Street	A4	Russell Rise
A2	Dallow Road	B4	Russell Street
C1	Dudley Street	C3	St Mary's Road
B4	Dumfries Street	A4	Salisbury Road
A1	Dunstable Road	B4	Stanley Street
B4	Farley Hill	C2	Station Road
C3	Flowers Way	D4	Strathmore Ave
B1	Frederick Street	B3	Stuart Street
B3	George Street	C4	Surrey Street
B3	George Street West	B4	Tavistock Street
B3	Gordon Street	B2	Telford Way
A3	Grove Road	B3	Upper George Street
B2	Guildford Street	D3	Vicarage Street
D2	Hart Hill Drive	A1	Waldeck Road
D2	Hart Hill Lane	B4	Wellington Street
D2	Hartley Road	C1	Wenlock Street
B4	Hastings Street	D3	Windmill Road
A2	Hatters Way	B4	Windsor Street
C1	Havelock Road	A4	Winsdon Road
A2	Hazelbury Crescent	C1	York Street

Maidstone

Maidstone is found on atlas page **38 C10**

D1	Albany Street	B2	Market Buildings
D2	Albion Place	C2	Marsham Street
D1	Allen Street	D4	Meadow Walk
D3	Ashford Road	B3	Medway Street
B3	Bank Street	C4	Melville Road
B4	Barker Road	B3	Mill Street
A3	Bedford Place	D3	Mote Avenue
B3	Bishops Way	D3	Mote Road
C2	Brewer Street	D2	Old School Place
A3	Broadway	C4	Orchard Street
B3	Broadway	C3	Padsole Lane
C4	Brunswick Street	B3	Palace Avenue
A2	Buckland Hill	D1	Princes Street
A2	Buckland Road	C4	Priory Road
C1	Camden Street	B2	Pudding Lane
D3	Chancery Lane	D2	Queen Anne Road
A4	Charles Street	A4	Reginald Road
C2	Church Street	A3	Rocky Hill
B4	College Avenue	C3	Romney Place
C4	College Road	B2	Rose Yard
C1	County Road	A4	Rowland Close
D4	Crompton Gardens	A2	St Anne Court
D2	Cromwell Road	B2	St Faith's Street
A4	Douglas Road	D1	St Luke's Avenue
B2	Earl Street	D1	St Luke's Road
D4	Elm Grove	A2	St Peters Street
B1	Fairmeadow	B1	Sandling Road
A4	Florence Road	D1	Sittingbourne Road
D1	Foley Street	D3	Square Hill Road
C4	Foster Street	B1	Stacey Street
C3	Gabriel's Hill	B1	Station Road
C4	George Street	A3	Terrace Road
D4	Greenside	A4	Tonbridge Road
A4	Hart Street	C2	Tufton Street
D4	Hastings Road	C2	Union Street
C4	Hayle Road	C4	Upper Stone Street
D1	Heathorn Street	A3	Victoria Street
C1	Hedley Street	D2	Vinters Road
B3	High Street	C3	Wat Tyler Way
D1	Holland Road	B1	Week Street
C1	James Street	C1	Well Road
C1	Jeffrey Street	A4	Westree Road
C3	King Street	C1	Wheeler Street
D4	Kingsley Road	C1	Woollett Street
C4	Knightrider Street	C2	Wyatt Street
A1	Lesley Place		
A3	London Road		
C3	Lower Stone Street		

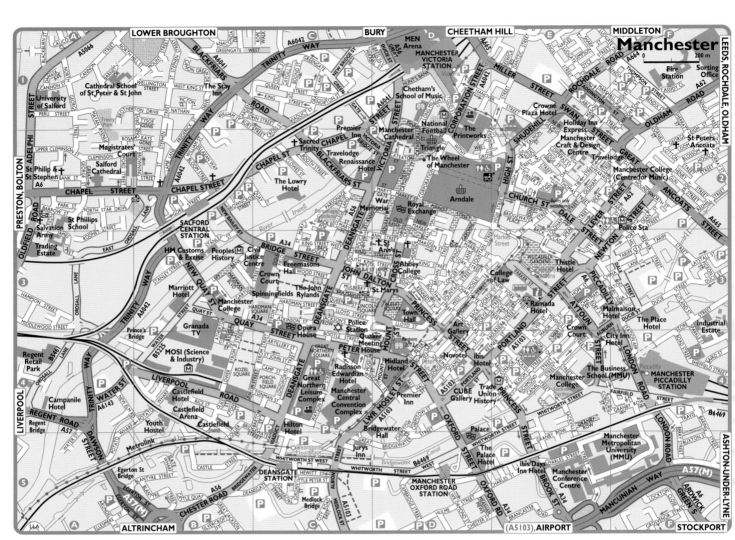

Manchester

Manchester is found on atlas page **82 H5**

E4	Abingdon Street	B2	Browning Street	A5	Dawson Street	E2	John Street	B2	New Bailey Street	C2	St Anns Square
E1	Addington Street	D3	Brown Street	C4	Deansgate	E2	Joiner Street	C1	New Bridge Street	C3	St Ann Street
A2	Adelphi Street	B1	Bury Street	D4	Dickinson Street	F3	Jutland Street	D2	New Cathedral Street	C3	St James Square
C5	Albion Street	B4	Byrom Street	B4	Duke Street	D3	Kennedy Street	A4	New Elm Road	D4	St James Street
E1	Angel Street	E1	Cable Street	F3	Dulcie Street	C1	King Street	E2	New George Street	C3	St Mary's Parsonage
F5	Ardwick Green South	D5	Cambridge Street	A3	East Ordsall Lane	C3	King Street	B3	New Quay Street	D4	St Peter's Square
C4	Artillery Street	C4	Camp Street	A5	Egerton Street	C3	King Street West	E3	Newton Street	B2	St Stephen Street
B4	Atherton Street	E4	Canal Street	F4	Fairfield Street	B2	Lamb Lane	E3	New York Street	F3	Store Street
C3	Atkinson Street	A1	Cannon Street	D4	Faulkner Street	F3	Laystall Street	D3	Nicholas Street	E1	Sharp Street
E4	Auburn Street	B1	Canon Green Drive	D1	Fennel Street	B3	Left Bank	A1	North George Street	E2	Shudehill
E3	Aytoun Street	B5	Castle Street	A2	Ford Street	E2	Lena Street	A1	North Hill Street	A1	Silk Street
E3	Back Piccadilly	D2	Cathedral Street	D3	Fountain Street	E2	Lever Street	A2	North Star Drive	E1	Simpson Street
A2	Bank Street	C4	Chadderton Street	B2	Frederick Street	E3	Little Lever Street	C1	Norton Street	C3	South King Street
F4	Baring Street	F1	Chapel Lane	B3	Gartside Street	C5	Little Peter Street	A3	Oldfield Road	E3	Spear Street
C4	Barton Street	A2	Chapel Street	F2	George Leigh Street	B4	Liverpool Road	F1	Oldham Road	D3	Spring Gardens
F4	Berry Street	E5	Charles Street	D4	George Street	C3	Lloyd Street	E2	Oldham Street	F3	Station Approach
B1	Blackfriars Road	D3	Charlotte Street	B2	Gore Street	F4	London Road	A4	Ordsall Lane	E1	Swan Street
C2	Blackfriars Street	E3	Chatham Street	E5	Granby Row	D1	Long Millgate	D5	Oxford Road	F3	Tariff Street
B5	Blantyre Street	D3	Cheapside	C1	Gravel Lane	C4	Longworth Street	D4	Oxford Street	E2	Thomas Street
B2	Bloom Street	B5	Chester Road	F2	Great Ancoats Street	B4	Lower Byrom Street	D3	Pall Mall	F1	Thompson Street
E4	Bloom Street	E3	China Lane	C5	Great Bridgewater Street	C4	Lower Mosley Street	E3	Parker Street	D3	Tib Lane
F2	Blossom Street	E4	Chorlton Street	D1	Great Ducie Street	D5	Lower Ormond Street	A1	Peru Street	E2	Tib Street
F4	Boad Street	E2	Church Street	A2	Great George Street	E1	Ludgate Street	C4	Peter Street	D1	Todd Street
C1	Boond Street	C5	City Road East	B5	Great Jackson Street	E4	Major Street	E3	Piccadilly	C4	Tonman Street
D3	Booth Street	A2	Cleminson Street	B4	Great John Street	E5	Mancunian Way	E3	Piccadilly Gardens	F4	Travis Street
C4	Bootle Street	C2	College Land	C1	Greengate	D3	Marble Street	D4	Portland Street	A4	Trinity Way
E5	Brancaster Road	C1	Collier Street	B1	Greengate West	D2	Market Street	F3	Port Street	E2	Turner Street
C3	Brazenose Street	C5	Commercial Street	F2	Gun Street	D3	Marsden Street	A5	Potato Wharf	A2	Upper Cleminson Street
F3	Brewer Street	F2	Copperas Street	D1	Hanover Street	E1	Marshall Street	D3	Princess Street	C2	Victoria Bridge Street
C3	Bridge Street	F2	Cornell Street	C3	Hardman Street	E1	Mason Street	B3	Quay Street	D2	Victoria Street
E2	Bridgewater Place	D2	Corporation Street	C5	Hewitt Street	A1	Mayan Avenue	C1	Queen Street	E2	Warwick Street
B4	Bridgewater Street	F2	Cotton Street	E2	High Street	C5	Medlock Street	C3	Queen Street	C4	Watson Street
B5	Bridgewater Viaduct	F1	Crosskeys Street	E3	Hood Street	A3	Middlewood Street	F2	Redhill Street	D2	Well Street
E5	Brook Street	C2	Cross Street	E3	Hope Street	E1	Miller Street	A4	Regent Road	B1	West King Street
A1	Brotherton Drive	D3	Cross Street	D5	Houndsworth Street	E3	Minshull Street	D4	Reyner Street	D3	West Mosley Street
B2	Browncross Street	E1	Dantzic Street	A3	Hulme Street	C1	Mirabel Street	B4	Rice Street	D5	Whitworth Street
				A3	James Street	D3	Mosley Street	E4	Richmond Street	C5	Whitworth Street West
				F2	Jersey Street	B1	Mount Street	E1	Rochdale Road	C4	Windmill Street
				C3	John Dalton Street	D4	Mount Street	A3	Rodney Street	D2	Withy Grove
				B1	John Street	C4	Museum Street	A2	Rosamond Drive	C3	Wood Street
						B1	Nathan Drive	E4	Sackville Street	D3	York Street

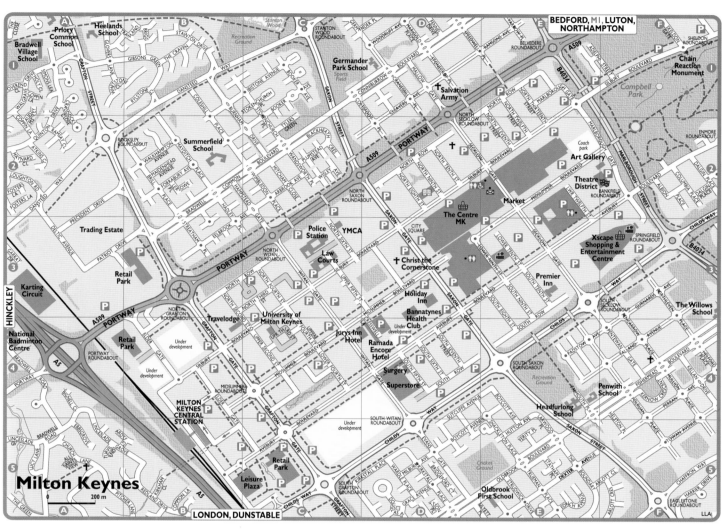

Milton Keynes

Milton Keynes is found on atlas page **49 N7**

E1	Adelphi Street
F2	Albion Place
A5	All Saints View
C2	Arbrook Avenue
A5	Ardys Court
E5	Arlott Close
F5	Arlott Crescent
A2	Atkins Close
A2	Audley Mews
C5	Avebury Boulevard
E2	Bankfield Roundabout
E1	Belvedere Roundabout
A4	Bignell Close
C2	Blackheath Crescent
C1	Booker Avenue
D5	Boycott Avenue
E4	Boycott Avenue
B2	Bradwell Common Boulevard
A4	Bradwell Road
A5	Bradwell Road
D5	Bridgeford Court
B2	Brill Place
B1	Burnham Drive
F5	Chaffron Way
C5	Childs Way
F3	Childs Way
A5	Church Lane
D3	City Square
D1	Cleavers Avenue
B1	Coleshill Place
C1	Coltsfoot Place
F2	Columbia Place
B5	Common Lane
C1	Conniburrow Boulevard

A2	Coppin Lane
A1	Craddocks Close
D1	Cranesbill Place
D3	Cresswell Lane
F2	Dalgin Place
A2	Dansteed Way
A3	Deltic Avenue
E5	Dexter Avenue
D5	Douglas Place
F5	Eaglestone Roundabout
A5	Ebbsgrove
E5	Edrich Avenue
B3	Eelbrook Avenue
B4	Elder Gate
F2	Enmore Roundabout
D5	Evans Gate
E4	Falmouth Place
D1	Fennel Drive
F4	Fishermead Boulevard
B2	Forrabury Avenue
A2	Fosters Lane
A3	Garrat Drive
C1	Germander Place
B1	Gibsons Green
A1	Glovers Lane
D5	Grace Avenue
B4	Grafton Gate
A1	Grafton Street
C5	Grafton Street
F3	Gurnards Avenue
B2	Hadley Place
B2	Hampstead Gate
F5	Harrier Drive
F4	Helford Place
F4	Helston Place

A1	Holy Close
E5	Hutton Avenue
C1	Ibistone Avenue
F4	Kellan Drive
F4	Kernow Crescent
B5	Kirkham Close
C5	Kirkstall Place
E5	Larwood Place
B2	Leasowe Place
A5	Linceslade Grove
A2	Loughton Road
C4	Lower Fourth Street
E3	Lower Ninth Street
E3	Lower Tenth Street
E2	Lower Twelfth Street
A5	Lucy Lane
B2	Maidenhead Avenue
D1	Mallow Gate
D1	Marigold Place
E1	Marlborough Gate
E2	Marlborough Gate
F2	Marlborough Street
B2	Mayditch Place
A2	Maynard Close
C4	Midsummer Boulevard
E2	Midsummer Boulevard
B4	Midsummer Roundabout
D5	Milburn Avenue
C2	Mitcham Close
F4	Mullion Place
D2	North Eighth Street
E1	North Eleventh Street
C3	North Fourth Street
B3	North Grafton Roundabout
D2	North Ninth Street
B3	North Row
D2	North Row
C2	North Saxon Roundabout

D1	North Secklow Roundabout
B3	North Second Street
C3	North Sixth Street
D2	North Tenth Street
C3	North Third Street
E1	North Thirteenth Street
E1	North Twelfth Street
C3	North Witan Roundabout
E5	Oldbrook Boulevard
A1	Overend Close
E4	Padstow Avenue
A3	Patriot Drive
F3	Pencarrow Place
F4	Pentewan Gate
F4	Perran Avenue
A5	Pitcher Lane
C2	Plumstead Avenue
F4	Polruan Place
F3	Porthleven Place
A4	Portway
A4	Portway Roundabout
A3	Precedent Drive
A2	Quinton Drive
A2	Ramsay Close
E1	Ramsons Avenue
B5	Redland Drive
A2	Rooksley Roundabout
B1	Rylstone Close
D2	Saxon Gate
C1	Saxon Street
D2	Secklow Gate
E5	Shackleton Place
F1	Sheldon Roundabout
B4	Silbury Boulevard
B4	Silbury Roundabout
A1	Simons Lea
F1	Skeldon Gate
E3	South Eighth Street
D4	South Fifth Street

C5	South Grafton Roundabout
E3	South Ninth Street
D4	South Row
E4	South Saxon Roundabout
F3	South Secklow Roundabout
D4	South Seventh Street
D4	South Sixth Street
E3	South Tenth Street
D5	South Witan Roundabout
D1	Speedwell Place
F3	Springfield Roundabout
B1	Stainton Drive
C1	Stanton Wood Roundabout
E5	Statham Place
C1	Stokenchurch Place
D1	Stonecrop Place
B3	Streatham Place
E5	Strudwick Drive
D4	Sutcliffe Avenue
F4	Talland Avenue
E5	The Boundary
A1	The Close
B1	The Craven
A5	The Green
F5	Towan Avenue
B1	Tranlands Brigg
E5	Trueman Place
A5	Turvil End
C2	Tylers Green
D5	Tyson Place
D5	Ulyett Place
C3	Upper Fifth Street
C4	Upper Fourth Street
C4	Upper Second Street
C4	Upper Third Street
E5	Verity Place
A1	Walgrave Drive
B2	Walkhampton Avenue
C2	Wandsworth Place

D5	Wardle Place
A1	Whetstone Close
C2	Wimbledon Place
C2	Wisely Avenue
C3	Witan Gate
D1	Woodruff Avenue
E1	Yarrow Place

Middlesbrough

Middlesbrough is found on atlas page **104 E7**

A4	Acklam Road	A3	Heywood Street
C3	Acton Street	B4	Kensington Road
B4	Aire Street	A4	Kildare Street
B3	Albany Street	D3	Laurel Street
C2	Albert Road	A2	Lees Road
C2	Amber Street	B4	Linthorpe Road
B3	Athol Street	A4	Longford Street
D3	Audrey Street	A3	Lorne Street
B4	Ayresome Park Road	D3	Lothian Road
A4	Ayresome Street	A2	Marsh Street
C2	Borough Road	D2	Marton Road
B2	Bretnall Street	D2	Melrose Street
C1	Bridge Street East	A1	Metz Bridge Road
C1	Bridge Street West	D3	Myrtle Street
B4	Bush Street	D3	Newlands Road
D2	Camden Street	A2	Newport Road
A2	Cannon Park Road	D3	Palm Street
A2	Cannon Park Way	C3	Park Lane
A2	Cannon Street	C4	Park Road North
A3	Carlow Street	C4	Park Road South
C2	Centre Square	D4	Park Vale Road
D4	Clairville Road	A3	Parliament Road
C3	Clarendon Road	C2	Pearl Street
B3	Clifton Street	C3	Pelham Street
D1	Corporation Road	B3	Portman Street
B4	Costa Street	B3	Princes Road
B3	Craven Street	A1	Riverside Park Road
A3	Crescent Road	C2	Ruby Street
D3	Croydon Road	D2	Russel Street
A2	Derwent Street	B2	St Pauls Road
B3	Diamond Road	C3	Southfield Road
D4	Egmont Road	C1	Station Street
C2	Emily Street	B3	Stowe Street
D3	Errol Street	B4	Tavistock Street
A4	Essex Street	B3	Tennyson Street
C2	Fairbridge Street	A3	Union Street
D3	Falmouth Street	C3	Victoria Road
B3	Finsbury Street	A3	Victoria Street
B2	Fleetham Street	B2	Warren Street
B2	Garnet Street	D3	Waterloo Road
B3	Glebe Road	B3	Waverley Street
B2	Grange Road	A3	Wembley Street
D2	Grange Road	B2	Wilson Street
C3	Granville Road	C3	Wilton Street
B3	Gresham Road	B2	Windsor Street
B3	Harewood Street	C3	Woodlands Road
B4	Harford Street	B4	Worcester Street
B2	Hartington Road	C1	Zetland Road

Newport

Newport is found on atlas page **31 K7**

B3	Albert Terrace	B3	Jones Street
A2	Allt-Yr-Yn Avenue	C4	Keynsham Avenue
B3	Bailey Street	C4	King Street
D2	Bedford Road	C2	Kingsway
B3	Blewitt Street	C4	Kingsway
C1	Bond Street	A3	Llanthewy Road
B2	Bridge Street	B1	Locke Street
A3	Bryngwyn Road	C4	Lower Dock Street
A4	Brynhyfryd Avenue	B1	Lucas Street
A4	Brynhyfryd Road	B2	Market Street
A4	Caerau Crescent	C4	Mellon Street
A3	Caerau Road	B2	Mill Street
B2	Cambrian Road	B3	North Street
D3	Caroline Street	A3	Oakfield Road
D2	Cedar Road	C4	Park Square
C3	Charles Street	C1	Pugsley Street
D1	Chepstow Road	B1	Queen's Hill
C1	Clarence Place	A1	Queen's Hill Crescent
B4	Clifton Place	C4	Queen Street
B4	Clifton Road	B2	Queensway
A3	Clyffard Crescent	A4	Risca Road
A2	Clytha Park Road	C2	Rodney Road
C4	Clytha Square	D1	Rudry Street
A1	Colts Foot Close	C4	Ruperra Lane
C4	Commercial Street	D4	Ruperra Street
D1	Corelli Street	B3	St Edward Street
C2	Corn Street	B4	St Julian Street
D2	Corporation Road	A2	St Mark's Crescent
B2	Devon Place	B3	St Mary Street
B4	Dewsland Park Road	C2	St Vincent Road
D4	Dumfries Place	B3	St Woolos Road
B3	East Street	C3	School Lane
C1	East Usk Road	A2	Serpentine Road
B1	Factory Road	C2	Skinner Street
A2	Fields Road	A1	Sorrel Drive
B4	Friars Field	A3	Spencer Road
B4	Friars Road	B3	Stow Hill
C3	Friar Street	B4	Stow Hill
D4	George Street	A4	Stow Park Avenue
A2	Godfrey Road	C3	Talbot Lane
A2	Gold Tops	D1	Tregare Street
C2	Grafton Road	A3	Tunnel Terrace
D4	Granville Lane	C3	Upper Dock Street
D4	Granville Street	C3	Upper Dock Street
B2	High Street	D3	Usk Way
C3	Hill Street	B3	Victoria Crescent
C3	John Frost Square	B3	West Street
D4	John Street	A4	York Place

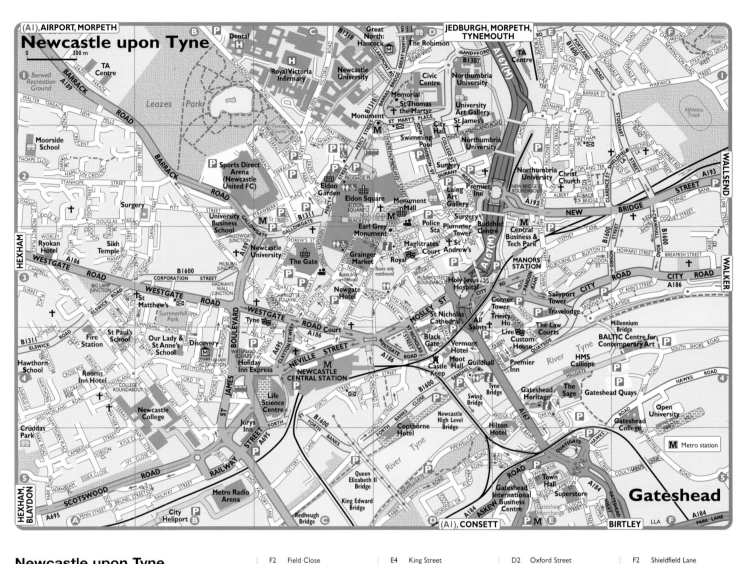

Newcastle upon Tyne

Newcastle upon Tyne is found on atlas page **113 K8**

F4	Abbots Hill	C4	Clayton Street West	F2	Field Close	E4	King Street	D2	Oxford Street	F2	Shieldfield Lane
E2	Albert Street	A4	Colby Court	D5	Fletcher Road	A4	Kirkdale Green	E3	Pandon	E2	Shield Street
E2	Argyle Street	A4	College Roundabout	C4	Forth Banks	A5	Kyle Close	E3	Pandon Bank	B5	Shot Factory Lane
D5	Askew Road	D2	College Street	D5	Forth Banks Close	E5	Lambton Street	F5	Park Lane	E2	Simpson Terrace
A2	Avision Street	A3	Cookson Close	C4	Forth Street	C2	Leazes Crescent	A5	Park Road	A4	Somerset Place
E2	Back New Bridge Street	E2	Copland Terrace	C3	Friars Street	C2	Leazes Lane	B4	Peel Lane	F4	South Shore Road
E1	Barker Street	E1	Coppice Way	B2	Gallowgate	C2	Leazes Park Road	A5	Penn Street	C4	South Street
A1	Barrack Road	F2	Coquet Street	B3	Gallowgate Junction	C2	Leazes Terrace	C2	Percy Street	A2	Stanhope Street
D1	Barras Bridge	B3	Corporation Street	E5	Gateshead Highway	A2	Liddle Road	D2	Pilgrim Street	F2	Stepney Bank
B3	Bath Lane	A3	Cottenham Street	B4	George Street	F2	Lime Street	C4	Pink Lane	E3	Stepney Lane
A4	Belgrave Parade	F5	Coulthards Lane	F3	Gibson Street	E4	Lombard Street	D5	Pipewellgate	F2	Stepney Road
A3	Big Lamp Junction	F2	Crawhall Road	E1	Gladstone Terrace	A2	Longley Street	B2	Pitt Street	F1	Stoddart Street
C2	Blackett Street	A4	Cross Parade	E1	Grainger Street	B4	Lord Street	E1	Portland Road	C3	Stowell Street
E3	Blagdon Street	C3	Cross Street	C3	Grainger Street	D3	Low Friar Street	F1	Portland Road	F1	Stratford Grove West
B4	Blandford Square	A2	Darnell Place	E1	Grantham Road	C3	Low Friar Street	C5	Pottery Lane	C2	Strawberry Place
B4	Blandford Street	D3	Dean Street	D1	Great North Road	B5	Maiden Street	A2	Prospect Place	B3	Summerhill Grove
E4	Bottle Bank	B2	Derby Street	D3	Grey Street	A3	Mansfield Street	C2	Prudhoe Place	A3	Summerhill Street
F2	Boyd Street	B3	Diana Street	C3	Groat Market	B5	Maple Street	F5	Quarryfield Road	B4	Summerhill Terrace
F3	Breamish Street	F1	Dinsdale Place	A2	Hamilton Crescent	A4	Maple Terrace	E5	Quayside	E5	Swinburne Street
E4	Bridge Street	F1	Dinsdale Road	C5	Hanover Street	D3	Market Street	F3	Quayside	F3	Tarset Road
E3	Broad Chare	A5	Dobson Close	E1	Harrison Place	A4	Mather Road	E4	Quayside	C2	Terrace Place
A5	Brunel Street	A2	Douglas Terrace	E5	Hawks Road	E3	Melbourne Street	E4	Queen Street	A2	Thorpe Close
B3	Buckingham Street	B4	Duke Street	A4	Hawthorn Place	F4	Mill Road	C1	Queen Victoria Road	A3	Tindal Street
E3	Buxton Street	A5	Dunn Street	A4	Hawthorn Terrace	E1	Milton Close	D5	Rabbit Banks Road	E3	Tower Street
E1	Byron Street	D2	Durant Road	E1	Helmsley Road	E1	Milton Place	B5	Railway Street	E4	Tyne Bridge
A5	Cambridge Street	E5	East Street	E2	Henry Square	A1	Monday Crescent	F2	Red Barnes	F2	Union Street
E2	Camden Street	A3	Edward Place	D3	High Bridge	D3	Mosley Street	B1	Richardson Road	A3	Vallum Way
A3	Campbell Place	C2	Eldon Square	D5	High Level Road	E1	Naper Street	E2	Rock Terrace	B4	Victoria Street
D3	Carliol Square	E5	Ellison Street	E5	High Street	C3	Nelson Street	E1	Rosedale Terrace	A1	Walter Terrace
C3	Charlotte Square	B4	Elswick East Terrace	E4	Hillgate	C3	Nelson Street	A4	Rye Hill	F1	Warwick Street
F1	Chelmsford Green	A3	Elswick Road	D3	Hood Street	C4	Neville Street	C3	St Andrew's Street	B4	Waterloo Square
E1	Chester Street	A3	Elswick Row	E5	Hopper Street	E2	New Bridge Street	F3	St Ann's Street	C4	Waterloo Street
E3	City Road	A5	Essex Close	A5	Hornbeam Place	C3	Newgate Street	B4	St James Boulevard	B2	Wellington Street
D1	Claremont Road	C3	Falconar's Court	A4	Houston Street	F1	Newington Road	D1	St Mary's Place	A3	Westgate Road
E2	Clarence Street	E2	Falconer Street	F3	Howard Street	A1	New Mills	D4	St Nicholas Street	A4	Westmorland Road
C3	Clayton Street	C3	Fenkle Street	E5	Hudson Street	D2	Northumberland Road	C2	St Thomas' Court	E5	West Street
				A5	Ivy Close	D2	Northumberland Street	C1	St Thomas' Street	C3	West Walls
				D1	Jesmond Road West	C3	Nun Street	E3	Sandgate	A3	Worley Close
				D2	John Dobson Street	C4	Oakwellgate	D4	Sandhill	D5	Worsdell Drive
				E3	Jubilee Road	C4	Orchard Street	D1	Sandyford Road	E2	Wretham Place
				C5	King Edward Bridge	B5	Ord Street	A5	Scotswood Road	A3	York Street

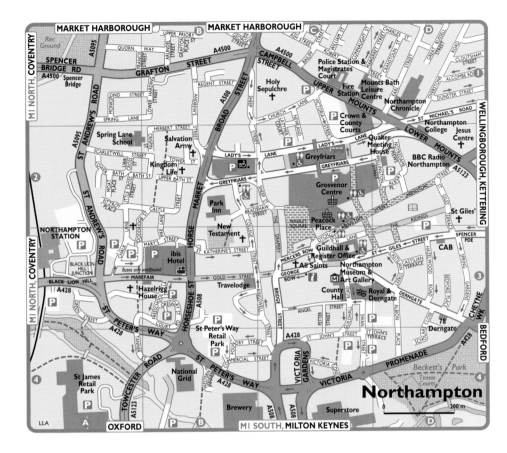

Northampton

Northampton is found on atlas page **60 G8**

C2	Abington Street	A2	Lower Bath Street
D2	Albert Place	A2	Lower Cross Street
D3	Albion Place	B1	Lower Harding Street
C3	Angel Street	D2	Lower Mounts
B1	Arundel Street	A3	Marefair
C1	Ash Street	C1	Margaret Street
C1	Bailiff Street	C2	Market Square
A3	Black Lion Hill	C3	Mercers Row
B2	Bradshaw Street	A2	Moat Place
C3	Bridge Street	A1	Monkspond Street
B1	Broad Street	C1	Newland
C1	Campbell Street	D2	Notredame Mews
D3	Castilian Street	D1	Overstone Road
B2	Castle Street	B3	Pike Lane
A3	Chalk Lane	A1	Quorn Way
D3	Cheyne Walk	B1	Regent Street
C1	Church Lane	C1	Robert Street
B2	College Street	A2	St Andrew's Road
B4	Commercial Street	B1	St Andrew's Street
C1	Connaught Street	D3	St Giles Street
B3	Court Road	D2	St Giles' Terrace
D1	Cranstoun Street	C4	St John's Street
B2	Crispin Street	B3	St Katherine's Street
D3	Derngate	A3	St Mary's Street
A3	Doddridge Street	D1	St Michael's Road
D1	Dunster Street	B4	St Peter's Way
D1	Dychurch Lane	A2	Scarletwell Street
D1	Earl Street	D4	Scholars Close
D2	Fetter Street	B1	Sheep Street
A2	Fitzroy Place	C2	Sheep Street
B4	Foundry Street	A1	Spencer Bridge Road
A1	Francis Street	D3	Spencer Parade
B3	Freeschool Lane	D3	Spring Gardens
C3	George Row	A1	Spring Lane
B3	Gold Street	C3	Swan Street
A1	Grafton Street	A4	Tanner Street
D1	Great Russell Street	C2	The Drapery
A3	Green Street	D2	The Ridings
B3	Gregory Street	A4	Towcester Road
B2	Greyfriars	B2	Tower Street
C3	Guildhall Road	B2	Upper Bath Street
D3	Hazelwood Road	C1	Upper Mounts
B2	Herbert Street	B1	Upper Priory Street
B3	Horse Market	C4	Victoria Gardens
B3	Horseshoe Street	C4	Victoria Promenade
C3	Kingswell Street	C1	Victoria Street
B2	Lady's Lane	D2	Wellington Street
A2	Little Cross Street	B4	Western Wharf

Norwich

Norwich is found on atlas page **77 J10**

B4	All Saints Green	A2	Pottergate
C2	Bank Plain	C2	Prince of Wales Road
A1	Barn Road	C2	Princes Street
C1	Bedding Lane	C1	Quay Side
B2	Bedford Street	B4	Queens Road
C4	Ber Street	C2	Queen Street
A3	Bethel Street	B3	Rampant Horse Street
D1	Bishopgate	D2	Recorder Road
B3	Brigg Street	B3	Red Lion Street
B1	Calvert Street	D3	Riverside Road
C3	Castle Meadow	D1	Riverside Walk
D2	Cathedral Street	C3	Rose Lane
C3	Cattle Market Street	C3	Rouen Road
B3	Chantry Road	A4	Rupert Street
A3	Chapelfield East	B2	St Andrews Street
A3	Chapelfield North	A2	St Benedicts Street
A3	Chapelfield Road	D2	St Faiths Lane
A3	Cleveland Road	B1	St Georges Street
B1	Colegate	A2	St Giles Street
A3	Convent Road	C4	St Julians Alley
B2	Coslany Street	B1	St Marys Plain
A2	Cow Hill	B3	St Peters Street
B3	Davey Place	B4	St Stephens Road
B2	Dove Street	A4	St Stephens Square
B1	Duke Street	B4	St Stephens Street
C2	Elm Hill	A2	St Swithins Road
B2	Exchange Street	D2	St Verdast Street
C3	Farmers Avenue	B4	Surrey Street
D2	Ferry Lane	A2	Ten Bell Lane
C1	Fishergate	B3	Theatre Street
B1	Friars Quay	C4	Thorn Lane
B3	Gentlemans Walk	C2	Tombland
C3	Goldenball Street	A1	Unicorn Yard
A2	Grapes Hill	A4	Union Street
B3	Haymarket	A3	Unthank Road
A1	Heigham Street	B2	Upper Goat Lane
C2	King Street	C2	Upper King Street
B2	London Street	A2	Upper St Giles Street
B2	Lower Goat Lane	A3	Vauxhall Street
C1	Magdalen Street	A3	Walpole Street
C3	Market Avenue	C1	Wensum Street
A1	Mills Yard	A4	Wessex Street
D3	Mountergate	B3	Westlegate
D4	Music House Lane	A1	Westwick Street
B1	Muspole Street	D4	Wherry Road
A4	Norfolk Street	C1	Whitefriars
A1	Oak Street	B3	White Lion Street
C1	Palace Street	A2	Willow Lane

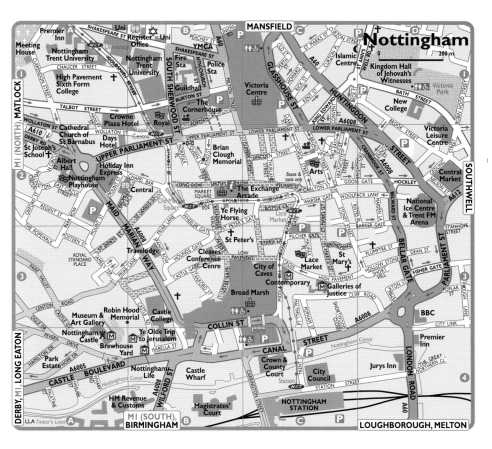

Nottingham

Nottingham is found on atlas page **72 F3**

B3	Albert Street	A3	Lenton Road
D2	Barker Gate	C2	Lincoln Street
D1	Bath Street	B3	Lister Gate
D3	Bellar Gate	D4	London Road
D2	Belward Street	B2	Long Row
C2	Broad Street	C2	Lower Parliament Street
C3	Broadway	B3	Low Pavement
A2	Bromley Place	A2	Maid Marian Way
D1	Brook Street	B2	Market Street
B1	Burton Street	C3	Middle Hill
C4	Canal Street	B1	Milton Street
C2	Carlton Street	A3	Mount Street
C4	Carrington Street	B2	Norfolk Place
A4	Castle Boulevard	A2	North Circus Street
B3	Castle Gate	A3	Park Row
B3	Castle Road	D3	Parliament Street
B2	Chapel Bar	C2	Pelham Street
A1	Chaucer Street	A4	Peveril Drive
A1	Clarendon Street	C3	Pilcher Gate
C3	Cliff Road	C3	Popham Street
B4	Collin Street	B2	Poultry
D2	Cranbrook Street	B2	Queen Street
C2	Cumber Street	A2	Regent Street
C1	Curzon Place	D1	St Ann's Well Road
A2	Derby Road	A3	St James's Street
B2	Exchange Walk	C3	St Marks Gate
D3	Fisher Gate	C1	St Marks Street
C3	Fletcher Gate	C3	St Mary's Gate
B1	Forman Street	B3	St Peter's Gate
A3	Friar Lane	A1	Shakespeare Street
D2	Gedling Street	B2	Smithy Row
C2	George Street	B2	South Parade
C1	Glasshouse Street	B1	South Sherwood Street
A1	Goldsmith Street	B3	Spaniel Row
C2	Goose Gate	C4	Station Street
C3	Halifax Place	C2	Stoney Street
C2	Heathcote Street	A1	Talbot Street
C2	High Cross Street	C2	Thurland Street
C3	High Pavement	C4	Trent Street
D2	Hockley	A2	Upper Parliament Street
D3	Hollow Stone	C2	Victoria Street
A4	Hope Drive	C2	Warser Gate
B3	Hounds Gate	C3	Weekday Cross
C1	Howard Street	A2	Wellington Circus
C1	Huntingdon Street	B2	Wheeler Gate
C1	Kent Street	B4	Wilford Street
C1	King Edward Street	A1	Wollaton Street
B2	King Street	C2	Woolpack Lane

Oldham

Oldham is found on atlas page **83 K4**

B3	Ascroft Street	D1	Mortimer Street
B1	Bar Gap Road	A4	Napier Street East
D4	Barlow Street	A2	New Radcliffe Street
B3	Barn Street	A3	Oldham Way
D2	Beever Street	B4	Park Road
D2	Bell Street	A4	Park Street
B1	Belmont Street	B3	Peter Street
A3	Booth Street	C3	Queen Street
C3	Bow Street	B1	Radcliffe Street
D2	Brook Street	B1	Raleigh Close
B3	Brunswick Street	A1	Ramsden Street
C2	Cardinal Street	D2	Regent Street
A1	Chadderton Way	C3	Rhodes Bank
B3	Chaucer Street	C2	Rhodes Street
C3	Clegg Street	B1	Rifle Street
B1	Coldhurst Road	A1	Rochdale Road
B4	Cromwell Street	B2	Rock Street
B4	Crossbank Street	C3	Roscoe Street
B2	Curzon Street	A1	Ruskin Street
A1	Dunbar Street	A1	St Hilda's Drive
B2	Eden Street	B1	St Marys Street
C2	Egerton Street	B2	St Mary's Way
C3	Firth Street	D1	Shaw Road
B2	Fountain Street	C1	Shaw Street
B1	Franklin Street	C1	Siddall Street
D2	Gower Street	B3	Silver Street
A2	Grange Street	C3	Southgate Street
C3	Greaves Street	D4	South Hill Street
D4	Greengate Street	D3	Southlink
D3	Hamilton Street	D2	Spencer Street
D4	Hardy Street	B1	Sunfield Road
C4	Harmony Street	D1	Thames Street
B2	Henshaw Street	A1	Trafalgar Street
C1	Higginshaw Road	B1	Trinity Street
A2	Highfield Street	A1	Tulbury Street
B3	High Street	B3	Union Street
B3	Hobson Street	A4	Union Street West
D4	Hooper Street	B3	Union Street West
C1	Horsedge Street	D2	Wallshaw Street
A3	John Street	B4	Wall Street
B3	King Street	A1	Ward Street
D2	Lemnos Street	C3	Waterloo Street
C1	Malby Street	B4	Wellington Street
A4	Malton Street	A2	West End Street
A3	Manchester Street	B3	West Street
B3	Market Place	D2	Willow Street
C4	Marlborough Street	C4	Woodstock Street
A3	Middleton Road	C3	Yorkshire Street

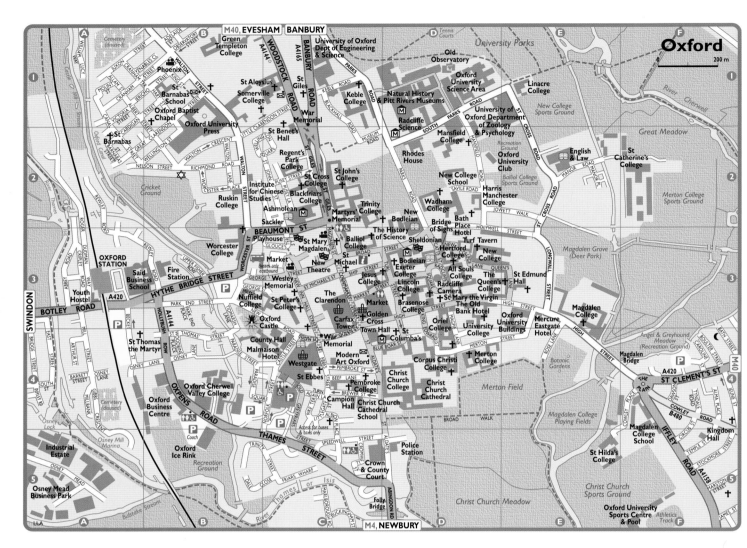

Oxford

Oxford is found on atlas page **34 F3**

A3	Abbey Road	B5	Dale Close	A4	Millbank	E2	St Cross Road
D5	Abingdon Road	F4	Dawson Street	A4	Mill Street	C4	St Ebbes Street
B1	Adelaide Street	A4	East Street	A1	Mount Street	C2	St Giles
A1	Albert Street	C5	Folly Bridge	C2	Museum Road	C2	St John Street
A1	Allam Street	C5	Friars Wharf	A2	Nelson Street	C3	St Michael's Street
F4	Alma Place	B3	George Street	D3	New College Lane	B4	St Thomas' Street
A4	Arthur Street	B3	George Street Mews	C3	New Inn Hall Street	D2	Savile Road
C1	Banbury Road	A4	Gibbs Crescent	B3	New Road	C3	Ship Street
A4	Barrett Street	C3	Gloucester Street	C4	Norfolk Street	D2	South Parks Road
F4	Bath Street	A2	Great Clarendon Street	B1	Observatory Street	A4	South Street
C3	Beaumont Street	B1	Hart Street	C4	Old Greyfriars Street	C5	Speedwell Street
A3	Becket Street	D3	High Street	A4	Osney Lane	F5	Stockmore Street
C4	Beef Lane	E4	High Street	B4	Osney Lane	F5	Temple Street
C1	Blackhall Road	B3	Hollybush Row	A5	Osney Mead	C5	Thames Street
C4	Blue Boar Street	D2	Holywell Street	B4	Oxpens Road	F4	The Plain
C4	Bonn Square	B3	Hythe Bridge Street	B4	Paradise Square	B3	Tidmarsh Lane
A3	Botley Road	F4	Iffley Road	B4	Paradise Street	B5	Trinity Street
F4	Boulter Street	F5	James Street	B3	Park End Street	D3	Turl Street
C4	Brewer Street	A1	Jericho Street	C1	Parks Road	C4	Turn Again Lane
A4	Bridge Street	D2	Jowett Walk	D2	Parks Road	F4	Tyndale Road
C3	Broad Street	A1	Juxon Street	C4	Pembroke Street	B3	Upper Fisher Row
D4	Broad Walk	C1	Keble Road	C4	Pike Terrace	A1	Venables Close
C5	Buckingham Street	D3	King Edward Street	C2	Pusey Lane	A1	Victoria Street
A1	Canal Street	B1	King Street	C2	Pusey Street	B2	Walton Crescent
A2	Cardigan Street	B2	Little Clarendon Street	D3	Queen's Lane	B2	Walton Lane
F4	Caroline Street	C4	Littlegate Street	C4	Queen Street	B1	Walton Street
C4	Castle Street	E3	Longwall Street	D3	Radcliffe Square	B2	Wellington Square
D3	Catte Street	E4	Magdalen Bridge	A2	Rewley Road	B2	Wellington Street
F5	Circus Street	C3	Magdalen Street	B3	Rewley Road	A1	William Lucy Way
C3	Cornmarket Street	D3	Magpie Lane	B2	Richmond Road	B4	Woodbine Place
F4	Cowley Place	E2	Manor Place	A3	Roger Dudman Way	C1	Woodstock Road
F4	Cowley Road	E2	Manor Road	E4	Rose Lane	B2	Worcester Place
A1	Cranham Street	D2	Mansfield Road	C4	St Aldate's	B3	Worcester Street
A1	Cranham Terrace	C3	Market Street	D5	St Aldate's		
A3	Cripley Road	C5	Marlborough Road	A2	St Barnabas Street		
C5	Cromwell Street	F5	Marston Street	F4	St Clement's Street		
		D4	Merton Street	E1	St Cross Road		

University Colleges

D3	All Souls College
C3	Balliol College
D3	Brasenose College
D4	Christ Church College
D4	Corpus Christi College
D3	Exeter College
D2	Harris Manchester College
D3	Hertford College
C3	Jesus College
C1	Keble College
E1	Linacre College
D3	Lincoln College
E3	Magdalen College
D2	Mansfield College
D4	Merton College
D3	New College
B3	Nuffield College
D3	Oriel College
C4	Pembroke College
B2	Ruskin College
F2	St Catherine's College
C3	St Cross College
E5	St Hilda's College
C2	St John's College
C3	St Peter's College
B1	Somerville College
D3	The Queen's College
C2	Trinity College
D3	University College
D2	Wadham College
B3	Worcester College

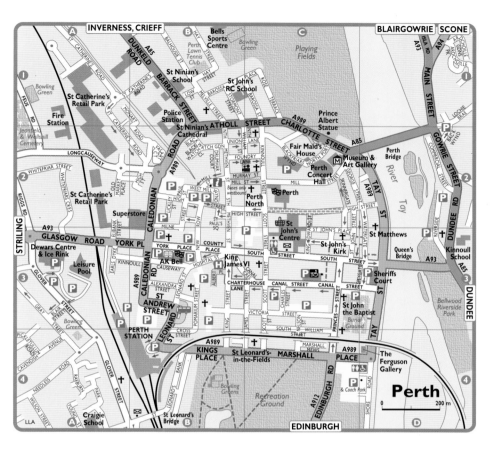

Perth

Perth is found on atlas page **134 E3**

B3	Albert Place	B1	Melville Street
B3	Alexandra Street	B2	Mill Street
D1	Ardchoille Park	C2	Mill Street
B1	Atholl Street	B2	Milne Street
D2	Back Wynd	A1	Monart Road
B1	Balhousie Street	B2	Murray Street
B1	Barossa Place	A4	Needless Road
B1	Barrack Street	B3	New Row
C2	Blackfriars Wynd	B2	North Methven Street
B2	Black Watch Garden	C2	North Port
B2	Caledonian Road	B2	North William Street
B3	Caledonian Road	A2	Old Market Place
C3	Canal Street	B2	Paul Street
A4	Cavendish Avenue	D2	Perth Bridge
C3	Charles Street	A4	Pickletullum Road
C2	Charlotte Street	B3	Pomarium Street
B3	Charterhouse Lane	C3	Princes Street
D2	Commercial Street	D3	Queen's Bridge
B3	County Place	A4	Raeburn Park
B4	Cross Street	A2	Riggs Road
D3	Dundee Road	D3	Riverside
B1	Dunkeld Road	C1	Rose Terrace
A3	Earls Dyke	B3	St Andrew Street
C4	Edinburgh Road	A1	St Catherine's Road
A1	Feus Road	C3	St John's Place
B2	Foundry Lane	C3	St John Street
C2	George Street	B4	St Leonard's Bank
A3	Glasgow Road	B2	St Paul's Square
A3	Glover Street	C2	Scott Street
A4	Glover Street	C3	Scott Street
D2	Gowrie Street	D4	Shore Road
A3	Gray Street	C2	Skinnergate
B1	Hay Street	B2	South Methven Street
B2	High Street	C3	South Street
C2	High Street	C4	South William Street
B3	Hospital Street	D3	Speygate
D1	Isla Road	B1	Stormont Street
C3	James Street	D2	Tay Street
C3	King Edward Street	D4	Tay Street
B4	Kings Place	B2	Union Lane
B3	King Street	C3	Victoria Street
A3	Kinnoull Causeway	D2	Watergate
C2	Kinnoull Street	B2	West Mill Wynd
B3	Leonard Street	A2	Whitefriars Crescent
D1	Lochie Brae	A2	Whitefriar Street
A2	Longcauseway	A4	Wilson Street
D1	Main Street	A3	York Place
C4	Marshall Place	B3	York Place

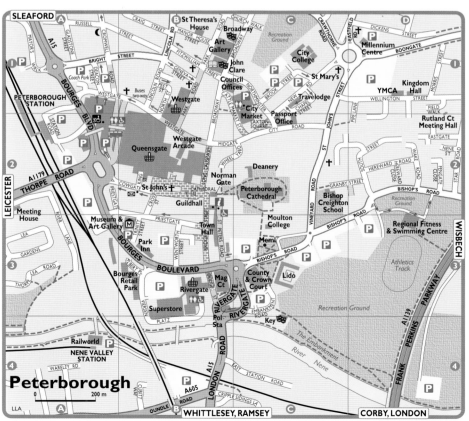

Peterborough

Peterborough is found on atlas page **74 C11**

B3	Albert Place	C1	New Road
C3	Bishop's Road	C1	Northminster
D1	Boongate	B1	North Street
A1	Bourges Boulevard	B4	Oundle Road
B3	Bridge Street	B1	Park Road
A1	Bright Street	B1	Peet Street
B2	Broadway	D2	Pipe Lane
C1	Brook Street	A2	Priestgate
B2	Cathedral Square	B3	Rivergate
B1	Cattle Market Street	A2	River Lane
C1	Chapel Street	A1	Russell Street
B2	Church Street	C2	St John's Street
C1	Church Walk	B3	St Peters Road
C2	City Road	D2	South Street
B2	Cowgate	D2	Star Road
B1	Craig Street	A2	Station Road
C1	Crawthorne Road	A3	Thorpe Lea Road
B4	Cripple Sidings Lane	A2	Thorpe Road
A1	Cromwell Road	B3	Trinity Street
B2	Cross Street	B3	Viersen Platz
B4	Cubitt Way	C3	Vineyard Road
A1	Deacon Street	D2	Wake Road
D1	Dickens Street	A4	Wareley Road
D1	Eastfield Road	D1	Wellington Street
D2	Eastgate	B3	Wentworth Street
C4	East Station Road	A1	Westgate
C3	Embankment Road		
B2	Exchange Street		
D2	Fengate Close		
D1	Field Walk		
B1	Fitzwilliam Street		
D4	Frank Perkins Parkway		
B1	Geneva Street		
A1	Gladstone Street		
C2	Granby Street		
D2	Hereward Close		
D2	Hereward Road		
B2	King Street		
C2	Laxton Square		
A3	Lea Gardens		
B1	Lincoln Road		
B4	London Road		
B2	Long Causeway		
B1	Manor House Street		
A1	Mayor's Walk		
B2	Midgate		
D1	Morris Street		
D2	Nene Street		

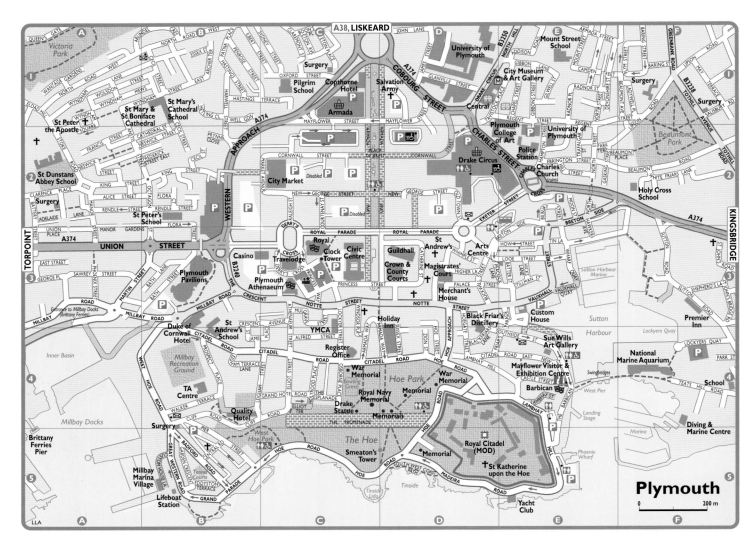

Plymouth

Plymouth is found on atlas page **6 D8**

E1	Addison Road	C1	Claremont Street
A2	Adelaide Lane	A2	Clarence Place
C4	Alfred Street	B4	Cliff Road
A2	Alice Street	D1	Cobourg Street
A2	Anstis Street	C2	Cornwall Street
B1	Archer Terrace	C3	Courtenay Street
E1	Armada Street	B3	Crescent Avenue
C2	Armada Way	B5	Custom House Lane
C4	Armada Way	C3	Derry's Cross
A1	Arundel Crescent	E1	Devonshire Street
C3	Athenaeum Street	D1	Drake Circus
F1	Baring Street	A3	East Street
B3	Bath Lane	E2	Ebrington Street
B3	Bath Street	B5	Eddystone Terrace
E3	Batter Street	A1	Eldad Hill
A2	Battery Street	C4	Elliot Road
F1	Beaumont Avenue	C4	Elliot Terrace
E2	Beaumont Place	B1	Essex Street
F2	Beaumont Road	C1	Eton Avenue
E2	Bilbury Street	C1	Eton Place
D4	Blackfriars Lane	D2	Exeter Street
C1	Boon's Place	B2	Flora Court
D3	Breton Side	B2	Flora Street
D3	Buckwell Street	A2	Francis Street
E1	Camden Street	B2	Frederick Street East
C1	Castle Street	D4	Friar's Parade
E4	Castle Street	B5	Garden Crescent
A2	Cathedral Street	E2	Gasking Street
D3	Catherine Street	A3	George Place
B1	Cecil Street	E1	Gibbon Lane
B5	Central Road	E1	Gibbons Street
E1	Chapel Street	E1	Gilwell Street
E2	Charles Cross	D1	Glanville Street
D2	Charles Street	C4	Grand Hotel Road
B4	Citadel Road	B5	Grand Parade
C4	Citadel Road	B5	Great Western Road
D4	Citadel Road East		

F1	Greenbank Road	A2	Neswick Street
E2	Hampton Street	C2	New George Street
B1	Harwell Street	E4	New Street
B1	Hastings Street	E1	North Hill
B1	Hastings Terrace	A1	North Road West
E2	Hawkers Avenue	E2	North Street
B1	Hetling Close	C3	Notte Street
E3	Hicks Lane	B2	Octagon Street
D3	Higher Lane	D2	Old Town Street
E2	Hill Street	C4	Osborne Place
D4	Hoe Approach	C1	Oxford Street
D3	Hoegate Street	D3	Palace Street
C5	Hoe Road	E2	Park Terrace
D3	Hoe Street	F4	Parr Street
C4	Holyrood Place	B1	Patna Place
E3	How Street	D3	Peacock Lane
B1	Ilbert Street	B1	Penrose Street
D1	James Street	A3	Phoenix Street
D1	John Lane	B5	Pier Street
A2	King Street	C2	Place de Brest
F1	Ladywell Place	F1	Plym Street
D4	Lambhay Hill	C3	Princess Street
E4	Lambhay Street	C3	Princess Way
B4	Leigham Street	B4	Prospect Place
B4	Leigham Terrace Lane	B2	Prynne Close
F1	Lipson Road	A1	Queen's Gate
F4	Lockyers Quay	B5	Radford Road
C3	Lockyer Street	E1	Radnor Place
E3	Looe Street	E1	Radnor Street
D5	Madeira Road	C2	Raleigh Street
A3	Manor Gardens	E1	Regent Street
A2	Manor Street	A2	Rendle Street
C2	Market Avenue	C3	Royal Parade
A3	Martin Street	B4	St James Place
C1	Mayflower Street	F3	St John's Bridge Road
D1	Mayflower Street	F3	St John's Road
F1	May Terrace	F1	Salisbury Road
A3	Millbay Road	A3	Sawrey Street
E2	Moon Street	F3	Shepherd's Lane
E1	Mount Street	D4	Southside Street
C3	Mulgrave Street	D5	South West Coast Path

E3	Stillman Street
A2	Stoke Road
D3	Sussex Street
F3	Sutton Road
B1	Sydney Street
D1	Tavistock Place
F4	Teats Hill Road
E4	The Barbican
B3	The Crescent
C4	The Esplanade
C4	The Promenade
E3	Tin Lane
F1	Tothill Avenue
F2	Tothill Road
E2	Trafalgar Street
A3	Union Place
A3	Union Street
E3	Vauxhall Quay
E3	Vauxhall Street
B4	Walker Terrace
A1	Wantage Gardens
B1	Well Garden
B2	Western Approach
A4	West Hoe Road
E3	Wharf Quay
D3	Whimple Street
F2	White Friars Lane
C3	Windsor Place
A1	Wolsdon Street
A1	Wyndham Lane
A1	Wyndham Mews
A1	Wyndham Square
A1	Wyndham Street East
D4	Zion Street

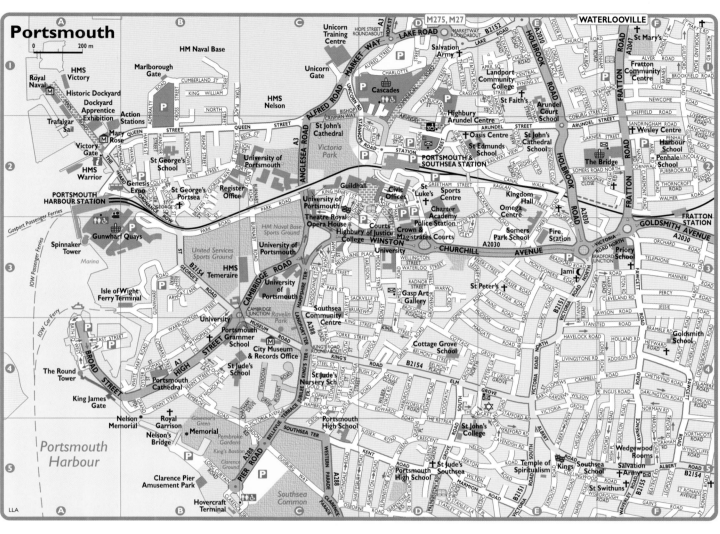

Portsmouth

Portsmouth is found on atlas page **14 H7**

F4	Addison Road	C4	Castle Road
B2	Admiralty Road	E5	Cavendish Road
E5	Albany Road	E1	Central Street
E5	Albert Grove	D1	Charlotte Street
E5	Albert Road	E5	Chelsea Road
D3	Alec Rose Lane	E5	Chester Place
E1	Alexandra Road	F4	Chetwynd Road
C1	Alfred Road	E1	Church Road
D1	Alfred Street	F2	Claremont Road
F1	Alver Road	C5	Clarence Parade
C2	Anglesea Road	F3	Cleveland Road
F2	Ariel Road	F1	Clive Road
B3	Armory Lane	B2	Clock Street
D2	Arundel Street	B2	College Street
E2	Arundel Street	E5	Collingwood Road
D5	Ashburton Road	D1	Commercial Road
E3	Bailey's Road	F2	Cornwall Road
A4	Bath Square	D4	Cottage Grove
C5	Bellevue Terrace	E2	Cottage View
D4	Belmont Place	D1	Crasswell Street
B2	Bishop Street	B2	Cross Street
C2	Bishop Crispian Way	B1	Cumberland Street
E2	Blackfriars Road	B2	Curzon Howe Road
C4	Blount Road	F4	Darlington Road
F5	Boulton Road	E1	Drummond Road
F4	Bramble Road	C5	Duisburg Way
E2	Bridgeside Close	E5	Duncan Road
B2	Britain Street	D3	Earlsdon Street
A4	Broad Street	A4	East Street
F1	Brookfield Road	D4	Eldon Street
C3	Brunswick Street	D4	Elm Grove
D1	Buckingham Street	D5	Elphinstone Road
C3	Cambridge Road	E5	Exmouth Road
E2	Campbell Road	F3	Fawcett Road
E2	Canal Walk	F4	Fawcett Road
E2	Carlisle Road	C4	Flint Street
E1	Foster Road	D1	Lake Road
F2	Fratton Road	E1	Landport Street
F5	Gain's Road	D2	Landport Terrace
E2	Garnier Street	C3	Landsdowne Street
F3	Goldsmith Avenue	F5	Lawrence Road
C4	Gold Street	F3	Lawson Road
E5	Goodwood Road	F5	Leopold Street
C5	Gordon Road	F2	Lincoln Road
C4	Great Southsea Street	C4	Little Southsea Street
D4	Green Road	E4	Livingstone Road
D2	Greetham Street	B4	Lombard Street
D3	Grosvenor Street	F4	Londesborough Road
D4	Grove Road North	E1	Lords Street
D5	Grove Road South	F4	Lorne Road
F1	Guildford Road	A1	Main Road
C2	Guildhall Walk	F3	Manners Road
B3	Gunwharf Road	D4	Margate Road
C4	Hambrook Street	D5	Marmion Road
C3	Hampshire Terrace	D2	Mary Rose Street
F5	Harold Road	C3	Melbourne Place
B2	Havant Street	D5	Merton Road
E4	Havelock Road	D3	Middle Street
E5	Hereford Road	E2	Milford Road
B4	Highbury Street	E3	Montgomerie Road
B4	High Street	F1	Moorland Road
E1	Holbrook Road	C4	Museum Road
D4	Holland Road	E5	Napier Road
F4	Hyde Park Road	D5	Nelson Road
F3	Inglis Road	F1	Newcome Road
F3	Jessie Road	C5	Nightingale Road
C4	Jubilee Terrace	D4	Norfolk Street
D5	Kent Road	F4	Norman Road
B2	Kent Street	F1	Olinda Street
E1	King Albert Street	F3	Orchard Road
C2	King Henry I Street	B2	Ordnance Row
C4	King's Road	C5	Osborne Road
C4	King's Terrace	E4	Outram Road
C4	King Street	F5	Oxford Road
B1	King William Street	B4	Oyster Street
		E3	Pains Road
D1	Lake Road	E1	Stamford Street
E1	Landport Street	D2	Stanhope Road
B3	Park Road	E4	Stansted Road
D4	Pelham Road	D2	Station Street
B4	Pembroke Road	C4	Steel Street
F2	Penhale Road	C4	Stone Street
B4	Penny Street	D5	Sussex Road
F3	Percy Road	F4	Sutherland Road
C5	Pier Road	F4	Talbot Road
E3	Playfair Road	F3	Telephone Road
D5	Portland Road	D1	Temple Street
F2	Purbrook Road	A2	The Hard
D5	Queens Crescent	D5	The Retreat
B2	Queen Street	D4	The Thicket
E2	Raglan Street	F2	Thorncroft Road
E2	Railway View	F1	Tottenham Road
D5	Richmond Place	F4	Trevor Road
D3	Rivers Street	C1	Unicorn Road
E3	Rugby Road	D2	Upper Arundel Street
C3	Sackville Street	C5	Victoria Avenue
E4	St Andrews Road	E4	Victoria Grove
E4	St Bartholomews Gardens	E4	Victoria Road North
E4	St Davids Road	F3	Victoria Road North
D4	St Edwards Road	E5	Victoria Road South
D1	St Faith's Road	F2	Vivash Road
B3	St George's Road	F2	Walmer Road
B2	St George's Square	B4	Warblington Street
B2	St George's Way	D3	Warwick Crescent
D3	St James's Road	D3	Waterloo Street
B2	St James's Street	F5	Waverley Road
B4	St Nicholas Street	C5	Western Parade
C3	St Paul's Road	A4	West Street
E4	St Peters Grove	B4	White Hart Road
B4	St Thomas's Street	E4	Wilson Grove
C2	Sandringham Road	C3	Wiltshire Street
F2	Shaftesbury Road	D3	Winston Churchill Avenue
D4	Somers Road	E5	Wisborough Road
E3	Somers Road	D4	Woodpath
E2	Somers Road North	C4	Woodville Drive
C5	Southsea Terrace	C4	Yarborough Road
E4	Stafford Road	C4	Yorke Street

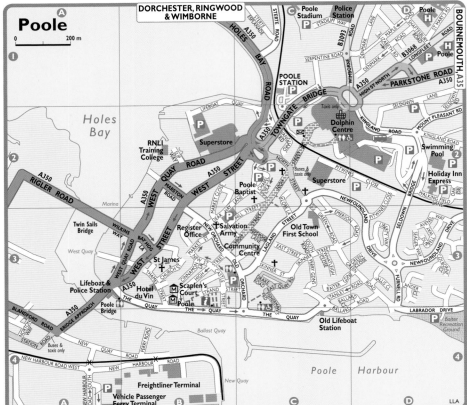

Poole

Poole is found on atlas page **12 H6**

D3	Avenel Way	A4	New Quay Road
C3	Baiter Gardens	B3	New Street
C3	Ballard Close	C2	North Street
C4	Ballard Road	A4	Norton Way
B3	Bay Hog Lane	D2	Oak Drive
A3	Blandford Road	B3	Old Orchard
A4	Bridge Approach	D1	Parkstone Road
B3	Castle Street	C3	Perry Gardens
C2	Chapel Lane	C2	Pitwines Close
B3	Church Street	A3	Poole Bridge
B3	Cinnamon Lane	A2	Rigler Road
D3	Colborne Close	D1	St Mary's Road
B3	Dear Hay Lane	D3	Seager Way
D1	Denmark Lane	D3	Seldown Bridge
D1	Denmark Road	D2	Seldown Lane
C3	Drake Road	D2	Seldown Road
D3	Durrell Way	C1	Serpentine Road
C3	East Quay Road	D1	Shaftesbury Road
C3	East Street	C3	Skinner Street
D1	Elizabeth Road	B2	Slip Way
C3	Emerson Road	C3	South Road
B4	Ferry Road	C1	Stadium Way
C3	Fisherman's Road	C3	Stanley Road
D3	Furnell Road	C1	Sterte Esplanade
C2	Globe Lane	C1	Sterte Road
D3	Green Close	B3	Strand Street
C3	Green Road	B3	Thames Street
B3	High Street	B3	The Quay
D1	High Street North	C2	Towngate Bridge
C3	Hill Street	A3	Twin Sails Bridge
C1	Holes Bay Road	D3	Vallis Close
D2	Kingland Road	C2	Vanguard Road
D4	Labrador Drive	D2	Walking Field Lane
C3	Lagland Street	C3	Westons Lane
D3	Lander Close	B3	West Quay Road
D3	Liberty Way	B3	West Street
B2	Lifeboat Quay	C3	Whatleigh Close
D1	Longfleet Road	A3	Wilkins Way
D1	Maple Road	D1	Wimborne Road
B2	Market Close		
B3	Market Street		
B2	Marston Road		
D2	Mount Pleasant Road		
C2	Newfoundland Drive		
A4	New Harbour Road		
A4	New Harbour Road South		
A4	New Harbour Road West		
B3	New Orchard		

Preston

Preston is found on atlas page **88 G5**

A1	Adelphi Street	C2	Lancaster Road
A3	Arthur Street	C1	Lancaster Road North
C4	Avenham Lane	C4	Latham Street
C3	Avenham Road	B1	Lawson Street
C3	Avenham Street	A2	Leighton Street
C4	Berwick Road	C1	Lund Street
C2	Birley Street	B3	Lune Street
C3	Boltons Court	D3	Manchester Road
A3	Bow Lane	C2	Market Street
B3	Butler Street	B2	Market Street West
C2	Carlisle Road	A2	Marsh Lane
C4	Chaddock Street	A1	Maudland Bank
B3	Chapel Street	A1	Maudland Road
D4	Charlotte Street	C1	Meadow Street
C3	Cheapside	B1	Moor Lane
A3	Christ Church Street	B3	Mount Street
C3	Church Street	C1	North Road
D4	Clarendon Street	D3	Oak Street
B2	Corporation Street	C2	Ormskirk Road
B3	Corporation Street	C3	Oxford Street
B1	Craggs Row	A1	Pedder Street
C3	Cross Street	D2	Percy Street
B1	Crown Street	A3	Pitt Street
D1	Deepdale Road	D2	Pole Street
D2	Derby Street	D1	Pump Street
C2	Earl Street	D3	Queen Street
B4	East Cliff	B4	Ribblesdale Place
D1	East Street	B2	Ring Way
D2	Edmund Street	D3	Rose Street
A2	Edward Street	D3	St Austin's Road
B1	Elizabeth Street	D1	St Paul's Road
B3	Fishergate	D1	St Paul's Square
A4	Fishergate Hill	B1	St Peter's Street
B3	Fleet Street	C1	Sedgwick Street
B3	Fox Street	D3	Shepherd Street
B2	Friargate	B2	Snow Hill
A1	Fylde Road	D1	Stanleyfield Road
C3	Glover Street	C4	Starkie Street
C4	Great Avenham Street	C3	Syke Street
B2	Great Shaw Street	C2	Tithebarn Street
D2	Grimshaw Street	B1	Walker Street
C3	Guildhall Street	A3	Walton's Parade
B1	Harrington Street	C2	Ward's End
B2	Heatley Street	B1	Warwick Street
D4	Herschell Street	A4	West Cliff
D1	Holstein Street	A4	West Cliff Terrace
D2	Hopwood Street	B3	Winkley Square
D1	Jutland Street		

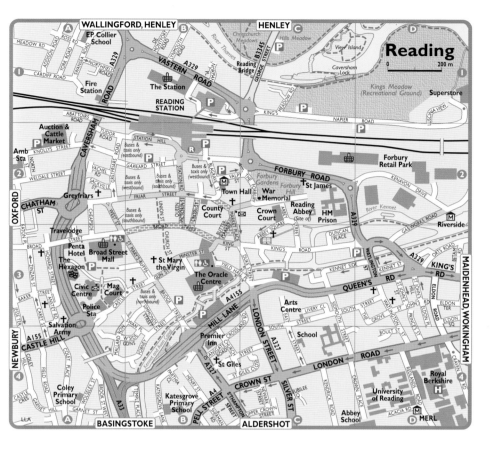

Reading

Reading is found on atlas page **35 K10**

C3	Abbey Square		D3	King's Road
C2	Abbey Street		B3	King Street
A1	Addison Road		A2	Knollys Street
A3	Anstey Road		C3	Livery Close
A3	Baker Street		C4	London Road
B2	Blagrave Street		C3	London Street
D4	Boult Street		A4	Mallard Row
B3	Bridge Street		B2	Market Place
A3	Broad Street		B4	Mill Lane
A4	Brook Street West		B3	Minster Street
B3	Buttermarket		C1	Napier Road
A1	Cardiff Road		C4	Newark Street
A3	Carey Street		A1	Northfield Road
A4	Castle Hill		B4	Parthia Close
A3	Castle Street		B4	Pell Street
A2	Caversham Road		D3	Prince's Street
A2	Chatham Street		C3	Queen's Road
A2	Cheapside		B2	Queen Victoria Street
B3	Church Street		D4	Redlands Road
B4	Church Street		A1	Ross Road
A4	Coley Place		A2	Sackville Street
D4	Craven Road		B4	St Giles Close
B4	Crossland Road		D3	St John's Road
B2	Cross Street		B3	St Mary's Butts
C4	Crown Street		C3	Sidmouth Street
B4	Deansgate Road		C4	Silver Street
C3	Duke Street		B3	Simmonds Street
C3	Duncan Place		A4	Southampton Street
C3	East Street		C3	South Street
D3	Eldon Road		B2	Station Hill
A4	Field Road		B2	Station Road
B4	Fobney Street		B3	Swan Place
C2	Forbury Road		A1	Swansea Road
B2	Friar Street		C2	The Forbury
A4	Garnet Street		A2	Tudor Road
B2	Garrard Street		B2	Union Street
D3	Gas Works Road		C4	Upper Crown Street
C1	George Street		A2	Vachel Road
A2	Greyfriars Road		B2	Valpy Street
B3	Gun Street		B1	Vastern Road
B4	Henry Street		B4	Waterside Gardens
A3	Howard Street		D3	Watlington Street
B4	Katesgrove Lane		A2	Weldale Street
D2	Kenavon Drive		A2	West Street
C4	Kendrick Road		A4	Wolseley Street
C3	Kennet Side		B3	Yield Hall Place
D3	Kennet Street		A1	York Road
C1	King's Meadow Road		A3	Zinzan Street

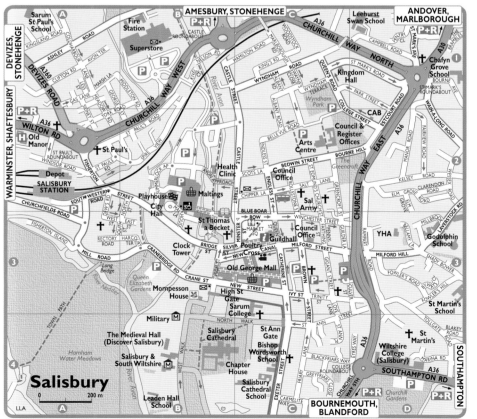

Salisbury

Salisbury is found on atlas page **21 M9**

C1	Albany Road		A1	Kingsland Road
A1	Ashley Road		C1	King's Road
B2	Avon Approach		D3	Laverstock Road
C2	Bedwin Street		B3	Malthouse Lane
C2	Belle Vue Road		D2	Manor Road
C4	Blackfriars Way		C1	Marlborough Road
C3	Blue Boar Row		A1	Meadow Road
D1	Bourne Avenue		A1	Middleton Road
C2	Bourne Hill		D3	Milford Hill
B3	Bridge Street		C3	Milford Street
C3	Brown Street		A3	Mill Road
D1	Campbell Road		C3	Minster Street
B1	Castle Street		B1	Nelson Road
C3	Catherine Street		B3	New Canal
C2	Chipper Lane		B3	New Street
A2	Churchfields Road		B3	North Street
D3	Churchill Way East		D1	Park Street
C1	Churchill Way North		D1	Pennyfarthing Street
C4	Churchill Way South		C1	Queen's Road
B2	Churchill Way West		C3	Queen Street
D2	Clarendon Road		D3	Rampart Road
A1	Clifton Road		A3	Rectory Road
C1	Coldharbour Lane		C2	Rollestone Street
C1	College Street		C4	St Ann Street
B3	Cranebridge Road		C2	St Edmund's Church Street
B3	Crane Street		D1	St Mark's Avenue
A1	Devizes Road		D1	St Mark's Road
A3	Dew's Road		B2	St Paul's Road
B3	East Street		C2	Salt Lane
D2	Elm Grove		C2	Scots Lane
D2	Elm Grove Road		A1	Sidney Street
C2	Endless Street		B3	Silver Street
D2	Estcourt Road		D4	Southampton Road
C4	Exeter Street		A3	South Street
D4	Eyres Way		A2	South Western Road
D2	Fairview Road		B2	Spire View
A2	Fisherton Street		B2	Summerlock Approach
D3	Fowler's Road		D4	Tollgate Road
C4	Friary Lane		C3	Trinity Street
A1	Gas Lane		D1	Wain-A-Long Road
A1	George Street		D2	Wessex Road
C3	Gigant Street		A3	West Street
C2	Greencroft Street		A2	Wilton Road
C3	Guilder Lane		A3	Winchester Street
C1	Hamilton Road		A2	Windsor Road
B3	High Street		C1	Woodstock Road
C3	Ivy Street		C1	Wyndham Road
D2	Kelsey Road		A2	York Road

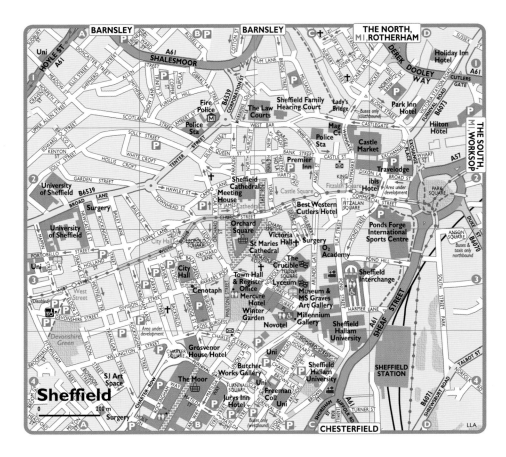

Sheffield

Sheffield is found on atlas page **84 E3**

C2	Angel Street	C4	Howard Street
C3	Arundel Gate	A1	Hoyle Street
C4	Arundel Street	C2	King Street
B3	Backfields	B1	Lambert Street
A2	Bailey Street	B3	Leopold Street
B3	Balm Green	A3	Mappin Street
C2	Bank Street	B4	Matilda Street
B3	Barkers Pool	C2	Meetinghouse Lane
A2	Broad Lane	C2	Mulberry Street
D2	Broad Street	A2	Newcastle Street
C4	Brown Street	C2	New Street
B3	Cambridge Street	C3	Norfolk Street
B2	Campo Lane	B2	North Church Street
B3	Carver Street	B3	Orchard Street
C1	Castlegate	B2	Paradise Street
C2	Castle Street	B3	Pinstone Street
B4	Charles Street	C3	Pond Hill
A4	Charter Row	C3	Pond Street
B2	Church Street	A3	Portobello Street
C2	Commercial Street	A2	Queen Street
B1	Corporation Street	A2	Rockingham Street
B3	Cross Burgess Street	B2	St James Street
D1	Cutlers Gate	C2	Scargill Croft
D1	Derek Dooley Way	A1	Scotland Street
A3	Devonshire Street	B1	Shalesmoor
A3	Division Street	D4	Sheaf Street
C2	Dixon Lane	C4	Shoreham Street
D2	Duke Street	D4	Shrewsbury Road
D2	Exchange Street	B2	Silver Street
B4	Eyre Street	A1	Smithfield
C2	Fig Tree Lane	C2	Snig Hill
A4	Fitzwilliam Street	A2	Solly Street
C3	Flat Street	C4	Suffolk Road
B1	Furnace Hill	C3	Surrey Street
B4	Furnival Gate	D4	Talbot Street
D1	Furnival Road	B2	Tenter Street
C4	Furnival Street	B2	Townhead Street
A2	Garden Street	A4	Trafalgar Street
C2	George Street	B3	Trippet Lane
B1	Gibralter Street	B2	Union Street
C3	Harmer Lane	B2	Vicar Lane
C2	Harts Head	D1	Victoria Station Road
B2	Hawley Street	C2	Waingate
C2	Haymarket	A4	Wellington Street
C2	High Street	B2	West Bar
A3	Holland Street	A3	West Street
A2	Hollis Croft	A2	White Croft
B3	Holly Street	C2	York Street

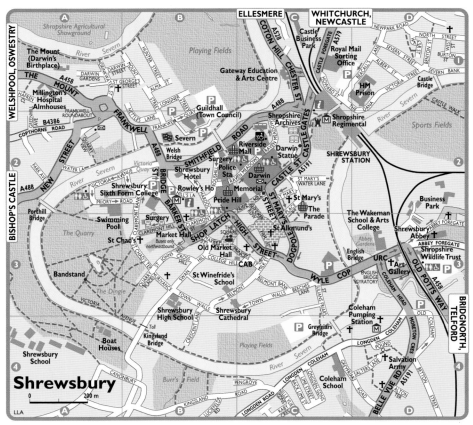

Shrewsbury

Shrewsbury is found on atlas page **56 H2**

D3	Abbey Foregate	B1	Longner Street
D1	Albert Street	B4	Luciefelde Road
B1	Alma Street	B2	Mardol
C4	Back Lime Street	B3	Market Street
B2	Barker Street	C3	Milk Street
D1	Beacall's Lane	D4	Moreton Crescent
C3	Beeches Lane	B1	Mount Street
C4	Belle Vue Gardens	B3	Murivance
D4	Belle Vue Road	B1	Nettles Lane
B3	Belmont	D1	Newpark Road
C3	Belmont Bank	A2	New Street
D1	Benyon Street	D1	North Street
D4	Betton Street	D3	Old Coleham
B2	Bridge Street	D3	Old Potts Way
D1	Burton Street	A2	Park Avenue
C2	Butcher Row	C4	Pengrove
A4	Canonbury	D4	Pound Close
C1	Castle Foregate	C2	Pride Hill
C2	Castle Gates	B3	Princess Street
C2	Castle Street	A2	Priory Road
C1	Chester Street	A2	Quarry Place
B3	Claremont Bank	A2	Quarry View
B3	Claremont Hill	C4	Raby Crescent
B3	Claremont Street	B2	Raven Meadows
D3	Coleham Head	B2	Roushill
B3	College Hill	B3	St Chad's Terrace
A2	Copthorne Road	A1	St George's Street
C1	Coton Hill	B3	St Johns Hill
B4	Crescent Lane	B3	St Julians Friars
B3	Cross Hill	C2	St Mary's Place
A1	Darwin Gardens	C2	St Mary's Street
A1	Darwin Street	C2	St Mary's Water Lane
C3	Dogpole	D4	Salters Lane
A1	Drinkwater Street	D1	Severn Bank
C3	Fish Street	D1	Severn Street
A2	Frankwell	B3	Shop Latch
B2	Frankwell Quay	B3	Smithfield Road
A2	Greenhill Avenue	B3	Swan Hill
C4	Greyfriars Road	D1	The Dana
C3	High Street	A1	The Mount
B2	Hill's Lane	B3	The Square
C1	Howard Street	B3	Town Walls
B1	Hunter Street	A2	Victoria Avenue
B4	Kingsland Road	D1	Victoria Street
C4	Lime Street	A2	Water Lane
C4	Longden Coleham	D1	Water Street
C4	Longden Gardens	D1	West Street
C4	Longden Road	C3	Wyle Cop

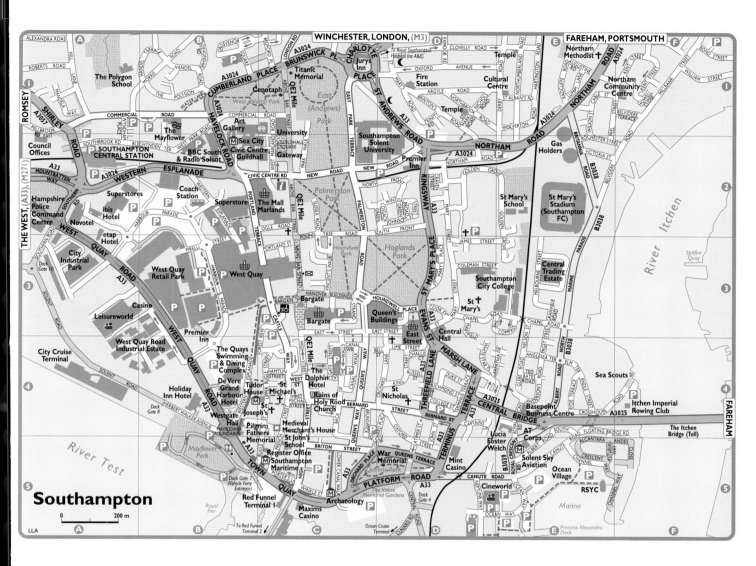

Southampton

Southampton is found on atlas page **14 D4**

C1	Above Bar Street
E4	Albert Road North
E5	Albert Road South
E5	Alcantara Crescent
A1	Alexandra Road
E4	Anderson's Road
F5	Andes Close
E4	Anglesea Terrace
D1	Argyle Road
E5	Asturias Way
E1	Augustine Road
C4	Back Of The Walls
C3	Bargate Street
C1	Bedford Place
D4	Bell Street
E2	Belvidere Road
F1	Belvidere Terrace
C4	Bernard Street
B2	Blechynden Terrace
F1	Bond Street
D1	Brinton's Road
E1	Britannia Road
C5	Briton Street
D2	Broad Green
C1	Brunswick Place
C4	Brunswick Square
C5	Bugle Street
E1	Cable Street
C4	Canal Walk
D5	Canute Road
D4	Captains Place
D4	Carpathia Drive
C3	Castle Way
D4	Central Bridge
D5	Central Road
D4	Challis Court

E5	Channel Way
D3	Chapel Road
C1	Charlotte Place
B2	Civic Centre Road
D1	Clovelly Road
D3	Coleman Street
D4	College Street
A1	Commercial Road
D3	Cook Street
D2	Cossack Green
D2	Craven Street
E4	Crosshouse Road
B1	Cumberland Place
D5	Cunard Road
E1	Derby Road
B1	Devonshire Road
D4	Duke Street
C1	East Park Terrace
C3	East Street
E4	Elm Terrace
E4	Endle Street
D3	Evans Street
D1	Exmoor Road
E4	Floating Bridge Road
C4	Forest View
C5	French Street
E4	Glebe Road
D2	Golden Grove
E3	Granville Road
B1	Grosvenor Square
C4	Hamtun Street
B1	Handel Road
B1	Handel Terrace
C3	Hanover Buildings
B2	Harbour Parade

E1	Hartington Road
B1	Havelock Road
B4	Herbert Walker Avenue
C4	High Street
A1	Hill Lane
D3	Houndwell Place
F1	Howell Close
F4	Itchen Bridge
D3	James Street
D2	Johnson Street
D5	John Street
F1	Kent Street
D4	King Street
D2	Kingsway
D5	Latimer Street
D4	Lime Street
C1	London Road
C5	Lower Canal Walk
E1	Lumpy Lane
A1	Mandela Way
E3	Marine Parade
D4	Marsh Lane
D3	Maryfield
B4	Mayflower Roundabout
E3	Melbourne Street
F1	Millbank Street
A1	Millbrook Road East
B1	Morris Road
A2	Mountbatten Way
E4	Nelson Street
D5	Neptune Way
C2	New Road
D1	Nichols Road
D2	Northam Road
D1	Northbrook Road
C2	North Front

E1	Northumberland Road
D5	Ocean Way
C2	Ogle Road
C5	Orchard Place
D1	Oxford Avenue
D4	Oxford Street
E4	Paget Street
C2	Palmerston Road
C2	Park Walk
E1	Peel Street
B3	Pirelli Street
C5	Platform Road
C3	Portland Street
B2	Portland Terrace
C3	Pound Tree Road
D5	Queens Terrace
C4	Queen's Way
E1	Radcliffe Road
D4	Richmond Street
A1	Roberts Road
E2	Rochester Street
E5	Royal Crescent Road
D4	Russell Street
E4	Ryde Terrace
E1	St Alban's Road
D1	St Andrews Road
D1	St Marks Road
D3	St Mary's Place
D1	St Mary's Road
D2	St Mary Street
C4	St Michael Street
A1	Shirley Road
A3	Solent Road
A2	Southbrook Road
A2	Southern Road

C2	South Front
C3	Strand
C2	Sussex Road
E4	Ted Bates Road
D5	Terminus Terrace
D3	The Compass
B1	The Polygon
D4	Threefield Lane
B5	Town Quay
D1	Trinity Road
C4	Upper Bugle Street
E2	Victoria Street
C3	Vincent's Walk
B1	Water Lane
A2	Western Esplanade
B4	Western Esplanade
C2	West Marlands Road
B1	West Park Road
A2	West Quay Road
C4	West Street
D4	White Star Place
F1	William Street
E1	Wilson Street
C5	Winkle Street
D2	Winton Street
E1	Wolverton Road
A1	Wyndham Place

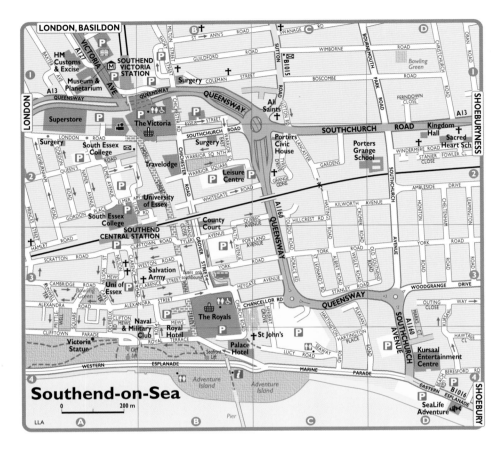

Southend-on-Sea

Southend-on-Sea is found on atlas page **38 E4**

C3	Albert Road	D4	Kursaal Way
A3	Alexandra Road	C2	Lancaster Gardens
A3	Alexandra Street	D2	Leamington Road
D2	Ambleside Drive	A2	London Road
A2	Ashburnham Road	C4	Lucy Road
B3	Baltic Avenue	A2	Luker Road
A1	Baxter Avenue	C4	Marine Parade
D4	Beach Road	B1	Milton Street
D4	Beresford Road	A2	Napier Avenue
C1	Boscombe Road	A3	Nelson Street
D1	Bournemouth Park Road	D1	Oban Road
A3	Cambridge Road	D3	Old Southend Road
A3	Capel Terrace	D3	Outing Close
B3	Chancellor Road	B2	Pitmans Close
D2	Cheltenham Road	C3	Pleasant Road
B1	Chichester Road	B3	Portland Avenue
D1	Christchurch Road	A2	Princes Street
B3	Church Road	A3	Prittlewell Square
A3	Clarence Road	B2	Quebec Avenue
B3	Clarence Street	A2	Queen's Road
A4	Clifftown Parade	A1	Queensway
B3	Clifftown Road	B4	Royal Terrace
B1	Coleman Street	A3	Runwell Terrace
C2	Cromer Road	B1	St Ann's Road
A4	Devereux Road	C3	St Leonard's Road
D4	Eastern Esplanade	A3	Scratton Road
A2	Elmer Approach	B1	Short Street
A2	Elmer Avenue	D2	Southchurch Avenue
B1	Essex Street	B2	Southchurch Road
D1	Ferndown Close	D2	Stanier Close
D2	Fowler Close	C3	Stanley Road
A2	Gordon Place	C1	Sutton Road
A2	Gordon Road	C1	Swanage Road
C2	Grange Gardens	C2	Toledo Road
B3	Grover Street	B3	Tylers Avenue
B1	Guildford Road	C2	Tyrel Drive
A3	Hamlet Road	A1	Victoria Avenue
C4	Hartington Place	B2	Warrior Square East
C3	Hartington Road	B2	Warrior Square North
C2	Hastings Road	B2	Warrior Square
D4	Hawtree Close	C3	Wesley Road
C3	Herbert Grove	A4	Western Esplanade
B3	Heygate Avenue	B3	Weston Road
B2	High Street	B2	Whitegate Road
C2	Hillcrest Road	C1	Wimborne Road
D2	Honiton Road	D2	Windermere Road
C3	Horace Road	D3	Woodgrange Drive
C2	Kilworth Avenue	B3	York Road

Stirling

Stirling is found on atlas page **133 M9**

D2	Abbey Road	C3	King Street
D1	Abbotsford Place	C1	Lovers Walk
B4	Abercromby Place	B1	Lower Bridge Street
B3	Academy Road	B2	Lower Castlehill
A3	Albert Place	B2	Mar Place
D1	Alexandra Place	C3	Maxwell Place
B4	Allan Park	D4	Meadowforth Road
D2	Argyll Avenue	D1	Millar Place
A1	Back O' Hill Road	B3	Morris Terrace
B3	Baker Street	C3	Murray Place
A1	Ballengeich Road	C4	Ninians Road
A3	Balmoral Place	C2	Park Lane
B3	Bank Street	B4	Park Terrace
B2	Barn Road	C4	Pitt Terrace
C2	Barnton Street	D4	Players Road
B1	Bayne Street	C4	Port Street
B3	Bow Street	B3	Princes Street
B3	Broad Street	D1	Queenshaugh Drive
B1	Bruce Street	A4	Queens Road
C1	Burghmuir Road	B2	Queen Street
B2	Castle Court	A2	Raploch Road
B4	Clarendon Place	C2	Ronald Place
B3	Clarendon Road	C2	Rosebery Place
B3	Corn Exchange Road	C2	Rosebery Terrace
B1	Cowane Street	A3	Royal Gardens
C4	Craigs Roundabout	B3	St John Street
B2	Crofthead Court	B2	St Mary's Wynd
C1	Customs Roundabout	C3	Seaforth Place
D1	Dean Crescent	D1	Shiphaugh Place
C2	Douglas Street	C2	Shore Road
A1	Duff Crescent	B3	Spittal Street
B4	Dumbarton Road	D2	Sutherland Avenue
D1	Edward Avenue	B2	Tannery Lane
C1	Edward Road	B1	Union Street
D2	Forrest Road	B2	Upper Bridge Street
C2	Forth Crescent	A2	Upper Castlehill
C1	Forth Street	C2	Upper Craigs
C1	Forth View	A4	Victoria Place
B4	Glebe Avenue	B3	Victoria Road
B4	Glebe Crescent	A4	Victoria Square
A1	Glendevon Drive	C2	Wallace Street
C2	Goosecroft Road	D1	Waverley Crescent
A1	Gowanhill Gardens	C4	Wellgreen Lane
A3	Greenwood Avenue	C4	Wellgreen Road
B1	Harvey Wynd	B2	Whinwell Road
B2	Irvine Place	B4	Windsor Place
C2	James Street		
B4	Kings Park Road		

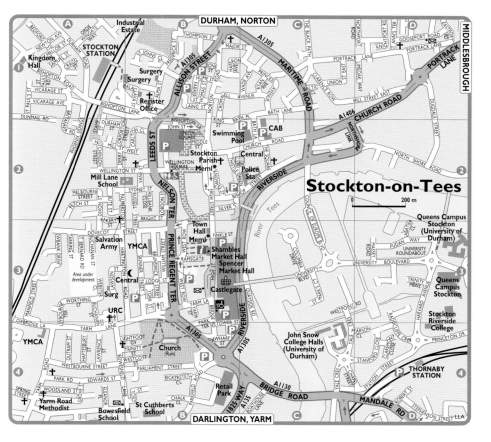

Stockton-on-Tees

Stockton-on-Tees is found on atlas page **104 D7**

B4	1825 Way	D3	Massey Road
B1	Allison Street	A2	Melbourne Street
B1	Alma Street	B2	Middle Street
C1	Bath Lane	A2	Mill Street West
A1	Bedford Street	B2	Nelson Terrace
B2	Bishop Street	D2	North Shore Road
A1	Bishopton Lane	D1	Northport Road
A1	Bishopton Road	C2	Northshore Link
A4	Bowesfield Lane	B1	Norton Road
B3	Bridge Road	A2	Palmerston Street
C4	Bridge Road	A4	Park Road
B2	Bright Street	C3	Park Terrace
A1	Britannia Road	B4	Parkfield Road
B3	Brunswick Street	B4	Parliament Street
A2	Bute Street	D1	Portrack Lane
D1	Church Road	B3	Prince Regent Terrace
C1	Clarence Row	C1	Princess Avenue
A2	Corportion Street	D4	Princeton Drive
C2	Council of Europe	C3	Quayside Road
	Boulevard	D3	Raddcliffe Crescent
B1	Cromwell Avenue	B3	Ramsgate
A2	Dixon Street	C4	Riverside
A3	Dovecot Street	B2	Russell Street
D1	Dugdale Street	A1	St Paul's Street
A1	Durham Road	B2	Silver Street
A2	Durham Street	B3	Skinner Street
A4	Edwards Street	D4	Station Street
B1	Farrer Street	B2	Sydney Street
C3	Finkle Street	D2	The Square
B1	Frederick Street	C2	Thistle Green
D3	Fudan Way	B1	Thomas Street
D1	Gooseport Road	B1	Thompson Street
A3	Hartington Road	B4	Tower Street
D3	Harvard Avenue	C1	Union Street East
B2	High Street	C3	University Boulevard
D1	Hill Street East	B2	Vane Street
B1	Hume Street	A1	Vicarage Street
A2	Hutchinson Street	A2	Wellington Street
B2	John Street	B3	West Row
B2	King Street	A4	Westbourne Street
D1	Knightport Road	C3	Westpoint Road
C2	Knowles Street	B4	Wharf Street
B1	Laing Street	B3	William Street
B2	Leeds Street	A4	Woodland Street
B2	Lobdon Street	A3	Worthing Street
B3	Lodge Street	C4	Yale Crescent
D4	Mandale Road	A4	Yarm Lane
C1	Maritime Road	A4	Yarm Road

Stoke-on-Trent (Hanley)

Stoke-on-Trent (Hanley) is found on atlas page **70 F5**

B3	Albion Street	C3	Lichfield Street
B3	Bagnall Street	D2	Linfield Road
D3	Balfour Street	D1	Lower Mayer Street
D1	Baskerville Road	A1	Lowther Street
B4	Bathesda Street	D3	Ludlow Street
C4	Bernard Street	B1	Malam Street
B3	Bethesda Street	B2	Marsh Street
C3	Birch Terrace	B2	Marsh Street North
C3	Botteslow Street	B3	Marsh Street South
B3	Broad Street	C1	Mayer Street
C1	Broom Street	B3	Mersey Street
B3	Brunswick Street	A4	Milton Street
B1	Bryan Street	A4	Mount Pleasant
C2	Bucknall New Road	D1	Mynors Street
D2	Bucknall Old Road	B2	New Hall Street
B4	Cardiff Grove	C4	Ogden Road
A1	Century Street	C3	Old Hall Street
C3	Charles Street	C1	Old Town Road
B3	Cheapside	B3	Pall Mall
A1	Chelwood Street	C2	Percy Street
A3	Clough Street	B3	Piccadilly
A4	Clyde Street	A1	Portland Street
D3	Commercial Road	B1	Potteries Way
A1	Denbigh Street	B2	Quadrant Road
C4	Derby Street	C4	Regent Road
D2	Dyke Street	A1	Rutland Street
C4	Eastwood Road	D1	St John Street
D2	Eaton Street	D3	St Luke Street
A2	Etruria Road	B1	Sampson Street
C1	Festing Street	A4	Sheaf Street
B2	Foundry Street	A4	Slippery Lane
C2	Garth Street	A4	Snow Hill
C3	Gilman Street	B2	Stafford Street
C2	Goodson Street	A4	Sun Street
C1	Grafton Street	C3	Tontine Street
B1	Hanover Street	C2	Town Road
C4	Harley Street	B1	Trafalgar Street
C2	Hillchurch	B2	Trinity Street
C2	Hillcrest Street	B1	Union Street
B4	Hinde Street	C2	Upper Hillchurch Street
B1	Hope Street	C2	Upper Huntbach Street
C3	Hordley Street	B3	Warner Street
C2	Huntbach Street	D3	Waterloo Street
C4	Jasper Street	D3	Well Street
D1	Jervis Street	D3	Wellington Road
D1	John Bright Street	D3	Wellington Street
B3	John Street	A4	Yates Street
D1	Keelings Road	B1	York Street

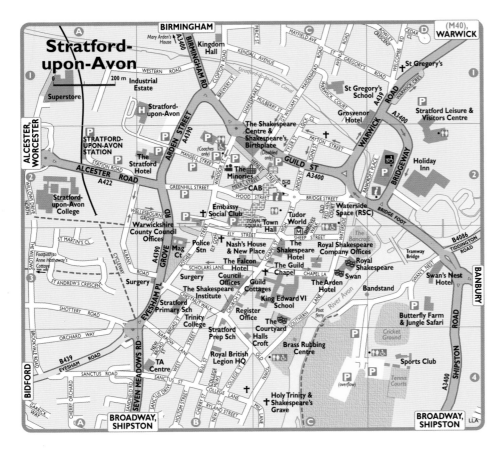

Stratford-upon-Avon

Stratford-upon-Avon is found on atlas page **47 P3**

A3	Albany Road	C2	Old Red Hen Court
A2	Alcester Road	C4	Old Town
B2	Arden Street	A4	Orchard Way
C1	Avenue Road	C2	Payton Street
C2	Bancroft Place	C1	Percy Street
B1	Birmingham Road	B3	Rother Street
B1	Brewery Street	D1	Rowley Crescent
D2	Bridge Foot	B4	Ryland Street
C2	Bridge Street	A3	St Andrew's Crescent
D2	Bridgeway	C1	St Gregory's Road
B4	Broad Street	A3	St Martin's Close
A4	Brookvale Road	B4	Sanctus Drive
B4	Bull Street	A4	Sanctus Road
D1	Cedar Close	B4	Sanctus Street
C3	Chapel Lane	A4	Sandfield Road
C3	Chapel Street	B3	Scholars Lane
A4	Cherry Orchard	A4	Seven Meadows Road
B4	Cherry Street	B1	Shakespeare Street
B3	Chestnut Walk	C3	Sheep Street
B3	Church Street	D4	Shipston Road
B1	Clopton Road	A3	Shottery Road
B4	College Lane	C3	Shrieves Walk
B4	College Mews	C3	Southern Lane
B4	College Street	A2	Station Road
B3	Ely Gardens	D3	Swan's Nest
B3	Ely Street	A3	The Willows
B3	Evesham Place	D3	Tiddington Road
A4	Evesham Road	B2	Town Square
A4	Garrick Way	D3	Tramway Bridge
C1	Great William Street	C2	Tyler Street
B2	Greenhill Street	C2	Union Street
B3	Grove Road	C1	Warwick Court
C2	Guild Street	D1	Warwick Crescent
B2	Henley Street	C2	Warwick Road
C3	High Street	C3	Waterside
B4	Holtom Street	D1	Welcombe Road
C2	John Street	B2	Wellesbourne Grove
B1	Kendall Avenue	B1	Western Road
C2	Lock Close	B4	West Street
C1	Maidenhead Road	A2	Willows Drive North
B2	Mansell Street	B2	Windsor Street
C1	Mayfield Avenue	B2	Wood Street
B2	Meer Street		
C4	Mill Lane		
C1	Mulberry Street		
B4	Narrow Lane		
B4	New Broad Street		
B4	New Street		

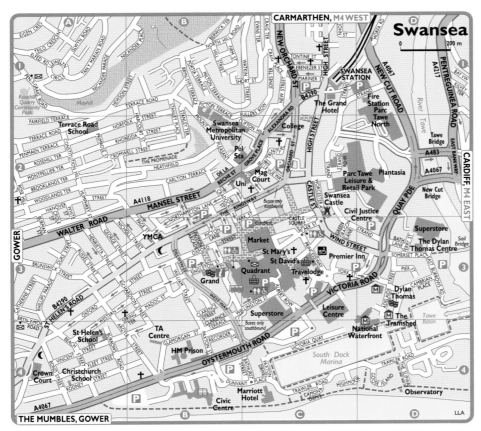

Swansea

Swansea is found on atlas page **29 J6**

D3	Adelaide Street	C1	New Orchard Street
C2	Alexandra Road	C1	New Street
A4	Argyle Street	A1	Nicander Parade
D3	Bath Lane	A3	Nicholl Street
A4	Beach Street	A2	Norfolk Street
A4	Bond Street	B1	North Hill Road
A3	Brunswick Street	B2	Northampton Lane
A4	Burrows Road	C2	Orchard Street
C3	Caer Street	A3	Oxford Street
B2	Carlton Terrace	B4	Oystermouth Road
C2	Castle Street	B3	Page Street
A3	Catherine Street	B3	Park Street
B3	Clarence Street	B4	Paxton Street
C2	Clifton Hill	D1	Pentreguinea Road
A2	Constituion Hill	A1	Pen-Y-Graig Road
B2	Cradock Street	B3	Picton Lane
C1	Craig Place	D3	Pier Street
A2	Cromwell Street	A2	Primrose Street
B2	De La Beche Street	C3	Princess Way
B3	Dillwyn Street	D2	Quay Parade
A3	Duke Street	B4	Recorder Street
B4	Dunvant Place	A2	Rhondda Street
D2	East Bank Way	A3	Richardson Street
D3	East Burrows Road	A4	Rodney Street
C1	Ebenezer Street	A2	Rose Hill
A1	Elfed Road	A3	Russel Street
D3	Ferry Street	A3	St Helen's Road
B1	Firm Street	B1	Short Street
A4	Fleet Street	B3	Singleton Street
A3	George Street	D3	Somerset Place
B4	Glamorgan Street	C1	Strand
C3	Green Lane Dragon	A1	Tan Y Marian Road
C2	Grove Place	A1	Teilo Crescent
A2	Hanover Street	A2	Terrace Road
B2	Harcourt Street	B2	The Kingsway
B2	Heathfield	C1	Tontine Street
A3	Henrietta Street	C4	Trawler Road
A1	Hewson Street	C4	Victoria Quay
C2	High Street	C3	Victoria Road
B1	Hill Street	A4	Vincent Street
A2	Humphrey Street	A3	Walter Road
A1	Islwyn Road	C1	Watkin Street
A1	Llewelyn Circle	C3	Wellington Street
B3	Madoc Street	B3	West Way
B2	Mansel Street	A4	Western Street
C1	Mariner Street	B3	William Street
B2	Mount Pleasant	C3	Wind Street
D1	New Cut Road	C3	York Street

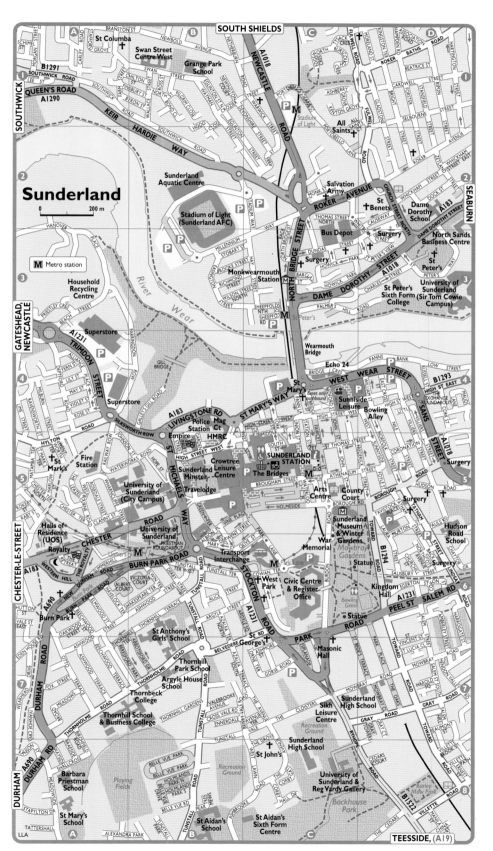

B7	Abbotsford Green
C2	Abbs Street
B6	Albion Place
B6	Alice Street
A4	Alliance Place
D6	Amberley Street
B6	Argyle Square
B6	Argyle Street
B8	Ashbrooke Road
C7	Ashmore Street
A7	Ashwood Street
A7	Ashwood Terrace
D1	Association Road
C5	Athenaeum Street
B6	Azalea Terrace North
B7	Azalea Terrace South
C3	Back North Bridge Street
A3	Beach Street
D7	Beaumont Street
C4	Bedford Street
A6	Beechwood Street
A7	Beechwood Terrace
B7	Belvedere Road
A7	Beresford Park
A7	Birchfield Road
D5	Borough Road
C4	Bridge Crescent
C4	Bridge Street
C7	Briery Vale Road
D1	Bright Street
B3	Brooke Street
C5	Brougham Street
C5	Burdon Road
B6	Burn Park Road
D1	Cardwell Street
A1	Carley Road
D3	Charles Street
A6	Chester Road
D6	Churchill Street
D2	Church Street North
A5	Clanny Street
D4	Cork Street
D5	Coronation Street
C6	Cowan Terrace
B7	Cross Vale Road
B1	Crozier Street
C3	Dame Dorothy Street
A4	Deptford Road
B6	Derby Street
B6	Derwent Street
B1	Devonshire Street
D2	Dock Street
C3	Dundas Street
A7	Durham Road
B3	Easington Street
D4	East Cross Street
A7	Eden House Road
D6	Egerton Street
B1	Eglinton Street
B1	Eglinton Street North
A6	Elmwood Street
B7	Ennerdale
A1	Farm Street
B4	Farringdon Row
C4	Fawcett Street
D1	Forster Street
A7	Fox Street
D5	Foyle Street
D5	Frederick Street
C1	Fulwell Road
B4	Galley's Gill Road
D1	Gladstone Street
C7	Gorse Road
D7	Gray Road
B5	Green Terrace
D1	Hampden Road
A2	Hanover Place
A5	Harlow Street
D6	Harrogate Street
D1	Hartington Street
A6	Havelock Terrace
C3	Hay Street
D7	Hendon Valley Road
D4	High Street East
B5	High Street West
C5	Holmeside
B5	Hope Street
C3	Howick Park
D5	Hudson Road
A5	Hylton Road
A5	Johnson Street
C4	John Street
A1	Keir Hardie Way
D5	Laura Street
A4	Lime Street
D6	Lindsay Road
D4	Little Villiers Street
B4	Livingstone Road
D4	Low Street
B6	Mary Street
D4	Mauds Lane

A8	Meadowside
C5	Middle Street
A4	Milburn Street
B3	Millennium Way
C2	Monk Street
D1	Moreland Street
A1	Morgan Street
D7	Mowbray Road
B1	Netherburn Road
B1	Newbold Avenue
C1	Newcastle Road
A6	New Durham Road
D4	Nile Street
D5	Norfolk Street
C3	North Bridge Street
D6	Northcote Avenue
B1	North Street
A6	Oakwood Street
B6	Olive Street
A7	Otto Terrace
C3	Palmer's Hill Road
D4	Panns Bank
C5	Park Lane
D6	Park Place
C6	Park Road
D5	Pauls Road
D6	Peel Street
C1	Portobello Lane
A1	Queen's Road
A5	Railway Row
A4	Ravensworth Street
B3	Richmond Street
D1	Ripon Street
C2	Roker Avenue
D1	Roker Baths Road
A5	Rosedale Street
B1	Ross Street
D4	Russell Street
C7	Ryhope Road
D7	St Bede's Terrace
C3	St Mary's Way
B5	St Michaels Way
D3	St Peter's View
C5	St Thomas' Street
D6	Salem Road
D6	Salem Street
D7	Salem Street South
D6	Salisbury Road
D4	Sans Street
D1	Selbourne Street
A6	Shakespeare Terrace
A8	Shallcross
C3	Sheepfolds Road
A4	Silksworth Row
C5	South Street
A1	Southwick Road
C2	Stadium Way
D1	Stansfield Street
C4	Station Street
B3	Stobart Street
C6	Stockton Road
B1	Swan Street
D5	Tatham Street
D5	Tatham Street Back
C7	The Avenue
C7	The Cloisters
A6	The Royalty
C2	Thomas Street North
B6	Thornhill Terrace
A7	Thornholme Road
D5	Toward Road
A4	Trimdon Street
B7	Tunstall Road
B6	Tunstall Terrace
B6	Tunstall Terrace West
B8	Tunstall Vale
C4	Union Street
B7	Valebrooke Avenue
D8	Villette Road
D4	Villiers Street
B5	Vine Place
B1	Wallace Street
C1	Warwick Street
C5	Waterloo Place
A5	Waterworks Road
A6	Wayman Street
A7	Wearhead Drive
A5	Westbourne Road
A6	Western Hill
C8	West Lawn
C5	West Street
D4	West Sunniside
C4	West Wear Street
A5	Wharncliffe Street
D2	Whickham Street
D2	Whickham Street East
D3	Whitburn Street
D4	William Street
B3	Wilson Street North
C4	York Street
D2	Zetland Street

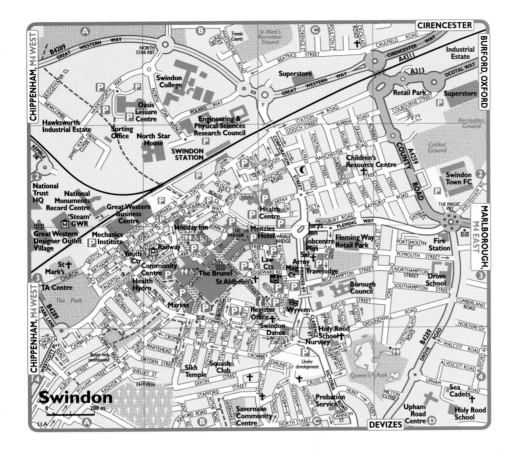

Swindon

Swindon is found on atlas page **33 M8**

A4 Albion Street	C3 Islington Street
C2 Alfred Street	B3 John Street
B4 Ashford Road	B3 King Street
B2 Aylesbury Street	A3 London Street
C2 Bathurst Road	C2 Manchester Road
C3 Beckhampton Street	B3 Market Street
B2 Bridge Street	A3 Maxwell Street
A3 Bristol Street	C2 Medgbury Road
C2 Broad Street	B2 Milford Street
A4 Cambria Bridge Road	B3 Milton Road
B3 Canal Walk	B3 Morley Street
C2 Carfax Street	B4 Morse Street
B3 Carr Street	D3 Newcastle Street
A3 Chester Street	A1 Newcombe Drive
A3 Church Place	B4 Newhall Street
D1 Cirencester Way	D3 Northampton Street
C3 Clarence Street	B1 North Star Avenue
B3 College Street	D1 Ocotal Way
B3 Commercial Road	A3 Park Lane
C2 Corporation Street	D3 Plymouth Street
D2 County Road	B1 Polaris Way
B4 Crombey Street	C2 Ponting Street
A4 Curtis Street	D3 Portsmouth Street
B4 Deacon Street	C3 Princes Street
B4 Dixon Street	C4 Prospect Hill
C4 Dover Street	B3 Queen Street
B4 Dowling Street	A4 Radnor Street
D4 Drove Road	C3 Regent Place
A4 Dryden Street	B3 Regent Street
C4 Eastcott Hill	C2 Rosebery Street
B2 East Street	C2 Salisbury Street
B3 Edgeware Road	B3 Sanford Street
C1 Elmina Road	B2 Sheppard Street
A3 Emlyn Square	D3 Southampton Street
C3 Euclid Street	B4 Stafford Street
A3 Faringdon Road	B4 Stanier Street
B3 Farnsby Street	B2 Station Road
B2 Fleet Street	C4 Swindon Road
C3 Fleming Way	A3 Tennyson Street
C2 Gladstone Street	A3 Theobald Street
C2 Gooch Street	C4 Victoria Road
C2 Graham Street	B3 Villett Street
A1 Great Western Way	A4 Westcott Place
C3 Groundwell Road	C4 Western Street
B3 Havelock Street	B4 Whitehead Street
A1 Hawksworth Way	B4 Whitney Street
C2 Haydon Street	A4 William Street
B2 Holbrook Way	D3 York Road

Taunton

Taunton is found on atlas page **18 H10**

B2 Albemarle Road	A3 Northfield Road
D3 Alfred Street	B3 North Street
C4 Alma Street	C1 Obridge Road
B2 Belvedere Road	D2 Obridge Viaduct
C4 Billetfield	B4 Old Pig Market
C4 Billet Street	A4 Parkfield Road
B2 Bridge Street	A4 Park Street
B2 Canal Road	B4 Paul Street
A4 Cann Street	C1 Plais Street
C3 Canon Street	A3 Portland Street
A4 Castle Street	B1 Priorswood Road
B1 Cheddon Road	C3 Priory Avenue
A1 Chip Lane	C2 Priory Bridge Road
D4 Church Road	D4 Queen Street
A3 Clarence Street	B1 Railway Street
A3 Cleveland Street	C3 Ranmer Road
A4 Compass Hill	A1 Raymond Street
D2 Critchard Way	A1 Rupert Street
A1 Cyril Street	B1 St Andrew's Road
B2 Deller's Wharf	C3 St Augustine Street
C3 Duke Street	B3 St James Street
C3 Eastbourne Road	A4 St John's Road
D4 Eastleigh Road	A1 Samuels Court
D3 East Reach	C4 South Road
C4 East Street	D4 South Street
B4 Fore Street	A2 Staplegrove Road
A1 Fowler Street	B2 Station Road
A2 French Weir Avenue	C3 Stephen Street
C3 Gloucester Road	C3 Stephen Way
D3 Grays Street	C3 Tancred Street
A1 Greenway Avenue	A2 The Avenue
C3 Gyffarde Street	B3 The Bridge
B4 Hammet Street	B4 The Crescent
C3 Haydon Road	C1 The Triangle
B1 Herbert Street	B1 Thomas Street
B4 High Street	D2 Toneway
C3 Hugo Street	D4 Tower Street
C4 Hurdle Way	D4 Trinity Road
C3 Laburnum Street	D4 Trinity Street
D2 Lambrook Road	B4 Upper High Street
C1 Lansdowne Road	D3 Victoria Gate
A1 Leslie Avenue	D3 Victoria Street
A2 Linden Grove	D4 Viney Street
B3 Lower Middle Street	A4 Wellington Road
B3 Magdalene Street	C3 Wilfred Road
B4 Mary Street	B1 William Street
A1 Maxwell Street	C2 Winchester Street
B3 Middle Street	B3 Wood Street

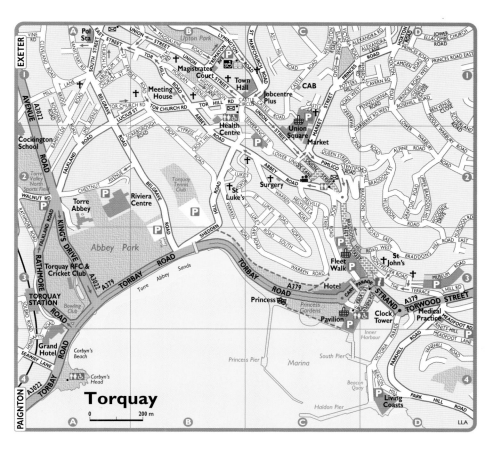

Torquay

Torquay is found on atlas page **7 N6**

B1	Abbey Road		D1	Middle Warbury Road
C1	Alexandra Road		A1	Mill Lane
C2	Alpine Road		D3	Montpellier Road
C1	Ash Hill Road		B1	Morgan Avenue
A1	Avenue Road		D3	Museum Road
A2	Bampfylde Road		B1	Palm Road
D4	Beacon Hill		D4	Parkhill Road
A1	Belgrave Road		C1	Pembroke Road
D3	Braddons Hill Road East		D1	Pennsylvania Road
C2	Braddons Hill Road West		C2	Pimlico
D2	Braddons Street		C1	Potters Hill
A1	Bridge Road		C1	Princes Road
D1	Camden Road		C2	Queen Street
C3	Cary Parade		A2	Rathmore Road
C3	Cary Road		C2	Rock Road
C1	Castle Lane		D1	Rosehill Road
C1	Castle Road		A1	St Efride's Road
D1	Cavern Road		B2	St Luke's Road
A2	Chestnut Avenue		C1	St Marychurch Road
A1	Church Lane		B2	Scarborough Road
A1	Church Street		A4	Seaway Lane
A1	Cleveland Road		B3	Shedden Hill Road
B2	Croft Hill		A3	Solbro Road
B2	Croft Road		D3	South Hill Road
A1	East Street		A1	South Street
C1	Ellacombe Road		C2	Stentiford Hill Road
A2	Falkland Road		D3	Strand
C3	Fleet Street		D1	Sutherland Road
D2	Grafton Road		C2	Temperance Street
A4	Hennapyn Road		D3	The Terrace
B1	Higher Union Lane		A4	Torbay Road
D2	Hillesdon Road		A1	Tor Church Road
D1	Hoxton Road		B1	Tor Hill Road
D3	Hunsdon Road		D3	Torwood Street
A3	King's Drive		B1	Trematon Ave
A1	Laburnum Street		D3	Trinity Hill
A2	Lime Avenue		B1	Union Street
D1	Lower Ellacombe Church		D2	Upper Braddons Hill
	Road		D4	Vanehill Road
C2	Lower Union Lane		A1	Vansittart Road
D2	Lower Warbury Road		C3	Vaughan Parade
A1	Lucius Street		D4	Victoria Parade
B1	Lymington Road		C1	Victoria Road
B1	Magdalene Road		A1	Vine Road
C2	Market Street		A2	Walnut Road
D4	Meadfoot Lane		C1	Warberry Road West
C2	Melville Lane		B2	Warren Road
C2	Melville Street		C1	Wellington Road

Tunbridge Wells

Tunbridge Wells is found on atlas page **25 N3**

C1	Albert Street		B4	High Street
C4	Arundel Road		C2	Lansdowne Road
D2	Bayhall Road		B1	Lime Hill Road
C1	Belgrave Road		A4	Linden Park Road
B4	Berkeley Road		B4	Little Mount Sion
A1	Boyne Park		A2	London Road
C4	Buckingham Road		B2	Lonsdale Gardens
C3	Calverley Gardens		B4	Madeira Park
C2	Calverley Park		A4	Major York's Road
D2	Calverley Park Gardens		B1	Meadow Road
C2	Calverley Road		A1	Molyneux Park Road
C1	Calverley Street		C2	Monson Road
D4	Cambridge Gardens		B2	Monson Way
D3	Cambridge Street		A3	Mount Edgcumbe Road
D3	Camden Hill		A2	Mount Ephraim
D3	Camden Park		B1	Mount Ephraim Road
C1	Camden Road		C3	Mountfield Gardens
D2	Carlton Road		C3	Mountfield Road
A2	Castle Road		B2	Mount Pleasant Avenue
B3	Castle Street		B2	Mount Pleasant Road
B4	Chapel Place		B4	Mount Sion
B3	Christchurch Avenue		B4	Nevill Street
A2	Church Road		B1	Newton Road
B2	Civic Way		C4	Norfolk Road
C4	Claremont Gardens		D2	North Street
C4	Claremont Road		D3	Oakfield Court Road
B2	Clarence Road		D3	Park Street
B2	Crescent Road		D2	Pembury Road
B1	Culverden Street		C4	Poona Road
C1	Dale Street		D3	Prince's Street
B1	Dudley Road		D3	Prospect Road
B4	Eden Road		B1	Rock Villa Road
A4	Eridge Road		A1	Royal Chase
C4	Farmcombe Lane		D1	St James' Road
C4	Farmcombe Road		D1	Sandrock Road
D1	Ferndale		A1	Somerville Gardens
A4	Frant Road		B3	South Green
B4	Frog Lane		B3	Station Approach
C1	Garden Road		D1	Stone Street
C1	Garden Street		C3	Sutherland Road
D3	George Street		C1	Tunnel Road
B1	Goods Station Road		B1	Upper Grosvenor Road
C4	Grecian Road		B3	Vale Avenue
B1	Grosvenor Road		B3	Vale Road
C3	Grove Hill Gardens		C1	Victoria Road
C3	Grove Hill Road		B4	Warwick Park
C3	Guildford Road		C1	Wood Street
B1	Hanover Road		B2	York Road

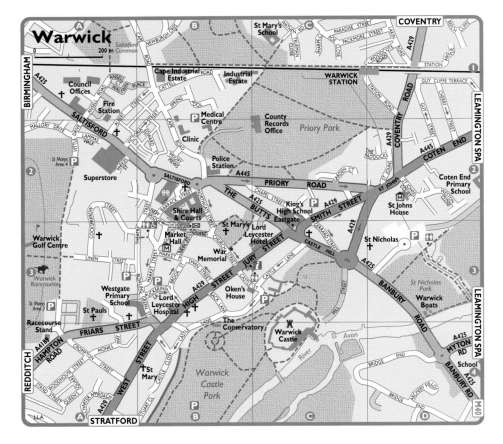

Warwick

Warwick is found on atlas page **59 L11**

A2	Albert Street	C1	Packmore Street
A1	Ansell Court	C1	Paradise Street
A1	Ansell Road	A2	Parkes Street
D4	Archery Fields	B2	Priory Mews
B3	Back Lane	C2	Priory Road
D3	Banbury Road	B3	Puckering's Lane
B2	Barrack Street	A4	Queen's Square
D1	Beech Cliffe	C1	Roe Close
B3	Bowling Green Street	D2	St Johns
D4	Bridge End	D2	St Johns Court
B3	Brook Street	A1	Saltisford
B1	Cape Road	C1	Sharpe Close
B4	Castle Close	C2	Smith Street
C3	Castle Hill	B1	Spring Pool
B4	Castle Lane	A4	Stand Street
B3	Castle Street	D1	Station Avenue
B1	Cattell Road	D1	Station Road
C2	Chapel Street	B4	Stuart Close
A4	Charter Approach	B3	Swan Street
D1	Cherry Street	B3	Theatre Street
B3	Church Street	B2	The Butts
A3	Cocksparrow Street	D2	The Paddocks
D2	Coten End	C1	Trueman Close
D2	Coventry Road	A2	Victoria Street
A4	Crompton Street	A2	Vittle Drive
B2	Edward Street	A1	Wallwin Place
A4	Friars Street	C1	Wathen Road
C2	Garden Court	D2	Weston Close
C3	Gerrard Street	A4	West Street
D1	Guy Cliffe Terrace	D1	Woodcote Road
D1	Guy Street	A4	Woodhouse Street
A4	Hampton Road		
B3	High Street		
B3	Jury Street		
D1	Lakin Road		
A2	Lammas Walk		
A3	Linen Street		
A2	Mallory Drive		
B3	Market Place		
B3	Market Street		
C3	Mill Street		
A4	Monks Way		
D4	Myton Road		
B2	New Bridge		
B1	Newburgh Crescent		
B3	New Street		
B2	Northgate Street		
B3	Old Square		

Watford

Watford is found on atlas page **50 D11**

B3	Addiscombe Road	B4	Market Street
B2	Albert Road North	B3	Marlborough Road
B2	Albert Road South	B3	Merton Road
A1	Alexandra Road	A3	Mildred Avenue
D1	Anglian Close	D1	Monica Close
C3	Beechen Grove	B1	Nascot Street
D2	Brocklesbury Close	D4	New Road
A4	Burton Avenue	C3	New Street
A2	Cassiobury Drive	C1	Orphanage Road
A3	Cassio Road	A3	Park Avenue
C3	Charter Way	A2	Peace Prospect
A4	Chester Road	B3	Percy Road
A4	Chester Street	A4	Pretoria Road
C1	Clarendon Road	C2	Prince Street
C2	Cross Street	C2	Queen's Road
A1	Denmark Road	C3	Queen Street
C3	Derby Road	D2	Radlett Road
C2	Duke Street	D1	Raphael Drive
A4	Durban Road East	C1	Reeds Crescent
A4	Durban Road West	A3	Rickmansworth Road
C3	Earl Street	B3	Rosslyn Road
D2	Ebury Road	B1	St Albans Road
A1	Essex Road	B1	St John's Road
C2	Estcourt Road	B4	St Mary's Road
B3	Exchange Road	D1	St Pauls Way
B4	Farraline Road	B1	Shady Lane
B4	Feranley Street	D2	Shaftesbury Road
B3	Francis Street	C4	Smith Street
B1	Franklin Road	C2	Sotheron Road
C2	Gartlet Road	A4	Southsea Avenue
B2	Gaumont Approach	C3	Stanley Road
C4	George Street	B1	Station Road
D3	Gladstone Road	D3	Stephenson Way
C4	Granville Road	C2	Sutton Road
C3	Grosvenor Road	A1	The Avenue
B2	Halsey Road	C3	The Broadway
A4	Harwoods Road	C4	The Crescent
A1	Hempstead Road	B2	The Parade
C3	Hyde Road	B3	Upton Road
A2	Hyde Road	B4	Vicarage Road
C1	Keele Close	D4	Water Lane
C4	King Street	B1	Wellington Road
C4	Lady's Close	B3	Wellstone Street
D1	Link Road	B1	Westland Road
C3	Loates Lane	B1	West Street
C3	Lord Street	A4	Whippendell Road
D4	Lower High Street	B4	Wiggenhall Road
A1	Malden Road	C1	Woodford Road

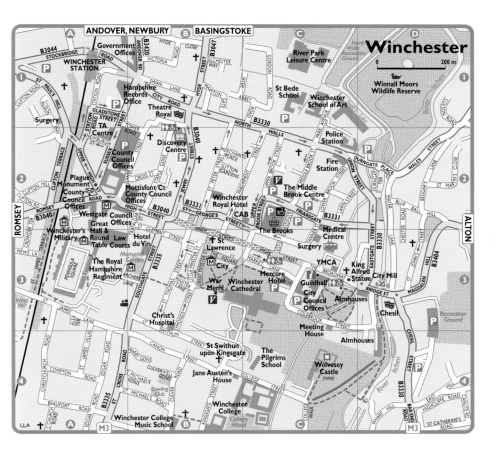

Winchester

Winchester is found on atlas page **22 E9**

A3	Alex Terrace	C3	Market Lane
A1	Alison Way	B1	Marston Gate
B1	Andover Road	B2	Merchants Place
A3	Archery Lane	A3	Mews Lane
D4	Bar End Road	C2	Middle Brook Street
A4	Beaufort Road	B3	Minster Lane
D2	Beggar's Lane	A2	Newburgh Street
D2	Blue Ball Hill	B1	North Walls
D3	Bridge Street	B2	Parchment Street
B4	Canon Street	C2	Park Avenue
D4	Canute Road	A2	Romsey Road
D3	Chesil Street	D4	St Catherine's Road
D2	Chester Road	B2	St Clement Street
A4	Christchurch Road	A4	St Cross Road
B1	City Road	B2	St George's Street
A2	Clifton Hill	A3	St James' Lane
A1	Clifton Road	A3	St James Terrace
A2	Clifton Terrace	A4	St James' Villas
C3	Colebrook Street	D3	St John's Street
B4	College Street	D2	St Martin's Close
C4	College Walk	B4	St Michael's Gardens
D1	Colson Road	B4	St Michael's Road
A4	Compton Road	A1	St Paul's Hill
B2	Cross Street	B2	St Peter Street
A3	Crowder Terrace	B3	St Swithun Street
B4	Culver Road	B3	St Thomas Street
B4	Culverwell Gardens	B1	Silchester Way
D2	Durngate Place	B3	Southgate Street
D2	Durngate Terrace	B2	Staple Gardens
D3	Eastgate Street	A1	Station Road
D4	East Hill	A1	Stockbridge Road
A4	Edgar Road	A2	Sussex Street
C2	Friarsgate	B2	Sutton Gardens
B4	Friary Gardens	B1	Swan Lane
A1	Gladstone Street	B3	Symonds Street
C1	Gordon Road	C3	Tanner Street
B3	Great Minster Street	C3	The Broadway
D4	Highcliffe Road	B3	The Square
B2	High Street	A1	Tower Road
B1	Hyde Abbey Road	A2	Tower Street
B1	Hyde Close	B3	Trafalgar Street
B1	Hyde Street	C2	Union Street
B2	Jewry Street	C2	Upper Brook Street
B4	Kingsgate Street	A2	Upper High Street
C2	Lawn Street	B1	Victoria Road
B3	Little Minster Street	D2	Wales Street
C2	Lower Brook Street	D3	Water Lane
D3	Magdalen Hill	D4	Wharf Hill

Wolverhampton

Wolverhampton is found on atlas page **58 D5**

A3	Alexander Street	B1	Park Road East
A1	Bath Avenue	A2	Park Road West
A2	Bath Road	B3	Peel Street
B3	Bell Street	B4	Penn Road
D3	Bilston Road	D2	Piper's Row
C3	Bilston Street	B3	Pitt Street
B2	Birch Street	D4	Powlett Street
C2	Broad Street	C2	Princess Street
C3	Castle Street	B2	Queen Square
A3	Chapel Ash	C2	Queen Street
B4	Church Lane	D4	Raby Street
B4	Church Street	A3	Raglan Street
B2	Clarence Road	D2	Railway Drive
B2	Clarence Street	B2	Red Lion Street
D4	Cleveland Road	A4	Retreat Street
B3	Cleveland Street	A2	Ring Road St Andrews
D2	Corn Hill	D2	Ring Road St Davids
D1	Culwell Street	C4	Ring Road St Georges
A4	Dale Street	B4	Ring Road St Johns
B3	Darlington Street	B3	Ring Road St Marks
C4	Dudley Road	C1	Ring Road St Patricks
C2	Dudley Street	B2	Ring Road St Peters
B3	Fold Street	A4	Russell Street
C2	Fryer Street	C4	St John's Square
C3	Garrick Street	A3	St Mark's Road
C3	George's Parade	A3	St Mark's Street
A4	Graiseley Street	B3	Salop Street
A4	Great Brickiln Street	B3	School Street
C1	Great Western Street	B3	Skinner Street
D1	Grimstone Street	C3	Snow Hill
A3	Herrick Street	C1	Stafford Street
D2	Horseley Fields	A3	Stephenson Street
D4	Hospital Street	B4	Stewart Street
A1	Lansdown Road	B3	Summer Row
C4	Lever Street	D4	Sutherland Place
C2	Lichfield Street	B3	Temple Street
C1	Little's Lane	B4	Thomas Street
C2	Long Street	C3	Tower Street
A3	Lord Street	D4	Vicarage Road
A4	Mander Street	B3	Victoria Street
C3	Market Street	B1	Waterloo Road
A4	Merridale Street	D1	Wednesfield Road
D3	Middle Cross	C2	Westbury Street
B2	Mitre Fold	B1	Whitemore Hill
B1	Molineux Street	C2	Whitmore Street
A1	New Hampton Road East	B4	Worcester Street
B2	North Street	C2	Wulfruna Street
A1	Park Avenue	A4	Zoar Street

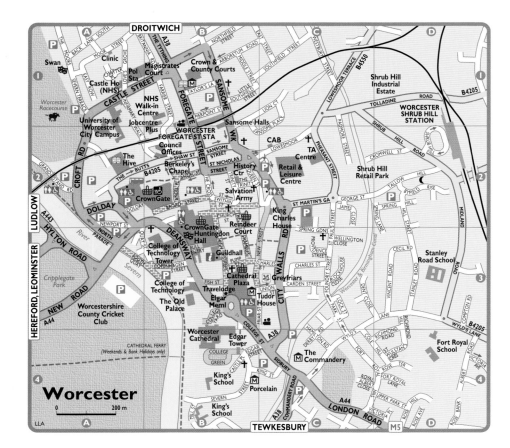

Worcester

Worcester is found on atlas page **46 G4**

D4 Albert Road	B1 Middle Street
B2 Angel Street	D2 Midland Road
B1 Arboretum Road	B4 Mill Street
A1 Back Lane South	A1 Moor Street
C3 Blockhouse Close	A2 Newport Street
A1 Britannia Road	A3 New Road
B2 Broad Street	C3 New Street
D2 Byfield Rise	B1 Northfield Street
C3 Carden Street	A3 North Parade
A1 Castle Street	C1 Padmore Street
A4 Cathedral Ferry	C3 Park Street
D3 Cecil Road	C2 Pheasant Street
C3 Charles Street	B1 Pierpoint Street
A1 Charter Place	C3 Providence Street
B2 Church Street	B3 Pump Street
C3 City Walls Road	A3 Quay Street
C4 Cole Hill	B2 Queen Street
B3 College Street	D4 Richmond Road
C4 Commandery Road	D4 Rose Hill
D3 Compton Road	D4 Rose Terrace
B3 Copenhagen Street	C2 St Martin's Gate
A2 Croft Road	B2 St Nicholas Street
D2 Cromwell Street	C3 St Paul's Street
B3 Deansway	B2 St Swithin Street
C3 Dent Close	B1 Sansome Walk
C4 Derby Road	B4 Severn Street
A2 Dolday	A1 Severn Terrace
B1 East Street	B2 Shaw Street
B4 Edgar Street	D2 Shrub Hill Road
B1 Farrier Street	C4 Sidbury
B3 Fish Street	C1 Southfield Street
B1 Foregate Street	D2 Spring Hill
C4 Fort Royal Hill	D3 Stanley Road
C3 Foundry Street	D2 Tallow Hill
C3 Friar Street	B1 Taylor's Lane
C2 George Street	A2 The Butts
A2 Grandstand Road	B2 The Cross
C3 Hamilton Road	A1 The Moors
B3 High Street	B2 The Shambles
D2 Hill Street	B1 The Tything
A3 Hylton Road	C1 Tolladine Road
B4 King Street	B2 Trinity Street
B1 Little Southfield Street	C3 Union Street
C3 Lock Street	D4 Upper Park Street
C4 London Road	D3 Vincent Road
A1 Love's Grove	C3 Wellington Close
C2 Lowesmoor	C1 Westbury Street
C1 Lowesmoor Terrace	C4 Wyld's Lane

York

York is found on atlas page **98 C10**

C2 Aldwark	C3 Lower Ousegate
D4 Barbican Road	B3 Lower Priory Street
B4 Bishopgate Street	C2 Low Petergate
B3 Bishophill Senior	D3 Margaret Street
D2 Black Horse Lane	C2 Market Street
B2 Blake Street	A3 Micklegate
A4 Blossom Street	B1 Minster Yard
B1 Bootham	C1 Monkgate
B3 Bridge Street	B2 Museum Street
B3 Buckingham Street	D3 Navigation Road
D4 Cemetery Road	B2 New Street
C2 Church Street	B2 North Street
C3 Clifford Street	A3 Nunnery Lane
C1 College Street	C1 Ogleforth
C2 Colliergate	D2 Palmer Lane
B2 Coney Street	D2 Palmer Street
C3 Coppergate	D4 Paragon Street
B4 Cromwell Road	C2 Parliament Street
B2 Davygate	C2 Pavement
C1 Deangate	D2 Peasholme Green
B4 Dove Street	D3 Percy's Lane
B2 Duncombe Place	C3 Piccadilly
D2 Dundas Street	B4 Price's Lane
B3 Fairfax Street	C3 Priory Street
D4 Fawcett Street	A3 Queen Street
C2 Feasegate	B2 Rougier Street
B3 Fetter Lane	C2 St Andrewgate
C2 Finkle Street	D3 St Denys' Road
C4 Fishergate	B1 St Leonard's Place
D1 Foss Bank	B3 St Martins Lane
C3 Fossgate	C1 St Maurice's Road
D2 Foss Islands Road	C2 St Saviourgate
D3 George Street	C2 St Saviours Place
B1 Gillygate	A4 Scarcroft Road
C2 Goodramgate	C2 Shambles
B4 Hampden Street	B3 Skeldergate
C3 High Ousegate	B2 Spen Lane
B1 High Petergate	B2 Spurriergate
A4 Holgate Road	A3 Station Road
D4 Hope Street	B3 Stonegate
D2 Hungate	C2 Swinegate
D1 Jewbury	C2 The Stonebow
D4 Kent Street	A3 Toft Green
C3 King Street	C3 Tower Street
B4 Kyme Street	B3 Trinity Lane
B2 Lendal	B4 Victor Street
D4 Long Close Lane	D3 Walmgate
C1 Lord Mayor's Walk	B2 Wellington Road

Major airports

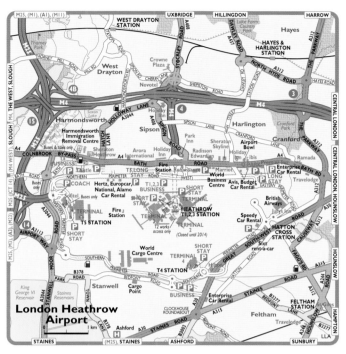

London Heathrow Airport

London Heathrow Airport – 16 miles west of London

Telephone: 0844 335 1801 or visit *www.heathrowairport.com*
Parking: short-stay, long-stay and business parking is available.
For booking and charges tel: 0844 335 1000
Public Transport: coach, bus, rail and London Underground.
There are several 4-star and 3-star hotels within easy reach of the airport.
Car hire facilities are available.

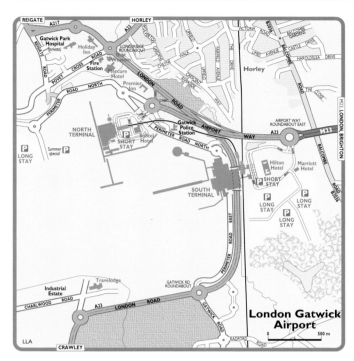

London Gatwick Airport

London Gatwick Airport – 35 miles south of London

Telephone: 0844 892 0322 or visit *www.gatwickairport.com*
Parking: short and long-stay parking is available at both the North and South terminals.
For booking and charges tel: 0844 811 8311.
Public Transport: coach, bus and rail.
There are several 4-star and 3-star hotels within easy reach of the airport.
Car hire facilities are available.

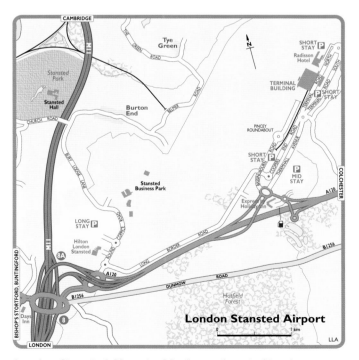

London Stansted Airport

London Stansted Airport – 36 miles north east of London

Telephone: 0844 335 1803 or visit *www.stanstedairport.com*
Parking: short, mid and long-stay open-air parking is available.
For booking and charges tel: 0844 335 1000
Public Transport: coach, bus and direct rail link to London on the Stansted Express.
There are several hotels within easy reach of the airport.
Car hire facilities are available.

London Luton Airport

London Luton Airport – 33 miles north of London

Telephone: 01582 405100 or visit *www.london-luton.co.uk*
Parking: short-term, mid-term and long-stay parking is available.
For booking and charges tel: 01582 405 100
Public Transport: coach, bus and rail.
There are several hotels within easy reach of the airport.
Car hire facilities are available.

Major airports

London City Airport – 7 miles east of London

Telephone: 020 7646 0088 or visit *www.londoncityairport.com*
Parking: short and long-stay open-air parking is available.
For booking and charges tel: 0871 360 1390
Public Transport: easy access to the rail network, Docklands Light Railway and the London Underground.
There are 5-star, 4-star and 3-star hotels within easy reach of the airport.
Car hire facilities are available.

Birmingham International Airport – 8 miles east of Birmingham

Telephone: 0844 576 6000 or visit *www.birminghamairport.co.uk*
Parking: short, mid-term and long-stay parking is available.
For booking and charges tel: 0844 576 6000
Public Transport: Air-Rail Link service operates every 2 minutes to and from Birmingham International Railway Station & Interchange.
There is one 3-star hotel adjacent to the airport and several 4 and 3-star hotels within easy reach of the airport. Car hire facilities are available.

East Midlands Airport – 15 miles south west of Nottingham, next to the M1 at junctions 23A and 24

Telephone: 0871 919 9000 or visit *www.eastmidlandsairport.com*
Parking: short and long-stay parking is available.
For booking and charges tel: 0871 310 3300
Public Transport: bus and coach services to major towns and cities in the East Midlands.
Call 0870 608 2608 for information.
There are several 3-star hotels within easy reach of the airport.
Car hire facilities are available.

Manchester Airport – 10 miles south of Manchester

Telephone: 0871 271 0711 or visit *www.manchesterairport.co.uk*
Parking: short and long-stay parking is available.
For booking and charges tel: 0871 310 2200
Public Transport: bus, coach and rail.
There are several 4-star and 3-star hotels within easy reach of the airport.
Car hire facilities are available.

Major airports

Leeds Bradford International Airport – 7 miles north east of Bradford and 9 miles north west of Leeds

Telephone: 0113 250 9696 or visit *www.leedsbradfordairport.co.uk*
Parking: short, mid-term and long-stay parking is available.
For booking and charges tel: 0113 250 9696
Public Transport: bus service operates every 30 minutes from Bradford, Leeds and Otley.
There are several 4-star and 3-star hotels within easy reach of the airport.
Car hire facilities are available.

Aberdeen Airport – 7 miles north west of Aberdeen

Telephone: 0844 481 6666 or visit *www.aberdeenairport.com*
Parking: short and long-stay parking is available.
For booking and charges tel: 0844 335 1000
Public Transport: regular bus service to central Aberdeen.
There are several 4-star and 3-star hotels within easy reach of the airport.
Car hire facilities are available.

Edinburgh Airport – 7 miles west of Edinburgh

Telephone: 0844 481 8989 or visit *www.edinburghairport.com*
Parking: short and long-stay parking is available.
For booking and charges tel: 0844 335 1000
Public Transport: regular bus services to central Edinburgh.
There are several 4-star and 3-star hotels within easy reach of the airport.
Car hire facilities are available.

Glasgow Airport – 8 miles west of Glasgow

Telephone: 0844 481 5555 or visit *www.glasgowairport.com*
Parking: short and long-stay parking is available.
For booking and charges tel: 0844 335 1000
Public Transport: regular coach services operate direct to central Glasgow and Edinburgh.
There are several 3-star hotels within easy reach of the airport.
Car hire facilities are available.

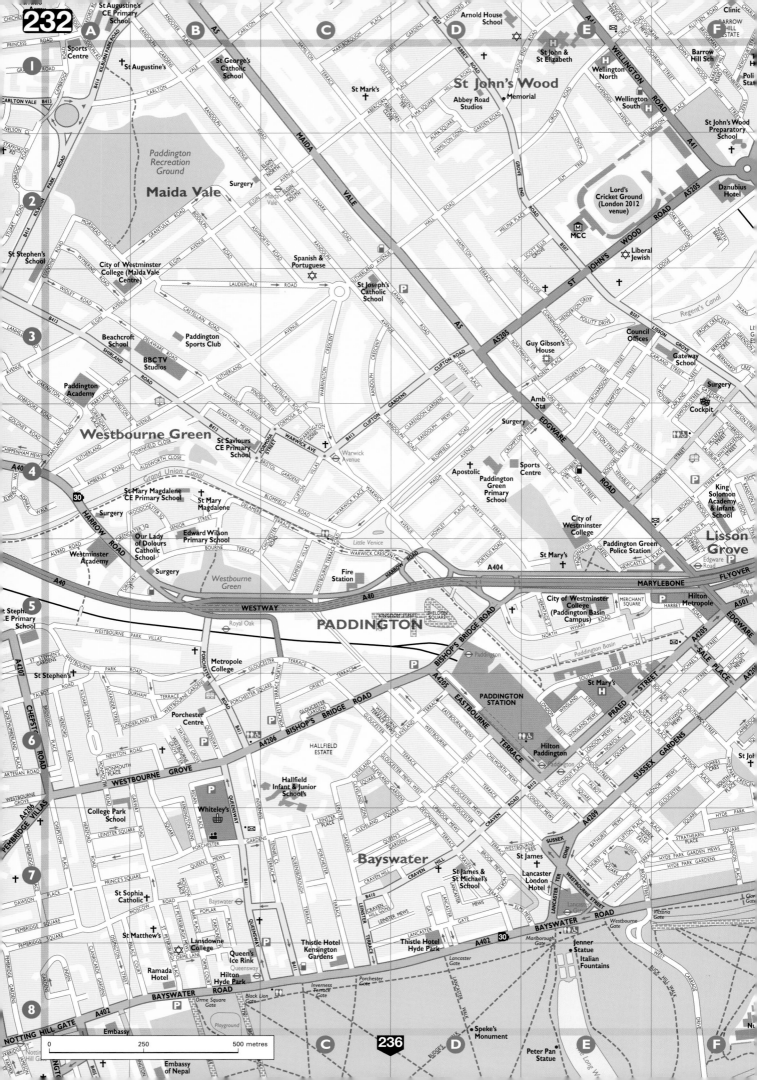

Central London street index

In this index, street and station names are listed in alphabetical order and written in full, but may be abbreviated on the map. Each entry is followed by its Postcode District and each street name is preceded by the page number and the grid reference to the square in which the name is found. Names are asterisked (*) in the index where there is insufficient space to show them on the map.

A

232 C1 **Abbey Gardens** NW8
238 B4 **Abbey Orchard Street** SW1P
232 D1 **Abbey Road** NW8
240 B7 **Abbey Street** SE1
235 L7 **Abchurch Lane** EC4N
232 C1 **Abercorn Close** NW8
232 C1 **Abercorn Place** NW8
232 E3 **Aberdeen Place** NW8
239 M5 **Aberdour Street** SE1
236 A4 **Abingdon Road** W8
238 C3 **Abingdon Street** SW1P
236 A4 **Abingdon Villas** W8
241 L1 **Ackroyd Drive** E3
241 K5 **Acorn Walk** SE16
234 E2 **Acton Street** WC1X
236 A3 **Adam and Eve Mews** W8
233 K8 **Adam's Row** W1K
234 D8 **Adam Street** WC2N
235 H7 **Addle Hill** EC4V
240 F1 **Adelina Grove** E1
234 B5 **Adeline Place** WC1B
240 D2 **Adler Street** E1
241 K5 **Admiral Place** SE16
232 A4 **Admiral Walk** W9
232 E4 **Adpar Street** W2
234 D8 **Agar Street** WC2N
235 H3 **Agdon Street** EC1V
241 L2 **Agnes Street** E14
241 G6 **Ainsty Street** SE16
234 A8 **Air Street** W1B
238 F2 **Alaska Street** SE1
239 L8 **Albany Road** SE5
233 L1 **Albany Street** NW1
233 L8 **Albemarle Street** W1S
235 H4 **Albermarle Way** EC1V
239 H6 **Alberta Street** SE17
239 G3 **Albert Bridge** SW3
238 D7 **Albert Embankment** SE1
241 H3 **Albert Gardens** E1
237 H2 **Albert Gate** SW1X
236 C3 **Albert Place** W8
233 G7 **Albion Gate** W2
235 H4 **Albion Place** EC1M
241 G7 **Albion Street** SE16
233 G7 **Albion Street** W2
234 A1 **Aldenham Street** NW1
235 K6 **Aldermanbury** EC2V
239 L6 **Alderney Mews** SE1
237 L6 **Alderney Street** SW1V
235 J4 **Aldersgate Street** EC1A
233 J8 **Alford Street** W1K
240 B3 **Aldgate** EC3M
240 B2 **Aldgate** ⊖ EC3N
240 C2 **Aldgate East** ⊖ E1
240 B3 **Aldgate High Street** EC3N
232 B4 **Aldsworth Close** W9
234 E7 **Aldwych** WC2E
236 F5 **Alexander Place** SW7
232 A6 **Alexander Street** W2
236 E3 **Alexandra Gate** SW7
234 B4 **Alfred Mews** WC1E
234 B4 **Alfred Place** WC1E
232 A5 **Alfred Road** W2
239 M4 **Alice Street** SE1
240 C3 **Alie Street** E1
236 A4 **Allen Street** W8
235 L8 **Allhallows Lane** EC4R
237 L4 **Allington Street** SW1E
232 F1 **Allitsen Road** NW8
233 H4 **Allsop Place** NW1
232 D1 **Alma Square** NW8
237 G8 **Alpha Place** SW3
239 M7 **Alsace Road** SE17
240 C8 **Alscot Road** SE1
239 M6 **Alvey Street** SE17
239 H7 **Ambergate Street** SE17
232 A4 **Amberley Road** W9
238 A4 **Ambrosden Avenue** SW1P
239 J6 **Amelia Street** SE17
240 B3 **America Square** EC3N
239 J2 **America Street** SE1
234 F2 **Ampton Street** WC1X
234 F2 **Amwell Street** EC1R
241 M6 **Anchorage Point** E14
232 B1 **Andover Place** NW6
235 G1 **Angel** ⊖ N1
235 L8 **Angel Lane** EC4R
235 J6 **Angel Street** EC1A
240 F8 **Ann Moss Way** SE16
237 J3 **Ann's Close** SW1X
236 B4 **Ansdell Street** W8
241 H2 **Antill Terrace** E1
240 E1 **Antizan Street** E1
234 A8 **Apple Tree Yard** SW1Y
235 M4 **Appold Street** EC2A
237 J2 **Apsley Gate** W1J
239 G1 **Aquinas Street** SE1
241 H2 **Arbour Square** E1
241 J7 **Archangels** SE16
234 B7 **Archer Street** W1B
239 J4 **Arch Street** SE1
235 M1 **Arden Estate** N1
234 D2 **Argyle Square** WC1H
234 D2 **Argyle Street** WC1H
236 A3 **Argyll Road** W8
233 M6 **Argyll Street** W1F
237 M1 **Arlington Street** SW1A
235 G2 **Arlington Way** EC1R
234 D6 **Arne Street** WC2H
241 M8 **Arnhem Place** E14
240 C7 **Arnold Estate** SE1
239 K8 **Arnside Street** SE17
232 A6 **Artesian Road** W11
235 L7 **Arthur Street** EC4V
240 E4 **Artichoke Hill** E1W
240 A1 **Artillery Lane** E1
238 B4 **Artillery Row** SW1P
234 F7 **Arundel Street** WC2R
232 F4 **Ashbridge Street** NW8
236 C5 **Ashburn Gardens** SW7
236 C5 **Ashburn Place** SW7
235 H2 **Ashby Street** EC1V
240 D4 **Asher Way** E1W
240 E2 **Ashfield Street** E1
235 M2 **Ashford Street** N1
237 M4 **Ashley Place** SW1P
232 F4 **Ashmill Street** NW1
238 F8 **Ashmole Street** SW8
232 B2 **Ashworth Road** W9
240 C2 **Assam Street** E1
241 G1 **Assembly Place** E1
237 G6 **Astell Street** SW3
241 K1 **Aston Street** E14
236 C5 **Astwood Mews** SW7
236 D5 **Atherstone Mews** SW7
238 C6 **Atterbury Street** SW1P
234 F3 **Attneave Street** WC1X
233 L1 **Augustus Street** NW1
239 G7 **Aulton Place** SE11
235 L6 **Austin Friars** EC2N
237 M3 **Australia Gate** SW1A
239 H5 **Austral Street** SE11
238 F7 **Aveline Street** SE11
235 H6 **Ave Maria Lane** EC1A
241 J6 **Avenue Dock Hill** SE16
237 K6 **Avery Farm Row** SW1W
233 L7 **Avery Row** W1K
233 J5 **Aybrook Street** W1U
239 L7 **Aylesbury Road** SE17
235 H4 **Aylesbury Street** EC1R
238 B7 **Aylesford Street** SW1V
241 G2 **Aylward Street** E1
239 K2 **Ayres Street** SE1

B

234 B8 **Babmaes Street** SW1Y
235 L2 **Bache's Street** N1
240 D3 **Back Church Lane** E1
235 G4 **Back Hill** EC1R
240 B8 **Bacon Grove** SE1
234 C6 **Bainbridge Street** WC1A
233 J6 **Bakers Mews** W1U
235 G4 **Baker's Row** EC1R
233 H4 **Baker Street** NW1
233 J5 **Baker Street** W1U
233 H4 **Baker Street** ⊖ NW1
233 G3 **Balcombe Street** NW1
233 J7 **Balderton Street** W1K
234 F5 **Baldwin's Gardens** EC1N
235 L2 **Baldwin Street** EC1V
241 J1 **Bale Road** E1
234 D1 **Balfe Street** N1
233 K8 **Balfour Mews** W1K
233 J8 **Balfour Place** W1K
239 K5 **Balfour Street** SE17
235 J3 **Baltic Street East** EC1Y
235 J4 **Baltic Street West** EC1Y
235 L6 **Bank** ⊖ ⊖ EC2R
239 K1 **Bank End** SE1
239 J1 **Bankside** SE1
235 K3 **Banner Street** EC1Y
240 E8 **Banyard Road** SE16
235 J4 **Barbican** ⊖ EC1A
235 J5 **Barbican Estate** EC2Y
239 G1 **Barge House Street** SE1
232 B7 **Bark Place** W2
236 B6 **Barkston Gardens** SW5
241 L4 **Barley Corn Way** E14
239 M5 **Barlow/Congreve Estate** SE17
233 L7 **Barlow Place** W1J
239 L5 **Barlow Street** SE17
241 H3 **Barnardo Street** E1
234 A1 **Barnby Street** NW1
241 J2 **Barnes Street** E14
240 A6 **Barnham Street** SE1
239 G3 **Baron's Place** SE1
235 G1 **Baron Street** N1
233 K6 **Barrett Street** W1U
232 F1 **Barrow Hill Estate** NW8
232 F1 **Barrow Hill Road** NW8
234 D5 **Barter Street** WC1A
235 J5 **Bartholomew Close** EC1A
235 L6 **Bartholomew Lane** EC2R
239 L5 **Bartholomew Street** SE1
235 G6 **Bartlett Court** EC4A
238 C4 **Barton Street** SW1P
237 H4 **Basil Street** SW3
241 K3 **Basin Approach** E14
235 K5 **Basinghall Lane** EC2V
235 K5 **Basinghall Street** EC2V
235 J3 **Bastwick Street** EC1V
234 B6 **Bateman's Buildings** W1D
234 B6 **Bateman Street** W1D
235 K2 **Bath Street** EC1V
239 J4 **Bath Terrace** SE1
232 E7 **Bathurst Mews** W2
232 E7 **Bathurst Street** W2
239 M1 **Battle Bridge Lane** SE1
240 D2 **Batty Street** E1
234 B5 **Bayley Street** WC1B
238 F3 **Baylis Road** SE1
232 B7 **Bayswater** ⊖ W2
232 D7 **Bayswater Road** W2
241 L1 **Baythorne Street** E3
239 M7 **Beaconsfield Road** SE17
234 A7 **Beak Street** W1F
239 J1 **Bear Grove** SE1
239 H1 **Bear Lane** SE1
237 G4 **Beauchamp Place** SW3
237 G4 **Beaufort Gardens** SW3
236 E8 **Beaufort Street** SW3
234 A3 **Beaumont Place** W1T
233 K4 **Beaumont Street** W1G
241 M3 **Beccles Street** E14
239 L3 **Beckett Street** SE1
239 M6 **Beckway Street** SE17
239 L1 **Bedale Street** SE1
234 C5 **Bedford Avenue** WC1B
234 C7 **Bedfordbury** WC2N
236 A2 **Bedford Gardens** W8
234 D4 **Bedford Place** WC1N
234 E4 **Bedford Row** WC1R
234 B5 **Bedford Square** WC1B
234 D7 **Bedford Street** WC2E
234 C3 **Bedford Way** WC1H
232 F3 **Bedlow Close** NW8
235 J4 **Beech Street** EC2Y
237 L4 **Beeston Place** SW1W
237 J3 **Belgrave Mews North** * SW1X
237 K4 **Belgrave Mews South** * SW1X
237 J4 **Belgrave Place** SW1X
237 L5 **Belgrave Road** SW1V
238 A6 **Belgrave Road** SW1V
237 J3 **Belgrave Square** SW1X
241 J2 **Belgrave Street** E1
234 D2 **Belgrove Street** WC1H
240 B1 **Bell Lane** E1
232 F4 **Bell Street** NW1
234 F6 **Bell Yard** WC2A
238 E2 **Belvedere Road** SE1
235 H4 **Benjamin Street** EC1M
241 J1 **Ben Jonson Road** E1
237 M1 **Bennett Street** SW1A
240 D7 **Ben Smith Way** SE16
240 F4 **Benson Quay** E1W
233 K6 **Bentinck Mews** W1U
233 K6 **Bentinck Street** W1U
241 H3 **Bere Street** E1W
241 K8 **Bergen Square** SE16
233 H6 **Berkeley Mews** W1H
233 L8 **Berkeley Square** W1J
233 L8 **Berkeley Street** W1J
240 E7 **Bermondsey** ⊖ ⊖ SE16
240 C8 **Bermondsey Spa** SE16
240 A8 **Bermondsey Square** SE1
240 A6 **Bermondsey Street** SE1
240 E7 **Bermondsey Wall East** SE16
240 D7 **Bermondsey Wall Estate** SE16
240 C6 **Bermondsey Wall West** SE16
234 D4 **Bernard Street** WC1N
234 A5 **Berners Mews** W1T
234 A6 **Berners Place** W1F
234 A5 **Berners Street** W1T
232 F3 **Bernhardt Crescent** NW8
239 J6 **Berryfield Road** SE17
235 H3 **Berry Street** EC1V
234 A6 **Berwick Street** W1F
238 B6 **Bessborough Gardens** SW1V
238 B6 **Bessborough Street** SW1V
234 D6 **Betterton Street** WC2H
235 L2 **Bevenden Street** N1
241 J5 **Bevin Close** SE16
240 D7 **Bevington Street** SE16
234 F1 **Bevin Way** WC1X
240 A2 **Bevis Marks** EC3A
240 F3 **Bewley Street** E1
233 H4 **Bickenhall Street** W1U
234 C2 **Bidborough Street** WC1H
232 B2 **Biddulph Road** W9
240 E3 **Bigland Street** E1
240 A3 **Billiter Square** EC3M
240 A3 **Billiter Street** EC3M
236 C6 **Bina Gardens** SW5
233 J4 **Bingham Place** W1U
233 K7 **Binney Street** W1K
241 M3 **Birchfield Street** E14
235 L7 **Birchin Lane** EC3V
238 A3 **Birdcage Walk** SW1H
235 H6 **Birde Lane** EC4Y
233 K6 **Bird Street** W1C
234 D1 **Birkenhead Street** N1
232 C6 **Bishop's Bridge Road** W2
240 A2 **Bishopsgate** EC2M
240 B1 **Bishops Square** E1
239 G5 **Bishop's Terrace** SE11
239 J3 **Bittern Street** SE1
235 M3 **Blackall Street** EC2A
233 J7 **Blackburne's Mews** W1K
235 H7 **Blackfriars** ⇌ ⊖ EC4V
235 H8 **Blackfriars Bridge** SE1
235 H7 **Black Friars Lane** EC4V
239 H3 **Blackfriars Road** SE1
239 L4 **Blackhorse Court** SE1
232 B8 **Black Lion Gate** W2
238 E6 **Black Prince Road** SE11
239 K6 **Blackwood Street** SE17
233 H5 **Blandford Street** W1U
233 L7 **Blenheim Street** W1S
235 K1 **Bletchley Street** N1
232 C4 **Blomfield Road** W9
235 M5 **Blomfield Street** EC2M
232 C5 **Blomfield Villas** W2
237 J6 **Bloomfield Terrace** SW1W
234 D5 **Bloomsbury Square** WC1A
234 C5 **Bloomsbury Street** WC1B
234 C5 **Bloomsbury Way** WC1A
241 K2 **Blount Street** E14
237 M1 **Blue Ball Yard** SW1A
241 J1 **Bohn Road** E1
233 L4 **Bolsover Street** W1W
236 B6 **Bolton Gardens** SW5
237 L1 **Bolton Street** W1J
233 K6 **Bond Street** ⊖ W1C
238 D8 **Bondway** SW8
235 L4 **Bonhill Street** EC2A
238 E8 **Bonnington Square** SW8
235 M2 **Boot Street** N1
239 K3 **Borough** ⊖ SE1
239 K3 **Borough High Street** SE1
239 H3 **Borough Road** SE1
237 K5 **Boscobel Place** SW1W
232 E4 **Boscobel Street** NW8
240 B6 **Boss Street** SE1
233 G3 **Boston Place** NW1
235 M7 **Botolph Lane** EC3R
239 K8 **Boundary Lane** SE17
239 G2 **Boundary Row** SE1
233 L7 **Bourdon Street** W1K
233 M5 **Bourlet Close** W1W
234 F4 **Bourne Estate** EC1N
237 J6 **Bourne Street** SW1W
232 B5 **Bourne Terrace** W2
232 F6 **Bouverie Place** W2
235 G6 **Bouverie Street** EC4Y
237 J3 **Bowland Yard** * SW1X
235 K6 **Bow Lane** EC4M
235 G3 **Bowling Green Lane** EC1R
239 L2 **Bowling Green Place** SE1
238 F8 **Bowling Green Street** SE11
235 M2 **Bowling Green Walk** N1
234 D4 **Bowsell Street** WC1N
234 D7 **Bow Street** WC2E
240 D3 **Boyd Street** E1
239 H3 **Boyfield Street** SE1
233 M7 **Boyle Street** W1S
239 K8 **Boyson Road** SE17
237 H6 **Brackland Terrace** SW3
235 J4 **Brackley Street** EC1Y
239 K8 **Bradenham Close** SE17
239 G2 **Brad Street** SE1
239 H7 **Braganza Street** SE17
240 C3 **Braham Street** E1
236 F7 **Bramerton Street** SW3
236 B6 **Bramham Gardens** SW5
241 J3 **Branch Road** E14
239 H8 **Brandon Estate** SE17
239 K6 **Brandon Street** SE17
238 F7 **Brangton Road** SE11
241 H6 **Bray Crescent** SE16
237 H6 **Bray Place** SW3
235 K7 **Bread Street** EC4M
234 F6 **Bream's Buildings** EC4A
236 D6 **Brechin Place** SW7
240 D4 **Breezer's Hill** E1W
233 G5 **Brendon Street** W1H
237 L4 **Bressenden Place** SW1W
239 L7 **Brettell Street** SE17
238 A3 **Brewers Green** SW1H
234 A7 **Brewer Street** W1F
240 F6 **Brewhouse Lane** E1W
241 J5 **Brewhouse Walk** SE16
234 D6 **Brick Court** WC2R
240 C1 **Brick Lane** E1
237 K2 **Brick Street** W1J
235 H7 **Bridewell Place** EC4V
232 F1 **Bridgeman Street** NW8
237 L5 **Bridge Place** SW1V
240 D4 **Bridgeport Place** E1W
235 J7 **Bridge Street** EC4V
238 D3 **Bridge Street** SW1A
235 J4 **Bridgewater Street** EC2Y
234 A1 **Bridgeway Street** NW1
234 A7 **Bridle Lane** W1F
232 A6 **Bridstow Place** W2
241 L4 **Brightlingsea Place** E14
234 C1 **Brill Place** NW1
235 H4 **Briset Street** EC1M
232 B4 **Bristol Gardens** W9
234 E2 **Britannia Street** WC1X
235 L2 **Britannia Walk** N1
235 L1 **Britannia Way** N1
236 F7 **Britten Street** SW3
235 H4 **Britton Street** EC1M
233 L7 **Broadbent Street** W1K
235 M5 **Broadgate Circle** EC2M
232 F4 **Broadley Street** NW8
232 F4 **Broadley Terrace** NW1
233 J5 **Broadstone Place** W1U
233 K1 **Broad Walk** NW1
233 H7 **Broad Walk** W2
239 G1 **Broadwall** SE1
238 B4 **Broadway** SW1H
234 A7 **Broadwick Street** W1F
239 K4 **Brockham Street** SE1
241 H3 **Brodlove Lane** E1W
241 J2 **Bromley Street** E1
237 G4 **Brompton Road** SW3
236 F5 **Brompton Road** SW7
236 F4 **Brompton Square** SW3
239 K7 **Bronti Close** SE17
239 G5 **Brook Drive** SE11
234 F5 **Brooke Street** EC1N
233 H8 **Brook Gate** W2
232 D7 **Brook Mews North** W2
233 K7 **Brook's Mews** W1K
233 K7 **Brook Street** W1K
232 E7 **Brook Street** W2
233 K7 **Brown Heart Gardens** W1K
233 K5 **Browning Mews** W1G
239 K6 **Browning Street** SE17
234 E3 **Brownlow Mews** WC1N
234 E5 **Brownlow Street** WC1V
233 G6 **Brown Street** W1H
241 G6 **Brunel Road** SE16
240 B1 **Brune Street** E1
240 A6 **Brunswick Close** SE1
236 A1 **Brunswick Gardens** W8
235 L2 **Brunswick Place** N1
241 J8 **Brunswick Quay** SE16
234 D3 **Brunswick Square** WC1N
234 D3 **Brunswick Street** WC1N
241 K3 **Brunton Place** E14
240 E3 **Brushfield Street** E1
233 L8 **Bruton Lane** W1J
233 L7 **Bruton Place** W1J
233 L8 **Bruton Street** W1J
241 K6 **Bryan Road** SE16
233 G5 **Bryanstone Mews West** W1H
233 H5 **Bryanston Mews East** W1H
233 G5 **Bryanston Place** W1H
233 H5 **Bryanston Square** W1H
233 H7 **Bryanston Street** W1C
232 E8 **Buck Hill Walk** W2
237 L3 **Buckingham Gate** SW1E
237 M3 **Buckingham Mews** SW1E
237 L5 **Buckingham Palace Road** SW1W
237 M4 **Buckingham Place** SW1E
235 L1 **Buckland Street** N1
240 C2 **Buckle Street** E1
241 J5 **Buckters Rents** SE16
236 D2 **Budge's Walk** W2
237 L5 **Bulleid Way** SW1V
233 K5 **Bulstrode Street** W1U
235 L3 **Bunhill Row** EC1Y
241 M1 **Burdett Estate** E14
241 L2 **Burdett Road** E14
238 F3 **Burdett Street** SE1
241 M1 **Burgess Street** E14
239 L4 **Burge Street** SE1
233 M8 **Burlington Arcade** W1J
233 M8 **Burlington Gardens** W1S
237 J6 **Burnhouse Place** SW1W
237 G7 **Burnsall Street** SW3
241 J5 **Burnside Close** SE16
239 H1 **Burrell Street** SE1
240 D3 **Burslem Street** E1
239 L7 **Burton Grove** SE17
234 C3 **Burton Street** WC1H
233 G6 **Burwood Place** W2
241 H5 **Bury Close** SE16
240 A2 **Bury Court** EC3A
234 D5 **Bury Place** WC1A
240 A2 **Bury Street** EC3A
238 A1 **Bury Street** SW1Y
236 F6 **Bury Walk** SW3
240 D5 **Bushell Street** E1W
235 L7 **Bush Lane** EC4V
241 J3 **Butcher Row** E14
236 E5 **Bute Street** SW7
238 B4 **Butler Place** SW1H
240 C6 **Butler's Wharf** SE1
235 L2 **Buttesland Street** N1
241 K6 **Byefield Close** SE16
241 J5 **Bylands Close** SE16
234 B4 **Byng Place** WC1E
241 M6 **Byng Street** E14
240 A4 **Byward Street** EC3R
241 K5 **Bywater Place** SE16
237 G6 **Bywater Street** SW3

C

232 F5 **Cabbell Street** NW1
240 F3 **Cable Street** E1
239 K7 **Cadiz Street** SE17
237 H5 **Cadogan Gardens** SW3
237 H5 **Cadogan Gate** SW1X
237 J4 **Cadogan Lane** SW1X
237 J4 **Cadogan Place** SW1X
237 H5 **Cadogan Square** SW1X
237 G6 **Cadogan Street** SW3
234 D1 **Caledonian Road** N1
234 D1 **Caledonia Street** N1
236 F6 **Cale Street** SW3
236 D7 **Callow Street** SW3
234 E1 **Calshot Street** N1
234 F3 **Calthorpe Street** WC1X
234 C7 **Cambridge Circus** WC2H
232 A1 **Cambridge Gardens** NW6
233 L3 **Cambridge Gate** NW1
232 A1 **Cambridge Road** NW6
232 A2 **Cambridge Road** NW6
232 F6 **Cambridge Square** W2
237 L6 **Cambridge Street** SW1V
233 L2 **Cambridge Terrace** NW1
233 L3 **Cambridge Terrace Mews** NW1
241 K2 **Camdenhurst Street** E14
236 D8 **Camera Place** SW10
240 A2 **Camomile Street** EC3A
236 A2 **Campden Grove** W8
236 A2 **Campden Hill Road** W8
236 A1 **Campden Street** W8
240 C3 **Camperdown Street** E1
241 G7 **Canada Estate** SE16
237 M3 **Canada Gate** SW1A
241 H7 **Canada Street** SE16
241 G7 **Canada Water** ⊖ ⊖ SE16
241 L5 **Canada Wharf** SE16
239 L8 **Canal Street** SE5
241 L4 **Canary Riverside** E14
241 K1 **Candle Street** E1
236 C4 **Canning Place** W8
241 M4 **Cannon Drive** E14
235 K7 **Cannon Street** EC4N
235 K7 **Cannon Street** ⇌ ⊖ EC4R
240 E3 **Cannon Street Road** E1
241 G6 **Canon Beck Road** SE16
238 D3 **Canon Row** SW1A
241 M3 **Canton Street** E14
237 J3 **Capeners Close** * SW1X
232 E3 **Capland Street** NW8
234 A4 **Capper Street** WC1E
241 K5 **Capstan Way** SE16
241 L2 **Carbis Road** E14
233 L4 **Carburton Street** W1W
238 F6 **Cardigan Street** SE11
234 A2 **Cardington Street** NW1
234 F6 **Carey Street** WC2A

Carlisle Avenue - Eyre Sreet Hill 243

240 B3 Carlisle Avenue EC3N
238 F4 Carlisle Lane SE1
237 M5 Carlisle Place SW1P
234 B6 Carlisle Street W1D
233 K7 Carlos Place W1K
238 B2 Carlton Gardens SW1Y
232 B1 Carlton Hill NW6
238 B1 Carlton House Terrace SW1Y
237 L1 Carlton Street W1J
232 A1 Carlton Vale NW6
232 B1 Carlton Vale NW6
236 F7 Carlyle Square SW3
235 G7 Carmelite Street EC4Y
233 M7 Carnaby Street W1F
232 B7 Caroline Place W2
241 H3 Caroline Street E1
237 J5 Caroline Terrace SW1W
233 K7 Carpenter Street W1K
237 L1 Carrington Street W1J
241 K1 Carr Street E14
238 B3 Carteret Street SW1H
235 H7 Carter Lane EC4V
239 K7 Carter Place SE17
239 J7 Carter Street SE17
235 J4 Carthusian Street EC1M
234 D8 Carting Lane WC2R
234 C2 Cartwright Gardens WC1H
240 C4 Cartwright Street E1
232 F3 Casey Close NW8
240 C1 Casson Street E1
232 B3 Castellain Road W9
239 G5 Castlebrook Close SE11
237 M4 Castle Lane SW1E
239 L6 Catesby Street SE17
240 F7 Cathay Street SE16
236 C8 Cathcart Road SW10
237 M4 Cathedral Walk SW1E
237 M4 Catherine Place SW1E
234 D7 Catherine Street WC2E
233 G5 Cato Street W1H
238 B6 Causton Street SW1P
240 F1 Cavell Street E1
232 E1 Cavendish Avenue NW8
233 L6 Cavendish Place W1G
233 L6 Cavendish Square W1G
235 L1 Cavendish Street N1
237 G8 Caversham Street SW3
238 B4 Caxton Street SW1H
235 K2 Cayton Street EC1V
238 F4 Centaur Street SE1
235 J2 Central Street EC1V
235 G1 Chadwell Street EC1R
238 B4 Chadwick Street SW1P
233 H4 Chagford Street NW1
234 B1 Chalton Street NW1
240 D7 Chambers Street SE16
240 C3 Chamber Street E1
240 D6 Chambers Wharf SE16
239 H1 Chancel Street SE1
234 F5 Chancery Lane WC2A
234 F5 Chancery Lane ⊖ WC1V
234 C8 Chandos Place WC2N
233 L5 Chandos Street W1G
236 B4 Chantry Square W8
234 F1 Chapel Market N1
232 F5 Chapel Street NW1
237 K3 Chapel Street SW1X
239 G3 Chaplin Close SE1
240 E3 Chapman Street E1
239 H7 Chapter Road SE17
238 B6 Chapter Street SW1P
241 H6 Chargrove Close SE16
238 D1 Charing Cross ⇌ ⊖ WC2N
234 B6 Charing Cross Road WC2H
234 C8 Charing Cross Road WC2N
232 F1 Charlbert Street NW8
234 B8 Charles II Street SW1Y
235 M2 Charles Square N1
237 K1 Charles Street W1J
239 K6 Charleston Street SE17
235 M3 Charlotte Road EC2A
234 A4 Charlotte Street W1T
238 A6 Charlwood Place SW1V
237 M7 Charlwood Street SW1V
238 A6 Charlwood Street SW1V
234 B1 Charrington Street NW1
235 H4 Charterhouse Square EC1M
235 G5 Charterhouse Street EC1M
235 L2 Chart Street N1
241 J2 Chaseley Street E14
239 L5 Chatham Street SE17
235 K6 Cheapside EC2V
237 K8 Chelsea Bridge SW1W
237 J7 Chelsea Bridge Road SW1W
237 G8 Chelsea Embankment SW3
236 F7 Chelsea Manor Gardens SW3
237 G7 Chelsea Manor Street SW3
236 E8 Chelsea Park Gardens SW3
236 E7 Chelsea Square SW3
237 H6 Cheltenham Terrace SW3
234 B4 Chenies Mews WC1E
234 B4 Chenies Street WC1E
236 A4 Cheniston Gardens W8
232 A7 Chepstow Place W2
232 A6 Chepstow Road W2
235 K3 Chequer Street EC1Y
235 L1 Cherbury Street N1
240 E7 Cherry Garden Street SE16
237 J4 Chesham Close SW1X
237 J4 Chesham Place SW1X
237 J4 Chesham Street SW1X
237 K3 Chester Close SW1X
233 L2 Chester Close North NW1
233 L2 Chester Close South NW1
237 K1 Chesterfield Gardens W1J
233 K8 Chesterfield Hill W1J
237 K1 Chesterfield Street W1J
233 L2 Chester Gate NW1
237 K3 Chester Mews SW1X
233 L1 Chester Place NW1
233 L2 Chester Road NW1
237 K5 Chester Row SW1W
237 K5 Chester Square SW1W
237 K4 Chester Square Mews SW1W
237 K4 Chester Street SW1X
233 L2 Chester Terrace NW1
239 G6 Chester Way SE11
240 C2 Cheval Place SW7
241 M7 Cheval Street E14
237 G8 Cheyne Gardens SW3
236 F8 Cheyne Row SW3
236 F8 Cheyne Walk SW3
238 E2 Chicheley Street SE1
232 A1 Chichester Road NW6
232 C5 Chichester Road W2
238 A7 Chichester Street SW1V
240 C1 Chicksand Street E1
240 E4 Chigwell Hill E1W
236 A5 Child's Place SW5
236 A5 Child's Street SW5
233 J4 Chiltern Street W1U
232 D6 Chilworth Mews W2
232 D6 Chilworth Street W2
241 G8 China Hall Mews SE16
232 A4 Chippenham Mews W9
235 K4 Chiswell Street EC1Y
234 A4 Chitty Street W1T
237 G8 Christchurch Street SW3
240 D3 Christian Street E1
235 M3 Christina Street EC2A
241 H6 Christopher Close SE16
235 L4 Christopher Street EC2A
241 H2 Chudleigh Street E1
239 M8 Chumleigh Street SE5
237 L7 Churchill Gardens Road SW1V
232 F4 Church Street NW8
234 B2 Church Way NW1
239 H5 Churchyard Row SE1
238 A6 Churton Place SW1V
238 A6 Churton Street SW1V
232 E1 Circus Road NW8
232 A5 Cirencester Square W2
235 J1 City Garden Row N1
235 J1 City Road EC1V
235 L3 City Road EC1Y
235 H6 City Thameslink ⇌ EC4M
237 H5 Clabon Mews SW1X
241 G7 Clack Street SE16
232 A8 Clanricarde Gardens W2
234 F1 Claremont Square N1
233 L2 Clarence Gardens NW1
241 G6 Clarence Mews SE16
232 D4 Clarendon Gardens W9
232 F7 Clarendon Gate W2
232 F7 Clarendon Place W2
237 L6 Clarendon Street SW1V
236 D6 Clareville Grove SW7
236 D6 Clareville Street SW7
237 L1 Clarges Mews W1J
237 L1 Clarges Street W1J
240 F2 Clark Street E1
238 A7 Claverton Street SW1V
240 F5 Clave Street E1W
233 H5 Clay Street W1U
238 F8 Clayton Street SE11
239 G7 Cleaver Square SE11
239 G7 Cleaver Street SE11
240 F5 Clegg Street E1W
241 L2 Clemence Street E14
235 L7 Clements Lane EC4N
240 E8 Clement's Road SE16
233 H6 Clenston Mews W1H
235 L3 Clere Street EC2A
235 G4 Clerkenwell Grove EC1R
235 G3 Clerkenwell Lane EC1R
235 G4 Clerkenwell Road EC1M
232 C6 Cleveland Gardens W2
233 M4 Cleveland Mews W1T
238 A1 Cleveland Place SW1Y
238 A2 Cleveland Row SW1A
232 C6 Cleveland Square W2
233 M4 Cleveland Street W1T
232 D6 Cleveland Terrace W2
233 M7 Clifford Street W1S
232 C4 Clifton Gardens W9
241 G6 Clifton Place SE16
232 E7 Clifton Place W2
232 D3 Clifton Road W9
235 M3 Clifton Street EC2A
232 C4 Clifton Villas W9
239 K1 Clink Street SE1
241 H6 Clipper Close SE16
233 M4 Clipstone Mews W1W
233 L4 Clipstone Street W1W
237 J5 Cliveden Place SW1W
235 K7 Cloak Lane EC4R
235 J5 Cloth Fair EC1A
235 J5 Cloth Street EC1A
240 A8 Cluny Place SE1
240 B2 Cobb Street E1
234 A2 Cobourg Street NW1
238 A5 Coburg Close SW1P
232 E1 Cochrane Mews NW8
232 E1 Cochrane Street NW8
235 H5 Cock Lane EC1A
238 C1 Cockspur Street SW1Y
240 D5 Codling Close * E1W
239 G1 Coin Street SE1
240 D2 Coke Street E1
236 C6 Colbeck Mews SW7
235 H1 Colebrook Row N1
236 B7 Coleherne Road SW10
235 L6 Coleman Street EC2R
239 K3 Cole Street SE1
234 F3 Coley Street WC1X
235 K7 College Hill EC4R
235 K7 College Street EC4R
240 D8 Collett Road SE16
234 E1 Collier Street N1
236 B6 Collingham Gardens SW5
236 B5 Collingham Place SW5
236 B5 Collingham Road SW5
239 H4 Colnbrook Street SE1
239 H1 Colombo Street SE1
234 D4 Colonnade WC1N
241 K2 Coltman Street E14
240 D2 Commercial Road E1
241 K3 Commercial Road E14
240 B1 Commercial Street E1
235 H3 Compton Street EC1V
238 E2 Concert Hall Approach SE1
241 K2 Conder Street E14
232 E6 Conduit Mews W2
232 E6 Conduit Place W2
233 L7 Conduit Street W1S
239 M5 Congreve Street SE17
232 F7 Connaught Close W2
233 G7 Connaught Place W2
233 G6 Connaught Square W2
233 G6 Connaught Street W2
239 G2 Cons Street SE1
237 L3 Constitution Hill SW1A
239 K5 Content Street SE17
233 M4 Conway Street W1T
241 H6 Cookham Crescent SE16
239 H8 Cook's Road SE17
235 J1 Coombs Street N1
234 B1 Cooper's Lane Estate NW1
240 B3 Cooper's Road EC3N
241 L2 Copenhagen Place E14
236 A4 Cope Place W8
239 J8 Copley Court SE17
241 H2 Copley Street E1
241 K1 Copperfield Road E3
239 J2 Copperfield Street SE1
235 L6 Copthall Avenue EC2R
234 C5 Coptic Street WC1A
239 G3 Coral Street SE1
234 C3 Coram Street WC1H
240 E5 Cork Square E1W
233 M8 Cork Street W1S
232 F4 Corlett Street NW1
235 L6 Cornhill EC3V
236 C4 Cornwall Gardens SW7
236 C5 Cornwall Mews South SW7
238 F1 Cornwall Road SE1
239 G2 Cornwall Road SE1
240 E3 Cornwall Street E1
233 H4 Cornwall Terrace Mews NW1
241 G2 Cornwood Drive E1
235 M2 Coronet Street N1
235 G3 Corporation Row EC1R
235 L2 Corsham Street N1
238 F4 Cosser Street SE1
233 G4 Cosway Street NW1
236 F4 Cottage Place SW3
236 B4 Cottesmore Gardens W8
239 M1 Cottons Lane SE1
237 H6 Coulson Street SW3
239 M1 Counter Street SE1
239 K5 County Street SE1
238 F7 Courtenay Square SE11
238 F6 Courtenay Street SE11
236 B5 Courtfield Gardens SW5
236 C5 Courtfield Road SW7
240 E1 Court Street E1
235 K8 Cousin Lane SE1
234 D7 Covent Garden WC2E
234 D7 Covent Garden ⊖ WC2E
234 B8 Coventry Street W1D
235 H4 Cowcross Street EC1M
235 L3 Cowper Street EC2A
239 L5 Crail Row SE17
233 J5 Cramer Street W1U
239 J6 Crampton Street SE17
234 C7 Cranbourn Street WC2H
234 A1 Cranleigh Street NW1
236 D6 Cranley Gardens SW7
236 D6 Cranley Mews SW7
236 E6 Cranley Place SW7
235 L1 Cranston Estate N1
235 L2 Cranwood Street EC1V
232 C7 Craven Hill W2
232 D7 Craven Hill W2
232 C7 Craven Hill Gardens W2
232 D7 Craven Road W2
238 D1 Craven Street WC2N
232 D7 Craven Terrace W2
235 G3 Crawford Passage EC1R
233 G5 Crawford Place W1H
233 G5 Crawford Street W1H
240 A3 Creechurch Lane EC3A
235 H7 Creed Lane EC4V
236 D6 Cresswell Place SW10
241 G1 Cressy Place E1
234 D2 Crestfield Street WC1H
240 A8 Crimscott Street SE1
240 B1 Crispin Street E1
234 D2 Cromer Street WC1H
232 D4 Crompton Street W2
236 E5 Cromwell Place SW7
236 B5 Cromwell Road SW5
236 E5 Cromwell Road SW7
235 M1 Crondall Court N1
235 L1 Crondall Street N1
235 K1 Cropley Street N1
239 L3 Crosby Row SE1
240 A4 Cross Lane EC3R
240 B3 Crosswall EC3N
240 E3 Crowder Street E1
240 A6 Crucifix Lane SE1
234 F1 Cruikshank Street WC1X
240 A3 Crutched Friars EC3N
241 M6 Cuba Street E14
234 E2 Cubitt Street WC1X
237 H6 Culford Gardens SW3
240 F7 Culling Road SE16
235 M7 Cullum Street EC3M
233 J8 Culross Street W1K
232 F1 Culworth Street NW8
234 F2 Cumberland Gardens WC1X
233 G7 Cumberland Gate W2
233 L2 Cumberland Market NW1
237 L6 Cumberland Street SW1V
233 K1 Cumberland Terrace NW1
233 L1 Cumberland Terrace Mews NW1
241 G6 Cumberland Wharf SE16
234 E1 Cumming Street N1
237 K6 Cundy Street SW1W
232 E3 Cunningham Place NW8
238 C6 Cureton Street SW1P
240 B6 Curlew Street SE1
234 F6 Cursitor Street EC4A
235 M3 Curtain Road EC2A
235 M4 Curtain Road EC2A
237 K2 Curzon Gate W2
237 K1 Curzon Street W1J
232 E4 Cuthbert Street W2
240 A2 Cutler Street EC3A
234 F1 Cynthia Street N1
234 A4 Cypress Place W1T
235 H3 Cyrus Street EC1V

D

238 B3 Dacre Street SW1H
241 J1 Dakin Place E1
235 H3 Dallington Street EC1V
240 F2 Damien Street E1
234 E5 Dane Street WC1R
233 M7 Dansey Place W1D
239 H5 Dante Road SE11
236 F8 Danvers Street SW3
234 A6 D'Arblay Street W1F
239 K8 Dartford Street SE17
238 B3 Dartmouth Street SW1H
239 L5 Darwin Street SE17
239 K7 Date Street SE17
240 D1 Davenant Street E1
232 F4 Daventry Street NW1
239 H3 Davidge Street SE1
233 K7 Davies Mews W1K
233 K7 Davies Street W1K
239 L6 Dawes Street SE17
232 A7 Dawson Place W2
239 J5 Deacon Way SE17
241 G8 Deal Porters Way SE16
240 D1 Deal Street E1
238 C5 Dean Bradley Street SW1P
241 H6 Dean Close SE16
240 F3 Deancross Street E1
237 K1 Deanery Street W1K
238 B3 Dean Farrar Street SW1H
238 C5 Dean Ryle Street SW1P
239 L6 Dean's Buildings SE17
238 C4 Dean Stanley Street SW1P
234 B6 Dean Street W1D
238 C4 Dean Yard SW1P
239 M4 Decima Street SE1
241 J6 Deck Close SE16
241 K7 Defoe Close SE16
232 B4 Delamere Terrace W2
239 H7 De Laune Street SE17
232 B3 Delaware Road W9
240 F3 Dellow Street E1
239 H7 Delverton Road SE17
237 M6 Denbigh Place SW1V
234 B7 Denman Street W1D
234 C6 Denmark Street WC2H
239 G6 Denny Close SE11
237 G5 Denyer Street SW3
238 D3 Derby Gate SW1A
237 K1 Derby Street W1J
233 L6 Dering Street W1S
236 B3 Derry Street W8
236 C3 De Vere Gardens W8
239 L4 Deverell Street SE1
241 G3 Devonport Street E1
233 K4 Devonshire Close W1G
233 K4 Devonshire Mews South W1G
233 K4 Devonshire Mews West W1G
233 K4 Devonshire Place W1G
233 K4 Devonshire Place Mews W1G
240 A2 Devonshire Row EC2M
240 A2 Devonshire Square EC2M
233 K4 Devonshire Street W1G
232 D7 Devonshire Terrace W2
233 K5 De Walden Street W1G
240 D7 Dickens Estate SE16
239 K4 Dickens Square SE1
237 H8 Dilke Street SW3
235 K2 Dingley Place EC1V
235 J2 Dingley Road EC1V
240 E5 Discovery Walk E1W
239 K2 Disney Place SE1
235 J7 Distaff Lane EC4V
238 F6 Distin Street SE11
240 C7 Dockhead SE1
240 D8 Dockley Road SE16
240 D4 Dock Street E1
239 H7 Doddington Grove SE17
239 H8 Doddington Place SE17
239 G3 Dodson Street SE1
241 M2 Dod Street E14
239 H2 Dolben Street SE1
238 E7 Dolland Street SE11
238 A7 Dolphin Square SW1V
238 B7 Dolphin Square SW1V
234 E4 Dombey Street WC1N
235 L5 Dominion Street EC2A
234 F1 Donegal Street N1
241 J1 Dongola Road E1
237 G5 Donne Place SW3
238 F1 Doon Street SE1
241 L2 Dora Street E14
234 B2 Doric Way NW1
235 G7 Dorset Rise EC4Y
233 H4 Dorset Square NW1
233 H5 Dorset Street W1U
234 E3 Doughty Mews WC1N
234 E3 Doughty Street WC1N
238 B6 Douglas Street SW1P
236 C3 Douro Place W8
240 D5 Douthwaite Square * E1W
236 E6 Dovehouse Street SW3
237 L1 Dover Street W1J
233 L8 Dover Street W1S
235 K7 Dowgate Hill EC4R
232 B4 Downfield Close W9
238 C2 Downing Street SW1A
237 K2 Down Street W1J
241 K6 Downtown Road SE16
237 J5 D'Oyley Street SW1X
239 J8 Draco Street SE17
241 H6 Drake Close SE16
237 G5 Draycott Avenue SW3
237 H6 Draycott Place SW3
237 H5 Draycott Terrace SW3
236 A3 Drayson Mews W8
236 D6 Drayton Gardens SW10
240 A6 Druid Street SE1
240 B6 Druid Street SE1
234 B2 Drummond Crescent NW1
240 E8 Drummond Road SE16
234 A3 Drummond Street NW1
234 D6 Drury Lane WC2B
239 G5 Dryden Court SE11
234 D6 Dryden Street WC2B
233 L5 Duchess Mews W1G
233 L5 Duchess Street W1B
239 G1 Duchy Street SE1
241 J1 Duckett Street E1
234 B6 Duck Lane W1F
235 K4 Dufferin Street EC1Y
237 K3 Duke of Wellington Place SW1W
237 H6 Duke of York Square SW3
234 A8 Duke of York Street SW1Y
241 K4 Duke Shore Wharf E14
236 A2 Duke's Lane W8
240 B2 Duke's Place EC3A
234 C2 Duke's Road WC1H
233 K7 Duke Street W1K
233 J6 Duke Street W1U
239 L1 Duke Street Hill SE1
238 A1 Duke Street St James's SW1Y
241 L4 Dunbar Wharf E14
234 C8 Duncannon Street WC2N
235 H1 Duncan Terrace N1
240 E5 Dundee Street E1W
241 L4 Dundee Wharf E14
241 H2 Dunelm Street E1
240 C8 Dunlop Place SE16
233 H7 Dunraven Street W1K
240 A3 Dunster Court EC3R
237 H3 Duplex Ride SW1X
241 L6 Durand's Wharf SE16
241 J1 Durham Row E1
238 E7 Durham Street SE11
232 A6 Durham Terrace W2
234 C6 Dyott Street WC1A
235 M4 Dysart Street EC2A

E

235 H4 Eagle Close EC1M
234 E5 Eagle Street WC1R
236 A7 Eardley Crescent SW5
234 C7 Earlham Street WC2H
236 A6 Earl's Court ⇌ ⊖ SW5
236 B6 Earl's Court Gardens SW5
236 A6 Earl's Court Road SW5
236 A6 Earl's Court Square SW5
235 H2 Earlstoke Street EC1V
235 M4 Earl Street EC2A
234 C6 Earnshaw Street WC2H
241 H2 East Arbour Street E1
232 D6 Eastbourne Mews W2
232 D6 Eastbourne Terrace W2
234 A6 Eastcastle Street W1W
235 M7 Eastcheap EC3M
241 K1 Eastfield Street E14
241 M3 East India Dock Road E14
240 D6 East Lane SE16
234 F3 Easton Street WC1X
235 H5 East Poultry Avenue EC1A
235 L2 East Road N1
240 C4 East Smithfield E1W
239 L6 East Street SE17
237 J5 Eaton Close SW1W
237 J5 Eaton Gate SW1W
237 L4 Eaton Lane SW1W
237 J5 Eaton Mews North SW1W
237 K5 Eaton Mews South SW1W
237 K5 Eaton Mews West SW1W
237 J4 Eaton Place SW1X
237 K4 Eaton Row SW1W
237 K5 Eaton Square SW1W
237 J5 Eaton Terrace SW1W
238 E8 Ebbisham Drive SW8
237 K6 Ebury Bridge SW1W
237 K7 Ebury Bridge Road SW1W
237 K5 Ebury Mews SW1W
237 K6 Ebury Square SW1W
237 K5 Ebury Street SW1W
237 L5 Eccleston Bridge SW1W
237 K4 Eccleston Mews SW1X
237 L5 Eccleston Place SW1W
237 L6 Eccleston Square SW1V
237 K4 Eccleston Street SW1X
232 A3 Edbrooke Road W9
236 A1 Edge Street W8
232 F5 Edgware Road W2
232 F5 Edgware Road ⊖ NW1
237 H3 Edinburgh Gate SW1X
236 C8 Edith Grove SW10
233 J6 Edwards Mews W1H
236 F5 Egerton Crescent SW3
236 F5 Egerton Gardens SW3
237 G4 Egerton Terrace SW3
239 J7 Eglington Court SE17
239 K5 Elba Place SE17
235 L5 Eldon Place EC2M
236 B4 Eldon Road W8
241 H6 Eleanor Close SE16
239 J4 Elephant & Castle SE1
239 J5 Elephant & Castle ⇌ ⊖ SE1
240 F6 Elephant Lane SE16
239 J5 Elephant Road SE17
241 G3 Elf Row E1W
241 K7 Elgar Street SE16
232 B2 Elgin Avenue W9
232 C2 Elgin Mews North W9
232 C2 Elgin Mews South W9
235 H1 Elia Mews N1
235 H1 Elia Street N1
239 M3 Elim Estate SE1
239 M3 Elim Street SE1
237 K5 Elizabeth Street SW1W
240 D3 Ellen Street E1
239 H5 Elliott's Row SE11
237 J5 Ellis Street SW1X
232 A4 Elmfield Way W9
236 E7 Elm Park Gardens SW10
236 E7 Elm Park Lane SW3
236 E8 Elm Park Road SW3
236 E7 Elm Place SW7
232 D7 Elms Mews W2
234 F4 Elm Street WC1X
232 E2 Elm Tree Road NW8
232 B4 Elnathan Mews W9
241 J1 Elsa Street E1
239 L6 Elsted Street SE17
236 D4 Elvaston Mews SW7
236 D4 Elvaston Place SW7
238 B5 Elverton Street SW1P
235 G5 Ely Place EC1N
237 G6 Elystan Place SW3
236 F6 Elystan Street SW3
238 D1 Embankment ⊖ WC2N
237 H8 Embankment Gardens SW3
238 D1 Embankment Place WC2N
240 D7 Emba Street SE16
234 E4 Emerald Street WC1N
239 J1 Emerson Street SE1
238 A5 Emery Hill Street SW1P
239 G3 Emery Street SE1
236 C5 Emperor's Gate SW7
239 L3 Empire Square SE1
236 A7 Empress Place SW6
234 C6 Endell Street WC2H
234 B3 Endsleigh Gardens WC1H
234 B3 Endsleigh Place WC1H
234 B3 Endsleigh Street WC1H
233 G5 Enford Street W1H
239 M1 English Grounds SE1
240 C8 Enid Street SE16
236 F3 Ennismore Gardens SW7
236 F3 Ennismore Gardens Mews SW7
236 F3 Ennismore Mews SW7
236 F4 Ennismore Street SW7
239 G6 Enny Street SE11
240 D4 Ensign Street E1
235 L3 Epworth Street EC2A
238 C6 Erasmus Street SW1P
235 K4 Errol Street EC1Y
232 A3 Essendine Road W9
234 F7 Essex Street WC2R
236 A3 Essex Villas W8
235 J2 Europa Place EC1V
234 B2 Euston ⇌ ⊖ ⊖ NW1
234 B3 Euston Road NW1
234 B2 Euston Square NW1
234 A3 Euston Square ⊖ NW1
234 A3 Euston Street NW1
236 D7 Evelyn Gardens SW7
235 L1 Evelyn Way N1
234 A1 Eversholt Street NW1
233 M2 Everton Buildings NW1
239 J2 Ewer Street SE1
241 G1 Ewhurst Close E1
235 M4 Exchange Square EC2A
234 D7 Exeter Street WC2E
236 E3 Exhibition Road SW7
235 G3 Exmouth Market EC1R
239 M6 Exon Street SE17
238 F2 Exton Street SE1
234 F4 Eyre Street Hill EC1R

244 Fairclough Street - Kirby Street

F

240 D3 Fairclough Street E1
240 B6 Fair Street SE1
239 K4 Falmouth Road SE1
235 J4 Fann Street EC1M
235 M1 Fanshaw Street N1
234 B6 Fareham Street W1D
236 A1 Farmer Street W8
236 A8 Farm Lane SW6
233 K8 Farm Street W1K
239 J1 Farnham Place SE1
241 M3 Farrance Street E14
235 G4 Farringdon ⇌ ⊖ EC1M
235 G4 Farringdon Lane EC1R
234 F3 Farringdon Road EC1R
235 H5 Farringdon Street EC1M
241 J5 Farrins Rents SE16
241 K7 Farrow Place SE16
240 F5 Farthing Fields * E1W
240 B1 Fashion Street E1
239 H7 Faunce Street SE17
236 C8 Fawcett Street SW10
235 L3 Featherstone Street EC1Y
240 A3 Fenchurch Avenue EC3M
240 A3 Fenchurch Buildings EC3M
240 A3 Fenchurch Place EC3M
240 A3 Fenchurch Street EC3M
240 A3 Fenchurch Street ⇌ EC3M
240 B8 Fendall Street SE1
239 M2 Fenning Street SE1
238 D8 Fentiman Road SW8
234 F2 Fernsbury Street WC1X
235 G6 Fetter Lane EC4A
240 D2 Fieldgate Street E1
239 J7 Fielding Street SE17
234 E1 Field Street WC1X
236 B8 Finborough Road SW10
235 L6 Finch Lane EC3V
241 K8 Finland Street SE16
235 L5 Finsbury Circus EC2M
235 G3 Finsbury Estate EC1R
235 M4 Finsbury Market EC2A
235 L4 Finsbury Square EC2A
235 L4 Finsbury Street EC2Y
237 G5 First Street SW3
241 J6 Fishermans Drive SE16
234 D5 Fisher Street WC1R
232 E3 Fisherton Street NW8
235 L7 Fish Street Hill EC3R
238 F5 Fitzalan Street SE11
233 J6 Fitzhardinge Street W1H
233 M4 Fitzroy Square W1T
233 M4 Fitzroy Street W1T
241 J3 Flamborough Street E14
240 C4 Flank Street E1
234 C3 Flaxman Terrace WC1H
235 G6 Fleet Street EC4A
239 H8 Fleming Road SE17
240 D3 Fletcher Street E1
239 L6 Flint Street SE17
234 C6 Flitcroft Street WC2H
240 D7 Flockton Street SE16
237 G7 Flood Street SW3
237 G7 Flood Walk SW3
234 D7 Floral Street WC2E
233 M5 Foley Street W1W
240 D3 Forbes Street E1
240 D2 Fordham Street E1
240 F2 Ford Square E1
235 K5 Fore Street EC2Y
232 C4 Formosa Street W9
236 G7 Forset Street W1H
239 H8 Forsyth Gardens SE17
240 B1 Fort Street E1
235 K4 Fortune Street EC1Y
235 J6 Foster Lane EC2V
236 E6 Foulis Terrace SW7
241 J5 Foundry Close SE16
240 B1 Fournier Street E1
240 E5 Fowey Close E1W
232 E4 Frampton Street NW8
238 A5 Francis Street SW1P
240 F8 Frankland Close SE16
237 H6 Franklin's Row SW3
239 G3 Frazier Street SE1
240 C8 Frean Street SE16
233 G7 Frederick Close W2
234 E2 Frederick Street WC1X
237 J3 Frederic Mews * SW1X
239 M6 Freemantle Street SE17
235 H2 Friend Street EC1V
234 B6 Frith Street W1D
240 E1 Fulbourne Street E1
240 F7 Fulford Street SE16
236 D8 Fulham Road SW10
236 F6 Fulham Road SW3
234 F5 Furnival Street EC4A
238 B5 Fynes Street SW1P

G

239 G1 Gabriel's Wharf SE1
240 B6 Gainsford Street SE1
241 G6 Galleon Close SE16
241 K2 Galsworthy Avenue E14
235 K2 Galway Street EC1V
239 H2 Gambia Street SE1
232 D1 Garden Road NW8
239 H4 Garden Row SE1
241 H1 Garden Street E1
235 M3 Garden Walk EC2A
235 J2 Gard Street EC1V
241 M4 Garford Street E14
235 G3 Garnault Place EC1R
240 F4 Garnet Street E1W
235 K3 Garrett Street EC1Y
234 C7 Garrick Street WC2E
241 H7 Garterway SE16
232 B6 Garway Road W2
240 E8 Gataker Street * SE16
236 F6 Gate Mews SW7
232 F3 Gateforth Street NW8
233 L3 Gate Mews NW1
235 M3 Gatesborough Street * EC2A
234 E5 Gate Street WC2A
237 K7 Gatliff Road SW1W
239 J4 Gaunt Street SE1
238 C4 Gayfere Street SW1P
239 H4 Gaywood Street SE1
239 H7 Gaza Street SE17
240 C7 Gedling Place SE1
235 J2 Gee Street EC1V
239 H5 George Mathers Road SE11
240 C7 George Row SE16
233 H6 George Street W1H
233 K7 George Yard W1K
239 H4 Geraldine Street SE1
237 K5 Gerald Road SW1W
234 B7 Gerrard Road W1D
239 G3 Gerridge Street SE1
236 D8 Gertrude Street SW10
238 E5 Gibson Road SE11
234 C5 Gilbert Place WC1A
239 G5 Gilbert Road SE11
233 K7 Gilbert Street W1K
233 L5 Gildea Street W1W
237 M5 Gillingham Street SW1V
241 L3 Gill Street E14
236 D7 Gilston Road SW10
235 H5 Giltspur Street EC1A
239 H4 Gladstone Street SE1
241 G4 Glamis Place E1W
241 G4 Glamis Road E1W
237 M7 Glasgow Terrace SW1V
239 J3 Glasshill Street SE1
234 A8 Glasshouse Street W1B
238 D7 Glasshouse Walk SE11
236 F7 Glebe Place SW3
236 C6 Gledhow Road SW5
233 H4 Glentworth Street NW1
241 J5 Globe Pond Road SE16
239 K3 Globe Street SE1
240 A4 Gloucester Court * EC3R
232 C6 Gloucester Gardens W2
232 D6 Gloucester Mews W2
232 C6 Gloucester Mews West W2
233 H3 Gloucester Place NW1
233 H5 Gloucester Place W1U
233 H5 Gloucester Place Mews W1U
236 C4 Gloucester Road SW7
236 D6 Gloucester Road SW7
236 C5 Gloucester Road ⊖ SW7
232 F6 Gloucester Square W2
237 M7 Gloucester Street SW1V
232 B5 Gloucester Terrace W2
232 D6 Gloucester Terrace W2
236 A2 Gloucester Walk W8
235 G2 Gloucester Way EC1R
238 E7 Glyn Street SE11
237 G6 Godfrey Street SW3
238 D7 Goding Street SE11
235 J7 Godliman Street EC4V
235 K1 Godwin Close N1
238 D1 Golden Jubilee Bridge WC2N
235 J4 Golden Lane EC1Y
234 A7 Golden Square W1F
240 E3 Golding Street E1
232 A4 Goldney Road W9
235 K6 Goldsmith Street EC2V
241 G8 Gomm Road SE16
234 A5 Goodge Place W1T
234 A5 Goodge Street W1T
234 B5 Goodge Street ⊖ W1T
240 C8 Goodwin Close SE16
236 A2 Gordon Place W8
234 B3 Gordon Square WC1H
234 B3 Gordon Street WC1H
236 D4 Gore Street SW7
240 A2 Goring Street * EC3A
233 L5 Gosfield Street W1W
234 B6 Goslett Yard WC2H
235 H1 Goswell Road EC1V
234 F3 Gough Street WC1X
240 B2 Goulston Street E1
234 B5 Gower Mews WC1E
234 A3 Gower Place NW1
234 B3 Gower Street WC1E
240 D2 Gower's Walk E1
235 M7 Gracechurch Street EC3V
234 B2 Grafton Place NW1
233 L8 Grafton Street W1S
234 A4 Grafton Way W1T
235 J1 Graham Street N1
237 J6 Graham Terrace SW1W
233 M1 Granby Terrace NW1
235 H5 Grand Avenue EC1A
240 B8 Grange Road SE1
240 A8 Grange Walk SE1
240 B8 Grange Yard SE1
232 B2 Grantully Road W9
233 J6 Granville Place W1H
232 A1 Granville Road NW6
234 F2 Granville Square WC1X
234 C6 Grape Street WC2H
240 B2 Gravel Lane E1
234 D2 Gray's Inn Road WC1X
234 F5 Gray's Inn Square WC1R
239 G3 Gray Street SE1
233 L6 Great Castle Street W1G
233 G4 Great Central Street NW1
234 B6 Great Chapel Street W1D
238 C4 Great College Street SW1P
233 H6 Great Cumberland Place W1H
239 K3 Great Dover Street SE1
235 M3 Great Eastern Street EC2A
238 C3 Great George Street SW1P
239 J1 Great Guildford Street SE1
234 E4 Great James Street WC1N
233 M7 Great Marlborough Street W1F
239 L2 Great Maze Pond SE1
234 C7 Great New Portland Street WC2H
240 D1 Greatorex Street E1
234 D4 Great Ormond Street WC1N
234 F2 Great Percy Street WC1X
238 B4 Great Peter Street SW1P
233 L4 Great Portland Street W1W
233 L4 Great Portland Street ⊖ W1W
234 A7 Great Pulteney Street W1F
234 D6 Great Queen Street WC2B
234 C5 Great Russell Street WC1B
238 C1 Great Scotland Yard SW1A
238 C4 Great Smith Street SW1P
239 H2 Great Suffolk Street SE1
235 H4 Great Sutton Street EC1V
235 L6 Great Swan Alley EC2R
233 M4 Great Titchfield Street W1W
235 M7 Great Tower Street EC3M
240 A4 Great Tower Street EC3R
235 L6 Great Winchester Street EC2N
234 B7 Great Windmill Street W1D
234 B6 Greek Street W1D
241 J6 Greenacre Square SE16
240 E5 Green Bank E1W
232 F1 Greenberry Street NW8
238 A5 Greencoat Place SW1P
238 A4 Green Coat Row SW1P
240 D2 Greenfield Road E1
238 F3 Greenham Close SE1
237 M1 Green Park ⊖ W1J
233 J7 Green Street W1K
233 L4 Greenwell Street W1W
239 G2 Greet Street SE1
241 L4 Grenade Street E14
232 F3 Grendon Street NW8
236 C5 Grenville Place SW7
235 J6 Gresham Street EC2V
234 B5 Gresse Street W1T
235 G5 Greville Street EC1N
238 B4 Greycoat Place SW1P
238 B4 Greycoat Street SW1P
240 A8 Grigg's Place SE1
237 L8 Grosvenor Bridge SW8
237 J3 Grosvenor Crescent SW1X
237 J3 Grosvenor Crescent Mews SW1X
237 L4 Grosvenor Gardens SW1W
237 L4 Grosvenor Gardens Mews East SW1W
237 L4 Grosvenor Gardens Mews North SW1W
237 L4 Grosvenor Gardens Mews South * SW1W
233 H8 Grosvenor Gate W2
233 L7 Grosvenor Hill W1K
237 K3 Grosvenor Place SW1X
237 L8 Grosvenor Road SW1V
233 J7 Grosvenor Square W1K
233 K7 Grosvenor Street W1K
239 J8 Grosvenor Terrace SE5
232 D2 Grove End Road NW8
237 M5 Guildhouse Street SW1V
234 D4 Guilford Street WC1N
239 M5 Guinness Square SE1
241 K8 Gulliver Street SE16
235 G6 Gunpowder Square EC4A
240 B1 Gun Street E1
240 C2 Gunthorpe Street E1
235 J6 Gutter Lane EC2V
239 L3 Guy Street SE1

H

235 L2 Haberdasher Street N1
239 M4 Haddonhall Estate SE1
240 F3 Hainton Close E1
240 F2 Halcrow Street * E1
237 L1 Half Moon Street W1J
236 A8 Halford Road SW6
237 J4 Halkin Place SW1X
237 K3 Halkin Street SW1X
233 L5 Hallam Street W1W
241 K1 Halley Street E14
232 C6 Hallfield Estate W2
232 E4 Hall Place W2
232 D2 Hall Road NW8
235 H2 Hall Street EC1V
239 M6 Halpin Place SE17
237 G5 Halsey Street SW3
232 D2 Hamilton Close NW8
241 K7 Hamilton Close SE16
232 D2 Hamilton Gardens NW8
237 K2 Hamilton Place W1J
232 C1 Hamilton Terrace NW8
239 L3 Hamlet Way SE1
240 B4 Hammett Street EC3N
234 B1 Hampden Close NW1
233 H6 Hampden Gurney Street W2
233 M2 Hampstead Road NW1
239 J6 Hampton Street SE17
240 C1 Hanbury Street E1
234 E5 Hand Court WC1V
234 D3 Handel Street WC1N
239 L3 Hankey Place SE1
241 G1 Hannibal Road E1
233 L6 Hanover Square W1S
233 L7 Hanover Street W1S
237 H3 Hans Crescent SW3
233 M4 Hanson Street W1W
237 H4 Hans Place SW1X
237 G4 Hans Road SW3
237 H4 Hans Street SW1X
234 B6 Hanway Place W1T
234 B6 Hanway Street W1T
232 F5 Harbet Road W2
234 E4 Harbour Street WC1N
233 G5 Harcourt Street W1H
236 C7 Harcourt Terrace SW10
241 G3 Harding Street E1W
235 G2 Hardwick Street EC1R
239 M2 Hardwidge Street SE1
241 H6 Hardy Close SE16
233 L6 Harewood Place W1G
233 G4 Harewood Row NW1
233 G4 Harewoood Avenue NW1
241 J1 Harford Street E1
238 E8 Harleyford Road SE11
236 D7 Harley Gardens SW10
233 K4 Harley Street W1G
239 G7 Harmsworth Street SE17
240 A8 Harold Estate SE1
239 K4 Harper Road SE1
237 H3 Harriet Street SW1X
237 H3 Harriet Walk SW1X
236 C6 Harrington Gardens SW7
236 E5 Harrington Road SW7
233 M1 Harrington Square NW1
233 M2 Harrington Street NW1
234 D2 Harrison Street WC1H
233 G6 Harrowby Street W1H
240 B2 Harrow Place E1
232 A4 Harrow Road W2
240 A3 Hart Street EC3R
237 G5 Hasker Street SW3
234 C2 Hastings Street WC1H
239 G1 Hatfields SE1
232 B6 Hatherley Grove W2
241 G6 Hatteraick Road SE16
235 G4 Hatton Garden EC1N
232 E4 Hatton Street W2
235 G4 Hatton Wall EC1N
241 H3 Havering Street E1
235 J1 Haverstock Street N1
241 H6 Hawke Place * SE16
240 B3 Haydon Street EC3N
233 G4 Hayes Place NW1
233 L8 Hay Hill W1J
239 H5 Hayles Street SE11
234 B8 Haymarket SW1Y
235 J4 Hayne Street EC1A
239 M1 Hay's Lane SE1
233 L8 Hay's Mews W1J
235 H3 Haywood Place EC1R
237 K3 Headfort Place SW1X
241 H2 Head Street E1
241 K2 Hearnshaw Street E14
235 M4 Hearn Street EC2A
234 E3 Heathcote Street WC1N
233 M7 Heddon Street W1B
234 A7 Heddon Street W1S
239 H5 Hedger Street SE11
239 J8 Heiron Street SE17
240 D5 Hellings Street E1W
235 K3 Helmet Row EC1V
241 L8 Helsinki Square SE16
232 E3 Henderson Drive NW8
240 A3 Heneage Lane EC3A
240 C1 Heneage Street E1
233 L6 Henrietta Place W1G
234 D7 Henrietta Street WC2E
240 D2 Henriques Street E1
239 L5 Henshaw Street SE17
235 G4 Herbal Hill EC1R
237 H4 Herbert Crescent SW1X
234 C3 Herbrand Street WC1H
238 F4 Hercules Road SE1
232 A6 Hereford Road W2
236 D6 Hereford Square SW7
232 E5 Hermitage Street W2
240 D5 Hermitage Wall E1W
235 H2 Hermit Street EC1V
241 K5 Heron Place SE16
241 M5 Heron Quay E14
238 C6 Herrick Street SW1P
237 K2 Hertford Street W1J
241 M4 Hertsmere Road E14
236 B6 Hesper Mews SW5
240 E3 Hessel Street E1
235 M3 Hewett Street EC2A
239 J5 Heygate Estate SE17
239 J5 Heygate Street SE17
238 B6 Hide Place SW1P
234 E5 High Holborn WC1V
236 A3 High Street Kensington ⊖ W8
236 A8 Hildyard Road SW6
240 F5 Hilliards Court E1W
239 J8 Hillingdon Street SE17
232 D1 Hill Road NW8
233 M6 Hills Place W1F
233 K8 Hill Street W1J
233 K6 Hinde Street W1U
241 M3 Hind Grove E14
241 M3 Hindgrove Area E14
241 G8 Hithe Grove SE16
237 K4 Hobart Place SW1W
236 D8 Hobury Street SW10
236 B6 Hogarth Road SW5
237 J6 Holbein Mews SW1W
237 J6 Holbein Place SW1W
235 G5 Holborn EC1N
234 E5 Holborn ⊖ WC2B
235 G5 Holborn Viaduct EC1A
234 F2 Holford Street WC1X
239 H1 Holland Street SE1
236 A3 Holland Street W8
234 A6 Hollen Street W1F
233 L6 Holles Street W1C
236 C8 Hollywood Road SW10
239 H5 Holyoak Road SE11
239 M2 Holyrood Street SE1
240 A6 Holyrood Street SE1
235 M4 Holywell Row EC2A
235 M1 Homefield Street * N1
233 G5 Homer Row W1H
233 G5 Homer Street W1H
240 D3 Hooper Street E1
240 C1 Hopetown Street E1
234 A7 Hopkins Street W1F
239 H1 Hopton Street SE1
239 L8 Hopwood Road SE17
236 A3 Hornton Place W8
236 A2 Hornton Street W8
234 B7 Horse & Dolphin Yard W1D
241 J3 Horseferry Road E14
238 B4 Horseferry Road SW1P
238 C2 Horse Guards Avenue SW1A
238 C2 Horse Guards Parade SW1A
238 C2 Horse Guards Road SW1A
240 B6 Horselydown Lane SE1
239 K8 Horsley Street SE17
235 H5 Hosier Lane EC1A
241 G8 Hothfield Place SE16
238 F6 Hotspur Street SE11
234 E6 Houghton Street WC2A
240 A2 Houndsditch EC3A
238 A4 Howick Place SW1E
234 A4 Howland Street W1T
241 K7 Howland Way SE16
232 D4 Howley Place W2
235 M2 Hoxton Square N1
235 M1 Hoxton Street N1
237 L6 Hugh Mews SW1V
237 L6 Hugh Street SW1V
237 L6 Hugh Street SW1V
241 J6 Hull Close SE16
235 J2 Hull Street EC1V
238 E1 Hungerford Bridge SE1
239 M4 Hunter Close SE1
234 D3 Hunter Street WC1N
234 A4 Huntley Street WC1E
239 M6 Huntsman Street SE17
233 H3 Huntsworth Mews NW1
241 H6 Hurley Crescent SE16
241 M7 Hutching's Street E14
235 G7 Hutton Street EC4Y
237 K2 Hyde Park Corner W1J
237 K2 Hyde Park Corner ⊖ W1J
236 D3 Hyde Park Court SW7
232 F6 Hyde Park Crescent W2
232 F7 Hyde Park Garden Mews W2
232 F7 Hyde Park Gardens W2
236 C3 Hyde Park Gate SW7
236 D3 Hyde Park Gate SW7
232 F7 Hyde Park Square W2
232 F7 Hyde Park Street W2

I

235 M7 Idol Lane EC3R
236 B8 Ifield Road SW10
239 J6 Iliffe Street SE17
239 J6 Iliffe Yard SE17
236 D4 Imperial College Road SW7
240 B3 India Street EC3N
234 A7 Ingestre Place W1F
234 F2 Inglebert Street EC1R
238 E5 Ingram Close SE11
233 J2 Inner Circle NW1
232 B6 Inverness Terrace W2
232 C8 Inverness Terrace Gate W2
239 H1 Invicta Plaza SE1
239 L7 Inville Road SE17
235 K6 Ironmonger Lane EC2V
235 K2 Ironmonger Row EC1V
234 C2 Irving Street WC2N
241 G6 Isambard Place SE16
241 K3 Island Row E14
236 A4 Iverna Court W8
236 A4 Iverna Gardens W8
237 G5 Ives Street SW3
233 G4 Ivor Place NW1
236 F6 Ixworth Place SW3

J

240 C6 Jacob Street SE1
240 F8 Jamaica Gate SE16
240 C7 Jamaica Road SE1
240 E7 Jamaica Road SE16
241 G2 Jamaica Street E1
240 C6 Jamaica Wharf SE1
233 K6 James Street W1U
234 D7 James Street WC2E
236 A1 Jameson Street W8
241 K1 Jamuna Close E14
240 D7 Janeway Street SE16
241 J4 Jardine Road E1W
240 C6 Java Wharf SE1
236 D3 Jay Mews SW7
234 A8 Jermyn Street SW1Y
232 F3 Jerome Crescent NW8
240 B3 Jewery Street EC3N
239 G2 Joan Street SE1
234 E4 Jockey's Fields WC1R
238 F3 Johanna Street SE1
234 D8 John Adam Street WC2N
235 G7 John Carpenter Street EC4Y
240 D7 John Felton Road SE16
240 C4 John Fisher Street E1
238 C5 John Islip Street SW1P
233 L6 John Prince's Street W1G
240 D7 John Roll Way SE16
239 J8 John Ruskin Street SE5
238 C6 John Slip Street SW1P
234 E4 John's Mews WC1N
238 A7 Johnson's Place SW1V
241 G3 Johnson Street E1
234 E4 John Street WC1N
239 L1 Joiner Street SE1
238 E6 Jonathan Street SE11
237 G6 Jubilee Place SW3
241 G2 Jubilee Street E1
236 B1 Jubilee Walk W8
234 C2 Judd Street WC1H
232 F5 Junction Mews W2
238 E5 Juxon Street SE11

K

241 H5 Katherine Close SE16
234 E6 Kean Street WC2B
241 J6 Keel Close SE16
234 E6 Keeley Street WC2B
240 E7 Keeton's Road SE16
239 H3 Kell Street SE1
236 B4 Kelso Place W8
234 E6 Kemble Street WC2B
236 A7 Kempsford Gardens SW5
239 G6 Kempsford Road SE11
233 J5 Kendall Place W1U
233 G6 Kendal Street W2
240 D5 Kennet Street E1W
241 G6 Kenning Street SE16
239 G7 Kennings Way SE11
239 H7 Kennington ⊖ SE11
238 E7 Kennington Lane SE11
238 E8 Kennington Oval SE11
239 G8 Kennington Park Gardens SE11
239 G7 Kennington Park Place SE11
239 G7 Kennington Park Road SE11
238 F4 Kennington Road SE1
239 G5 Kennington Road SE11
238 F8 Kennnington Oval SE11
233 J5 Kenrick Place W1U
236 A1 Kensington Church Street W8
236 B3 Kensington Court W8
232 B6 Kensington Gardens Square W2
236 C4 Kensington Gate W8
236 D3 Kensington Gore SW7
236 A4 Kensington High Street W8
236 B1 Kensington Palace Gardens W8
236 B2 Kensington Palace Gardens W8
236 A1 Kensington Place W8
237 G3 Kensington Road SW7
236 B3 Kensington Road W8
236 B3 Kensington Square W8
234 C3 Kenton Street WC1H
236 A6 Kenway Road SW5
234 D1 Keystone Close N1
239 H4 Keyworth Street SE1
232 A2 Kilburn Park Road NW6
232 A6 Kildare Terrace W2
234 E1 Killick Street N1
241 H6 Kinburn Street SE16
240 E2 Kinder Street E1
241 H5 King & Queen Wharf SE16
239 K6 King and Queen Street SE17
238 C2 King Charles Street SW1A
232 C5 Kingdom Street W2
235 J6 King Edward Street EC1A
239 G4 King Edward Walk SE1
239 H3 King James Street SE1
233 M7 Kingly Street W1F
235 L6 King's Arms Yard EC2R
239 H2 King's Bench Street SE1
235 H7 Kingscote Street EC4V
234 D1 King's Cross ⇌ N1C
234 E2 King's Cross Road WC1X
234 D1 King's Cross St Pancras ⊖ N1C
239 L1 King's Head Yard SE1
234 F4 King's Mews WC1N
232 E1 Kingsmill Terrace NW8
235 J2 King Square EC1V
236 E8 King's Road SW3
237 M5 King's Scholars Passage SW1P
240 F6 King's Stairs Close SE16
234 D7 King Street WC2E
238 A1 King Street SW1Y
235 K6 King Street EC2V
234 E6 Kingsway WC2B
235 L7 King William Street EC4N
237 J3 Kinnerton Place North * SW1X
237 J3 Kinnerton Place South * SW1X
237 J3 Kinnerton Street SW1X
237 J3 Kinnerton Yard * SW1X
239 L3 Kipling Estate SE1
239 L3 Kipling Street SE1
240 D7 Kirby Estate SE16
239 M3 Kirby Grove SE1
235 G4 Kirby Street EC1N

236 B5 Knaresborough Place SW5
235 H7 Knightrider Street EC4V
237 H3 Knightsbridge SW1X
237 H3 Knightsbridge ⊖ SW3
233 H4 Knox Street W1H
236 C4 Kynance Mews SW7
236 C4 Kynance Place SW7

L

235 L4 Lackington Street EC2A
240 B6 Lafone Street SE1
241 H5 Lagado Mews SE16
238 D5 Lambeth Bridge SW1P
238 E5 Lambeth High Street SE1
235 J7 Lambeth Hill EC4V
238 F3 Lambeth North ⊖ SE1
238 E4 Lambeth Palace Road SE1
238 F4 Lambeth Road SE1
238 F5 Lambeth Walk SE11
234 E4 Lamb's Conduit Street WC1N
235 K4 Lamb's Passage EC1Y
240 B1 Lamb Street E1
240 A7 Lamb Way SE1
239 H5 Lamlash Street SE11
232 D3 Lanark Place W9
232 B1 Lanark Road W9
232 D7 Lancaster Gate W2
232 D8 Lancaster Gate ⊖ W2
232 E7 Lancaster Gate ⊖ W2
232 D7 Lancaster Mews W2
234 E7 Lancaster Place WC2E
239 H3 Lancaster Street SE1
232 E7 Lancaster Terrace W2
232 D8 Lancaster Walk W2
237 G3 Lancelot Place SW7
234 B2 Lancing Street NW1
237 J3 Lanesborough Place * SW1X
240 E1 Langdale Street E1
232 D1 Langford Street NW8
233 L5 Langham Place W1B
233 L5 Langham Street W1W
233 M5 Langham Street W1W
238 D8 Langley Lane SW8
234 C7 Langley Street WC2H
234 E3 Langton Close WC1X
232 A3 Lanhill Road W9
239 L4 Lansdowne Place SE1
239 J3 Lant Street SE1
239 K6 Larcom Street SE17
232 B3 Lauderdale Road W9
238 E7 Laud Street SE11
237 F3 Launcelot Street SE1
236 C4 Launceston Place W8
235 L7 Laurence Pountney
        Lane EC4V
241 K5 Lavender Road SE16
241 K6 Lavender Wharf SE16
239 J1 Lavington Street SE1
238 D8 Lawn Lane SW8
236 F8 Lawrence Street SW3
241 L6 Lawrence Wharf SE16
239 L4 Law Street SE1
233 L3 Laxton Place NW1
234 F4 Laystall Street EC1R
240 A3 Leadenhall Street EC3A
235 M6 Leadenhall Street EC3V
238 E2 Leake Street SE1
234 E2 Leather Lane EC1N
239 M3 Leathermarket Street SE1
234 E2 Leeke Street WC1X
233 J7 Lees Place W1K
234 B7 Leicester Square W1D
234 B7 Leicester Square ⊖ WC2H
234 B7 Leicester Street WC2H
234 C3 Leigh Street WC1H
232 C6 Leinster Gardens W2
232 C7 Leinster Mews W2
232 C7 Leinster Place W2
232 A7 Leinster Square W2
232 C7 Leinster Terrace W2
240 C3 Leman Street E1
237 G3 Lennox Gardens SW1X
237 G5 Lennox Gardens Mews SW1X
235 L3 Leonard Street EC2A
241 M1 Leopold Estate E3
241 L1 Leopold Street E3
239 M5 Leroy Street SE1
235 J2 Lever Street EC1V
238 B3 Lewisham Street SW1H
236 A5 Lexham Gardens W8
236 A5 Lexham Mews W8
234 A7 Lexington Street W1F
240 B2 Leyden Street E1
241 H5 Leydon Close SE16
239 H3 Library Street SE1
234 A1 Lidlington Place NW1
232 F3 Lilestone Street NW8
240 D5 Lilley Close E1W
236 A7 Lillie Road SW6
236 A7 Lillie Yard SW6
235 H6 Limeburner Lane EC4M
240 D5 Lime Close E1W
241 L4 Limehouse Causeway E14
241 L3 Limehouse Link E14
241 J3 Limehouse ⇌ ⊖ E14
236 D8 Limerston Street SW10
235 M7 Lime Street EC3M
234 E6 Lincoln's Inn Fields WC2A
232 A8 Linden Gardens W2
240 F1 Lindley Street E1
238 B7 Lindsay Square SW1V
235 H4 Lindsey Street EC1A
233 D3 Linhope Street NW1
240 D8 Linsey Street SE16
234 B7 Lisle Street WC2H
232 F3 Lisson Green Estate NW8
233 G4 Lisson Grove NW1
232 F3 Lisson Grove NW8
234 C7 Litchfield Street WC2H
233 M6 Little Argyll Street W1F
235 J5 Little Britain EC1A
237 K4 Little Chester Street SW1X
238 C3 Little George Street SW1P
234 A7 Little Marlborough
        Street W1F
235 G6 Little New Street EC4A
233 L6 Little Portland Street W1G
233 L6 Little Russell Street WC1B
237 M2 Little St James's Street SW1A
238 C3 Little Sanctuary SW1A
234 C7 Little Somerset Street E1
239 M5 Little Titchfield Street W1W
239 K7 Liverpool Grove SE17
235 M5 Liverpool Street EC2M
235 M5 Liverpool Street ⇌ EC2M
235 K3 Lizard Street EC1V
240 D7 Llewellyn Street SE16

234 F2 Lloyd Baker Street WC1X
240 B3 Lloyd's Avenue EC3N
234 F2 Lloyd Square WC1X
235 G2 Lloyds Row EC1R
234 F2 Lloyd's Street WC1X
241 L2 Locksley Estate E14
241 L1 Locksley Street E14
239 L3 Lockyer Street SE1
232 F3 Lodge Road NW8
240 D7 Loftie Street SE16
236 A5 Logan Place W8
238 B1 Lolesworth Close E1
238 F5 Lollard Street SE11
238 F6 Lollard Street SE11
239 J2 Loman Street SE1
240 D1 Lomas Street E1
235 G6 London EC4Y
235 L7 Lombard Street EC3V
235 L8 London Bridge EC4R
235 L1 London Bridge ⇌ ⊖ SE1
239 L1 London Bridge Street SE1
232 E6 London Mews W2
239 H4 London Road SE1
240 A3 London Street EC3R
232 E6 London Street W2
235 K5 London Wall EC2M
234 D7 Long Acre WC2E
235 J3 Longford Street NW1
235 J5 Long Lane EC1A
239 L3 Long Lane SE1
237 M5 Longmoore Street SW1V
236 A5 Longridge Road SW5
239 H5 Longville Road SE11
240 A8 Long Walk SE1
234 E4 Long Yard WC1N
238 C4 Lord North Street SW1P
234 F1 Lorenzo Street WC1X
239 J8 Lorrimore Road SE17
239 H8 Lorrimore Square SE17
235 L6 Lothbury EC2R
238 F7 Loughborough Street SE11
235 M7 Lovat Lane EC3R
235 K6 Love Lane EC2V
241 K7 Lovell Place SE16
241 K2 Lovell Street E14
237 K4 Lower Belgrave
        Street SW1W
237 L4 Lower Grosvenor
        Place SW1W
234 A7 Lower James Street W1F
234 A7 Lower John Street W1F
238 F3 Lower Marsh SE1
241 G7 Lower Road SE16
237 J6 Lower Sloane Street SW1W
240 A4 Lower Thames
        Street EC3R
237 J4 Lowndes Close * SW1X
237 J4 Lowndes Place SW1X
237 H3 Lowndes Square SW1X
237 J4 Lowndes Street SW1X
236 F5 Lucan Place SW3
240 C8 Lucey Road SE16
235 H6 Ludgate Circus EC4M
235 H6 Ludgate Hill EC4M
241 G3 Lukin Street E1
233 K7 Lumley Street W1K
237 L7 Lupus Street SW1V
238 B7 Lupus Street SW1V
232 E4 Luton Street NW8
233 J4 Luxborough Street W1U
237 J4 Lyall Mews SW1X
237 J4 Lyall Street SW1X
232 E3 Lyons Place NW8
239 K7 Lytham Street SE17

M

235 J2 Macclesfield Road EC1V
234 B7 Macclesfield Street * W1D
240 E5 Mace Close E1W
236 D2 Macklin Street WC2B
233 M2 Mackworth Street NW1
239 K7 Macleod Street SE17
233 M7 Maddox Street W1S
239 M2 Magdalen Street SE1
238 F8 Magee Street SE11
240 C6 Maguire Street SE1
232 D4 Maida Avenue W9
232 C2 Maida Vale W9
232 C2 Maida Vale ⊖ W9
239 K1 Maiden Lane SE1
234 D7 Maiden Lane WC2E
240 D7 Major Road SE16
237 G6 Makins Street SW3
234 B4 Malet Street WC1E
236 E8 Mallord Street SW3
232 F3 Mallory Street NW8
235 L3 Mallow Street EC1Y
235 H3 Malta Street EC1V
240 B7 Maltby Street SE1
233 J6 Manchester Square W1U
233 J5 Manchester Street W1U
239 L3 Manciple Street SE1
233 K6 Mandeville Place W1U
234 B6 Manette Street W1D
241 M6 Manilla Street E14
235 H2 Manningford Close EC1V
239 J7 Manor Place SE17
236 F7 Manresa Road SW3
240 C3 Mansell Street E1
233 K5 Mansfield Mews W1G
233 L5 Mansfield Street W1G
235 K7 Mansion House EC4V
235 L7 Mansion House ⊖ EC4R
236 D5 Manson Mews SW7
236 D6 Manson Place SW7
241 J6 Mapleleaf Square SE16
240 F1 Maples Place E1
233 M4 Maple Street W1T
233 H7 Marble Arch W1C
234 C3 Marchmont Street WC1H
233 L6 Margaret Street W1W
236 F8 Margaretta Terrace SW3
234 B7 Margery Street WC1X
240 E7 Marigold Street SE16
234 E3 Marine Street SE16
237 K1 Market Mews W1J
233 M6 Market Place W1W
237 G6 Markham Square SW3
237 G6 Markham Street SW3
240 A4 Mark Lane EC3R
232 E7 Marlborough Gate W2
233 C1 Marlborough Place NW8
238 A2 Marlborough Road SW1A
232 F6 Marlborough Street SW3
236 B4 Marloes Road W8
241 H6 Marlow Way SE16
241 K2 Maroon Street E14
234 A7 Marshall Street W1F

239 J2 Marshalsea Road SE1
238 C5 Marsham Street SW1P
241 M5 Marsh Wall E14
235 K3 Martha's Buildings EC1V
240 F3 Martha Street E1
235 L7 Martin Lane EC4V
232 A4 Marylands Road W9
232 A4 Marylands Road W9
233 K4 Marylebone ⇌ ⊖ NW1
233 K4 Marylebone
        High Street W1U
233 K6 Marylebone Lane W1U
233 J4 Marylebone Road NW1
233 K5 Marylebone Street W1G
238 F6 Marylee Way SE11
241 M2 Masjid Lane E14
239 M5 Mason Street SE17
239 M6 Massinger Street SE17
241 J1 Masters Street E1
241 J2 Matlock Street E14
238 C3 Matthew Parker
        Street SW1H
238 B5 Maunsel Street SW1P
237 L1 Mayfair Place W1J
240 F7 Mayflower Street SE16
234 A1 Mayford Estate NW1
240 F4 Maynards Quay E1W
234 C8 May's Court WC2N
237 M4 McAuley Close SE1
236 C5 McLeod's Mews SW7
239 G8 Meadcroft Road SE11
239 H8 Meadcroft Road SE11
238 E8 Meadow Road SW8
239 J5 Meadow Row SE1
238 F4 Mead Row SE1
239 M4 Meakin Estate SE1
234 E3 Mecklenburgh
        Square WC1N
238 B5 Medway Street SW1P
240 E5 Meeting House Alley E1W
233 G4 Melcombe Place NW1
233 H4 Melcombe Street NW1
232 D2 Melina Place NW8
239 M2 Melior Street SE1
234 A1 Melton Street NW1
237 K3 Memorial Gates SW1W
238 E7 Mepham Street SE1
234 C7 Mercer Street WC2H
232 E5 Merchant Square W2
234 F2 Merlin Street EC1R
239 K2 Mermaid Court SE1
239 K4 Merrick Square SE1
239 H8 Merrington Road SW6
239 L7 Merrow Street SE17
239 G7 Methley Street SE11
239 G2 Meymott Street SE1
235 K1 Micawber Street N1
236 A8 Micklethwaite Lane SW6
240 A1 Middlesex Street E1
240 B2 Middlesex Street E1
235 J5 Middle Temple WC2R
234 F7 Middle Temple Lane EC4Y
241 H6 Middleton Drive SE16
234 C1 Midland Road NW1
241 H6 Midship Close SE16
236 D7 Milborne Grove SW10
239 H3 Milcote Street SE1
238 D8 Miles Street SW8
234 F7 Milford Lane WC2R
235 K6 Milk Street EC2V
241 G4 Milk Yard E1W
238 D4 Millbank SW1P
235 J8 Millennium Bridge SE1
241 M6 Millennium Harbour E14
234 L4 Milligan Street E14
234 E4 Millman Mews WC1N
234 E4 Millman Street WC1N
241 K3 Mill Place E14
240 B7 Millstream Road SE1
240 C6 Mill Street SE1
233 L7 Mill Street W1S
237 G5 Milner Street SW3
235 K4 Milton Street EC2Y
239 G7 Milverton Street SE11
240 A4 Mincing Lane EC3M
237 J5 Minera Mews SW1W
240 B3 Minories EC3N
235 J3 Mitchell Street EC1V
239 G2 Mitre Road SE1
240 A3 Mitre Street EC3A
238 C4 Molyneux Street W1H
235 G5 Monck Street SW1P
235 K5 Monkton Street SE11
235 K5 Monkwell Square EC2Y
232 A6 Monmouth Place W2
232 A6 Monmouth Road W2
234 C6 Monmouth Street WC2H
239 L1 Montague Close SE1
234 C5 Montague Place EC3R
234 C5 Montague Street WC1B
233 H5 Montagu Mansions W1U
233 H5 Montagu Mews North W1H
233 H5 Montagu Mews West W1H
233 H5 Montagu Place W1H
233 H5 Montagu Row W1U
233 H5 Montagu Square W1H
233 H6 Montagu Street W1H
238 F7 Montford Place SE11
240 C1 Monthorpe Road E1
237 G3 Montpelier Square SW7
237 G3 Montpelier Street SW7
237 G3 Montpelier Walk SW7
237 K3 Montrose Place SW1X
235 L7 Monument ⊖ EC4R
235 L7 Monument Street EC3R
235 M7 Monument Street EC3R
241 G4 Monza Street E1W
241 G7 Moodkee Street SE16
237 H5 Moore Street SW3
235 L5 Moorfields EC2Y
235 L6 Moorgate EC2R
234 L5 Moorgate ⇌ ⊖ EC2Y
235 K5 Moor Lane EC2Y
234 C7 Moor Street W1D
235 K2 Mora Street EC1V
239 K6 Morecambe Street SE17
235 H2 Moreland Street EC1V
240 A5 More London SE1
238 A6 Moreton Place SW1V
238 B6 Moreton Street SW1V
238 A6 Moreton Terrace SW1V
239 M2 Morgan's Lane SE1
240 A5 Morgan's Lane SE1
239 G3 Morley Street SE1
233 M1 Mornington
        Crescent NW1
233 L1 Mornington Place NW1
233 L1 Mornington Terrace NW1
240 A7 Morocco Street SE1
237 M5 Morpeth Terrace SW1P

240 F3 Morris Street E1
232 A2 Morshead Road W9
234 A4 Mortimer Market WC1E
234 A5 Mortimer Street W1T
233 M5 Mortimer Street W1W
238 F4 Morton Place SE1
234 B5 Morwell Street WC1B
232 B7 Moscow Place W2
232 B7 Moscow Road W2
237 G5 Mossop Street SW3
237 J4 Motcomb Street SW1X
236 E2 Mount Gate W2
233 J3 Mount Mills EC1V
234 F4 Mount Pleasant WC1X
233 K8 Mount Row W1K
233 K8 Mount Street W1K
233 K8 Mount Street Mews W1K
240 E1 Mount Terrace E1
233 J5 Moxon Street W1U
240 D2 Mulberry Street E1
236 E8 Mulberry Walk SW3
232 F4 Mulready Street NW8
235 M2 Mundy Street N1
233 L3 Munster Square NW1
239 K5 Munton Road SE17
238 F3 Murphy Street SE1
235 K1 Murray Grove N1
241 G2 Musbury Street E1
240 A4 Muscovy Street EC3N
234 C5 Museum Street WC1A
235 G3 Myddelton Passage EC1R
235 G1 Myddelton Square EC1R
235 G3 Myddelton Street EC1R
240 D2 Myrdle Street E1

N

234 F2 Naoroji Street WC1X
235 K1 Napier Grove N1
241 K4 Narrow Street E14
233 L2 Nash Street NW1
233 M5 Nassau Street W1W
240 C7 Nathaniel Close * E1
234 C6 Neal Street WC2H
240 C8 Neckinger SE1
241 H7 Needleman Street SE16
232 A1 Nelson Close NW6
235 H1 Nelson Place N1
239 H1 Nelson Square SE1
240 E2 Nelson Street E1
235 H1 Nelson Terrace N1
241 G7 Neptune Street SE16
240 D4 Nesham Street E1W
236 A6 Netherton Grove SW10
233 M2 Netley Street NW1
236 A6 Nevern Place SW5
236 A6 Nevern Square SW5
236 E6 Neville Street SW7
240 E2 Newark Street E1
241 M8 New Atlas Wharf E14
233 L7 New Bond Street W1S
233 L8 New Bond Street W1S
235 H6 New Bridge Street EC4V
235 M5 New Broad Street EC2M
233 M7 New Burlington Street W1S
238 F7 Newburn Street SE11
235 J5 Newbury Street EC1A
232 E5 Newcastle Place W2
235 K5 New Cavendish Street W1G
235 J6 New Change EC4M
239 L8 New Church Road SE5
239 K2 Newcomen Street SE1
232 F1 Newcourt Street NW8
241 J3 Newell Street E14
235 G6 New Fetter Lane EC4A
235 H6 Newgate Street EC1A
240 C1 New Goulston Street E1
234 A5 Newman's Row WC1A
239 H6 Newington Butts SE1
239 J4 Newington Causeway SE1
239 H5 New Kent Road SE1
240 F4 Newlands Quay E1W
234 A5 Newman Street W1T
235 M3 New North Place EC2A
235 L1 New North Road N1
234 D4 New North Street WC1N
234 C5 New Oxford Street WC1A
238 E5 Newport Street SE11
233 H6 New Quebec Street W1H
236 E3 New Ride SW7
240 E2 New Road E1
234 C7 New Row WC2N
238 D7 New Spring
        Gardens Walk SE1
235 M2 New Square WC2A
235 M2 New Street EC2M
235 G6 New Street Square EC4A
232 A6 Newton Road W2
234 D5 Newton Street WC2B
235 K5 New Union Street EC2Y
235 L7 Nicholas Lane EC3V
239 H1 Nicholson Street SE1
236 D8 Nightingale Place SW10
235 K2 Nile Street N1
238 C8 Nine Elms Lane SW8
235 J6 Noble Street EC2V
235 J1 Noel Road N1
234 N4 Noel Street W1F
241 L2 Norbiton Road E14
233 G6 Norfolk Crescent W2
232 E6 Norfolk Place W2
232 E6 Norfolk Square W2
235 J3 Norman Street EC1V
234 B8 Norris Street SW1Y
235 G3 Northampton Road EC1R
235 H3 Northampton Square EC1V
233 J7 North Audley Street W1K
232 F2 North Bank NW8
235 H3 Northburgh Street EC1V
236 F7 North Carriage Drive W2
234 D1 Northdown Street N1
235 K4 Northey Street E14
232 A6 North Gower Street NW1
234 C1 North Mews WC1N
234 E4 North Mews WC1N
233 G7 North Ride W2
233 J7 North Row W1K
240 C3 North Tenter Street E1
236 F5 North Terrace SW3
240 B3 Northumberland
        Alley EC3N
234 C8 Northumberland
        Avenue WC2N
232 A6 Northumberland Place W2
238 C1 Northumberland
        Street WC2N
232 E5 North Wharf Road W2
240 D3 Northwick Terrace NW8
241 K7 Norway Gate SE16

241 L3 Norway Place E14
234 F5 Norwich Street EC4A
233 J4 Nottingham Place W1U
233 J4 Nottingham Street W1U
232 A8 Notting Hill Gate W11
236 A1 Notting Hill Gate ⊖ W11
232 D1 Nugent Terrace NW8
233 G6 Nutford Place W1H

O

239 G5 Oakden Street SE11
232 A3 Oakington Road W9
241 L3 Oak Lane E14
235 H1 Oakley Close EC1V
237 G8 Oakley Gardens SW3
234 A1 Oakley Square NW1
236 F8 Oakley Street SW3
232 F2 Oak Tree Road NW8
235 J5 Oat Lane EC2V
239 J6 Occupation Road SE17
241 J1 Ocean Square N1
241 L7 Odessa Street SE16
233 M5 Ogle Street W1W
235 H6 Old Bailey EC4M
233 J7 Old Barrack Yard SW1X
233 M8 Old Bond Street W1S
235 M6 Old Broad Street EC2N
236 B6 Old Brompton Road SW5
236 D6 Old Brompton Road SW7
233 M7 Old Burlington Street W1S
233 J4 Oldbury Place W1U
240 B2 Old Castle Street E1
233 L6 Old Cavendish Street W1G
241 H2 Old Church Road E1
236 F7 Old Church Street SW3
234 B7 Old Compton Street W1D
235 B3 Old Court Place W8
234 D4 Old Gloucester Street WC1N
240 C7 Old Jamaica Road SE16
235 K6 Old Jewry EC2R
239 M5 Old Kent Road SE1
233 G5 Old Marylebone Road NW1
240 C1 Old Montague Street E1
234 E5 Old North Street WC1X
238 E5 Old Paradise Street SE11
237 K2 Old Park Lane W1J
238 B4 Old Pye Street SW1P
238 B3 Old Queen Street SW1H
234 F6 Old Square WC2A
235 J3 Old Street EC1V
235 L3 Old Street EC1Y
235 L3 Old Street ⇌ ⊖ EC1Y
235 L3 Oliver's Yard EC1Y
239 J8 Olney Road SE17
239 K2 O'Meara Street SE1
234 D1 Omega Place N1
241 J8 Omega Gate SE16
236 A8 Ongar Road SW6
236 D6 Onslow Gardens SW7
236 E5 Onslow Square SW7
236 D5 Onslow Square SW7
239 J4 Ontario Street SE1
234 M4 Ontario Way E14
239 H6 Opal Street SE11
241 G8 Orange Place SE16
237 K6 Orange Square SW1W
240 D5 Orange Street E1W
234 B8 Orange Street WC2H
235 L6 Orb Street SE17
232 E4 Orchardson Street NW8
233 J6 Orchard Street W1H
234 E4 Ordehall Street WC1N
239 H5 Orient Street SE11
232 B8 Orme Court W2
232 B8 Orme Lane W2
232 B8 Orme Square Gate W2
234 D4 Ormond Close WC1N
237 H7 Ormonde Gate SW3
234 A8 Ormond Yard SW1Y
238 E6 Orsett Street SE11
232 C6 Orsett Terrace W2
240 D5 Orton Street E1W
238 B6 Osbert Street SW1V
240 C2 Osborn Street E1
241 K7 Oslo Square SE16
233 L3 Osnaburgh Street NW1
233 L3 Osnaburgh Terrace NW1
235 J5 Ossington Buildings W1U
232 A7 Ossington Street W2
234 B1 Ossulston Street NW1
239 H5 Oswin Street SE11
239 H6 Othello Close SE1
239 H8 Otto Street SE17
233 H3 Outer Circle NW1
233 K1 Outer Circle NW1
238 F8 Oval ⊖ SE11
238 E7 Oval Way SE11
237 G4 Ovington Square SW3
237 G5 Ovington Street SW3
235 G1 Owen Street EC1V
234 B8 Oxendon Street SW1Y
233 M6 Oxford Circus ⊖ W1B
232 A1 Oxford Road NW6
232 F6 Oxford Square W2
233 L6 Oxford Street W1C
234 A6 Oxford Street WC1A

P

240 E3 Pace Place E1
241 H6 Pacific Wharf SE16
232 D6 Paddington ⇌ ⊖ W2
232 E5 Paddington Green W2
233 J5 Paddington Street W1U
241 K5 Pageant Crescent SE16
238 B5 Page Street SW1P
235 H2 Paget Street EC1V
235 M2 Pakenham Street WC1X
236 B2 Palace Avenue W8
232 A7 Palace Court W2
236 A1 Palace Gardens Crescce W8
236 C3 Palace Gate W8
236 B2 Palace Green W8
237 M4 Palace Place SW1E
237 M4 Palace Street SW1E
238 A1 Pall Mall SW1Y
238 B1 Pall Mall East SW1Y
238 B3 Palmer Street SW1H
235 K6 Pancras Lane EC4N
234 B8 Panton Street SW1Y
240 E7 Paradise Street SE16
237 H8 Paradise Walk SW3
235 H3 Pardon Street EC1V
240 D2 Parfett Street E1
239 G1 Paris Garden SE1
233 K4 Park Crescent W1B

240 C7	**Parker's Row** SE1	
234 D6	**Parker Street** WC2B	
233 H7	**Park Lane** W1K	
237 J1	**Park Lane** W2	
237 M1	**Park Place** SW1A	
233 H3	**Park Road** NW1	
233 L3	**Park Square East** NW1	
233 K3	**Park Square Mews** NW1	
233 K3	**Park Square West** NW1	
239 K1	**Park Street** SE1	
233 J7	**Park Street** W1K	
233 L1	**Park Village East** NW1	
236 D8	**Park Walk** SW10	
233 G6	**Park West Place** W2	
238 C2	**Parliament Street** SW1A	
238 D8	**Parry Street** SW8	
237 J6	**Passmore Street** SW1W	
235 J6	**Paternoster Square** EC1A	
236 A4	**Pater Street** W8	
241 K5	**Pattina Walk** SE16	
235 M3	**Paul Street** EC2A	
236 E8	**Paultons Square** SW3	
233 G3	**Paveley Street** NW1	
237 H3	**Pavilion Road** SW1X	
237 H4	**Pavilion Street** SW1X	
237 L7	**Paxton Terrace** SW1V	
237 L7	**Peabody Avenue** SW1V	
239 J1	**Peabody Estate** SE1	
239 J6	**Peacock Street** SE17	
240 F5	**Pearl Street** E1W	
239 G3	**Pearman Street** SE1	
235 G3	**Pear Tree Court** EC1R	
241 G4	**Peartree Lane** E1W	
235 J3	**Pear Tree Street** EC1V	
236 A1	**Peel Street** W8	
235 K2	**Peerless Street** EC1V	
237 F6	**Pelham Crescent** SW7	
236 F5	**Pelham Place** SW7	
236 F5	**Pelham Street** SW7	
239 K8	**Pelier Street** SE17	
235 G6	**Pemberton Row** EC4A	
232 A8	**Pembridge Gardens** W2	
232 A7	**Pembridge Place** W2	
232 A7	**Pembridge Square** W2	
232 A7	**Pembridge Villas** W11	
237 J3	**Pembroke Close** SW1X	
240 F5	**Penang Street** E1W	
232 F5	**Penfold Place** NW8	
232 E4	**Penfold Street** NW8	
236 B5	**Pennant Mews** W8	
240 D4	**Pennington Street** E1W	
241 M4	**Pennyfields** E14	
239 J7	**Penrose Grove** SE17	
239 J7	**Penrose Street** SE17	
240 E7	**Penryn Road** SE16	
239 H6	**Penton Place** SE17	
234 E2	**Penton Rise** WC1X	
234 F1	**Penton Street** N1	
234 E1	**Pentonville Road** N1	
236 A6	**Penywern Road** SW5	
239 J2	**Pepper Street** SE1	
240 A4	**Pepys Street** EC3N	
235 H3	**Percival Street** EC1V	
234 F2	**Percy Circus** WC1X	
234 B5	**Percy Street** W1T	
238 B4	**Perkin's Rent** SW1P	
236 D4	**Petersham Mews** SW7	
236 C4	**Petersham Place** SW7	
234 B7	**Peter Street** W1F	
233 L3	**Peto Place** NW1	
240 B2	**Petticoat Lane** E1	
238 A3	**Petty France** SW1H	
240 A4	**Petty Wales** EC3R	
237 G6	**Petyward** SW3	
239 L7	**Phelp Street** SE17	
237 G8	**Phene Street** SW3	
236 A3	**Phillimore Walk** W8	
235 M7	**Philpot Lane** EC3M	
240 E2	**Philpot Street** E1	
237 L5	**Phipp's Mews** SW1W	
235 M3	**Phipp Street** EC2A	
234 F3	**Phoenix Place** WC1X	
234 B1	**Phoenix Road** NW1	
234 C6	**Phoenix Street** WC2H	
234 A8	**Piccadilly** W1J	
237 L2	**Piccadilly** W1J	
237 M1	**Piccadilly Arcade** SW1Y	
234 A8	**Piccadilly Circus** W1B	
234 B8	**Piccadilly Circus** ⊖ W1J	
235 J2	**Pickard Street** EC1V	
233 K6	**Picton Place** W1U	
240 E6	**Pier Head** E1W	
241 M3	**Pigott Street** E14	
239 L3	**Pilgrimage Street** SE1	
238 B6	**Pimlico** ⊖ SW1V	
237 J6	**Pimlico Road** SW1W	
240 D3	**Pinchin Street** E1	
235 M4	**Pindar Street** EC2A	
232 B3	**Pindock Mews** W9	
234 F3	**Pine Street** EC1R	
235 M1	**Pitfield Street** N1	
241 H3	**Pitsea Street** E1	
237 K2	**Pitt's Head Mews** W1J	
236 A2	**Pitt Street** W8	
241 L2	**Pixley Street** E14	
235 L3	**Platina Street** * EC2A	
241 K8	**Plover Way** SE16	
240 D2	**Plumbers Row** E1	
235 G5	**Plumtree Court** EC4A	
232 F4	**Plympton Street** NW8	
239 H2	**Pocock Street** SE1	
234 A6	**Poland Street** W1F	
233 L7	**Pollen Street** W1S	
232 E3	**Pollitt Drive** NW8	
235 G5	**Polperrom** SE1	
234 B1	**Polygon Road** NW1	
236 F6	**Pond Place** SW3	
240 E3	**Ponler Street** E1	
238 C6	**Ponsonby Place** SW1P	
238 C6	**Ponsonby Terrace** SW1P	
238 B8	**Ponton Road** SW1V	
237 H4	**Pont Street** SW1X	
241 H6	**Poolmans Street** SE16	
240 B7	**Pope Street** SE1	
232 B7	**Poplar Place** W2	
235 H6	**Poppin's Court** EC4A	
232 B7	**Porchester Gardens** W2	
232 C8	**Porchester Gate** W2	
233 G6	**Porchester Place** W2	
232 B5	**Porchester Road** W2	
232 B6	**Porchester Square** W2	
232 C7	**Porchester Terrace** W2	
232 C6	**Porchester Terrace North** W2	
239 L3	**Porlock Street** SE1	
233 H4	**Porter Street** NW1	
232 D5	**Porteus Road** W2	
233 L4	**Portland Place** W1B	
233 L4	**Portland Place** W1B	
240 E5	**Portland Square** E1W	
239 L7	**Portland Street** SE17	
233 J6	**Portman Close** W1H	
233 J6	**Portman Mews South** W1H	
233 J6	**Portman Square** W1H	
233 J6	**Portman Street** W1H	
234 F4	**Portpool Lane** EC1N	
233 G6	**Portsea Place** W2	
234 E6	**Portsmouth Street** WC2A	
240 B3	**Portsoken Street** E1	
234 E6	**Portugal Street** WC2A	
239 L4	**Potier Street** SE1	
240 B6	**Potters Fields** SE1	
240 F7	**Pottery Street** SE16	
235 K6	**Poultry** EC2V	
234 D4	**Powis Street** WC1N	
232 E6	**Praed Mews** W2	
232 E6	**Praed Street** W2	
238 E5	**Pratt Walk** SE1	
241 M4	**Premier Place** E14	
240 C3	**Prescot Street** E1	
239 M5	**Preston Close** SE1	
239 J1	**Price's Street** SE1	
234 F2	**Prideaux Place** WC1X	
240 A1	**Primrose Street** EC2A	
232 F1	**Prince Albert Road** NW8	
236 D3	**Prince Consort Road** SW7	
240 C1	**Princelet Street** E1	
236 F3	**Prince of Wales Gate** SW7	
234 A8	**Princes Arcade** SW1Y	
236 E3	**Prince's Gardens** SW7	
236 E3	**Prince's Gate** SW7	
240 F7	**Prince's Gate Mews** SW16	
241 H5	**Princes Riverside Road** SE16	
232 A7	**Prince's Square** W2	
232 A1	**Princess Road** NW6	
239 H4	**Princess Street** SE1	
233 L6	**Princes Street** W1B	
235 L6	**Prince's Street** EC2R	
234 E5	**Princeton Street** WC1R	
239 L4	**Prioress Street** SE1	
234 E1	**Priory Green Estate** N1	
236 D7	**Priory Walk** SW10	
234 E5	**Proctor Street** WC1V	
241 G5	**Prospect Place** E1W	
240 F7	**Prospect Street** SE16	
233 J7	**Provident Court** W1K	
235 L1	**Provost Street** N1	
240 F1	**Prusom Street** E1W	
235 M7	**Pudding Lane** EC3R	
240 D3	**Pumphouse Mews** E1W	
240 A7	**Purbrook Street** SE1	
235 M1	**Purcell Street** N1	
234 B1	**Purchese Street** NW1	

Q

241 J7	**Quebec Way** SE16	
238 B3	**Queen Anne's Gate** SW1H	
233 K5	**Queen Ann Street** W1G	
240 B6	**Queen Elizabeth Street** SE1	
237 J2	**Queen Mother Gate** W2	
232 C7	**Queensborough Terrace** W2	
236 E3	**Queensberry Place** SW7	
232 C7	**Queen's Gardens** W2	
236 D3	**Queen's Gate** SW7	
236 D3	**Queen's Gate** SW7	
236 D5	**Queen's Gate Gardens** SW7	
236 D4	**Queen's Gate Mews** SW7	
236 D4	**Queen's Gate Place** SW7	
236 D4	**Queen's Gate** **Place Mews** SW7	
236 C4	**Queen's Gate Terrace** SW7	
239 L2	**Queen's Head Yard** SE1	
232 B7	**Queen's Mews** W2	
234 D4	**Queen Square** WC1N	
239 K7	**Queen's Row** SE17	
235 K7	**Queen Street** EC4N	
237 L1	**Queen Street** W1J	
235 K7	**Queen Street Place** EC4R	
240 A5	**Queen's Walk** SE1	
237 M2	**Queen's Walk** SW1A	
232 B6	**Queensway** W2	
232 B8	**Queensway** ⊖ W2	
235 J7	**Queen Victoria Street** EC4V	
235 H1	**Quick Street** N1	

R

241 K2	**Raby Street** E14	
240 B8	**Radcliffe Road** SE1	
239 G7	**Radcot Street** SE11	
232 E6	**Radnor Mews** W2	
232 F6	**Radnor Place** W2	
235 K3	**Radnor Street** EC1V	
232 G7	**Radnor Walk** SW3	
239 L1	**Railway Approach** SE1	
241 G6	**Railway Avenue** SE16	
234 D1	**Railway Street** N1	
240 F5	**Raine Street** E1W	
237 H7	**Ralston Street** SW3	
233 M6	**Ramillies Place** W1F	
233 M6	**Ramillies Street** W1F	
240 E2	**Rampart Street** E1	
238 B6	**Rampayne Street** SW1V	
238 D6	**Randall Road** SE11	
238 E6	**Randall Row** SE11	
232 C3	**Randolph Avenue** W9	
232 C3	**Randolph Crescent** W9	
232 B1	**Randolph Gardens** NW6	
232 D4	**Randolph Mews** W9	
232 C4	**Randolph Road** W9	
237 K6	**Ranelagh Grove** SW1W	
238 A7	**Ranelagh Road** SW1V	
240 B3	**Rangoon Street** * EC3N	
232 F4	**Ranston Street** NW8	
237 G3	**Raphael Street** SW7	
241 J3	**Ratcliffe Cross Street** E1W	
241 J3	**Ratcliffe Lane** E14	
234 B5	**Rathbone Place** W1T	
234 A5	**Rathbone Street** W1T	
240 F1	**Raven Row** E1	
239 G7	**Ravensdon Street** SE11	
235 M3	**Raven Street** EC2A	
237 G5	**Rawlings Street** SW3	
235 H2	**Rawstone Street** EC1V	
235 G4	**Ray Street** EC1R	
240 E5	**Reardon Place** E1W	
240 E5	**Reardon Street** E1W	
241 H1	**Rectory Square** E1	
232 B2	**Redan Place** W2	
237 G7	**Redburn Street** SW3	
241 G4	**Redcastle Close** E1W	
236 B7	**Redcliffe Gardens** SW10	
236 B7	**Redcliffe Mews** SW10	
236 C8	**Redcliffe Place** SW10	
236 B7	**Redcliffe Road** SW10	
236 B8	**Redcliffe Square** SW10	
236 B8	**Redcliffe Street** SW10	
239 K2	**Redcross Way** SE1	
237 G7	**Redesdale Street** SW3	

236 A5	**Redfield Lane** SW5	
239 L1	**Redhill Street** NW1	
239 M4	**Red Lion Row** SE5	
234 E5	**Red Lion Square** WC1R	
234 E5	**Red Lion Street** WC2B	
241 G1	**Redman's Road** E1	
233 J7	**Red Place** W1K	
241 J8	**Rediff Road** SE16	
239 G6	**Reedworth Street** SE11	
233 J8	**Reeves Mews** W1K	
240 D1	**Regal Close** E1	
235 M1	**Regan Way** N1	
238 B5	**Regency Street** SW1P	
234 A7	**Regent Place** W1B	
233 L4	**Regent's Park** ⊖ W1B	
233 L2	**Regent's Park Estate** NW1	
234 D2	**Regent Square** WC1H	
234 B8	**Regent Street** SW1Y	
234 M7	**Regent Street** W1S	
237 G4	**Relton Mews** SW7	
235 H1	**Remington Street** N1	
234 E6	**Remnant Street** WC2A	
241 G7	**Renforth Street** SE16	
239 H1	**Rennie Street** SE1	
239 M4	**Rephidim Street** SE1	
241 K7	**Repton Street** E14	
241 K7	**Reveley Square** SE16	
233 J8	**Rex Place** W1K	
241 L2	**Rhodeswell Road** E14	
241 M3	**Rich Street** E14	
236 A8	**Rickett Street** SW6	
234 B4	**Ridgmount Street** WC1E	
234 B4	**Ridgmount Gardens** WC1E	
233 M5	**Riding House Street** W1W	
240 B7	**Riley Road** SE1	
239 J2	**Risborough Street** SE1	
241 G7	**Risdon Street** SE16	
234 F1	**Rissinghill Street** N1	
234 F2	**River Street** EC1R	
235 M3	**Rivington Street** EC2A	
233 J6	**Robert Adam Street** W1U	
241 J7	**Roberts Close** SE16	
233 L2	**Robert Street** NW1	
238 A5	**Rochester Row** SW1P	
238 B5	**Rochester Street** SW1P	
239 J4	**Rockingham Street** SE1	
235 H1	**Rocliffe Street** N1	
240 D5	**Roding Mews** E1W	
239 H5	**Rodmarton Street** W1U	
239 K5	**Rodney Place** SE17	
239 K5	**Rodney Road** SE17	
234 E1	**Rodney Street** N1	
234 E4	**Roger Street** WC1N	
239 L7	**Roland Way** SE17	
236 D6	**Roland Gardens** SW7	
240 E2	**Romford Street** E1	
234 B7	**Romilly Street** W1D	
238 C5	**Romney Street** SW1P	
235 M7	**Rood Lane** EC3M	
241 K7	**Ropemaker Road** SE16	
235 L4	**Ropemaker Street** EC2Y	
240 B7	**Roper Lane** SE1	
241 K8	**Rope Street** SE16	
240 E2	**Rope Walk Gardens** E1	
236 D6	**Rosary Gardens** SW7	
235 K3	**Roscoe Street** EC1Y	
235 K8	**Rose Alley** SE1	
234 F3	**Rosebery Avenue** EC1R	
237 F6	**Rosemoor Street** SW3	
234 C7	**Rose Street** WC2E	
233 H3	**Rossmore Road** NW1	
239 H3	**Rotary Street** SE1	
241 G6	**Rotherhithe** ⊖ SE16	
241 G6	**Rotherhithe Street** SE16	
241 J4	**Rotherhithe Street** SE16	
241 H5	**Rotherhithe Tunnel** SE16	
239 M4	**Rothsay Street** SE1	
236 F2	**Rotten Row** W2	
240 C8	**Rouel Road** SE16	
239 G2	**Roupell Street** SE1	
237 H6	**Royal Avenue** SW3	
237 H7	**Royal Hospital Road** SW3	
240 C4	**Royal Mint Street** E1	
232 B5	**Royal Oak** ⊖ W2	
240 A7	**Royal Oak Yard** SE1	
239 H8	**Royal Road** SE17	
238 E3	**Royal Street** SE1	
232 A1	**Rudolph Road** NW6	
234 E4	**Rugby Street** WC1N	
240 F4	**Rum Close** E1W	
240 F7	**Rupack Street** SE16	
234 B7	**Rupert Street** W1D	
239 H2	**Rushworth Street** SE1	
238 A2	**Russell Court** SW1A	
234 C4	**Russell Square** WC1B	
234 D4	**Russell Square** ⊖ WC1N	
234 D7	**Russell Street** WC2B	
241 K6	**Russia Dock Road** SE16	
238 B5	**Rutherford Street** SW1P	
237 G3	**Rutland Gardens** SW7	
236 F3	**Rutland Gate** SW7	
236 F4	**Rutland Mews** SW7	
236 F4	**Rutland Street** SW7	
238 A1	**Ryder Street** SW1Y	

S

234 A8	**Sackville Street** W1S	
235 G4	**Saffron Hill** EC1N	
235 G4	**Saffron Street** EC1N	
238 F5	**Sail Street** SE11	
239 G8	**St Agnes Place** SE11	
236 B4	**St Alban's Grove** W8	
234 B8	**St Alban's Street** * W1D	
235 K5	**St Alphage Garden** EC2Y	
235 H7	**St Andrews Hill** EC4V	
233 L1	**St Andrew's Place** NW1	
235 G5	**St Andrew Street** EC4A	
236 B5	**St Anne's Court** W1F	
238 C4	**St Ann's Street** SW1P	
235 K7	**St Anselm's Place** W1K	
237 K6	**St Barnabas Street** SW1W	
235 B2	**St Botolph Street** EC3N	
235 G6	**St Bride Street** EC4A	
234 D2	**St Chad's Street** WC1H	
240 B3	**St Clare Street** EC3N	
234 E6	**St Clements Lane** WC2A	
235 G1	**St Cross Street** EC1N	
235 M8	**St Dunstan's Hill** EC3R	
235 M7	**St Dunstan's Lane** EC3R	
241 J7	**St Elmos Road** SE16	
238 B3	**St Ermin's Hill** SW1H	
239 H3	**St George's Circus** SE1	
237 M6	**St George's Drive** SW1V	
240 D3	**St George's Lane** * EC3R	
235 M7	**St George's Lane** * EC3R	
239 G4	**St George's Road** SE1	
238 B7	**St George's Square** SW1V	

233 L7	**St George Street** W1S	
234 C6	**St Giles High Street** WC2H	
233 M6	**St Helen's Place** EC3A	
238 B8	**St James Market** * SW1Y	
238 B3	**St James's Park** ⊖ SW1H	
237 M2	**St James's Place** SW1A	
238 A1	**St James's Road** SE16	
237 M1	**St James's Square** SW1Y	
235 G3	**St James Way** EC1R	
235 H4	**St John's Lane** EC1M	
235 H4	**St John's Place** EC1M	
235 H4	**St John's Square** EC1V	
235 H2	**St John Street** EC1V	
232 F1	**St John's Wood** **High Street** NW8	
232 E3	**St John's Wood Road** NW8	
240 C5	**St Katharine's Way** E1W	
237 H7	**St Leonard's Terrace** SW3	
237 G8	**St Loo Avenue** SW3	
235 K3	**St Luke's Close** EC1V	
236 F6	**St Luke's Street** SW3	
240 C2	**St Manningtree** E1	
240 C3	**St Mark Street** E1	
234 B7	**St Martin's Lane** WC2N	
235 J6	**St Martin's le Grand** EC1A	
235 M8	**St Mary at Hill** EC3R	
240 A3	**St Mary Axe** EC3A	
240 F7	**St Mary Church Street** SE16	
232 D4	**St Mary's Grove** SE11	
232 D4	**St Mary's Terrace** W2	
232 G5	**St Mary's Way** SE11	
238 B4	**St Matthew Street** SW1P	
232 F6	**St Michael's Street** W2	
240 F7	**St Olav's Square** SE16	
238 E7	**St Oswald's Place** SE11	
234 C1	**St Pancras** **International** ⇌ N1C	
235 J6	**St Paul's** ⊖ EC1A	
241 J5	**St Paul's Avenue** SE16	
235 J6	**St Paul's Churchyard** EC4M	
234 L1	**St Paul's Way** E3	
232 B7	**St Petersburgh Mews** W2	
232 B7	**St Petersburgh Place** W2	
240 C6	**St Saviours Wharf** SE1	
232 A5	**St Stephen's Gardens** W2	
235 L7	**St Swithin's Lane** EC4N	
239 L2	**St Thomas Street** SE1	
233 J5	**St Vincent Street** W1U	
238 D6	**Salamanca Street** SE1	
232 B7	**Salem Road** W2	
232 F5	**Sale Place** W2	
235 J6	**Salisbury Court** EC4Y	
233 H4	**Salisbury Place** W1H	
232 F4	**Salisbury Street** NW8	
241 J2	**Salmon Lane** E14	
241 J5	**Salter Road** SE16	
241 M4	**Salter Street** E14	
232 F4	**Sampson Street** NW8	
240 D5	**Sampson Street** E1W	
238 F6	**Sancroft Street** SE11	
239 L6	**Sandford Row** SE17	
234 E5	**Sandland Street** WC1R	
241 L6	**Sandpiper Close** SE16	
234 C2	**Sandwich Street** WC1H	
240 B1	**Sandy's Row** E1	
235 G3	**Sans Walk** EC1R	
234 E6	**Sardinia Street** WC2A	
240 B3	**Savage Gardens** EC3N	
233 M7	**Savile Row** W1S	
234 E8	**Savoy Hill** WC2R	
234 D8	**Savoy Place** WC2R	
234 E7	**Savoy Street** WC2E	
239 J2	**Sawyer Street** SE1	
234 A5	**Scala Street** W1T	
240 C5	**Scandrett Street** E1W	
240 C3	**Scarborough Street** E1	
236 A4	**Scarsdale Villas** W8	
241 H6	**Schooner Close** * SE16	
239 H2	**Scoresby Street** SE1	
237 H3	**Scotch House Junction** SW1X	
238 C1	**Scotland Place** SW1A	
232 E2	**Scott Ellis Grove** NW8	
240 D7	**Scott Lidgett Crescent** SE16	
235 M3	**Scrutton Street** EC2A	
234 D2	**Seaford Street** WC1H	
236 A8	**Seagrave Road** SW6	
239 L5	**Searles Road** SE1	
235 K1	**Sebastian Street** EC1V	
238 F2	**Secker Street** SE1	
239 M6	**Sedan Way** SE17	
237 J5	**Sedding Street** SW1X	
234 E3	**Seddon Street** WC1X	
234 A4	**Seething Lane** EC3N	
235 H3	**Sekforde Street** EC1R	
235 M1	**Selsey Street** E14	
236 E6	**Selwood Place** SW7	
237 K6	**Semley Place** SW1W	
232 B4	**Senior Street** W2	
241 H2	**Senrab Street** E1	
234 F6	**Serle Street** WC2A	
236 E1	**Serpentine Bridge** W2	
236 E1	**Serpentine Road** W2	
241 G7	**Seth Street** SE16	
240 D2	**Settles Street** E1	
233 J6	**Seven Dials** WC2H	
237 H3	**Seville Street** SW1X	
232 A3	**Sevington Street** W9	
235 J3	**Seward Street** EC1V	
233 J6	**Seymour Mews** W1H	
233 G5	**Seymour Place** W1H	
233 H6	**Seymour Place** W1H	
233 G7	**Seymour Street** W1H	
236 C7	**Seymour Walk** SW10	
240 B6	**Shad Thames** SE1	
240 C6	**Shad Thames** SE1	
240 F3	**Shadwell** ⊖ ⊖ SE1	
240 F3	**Shadwell Gardens** E1	
234 B7	**Shaftesbury Avenue** W1D	
234 C6	**Shaftesbury Avenue** WC2H	
235 K1	**Shaftesbury Street** N1	
240 A6	**Shand Street** SE1	
239 H7	**Sharsted Street** SE17	
241 K2	**Shaw Crescent** E14	
237 G7	**Shawfield Street** SW3	
236 A2	**Sheffield Terrace** W8	
232 D5	**Sheldon Square** W2	
234 M1	**Shelmerdine Close** E3	
234 D6	**Shelton Street** WC2H	
235 K1	**Shepherdess Walk** N1	
233 K7	**Shepherd Street** W1J	
236 B6	**Sherbrand Street** W1F	
235 L7	**Sherborne Lane** EC4N	
239 M2	**Ship and Mermaid Row** SE1	
241 K7	**Shipwright Road** SE16	
232 A3	**Shirland Road** W9	
235 G5	**Shoe Lane** EC4A	
236 B4	**Shorter Street** EC3N	
234 C6	**Shorts Gardens** WC2H	
239 G2	**Short Street** SE1	
241 K4	**Shoulder of Mutton Alley** E14	

233 G5	**Shouldham Street** W1H	
232 F4	**Shroton Street** NW1	
233 H4	**Siddons Lane** W1H	
234 D3	**Sidmouth Street** WC1N	
240 F3	**Sidney Square** E1	
240 F1	**Sidney Street** E1	
239 H3	**Silex Street** SE1	
235 K4	**Silk Street** EC2Y	
241 K5	**Silver Walk** SE16	
239 K3	**Silvester Street** SE1	
235 L3	**Singer Street** EC2A	
237 J6	**Skinner Place** * SW1W	
234 C4	**Skinners Lane** EC4V	
235 G3	**Skinner Street** EC1R	
240 F8	**Slippers Place** SE16	
237 G6	**Sloane Avenue** SW3	
237 J6	**Sloane Court SW3**	
237 J6	**Sloane Court East** SW3	
237 J6	**Sloane Gardens** SW1W	
237 J6	**Sloane Square** SW1W	
237 J6	**Sloane Square** ⊖ SW1X	
237 H3	**Sloane Street** SW1X	
237 J5	**Sloane Terrace** SW1X	
240 C3	**Smeaton Street** E1W	
235 H5	**Smithfield Street** EC1A	
238 C4	**Smith Square** SW1P	
237 G7	**Smith Street** SW3	
237 G7	**Smith Terrace** SW3	
241 G1	**Smithy Street** E1	
235 M4	**Snowden Street** EC2A	
235 H5	**Snow Hill** EC1A	
239 L6	**Snowsfields** SE1	
234 B6	**Soho Square** W1D	
234 B6	**Soho Street** W1D	
241 K7	**Somerford Way** SE16	
232 F6	**Somers Crescent** W2	
234 A1	**Somerstown Estate** NW1	
239 L7	**Sondes Street** SE17	
238 C4	**South & West Africa** **Gate** SW1A	
239 L3	**Southall Place** SE1	
234 F5	**Southampton** **Buildings** WC2A	
234 D5	**Southampton Place** WC1A	
234 C6	**Southampton Row** WC1B	
234 D7	**Southampton Street** WC2E	
233 K8	**South Audley Street** W1K	
237 H3	**South Carriage Drive** SW1X	
236 F3	**South Carriage Drive** SW7	
237 J5	**South Eaton Place** SW1W	
234 E1	**Southern Street** N1	
236 E4	**South Kensington** SW7	
236 E5	**South Kensington** ⊖ SW7	
238 D8	**South Lambeth Road** SW8	
233 K7	**South Molton Lane** W1K	
233 K7	**South Molton Street** W1K	
236 E7	**South Parade** SW3	
235 L5	**South Place** EC2M	
241 L8	**South Sea Street** SE16	
234 F5	**South Square** WC1R	
237 J1	**South Street** W1K	
240 C3	**South Tenter Street** E1	
236 F5	**South Terrace** SW7	
239 H2	**Southwark** ⊖ SE1	
235 K8	**Southwark Bridge** SE1	
239 J3	**Southwark Bridge Road** SE1	
240 E8	**Southwark Park Road** SE16	
239 H1	**Southwark Street** SE1	
236 C5	**Southwell Gardens** SW7	
232 E6	**South Wharf Road** W2	
232 F6	**Southwick Mews** W2	
232 F6	**Southwick Place** W2	
232 F6	**Southwick Street** W2	
240 F4	**Sovereign Close** E1W	
241 J4	**Sovereign Crescent** SE16	
233 J5	**Spanish Place** W1U	
240 C8	**Spa Road** SE16	
236 C8	**Spear Mews** SW5	
240 C1	**Spelman Street** E1	
235 K7	**Spence Close** SE16	
235 H2	**Spencer Street** EC1V	
238 A4	**Spenser Street** SW1E	
241 J4	**Spert Street** E14	
240 A1	**Spital Square** E1	
238 C1	**Spring Gardens** SW1A	
232 E6	**Spring Street** W2	
239 L4	**Spurgeon Street** SE1	
238 F3	**Spur Road** SE1	
238 F7	**Stables Way** SE11	
238 A2	**Stable Yard Road** SW1A	
234 C6	**Stacey Street** WC2H	
237 M3	**Stafford Place** SW1E	
232 A2	**Stafford Road** NW6	
234 M8	**Stafford Street** W1S	
236 A3	**Stafford Terrace** W8	
239 L2	**Stainer Street** SE1	
241 M2	**Stainsby Road** E14	
240 F8	**Stalham Street** SE16	
239 G1	**Stamford Street** SE1	
239 M6	**Stanford Place** SE1	
236 B4	**Stanford Road** W8	
241 H6	**Stanhope Close** * SE16	
236 D5	**Stanhope Gardens** SW7	
237 K1	**Stanhope Gate** W1K	
236 D5	**Stanhope Mews** SW7	
236 D5	**Stanhope Mews East** SW7	
236 D5	**Stanhope Mews West** SW7	
233 G7	**Stanhope Place** W2	
233 G7	**Stanhope Place Gate** W2	
237 K1	**Stanhope Row** W1J	
233 M1	**Stanhope Street** NW1	
232 E7	**Stanhope Terrace** W2	
239 G7	**Stannary Street** SE11	
241 J5	**Staples Close** SE16	
239 L3	**Staple Street** SE1	
234 A2	**Starcross Street** NW1	
232 F6	**Star Street** W2	
241 J5	**Stave Yard Road** SE16	
239 K6	**Stead Street** SE17	
239 K5	**Steedman Street** SE17	
241 G3	**Steel's Lane** E1	
241 K7	**Steeres Way** SE16	
234 A3	**Stephenson Way** NW1	
234 B5	**Stephen Street** W1T	
241 H1	**Stepney Green** E1	
241 J1	**Stepney High Street** E1	
240 E1	**Stepney Way** E1	
237 G3	**Sterling Street** SW7	
240 E5	**Stevedore Street** E1W	
240 A7	**Stevens Street** SE1	
240 B1	**Steward Street** * E1	
236 F6	**Stewart's Grove** SW3	
235 J7	**Stew Lane** EC4V	
238 A5	**Stillington Street** SW1P	
240 D5	**Stockholm Way** E1W	
241 M3	**Stocks Place** E14	
234 F5	**Stone Buildings** WC2A	
235 G6	**Stonecutter Street** EC4A	
240 B2	**Stoney Lane** E1	
239 K1	**Stoney Street** SE1	
239 J7	**Stopford Road** SE17	

234	B5	Store Street WC1E
238	C3	Storey's Gate SW1H
240	D8	Storks Road SE16
238	E6	Stoughton Close SE11
233	G5	Stourcliffe Street W1H
241	M6	Strafford Street E14
234	D8	Strand WC2R
233	K6	Stratford Place W1C
236	A5	Stratford Road W8
232	F7	Strathearn Place W2
237	L1	Stratton Street W1J
240	B2	Strype Street E1
232	A2	Stuart Road NW6
234	D6	Stukeley Street WC2B
239	J7	Sturgeon Road SE17
239	J3	Sturge Street SE1
235	K1	Sturt Street N1
240	D3	Stutfield Street E1
235	H1	Sudley Street N1
239	J3	Sudrey Street SE1
235	L7	Suffolk Lane EC4V
234	B8	Suffolk Street SW1Y
240	A4	Sugar Quay Walk EC3R
239	G5	Sullivan Road SE11
241	G2	Summercourt Road E1
236	E6	Summer Place SW7
234	F4	Summers Street EC1R
239	J1	Sumner Street SE1
232	A6	Sunderland Terrace W2
240	D8	Sun Passage SE16
235	M4	Sun Street EC2M
232	A4	Surrendale Place W9
241	H7	Surrey Quays Road SE16
239	H2	Surrey Row SE1
239	M6	Surrey Square SE17
234	E7	Surrey Street WC2E
241	H6	Surrey Water Road SE16
232	E6	Sussex Gardens W2
232	E7	Sussex Mews East W2
233	H3	Sussex Place NW1
232	E6	Sussex Place W2
232	E7	Sussex Square W2
237	L7	Sussex Street SW1V
232	A4	Sutherland Avenue W9
237	L6	Sutherland Row SW1V
239	J7	Sutherland Square SE17
237	L7	Sutherland Street SW1V
234	B6	Sutton Row W1D
241	G3	Sutton Street E1
235	K4	Suttons Way EC1Y
232	F3	Swain Street NW8
233	L6	Swallow Place W1B
234	A8	Swallow Street W1B
235	L8	Swan Lane EC4R
239	M4	Swan Mead SE1
241	G6	Swan Road SE16
239	K3	Swan Street SE1
237	H8	Swan Walk SW3
240	E4	Swedenborg Gardens E1
240	C7	Sweeney Crescent SE1
234	E2	Swinton Street WC1X
236	F6	Sydney Street SW3
237	H6	Symons Street SW3

T

239	L3	Tabard Gardens Estate SE1
239	L3	Tabard Street SE1
235	L5	Tabernacle Street EC2A
238	A6	Tachbrook Street SW1V
232	A6	Talbot Road W2
232	E6	Talbot Square W2
235	G7	Tallis Street EC4Y
236	A8	Tamworth Street SW6
240	A7	Tanner Street SE1
235	K1	Taplow Street N1
240	F3	Tarling Street E1
239	H7	Tarver Road SE17
239	M6	Tatum Street SE17
233	G3	Taunton Place NW1
234	C3	Tavistock Place WC1H
234	C3	Tavistock Square WC1H
234	D7	Tavistock Street WC2E
234	B3	Taviton Street WC1H
241	K6	Teak Close SE16
237	G7	Tedworth Square SW3
237	M7	Telford Terrace SW1V
241	G6	Temeraire Street SE16
234	F7	Temple ⊖ WC2R
235	G7	Temple Avenue EC4Y
235	G7	Temple Lane EC4Y
234	F7	Temple Place WC2R
236	A5	Templeton Place SW5
240	E5	Tench Street E1W
232	C7	Tenniel Close W2
239	L2	Tennis Street SE1
233	L6	Tenterden Street W1S
240	B1	Tenterground E1
241	J8	Teredo Street SE16
237	L4	Terminus Place SW1V
241	H6	Thame Road SE16
234	C2	Thanet Street WC1H
235	G6	Thavies Inn EC4A
233	K5	Thayer Street W1U
234	D8	The Arches WC2N
236	C7	The Boltons SW10
232	B8	The Broad Walk W2
236	C2	The Broad Walk W8
239	G2	The Cut SE1
239	G2	Theed Street SE1
236	D3	The Flower Walk W2
240	B8	The Grange SE1
240	E4	The Highway E1W
236	C7	The Little Boltons SW10
238	B2	The Mall SW1A
241	L3	The Mitre E14
234	E4	Theobald's Road WC1X
239	L5	Theobald Street SE1
236	E8	The Vale SW3
238	A4	Thirleby Road SW1P
240	D4	Thomas More Street E1W
241	M2	Thomas Road E14
235	K1	Thoresby Street N1
238	C5	Thorney Street SW1P
233	H4	Thornton Place W1H
239	K1	Thrale Street SE1
240	C1	Thrawl Street E1
235	L6	Threadneedle Street EC2R
241	L3	Three Colt Street E14
240	B6	Three Oak Lane SE1
235	L6	Throgmorton Avenue EC2N
235	L6	Throgmorton Street EC2N
240	D8	Thurland Road SE16
236	F5	Thurloe Place SW7
236	F5	Thurloe Square SW7
236	E5	Thurloe Street SW7
239	M7	Thurlow Street SE17

232	F6	Tichbourne Row W2
241	M8	Tiller Road E14
240	E3	Tilman Street E1
237	K1	Tilney Street W1J
241	J6	Timber Pond Road SE16
241	G1	Tinsley Road E1
238	D6	Tinworth Street SE11
239	L6	Tisdall Place SE17
237	H8	Tite Street SW3
239	J4	Tiverton Street SE1
235	L6	Token House Yard EC2R
234	A3	Tolmer's Square NW1
241	K2	Tomlin's Terrace E14
234	D2	Tonbridge Street WC1H
239	L1	Tooley Street SE1
240	B6	Tooley Street SE1
236	A2	Tor Gardens W8
232	A5	Torquay Street W2
235	G1	Torrens Street EC1V
240	D5	Torrington Place E1W
234	B4	Torrington Place WC1E
234	B4	Torrington Square WC1E
238	B3	Tothill Street SW1H
234	A4	Tottenham Court Road W1T
234	B6	Tottenham Court Road ⊖ W1D
234	A5	Tottenham Street W1T
239	J3	Toulmin Street SE1
240	B5	Tower Bridge EC3N
240	B5	Tower Bridge Approach EC3N
240	A7	Tower Bridge Road SE1
240	C5	Tower Bridge Wharf E1W
240	B4	Tower Gateway ⊖ EC3N
240	B4	Tower Hill EC3R
240	B4	Tower Hill ⊖ EC3N
240	A4	Tower Place EC3R
234	C7	Tower Street WC2H
239	M5	Townsend Street SE17
240	B1	Toynbee Street E1
241	H1	Trafalgar Gardens E1
238	C1	Trafalgar Square WC2N
239	L7	Trafalgar Street SE17
232	F5	Transept Street NW1
237	L1	Trebeck Street W1J
234	A6	Trebovir Road SW5
236	C7	Tregunter Road SW10
240	E8	Trenton Road SE16
232	F3	Tresham Crescent NW8
237	G3	Trevor Place SW7
237	G3	Trevor Square SW7
237	G3	Trevor Street SW7
241	M4	Trinidad Street E14
239	K3	Trinity Church Square SE1
240	B4	Trinity Square EC3N
239	K3	Trinity Street SE1
235	K6	Trump Street EC2V
235	G7	Tudor Street EC4Y
238	C4	Tufton Street SW1P
241	G6	Tunnel Road SE16
237	J6	Turks Row SW3
241	L2	Turner's Road E3
240	E2	Turner Street E1
235	G4	Turnmill Street EC1N
237	L7	Turpentine Lane SW1V
239	K6	Turquand Street SE17
239	M3	Tyers Gate SE1
238	E7	Tyers Street SE11
238	E7	Tyers Terrace SE11
237	H6	Tyron Street SW3
235	G3	Tysoe Street EC1R

U

238	A5	Udall Street SW1P
239	G3	Ufford Street SE1
233	K4	Ulster Place NW1
240	E2	Umberston Street E1
240	A2	Undershaft EC3A
235	K2	Underwood Road N1
235	K1	Underwood Street N1
239	H2	Union Street SE1
234	A4	University Street WC1E
232	D6	Upbrook Mews W2
237	K4	Upper Belgrave Street SW1X
233	H6	Upper Berkeley Street W1H
233	J7	Upper Brook Street W1K
236	F8	Upper Cheyne Row SW3
233	J8	Upper Grosvenor Street W1K
238	F1	Upper Ground SE1
233	K3	Upper Harley Street NW1
234	A7	Upper James Street W1F
234	A7	Upper John Street W1F
238	E3	Upper Marsh SE1
233	H5	Upper Montagu Street W1H
234	C7	Upper St Martin's WC2H
238	A5	Upper Tachbrook Street SW1V
235	J7	Upper Thames Street EC4V
233	K4	Upper Wimpole Street W1G
234	B2	Upper Woburn Place WC1H
239	J8	Urlwin Street SE5
236	A1	Uxbridge Street W8

V

239	G3	Valentine Place SE1
238	A3	Vandon Passage SW1H
238	A4	Vandon Street SW1H
235	M4	Vandy Street EC2A
240	E2	Varden Street E1
233	M2	Varndell Street NW1
240	C8	Vauban Street SE16
241	L7	Vaughan Street SE16
240	D5	Vaughan Way E1W
238	D7	Vauxhall ≠ ⊖ SW8
238	D7	Vauxhall Bridge SW1V
238	D7	Vauxhall Bridgefoot SE1
237	M5	Vauxhall Bridge Road SW1V
238	D8	Vauxhall Grove SW8
238	E6	Vauxhall Street SE11
238	E6	Vauxhall Walk SE11
232	E4	Venables Street W2
233	K6	Vere Street W1G
234	D5	Vernon Place WC1A
234	E2	Vernon Rise WC1X
234	F4	Verulam Street WC1X
235	L2	Vestry Street N1
237	L5	Victoria ≠ ⊖ SW1V
238	D2	Victoria Embankment SW1A
234	F7	Victoria Embankment WC2R
232	F7	Victoria Gate W2
236	C4	Victoria Road W8

237	L4	Victoria Square SW1W
237	L4	Victoria Street SW1E
239	K5	Victory Place SE17
241	K7	Victory Way SE16
233	M8	Vigo Street W1S
239	L7	Villa Street SE17
234	D8	Villiers Street WC2N
241	K7	Vincent Close SE16
238	B5	Vincent Square SW1P
238	B5	Vincent Street SW1P
237	H1	Vincent Terrace N1
235	L2	Vince Street EC1V
240	D1	Vine Court E1
240	E7	Vinegar Street E1W
234	F4	Vine Hill EC1R
240	A6	Vine Lane SE1
240	B3	Vine Street EC3N
232	C1	Violet Hill NW8
238	F4	Virgil Street SE1
240	D4	Virginia Street E1W
235	J4	Viscount Street EC2Y

W

239	K6	Wadding Street SE17
234	D3	Wakefield Street WC1H
241	J3	Wakeling Street E14
235	H2	Wakley Street EC1V
235	L7	Walbrook EC4N
239	K6	Walcorde Avenue SE17
239	G5	Walcot Square SE11
240	E2	Walden Street E1
241	M1	Wallwood Street E14
238	F5	Walnut Tree Walk SE11
237	H6	Walpole Street SW3
241	H2	Walter Terrace E1
237	H4	Walton Place SW3
237	G4	Walton Street SW3
239	K7	Walworth Place SE17
239	J5	Walworth Road SE17
238	C8	Wandsworth Road SW8
239	J6	Wansey Street SE17
240	F5	Wapping ⊖ E1W
240	E6	Wapping High Street E1W
240	F4	Wapping Lane E1W
241	G5	Wapping Wall E1W
239	J2	Warden's Grove SE1
234	B6	Wardour Street W1F
234	F4	Warner Street EC1R
233	M4	Warren Street W1T
233	M3	Warren Street ⊖ NW1
232	C3	Warrington Crescent W9
232	C4	Warrington Gardens W9
232	B3	Warwick Avenue W9
232	C4	Warwick Avenue ⊖ W9
232	C5	Warwick Crescent W2
238	B1	Warwick House Street SW1Y
235	H6	Warwick Lane EC4M
232	C4	Warwick Place W9
236	A6	Warwick Road SW5
237	L4	Warwick Row SW1E
237	M6	Warwick Square SW1V
234	A7	Warwick Street W1B
237	L6	Warwick Way SW1V
234	F5	Waterhouse Square EC1N
238	F2	Waterloo ≠ ⊖ SE1
238	E1	Waterloo Bridge SE1
234	E8	Waterloo Bridge WC2R
239	G2	Waterloo East ≠ SE1
238	B1	Waterloo Place SW1Y
238	F1	Waterloo Road SE1
239	G2	Waterloo Road SE1
240	E5	Waterman Way E1W
240	D7	Waterside Close SE16
235	K7	Watling Street EC4N
240	F3	Watney Street E1
240	E5	Watts Street E1W
240	D5	Waveney Close E1W
233	K8	Waverton Street W1J
240	A6	Weavers Lane SE1
239	G3	Webber Row SE1
239	H3	Webber Street SE1
240	A8	Webb Street SE1
240	D8	Webster Road SE16
233	K7	Weigh House Street W1K
233	K5	Welbeck Street W1G
233	K6	Welbeck Way W1G
240	E5	Welland Mews E1W
240	D4	Wellclose Square E1
241	H2	Wellesley Street E1
235	K2	Wellesley Terrace N1
237	H6	Wellington Square SW3
232	E2	Wellington Place NW8
232	E1	Wellington Road NW8
234	D7	Wellington Street WC2E
234	A5	Wells Mews W1T
234	A5	Wells Street W1T
239	M8	Wells Way SE5
235	K1	Wenlock Road N1
235	K1	Wenlock Street N1
240	B2	Wentworth Street E1
234	A1	Werrington Street NW1
233	K5	Wesley Street W1G
241	G2	West Arbour Street E1
232	D7	Westbourne Crescent W2
232	B6	Westbourne Gardens W2
232	E7	Westbourne Gate W2
232	A6	Westbourne Grove W2
232	B6	Westbourne Grove Terrace W2
232	A5	Westbourne Park Road W2
232	A5	Westbourne Park Villas W2
232	E7	Westbourne Street W2
232	B6	Westbourne Terrace W2
232	C6	Westbourne Terrace Mews W2
232	C5	Westbourne Terrace Road W2
236	A7	West Brompton ≠ ⊖ ⊖ SW5
236	E2	West Carriage Drive W2
239	H8	Westcott Road SE17
236	A5	West Cromwell Road SW5
241	G6	Western Place SE16
241	M4	Westferry ⊖ E14
241	M5	Westferry Circus E14
241	M5	Westferry Road E14
240	F4	West Gardens E1W
236	B7	Westgate Terrace SW10
237	J4	West Halkin Street SW1X
241	M5	West India Avenue E14
241	M3	West India Dock Road E14
235	K2	Westland Place N1
240	E7	West Lane SE16
238	D3	Westminster ⊖ SW1A
238	D3	Westminster Bridge SW1A
238	F3	Westminster Bridge Road SE1
237	L7	Westmoreland Place SW1V
239	K8	Westmoreland Road SE17

233	K5	Westmoreland Street W1G
237	L7	Westmoreland Terrace SW1V
234	E1	Weston Rise WC1X
239	M2	Weston Street SE1
239	M3	Weston Street SE1
241	H2	Westport Street E1
235	H5	West Poultry Avenue EC1A
237	H7	West Road SW3
235	H5	West Smithfield EC1A
239	H4	West Square SE11
234	C7	West Street WC2H
240	C3	West Tenter Street E1
237	M6	West Warwick Place SW1V
232	B5	Westway W2
236	C6	Wetherby Gardens SW5
240	D2	Weyhill Road E1
233	L5	Weymouth Mews W1G
233	K5	Weymouth Street W1G
234	D1	Wharfdale Road N1
236	B7	Wharfedale Street SW10
235	J1	Wharf Road N1
234	F2	Wharton Street WC1X
233	K5	Wheatley Street W1G
234	E5	Whetstone Park WC2A
234	D2	Whidborne Street WC1H
235	G2	Whiskin Street EC1R
234	B8	Whitcomb Street WC2H
240	E1	Whitechapel ≠ ⊖ ⊖ E1
240	C4	Whitechapel Estate E1
240	C2	Whitechapel High Street E1
240	D1	Whitechapel Road E1
235	K3	Whitecross Street EC1Y
235	G6	Whitefriars Street EC4Y
238	C2	Whitehall SW1A
238	D2	Whitehall Court SW1A
238	D1	Whitehall Place SW1A
239	G6	White Hart Street SE11
239	L2	White Hart Yard SE1
232	F4	Whitehaven Street NW8
237	G6	Whitehead's Grove SW3
241	H1	White Horse Lane E1
241	J1	Whitehorse Road E1
241	J3	Whitehorse Road E1
237	L1	White Horse Street W1J
240	B2	White Kennett Street E1
235	H7	White Lion Hill EC4V
234	F1	White Lion Street N1
240	A7	White's Grounds SE1
240	B1	White's Row E1
241	J1	White Tower Way E1
234	A4	Whitfield Place W1T
234	A4	Whitfield Street W1T
238	E5	Whitgift Street SE11
237	J6	Whittaker Street SW1W
239	G2	Whittlesey Street SE1
240	E3	Wicker Street E1
241	G1	Wickham Close E1
238	E7	Wickham Street SE11
234	E2	Wicklow Street WC1X
240	A1	Widegate Street E1
232	A3	Widley Road W9
233	K5	Wigmore Place W1G
233	K6	Wigmore Street W1U
239	G7	Wigton Place SE11
237	J5	Wilbraham Place SW1X
234	E6	Wild Court WC2B
239	M4	Wild's Rents SE1
234	D6	Wild Street WC2B
237	M4	Wilfred Street SW1E
240	B1	Wilkes Street E1
234	C8	William IV Street WC2N
237	H3	William Mews SW1X
233	M3	William Road NW1
238	A5	Willow Place SW1P
235	M3	Willow Street EC2A
234	F3	Wilmington Square WC1X
234	F2	Wilmington Street WC1X
240	E7	Wilson Grove SE16
235	L4	Wilson Street EC2A
237	J3	Wilton Crescent SW1X
237	K4	Wilton Mews SW1X
237	J3	Wilton Place SW1X
237	L4	Wilton Road SW1V
237	J3	Wilton Row SW1X
237	K4	Wilton Street SW1X
233	K5	Wimpole Mews W1G
233	K5	Wimpole Street W1G
237	L6	Winchester Street SW1V
239	K1	Winchester Walk SE1
235	G5	Wincott Street SE11
238	F7	Windmill Road SE11
234	B5	Windmill Street W1T
241	H6	Windrose Close SE16
235	K1	Windsor Terrace N1
240	F5	Wine Close E1W
234	B7	Winnett Street W1D
232	E6	Winsland Mews W2
232	E6	Winsland Street W2
234	A6	Winsley Street W1W
240	E1	Winthrop Street E1
234	C3	Woburn Place WC1H
234	C4	Woburn Square WC1H
240	E1	Wodeham Gardens E1
241	H7	Wolfe Crescent SE16
240	C6	Wolseley Street SE1
235	G3	Woodbridge Street EC1R
232	A4	Woodchester Square W9
237	H7	Woodfall Street SW3
241	H7	Woodland Crescent SE16
240	C1	Woodseer Street E1
233	J7	Woods Mews W1K
240	A8	Woods Place SE1
233	K6	Woodstock Street W1C
235	K6	Wood Street EC2V
239	J5	Woolaston Close SE1
239	L7	Wooler Street SE17
239	G2	Wooton Street SE1
238	E6	Worgan Street SE11
241	H8	Worgan Street SE16
235	M5	Wormwood Street EC2M
235	M4	Worship Street EC2A
234	F2	Wren Street WC1X
236	A3	Wright's Lane W8
241	J7	Wyatt Close SE16
235	H2	Wyclif Street EC1V
232	A2	Wymering Road W9
238	F7	Wynard Terrace SE11
233	H5	Wyndham Place W1H
233	G4	Wyndham Street W1H
234	A4	Wynnstay Gardens W8
235	H2	Wynyat Street EC1V
233	H6	Wythburn Place W1H

Y

240	C8	Yalding Road SE16
234	F2	Yardley Street WC1X
237	G4	Yeomans Row SW3
234	D8	York Boulevard WC2N

233	J3	York Bridge NW1
233	J4	York Gate NW1
238	E2	York Road SE1
241	K3	Yorkshire Road E14
241	J2	York Square E14
233	G5	York Street W1H
233	J4	York Terrace East NW1
233	J4	York Terrace West NW1
234	D1	York Way N1

Z

239	J1	Zoar Street SE1

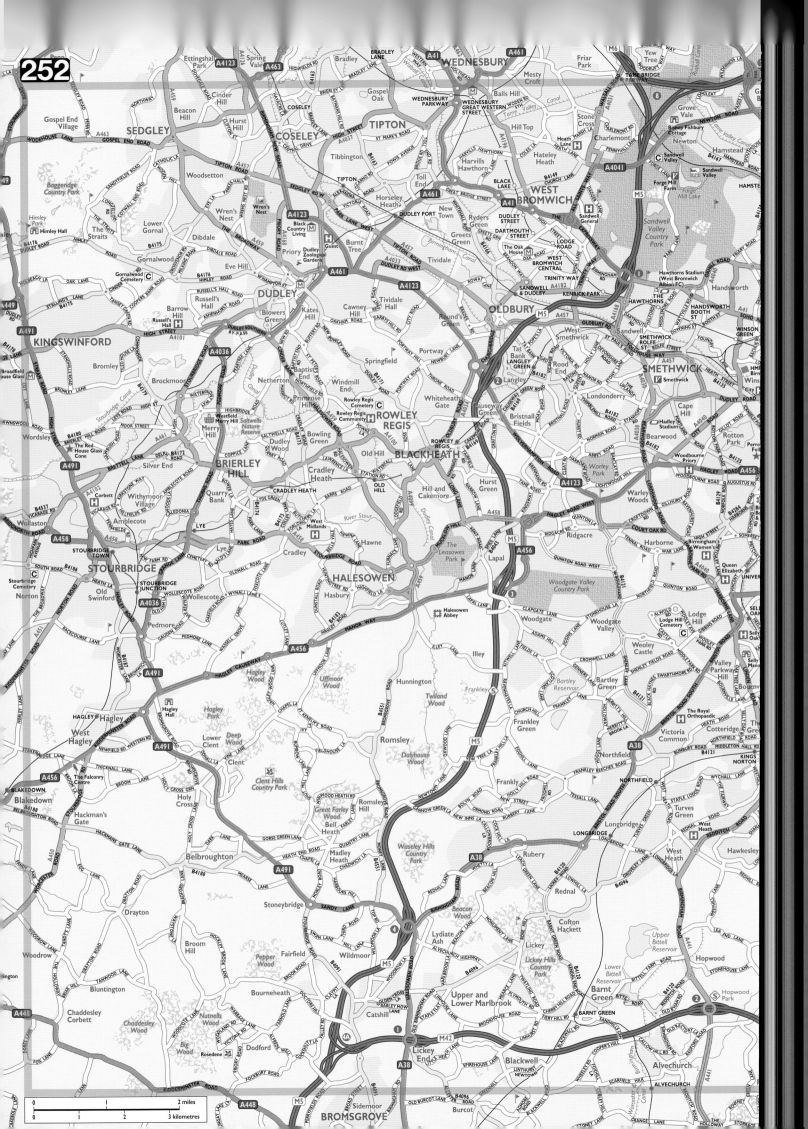

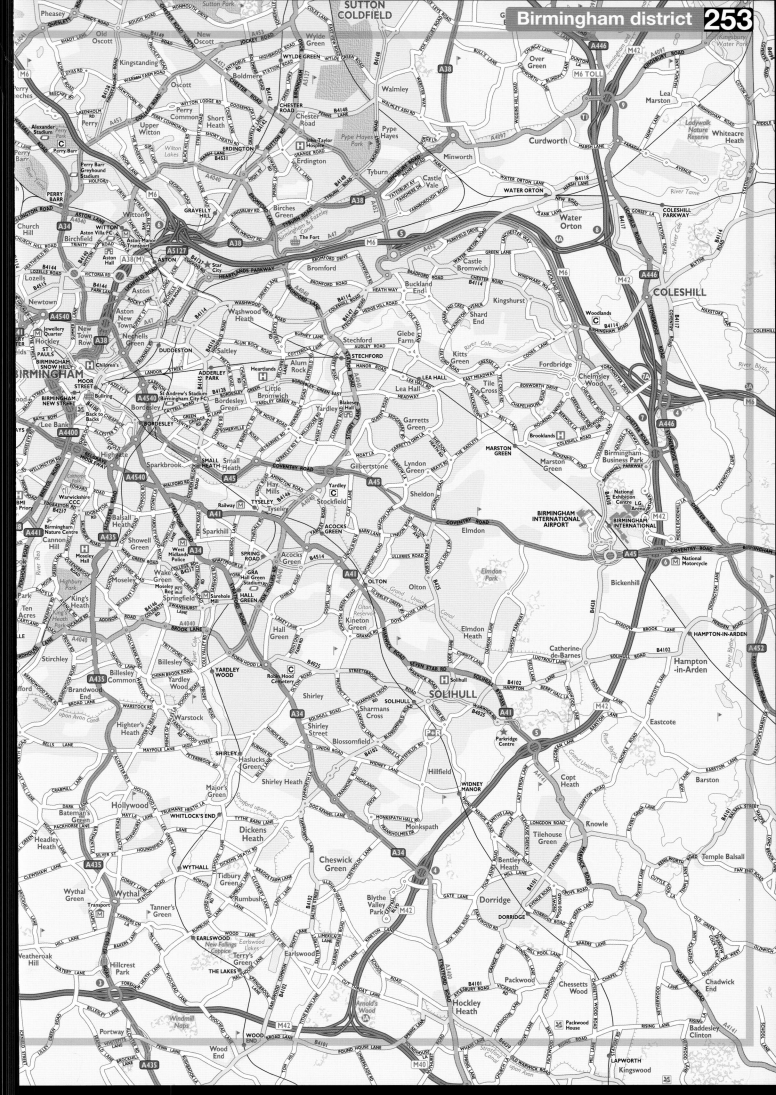

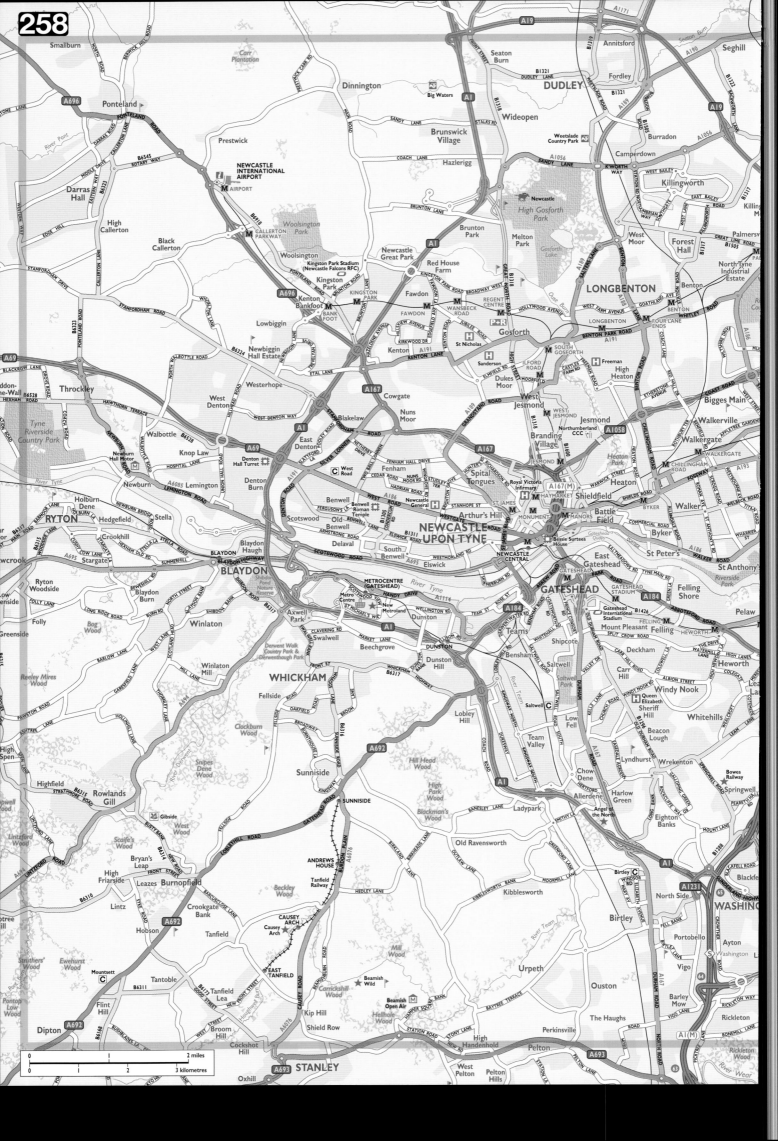

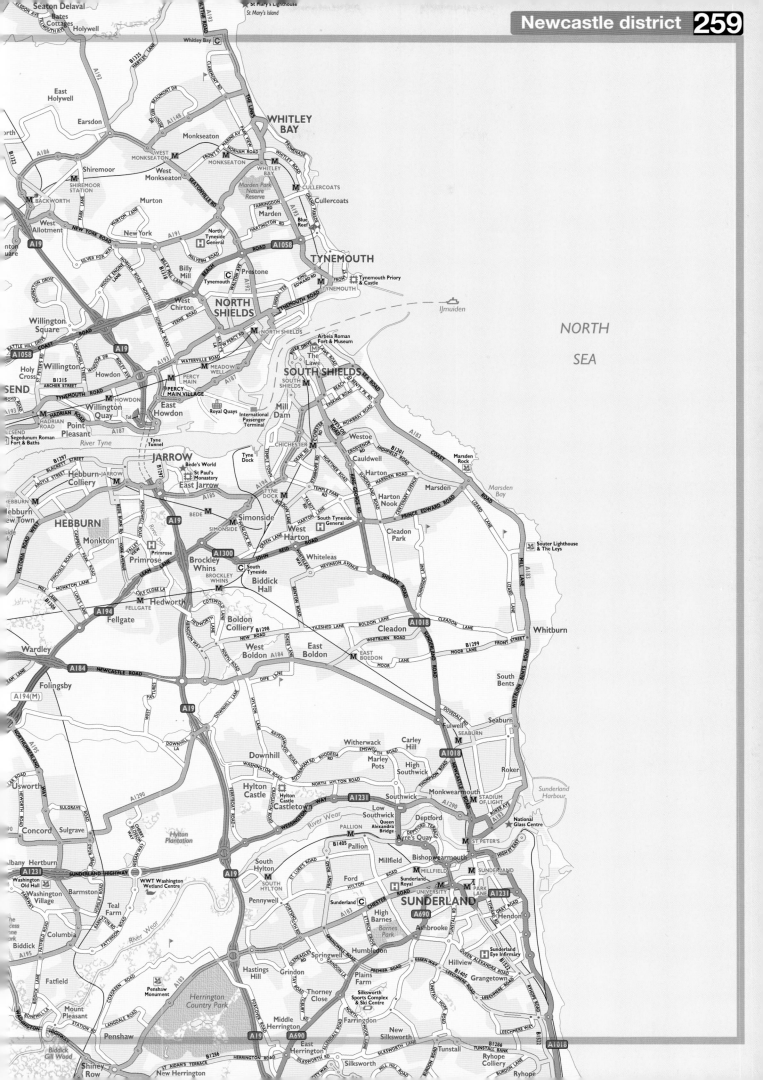

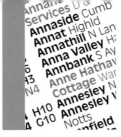

Index to place names

This index lists places appearing in the main-map section of the atlas in alphabetical order. The reference before each name gives the atlas page number and grid reference of the square in which the place appears. The map shows counties, unitary authorities and administrative areas, together with a list of the abbreviated name forms used in the index.

The top 100 places of tourist interest are indexed in **red** (or **green** if a World Heritage site), motorway service areas in **blue** and airports in blue *italic*.

Scotland

Abers	**Aberdeenshire**
Ag & B	**Argyll and Bute**
Angus	**Angus**
Border	**Scottish Borders**
C Aber	**City of Aberdeen**
C Dund	**City of Dundee**
C Edin	**City of Edinburgh**
C Glas	**City of Glasgow**
Clacks	**Clackmannanshire (1)**
D & G	**Dumfries & Galloway**
E Ayrs	**East Ayrshire**
E Duns	**East Dunbartonshire (2)**
E Loth	**East Lothian**
E Rens	**East Renfrewshire (3)**
Falk	**Falkirk**
Fife	**Fife**
Highld	**Highland**
Inver	**Inverclyde (4)**
Mdloth	**Midlothian (5)**
Moray	**Moray**
N Ayrs	**North Ayrshire**
N Lans	**North Lanarkshire (6)**
Ork	**Orkney Islands**
P & K	**Perth & Kinross**
Rens	**Renfrewshire (7)**
S Ayrs	**South Ayrshire**
Shet	**Shetland Islands**
S Lans	**South Lanarkshire**
Stirlg	**Stirling**
W Duns	**West Dunbartonshire (8)**
W Isls	**Western Isles (Na h-Eileanan an Iar)**
W Loth	**West Lothian**

Wales

Blae G	**Blaenau Gwent (9)**
Brdgnd	**Bridgend (10)**
Caerph	**Caerphilly (11)**
Cardif	**Cardiff**
Carmth	**Carmarthenshire**
Cerdgn	**Ceredigion**
Conwy	**Conwy**
Denbgs	**Denbighshire**
Flints	**Flintshire**
Gwynd	**Gwynedd**
IoA	**Isle of Anglesey**
Mons	**Monmouthshire**
Myr Td	**Merthyr Tydfil (12)**
Neath	**Neath Port Talbot (13)**
Newpt	**Newport (14)**
Pembks	**Pembrokeshire**
Powys	**Powys**
Rhondd	**Rhondda Cynon Taff (15)**
Swans	**Swansea**
Torfn	**Torfaen (16)**
V Glam	**Vale of Glamorgan (17)**
Wrexhm	**Wrexham**

Channel Islands & Isle of Man

Guern	**Guernsey**
Jersey	**Jersey**
IoM	**Isle of Man**

England

BaNES	**Bath & N E Somerset (18)**
Barns	**Barnsley (19)**
Bed	**Bedford**
Birm	**Birmingham**
Bl w D	**Blackburn with Darwen (20)**
Bmouth	**Bournemouth**
Bolton	**Bolton (21)**
Bpool	**Blackpool**
Br & H	**Brighton & Hove (22)**
Br For	**Bracknell Forest (23)**
Bristl	**City of Bristol**
Bucks	**Buckinghamshire**
Bury	**Bury (24)**
C Beds	**Central Bedfordshire**
C Brad	**City of Bradford**
C Derb	**City of Derby**
C KuH	**City of Kingston upon Hull**
C Leic	**City of Leicester**
C Nott	**City of Nottingham**
C Pete	**City of Peterborough**
C Plym	**City of Plymouth**
C Port	**City of Portsmouth**
C Sotn	**City of Southampton**
C Stke	**City of Stoke-on-Trent**
C York	**City of York**
Calder	**Calderdale (25)**
Cambs	**Cambridgeshire**
Ches E	**Cheshire East**
Ches W	**Cheshire West and Chester**
Cnwll	**Cornwall**
Covtry	**Coventry**
Cumb	**Cumbria**
Darltn	**Darlington (26)**
Derbys	**Derbyshire**
Devon	**Devon**
Donc	**Doncaster (27)**
Dorset	**Dorset**
Dudley	**Dudley (28)**
Dur	**Durham**
E R Yk	**East Riding of Yorkshire**

E Susx	**East Sussex**
Essex	**Essex**
Gatesd	**Gateshead (29)**
Gloucs	**Gloucestershire**
Gt Lon	**Greater London**
Halton	**Halton (30)**
Hants	**Hampshire**
Hartpl	**Hartlepool (31)**
Herefs	**Herefordshire**
Herts	**Hertfordshire**
IoS	**Isles of Scilly**
IoW	**Isle of Wight**
Kent	**Kent**
Kirk	**Kirklees (32)**
Knows	**Knowsley (33)**
Lancs	**Lancashire**
Leeds	**Leeds**
Leics	**Leicestershire**
Lincs	**Lincolnshire**
Lpool	**Liverpool**
Luton	**Luton**
M Keyn	**Milton Keynes**
Manch	**Manchester**
Medway	**Medway**
Middsb	**Middlesbrough**
NE Lin	**North East Lincolnshire**
N Linc	**North Lincolnshire**
N Som	**North Somerset (34)**
N Tyne	**North Tyneside (35)**
N u Ty	**Newcastle upon Tyne**
N York	**North Yorkshire**
Nhants	**Northamptonshire**
Norfk	**Norfolk**
Notts	**Nottinghamshire**
Nthumb	**Northumberland**
Oldham	**Oldham (36)**
Oxon	**Oxfordshire**
Poole	**Poole**
R & Cl	**Redcar & Cleveland**
Readg	**Reading**
Rochdl	**Rochdale (37)**
Rothm	**Rotherham (38)**
Rutlnd	**Rutland**
S Glos	**South Gloucestershire (39)**
S on T	**Stockton-on-Tees (40)**
S Tyne	**South Tyneside (41)**
Salfd	**Salford (42)**
Sandw	**Sandwell (43)**
Sefton	**Sefton (44)**
Sheff	**Sheffield**
Shrops	**Shropshire**
Slough	**Slough (45)**
Solhll	**Solihull (46)**
Somset	**Somerset**
St Hel	**St Helens (47)**
Staffs	**Staffordshire**
Sthend	**Southend-on-Sea**
Stockp	**Stockport (48)**
Suffk	**Suffolk**
Sundld	**Sunderland**
Surrey	**Surrey**
Swindn	**Swindon**
Tamesd	**Tameside (49)**
Thurr	**Thurrock (50)**
Torbay	**Torbay**
Traffd	**Trafford (51)**
W & M	**Windsor and Maidenhead (52)**
W Berk	**West Berkshire**
W Susx	**West Sussex**
Wakefd	**Wakefield (53)**
Warrtn	**Warrington (54)**
Warwks	**Warwickshire**
Wigan	**Wigan (55)**
Wilts	**Wiltshire**
Wirral	**Wirral (56)**
Wokham	**Wokingham (57)**
Wolves	**Wolverhampton (58)**
Worcs	**Worcestershire**
Wrekin	**Telford & Wrekin (59)**
Wsall	**Walsall (60)**

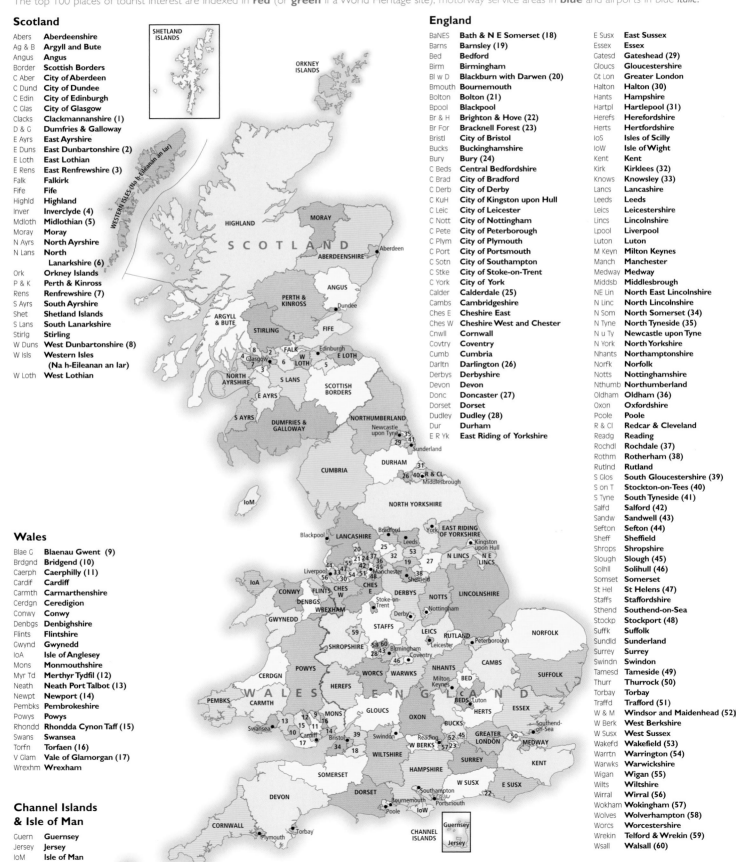

Abbas Combe - Ansteadbrook 261

A

20 D10 Abbas Combe Somset
57 P11 Abberley Worcs
57 N11 Abberley Common Worcs
52 H8 Abberton Essex
47 J4 Abberton Worcs
119 M8 Abberwick Nthumb
51 N8 Abbess Roding Essex
10 C2 Abbey Devon
55 P10 Abbey-Cwm-Hir Powys
84 D4 Abbeydale Sheff
45 M8 Abbey Dore Herefs
70 H3 Abbey Green Staffs
19 J11 Abbey Hill Somset
129 K7 Abbey St Bathans Border
95 M10 Abbeystead Lancs
110 C10 Abbey Town Cumb
89 J6 Abbey Village Lancs
37 L5 Abbey Wood Gt Lon
118 B8 Abbotrule Border
16 F9 Abbots Bickington Devon
71 K10 Abbots Bromley Staffs
11 M7 Abbotsbury Dorset
83 M6 Abbot's Chair Derbys
134 E5 Abbots Deuglie P & K
16 G6 Abbotsham Devon
7 M5 Abbotskerswell Devon
50 C10 Abbots Langley Herts
7 L9 Abbotsleigh Devon
31 P10 Abbots Leigh N Som
62 B9 Abbotsley Cambs
47 K3 Abbots Morton Worcs
62 B5 Abbots Ripton Cambs
47 L4 Abbot's Salford Warwks
22 G8 Abbotstone Hants
22 C10 Abbotswood Hants
22 E8 Abbots Worthy Hants
22 B6 Abbotts Ann Hants
12 G4 Abbott Street Dorset
56 F9 Abcott Shrops
57 K7 Abdon Shrops
46 C11 Abenhall Gloucs
43 J2 Aberaeron Cerdgn
30 D4 Aberaman Rhondd
55 J2 Aberangell Gwynd
42 F6 Aber-arad Carmth
147 Q2 Aberarder Highld
134 F4 Aberargie P & K
43 J2 Aberarth Cerdgn
29 K7 Aberavon Neath
42 G6 Aber-banc Cerdgn
30 G4 Aberbargoed Caerph
30 H4 Aberbeeg Blae G
30 E4 Abercanaid Myr Td
30 H6 Abercarn Caerph
40 G4 Abercastle Pembks
55 J4 Abercegir Powys
147 J7 Aberchalder Lodge Highld
158 F7 Aberchirder Abers
44 G10 Aber Clydach Powys
29 M2 Abercraf Powys
29 M5 Abercregan Neath
30 D5 Abercwmboi Rhondd
41 P2 Abercych Pembks
30 E6 Abercynon Rhondd
134 D3 Aberdalgie P & K
30 D4 Aberdare Rhondd
66 B9 Aberdaron Gwynd
151 N6 Aberdeen C Aber
151 M5 Aberdeen Airport C Aber
151 M6 Aberdeen Crematorium C Aber
66 G4 Aberdesach Gwynd
134 F10 Aberdour Fife
29 L5 Aberdulais Neath
54 E5 Aberdyfi Gwynd
44 F5 Aberedw Powys
40 E4 Abereiddy Pembks
66 F7 Abererch Gwynd
30 E4 Aberfan Myr Td
141 L8 Aberfeldy P & K
78 F11 Aberffraw IoA
54 F9 Aberffrwd Cerdgn
91 L3 Aberford Leeds
132 G7 Aberfoyle Stirlg
29 P8 Abergarw Brdgnd
29 M4 Abergarwed Neath
31 J2 Abergavenny Mons
80 C9 Abergele Conwy
43 K6 Aber-giar Carmth
43 L8 Abergorlech Carmth
44 B4 Abergwesyn Powys
42 H10 Abergwili Carmth
54 H4 Abergwydol Powys
29 N5 Abergwynfi Neath
79 M10 Abergwyngregyn Gwynd
54 F3 Abergynolwyn Gwynd
55 P6 Aberhafesp Powys
55 J5 Aberhosan Powys
29 N8 Aberkenfig Brdgnd
128 D4 Aberlady E Loth
143 J6 Aberlemno Angus
54 H3 Aberllefenni Gwynd
44 H7 Aberllynfi Powys
157 P9 Aberlour Moray
54 F10 Aber-Magwr Cerdgn
43 L3 Aber-meurig Cerdgn
69 K3 Abermorddu Flints
56 B6 Abermule Powys
42 F10 Abernant Carmth
30 D4 Aber-nant Rhondd
134 F4 Abernethy P & K
142 D11 Abernyte P & K
42 E4 Aberporth Cerdgn
66 E9 Abersoch Gwynd
31 J4 Abersychan Torfn
30 D10 Aberthin V Glam
30 H4 Abertillery Blae G
30 F7 Abertridwr Caerph
68 D11 Abertridwr Powys
30 F3 Abertysswg Caerph
134 B4 Aberuthven P & K
44 D9 Aberyscir Powys
54 D8 Aberystwyth Cerdgn
54 E8 Aberystwyth Crematorium Cerdgn
34 E5 Abingdon-on-Thames Oxon
36 D11 Abinger Common Surrey
36 C11 Abinger Hammer Surrey
60 G8 Abington Nhants
116 C6 Abington S Lans
50 H2 Abington Pigotts Cambs
116 C6 Abington Services S Lans
24 D7 Abingworth W Susx
73 J6 Ab Kettleby Leics
47 K4 Ab Lench Worcs
33 M3 Ablington Gloucs
21 N5 Ablington Wilts
83 Q8 Abney Derbys
71 J4 Above Church Staffs
150 E8 Aboyne Abers
82 D4 Abram Wigan
155 Q10 Abriachan Highld
51 L11 Abridge Essex
126 D2 Abronhill N Lans
32 D10 Abson S Glos
48 H5 Abthorpe Nhants
87 M5 Aby Lincs
98 B11 Acaster Malbis C York
91 P2 Acaster Selby N York
89 M5 Accrington Lancs
89 M5 Accrington Crematorium Lancs
136 F5 Acha Ag & B
123 N4 Achahoish Ag & B
141 R8 Achalader P & K
138 G11 Achaleven Ag & B
168 i5 Acha Mor W Isls
155 J5 Achanalt Highld
156 A3 Achandunie Highld
162 D6 Achany Highld
138 B4 Acharacle Highld
138 C7 Acharn Highld
141 J9 Acharn P & K
167 L8 Achavanich Highld
160 G6 Achduart Highld
164 G9 Achfary Highld
144 C6 A'Chill Highld
160 G5 Achiltibuie Highld
166 B4 Achina Highld
120 E8 Achinhoan Ag & B
154 B9 Achintee Highld
153 Q10 Achintraid Highld
160 H2 Achmelvich Highld
153 R11 Achmore Highld
168 i5 Achmore W Isls
164 B10 Achnacarnin Highld
146 F10 Achnacarry Highld
145 J6 Achnacloich Highld
147 L4 Achnaconeran Highld
138 F9 Achnacroish Ag & B
137 M5 Achnadrish House Ag & B
141 L10 Achnafauld P & K
156 B3 Achnagarron Highld
137 M2 Achnaha Highld
160 G4 Achnahaird Highld
162 D4 Achnairn Highld
138 F5 Achnalea Highld
130 F10 Achnamara Ag & B
154 G6 Achnasheen Highld
154 D8 Achnashellach Lodge Highld
157 P11 Achnastank Moray
137 L2 Achosnich Highld
138 C8 Achranich Highld
166 H3 Achreamie Highld
139 L4 Achriabhach Highld
164 G6 Achriesgill Highld
165 Q4 Achtoty Highld
61 M4 Achurch Nhants
162 G8 Achvaich Highld
166 G4 Achvarasdal Highld
167 Q6 Ackergill Highld
104 E7 Acklam Middsb
98 F8 Acklam N York
57 P5 Ackleton Shrops
119 P10 Acklington Nthumb
91 L6 Ackton Wakefd
91 L7 Ackworth Moor Top Wakefd
77 N9 Acle Norfk
58 H8 Acock's Green Birm
39 P8 Acol Kent
98 B10 Acomb C York
112 D7 Acomb Nthumb
10 D2 Acombe Somset
45 Q8 Aconbury Herefs
89 M6 Acre Lancs
69 J6 Acrefair Wrexhm
70 A4 Acton Ches E
12 G9 Acton Dorset
36 F4 Acton Gt Lon
56 E8 Acton Shrops
70 E6 Acton Staffs
52 E2 Acton Suffk
58 B11 Acton Worcs
46 C4 Acton Beauchamp Herefs
82 C9 Acton Bridge Ches W
57 J4 Acton Burnell Shrops
46 C4 Acton Green Herefs
69 K4 Acton Park Wrexhm
57 J4 Acton Pigott Shrops
57 L5 Acton Round Shrops
56 H7 Acton Scott Shrops
70 G11 Acton Trussell Staffs
32 F8 Acton Turville S Glos
70 D9 Adbaston Staffs
19 Q10 Adber Dorset
72 F3 Adbolton Notts
48 E7 Adderbury Oxon
70 B7 Adderley Shrops
119 M4 Adderstone Nthumb
126 H5 Addiewell W Loth
96 G11 Addingham C Brad
49 K9 Addington Bucks
37 J8 Addington Gt Lon
37 Q9 Addington Kent
36 H7 Addiscombe Gt Lon
36 C8 Addlestone Surrey
36 C7 Addlestonemoor Surrey
87 P7 Addlethorpe Lincs
70 B11 Adeney Wrekin
50 C9 Adeyfield Herts
55 P4 Adfa Powys
56 G10 Adforton Herefs
39 M11 Adisham Kent
47 P9 Adlestrop Gloucs
92 D6 Adlingfleet E R Yk
83 K8 Adlington Ches E
89 J8 Adlington Lancs
71 J10 Admaston Staffs
57 L2 Admaston Wrekin
47 P5 Admington Warwks
42 F6 Adpar Cerdgn
19 J9 Adsborough Somset
18 G7 Adscombe Somset
49 K9 Adstock Bucks
48 G4 Adstone Nhants
83 J7 Adswood Stockp
24 C6 Adversane W Susx
157 L11 Advie Highld
90 G5 Adwalton Leeds
35 J5 Adwell Oxon
91 N9 Adwick Le Street Donc
91 M10 Adwick upon Dearne Donc
109 L3 Ae D & G
109 M3 Ae Bridgend D & G
29 N5 Afan Forest Park Neath
89 M8 Affetside Bury
158 E9 Affleck Abers
12 D6 Affpuddle Dorset
146 F3 Affric Lodge Highld
80 G10 Afon-wen Flints
7 L6 Afton Devon
13 P7 Afton IoW
82 H4 Agecroft Crematorium Salfd
96 G3 Agglethorpe N York
81 M7 Aigburth Lpool
99 L11 Aike E R Yk
111 J11 Aiketgate Cumb
110 D11 Aikhead Cumb
110 E10 Aikton Cumb
87 M5 Ailby Lincs
45 L5 Ailey Herefs
74 B11 Ailsworth C Pete
97 M4 Ainderby Quernhow N York
97 M2 Ainderby Steeple N York
53 K7 Aingers Green Essex
88 C8 Ainsdale Sefton
88 B8 Ainsdale-on-Sea Sefton
111 K11 Ainstable Cumb
89 M8 Ainsworth Bury
105 K9 Ainthorpe N York
81 M5 Aintree Sefton
127 L5 Ainville W Loth
130 F7 Aird Ag & B
106 E5 Aird D & G
168 k4 Aird W Isls
168 g6 Aird a Mhulaidh W Isls
168 g7 Aird Asaig W Isls
153 N9 Aird Dhubh Highld
131 K2 Airdeny Ag & B
137 N10 Aird of Kinloch Ag & B
145 J7 Aird of Sleat Highld
126 D4 Airdrie N Lans
126 D4 Airdriehill N Lans
108 E6 Airds of Kells D & G
168 f4 Aird Uig W Isls
168 h6 Airidh a bhruaich W Isls
108 G9 Airieland D & G
142 E7 Airlie Angus
92 B6 Airmyn E R Yk
141 Q10 Airntully P & K
145 M6 Airor Highld
133 Q10 Airth Falk
96 D9 Airton N York
73 Q3 Aisby Lincs
85 Q2 Aisby Lincs
102 E11 Aisgill Cumb
6 H6 Aish Devon
7 L7 Aish Devon
18 G7 Aisholt Somset
97 L3 Aiskew N York
98 F3 Aislaby N York
105 N9 Aislaby N York
104 D8 Aislaby S on T
86 B4 Aisthorpe Lincs
169 q8 Aith Shet
119 J5 Akeld Nthumb
49 K7 Akeley Bucks
53 K2 Akenham Suffk
5 Q7 Albaston Cnwll
56 F2 Alberbury Shrops
24 G7 Albourne W Susx
24 G7 Albourne Green W Susx
57 Q4 Albrighton Shrops
69 N11 Albrighton Shrops
65 K4 Alburgh Norfk
51 K6 Albury Herts
35 J3 Albury Oxon
36 B11 Albury Surrey
51 K6 Albury End Herts
36 C11 Albury Heath Surrey
76 H5 Alby Hill Norfk
155 Q6 Alcaig Highld
56 H7 Alcaston Shrops
47 L3 Alcester Warwks
58 G8 Alcester Lane End Birm
25 M9 Alciston E Susx
18 C5 Alcombe Somset
32 F11 Alcombe Wilts
61 Q5 Alconbury Cambs
61 Q5 Alconbury Weston Cambs
97 P7 Aldborough N York
76 H5 Aldborough Norfk
33 Q9 Aldbourne Wilts
93 M3 Aldbrough E R Yk
103 P8 Aldbrough St John N York
35 Q2 Aldbury Herts
95 K8 Aldcliffe Lancs
141 L5 Aldclune P & K
65 P10 Aldeburgh Suffk
65 N3 Aldeby Norfk
50 D11 Aldenham Herts
21 N9 Alderbury Wilts
84 F11 Aldercar Derbys
76 G8 Alderford Norfk
13 K2 Alderholt Dorset
32 E6 Alderley Gloucs
82 H9 Alderley Edge Ches E
59 N8 Aldermans Green Covtry
34 G11 Aldermaston W Berk
47 P5 Alderminster Warwks
71 N9 Alder Moor Staffs
69 N3 Aldersey Green Ches W
23 N4 Aldershot Hants
47 K8 Alderton Gloucs
49 K5 Alderton Nhants
69 N10 Alderton Shrops
53 P3 Alderton Suffk
32 F8 Alderton Wilts
71 Q4 Alderwasley Derbys
97 L7 Aldfield N York
69 M3 Aldford Ches W
73 P10 Aldgate Rutlnd
52 F6 Aldham Essex
52 J2 Aldham Suffk
15 P5 Aldingbourne W Susx
94 F6 Aldingham Cumb
27 J4 Aldington Kent
47 L6 Aldington Worcs
27 J4 Aldington Corner Kent
150 B2 Aldivalloch Moray
132 D9 Aldochlay Ag & B
56 G9 Aldon Shrops
109 P11 Aldoth Cumb
62 F6 Aldreth Cambs
58 G4 Aldridge Wsall
65 N9 Aldringham Suffk
98 G8 Aldro N York
33 N3 Aldsworth Gloucs
15 L5 Aldsworth W Susx
150 B2 Aldunie Moray
84 B9 Aldwark Derbys
97 Q8 Aldwark N York
15 P7 Aldwick W Susx
61 M4 Aldwincle Nhants
34 G9 Aldworth W Berk
125 K2 Alexandria W Duns
18 G7 Aley Somset
16 D9 Alfardisworthy Devon
10 C5 Alfington Devon
24 B4 Alfold Surrey
24 B4 Alfold Bars W Susx
24 B3 Alfold Crossways Surrey
150 F4 Alford Abers
87 N5 Alford Lincs
20 B8 Alford Somset
87 M5 Alford Crematorium Lincs
84 F9 Alfreton Derbys
46 D4 Alfrick Worcs
46 D4 Alfrick Pound Worcs
25 M10 Alfriston E Susx
74 E3 Algarkirk Lincs
20 B8 Alhampton Somset
92 E6 Alkborough N Linc
32 E3 Alkerton Gloucs
48 C6 Alkerton Oxon
27 N3 Alkham Kent
69 P7 Alkington Shrops
71 M7 Alkmonton Derbys
7 L8 Allaleigh Devon
149 L9 Allanaquoich Abers
126 E6 Allanbank N Lans
129 M9 Allanton Border
126 E6 Allanton N Lans
126 C7 Allanton S Lans
32 B4 Allaston Gloucs
22 E10 Allbrook Hants
21 L2 All Cannings Wilts
112 B9 Allendale Nthumb
59 J5 Allen End Warwks
112 C11 Allenheads Nthumb
112 G10 Allensford Dur
51 L7 Allen's Green Herts
45 P8 Allensmore Herefs
72 B4 Allenton C Derb
17 P6 Aller Devon
19 M9 Aller Somset
100 E3 Allerby Cumb
9 P6 Allercombe Devon
18 B5 Allerford Somset
98 H4 Allerston N York
98 F11 Allerthorpe E R Yk
90 E4 Allerton C Brad
156 D4 Allerton Highld
81 M7 Allerton Lpool
91 L5 Allerton Bywater Leeds
97 P9 Allerton Mauleverer N York
59 M8 Allesley Covtry
72 A3 Allestree C Derb
3 K4 Allet Common Cnwll
73 L10 Allexton Leics
83 L11 Allgreave Ches E
38 D6 Allhallows Medway
38 D6 Allhallows-on-Sea Medway
153 Q6 Alligin Shuas Highld
70 F11 Allimore Green Staffs
11 K6 Allington Dorset
38 C10 Allington Kent
73 M2 Allington Lincs
21 L2 Allington Wilts
21 P7 Allington Wilts
32 G9 Allington Wilts
94 H5 Allithwaite Cumb
133 P9 Alloa Clacks
100 E2 Allonby Cumb
82 F10 Allostock Ches W
114 F4 Alloway S Ayrs
10 H2 Allowenshay Somset
65 L5 All Saints South Elmham Suffk
57 N5 Allscott Shrops
57 L2 Allscott Wrekin
56 H5 All Stretton Shrops
81 K11 Alltami Flints
139 M7 Alltchaorunn Highld
44 F5 Alltmawr Powys
42 H8 Alltwalis Carmth
29 K4 Alltwen Neath
43 K5 Alltyblaca Cerdgn
11 P2 Allweston Dorset
64 E7 Allwood Green Suffk
45 L4 Almeley Herefs
45 L4 Almeley Wooton Herefs
12 F5 Almer Dorset
91 P9 Almholme Donc
70 C8 Almington Staffs
15 M7 Almodington W Susx
134 D2 Almondbank P & K
90 F8 Almondbury Kirk
32 B8 Almondsbury S Glos
97 Q7 Alne N York
156 B4 Alness Highld
119 J8 Alnham Nthumb
119 P8 Alnmouth Nthumb
119 N8 Alnwick Nthumb
36 E4 Alperton Gt Lon
52 E4 Alphamstone Essex
64 B11 Alpheton Suffk
9 M6 Alphington Devon
77 K11 Alpington Norfk
84 B8 Alport Derbys
69 Q3 Alpraham Ches E
53 J7 Alresford Essex
59 J2 Alrewas Staffs
70 D3 Alsager Ches E
70 D5 Alsagers Bank Staffs
71 M4 Alsop en le Dale Derbys
111 P11 Alston Cumb
10 G4 Alston Devon
47 J8 Alstone Gloucs
19 K5 Alstone Somset
71 L3 Alstonefield Staffs
19 M4 Alston Sutton Somset
17 N7 Alswear Devon
83 K4 Alt Oldham
160 F4 Altandhu Highld
5 L5 Altarnun Cnwll
162 C6 Altass Highld
138 B10 Altcreich Ag & B
124 C3 Altgaltraig Ag & B
89 M4 Altham Lancs
38 F2 Althorne Essex
92 D9 Althorpe N Linc
166 H7 Altnabreac Station Highld
165 N9 Altnaharra Highld
91 K6 Altofts Wakefd
84 E8 Alton Derbys
23 K7 Alton Hants
71 K6 Alton Staffs
21 N5 Alton Wilts
21 M2 Alton Barnes Wilts
11 Q4 Alton Pancras Dorset
21 M2 Alton Priors Wilts
71 K6 Alton Towers Staffs
82 G7 Altrincham Traffd
82 F7 Altrincham Crematorium Traffd
132 F7 Altskeith Hotel Stirlg
133 P8 Alva Clacks
81 P10 Alvanley Ches W
72 B4 Alvaston C Derb
58 F10 Alvechurch Worcs
59 K4 Alvecote Warwks
21 J10 Alvediston Wilts
57 P8 Alveley Shrops
17 J6 Alverdiscott Devon
14 H7 Alverstoke Hants
14 G9 Alverstone IoW
91 J6 Alverthorpe Wakefd
73 K2 Alverton Notts
157 L5 Alves Moray
33 Q4 Alvescot Oxon
32 B7 Alveston S Glos
47 P3 Alveston Warwks
87 L2 Alvingham Lincs
32 B4 Alvington Gloucs
74 B11 Alwalton C Pete
118 H9 Alwinton Nthumb
90 H2 Alwoodley Leeds
91 J2 Alwoodley Gates Leeds
142 C8 Alyth P & K
84 D10 Ambergate Derbys
86 H11 Amber Hill Lincs
32 G4 Amberley Gloucs
24 B8 Amberley W Susx
84 E9 Amber Row Derbys
25 N8 Amberstone E Susx
119 Q10 Amble Nthumb
58 C7 Amblecote Dudley
90 D5 Ambler Thorn C Brad
101 L10 Ambleside Cumb
41 K5 Ambleston Pembks
48 H11 Ambrosden Oxon
92 E8 Amcotts N Linc
62 F5 America Cambs
35 Q5 Amersham Bucks
35 Q5 Amersham Common Bucks
35 Q5 Amersham Old Town Bucks
35 Q5 Amersham on the Hill Bucks
70 H9 Amerton Staffs
21 N6 Amesbury Wilts
168 f7 Amhuinnsuidhe W Isls
59 K4 Amington Staffs
109 M4 Amisfield Town D & G
78 G6 Amlwch IoA
28 H2 Ammanford Carmth
98 E6 Amotherby N York
22 D10 Ampfield Hants
98 B5 Ampleforth N York
33 L4 Ampney Crucis Gloucs
33 L4 Ampney St Mary Gloucs
33 L4 Ampney St Peter Gloucs
22 B6 Amport Hants
50 B3 Ampthill C Beds
64 B7 Ampton Suffk
41 N9 Amroth Pembks
141 L10 Amulree P & K
50 E8 Amwell Herts
138 E5 Anaheilt Highld
73 P2 Ancaster Lincs
56 B7 Anchor Shrops
129 P11 Ancroft Nthumb
118 B6 Ancrum Border
15 Q6 Ancton W Susx
87 P5 Anderby Lincs
19 K8 Andersea Somset
18 H8 Andersfield Somset
12 E5 Anderson Dorset
82 D9 Anderton Ches W
6 C8 Anderton Cnwll
22 C5 Andover Hants
47 K11 Andoversford Gloucs
80 f2 Andreas IoM
66 B9 Anelog Gwynd
36 H7 Anerley Gt Lon
81 M6 Anfield Lpool
81 M6 Anfield Crematorium Lpool
2 F6 Angarrack Cnwll
3 K6 Angarrick Cnwll
57 K9 Angelbank Shrops
18 G11 Angersleigh Somset
110 D9 Angerton Cumb
40 G10 Angle Pembks
78 G8 Anglesey IoA
24 C10 Angmering W Susx
97 R11 Angram N York
102 G11 Angram N York
2 H10 Angrouse Cnwll
112 D7 Anick Nthumb
156 E3 Ankerville Highld
73 K7 Ankle Hill Leics
92 H5 Anlaby E R Yk
75 P5 Anmer Norfk
15 J4 Anmore Hants
110 C7 Annan D & G
109 P2 Annandale Water Services D & G
94 B3 Annaside Cumb
154 A7 Annat Highld
126 C3 Annathill N Lans
22 C6 Anna Valley Hants
114 H3 Annbank S Ayrs
47 N4 Anne Hathaway's Cottage Warwks
84 H10 Annesley Notts
84 G10 Annesley Woodhouse Notts
113 J10 Annfield Plain Dur
125 N4 Anniesland C Glas
113 L6 Annitsford N Tyne
56 H3 Annscroft Shrops
88 C5 Ansdell Lancs
20 B8 Ansford Somset
59 M6 Ansley Warwks
71 N9 Anslow Staffs
71 M10 Anslow Gate Staffs
71 N10 Anslow Lees Staffs
23 P8 Ansteadbrook Surrey

23 K6 **Anstey** Hants
51 K4 **Anstey** Herts
72 F9 **Anstey** Leics
135 P7 **Anstruther** Fife
24 G6 **Ansty** W Susx
59 P8 **Ansty** Warwks
21 J9 **Ansty** Wilts
12 C4 **Ansty Cross** Dorset
14 H4 **Anthill Common** Hants
36 B8 **Anthonys** Surrey
110 C9 **Anthorn** Cumb
77 K11 **Antingham** Norfk
168 f9 **An t-Ob** W Isls
87 K11 **Anton's Gowt** Lincs
5 Q11 **Antony** Cnwll
82 D9 **Antrobus** Ches W
16 F11 **Anvil Corner** Devon
27 K2 **Anvil Green** Kent
86 F10 **Anwick** Lincs
108 C9 **Anwoth** D & G
37 K9 **Aperfield** Gt Lon
58 E10 **Apes Dale** Worcs
73 Q11 **Apethorpe** Nhants
70 F11 **Apeton** Staffs
86 F5 **Apley** Lincs
84 E5 **Apperknowle** Derbys
46 G6 **Apperley** Gloucs
90 F3 **Apperley Bridge** C Brad
112 G9 **Apperley Dene** Nthumb
96 C2 **Appersett** N York
138 G8 **Appin** Ag & B
92 G8 **Appleby** N Linc
102 C6 **Appleby-in-Westmorland** Cumb
59 M3 **Appleby Magna** Leics
59 M3 **Appleby Parva** Leics
50 H10 **Appleby Street** Herts
153 N9 **Applecross** Highld
9 Q2 **Appledore** Devon
16 H5 **Appledore** Devon
26 G6 **Appledore** Kent
26 G5 **Appledore Heath** Kent
34 F6 **Appleford** Oxon
109 P4 **Applegarth Town** D & G
91 K8 **Applehaigh** Wakefd
22 B5 **Appleshaw** Hants
101 J5 **Applethwaite** Cumb
81 Q7 **Appleton** Halton
34 D4 **Appleton** Oxon
82 D8 **Appleton** Warrtn
98 E3 **Appleton-le-Moors** N York
98 E6 **Appleton-le-Street** N York
91 P2 **Appleton Roebuck** N York
82 D8 **Appleton Thorn** Warrtn
104 C10 **Appleton Wiske** N York
117 Q7 **Appletreehall** Border
96 C8 **Appletreewick** N York
18 E10 **Appley** Somset
88 C9 **Appley Bridge** Lancs
14 G10 **Apse Heath** IoW
50 D4 **Apsley End** C Beds
15 M6 **Apuldram** W Susx
156 E2 **Arabella** Highld
143 L9 **Arbirlot** Angus
163 K10 **Arboll** Highld
35 L11 **Arborfield** Wokham
35 L11 **Arborfield Cross** Wokham
84 E3 **Arbourthorne** Sheff
143 L9 **Arbroath** Angus
143 P2 **Arbuthnott** Abers
26 K4 **Arcadia** Kent
28 D4 **Archddu** Carmth
103 Q7 **Archdeacon Newton** Darltn
132 E11 **Archencarroch** W Duns
157 N9 **Archiestown** Moray
11 C1 **Archirondel** Jersey
70 D2 **Arclid Green** Ches E
159 P10 **Ardachie** Highld
131 M3 **Ardanaiseig Hotel** Ag & B
153 Q10 **Ardaneaskan** Highld
153 Q10 **Ardarroch** Highld
122 F10 **Ardbeg** Ag & B
124 D4 **Ardbeg** Ag & B
131 P11 **Ardbeg** Ag & B
161 K9 **Ardcharnich** Highld
137 K12 **Ardchiavaig** Ag & B
131 K5 **Ardchonnel** Ag & B
132 H5 **Ardchullarie More** Stirlg
131 Q9 **Arddarroch** Ag & B
69 J11 **Arddleen** Powys
146 E9 **Ardechive** Highld
124 H9 **Ardeer** N Ayrs
50 H5 **Ardeley** Herts
145 Q2 **Ardelve** Highld
132 D11 **Arden** Ag & B
47 M4 **Ardens Grafton** Warwks
130 G3 **Ardentallen** Ag & B
131 P10 **Ardentinny** Ag & B
124 C3 **Ardentraive** Ag & B
140 G10 **Ardeonaig** Stirlg
156 D7 **Ardersier** Highld
160 H9 **Ardessie** Highld
130 G7 **Ardfern** Ag & B
123 J9 **Ardfernal** Ag & B
162 D8 **Ardgay** Highld
139 J5 **Ardgour** Highld
124 G3 **Ardgowan** Inver
124 F3 **Ardhallow** Ag & B
168 g7 **Ardhasig** W Isls
153 P6 **Ardheslaig** Highld
161 K9 **Ardindrean** Highld
24 H5 **Ardingly** W Susx
34 D7 **Ardington** Oxon
34 D7 **Ardington Wick** Oxon
124 B4 **Ardlamont** Ag & B
53 J6 **Ardleigh** Essex
52 H5 **Ardleigh Heath** Essex
142 D9 **Ardler** P & K
48 F9 **Ardley** Oxon
51 M8 **Ardley End** Essex
132 C4 **Ardlui** Ag & B
130 C10 **Ardlussa** Ag & B
161 J7 **Ardmair** Highld
124 D4 **Ardmaleish** Ag & B
123 K10 **Ardminish** Ag & B
138 C3 **Ardmolich** Highld
125 J2 **Ardmore** Ag & B
162 G9 **Ardmore** Highld
131 P11 **Ardnadam** Ag & B
155 P8 **Ardnagrask** Highld
154 A10 **Ardnarff** Highld
138 E5 **Ardnastang** Highld
123 N8 **Ardpatrick** Ag & B
130 F10 **Ardrishaig** Ag & B
155 R3 **Ardross** Highld
124 G9 **Ardrossan** N Ayrs

91 K9 **Ardsley** Barns
91 J5 **Ardsley East** Leeds
137 P3 **Ardslignish** Highld
122 G9 **Ardtalla** Ag & B
138 A3 **Ardtoe** Highld
130 F5 **Arduaine** Ag & B
155 Q5 **Ardullie** Highld
145 K7 **Ardvasar** Highld
133 J3 **Ardvorlich** P & K
168 g6 **Ardvourlie** W Isls
106 F8 **Ardwell** D & G
83 J5 **Ardwick** Manch
57 P10 **Areley Kings** Worcs
138 B4 **Arevegaig** Highld
23 M7 **Arford** Hants
30 G5 **Argoed** Caerph
69 K10 **Argoed** Shrops
44 D2 **Argoed Mill** Powys
25 N5 **Argos Hill** E Susx
131 Q7 **Argyll Forest Park** Ag & B
168 h6 **Aribruach** W Isls
137 J11 **Aridhglas** Ag & B
136 F5 **Arileod** Ag & B
136 G4 **Arinagour** Ag & B
130 H2 **Ariogan** Ag & B
145 L10 **Arisaig** Highld
145 L11 **Arisaig House** Highld
97 N8 **Arkendale** N York
51 L4 **Arkesden** Essex
95 M6 **Arkholme** Lancs
100 F3 **Arkleby** Cumb
110 G2 **Arkleton** D & G
103 K10 **Arkle Town** N York
50 F11 **Arkley** Gt Lon
91 P9 **Arksey** Donc
84 F6 **Arkwright Town** Derbys
46 H10 **Arle** Gloucs
100 D7 **Arlecdon** Cumb
48 C5 **Arlescote** Warwks
50 E3 **Arlesey** C Beds
57 M2 **Arleston** Wrekin
82 E8 **Arley** Ches E
59 L6 **Arley** Warwks
32 D2 **Arlingham** Gloucs
17 L3 **Arlington** Devon
25 M9 **Arlington** E Susx
33 M3 **Arlington** Gloucs
17 L3 **Arlington Beccott** Devon
145 K7 **Armadale** Highld
166 C4 **Armadale** Highld
126 G4 **Armadale** W Loth
100 G5 **Armaside** Cumb
111 K11 **Armathwaite** Cumb
77 K11 **Arminghall** Norfk
71 K11 **Armitage** Staffs
90 E8 **Armitage Bridge** Kirk
90 H4 **Armley** Leeds
47 P6 **Armscote** Warwks
70 G5 **Armshead** Staffs
61 N3 **Armston** Nhants
91 Q10 **Armthorpe** Donc
136 G3 **Arnabost** Ag & B
94 D4 **Arnaby** Cumb
96 D6 **Arncliffe** N York
96 D6 **Arncliffe Cote** N York
135 N6 **Arncroach** Fife
157 P8 **Arndilly House** Moray
12 G7 **Arne** Dorset
60 D2 **Arnesby** Leics
134 E5 **Arngask** P & K
145 P5 **Arnisdale** Highld
153 K8 **Arnish** Highld
127 Q5 **Arniston** Mdloth
168 i3 **Arnol** W Isls
93 K2 **Arnold** E R Yk
85 J11 **Arnold** Notts
133 J9 **Arnprior** Stirlg
95 K5 **Arnside** Cumb
137 P6 **Aros** Ag & B
69 N7 **Arowry** Wrexhm
94 G4 **Arrad Foot** Cumb
92 H2 **Arram** E R Yk
120 H4 **Arran** N Ayrs
97 K2 **Arrathorne** N York
14 F9 **Arreton** IoW
153 N6 **Arrina** Highld
62 D10 **Arrington** Cambs
132 B7 **Arrochar** Ag & B
47 L3 **Arrow** Warwks
58 F10 **Arrowfield Top** Worcs
56 G3 **Arscott** Shrops
156 A4 **Artafallie** Highld
90 H2 **Arthington** Leeds
60 G4 **Arthingworth** Nhants
54 E2 **Arthog** Gwynd
159 N10 **Arthrath** Abers
91 K3 **Arthursdale** Leeds
159 P11 **Artrochie** Abers
24 B9 **Arundel** W Susx
100 E6 **Asby** Cumb
124 E5 **Ascog** Ag & B
35 P11 **Ascot** W & M
88 F9 **Ascott** Warwks
24 E7 **Ascott Earl** Oxon
48 B11 **Ascott-under-Wychwood** Oxon
97 N5 **Asenby** N York
73 J7 **Asfordby** Leics
73 J7 **Asfordby Hill** Leics
86 F11 **Asgarby** Lincs
87 K7 **Asgarby** Lincs
7 L9 **Ash** Devon
17 J10 **Ash** Devon
12 E2 **Ash** Dorset
37 P8 **Ash** Kent
39 N10 **Ash** Kent
19 J10 **Ash** Somset
19 N10 **Ash** Somset
23 P4 **Ash** Surrey
34 G9 **Ashampstead** W Berk
34 G9 **Ashampstead Green** W Berk
64 H11 **Ashbocking** Suffk
71 M5 **Ashbourne** Derbys
18 E10 **Ashbrittle** Somset
25 Q8 **Ashburnham Place** E Susx
7 K4 **Ashburton** Devon
8 D5 **Ashbury** Devon
33 Q7 **Ashbury** Oxon
92 E9 **Ashby** N Linc
87 M7 **Ashby by Partney** Lincs
93 N10 **Ashby cum Fenby** NE Lin
86 E9 **Ashby de la Launde** Lincs
72 B7 **Ashby-de-la-Zouch** Leics
73 J8 **Ashby Folville** Leics
60 C2 **Ashby Magna** Leics
60 B3 **Ashby Parva** Leics
87 K6 **Ashby Puerorum** Lincs
60 C7 **Ashby St Ledgers** Nhants

77 L11 **Ashby St Mary** Norfk
46 H8 **Ashchurch** Gloucs
9 M9 **Ashcombe** Devon
19 K2 **Ashcombe** N Som
19 M7 **Ashcott** Somset
51 N2 **Ashdon** Essex
22 F4 **Ashe** Hants
52 G11 **Asheldham** Essex
52 B3 **Ashen** Essex
35 K2 **Ashendon** Bucks
35 P4 **Asheridge** Bucks
22 C11 **Ashfield** Hants
46 A10 **Ashfield** Herefs
133 M7 **Ashfield** Stirlg
65 J9 **Ashfield cum Thorpe** Suffk
65 N9 **Ashfield Green** Suffk
65 K7 **Ashfield Green** Suffk
24 F5 **Ashfold Crossways** W Susx
6 H9 **Ashford** Devon
17 J4 **Ashford** Devon
26 H3 **Ashford** Kent
36 C6 **Ashford** Surrey
57 J10 **Ashford Bowdler** Shrops
57 J10 **Ashford Carbonell** Shrops
22 G2 **Ashford Hill** Hants
83 Q11 **Ashford in the Water** Derbys
126 D7 **Ashgill** S Lans
23 P5 **Ash Green** Surrey
59 M8 **Ash Green** Warwks
10 B2 **Ashill** Devon
76 B11 **Ashill** Norfk
19 K11 **Ashill** Somset
38 E3 **Ashingdon** Essex
113 L3 **Ashington** Nthumb
12 H5 **Ashington** Poole
19 Q10 **Ashington** Somset
24 D7 **Ashington** W Susx
117 P6 **Ashkirk** Border
14 E6 **Ashlett** Hants
46 F9 **Ashleworth** Gloucs
46 F9 **Ashleworth Quay** Gloucs
63 L8 **Ashley** Cambs
82 G8 **Ashley** Ches E
17 M9 **Ashley** Devon
13 K4 **Ashley** Dorset
32 H6 **Ashley** Gloucs
13 N5 **Ashley** Hants
22 C8 **Ashley** Hants
27 P2 **Ashley** Kent
60 G2 **Ashley** Nhants
70 D7 **Ashley** Staffs
32 F11 **Ashley** Wilts
35 Q3 **Ashley Green** Bucks
71 P4 **Ashleyhay** Derbys
13 K4 **Ashley Heath** Dorset
56 H11 **Ashley Moor** Herefs
69 Q7 **Ash Magna** Shrops
22 D3 **Ashmansworth** Hants
16 E8 **Ashmansworthy** Devon
32 E5 **Ashmead Green** Gloucs
5 P2 **Ashmill** Devon
17 P7 **Ash Mill** Devon
20 H11 **Ashmore** Dorset
34 F11 **Ashmore Green** W Berk
48 B3 **Ashorne** Warwks
84 D8 **Ashover** Derbys
84 D8 **Ashover Hay** Derbys
59 M10 **Ashow** Warwks
69 Q7 **Ash Parva** Shrops
46 B6 **Ashperton** Herefs
7 L7 **Ashprington** Devon
18 G9 **Ash Priors** Somset
17 L9 **Ashreigney** Devon
52 H2 **Ash Street** Suffk
36 F9 **Ashtead** Surrey
9 P2 **Ash Thomas** Devon
74 B9 **Ashton** C Pete
81 Q11 **Ashton** Ches W
2 G8 **Ashton** Cnwll
9 L8 **Ashton** Devon
22 F11 **Ashton** Hants
45 Q2 **Ashton** Herefs
124 G2 **Ashton** Inver
61 N3 **Ashton** Nhants
49 M5 **Ashton** Nhants
19 M5 **Ashton** Somset
20 G3 **Ashton Common** Wilts
20 H3 **Ashton Hill** Wilts
82 C5 **Ashton-in-Makerfield** Wigan
33 K6 **Ashton Keynes** Wilts
47 J7 **Ashton under Hill** Worcs
83 K5 **Ashton-under-Lyne** Tamesd
82 G6 **Ashton upon Mersey** Traffd
13 P2 **Ashurst** Hants
25 M3 **Ashurst** Kent
88 F9 **Ashurst** Lancs
24 E7 **Ashurst** W Susx
25 K3 **Ashurstwood** W Susx
23 N4 **Ash Vale** Surrey
5 P2 **Ashwater** Devon
50 G3 **Ashwell** Herts
73 M8 **Ashwell** Rutlnd
19 L11 **Ashwell** Somset
50 G2 **Ashwell End** Herts
64 G2 **Ashwellthorpe** Norfk
20 B5 **Ashwick** Somset
75 P7 **Ashwicken** Norfk
58 C7 **Ashwood** Staffs
94 E5 **Askam in Furness** Cumb
91 P8 **Askern** Donc
11 L6 **Askerswell** Dorset
35 M3 **Askett** Bucks
101 P6 **Askham** Cumb
85 M6 **Askham** Notts
98 B11 **Askham Bryan** C York
98 A11 **Askham Richard** C York
131 J9 **Asknish** Ag & B
96 D2 **Askrigg** N York
97 J11 **Askwith** N York
74 A4 **Aslackby** Lincs
64 H3 **Aslacton** Norfk
73 J3 **Aslockton** Notts
19 N7 **Asney** Somset
64 H9 **Aspall** Suffk
100 F2 **Aspatria** Cumb
51 J5 **Aspenden** Herts
83 M7 **Aspenshaw** Derbys
74 E3 **Asperton** Lincs
70 E8 **Aspley** Staffs
49 P7 **Aspley Guise** C Beds
49 P8 **Aspley Heath** C Beds
58 G10 **Aspley Heath** Warwks
89 J9 **Aspull** Wigan

82 D5 **Aspull Common** Wigan
92 B5 **Asselby** E R Yk
87 N5 **Asserby** Lincs
87 N5 **Asserby Turn** Lincs
63 N10 **Assington** Suffk
63 N10 **Assington Green** Suffk
70 E2 **Astbury** Ches E
49 J4 **Astcote** Nhants
87 J5 **Asterby** Lincs
56 F3 **Asterley** Shrops
56 F4 **Asterton** Shrops
48 G7 **Asthall** Oxon
34 B2 **Asthall Leigh** Oxon
162 G8 **Astle** Highld
69 P11 **Astley** Shrops
59 M7 **Astley** Warwks
82 F4 **Astley** Wigan
57 P11 **Astley** Worcs
57 N5 **Astley Abbotts** Shrops
89 L8 **Astley Bridge** Bolton
57 Q11 **Astley Cross** Worcs
22 F5 **Astley Green** Wigan
58 G7 **Aston** Birm
69 R5 **Aston** Ches E
82 C9 **Aston** Ches W
83 Q8 **Aston** Derbys
81 L11 **Aston** Flints
45 P2 **Aston** Herefs
50 G6 **Aston** Herts
34 B4 **Aston** Oxon
84 G3 **Aston** Rothm
57 Q6 **Aston** Shrops
69 P9 **Aston** Shrops
70 D6 **Aston** Staffs
70 F10 **Aston** Staffs
35 L8 **Aston** Wokham
57 L3 **Aston** Wrekin
49 M10 **Aston Abbotts** Bucks
57 L8 **Aston Botterell** Shrops
70 G8 **Aston-by-Stone** Staffs
47 M2 **Aston Cantlow** Warwks
35 N2 **Aston Clinton** Bucks
46 C10 **Aston Crews** Herefs
46 H8 **Aston Cross** Gloucs
50 G6 **Aston End** Herts
57 M6 **Aston-Eyre** Shrops
58 E11 **Aston Fields** Worcs
59 Q6 **Aston Flamville** Leics
82 C9 **Aston Heath** Ches W
46 C10 **Aston Ingham** Herefs
70 A3 **Aston juxta Mondrum** Ches E
48 E4 **Aston le Walls** Nhants
47 N7 **Aston Magna** Gloucs
57 J7 **Aston Munslow** Shrops
56 F8 **Aston on Clun** Shrops
56 E3 **Aston Pigott** Shrops
56 E3 **Aston Rogers** Shrops
35 K5 **Aston Rowant** Oxon
35 L3 **Aston Sandford** Bucks
47 K7 **Aston Somerville** Worcs
47 M6 **Aston-sub-Edge** Gloucs
34 G7 **Aston Tirrold** Oxon
72 C5 **Aston-upon-Trent** Derbys
34 G7 **Aston Upthorpe** Oxon
48 F7 **Astrop** Nhants
35 N2 **Astrope** Herts
50 F3 **Astwick** C Beds
84 F8 **Astwith** Derbys
49 Q5 **Astwood** M Keyn
59 D11 **Astwood** Worcs
47 K2 **Astwood Bank** Worcs
46 G3 **Astwood Crematorium** Worcs
73 R3 **Aswarby** Lincs
87 L6 **Aswardby** Lincs
57 J3 **Atcham** Shrops
57 K4 **Atch Lench** Worcs
12 C6 **Athelhampton** Dorset
65 J7 **Athelington** Suffk
19 K9 **Athelney** Somset
128 E4 **Athelstaneford** E Loth
14 E11 **Atherfield Green** IoW
17 K7 **Atherington** Devon
24 B10 **Atherington** W Susx
19 L11 **Atherstone** Somset
59 M5 **Atherstone** Warwks
47 P4 **Atherstone on Stour** Warwks
82 E4 **Atherton** Wigan
103 Q10 **Atley Hill** N York
71 N5 **Atlow** Derbys
154 B10 **Attadale** Highld
72 E4 **Attenborough** Notts
86 C2 **Atterby** Lincs
84 E3 **Attercliffe** Sheff
57 L5 **Atterley** Shrops
72 B11 **Atterton** Leics
64 E2 **Attleborough** Norfk
59 N6 **Attleborough** Warwks
76 E8 **Attlebridge** Norfk
63 M10 **Attleton Green** Suffk
99 P11 **Atwick** E R Yk
32 G11 **Atworth** Wilts
45 P5 **Auberrow** Herefs
86 B8 **Aubourn** Lincs
149 N2 **Auchbreck** Moray
159 L11 **Auchedly** Abers
143 N2 **Auchenblae** Abers
133 M10 **Auchenbowie** Stirlg
108 G10 **Auchencairn** D & G
109 L4 **Auchencairn** D & G
121 K6 **Auchencairn** N Ayrs
129 M7 **Auchencrow** Border
127 P5 **Auchendinny** Mdloth
126 H7 **Auchengray** S Lans
157 R5 **Auchenhalrig** Moray
126 E9 **Auchenheath** S Lans
115 R8 **Auchenhessnane** D & G
125 R8 **Auchenlochan** Ag & B
125 K8 **Auchenmade** N Ayrs
106 H7 **Auchenmalg** D & G
125 K8 **Auchentiber** N Ayrs
131 L7 **Auchindrain** Ag & B
161 K10 **Auchindrean** Highld
158 G8 **Auchininna** Abers
135 L3 **Auchinleck** E Ayrs
126 B3 **Auchinloch** N Lans
126 C2 **Auchinstarry** N Lans
139 K3 **Auchintore** Highld
159 Q10 **Auchiries** Abers
148 F8 **Auchlean** Highld
151 M8 **Auchlee** Abers
150 G3 **Auchleven** Abers
126 E10 **Auchlochan** S Lans
150 F7 **Auchlossan** Abers
150 F3 **Auchlyne** Stirlg
115 K2 **Auchmillan** E Ayrs
143 M9 **Auchmithie** Angus
134 G7 **Auchmuirbridge** Fife

142 H5 **Auchnacree** Angus
159 M9 **Auchnagatt** Abers
149 N3 **Auchnarrow** Moray
106 C5 **Auchnotteroch** D & G
157 Q7 **Auchroisk** Moray
133 Q5 **Auchterarder** P & K
147 K6 **Auchteraw** Highld
148 C3 **Auchterblair** Highld
152 D2 **Auchtercairn** Highld
134 G8 **Auchterderran** Fife
142 H10 **Auchterhouse** Angus
158 H9 **Auchterless** Abers
134 G5 **Auchtermuchty** Fife
155 N6 **Auchterneed** Highld
134 G9 **Auchtertool** Fife
145 P2 **Auchtertyre** Highld
132 H3 **Auchtubh** Stirlg
167 Q3 **Auckengill** Highld
91 Q10 **Auckley** Donc
83 K5 **Audenshaw** Tamesd
70 B6 **Audlem** Ches E
70 D4 **Audley** Staffs
51 M8 **Audley End** Essex
52 D4 **Audley End** Essex
64 B11 **Audley End** Suffk
51 M3 **Audley End House** Essex
70 D4 **Audmore** Staffs
58 C7 **Audnam** Dudley
101 J3 **Aughertree** Cumb
92 B3 **Aughton** E R Yk
88 D9 **Aughton** Lancs
95 M7 **Aughton** Lancs
84 G3 **Aughton** Rothm
21 P3 **Aughton** Wilts
88 E9 **Aughton Park** Lancs
156 G6 **Auldearn** Highld
45 P4 **Aulden** Herefs
109 K3 **Auldgirth** D & G
125 Q7 **Auldhouse** S Lans
146 A3 **Ault a' chruinn** Highld
160 D9 **Aultbea** Highld
160 A9 **Aultgrishin** Highld
155 L3 **Aultguish Inn** Highld
84 G7 **Ault Hucknall** Derbys
158 B7 **Aultmore** Moray
147 N3 **Aultnagoire** Highld
162 F10 **Aultnamain Inn** Highld
73 Q8 **Aunby** Lincs
9 P4 **Aunk** Devon
73 Q3 **Aunsby** Lincs
31 Q7 **Aust** S Glos
74 E6 **Austendike** Lincs
85 L2 **Austerfield** Donc
90 B9 **Austerlands** Oldham
91 K4 **Austhorpe** Leeds
90 E9 **Austonley** Kirk
59 L3 **Austrey** Warwks
95 R7 **Austwick** N York
87 L4 **Authorpe** Lincs
87 P6 **Authorpe Row** Lincs
33 M11 **Avebury** Wilts
33 L11 **Avebury Trusloe** Wilts
37 N4 **Aveley** Thurr
32 G5 **Avening** Gloucs
85 N10 **Averham** Notts
6 H9 **Aveton Gifford** Devon
148 F5 **Aviemore** Highld
34 C11 **Avington** W Berk
156 C6 **Avoch** Highld
13 K5 **Avon** Hants
126 G3 **Avonbridge** Falk
48 D4 **Avon Dassett** Warwks
31 P9 **Avonmouth** Bristl
7 J7 **Avonwick** Devon
22 B10 **Awbridge** Hants
31 Q7 **Awkley** S Glos
10 C4 **Awliscombe** Devon
32 D3 **Awre** Gloucs
72 D2 **Awsworth** Notts
59 C9 **Axborough** Worcs
19 M4 **Axbridge** Somset
22 H6 **Axford** Hants
33 P10 **Axford** Wilts
10 F5 **Axminster** Devon
10 F6 **Axmouth** Devon
80 G8 **Axton** Flints
103 Q6 **Aycliffe** Dur
112 F7 **Aydon** Nthumb
32 B4 **Aylburton** Gloucs
111 P11 **Ayle** Nthumb
9 P6 **Aylesbeare** Devon
35 M2 **Aylesbury** Bucks
93 M9 **Aylesby** NE Lin
38 B10 **Aylesford** Kent
39 M11 **Aylesham** Kent
72 F10 **Aylestone** C Leic
72 F10 **Aylestone Park** C Leic
76 H4 **Aylmerton** Norfk
76 H6 **Aylsham** Norfk
46 C7 **Aylton** Herefs
46 E10 **Aylworth** Gloucs
56 G11 **Aymestrey** Herefs
48 F8 **Aynho** Nhants
50 F8 **Ayot Green** Herts
50 E7 **Ayot St Lawrence** Herts
50 F7 **Ayot St Peter** Herts
114 F3 **Ayr** S Ayrs
96 F3 **Aysgarth** N York
18 D11 **Ayshford** Devon
94 H4 **Ayside** Cumb
73 M10 **Ayston** Rutlnd
51 N7 **Aythorpe Roding** Essex
129 N7 **Ayton** Border
97 L6 **Azerley** N York

B

7 N5 **Babbacombe** Torbay
72 D2 **Babbington** Notts
69 K9 **Babbinswood** Shrops
51 J7 **Babbs Green** Herts
19 Q9 **Babcary** Somset
44 A7 **Babel** Carmth
63 M11 **Babel Green** Suffk
80 H10 **Babell** Flints
8 G2 **Babeny** Devon
34 D4 **Bablock Hythe** Oxon
62 H10 **Babraham** Cambs
85 L4 **Babworth** Notts
78 G8 **Bachau** IoA
56 H8 **Bache** Shrops
56 C6 **Bacheldre** Powys
26 D9 **Bachelor's Bump** E Susx
169 e3 **Backaland** Ork
94 H4 **Backbarrow** Cumb
41 Q7 **Backe** Carmth
159 P7 **Backfolds** Abers
81 M10 **Backford** Ches W

Backford Cross - Beattock 263

81 M10 **Backford Cross** Ches W
163 J6 **Backies** Highld
145 L10 **Back of Keppoch** Highld
71 K4 **Back o' th' Brook** Staffs
63 M9 **Back Street** Suffk
31 N11 **Backwell** N Som
113 M6 **Backworth** N Tyne
59 J7 **Bacon's End** Solhll
76 G4 **Baconsthorpe** Norfk
45 M8 **Bacton** Herefs
77 L5 **Bacton** Norfk
64 F8 **Bacton** Suffk
64 E8 **Bacton Green** Suffk
89 P6 **Bacup** Lancs
153 P3 **Badachro** Highld
33 N8 **Badbury** Swindn
60 C9 **Badby** Nhants
164 E8 **Badcall** Highld
164 F5 **Badcall** Highld
160 G8 **Badcaul** Highld
70 G4 **Baddeley Edge** C Stke
70 G4 **Baddeley Green** C Stke
59 K10 **Baddesley Clinton** Warwks
59 L5 **Baddesley Ensor** Warwks
160 H2 **Baddidarrach** Highld
127 L7 **Baddinsgill** Border
158 G10 **Badenscoth** Abers
149 Q4 **Badenyon** Abers
5 L4 **Badgall** Cnwll
74 H11 **Badgeney** Cambs
57 P5 **Badger** Shrops
2 D7 **Badger's Cross** Cnwll
37 L8 **Badgers Mount** Kent
46 H11 **Badgeworth** Gloucs
19 L4 **Badgworth** Somset
5 M4 **Badharlick** Cnwll
145 N2 **Badicaul** Highld
65 L8 **Badingham** Suffk
38 H11 **Badlesmere** Kent
116 F7 **Badlieu** Border
167 M7 **Badlipster** Highld
160 F8 **Badluachrach** Highld
162 H8 **Badninish** Highld
160 H8 **Badrallach** Highld
47 L6 **Badsey** Worcs
23 N5 **Badshot Lea** Surrey
91 M8 **Badsworth** Wakefd
64 D8 **Badwell Ash** Suffk
64 E8 **Badwell Green** Suffk
12 C2 **Bagber** Dorset
97 Q4 **Bagby** N York
87 L6 **Bag Enderby** Lincs
33 K3 **Bagendon** Gloucs
57 M8 **Bagginswood** Shrops
100 G2 **Baggrow** Cumb
168 b18 **Bagh a Chaisteil** W Isls
39 J11 **Bagham** Kent
168 c17 **Bagh a Tuath** W Isls
81 J9 **Bagillt** Flints
59 M10 **Baginton** Warwks
29 K6 **Baglan** Neath
90 G3 **Bagley** Leeds
69 M9 **Bagley** Shrops
19 N5 **Bagley** Somset
23 J6 **Bagmore** Hants
70 G4 **Bagnall** Staffs
34 E11 **Bagnor** W Berk
57 K10 **Bagot** Shrops
23 P2 **Bagshot** Surrey
34 B11 **Bagshot** Wilts
32 C7 **Bagstone** S Glos
84 G10 **Bagthorpe** Notts
72 C9 **Bagworth** Leics
45 N9 **Bagwy Llydiart** Herefs
90 F3 **Baildon** C Brad
90 E3 **Baildon Green** C Brad
168 h5 **Baile Ailein** W Isls
168 c12 **Baile a Mhanaich** W Isls
136 H11 **Baile Mor** Ag & B
23 J9 **Bailey Green** Hants
111 K5 **Baileyhead** Cumb
90 E5 **Bailiff Bridge** Calder
126 B5 **Baillieston** C Glas
95 K9 **Bailrigg** Lancs
96 D2 **Bainbridge** N York
158 F10 **Bainshole** Abers
74 A9 **Bainton** C Pete
99 K10 **Bainton** E R Yk
48 G9 **Bainton** Oxon
135 K7 **Baintown** Fife
118 C7 **Bairnkine** Border
51 J7 **Baker's End** Herts
37 P4 **Baker Street** Thurr
84 B7 **Bakewell** Derbys
68 B7 **Bala** Gwynd
168 h5 **Balallan** W Isls
155 M11 **Balbeg** Highld
134 F2 **Balbeggie** P & K
155 P8 **Balblair** Highld
156 C4 **Balblair** Highld
91 P10 **Balby** Donc
108 H11 **Balcary** D & G
155 P9 **Balchraggan** Highld
164 E4 **Balchreick** Highld
24 H4 **Balcombe** W Susx
24 H4 **Balcombe Lane** W Susx
135 Q6 **Balcomie Links** Fife
97 N5 **Baldersby** N York
97 N5 **Baldersby St James** N York
89 J4 **Balderstone** Lancs
89 Q8 **Balderstone** Rochdl
85 P10 **Balderton** Notts
3 K5 **Baldhu** Cnwll
135 L5 **Baldinnie** Fife
134 C4 **Baldinnies** P & K
50 F4 **Baldock** Herts
50 F3 **Baldock Services** Herts
142 H11 **Baldovie** C Dund
80 f5 **Baldrine** IoM
26 D9 **Baldslow** E Susx
80 e5 **Baldwin** IoM
110 F10 **Baldwinholme** Cumb
70 D7 **Baldwin's Gate** Staffs
25 J3 **Baldwin's Hill** W Susx
76 E4 **Bale** Norfk
142 D11 **Baledgarno** P & K
136 B7 **Balemartine** Ag & B
127 M4 **Balerno** C Edin
134 H7 **Balfarg** Fife
143 J4 **Balfield** Angus
169 d5 **Balfour** Ork
132 G10 **Balfron** Stirlg
158 G9 **Balgaveny** Abers
134 C9 **Balgonar** Fife
106 F9 **Balgowan** D & G
147 Q9 **Balgowan** Highld
152 F4 **Balgown** Highld
106 C5 **Balgracie** D & G
116 B6 **Balgray** S Lans
36 G6 **Balham** Gt Lon
142 D8 **Balhary** P & K
142 A10 **Balholmie** P & K
166 E3 **Baligill** Highld
142 D6 **Balintore** Angus
156 F2 **Balintore** Highld
156 C3 **Balintraid** Highld
168 c12 **Balivanich** W Isls
97 Q4 **Balk** N York
142 E9 **Balkeerie** Angus
92 C5 **Balkholme** E R Yk
80 c7 **Ballabeg** IoM
139 K6 **Ballachulish** Highld
80 b7 **Ballafesson** IoM
80 g3 **Ballajora** IoM
80 b7 **Ballakilpheric** IoM
80 c7 **Ballamodha** IoM
124 C5 **Ballanlay** Ag & B
114 A11 **Ballantrae** S Ayrs
38 F3 **Ballards Gore** Essex
59 L6 **Ballards Green** Warwks
80 c7 **Ballasalla** IoM
150 B8 **Ballater** Abers
80 d3 **Ballaugh** IoM
156 D2 **Ballchraggan** Highld
128 D4 **Ballencrieff** E Loth
136 B6 **Ballevullin** Ag & B
70 F4 **Ball Green** C Stke
70 H3 **Ball Haye Green** Staffs
22 D2 **Ball Hill** Hants
71 N4 **Ballidon** Derbys
120 G4 **Balliekine** N Ayrs
131 N8 **Balliemore** Ag & B
114 D9 **Balligmorrie** S Ayrs
132 G4 **Ballimore** Stirlg
157 M10 **Ballindalloch** Moray
134 H2 **Ballindean** P & K
52 E3 **Ballingdon** Suffk
35 P4 **Ballinger Common** Bucks
46 A8 **Ballingham** Herefs
134 F8 **Ballingry** Fife
141 N7 **Ballinluig** P & K
142 G7 **Ballinshoe** Angus
141 R6 **Ballintuim** P & K
156 C8 **Balloch** Highld
126 C3 **Balloch** N Lans
133 N4 **Balloch** P & K
114 F8 **Balloch** S Ayrs
132 D11 **Balloch** W Duns
23 Q9 **Balls Cross** W Susx
25 L3 **Balls Green** E Susx
32 G5 **Ball's Green** Gloucs
137 L7 **Ballygown** Ag & B
122 E6 **Ballygrant** Ag & B
136 F4 **Ballyhaugh** Ag & B
145 P2 **Balmacara** Highld
108 E5 **Balmaclellan** D & G
108 E12 **Balmae** D & G
132 E9 **Balmaha** Stirlg
135 J6 **Balmalcolm** Fife
108 D11 **Balmangan** D & G
151 P4 **Balmedie** Abers
69 M8 **Balmer Heath** Shrops
135 K3 **Balmerino** Fife
13 P4 **Balmerlawn** Hants
120 H5 **Balmichael** N Ayrs
149 P9 **Balmoral Castle Grounds** Abers
125 P3 **Balmore** E Duns
163 K11 **Balmuchy** Highld
134 G10 **Balmule** Fife
135 L3 **Balmullo** Fife
163 J4 **Balnacoil Lodge** Highld
154 C8 **Balnacra** Highld
149 P9 **Balnacroft** Abers
156 B10 **Balnafoich** Highld
141 M7 **Balnaguard** P & K
136 c2 **Balnahard** Ag & B
137 M9 **Balnahard** Ag & B
155 M11 **Balnain** Highld
165 J3 **Balnakeil** Highld
91 P7 **Balne** N York
141 P10 **Balquharn** P & K
132 G3 **Balquhidder** Stirlg
59 K9 **Balsall Common** Solhll
58 G8 **Balsall Heath** Birm
59 K9 **Balsall Street** Solhll
48 C6 **Balscote** Oxon
63 J10 **Balsham** Cambs
169 t3 **Baltasound** Shet
70 D4 **Balterley** Staffs
70 D4 **Balterley Green** Staffs
70 C4 **Balterley Heath** Staffs
107 M5 **Baltersan** D & G
19 P8 **Baltonsborough** Somset
130 F4 **Balvicar** Ag & B
145 P4 **Balvraid** Highld
156 E11 **Balvraid** Highld
2 F7 **Balwest** Cnwll
88 H5 **Bamber Bridge** Lancs
51 N6 **Bamber's Green** Essex
119 N4 **Bamburgh** Nthumb
119 N3 **Bamburgh Castle** Nthumb
84 B4 **Bamford** Derbys
89 P8 **Bamford** Rochdl
101 P7 **Bampton** Cumb
18 C10 **Bampton** Devon
34 B4 **Bampton** Oxon
101 P7 **Bampton Grange** Cumb
139 L2 **Banavie** Highld
48 E6 **Banbury** Oxon
48 E6 **Banbury Crematorium** Oxon
28 E2 **Bancffosfelen** Carmth
150 H8 **Banchory** Abers
151 N7 **Banchory-Devenick** Abers
28 D2 **Bancycapel** Carmth
42 F11 **Bancyfelin** Carmth
42 H7 **Banc-y-ffordd** Carmth
142 C11 **Bandirran** P & K
94 G3 **Bandrake Head** Cumb
158 G5 **Banff** Abers
79 K10 **Bangor** Gwynd
79 K10 **Bangor Crematorium** Gwynd
69 L5 **Bangor-is-y-coed** Wrexhm
5 L2 **Bangors** Cnwll
88 D9 **Bangor's Green** Lancs
64 C7 **Bangrove** Suffk
64 F4 **Banham** Norfk
13 N3 **Bank** Hants
109 M7 **Bankend** D & G
141 Q10 **Bankfoot** P & K
115 L5 **Bankglen** E Ayrs
101 K11 **Bank Ground** Cumb
151 N6 **Bankhead** C Aber
116 D2 **Bankhead** S Lans
96 D10 **Bank Newton** N York
126 D2 **Banknock** Falk
111 L8 **Banks** Cumb
88 D6 **Banks** Lancs
58 E11 **Banks Green** Worcs
110 C4 **Bankshill** D & G
46 B2 **Bank Street** Worcs
90 E6 **Bank Top** Calder
88 G9 **Bank Top** Lancs
77 J6 **Banningham** Norfk
51 Q6 **Bannister Green** Essex
133 N9 **Bannockburn** Stirlg
36 G9 **Banstead** Surrey
6 H10 **Bantham** Devon
126 C2 **Banton** N Lans
19 L3 **Banwell** N Som
38 F9 **Bapchild** Kent
21 J7 **Bapton** Wilts
168 i3 **Barabhas** W Isls
125 J11 **Barassie** S Ayrs
156 C3 **Barbaraville** Highld
83 P8 **Barber Booth** Derbys
94 H4 **Barber Green** Cumb
114 H4 **Barbieston** S Ayrs
95 N4 **Barbon** Cumb
69 R3 **Barbridge** Ches E
17 N2 **Barbrook** Devon
60 B6 **Barby** Nhants
138 H9 **Barcaldine** Ag & B
47 Q7 **Barcheston** Warwks
110 H8 **Barclose** Cumb
25 K8 **Barcombe** E Susx
25 K7 **Barcombe Cross** E Susx
90 C3 **Barcroft** C Brad
96 H2 **Barden** N York
37 N11 **Barden Park** Kent
51 P4 **Bardfield End Green** Essex
51 Q5 **Bardfield Saling** Essex
86 F7 **Bardney** Lincs
72 C8 **Bardon** Leics
111 Q8 **Bardon Mill** Nthumb
125 P3 **Bardowie** E Duns
25 Q5 **Bardown** E Susx
125 J3 **Bardrainney** Inver
94 G6 **Bardsea** Cumb
91 K2 **Bardsey** Leeds
66 A10 **Bardsey Island** Gwynd
83 K4 **Bardsley** Oldham
64 C7 **Bardwell** Suffk
95 K8 **Bare** Lancs
3 K8 **Bareppa** Cnwll
107 K4 **Barfad** D & G
76 G10 **Barford** Norfk
47 Q2 **Barford** Warwks
48 D8 **Barford St John** Oxon
21 L8 **Barford St Martin** Wilts
48 D8 **Barford St Michael** Oxon
39 N11 **Barfrestone** Kent
84 E11 **Bargate** Derbys
126 B5 **Bargeddie** N Lans
30 G5 **Bargoed** Caerph
107 L2 **Bargrennan** D & G
61 P5 **Barham** Cambs
39 M11 **Barham** Kent
64 G11 **Barham** Suffk
27 M2 **Barham Crematorium** Kent
62 E8 **Bar Hill** Cambs
74 A8 **Barholm** Lincs
72 G9 **Barkby** Leics
72 G9 **Barkby Thorpe** Leics
69 P9 **Barkers Green** Shrops
73 K4 **Barkestone-le-Vale** Leics
35 L11 **Barkham** Wokham
37 K4 **Barking** Gt Lon
64 F11 **Barking** Suffk
37 K3 **Barkingside** Gt Lon
64 F11 **Barking Tye** Suffk
90 D7 **Barkisland** Calder
3 J3 **Barkla Shop** Cnwll
73 N2 **Barkston** Lincs
91 M3 **Barkston Ash** N York
51 J3 **Barkway** Herts
126 B5 **Barlanark** C Glas
70 F7 **Barlaston** Staffs
23 Q11 **Barlavington** W Susx
84 G5 **Barlborough** Derbys
91 Q4 **Barlby** N York
72 C9 **Barlestone** Leics
51 K3 **Barley** Herts
89 N2 **Barley** Lancs
51 K5 **Barleycroft End** Herts
91 K11 **Barley Hole** Rothm
73 L9 **Barleythorpe** Rutlnd
38 F4 **Barling** Essex
86 E6 **Barlings** Lincs
108 H9 **Barlochan** D & G
84 D6 **Barlow** Derbys
113 J8 **Barlow** Gatesd
91 Q5 **Barlow** N York
98 F11 **Barmby Moor** E R Yk
92 A5 **Barmby on the Marsh** E R Yk
75 R4 **Barmer** Norfk
38 B10 **Barming Heath** Kent
120 F3 **Barmollack** Ag & B
67 L11 **Barmouth** Gwynd
104 B7 **Barmpton** Darltn
99 P9 **Barmston** E R Yk
65 P5 **Barnaby Green** Suffk
131 L9 **Barnacarry** Ag & B
74 A9 **Barnack** C Pete
59 N8 **Barnacle** Warwks
103 L7 **Barnard Castle** Dur
34 D2 **Barnard Gate** Oxon
63 M11 **Barnardiston** Suffk
108 H9 **Barnbarroch** D & G
91 M10 **Barnburgh** Donc
65 P4 **Barnby** Suffk
91 Q9 **Barnby Dun** Donc
85 Q10 **Barnby in the Willows** Notts
85 L4 **Barnby Moor** Notts
106 E10 **Barncorkrie** D & G
37 L5 **Barnehurst** Gt Lon
36 F5 **Barnes** Gt Lon
37 P11 **Barnes Street** Kent
50 F11 **Barnet** Gt Lon
93 J9 **Barnetby le Wold** N Linc
50 F11 **Barnet Gate** Gt Lon
76 D5 **Barney** Norfk
64 B6 **Barnham** Suffk
15 Q6 **Barnham** W Susx
76 F10 **Barnham Broom** Norfk
143 M6 **Barnhead** Angus
142 H11 **Barnhill** C Dund
69 N4 **Barnhill** Ches W
157 L6 **Barnhill** Moray
106 C3 **Barnhills** D & G
103 L8 **Barningham** Dur
64 D6 **Barningham** Suffk
93 M10 **Barnoldby le Beck** NE Lin
96 C11 **Barnoldswick** Lancs
91 N8 **Barnsdale Bar** Donc
24 D5 **Barns Green** W Susx
91 J9 **Barnsley** Barns
33 L4 **Barnsley** Gloucs
91 K9 **Barnsley Crematorium** Barns
39 N10 **Barnsole** Kent
17 K5 **Barnstaple** Devon
51 P7 **Barnston** Essex
81 K8 **Barnston** Wirral
73 J3 **Barnstone** Notts
58 F10 **Barnt Green** Worcs
127 M3 **Barnton** C Edin
82 D10 **Barnton** Ches W
61 M4 **Barnwell All Saints** Nhants
61 N4 **Barnwell St Andrew** Nhants
46 G11 **Barnwood** Gloucs
45 P3 **Baron's Cross** Herefs
101 P2 **Baronwood** Cumb
114 E9 **Barr** S Ayrs
168 b17 **Barra** W Isls
168 c17 **Barra Airport** W Isls
107 L8 **Barrachan** D & G
168 b17 **Barraigh** W Isls
136 A7 **Barrapoll** Ag & B
102 F8 **Barras** Cumb
112 D6 **Barrasford** Nthumb
80 d4 **Barregarrow** IoM
69 Q3 **Barrets Green** Ches E
125 M6 **Barrhead** E Rens
114 D11 **Barrhill** S Ayrs
62 E11 **Barrington** Cambs
19 L11 **Barrington** Somset
2 G6 **Barripper** Cnwll
125 K7 **Barrmill** N Ayrs
167 N2 **Barrock** Highld
46 G10 **Barrow** Gloucs
89 L3 **Barrow** Lancs
73 M7 **Barrow** Rutlnd
57 M4 **Barrow** Shrops
20 D8 **Barrow** Somset
63 N8 **Barrow** Suffk
75 L10 **Barroway Drove** Norfk
89 K8 **Barrow Bridge** Bolton
118 G8 **Barrow Burn** Nthumb
73 M3 **Barrowby** Lincs
73 N10 **Barrowden** Rutlnd
89 P3 **Barrowford** Lancs
31 P11 **Barrow Gurney** N Som
93 J6 **Barrow Haven** N Linc
84 F5 **Barrow Hill** Derbys
94 E7 **Barrow-in-Furness** Cumb
94 D7 **Barrow Island** Cumb
81 N4 **Barrow Nook** Lancs
70 B3 **Barrow's Green** Ches E
20 F8 **Barrow Street** Wilts
93 J6 **Barrow-upon-Humber** N Linc
72 F7 **Barrow upon Soar** Leics
72 B5 **Barrow upon Trent** Derbys
20 B2 **Barrow Vale** BaNES
143 J11 **Barry** Angus
30 F11 **Barry** V Glam
30 F11 **Barry Island** V Glam
72 H8 **Barsby** Leics
65 M4 **Barsham** Suffk
59 K9 **Barston** Solhll
45 R6 **Bartestree** Herefs
159 K11 **Barthol Chapel** Abers
52 B7 **Bartholomew Green** Essex
70 D4 **Barthomley** Ches E
13 P2 **Bartley** Hants
58 F8 **Bartley Green** Birm
63 J11 **Bartlow** Cambs
62 F9 **Barton** Cambs
69 M4 **Barton** Ches W
47 L9 **Barton** Gloucs
45 K3 **Barton** Herefs
88 D9 **Barton** Lancs
88 G3 **Barton** Lancs
103 P9 **Barton** N York
34 G3 **Barton** Oxon
7 N5 **Barton** Torbay
47 M4 **Barton** Warwks
75 P9 **Barton Bendish** Norfk
32 F5 **Barton End** Gloucs
71 M11 **Barton Green** Staffs
48 H8 **Barton Hartshorn** Bucks
98 E8 **Barton Hill** N York
72 E4 **Barton in Fabis** Notts
72 B9 **Barton in the Beans** Leics
50 C4 **Barton-le-Clay** C Beds
98 E6 **Barton-le-Street** N York
98 E8 **Barton-le-Willows** N York
63 M6 **Barton Mills** Suffk
13 M6 **Barton-on-Sea** Hants
47 Q8 **Barton-on-the-Heath** Warwks
19 P8 **Barton St David** Somset
61 J5 **Barton Seagrave** Nhants
22 D6 **Barton Stacey** Hants
17 M3 **Barton Town** Devon
77 M7 **Barton Turf** Norfk
71 M11 **Barton-under-Needwood** Staffs
92 H6 **Barton-upon-Humber** N Linc
82 G5 **Barton upon Irwell** Salfd
92 H6 **Barton Waterside** N Linc
91 J9 **Barugh** Barns
91 J9 **Barugh Green** Barns
168 i3 **Barvas** W Isls
63 J5 **Barway** Cambs
72 C11 **Barwell** Leics
17 K10 **Barwick** Devon
51 J7 **Barwick** Herts
11 M2 **Barwick** Somset
91 L3 **Barwick in Elmet** Leeds
69 M10 **Baschurch** Shrops
48 D2 **Bascote** Warwks
48 C2 **Bascote Heath** Warwks
64 E9 **Base Green** Suffk
70 H4 **Basford Green** Staffs
89 K2 **Bashall Eaves** Lancs
89 L2 **Bashall Town** Lancs
13 M5 **Bashley** Hants
38 B4 **Basildon** Essex
38 C4 **Basildon & District Crematorium** Essex
22 H4 **Basingstoke** Hants
22 G5 **Basingstoke Crematorium** Hants
84 C6 **Baslow** Derbys
19 K5 **Bason Bridge** Somset
31 J7 **Bassaleg** Newpt
128 G10 **Bassendean** Border
100 H4 **Bassenthwaite** Cumb
22 D11 **Bassett** C Sotn
50 H2 **Bassingbourn** Cambs
73 G3 **Bassingfield** Notts
86 B9 **Bassingham** Lincs
73 P5 **Bassingthorpe** Lincs
50 H5 **Bassus Green** Herts
37 P9 **Basted** Kent
74 B8 **Baston** Lincs
77 N8 **Bastwick** Norfk
19 K3 **Batch** Somset
36 C2 **Batchworth** Herts
36 C2 **Batchworth Heath** Herts
11 N4 **Batcombe** Dorset
20 C7 **Batcombe** Somset
82 E9 **Bate Heath** Ches E
50 D7 **Batford** Herts
20 D2 **Bath** BaNES
32 E11 **Bathampton** BaNES
18 E10 **Bathealton** Somset
32 E11 **Batheaston** BaNES
32 E11 **Bathford** BaNES
126 H4 **Bathgate** W Loth
85 N9 **Bathley** Notts
5 M7 **Bathpool** Cnwll
19 J9 **Bathpool** Somset
53 N5 **Bath Side** Essex
126 G4 **Bathville** W Loth
19 Q4 **Bathway** Somset
90 G6 **Batley** Kirk
47 N8 **Batsford** Gloucs
7 J11 **Batson** Devon
104 G9 **Battersby** N York
36 G5 **Battersea** Gt Lon
6 F9 **Battisborough Cross** Devon
64 F11 **Battisford** Suffk
64 E11 **Battisford Tye** Suffk
26 C8 **Battle** E Susx
44 E8 **Battle** Powys
19 K4 **Battleborough** Somset
47 J10 **Battledown** Gloucs
142 H6 **Battledykes** Angus
69 P11 **Battlefield** Shrops
86 H9 **Battle of Britain Memorial Flight** Lincs
38 C3 **Battlesbridge** Essex
49 Q9 **Battlesden** C Beds
18 B9 **Battleton** Somset
64 C9 **Battlies Green** Suffk
13 P5 **Battramsley Cross** Hants
23 M6 **Batt's Corner** Hants
46 G6 **Baughton** Worcs
22 G2 **Baughurst** Hants
150 G9 **Baulds** Abers
34 B6 **Baulking** Oxon
86 H6 **Baumber** Lincs
33 K4 **Baunton** Gloucs
57 M9 **Baveney Wood** Shrops
21 K8 **Baverstock** Wilts
76 H10 **Bawburgh** Norfk
76 E7 **Bawdeswell** Norfk
19 K7 **Bawdrip** Somset
53 P3 **Bawdsey** Suffk
75 N6 **Bawsey** Norfk
85 K2 **Bawtry** Donc
89 M5 **Baxenden** Lancs
59 L5 **Baxterley** Warwks
63 N9 **Baxter's Green** Suffk
152 D7 **Bay** Highld
168 k4 **Bayble** W Isls
22 F10 **Baybridge** Hants
112 E10 **Baybridge** Nthumb
94 F6 **Baycliff** Cumb
33 Q9 **Baydon** Wilts
50 H9 **Bayford** Herts
20 D9 **Bayford** Somset
168 c11 **Bayhead** W Isls
95 K10 **Bay Horse** Lancs
37 M10 **Bayley's Hill** Kent
64 G11 **Baylham** Suffk
48 F9 **Baynard's Green** Oxon
104 H9 **Baysdale Abbey** N York
45 R9 **Baysham** Herefs
56 H3 **Bayston Hill** Shrops
52 B3 **Baythorne End** Essex
57 M10 **Bayton** Worcs
57 N10 **Bayton Common** Worcs
34 E4 **Bayworth** Oxon
32 D10 **Beach** S Glos
49 L7 **Beachampton** Bucks
75 Q9 **Beachamwell** Norfk
31 Q6 **Beachley** Gloucs
25 N11 **Beachy Head** E Susx
10 D3 **Beacon** Devon
52 G7 **Beacon End** Essex
25 M4 **Beacon Hill** E Susx
26 D5 **Beacon Hill** Kent
85 P10 **Beacon Hill** Notts
23 N7 **Beacon Hill** Surrey
35 L5 **Beacon's Bottom** Bucks
35 P6 **Beaconsfield** Bucks
35 Q7 **Beaconsfield Services** Bucks
98 D4 **Beadlam** N York
50 D3 **Beadlow** C Beds
119 P5 **Beadnell** Nthumb
17 K8 **Beaford** Devon
91 N5 **Beal** N York
119 L2 **Beal** Nthumb
5 P8 **Bealbury** Cnwll
5 P6 **Bealsmill** Cnwll
71 N9 **Beam Hill** Staffs
71 K7 **Beamhurst** Staffs
11 K4 **Beaminster** Dorset
113 K10 **Beamish** Dur
96 G10 **Beamsley** N York
37 N6 **Bean** Kent
32 H11 **Beanacre** Wilts
119 L7 **Beanley** Nthumb
8 D8 **Beardon** Devon
89 K5 **Beardwood** Bl w D
9 N4 **Beare** Devon
24 E2 **Beare Green** Surrey
47 N2 **Bearley** Warwks
47 N2 **Bearley Cross** Warwks
103 P2 **Bearpark** Dur
125 N3 **Bearsden** E Duns
38 D10 **Bearsted** Kent
70 C7 **Bearstone** Shrops
58 F7 **Bearwood** Birm
45 M3 **Bearwood** Herefs
12 H5 **Bearwood** Poole
116 F10 **Beattock** D & G

264 Beauchamp Roding - Blackcraig

51 N9 Beauchamp Roding Essex
84 D4 Beauchief Sheff
59 J11 Beaudesert Warwks
30 G2 Beaufort Blae G
14 C6 Beaulieu Hants
14 C6 Beaulieu House Hants
13 P3 Beaulieu Road Station Hants
155 P8 Beauly Highld
79 L9 Beaumaris IoA
110 F9 Beaumont Cumb
53 L7 Beaumont Essex
11 b2 Beaumont Jersey
103 Q7 Beaumont Hill Darltn
59 K10 Beausale Warwks
22 G9 Beauworth Hants
8 C5 Beaworthy Devon
52 B6 Beazley End Essex
81 L8 Bebington Wirral
113 L4 Bebside Nthumb
65 N4 Beccles Suffk
88 F6 Becconsall Lancs
57 P4 Beckbury Shrops
37 J7 Beckenham Gt Lon
37 J7 Beckenham Crematorium Gt Lon
100 D9 Beckermet Cumb
75 Q11 Beckett End Norfk
94 D3 Beckfoot Cumb
100 G10 Beckfoot Cumb
102 B11 Beck Foot Cumb
109 N11 Beckfoot Cumb
47 J7 Beckford Worcs
33 L11 Beckhampton Wilts
105 M10 Beck Hole N York
85 Q10 Beckingham Lincs
85 N3 Beckingham Notts
20 F4 Beckington Somset
56 F9 Beckjay Shrops
26 E7 Beckley E Susx
13 M5 Beckley Hants
34 G2 Beckley Oxon
63 L5 Beck Row Suffk
96 F11 Becks C Brad
94 E4 Beck Side Cumb
94 H4 Beck Side Cumb
37 K4 Beckton Gt Lon
97 L10 Beckwithshaw N York
37 L3 Becontree Gt Lon
11 b1 Becquet Vincent Jersey
97 L3 Bedale N York
103 L4 Bedburn Dur
20 G11 Bedchester Dorset
30 E7 Beddau Rhondd
67 K5 Beddgelert Gwynd
25 K9 Beddingham E Susx
36 H7 Beddington Gt Lon
36 G7 Beddington Corner Gt Lon
65 J8 Bedfield Suffk
65 J8 Bedfield Little Green Suffk
61 M11 Bedford Bed
61 N10 Bedford Crematorium Bed
26 B5 Bedgebury Cross Kent
24 B6 Bedham W Susx
15 K5 Bedhampton Hants
64 H8 Bedingfield Suffk
64 H8 Bedingfield Green Suffk
97 L8 Bedlam N York
113 L4 Bedlington Nthumb
30 E4 Bedlinog Myr Td
31 Q10 Bedminster Bristl
31 Q10 Bedminster Down Bristl
50 C10 Bedmond Herts
70 H11 Bednall Staffs
118 B7 Bedrule Border
56 F9 Bedstone Shrops
30 G7 Bedwas Caerph
30 G4 Bedwellty Caerph
59 N7 Bedworth Warwks
59 M7 Bedworth Woodlands Warwks
72 H9 Beeby Leics
23 J7 Beech Hants
70 F7 Beech Staffs
23 J2 Beech Hill W Berk
21 L3 Beechingstoke Wilts
34 E9 Beedon W Berk
34 E9 Beedon Hill W Berk
99 N10 Beeford E R Yk
84 C7 Beeley Derbys
93 M10 Beelsby NE Lin
34 G11 Beenham W Berk
35 M9 Beenham's Heath W & M
5 J3 Beeny Cnwll
10 E7 Beer Devon
19 M8 Beer Somset
19 K10 Beercrocombe Somset
11 N2 Beer Hackett Dorset
7 L10 Beesands Devon
87 N4 Beesby Lincs
7 L10 Beeson Devon
61 Q11 Beeston C Beds
69 P3 Beeston Ches W
90 H4 Beeston Leeds
76 C8 Beeston Norfk
72 E3 Beeston Notts
76 H3 Beeston Regis Norfk
109 J7 Beeswing D & G
95 K5 Beetham Cumb
10 F2 Beetham Somset
76 D8 Beetley Norfk
30 H8 Began Cardif
34 E2 Begbroke Oxon
75 J9 Begdale Cambs
41 M9 Begelly Pembks
90 H6 Beggarington Hill Leeds
45 K2 Beggar's Bush Powys
56 B9 Beguildy Powys
77 M10 Beighton Norfk
84 F4 Beighton Sheff
168 d12 Beinn Na Faoghla W Isls
125 K7 Beith N Ayrs
39 L10 Bekesbourne Kent
39 L10 Bekesbourne Hill Kent
77 K8 Belaugh Norfk
58 D9 Belbroughton Worcs
12 C3 Belchalwell Dorset
12 C3 Belchalwell Street Dorset
52 D3 Belchamp Otten Essex
52 C3 Belchamp St Paul Essex
52 D3 Belchamp Walter Essex
87 J5 Belchford Lincs
119 M4 Belford Nthumb
72 F9 Belgrave C Leic
128 H4 Belhaven E Loth
151 N4 Belhelvie Abers
150 D2 Belhinnie Abers
150 B5 Bellabeg Abers
45 M6 Bellamore Herefs
130 F9 Bellanoch Ag & B
92 D5 Bellasize E R Yk
142 C6 Bellaty Angus
50 G9 Bell Bar Herts
96 D9 Bell Busk N York
87 M5 Belleau Lincs
58 D9 Bell End Worcs
96 H2 Bellerby N York
8 G9 Bellever Devon
110 G9 Belle Vue Cumb
91 J7 Belle Vue Wakefd
116 D6 Bellfield S Lans
126 E11 Bellfield S Lans
58 D9 Bell Heath Worcs
23 K10 Bell Hill Hants
35 P3 Bellingdon Bucks
112 B4 Bellingham Nthumb
120 C4 Belloch Ag & B
120 C5 Bellochantuy Ag & B
69 P5 Bell o' th' Hill Ches W
13 J2 Bellows Cross Dorset
64 H11 Bells Cross Suffk
126 C5 Bellshill N Lans
119 M4 Bellshill Nthumb
126 E6 Bellside N Lans
127 J4 Bellsquarry W Loth
25 P3 Bells Yew Green E Susx
20 B2 Belluton BaNES
156 A6 Belmaduthy Highld
73 Q8 Belmesthorpe Rutlnd
89 K7 Belmont Bl w D
36 G8 Belmont Gt Lon
114 F4 Belmont S Ayrs
169 s3 Belmont Shet
150 B4 Belnacraig Abers
4 F9 Belowda Cnwll
84 D11 Belper Derbys
84 D11 Belper Lane End Derbys
84 H5 Belph Derbys
112 G5 Belsay Nthumb
117 R5 Belses Border
7 K7 Belsford Devon
50 B10 Belsize Herts
53 K3 Belstead Suffk
8 F6 Belstone Devon
89 L6 Belthorn Lancs
39 L8 Beltinge Kent
111 Q8 Beltingham Nthumb
92 D9 Beltoft N Linc
72 C6 Belton Leics
73 N3 Belton Lincs
92 C9 Belton N Linc
77 P11 Belton Norfk
73 L10 Belton Rutlnd
37 Q11 Beltring Kent
37 L5 Belvedere Gt Lon
73 L4 Belvoir Leics
73 L4 Belvoir Castle Leics
14 H9 Bembridge IoW
21 M8 Bemerton Wilts
99 P6 Bempton E R Yk
65 Q5 Benacre Suffk
168 d12 Benbecula W Isls
168 c12 Benbecula Airport W Isls
115 P8 Benbuie D & G
138 G10 Benderloch Ag & B
26 D5 Benenden Kent
112 G10 Benfieldside Dur
77 L6 Bengates Norfk
50 H8 Bengeo Herts
47 K6 Bengeworth Worcs
65 M9 Benhall Green Suffk
65 M9 Benhall Street Suffk
143 Q4 Benholm Abers
98 A9 Beningbrough N York
50 G6 Benington Herts
87 L11 Benington Lincs
87 M11 Benington Sea End Lincs
79 J8 Benllech IoA
131 N10 Benmore Ag & B
5 M3 Bennacott Cnwll
121 J7 Bennan N Ayrs
101 M6 Bennet Head Cumb
92 D5 Bennetland E R Yk
35 L5 Bennett End Bucks
139 M3 Ben Nevis Highld
86 H4 Benniworth Lincs
26 B2 Benover Kent
96 H11 Ben Rhydding C Brad
125 J9 Benslie N Ayrs
34 H6 Benson Oxon
51 M5 Bentfield Green Essex
57 M4 Benthall Shrops
46 H11 Bentham Gloucs
151 L7 Benthoul C Aber
56 E4 Bentlawn Shrops
91 P9 Bentley Donc
92 H3 Bentley E R Yk
23 L6 Bentley Hants
53 K4 Bentley Suffk
59 L5 Bentley Warwks
51 N11 Bentley Crematorium Essex
50 G11 Bentley Heath Herts
59 J9 Bentley Heath Solhll
17 M4 Benton Devon
110 F2 Bentpath D & G
17 N5 Bentwichen Devon
23 J6 Bentworth Hants
142 E11 Benvie Angus
11 L4 Benville Dorset
62 D2 Benwick Cambs
58 G11 Beoley Worcs
145 L9 Beoraidbeg Highld
23 N11 Bepton W Susx
51 L5 Berden Essex
40 E4 Berea Pembks
6 C5 Bere Alston Devon
6 D6 Bere Ferrers Devon
2 H9 Berepper Cnwll
12 D6 Bere Regis Dorset
77 L11 Bergh Apton Norfk
19 M7 Berhill Somset
34 G5 Berinsfield Oxon
32 C5 Berkeley Gloucs
32 C5 Berkeley Heath Gloucs
32 D4 Berkeley Road Gloucs
35 Q3 Berkhamsted Herts
20 F5 Berkley Somset
59 K9 Berkswell Solhll
36 H5 Bermondsey Gt Lon
59 N7 Bermuda Warwks
145 P3 Bernera Highld
152 G7 Bernisdale Highld
34 H6 Berrick Prior Oxon
34 H6 Berrick Salome Oxon
163 Q2 Berriedale Highld
101 L5 Berrier Cumb
56 B4 Berriew Powys
119 K2 Berrington Nthumb
57 J3 Berrington Shrops
57 K11 Berrington Worcs
57 K11 Berrington Green Worcs
19 J4 Berrow Somset
46 E8 Berrow Worcs
46 D3 Berrow Green Worcs
90 E8 Berry Brow Kirk
16 H9 Berry Cross Devon
17 K3 Berry Down Cross Devon
31 Q2 Berry Hill Gloucs
41 L2 Berry Hill Pembks
158 D5 Berryhillock Moray
158 D7 Berryhillock Moray
17 K2 Berrynarbor Devon
7 L6 Berry Pomeroy Devon
37 K9 Berry's Green Gt Lon
69 K5 Bersham Wrexhm
80 G9 Berthengam Flints
25 M9 Berwick E Susx
33 L10 Berwick Bassett Wilts
113 J5 Berwick Hill Nthumb
21 L7 Berwick St James Wilts
20 H10 Berwick St John Wilts
20 H8 Berwick St Leonard Wilts
129 P9 Berwick-upon-Tweed Nthumb
73 L5 Bescaby Leics
88 D8 Bescar Lancs
69 Q9 Besford Shrops
46 H6 Besford Worcs
91 Q10 Bessacarr Donc
34 E4 Bessels Leigh Oxon
89 N9 Besses o' th' Barn Bury
99 P7 Bessingby E R Yk
76 H4 Bessingham Norfk
25 P4 Bestbeech Hill E Susx
64 F2 Besthorpe Norfk
85 P8 Besthorpe Notts
85 J11 Bestwood Village Notts
99 L11 Beswick E R Yk
56 G5 Betchcott Shrops
36 F10 Betchworth Surrey
43 L2 Bethania Cerdgn
67 N6 Bethania Gwynd
53 J7 Beth Chatto Garden Essex
68 C7 Bethel Gwynd
79 J11 Bethel Gwynd
78 F10 Bethel IoA
68 F10 Bethel Powys
26 F3 Bethersden Kent
79 L11 Bethesda Gwynd
41 L7 Bethesda Pembks
43 N9 Bethlehem Carmth
36 H4 Bethnal Green Gt Lon
70 D5 Betley Staffs
37 P6 Betsham Kent
39 P11 Betteshanger Kent
10 H4 Bettiscombe Dorset
69 N7 Bettisfield Wrexhm
70 B7 Betton Shrops
57 J3 Betton Strange Shrops
31 J6 Bettws Newpt
43 L4 Bettws Bledrws Cerdgn
55 Q5 Bettws Cedewain Powys
42 F5 Bettws Evan Cerdgn
31 L3 Bettws-Newydd Mons
166 B4 Bettyhill Highld
29 P7 Betws Brdgnd
28 H2 Betws Carmth
67 J3 Betws Garmon Gwynd
68 D5 Betws Gwerfil Goch Denbgs
67 P3 Betws-y-Coed Conwy
80 C10 Betws-yn-Rhos Conwy
42 E5 Beulah Cerdgn
44 C4 Beulah Powys
24 H9 Bevendean Br & H
85 L6 Bevercotes Notts
92 H3 Beverley E R Yk
32 G6 Beverston Gloucs
32 C5 Bevington Gloucs
100 H4 Bewaldeth Cumb
111 L6 Bewcastle Cumb
57 P9 Bewdley Worcs
97 J7 Bewerley N York
99 P11 Bewholme E R Yk
25 Q4 Bewlbridge Kent
26 B10 Bexhill E Susx
37 L6 Bexley Gt Lon
37 L5 Bexleyheath Gt Lon
23 P9 Bexleyhill W Susx
38 E10 Bexon Kent
75 M10 Bexwell Norfk
64 C9 Beyton Suffk
64 C9 Beyton Green Suffk
168 f4 Bhaltos W Isls
168 b18 Bhatarsaigh W Isls
32 C6 Bibstone S Glos
33 M3 Bibury Gloucs
48 G10 Bicester Oxon
59 J8 Bickenhill Solhll
74 D3 Bicker Lincs
74 D3 Bicker Bar Lincs
74 D3 Bicker Gauntlet Lincs
82 D4 Bickershaw Wigan
81 N4 Bickerstaffe Lancs
69 P4 Bickerton Ches E
7 L11 Bickerton Devon
97 Q10 Bickerton N York
119 J10 Bickerton Nthumb
58 C2 Bickford Staffs
7 L4 Bickington Devon
17 J5 Bickington Devon
6 E6 Bickleigh Devon
9 M3 Bickleigh Devon
17 J5 Bickleton Devon
69 P5 Bickley Ches W
37 K7 Bickley Gt Lon
99 J2 Bickley N York
57 L10 Bickley Worcs
69 P5 Bickley Moss Ches W
52 C11 Bicknacre Essex
18 F7 Bicknoller Somset
38 E10 Bicknor Kent
13 K2 Bickton Hants
45 P2 Bicton Herefs
56 D8 Bicton Shrops
69 M11 Bicton Shrops
25 N2 Bidborough Kent
23 K5 Bidden Hants
26 E4 Biddenden Kent
26 E3 Biddenden Green Kent
61 M10 Biddenham Bed
32 G10 Biddestone Wilts
19 L4 Biddisham Somset
48 H7 Biddlesden Bucks
119 J9 Biddlestone Nthumb
70 F3 Biddulph Staffs
70 G3 Biddulph Moor Staffs
16 H6 Bideford Devon
47 M4 Bidford-on-Avon Warwks
81 K6 Bidston Wirral
92 C2 Bielby E R Yk
151 M7 Bieldside C Aber
14 F11 Bierley IoW
49 M11 Bierton Bucks
107 L9 Big Balcraig D & G
6 H9 Bigbury Devon
6 H10 Bigbury-on-Sea Devon
93 J9 Bigby Lincs
115 N8 Big Carlae D & G
94 D7 Biggar Cumb
116 E3 Biggar S Lans
71 M3 Biggin Derbys
71 P5 Biggin Derbys
91 N4 Biggin N York
37 K9 Biggin Hill Gt Lon
37 K8 Biggin Hill Airport Gt Lon
50 E2 Biggleswade C Beds
110 F4 Bigholms D & G
166 E4 Bighouse Highld
22 H8 Bighton Hants
110 E10 Biglands Cumb
15 Q4 Bignor W Susx
30 H3 Big Pit Blaenavon Torfn
100 D8 Bigrigg Cumb
160 B11 Big Sand Highld
169 q11 Bigton Shet
72 E2 Bilborough C Nott
18 D6 Bilbrook Somset
58 C4 Bilbrook Staffs
98 A11 Bilbrough N York
167 N6 Bilbster Highld
103 P6 Bildershaw Dur
52 G2 Bildeston Suffk
5 M3 Billacott Cnwll
37 Q2 Billericay Essex
73 J10 Billesdon Leics
47 M3 Billesley Warwks
74 B4 Billingborough Lincs
82 B4 Billinge St Hel
64 H6 Billingford Norfk
76 E7 Billingford Norfk
104 E6 Billingham S on T
86 G10 Billinghay Lincs
91 L10 Billingley Barns
24 C5 Billingshurst W Susx
57 N8 Billingsley Shrops
49 P10 Billington C Beds
89 L3 Billington Lancs
70 F10 Billington Staffs
77 N9 Billockby Norfk
103 N3 Billy Row Dur
88 G3 Bilsborrow Lancs
87 N5 Bilsby Lincs
15 Q6 Bilsham W Susx
26 H5 Bilsington Kent
85 K8 Bilsthorpe Notts
85 L8 Bilsthorpe Moor Notts
127 P5 Bilston Mdloth
58 E5 Bilston Wolves
72 B9 Bilstone Leics
27 J2 Bilting Kent
93 L4 Bilton E R Yk
97 M9 Bilton N York
97 Q11 Bilton N York
119 P8 Bilton Nthumb
59 Q10 Bilton Warwks
119 P8 Bilton Banks Nthumb
86 H2 Binbrook Lincs
103 P4 Binchester Blocks Dur
11 P8 Bincombe Dorset
20 B5 Binegar Somset
24 E7 Bines Green W Susx
35 M10 Binfield Br For
35 K9 Binfield Heath Oxon
112 E6 Bingfield Nthumb
73 J3 Bingham Notts
12 C4 Bingham's Melcombe Dorset
90 E3 Bingley C Brad
69 P11 Bings Shrops
76 D4 Binham Norfk
59 N9 Binley Covtry
22 D4 Binley Hants
59 N9 Binley Woods Warwks
12 E7 Binnegar Dorset
126 F3 Binniehill Falk
23 Q5 Binscombe Surrey
34 E3 Binsey Oxon
14 G8 Binstead IoW
23 L6 Binsted Hants
15 Q5 Binsted W Susx
47 M4 Binton Warwks
76 E7 Bintree Norfk
56 E4 Binweston Shrops
52 F8 Birch Essex
89 P9 Birch Rochdl
75 Q4 Bircham Newton Norfk
75 Q4 Bircham Tofts Norfk
51 M6 Birchanger Essex
51 M6 Birchanger Green Services Essex
71 L8 Birch Cross Staffs
90 E7 Birchencliffe Kirk
56 H11 Bircher Herefs
58 G6 Birchfield Birm
52 F8 Birch Green Essex
50 G8 Birch Green Herts
46 G5 Birch Green Worcs
30 G9 Birchgrove Cardif
29 K5 Birchgrove Swans
25 K5 Birchgrove W Susx
69 P2 Birch Heath Ches W
81 Q10 Birch Hill Ches W
39 P8 Birchington Kent
59 L6 Birchley Heath Warwks
59 L4 Birchmoor Warwks
49 Q8 Birchmoor Green C Beds
84 B8 Birchover Derbys
89 N9 Birch Services Rochdl
83 M7 Birch Vale Derbys
86 B7 Birchwood Lincs
10 E2 Birch Wood Somset
82 E6 Birchwood Warrtn
85 K2 Bircotes Notts
52 B3 Birdbrook Essex
97 Q5 Birdforth N York
15 M6 Birdham W Susx
59 P11 Birdingbury Warwks
32 H2 Birdlip Gloucs
111 M7 Birdoswald Cumb
98 G7 Birdsall N York
90 G9 Birds Edge Kirk
51 N9 Birds Green Essex
57 P7 Birdsgreen Shrops
10 H4 Birdsmoorgate Dorset
64 E11 Bird Street Suffk
91 J10 Birdwell Barns
46 D11 Birdwood Gloucs
118 E3 Birgham Border
162 H8 Birichin Highld
88 H8 Birkacre Lancs
104 B10 Birkby N York
88 C8 Birkdale Sefton
158 D4 Birkenbog Abers
81 L7 Birkenhead Wirral
158 H8 Birkenhills Abers
90 G5 Birkenshaw Kirk
149 Q9 Birkhall Abers
142 F11 Birkhill Angus
117 J7 Birkhill D & G
73 P6 Birkholme Lincs
91 N5 Birkin N York
90 H5 Birks Leeds
111 Q7 Birkshaw Nthumb
45 P4 Birley Herefs
84 D2 Birley Carr Sheff
37 Q8 Birling Kent
119 P9 Birling Nthumb
25 N11 Birling Gap E Susx
46 H6 Birlingham Worcs
58 G7 Birmingham Birm
59 J8 Birmingham Airport Solhll
141 P9 Birnam P & K
159 N11 Birness Abers
150 F8 Birse Abers
150 E8 Birsemore Abers
90 G5 Birstall Kirk
72 F9 Birstall Leics
97 K9 Birstwith N York
74 B4 Birthorpe Lincs
113 L9 Birtley Gatesd
56 F11 Birtley Herefs
112 C5 Birtley Nthumb
113 L9 Birtley Crematorium Gatesd
46 E7 Birts Street Worcs
73 M11 Bisbrooke Rutlnd
86 H4 Biscathorpe Lincs
3 R3 Biscovey Cnwll
35 M7 Bisham W & M
47 J4 Bishampton Worcs
17 N6 Bish Mill Devon
103 P5 Bishop Auckland Dur
86 D2 Bishopbridge Lincs
125 Q3 Bishopbriggs E Duns
92 G3 Bishop Burton E R Yk
104 B4 Bishop Middleham Dur
157 N5 Bishopmill Moray
97 M7 Bishop Monkton N York
86 C2 Bishop Norton Lincs
39 L11 Bishopsbourne Kent
21 K2 Bishops Cannings Wilts
56 E7 Bishop's Castle Shrops
11 P2 Bishop's Caundle Dorset
47 J9 Bishop's Cleeve Gloucs
46 C5 Bishop's Frome Herefs
35 Q10 Bishops Gate Surrey
51 P7 Bishop's Green Essex
22 F2 Bishop's Green Hants
18 H10 Bishops Hull Somset
48 C3 Bishop's Itchington Warwks
18 G9 Bishops Lydeard Somset
46 F10 Bishop's Norton Gloucs
17 P7 Bishop's Nympton Devon
70 D9 Bishop's Offley Staffs
51 L6 Bishop's Stortford Herts
22 H8 Bishop's Sutton Hants
48 B2 Bishop's Tachbrook Warwks
17 K6 Bishop's Tawton Devon
7 N4 Bishopsteignton Devon
22 E11 Bishopstoke Hants
28 G7 Bishopston Swans
35 M2 Bishopstone Bucks
25 L10 Bishopstone E Susx
45 N6 Bishopstone Herefs
39 M8 Bishopstone Kent
33 P8 Bishopstone Swindn
21 L9 Bishopstone Wilts
20 G6 Bishopstrow Wilts
19 Q3 Bishop Sutton BaNES
22 G11 Bishop's Waltham Hants
10 F2 Bishopswood Somset
58 B3 Bishop's Wood Staffs
31 Q11 Bishopsworth Bristl
97 L8 Bishop Thornton N York
98 B11 Bishopthorpe C York
104 C6 Bishopton Darltn
125 L3 Bishopton Rens
47 N3 Bishopton Warwks
98 F9 Bishop Wilton E R Yk
31 L7 Bishton Newpt
71 J10 Bishton Staffs
32 H3 Bisley Gloucs
23 Q3 Bisley Surrey
23 P3 Bisley Camp Surrey
88 C2 Bispham Bpool
88 F8 Bispham Green Lancs
3 K5 Bissoe Cnwll
13 K4 Bisterne Hants
37 N10 Bitchet Green Kent
73 P5 Bitchfield Lincs
17 J3 Bittadon Devon
6 H7 Bittaford Devon
76 C8 Bittering Norfk
57 K9 Bitterley Shrops
14 E4 Bitterne C Sotn
60 B3 Bitteswell Leics
32 C11 Bitton S Glos
35 K8 Bix Oxon
169 q8 Bixter Shet
72 F11 Blaby Leics
129 L9 Blackadder Border
7 L8 Blackawton Devon
100 D9 Blackbeck Cumb
10 B3 Blackborough Devon
75 N7 Blackborough End Norfk
33 Q4 Black Bourton Oxon
25 M6 Blackboys E Susx
84 D11 Blackbrook Derbys
82 B5 Blackbrook St Hel
70 D7 Blackbrook Staffs
36 E11 Blackbrook Surrey
151 L5 Blackburn Abers
89 K5 Blackburn Bl w D
84 E2 Blackburn Rothm
126 H4 Blackburn W Loth
89 K6 Blackburn with Darwen Services Bl w D
113 J7 Black Callerton N u Ty
64 F2 Black Car Norfk
24 G3 Black Corner W Susx
115 M6 Blackcraig E Ayrs

Black Crofts - Bracebridge Heath 265

138 G11 Black Crofts Ag & B
4 E9 Black Cross Cnwll
82 G10 Blackden Heath Ches E
151 P5 Blackdog Abers
9 K3 Black Dog Devon
8 D9 Blackdown Devon
10 H4 Blackdown Dorset
109 P10 Blackdyke Cumb
91 J9 Blacker Barns
91 K10 Blacker Hill Barns
37 L6 Blackfen Gt Lon
14 D6 Blackfield Hants
110 G8 Blackford Cumb
133 P6 Blackford P & K
19 M5 Blackford Somset
20 C9 Blackford Somset
72 A7 Blackfordby Leics
14 E11 Blackgang IoW
127 M2 Blackhall C Edin
104 E3 Blackhall Dur
104 E3 Blackhall Colliery Dur
112 H9 Blackhall Mill Gatesd
117 N3 Blackhaugh Border
52 H7 Blackheath Essex
37 J5 Blackheath Gt Lon
58 E7 Blackheath Sandw
65 N7 Blackheath Suffk
36 B11 Blackheath Surrey
112 G5 Black Heddon Nthumb
159 Q6 Blackhill Abers
159 Q9 Blackhill Abers
112 G10 Blackhill Dur
159 M8 Blackhill of Clackriach Abers
9 N6 Blackhorse Devon
74 E3 Blackjack Lincs
33 K11 Blackland Wilts
89 Q2 Black Lane Ends Lancs
116 E9 Blacklaw D & G
83 J4 Blackley Manch
82 H4 Blackley Crematorium Manch
142 A5 Blacklunans P & K
45 Q7 Blackmarstone Herefs
29 P7 Blackmill Brdgnd
23 L8 Blackmoor Hants
90 H3 Black Moor Leeds
19 N2 Blackmoor N Som
90 D8 Blackmoorfoot Kirk
51 P10 Blackmore Essex
52 B5 Blackmore End Essex
50 E7 Blackmore End Herts
127 K2 Blackness Falk
23 L6 Blacknest Hants
35 Q11 Blacknest W & M
52 C7 Black Notley Essex
89 P2 Blacko Lancs
28 H6 Black Pill Swans
88 C3 Blackpool Bpool
7 L4 Blackpool Devon
7 M9 Blackpool Devon
88 C4 Blackpool Airport Lancs
111 K5 Blackpool Gate Cumb
126 F4 Blackridge W Loth
2 H7 Blackrock Cnwll
30 H2 Blackrock Mons
89 J8 Blackrod Bolton
157 M10 Blacksboat Moray
109 M7 Blackshaw D & G
90 B5 Blackshaw Head Calder
64 G8 Blacksmith's Green Suffk
89 L6 Blacksnape Bl w D
24 F7 Blackstone W Susx
65 Q4 Black Street Suffk
41 J9 Black Tar Pembks
48 H11 Blackthorn Oxon
64 C9 Blackthorpe Suffk
92 D6 Blacktoft E R Yk
151 M7 Blacktop C Aber
8 C3 Black Torrington Devon
71 P5 Blackwall Derbys
3 J4 Blackwater Cnwll
23 M3 Blackwater Hants
14 F9 Blackwater IoW
19 J11 Blackwater Somset
120 H6 Blackwaterfoot N Ayrs
110 H10 Blackwell Cumb
103 Q8 Blackwell Darltn
83 P10 Blackwell Derbys
84 F9 Blackwell Derbys
47 P6 Blackwell Warwks
58 E10 Blackwell Worcs
46 E9 Blackwellsend Green Gloucs
30 G5 Blackwood Caerph
109 K3 Blackwood D & G
126 D9 Blackwood S Lans
70 G3 Blackwood Hill Staffs
81 M11 Blacon Ches W
27 L2 Bladbean Kent
107 M7 Bladnoch D & G
34 E2 Bladon Oxon
19 M10 Bladon Somset
42 D5 Blaenannerch Cerdgn
67 N5 Blaenau Ffestiniog Gwynd
31 J3 Blaenavon Torfn
44 C7 Blaen Dyryn Powys
41 N3 Blaenffos Pembks
29 P6 Blaengarw Brdgnd
54 E8 Blaengeuffordd Cerdgn
29 N3 Blaengwrach Neath
29 N5 Blaengwynfi Neath
30 D5 Blaenllechau Rhondd
43 M2 Blaenpennal Cerdgn
54 D9 Blaenplwyf Cerdgn
42 E5 Blaenporth Cerdgn
29 P5 Blaenrhondda Rhondd
41 P5 Blaenwaun Carmth
42 F9 Blaen-y-Coed Carmth
30 F2 Blaen-y-cwm Blae G
55 J9 Blaenycwm Cerdgn
29 P5 Blaen-y-cwm Rhondd
19 P3 Blagdon N Som
18 H11 Blagdon Somset
7 M6 Blagdon Torbay
18 H11 Blagdon Hill Somset
111 P11 Blagill Cumb
88 F9 Blaguegate Lancs
139 J2 Blaich Highld
138 B4 Blain Highld
30 H3 Blaina Blae G
141 L4 Blair Atholl P & K
133 L8 Blair Drummond Stirlg
142 B8 Blairgowrie P & K
134 B10 Blairhall Fife
134 B8 Blairingone P & K
133 N8 Blairlogie Stirlg
131 P11 Blairmore Ag & B
164 E5 Blairmore Highld
124 B4 Blair's Ferry Ag & B
46 D11 Blaisdon Gloucs
57 Q9 Blakebrook Worcs
58 C9 Blakedown Worcs
52 B7 Blake End Essex
70 H5 Blakeley Lane Staffs
82 C10 Blakemere Ches W
45 M6 Blakemere Herefs
7 K6 Blakemore Devon
58 F4 Blakenall Heath Wsall
32 C3 Blakeney Gloucs
76 E3 Blakeney Norfk
70 C5 Blakenhall Ches E
58 D5 Blakenhall Wolves
58 B8 Blakeshall Worcs
48 H4 Blakesley Nhants
112 E10 Blanchland Nthumb
12 F3 Blandford Camp Dorset
12 E3 Blandford Forum Dorset
12 E3 Blandford St Mary Dorset
97 K10 Bland Hill N York
125 N2 Blanefield Stirlg
86 E8 Blankney Lincs
126 B6 Blantyre S Lans
139 L4 Blar a' Chaorainn Highld
147 Q9 Blargie Highld
139 K4 Blarmachfoldach Highld
13 L3 Blashford Hants
73 L11 Blaston Leics
73 P11 Blatherwycke Nhants
94 F3 Blawith Cumb
108 D4 Blawquhairn D & G
65 M10 Blaxhall Suffk
91 R10 Blaxton Donc
113 J8 Blaydon Gatesd
19 N5 Bleadney Somset
19 K3 Bleadon N Som
20 E8 Bleak Street Somset
39 K9 Blean Kent
86 F4 Bleasby Lincs
85 M11 Bleasby Notts
95 M11 Bleasdale Lancs
102 D8 Bleatarn Cumb
57 K10 Bleathwood Herefs
135 L4 Blebocraigs Fife
56 C11 Bleddfa Powys
47 P10 Bledington Gloucs
35 L4 Bledlow Bucks
35 L5 Bledlow Ridge Bucks
20 G3 Bleet Wilts
128 D7 Blegbie E Loth
102 B4 Blencarn Cumb
110 C11 Blencogo Cumb
15 K4 Blendworth Hants
100 G2 Blennerhasset Cumb
48 F11 Bletchingdon Oxon
36 H10 Bletchingley Surrey
49 N8 Bletchley M Keyn
69 R8 Bletchley Shrops
41 L6 Bletherston Pembks
61 M9 Bletsoe Bed
34 F7 Blewbury Oxon
76 H6 Blickling Norfk
85 J9 Blidworth Notts
85 J10 Blidworth Bottoms Notts
118 F8 Blindburn Nthumb
100 F4 Blindcrake Cumb
37 J11 Blindley Heath Surrey
5 J7 Blisland Cnwll
13 L2 Blissford Hants
57 N10 Bliss Gate Worcs
49 K4 Blisworth Nhants
71 K11 Blithbury Staffs
109 P10 Blitterlees Cumb
47 N8 Blockley Gloucs
77 L10 Blofield Norfk
77 L9 Blofield Heath Norfk
64 E6 Blo Norton Norfk
118 A6 Bloomfield Border
70 C8 Blore Staffs
71 L5 Blore Staffs
23 K5 Blounce Hants
71 K8 Blounts Green Staffs
88 D7 Blowick Sefton
48 D7 Bloxham Oxon
86 E10 Bloxholm Lincs
58 E4 Bloxwich Wsall
12 E6 Bloxworth Dorset
97 J9 Blubberhouses N York
4 E10 Blue Anchor Cnwll
18 D6 Blue Anchor Somset
38 B9 Blue Bell Hill Kent
83 P8 Blue John Cavern Derbys
81 L5 Blundellsands Sefton
65 Q2 Blundeston Suffk
61 Q10 Blunham C Beds
33 M7 Blunsdon St Andrew Swindn
58 D10 Bluntington Worcs
62 E6 Bluntisham Cambs
5 N9 Blunts Cnwll
58 H11 Blunts Green Warwks
70 F6 Blurton C Stke
86 B2 Blyborough Lincs
65 N6 Blyford Suffk
57 Q2 Blymhill Staffs
57 Q2 Blymhill Lawn Staffs
85 K3 Blyth Notts
113 M4 Blyth Nthumb
127 L8 Blyth Bridge Border
65 N6 Blythburgh Suffk
113 M4 Blyth Crematorium Nthumb
128 F10 Blythe Border
70 H6 Blythe Bridge Staffs
59 K6 Blythe End Warwks
70 H6 Blythe Marsh Staffs
85 Q2 Blyton Lincs
135 P5 Boarhills Fife
14 H5 Boarhunt Hants
38 C10 Boarley Kent
89 N6 Boarsgreave Lancs
25 M4 Boarshead E Susx
88 H9 Boar's Head Wigan
34 E4 Boars Hill Oxon
34 H2 Boarstall Bucks
8 D6 Boasley Cross Devon
155 Q3 Boath Highld
148 G4 Boat of Garten Highld
38 E8 Bobbing Kent
57 Q6 Bobbington Staffs
51 M9 Bobbingworth Essex
5 K10 Bocaddon Cnwll
52 C7 Bocking Essex
52 C6 Bocking Churchstreet Essex
46 A2 Bockleton Worcs
5 J9 Boconnoc Cnwll
159 R9 Boddam Abers
169 q12 Boddam Shet
46 G9 Boddington Gloucs
78 E8 Bodedern IoA
80 E9 Bodelwyddan Denbgs
45 Q4 Bodenham Herefs
21 N9 Bodenham Wilts
45 Q4 Bodenham Moor Herefs
78 G6 Bodewryd IoA
80 F10 Bodfari Denbgs
78 G9 Bodffordd IoA
66 E7 Bodfuan Gwynd
76 G3 Bodham Norfk
26 C6 Bodiam E Susx
26 C6 Bodiam Castle E Susx
48 E7 Bodicote Oxon
4 F7 Bodieve Cnwll
5 J11 Bodinnick Cnwll
25 Q8 Bodle Street Green E Susx
4 H8 Bodmin Cnwll
5 K6 Bodmin Moor Cnwll
79 Q10 Bodnant Garden Conwy
64 A2 Bodney Norfk
78 F11 Bodorgan IoA
27 K2 Bodsham Kent
4 G9 Bodwen Cnwll
59 J5 Bodymoor Heath Warwks
156 A7 Bogallan Highld
159 P10 Bogbrae Abers
125 L11 Bogend S Ayrs
128 C5 Boggs Holdings E Loth
127 N4 Boghall Mdloth
126 H4 Boghall W Loth
126 D9 Boghead S Lans
157 R5 Bogmoor Moray
143 L3 Bogmuir Abers
158 E8 Bogniebrae Abers
15 P7 Bognor Regis W Susx
148 G3 Bogroy Highld
108 D4 Bogue D & G
5 Q8 Bohetherick Cnwll
3 M7 Bohortha Cnwll
146 H11 Bohuntine Highld
2 B7 Bojewyan Cnwll
4 H9 Bokiddick Cnwll
103 N6 Bolam Dur
112 H4 Bolam Nthumb
6 H11 Bolberry Devon
82 B7 Bold Heath St Hel
58 H6 Boldmere Birm
113 M8 Boldon Colliery S Tyne
13 P5 Boldre Hants
103 K8 Boldron Dur
85 N3 Bole Notts
84 C9 Bolehill Derbys
84 D6 Bole Hill Derbys
2 H6 Bolenowe Cnwll
18 C11 Bolham Devon
10 D2 Bolham Water Devon
3 K3 Bolingey Cnwll
83 K9 Bollington Ches E
83 K9 Bollington Cross Ches E
32 D2 Bollow Gloucs
24 G6 Bolney W Susx
61 N9 Bolnhurst Bed
143 L7 Bolshan Angus
84 G6 Bolsover Derbys
90 D7 Bolster Moor Kirk
90 H11 Bolsterstone Sheff
97 Q3 Boltby N York
150 C5 Boltenstone Abers
35 L6 Bolter End Bucks
89 L9 Bolton Bolton
102 B6 Bolton Cumb
128 E6 Bolton E Loth
98 F10 Bolton E R Yk
119 M8 Bolton Nthumb
96 G10 Bolton Abbey N York
96 G10 Bolton Bridge N York
96 A11 Bolton by Bowland Lancs
111 J7 Boltonfellend Cumb
100 H2 Boltongate Cumb
95 K7 Bolton le Sands Lancs
100 H2 Bolton Low Houses Cumb
100 H2 Bolton New Houses Cumb
103 Q11 Bolton-on-Swale N York
91 N2 Bolton Percy N York
95 K7 Bolton Town End Lancs
91 M10 Bolton Upon Dearne Barns
89 J8 Bolton West Services Lancs
5 K6 Bolventor Cnwll
113 L4 Bomarsund Nthumb
69 N11 Bomere Heath Shrops
162 E8 Bonar Bridge Highld
139 J11 Bonawe Ag & B
92 H7 Bonby N Linc
41 P3 Boncath Pembks
118 A8 Bonchester Bridge Border
14 G11 Bonchurch IoW
8 G4 Bondleigh Devon
88 F2 Bonds Lancs
8 H9 Bonehill Devon
59 J4 Bonehill Staffs
134 C11 Bo'ness Falk
58 F2 Boney Hay Staffs
125 K2 Bonhill W Duns
57 Q4 Boningale Shrops
118 C6 Bonjedward Border
126 E6 Bonkle N Lans
143 K10 Bonnington Angus
27 J4 Bonnington Kent
135 K7 Bonnybank Fife
126 E2 Bonnybridge Falk
159 L7 Bonnykelly Abers
127 Q4 Bonnyrigg Mdloth
142 E10 Bonnyton Angus
84 C9 Bonsall Derbys
110 D6 Bonshaw Tower D & G
45 M11 Bont Mons
67 M11 Bontddu Gwynd
55 K4 Bont-Dolgadfan Powys
54 F7 Bont-goch or Elerch Cerdgn
87 N6 Bonthorpe Lincs
54 E11 Bontnewydd Cerdgn
66 H3 Bontnewydd Gwynd
68 E3 Bontuchel Denbgs
30 E10 Bonvilston V Glam
68 F6 Bonwm Denbgs
29 J5 Bon-y-maen Swans
17 J4 Boode Devon
35 M6 Booker Bucks
69 Q9 Booley Shrops
128 F10 Boon Border
70 E4 Boon Hill Staffs
14 F4 Boorley Green Hants
105 J7 Boosbeck R & Cl
52 D5 Boose's Green Essex
100 G10 Boot Cumb
90 C5 Booth Calder
86 C9 Boothby Graffoe Lincs
73 P4 Boothby Pagnell Lincs
92 B5 Boothferry E R Yk
83 K8 Booth Green Ches E
82 F4 Boothstown Salfd
90 D5 Booth Town Calder
60 G8 Boothville Nhants
94 C3 Bootle Cumb
81 L5 Bootle Sefton
82 G10 Boots Green Ches W
53 M2 Boot Street Suffk
103 K10 Booze N York
57 L11 Boraston Shrops
10 c1 Bordeaux Guern
38 E9 Borden Kent
23 M10 Borden W Susx
10 C10 Border Cumb
111 M4 Border Forest Park
117 R4 Borders Crematorium Border
96 D7 Bordley N York
23 L7 Bordon Camp Hants
52 C10 Boreham Essex
20 G6 Boreham Wilts
25 Q8 Boreham Street E Susx
50 E11 Borehamwood Herts
110 C2 Boreland D & G
152 B7 Boreraig Highld
57 J3 Boreton Shrops
168 b17 Borgh W Isls
168 j2 Borgh W Isls
165 Q5 Borgie Highld
108 D11 Borgue D & G
167 K11 Borgue Highld
52 D3 Borley Essex
52 D3 Borley Green Essex
64 D9 Borley Green Suffk
152 F3 Borneskitaig Highld
108 D11 Borness D & G
97 N7 Boroughbridge N York
37 P9 Borough Green Kent
69 L4 Borras Head Wrexhm
72 C4 Borrowash Derbys
97 P3 Borrowby N York
105 L7 Borrowby N York
134 B11 Borrowstoun Falk
38 B8 Borstal Medway
54 E6 Borth Cerdgn
117 N8 Borthwickbrae Border
117 N7 Borthwickshiels Border
67 K7 Borth-y-Gest Gwynd
152 G8 Borve Highld
168 b17 Borve W Isls
168 f8 Borve W Isls
168 j2 Borve W Isls
95 L6 Borwick Lancs
101 K11 Borwick Lodge Cumb
94 D5 Borwick Rails Cumb
2 B7 Bosavern Cnwll
46 C6 Bosbury Herefs
4 G8 Boscarne Cnwll
4 H3 Boscastle Cnwll
13 K6 Boscombe Bmouth
21 P7 Boscombe Wilts
3 Q3 Boscoppa Cnwll
15 M6 Bosham W Susx
15 M6 Bosham Hoe W Susx
41 J12 Bosherston Pembks
2 C7 Boskednan Cnwll
2 C9 Boskenna Cnwll
83 K11 Bosley Ches E
4 D9 Bosoughan Cnwll
98 E8 Bossall N York
4 H4 Bossiney Cnwll
27 L2 Bossingham Kent
18 A5 Bossington Somset
82 E11 Bostock Green Ches W
74 F2 Boston Lincs
87 K11 Boston Crematorium Lincs
97 P11 Boston Spa Leeds
2 C7 Boswarthan Cnwll
3 P5 Boswinger Cnwll
2 B7 Botallack Cnwll
50 G11 Botany Bay Gt Lon
72 D10 Botcheston Leics
64 E6 Botesdale Suffk
113 K3 Bothal Nthumb
34 F9 Bothampstead W Berk
85 L6 Bothamsall Notts
100 G3 Bothel Cumb
11 K6 Bothenhampton Dorset
126 C6 Bothwell S Lans
126 C6 Bothwell Services S Lans
35 Q4 Botley Bucks
14 F4 Botley Hants
34 E3 Botley Oxon
49 K10 Botolph Claydon Bucks
24 E9 Botolphs W Susx
27 K5 Botolph's Bridge Kent
73 L3 Bottesford Leics
92 E9 Bottesford N Linc
62 H8 Bottisham Cambs
135 K3 Bottomcraig Fife
88 F5 Bottom of Hutton Lancs
89 K8 Bottom o' th' Moor Bolton
89 Q6 Bottoms Calder
2 B9 Bottoms Cnwll
59 K6 Botts Green Warwks
5 Q9 Botusfleming Cnwll
66 D8 Botwnnog Gwynd
37 L11 Bough Beech Kent
44 G7 Boughrood Powys
31 Q5 Boughspring Gloucs
60 G7 Boughton Nhants
75 P10 Boughton Norfk
85 L7 Boughton Notts
26 H2 Boughton Aluph Kent
49 Q7 Boughton End C Beds
38 C11 Boughton Green Kent
26 E2 Boughton Malherbe Kent
38 C11 Boughton Monchelsea Kent
39 J10 Boughton Street Kent
105 L7 Boulby R & Cl
90 C6 Boulder Clough Calder
14 C9 Bouldnor IoW
57 J7 Bouldon Shrops
119 Q8 Boulmer Nthumb
41 J8 Boulston Pembks
86 C7 Boultham Lincs
62 D9 Bourn Cambs
74 A6 Bourne Lincs
37 M2 Bournebridge Essex
58 F8 Bournebrook Birm
61 M8 Bourne End Bed
35 N7 Bourne End Bucks
49 Q6 Bourne End C Beds
50 B9 Bourne End Herts
13 J6 Bournemouth Bmouth
13 K5 Bournemouth Airport Dorset
13 K6 Bournemouth Crematorium Bmouth
32 H4 Bournes Green Gloucs
38 F4 Bournes Green Sthend
58 E10 Bournheath Worcs
113 M10 Bournmoor Dur
32 D6 Bournstream Gloucs
58 F8 Bournville Birm
20 E8 Bourton Dorset
19 L2 Bourton N Som
33 P7 Bourton Oxon
57 K5 Bourton Shrops
21 K2 Bourton Wilts
59 P10 Bourton on Dunsmore Warwks
47 N8 Bourton-on-the-Hill Gloucs
47 N10 Bourton-on-the-Water Gloucs
136 H3 Bousd Ag & B
110 E9 Boustead Hill Cumb
94 G3 Bouth Cumb
96 H6 Bouthwaite N York
47 K3 Bouts Worcs
35 P9 Boveney Bucks
13 J2 Boveridge Dorset
9 K9 Bovey Tracey Devon
50 B10 Bovingdon Herts
35 M7 Bovingdon Green Bucks
51 M9 Bovinger Essex
12 D7 Bovington Dorset
12 D7 Bovington Camp Dorset
12 D7 Bovington Tank Museum Dorset
110 F9 Bow Cumb
7 L7 Bow Devon
8 H4 Bow Devon
37 J4 Bow Gt Lon
169 c7 Bow Ork
102 H6 Bowbank Dur
49 P8 Bow Brickhill M Keyn
32 G3 Bowbridge Gloucs
104 B3 Bowburn Dur
14 E9 Bowcombe IoW
10 C6 Bowd Devon
117 R4 Bowden Border
7 L9 Bowden Devon
32 H11 Bowden Hill Wilts
82 G7 Bowdon Traffd
167 M4 Bower Highld
31 Q10 Bower Ashton Bristl
21 K10 Bowerchalke Wilts
20 H2 Bowerhill Wilts
19 N11 Bower Hinton Somset
52 G3 Bower House Tye Suffk
167 M4 Bowermadden Highld
70 E7 Bowers Staffs
38 C4 Bowers Gifford Essex
134 D9 Bowershall Fife
91 L5 Bower's Row Leeds
103 J8 Bowes Dur
88 F2 Bowgreave Lancs
109 M7 Bowhouse D & G
5 K5 Bowithick Cnwll
81 N4 Bowker's Green Lancs
117 P2 Bowland Border
95 J3 Bowland Bridge Cumb
45 Q4 Bowley Herefs
45 Q4 Bowley Town Herefs
23 P7 Bowlhead Green Surrey
90 F4 Bowling C Brad
125 L3 Bowling W Duns
69 L5 Bowling Bank Wrexhm
46 F4 Bowling Green Worcs
101 K11 Bowmanstead Cumb
122 D8 Bowmore Ag & B
110 D8 Bowness-on-Solway Cumb
101 M11 Bowness-on-Windermere Cumb
135 J5 Bow of Fife Fife
143 J8 Bowriefauld Angus
101 L4 Bowscale Cumb
119 J2 Bowsden Nthumb
101 N11 Bowston Cumb
54 E7 Bow Street Cerdgn
64 E2 Bow Street Norfk
76 H10 Bowthorpe Norfk
32 G4 Box Gloucs
32 F11 Box Wilts
32 D2 Boxbush Gloucs
46 C10 Boxbush Gloucs
61 M11 Box End Bed
52 G3 Boxford Suffk
34 D10 Boxford W Berk
15 P5 Boxgrove W Susx
36 E10 Box Hill Surrey
38 C10 Boxley Kent
50 B9 Boxmoor Herts
16 C11 Box's Shop Cnwll
52 G5 Boxted Essex
52 H5 Boxted Essex
64 A11 Boxted Suffk
52 H5 Boxted Cross Essex
32 F6 Boxwell Gloucs
62 D8 Boxworth Cambs
62 E7 Boxworth End Cambs
63 M9 Boyden End Suffk
39 M8 Boyden Gate Kent
71 M7 Boylestone Derbys
158 F5 Boyndie Abers
159 M5 Boyndlie Abers
99 N7 Boynton E R Yk
143 L8 Boysack Angus
11 P2 Boys Hill Dorset
84 E7 Boythorpe Derbys
5 N3 Boyton Cnwll
53 Q2 Boyton Suffk
21 J7 Boyton Wilts
51 P9 Boyton Cross Essex
52 B3 Boyton End Suffk
61 K9 Bozeat Nhants
80 d6 Braaid IoM
65 K9 Brabling Green Suffk
27 K3 Brabourne Kent
27 J3 Brabourne Lees Kent
167 P3 Brabstermire Highld
152 F10 Bracadale Highld
74 A8 Braceborough Lincs
86 C7 Bracebridge Heath Lincs

86 C7 **Bracebridge Low Fields** Lincs
73 Q3 **Braceby** Lincs
96 C11 **Bracewell** Lancs
84 E9 **Brackenfield** Derbys
126 C4 **Brackenhirst** N Lans
110 E11 **Brackenthwaite** Cumb
97 L10 **Brackenthwaite** N York
15 M7 **Bracklesham** W Susx
146 F11 **Brackletter** Highld
48 G7 **Brackley** Nhants
48 H6 **Brackley Hatch** Nhants
35 N11 **Bracknell** Br For
133 N6 **Braco** P & K
158 D7 **Bracobrae** Moray
64 H2 **Bracon Ash** Norfk
145 M9 **Bracora** Highld
145 M9 **Bracorina** Highld
5 P3 **Bradaford** Devon
71 N4 **Bradbourne** Derbys
104 B5 **Bradbury** Dur
48 H5 **Bradden** Nhants
5 K9 **Braddock** Cnwll
70 F4 **Bradeley** C Stke
35 M5 **Bradenham** Bucks
33 K9 **Bradenstoke** Wilts
9 Q3 **Bradfield** Devon
53 K5 **Bradfield** Essex
77 K5 **Bradfield** Norfk
84 C2 **Bradfield** Sheff
34 H10 **Bradfield** W Berk
64 B10 **Bradfield Combust** Suffk
70 B3 **Bradfield Green** Ches E
53 K5 **Bradfield Heath** Essex
64 C10 **Bradfield St Clare** Suffk
64 C10 **Bradfield St George** Suffk
90 F4 **Bradford** C Brad
5 J6 **Bradford** Cnwll
16 G10 **Bradford** Devon
112 G5 **Bradford** Nthumb
119 N4 **Bradford** Nthumb
11 M2 **Bradford Abbas** Dorset
20 F2 **Bradford Leigh** Wilts
20 F2 **Bradford-on-Avon** Wilts
18 G10 **Bradford-on-Tone** Somset
11 P6 **Bradford Peverell** Dorset
17 K5 **Bradiford** Devon
14 H9 **Brading** IoW
71 N5 **Bradley** Derbys
22 H6 **Bradley** Hants
90 F6 **Bradley** Kirk
96 F4 **Bradley** N York
93 M9 **Bradley** NE Lin
70 F11 **Bradley** Staffs
58 E5 **Bradley** Wolves
47 J2 **Bradley** Worcs
69 K4 **Bradley** Wrexhm
69 P5 **Bradley Common** Ches W
19 J7 **Bradley Green** Somset
59 L4 **Bradley Green** Warwks
47 J2 **Bradley Green** Worcs
71 K6 **Bradley in the Moors** Staffs
32 B8 **Bradley Stoke** S Glos
72 F4 **Bradmore** Notts
19 K7 **Bradney** Somset
9 N4 **Bradninch** Devon
17 L5 **Bradninch** Devon
71 J3 **Bradnop** Staffs
45 K3 **Bradnor Green** Herefs
11 K6 **Bradpole** Dorset
89 L8 **Bradshaw** Bolton
90 D5 **Bradshaw** Calder
90 D8 **Bradshaw** Kirk
5 P5 **Bradstone** Devon
70 D2 **Bradwall Green** Ches E
83 Q8 **Bradwell** Derbys
17 J3 **Bradwell** Devon
52 D7 **Bradwell** Essex
49 M6 **Bradwell** M Keyn
77 Q11 **Bradwell** Norfk
70 F5 **Bradwell Crematorium** Staffs
52 H10 **Bradwell-on-Sea** Essex
52 G10 **Bradwell Waterside** Essex
16 E9 **Bradworthy** Devon
156 B5 **Brae** Highld
169 q7 **Brae** Shet
133 M11 **Braeface** Falk
143 M7 **Braehead** Angus
107 M7 **Braehead** D & G
126 H7 **Braehead** S Lans
149 M9 **Braemar** Abers
161 K11 **Braemore** Highld
167 J11 **Braemore** Highld
147 J9 **Brae Roy Lodge** Highld
124 G3 **Braeside** Inver
142 D6 **Braes of Coul** Angus
158 A6 **Braes of Enzie** Moray
169 f3 **Braeswick** Ork
131 K6 **Braevallich** Ag & B
103 Q6 **Brafferton** Darltn
97 P6 **Brafferton** N York
60 H9 **Brafield-on-the-Green** Nhants
168 h3 **Bragar** W Isls
50 G6 **Bragbury End** Herts
126 E8 **Braidwood** S Lans
71 P6 **Brailsford** Derbys
71 P6 **Brailsford Green** Derbys
32 C3 **Brain's Green** Gloucs
52 C7 **Braintree** Essex
64 C7 **Braiseworth** Suffk
22 C9 **Braishfield** Hants
90 C2 **Braithwaite** C Brad
100 H6 **Braithwaite** Cumb
84 H2 **Braithwell** Donc
91 L7 **Braken Hill** Wakefd
24 E8 **Bramber** W Susx
22 E10 **Brambridge** Hants
72 E3 **Bramcote** Notts
59 P7 **Bramcote** Warwks
72 E3 **Bramcote Crematorium** Notts
22 H9 **Bramdean** Hants
77 K11 **Bramerton** Norfk
50 G7 **Bramfield** Herts
65 M7 **Bramfield** Suffk
53 K2 **Bramford** Suffk
83 J8 **Bramhall** Stockp
91 L2 **Bramham** Leeds
90 H2 **Bramhope** Leeds
23 J3 **Bramley** Hants
90 G3 **Bramley** Leeds
84 G2 **Bramley** Rothm
24 B2 **Bramley** Surrey
72 H3 **Bramley Corner** Hants
23 J3 **Bramley Green** Hants

96 H9 **Bramley Head** N York
39 M10 **Bramling** Kent
9 M5 **Brampford Speke** Devon
62 B6 **Brampton** Cambs
102 C6 **Brampton** Cumb
111 K8 **Brampton** Cumb
85 P5 **Brampton** Lincs
77 J7 **Brampton** Norfk
91 L10 **Brampton** Rothm
65 N5 **Brampton** Suffk
46 B9 **Brampton Abbotts** Herefs
60 G3 **Brampton Ash** Nhants
56 F10 **Brampton Bryan** Herefs
84 G3 **Brampton-en-le-Morthen** Rothm
71 K8 **Bramshall** Staffs
21 Q11 **Bramshaw** Hants
23 K2 **Bramshill** Hants
23 M8 **Bramshott** Hants
19 M9 **Bramwell** Somset
137 N2 **Branault** Highld
75 Q2 **Brancaster** Norfk
75 Q2 **Brancaster Staithe** Norfk
103 P3 **Brancepeth** Dur
157 K7 **Branchill** Moray
87 L11 **Brand End** Lincs
157 N3 **Branderburgh** Moray
99 N11 **Brandesburton** E R Yk
65 J9 **Brandeston** Suffk
46 D9 **Brand Green** Gloucs
16 G11 **Brandis Corner** Devon
76 G7 **Brandiston** Norfk
103 P2 **Brandon** Dur
86 B11 **Brandon** Lincs
119 K7 **Brandon** Nthumb
63 N3 **Brandon** Suffk
59 P9 **Brandon** Warwks
63 K3 **Brandon Bank** Norfk
63 K2 **Brandon Creek** Norfk
76 F10 **Brandon Parva** Norfk
98 B6 **Brandsby** N York
92 H11 **Brandy Wharf** Lincs
2 C8 **Brane** Cnwll
51 Q5 **Bran End** Essex
12 H6 **Branksome** Poole
12 J6 **Branksome Park** Poole
22 D6 **Bransbury** Hants
85 Q5 **Bransby** Lincs
10 D7 **Branscombe** Devon
46 E4 **Bransford** Worcs
13 L5 **Bransgore** Hants
93 K4 **Bransholme** C KuH
57 M9 **Bransley** Shrops
58 G10 **Branson's Cross** Worcs
73 L5 **Branston** Leics
86 D7 **Branston** Lincs
71 N10 **Branston** Staffs
86 E7 **Branston Booths** Lincs
14 G10 **Branstone** IoW
86 B10 **Brant Broughton** Lincs
53 K5 **Brantham** Suffk
100 E6 **Branthwaite** Cumb
101 J3 **Branthwaite** Cumb
92 F5 **Brantingham** E R Yk
91 Q10 **Branton** Donc
119 K7 **Branton** Nthumb
97 P8 **Branton Green** N York
118 C4 **Branxton** Nthumb
69 P2 **Brassey Green** Ches W
71 N4 **Brassington** Derbys
37 L9 **Brasted** Kent
37 L10 **Brasted Chart** Kent
150 H8 **Brathens** Abers
87 N8 **Bratoft** Lincs
86 B4 **Brattleby** Lincs
18 B5 **Bratton** Somset
20 H4 **Bratton** Wilts
57 L2 **Bratton** Wrekin
8 C6 **Bratton Clovelly** Devon
17 L4 **Bratton Fleming** Devon
20 C9 **Bratton Seymour** Somset
51 J5 **Braughing** Herts
51 K6 **Braughing Friars** Herts
60 B7 **Braunston** Nhants
73 L9 **Braunston** Rutlnd
72 F10 **Braunstone** Leics
16 H4 **Braunton** Devon
98 E5 **Brawby** N York
166 D3 **Brawl** Highld
104 F9 **Braworth** N York
35 P9 **Bray** W & M
60 G4 **Braybrooke** Nhants
33 K7 **Braydon** Wilts
33 J6 **Braydon Brook** Wilts
33 K7 **Braydon Side** Wilts
17 M5 **Brayford** Devon
25 Q8 **Bray's Hill** E Susx
5 N7 **Bray Shop** Cnwll
100 D9 **Braystones** Cumb
97 K11 **Braythorn** N York
91 Q4 **Brayton** N York
35 N9 **Braywick** W & M
35 N9 **Braywoodside** W & M
5 M3 **Brazacott** Cnwll
27 L2 **Breach** Kent
38 D8 **Breach** Kent
50 E6 **Breachwood Green** Herts
69 M7 **Breaden Heath** Shrops
72 B3 **Breadsall** Derbys
32 D4 **Breadstone** Gloucs
45 K4 **Breadward** Herefs
2 G8 **Breage** Cnwll
155 N9 **Breakachy** Highld
36 C3 **Breakspear Crematorium** Gt Lon
162 C8 **Brealangwell Lodge** Highld
32 B3 **Bream** Gloucs
21 N11 **Breamore** Hants
19 J3 **Brean** Somset
168 e5 **Breanais** W Isls
90 C5 **Brearley** Calder
97 M8 **Brearton** N York
168 h4 **Breascleit** W Isls
168 h4 **Breasclete** W Isls
72 D4 **Breaston** Derbys
43 K8 **Brechfa** Carmth
143 L5 **Brechin** Angus
64 D3 **Breckles** Norfk
44 E9 **Brecon** Powys
44 E10 **Brecon Beacons National Park**
83 K6 **Bredbury** Stockp
26 D8 **Brede** E Susx
46 B3 **Bredenbury** Herefs
65 K11 **Bredfield** Suffk
38 E9 **Bredgar** Kent
38 C9 **Bredhurst** Kent
46 H7 **Bredon** Worcs

46 H7 **Bredon's Hardwick** Worcs
46 H7 **Bredon's Norton** Worcs
45 L6 **Bredwardine** Herefs
72 C6 **Breedon on the Hill** Leics
126 H5 **Breich** W Loth
89 L9 **Breightmet** Bolton
92 B4 **Breighton** E R Yk
45 P7 **Breinton** Herefs
33 J10 **Bremhill** Wilts
17 M6 **Bremridge** Devon
25 Q2 **Brenchley** Kent
16 F10 **Brendon** Devon
17 P2 **Brendon** Devon
18 D8 **Brendon Hill** Somset
123 P3 **Brenfield** Ag & B
168 e5 **Brenish** W Isls
113 K5 **Brenkley** N u Ty
52 F2 **Brent Eleigh** Suffk
36 E5 **Brentford** Gt Lon
73 K7 **Brentingby** Leics
19 K4 **Brent Knoll** Somset
6 H7 **Brent Mill** Devon
51 K4 **Brent Pelham** Herts
26 H6 **Brentwood** Essex
26 H6 **Brenzett** Kent
26 H6 **Brenzett Green** Kent
71 K11 **Brereton** Staffs
70 D2 **Brereton Green** Ches E
82 H11 **Brereton Heath** Ches E
71 K11 **Brereton Hill** Staffs
169 s9 **Bressay** Shet
64 F5 **Bressingham** Norfk
64 F5 **Bressingham Common** Norfk
71 P10 **Bretby** Derbys
71 P10 **Bretby Crematorium** Derbys
59 P9 **Bretford** Warwks
47 L6 **Bretforton** Worcs
88 F6 **Bretherton** Lancs
169 r8 **Brettabister** Shet
64 C5 **Brettenham** Norfk
64 D11 **Brettenham** Suffk
84 B5 **Bretton** Derbys
69 L2 **Bretton** Flints
51 N6 **Brewers End** Essex
36 H10 **Brewer Street** Surrey
58 C3 **Brewood** Staffs
12 D6 **Briantspuddle** Dorset
51 N5 **Brick End** Essex
50 H9 **Brickendon** Herts
50 D10 **Bricket Wood** Herts
84 D4 **Brick Houses** Sheff
52 B5 **Brickkiln Green** Essex
47 J6 **Bricklehampton** Worcs
80 f1 **Bride** IoM
100 F4 **Bridekirk** Cumb
41 N2 **Bridell** Pembks
8 D7 **Bridestowe** Devon
158 E10 **Brideswell** Abers
9 K7 **Bridford** Devon
39 L11 **Bridge** Kent
94 D4 **Bridge End** Cumb
110 C11 **Bridge End** Cumb
6 H9 **Bridge End** Devon
103 K3 **Bridge End** Dur
51 Q4 **Bridge End** Essex
74 B3 **Bridge End** Lincs
100 E5 **Bridgefoot** Cumb
51 L3 **Bridge Green** Essex
19 Q10 **Bridgehampton** Somset
97 M6 **Bridge Hewick** N York
112 G10 **Bridgehill** Dur
97 J7 **Bridgehouse Gate** N York
14 G6 **Bridgemary** Hants
70 C5 **Bridgemere** Ches E
158 D10 **Bridgend** Abers
120 E4 **Bridgend** Ag & B
122 D7 **Bridgend** Ag & B
143 J4 **Bridgend** Angus
29 P9 **Bridgend** Brdgnd
42 C5 **Bridgend** Cerdgn
101 M8 **Bridgend** Cumb
116 F9 **Bridgend** D & G
6 F9 **Bridgend** Devon
135 K5 **Bridgend** Fife
158 A11 **Bridgend** Moray
134 E3 **Bridgend** P & K
127 J2 **Bridgend** W Loth
142 D7 **Bridgend of Lintrathen** Angus
150 F4 **Bridge of Alford** Abers
133 M8 **Bridge of Allan** Stirlg
149 M3 **Bridge of Avon** Moray
157 M10 **Bridge of Avon** Moray
140 E8 **Bridge of Balgie** P & K
142 B5 **Bridge of Brewlands** Angus
149 L3 **Bridge of Brown** Highld
142 A7 **Bridge of Cally** P & K
150 H8 **Bridge of Canny** Abers
142 D7 **Bridge of Craigisla** Angus
108 F9 **Bridge of Dee** D & G
151 N6 **Bridge of Don** C Aber
150 H10 **Bridge of Dulsie** Highld
134 E4 **Bridge of Earn** P & K
140 D6 **Bridge of Ericht** P & K
151 J9 **Bridge of Feugh** Abers
166 H3 **Bridge of Forss** Highld
150 B8 **Bridge of Gairn** Abers
140 D6 **Bridge of Gaur** P & K
158 E7 **Bridge of Marnoch** Abers
139 P10 **Bridge of Orchy** Ag & B
141 L4 **Bridge of Tilt** P & K
158 A5 **Bridge of Tynet** Moray
169 p8 **Bridge of Walls** Shet
125 K4 **Bridge of Weir** Rens
17 M9 **Bridge Reeve** Devon
8 D11 **Bridgerule** Devon
56 F5 **Bridges** Shrops
45 N6 **Bridge Sollers** Herefs
52 E2 **Bridge Street** Suffk
5 N4 **Bridgetown** Cnwll
18 B8 **Bridgetown** Somset
81 P10 **Bridge Trafford** Ches W
32 C10 **Bridge Yate** S Glos
57 N6 **Bridgham** Norfk
57 N6 **Bridgnorth** Shrops
19 K8 **Bridgwater** Somset
19 K8 **Bridgwater Services** Somset
99 P7 **Bridlington** E R Yk
11 K6 **Bridport** Dorset
46 A10 **Bridstow** Herefs
89 N3 **Brierfield** Lancs
91 L8 **Brierley** Barns
46 B11 **Brierley** Gloucs
45 P3 **Brierley** Herefs

58 D7 **Brierley Hill** Dudley
104 E4 **Brierton** Hartpl
101 J6 **Briery** Cumb
77 L6 **Briggate** Norfk
105 N9 **Briggswath** N York
100 E4 **Brigham** Cumb
101 J6 **Brigham** Cumb
99 M10 **Brigham** E R Yk
90 E6 **Brighouse** Calder
14 D10 **Brighstone** IoW
84 C9 **Brightgate** Derbys
34 C4 **Brighthampton** Oxon
90 H11 **Brightholmlee** Sheff
8 F5 **Brightley** Devon
25 Q6 **Brightling** E Susx
53 J8 **Brightlingsea** Essex
24 H10 **Brighton** Br & H
1 N3 **Brighton** Cnwll
81 L5 **Brighton le Sands** Sefton
126 G2 **Brightons** Falk
34 D9 **Brightwalton** W Berk
34 D9 **Brightwalton Green** W Berk
34 D9 **Brightwalton Holt** W Berk
53 N3 **Brightwell** Suffk
35 J5 **Brightwell Baldwin** Oxon
34 G6 **Brightwell-cum-Sotwell** Oxon
35 J6 **Brightwell Upperton** Oxon
103 L8 **Brignall** Dur
132 G6 **Brig o'Turk** Stirlg
93 N10 **Brigsley** NE Lin
95 K3 **Brigsteer** Cumb
61 K3 **Brigstock** Nhants
35 J2 **Brill** Bucks
3 J8 **Brill** Cnwll
45 K5 **Brilley** Herefs
57 J11 **Brimfield** Herefs
57 J11 **Brimfield Cross** Herefs
84 F6 **Brimington** Derbys
9 K9 **Brimley** Devon
32 H2 **Brimpsfield** Gloucs
22 G2 **Brimpton** W Berk
22 G2 **Brimpton Common** W Berk
32 G4 **Brimscombe** Gloucs
81 L8 **Brimstage** Wirral
84 D4 **Brincliffe** Sheff
92 B4 **Brind** E R Yk
19 P7 **Brindham** Somset
88 H6 **Brindle** Lancs
57 Q2 **Brineton** Staffs
60 H2 **Bringhurst** Leics
46 D3 **Bringsty Common** Herefs
61 N5 **Brington** Cambs
76 E5 **Briningham** Norfk
85 M10 **Brinkhill** Lincs
63 K10 **Brinkley** Cambs
59 P9 **Brinklow** Warwks
33 K8 **Brinkworth** Wilts
89 J6 **Brinscall** Lancs
19 M4 **Brinscombe** Somset
19 M2 **Brinsea** N Som
84 G11 **Brinsley** Notts
45 N6 **Brinsop** Herefs
84 F3 **Brinsworth** Rothm
76 E4 **Brinton** Norfk
169 d4 **Brinyan** Ork
110 H10 **Brisco** Cumb
76 C7 **Brisley** Norfk
32 B10 **Brislington** Bristl
26 F4 **Brissenden Green** Kent
31 Q10 **Bristol** Bristl
31 P11 **Bristol Airport** N Som
31 Q10 **Bristol Zoo** Bristl
76 F5 **Briston** Norfk
6 F5 **Brisworthy** Devon
89 P6 **Britannia** Lancs
21 N9 **Britford** Wilts
30 F4 **Brithdir** Caerph
67 P11 **Brithdir** Gwynd
38 B10 **British Legion Village** Kent
29 K6 **Briton Ferry** Neath
35 J6 **Britwell Salome** Oxon
7 N7 **Brixham** Torbay
6 F8 **Brixton** Devon
36 H5 **Brixton** Gt Lon
20 G7 **Brixton Deverill** Wilts
60 F6 **Brixworth** Nhants
33 Q3 **Brize Norton** Oxon
33 Q3 **Brize Norton Airport** Oxon
58 C11 **Broad Alley** Worcs
33 M6 **Broad Blunsdon** Swindn
83 L6 **Broadbottom** Tamesd
15 M5 **Broadbridge** W Susx
24 D4 **Broadbridge Heath** W Susx
47 N7 **Broad Campden** Gloucs
90 D7 **Broad Carr** Calder
21 K9 **Broad Chalke** Wilts
89 P6 **Broad Clough** Lancs
9 N5 **Broadclyst** Devon
125 J3 **Broadfield** Inver
41 M10 **Broadfield** Pembks
145 K3 **Broadford** Highld
26 B4 **Broad Ford** Kent
24 C6 **Broadford Bridge** W Susx
117 J8 **Broadgairhill** Border
64 D9 **Broadgrass Green** Suffk
63 L8 **Broad Green** Cambs
52 E7 **Broad Green** Essex
46 E3 **Broad Green** Worcs
58 E10 **Broad Green** Worcs
129 M9 **Broadhaugh** Border
40 G7 **Broad Haven** Pembks
82 G7 **Broadheath** Traffd
57 M11 **Broadheath** Worcs
10 C4 **Broadhembury** Devon
7 L5 **Broadhempston** Devon
63 J5 **Broad Hill** Cambs
33 M9 **Broad Hinton** Wilts
85 Q6 **Broadholme** Lincs
26 D8 **Broadland Row** E Susx
28 C3 **Broadlay** Carmth
22 D2 **Broad Layings** Hants
51 K9 **Broadley** Essex
89 P7 **Broadley** Lancs
158 A5 **Broadley** Moray
51 K9 **Broadley Common** Essex
47 M8 **Broad Marston** Worcs
12 B7 **Broadmayne** Dorset
70 E5 **Broad Meadow** Staffs
22 H5 **Broadmere** Hants

46 B11 **Broadmoor** Gloucs
41 L9 **Broadmoor** Pembks
8 H4 **Broadnymett** Devon
94 C2 **Broad Oak** Cumb
11 J5 **Broadoak** Dorset
25 P6 **Broad Oak** E Susx
26 B8 **Broad Oak** E Susx
32 C2 **Broadoak** Gloucs
23 L4 **Broad Oak** Hants
45 P10 **Broad Oak** Herefs
39 L9 **Broad Oak** Kent
82 B5 **Broad Oak** St Hel
69 L3 **Broadoak** Wrexhm
65 K6 **Broad Road** Suffk
51 Q8 **Broad's Green** Essex
39 Q8 **Broadstairs** Kent
31 P4 **Broadstone** Mons
12 H5 **Broadstone** Poole
57 J7 **Broadstone** Shrops
26 E8 **Broad Street** E Susx
51 N7 **Broad Street** Essex
27 K3 **Broad Street** Kent
38 D10 **Broad Street** Kent
38 C7 **Broad Street** Medway
21 M3 **Broad Street** Wilts
52 E10 **Broad Street Green** Essex
33 L9 **Broad Town** Wilts
46 E3 **Broadwas** Worcs
50 F6 **Broadwater** Herts
24 D10 **Broadwater** W Susx
58 B9 **Broadwaters** Worcs
28 C3 **Broadway** Carmth
41 Q8 **Broadway** Carmth
40 G8 **Broadway** Pembks
19 K11 **Broadway** Somset
65 M6 **Broadway** Suffk
47 L7 **Broadway** Worcs
32 Q2 **Broadwell** Gloucs
47 P9 **Broadwell** Gloucs
33 Q4 **Broadwell** Oxon
59 Q11 **Broadwell** Warwks
11 P8 **Broadwey** Dorset
11 J4 **Broadwindsor** Dorset
8 F3 **Broadwood Kelly** Devon
5 Q4 **Broadwoodwidger** Devon
45 L6 **Brobury** Herefs
153 K8 **Brochel** Highld
139 J11 **Brochroy** Ag & B
88 G2 **Brock** Lancs
46 E4 **Brockamin** Worcs
22 H11 **Brockbridge** Hants
65 J6 **Brockdish** Norfk
58 C10 **Brockencote** Worcs
13 P4 **Brockenhurst** Hants
126 E10 **Brocketsbrae** S Lans
64 G8 **Brockford Green** Suffk
64 G8 **Brockford Street** Suffk
60 D8 **Brockhall** Nhants
36 E11 **Brockham** Surrey
46 H9 **Brockhampton** Gloucs
47 K10 **Brockhampton** Gloucs
15 K5 **Brockhampton** Hants
46 A8 **Brockhampton** Herefs
46 C3 **Brockhampton Estate** Herefs
11 Q3 **Brockhampton Green** Dorset
90 F8 **Brockholes** Kirk
84 D8 **Brockhurst** Derbys
59 Q8 **Brockhurst** Warwks
101 K2 **Brocklebank** Cumb
93 K8 **Brocklesby** Lincs
31 N11 **Brockley** N Som
64 A7 **Brockley** Suffk
63 M11 **Brockley Green** Suffk
64 A11 **Brockley Green** Suffk
101 N3 **Brockleymoor** Cumb
58 D7 **Brockmoor** Dudley
8 C5 **Brockscombe** Devon
22 F2 **Brock's Green** Hants
56 E4 **Brockton** Shrops
56 E7 **Brockton** Shrops
57 K6 **Brockton** Shrops
57 N4 **Brockton** Shrops
70 E8 **Brockton** Staffs
31 P4 **Brockweir** Gloucs
22 H9 **Brockwood Park** Hants
46 G11 **Brockworth** Gloucs
4 G8 **Brocton** Cnwll
70 H11 **Brocton** Staffs
121 K4 **Brodick** N Ayrs
156 H6 **Brodie** Moray
91 N9 **Brodsworth** Donc
152 H4 **Brogaig** Highld
49 Q7 **Brogborough** C Beds
32 H7 **Brokenborough** Wilts
83 J10 **Broken Cross** Ches E
82 E10 **Broken Cross** Ches W
20 F4 **Brokerswood** Wilts
81 M8 **Bromborough** Wirral
64 G6 **Brome** Suffk
64 H6 **Brome Street** Suffk
65 L11 **Bromeswell** Suffk
110 C11 **Bromfield** Cumb
56 H7 **Bromfield** Shrops
61 M10 **Bromham** Bed
33 J11 **Bromham** Wilts
91 J11 **Bromley** Barns
58 D7 **Bromley** Dudley
37 K7 **Bromley** Gt Lon
57 N5 **Bromley** Shrops
37 K7 **Bromley Common** Gt Lon
53 J6 **Bromley Cross** Essex
26 G4 **Bromley Green** Kent
56 E4 **Bromlow** Shrops
38 C8 **Brompton** Medway
104 C11 **Brompton** N York
99 J4 **Brompton-by-Sawdon** N York
103 P11 **Brompton-on-Swale** N York
18 E8 **Brompton Ralph** Somset
18 C8 **Brompton Regis** Somset
46 C10 **Bromsash** Herefs
46 B9 **Bromsberrow** Gloucs
46 D8 **Bromsberrow Heath** Gloucs
58 E10 **Bromsgrove** Worcs
70 H11 **Bromstead Heath** Staffs
46 C4 **Bromyard** Herefs
46 C4 **Bromyard Downs** Herefs
67 N8 **Bronaber** Gwynd
54 E11 **Bronant** Cerdgn
57 J7 **Broncroft** Shrops
42 F5 **Brongest** Cerdgn
69 N7 **Bronington** Wrexhm
44 G8 **Bronllys** Powys
43 H10 **Bronwydd** Carmth
42 J5 **Bronydd** Powys

69	J7	**Bronygarth** Shrops
79	Q9	**Bron-y-Nant Crematorium** Conwy
41	Q9	**Brook** Carmth
13	N2	**Brook** Hants
22	B9	**Brook** Hants
14	C10	**Brook** IoW
27	J3	**Brook** Kent
23	P7	**Brook** Surrey
36	C11	**Brook** Surrey
65	K2	**Brooke** Norfk
73	L9	**Brooke** Rutlnd
93	M11	**Brookenby** Lincs
61	N8	**Brook End** Bed
61	Q11	**Brook End** C Beds
61	N6	**Brook End** Cambs
49	P6	**Brook End** M Keyn
125	L5	**Brookfield** Rens
34	H5	**Brookhampton** Oxon
20	B9	**Brookhampton** Somset
13	N2	**Brook Hill** Hants
80	F11	**Brook House** Denbgs
95	L8	**Brookhouse** Lancs
84	H3	**Brookhouse** Rothm
70	E2	**Brookhouse Green** Ches E
83	M7	**Brookhouses** Derbys
26	G6	**Brookland** Kent
82	G6	**Brooklands** Traffd
50	F10	**Brookmans Park** Herts
55	Q5	**Brooks** Powys
72	H7	**Brooksby** Leics
39	N8	**Brooks End** Kent
24	D6	**Brooks Green** W Susx
37	N2	**Brook Street** Essex
26	F5	**Brook Street** Kent
52	D2	**Brook Street** Suffk
24	H5	**Brook Street** W Susx
32	F2	**Brookthorpe** Gloucs
75	P11	**Brookville** Norfk
23	Q3	**Brookwood** Surrey
50	E2	**Broom** C Beds
84	F2	**Broom** Rothm
47	L4	**Broom** Warwks
65	M3	**Broome** Norfk
56	G8	**Broome** Shrops
58	D9	**Broome** Worcs
82	F7	**Broomedge** Warrtn
119	M8	**Broome Park** Nthumb
24	D6	**Broomer's Corner** W Susx
24	C7	**Broomershill** W Susx
52	B9	**Broomfield** Essex
38	D11	**Broomfield** Kent
39	L8	**Broomfield** Kent
18	H8	**Broomfield** Somset
69	M11	**Broomfields** Shrops
92	E5	**Broomfleet** E R Yk
76	D7	**Broom Green** Norfk
35	Q11	**Broomhall** W & M
112	F8	**Broomhaugh** Nthumb
91	L10	**Broom Hill** Barns
12	H4	**Broom Hill** Dorset
84	H11	**Broom Hill** Notts
119	P10	**Broomhill** Nthumb
58	D9	**Broom Hill** Worcs
70	A5	**Broomhill Green** Ches E
112	F8	**Bromley** Nthumb
103	P2	**Broompark** Dur
46	D8	**Broom's Green** Gloucs
76	A6	**Broomsthorpe** Norfk
38	H9	**Broom Street** Kent
163	L6	**Brora** Highld
57	M4	**Broseley** Shrops
74	E8	**Brotherhouse Bar** Lincs
102	H3	**Brotherlee** Dur
87	J11	**Brothertoft** Lincs
91	M5	**Brotherton** N York
105	J7	**Brotton** R & Cl
166	H5	**Broubster** Highld
102	E8	**Brough** Cumb
83	Q8	**Brough** Derbys
92	F5	**Brough** E R Yk
167	M2	**Brough** Highld
85	P9	**Brough** Notts
169	s7	**Brough** Shet
69	Q6	**Broughall** Shrops
169	s4	**Brough Lodge** Shet
102	E8	**Brough Sowerby** Cumb
116	G3	**Broughton** Border
35	M2	**Broughton** Bucks
62	C5	**Broughton** Cambs
69	K2	**Broughton** Flints
22	B8	**Broughton** Hants
88	G4	**Broughton** Lancs
49	N7	**Broughton** M Keyn
92	G9	**Broughton** N Linc
96	D10	**Broughton** N York
98	F6	**Broughton** N York
60	H5	**Broughton** Nhants
48	D7	**Broughton** Oxon
82	H4	**Broughton** Salfd
70	D8	**Broughton** Staffs
29	P10	**Broughton** V Glam
60	B2	**Broughton Astley** Leics
94	F4	**Broughton Beck** Cumb
20	G2	**Broughton Gifford** Wilts
47	J2	**Broughton Green** Worcs
46	H4	**Broughton Hackett** Worcs
94	E3	**Broughton-in-Furness** Cumb
107	N8	**Broughton Mains** D & G
94	E2	**Broughton Mills** Cumb
100	E4	**Broughton Moor** Cumb
33	P4	**Broughton Poggs** Oxon
94	E3	**Broughton Tower** Cumb
142	H11	**Broughty Ferry** C Dund
94	F6	**Brow End** Cumb
102	D9	**Brownber** Cumb
22	G7	**Brown Candover** Hants
88	D8	**Brown Edge** Lancs
70	G4	**Brown Edge** Staffs
69	N2	**Brown Heath** Ches W
69	N9	**Brownheath** Shrops
159	L9	**Brownhill** Abers
135	N4	**Brownhills** Fife
58	F3	**Brownhills** Wsall
119	N6	**Brownieside** Nthumb
22	G3	**Browninghill Green** Hants
70	F3	**Brown Lees** Staffs
70	E2	**Brownlow Heath** Ches E
100	D6	**Brownrigg** Cumb
110	C10	**Brownrigg** Cumb
12	H7	**Brownsea Island** Dorset
58	G6	**Brown's Green** Birm
16	D6	**Brownsham** Devon
32	G4	**Browns Hill** Gloucs
60	B5	**Brownsover** Warwks
6	H8	**Brownston** Devon
64	F9	**Brown Street** Suffk
75	N7	**Brow-of-the-Hill** Norfk
77	P11	**Browston Green** Norfk
99	J2	**Broxa** N York
51	J9	**Broxbourne** Herts
128	H4	**Broxburn** E Loth
127	K3	**Broxburn** W Loth
119	P7	**Broxfield** Nthumb
51	N5	**Broxted** Essex
69	N4	**Broxton** Ches W
25	L8	**Broyle Side** E Susx
167	P9	**Bruan** Highld
141	K4	**Bruar** P & K
163	K8	**Brucefield** Highld
124	E6	**Bruchag** Ag & B
69	M2	**Bruera** Ches W
47	Q10	**Bruern Abbey** Oxon
122	C7	**Bruichladdich** Ag & B
65	L8	**Bruisyard** Suffk
65	L8	**Bruisyard Street** Suffk
92	E9	**Brumby** N Linc
71	L2	**Brund** Staffs
77	L10	**Brundall** Norfk
65	K8	**Brundish** Suffk
65	K7	**Brundish Street** Suffk
138	C3	**Brunery** Highld
2	E6	**Brunnion** Cnwll
56	F8	**Brunslow** Shrops
113	K6	**Brunswick Village** N u Ty
90	H5	**Bruntcliffe** Leeds
96	G11	**Brunthwaite** C Brad
60	D3	**Bruntingthorpe** Leics
135	J3	**Brunton** Fife
119	P6	**Brunton** Nthumb
21	P3	**Brunton** Wilts
17	M10	**Brushford** Devon
18	B9	**Brushford** Somset
20	C7	**Bruton** Somset
58	C11	**Bryan's Green** Worcs
12	E3	**Bryanston** Dorset
35	N5	**Bryant's Bottom** Bucks
110	C6	**Brydekirk** D & G
2	b2	**Bryher** IoS
69	J4	**Brymbo** Wrexhm
19	P11	**Brympton** Somset
28	F4	**Bryn** Carmth
82	D10	**Bryn** Ches W
29	M6	**Bryn** Neath
56	D7	**Bryn** Shrops
82	C4	**Bryn** Wigan
29	K2	**Brynamman** Carmth
41	M3	**Brynberian** Pembks
29	L6	**Brynbryddan** Neath
67	L7	**Bryn-bwbach** Gwynd
30	C8	**Bryncae** Rhondd
29	P8	**Bryncethin** Brdgnd
66	H6	**Bryncir** Gwynd
29	K5	**Bryn-coch** Neath
66	C8	**Bryncroes** Gwynd
54	E4	**Bryncrug** Gwynd
78	E10	**Bryn Du** IoA
67	N9	**Bryn-Eden** Gwynd
68	F5	**Bryneglwys** Denbgs
69	K6	**Brynfields** Wrexhm
80	H10	**Brynford** Flints
82	C4	**Bryn Gates** Wigan
30	D7	**Bryn Golau** Rhondd
78	F9	**Bryngwran** IoA
31	L3	**Bryngwyn** Mons
44	H5	**Bryngwyn** Powys
41	K3	**Bryn-Henllan** Pembks
42	F4	**Brynhoffnant** Cerdgn
88	E5	**Bryning** Lancs
30	H4	**Brynithel** Blae G
30	G2	**Brynmawr** Blae G
66	C8	**Bryn-mawr** Gwynd
29	P8	**Brynmenyn** Brdgnd
28	H6	**Brynmill** Swans
30	C8	**Brynna** Rhondd
55	Q4	**Bryn-penarth** Powys
67	K2	**Brynrefail** Gwynd
78	H7	**Brynrefail** IoA
30	D8	**Brynsadler** Rhondd
68	E4	**Bryn Saith Marchog** Denbgs
78	H11	**Brynsiencyn** IoA
78	H8	**Brynteg** IoA
69	J2	**Bryn-y-bal** Flints
79	Q9	**Bryn-y-Maen** Conwy
69	J6	**Bryn-yr-Eos** Wrexhm
144	F3	**Bualintur** Highld
80	H9	**Buarth-draw** Flints
59	N10	**Bubbenhall** Warwks
92	B3	**Bubwith** E R Yk
117	L8	**Buccleuch** Border
132	F10	**Buchanan Smithy** Stirlg
159	R8	**Buchanhaven** Abers
133	Q2	**Buchanty** P & K
133	L7	**Buchany** Stirlg
132	H9	**Buchlyvie** Stirlg
110	G11	**Buckabank** Cumb
61	Q7	**Buckden** Cambs
96	D5	**Buckden** N York
77	M10	**Buckenham** Norfk
10	C4	**Buckerell** Devon
7	J5	**Buckfast** Devon
7	J5	**Buckfastleigh** Devon
135	K8	**Buckhaven** Fife
45	Q11	**Buckholt** Mons
5	P2	**Buckhorn** Devon
20	E10	**Buckhorn Weston** Dorset
37	K2	**Buckhurst Hill** Essex
158	B4	**Buckie** Moray
49	J8	**Buckingham** Bucks
35	N2	**Buckland** Bucks
6	H10	**Buckland** Devon
47	L7	**Buckland** Gloucs
13	P5	**Buckland** Hants
51	J4	**Buckland** Herts
27	P3	**Buckland** Kent
34	B5	**Buckland** Oxon
36	F10	**Buckland** Surrey
16	G2	**Buckland Brewer** Devon
35	P3	**Buckland Common** Bucks
20	E4	**Buckland Dinham** Somset
16	H10	**Buckland Filleigh** Devon
7	J4	**Buckland in the Moor** Devon
6	D5	**Buckland Monachorum** Devon
11	P3	**Buckland Newton** Dorset
11	P3	**Buckland Ripers** Dorset
10	F2	**Buckland St Mary** Somset
7	K9	**Buckland-Tout-Saints** Devon
34	G10	**Bucklebury** W Berk
14	D6	**Bucklers Hard** Hants
53	M3	**Bucklesham** Suffk
69	J2	**Buckley** Flints
59	J11	**Buckley Green** Warwks
82	F8	**Bucklow Hill** Ches E
73	M6	**Buckminster** Leics
70	G5	**Bucknall** C Stke
86	G7	**Bucknall** Lincs
48	G9	**Bucknell** Oxon
56	F10	**Bucknell** Shrops
158	B4	**Buckpool** Moray
151	M6	**Bucksburn** C Aber
16	F7	**Buck's Cross** Devon
24	C4	**Bucks Green** W Susx
88	H6	**Buckshaw Village** Lancs
50	C10	**Bucks Hill** Herts
23	M6	**Bucks Horn Oak** Hants
16	F7	**Buck's Mills** Devon
99	P6	**Buckton** E R Yk
56	F10	**Buckton** Herefs
119	L3	**Buckton** Nthumb
61	P5	**Buckworth** Cambs
85	K7	**Budby** Notts
70	C5	**Buddileigh** Staffs
16	C10	**Bude** Cnwll
5	N10	**Budge's Shop** Cnwll
9	N4	**Budlake** Devon
119	N3	**Budle** Nthumb
9	Q8	**Budleigh Salterton** Devon
25	L6	**Budlett's Common** E Susx
3	K7	**Budock Water** Cnwll
70	B6	**Buerton** Ches E
60	E9	**Bugbrooke** Nhants
7	L8	**Bugford** Devon
70	F2	**Buglawton** Ches E
4	G10	**Bugle** Cnwll
20	E10	**Bugley** Dorset
98	F9	**Bugthorpe** E R Yk
57	L4	**Buildwas** Shrops
44	E4	**Builth Road** Powys
44	E4	**Builth Wells** Powys
35	P2	**Bulbourne** Herts
21	L8	**Bulbridge** Wilts
73	R5	**Bulby** Lincs
21	N6	**Bulford** Wilts
21	N6	**Bulford Camp** Wilts
69	P4	**Bulkeley** Ches E
59	N7	**Bulkington** Warwks
20	H3	**Bulkington** Wilts
16	F9	**Bulkworthy** Devon
97	N2	**Bullamoor** N York
78	G6	**Bull Bay** IoA
84	E10	**Bullbridge** Derbys
35	N11	**Bullbrook** Br For
50	F9	**Bullen's Green** Herts
46	E11	**Bulley** Gloucs
100	E3	**Bullgill** Cumb
45	Q7	**Bullinghope** Herefs
22	E6	**Bullington** Hants
86	E5	**Bullington** Lincs
39	L8	**Bullockstone** Kent
65	M3	**Bull's Green** Herts
65	N3	**Bull's Green** Norfk
52	D3	**Bulmer** Essex
98	D7	**Bulmer** N York
52	D4	**Bulmer Tye** Essex
37	P3	**Bulphan** Thurr
10	D7	**Bulstone** Devon
50	B10	**Bulstrode** Herts
26	C10	**Bulverhythe** E Susx
159	M8	**Bulwark** Abers
72	E2	**Bulwell** C Nott
61	L2	**Bulwick** Nhants
51	K9	**Bumble's Green** Essex
145	L10	**Bunacaimb** Highld
146	F10	**Bunarkaig** Highld
69	Q3	**Bunbury** Ches E
69	Q3	**Bunbury Heath** Ches E
155	R8	**Bunchrew** Highld
24	D8	**Buncton** W Susx
145	Q2	**Bundalloch** Highld
137	K11	**Bunessan** Ag & B
65	L4	**Bungay** Suffk
87	J10	**Bunker's Hill** Lincs
122	F5	**Bunnahabhain** Ag & B
72	F5	**Bunny** Notts
155	M11	**Buntait** Highld
51	J5	**Buntingford** Herts
64	G3	**Bunwell** Norfk
64	G3	**Bunwell Hill** Norfk
71	N7	**Bupton** Derbys
83	M10	**Burbage** Derbys
59	P6	**Burbage** Leics
21	P2	**Burbage** Wilts
45	L2	**Burcher** Herefs
25	L9	**Burchett's Green** E Susx
35	M8	**Burchett's Green** W & M
21	L8	**Burcombe** Wilts
34	G5	**Burcot** Oxon
58	E10	**Burcot** Worcs
57	N5	**Burcote** Shrops
49	M11	**Burcott** Bucks
49	N10	**Burcott** Bucks
98	H8	**Burdale** N York
52	F5	**Bures** Essex
33	Q2	**Burford** Oxon
57	K11	**Burford** Shrops
137	K6	**Burg** Ag & B
64	F6	**Burgate** Suffk
23	L9	**Burgates** Hants
50	D4	**Burge End** Herts
24	H7	**Burgess Hill** W Susx
65	J11	**Burgh** Suffk
110	F9	**Burgh by Sands** Cumb
77	P10	**Burgh Castle** Norfk
22	E2	**Burghclere** Hants
157	L4	**Burghead** Moray
35	J11	**Burghfield** W Berk
35	J11	**Burghfield Common** W Berk
36	F9	**Burgh Heath** Surrey
25	B6	**Burgh Hill** E Susx
45	N6	**Burghill** Herefs
6	G10	**Burgh Island** Devon
87	P7	**Burgh le Marsh** Lincs
77	J6	**Burgh next Aylsham** Norfk
86	H3	**Burgh on Bain** Lincs
77	N9	**Burgh St Margaret** Norfk
65	P3	**Burgh St Peter** Norfk
91	M4	**Burghwallis** Donc
38	B9	**Burham** Kent
23	K11	**Buriton** Hants
69	R4	**Burland** Ches E
4	F7	**Burlawn** Cnwll
32	G4	**Burleigh** Gloucs
18	E11	**Burlescombe** Devon
12	C6	**Burleston** Dorset
7	L9	**Burlestone** Devon
13	M4	**Burley** Hants
73	M8	**Burley** Rutlnd
56	H8	**Burley** Shrops
59	R6	**Burleydam** Ches E
46	A5	**Burley Gate** Herefs
97	J11	**Burley in Wharfedale** C Brad
13	M4	**Burley Lawn** Hants
13	M4	**Burley Street** Hants
90	F2	**Burley Wood Head** C Brad
77	M9	**Burlingham Green** Norfk
45	K3	**Burlingjobb** Powys
57	P2	**Burlington** Shrops
69	N9	**Burlton** Shrops
27	K5	**Burmarsh** Kent
47	Q7	**Burmington** Warwks
91	P5	**Burn** N York
83	J6	**Burnage** Manch
71	P8	**Burnaston** Derbys
101	P7	**Burnbanks** Cumb
126	F6	**Burnbrae** N Lans
98	G11	**Burnby** E R Yk
91	J11	**Burn Cross** Sheff
15	Q6	**Burndell** W Susx
89	L9	**Burnden** Bolton
89	Q8	**Burnedge** Rochdl
101	P11	**Burneside** Cumb
97	M4	**Burneston** N York
32	C11	**Burnett** BaNES
117	N8	**Burnfoot** Border
117	Q7	**Burnfoot** Border
109	L2	**Burnfoot** D & G
110	F3	**Burnfoot** D & G
117	M11	**Burnfoot** D & G
134	B7	**Burnfoot** P & K
35	P8	**Burnham** Bucks
93	J7	**Burnham** N Linc
75	R2	**Burnham Deepdale** Norfk
50	G7	**Burnham Green** Herts
76	A3	**Burnham Market** Norfk
76	A3	**Burnham Norton** Norfk
38	F2	**Burnham-on-Crouch** Essex
19	K5	**Burnham-on-Sea** Somset
76	A3	**Burnham Overy** Norfk
76	A3	**Burnham Overy Staithe** Norfk
76	B3	**Burnham Thorpe** Norfk
159	R9	**Burnhaven** Abers
116	B11	**Burnhead** D & G
151	J4	**Burnhervie** Abers
57	P4	**Burnhill Green** Staffs
113	J11	**Burnhope** Dur
125	K7	**Burnhouse** N Ayrs
99	L2	**Burniston** N York
89	N4	**Burnley** Lancs
89	N4	**Burnley Crematorium** Lancs
129	P7	**Burnmouth** Border
88	C2	**Burn Naze** Lancs
133	L7	**Burn of Cambus** Stirlg
113	L7	**Burnopfield** Dur
111	J9	**Burnrigg** Cumb
96	F8	**Burnsall** N York
142	G6	**Burnside** Angus
143	J7	**Burnside** Angus
134	F6	**Burnside** Fife
157	M4	**Burnside** Moray
127	K2	**Burnside** W Loth
142	G11	**Burnside of Duntrune** Angus
36	B10	**Burntcommon** Surrey
71	N8	**Burntheath** Derbys
53	J6	**Burnt Heath** Essex
34	G10	**Burnt Hill** W Berk
3	K6	**Burnthouse** Cnwll
103	M6	**Burnt Houses** Dur
134	G10	**Burntisland** Fife
25	M5	**Burnt Oak** E Susx
58	G3	**Burntwood** Staffs
58	G3	**Burntwood Green** Staffs
97	L8	**Burnt Yates** N York
18	G11	**Burnworthy** Somset
36	B10	**Burpham** Surrey
24	B9	**Burpham** W Susx
113	L6	**Burradon** N Tyne
119	J9	**Burradon** Nthumb
169	t2	**Burrafirth** Shet
2	H7	**Burras** Cnwll
5	Q8	**Burraton** Cnwll
169	s5	**Burravoe** Shet
102	C7	**Burrells** Cumb
142	C10	**Burrelton** P & K
10	G3	**Burridge** Devon
17	K4	**Burridge** Devon
14	F4	**Burridge** Hants
97	K3	**Burrill** N York
92	D9	**Burringham** N Linc
17	L8	**Burrington** Devon
56	G10	**Burrington** Herefs
19	N3	**Burrington** N Som
63	K9	**Burrough End** Cambs
63	K9	**Burrough Green** Cambs
73	K8	**Burrough on the Hill** Leics
95	N6	**Burrow** Lancs
18	B6	**Burrow** Somset
19	L8	**Burrow Bridge** Somset
23	Q2	**Burrowhill** Surrey
36	C11	**Burrows Cross** Surrey
28	E6	**Burry** Swans
28	D4	**Burry Green** Swans
28	D4	**Burry Port** Carmth
88	E8	**Burscough** Lancs
88	E8	**Burscough Bridge** Lancs
92	D4	**Bursea** E R Yk
99	M11	**Burshill** E R Yk
14	E5	**Bursledon** Hants
70	F5	**Burslem** C Stke
53	J3	**Burstall** Suffk
11	J4	**Burstock** Dorset
64	G5	**Burston** Norfk
70	G8	**Burston** Staffs
24	H2	**Burstow** Surrey
93	M5	**Burstwick** E R Yk
96	C3	**Burtersett** N York
111	K8	**Burtholme** Cumb
63	N8	**Burthorpe Green** Suffk
110	H11	**Burthwaite** Cumb
4	E10	**Burthy** Cnwll
19	L6	**Burtle** Somset
74	E3	**Burtoft** Lincs
69	R4	**Burton** Ches W
81	L10	**Burton** Ches W
11	P6	**Burton** Dorset
13	L6	**Burton** Dorset
86	C6	**Burton** Lincs
119	N4	**Burton** Nthumb
41	J9	**Burton** Pembks
11	L2	**Burton** Somset
18	G6	**Burton** Somset
20	F8	**Burton** Wilts
32	F9	**Burton** Wilts
99	N8	**Burton Agnes** E R Yk
11	K7	**Burton Bradstock** Dorset
73	P5	**Burton Coggles** Lincs
93	L3	**Burton Constable Hall** E R Yk
48	C4	**Burton Dassett** Warwks
51	M6	**Burton End** Essex
63	L11	**Burton End** Suffk
99	M6	**Burton Fleming** E R Yk
59	L9	**Burton Green** Warwks
69	K3	**Burton Green** Wrexhm
59	P7	**Burton Hastings** Warwks
95	L5	**Burton-in-Kendal** Cumb
95	L5	**Burton-in-Kendal Services** Cumb
95	P6	**Burton in Lonsdale** N York
72	G2	**Burton Joyce** Notts
61	K6	**Burton Latimer** Nhants
73	K7	**Burton Lazars** Leics
97	M8	**Burton Leonard** N York
72	F6	**Burton on the Wolds** Leics
72	H11	**Burton Overy** Leics
74	B2	**Burton Pedwardine** Lincs
93	M4	**Burton Pidsea** E R Yk
91	M5	**Burton Salmon** N York
52	D6	**Burton's Green** Essex
92	E7	**Burton upon Stather** N Linc
71	N10	**Burton upon Trent** Staffs
86	B6	**Burton Waters** Lincs
82	C6	**Burtonwood** Warrtn
82	C6	**Burtonwood Services** Warrtn
69	P3	**Burwardsley** Ches W
57	L7	**Burwarton** Shrops
25	Q6	**Burwash** E Susx
25	P6	**Burwash Common** E Susx
25	Q6	**Burwash Weald** E Susx
63	J7	**Burwell** Cambs
87	L5	**Burwell** Lincs
78	G6	**Burwen** IoA
169	d8	**Burwick** Ork
89	N8	**Bury** Bury
62	C4	**Bury** Cambs
18	B9	**Bury** Somset
24	B8	**Bury** W Susx
50	D3	**Bury End** C Beds
51	L6	**Bury Green** Herts
64	B9	**Bury St Edmunds** Suffk
98	F7	**Burythorpe** N York
125	P6	**Busby** E Rens
97	N4	**Busby Stoop** N York
33	P5	**Buscot** Oxon
143	P4	**Bush** Abers
16	C10	**Bush** Cnwll
45	P4	**Bush Bank** Herefs
58	D4	**Bushbury** Wolves
58	D4	**Bushbury Crematorium** Wolves
72	H10	**Bushby** Leics
50	D11	**Bushey** Herts
36	C10	**Bushey Heath** Herts
65	J4	**Bush Green** Norfk
64	C10	**Bush Green** Suffk
50	H11	**Bush Hill Park** Gt Lon
46	E8	**Bushley** Worcs
46	E8	**Bushley Green** Worcs
61	P8	**Bushmead** Bed
56	G7	**Bushmoor** Shrops
33	L9	**Bushton** Wilts
102	B2	**Busk** Cumb
86	E3	**Buslingthorpe** Lincs
32	G4	**Bussage** Gloucs
19	L7	**Bussex** Somset
25	N5	**Butcher's Cross** E Susx
19	P2	**Butcombe** N Som
124	F4	**Bute** Ag & B
19	P8	**Butleigh** Somset
19	P7	**Butleigh Wootton** Somset
35	M3	**Butler's Cross** Bucks
84	H11	**Butler's Hill** Notts
48	B4	**Butlers Marston** Warwks
65	M11	**Butley** Suffk
53	Q2	**Butley High Corner** Suffk
98	E9	**Buttercrambe** N York
129	K2	**Butterdean** Border
103	M5	**Butterknowle** Dur
9	N3	**Butterleigh** Devon
84	F10	**Butterley** Derbys
100	G7	**Buttermere** Cumb
22	B2	**Buttermere** Wilts
70	E4	**Butters Green** Staffs
90	E5	**Buttershaw** C Brad
141	Q8	**Butterstone** P & K
70	E6	**Butterton** Staffs
71	K3	**Butterton** Staffs
104	C4	**Butterwick** Dur
87	L11	**Butterwick** Lincs
98	E5	**Butterwick** N York
99	K6	**Butterwick** N York
70	B4	**Butt Green** Ches E
56	C3	**Buttington** Powys
57	M9	**Buttonbridge** Shrops
57	P9	**Buttonoak** Shrops
14	D5	**Buttsash** Hants
16	D11	**Buttsbear Cross** Cnwll
52	C11	**Butt's Green** Essex
64	E10	**Buxhall** Suffk
64	E10	**Buxhall Fen Street** Suffk
25	L6	**Buxted** E Susx
83	N10	**Buxton** Derbys
77	J7	**Buxton** Norfk
76	H7	**Buxton Heath** Norfk
44	H10	**Bwlch** Powys
69	J4	**Bwlchgwyn** Wrexhm
43	L3	**Bwlchllan** Cerdgn
42	G10	**Bwlchnewydd** Carmth
66	E9	**Bwlchtocyn** Gwynd
68	G11	**Bwlch-y-cibau** Powys
68	G10	**Bwlch-y-Ddar** Powys
42	H5	**Bwlchyfadfa** Cerdgn
55	P5	**Bwlch-y-ffridd** Powys
41	P3	**Bwlch-y-groes** Pembks
28	G5	**Bwlchymyrdd** Swans
55	N10	**Bwlch-y-sarnau** Powys
113	J9	**Byermoor** Gatesd
103	P4	**Byers Green** Dur
48	F4	**Byfield** Nhants
36	C8	**Byfleet** Surrey
45	M6	**Byford** Herefs
50	G3	**Bygrave** Herts

268 Byker - Causewayhead

113 L8 Byker N u Ty
98 A5 Byland Abbey N York
68 C2 Bylchau Conwy
82 F11 Byley Ches W
28 F5 Bynea Carmth
118 E10 Byrness Nthumb
9 P8 Bystock Devon
61 N5 Bythorn Cambs
45 M2 Byton Herefs
112 F8 Bywell Nthumb
23 Q10 Byworth W Susx

C

16 G7 Cabbacott Devon
93 K10 Cabourne Lincs
122 G7 Cabrach Ag & B
150 B2 Cabrach Moray
95 K11 Cabus Lancs
25 L5 Cackle Street E Susx
25 Q7 Cackle Street E Susx
26 D8 Cackle Street E Susx
9 M3 Cadbury Devon
17 M8 Cadbury Barton Devon
125 Q3 Cadder E Duns
50 C7 Caddington C Beds
117 P3 Caddonfoot Border
91 N10 Cadeby Donc
72 C10 Cadeby Leics
9 M3 Cadeleigh Devon
25 P6 Cade Street E Susx
3 J11 Cadgwith Cnwll
134 H7 Cadham Fife
82 F6 Cadishead Salfd
28 H5 Cadle Swans
88 G4 Cadley Lancs
21 P4 Cadley Wilts
33 P11 Cadley Wilts
35 L6 Cadmore End Bucks
13 P2 Cadnam Hants
92 H10 Cadney N Linc
68 H2 Cadole Flints
30 F11 Cadoxton V Glam
29 L5 Cadoxton Juxta-Neath Neath
68 D7 Cadwst Denbgs
67 J2 Caeathro Gwynd
29 M2 Caehopkin Powys
86 C3 Caenby Lincs
43 N6 Caeo Carmth
29 N6 Caerau Brdgnd
30 F9 Caerau Cardif
29 M2 Cae'r-bont Powys
28 G2 Cae'r bryn Carmth
67 M11 Caerdeon Gwynd
40 E5 Caer Farchell Pembks
78 E9 Caergeiliog IoA
69 K3 Caergwrle Flints
79 P10 Caerhun Conwy
117 M10 Caerlanrig Border
31 K6 Caerleon Newpt
31 K6 Caerleon Roman Amphitheatre Newpt
66 H2 Caernarfon Gwynd
66 H2 Caernarfon Castle Gwynd
30 G7 Caerphilly Caerph
55 N6 Caersws Powys
42 G3 Caerwedros Cerdgn
31 N6 Caerwent Mons
80 G10 Caerwys Flints
67 P11 Caerynwch Gwynd
45 M11 Caggle Street Mons
79 L8 Caim IoA
168 d11 Cairinis W Isls
130 G9 Cairnbaan Ag & B
159 P4 Cairnbulg Abers
129 M7 Cairncross Border
125 J3 Cairncurran Inver
131 P5 Cairndow Ag & B
134 C10 Cairneyhill Fife
106 E8 Cairngarroch D & G
149 K7 Cairngorms National Park
158 C9 Cairnie Abers
159 L9 Cairnorrie Abers
106 E3 Cairnryan D & G
157 Q7 Cairnty Moray
77 Q9 Caister-on-Sea Norfk
93 K10 Caistor Lincs
77 J11 Caistor St Edmund Norfk
58 C10 Cakebole Worcs
64 F3 Cake Street Norfk
52 G4 Calais Street Suffk
168 h4 Calanais W Isls
14 D9 Calbourne IoW
87 L5 Calceby Lincs
80 H10 Calcot Flints
33 L2 Calcot Gloucs
35 J10 Calcot W Berk
35 J10 Calcot Row W Berk
157 P5 Calcots Moray
39 L9 Calcott Kent
56 G2 Calcott Shrops
97 M9 Calcutt N York
33 M6 Calcutt Wilts
101 K2 Caldbeck Cumb
96 G3 Caldbergh N York
61 P3 Caldecote Cambs
62 D9 Caldecote Cambs
50 F3 Caldecote Herts
49 J4 Caldecote Nhants
62 E9 Caldecote Highfields Cambs
61 L7 Caldecott Nhants
34 E5 Caldecott Oxon
61 J2 Caldecott Rutlnd
49 N7 Caldecotte M Keyn
100 D10 Calder Cumb
126 D5 Calderbank N Lans
100 D9 Calder Bridge Cumb
89 Q7 Calderbrook Rochdl
126 E4 Caldercruix N Lans
91 J7 Calder Grove Wakefd
126 B9 Caldermill S Lans
89 Q7 Caldermore Rochdl
95 L11 Calder Vale Lancs
126 B6 Calderwood S Lans
41 M11 Caldey Island Pembks
31 N7 Caldicot Mons
58 F5 Caldmore Wsall
103 N8 Caldwell N York
81 J7 Caldy Wirral
43 N9 Caledfwlch Carmth
3 L5 Calenick Cnwll
80 a8 Calf of Man IoM
63 M11 Calford Green Suffk
169 e3 Calfsound Ork
137 K5 Calgary Ag & B
157 K6 Califer Moray
126 G2 California Falk
77 Q8 California Norfk
7 J8 California Cross Devon
72 B6 Calke Derbys
153 M6 Callakille Highld
133 J6 Callander Stirlg
168 h4 Callanish W Isls
57 L5 Callaughton Shrops
3 K3 Callestick Cnwll
145 K7 Calligarry Highld
5 P8 Callington Cnwll
71 M10 Callingwood Staffs
45 P8 Callow Herefs
46 F4 Callow End Worcs
33 K8 Callow Hill Wilts
47 K2 Callow Hill Worcs
57 N10 Callow Hill Worcs
57 K11 Callows Grave Worcs
13 P2 Calmore Hants
33 K3 Calmsden Gloucs
33 J10 Calne Wilts
84 F6 Calow Derbys
14 E6 Calshot Hants
6 C5 Calstock Cnwll
33 K11 Calstone Wellington Wilts
76 H5 Calthorpe Norfk
77 N6 Calthorpe Street Norfk
101 N2 Calthwaite Cumb
96 D9 Calton N York
71 L5 Calton Staffs
69 Q3 Calveley Ches E
84 B6 Calver Derbys
69 R7 Calverhall Shrops
45 M5 Calver Hill Herefs
9 M2 Calverleigh Devon
90 G3 Calverley Leeds
84 B6 Calver Sough Derbys
49 J10 Calvert Bucks
49 L7 Calverton M Keyn
85 K11 Calverton Notts
141 K4 Calvine P & K
109 P10 Calvo Cumb
116 G3 Calzeat Border
32 E5 Cam Gloucs
138 D5 Camasachoirce Highld
138 D5 Camasine Highld
146 A2 Camas Luinie Highld
153 J10 Camastianavaig Highld
155 P9 Camault Muir Highld
26 G8 Camber E Susx
23 N2 Camberley Surrey
36 H5 Camberwell Gt Lon
91 Q5 Camblesforth N York
112 F3 Cambo Nthumb
113 M4 Cambois Nthumb
2 G5 Camborne Cnwll
62 D9 Cambourne Cambs
62 G9 Cambridge Cambs
32 D4 Cambridge Gloucs
62 G9 Cambridge Airport Cambs
62 E8 Cambridge City Crematorium Cambs
2 H4 Cambrose Cnwll
133 P9 Cambus Clacks
162 H7 Cambusavie Platform Highld
133 M9 Cambusbarron Stirlg
133 N9 Cambuskenneth Stirlg
125 Q5 Cambuslang S Lans
150 C8 Cambus o' May Abers
116 E3 Cambuswallace S Lans
36 G4 Camden Town Gt Lon
20 B3 Cameley BaNES
5 J5 Camelford Cnwll
133 P11 Camelon Falk
157 J11 Camerory Highld
46 E7 Camer's Green Worcs
20 C3 Camerton BaNES
100 D4 Camerton Cumb
140 E6 Camghouran P & K
117 R4 Camieston Border
151 N8 Cammachmore Abers
86 B4 Cammeringham Lincs
162 H9 Camore Highld
120 D7 Campbeltown Ag & B
120 C7 Campbeltown Airport Ag & B
113 L6 Camperdown N Tyne
109 J2 Cample D & G
142 C10 Campmuir P & K
127 K4 Camps W Loth
91 N8 Campsall Donc
65 L10 Campsea Ash Suffk
51 P2 Camps End Cambs
50 D3 Campton C Beds
118 C8 Camptown Border
40 H6 Camrose Pembks
141 K8 Camserney P & K
139 K3 Camusnagaul Highld
160 H9 Camusnagaul Highld
153 N9 Camusteel Highld
153 N9 Camusterrach Highld
21 Q11 Canada Hants
94 G5 Canal Foot Cumb
41 L7 Canaston Bridge Pembks
149 Q8 Candacraig Abers
87 N7 Candlesby Lincs
64 E7 Candle Street Suffk
57 J3 Candover Green Shrops
116 F2 Candy Mill Border
35 J9 Cane End Oxon
38 F3 Canewdon Essex
12 H4 Canford Bottom Dorset
13 J7 Canford Cliffs Poole
31 Q9 Canford Crematorium Bristl
12 H6 Canford Heath Poole
12 H5 Canford Magna Poole
64 F8 Canhams Green Suffk
167 P2 Canisbay Highld
84 F2 Canklow Rothm
59 M9 Canley Covtry
59 M9 Canley Crematorium Covtry
20 G10 Cann Dorset
144 B6 Canna Highld
155 K11 Cannich Highld
19 J7 Cannington Somset
37 K4 Canning Town Gt Lon
58 E2 Cannock Staffs
70 H11 Cannock Chase Staffs
58 F2 Cannock Wood Staffs
45 N6 Cannon Bridge Herefs
110 G5 Canonbie D & G
46 B6 Canon Frome Herefs
45 P5 Canon Pyon Herefs
48 G4 Canons Ashby Nhants
2 E6 Canonstown Cnwll
39 K10 Canterbury Kent
39 L10 Canterbury Cathedral Kent
77 M11 Cantley Norfk
57 J3 Cantlop Shrops
30 G9 Canton Cardif
156 D8 Cantraywood Highld
95 N6 Cantsfield Lancs
38 C5 Canvey Island Essex
86 C7 Canwick Lincs
5 L3 Canworthy Water Cnwll
139 L2 Caol Highld
168 h8 Caolas Scalpaigh W Isls
136 D6 Caoles Ag & B
146 D9 Caonich Highld
25 P2 Capel Kent
24 E2 Capel Surrey
54 F8 Capel Bangor Cerdgn
43 M3 Capel Betws Lleucu Cerdgn
78 H8 Capel Coch IoA
67 N3 Capel Curig Conwy
42 G5 Capel Cynon Cerdgn
43 J10 Capel Dewi Carmth
43 J6 Capel Dewi Cerdgn
54 E8 Capel-Dewi Cerdgn
67 Q3 Capel Garmon Conwy
53 Q2 Capel Green Suffk
43 J10 Capel Gwyn Carmth
78 E9 Capel Gwyn IoA
43 P10 Capel Gwynfe Carmth
28 G2 Capel Hendre Carmth
43 L9 Capel Isaac Carmth
41 Q3 Capel Iwan Carmth
27 N4 Capel le Ferne Kent
10 c1 Capelles Guern
30 E9 Capel Llanilltern Cardif
78 G10 Capel Mawr IoA
78 G7 Capel Parc IoA
53 Q2 Capel St Andrew Suffk
53 J4 Capel St Mary Suffk
54 E9 Capel Seion Cerdgn
54 G9 Capel Trisant Cerdgn
66 G5 Capeluchaf Gwynd
79 N9 Capelulo Conwy
45 K8 Capel-y-ffin Powys
79 J11 Capel-y-graig Gwynd
81 M10 Capenhurst Ches W
95 L6 Capernwray Lancs
112 F4 Capheaton Nthumb
125 L6 Caplaw E Rens
65 K8 Capon's Green Suffk
117 J6 Cappercleuch Border
38 C8 Capstone Medway
7 L8 Capton Devon
18 E7 Capton Somset
141 Q9 Caputh P & K
5 M7 Caradon Town Cnwll
125 N2 Carbeth Inn Stirlg
4 G10 Carbis Cnwll
2 E6 Carbis Bay Cnwll
152 F11 Carbost Highld
152 G8 Carbost Highld
84 E3 Carbrook Sheff
76 C11 Carbrooke Norfk
85 K6 Carburton Notts
3 Q3 Carclaze Cnwll
73 J2 Car Colston Notts
91 N9 Carcroft Donc
134 G8 Cardenden Fife
56 F2 Cardeston Shrops
110 G10 Cardewlees Cumb
157 M9 Cardhu Moray
30 G9 Cardiff Cardif
30 E11 Cardiff Airport V Glam
30 H8 Cardiff Gate Services Cardif
30 E9 Cardiff West Services Cardif
42 C5 Cardigan Cerdgn
63 K11 Cardinal's Green Cambs
61 N11 Cardington Bed
57 J5 Cardington Shrops
5 J8 Cardinham Cnwll
106 F11 Cardrain D & G
117 L3 Cardrona Border
125 J2 Cardross Ag & B
125 J2 Cardross Crematorium Ag & B
106 F11 Cardryne D & G
110 C9 Cardurnock Cumb
73 Q7 Careby Lincs
143 J5 Careston Angus
41 K10 Carew Pembks
41 K10 Carew Cheriton Pembks
41 K10 Carew Newton Pembks
45 R8 Carey Herefs
126 D6 Carfin N Lans
128 E9 Carfraemill Border
77 M9 Cargate Green Norfk
109 L5 Cargenbridge D & G
142 B10 Cargill P & K
110 G9 Cargo Cumb
6 C6 Cargreen Cnwll
3 M6 Cargurrel Cnwll
118 E3 Carham Nthumb
18 D6 Carhampton Somset
3 J5 Carharrack Cnwll
140 F6 Carie P & K
168 d11 Carinish W Isls
14 E9 Carisbrooke IoW
94 H5 Cark Cumb
5 Q3 Carkeel Cnwll
168 h3 Carlabhagh W Isls
3 M3 Carland Cross Cnwll
103 P7 Carlbury Darltn
73 Q8 Carlby Lincs
118 F8 Carlcroft Nthumb
83 Q4 Carlecotes Barns
2 G7 Carleen Cnwll
97 K6 Carlesmoor N York
100 D9 Carleton Cumb
101 P5 Carleton Cumb
110 H10 Carleton Cumb
88 C3 Carleton Lancs
96 E11 Carleton N York
91 M6 Carleton Wakefd
88 C3 Carleton Crematorium Bpool
76 F10 Carleton Forehoe Norfk
64 G3 Carleton Rode Norfk
77 L11 Carleton St Peter Norfk
3 K8 Carlidnack Cnwll
158 G9 Carlincraig Abers
20 C3 Carlingcott BaNES
105 K7 Carlin How R & Cl
110 G9 Carlisle Cumb
111 J8 Carlisle Airport Cumb
110 G10 Carlisle Crematorium Cumb
4 D8 Carloggas Cnwll
127 M6 Carlops Border
168 h3 Carloway W Isls
91 K8 Carlton Barns
61 L9 Carlton Bed
63 K10 Carlton Cambs
91 J5 Carlton Leeds
72 B10 Carlton Leics
91 Q6 Carlton N York
96 G4 Carlton N York
98 C3 Carlton N York
72 G2 Carlton Notts
104 C6 Carlton S on T
65 M9 Carlton Suffk
65 Q4 Carlton Colville Suffk
72 H11 Carlton Curlieu Leics
63 K10 Carlton Green Cambs
97 Q5 Carlton Husthwaite N York
104 F10 Carlton-in-Cleveland N York
85 J4 Carlton in Lindrick Notts
86 B9 Carlton-le-Moorland Lincs
97 N4 Carlton Miniott N York
85 N8 Carlton-on-Trent Notts
86 B11 Carlton Scroop Lincs
126 E7 Carluke S Lans
3 R3 Carlyon Bay Cnwll
115 Q2 Carmacoup S Lans
42 H10 Carmarthen Carmth
43 L11 Carmel Carmth
80 H9 Carmel Flints
66 H4 Carmel Gwynd
116 C3 Carmichael S Lans
70 G5 Carmountside Crematorium C Stke
125 P6 Carmunnock C Glas
125 Q5 Carmyle C Glas
143 J9 Carmyllie Angus
99 N7 Carnaby E R Yk
135 N6 Carnbee Fife
134 D7 Carnbo P & K
2 H5 Carn Brea Cnwll
151 M2 Carnbrogie Abers
145 Q2 Carndu Highld
126 B8 Carnduff S Lans
3 K6 Carne Cnwll
3 N6 Carne Cnwll
4 F10 Carne Cnwll
125 M11 Carnell E Ayrs
4 D8 Carnewas Cnwll
95 K6 Carnforth Lancs
146 B3 Carn-gorm Highld
40 F5 Carnhedryn Pembks
2 G6 Carnhell Green Cnwll
151 L6 Carnie Abers
2 H5 Carnkie Cnwll
3 J7 Carnkie Cnwll
3 K3 Carnkiet Cnwll
55 M5 Carno Powys
134 C10 Carnock Fife
3 K5 Carnon Downs Cnwll
158 G7 Carnousie Abers
143 K11 Carnoustie Angus
4 G10 Carnsmerry Cnwll
126 H8 Carnwath S Lans
2 B7 Carnyorth Cnwll
59 L9 Carol Green Solhll
3 P3 Carpalla Cnwll
96 F3 Carperby N York
84 H2 Carr Rothm
120 F4 Carradale Ag & B
148 G3 Carrbridge Highld
83 L4 Carrbrook Tamesd
11 b1 Carrefour Jersey
78 F7 Carreglefn IoA
91 J6 Carr Gate Wakefd
92 C9 Carrhouse N Linc
131 J10 Carrick Ag & B
131 P9 Carrick Castle Ag & B
134 C11 Carriden Falk
87 K9 Carrington Lincs
127 Q5 Carrington Mdloth
82 F6 Carrington Traffd
67 P5 Carrog Conwy
68 F6 Carrog Denbgs
133 P11 Carron Falk
157 N9 Carron Moray
116 B11 Carronbridge D & G
133 L11 Carron Bridge Stirlg
133 P11 Carronshore Falk
31 M6 Carrow Hill Mons
112 B11 Carr Shield Nthumb
109 P6 Carrutherstown D & G
125 K4 Carruth House Inver
84 G7 Carr Vale Derbys
104 B2 Carrville Dur
137 N11 Carsaig Ag & B
107 K4 Carseriggan D & G
109 L9 Carsethorn D & G
36 G8 Carshalton Gt Lon
71 P4 Carsington Derbys
120 C10 Carskey Ag & B
107 N7 Carsluith D & G
115 L9 Carsphairn D & G
126 G8 Carstairs S Lans
126 H8 Carstairs Junction S Lans
34 B5 Carswell Marsh Oxon
22 B10 Carter's Clay Hants
51 M8 Carters Green Essex
33 Q3 Carterton Oxon
112 F10 Carterway Heads Nthumb
4 G10 Carthew Cnwll
97 M4 Carthorpe N York
119 K10 Cartington Nthumb
126 F8 Cartland S Lans
84 D5 Cartledge Derbys
94 H5 Cartmel Cumb
95 J3 Cartmel Fell Cumb
28 E3 Carway Carmth
110 H6 Carwinley Cumb
32 F3 Cashe's Green Gloucs
12 G2 Cashmoor Dorset
34 E2 Cassington Oxon
104 B3 Cassop Colliery Dur
2 D8 Castallack Cnwll
10 b2 Castel Guern
79 P11 Castell Conwy
31 J6 Castell-y-bwch Torfn
95 N5 Casterton Cumb
4 H10 Castle Cnwll
75 R7 Castle Acre Norfk
61 J9 Castle Ashby Nhants
168 b18 Castlebay W Isls
96 F2 Castle Bolton N York
58 H7 Castle Bromwich Solhll
73 P7 Castle Bytham Lincs
41 K5 Castlebythe Pembks
56 B3 Castle Caereinion Powys
51 P2 Castle Camps Cambs
111 K9 Castle Carrock Cumb
126 D2 Castlecary Falk
20 B8 Castle Cary Somset
32 F9 Castle Combe Wilts
72 C5 Castle Donington Leics
108 G8 Castle Douglas D & G
33 M5 Castle Eaton Swindn
104 D3 Castle Eden Dur
74 B9 Castle End C Pete
91 L5 Castleford Wakefd
46 C5 Castle Frome Herefs
2 D7 Castle Gate Cnwll
95 L2 Castle Green Cumb
23 Q2 Castle Green Surrey
71 P11 Castle Gresley Derbys
52 C4 Castle Hedingham Essex
117 J3 Castlehill Border
167 L3 Castlehill Highld
25 Q2 Castle Hill Kent
53 K2 Castle Hill Suffk
125 K2 Castlehill W Duns
106 F6 Castle Kennedy D & G
131 L8 Castle Lachlan Ag & B
40 H11 Castlemartin Pembks
125 P6 Castlemilk C Glas
40 H4 Castle Morris Pembks
46 E7 Castlemorton Worcs
46 E7 Castlemorton Common Worcs
110 D2 Castle O'er D & G
56 G4 Castle Pulverbatch Shrops
101 J6 Castlerigg Stone Circle Cumb
75 N6 Castle Rising Norfk
112 G11 Castleside Dur
156 C8 Castle Stuart Highld
49 M6 Castlethorpe M Keyn
92 G9 Castlethorpe N Linc
111 K3 Castleton Border
83 Q8 Castleton Derbys
105 J9 Castleton N York
31 J8 Castleton Newpt
89 P8 Castleton Rochdl
11 P10 Castletown Dorset
167 L3 Castletown Highld
80 c8 Castletown IoM
113 N9 Castletown Sundld
97 L11 Castley N York
64 D2 Caston Norfk
74 B11 Castor C Pete
28 G7 Caswell Bay Swans
123 R10 Catacol N Ayrs
83 M10 Cat and Fiddle Derbys
31 Q8 Catbrain S Glos
31 P4 Catbrook Mons
81 J10 Catch Flints
2 C8 Catchall Cnwll
59 L9 Catchem's Corner Solhll
113 J10 Catchgate Dur
84 F3 Catcliffe Rothm
33 K9 Catcomb Wilts
19 L7 Catcott Somset
19 M6 Catcott Burtle Somset
36 H9 Caterham Surrey
77 M7 Catfield Norfk
77 N7 Catfield Common Norfk
37 J6 Catford Gt Lon
88 F3 Catforth Lancs
125 P5 Cathcart C Glas
44 G9 Cathedine Powys
59 J8 Catherine-de-Barnes Solhll
90 D5 Catherine Slack C Brad
15 J4 Catherington Hants
10 H6 Catherston Leweston Dorset
57 M9 Catherton Shrops
14 G5 Catisfield Hants
46 C6 Catley Herefs
89 P7 Catley Lane Head Rochdl
147 Q9 Catlodge Highld
89 P3 Catlow Lancs
111 J5 Catlowdy Cumb
51 L3 Catmere End Essex
34 E8 Catmore W Berk
7 K4 Caton Devon
95 L8 Caton Lancs
95 M7 Caton Green Lancs
8 G9 Cator Court Devon
115 K2 Catrine E Ayrs
31 L6 Cat's Ash Newpt
26 B9 Catsfield E Susx
26 B9 Catsfield Stream E Susx
19 P9 Catsgore Somset
19 Q8 Catsham Somset
58 E10 Catshill Worcs
57 N5 Catstree Shrops
120 C9 Cattadale Ag & B
97 P10 Cattal N York
53 K5 Cattawade Suffk
88 F2 Catterall Lancs
69 Q6 Catteralslane Shrops
103 P11 Catterick N York
103 P11 Catterick Bridge N York
103 N11 Catterick Garrison N York
101 N4 Catterlen Cumb
143 R2 Catterline Abers
97 R11 Catterton N York
23 Q6 Catteshall Surrey
60 C5 Catthorpe Leics
64 B8 Cattishall Suffk
11 M5 Cattistock Dorset
97 N5 Catton N York
112 B9 Catton Nthumb
99 N11 Catwick E R Yk
61 N6 Catworth Cambs
32 H2 Caudle Green Gloucs
50 B2 Caulcott C Beds
48 F10 Caulcott Oxon
143 M8 Cauldcots Angus
133 J9 Cauldhame Stirlg
117 Q7 Cauldmill Border
71 K5 Cauldon Staffs
71 K5 Cauldon Lowe Staffs
71 P11 Cauldwell Derbys
109 K9 Caulkerbush D & G
110 H4 Caulside D & G
11 P2 Caundle Marsh Dorset
58 C8 Caunsall Worcs
85 M8 Caunton Notts
23 K10 Causeway Hants
95 K3 Causeway End Cumb
107 M6 Causeway End D & G
51 Q7 Causeway End Essex
116 E3 Causewayend S Lans
109 P10 Causewayhead Cumb
133 N8 Causewayhead Stirlg

151 N4 **Causeyend** Abers
113 J2 **Causey Park** Nthumb
113 J2 **Causey Park Bridge** Nthumb
63 P11 **Cavendish** Suffk
63 N6 **Cavenham** Suffk
48 G9 **Caversfield** Oxon
35 K10 **Caversham** Readg
70 H6 **Caverswall** Staffs
118 D5 **Caverton Mill** Border
92 C4 **Cavil** E R Yk
156 E7 **Cawdor** Highld
87 J5 **Cawkwell** Lincs
91 P3 **Cawood** N York
6 C8 **Cawsand** Cnwll
76 G7 **Cawston** Norfk
59 Q10 **Cawston** Warwks
98 F3 **Cawthorn** N York
90 H9 **Cawthorne** Barns
98 C5 **Cawton** N York
62 D9 **Caxton** Cambs
62 D9 **Caxton End** Cambs
62 C8 **Caxton Gibbet** Cambs
57 K10 **Caynham** Shrops
86 B11 **Caythorpe** Lincs
85 L11 **Caythorpe** Notts
99 M4 **Cayton** N York
168 c11 **Ceann a Bhaigh** W Isls
146 G5 **Ceannacroc Lodge** Highld
168 i5 **Cearsiadar** W Isls
31 P4 **Ceciliford** Mons
31 J7 **Cefn** Newpt
80 D11 **Cefn Berain** Conwy
68 B4 **Cefn-brith** Conwy
29 K2 **Cefn Byrle** Powys
29 M2 **Cefn Byrle** Powys
68 H8 **Cefn Canel** Powys
68 F9 **Cefn Coch** Powys
30 D3 **Cefn-coed-y-cymmer** Myr Td
29 N8 **Cefn Cribwr** Brdgnd
29 N8 **Cefn Cross** Brdgnd
68 C7 **Cefn-ddwysarn** Gwynd
56 D7 **Cefn-Einion** Shrops
28 G2 **Cefneithin** Carmth
44 C5 **Cefngorwydd** Powys
69 J6 **Cefn-mawr** Wrexhm
30 D4 **Cefnpennar** Rhondd
69 K3 **Cefn-y-bedd** Flints
41 N5 **Cefn-y-pant** Carmth
78 H9 **Ceint** IoA
43 M5 **Cellan** Cerdgn
135 P7 **Cellardyke** Fife
70 H5 **Cellarhead** Staffs
101 N5 **Celleron** Cumb
30 H5 **Celynen** Caerph
78 F6 **Cemaes** IoA
55 J3 **Cemmaes** Powys
55 J4 **Cemmaes Road** Powys
41 Q2 **Cenarth** Cerdgn
40 F5 **Cerbyd** Pembks
135 L5 **Ceres** Fife
11 P4 **Cerne Abbas** Dorset
33 L5 **Cerney Wick** Gloucs
78 G10 **Cerrigceinwen** IoA
68 C5 **Cerrigydrudion** Conwy
77 N8 **Cess** Norfk
67 J2 **Ceunant** Gwynd
46 G8 **Chaceley** Gloucs
3 K5 **Chacewater** Cnwll
49 J7 **Chackmore** Bucks
48 E6 **Chacombe** Nhants
47 K5 **Chadbury** Worcs
89 Q9 **Chadderton** Oldham
89 Q9 **Chadderton Fold** Oldham
72 B3 **Chaddesden** C Derb
58 C10 **Chaddesley Corbett** Worcs
8 C10 **Chaddlehanger** Devon
34 D9 **Chaddleworth** W Berk
48 B10 **Chadlington** Oxon
48 B4 **Chadshunt** Warwks
73 K6 **Chadwell** Leics
57 P2 **Chadwell** Shrops
61 N7 **Chadwell End** Bed
37 L3 **Chadwell Heath** Gt Lon
37 P5 **Chadwell St Mary** Thurr
58 B11 **Chadwick** Worcs
59 K10 **Chadwick End** Solhll
82 B5 **Chadwick Green** St Hel
10 H2 **Chaffcombe** Somset
37 P5 **Chafford Hundred** Thurr
8 H7 **Chagford** Devon
25 J7 **Chailey** E Susx
74 H10 **Chainbridge** Cambs
26 B2 **Chainhurst** Kent
12 H3 **Chalbury** Dorset
12 H3 **Chalbury Common** Dorset
36 H9 **Chaldon** Surrey
14 E11 **Chale** IoW
14 E11 **Chale Green** IoW
36 B2 **Chalfont Common** Bucks
35 Q6 **Chalfont St Giles** Bucks
36 B2 **Chalfont St Peter** Bucks
32 G4 **Chalford** Gloucs
35 K4 **Chalford** Oxon
20 G4 **Chalford** Wilts
50 B5 **Chalgrave** C Beds
34 H5 **Chalgrove** Oxon
37 Q6 **Chalk** Kent
51 P8 **Chalk End** Essex
35 K9 **Chalkhouse Green** Oxon
10 H3 **Chalkway** Somset
38 E9 **Chalkwell** Kent
6 H10 **Challaborough** Devon
17 M3 **Challacombe** Devon
107 L4 **Challoch** D & G
38 H11 **Challock** Kent
11 M4 **Chalmington** Dorset
50 B5 **Chalton** C Beds
61 P10 **Chalton** C Beds
23 K11 **Chalton** Hants
35 Q9 **Chalvey** Slough
25 M9 **Chalvington** E Susx
26 F3 **Chambers Green** Kent
50 C11 **Chandler's Cross** Herts
46 C7 **Chandlers Cross** Worcs
22 D11 **Chandler's Ford** Hants
61 P9 **Channel's End** Bed
93 J4 **Chanterlands Crematorium** C KuH
20 D5 **Chantry** Somset
53 K3 **Chantry** Suffk
100 H4 **Chapel** Cumb
134 H9 **Chapel** Fife
91 J3 **Chapel Allerton** Leeds
19 M4 **Chapel Allerton** Somset
4 F6 **Chapel Amble** Cnwll

60 F7 **Chapel Brampton** Nhants
62 C2 **Chapelbridge** Cambs
70 E7 **Chapel Chorlton** Staffs
25 P6 **Chapel Cross** E Susx
61 P9 **Chapel End** Bed
50 C2 **Chapel End** C Beds
61 P4 **Chapel End** Cambs
59 M6 **Chapel End** Warwks
52 B4 **Chapelend Way** Essex
83 N8 **Chapel-en-le-Frith** Derbys
89 M9 **Chapel Field** Bury
74 H6 **Chapelgate** Lincs
48 E2 **Chapel Green** Warwks
59 L7 **Chapel Green** Warwks
91 P5 **Chapel Haddlesey** N York
126 D5 **Chapelhall** N Lans
159 Q10 **Chapel Hill** Abers
86 H10 **Chapel Hill** Lincs
31 P5 **Chapel Hill** Mons
97 M11 **Chapel Hill** N York
117 J7 **Chapelhope** Border
110 F6 **Chapelknowe** D & G
56 E9 **Chapel Lawn** Shrops
95 Q5 **Chapel le Dale** N York
18 F9 **Chapel Leigh** Somset
83 N8 **Chapel Milton** Derbys
151 J3 **Chapel of Garioch** Abers
106 F9 **Chapel Rossan** D & G
25 P8 **Chapel Row** E Susx
52 C11 **Chapel Row** Essex
34 G11 **Chapel Row** W Berk
94 E4 **Chapels** Cumb
87 Q6 **Chapel St Leonards** Lincs
101 K9 **Chapel Stile** Cumb
143 L8 **Chapelton** Angus
17 K6 **Chapelton** Devon
126 B8 **Chapelton** S Lans
89 L7 **Chapeltown** Bl w D
4 D10 **Chapel Town** Cnwll
149 N3 **Chapeltown** Moray
91 K11 **Chapeltown** Sheff
20 F5 **Chapmanslade** Wilts
5 P3 **Chapmans Well** Devon
50 H7 **Chapmore End** Herts
52 E6 **Chappel** Essex
5 N8 **Charaton** Cnwll
10 G3 **Chard** Somset
10 G2 **Chard Junction** Somset
10 G2 **Chardleigh Green** Somset
10 G4 **Chardstock** Devon
32 D6 **Charfield** S Glos
46 H11 **Chargrove** Gloucs
26 G2 **Charing** Kent
26 G2 **Charing Crematorium** Kent
26 F2 **Charing Heath** Kent
38 G11 **Charing Hill** Kent
47 N7 **Charingworth** Gloucs
48 C11 **Charlbury** Oxon
32 D11 **Charlcombe** BaNES
33 J9 **Charlcutt** Wilts
47 Q3 **Charlecote** Warwks
58 F6 **Charlemont** Sandw
17 M5 **Charles** Devon
23 N6 **Charleshill** Surrey
142 F8 **Charleston** Angus
151 N7 **Charlestown** C Aber
90 F3 **Charlestown** C Brad
90 B5 **Charlestown** Calder
3 Q3 **Charlestown** Cnwll
83 M6 **Charlestown** Derbys
11 P9 **Charlestown** Dorset
134 D11 **Charlestown** Fife
153 Q3 **Charlestown** Highld
156 A8 **Charlestown** Highld
82 H4 **Charlestown** Salfd
64 E11 **Charles Tye** Suffk
83 M6 **Charlesworth** Derbys
18 H7 **Charlinch** Somset
134 H5 **Charlottetown** Fife
37 K5 **Charlton** Gt Lon
22 C5 **Charlton** Hants
50 E5 **Charlton** Herts
48 F7 **Charlton** Nhants
112 B4 **Charlton** Nthumb
34 D7 **Charlton** Oxon
19 J9 **Charlton** Somset
20 B6 **Charlton** Somset
20 C4 **Charlton** Somset
36 C7 **Charlton** Surrey
15 N4 **Charlton** W Susx
20 H10 **Charlton** Wilts
33 J7 **Charlton** Wilts
47 K5 **Charlton** Worcs
58 B10 **Charlton** Worcs
57 K2 **Charlton** Wrekin
47 K10 **Charlton Abbots** Gloucs
19 P9 **Charlton Adam** Somset
21 N10 **Charlton-All-Saints** Wilts
11 P5 **Charlton Down** Dorset
57 K3 **Charlton Hill** Shrops
20 C10 **Charlton Horethorne** Somset
47 J11 **Charlton Kings** Gloucs
19 P9 **Charlton Mackrell** Somset
12 F4 **Charlton Marshall** Dorset
20 D9 **Charlton Musgrove** Somset
48 G11 **Charlton-on-Otmoor** Oxon
12 E4 **Charlton on the Hill** Dorset
21 M3 **Charlton St Peter** Wilts
23 J8 **Charlwood** Hants
24 F2 **Charlwood** Surrey
11 P6 **Charminster** Dorset
10 H6 **Charmouth** Dorset
49 J10 **Charndon** Bucks
34 C6 **Charney Bassett** Oxon
88 H7 **Charnock Green** Lancs
88 H7 **Charnock Richard** Lancs
88 H7 **Charnock Richard Crematorium** Lancs
88 G7 **Charnock Richard Services** Lancs
65 K10 **Charsfield** Suffk
38 C11 **Chart Corner** Kent
22 G3 **Charter Alley** Hants
129 K10 **Charterhall** Border
19 N3 **Charterhouse** Somset
133 M9 **Chartershall** Stirlg
34 B2 **Charterville Allotments** Oxon
39 K11 **Chartham** Kent
39 K10 **Chartham Hatch** Kent
26 C2 **Chart Hill** Kent
35 P4 **Chartridge** Bucks
26 D2 **Chart Sutton** Kent

38 D11 **Chartway Street** Kent
35 L9 **Charvil** Wokham
60 B9 **Charwelton** Nhants
58 F3 **Chase Terrace** Staffs
58 F3 **Chasetown** Staffs
47 P9 **Chastleton** Oxon
16 E11 **Chasty** Devon
89 M2 **Chatburn** Lancs
70 D8 **Chatcull** Staffs
30 H7 **Chatham** Caerph
38 C8 **Chatham** Medway
52 B8 **Chatham Green** Essex
119 N5 **Chathill** Nthumb
46 G2 **Chatley** Worcs
84 C6 **Chatsworth House** Derbys
38 C7 **Chattenden** Medway
51 L5 **Chatter End** Essex
62 E3 **Chatteris** Cambs
89 M7 **Chatterton** Lancs
53 J3 **Chattisham** Suffk
118 E7 **Chatto** Border
119 L5 **Chatton** Nthumb
50 C6 **Chaul End** C Beds
17 N9 **Chawleigh** Devon
34 E4 **Chawley** Oxon
61 Q9 **Chawston** Bed
23 K7 **Chawton** Hants
32 D2 **Chaxhill** Gloucs
35 J9 **Chazey Heath** Oxon
71 J6 **Cheadle** Staffs
83 J7 **Cheadle** Stockp
83 J7 **Cheadle Heath** Stockp
83 J7 **Cheadle Hulme** Stockp
36 F8 **Cheam** Gt Lon
35 P11 **Cheapside** W & M
35 K2 **Chearsley** Bucks
70 F9 **Chebsey** Staffs
35 J8 **Checkendon** Oxon
70 C5 **Checkley** Ches E
46 A7 **Checkley** Herefs
71 J7 **Checkley** Staffs
70 C5 **Checkley Green** Ches E
63 N9 **Chedburgh** Suffk
19 N4 **Cheddar** Somset
49 P11 **Cheddington** Bucks
70 H4 **Cheddleton** Staffs
70 H4 **Cheddleton Heath** Staffs
18 H9 **Cheddon Fitzpaine** Somset
32 H6 **Chedglow** Wilts
65 M2 **Chedgrave** Norfk
11 K3 **Chedington** Dorset
65 M6 **Chediston** Suffk
65 M6 **Chediston Green** Suffk
33 L2 **Chedworth** Gloucs
19 K7 **Chedzoy** Somset
26 H4 **Cheeseman's Green** Kent
82 H4 **Cheetham Hill** Manch
8 H2 **Cheldon** Devon
82 H10 **Chelford** Ches E
72 B4 **Chellaston** C Derb
61 L9 **Chellington** Bed
57 N7 **Chelmarsh** Shrops
56 H6 **Chelmick** Shrops
53 M4 **Chelmondiston** Suffk
83 P11 **Chelmorton** Derbys
52 B10 **Chelmsford** Essex
51 Q9 **Chelmsford Crematorium** Essex
59 J7 **Chelmsley Wood** Solhll
36 G5 **Chelsea** Gt Lon
37 L8 **Chelsfield** Gt Lon
37 J9 **Chelsham** Surrey
18 G10 **Chelston** Somset
52 G2 **Chelsworth** Suffk
46 H10 **Cheltenham** Gloucs
47 J10 **Cheltenham Crematorium** Gloucs
61 L7 **Chelveston** Nhants
31 N11 **Chelvey** N Som
20 B2 **Chelwood** BaNES
25 K5 **Chelwood Common** E Susx
25 K4 **Chelwood Gate** E Susx
33 J6 **Chelworth** Wilts
33 L6 **Chelworth Lower Green** Wilts
33 L6 **Chelworth Upper Green** Wilts
56 G8 **Cheney Longville** Shrops
50 B11 **Chenies** Bucks
31 P6 **Chepstow** Mons
89 K9 **Chequerbent** Bolton
75 J9 **Chequers Corner** Norfk
33 K10 **Cherhill** Wilts
32 H5 **Cherington** Gloucs
47 Q7 **Cherington** Warwks
17 N2 **Cheriton** Devon
22 G9 **Cheriton** Hants
27 M4 **Cheriton** Kent
28 E6 **Cheriton** Swans
9 J6 **Cheriton Bishop** Devon
9 L3 **Cheriton Fitzpaine** Devon
41 J11 **Cheriton or Stackpole Elidor** Pembks
70 B11 **Cherrington** Wrekin
92 G2 **Cherry Burton** E R Yk
62 G9 **Cherry Hinton** Cambs
46 G4 **Cherry Orchard** Worcs
86 D6 **Cherry Willingham** Lincs
36 B7 **Chertsey** Surrey
48 F9 **Cherwell Valley Services** Oxon
12 C5 **Cheselbourne** Dorset
35 Q4 **Chesham** Bucks
89 N8 **Chesham** Bury
35 Q5 **Chesham Bois** Bucks
51 J10 **Cheshunt** Herts
11 N9 **Chesil Beach** Dorset
58 E3 **Chesley** Kent
58 E3 **Cheslyn Hay** Staffs
47 P3 **Chessetts Wood** Warwks
36 E8 **Chessington** Gt Lon
36 E8 **Chessington World of Adventures** Gt Lon
81 N11 **Chester** Ches W
20 C6 **Chesterblade** Somset
81 N11 **Chester Cathedral** Ches W
81 M11 **Chester Crematorium** Ches W
84 E6 **Chesterfield** Derbys
58 G3 **Chesterfield** Staffs
84 E6 **Chesterfield Crematorium** Derbys
84 F8 **Chesterfield Services** Derbys
128 B7 **Chesterhill** Mdloth

113 L10 **Chester-le-Street** Dur
113 L11 **Chester Moor** Dur
118 B6 **Chesters** Border
118 B8 **Chesters** Border
81 P10 **Chester Services** Ches W
62 G3 **Chesterton** Cambs
74 B11 **Chesterton** Cambs
33 K4 **Chesterton** Gloucs
48 G10 **Chesterton** Oxon
57 N5 **Chesterton** Shrops
70 E5 **Chesterton** Staffs
48 C3 **Chesterton Green** Warwks
112 B7 **Chesterwood** Nthumb
81 N10 **Chester Zoo** Ches W
39 K8 **Chestfield** Kent
38 E9 **Chestnut Street** Kent
6 H7 **Cheston** Devon
70 C8 **Cheswardine** Shrops
129 Q10 **Cheswick** Nthumb
58 H9 **Cheswick Green** Solhll
11 N3 **Chetnole** Dorset
9 N2 **Chettiscombe** Devon
62 H4 **Chettisham** Cambs
12 G2 **Chettle** Dorset
57 M6 **Chetton** Shrops
48 H9 **Chetwode** Bucks
70 C10 **Chetwynd** Wrekin
70 D11 **Chetwynd Aston** Wrekin
63 L8 **Cheveley** Cambs
37 L9 **Chevening** Kent
14 E10 **Cheverton** IoW
63 N9 **Chevington** Suffk
18 E9 **Cheviot Hills**
15 N5 **Chevithorne** Devon
19 Q2 **Chew Magna** BaNES
89 K9 **Chew Moor** Bolton
19 Q2 **Chew Stoke** BaNES
32 C11 **Chewton Keynsham** BaNES
19 Q4 **Chewton Mendip** Somset
49 F5 **Chichacott** Devon
15 N6 **Chicheley** M Keyn
15 N5 **Chichester** W Susx
15 N5 **Chichester Crematorium** W Susx
11 N8 **Chickerell** Dorset
65 J6 **Chickering** Suffk
20 H8 **Chicklade** Wilts
45 K4 **Chickward** Herefs
23 J11 **Chidden** Hants
23 Q7 **Chiddingfold** Surrey
25 M8 **Chiddingly** E Susx
37 M12 **Chiddingstone** Kent
37 M11 **Chiddingstone Causeway** Kent
11 J5 **Chideock** Dorset
15 L6 **Chidham** W Susx
90 H6 **Chidswell** Kirk
34 E10 **Chieveley** W Berk
51 Q8 **Chignall St James** Essex
51 Q8 **Chignall Smealy** Essex
37 K2 **Chigwell** Essex
37 L2 **Chigwell Row** Essex
22 C6 **Chilbolton** Hants
22 F9 **Chilcomb** Hants
11 L6 **Chilcombe** Dorset
20 B4 **Chilcompton** Somset
59 L2 **Chilcote** Leics
81 M9 **Childer Thornton** Ches W
12 D2 **Child Okeford** Dorset
34 C7 **Childrey** Oxon
70 B9 **Child's Ercall** Shrops
47 L7 **Childswickham** Worcs
81 N7 **Childwall** Lpool
50 D8 **Childwick Bury** Herts
50 D8 **Childwick Green** Herts
11 M5 **Chilfrome** Dorset
15 M4 **Chilgrove** W Susx
39 J11 **Chilham** Kent
8 B4 **Chilla** Devon
8 B8 **Chillaton** Devon
39 N11 **Chillenden** Kent
14 E10 **Chillerton** IoW
65 M11 **Chillesford** Suffk
119 L5 **Chillingham** Nthumb
7 K10 **Chillington** Devon
10 H2 **Chillington** Somset
21 J8 **Chilmark** Wilts
26 G3 **Chilmington Green** Kent
48 B11 **Chilson** Oxon
5 Q7 **Chilsworthy** Cnwll
16 E10 **Chilsworthy** Devon
50 B11 **Chiltern Green** C Beds
35 L5 **Chiltern Hills**
35 P5 **Chilterns Crematorium** Bucks
19 P11 **Chilthorne Domer** Somset
35 J2 **Chilton** Bucks
9 L4 **Chilton** Devon
103 Q5 **Chilton** Dur
27 N3 **Chilton** Kent
34 E7 **Chilton** Oxon
52 E3 **Chilton** Suffk
22 G6 **Chilton Candover** Hants
19 Q10 **Chilton Cantelo** Somset
34 B10 **Chilton Foliat** Wilts
19 L6 **Chilton Polden** Somset
63 N11 **Chilton Street** Suffk
19 J7 **Chilton Trinity** Somset
72 E3 **Chilwell** Notts
22 D11 **Chilworth** Hants
36 B11 **Chilworth** Surrey
34 C4 **Chimney** Oxon
23 J3 **Chineham** Hants
37 J2 **Chingford** Gt Lon
83 M8 **Chinley** Derbys
35 L4 **Chinnor** Oxon
112 C5 **Chipchase Castle** Nthumb
70 B8 **Chipnall** Shrops
63 L7 **Chippenham** Cambs
33 J8 **Chippenham** Wilts
50 B10 **Chipperfield** Herts
51 J4 **Chipping** Herts
89 J2 **Chipping** Lancs
47 N7 **Chipping Campden** Gloucs
52 D8 **Chipping Hill** Essex
48 B9 **Chipping Norton** Oxon
51 N10 **Chipping Ongar** Essex
32 D8 **Chipping Sodbury** S Glos
48 E5 **Chipping Warden** Nhants
18 D9 **Chipstable** Somset
37 M9 **Chipstead** Kent
36 G9 **Chipstead** Surrey
56 D5 **Chirbury** Shrops
69 J7 **Chirk** Wrexhm
129 M8 **Chirnside** Border

129 M8 **Chirnsidebridge** Border
21 L3 **Chirton** Wilts
33 Q11 **Chisbury** Wilts
11 K2 **Chiselborough** Somset
33 N8 **Chiseldon** Swindn
34 N8 **Chiselhampton** Oxon
117 N8 **Chisholme** Border
37 K6 **Chislehurst** Gt Lon
39 M9 **Chislet** Kent
90 C5 **Chisley** Calder
50 D10 **Chiswell Green** Herts
36 F5 **Chiswick** Gt Lon
62 E11 **Chiswick End** Cambs
83 L6 **Chisworth** Derbys
26 D7 **Chithurst** W Susx
23 M10 **Chithurst** W Susx
62 G7 **Chittering** Cambs
21 J5 **Chitterne** Wilts
17 M7 **Chittlehamholt** Devon
17 L6 **Chittlehampton** Devon
33 J11 **Chittoe** Wilts
7 K11 **Chivelstone** Devon
17 J5 **Chivenor** Devon
106 F5 **Chlenry** D & G
23 Q2 **Chobham** Surrey
21 P6 **Cholderton** Wilts
35 P3 **Cholesbury** Bucks
112 D6 **Chollerford** Nthumb
112 D6 **Chollerton** Nthumb
70 A3 **Cholmondeston** Ches E
34 G7 **Cholsey** Oxon
45 P3 **Cholstrey** Herefs
104 G11 **Chop Gate** N York
113 L4 **Choppington** Nthumb
112 H9 **Chopwell** Gatesd
69 Q4 **Chorley** Ches E
88 H7 **Chorley** Lancs
57 M8 **Chorley** Shrops
58 G2 **Chorley** Staffs
50 B11 **Chorleywood** Herts
50 B11 **Chorleywood West** Herts
70 C4 **Chorlton** Ches E
82 H6 **Chorlton-cum-Hardy** Manch
69 N5 **Chorlton Lane** Ches W
56 F7 **Choulton** Shrops
69 N3 **Chowley** Ches W
51 K3 **Chrishall** Essex
124 G3 **Chrisswell** Inver
75 J11 **Christchurch** Cambs
13 L6 **Christchurch** Dorset
31 Q2 **Christchurch** Gloucs
31 K7 **Christchurch** Newpt
33 J9 **Christian Malford** Wilts
81 N11 **Christleton** Ches W
35 K6 **Christmas Common** Oxon
19 L3 **Christon** N Som
119 P6 **Christon Bank** Nthumb
9 K7 **Christow** Devon
24 D5 **Christ's Hospital** W Susx
25 L4 **Chuck Hatch** E Susx
9 L9 **Chudleigh** Devon
9 K9 **Chudleigh Knighton** Devon
17 M9 **Chulmleigh** Devon
83 M6 **Chunal** Derbys
89 L5 **Church** Lancs
46 E11 **Churcham** Gloucs
70 C11 **Church Aston** Wrekin
60 F7 **Church Brampton** Nhants
102 E8 **Church Brough** Cumb
71 N8 **Church Broughton** Derbys
3 J11 **Church Cove** Cnwll
23 M4 **Church Crookham** Hants
46 G11 **Churchdown** Gloucs
70 E11 **Church Eaton** Staffs
61 N9 **Church End** Bed
61 P9 **Church End** Bed
35 K3 **Church End** Bucks
49 Q10 **Church End** C Beds
50 B4 **Church End** C Beds
50 B7 **Church End** C Beds
61 Q10 **Church End** C Beds
61 N6 **Church End** Cambs
62 B4 **Church End** Cambs
62 G9 **Church End** Cambs
38 H3 **Churchend** Essex
51 P6 **Church End** Essex
52 B6 **Church End** Essex
52 B8 **Church End** Essex
46 G7 **Church End** Gloucs
36 F2 **Church End** Gt Lon
23 J3 **Church End** Hants
50 D8 **Church End** Herts
50 G4 **Church End** Herts
51 K6 **Church End** Herts
74 D4 **Church End** Lincs
93 R11 **Church End** Lincs
59 K6 **Church End** Warwks
59 L6 **Church End** Warwks
48 C9 **Church Enstone** Oxon
91 N3 **Church Fenton** N York
58 F6 **Churchfield** Sandw
50 H10 **Churchgate** Herts
51 L8 **Churchgate Street** Essex
10 D5 **Church Green** Devon
71 P11 **Church Gresley** Derbys
34 B11 **Church Hanborough** Oxon
58 F2 **Church Hill** Staffs
105 J11 **Church Houses** N York
10 F4 **Churchill** Devon
17 K3 **Churchill** Devon
19 M3 **Churchill** N Som
47 Q10 **Churchill** Oxon
46 H4 **Churchill** Worcs
58 C9 **Churchill** Worcs
10 E2 **Churchinford** Somset
12 F8 **Church Knowle** Dorset
85 P5 **Church Laneham** Notts
60 F2 **Church Langton** Leics
59 Q9 **Church Lawford** Warwks
70 E3 **Church Lawton** Ches E
71 J7 **Church Leigh** Staffs
47 K4 **Church Lench** Worcs
71 M6 **Church Mayfield** Staffs
70 B3 **Church Minshull** Ches E
15 N7 **Church Norton** W Susx
60 B4 **Churchover** Warwks
57 J5 **Church Preen** Shrops
56 G4 **Church Pulverbatch** Shrops
10 D2 **Churchstanton** Somset
56 D6 **Churchstoke** Powys

270 Churchstow - Compton

7 J9 **Churchstow** Devon
60 D9 **Church Stowe** Nhants
52 C3 **Church Street** Essex
38 B7 **Church Street** Kent
65 P5 **Church Street** Suffk
56 H6 **Church Stretton** Shrops
93 P11 **Churchthorpe** Lincs
88 C2 **Churchtown** Bpool
4 H6 **Churchtown** Cnwll
84 C8 **Churchtown** Derbys
17 M3 **Churchtown** Devon
80 f3 **Churchtown** IoM
88 F2 **Churchtown** Lancs
92 C9 **Church Town** N Linc
88 D7 **Churchtown** Sefton
30 E7 **Church Village** Rhondd
85 J7 **Church Warsop** Notts
72 C4 **Church Wilne** Derbys
111 N5 **Churnsike Lodge** Nthumb
7 N7 **Churston Ferrers** Torbay
23 N7 **Churt** Surrey
69 M3 **Churton** Ches W
90 H5 **Churwell** Leeds
66 G7 **Chwilog** Gwynd
2 D7 **Chyandour** Cnwll
2 H9 **Chyanvounder** Cnwll
3 K5 **Chyeowling** Cnwll
2 D7 *Chysauster* Cnwll
2 H9 **Chyvarloe** Cnwll
56 B4 **Cil** Powys
80 H11 **Cilcain** Flints
43 K2 **Cilcennin** Cerdgn
56 C4 **Cilcewydd** Powys
29 L4 **Cilfrew** Neath
30 E6 **Cilfynydd** Rhondd
41 N2 **Cilgerran** Pembks
43 P9 **Cilgwyn** Carmth
66 H4 **Cilgwyn** Gwynd
43 K3 **Ciliau-Aeron** Cerdgn
29 K3 **Cilmaengwyn** Neath
44 E4 **Cilmery** Powys
41 Q4 **Cilrhedyn** Pembks
43 L10 **Cilsan** Carmth
68 A6 **Ciltalgarth** Gwynd
43 Q7 **Cilycwm** Carmth
29 L5 **Cimla** Neath
32 C2 **Cinderford** Gloucs
58 D6 **Cinder Hill** Wolves
35 Q8 **Cippenham** Slough
33 K4 **Cirencester** Gloucs
103 P11 **Citadilla** N York
36 H4 **City** Gt Lon
30 C9 **City** V Glam
37 K4 *City Airport* Gt Lon
78 H7 **City Dulas** IoA
37 K3 **City of London Crematorium** Gt Lon
136 F4 **Clabhach** Ag & B
131 N11 **Clachaig** Ag & B
123 N8 **Clachan** Ag & B
130 F4 **Clachan** Ag & B
138 F9 **Clachan** Ag & B
153 J10 **Clachan** Highld
168 d11 **Clachan-a-Luib** W Isls
136 B6 **Clachan Mor** Ag & B
168 d11 **Clachan na Luib** W Isls
125 Q2 **Clachan of Campsie** E Duns
130 F4 **Clachan-Seil** Ag & B
156 A8 **Clachnaharry** Highld
164 B11 **Clachtoll** Highld
142 A5 **Clackavoid** P & K
37 K10 *Clacket Lane Services* Surrey
133 Q9 **Clackmannan** Clacks
157 N6 **Clackmarras** Moray
53 L8 **Clacton-on-Sea** Essex
131 M3 **Cladich** Ag & B
47 L3 **Cladswell** Worcs
138 C8 **Claggan** Highld
152 C7 **Claigan** Highld
20 C3 **Clandown** BaNES
23 J11 **Clanfield** Hants
33 Q4 **Clanfield** Oxon
8 H4 **Clannaborough** Devon
22 B5 **Clanville** Hants
20 B8 **Clanville** Somset
123 Q8 **Claonaig** Ag & B
12 H4 **Clapgate** Dorset
51 K6 **Clapgate** Herts
61 M10 **Clapham** Bed
9 L7 **Clapham** Devon
36 G5 **Clapham** Gt Lon
95 Q7 **Clapham** N York
24 C9 **Clapham** W Susx
61 M10 **Clapham Green** Bed
27 J4 **Clap Hill** Kent
101 L10 **Clappersgate** Cumb
11 J3 **Clapton** Somset
20 B4 **Clapton** Somset
31 N10 **Clapton-in-Gordano** N Som
47 N11 **Clapton-on-the-Hill** Gloucs
17 M7 **Clapworthy** Devon
54 E8 **Clarach** Cerdgn
112 H8 **Claravale** Gatesd
41 L6 **Clarbeston** Pembks
41 K6 **Clarbeston Road** Pembks
85 M4 **Clarborough** Notts
63 N11 **Clare** Suffk
108 G7 **Clarebrand** D & G
109 N7 **Clarencefield** D & G
112 F7 **Clarewood** Nthumb
117 Q7 **Clarilaw** Border
22 G4 **Clarken Green** Hants
24 E3 **Clark's Green** Surrey
125 P6 **Clarkston** E Rens
162 G9 **Clashmore** Highld
164 B10 **Clashmore** Highld
164 C10 **Clashnessie** Highld
149 N3 **Clashnoir** Moray
134 B3 **Clathy** P & K
134 C3 **Clathymore** P & K
150 E2 **Clatt** Abers
55 M6 **Clatter** Powys
51 P8 **Clatterford End** Essex
18 E8 **Clatworthy** Somset
88 G2 **Claughton** Lancs
95 M7 **Claughton** Lancs
81 L7 **Claughton** Wirral
19 J8 **Clavelshay** Somset
59 J11 **Claverdon** Warwks
31 N11 **Claverham** N Som
51 L4 **Clavering** Essex
57 P6 **Claverley** Shrops
20 E2 **Claverton** BaNES
20 E2 **Claverton Down** BaNES
30 E9 **Clawdd-coch** V Glam
68 E4 **Clawdd-newydd** Denbgs
95 L5 **Clawthorpe** Cumb
5 P2 **Clawton** Devon
86 F2 **Claxby** Lincs
87 N6 **Claxby** Lincs
98 D9 **Claxton** N York
77 L11 **Claxton** Norfk
59 Q7 **Claybrooke Magna** Leics
65 P5 **Clay Common** Suffk
60 C5 **Clay Coton** Nhants
84 E8 **Clay Cross** Derbys
48 E5 **Claydon** Oxon
53 K2 **Claydon** Suffk
50 H6 **Clay End** Herts
110 G5 **Claygate** D & G
26 B3 **Claygate** Kent
36 E8 **Claygate** Surrey
37 P9 **Claygate Cross** Kent
37 K2 **Clayhall** Gt Lon
18 D10 **Clayhanger** Devon
58 F4 **Clayhanger** Wsall
18 G11 **Clayhidon** Devon
26 D7 **Clayhill** E Susx
13 P3 **Clayhill** Hants
62 H8 **Clayhithe** Cambs
167 L5 **Clayock** Highld
62 E10 **Claypit Hill** Cambs
32 E3 **Claypits** Gloucs
85 P11 **Claypole** Lincs
87 M5 **Claythorpe** Lincs
90 E4 **Clayton** C Brad
91 M9 **Clayton** Donc
24 G8 **Clayton** W Susx
88 H6 **Clayton Green** Lancs
89 M4 **Clayton-le-Moors** Lancs
88 H6 **Clayton-le-Woods** Lancs
90 H8 **Clayton West** Kirk
85 M3 **Clayworth** Notts
144 G10 **Cleadale** Highld
113 N8 **Cleadon** S Tyne
6 E5 **Clearbrook** Devon
31 Q3 **Clearwell** Gloucs
31 Q3 **Clearwell Meend** Gloucs
103 Q8 **Cleasby** N York
169 d8 **Cleat** Ork
103 M7 **Cleatlam** Dur
100 D8 **Cleator** Cumb
100 D7 **Cleator Moor** Cumb
90 F5 **Cleckheaton** Kirk
57 K8 **Cleedownton** Shrops
57 K9 **Cleehill** Shrops
126 D6 **Cleekhimin** N Lans
57 K8 **Clee St Margaret** Shrops
57 K9 **Cleestanton** Shrops
93 P9 **Cleethorpes** NE Lin
57 L9 **Cleeton St Mary** Shrops
31 N11 **Cleeve** N Som
34 H8 **Cleeve** Oxon
47 J9 **Cleeve Hill** Gloucs
47 L5 **Cleeve Prior** Worcs
128 F3 **Cleghornie** E Loth
45 N7 **Clehonger** Herefs
134 D8 **Cleish** P & K
126 D6 **Cleland** N Lans
50 B8 **Clement's End** C Beds
37 M6 **Clement Street** Kent
131 J2 **Clenamacrie** Ag & B
33 N11 **Clench Common** Wilts
75 L6 **Clenchwarton** Norfk
159 J5 **Clenerty** Abers
58 D9 **Clent** Worcs
57 M9 **Cleobury Mortimer** Shrops
57 L7 **Cleobury North** Shrops
120 C5 **Cleongart** Ag & B
156 E7 **Clephanton** Highld
117 K11 **Clerkhill** D & G
115 R7 **Cleuch-head** D & G
33 L9 **Clevancy** Wilts
31 M10 **Clevedon** N Som
48 C10 **Cleveley** Oxon
88 C2 **Cleveleys** Lancs
33 J7 **Cleverton** Wilts
19 M4 **Clewer** Somset
76 E3 **Cley next the Sea** Norfk
101 Q6 **Cliburn** Cumb
22 H5 **Cliddesden** Hants
59 K5 **Cliff** Warwks
89 L4 **Cliffe** Lancs
38 B6 **Cliffe** Medway
91 R4 **Cliffe** N York
103 P7 **Cliffe** N York
26 E9 **Cliff End** E Susx
38 B7 **Cliffe Woods** Medway
45 J5 **Clifford** Herefs
91 L2 **Clifford** Leeds
47 N4 **Clifford Chambers** Warwks
46 D10 **Clifford's Mesne** Gloucs
39 P9 **Cliffsend** Kent
31 Q10 **Clifton** Bristl
50 E3 **Clifton** C Beds
72 E4 **Clifton** C Nott
98 B10 **Clifton** C York
90 F6 **Clifton** Calder
101 P5 **Clifton** Cumb
71 M6 **Clifton** Derbys
17 L3 **Clifton** Devon
91 N11 **Clifton** Donc
88 F4 **Clifton** Lancs
97 J11 **Clifton** N York
113 K4 **Clifton** Nthumb
48 E8 **Clifton** Oxon
82 G4 **Clifton** Salfd
46 F5 **Clifton** Worcs
59 L2 **Clifton Campville** Staffs
34 F5 **Clifton Hampden** Oxon
49 P4 **Clifton Reynes** M Keyn
60 B5 **Clifton upon Dunsmore** Warwks
46 D2 **Clifton upon Teme** Worcs
39 Q7 **Cliftonville** Kent
15 Q6 **Climping** W Susx
20 E5 **Clink** Somset
97 L9 **Clint** N York
151 L5 **Clinterty** C Aber
76 E9 **Clint Green** Norfk
118 B4 **Clintmains** Border
55 J2 **Clipiau** Gwynd
77 N9 **Clippesby** Norfk
73 P7 **Clipsham** Rutlnd
60 F4 **Clipston** Nhants
72 G4 **Clipston** Notts
49 P9 **Clipstone** C Beds
85 J8 **Clipstone** Notts
89 L2 **Clitheroe** Lancs
69 P10 **Clive** Shrops
93 J10 **Clixby** Lincs
33 J6 **Cloatley** Wilts
68 E4 **Clocaenog** Denbgs
158 B5 **Clochan** Moray
82 B6 **Clock Face** St Hel
56 C3 **Cloddiau** Powys
45 L9 **Clodock** Herefs
20 D6 **Cloford** Somset
159 P9 **Clola** Abers
50 C3 **Clophill** C Beds
61 N4 **Clopton** Nhants
65 J11 **Clopton** Suffk
65 J11 **Clopton Corner** Suffk
63 N10 **Clopton Green** Suffk
64 D10 **Clopton Green** Suffk
10 c1 **Clos du Valle** Guern
109 J2 **Closeburn** D & G
109 K2 **Closeburnmill** D & G
80 c6 **Closeclark** IoM
11 M2 **Closworth** Somset
50 G4 **Clothall** Herts
69 P2 **Clotton** Ches W
59 Q7 **Cloudesley Bush** Warwks
46 A7 **Clouds** Herefs
89 Q9 **Clough** Oldham
89 Q6 **Clough Foot** Calder
90 D7 **Clough Head** Calder
99 L2 **Cloughton** N York
105 R11 **Cloughton Newlands** N York
169 q8 **Clousta** Shet
142 E3 **Clova** Angus
16 E7 **Clovelly** Devon
117 P3 **Clovenfords** Border
139 J5 **Clovulin** Highld
89 N5 **Clow Bridge** Lancs
84 G5 **Clowne** Derbys
57 N10 **Clows Top** Worcs
69 L6 **Cloy** Wrexhm
146 D5 **Cluanie Inn** Highld
146 D5 **Cluanie Lodge** Highld
5 M3 **Clubworthy** Cnwll
107 L6 **Clugston** D & G
56 E8 **Clun** Shrops
156 F8 **Clunas** Highld
56 F8 **Clunbury** Shrops
41 M7 **Clunderwen** Carmth
148 D2 **Clune** Highld
146 F10 **Clunes** Highld
56 F9 **Clungunford** Shrops
141 R9 **Clunie** P & K
56 E8 **Clunton** Shrops
134 G8 **Cluny** Fife
20 B3 **Clutton** BaNES
69 N4 **Clutton** Ches W
20 B3 **Clutton Hill** BaNES
67 K2 **Clwt-y-bont** Gwynd
30 H2 **Clydach** Mons
29 J4 **Clydach** Swans
30 C6 **Clydach Vale** Rhondd
125 M3 **Clydebank** W Duns
125 M3 **Clydebank Crematorium** W Duns
41 Q3 **Clydey** Pembks
33 L9 **Clyffe Pypard** Wilts
131 Q11 **Clynder** Ag & B
29 M4 **Clyne** Neath
66 G5 **Clynnog-fawr** Gwynd
45 J6 **Clyro** Powys
9 N6 **Clyst Honiton** Devon
9 P4 **Clyst Hydon** Devon
9 N7 **Clyst St George** Devon
9 P4 **Clyst St Lawrence** Devon
9 N6 **Clyst St Mary** Devon
168 j4 **Cnoc** W Isls
54 F10 **Cnwch Coch** Cerdgn
5 M6 **Coad's Green** Cnwll
84 E5 **Coal Aston** Derbys
30 G3 **Coalbrookvale** Blae G
126 E11 **Coalburn** S Lans
112 H8 **Coalburns** Gatesd
32 E4 **Coaley** Gloucs
38 C2 **Coalhill** Essex
57 M3 **Coalmoor** Wrekin
32 C8 **Coalpit Heath** S Glos
58 F5 **Coal Pool** Wsall
57 M4 **Coalport** Wrekin
133 Q8 **Coalsnaughton** Clacks
65 J7 **Coal Street** Suffk
134 H8 **Coaltown of Balgonie** Fife
135 J8 **Coaltown of Wemyss** Fife
72 C8 **Coalville** Leics
111 N9 **Coanwood** Nthumb
19 N10 **Coat** Somset
126 C4 **Coatbridge** N Lans
126 C4 **Coatdyke** N Lans
33 N8 **Coate** Swindn
21 K2 **Coate** Wilts
74 F11 **Coates** Cambs
33 J4 **Coates** Gloucs
86 B4 **Coates** Lincs
85 P4 **Coates** Notts
23 Q11 **Coates** W Susx
104 G5 **Coatham** R & Cl
103 Q6 **Coatham Mundeville** Darltn
17 L6 **Cobbaton** Devon
47 J11 **Coberley** Gloucs
45 P7 **Cobhall Common** Herefs
37 Q7 **Cobham** Kent
36 D8 **Cobham** Surrey
36 D9 *Cobham Services* Surrey
51 Q7 **Coblers Green** Essex
21 K10 **Cobley** Dorset
45 P2 **Cobnash** Herefs
10 b1 **Cobo** Guern
70 F5 **Cobridge** C Stke
159 M5 **Coburby** Abers
84 F6 **Cock Alley** Derbys
104 H11 **Cockayne** N York
62 C11 **Cockayne Hatley** C Beds
69 L5 **Cock Bank** Wrexhm
47 L4 **Cock Bevington** Warwks
149 P6 **Cock Bridge** Abers
129 K5 **Cockburnspath** Border
52 D11 **Cock Clarks** Essex
63 M10 **Cock & End** Suffk
128 C4 **Cockenzie and Port Seton** E Loth
88 G6 **Cocker Bar** Lancs
89 L5 **Cocker Brook** Lancs
95 K10 **Cockerham** Lancs
100 F4 **Cockermouth** Cumb
50 D6 **Cockernhoe** Herts
90 G5 **Cockersdale** Leeds
28 H6 **Cockett** Swans
103 M6 **Cockfield** Dur
64 C11 **Cockfield** Suffk
50 G11 **Cockfosters** Gt Lon
51 Q7 **Cock Green** Essex
23 N11 **Cocking** W Susx
23 N11 **Cocking Causeway** W Susx
7 M6 **Cockington** Torbay
19 M5 **Cocklake** Somset
100 H10 **Cockley Beck** Cumb
75 Q10 **Cockley Cley** Norfk
26 E8 **Cock Marling** E Susx
35 L8 **Cockpole Green** Wokham
3 K3 **Cocks** Cnwll
57 K7 **Cockshutford** Shrops
69 M9 **Cockshutt** Shrops
38 C11 **Cock Street** Kent
76 D3 **Cockthorpe** Norfk
2 E7 **Cockwells** Cnwll
9 N8 **Cockwood** Devon
18 H6 **Cockwood** Somset
83 M9 **Cockyard** Derbys
45 N8 **Cockyard** Herefs
64 G11 **Coddenham** Suffk
69 N3 **Coddington** Ches W
46 D6 **Coddington** Herefs
85 P10 **Coddington** Notts
21 J7 **Codford St Mary** Wilts
21 J7 **Codford St Peter** Wilts
50 F7 **Codicote** Herts
24 C6 **Codmore Hill** W Susx
84 F11 **Codnor** Derbys
32 D9 **Codrington** S Glos
58 C4 **Codsall** Staffs
58 B4 **Codsall Wood** Staffs
30 D7 **Coedely** Rhondd
31 J8 **Coedkernew** Newpt
31 L2 **Coed Morgan** Mons
69 J4 **Coedpoeth** Wrexhm
69 J3 **Coed Talon** Flints
69 K11 **Coedway** Powys
42 G5 **Coed-y-Bryn** Cerdgn
31 L6 **Coed-y-caerau** Newpt
31 K5 **Coed-y-paen** Mons
44 H10 **Coed-yr-ynys** Powys
67 K10 **Coed Ystumgwern** Gwynd
29 N2 **Coelbren** Powys
7 M5 **Coffinswell** Devon
61 M9 **Coffle End** Bed
9 N8 **Cofton** Devon
58 F9 **Cofton Hackett** Worcs
30 G10 **Cogan** V Glam
60 H8 **Cogenhoe** Nhants
34 C3 **Cogges** Oxon
52 E7 **Coggeshall** Essex
25 N5 **Coggin's Mill** E Susx
148 C4 **Coignafearn** Highld
149 Q8 **Coilacriech** Abers
132 H6 **Coilantogle** Stirlg
152 F10 **Coillore** Highld
29 P8 **Coity** Brdgnd
168 j4 **Col** W Isls
162 D4 **Colaboll** Highld
4 D9 **Colan** Cnwll
10 B7 **Colaton Raleigh** Devon
152 C8 **Colbost** Highld
103 N11 **Colburn** N York
102 C6 **Colby** Cumb
80 b7 **Colby** IoM
77 J5 **Colby** Norfk
52 G6 **Colchester** Essex
52 G7 **Colchester Crematorium** Essex
34 F11 **Cold Ash** W Berk
60 E5 **Cold Ashby** Nhants
32 E10 **Cold Ashton** S Glos
47 M11 **Cold Aston** Gloucs
165 P4 **Coldbackie** Highld
102 D10 **Coldbeck** Cumb
41 M8 **Cold Blow** Pembks
49 P4 **Cold Brayfield** M Keyn
95 Q6 **Cold Cotes** N York
24 H9 **Coldean** Br & H
7 L4 **Coldeast** Devon
90 B5 **Colden** Calder
22 E10 **Colden Common** Hants
65 N9 **Coldfair Green** Suffk
74 H10 **Coldham** Cambs
86 D4 **Cold Hanworth** Lincs
3 K4 **Coldharbour** Cnwll
9 Q2 **Coldharbour** Devon
31 Q4 **Coldharbour** Gloucs
50 D7 **Cold Harbour** Herts
34 H9 **Cold Harbour** Oxon
24 D2 **Coldharbour** Surrey
20 G5 **Cold Harbour** Wilts
70 A10 **Cold Hatton** Wrekin
70 A10 **Cold Hatton Heath** Wrekin
113 P11 **Cold Hesledon** Dur
91 K8 **Cold Hiendley** Wakefd
49 J4 **Cold Higham** Nhants
129 N6 **Coldingham** Border
98 A4 **Cold Kirby** N York
70 F8 **Coldmeece** Staffs
73 J9 **Cold Newton** Leics
5 L4 **Cold Northcott** Cnwll
52 E11 **Cold Norton** Essex
73 L8 **Cold Overton** Leics
27 N2 **Coldred** Kent
17 M10 **Coldridge** Devon
118 F3 **Coldstream** Border
24 B7 **Coldwaltham** W Susx
45 N7 **Coldwell** Herefs
159 N10 **Coldwells** Abers
57 K8 **Cold Weston** Shrops
20 C8 **Cole** Somset
56 E7 **Colebatch** Shrops
6 E7 **Colebrook** C Plym
9 P3 **Colebrook** Devon
9 J5 **Colebrooke** Devon
86 C8 **Coleby** Lincs
92 E7 **Coleby** N Linc
59 K7 **Cole End** Warwks
9 J4 **Coleford** Devon
31 Q2 **Coleford** Gloucs
20 C5 **Coleford** Somset
18 F8 **Coleford Water** Somset
64 H4 **Colegate End** Norfk
50 G8 **Cole Green** Herts
51 K4 **Cole Green** Herts
22 E4 **Cole Henley** Hants
12 H4 **Colehill** Dorset
50 E8 **Coleman Green** Herts
25 K4 **Coleman's Hatch** E Susx
69 M8 **Colemere** Shrops
23 K8 **Colemore** Hants
57 N5 **Colemore Green** Shrops
134 E2 **Colenden** P & K
72 C7 **Coleorton** Leics
32 F10 **Colerne** Wilts
33 K2 **Colesbourne** Gloucs
7 K9 **Cole's Cross** Devon
10 H4 **Coles Cross** Dorset
61 P9 **Colesden** Bed
53 K3 **Coles Green** Suffk
35 P5 **Coleshill** Bucks
33 P6 **Coleshill** Oxon
59 K7 **Coleshill** Warwks
10 B4 **Colestocks** Devon
19 Q3 **Coley** BaNES
24 F4 **Colgate** W Susx
135 M7 **Colinsburgh** Fife
127 N4 **Colinton** C Edin
124 C3 **Colintraive** Ag & B
76 C6 **Colkirk** Norfk
136 G4 **Coll** Ag & B
142 C11 **Collace** P & K
169 q5 **Collafirth** Shet
136 F4 *Coll Airport* Ag & B
7 J11 **Collaton** Devon
7 M6 **Collaton St Mary** Torbay
157 L4 **College of Roseisle** Moray
23 N2 **College Town** Br For
134 H5 **Collessie** Fife
17 M8 **Colleton Mills** Devon
37 M2 **Collier Row** Gt Lon
51 J6 **Collier's End** Herts
26 C7 **Collier's Green** E Susx
26 C4 **Colliers Green** Kent
26 B2 **Collier Street** Kent
113 M11 **Colliery Row** Sundld
151 Q2 **Collieston** Abers
109 M5 **Collin** D & G
21 P4 **Collingbourne Ducis** Wilts
21 P3 **Collingbourne Kingston** Wilts
97 N11 **Collingham** Leeds
85 P8 **Collingham** Notts
46 B2 **Collington** Herefs
60 G9 **Collingtree** Nhants
82 C6 **Collins Green** Warrtn
46 D3 **Collins Green** Worcs
143 L8 **Colliston** Angus
10 B4 **Colliton** Devon
73 P10 **Collyweston** Nhants
114 B10 **Colmonell** S Ayrs
61 P9 **Colmworth** Bed
36 B5 **Colnbrook** Slough
62 E5 **Colne** Cambs
89 P3 **Colne** Lancs
90 F6 **Colne Bridge** Kirk
89 P2 **Colne Edge** Lancs
52 D5 **Colne Engaine** Essex
76 H10 **Colney** Norfk
50 F9 **Colney Heath** Herts
50 E10 **Colney Street** Herts
33 L3 **Coln Rogers** Gloucs
33 M3 **Coln St Aldwyns** Gloucs
33 L2 **Coln St Dennis** Gloucs
136 b2 **Colonsay** Ag & B
136 b3 *Colonsay Airport* Ag & B
158 F11 **Colpy** Abers
117 L2 **Colquhar** Border
4 H7 **Colquite** Cnwll
16 F9 **Colscott** Devon
96 H4 **Colsterdale** N York
73 N6 **Colsterworth** Lincs
73 J4 **Colston Bassett** Notts
157 L5 **Coltfield** Moray
23 L4 **Colt Hill** Hants
77 K8 **Coltishall** Norfk
94 G3 **Colton** Cumb
91 K4 **Colton** Leeds
91 N2 **Colton** N York
76 G10 **Colton** Norfk
71 J10 **Colton** Staffs
25 P2 **Colt's Hill** Kent
9 N5 **Columbjohn** Devon
44 H4 **Colva** Powys
109 J10 **Colvend** D & G
46 E6 **Colwall** Herefs
112 E5 **Colwell** Nthumb
71 J10 **Colwich** Staffs
72 G2 **Colwick** Notts
29 P9 **Colwinston** V Glam
15 P6 **Colworth** W Susx
80 B9 **Colwyn Bay** Conwy
10 F6 **Colyford** Devon
10 E6 **Colyton** Devon
7 J11 **Combe** Devon
45 L2 **Combe** Herefs
48 D11 **Combe** Oxon
22 C2 **Combe** W Berk
12 G5 **Combe Almer** Dorset
23 P7 **Combe Common** Surrey
20 E2 **Combe Down** BaNES
7 L5 **Combe Fishacre** Devon
18 G8 **Combe Florey** Somset
20 D3 **Combe Hay** BaNES
7 N4 **Combeinteignhead** Devon
17 K2 **Combe Martin** Devon
10 D4 **Combe Raleigh** Devon
82 D9 **Comberbach** Ches W
59 J3 **Comberford** Staffs
62 E9 **Comberton** Cambs
56 H11 **Comberton** Herefs
10 G2 **Combe St Nicholas** Somset
10 F6 **Combpyne** Devon
71 K8 **Combridge** Staffs
48 B4 **Combrook** Warwks
83 M9 **Combs** Derbys
64 E10 **Combs** Suffk
64 E10 **Combs Ford** Suffk
19 J6 **Combwich** Somset
150 H6 **Comers** Abers
58 B11 **Comhampton** Worcs
63 J8 **Commercial End** Cambs
55 J4 **Commins Coch** Powys
105 J8 **Commondale** N York
88 C4 **Common Edge** Bpool
100 D6 **Common End** Cumb
5 L8 **Common Moor** Cnwll
33 M7 **Common Platt** Wilts
82 B10 **Commonside** Ches W
71 N6 **Commonside** Derbys
84 D5 **Common Side** Derbys
69 N9 **Commonwood** Shrops
69 L4 **Commonwood** Wrexhm
19 J8 **Compass** Somset
83 L6 **Compstall** Stockp
108 E10 **Compstonend** D & G
7 M6 **Compton** Devon
22 B9 **Compton** Hants
22 E9 **Compton** Hants
57 Q8 **Compton** Staffs
23 Q5 **Compton** Surrey
34 F8 **Compton** W Berk
15 L4 **Compton** W Susx
21 M4 **Compton** Wilts

20 G11	**Compton Abbas** Dorset	9 J4	**Copplestone** Devon
47 L11	**Compton Abdale** Gloucs	88 H8	**Coppull** Lancs
33 K10	**Compton Bassett** Wilts	88 H8	**Coppull Moor** Lancs
33 Q7	**Compton Beauchamp** Oxon	24 E6	**Copsale** W Susx
19 L3	**Compton Bishop** Somset	89 K4	**Copster Green** Lancs
21 K9	**Compton Chamberlayne** Wilts	59 Q7	**Copston Magna** Warwks
20 B2	**Compton Dando** BaNES	39 N9	**Cop Street** Kent
19 N8	**Compton Dundon** Somset	51 K10	**Copthall Green** Essex
19 M11	**Compton Durville** Somset	59 J9	**Copt Heath** Solhll
31 Q8	**Compton Greenfield** S Glos	97 M6	**Copt Hewick** N York
19 P3	**Compton Martin** BaNES	5 M3	**Copthorne** Cnwll
20 B9	**Compton Pauncefoot** Somset	24 H3	**Copthorne** W Susx
11 M6	**Compton Valence** Dorset	72 D8	**Copt Oak** Leics
48 B4	**Compton Verney** Warwks	76 C4	**Copy's Green** Norfk
134 C10	**Comrie** Fife	13 P2	**Copythorne** Hants
133 M3	**Comrie** P & K	52 H3	**Coram Street** Suffk
139 J4	**Conaglen House** Highld	37 N3	**Corbets Tey** Gt Lon
145 Q2	**Conchra** Highld	11 a2	**Corbiere** Jersey
141 Q9	**Concraigie** P & K	112 E8	**Corbridge** Nthumb
95 K9	**Conder Green** Lancs	61 J3	**Corby** Nhants
47 J7	**Conderton** Worcs	73 Q6	**Corby Glen** Lincs
47 N9	**Condicote** Gloucs	111 J9	**Corby Hill** Cumb
126 C3	**Condorrat** N Lans	121 K5	**Cordon** N Ayrs
56 H3	**Condover** Shrops	84 D5	**Cordwell** Derbys
46 G11	**Coney Hill** Gloucs	57 L10	**Coreley** Shrops
24 D6	**Coneyhurst Common** W Susx	35 P7	**Cores End** Bucks
98 E6	**Coneysthorpe** N York	18 H11	**Corfe** Somset
97 N9	**Coneythorpe** N York	12 G8	**Corfe Castle** Dorset
64 D6	**Coney Weston** Suffk	12 G5	**Corfe Mullen** Dorset
23 M8	**Conford** Hants	56 H7	**Corfton** Shrops
5 M6	**Congdon's Shop** Cnwll	149 P6	**Corgarff** Abers
72 B9	**Congerstone** Leics	22 H10	**Corhampton** Hants
75 P6	**Congham** Norfk	25 Q2	**Corks Pond** Kent
70 F2	**Congleton** Ches E	59 M7	**Corley** Warwks
67 N6	**Congl-y-wal** Gwynd	59 L7	**Corley Ash** Warwks
19 M2	**Congresbury** N Som	59 L8	**Corley Moor** Warwks
58 D2	**Congreve** Staffs	59 M7	**Corley Services** Warwks
109 L7	**Conheath** D & G	142 K4	**Cormuir** Angus
156 H1	**Conicavel** Moray	52 F3	**Cornard Tye** Suffk
86 H9	**Coningsby** Lincs	8 G7	**Corndon** Devon
61 Q3	**Conington** Cambs	88 E4	**Corner Row** Lancs
62 D7	**Conington** Cambs	94 C2	**Corney** Cumb
91 N11	**Conisbrough** Donc	104 B4	**Cornforth** Dur
93 R11	**Conisholme** Lincs	158 E6	**Cornhill** Abers
101 K11	**Coniston** Cumb	118 G3	**Cornhill-on-Tweed** Nthumb
93 L3	**Coniston** E R Yk	89 Q5	**Cornholme** Calder
96 D10	**Coniston Cold** N York	51 Q3	**Cornish Hall End** Essex
96 E7	**Conistone** N York	136 B6	**Cornoigmore** Ag & B
81 K11	**Connah's Quay** Flints	102 F2	**Cornriggs** Dur
138 G11	**Connel** Ag & B	103 M2	**Cornsay** Dur
115 M5	**Connel Park** E Ayrs	103 N2	**Cornsay Colliery** Dur
2 F6	**Connor Downs** Cnwll	155 Q6	**Corntown** Highld
155 P6	**Conon Bridge** Highld	29 P9	**Corntown** V Glam
96 E11	**Cononley** N York	47 Q9	**Cornwell** Oxon
70 H5	**Consall** Staffs	6 G7	**Cornwood** Devon
112 H10	**Consett** Dur	7 L7	**Cornworthy** Devon
97 J2	**Constable Burton** N York	139 K2	**Corpach** Highld
89 N6	**Constable Lee** Lancs	76 G6	**Corpusty** Norfk
3 J8	**Constantine** Cnwll	150 D7	**Corrachree** Abers
4 D7	**Constantine Bay** Cnwll	139 J5	**Corran** Highld
155 N6	**Contin** Highld	145 P6	**Corran** Highld
79 P9	**Conwy** Conwy	80 g4	**Corrany** IoM
38 G9	**Conyer** Kent	110 D3	**Corrie** D & G
64 B8	**Conyer's Green** Suffk	121 K3	**Corrie** N Ayrs
26 B10	**Cooden** E Susx	120 H7	**Corriecravie** N Ayrs
16 G10	**Cookbury** Devon	121 K4	**Corriegills** N Ayrs
16 F10	**Cookbury Wick** Devon	146 H9	**Corriegour Lodge Hotel** Highld
35 N7	**Cookham** W & M	155 L5	**Corriemoille** Highld
35 N7	**Cookham Dean** W & M	155 L11	**Corrimony** Highld
35 N7	**Cookham Rise** W & M	85 Q2	**Corringham** Lincs
47 L3	**Cookhill** Worcs	38 B5	**Corringham** Thurr
65 L6	**Cookley** Suffk	54 H3	**Corris** Gwynd
58 B8	**Cookley** Worcs	54 G3	**Corris Uchaf** Gwynd
35 J6	**Cookley Green** Oxon	131 P7	**Corrow** Ag & B
151 M9	**Cookney** Abers	145 K3	**Corry** Highld
25 K8	**Cooksbridge** E Susx	8 F5	**Corscombe** Devon
58 D11	**Cooksey Green** Worcs	11 L3	**Corscombe** Dorset
53 L8	**Cook's Green** Essex	46 E9	**Corse** Gloucs
64 D11	**Cooks Green** Suffk	46 F8	**Corse Lawn** Gloucs
70 G6	**Cookshill** Staffs	32 G10	**Corsham** Wilts
4 H8	**Cooksland** Cnwll	150 H6	**Corsindae** Abers
51 P9	**Cooksmill Green** Essex	20 F5	**Corsley** Wilts
82 C10	**Cookson Green** Ches W	20 F5	**Corsley Heath** Wilts
24 D6	**Coolham** W Susx	108 G5	**Corsock** D & G
38 C6	**Cooling** Medway	32 C11	**Corston** BaNES
38 B7	**Cooling Street** Medway	32 H8	**Corston** Wilts
2 G5	**Coombe** Cnwll	127 M3	**Corstorphine** C Edin
3 L5	**Coombe** Cnwll	67 L10	**Cors-y-Gedol** Gwynd
3 N3	**Coombe** Cnwll	142 F6	**Cortachy** Angus
7 N4	**Coombe** Devon	65 Q2	**Corton** Suffk
9 K8	**Coombe** Devon	20 H6	**Corton** Wilts
10 C6	**Coombe** Devon	20 B10	**Corton Denham** Somset
32 E6	**Coombe** Gloucs	139 K4	**Coruanan** Highld
23 J10	**Coombe** Hants	68 E6	**Corwen** Denbgs
21 M4	**Coombe** Wilts	11 N7	**Coryates** Dorset
21 M9	**Coombe Bissett** Wilts	8 C8	**Coryton** Devon
7 N4	**Coombe Cellars** Devon	38 B5	**Coryton** Thurr
23 J10	**Coombe Cross** Hants	72 E11	**Cosby** Leics
46 G9	**Coombe Hill** Gloucs	58 D6	**Coseley** Dudley
12 D8	**Coombe Keynes** Dorset	57 Q3	**Cosford** Shrops
7 N5	**Coombe Pafford** Torbay	49 L6	**Cosgrove** Nhants
24 E9	**Coombes** W Susx	15 J5	**Cosham** C Port
45 M2	**Coombes-Moor** Herefs	41 K10	**Cosheston** Pembks
20 E8	**Coombe Street** Somset	141 J8	**Coshieville** P & K
58 E7	**Coombeswood** Dudley	72 D2	**Cossall** Notts
51 L10	**Coopersale Common** Essex	72 D2	**Cossall Marsh** Notts
51 L10	**Coopersale Street** Essex	72 G8	**Cossington** Leics
37 L11	**Cooper's Corner** Kent	19 L6	**Cossington** Somset
25 L6	**Coopers Green** E Susx	76 H9	**Costessey** Norfk
50 E9	**Coopers Green** Herts	72 F5	**Costock** Notts
39 P9	**Cooper Street** Kent	73 L6	**Coston** Leics
89 J9	**Cooper Turning** Bolton	76 F10	**Coston** Norfk
24 C8	**Cootham** W Susx	34 C4	**Cote** Oxon
53 K3	**Copdock** Suffk	19 K6	**Cote** Somset
52 F7	**Copford Green** Essex	82 C11	**Cotebrook** Ches W
97 M8	**Copgrove** N York	111 J10	**Cotehill** Cumb
169 r6	**Copister** Shet	95 K3	**Cotes** Cumb
61 P11	**Cople** Bed	72 F6	**Cotes** Leics
90 D6	**Copley** Calder	70 E8	**Cotes** Staffs
103 L5	**Copley** Dur	60 B4	**Cotesbach** Leics
83 L5	**Copley** Tamesd	70 E8	**Cotes Heath** Staffs
83 Q9	**Coplow Dale** Derbys	18 H2	**Cotford St Luke** Somset
98 B11	**Copmanthorpe** C York	72 G3	**Cotgrave** Notts
70 E9	**Copmere End** Staffs	151 M4	**Cothal** Abers
88 E3	**Copp** Lancs	85 N11	**Cotham** Notts
16 C11	**Coppathorne** Cnwll	18 G8	**Cothelstone** Somset
70 G11	**Coppenhall** Staffs	103 K7	**Cotherstone** Dur
70 C3	**Coppenhall Moss** Ches E	34 E5	**Cothill** Oxon
2 F6	**Copperhouse** Cnwll	10 E4	**Cotleigh** Devon
57 N8	**Coppicegate** Shrops	72 D2	**Cotmanhay** Derbys
61 Q5	**Coppingford** Cambs	62 F9	**Coton** Cambs
26 F2	**Coppins Corner** Kent	60 E6	**Coton** Nhants
		69 P8	**Coton** Shrops
		59 J4	**Coton** Staffs
		70 E10	**Coton** Staffs
		70 H8	**Coton** Staffs
		70 F10	**Coton Clanford** Staffs
		70 H8	**Coton Hayes** Staffs

56 H2	**Coton Hill** Shrops	51 N11	**Coxtie Green** Essex
71 M9	**Coton in the Clay** Staffs	98 A5	**Coxwold** N York
71 N11	**Coton in the Elms** Derbys	29 P9	**Coychurch** Brdgnd
71 P11	**Coton Park** Derbys	29 P9	**Coychurch Crematorium** Brdgnd
33 J3	**Cotswolds**	114 H4	**Coylton** S Ayrs
7 K6	**Cott** Devon	148 G5	**Coylumbridge** Highld
22 D6	**Cottage End** Hants	29 N7	**Coytrahen** Brdgnd
88 G4	**Cottam** Lancs	51 F3	**Crabbs Cross** Worcs
85 P5	**Cottam** Notts	13 J3	**Crab Orchard** Dorset
62 F7	**Cottenham** Cambs	7 L4	**Crabtree** W Susx
96 B2	**Cotterdale** N York	69 K6	**Crabtree Green** Wrexhm
50 H5	**Cottered** Herts	102 C6	**Crackenthorpe** Cumb
58 F8	**Cotteridge** Birm	5 J2	**Crackington Haven** Cnwll
61 M2	**Cotterstock** Nhants	70 E4	**Crackley** Staffs
60 F6	**Cottesbrooke** Nhants	59 L10	**Crackley** Warwks
73 N8	**Cottesmore** Rutlnd	57 P2	**Crackleybank** Shrops
92 H4	**Cottingham** E R Yk	103 J11	**Crackpot** N York
60 H2	**Cottingham** Nhants	96 E8	**Cracoe** N York
90 E3	**Cottingley** C Brad	10 B2	**Craddock** Devon
90 M4	**Cottingley Hall Crematorium** Leeds	51 L6	**Cradle End** Herts
48 G8	**Cottisford** Oxon	58 D7	**Cradley** Dudley
64 F8	**Cotton** Suffk	45 N6	**Cradley** Herefs
61 N11	**Cotton End** Bed	58 D7	**Cradley Heath** Sandw
89 Q3	**Cotton Tree** Lancs	44 E8	**Cradoc** Powys
150 E2	**Cottown** Abers	5 P11	**Crafthole** Cnwll
151 K4	**Cottown** Abers	49 N11	**Crafton** Bucks
159 K9	**Cottown of Gight** Abers	95 K6	**Crag Foot** Lancs
6 C5	**Cotts** Devon	149 J2	**Craggan** Highld
69 R11	**Cotwall** Wrekin	90 G3	**Cragg Hill** Leeds
70 G8	**Cotwalton** Staffs	113 K10	**Craghead** Dur
5 J10	**Couch's Mill** Cnwll	44 B10	**Crai** Powys
46 A10	**Coughton** Herefs	158 C6	**Craibstone** Moray
47 L2	**Coughton** Warwks	143 J8	**Craichie** Angus
123 M6	**Coulaghailtro** Ag & B	143 J6	**Craig** Angus
154 C9	**Coulags** Highld	154 D8	**Craig** Highld
100 C9	**Coulderton** Cumb	115 L5	**Craigbank** E Ayrs
150 E7	**Coull** Abers	127 N7	**Craigburn** Border
131 Q10	**Coulport** Ag & B	110 F3	**Craigcleuch** D & G
36 G9	**Coulsdon** Gt Lon	159 K11	**Craigdam** Abers
21 J4	**Coulston** Wilts	130 G6	**Craigdhu** Ag & B
116 E4	**Coulter** S Lans	151 J5	**Craigearn** Abers
23 Q11	**Coultershaw Bridge** W Susx	157 P9	**Craigellachie** Moray
18 H6	**Coultings** Somset	134 E3	**Craigend** P & K
98 C6	**Coulton** N York	125 M3	**Craigend** Rens
135 K3	**Coultra** Fife	132 C11	**Craigendoran** Ag & B
57 K3	**Cound** Shrops	125 L4	**Craigends** Rens
57 K4	**Coundlane** Shrops	107 K5	**Craighlaw** D & G
103 P5	**Coundon** Dur	122 H6	**Craighouse** Ag & B
103 P5	**Coundon Grange** Dur	141 R9	**Craigie** P & K
96 D3	**Countersett** N York	125 L11	**Craigie** S Ayrs
21 N6	**Countess** Wilts	159 M4	**Craigiefold** Abers
52 E5	**Countess Cross** Essex	108 G9	**Craigley** D & G
9 M7	**Countess Wear** Devon	29 K4	**Craig Llangiwg** Neath
72 F11	**Countesthorpe** Leics	127 N3	**Craiglockhart** C Edin
17 N2	**Countisbury** Devon	127 Q3	**Craigmillar** C Edin
142 C10	**Coupar Angus** P & K	69 J7	**Craignant** Shrops
88 H5	**Coup Green** Lancs	115 Q10	**Craigneston** D & G
102 D7	**Coupland** Cumb	126 D4	**Craigneuk** N Lans
118 H4	**Coupland** Nthumb	126 D6	**Craigneuk** N Lans
123 P10	**Cour** Ag & B	138 C10	**Craignure** Ag & B
27 J4	**Court-at-Street** Kent	143 M5	**Craigo** Angus
145 L8	**Courteachan** Highld	30 D7	**Craig Penllyn** V Glam
49 L4	**Courteenhall** Nhants	135 K5	**Craigrothie** Fife
43 L10	**Court Henry** Carmth	132 F3	**Craigruie** Stirlg
38 H3	**Courtsend** Essex	52 B4	**Craig's End** Essex
18 H8	**Courtway** Somset	143 J10	**Craigton** Angus
128 B6	**Cousland** Mdloth	151 L7	**Craigton** C Aber
25 Q4	**Cousley Wood** E Susx	125 M7	**Craigton** E Rens
131 Q11	**Cove** Ag & B	125 N5	**Craigton Crematorium** C Glas
129 K5	**Cove** Border	142 E7	**Craigton of Airlie** Angus
18 C11	**Cove** Devon	29 K4	**Craig-y-Duke** Neath
23 N3	**Cove** Hants	44 A11	**Craig-y-nos** Powys
160 C8	**Cove** Highld	135 Q6	**Crail** Fife
65 P6	**Cove Bottom** Suffk	118 C6	**Crailing** Border
151 P7	**Cove Bay** C Aber	92 C11	**Craiselound** N Linc
65 P6	**Cove Bottom** Suffk	97 K3	**Crakehall** N York
65 Q5	**Covehithe** Suffk	97 P6	**Crakehill** N York
58 D3	**Coven** Staffs	71 K7	**Crakemarsh** Staffs
62 G4	**Coveney** Cambs	98 E8	**Crambe** N York
87 K2	**Covenham St Bartholomew** Lincs	113 L5	**Cramlington** Nthumb
87 K2	**Covenham St Mary** Lincs	127 M2	**Cramond** C Edin
58 D3	**Coven Heath** Staffs	127 M2	**Cramond Bridge** C Edin
59 M9	**Coventry** Covtry	22 C10	**Crampmoor** Hants
59 N10	**Coventry Airport** Warwks	82 G11	**Cranage** Ches E
3 K10	**Coverack** Cnwll	71 P7	**Cranberry** Staffs
2 H7	**Coverack Bridges** Cnwll	13 J2	**Cranborne** Dorset
96 H3	**Coverham** N York	35 P10	**Cranbourne** Br For
61 N6	**Covington** Cambs	26 C4	**Cranbrook** Kent
116 D3	**Covington** S Lans	26 C4	**Cranbrook Common** Kent
95 N5	**Cowan Bridge** Lancs	91 J10	**Crane Moor** Barns
25 P8	**Cowbeech** E Susx	76 C9	**Crane's Corner** Norfk
74 E7	**Cowbit** Lincs	49 Q6	**Cranfield** C Beds
30 C10	**Cowbridge** V Glam	16 E7	**Cranford** Gt Lon
83 N10	**Cowdale** Derbys	36 D5	**Cranford** Gt Lon
25 L2	**Cowden** Kent	61 K5	**Cranford St Andrew** Nhants
134 F9	**Cowdenbeath** Fife	61 K5	**Cranford St John** Nhants
25 L2	**Cowden Pound** Kent	32 G2	**Cranham** Gloucs
25 L2	**Cowden Station** Kent	37 N3	**Cranham** Gt Lon
71 Q5	**Cowers Lane** Derbys	47 M4	**Cranhill** Warwks
14 E7	**Cowes** IoW	81 Q5	**Crank** St Hel
97 Q3	**Cowesby** N York	24 C3	**Cranleigh** Surrey
21 Q10	**Cowesfield Green** Wilts	64 C7	**Cranmer Green** Suffk
24 F6	**Cowfold** W Susx	14 C8	**Cranmore** IoW
95 R3	**Cowgill** Cumb	20 C6	**Cranmore** Somset
64 F8	**Cow Green** Suffk	73 K11	**Cranoe** Leics
32 B6	**Cowhill** S Glos	65 L9	**Cransford** Suffk
133 N10	**Cowie** Stirlg	128 H7	**Cranshaws** Border
99 K7	**Cowlam** E R Yk	80 g1	**Cranstal** IoM
9 M5	**Cowley** Devon	99 L10	**Cranswick** E R Yk
33 J2	**Cowley** Gloucs	4 B9	**Crantock** Cnwll
36 C4	**Cowley** Gt Lon	86 D11	**Cranwell** Lincs
34 F4	**Cowley** Oxon	63 N2	**Cranwich** Norfk
88 H7	**Cowling** N York	76 D11	**Cranworth** Norfk
90 B2	**Cowling** N York	130 F6	**Craobh Haven** Ag & B
97 K3	**Cowling** N York	6 E5	**Crapstone** Devon
63 M10	**Cowlinge** Suffk	131 K8	**Crarae** Ag & B
90 F7	**Cowmes** Kirk	162 C2	**Crask Inn** Highld
89 N6	**Cowpe** Lancs	155 N9	**Crask of Aigas** Highld
113 L4	**Cowpen** Nthumb	119 Q7	**Craster** Nthumb
104 E6	**Cowpen Bewley** S on T	45 K7	**Craswall** Herefs
15 J4	**Cowplain** Hants	58 D3	**Crateford** Staffs
102 G2	**Cowshill** Dur	65 L6	**Cratfield** Suffk
19 N2	**Cowslip Green** N Som	151 K8	**Crathes** Abers
97 P10	**Cowthorpe** N York	151 J8	**Crathes Castle** Abers
56 F10	**Coxall** Herefs	149 P8	**Crathie** Abers
70 B6	**Coxbank** Ches E	147 P9	**Crathie** Highld
72 B2	**Coxbench** Derbys	104 D9	**Crathorne** N York
19 P7	**Coxbridge** Somset	56 G8	**Craven Arms** Shrops
65 N5	**Cox Common** Suffk	112 H8	**Crawcrook** Gatesd
5 K2	**Coxford** Cnwll	81 P4	**Crawford** Lancs
76 B6	**Coxford** Norfk	116 B6	**Crawford** S Lans
57 Q2	**Coxgreen** Staffs	116 B7	**Crawfordjohn** S Lans
38 B11	**Coxheath** Kent	22 H7	**Crawley** Hants
104 B3	**Coxhoe** Dur	34 B2	**Crawley** Oxon
19 P6	**Coxley** Somset	24 G3	**Crawley** W Susx
90 H7	**Coxley** Wakefd	24 H3	**Crawley Down** W Susx
19 P6	**Coxley Wick** Somset	103 J2	**Crawleyside** Dur
5 Q7	**Coxpark** Cnwll	89 N5	**Crawshawbooth** Lancs
		143 R2	**Crawton** Abers
		52 F8	**Craxe's Green** Essex
		96 C5	**Cray** N York
		37 M5	**Crayford** Gt Lon
		98 B6	**Crayke** N York
		76 F5	**Craymere Beck** Norfk
		38 B3	**Crays Hill** Essex
		34 H8	**Cray's Pond** Oxon
		71 N9	**Craythorne** Staffs
		9 N2	**Craze Lowman** Devon
		35 L8	**Crazies Hill** Wokham
		17 Q8	**Creacombe** Devon
		138 H9	**Creagan Inn** Ag & B
		168 c13	**Creag Ghoraidh** W Isls
		168 c13	**Creagorry** W Isls
		139 Q4	**Creaguaineach Lodge** Highld
		69 P8	**Creamore Bank** Shrops
		60 F6	**Creaton** Nhants
		110 D6	**Creca** D & G
		45 P6	**Credenhill** Herefs
		9 K4	**Crediton** Devon
		107 K2	**Creebank** D & G
		107 M4	**Creebridge** D & G
		12 F8	**Creech** Dorset
		19 J9	**Creech Heathfield** Somset
		19 J9	**Creech St Michael** Somset
		3 N4	**Creed** Cnwll
		37 L4	**Creekmouth** Gt Lon
		38 F7	**Creeksea** Essex
		64 F10	**Creeting St Mary** Suffk
		73 Q6	**Creeton** Lincs
		107 N6	**Creetown** D & G
		80 a8	**Cregneash** IoM
		80 e5	**Cregny Baa** IoM
		44 G4	**Cregrina** Powys
		135 J3	**Creich** Fife
		30 E8	**Creigiau** Cardif
		6 D8	**Cremyll** Cnwll
		57 K4	**Cressage** Shrops
		83 Q10	**Cressbrook** Derbys
		41 L9	**Cresselly** Pembks
		35 M6	**Cressex** Bucks
		52 C7	**Cressing** Essex
		113 L2	**Cresswell** Nthumb
		41 L9	**Cresswell** Pembks
		70 H7	**Cresswell** Staffs
		84 H6	**Creswell** Derbys
		58 G2	**Creswell Green** Staffs
		65 J9	**Cretingham** Suffk
		123 M6	**Cretshengan** Ag & B
		70 C3	**Crewe** Ches E
		69 M4	**Crewe** Ches W
		70 C3	**Crewe Crematorium** Ches E
		70 C3	**Crewe Green** Ches E
		69 K11	**Crew Green** Powys
		11 J3	**Crewkerne** Somset
		50 H10	**Crews Hill Station** Gt Lon
		72 B4	**Crewton** C Derb
		132 D2	**Crianlarich** Stirlg
		43 K4	**Cribyn** Cerdgn
		66 H7	**Criccieth** Gwynd
		84 D10	**Crich** Derbys
		84 D10	**Crich Carr** Derbys
		128 B7	**Crichton** Mdloth
		31 N6	**Crick** Mons
		60 C6	**Crick** Nhants
		44 F6	**Crickadarn** Powys
		10 H3	**Cricket St Thomas** Somset
		69 J10	**Crickheath** Shrops
		45 J11	**Crickhowell** Powys
		33 L6	**Cricklade** Wilts
		36 F3	**Cricklewood** Gt Lon
		91 N6	**Cridling Stubbs** N York
		133 P3	**Crieff** P & K
		4 G9	**Criggan** Cnwll
		69 J11	**Criggion** Powys
		91 J7	**Crigglestone** Wakefd
		89 P8	**Crimble** Rochdl
		159 Q6	**Crimond** Abers
		75 N10	**Crimplesham** Norfk
		47 P5	**Crimscote** Warwks
		155 M9	**Crinaglack** Highld
		130 F9	**Crinan** Ag & B
		126 E6	**Crindledyke** N Lans
		76 H10	**Cringleford** Norfk
		96 F11	**Cringles** C Brad
		41 M8	**Crinow** Pembks
		2 E6	**Crippleease** Cnwll
		13 J2	**Cripplestyle** Dorset
		26 C7	**Cripp's Corner** E Susx
		148 B2	**Croachy** Highld
		4 G7	**Croanford** Cnwll
		72 E11	**Croft** Leics
		87 P11	**Croft** Lincs
		82 D6	**Croft** Warrtn
		132 F10	**Croftamie** Stirlg
		2 H6	**Croft Mitchell** Cnwll
		110 F10	**Crofton** Cumb
		91 K7	**Crofton** Wakefd
		21 Q5	**Crofton** Wilts
		103 Q9	**Croft-on-Tees** N York
		161 K10	**Croftown** Highld
		157 P7	**Crofts** Moray
		82 G5	**Crofts Bank** Traffd
		157 N10	**Crofts of Dipple** Moray
		159 P5	**Crofts of Savoch** Abers
		28 H6	**Crofty** Swans
		31 K6	**Crogen** Gwynd
		130 E2	**Croggan** Ag & B
		111 L11	**Croglin** Cumb
		162 B8	**Croick** Highld
		156 D4	**Cromarty** Highld

134 D11	**Crombie**	Fife
149 K2	**Cromdale**	Highld
50 G5	**Cromer**	Herts
77 J3	**Cromer**	Norfk
84 C9	**Cromford**	Derbys
32 C6	**Cromhall**	S Glos
32 C7	**Cromhall Common**	S Glos
168 j5	**Cromor**	W Isls
89 Q9	**Crompton Fold**	Oldham
85 N8	**Cromwell**	Notts
115 M3	**Cronberry**	E Ayrs
23 L5	**Crondall**	Hants
80 e6	**Cronkbourne**	IoM
80 d4	**Cronk-y-Voddy**	IoM
81 P7	**Cronton**	Knows
101 N11	**Crook**	Cumb
103 N3	**Crook**	Dur
100 G2	**Crookdake**	Cumb
88 H9	**Crooke**	Wigan
46 B11	**Crooked End**	Gloucs
125 M10	**Crookedholm**	E Ayrs
34 B10	**Crooked Soley**	Wilts
84 D3	**Crookes**	Sheff
112 H10	**Crookhall**	Dur
118 H3	**Crookham**	Nthumb
22 F2	**Crookham**	W Berk
23 L4	**Crookham Village**	Hants
116 G5	**Crook Inn**	Border
95 L4	**Crooklands**	Cumb
134 C7	**Crook of Devon**	P & K
71 N7	**Cropper**	Derbys
48 E5	**Cropredy**	Oxon
72 F8	**Cropston**	Leics
47 J5	**Cropthorne**	Worcs
98 F3	**Cropton**	N York
72 H3	**Cropwell Bishop**	Notts
72 H3	**Cropwell Butler**	Notts
168 k1	**Cros**	W Isls
168 i5	**Crosbost**	W Isls
100 E3	**Crosby**	Cumb
80 d6	**Crosby**	IoM
92 E8	**Crosby**	N Linc
81 L5	**Crosby**	Sefton
102 D9	**Crosby Garret**	Cumb
102 B8	**Crosby Ravensworth** Cumb	
100 E3	**Crosby Villa**	Cumb
19 Q6	**Croscombe**	Somset
69 M9	**Crosemere**	Shrops
90 E8	**Crosland Edge**	Kirk
90 E8	**Crosland Hill**	Kirk
19 M4	**Cross**	Somset
123 P9	**Crossaig**	Ag & B
136 B7	**Crossapoll**	Ag & B
45 N11	**Cross Ash**	Mons
26 C2	**Cross-at-Hand**	Kent
24 B9	**Crossbush**	W Susx
100 E3	**Crosscanonby**	Cumb
3 J3	**Cross Coombe**	Cnwll
77 J4	**Crossdale Street**	Norfk
61 N9	**Cross End**	Bed
52 E5	**Cross End**	Essex
88 D6	**Crossens**	Sefton
90 E2	**Cross Flatts**	C Brad
134 D10	**Crossford**	Fife
126 E8	**Crossford**	S Lans
5 N4	**Crossgate**	Cnwll
74 D5	**Crossgate**	Lincs
70 G7	**Crossgate**	Staffs
128 B6	**Crossgatehall**	E Loth
125 K9	**Crossgates**	E Ayrs
134 E10	**Crossgates**	Fife
91 K4	**Cross Gates**	Leeds
99 L4	**Crossgates**	N York
44 F2	**Crossgates**	Powys
95 M8	**Crossgill**	Lancs
5 P4	**Cross Green**	Devon
91 J4	**Cross Green**	Leeds
58 D3	**Cross Green**	Staffs
64 A11	**Cross Green**	Suffk
64 B10	**Cross Green**	Suffk
64 D11	**Cross Green**	Suffk
28 G2	**Cross Hands**	Carmth
41 N6	**Crosshands**	Carmth
125 M11	**Crosshands**	E Ayrs
41 L8	**Cross Hands**	Pembks
84 F11	**Cross Hill**	Derbys
134 F8	**Crosshill**	Fife
114 F6	**Crosshill**	S Ayrs
96 F11	**Cross Hills**	N York
125 K10	**Crosshouse**	E Ayrs
57 J3	**Cross Houses**	Shrops
57 M6	**Cross Houses**	Shrops
25 N6	**Cross in Hand**	E Susx
42 G3	**Cross Inn**	Cerdgn
43 K2	**Cross Inn**	Cerdgn
41 M9	**Cross Inn**	Pembks
30 E8	**Cross Inn**	Rhondd
132 C10	**Cross Keys**	Ag & B
30 H6	**Crosskeys**	Caerph
32 G10	**Cross Keys**	Wilts
166 H3	**Crosskirk**	Highld
94 G3	**Crosslands**	Cumb
14 F9	**Cross Lane**	IoW
57 N5	**Cross Lane Head**	Shrops
2 H9	**Cross Lanes**	Cnwll
3 K5	**Cross Lanes**	Cnwll
98 A8	**Cross Lanes**	N York
69 K11	**Crosslanes**	Shrops
69 L5	**Cross Lanes**	Wrexhm
125 L4	**Crosslee**	Rens
90 G6	**Crossley**	Kirk
108 F7	**Crossmichael**	D & G
44 G10	**Cross Oak**	Powys
158 H11	**Cross of Jackston**	Abers
71 P5	**Cross o' th' hands**	Derbys
24 G6	**Crosspost**	W Susx
150 F6	**Crossroads**	Abers
151 K9	**Crossroads**	Abers
64 H6	**Cross Street**	Suffk
143 J6	**Crosston**	Angus
82 G9	**Cross Town**	Ches E
45 N11	**Crossway**	Mons
44 F3	**Crossway**	Powys
31 P6	**Crossway Green**	Mons
58 B11	**Crossway Green**	Worcs
12 C7	**Crossways**	Dorset
41 M3	**Crosswell**	Pembks
95 J2	**Crosthwaite**	Cumb
88 F7	**Croston**	Lancs
77 K8	**Crostwick**	Norfk
77 L6	**Crostwight**	Norfk
37 P9	**Crouch**	Kent
39 J10	**Crouch**	Kent
36 H3	**Crouch End**	Gt Lon
21 L9	**Croucheston**	Wilts
11 Q2	**Crouch Hill**	Dorset
37 K11	**Crough House Green** Kent	
48 F8	**Croughton**	Nhants
159 K4	**Crovie**	Abers
13 L4	**Crow**	Hants
2 G7	**Crowan**	Cnwll
25 M4	**Crowborough**	E Susx
25 M4	**Crowborough Town** E Susx	
18 F7	**Crowcombe**	Somset
83 P11	**Crowdecote**	Derbys
83 N5	**Crowden**	Derbys
8 C5	**Crowden**	Devon
22 E10	**Crowdhill**	Hants
37 N9	**Crowdleham**	Kent
83 Q4	**Crow Edge**	Barns
85 K5	**Crowell**	Oxon
62 D9	**Crow End**	Cambs
48 H6	**Crowfield**	Nhants
64 G10	**Crowfield**	Suffk
64 G10	**Crowfield Green**	Suffk
77 L7	**Crowgate Street**	Norfk
51 N11	**Crow Green**	Essex
129 J5	**Crowhill**	E Loth
46 B9	**Crow Hill**	Herefs
84 D5	**Crowhole**	Derbys
26 C9	**Crowhurst**	E Susx
37 J11	**Crowhurst**	Surrey
37 J11	**Crowhurst Lane End** Surrey	
74 D8	**Crowland**	Lincs
64 E7	**Crowland**	Suffk
2 E7	**Crowlas**	Cnwll
92 C8	**Crowle**	N Linc
46 H3	**Crowle**	Worcs
46 H3	**Crowle Green**	Worcs
34 H7	**Crowmarsh Gifford**	Oxon
65 K7	**Crown Corner**	Suffk
6 D7	**Crownhill**	C Plym
49 M7	**Crownhill Crematorium** M Keyn	
23 Q6	**Crownpits**	Surrey
76 F11	**Crownthorpe**	Norfk
2 G7	**Crowntown**	Cnwll
2 B8	**Crows-an-Wra**	Cnwll
51 Q5	**Crow's Green**	Essex
76 D10	**Crowshill**	Norfk
5 M8	**Crow's Nest**	Cnwll
56 F4	**Crowsnest**	Shrops
23 M2	**Crowthorne**	Wokham
82 C10	**Crowton**	Ches W
59 J2	**Croxall**	Staffs
93 L11	**Croxby**	Lincs
103 Q3	**Croxdale**	Dur
71 K7	**Croxden**	Staffs
50 C11	**Croxley Green**	Herts
81 N5	**Croxteth**	Lpool
62 B8	**Croxton**	Cambs
93 J8	**Croxton**	N Linc
64 B4	**Croxton**	Norfk
76 D5	**Croxton**	Norfk
70 D8	**Croxton**	Staffs
70 D8	**Croxtonbank**	Staffs
69 Q4	**Croxton Green**	Ches E
73 L5	**Croxton Kerrial**	Leics
156 D8	**Croy**	Highld
126 C2	**Croy**	N Lans
16 G4	**Croyde**	Devon
16 G4	**Croyde Bay**	Devon
62 D11	**Croydon**	Cambs
36 H7	**Croydon**	Gt Lon
36 H7	**Croydon Crematorium** Gt Lon	
148 B9	**Crubenmore**	Highld
56 G3	**Cruckmeole**	Shrops
56 G2	**Cruckton**	Shrops
159 Q10	**Cruden Bay**	Abers
70 A11	**Crudgington**	Wrekin
33 J6	**Crudwell**	Wilts
8 D5	**Cruft**	Devon
56 B10	**Crug**	Powys
4 E6	**Crugmeer**	Cnwll
43 N7	**Crugybar**	Carmth
56 B8	**Crug-y-byddar**	Powys
30 H5	**Crumlin**	Caerph
5 L11	**Crumplehorn**	Cnwll
82 H4	**Crumpsall**	Manch
27 J2	**Crundale**	Kent
41 J7	**Crundale**	Pembks
41 N8	**Crunwear**	Pembks
9 L2	**Cruwys Morchard**	Devon
22 D3	**Crux Easton**	Hants
11 N5	**Cruxton**	Dorset
28 E2	**Crwbin**	Carmth
35 N5	**Cryers Hill**	Bucks
41 N4	**Crymmych**	Pembks
29 L4	**Crynant**	Neath
36 H6	**Crystal Palace**	Gt Lon
153 N6	**Cuaig**	Highld
130 F5	**Cuan**	Ag & B
59 M11	**Cubbington**	Warwks
4 B10	**Cubert**	Cnwll
90 G10	**Cubley**	Barns
49 M10	**Cublington**	Bucks
45 N7	**Cublington**	Herefs
24 H5	**Cuckfield**	W Susx
20 E9	**Cucklington**	Somset
85 J6	**Cuckney**	Notts
74 D6	**Cuckoo Bridge**	Lincs
23 K6	**Cuckoo's Corner**	Hants
69 L2	**Cuckoo's Nest**	Ches W
34 G4	**Cuddesdon**	Oxon
35 K2	**Cuddington**	Bucks
82 C10	**Cuddington**	Ches W
69 N5	**Cuddington Heath** Ches W	
88 F3	**Cuddy Hill**	Lancs
37 K9	**Cudham**	Gt Lon
8 D9	**Cudliptown**	Devon
13 J5	**Cudnell**	Bmouth
91 K9	**Cudworth**	Barns
10 H2	**Cudworth**	Somset
82 B7	**Cuerdley Cross**	Warrtn
23 J3	**Cufaude**	Hants
50 H10	**Cuffley**	Herts
138 H6	**Cuil**	Highld
155 R6	**Culbokie**	Highld
17 Q2	**Culbone**	Somset
155 N9	**Culburnie**	Highld
156 B9	**Culcabock**	Highld
156 F7	**Culcharry**	Highld
82 E6	**Culcheth**	Warrtn
158 D11	**Culdrain**	Abers
153 N9	**Culduie**	Highld
64 A7	**Culford**	Suffk
102 B5	**Culgaith**	Cumb
34 F5	**Culham**	Oxon
164 B10	**Culkein**	Highld
164 B10	**Culkein Drumbeg**	Highld
32 H5	**Culkerton**	Gloucs
158 D4	**Cullen**	Moray
113 N6	**Cullercoats**	N Tyne
151 K7	**Cullerlie**	Abers
156 A5	**Cullicudden**	Highld
90 D3	**Cullingworth**	C Brad
144 G3	**Cuillin Hills**	Highld
130 E5	**Cullipool**	Ag & B
169 s3	**Cullivoe**	Shet
156 C8	**Culloden**	Highld
9 P3	**Cullompton**	Devon
9 P3	**Cullompton Services** Devon	
18 F11	**Culm Davy**	Devon
56 H8	**Culmington**	Shrops
10 C2	**Culmstock**	Devon
160 H6	**Culnacraig**	Highld
108 G10	**Culnaightrie**	D & G
153 J5	**Culnaknock**	Highld
53 M2	**Culpho**	Suffk
162 D8	**Culrain**	Highld
134 B10	**Culross**	Fife
114 F5	**Culroy**	S Ayrs
158 G11	**Culsalmond**	Abers
107 N8	**Culscadden**	D & G
107 K7	**Culshabbin**	D & G
169 p9	**Culswick**	Shet
151 N3	**Cultercullen**	Abers
48 F5	**Cults**	C Aber
114 D5	**Culverstone Green**	Kent
73 Q2	**Culverthorpe**	Lincs
48 F5	**Culworth**	Nhants
114 D5	**Culzean Castle & Country Park** S Ayrs	
126 D3	**Cumbernauld**	N Lans
126 D2	**Cumbernauld Village** N Lans	
87 P6	**Cumberworth**	Lincs
110 F11	**Cumdivock**	Cumb
159 K7	**Cuminestown**	Abers
129 K8	**Cumledge**	Border
110 G10	**Cummersdale**	Cumb
109 P7	**Cummertrees**	D & G
157 L4	**Cummingstown**	Moray
115 L3	**Cumnock**	E Ayrs
34 E4	**Cumnor**	Oxon
111 L10	**Cumrew**	Cumb
109 N3	**Cumrue**	D & G
111 J10	**Cumwhinton**	Cumb
111 K10	**Cumwhitton**	Cumb
97 P6	**Cundall**	N York
125 K9	**Cunninghamhead**	N Ayrs
169 r10	**Cunningsburgh**	Shet
135 K5	**Cupar**	Fife
135 K5	**Cupar Muir**	Fife
84 C6	**Curbar**	Derbys
14 F4	**Curbridge**	Hants
34 B3	**Curbridge**	Oxon
14 F4	**Curdridge**	Hants
59 J6	**Curdworth**	Warwks
19 J11	**Curland**	Somset
34 E10	**Curridge**	W Berk
127 M4	**Currie**	C Edin
19 K10	**Curry Mallet**	Somset
19 L9	**Curry Rivel**	Somset
26 E4	**Curteis Corner**	Kent
26 B3	**Curtisden Green**	Kent
7 J8	**Curtisknowle**	Devon
2 H9	**Cury**	Cnwll
150 E5	**Cushnie**	Abers
18 G8	**Cushuish**	Somset
45 J6	**Cusop**	Herefs
107 N11	**Cutcloy**	D & G
18 B7	**Cutcombe**	Somset
89 P8	**Cutgate**	Rochdl
162 H3	**Cuthill**	Highld
67 L11	**Cutiau**	Gwynd
51 N4	**Cutler's Green**	Essex
4 H9	**Cutmadoc**	Cnwll
5 N9	**Cutmere**	Cnwll
58 C11	**Cutnall Green**	Worcs
47 L3	**Cutsdean**	Gloucs
91 L6	**Cutsyke**	Wakefd
84 D6	**Cutthorpe**	Derbys
5 P9	**Cuttivett**	Cnwll
35 J5	**Cuxham**	Oxon
38 B8	**Cuxton**	Medway
93 L10	**Cuxwold**	Lincs
30 G3	**Cwm**	Blae G
80 F9	**Cwm**	Denbgs
29 L6	**Cwmafan**	Neath
30 D5	**Cwmaman**	Rhondd
43 L5	**Cwmann**	Carmth
31 J3	**Cwmavon**	Torfn
28 E4	**Cwm-bach**	Carmth
41 Q5	**Cwmbach**	Carmth
44 H7	**Cwmbach**	Powys
30 D4	**Cwmbach**	Rhondd
44 E4	**Cwmbach Llechrhyd** Powys	
55 L8	**Cwmbelan**	Powys
31 J6	**Cwmbran**	Torfn
54 G8	**Cwmbrwyno**	Cerdgn
28 E4	**Cwm Capel**	Carmth
30 H6	**Cwmcarn**	Caerph
31 N3	**Cwmcarvan**	Mons
30 H3	**Cwm-celyn**	Blae G
55 K2	**Cwm-Cewydd**	Gwynd
42 Q2	**Cwm-cou**	Cerdgn
44 G11	**Cwm Crawnon**	Powys
30 C4	**Cwmdare**	Rhondd
43 M8	**Cwmdu**	Carmth
44 H10	**Cwmdu**	Powys
28 H6	**Cwmdu**	Swans
42 G8	**Cwmduad**	Carmth
28 H4	**Cwm Dulais**	Swans
43 P8	**Cwmdwr**	Carmth
29 N7	**Cwmfelin**	Brdgnd
30 E4	**Cwmfelin**	Myr Td
41 N7	**Cwmfelin Boeth**	Carmth
30 G6	**Cwmfelinfach**	Caerph
41 P6	**Cwmfelin Mynach** Carmth	
42 H11	**Cwmffrwd**	Carmth
29 L2	**Cwmgiedd**	Powys
29 G2	**Cwmgorse**	Carmth
28 G2	**Cwmgwili**	Carmth
42 F7	**Cwmgwrach**	Neath
42 F7	**Cwmhiraeth**	Carmth
43 N9	**Cwm-Ifor**	Carmth
44 B5	**Cwm Irfon**	Powys
43 J11	**Cwmisfael**	Carmth
55 J3	**Cwm Llinau**	Powys
29 K2	**Cwmllynfell**	Neath
28 F2	**Cwmmawr**	Carmth
41 Q4	**Cwm Morgan**	Carmth
29 P5	**Cwmparc**	Rhondd
42 G7	**Cwmpengraig**	Carmth
67 P5	**Cwm Penmachno**	Conwy
30 D4	**Cwmpennar**	Rhondd
44 H10	**Cwmrhos**	Powys
29 J5	**Cwmrhydyceirw**	Swans
43 J5	**Cwmsychbant**	Cerdgn
30 H3	**Cwmtillery**	Blae G
29 L2	**Cwm-twrch Isaf**	Powys
29 L2	**Cwm-twrch Uchaf**	Powys
28 G2	**Cwm-y-glo**	Carmth
67 K2	**Cwm-y-glo**	Gwynd
45 K10	**Cwmyoy**	Mons
54 H10	**Cwmystwyth**	Cerdgn
54 F5	**Cwrt**	Gwynd
43 J5	**Cwrt-newydd**	Cerdgn
45 J11	**Cwrt-y-gollen**	Powys
55 Q3	**Cyfronydd**	Powys
29 K4	**Cylibebyll**	Neath
29 N5	**Cymer**	Neath
30 D6	**Cymmer**	Rhondd
43 R6	**Cynghordy**	Carmth
28 E3	**Cynheidre**	Carmth
29 M5	**Cynonville**	Neath
68 E6	**Cynwyd**	Denbgs
42 G9	**Cynwyl Elfed**	Carmth

D

7 N5	**Daccombe**	Devon
101 N5	**Dacre**	Cumb
97 J8	**Dacre**	N York
97 J8	**Dacre Banks**	N York
102 G3	**Daddry Shield**	Dur
49 J7	**Dadford**	Bucks
72 C11	**Dadlington**	Leics
28 F4	**Dafen**	Carmth
76 D10	**Daffy Green**	Norfk
37 M4	**Dagenham**	Gt Lon
33 J3	**Daglingworth**	Gloucs
49 Q11	**Dagnall**	Bucks
64 E9	**Dagworth**	Suffk
114 E7	**Dailly**	S Ayrs
7 M5	**Dainton**	Devon
135 L4	**Dairsie**	Fife
82 E4	**Daisy Hill**	Bolton
90 H5	**Daisy Hill**	Leeds
168 c15	**Dalabrog**	W Isls
131 K5	**Dalavich**	Ag & B
108 H8	**Dalbeattie**	D & G
71 P8	**Dalbury**	Derbys
80 b6	**Dalby**	IoM
87 M7	**Dalby**	Lincs
98 C6	**Dalby**	N York
141 N7	**Dalcapon**	P & K
163 L5	**Dalchalm**	Highld
146 H5	**Dalchreichart**	Highld
133 L4	**Dalchruin**	P & K
134 C2	**Dalcrue**	P & K
87 J7	**Dalderby**	Lincs
9 P8	**Dalditch**	Devon
126 B5	**Daldowie Crematorium** C Glas	
101 P2	**Dale**	Cumb
72 C3	**Dale**	Derbys
40 F9	**Dale**	Pembks
101 J6	**Dale Bottom**	Cumb
84 B8	**Dale End**	Derbys
96 E11	**Dale End**	N York
26 B5	**Dale Hill**	E Susx
105 L7	**Dalehouse**	N York
138 C4	**Dalelia**	Highld
124 H8	**Dalgarven**	N Ayrs
134 F11	**Dalgety Bay**	Fife
115 L5	**Dalgig**	E Ayrs
133 M3	**Dalginross**	P & K
141 N8	**Dalguise**	P & K
166 E6	**Dalhalvaig**	Highld
63 M8	**Dalham**	Suffk
168 c15	**Daliburgh**	W Isls
127 Q4	**Dalkeith**	Mdloth
157 L7	**Dallas**	Moray
65 K10	**Dallinghoo**	Suffk
25 Q7	**Dallington**	E Susx
60 F8	**Dallington**	Nhants
97 J6	**Dallow**	N York
131 P2	**Dalmally**	Ag & B
132 G8	**Dalmary**	Stirlg
115 J6	**Dalmellington**	E Ayrs
127 L2	**Dalmeny**	C Edin
156 B4	**Dalmore**	Highld
125 M3	**Dalmuir**	W Duns
138 C4	**Dalnabreck**	Highld
140 H3	**Dalnacardoch**	P & K
148 F4	**Dalnahaitnach**	Highld
140 F3	**Dalnaspidal**	P & K
166 H8	**Dalnawillan Lodge** Highld	
141 J6	**Daloist**	P & K
134 D7	**Dalqueich**	P & K
114 F8	**Dalquhairn**	S Ayrs
162 H5	**Dalreavoch Lodge**	Highld
124 H8	**Dalry**	N Ayrs
114 G5	**Dalrymple**	E Ayrs
126 D7	**Dalserf**	S Lans
120 B9	**Dalsmeran**	Ag & B
110 G10	**Dalston**	Cumb
36 H4	**Dalston**	Gt Lon
109 K3	**Dalswinton**	D & G
95 L5	**Dalton**	Cumb
109 P6	**Dalton**	D & G
88 F9	**Dalton**	Lancs
97 P5	**Dalton**	N York
103 M9	**Dalton**	N York
112 H6	**Dalton**	Nthumb
84 G3	**Dalton**	Rothm
94 E6	**Dalton-in-Furness**	Cumb
113 P11	**Dalton-le-Dale**	Dur
84 G2	**Dalton Magna**	Rothm
103 Q9	**Dalton-on-Tees**	N York
84 G2	**Dalton Parva**	Rothm
104 E4	**Dalton Piercy**	Hartpl
133 J3	**Dalveich**	Stirlg
147 Q11	**Dalwhinnie**	Highld
10 E4	**Dalwood**	Devon
50 G5	**Damask Green**	Herts
21 M11	**Damerham**	Hants
77 N10	**Damgate**	Norfk
64 A4	**Dam Green**	Norfk
26 C8	**Danaway**	Kent
52 C10	**Danbury**	Essex
105 K9	**Danby**	N York
105 J10	**Danby Bottom**	N York
104 H11	**Danby Wiske**	N York
157 P8	**Dandaleith**	Moray
127 Q4	**Danderhall**	Mdloth
83 L11	**Danebridge**	Ches E
50 H6	**Dane End**	Herts
25 N4	**Danegate**	E Susx
25 K5	**Danehill**	E Susx
72 F10	**Dane Hills**	C Leic
76 F10	**Danemoor Green**	Norfk
57 N6	**Danesford**	Shrops
84 F8	**Danesmoor**	Derbys
39 J11	**Dane Street**	Kent
26 G3	**Daniel's Water**	Kent
158 H6	**Danshillock**	Abers
128 F6	**Danskine**	E Loth
93 N4	**Danthorpe**	E R Yk
58 H11	**Danzey Green**	Warwks
71 J9	**Dapple Heath**	Staffs
23 M2	**Darby Green**	Hants
89 L9	**Darcy Lever**	Bolton
45 J11	**Dardy**	Powys
30 H2	**Daren-felen**	Mons
37 N6	**Darenth**	Kent
82 C8	**Daresbury**	Halton
91 L10	**Darfield**	Barns
85 J5	**Darfoulds**	Notts
39 J9	**Dargate**	Kent
5 M8	**Darite**	Cnwll
38 C8	**Darland**	Medway
69 L3	**Darland**	Wrexhm
58 E5	**Darlaston**	Wsall
58 E5	**Darlaston Green**	Wsall
97 K9	**Darley**	N York
72 B3	**Darley Abbey**	C Derb
84 C8	**Darley Bridge**	Derbys
84 C8	**Darley Dale**	Derbys
59 J10	**Darley Green**	Solhll
50 D6	**Darleyhall**	Herts
97 J9	**Darley Head**	N York
47 P6	**Darlingscott**	Warwks
103 Q8	**Darlington**	Darltn
103 Q8	**Darlington Crematorium** Darltn	
69 Q8	**Darliston**	Shrops
85 N6	**Darlton**	Notts
58 H3	**Darnford**	Staffs
117 Q4	**Darnick**	Border
55 J4	**Darowen**	Powys
158 H8	**Darra**	Abers
16 C8	**Darracott**	Devon
16 H4	**Darracott**	Devon
113 J6	**Darras Hall**	Nthumb
91 M7	**Darrington**	Wakefd
65 N8	**Darsham**	Suffk
20 B6	**Darshill**	Somset
37 M6	**Dartford**	Kent
7 K6	**Dartington**	Devon
6 H4	**Dartmeet**	Devon
8 G9	**Dartmoor National Park** Devon	
7 M8	**Dartmouth**	Devon
91 J8	**Darton**	Barns
125 P10	**Darvel**	E Ayrs
25 Q7	**Darwell Hole**	E Susx
89 K6	**Darwen**	Bl w D
35 Q9	**Datchet**	W & M
50 G7	**Datchworth**	Herts
50 G7	**Datchworth Green**	Herts
89 L9	**Daubhill**	Bolton
157 N9	**Daugh of Kinermony** Moray	
33 J8	**Dauntsey**	Wilts
157 J10	**Dava**	Highld
82 E10	**Davenham**	Ches W
83 K7	**Davenport**	Stockp
82 H9	**Davenport Green**	Ches E
82 H7	**Davenport Green**	Traffd
60 C8	**Daventry**	Nhants
127 N2	**Davidson's Mains**	C Edin
5 K4	**Davidstow**	Cnwll
37 P8	**David Street**	Kent
117 J10	**Davington**	D & G
38 H9	**Davington Hill**	Kent
151 J2	**Daviot**	Abers
156 C10	**Daviot**	Highld
156 C9	**Daviot House**	Highld
25 M7	**Davis's Town**	E Susx
158 C7	**Davoch of Grange**	Moray
82 G5	**Davyhulme**	Traffd
58 F4	**Daw End**	Wsall
36 F11	**Dawesgreen**	Surrey
57 M3	**Dawley**	Wrekin
9 N9	**Dawlish**	Devon
9 N9	**Dawlish Warren**	Devon
80 B10	**Dawn**	Conwy
18 G10	**Daws Green**	Somset
38 D4	**Daws Heath**	Essex
5 N5	**Daw's House**	Cnwll
74 H4	**Dawsmere**	Lincs
85 J11	**Daybrook**	Notts
70 D3	**Day Green**	Ches E
70 H8	**Dayhills**	Staffs
58 E9	**Dayhouse Bank**	Worcs
47 P9	**Daylesford**	Gloucs
80 G10	**Ddol**	Flints
68 G10	**Ddol-Cownwy**	Powys
39 Q11	**Deal**	Kent
100 E5	**Dean**	Cumb
7 J6	**Dean**	Devon
17 L2	**Dean**	Devon
17 N2	**Dean**	Devon
21 J11	**Dean**	Dorset
22 D8	**Dean**	Hants
22 G11	**Dean**	Hants
89 P5	**Dean**	Lancs
48 B10	**Dean**	Oxon
20 C6	**Dean**	Somset
37 N7	**Dean Bottom**	Kent
117 M8	**Deanburnhaugh**	Border
7 J6	**Deancombe**	Devon
34 E3	**Dean Court**	Oxon
89 K9	**Deane**	Bolton
22 F4	**Deane**	Hants
21 J11	**Dean End**	Dorset
90 H10	**Dean Head**	Barns
90 C7	**Deanhead**	Kirk
21 J11	**Deanland**	Dorset
15 K4	**Deanlane End**	W Susx
7 J6	**Dean Prior**	Devon
112 B8	**Deanraw**	Nthumb
83 J8	**Dean Row**	Ches E
127 J4	**Deans**	W Loth
100 E5	**Deanscales**	Cumb
49 L7	**Deanshanger**	Nhants
157 R7	**Deanshaugh**	Moray
133 L2	**Deanston**	Stirlg
100 E3	**Dearham**	Cumb
89 Q7	**Dearnley**	Rochdl
65 J11	**Debach**	Suffk
51 K11	**Debden**	Essex
51 N4	**Debden**	Essex
51 N4	**Debden Green**	Essex
64 H9	**Debenham**	Suffk
46 F5	**Deblin's Green**	Worcs
127 J3	**Dechmont**	W Loth
127 J3	**Dechmont Road**	W Loth
48 E8	**Deddington**	Oxon
53 J5	**Dedham**	Essex
53 J5	**Dedham Heath**	Essex
35 P9	**Dedworth**	W & M
61 K2	**Deene**	Nhants
61 L2	**Deenethorpe**	Nhants

90	H11	**Deepcar** Sheff
23	P3	**Deepcut** Surrey
95	Q4	**Deepdale** Cumb
96	C5	**Deepdale** N York
74	B9	**Deeping Gate** C Pete
74	C9	**Deeping St James** Lincs
74	D7	**Deeping St Nicholas** Lincs
46	G8	**Deerhurst** Gloucs
46	G9	**Deerhurst Walton** Gloucs
38	G9	**Deerton Street** Kent
46	H6	**Defford** Worcs
44	C9	**Defynnog** Powys
79	P9	**Deganwy** Conwy
130	F5	**Degnish** Ag & B
91	Q2	**Deighton** C York
104	C10	**Deighton** N York
67	K2	**Deiniolen** Gwynd
4	H5	**Delabole** Cnwll
82	C11	**Delamere** Ches W
151	P3	**Delfrigs** Abers
17	J7	**Delley** Devon
157	K11	**Delliefure** Highld
15	M6	**Dell Quay** W Susx
34	C2	**Delly End** Oxon
149	M4	**Delnabo** Moray
157	M10	**Delnashaugh Inn** Moray
156	C3	**Delny** Highld
90	B9	**Delph** Oldham
112	H11	**Delves** Dur
52	C4	**Delvin End** Essex
73	Q3	**Dembleby** Lincs
4	F9	**Demelza** Cnwll
91	M11	**Denaby** Donc
91	M11	**Denaby Main** Donc
36	D10	**Denbies** Surrey
80	F11	**Denbigh** Denbgs
135	K4	**Denbrae** Fife
7	L5	**Denbury** Devon
84	E11	**Denby** Derbys
84	E11	**Denby Bottles** Derbys
90	G9	**Denby Dale** Kirk
34	C6	**Denchworth** Oxon
94	E6	**Dendron** Cumb
50	B3	**Denel End** C Beds
134	B4	**Denfield** P & K
61	L5	**Denford** Nhants
52	G11	**Dengie** Essex
36	B3	**Denham** Bucks
63	N8	**Denham** Suffk
64	H7	**Denham** Suffk
63	N8	**Denham End** Suffk
36	B3	**Denham Green** Bucks
64	H7	**Denham Green** Suffk
159	N7	**Denhead** Abers
135	M5	**Denhead** Fife
142	F11	**Denhead of Gray** C Dund
117	R7	**Denholm** Border
90	D4	**Denholme** C Brad
90	D4	**Denholme Clough** C Brad
66	F7	**Denio** Gwynd
15	J4	**Denmead** Hants
151	N5	**Denmore** C Aber
24	E5	**Denne Park** W Susx
65	K8	**Dennington** Suffk
133	N11	**Denny** Falk
133	N11	**Dennyloanhead** Falk
134	H4	**Den of Lindores** Fife
90	B8	**Denshaw** Oldham
151	L8	**Denside** Abers
27	M3	**Densole** Kent
63	N10	**Denston** Suffk
71	K6	**Denstone** Staffs
39	K9	**Denstroude** Kent
95	Q3	**Dent** Cumb
61	Q3	**Denton** Cambs
103	P7	**Denton** Darltn
25	L10	**Denton** E Susx
27	M2	**Denton** Kent
37	Q6	**Denton** Kent
73	M4	**Denton** Lincs
96	H11	**Denton** N York
60	H9	**Denton** Nhants
65	K4	**Denton** Norfk
34	G4	**Denton** Oxon
83	K5	**Denton** Tamesd
75	M10	**Denver** Norfk
119	P8	**Denwick** Nthumb
76	E11	**Deopham** Norfk
64	E2	**Deopham Green** Norfk
63	N9	**Depden** Suffk
63	N9	**Depden Green** Suffk
37	J5	**Deptford** Gt Lon
21	K7	**Deptford** Wilts
72	B3	**Derby** C Derb
17	K5	**Derby** Devon
80	c8	**Derbyhaven** IoM
141	L7	**Derculich** P & K
76	D9	**Dereham** Norfk
30	F4	**Deri** Caerph
16	E11	**Derril** Devon
27	M2	**Derringstone** Kent
70	F10	**Derrington** Staffs
16	E11	**Derriton** Devon
33	J10	**Derry Hill** Wilts
92	D9	**Derrythorpe** N Linc
75	N4	**Dersingham** Norfk
137	L5	**Dervaig** Ag & B
68	E4	**Derwen** Denbgs
43	L10	**Derwen Fawr** Carmth
54	G5	**Derwenlas** Powys
101	J6	**Derwent Water** Cumb
43	M11	**Derwydd** Carmth
60	H4	**Desborough** Nhants
72	D10	**Desford** Leics
158	D5	**Deskford** Moray
119	L3	**Detchant** Nthumb
38	C10	**Detling** Kent
57	M7	**Deuxhill** Shrops
31	N5	**Devauden** Mons
54	G9	**Devil's Bridge** Cerdgn
59	L6	**Devitts Green** Warwks
21	K2	**Devizes** Wilts
6	D8	**Devonport** C Plym
133	Q8	**Devonside** Clacks
3	K6	**Devoran** Cnwll
128	B7	**Dewarton** Mdloth
12	C5	**Dewlish** Dorset
90	G6	**Dewsbury** Kirk
90	G6	**Dewsbury Moor** Kirk
90	G6	**Dewsbury Moor Crematorium** Kirk
68	H11	**Deytheur** Powys
31	P11	**Dial** N Som
23	P9	**Dial Green** W Susx
24	E7	**Dial Post** W Susx
11	K4	**Dibberford** Dorset
14	D5	**Dibden** Hants
14	D5	**Dibden Purlieu** Hants
58	H9	**Dickens Heath** Solhll
64	H5	**Dickleburgh** Norfk
47	L8	**Didbrook** Gloucs
34	F6	**Didcot** Oxon
34	F6	**Didcot Railway Centre** Oxon
61	Q7	**Diddington** Cambs
57	J7	**Diddlebury** Shrops
45	P8	**Didley** Herefs
23	M11	**Didling** W Susx
32	F7	**Didmarton** Gloucs
82	H6	**Didsbury** Manch
6	H6	**Didworthy** Devon
86	E10	**Digby** Lincs
152	H4	**Digg** Highld
90	C9	**Diggle** Oldham
88	F9	**Digmoor** Lancs
50	F7	**Digswell** Herts
50	G8	**Digswell Water** Herts
43	J3	**Dihewyd** Cerdgn
77	L6	**Dilham** Norfk
70	H6	**Dilhorne** Staffs
89	M5	**Dill Hall** Lancs
61	P7	**Dillington** Cambs
112	E8	**Dilston** Nthumb
20	G5	**Dilton** Wilts
20	F5	**Dilton Marsh** Wilts
45	N4	**Dilwyn** Herefs
89	L7	**Dimple** Bolton
84	C8	**Dimple** Derbys
41	Q4	**Dinas** Carmth
4	E7	**Dinas** Cnwll
66	D7	**Dinas** Gwynd
41	K3	**Dinas** Pembks
30	D6	**Dinas** Rhondd
66	G3	**Dinas Dinlle** Gwynd
67	N11	**Dinas-Mawddwy** Gwynd
30	G10	**Dinas Powys** V Glam
19	Q6	**Dinder** Somset
45	Q7	**Dinedor** Herefs
31	N2	**Dingestow** Mons
81	M7	**Dingle** Lpool
26	D5	**Dingleden** Kent
60	G3	**Dingley** Nhants
155	P6	**Dingwall** Highld
68	D6	**Dinmael** Conwy
150	H8	**Dinnet** Abers
113	K6	**Dinnington** N u Ty
84	H3	**Dinnington** Rothm
11	J2	**Dinnington** Somset
67	K2	**Dinorwic** Gwynd
35	L2	**Dinton** Bucks
21	K8	**Dinton** Wilts
109	P2	**Dinwoodie** D & G
16	E8	**Dinworthy** Devon
18	H10	**Dipford** Somset
23	K3	**Dipley** Hants
120	F4	**Dippen** Ag & B
121	K7	**Dippen** N Ayrs
23	M5	**Dippenhall** Surrey
8	B3	**Dippermill** Devon
8	B8	**Dippertown** Devon
157	Q6	**Dipple** Moray
114	D7	**Dipple** S Ayrs
7	J7	**Diptford** Devon
113	J10	**Dipton** Dur
112	D8	**Diptonmill** Nthumb
128	E3	**Dirleton** E Loth
112	C11	**Dirt Pot** Nthumb
45	K2	**Discoed** Powys
72	D6	**Diseworth** Leics
97	N6	**Dishforth** N York
83	L8	**Disley** Ches E
64	G5	**Diss** Norfk
44	E3	**Disserth** Powys
100	D6	**Distington** Cumb
100	D6	**Distington Hall Crematorium** Cumb
21	L8	**Ditchampton** Wilts
20	B7	**Ditcheat** Somset
65	L3	**Ditchingham** Norfk
24	H7	**Ditchling** E Susx
57	J2	**Ditherington** Shrops
7	M7	**Dittisham** Devon
38	B10	**Ditton** Kent
63	L9	**Ditton Green** Cambs
57	L7	**Ditton Priors** Shrops
47	J8	**Dixton** Gloucs
31	P2	**Dixton** Mons
5	K2	**Dizzard** Cnwll
90	B9	**Dobcross** Oldham
5	N9	**Dobwalls** Cnwll
9	J7	**Doccombe** Devon
155	R9	**Dochgarroch** Highld
23	M6	**Dockenfield** Surrey
95	M6	**Docker** Lancs
75	Q3	**Docking** Norfk
45	R3	**Docklow** Herefs
101	L6	**Dockray** Cumb
110	E11	**Dockray** Cumb
7	J10	**Dodbrooke** Devon
51	N11	**Doddinghurst** Essex
62	F2	**Doddington** Cambs
38	F10	**Doddington** Kent
85	Q6	**Doddington** Lincs
119	J4	**Doddington** Nthumb
57	J9	**Doddington** Shrops
9	L7	**Doddiscombsleigh** Devon
69	R6	**Dodd's Green** Ches E
75	N4	**Doddshill** Norfk
5	N9	**Doddy Cross** Cnwll
60	D8	**Dodford** Nhants
58	D10	**Dodford** Worcs
32	E8	**Dodington** S Glos
18	G6	**Dodington** Somset
69	L2	**Dodleston** Ches W
17	J8	**Dodscott** Devon
125	N7	**Dodside** E Rens
71	J8	**Dod's Leigh** Staffs
91	J9	**Dodworth** Barns
91	J10	**Dodworth Bottom** Barns
91	J10	**Dodworth Green** Barns
58	H10	**Doe Bank** Birm
84	G7	**Doe Lea** Derbys
86	H9	**Dogdyke** Lincs
90	F8	**Dogley Lane** Kirk
23	L4	**Dogmersfield** Hants
33	L7	**Dogridge** Wilts
74	C10	**Dogsthorpe** C Pete
9	N5	**Dog Village** Devon
55	P2	**Dolanog** Powys
55	Q11	**Dolau** Powys
43	N6	**Dolaucothi** Carmth
67	J6	**Dolbenmaen** Gwynd
70	C9	**Doley** Staffs
55	L4	**Dolfach** Powys
55	J3	**Dol-for** Powys
55	Q7	**Dolfor** Powys
79	P11	**Dolgarrog** Conwy
67	N11	**Dolgellau** Gwynd
54	F4	**Dolgoch** Gwynd
42	H8	**Dol-gran** Carmth
163	K6	**Doll** Highld
134	B8	**Dollar** Clacks
134	B8	**Dollarfield** Clacks
56	D11	**Dolley Green** Powys
54	F8	**Dollwen** Cerdgn
80	H10	**Dolphin** Flints
95	L10	**Dolphinholme** Lancs
127	L8	**Dolphinton** S Lans
17	K9	**Dolton** Devon
80	B10	**Dolwen** Conwy
67	N4	**Dolwyddelan** Conwy
54	E7	**Dolybont** Cerdgn
45	J3	**Dolyhir** Powys
69	J11	**Domgay** Powys
118	G2	**Donaldson's Lodge** Nthumb
91	P10	**Doncaster** Donc
91	P10	**Doncaster Carr** Donc
91	R8	**Doncaster North Services** Donc
20	H10	**Donhead St Andrew** Wilts
20	H10	**Donhead St Mary** Wilts
134	H10	**Donibristle** Fife
18	E6	**Doniford** Somset
74	D3	**Donington** Lincs
86	H4	**Donington on Bain** Lincs
72	D5	**Donington Park Services** Leics
74	D4	**Donington Southing** Lincs
59	M2	**Donisthorpe** Leics
27	K5	**Donkey Street** Kent
23	P7	**Donkey Town** Surrey
47	N9	**Donnington** Gloucs
46	D8	**Donnington** Herefs
57	K3	**Donnington** Shrops
34	E11	**Donnington** W Berk
15	N6	**Donnington** W Susx
57	N2	**Donnington** Wrekin
57	N2	**Donnington Wood** Wrekin
10	G2	**Donyatt** Somset
24	E5	**Doomsday Green** W Susx
114	F4	**Doonfoot** S Ayrs
149	K4	**Dorback Lodge** Highld
11	P6	**Dorchester** Dorset
34	G6	**Dorchester** Oxon
59	L4	**Dordon** Warwks
84	D4	**Dore** Sheff
155	Q11	**Dores** Highld
36	F11	**Dorking** Surrey
52	F4	**Dorking Tye** Suffk
25	K2	**Dormans Land** Surrey
25	J2	**Dormans Park** Surrey
46	A6	**Dormington** Herefs
47	J3	**Dormston** Worcs
35	P9	**Dorney** Bucks
145	Q2	**Dornie** Highld
162	H9	**Dornoch** Highld
110	D7	**Dornock** D & G
167	J6	**Dorrery** Highld
59	J10	**Dorridge** Solhll
86	E10	**Dorrington** Lincs
56	H4	**Dorrington** Shrops
70	C6	**Dorrington** Shrops
47	M5	**Dorsington** Warwks
45	L6	**Dorstone** Herefs
35	J2	**Dorton** Bucks
59	K5	**Dosthill** Staffs
78	F10	**Dothan** IoA
11	K5	**Dottery** Dorset
5	K9	**Doublebois** Cnwll
32	G6	**Doughton** Gloucs
80	e6	**Douglas** IoM
116	A4	**Douglas** S Lans
142	G11	**Douglas and Angus** C Dund
80	e6	**Douglas Borough Crematorium** IoM
131	P8	**Douglas Pier** Ag & B
142	G8	**Douglastown** Angus
116	B3	**Douglas Water** S Lans
126	E11	**Douglas West** S Lans
20	B6	**Doulting** Somset
169	b4	**Dounby** Ork
161	Q6	**Doune** Highld
133	L7	**Doune** Stirlg
114	C8	**Dounepark** S Ayrs
162	D8	**Dounie** Highld
6	E5	**Dousland** Devon
69	L10	**Dovaston** Shrops
84	G10	**Dove Green** Notts
83	N9	**Dove Holes** Derbys
100	E4	**Dovenby** Cumb
27	P3	**Dover** Kent
82	D4	**Dover** Wigan
27	P3	**Dover Castle** Kent
53	M5	**Dovercourt** Essex
58	C11	**Doverdale** Worcs
71	L8	**Doveridge** Derbys
36	G11	**Doversgreen** Surrey
141	P8	**Dowally** P & K
88	E4	**Dowbridge** Lancs
47	K11	**Dowdeswell** Gloucs
30	E3	**Dowlais** Myr Td
17	K9	**Dowland** Devon
10	H2	**Dowlish Ford** Somset
10	H2	**Dowlish Wake** Somset
33	L5	**Down Ampney** Gloucs
5	N11	**Downderry** Cnwll
37	K8	**Downe** Gt Lon
32	F5	**Downend** Gloucs
14	F9	**Downend** IoW
32	C9	**Downend** S Glos
34	E9	**Downend** W Berk
142	F11	**Downfield** C Dund
5	M7	**Downgate** Cnwll
5	P7	**Downgate** Cnwll
51	Q7	**Downham** Essex
37	J6	**Downham** Gt Lon
89	M2	**Downham** Lancs
75	M10	**Downham Market** Norfk
46	G10	**Down Hatherley** Gloucs
19	Q9	**Downhead** Somset
20	C5	**Downhead** Somset
4	D8	**Downhill** Cnwll
134	D2	**Downhill** P & K
3	P2	**Downholland Cross** Lancs
103	M11	**Downholme** N York
5	P3	**Downicarey** Devon
151	N9	**Downies** Abers
80	H9	**Downing** Flints
35	M5	**Downley** Bucks
8	H4	**Down St Mary** Devon
24	H9	**Downs Crematorium** Br & H
20	B4	**Downside** Somset
20	B6	**Downside** Somset
36	D9	**Downside** Surrey
6	E8	**Down Thomas** Devon
13	N6	**Downton** Hants
21	N10	**Downton** Wilts
74	B5	**Dowsby** Lincs
74	B5	**Dowsdale** Lincs
70	F10	**Doxey** Staffs
119	N6	**Doxford** Nthumb
32	D10	**Doynton** S Glos
30	H7	**Draethen** Caerph
126	D8	**Draffan** S Lans
92	F3	**Dragonby** N Linc
24	D6	**Dragons Green** W Susx
85	M2	**Drakeholes** Notts
57	Q8	**Drakelow** Worcs
124	H7	**Drakemyre** N Ayrs
46	H5	**Drakes Broughton** Worcs
6	C4	**Drakewalls** Cnwll
96	F10	**Draughton** N York
60	G5	**Draughton** Nhants
92	A5	**Drax** N York
91	R5	**Drax Hales** N York
59	P10	**Draycote** Warwks
33	N9	**Draycot Foliat** Swindn
72	C4	**Draycott** Derbys
47	N7	**Draycott** Gloucs
57	Q6	**Draycott** Shrops
19	N4	**Draycott** Somset
19	Q10	**Draycott** Somset
46	G5	**Draycott** Worcs
71	M9	**Draycott in the Clay** Staffs
70	H6	**Draycott in the Moors** Staffs
9	J2	**Drayford** Devon
15	J5	**Drayton** C Port
60	H2	**Drayton** Leics
74	D3	**Drayton** Lincs
76	H9	**Drayton** Norfk
34	K6	**Drayton** Oxon
48	D6	**Drayton** Oxon
19	M10	**Drayton** Somset
58	D9	**Drayton** Worcs
59	J4	**Drayton Bassett** Staffs
35	P2	**Drayton Beauchamp** Bucks
59	J4	**Drayton Manor Park** Staffs
49	M9	**Drayton Parslow** Bucks
34	G5	**Drayton St Leonard** Oxon
96	G9	**Drebley** N York
80	g3	**Dreemskerry** IoM
40	H8	**Dreen Hill** Pembks
28	F2	**Drefach** Carmth
42	G7	**Drefach** Carmth
43	J5	**Drefach** Carmth
42	G7	**Drefach** Cerdgn
42	A2	**Drefelin** Carmth
125	K10	**Dreghorn** N Ayrs
27	M3	**Drellingore** Kent
128	E4	**Drem** E Loth
70	G6	**Dresden** C Stke
8	H6	**Drewsteignton** Devon
87	L6	**Driby** Lincs
99	L9	**Driffield** E R Yk
33	L5	**Driffield** Gloucs
33	L5	**Driffield Cross Roads** Gloucs
2	C8	**Drift** Cnwll
100	E11	**Drigg** Cumb
90	G5	**Drighlington** Leeds
137	P5	**Drimnin** Highld
11	J4	**Drimpton** Dorset
138	H2	**Drimsallie** Highld
98	B11	**Dringhouses** C York
64	D9	**Drinkstone** Suffk
64	D9	**Drinkstone Green** Suffk
11	M3	**Drive End** Dorset
50	F6	**Driver's End** Herts
71	J9	**Droitton** Staffs
46	G2	**Droitwich** Worcs
134	E4	**Dron** P & K
84	E5	**Dronfield** Derbys
84	D5	**Dronfield Woodhouse** Derbys
114	H4	**Drongan** E Ayrs
142	E10	**Dronley** Angus
12	C3	**Droop** Dorset
84	E2	**Dropping Well** Rothm
22	H11	**Droxford** Hants
83	K5	**Droylsden** Tamesd
68	D6	**Druid** Denbgs
40	G7	**Druidston** Pembks
139	K3	**Druimarbin** Highld
139	J8	**Druimavuic** Ag & B
123	M5	**Druimdrishaig** Ag & B
145	L11	**Druimindarroch** Highld
124	A2	**Drum** Ag & B
134	C7	**Drum** P & K
116	C3	**Drumalbin** S Lans
164	D10	**Drumbeg** Highld
158	E9	**Drumblade** Abers
106	E9	**Drumbreddon** D & G
153	P11	**Drumbuie** Highld
110	E9	**Drumburgh** Cumb
109	J10	**Drumburn** D & G
125	N3	**Drumchapel** C Glas
140	G6	**Drumchastle** P & K
125	Q10	**Drumclog** S Lans
135	L7	**Drumeldrie** Fife
116	G4	**Drumelzier** Border
145	L4	**Drumfearn** Highld
151	L8	**Drumfrennie** Abers
142	G7	**Drumgley** Angus
148	D7	**Drumguish** Highld
157	M11	**Drumin** Moray
115	K8	**Drumjohn** D & G
107	J2	**Drumlamford** S Ayrs
151	J8	**Drumlasie** Abers
116	E10	**Drumleaning** Cumb
120	C8	**Drumlemble** Ag & B
115	K11	**Drumlithie** Abers
107	L8	**Drummoddie** D & G
104	G10	**Drummore** D & G
158	A9	**Drummuir** Moray
155	P11	**Drumnadrochit** Highld
158	D7	**Drumnagorrach** Moray
109	J5	**Drumpark** D & G
161	K6	**Drumrunie Lodge** Highld
114	E5	**Drumshang** S Ayrs
152	H8	**Drumuie** Highld
148	G3	**Drumuillie** Highld
133	K7	**Drumvaich** Stirlg
134	E6	**Drunzie** P & K
119	Q11	**Druridge** Nthumb
69	J2	**Drury** Flints
102	C7	**Drybeck** Cumb
158	B5	**Drybridge** Moray
125	K10	**Drybridge** N Ayrs
46	B11	**Drybrook** Gloucs
118	A4	**Dryburgh** Border
85	Q11	**Dry Doddington** Lincs
62	E8	**Dry Drayton** Cambs
132	F10	**Drymen** Stirlg
159	M8	**Drymuir** Abers
152	G11	**Drynoch** Highld
34	E4	**Dry Sandford** Oxon
43	L10	**Dryslwyn** Carmth
37	Q3	**Dry Street** Essex
57	K3	**Dryton** Shrops
159	J5	**Dubford** Abers
64	H8	**Dublin** Suffk
161	P3	**Duchally** Highld
50	C2	**Duck End** Bed
62	B8	**Duck End** Cambs
51	Q4	**Duck End** Essex
51	Q5	**Duck End** Essex
52	B7	**Duckend Green** Essex
69	N4	**Ducklington** Oxon
34	C3	**Ducklington** Oxon
61	P9	**Duck's Cross** Bed
51	L3	**Duddenhoe End** Essex
127	P3	**Duddingston** C Edin
73	P10	**Duddington** Nhants
18	H10	**Duddlestone** Somset
25	L5	**Duddlewick** Shrops
57	M8	**Duddlewick** Shrops
118	H2	**Duddo** Nthumb
69	P2	**Duddon** Ches W
94	D3	**Duddon Bridge** Cumb
81	Q11	**Duddon Common** Ches W
69	K7	**Dudleston** Shrops
69	L7	**Dudleston Heath** Shrops
58	D6	**Dudley** Dudley
113	L6	**Dudley** N Tyne
90	F4	**Dudley Hill** C Brad
58	D6	**Dudley Port** Sandw
57	L10	**Dudnill** Shrops
13	J5	**Dudsbury** Dorset
35	Q3	**Dudswell** Herts
72	A2	**Duffield** Derbys
29	M5	**Duffryn** Neath
157	Q9	**Dufftown** Moray
157	M4	**Duffus** Moray
102	C5	**Dufton** Cumb
98	H1	**Duggleby** N York
153	P11	**Duirinish** Highld
145	L11	**Duisdalemore** Highld
139	J2	**Duisky** Highld
30	F2	**Dukestown** Blae G
53	J3	**Duke Street** Suffk
83	K5	**Dukinfield** Tamesd
83	K5	**Dukinfield Crematorium** Tamesd
78	H7	**Dulas** IoA
19	Q6	**Dulcote** Somset
9	Q3	**Dulford** Devon
141	M8	**Dull** P & K
126	C2	**Dullatur** N Lans
63	K9	**Dullingham** Cambs
63	K9	**Dullingham Ley** Cambs
148	H3	**Dulnain Bridge** Highld
61	Q8	**Duloe** Bed
5	L10	**Duloe** Cnwll
18	B9	**Dulverton** Somset
36	H6	**Dulwich** Gt Lon
125	C4	**Dumbarton** W Duns
47	K7	**Dumbleton** Gloucs
109	L5	**Dumfries** D & G
132	G11	**Dumgoyne** Stirlg
22	G5	**Dummer** Hants
39	Q8	**Dumpton** Kent
143	M6	**Dun** Angus
140	H6	**Dunalastair** P & K
124	F3	**Dunan** Ag & B
145	J2	**Dunan** Highld
140	C6	**Dunan** P & K
120	C10	**Dunaverty** Ag & B
19	K6	**Dunball** Somset
128	H4	**Dunbar** E Loth
167	L11	**Dunbeath** Highld
138	F11	**Dunbeg** Ag & B
133	M7	**Dunblane** Stirlg
134	H4	**Dunbog** Fife
22	B9	**Dunbridge** Hants
155	Q6	**Duncanston** Highld
150	F2	**Duncanstone** Abers
9	L7	**Dunchideock** Devon
59	Q10	**Dunchurch** Warwks
49	J4	**Duncote** Nhants
109	L4	**Duncow** D & G
134	E3	**Duncrievie** P & K
23	Q11	**Duncton** W Susx
142	G11	**Dundee** C Dund
135	K2	**Dundee Airport** C Dund
142	F11	**Dundee Crematorium** C Dund
19	N8	**Dundon** Somset
125	K11	**Dundonald** S Lans
160	H9	**Dundonnell** Highld
110	D11	**Dundraw** Cumb
147	J5	**Dundreggan** Highld
108	F11	**Dundrennan** D & G
31	Q11	**Dundry** N Som
151	K6	**Dunecht** Abers
134	D10	**Dunfermline** Fife
134	E10	**Dunfermline Crematorium** Fife
33	M5	**Dunfield** Gloucs
83	Q4	**Dunford Bridge** Barns
38	F10	**Dungate** Kent
126	B10	**Dungavel** S Lans
20	G4	**Dunge** Wilts
27	J8	**Dungeness** Kent
84	C3	**Dungworth** Sheff
81	P10	**Dunham-on-the-Hill** Ches W
46	H11	**Dunhampstead** Worcs
58	B11	**Dunhampton** Worcs
82	F7	**Dunham Town** Traffd
82	F7	**Dunham Woodhouses** Traffd
86	D5	**Dunholme** Lincs
135	N5	**Dunino** Fife
133	N11	**Dunipace** Falk
141	P9	**Dunkeld** P & K
20	D3	**Dunkerton** BaNES
10	C3	**Dunkeswell** Devon
97	M11	**Dunkeswick** N York
81	M10	**Dunkirk** Ches W
39	J10	**Dunkirk** Kent
32	E7	**Dunkirk** S Glos
21	J1	**Dunkirk** Wilts

37 P10 Dunk's Green Kent
143 K4 Dunlappie Angus
22 E4 Dunley Hants
57 P11 Dunley Worcs
125 L8 Dunlop E Ayrs
147 P3 Dunmaglass Highld
4 G8 Dunmere Cnwll
133 P10 Dunmore Falk
167 M2 Dunnet Highld
143 J8 Dunnichen Angus
134 C5 Dunning P & K
98 D10 Dunnington C York
99 P10 Dunnington E R Yk
47 L4 Dunnington Warwks
89 N5 Dunnockshaw Lancs
38 C9 Dunn Street Kent
124 F2 Dunphail Moray
157 J8 Dunragit D & G
106 G6 Dunragit D & G
129 K9 Duns Border
84 B6 Dunsa Derbys
74 B5 Dunsby Lincs
89 L8 Dunscar Bolton
109 J4 Dunscore D & G
91 Q9 Dunscroft Donc
104 H7 Dunsdale R & Cl
35 K9 Dunsden Green Oxon
16 E10 Dunsdon Devon
24 B3 Dunsfold Surrey
9 K7 Dunsford Devon
134 G5 Dunshalt Fife
159 N8 Dunshillock Abers
84 G8 Dunsill Notts
105 N8 Dunsley N York
58 C8 Dunsley Staffs
35 N3 Dunsmore Bucks
95 P11 Dunsop Bridge Lancs
50 B6 Dunstable C Beds
71 M10 Dunstall Staffs
46 G6 Dunstall Common Worcs
63 M8 Dunstall Green Suffk
119 P7 Dunstan Nthumb
119 P6 Dunstan Steads Nthumb
18 C6 Dunster Somset
48 E9 Duns Tew Oxon
113 K8 Dunston Gatesd
86 E8 Dunston Lincs
77 J11 Dunston Norfk
70 G11 Dunston Staffs
6 F8 Dunstone Devon
8 H9 Dunstone Devon
70 G11 Dunston Heath Staffs
91 Q9 Dunsville Donc
93 J3 Dunswell E R Yk
127 K8 Dunsyre S Lans
5 P6 Dunterton Devon
48 C9 Dunthrop Oxon
33 J3 Duntisbourne Abbots Gloucs
33 J3 Duntisbourne Leer Gloucs
33 J3 Duntisbourne Rouse Gloucs
11 P3 Duntish Dorset
125 M3 Duntocher W Duns
49 M10 Dunton Bucks
50 F2 Dunton C Beds
76 B5 Dunton Norfk
60 B2 Dunton Bassett Leics
37 M9 Dunton Green Kent
37 Q2 Dunton Wayletts Essex
152 G3 Duntulm Highld
114 E4 Dunure S Ayrs
28 G6 Dunvant Swans
152 D8 Dunvegan Highld
65 P7 Dunwich Suffk
70 G3 Dunwood Staffs
110 H10 Durdar Cumb
3 K8 Durgan Cnwll
103 Q2 Durham Dur
103 Q2 Durham Cathedral Dur
103 Q2 Durham Crematorium Dur
104 B3 Durham Services Dur
104 C8 Durham Tees Valley Airport S on T
116 B10 Durisdeer D & G
116 B10 Durisdeermill D & G
91 J7 Durkar Wakefd
19 J7 Durleigh Somset
22 F11 Durley Hants
21 P2 Durley Wilts
22 F11 Durley Street Hants
39 N10 Durlock Kent
39 P9 Durlock Kent
46 B7 Durlow Common Herefs
89 Q7 Durn Rochdl
165 K3 Durness Highld
151 J2 Durno Abers
138 H6 Duror Highld
131 K6 Durran Ag & B
24 D9 Durrington W Susx
21 N6 Durrington Wilts
151 K8 Durris Abers
32 E5 Dursley Gloucs
46 C10 Dursley Cross Gloucs
19 J9 Durston Somset
12 E3 Durweston Dorset
60 F8 Duston Nhants
148 G3 Duthil Highld
56 C9 Dutlas Powys
51 P5 Duton Hill Essex
5 N4 Dutson Cnwll
82 C9 Dutton Ches W
62 G11 Duxford Cambs
34 C5 Duxford Oxon
62 G11 Duxford Aircraft Museum Cambs
79 N9 Dwygyfylchi Conwy
78 G11 Dwyran IoA
151 M5 Dyce C Aber
52 B4 Dyer's End Essex
28 E4 Dyfatty Carmth
54 F2 Dyffrydan Gwynd
29 N6 Dyffryn Brdgnd
30 E4 Dyffryn Myr Td
30 E10 Dyffryn V Glam
67 K10 Dyffryn Ardudwy Gwynd
54 H8 Dyffryn Castell Cerdgn
29 N2 Dyffryn Ceilwen Neath
74 B6 Dyke Lincs
156 H6 Dyke Moray
142 C7 Dykehead Angus
142 F6 Dykehead Angus
126 F6 Dykehead N Lans
132 H8 Dykehead Stirlg
143 N4 Dykelands Abers
142 D6 Dykends Angus
158 H9 Dykeside Abers
55 K6 Dylife Powys

27 K6 Dymchurch Kent
46 D8 Dymock Gloucs
32 D9 Dyrham S Glos
135 J9 Dysart Fife
80 F9 Dyserth Denbgs

E

58 E9 Eachway Worcs
112 H6 Eachwick Nthumb
95 J11 Eagland Hill Lancs
85 Q7 Eagle Lincs
85 Q7 Eagle Barnsdale Lincs
85 Q7 Eagle Moor Lincs
104 D7 Eaglescliffe S on T
100 E5 Eaglesfield Cumb
110 D6 Eaglesfield D & G
125 P7 Eaglesham E Rens
89 L8 Eagley Bolton
80 C6 Eairy IoM
85 L8 Eakring Notts
92 C8 Ealand N Linc
36 E4 Ealing Gt Lon
111 N9 Eals Nthumb
101 P5 Eamont Bridge Cumb
96 D11 Earby Lancs
89 K6 Earcroft Bl w D
57 N6 Eardington Shrops
45 N3 Eardisland Herefs
45 L5 Eardisley Herefs
69 L9 Eardiston Shrops
57 M11 Eardiston Worcs
62 E5 Earith Cambs
119 J5 Earle Nthumb
82 C5 Earlestown St Hel
35 K10 Earley Wokham
76 H10 Earlham Norfk
77 J10 Earlham Crematorium Norfk
152 F5 Earlish Highld
61 J8 Earls Barton Nhants
52 E6 Earls Colne Essex
47 J3 Earls Common Worcs
46 G6 Earl's Croome Worcs
57 L9 Earlsditton Shrops
59 M9 Earlsdon Covtry
25 P7 Earl's Down E Susx
135 M7 Earlsferry Fife
36 G6 Earlsfield Gt Lon
159 K11 Earlsford Abers
64 E8 Earl's Green Suffk
90 H6 Earlsheaton Kirk
72 D11 Earl Shilton Leics
65 J9 Earl Soham Suffk
83 N11 Earl Sterndale Derbys
117 R3 Earlston Border
125 L10 Earlston E Ayrs
64 G10 Earl Stonham Suffk
36 G11 Earlswood Surrey
58 H10 Earlswood Warwks
31 N6 Earlswood Common Mons
15 M7 Earnley W Susx
88 G6 Earnshaw Bridge Lancs
113 M6 Earsdon N Tyne
113 J2 Earsdon Nthumb
65 L4 Earsham Norfk
98 C9 Earswick C York
15 P5 Eartham W Susx
32 C7 Earthcott S Glos
104 G9 Easby N York
130 E4 Easdale Ag & B
23 P10 Easebourne W Susx
59 Q9 Easenhall Warwks
23 P6 Eashing Surrey
35 J2 Easington Bucks
104 D2 Easington Dur
93 Q7 Easington E R Yk
119 M4 Easington Nthumb
35 J5 Easington Oxon
105 K7 Easington R & Cl
104 D2 Easington Colliery Dur
113 N11 Easington Lane Sundld
98 A7 Easingwold N York
39 N11 Easole Street Kent
142 E9 Eassie and Nevay Angus
30 D11 East Aberthaw V Glam
7 K9 East Allington Devon
17 R6 East Anstey Devon
22 C5 East Anton Hants
103 P11 East Appleton N York
14 G9 East Ashey IoW
15 M5 East Ashling W Susx
22 D5 East Aston Hants
99 K3 East Ayton N York
5 M2 East Balsdon Cnwll
30 H3 East Bank Blae G
86 G4 East Barkwith Lincs
38 B11 East Barming Kent
105 M8 East Barnby N York
50 G11 East Barnet Gt Lon
129 J4 East Barns E Loth
76 C5 East Barsham Norfk
76 H4 East Beckham Norfk
36 C6 East Bedfont Gt Lon
53 J5 East Bergholt Suffk
90 F5 East Bierley Kirk
76 D8 East Bilney Norfk
25 L10 East Blatchington E Susx
12 C6 East Bloxworth Dorset
113 N8 East Boldon S Tyne
14 C6 East Boldre Hants
119 M7 East Bolton Nthumb
104 B8 Eastbourne Darltn
25 P11 Eastbourne E Susx
25 P10 Eastbourne Crematorium E Susx
19 K7 East Bower Somset
76 C10 East Bradenham Norfk
19 K4 East Brent Somset
65 P8 Eastbridge Suffk
72 H2 East Bridgford Notts
103 J7 East Briscoe Dur
30 G10 Eastbrook V Glam
17 M5 East Buckland Devon
9 Q8 East Budleigh Devon
90 C2 Eastburn C Brad
99 K9 Eastburn E R Yk
35 Q8 East Burnham Bucks
12 D7 East Burton Dorset
36 D2 Eastbury Herts
34 B9 Eastbury W Berk
112 H11 East Butsfield Dur
92 D9 East Butterwick N Linc
96 F10 Eastby N York
127 K4 East Calder W Loth
76 H11 East Carleton Norfk
90 G2 East Carlton Leeds

60 H3 East Carlton Nhants
12 C8 East Chaldon (Chaldon Herring) Dorset
34 C7 East Challow Oxon
7 K10 East Charleton Devon
11 M3 East Chelborough Dorset
25 J7 East Chiltington E Susx
11 K2 East Chinnock Somset
21 M4 East Chisenbury Wilts
21 Q5 East Cholderton Hants
38 G7 Eastchurch Kent
36 C10 East Clandon Surrey
49 K9 East Claydon Bucks
31 M10 East Clevedon N Som
11 L2 East Coker Somset
32 G4 Eastcombe Gloucs
18 G8 Eastcombe Somset
20 B6 East Compton Somset
7 L7 East Cornworthy Devon
109 P9 East Cote Cumb
36 D3 Eastcote Gt Lon
49 J4 Eastcote Nhants
59 J9 Eastcote Solhll
16 D8 Eastcott Cnwll
21 K3 Eastcott Wilts
92 B2 East Cottingwith E R Yk
21 P2 Eastcourt Wilts
33 J6 Eastcourt Wilts
14 F7 East Cowes IoW
91 R6 East Cowick E R Yk
104 B10 East Cowton N York
113 L5 East Cramlington Nthumb
20 C6 East Cranmore Somset
12 F8 East Creech Dorset
110 F11 East Curthwaite Cumb
25 N11 East Dean E Susx
46 C10 East Dean Gloucs
21 Q9 East Dean Hants
15 P4 East Dean W Susx
9 Q5 East Devon Crematorium Devon
7 L9 Eastdown Devon
17 L3 East Down Devon
85 N5 East Drayton Notts
36 H5 East Dulwich Gt Lon
31 Q11 East Dundry N Som
93 J5 East Ella C KuH
61 P9 East End Bed
49 Q6 East End C Beds
93 L4 East End E R Yk
93 N5 East End E R Yk
38 F3 Eastend Essex
51 K8 East End Essex
14 C7 East End Hants
22 D2 East End Hants
51 L5 East End Herts
26 D4 East End Kent
38 G7 East End Kent
49 P6 East End M Keyn
31 N10 East End N Som
48 C11 East End Oxon
20 C5 East End Somset
53 K4 East End Suffk
149 P9 Easter Balmoral Abers
31 Q8 Easter Compton S Glos
156 D7 Easter Dalziel Highld
15 P5 Eastergate W Susx
126 B4 Easterhouse C Glas
127 N5 Easter Howgate Mdloth
155 Q6 Easter Kinkell Highld
155 Q9 Easter Moniack Highld
59 L9 Eastern Green Covtry
151 L7 Easter Ord Abers
135 P6 Easter Pitkierie Fife
169 g9 Easter Skeld Shet
118 E4 Easter Softlaw Border
21 K4 Eastertown Wilts
19 K4 Eastertown Somset
21 P4 East Everleigh Wilts
38 B11 East Farleigh Kent
60 F4 East Farndon Nhants
92 D11 East Ferry Lincs
126 F5 Eastfield N Lans
99 L4 Eastfield N York
86 D3 East Firsby Lincs
128 E4 East Fortune E Loth
91 L4 East Garforth Leeds
34 C9 East Garston W Berk
103 J3 Eastgate Dur
74 B7 Eastgate Lincs
76 G7 Eastgate Norfk
34 D7 East Ginge Oxon
72 G8 East Goscote Leics
21 Q2 East Grafton Wilts
65 N8 East Green Suffk
21 P9 East Grimstead Wilts
25 J3 East Grinstead W Susx
26 F7 East Guldeford E Susx
60 E7 East Haddon Nhants
34 F7 East Hagbourne Oxon
93 K7 East Halton N Linc
37 K4 East Ham Gt Lon
81 M8 Eastham Wirral
81 M8 Eastham Ferry Wirral
35 M11 Easthampstead Park Crematorium Br For
45 N2 Easthampton Herefs
34 D6 East Hanney Oxon
52 C11 East Hanningfield Essex
91 M7 East Hardwick Wakefd
64 D4 East Harling Norfk
104 D10 East Harlsey N York
21 M9 East Harnham Wilts
19 Q3 East Harptree BaNES
104 D7 East Hartburn S on T
113 L5 East Hartford Nthumb
23 L11 East Harting W Susx
20 H9 East Hatch Wilts
62 C10 East Hatley Cambs
97 J2 East Hauxwell N York
143 K10 East Haven Angus
35 L11 Eastheath Wokham
74 C2 East Heckington Lincs
103 N2 East Hedleyhope Dur
163 N3 East Helmsdale Highld
34 E7 East Hendred Oxon
99 J5 East Heslerton N York
19 M2 East Hewish N Som
25 M7 East Hoathly E Susx
12 E7 East Holme Dorset
57 K5 Easthope Shrops
65 J2 Easthorpe Essex
52 F5 Easthorpe Essex
85 M10 Easthorpe Notts
19 Q5 East Horrington Somset
36 C10 East Horsley Surrey
119 K4 East Horton Nthumb
13 J5 East Howe Bmouth
98 C9 East Huntington C York
19 K5 East Huntspill Somset

50 D7 East Hyde C Beds
17 N2 East Ilkerton Devon
34 E8 East Ilsley W Berk
8 H3 Eastington Devon
32 E3 Eastington Gloucs
33 M2 Eastington Gloucs
87 L8 East Keal Lincs
33 M11 East Kennett Wilts
91 K2 East Keswick Leeds
125 Q7 East Kilbride S Lans
8 C5 East Kimber Devon
87 K8 East Kirkby Lincs
12 D7 East Knighton Dorset
17 Q7 East Knowstone Devon
20 G8 East Knoyle Wilts
19 M11 East Lambrook Somset
89 M9 East Lancashire Crematorium Bury
108 H6 Eastlands D & G
27 P2 East Langdon Kent
60 F2 East Langton Leics
15 N5 East Lavant W Susx
23 P11 East Lavington W Susx
103 N9 East Layton N York
33 P4 Eastleach Martin Gloucs
33 N3 Eastleach Turville Gloucs
72 F5 East Leake Notts
118 G3 East Learmouth Nthumb
8 H8 East Leigh Devon
7 K7 East Leigh Devon
8 G3 East Leigh Devon
22 E11 Eastleigh Hants
76 B8 East Lexham Norfk
38 G10 Eastling Kent
128 F4 East Linton E Loth
23 L9 East Liss Hants
34 D7 East Lockinge Oxon
37 J4 East London Crematorium Gt Lon
92 C11 East Lound N Linc
12 E8 East Lulworth Dorset
99 J7 East Lutton N York
18 G9 East Lydeard Somset
19 Q8 East Lydford Somset
38 B10 East Malling Kent
37 Q9 East Malling Heath Kent
15 M4 East Marden W Susx
85 M6 East Markham Notts
21 L11 East Martin Hants
96 D10 East Marton N York
23 J10 East Meon Hants
18 C11 East Mere Devon
52 H9 East Mersea Essex
72 D5 East Midlands Airport Leics
36 D7 East Molesey Surrey
75 P10 Eastmoor Norfk
12 F6 East Morden Dorset
90 D2 East Morton C Brad
116 B10 East Morton D & G
98 D5 East Ness N York
93 N3 East Newton E R Yk
15 J7 Eastney C Port
46 D7 Eastnor Herefs
73 K10 East Norton Leics
92 D7 Eastoft N Linc
7 L4 East Ogwell Devon
61 P6 Easton Cambs
110 E9 Easton Cumb
8 H7 Easton Devon
11 P10 Easton Dorset
22 F8 Easton Hants
73 N5 Easton Lincs
76 G9 Easton Norfk
19 P5 Easton Somset
65 K10 Easton Suffk
34 D10 Easton W Berk
32 G10 Easton Wilts
32 G7 Easton Grey Wilts
31 P9 Easton-in-Gordano N Som
61 J9 Easton Maudit Nhants
73 Q10 Easton-on-the-Hill Nhants
21 P2 Easton Royal Wilts
20 F11 East Orchard Dorset
129 P9 East Ord Nthumb
5 P3 East Panson Devon
13 J5 East Parley Dorset
37 Q11 East Peckham Kent
41 J10 East Pennar Pembks
19 Q7 East Pennard Somset
61 Q7 East Perry Cambs
7 K11 East Portlemouth Devon
7 K11 East Prawle Devon
24 C10 East Preston W Susx
11 Q3 East Pulham Dorset
16 F8 East Putford Devon
18 F6 East Quantoxhead Somset
38 D8 East Rainham Medway
113 M11 East Rainton Sundld
93 M11 East Ravendale NE Lin
76 B6 East Raynham Norfk
74 E11 Eastrea Cambs
99 L7 East Riding Crematorium E R Yk
110 D7 Eastriggs D & G
91 K2 East Rigton Leeds
92 C5 Eastrington E R Yk
19 L2 East Rolstone N Som
33 P6 Eastrop Swindn
104 D10 East Rounton N York
76 A6 East Rudham Norfk
76 H3 East Runton Norfk
77 L6 East Ruston Norfk
39 P11 Eastry Kent
128 D6 East Saltoun E Loth
23 N10 Eastshaw W Susx
34 C10 East Shefford W Berk
113 L4 East Sleekburn Nthumb
77 P8 East Somerton Norfk
85 N2 East Stockwith Lincs
12 E7 East Stoke Dorset
85 N11 East Stoke Notts
20 F10 East Stour Dorset
39 N9 East Stourmouth Kent
17 L6 East Stowford Devon
22 F6 East Stratton Hants
27 P2 East Studdal Kent
26 D2 East Sutton Kent
5 K9 East Taphouse Cnwll
16 H6 East-the-Water Devon
119 N10 East Thirston Nthumb
37 N5 East Tilbury Thurr
23 K8 East Tisted Hants
86 F4 East Torrington Lincs
76 F9 East Tuddenham Norfk
21 Q9 East Tytherley Hants

33 J10 East Tytherton Wilts
9 K3 East Village Devon
32 B10 East Village Bristl
87 M9 Eastville Lincs
57 J6 East Wall Shrops
75 P7 East Walton Norfk
19 P4 East Water Somset
8 G6 East Week Devon
73 K5 Eastwell Leics
22 B10 East Wellow Hants
135 J8 East Wemyss Fife
126 H4 East Whitburn W Loth
51 K8 Eastwick Herts
37 L5 East Wickham Gt Lon
41 L10 East Williamston Pembks
75 N7 East Winch Norfk
21 P8 East Winterslow Wilts
15 L7 East Wittering W Susx
96 H3 East Witton N York
84 G11 Eastwood Notts
38 B4 Eastwood Sthend
112 D3 East Woodburn Nthumb
62 F2 Eastwood End Cambs
22 D2 East Woodhay Hants
20 E6 East Woodlands Somset
23 L7 East Worldham Hants
64 C3 East Wretham Norfk
16 D8 East Youlstone Devon
59 N11 Eathorpe Warwks
83 J11 Eaton Ches E
69 Q2 Eaton Ches W
73 K5 Eaton Leics
77 J10 Eaton Norfk
85 M5 Eaton Notts
34 D4 Eaton Oxon
56 F7 Eaton Shrops
57 J7 Eaton Shrops
45 N7 Eaton Bishop Herefs
49 Q10 Eaton Bray C Beds
57 K3 Eaton Constantine Shrops
61 Q9 Eaton Ford Cambs
49 Q10 Eaton Green C Beds
33 Q5 Eaton Hastings Oxon
57 J3 Eaton Mascott Shrops
61 Q9 Eaton Socon Cambs
70 B10 Eaton upon Tern Shrops
82 D6 Eaves Brow Warrtn
59 L8 Eaves Green Solhll
98 H4 Ebberston N York
21 J10 Ebbesborne Wake Wilts
30 G3 Ebbw Vale Blae G
112 H9 Ebchester Dur
19 L2 Ebdon N Som
9 N7 Ebford Devon
32 F3 Ebley Gloucs
69 N5 Ebnal Ches W
45 P3 Ebnall Herefs
47 N6 Ebrington Gloucs
8 D6 Ebsworthy Devon
22 E3 Ecchinswell Hants
129 K6 Ecclaw Border
110 C6 Ecclefechan D & G
118 E2 Eccles Border
38 B9 Eccles Kent
82 G5 Eccles Salfd
84 D4 Ecclesall Sheff
82 F5 Eccles Crematorium Salfd
84 E2 Ecclesfield Sheff
45 M5 Eccles Green Herefs
70 E9 Eccleshall Staffs
90 F3 Eccleshill C Brad
127 K3 Ecclesmachan W Loth
77 N6 Eccles on Sea Norfk
64 E4 Eccles Road Norfk
69 M2 Eccleston Ches W
88 G7 Eccleston Lancs
81 P5 Eccleston St Hel
88 G7 Eccleston Green Lancs
151 J6 Echt Abers
118 D5 Eckford Border
84 F5 Eckington Derbys
46 H6 Eckington Worcs
60 H8 Ecton Nhants
71 K3 Ecton Staffs
83 P7 Edale Derbys
169 e3 Eday Ork
169 e3 Eday Airport Ork
24 F8 Edburton W Susx
109 P11 Edderside Cumb
162 G10 Edderton Highld
39 L8 Eddington Kent
127 N8 Eddleston Border
126 C7 Eddlewood S Lans
37 K11 Edenbridge Kent
89 N7 Edenfield Lancs
101 Q4 Edenhall Cumb
73 R6 Edenham Lincs
95 J5 Eden Mount Cumb
37 J7 Eden Park Gt Lon
3 Q3 Eden Project Cnwll
84 B7 Edensor Derbys
132 C9 Edentaggart Ag & B
91 Q9 Edenthorpe Donc
66 D7 Edern Gwynd
19 P7 Edgarley Somset
58 G8 Edgbaston Birm
3 J7 Edgcombe Cnwll
49 J10 Edgcott Bucks
17 Q4 Edgcott Somset
32 F3 Edge Gloucs
56 F3 Edge Shrops
69 Q10 Edgebolton Shrops
31 Q2 Edge End Gloucs
76 F5 Edgefield Norfk
76 F5 Edgefield Green Norfk
89 L8 Edgefold Bolton
69 N4 Edge Green Ches W
48 C5 Edgehill Warwks
69 L11 Edgerley Shrops
90 E7 Edgerton Kirk
89 N6 Edgeside Lancs
32 F3 Edgeworth Gloucs
9 K2 Edgeworthy Devon
7 M5 Edginswell Torbay
47 K2 Edgiock Worcs
70 C11 Edgmond Wrekin
70 C10 Edgmond Marsh Wrekin
56 F7 Edgton Shrops
36 E2 Edgware Gt Lon
89 L7 Edgworth Bl w D
152 E7 Edinbane Highld
127 P3 Edinburgh C Edin
127 L3 Edinburgh Airport C Edin
127 N2 Edinburgh Castle C Edin
127 N2 Edinburgh Royal Botanic Gardens C Edin
127 N3 Edinburgh Zoo C Edin
59 K2 Edingale Staffs

108 H8 Edingham D & G
85 L9 Edingley Notts
77 L5 Edingthorpe Norfk
77 L5 Edingthorpe Green Norfk
129 K7 Edington Border
113 J4 Edington Nthumb
19 L7 Edington Somset
20 H4 Edington Wilts
19 L6 Edington Burtle Somset
19 L4 Edingworth Somset
16 D7 Edistone Devon
19 K5 Edithmead Somset
73 N9 Edith Weston Rutlnd
49 Q11 Edlesborough Bucks
119 M9 Edlingham Nthumb
86 H6 Edlington Lincs
111 J9 Edmond Castle Cumb
13 J2 Edmondsham Dorset
113 K11 Edmondsley Dur
73 M7 Edmondthorpe Leics
4 F7 Edmonton Cnwll
36 H2 Edmonton Gt Lon
112 F10 Edmundbyers Dur
118 D3 Ednam Border
71 N6 Ednaston Derbys
141 L7 Edradynate P & K
129 L8 Edrom Border
69 P8 Edstaston Shrops
47 N2 Edstone Warwks
46 C3 Edvin Loach Herefs
72 F3 Edwalton Notts
52 F3 Edwardstone Suffk
30 E5 Edwardsville Myr Td
43 M8 Edwinsford Carmth
85 K7 Edwinstowe Notts
50 F2 Edworth C Beds
46 B3 Edwyn Ralph Herefs
143 L4 Edzell Angus
143 L4 Edzell Woods Abers
29 L5 Efail-fach Neath
30 E8 Efail Isaf Rhondd
66 F7 Efailnewydd Gwynd
68 G9 Efail-Rhyd Powys
41 M5 Efailwen Carmth
68 F3 Efenechtyd Denbgs
110 F2 Effgill D & G
36 D10 Effingham Surrey
71 M11 Efflinch Staffs
9 L4 Efford Devon
6 E7 Efford Crematorium C Plym
22 D4 Egbury Hants
23 Q10 Egdean W Susx
89 L8 Egerton Bolton
26 F2 Egerton Kent
26 E2 Egerton Forstal Kent
91 P6 Eggborough N York
6 E7 Eggbuckland C Plym
17 M9 Eggesford Devon
49 Q9 Eggington C Beds
71 P9 Egginton Derbys
104 D8 Egglescliffe S on T
103 J6 Eggleston Dur
36 B6 Egham Surrey
35 Q10 Egham Wick Surrey
73 M9 Egleton Rutlnd
119 M7 Eglingham Nthumb
4 G7 Egloshayle Cnwll
5 M4 Egloskerry Cnwll
79 Q10 Eglwysbach Conwy
30 D11 Eglwys-Brewis V Glam
69 N6 Eglwys Cross Wrexhm
54 F5 Eglwys Fach Cerdgn
41 M3 Eglwyswrw Pembks
85 M7 Egmanton Notts
100 D8 Egremont Cumb
81 L6 Egremont Wirral
105 M9 Egton N York
105 M10 Egton Bridge N York
35 Q7 Egypt Bucks
22 E6 Egypt Hants
144 G10 Eigg Highld
52 F6 Eight Ash Green Essex
145 P4 Eilanreach Highld
54 H8 Eisteddfa Gurig Cerdgn
44 B2 Elan Valley Powys
44 C2 Elan Village Powys
32 B7 Elberton S Glos
15 P6 Elbridge W Susx
6 E8 Elburton C Plym
33 M8 Elcombe Swindn
34 C11 Elcot W Berk
74 F11 Eldernell Cambs
46 E8 Eldersfield Worcs
125 L5 Elderslie Rens
51 N4 Elder Street Essex
103 P5 Eldon Dur
90 E2 Eldwick C Brad
151 L10 Elfhill Abers
119 N4 Elford Nthumb
59 J2 Elford Staffs
157 N5 Elgin Moray
144 H5 Elgol Highld
27 L3 Elham Kent
135 M7 Elie Fife
119 J9 Elilaw Nthumb
78 F8 Elim IoA
14 C4 Eling Hants
85 L5 Elkesley Notts
33 J2 Elkstone Gloucs
158 F6 Ella Abers
7 N6 Ellacombe Torbay
90 E6 Elland Calder
90 E6 Elland Lower Edge Calder
123 M4 Ellary Ag & B
71 L6 Ellastone Staffs
95 K9 Ellel Lancs
129 J7 Ellemford Border
130 E4 Ellenabeich Ag & B
100 D3 Ellenborough Cumb
82 F4 Ellenbrook Salfd
70 E9 Ellenhall Staffs
24 C3 Ellen's Green Surrey
104 D11 Ellerbeck N York
105 L8 Ellerby N York
69 R10 Ellerdine Heath Wrekin
9 N4 Ellerhayes Devon
139 J8 Elleric Ag & B
92 F5 Ellerker E R Yk
90 C2 Ellers N York
92 B3 Ellerton E R Yk
103 Q11 Ellerton N York
70 C9 Ellerton Shrops
35 M3 Ellesborough Bucks
69 L8 Ellesmere Shrops
81 N9 Ellesmere Port Ches W
13 K3 Ellingham Hants
65 M3 Ellingham Norfk

119 N5 Ellingham Nthumb
97 J4 Ellingstring N York
61 Q6 Ellington Cambs
113 L2 Ellington Nthumb
61 Q6 Ellington Thorpe Cambs
20 E5 Elliots Green Somset
22 H5 Ellisfield Hants
153 J4 Ellishader Highld
72 C8 Ellistown Leics
159 N11 Ellon Abers
101 M3 Ellonby Cumb
65 N4 Ellough Suffk
92 F5 Elloughton E R Yk
31 Q3 Ellwood Gloucs
75 J9 Elm Cambs
58 D11 Elmbridge Worcs
51 L3 Elmdon Essex
59 J8 Elmdon Solhll
59 J8 Elmdon Heath Solhll
15 Q6 Elmer W Susx
37 J7 Elmers End Gt Lon
88 G9 Elmer's Green Lancs
72 D11 Elmesthorpe Leics
52 C10 Elm Green Essex
58 H2 Elmhurst Staffs
47 J6 Elmley Castle Worcs
58 C11 Elmley Lovett Worcs
46 E11 Elmore Gloucs
46 E11 Elmore Back Gloucs
37 M3 Elm Park Gt Lon
16 C7 Elmscott Devon
53 J2 Elmsett Suffk
57 N11 Elms Green Worcs
53 J7 Elmstead Heath Essex
53 J7 Elmstead Market Essex
53 J7 Elmstead Row Essex
27 K3 Elmsted Kent
39 N9 Elmstone Kent
46 H9 Elmstone Hardwicke Gloucs
99 K9 Elmswell E R Yk
64 D9 Elmswell Suffk
84 H6 Elmton Derbys
161 L4 Elphin Highld
128 B6 Elphinstone E Loth
151 L6 Elrick Abers
107 K8 Elrig D & G
112 C8 Elrington Nthumb
112 D2 Elsdon Nthumb
91 K11 Elsecar Barns
51 M5 Elsenham Essex
34 F2 Elsfield Oxon
92 H8 Elsham N Linc
76 F8 Elsing Norfk
96 D11 Elslack N York
14 H6 Elson Hants
69 L7 Elson Shrops
116 F2 Elsrickle S Lans
23 P6 Elstead Surrey
23 M11 Elsted W Susx
73 R6 Elsthorpe Lincs
104 B6 Elstob Dur
88 H4 Elston Lancs
85 N11 Elston Notts
21 L6 Elston Wilts
17 M8 Elstone Devon
61 N11 Elstow Bed
50 E11 Elstree Herts
93 M4 Elstronwick E R Yk
88 E3 Elswick Lancs
113 K8 Elswick N u Ty
62 D8 Elsworth Cambs
101 K10 Elterwater Cumb
37 K6 Eltham Gt Lon
37 K6 Eltham Crematorium Gt Lon
62 C9 Eltisley Cambs
89 M8 Elton Bury
61 N2 Elton Cambs
81 P9 Elton Ches W
84 B8 Elton Derbys
32 D2 Elton Gloucs
56 H10 Elton Herefs
73 K3 Elton N York
104 D7 Elton S on T
81 P10 Elton Green Ches W
112 G8 Eltringham Nthumb
116 D7 Elvanfoot S Lans
72 C4 Elvaston Derbys
63 P4 Elveden Suffk
23 M3 Elvetham Heath Hants
128 D5 Elvingston E Loth
98 E11 Elvington C York
39 N11 Elvington Kent
17 M5 Elwell Devon
104 E4 Elwick Hartpl
119 M3 Elwick Nthumb
70 C2 Elworth Ches E
18 E8 Elworthy Somset
62 H4 Ely Cambs
30 F9 Ely Cardif
49 N5 Emberton M Keyn
100 G4 Embleton Cumb
104 D5 Embleton Dur
119 P6 Embleton Nthumb
163 J8 Embo Highld
20 B4 Emborough Somset
163 J8 Embo Street Highld
96 F10 Embsay N York
13 N3 Emery Down Hants
90 G8 Emley Kirk
90 G8 Emley Moor Kirk
35 M11 Emmbrook Wokham
35 K9 Emmer Green Readg
84 G5 Emmett Carr Derbys
35 K4 Emmington Oxon
75 J9 Emneth Norfk
75 K9 Emneth Hungate Norfk
73 N9 Empingham Rutlnd
23 L8 Empshott Hants
23 K8 Empshott Green Hants
57 J2 Emstrey Crematorium Shrops
15 K5 Emsworth Hants
34 D11 Enborne W Berk
22 D7 Enborne Row W Berk
57 J5 Enchmarsh Shrops
72 E11 Enderby Leics
95 L4 Endmoor Cumb
70 G4 Endon Staffs
70 G4 Endon Bank Staffs
51 J11 Enfield Gt Lon
50 H11 Enfield Crematorium Gt Lon
51 J11 Enfield Lock Gt Lon
51 J11 Enfield Wash Gt Lon
21 M4 Enford Wilts
32 C8 Engine Common S Glos
45 Q4 England's Gate Herefs
34 H10 Englefield W Berk

35 Q10 Englefield Green Surrey
70 D4 Engleseabrook Ches E
46 A11 English Bicknor Gloucs
20 D2 Englishcombe BaNES
69 N9 English Frankton Shrops
4 D7 Engollan Cnwll
22 C5 Enham-Alamein Hants
18 H7 Enmore Somset
12 H3 Enmore Green Dorset
100 E7 Ennerdale Bridge Cumb
141 Q5 Enochdhu P & K
137 K6 Ensay Ag & B
13 J5 Ensbury Bmouth
69 M11 Ensdon Shrops
17 K6 Ensis Devon
70 G9 Enson Staffs
48 C10 Enstone Oxon
116 B10 Enterkinfoot D & G
104 E9 Enterpen N York
58 B7 Enville Staffs
168 C17 Eolaigearraidh W Isls
32 E2 Epney Gloucs
85 L11 Epperstone Notts
51 L10 Epping Essex
51 K9 Epping Green Essex
50 G9 Epping Green Herts
51 K10 Epping Upland Essex
103 N8 Eppleby N York
92 H4 Eppleworth E R Yk
36 F8 Epsom Surrey
48 C6 Epwell Oxon
92 C10 Epworth N Linc
92 C10 Epworth Turbary N Linc
69 L6 Erbistock Wrexhm
58 H6 Erdington Birm
25 N3 Eridge Green E Susx
25 M4 Eridge Station E Susx
123 Q4 Erines Ag & B
138 G9 Eriska Ag & B
168 c17 Eriskay W Isls
63 M5 Eriswell Suffk
37 M5 Erith Gt Lon
21 J4 Erlestoke Wilts
6 G8 Ermington Devon
76 H5 Erpingham Norfk
38 F10 Erriottwood Kent
147 P3 Errogie Highld
134 G3 Errol P & K
125 M3 Erskine Rens
106 D4 Ervie D & G
53 M5 Erwarton Suffk
44 F6 Erwood Powys
104 B9 Eryholme N York
68 H3 Eryrys Denbgs
2 B8 Escalls Cnwll
103 N4 Escomb Dur
18 E7 Escott Somset
91 Q2 Escrick N York
42 G9 Esgair Carmth
54 D11 Esgair Cerdgn
54 H3 Esgairgeiliog Powys
43 M6 Esgerdawe Carmth
79 Q9 Esgyryn Conwy
103 N2 Esh Dur
36 D8 Esher Surrey
90 F2 Esholt C Brad
119 P11 Eshott Nthumb
96 D9 Eshton N York
103 N2 Esh Winning Dur
155 N9 Eskadale Highld
127 Q4 Eskbank Mdloth
100 F10 Eskdale Green Cumb
117 K11 Eskdalemuir D & G
93 Q11 Eskham Lincs
91 Q7 Eskholme N York
103 M6 Esperley Lane Ends Dur
88 E3 Esprick Lancs
73 Q8 Essendine Rutlnd
50 G9 Essendon Herts
156 A10 Essich Highld
58 E4 Essington Staffs
151 N2 Esslemont Abers
104 F7 Eston R & Cl
118 H3 Etal Nthumb
21 K2 Etchilhampton Wilts
26 B6 Etchingham E Susx
27 L4 Etchinghill Kent
71 J11 Etchinghill Staffs
25 M6 Etchingwood E Susx
76 E9 Etling Green Norfk
32 C3 Etloe Gloucs
35 Q9 Eton W & M
35 P9 Eton Wick W & M
70 F5 Etruria C Stke
148 B9 Etteridge Highld
102 G5 Ettersgill Dur
70 C2 Ettiley Heath Ches E
58 D5 Ettingshall Wolves
47 Q5 Ettington Warwks
74 B9 Etton C Pete
92 G2 Etton E R Yk
117 K8 Ettrick Border
117 M6 Ettrickbridge Border
117 K8 Ettrickhill Border
71 P8 Etwall Derbys
57 M7 Eudon George Shrops
64 B6 Euston Suffk
75 J11 Euximoor Drove Cambs
88 H7 Euxton Lancs
45 K2 Evancoyd Powys
155 R4 Evanton Highld
86 F11 Evedon Lincs
57 N3 Evelith Shrops
162 H8 Evelix Highld
45 K2 Evenjobb Powys
48 G3 Evenley Nhants
47 P9 Evenlode Gloucs
103 N6 Evenwood Dur
103 N6 Evenwood Gate Dur
20 B7 Evercreech Somset
92 D2 Everingham E R Yk
21 P4 Everleigh Wilts
99 K3 Everley N York
49 Q8 Eversholt C Beds
11 M4 Evershot Dorset
23 L2 Eversley Hants
23 L2 Eversley Cross Hants
92 F4 Everthorpe E R Yk
62 B10 Everton C Beds
13 N6 Everton Hants
81 L6 Everton Lpool
85 L2 Everton Notts
110 G5 Evertown D & G
46 C5 Evesbatch Herefs
47 K6 Evesham Worcs
72 G10 Evington C Leic
90 H11 Ewden Village Sheff
36 F8 Ewell Surrey

27 N3 Ewell Minnis Kent
34 H6 Ewelme Oxon
32 K5 Ewen Gloucs
29 P9 Ewenny V Glam
86 F11 Ewerby Lincs
86 F11 Ewerby Thorpe Lincs
24 C2 Ewhurst Surrey
26 C7 Ewhurst Green E Susx
24 C3 Ewhurst Green Surrey
81 L11 Ewloe Flints
81 K11 Ewloe Green Flints
89 K5 Ewood Bl w D
89 M6 Ewood Bridge Lancs
8 B5 Eworthy Devon
23 M5 Ewshot Hants
45 M9 Ewyas Harold Herefs
8 F4 Exbourne Devon
18 B10 Exbridge Somset
14 D6 Exbury Hants
25 M11 Exceat E Susx
97 L3 Exelby N York
9 M6 Exeter Devon
9 N6 Exeter Airport Devon
9 M6 Exeter & Devon Crematorium Devon
9 N6 Exeter Services Devon
17 R4 Exford Somset
56 H3 Exfordsgreen Shrops
47 M3 Exhall Warwks
59 N7 Exhall Warwks
35 J8 Exlade Street Oxon
90 C2 Exley Head C Brad
9 M7 Exminster Devon
17 R4 Exmoor National Park
9 P8 Exmouth Devon
63 K7 Exning Suffk
27 L3 Exted Kent
9 N7 Exton Devon
22 H10 Exton Hants
73 N8 Exton Rutlnd
18 B8 Exton Somset
9 M6 Exwick Devon
84 B5 Eyam Derbys
48 F5 Eydon Nhants
74 D10 Eye C Pete
45 P2 Eye Herefs
64 G7 Eye Suffk
74 D10 Eye Green C Pete
73 J7 Eye Kettleby Leics
129 N7 Eyemouth Border
62 C11 Eyeworth C Beds
38 D11 Eyhorne Street Kent
65 L11 Eyke Suffk
61 Q9 Eynesbury Cambs
37 M7 Eynsford Kent
34 D3 Eynsham Oxon
11 J6 Eype Dorset
152 G7 Eyre Highld
27 N2 Eythorne Kent
45 P2 Eyton Herefs
56 F2 Eyton Shrops
56 F7 Eyton Shrops
69 M10 Eyton Shrops
69 L6 Eyton Wrexhm
57 K3 Eyton on Severn Shrops
57 M2 Eyton upon the Weald Moors Wrekin

F

22 C3 Faccombe Hants
104 E10 Faceby N York
68 D11 Fachwen Powys
89 P7 Facit Lancs
84 G8 Fackley Notts
69 Q4 Faddiley Ches E
98 D3 Fadmoor N York
29 J4 Faerdre Swans
29 J4 Fagwyr Swans
125 M3 Faifley W Duns
31 P10 Failand N Som
115 J2 Failford S Ayrs
83 J4 Failsworth Oldham
54 E2 Fairbourne Gwynd
91 M5 Fairburn N York
83 N10 Fairfield Derbys
26 G6 Fairfield Kent
58 D9 Fairfield Worcs
33 N4 Fairford Gloucs
33 N4 Fairford Park Gloucs
109 J9 Fairgirth D & G
75 N7 Fair Green Norfk
88 C5 Fairhaven Lancs
169 t12 Fair Isle Shet
32 C3 Fairlands Surrey
124 C7 Fairlie N Ayrs
26 E9 Fairlight E Susx
10 B5 Fairmile Devon
36 D8 Fairmile Surrey
117 P4 Fairnilee Border
22 E11 Fair Oak Hants
70 D8 Fairoak Staffs
23 J2 Fair Oak Green Hants
37 P8 Fairseat Kent
52 C8 Fairstead Essex
75 M6 Fairstead Norfk
25 L5 Fairwarp E Susx
30 F9 Fairwater Cardif
16 G7 Fairy Cross Devon
76 C6 Fakenham Norfk
64 C6 Fakenham Magna Suffk
128 C7 Fala Mdloth
128 C7 Fala Dam Mdloth
48 G6 Falcut Nhants
86 E4 Faldingworth Lincs
11 c2 Faldouet Jersey
32 C6 Falfield S Glos
53 N4 Falkenham Suffk
133 P11 Falkirk Falk
133 P11 Falkirk Crematorium Falk
134 H6 Falkland Fife
116 D3 Fallburn S Lans
84 E8 Fallgate Derbys
133 N9 Fallin Stirlg
119 N6 Fallodon Nthumb
83 J6 Fallowfield Manch
112 D7 Fallowfield Nthumb
131 K5 Falls of Blarghour Ag & B
25 J9 Falmer E Susx
3 L1 Falmouth Cnwll
117 M9 Falnash Border
99 L3 Falsgrave N York
111 P3 Falstone Nthumb
164 E7 Fanagmore Highld
50 B5 Fancott C Beds
155 N9 Fanellan Highld

98 B2 Fangdale Beck N York
85 F10 Fangfoss E R Yk
137 L7 Fanmore Ag & B
154 H4 Fannich Lodge Highld
118 B2 Fans Border
49 N8 Far Bletchley M Keyn
62 B2 Farcet Cambs
60 G9 Far Cotton Nhants
57 K9 Farden Shrops
14 G5 Fareham Hants
101 K11 Far End Cumb
58 G2 Farewell Staffs
57 N9 Far Forest Worcs
87 K5 Farforth Lincs
32 E4 Far Green Gloucs
33 Q5 Faringdon Oxon
88 G5 Farington Lancs
111 L9 Farlam Cumb
31 P11 Farleigh N Som
37 J8 Farleigh Surrey
20 F3 Farleigh Hungerford Somset
22 H5 Farleigh Wallop Hants
87 N6 Farlesthorpe Lincs
95 L4 Farleton Cumb
95 M7 Farleton Lancs
84 C8 Farley Derbys
71 K6 Farley Staffs
21 P9 Farley Wilts
63 M10 Farley Green Suffk
36 C11 Farley Green Surrey
23 K7 Farley Hill Wokham
32 E2 Farleys End Gloucs
15 J3 Farlington C Port
98 C7 Farlington N York
57 L8 Farlow Shrops
20 C2 Farmborough BaNES
51 P8 Farmbridge End Essex
47 L9 Farmcote Gloucs
57 P6 Farmcote Shrops
43 M6 Farmers Carmth
47 M11 Farmington Gloucs
34 E3 Farmoor Oxon
82 B4 Far Moor Wigan
2 H7 Farms Common Cnwll
72 B7 Farm Town Leics
158 D7 Farmtown Moray
84 D11 Farnah Green Derbys
37 K8 Farnborough Gt Lon
23 N4 Farnborough Hants
34 D8 Farnborough W Berk
48 D5 Farnborough Warwks
23 N3 Farnborough Park Hants
23 N3 Farnborough Street Hants
23 Q6 Farncombe Surrey
61 K8 Farndish Bed
69 M4 Farndon Ches W
85 N10 Farndon Notts
119 Q3 Farne Islands Nthumb
143 L6 Farnell Angus
21 J11 Farnham Dorset
51 L6 Farnham Essex
97 M8 Farnham N York
65 M9 Farnham Suffk
23 M5 Farnham Surrey
35 Q7 Farnham Common Bucks
51 L5 Farnham Green Essex
35 Q8 Farnham Royal Bucks
37 M7 Farningham Kent
90 H4 Farnley Leeds
97 K11 Farnley N York
90 F8 Farnley Tyas Kirk
85 K9 Farnsfield Notts
82 D4 Farnworth Bolton
81 Q7 Farnworth Halton
32 H4 Far Oakridge Gloucs
148 E7 Farr Highld
156 B11 Farr Highld
166 B4 Farr Highld
147 P3 Farraline Highld
9 P6 Farringdon Devon
20 B3 Farrington Gurney BaNES
101 L11 Far Sawrey Cumb
90 G3 Farsley Leeds
52 D11 Farther Howegreen Essex
26 D2 Farthing Green Kent
48 F7 Farthinghoe Nhants
27 N3 Farthingloe Kent
48 H4 Farthingstone Nhants
37 K8 Farthing Street Gt Lon
90 F7 Fartown Kirk
90 F7 Fartown Leeds
10 D5 Farway Devon
139 J8 Fasnacloich Ag & B
147 J2 Fasnakyle Highld
139 J2 Fassfern Highld
113 L10 Fatfield Sundld
111 K10 Faugh Cumb
71 M9 Fauld Staffs
126 G5 Fauldhouse W Loth
52 C8 Faulkbourne Essex
20 D4 Faulkland Somset
69 Q8 Fauls Shrops
38 H9 Faversham Kent
97 P6 Fawdington N York
113 K7 Fawdon N u Ty
119 K7 Fawdon Nthumb
71 K7 Fawfieldhead Staffs
37 N7 Fawkham Green Kent
48 C11 Fawler Oxon
35 L7 Fawley Bucks
14 E6 Fawley Hants
34 C8 Fawley W Berk
46 A9 Fawley Chapel Herefs
81 J11 Fawnog Flints
60 C9 Fawsley Nhants
92 E6 Faxfleet E R Yk
24 F3 Faygate W Susx
81 M5 Fazakerley Lpool
59 K4 Fazeley Staffs
97 J4 Fearby N York
156 E2 Fearn Highld
140 H9 Fearnan P & K
153 N6 Fearnbeg Highld
82 D6 Fearnhead Warrtn
153 N5 Fearnmore Highld
124 A2 Fearnoch Ag & B
58 D3 Featherstone Staffs
91 L6 Featherstone Wakefd
47 K2 Feckenham Worcs
52 E7 Feering Essex
103 J11 Feetham N York
96 A7 Feizor N York
25 J3 Felbridge Surrey
77 J4 Felbrigg Norfk
25 J2 Felcourt Surrey
50 B10 Felden Herts

42 G7 Felindre Carmth
43 L10 Felindre Carmth
43 P9 Felindre Carmth
43 L3 Felindre Cerdgn
44 H10 Felindre Powys
56 B8 Felindre Powys
28 H4 Felindre Powys
41 M3 Felindre Farchog Pembks
43 K3 Felin Fach Cerdgn
44 F8 Felinfach Powys
28 F4 Felinfoel Carmth
43 K10 Felingwm Isaf Carmth
43 K10 Felingwm Uchaf Carmth
44 G7 Felin-newydd Powys
97 Q4 Felixkirk N York
53 P5 Felixstowe Suffk
53 P4 Felixstowe Ferry Suffk
118 H2 Felkington Nthumb
91 K8 Felkirk Wakefd
113 L8 Felling Gatesd
90 C2 Fell Lane C Brad
101 K3 Fell Side Cumb
61 L9 Felmersham Bed
77 K6 Felmingham Norfk
15 P7 Felpham W Susx
64 C10 Felsham Suffk
51 Q6 Felsted Essex
36 C6 Feltham Gt Lon
36 C6 Felthamhill Surrey
76 H3 Felthorpe Norfk
46 A5 Felton Herefs
31 P11 Felton N Som
119 N10 Felton Nthumb
69 L11 Felton Butler Shrops
63 M2 Feltwell Norfk
90 F7 Fenay Bridge Kirk
89 N3 Fence Lancs
84 F3 Fence Rothm
113 M11 Fence Houses Sundld
48 G11 Fencott Oxon
87 N8 Fendike Corner Lincs
62 G8 Fen Ditton Cambs
62 D7 Fen Drayton Cambs
74 D6 Fen End Lincs
59 K10 Fen End Solhll
119 L2 Fenham Nthumb
89 K5 Feniscliffe Bl w D
89 J5 Feniscowles Bl w D
10 C5 Feniton Devon
62 F2 Fenland Crematorium Cambs
57 N6 Fenn Green Shrops
38 C6 Fenn Street Medway
71 M5 Fenny Bentley Derbys
10 C5 Fenny Bridges Devon
48 D4 Fenny Compton Warwks
72 B11 Fenny Drayton Leics
49 N8 Fenny Stratford M Keyn
113 J2 Fenrother Nthumb
62 D7 Fenstanton Cambs
63 P10 Fenstead End Suffk
64 D2 Fen Street Norfk
64 H9 Fen Street Suffk
70 F6 Fenton C Stke
62 D5 Fenton Cambs
111 K9 Fenton Cumb
85 P5 Fenton Lincs
85 Q10 Fenton Lincs
85 N4 Fenton Notts
119 J4 Fenton Nthumb
128 E3 Fenton Barns E Loth
91 P7 Fenwick Donc
125 M9 Fenwick E Ayrs
112 G6 Fenwick Nthumb
119 L2 Fenwick Nthumb
3 L6 Feock Cnwll
122 F6 Feolin Ferry Ag & B
125 J9 Fergushill N Ayrs
152 B7 Feriniquarrie Highld
10 c2 Fermain Bay Guern
142 H5 Fern Angus
30 C5 Ferndale Rhondd
13 J4 Ferndown Dorset
156 H8 Ferness Highld
33 Q6 Fernham Oxon
46 G3 Fernhill Heath Worcs
23 N9 Fernhurst W Susx
135 J4 Fernie Fife
126 C7 Ferniegair S Lans
152 F11 Fernilea Highld
83 M9 Fernilee Derbys
85 P10 Fernwood Notts
97 N8 Ferrensby N York
92 G6 Ferriby Sluice N Linc
145 L6 Ferrindonald Highld
24 C10 Ferring W Susx
91 M6 Ferrybridge Wakefd
91 M6 Ferrybridge Services Wakefd
143 N6 Ferryden Angus
103 Q4 Ferryhill Dur
162 G9 Ferry Point Highld
28 C2 Ferryside Carmth
162 G9 Ferrytown Highld
64 F5 Fersfield Norfk
139 R2 Fersit Highld
148 F7 Feshiebridge Highld
36 D9 Fetcham Surrey
169 t4 Fetlar Shet
159 N7 Fetterangus Abers
143 M3 Fettercairn Abers
48 F9 Fewcott Oxon
97 J10 Fewston N York
43 M10 Ffairfach Carmth
54 G11 Ffair Rhos Cerdgn
43 M6 Ffald-y-Brenin Carmth
45 J11 Ffawyddog Powys
67 N6 Ffestiniog Gwynd
67 N6 Ffestiniog Railway Gwynd
68 F2 Ffordd-las Denbgs
28 G4 Fforest Carmth
45 K10 Fforest Mons
28 H5 Fforest Fach Swans
29 K4 Fforest Goch Neath
42 G5 Ffostrasol Cerdgn
69 J3 Ffrith Flints
42 G4 Ffynnonddewi Cerdgn
80 G8 Ffynnongroyw Flints
43 K4 Ffynnon-Oer Cerdgn
165 L11 Fiag Lodge Highld
37 J8 Fickleshole Surrey
46 H8 Fiddington Gloucs
18 H6 Fiddington Somset
12 D2 Fiddleford Dorset
4 C10 Fiddlers Green Cnwll
51 L10 Fiddlers Hamlet Essex
71 J8 Field Staffs
94 H4 Field Broughton Cumb

76 E4 Field Dalling Norfk
101 N3 Fieldhead Cumb
72 D9 Field Head Leics
20 E10 Fifehead Magdalen Dorset
12 C2 Fifehead Neville Dorset
12 C2 Fifehead St Quintin Dorset
158 B7 Fife Keith Moray
47 P11 Fifield Oxon
35 P9 Fifield W & M
21 M4 Fifield Wilts
21 N5 Figheldean Wilts
32 H7 Filands Wilts
77 P9 Filby Norfk
99 N4 Filey N York
49 N5 Filgrave M Keyn
33 P4 Filkins Oxon
8 H2 Filleigh Devon
17 M6 Filleigh Devon
86 B3 Fillingham Lincs
59 L7 Fillongley Warwks
23 J9 Filmore Hill Hants
32 B9 Filton S Glos
98 H8 Fimber E R Yk
142 H6 Finavon Angus
75 N9 Fincham Norfk
23 L2 Finchampstead Wokham
131 J7 Fincharn Ag & B
15 K4 Finchdean Hants
51 Q4 Finchingfield Essex
36 G2 Finchley Gt Lon
71 Q8 Findern Derbys
157 J5 Findhorn Moray
148 E2 Findhorn Bridge Highld
158 C4 Findochty Moray
134 C4 Findo Gask P & K
151 N8 Findon Abers
24 D9 Findon W Susx
155 R5 Findon Mains Highld
150 G7 Findrack House Abers
61 K6 Finedon Nhants
73 P11 Fineshade Nhants
65 J8 Fingal Street Suffk
134 F4 Fingask P & K
35 L6 Fingest Bucks
97 J3 Finghall N York
110 E9 Fingland Cumb
115 Q4 Fingland D & G
39 P11 Finglesham Kent
52 H7 Fingringhoe Essex
52 B3 Finkle Green Essex
91 J11 Finkle Street Barns
140 E11 Finlarig Stirlg
48 H8 Finmere Oxon
140 D6 Finnart P & K
64 F8 Finningham Suffk
91 R11 Finningley Donc
168 f9 Finsbay W Isls
58 E10 Finstall Worcs
94 H3 Finsthwaite Cumb
48 C11 Finstock Oxon
169 c5 Finstown Ork
159 J7 Fintry Abers
133 J10 Fintry Stirlg
150 G9 Finzean Abers
137 J11 Fionnphort Ag & B
168 f9 Fionnsbhagh W Isls
95 N2 Firbank Cumb
85 J3 Firbeck Rothm
97 L3 Firby N York
98 E7 Firby N York
89 Q8 Firgrove Rochdl
25 L9 Firle E Susx
87 N8 Firsby Lincs
21 P8 Firsdown Wilts
103 M4 Fir Tree Dur
14 G8 Fishbourne IoW
15 M6 Fishbourne W Susx
15 M5 Fishbourne Roman Palace W Susx
104 C4 Fishburn Dur
133 P8 Fishcross Clacks
15 N6 Fisher W Susx
158 G10 Fisherford Abers
127 Q3 Fisherrow E Loth
22 E10 Fisher's Pond Hants
95 J11 Fisher's Row Lancs
23 P8 Fisherstreet W Susx
156 C7 Fisherton Highld
114 K4 Fisherton S Ayrs
21 K7 Fisherton de la Mere Wilts
59 J3 Fisherwick Staffs
35 N8 Fishery Estate W & M
41 J3 Fishguard Pembks
91 R8 Fishlake Donc
8 D3 Fishleigh Devon
74 E3 Fishmere End Lincs
138 B9 Fishnish Pier Ag & B
10 H5 Fishpond Bottom Dorset
32 B9 Fishponds Bristl
74 G2 Fishtoft Lincs
87 K11 Fishtoft Drove Lincs
88 H5 Fishwick Lancs
152 E11 Fiskavaig Highld
86 D6 Fiskerton Lincs
85 M10 Fiskerton Notts
93 N4 Fitling E R Yk
21 M5 Fittleton Wilts
24 B7 Fittleworth W Susx
74 H4 Fitton End Cambs
69 M11 Fitz Shrops
18 H8 Fitzhead Somset
18 H8 Fitzroy Somset
91 L7 Fitzwilliam Wakefd
25 L6 Five Ash Down E Susx
25 N5 Five Ashes E Susx
18 E6 Five Bells Somset
46 B5 Five Bridges Herefs
82 B9 Fivecrosses Ches W
19 L10 Fivehead Somset
5 L5 Fivelanes Cnwll
31 M6 Five Lanes Mons
37 P11 Five Oak Green Kent
11 C2 Five Oaks Jersey
24 C5 Five Oaks W Susx
28 E3 Five Roads Carmth
38 D11 Five Wents Kent
52 C9 Flack's Green Essex
35 N7 Flackwell Heath Bucks
47 J3 Fladbury Worcs
169 r10 Fladdabister Shet
83 P11 Flagg Derbys
99 Q6 Flamborough E R Yk
99 R6 Flamborough Head E R Yk
98 F5 Flamingo Land Theme Park N York
50 C8 Flamstead Herts

15 Q6 Flansham W Susx
91 J6 Flanshaw Wakefd
90 D3 Flappit Spring C Brad
96 D9 Flasby N York
83 M11 Flash Staffs
152 E7 Flashader Highld
50 B10 Flaunden Herts
73 K2 Flawborough Notts
97 Q7 Flawith N York
31 P11 Flax Bourton N Som
97 N9 Flaxby N York
46 C11 Flaxley Gloucs
82 C10 Flaxmere Ches W
18 F7 Flaxpool Somset
23 N3 Flaxton N York
60 D2 Fleckney Leics
85 P6 Fledborough Notts
11 N8 Fleet Dorset
15 K6 Fleet Hants
23 M4 Fleet Hants
74 G6 Fleet Lincs
14 F5 Fleetend Hants
74 G6 Fleet Hargate Lincs
23 L3 Fleet Services Hants
94 G11 Fleetwood Lancs
30 D11 Flemingston V Glam
126 B6 Flemington S Lans
63 P7 Flempton Suffk
37 M11 Fletcher Green Kent
5 J8 Fletchersbridge Cnwll
100 H2 Fletchertown Cumb
25 K6 Fletching E Susx
30 G5 Fleur-de-lis Caerph
16 C10 Flexbury Cnwll
23 P4 Flexford Surrey
100 D4 Flimby Cumb
26 B5 Flimwell E Susx
81 J10 Flint Flints
85 M11 Flintham Notts
81 J10 Flint Mountain Flints
93 M3 Flinton E R Yk
59 J3 Flint's Green Solhll
26 C4 Flishinghurst Kent
75 P5 Flitcham Norfk
50 C3 Flitton C Beds
50 B4 Flitwick C Beds
92 E8 Flixborough N Linc
92 E8 Flixborough Stather N Linc
99 L5 Flixton N York
65 L4 Flixton Suffk
82 F6 Flixton Traffd
90 H7 Flockton Kirk
90 H7 Flockton Green Kirk
118 H3 Flodden Nthumb
152 H3 Flodigarry Highld
94 H5 Flookburgh Cumb
64 H2 Flordon Norfk
60 D8 Flore Nhants
119 J10 Flotterton Nthumb
25 P8 Flowers Green E Susx
53 J2 Flowton Suffk
90 H6 Flushdyke Wakefd
3 L7 Flushing Cnwll
10 B6 Fluxton Devon
47 J3 Flyford Flavell Worcs
38 B5 Fobbing Thurr
157 Q6 Fochabers Moray
30 F3 Fochriw Caerph
92 E7 Fockerby N Linc
19 Q9 Foddington Somset
55 M2 Foel Powys
28 F2 Foelgastell Carmth
29 N6 Foel y Dyffryn Brdgnd
92 C3 Foggathorpe E R Yk
129 K10 Fogo Border
157 N6 Fogwatt Moray
164 E7 Foindle Highld
142 B5 Folda Angus
71 J7 Fole Staffs
59 N8 Foleshill Covtry
11 P2 Folke Dorset
27 M4 Folkestone Kent
73 R4 Folkingham Lincs
25 N10 Folkington E Susx
61 P3 Folksworth Cambs
99 M5 Folkton N York
158 H11 Folla Rule Abers
97 M10 Follifoot N York
8 E5 Folly Gate Devon
23 M5 Folly Hill Surrey
30 D11 Fonmon V Glam
20 H8 Fonthill Bishop Wilts
20 H8 Fonthill Gifford Wilts
20 G11 Fontmell Magna Dorset
12 D2 Fontmell Parva Dorset
15 P5 Fontwell W Susx
30 E11 Font-y-gary V Glam
83 Q9 Foolow Derbys
37 L6 Foots Cray Gt Lon
150 B7 Forbestown Abers
103 N8 Forcett N York
130 H7 Ford Ag & B
35 L3 Ford Bucks
84 F4 Ford Derbys
6 G8 Ford Devon
7 K10 Ford Devon
16 G7 Ford Devon
47 L9 Ford Gloucs
118 H3 Ford Nthumb
56 E7 Ford Shrops
18 E9 Ford Somset
19 Q4 Ford Somset
71 K4 Ford Staffs
15 Q6 Ford W Susx
21 N8 Ford Wilts
32 F9 Ford Wilts
8 D6 Forda Devon
25 M2 Fordcombe Kent
56 C4 Forden Powys
51 Q7 Ford End Essex
7 K5 Forder Green Devon
95 K11 Ford Green Lancs
63 K6 Fordham Cambs
52 F6 Fordham Essex
75 M11 Fordham Norfk
52 F6 Fordham Heath Essex
56 G2 Ford Heath Shrops
13 K2 Fordingbridge Hants
99 L5 Fordon E R Yk
143 N2 Fordoun Abers
64 F8 Ford's Green Suffk
52 F6 Fordstreet Essex
18 G11 Ford Street Somset
9 K5 Fordton Devon
39 L10 Fordwich Kent
158 E5 Fordyce Abers

70 G10 Forebridge Staffs
72 A5 Foremark Derbys
10 b2 Forest Guern
103 Q10 Forest N York
96 A10 Forest Becks Lancs
119 L11 Forestburn Gate Nthumb
83 L10 Forest Chapel Ches E
24 D2 Forest Gate Gt Lon
113 L7 Forest Green Surrey
111 L9 Forest Head Cumb
37 J6 Forest Hill Gt Lon
34 G3 Forest Hill Oxon
102 G4 Forest-in-Teesdale Dur
97 M9 Forest Lane Head N York
134 B9 Forest Mill Clacks
32 B2 Forest of Dean Gloucs
37 L2 Forest Park Crematorium Gt Lon
25 K4 Forest Row E Susx
14 E9 Forest Side IoW
15 L4 Forestside W Susx
85 J8 Forest Town Notts
142 H7 Forfar Angus
134 D4 Forgandenny P & K
54 H5 Forge Powys
31 J5 Forge Hammer Torfn
30 H3 Forge Side Torfn
158 A7 Forgie Moray
158 B7 Forgieside Moray
158 F8 Forgue Abers
58 G9 Forhill Worcs
88 C9 Formby Sefton
64 G3 Forncett End Norfk
64 H3 Forncett St Mary Norfk
64 H3 Forncett St Peter Norfk
64 A8 Fornham All Saints Suffk
64 B8 Fornham St Martin Suffk
156 G7 Fornighty Highld
157 J6 Forres Moray
70 H6 Forsbrook Staffs
167 M10 Forse Highld
58 G10 Forshaw Heath Warwks
166 B11 Forsinard Highld
11 P5 Forston Dorset
147 K6 Fort Augustus Highld
134 D4 Forteviot P & K
126 G7 Forth S Lans
46 G8 Forthampton Gloucs
10 b1 Fort Hommet Guern
10 c1 Fort le Marchant Guern
22 D7 Forton Hants
95 K10 Forton Lancs
69 M11 Forton Shrops
18 G10 Forton Somset
70 D10 Forton Staffs
158 G8 Fortrie Abers
156 C6 Fortrose Highld
11 P10 Fortuneswell Dorset
139 L3 Fort William Highld
35 P6 Forty Green Bucks
50 H11 Forty Hill Gt Lon
64 G10 Forward Green Suffk
22 B3 Fosbury Wilts
47 P10 Foscot Oxon
49 J5 Foscote Nhants
74 F4 Fosdyke Lincs
74 F4 Fosdyke Bridge Lincs
141 J6 Foss P & K
33 L2 Fossebridge Gloucs
42 H2 Foss-y-ffin Cerdgn
91 R8 Fosterhouses Donc
51 L9 Foster Street Essex
71 M8 Foston Derbys
60 D2 Foston Leics
73 M2 Foston Lincs
98 D7 Foston N York
99 N9 Foston on the Wolds E R Yk
87 K2 Fotherby Lincs
100 D4 Fothergill Cumb
61 N2 Fotheringhay Nhants
169 k10 Foula Shet
110 H11 Foulbridge Cumb
91 K7 Fouldry Wakefd
129 N8 Foulden Border
75 Q11 Foulden Norfk
60 C6 Foul End Warwks
25 P7 Foul Mile E Susx
38 G3 Foulness Island Essex
10 b2 Foulon Vale Crematorium Guern
89 P2 Foulridge Lancs
76 E7 Foulsham Norfk
128 C10 Fountainhall Border
59 J9 Four Ashes Solhll
57 Q7 Four Ashes Staffs
58 D3 Four Ashes Staffs
64 E7 Four Ashes Suffk
10 b2 Four Cabots Guern
69 J11 Four Crosses Powys
58 E3 Four Crosses Staffs
37 L11 Four Elms Kent
19 Q8 Four Foot Somset
18 H7 Four Forks Somset
89 J9 Four Gates Bolton
75 J7 Four Gotes Cambs
69 Q2 Four Lane Ends Ches W
2 H6 Four Lanes Cnwll
70 E3 Fourlanes End Ches E
23 J7 Four Marks Hants
78 D9 Four Mile Bridge IoA
58 H5 Four Oaks Birm
26 E7 Four Oaks E Susx
46 C9 Four Oaks Gloucs
59 K8 Four Oaks Solhll
163 J8 Fourpenny Highld
34 G9 Four Points W Berk
28 D3 Four Roads Carmth
47 P8 Four Shire Stone Warwks
112 C7 Fourstones Nthumb
25 C6 Four Throws Kent
37 P10 Four Wents Kent
21 K9 Fovant Wilts
151 P3 Foveran Abers
5 J11 Fowey Cnwll
37 Q11 Fowlhall Kent
142 E11 Fowlis Angus
133 Q3 Fowlis Wester P & K
62 F11 Fowlmere Cambs
45 A8 Fownhope Herefs
125 M5 Foxbar Rens
8 C7 Foxcombe Head Devon
23 Q4 Fox Corner Surrey
47 K11 Foxcote Gloucs
20 D3 Foxcote Somset
80 c6 Foxdale IoM

52 D3 Foxearth Essex
37 P7 Foxendown Kent
94 E3 Foxfield Cumb
33 J9 Foxham Wilts
51 N11 Fox Hatch Essex
13 P2 Foxhills Hants
3 P3 Foxhole Cnwll
99 L6 Foxholes N York
25 M7 Foxhunt Green E Susx
48 H4 Foxley Nhants
76 E7 Foxley Norfk
32 G7 Foxley Wilts
58 F11 Foxlydiate Worcs
52 H6 Fox Street Essex
71 J5 Foxt Staffs
62 F11 Foxton Cambs
104 C6 Foxton Dur
60 F3 Foxton Leics
104 D11 Foxton N York
96 C5 Foxup N York
82 D11 Foxwist Green Ches W
57 L9 Foxwood Shrops
46 A9 Foy Herefs
147 M3 Foyers Highld
156 F7 Foynesfield Highld
2 F7 Fraddam Cnwll
4 E10 Fraddon Cnwll
59 J2 Fradley Staffs
70 H8 Fradswell Staffs
99 P8 Fraisthorpe E R Yk
25 L6 Framfield E Susx
77 K11 Framingham Earl Norfk
77 K11 Framingham Pigot Norfk
65 K9 Framlingham Suffk
11 N5 Frampton Dorset
74 F3 Frampton Lincs
32 C8 Frampton Cotterell S Glos
32 H4 Frampton Mansell Gloucs
32 D3 Frampton on Severn Gloucs
74 F2 Frampton West End Lincs
64 H10 Framsden Suffk
103 Q2 Framwellgate Moor Dur
57 Q9 Franche Worcs
82 D9 Frandley Ches W
5 P3 Frankaborough Devon
81 J7 Frankby Wirral
45 Q5 Franklands Gate Herefs
58 E8 Frankley Worcs
58 E8 Frankley Services Worcs
44 G3 Franksbridge Powys
59 P10 Frankton Warwks
25 N3 Frant E Susx
159 N4 Fraserburgh Abers
53 J7 Frating Essex
53 J7 Frating Green Essex
15 J6 Fratton C Port
5 P11 Freathy Cnwll
63 L6 Freckenham Suffk
88 E5 Freckleton Lancs
84 D6 Freebirch Derbys
73 L6 Freeby Leics
22 E5 Freefolk Hants
71 J6 Freehay Staffs
34 D2 Freeland Oxon
77 N10 Freethorpe Norfk
77 N11 Freethorpe Common Norfk
74 G2 Freiston Lincs
17 J5 Fremington Devon
103 K11 Fremington N York
32 B9 Frenchay S Glos
8 G7 Frenchbeer Devon
37 L10 French Street Kent
141 K6 Frenich P & K
23 M6 Frensham Surrey
88 B9 Freshfield Sefton
20 E2 Freshford Wilts
13 P7 Freshwater IoW
13 P7 Freshwater Bay IoW
41 K11 Freshwater East Pembks
65 K6 Fressingfield Suffk
53 L4 Freston Suffk
167 Q3 Freswick Highld
32 D2 Fretherne Gloucs
77 J8 Frettenham Norfk
134 H6 Freuchie Fife
41 J8 Freystrop Pembks
58 F6 Friar Park Sandw
25 L4 Friar's Gate E Susx
98 E3 Friars' Hill N York
11 N7 Friar Waddon Dorset
62 J10 Friday Bridge Cambs
65 L10 Friday Street Suffk
65 L11 Friday Street Suffk
65 M9 Friday Street Suffk
36 D11 Friday Street Surrey
98 H9 Fridaythorpe E R Yk
71 M2 Friden Derbys
90 B6 Friendly Calder
36 G2 Friern Barnet Gt Lon
86 B11 Frieston Lincs
86 B11 Friesthorpe Lincs
35 L6 Frieth Bucks
34 D5 Frilford Oxon
34 F10 Frilsham W Berk
23 N3 Frimley Surrey
23 N3 Frimley Green Surrey
38 B8 Frindsbury Medway
75 P4 Fring Norfk
48 H9 Fringford Oxon
38 E10 Frinsted Kent
53 M7 Frinton-on-Sea Essex
143 K8 Friockheim Angus
54 E2 Friog Gwynd
72 H7 Frisby on the Wreake Leics
87 N9 Friskney Lincs
87 N9 Friskney Eaudike Lincs
25 E7 Friston E Susx
65 N9 Friston Suffk
84 E10 Fritchley Derbys
13 M2 Fritham Hants
87 K11 Frith Bank Lincs
57 M11 Frith Common Worcs
16 H8 Frithelstock Devon
16 H8 Frithelstock Stone Devon
23 M7 Frithend Hants
50 B9 Frithsden Herts
87 K10 Frithville Lincs
26 D3 Frittenden Kent
7 L10 Frittiscombe Devon
77 N9 Fritton Norfk
77 P11 Fritton Norfk
48 F9 Fritwell Oxon

Frizinghall - Goodleigh 277

90 E3 Frizinghall C Brad
100 D7 Frizington Cumb
32 E4 Frocester Gloucs
57 J4 Frodesley Shrops
81 Q9 Frodsham Ches W
118 E5 Frogden Border
62 E11 Frog End Cambs
62 H9 Frog End Cambs
84 B5 Froggatt Derbys
71 J5 Froghall Staffs
13 L2 Frogham Hants
39 N11 Frogham Kent
7 K10 Frogmore Devon
74 C8 Frognall Lincs
3 K5 Frogpool Cnwll
57 Q11 Frog Pool Worcs
5 N8 Frogwell Cnwll
60 B2 Frolesworth Leics
20 E5 Frome Somset
11 M4 Frome St Quintin Dorset
46 C5 Fromes Hill Herefs
80 F11 Fron Denbgs
66 F7 Fron Gwynd
67 J4 Fron Gwynd
56 B5 Fron Powys
56 C4 Fron Powys
69 J6 Froncysyllte Denbgs
68 B7 Fron-goch Gwynd
69 J6 Fron Isaf Wrexhm
65 P5 Frostenden Suffk
103 K3 Frosterley Dur
49 Q8 Froxfield C Beds
33 Q11 Froxfield Wilts
23 K9 Froxfield Green Hants
22 D10 Fryern Hill Hants
51 P10 Fryerning Essex
98 D6 Fryton N York
137 Q6 Fuinary Highld
86 B10 Fulbeck Lincs
62 H9 Fulbourn Cambs
33 Q2 Fulbrook Oxon
22 E8 Fulflood Hants
98 C11 Fulford C York
18 H9 Fulford Somset
70 H7 Fulford Staffs
36 G5 Fulham Gt Lon
24 F8 Fulking W Susx
17 M4 Fullaford Devon
125 J10 Fullarton N Ayrs
51 M5 Fuller's End Essex
69 N4 Fuller's Moor Ches W
52 B8 Fuller Street Essex
37 N9 Fuller Street Kent
22 C7 Fullerton Hants
87 J6 Fulletby Lincs
47 Q5 Fullready Warwks
89 E9 Full Sutton E R Yk
125 L7 Fullwood E Ayrs
35 Q7 Fulmer Bucks
76 D5 Fulmodeston Norfk
86 E5 Fulnetby Lincs
74 E6 Fulney Lincs
90 F9 Fulstone Kirk
93 P11 Fulstow Lincs
48 C10 Fulwell Oxon
113 N9 Fulwell Sundld
88 G4 Fulwood Lancs
84 G9 Fulwood Notts
84 D3 Fulwood Sheff
18 H10 Fulwood Somset
64 H2 Fundenhall Norfk
15 M5 Funtington W Susx
14 G5 Funtley Hants
133 M2 Funtullich P & K
10 F4 Furley Devon
131 L7 Furnace Ag & B
28 F4 Furnace Carmth
54 F5 Furnace Cerdgn
59 K6 Furnace End Warwks
25 K5 Furner's Green E Susx
83 M8 Furness Vale Derbys
51 K5 Furneux Pelham Herts
26 E4 Further Quarter Kent
49 L6 Furtho Nhants
17 N2 Furzehill Devon
14 F2 Furzehill Dorset
87 J6 Furzehills Lincs
15 J4 Furzeley Corner Hants
35 N8 Furze Platt W & M
21 Q11 Furzley Hants
10 E2 Fyfett Somset
51 N9 Fyfield Essex
21 Q5 Fyfield Hants
34 D5 Fyfield Oxon
21 N2 Fyfield Wilts
33 M11 Fyfield Wilts
21 K9 Fyfield Bavant Wilts
105 P10 Fylingthorpe N York
23 M10 Fyning W Susx
159 J10 Fyvie Abers

G

125 M7 Gabroc Hill E Ayrs
72 H8 Gaddesby Leics
50 C8 Gaddesden Row Herts
78 H7 Gadfa IoA
114 H3 Gadgirth S Ayrs
69 L7 Gadlas Shrops
44 H10 Gaer Powys
31 M5 Gaer-llwyd Mons
78 H10 Gaerwen IoA
48 D9 Gagingwell Oxon
125 J10 Gailes N Ayrs
58 D2 Gailey Staffs
103 N7 Gainford Dur
85 P3 Gainsborough Lincs
52 B4 Gainsford End Essex
153 Q2 Gairloch Highld
146 F11 Gairlochy Highld
134 E8 Gairneybridge P & K
102 B9 Gaisgill Cumb
110 G11 Gaitsgill Cumb
117 P3 Galashiels Border
95 K9 Galgate Lancs
20 B9 Galhampton Somset
130 G2 Gallanachbeg Ag & B
130 G2 Gallanachmore Ag & B
69 P4 Gallantry Bank Ches E
134 H9 Gallatown Fife
59 M6 Galley Common Warwks
52 B11 Galleywood Essex
147 P10 Gallovie Highld
114 H10 Galloway Forest Park
142 G9 Gallowfauld Angus
142 B10 Gallowhill P & K
52 F6 Gallows Green Essex
46 H2 Gallows Green Worcs
35 J8 Gallowstree Common Oxon
145 P3 Galltair Highld
67 K2 Gallt-y-foel Gwynd
23 M4 Gally Hill Hants
25 L3 Gallypot Street E Susx
6 H10 Galmpton Devon
7 M7 Galmpton Torbay
97 L6 Galphay N York
125 N10 Galston E Ayrs
83 M11 Gamballs Green Staffs
102 B3 Gamblesby Cumb
52 C9 Gambles Green Essex
110 E10 Gamelsby Cumb
83 M6 Gamesley Derbys
62 B10 Gamlingay Cambs
62 B10 Gamlingay Cinques Cambs
62 B10 Gamlingay Great Heath Cambs
96 G4 Gammersgill N York
159 J5 Gamrie Abers
72 F3 Gamston Notts
85 M5 Gamston Notts
45 Q11 Ganarew Herefs
138 F11 Ganavan Bay Ag & B
5 N8 Gang Cnwll
67 N10 Ganllwyd Gwynd
143 K3 Gannachy Angus
93 K4 Ganstead E R Yk
98 D6 Ganthorpe N York
99 K5 Ganton N York
50 G11 Ganwick Corner Herts
9 L9 Gappah Devon
157 Q7 Garbity Moray
64 E5 Garboldisham Norfk
148 D3 Garbole Highld
149 Q5 Garchory Abers
81 L11 Garden City Flints
35 M11 Gardeners Green Wokham
159 K5 Gardenstown Abers
90 H11 Garden Village Sheff
169 q9 Garderhouse Shet
92 G2 Gardham E R Yk
20 E6 Gare Hill Somset
131 Q9 Garelochhead Ag & B
34 D5 Garford Oxon
91 L4 Garforth Leeds
96 D10 Gargrave N York
133 L9 Gargunnock Stirlg
79 M9 Garizim Conwy
65 J5 Garlic Street Norfk
107 N8 Garlieston D & G
39 P8 Garlinge Kent
39 K11 Garlinge Green Kent
151 K6 Garlogie Abers
159 K7 Garmond Abers
157 Q5 Garmouth Moray
57 L3 Garmston Shrops
29 J2 Garnant Carmth
66 H6 Garn-Dolbenmaen Gwynd
101 P11 Garnett Bridge Cumb
66 D8 Garnfadryn Gwynd
126 B4 Garnkirk N Lans
28 H3 Garnswllt Swans
30 H3 Garn-yr-erw Torfn
168 k4 Garrabost W Isls
115 K4 Garrallan E Ayrs
3 J9 Garras Cnwll
67 L6 Garreg Gwynd
102 D2 Garrigill Cumb
97 J2 Garriston N York
108 C4 Garroch D & G
106 F10 Garrochtrie D & G
124 D7 Garrochty Ag & B
152 H5 Garros Highld
95 Q3 Garsdale Cumb
96 A2 Garsdale Head Cumb
33 J7 Garsdon Wilts
70 H8 Garshall Green Staffs
34 G4 Garsington Oxon
95 K11 Garstang Lancs
50 D10 Garston Herts
81 N8 Garston Lpool
122 D7 Gartachossan Ag & B
126 B4 Gartcosh N Lans
29 N6 Garth Brdgnd
31 K6 Garth Mons
44 D5 Garth Powys
56 D10 Garth Powys
69 J6 Garth Wrexhm
126 B4 Garthamlock C Glas
44 E8 Garthbrengy Powys
43 L3 Gartheli Cerdgn
56 B5 Garthmyl Powys
73 L6 Garthorpe Leics
92 D7 Garthorpe N Linc
54 E8 Garth Penrhyncoch Cerdgn
101 P11 Garth Row Cumb
95 L3 Garths Cumb
158 D11 Gartly Abers
132 G8 Gartmore Stirlg
126 D5 Gartness N Lans
132 G10 Gartness Stirlg
132 E10 Gartocharn W Duns
93 N3 Garton E R Yk
99 K9 Garton-on-the-Wolds E R Yk
163 N4 Gartymore Highld
128 F5 Garvald E Loth
138 H2 Garvan Highld
136 b3 Garvard Ag & B
155 L5 Garve Highld
130 D5 Garvellachs Ag & B
76 E10 Garvestone Norfk
124 H3 Garvock Inver
45 P10 Garway Herefs
45 P10 Garway Common Herefs
45 N9 Garway Hill Herefs
168 i6 Garyvard W Isls
20 E8 Gasper Wilts
32 G11 Gastard Wilts
64 D5 Gasthorpe Norfk
51 L7 Gaston Green Essex
14 E9 Gatcombe IoW
95 L3 Gatebeck Cumb
85 P4 Gate Burton Lincs
85 J4 Gateford Notts
91 P5 Gateforth N York
125 K10 Gatehead E Ayrs
98 D9 Gate Helmsley N York
111 Q3 Gatehouse Nthumb
108 C9 Gatehouse of Fleet D & G
76 D7 Gateley Norfk
97 M3 Gatenby N York
100 G7 Gatesgarth Cumb
118 E6 Gateshaw Border
113 L8 Gateshead Gatesd
69 N2 Gates Heath Ches W
142 G9 Gateside Angus
125 M6 Gateside E Rens
134 F6 Gateside Fife
125 K7 Gateside N Ayrs
116 B10 Gateslack D & G
88 G9 Gathurst Wigan
82 H7 Gatley Stockp
36 G10 Gatton Surrey
117 Q3 Gattonside Border
24 G2 *Gatwick Airport* W Susx
55 M11 Gaufron Powys
72 H10 Gaulby Leics
135 K3 Gauldry Fife
142 C7 Gauldswell P & K
89 M5 Gaulkthorn Lancs
75 J9 Gaultree Norfk
69 Q5 Gaunton's Bank Ches E
12 H3 Gaunt's Common Dorset
51 N5 Gaunt's End Essex
86 G6 Gautby Lincs
129 K9 Gavinton Border
91 J9 Gawber Barns
49 J8 Gawcott Bucks
83 J11 Gawsworth Ches E
90 H6 Gawthorpe Wakefd
95 P3 Gawthrop Cumb
94 F4 Gawthwaite Cumb
52 C11 Gay Bowers Essex
48 C4 Gaydon Warwks
49 M5 Gayhurst M Keyn
96 C3 Gayle N York
103 M9 Gayles N York
24 C6 Gay Street W Susx
49 K4 Gayton Nhants
75 P7 Gayton Norfk
70 H9 Gayton Staffs
81 K8 Gayton Wirral
87 M4 Gayton le Marsh Lincs
75 P7 Gayton Thorpe Norfk
75 M6 Gaywood Norfk
63 M8 Gazeley Suffk
3 J9 Gear Cnwll
168 i6 Gearraidh Bhaird W Isls
152 D5 Geary Highld
64 C10 Gedding Suffk
61 J4 Geddington Nhants
72 G2 Gedling Notts
74 H6 Gedney Lincs
74 H6 Gedney Broadgate Lincs
75 J5 Gedney Drove End Lincs
74 H5 Gedney Dyke Lincs
74 F8 Gedney Hill Lincs
83 L6 Gee Cross Tamesd
73 P10 Geeston Rutlnd
65 M3 Geldeston Norfk
30 C6 Gelli Rhondd
31 J6 Gelli Torfn
68 F2 Gellifor Denbgs
30 F5 Gelligaer Caerph
30 G6 Gelligroes Caerph
29 K4 Gelligron Neath
67 M7 Gellilydan Gwynd
29 K4 Gellinudd Neath
41 L7 Gelly Pembks
141 Q10 Gellyburn P & K
41 Q6 Gellywen Carmth
108 G9 Gelston D & G
86 B11 Gelston Lincs
99 N9 Gembling E R Yk
58 G2 Gentleshaw Staffs
110 E2 Georgefield D & G
35 Q8 George Green Bucks
16 H4 Georgeham Devon
167 L5 Georgemas Junction Station Highld
17 N7 George Nympton Devon
30 G3 Georgetown Blae G
2 D6 Georgia Cnwll
169 c4 Georth Ork
79 L11 Gerlan Gwynd
8 B6 Germansweek Devon
2 F8 Germoe Cnwll
3 M6 Gerrans Cnwll
36 B3 Gerrards Cross Bucks
105 K8 Gerrick R & Cl
52 D4 Gestingthorpe Essex
56 C2 Geuffordd Powys
82 D9 Gib Hill Ches W
87 Q9 Gibraltar Lincs
85 M11 Gibsmere Notts
32 G10 Giddeahall Wilts
12 D7 Giddy Green Dorset
37 M2 Gidea Park Gt Lon
8 G7 Gidleigh Devon
125 P6 Giffnock E Rens
128 E6 Gifford E Loth
134 H5 Giffordtown Fife
96 B8 Giggleswick N York
123 K10 Gigha Ag & B
92 D5 Gilberdyke E R Yk
46 F6 Gilbert's End Worcs
22 H8 Gilbert Street Hants
128 D6 Gilchriston E Loth
100 F3 Gilcrux Cumb
90 G5 Gildersome Leeds
85 J3 Gildingwells Rothm
103 Q2 Gilesgate Moor Dur
30 D11 Gileston V Glam
30 G5 Gilfach Caerph
30 C6 Gilfach Goch Brdgnd
42 H3 Gilfachrheda Cerdgn
100 D6 Gilgarran Cumb
101 M5 Gill Cumb
98 D3 Gillamoor N York
3 K8 Gillan Cnwll
152 D6 Gillen Highld
110 C2 Gillesbie D & G
98 C5 Gilling East N York
20 F9 Gillingham Dorset
38 C8 Gillingham Medway
65 N3 Gillingham Norfk
103 N9 Gilling West N York
167 M5 Gillock Highld
70 F3 Gillow Heath Staffs
167 P2 Gills Highld
26 C5 Gill's Green Kent
117 L6 Gilmanscleuch Border
127 P4 Gilmerton C Edin
133 P3 Gilmerton P & K
103 J8 Gilmonby Dur
60 C3 Gilmorton Leics
72 F9 Gilroes Crematorium C Leic
111 M7 Gilsland Nthumb
59 J7 Gilson Warwks
90 E3 Gilstead C Brad
128 C8 Gilston Border
51 K8 Gilston Herts
51 K8 Gilston Park Herts
84 G11 Giltbrook Notts
30 H2 Gilwern Mons
77 K4 Gimingham Norfk
83 L9 Ginclough Ches E
25 P8 Gingers Green E Susx
64 F9 Gipping Suffk
87 J11 Gipsey Bridge Lincs
125 J9 Girdle Toll N Ayrs
90 E4 Girlington C Brad
169 r8 Girlsta Shet
104 C9 Girsby N York
61 J11 Girtford C Beds
108 D10 Girthon D & G
62 F8 Girton Cambs
85 P7 Girton Notts
114 C8 Girvan S Ayrs
96 B11 Gisburn Lancs
65 Q4 Gisleham Suffk
64 F7 Gislingham Suffk
64 H4 Gissing Norfk
10 C5 Gittisham Devon
45 J3 Gladestry Powys
128 D5 Gladsmuir E Loth
29 K4 Glais Swans
105 L9 Glaisdale N York
142 F8 Glamis Angus
67 L4 Glanaber Gwynd
41 J7 Glanafon Pembks
29 J2 Glanaman Carmth
76 E3 Glandford Norfk
43 K6 Glan-Duar Carmth
41 N5 Glandwr Pembks
66 H6 Glan-Dwyfach Gwynd
54 F5 Glandyfi Cerdgn
45 J11 Glangrwyney Powys
29 N6 Glanllynfi Brdgnd
56 B6 Glanmule Powys
41 M2 Glanrhyd Pembks
29 L3 Glan-rhyd Powys
119 L8 Glanton Nthumb
119 L8 Glanton Pike Nthumb
11 P3 Glanvilles Wootton Dorset
80 H9 Glan-y-don Flints
30 F8 Glan-y-llyn Rhondd
55 L8 Glan-y-nant Powys
68 B6 Glan-yr-afon Gwynd
68 D6 Glan-yr-afon Gwynd
79 L8 Glan-yr-afon IoA
28 H3 Glan-yr-afon Swans
61 M2 Glapthorn Nhants
84 G7 Glapwell Derbys
44 H7 Glasbury Powys
80 D10 Glascoed Denbgs
31 K4 Glascoed Mons
59 K3 Glascote Staffs
44 H4 Glascwm Powys
68 B4 Glasfryn Conwy
125 P4 Glasgow C Glas
125 M4 *Glasgow Airport* Rens
125 P4 Glasgow Science Centre C Glas
79 K11 Glasinfryn Gwynd
145 L8 Glasnacardoch Bay Highld
144 H5 Glasnakille Highld
54 G5 Glaspwll Powys
26 C4 Glassenbury Kent
126 C8 Glassford S Lans
91 L6 Glass Houghton Wakefd
46 D10 Glasshouse Gloucs
46 D10 Glasshouse Hill Gloucs
97 J8 Glasshouses N York
110 E8 Glasson Cumb
95 J9 Glasson Lancs
101 Q3 Glassonby Cumb
143 K7 Glasterlaw Angus
73 M10 Glaston Rutlnd
19 P7 Glastonbury Somset
61 Q3 Glatton Cambs
82 E6 Glazebrook Warrtn
82 E5 Glazebury Warrtn
57 N7 Glazeley Shrops
84 E4 Gleadless Sheff
82 H11 Gleadsmoss Ches E
94 F6 Gleaston Cumb
147 N4 Glebe Highld
91 J3 Gledhow Leeds
108 D10 Gledpark D & G
69 K7 Gledrid Shrops
52 D2 Glemsford Suffk
157 P9 Glenallachie Moray
145 L9 Glenancross Highld
137 P7 Glenaros House Ag & B
80 f3 Glen Auldyn IoM
120 C4 Glenbarr Ag & B
158 E7 Glenbarry Abers
137 P3 Glenbeg Highld
151 K11 Glenbervie Abers
126 C4 Glenboig N Lans
137 Q3 Glenborrodale Highld
131 N8 Glenbranter Ag & B
116 F6 Glenbreck Border
144 F3 Glenbrittle House Highld
115 P2 Glenbuck E Ayrs
142 F5 Glencally Angus
109 L7 Glencaple D & G
154 E7 Glencarron Lodge Highld
134 F3 Glencarse P & K
149 L11 Glen Clunie Lodge Abers
139 L6 Glencoe Highld
116 F5 Glencothe Border
134 F9 Glencraig Fife
115 Q10 Glencrosh D & G
152 B8 Glendale Highld
131 K11 Glendaruel Ag & B
134 B7 Glendevon P & K
147 L6 Glendoe Lodge Highld
134 G3 Glendoick P & K
134 H4 Glenduckie Fife
122 D9 Glenegedale Ag & B
145 P4 Glenelg Highld
157 J8 Glenerney Moray
134 E5 Glenfarg P & K
72 E9 Glenfield Leics
145 R11 Glenfinnan Highld
146 G10 Glenfintaig Lodge Highld
134 F4 Glenfoot P & K
131 Q4 Glenfyne Lodge Ag & B
125 J7 Glengarnock N Ayrs
167 K3 Glengolly Highld
137 L4 Glengorm Castle Ag & B
152 G9 Glengrasco Highld
116 G4 Glenholm Border
115 M10 Glenhoul D & G
142 C5 Glenisla Angus
131 N11 Glenkin Ag & B
150 C5 Glenkindie Abers
149 M2 Glenlivet Moray
108 F8 Glenlochar D & G
134 F7 Glenlomond P & K
106 G6 Glenluce D & G
131 N10 Glenmassen Ag & B
126 D4 Glenmavis N Lans
80 b6 Glen Maye IoM
80 g4 Glen Mona IoM
152 G9 Glenmore Highld
148 H6 Glenmore Lodge Highld
139 L3 Glen Nevis House Highld
133 P8 Glenochil Clacks
72 F11 Glen Parva Leics
142 G5 Glenquiech Angus
123 Q6 Glenralloch Ag & B
101 L7 Glenridding Cumb
134 H7 Glenrothes Fife
147 P9 Glenshero Lodge Highld
124 D2 Glenstriven Ag & B
86 D2 Glentham Lincs
114 H11 Glen Trool Lodge D & G
107 L2 Glentrool Village D & G
148 B9 Glentruim House Highld
86 B3 Glentworth Lincs
138 B2 Glenuig Highld
152 H10 Glenvarragill Highld
80 d6 Glen Vine IoM
106 G3 Glenwhilly D & G
115 R2 Glespin S Lans
45 R10 Glewstone Herefs
74 C9 Glinton C Pete
73 K11 Glooston Leics
83 M6 Glossop Derbys
119 Q10 Gloster Hill Nthumb
46 F11 Gloucester Gloucs
46 G11 Gloucester Crematorium Gloucs
46 G10 *Gloucestershire Airport* Gloucs
96 F11 Glusburn N York
166 H9 Glutt Lodge Highld
4 E9 Gluvian Cnwll
48 D10 Glympton Oxon
42 F5 Glynarthen Cerdgn
68 H7 Glyn Ceiriog Wrexhm
29 N5 Glyncorrwg Neath
25 L9 Glynde E Susx
25 L8 Glyndebourne E Susx
68 F6 Glyndyfrdwy Denbgs
29 N3 Glynneath Neath
4 H8 Glynn Valley Crematorium Cnwll
30 E7 Glyntaff Rhondd
30 E7 Glyntaff Crematorium Rhondd
44 A11 Glyntawe Powys
42 G7 Glynteg Carmth
70 E10 Gnosall Staffs
70 E10 Gnosall Heath Staffs
73 K11 Goadby Leics
73 K5 Goadby Marwood Leics
33 K9 Goatacre Wilts
26 D7 Goatham Green E Susx
20 C11 Goathill Dorset
105 M10 Goathland N York
19 J8 Goathurst Somset
37 L10 Goathurst Common Kent
26 H2 Goat Lees Kent
69 K8 Gobowen Shrops
23 Q6 Godalming Surrey
65 K8 Goddard's Corner Suffk
26 D5 Goddard's Green Kent
10 C4 Godford Cross Devon
48 H9 Godington Oxon
83 L5 Godley Tamesd
62 B6 Godmanchester Cambs
11 P5 Godmanstone Dorset
39 J11 Godmersham Kent
19 N6 Godney Somset
2 G7 Godolphin Cross Cnwll
29 L3 Godre'r-graig Neath
21 N11 Godshill Hants
14 F10 Godshill IoW
71 J8 Godstone Staffs
37 J10 Godstone Surrey
8 D9 Godsworthy Devon
13 L5 Godwinscroft Hants
31 K3 Goetre Mons
50 H10 Goff's Oak Herts
31 J2 Gofilon Mons
127 M3 Gogar C Edin
54 F8 Goginan Cerdgn
67 J6 Golan Gwynd
5 J11 Golant Cnwll
5 N7 Golberdon Cnwll
82 D5 Golborne Wigan
90 D7 Golcar Kirk
31 L8 Goldcliff Newpt
25 M8 Golden Cross E Susx
37 P11 Golden Green Kent
43 L11 Golden Grove Carmth
70 F4 Goldenhill C Stke
41 J10 Golden Hill Pembks
23 K6 Golden Pot Hants
84 F10 Golden Valley Derbys
36 F3 Golders Green Gt Lon
36 G3 Golders Green Crematorium Gt Lon
22 F2 Goldfinch Bottom W Berk
52 F10 Goldhanger Essex
62 H2 Gold Hill Cambs
12 D2 Gold Hill Dorset
57 J4 Golding Shrops
61 N10 Goldington Bed
97 N9 Goldsborough N York
105 M8 Goldsborough N York
58 E6 Golds Green Sandw
2 E7 Goldsithney Cnwll
39 N9 Goldstone Kent
70 C9 Goldstone Shrops
23 Q3 Goldsworth Park Surrey
91 M10 Goldthorpe Barns
16 F7 Goldworthy Devon
26 C4 Golford Kent
26 C4 Golford Green Kent
156 E7 Gollanfield Highld
96 H4 Gollinglith Foot N York
69 K3 Golly Wrexhm
18 D7 Golsoncott Somset
163 J6 Golspie Highld
21 N7 Gomeldon Wilts
90 G5 Gomersal Kirk
36 C11 Gomshall Surrey
85 L11 Gonalston Notts
73 N3 Gonerby Hill Foot Lincs
169 q7 Gonfirth Shet
6 E6 Goodameavy Devon
51 P8 Good Easter Essex
75 Q10 Gooderstone Norfk
17 L5 Goodleigh Devon

278 Goodmanham - Guide Bridge

92 E2 **Goodmanham** E R Yk
37 L3 **Goodmayes** Gt Lon
38 H9 **Goodnestone** Kent
39 N11 **Goodnestone** Kent
45 R11 **Goodrich** Herefs
46 A11 **Goodrich Castle** Herefs
7 M7 **Goodrington** Torbay
89 N5 **Goodshaw** Lancs
89 N5 **Goodshaw Fold** Lancs
7 K4 **Goodstone** Devon
40 H3 **Goodwick** Pembks
22 C6 **Goodworth Clatford** Hants
59 M7 **Goodyers End** Warwks
92 B6 **Goole** E R Yk
92 C6 **Goole Fields** E R Yk
47 K4 **Goom's Hill** Worcs
3 J4 **Goonbell** Cnwll
3 K3 **Goonhavern** Cnwll
3 J4 **Goonvrea** Cnwll
151 K11 **Goosecruives** Abers
8 G6 **Gooseford** Devon
53 K6 **Goose Green** Essex
26 D4 **Goose Green** Kent
37 P10 **Goose Green** Kent
32 C10 **Goose Green** S Glos
24 D7 **Goose Green** W Susx
82 C4 **Goose Green** Wigan
16 C8 **Gooseham** Cnwll
16 C8 **Gooseham Mill** Cnwll
46 H2 **Goosehill Green** Worcs
45 P7 **Goose Pool** Herefs
34 C6 **Goosey** Oxon
88 H3 **Goosnargh** Lancs
82 G10 **Goostrey** Ches E
31 P9 **Gordano Services** N Som
79 M10 **Gorddinog** Conwy
118 B2 **Gordon** Border
117 L5 **Gordon Arms Hotel** Border
158 E6 **Gordonstown** Abers
158 H10 **Gordonstown** Abers
45 K3 **Gore** Powys
127 Q5 **Gorebridge** Mdloth
74 H8 **Gorefield** Cambs
52 E8 **Gore Pit** Essex
21 M3 **Gores** Wilts
39 N8 **Gore Street** Kent
11 c2 **Gorey** Jersey
34 H8 **Goring** Oxon
24 D10 **Goring-by-Sea** W Susx
35 J9 **Goring Heath** Oxon
77 Q11 **Gorleston on Sea** Norfk
58 D6 **Gornal Wood Crematorium** Dudley
158 H6 **Gorrachie** Abers
3 P5 **Gorran Churchtown** Cnwll
3 Q5 **Gorran Haven** Cnwll
3 P5 **Gorran High Lanes** Cnwll
42 H6 **Gorrig** Cerdgn
54 E9 **Gors** Cerdgn
80 H9 **Gorsedd** Flints
33 N7 **Gorse Hill** Swindn
28 G5 **Gorseinon** Swans
71 P4 **Gorseybank** Derbys
43 J4 **Gorsgoch** Cerdgn
28 G2 **Gorslas** Carmth
46 C9 **Gorsley** Gloucs
46 C9 **Gorsley Common** Herefs
82 D10 **Gorstage** Ches W
155 L5 **Gorstan** Highld
69 L2 **Gorstella** Ches W
57 N10 **Gorst Hill** Worcs
71 L9 **Gorsty Hill** Staffs
138 C11 **Gorten** Ag & B
147 N3 **Gorthleck** Highld
83 J5 **Gorton** Manch
64 H10 **Gosbeck** Suffk
74 D4 **Gosberton** Lincs
74 C5 **Gosberton Clough** Lincs
52 C6 **Gosfield** Essex
10 C5 **Gosford** Devon
100 E10 **Gosforth** Cumb
113 K7 **Gosforth** N u Ty
19 P8 **Gosling Street** Somset
50 E5 **Gosmore** Herts
58 C6 **Gospel End** Staffs
23 P8 **Gospel Green** W Susx
14 H7 **Gosport** Hants
49 Q6 **Gossard's Green** C Beds
32 D4 **Gossington** Gloucs
119 L2 **Goswick** Nthumb
72 E4 **Gotham** Notts
47 J9 **Gotherington** Gloucs
18 H9 **Gotton** Somset
26 B4 **Goudhurst** Kent
87 J5 **Goulceby** Lincs
159 J9 **Gourdas** Abers
142 F11 **Gourdie** C Dund
143 Q3 **Gourdon** Abers
124 G2 **Gourock** Inver
125 N4 **Govan** C Glas
7 K9 **Goveton** Devon
91 Q6 **Gowdall** E R Yk
155 P6 **Gower** Highld
28 F6 **Gower** Swans
28 G5 **Gowerton** Swans
134 D10 **Gowkhall** Fife
98 F10 **Gowthorpe** E R Yk
93 L2 **Goxhill** E R Yk
93 K6 **Goxhill** N Linc
168 i6 **Grabhair** W Isls
74 A5 **Graby** Lincs
3 J11 **Grade** Cnwll
69 Q4 **Gradeley Green** Ches E
23 P11 **Graffham** W Susx
61 Q7 **Grafham** Cambs
24 B2 **Grafham** Surrey
45 P7 **Grafton** Herefs
97 P8 **Grafton** N York
33 Q4 **Grafton** Oxon
69 M11 **Grafton** Shrops
46 A2 **Grafton** Worcs
47 J7 **Grafton** Worcs
47 J3 **Grafton Flyford** Worcs
49 L5 **Grafton Regis** Nhants
61 K4 **Grafton Underwood** Nhants
26 E2 **Grafty Green** Kent
68 H3 **Graianrhyd** Denbgs
79 Q10 **Graig** Conwy
80 F10 **Graig** Denbgs
68 F4 **Graig-fechan** Denbgs
38 E6 **Grain** Medway
90 B9 **Grains Bar** Oldham
93 N11 **Grainsby** Lincs
93 Q11 **Grainthorpe** Lincs
3 N4 **Grampound** Cnwll
3 N3 **Grampound Road** Cnwll
168 d12 **Gramsdal** W Isls
168 d12 **Gramsdale** W Isls
49 L9 **Granborough** Bucks
73 K3 **Granby** Notts
59 Q11 **Grandborough** Warwks
11 c2 **Grand Chemins** Jersey
10 b1 **Grandes Rocques** Guern
72 C5 **Grand Prix Collection Donington** Leics
141 M7 **Grandtully** P & K
101 J7 **Grange** Cumb
38 C8 **Grange** Medway
134 H2 **Grange** P & K
81 J7 **Grange** Wirral
158 C7 **Grange Crossroads** Moray
157 K5 **Grange Hall** Moray
116 D2 **Grangehall** S Lans
37 K2 **Grange Hill** Essex
84 B9 **Grangemill** Derbys
90 G7 **Grange Moor** Kirk
133 Q11 **Grangemouth** Falk
134 H4 **Grange of Lindores** Fife
95 J5 **Grange-over-Sands** Cumb
134 C11 **Grangepans** Falk
104 F6 **Grangetown** R & Cl
113 P10 **Grangetown** Sundld
113 K8 **Grange Villa** Dur
99 N9 **Gransmoor** E R Yk
51 Q6 **Gransmore Green** Essex
40 G4 **Granston** Pembks
62 F9 **Grantchester** Cambs
73 N3 **Grantham** Lincs
73 N3 **Grantham Crematorium** Lincs
127 N2 **Granton** C Edin
149 J2 **Grantown-on-Spey** Highld
45 Q2 **Grantsfield** Herefs
129 L6 **Grantshouse** Border
82 D7 **Grappenhall** Warrtn
93 J10 **Grasby** Lincs
101 K9 **Grasmere** Cumb
83 L4 **Grasscroft** Oldham
81 M7 **Grassendale** Lpool
101 K2 **Grassgarth** Cumb
52 B4 **Grass Green** Essex
96 F8 **Grassington** N York
84 F7 **Grassmoor** Derbys
85 N7 **Grassthorpe** Notts
21 Q6 **Grateley** Hants
71 J8 **Gratwich** Staffs
62 C8 **Graveley** Cambs
50 F5 **Graveley** Herts
58 H6 **Gravelly Hill** Birm
56 E4 **Gravelsbank** Shrops
39 J9 **Graveney** Kent
37 Q6 **Gravesend** Kent
168 i6 **Gravir** W Isls
92 F11 **Grayingham** Lincs
101 Q11 **Grayrigg** Cumb
37 P5 **Grays** Thurr
23 N7 **Grayshott** Hants
100 C5 **Grayson Green** Cumb
23 P8 **Grayswood** Surrey
104 F5 **Graythorpe** Hartpl
35 J11 **Grazeley** Wokham
91 L11 **Greasbrough** Rothm
81 K7 **Greasby** Wirral
84 G11 **Greasley** Notts
62 H11 **Great Abington** Cambs
61 L5 **Great Addington** Nhants
47 M3 **Great Alne** Warwks
88 C9 **Great Altcar** Lancs
51 J8 **Great Amwell** Herts
102 C8 **Great Asby** Cumb
64 D8 **Great Ashfield** Suffk
104 G8 **Great Ayton** N York
52 B11 **Great Baddow** Essex
32 F8 **Great Badminton** S Glos
51 Q4 **Great Bardfield** Essex
61 P10 **Great Barford** Bed
58 F5 **Great Barr** Sandw
33 P2 **Great Barrington** Gloucs
81 P11 **Great Barrow** Ches W
64 B8 **Great Barton** Suffk
98 E5 **Great Barugh** N York
112 E4 **Great Bavington** Nthumb
53 M2 **Great Bealings** Suffk
21 Q2 **Great Bedwyn** Wilts
53 K7 **Great Bentley** Essex
60 H8 **Great Billing** Nhants
75 Q4 **Great Bircham** Norfk
64 G11 **Great Blakenham** Suffk
101 N4 **Great Blencow** Cumb
70 A10 **Great Bolas** Wrekin
36 D10 **Great Bookham** Surrey
2 C7 **Great Bosullow** Cnwll
48 E5 **Great Bourton** Oxon
60 F3 **Great Bowden** Leics
63 L10 **Great Bradley** Suffk
52 E9 **Great Braxted** Essex
64 E11 **Great Bricett** Suffk
49 P8 **Great Brickhill** Bucks
70 F9 **Great Bridgeford** Staffs
60 E7 **Great Brington** Nhants
53 J6 **Great Bromley** Essex
100 E4 **Great Broughton** Cumb
104 F9 **Great Broughton** N York
82 E9 **Great Budworth** Ches W
104 B7 **Great Burdon** Darltn
37 Q2 **Great Burstead** Essex
104 F9 **Great Busby** N York
51 N7 **Great Canfield** Essex
87 M3 **Great Carlton** Lincs
73 Q9 **Great Casterton** Rutlnd
20 G2 **Great Chalfield** Wilts
26 G3 **Great Chart** Kent
57 P2 **Great Chatwell** Staffs
70 F4 **Great Chell** C Stke
51 M2 **Great Chesterford** Essex
21 J4 **Great Cheverell** Wilts
51 K3 **Great Chishill** Cambs
53 L8 **Great Clacton** Essex
91 J7 **Great Cliffe** Wakefd
100 D5 **Great Clifton** Cumb
93 M9 **Great Coates** NE Lin
47 J6 **Great Comberton** Worcs
37 P9 **Great Comp** Kent
111 J10 **Great Corby** Cumb
52 E3 **Great Cornard** Suffk
93 M2 **Great Cowden** E R Yk
33 Q6 **Great Coxwell** Oxon
60 H5 **Great Cransley** Nhants
76 B11 **Great Cressingham** Norfk
101 J6 **Great Crosthwaite** Cumb
71 M7 **Great Cubley** Derbys
124 F6 **Great Cumbrae Island** N Ayrs
73 J8 **Great Dalby** Leics
61 J8 **Great Doddington** Nhants
45 Q11 **Great Doward** Herefs
76 B9 **Great Dunham** Norfk
51 P6 **Great Dunmow** Essex
21 M7 **Great Durnford** Wilts
51 P5 **Great Easton** Essex
60 H2 **Great Easton** Leics
88 E2 **Great Eccleston** Lancs
98 E4 **Great Edstone** N York
64 E2 **Great Ellingham** Norfk
20 D5 **Great Elm** Somset
60 C9 **Great Everdon** Nhants
62 E10 **Great Eversden** Cambs
97 L2 **Great Fencote** N York
33 L7 **Greatfield** Wilts
64 E10 **Great Finborough** Suffk
74 A8 **Greatford** Lincs
76 B9 **Great Fransham** Norfk
50 B8 **Great Gaddesden** Herts
71 K7 **Greatgate** Staffs
61 P4 **Great Gidding** Cambs
98 G10 **Great Givendale** E R Yk
65 L9 **Great Glemham** Suffk
72 H11 **Great Glen** Leics
73 M3 **Great Gonerby** Lincs
62 C9 **Great Gransden** Cambs
50 G2 **Great Green** Cambs
65 K4 **Great Green** Norfk
64 C10 **Great Green** Suffk
64 C8 **Great Green** Suffk
98 F5 **Great Habton** N York
74 B2 **Great Hale** Lincs
51 M7 **Great Hallingbury** Essex
23 L8 **Greatham** Hants
104 E5 **Greatham** Hartpl
24 B7 **Greatham** W Susx
35 M4 **Great Hampden** Bucks
61 J6 **Great Harrowden** Nhants
89 L4 **Great Harwood** Lancs
34 H4 **Great Haseley** Oxon
93 L2 **Great Hatfield** E R Yk
70 H10 **Great Haywood** Staffs
91 P6 **Great Heck** N York
52 E4 **Great Henny** Essex
20 H3 **Great Hinton** Wilts
64 D3 **Great Hockham** Norfk
53 M8 **Great Holland** Essex
35 N11 **Great Hollands** Br For
52 G5 **Great Horkesley** Essex
51 K5 **Great Hormead** Herts
90 E4 **Great Horton** C Brad
49 L8 **Great Horwood** Bucks
91 L9 **Great Houghton** Barns
60 G9 **Great Houghton** Nhants
83 Q9 **Great Hucklow** Derbys
99 N9 **Great Kelk** E R Yk
35 M3 **Great Kimble** Bucks
35 N5 **Great Kingshill** Bucks
101 J9 **Great Langdale** Cumb
103 Q11 **Great Langton** N York
52 B8 **Great Leighs** Essex
93 K9 **Great Limber** Lincs
49 N6 **Great Linford** M Keyn
64 B7 **Great Livermere** Suffk
84 B6 **Great Longstone** Derbys
113 L11 **Great Lumley** Dur
56 H3 **Great Lyth** Shrops
46 E5 **Great Malvern** Worcs
52 D5 **Great Maplestead** Essex
88 C3 **Great Marton** Bpool
75 Q6 **Great Massingham** Norfk
76 G10 **Great Melton** Norfk
81 J6 **Great Meols** Wirral
34 H4 **Great Milton** Oxon
35 N4 **Great Missenden** Bucks
89 L3 **Great Mitton** Lancs
39 Q11 **Great Mongeham** Kent
64 H3 **Great Moulton** Norfk
51 J6 **Great Munden** Herts
102 E8 **Great Musgrave** Cumb
69 L11 **Great Ness** Shrops
52 B7 **Great Notley** Essex
31 L2 **Great Oak** Mons
53 L6 **Great Oakley** Essex
61 J3 **Great Oakley** Nhants
50 D5 **Great Offley** Herts
102 D7 **Great Ormside** Cumb
110 F10 **Great Orton** Cumb
97 P8 **Great Ouseburn** N York
60 F4 **Great Oxendon** Nhants
51 Q9 **Great Oxney Green** Essex
76 A9 **Great Palgrave** Norfk
26 B3 **Great Pattenden** Kent
62 B8 **Great Paxton** Cambs
88 D4 **Great Plumpton** Lancs
77 L9 **Great Plumstead** Norfk
73 N4 **Great Ponton** Lincs
17 J9 **Great Potheridge** Devon
91 L5 **Great Preston** Leeds
48 F7 **Great Purston** Nhants
62 C4 **Great Raveley** Cambs
47 N11 **Great Rissington** Gloucs
48 B8 **Great Rollright** Oxon
41 J6 **Great Rudbaxton** Pembks
76 D6 **Great Ryburgh** Norfk
119 K8 **Great Ryle** Nthumb
56 H4 **Great Ryton** Shrops
51 Q5 **Great Saling** Essex
101 Q3 **Great Salkeld** Cumb
51 P3 **Great Sampford** Essex
58 E3 **Great Saredon** Staffs
81 M11 **Great Saughall** Ches W
63 N8 **Great Saxham** Suffk
34 C9 **Great Shefford** W Berk
62 G10 **Great Shelford** Cambs
104 B10 **Great Smeaton** N York
76 C5 **Great Snoring** Norfk
33 J8 **Great Somerford** Wilts
70 C9 **Great Soudley** Shrops
104 B6 **Great Stainton** Darltn
38 E3 **Great Stambridge** Essex
61 P8 **Great Staughton** Cambs
87 M8 **Great Steeping** Lincs
32 B8 **Great Stoke** S Glos
39 P10 **Great Stonar** Kent
27 J7 **Greatstone-on-Sea** Kent
101 Q6 **Great Strickland** Cumb
62 B6 **Great Stukeley** Cambs
86 H5 **Great Sturton** Lincs
81 M9 **Great Sutton** Ches W
57 J8 **Great Sutton** Shrops
112 D5 **Great Swinburne** Nthumb
48 D9 **Great Tew** Oxon
52 E6 **Great Tey** Essex
63 L10 **Great Thurlow** Suffk
16 H8 **Great Torrington** Devon
119 K10 **Great Tosson** Nthumb
52 E9 **Great Totham** Essex
52 E9 **Great Totham** Essex
86 H2 **Great Tows** Lincs
94 F6 **Great Urswick** Cumb
38 F4 **Great Wakering** Essex
52 F3 **Great Waldingfield** Suffk
76 C4 **Great Walsingham** Norfk
51 Q8 **Great Waltham** Essex
82 H9 **Great Warford** Ches E
37 N2 **Great Warley** Essex
47 J8 **Great Washbourne** Gloucs
8 H7 **Great Weeke** Devon
61 K3 **Great Weldon** Nhants
64 B10 **Great Welnetham** Suffk
53 J4 **Great Wenham** Suffk
112 F6 **Great Whittington** Nthumb
52 G8 **Great Wigborough** Essex
63 J9 **Great Wilbraham** Cambs
21 L7 **Great Wishford** Wilts
76 G7 **Great Witchingham** Norfk
32 H2 **Great Witcombe** Gloucs
57 P11 **Great Witley** Worcs
47 Q8 **Great Wolford** Warwks
48 G6 **Greatworth** Nhants
63 L11 **Great Wratting** Suffk
50 F5 **Great Wymondley** Herts
58 E3 **Great Wyrley** Staffs
69 Q11 **Great Wytheford** Shrops
77 Q10 **Great Yarmouth** Norfk
77 Q11 **Great Yarmouth Crematorium** Norfk
52 C4 **Great Yeldham** Essex
87 M7 **Grebby** Lincs
80 d5 **Greeba** IoM
80 F11 **Green** Denbgs
94 H4 **Green Bank** Cumb
126 G5 **Greenburn** W Loth
113 J11 **Greencroft Hall** Dur
23 N7 **Green Cross** Surrey
19 Q4 **Green Down** Somset
61 M11 **Green End** Bed
61 N8 **Green End** Bed
61 P10 **Green End** Bed
61 P8 **Green End** Bed
61 Q4 **Green End** Cambs
62 B6 **Green End** Cambs
62 E9 **Green End** Cambs
62 G7 **Green End** Cambs
62 G8 **Green End** Cambs
50 G4 **Green End** Herts
50 H4 **Green End** Herts
50 H6 **Green End** Herts
48 B10 **Greenend** Oxon
59 L7 **Green End** Warwks
131 Q9 **Greenfield** Ag & B
50 C4 **Greenfield** C Beds
80 H9 **Greenfield** Flints
146 G7 **Greenfield** Highld
83 L4 **Greenfield** Oldham
35 K6 **Greenfield** Oxon
36 D4 **Greenford** Gt Lon
126 D3 **Greengairs** N Lans
90 F3 **Greengates** C Brad
100 F3 **Greengill** Cumb
88 E3 **Greenhalgh** Lancs
18 E10 **Greenham** Somset
34 E11 **Greenham** W Berk
97 Q9 **Green Hammerton** N York
111 Q3 **Greenhaugh** Nthumb
110 G11 **Green Head** Cumb
111 N7 **Greenhead** Nthumb
58 E2 **Green Heath** Staffs
82 F4 **Greenheys** Salfd
109 P5 **Greenhill** D & G
126 E2 **Greenhill** Falk
46 D5 **Greenhill** Herefs
39 L8 **Greenhill** Kent
116 C4 **Greenhill** S Lans
33 L7 **Green Hill** Wilts
84 F11 **Greenhillocks** Derbys
37 N5 **Greenhithe** Kent
125 N10 **Greenholm** E Ayrs
101 Q9 **Greenholme** Cumb
117 R6 **Greenhouse** Border
96 H8 **Greenhow Hill** N York
167 M3 **Greenland** Highld
84 E3 **Greenland** Sheff
35 L7 **Greenlands** Bucks
9 J9 **Green Lane** Devon
47 L2 **Green Lane** Worcs
129 J10 **Greenlaw** Border
109 M5 **Greenlea** D & G
133 N6 **Greenloaning** P & K
90 H11 **Green Moor** Barns
89 M8 **Greenmount** Bury
92 D5 **Green Oak** E R Yk
124 H2 **Greenock** Inver
124 H2 **Greenock Crematorium** Inver
94 G4 **Greenodd** Cumb
19 Q4 **Green Ore** Somset
101 N10 **Green Quarter** Cumb
76 G8 **Greensgate** Norfk
116 E2 **Greenshields** S Lans
112 H8 **Greenside** Gatesd
90 F7 **Greenside** Kirk
49 J5 **Greens Norton** Nhants
52 H6 **Greenstead** Essex
52 D6 **Greenstead Green** Essex
51 M10 **Greensted** Essex
26 C9 **Green Street** E Susx
46 G11 **Green Street** Gloucs
50 E11 **Green Street** Herts
51 L6 **Green Street** Herts
46 G5 **Green Street** Worcs
37 L8 **Green Street Green** Gt Lon
37 N6 **Green Street Green** Kent
52 H2 **Greenstreet Green** Suffk
51 K7 **Green Tye** Herts
46 D8 **Greenway** Gloucs
19 K10 **Greenway** Somset
30 E10 **Greenway** V Glam
57 N10 **Greenway** Worcs
37 J5 **Greenwich** Gt Lon
47 K8 **Greet** Gloucs
57 K10 **Greete** Shrops
87 K6 **Greetham** Lincs
73 N8 **Greetham** Rutlnd
90 D6 **Greetland** Calder
88 H5 **Gregson Lane** Lancs
19 M7 **Greinton** Somset
80 C7 **Grenaby** IoM
61 J8 **Grendon** Nhants
59 L5 **Grendon** Warwks
46 A3 **Grendon Green** Herefs
49 J10 **Grendon Underwood** Bucks
6 D4 **Grenofen** Devon
84 D2 **Grenoside** Sheff
84 D2 **Grenoside Crematorium** Sheff
168 g8 **Greosabhagh** W Isls
69 K4 **Gresford** Wrexhm
76 H4 **Gresham** Norfk
152 E7 **Greshornish House Hotel** Highld
76 D8 **Gressenhall** Norfk
76 D8 **Gressenhall Green** Norfk
95 M7 **Gressingham** Lancs
70 C4 **Gresty Green** Ches E
103 L8 **Greta Bridge** Dur
110 F7 **Gretna** D & G
110 F7 **Gretna Green** D & G
110 F7 **Gretna Services** D & G
47 K8 **Gretton** Gloucs
61 J2 **Gretton** Nhants
57 J5 **Gretton** Shrops
97 K5 **Grewelthorpe** N York
65 P7 **Grey Friars** Suffk
97 J6 **Greygarth** N York
92 C9 **Grey Green** N Linc
19 L8 **Greylake** Somset
109 N3 **Greyrigg** D & G
35 K8 **Greys Green** Oxon
100 E5 **Greysouthen** Cumb
101 M4 **Greystoke** Cumb
143 J9 **Greystone** Angus
23 K4 **Greywell** Hants
10 H4 **Gribb** Dorset
92 C3 **Gribthorpe** E R Yk
59 N7 **Griff** Warwks
31 J5 **Griffithstown** Torfn
72 C7 **Griffydam** Leics
23 M8 **Griggs Green** Hants
89 J8 **Grimeford Village** Lancs
84 E3 **Grimesthorpe** Sheff
91 L9 **Grimethorpe** Barns
46 F2 **Grimley** Worcs
114 F5 **Grimmet** S Ayrs
87 L3 **Grimoldby** Lincs
69 L9 **Grimpo** Shrops
88 H4 **Grimsargh** Lancs
93 N8 **Grimsby** NE Lin
93 N9 **Grimsby Crematorium** NE Lin
49 J4 **Grimscote** Nhants
16 D10 **Grimscott** Cnwll
168 j5 **Grimshader** W Isls
89 L6 **Grimshaw** Bl w D
88 F8 **Grimshaw Green** Lancs
73 Q6 **Grimsthorpe** Lincs
93 N3 **Grimston** E R Yk
72 H6 **Grimston** Leics
75 P6 **Grimston** Norfk
11 N6 **Grimstone** Dorset
64 C8 **Grimstone End** Suffk
5 Q3 **Grinacombe Moor** Devon
99 N6 **Grindale** E R Yk
57 P4 **Grindle** Shrops
84 B5 **Grindleford** Derbys
95 R11 **Grindleton** Lancs
69 P6 **Grindley Brook** Shrops
83 Q9 **Grindlow** Derbys
118 H2 **Grindon** Nthumb
104 C5 **Grindon** S on T
71 K4 **Grindon** Staffs
112 B7 **Grindon Hill** Nthumb
118 H2 **Grindonrigg** Nthumb
85 M2 **Gringley on the Hill** Notts
110 G9 **Grinsdale** Cumb
69 P10 **Grinshill** Shrops
103 K11 **Grinton** N York
168 j5 **Griomaisiader** W Isls
168 d12 **Griomsaigh** W Isls
136 F4 **Grishipoll** Ag & B
25 K6 **Grisling Common** E Susx
99 M4 **Gristhorpe** N York
64 C2 **Griston** Norfk
169 e6 **Gritley** Ork
33 K8 **Grittenham** Wilts
32 G8 **Grittleton** Wilts
94 E4 **Grizebeck** Cumb
94 G2 **Grizedale** Cumb
72 E9 **Groby** Leics
68 D2 **Groes** Conwy
30 E8 **Groes-faen** Rhondd
66 D7 **Groesffordd** Gwynd
80 E10 **Groesffordd Marli** Denbgs
56 C2 **Groeslwyd** Powys
66 H3 **Groeslon** Gwynd
67 J2 **Groeslon** Gwynd
30 F7 **Groes-Wen** Caerph
168 c14 **Grogarry** W Isls
120 F3 **Grogport** Ag & B
168 c14 **Groigearraidh** W Isls
65 M10 **Gromford** Suffk
80 F8 **Gronant** Flints
25 M3 **Groombridge** E Susx
168 g8 **Grosebay** W Isls
45 N10 **Grosmont** Mons
105 M9 **Grosmont** N York
52 G3 **Groton** Suffk
83 L4 **Grotton** Oldham
11 c2 **Grouville** Jersey
49 P10 **Grove** Bucks
11 P10 **Grove** Dorset
39 M9 **Grove** Kent
85 M5 **Grove** Notts
34 D6 **Grove** Oxon
41 J10 **Grove** Pembks
38 C10 **Grove Green** Kent
26 B3 **Grovenhurst** Kent
37 K6 **Grove Park** Gt Lon
32 C7 **Grovesend** S Glos
28 G4 **Grovesend** Swans
37 N7 **Grubb Street** Kent
160 E9 **Gruinard** Highld
122 C6 **Gruinart** Ag & B
144 E2 **Grula** Highld
137 N7 **Gruline** Ag & B
2 C8 **Grumbla** Cnwll
65 J11 **Grundisburgh** Suffk
169 p9 **Gruting** Shet
139 L8 **Gualachulain** Highld
74 G8 **Guanockgate** Lincs
135 M4 **Guardbridge** Fife
46 F5 **Guarlford** Worcs
141 P8 **Guay** P & K
10 b2 *Guernsey Airport* Guern
26 E9 **Guestling Green** E Susx
26 E8 **Guestling Thorn** E Susx
76 F6 **Guestwick** Norfk
83 K5 **Guide Bridge** Tamesd

Guide Post - Hatch 279

113 L3 **Guide Post** Nthumb
50 G2 **Guilden Morden** Cambs
81 N11 **Guilden Sutton** Ches W
23 Q5 **Guildford** Surrey
23 Q5 **Guildford Crematorium** Surrey
38 D9 **Guildstead** Kent
142 A11 **Guildtown** P & K
60 E6 **Guilsborough** Nhants
56 C2 **Guilsfield** Powys
39 N10 **Guilton** Kent
114 G5 **Guiltreehill** S Ayrs
17 K4 **Guineaford** Devon
104 H7 **Guisborough** R & Cl
90 F2 **Guiseley** Leeds
76 E6 **Guist** Norfk
47 L10 **Guiting Power** Gloucs
128 D3 **Gullane** E Loth
64 A10 **Gulling Green** Suffk
2 D7 **Gulval** Cnwll
6 D4 **Gulworthy** Devon
41 M10 **Gumfreston** Pembks
60 E3 **Gumley** Leics
4 D10 **Gummow's Shop** Cnwll
92 B3 **Gunby** E R Yk
73 N6 **Gunby** Lincs
87 N7 **Gunby** Lincs
22 H8 **Gundleton** Hants
26 C5 **Gun Green** Kent
25 N8 **Gun Hill** E Susx
59 L7 **Gun Hill** Warwks
17 L5 **Gunn** Devon
103 J11 **Gunnerside** N York
112 D6 **Gunnerton** Nthumb
92 D8 **Gunness** N Linc
6 C4 **Gunnislake** Cnwll
169 s9 **Gunnista** Shet
74 C10 **Gunthorpe** C Pete
92 D11 **Gunthorpe** N Linc
76 E5 **Gunthorpe** Norfk
72 H2 **Gunthorpe** Notts
65 Q2 **Gunton** Suffk
2 H9 **Gunwalloe** Cnwll
18 C8 **Gupworthy** Somset
14 E7 **Gurnard** IoW
83 K10 **Gurnett** Ches E
20 B5 **Gurney Slade** Somset
29 L3 **Gurnos** Powys
38 H10 **Gushmere** Kent
12 H2 **Gussage All Saints** Dorset
12 G2 **Gussage St Andrew** Dorset
12 G2 **Gussage St Michael** Dorset
27 P3 **Guston** Kent
169 s4 **Gutcher** Shet
143 K7 **Guthrie** Angus
74 H10 **Guyhirn** Cambs
74 G10 **Guyhirn Gull** Cambs
20 F10 **Guy's Marsh** Dorset
119 P10 **Guyzance** Nthumb
80 F8 **Gwaenysgor** Flints
78 F9 **Gwalchmai** IoA
67 L3 **Gwastadnant** Gwynd
29 J2 **Gwaun-Cae-Gurwen** Carmth
42 C4 **Gwbert on Sea** Cerdgn
2 G5 **Gwealavellan** Cnwll
3 J8 **Gweek** Cnwll
31 L4 **Gwehelog** Mons
44 F6 **Gwenddwr** Powys
3 J5 **Gwennap** Cnwll
31 K5 **Gwent Crematorium** Mons
3 J10 **Gwenter** Cnwll
81 J11 **Gwernaffield** Flints
31 M4 **Gwernesney** Mons
43 K8 **Gwernogle** Carmth
68 H2 **Gwernymynydd** Flints
69 K4 **Gwersyllt** Wrexhm
80 G8 **Gwespyr** Flints
3 P3 **Gwindra** Cnwll
2 F6 **Gwinear** Cnwll
2 F5 **Gwithian** Cnwll
78 G7 **Gwredog** IoA
30 G5 **Gwrhay** Caerph
68 E5 **Gwyddelwern** Denbgs
43 J7 **Gwyddgrug** Carmth
69 J4 **Gwynfryn** Wrexhm
55 P11 **Gwystre** Powys
68 A2 **Gwytherin** Conwy
69 K5 **Gyfelia** Wrexhm
66 G5 **Gyrn-goch** Gwynd

H

56 F4 **Habberley** Shrops
57 Q9 **Habberley** Worcs
89 N4 **Habergham** Lancs
87 P7 **Habertoft** Lincs
23 M10 **Habin** W Susx
93 K8 **Habrough** NE Lin
74 B5 **Hacconby** Lincs
73 Q3 **Haceby** Lincs
65 L10 **Hacheston** Suffk
36 G7 **Hackbridge** Gt Lon
84 F4 **Hackenthorpe** Sheff
76 F11 **Hackford** Norfk
97 K2 **Hackforth** N York
70 A5 **Hack Green** Ches E
169 c4 **Hackland** Ork
60 H9 **Hackleton** Nhants
39 P11 **Hacklinge** Kent
58 C9 **Hackman's Gate** Worcs
99 K2 **Hackness** N York
19 K5 **Hackness** Somset
36 H4 **Hackney** Gt Lon
86 C4 **Hackthorn** Lincs
101 P6 **Hackthorpe** Cumb
37 N3 **Hacton** Gt Lon
118 E3 **Hadden** Border
35 K3 **Haddenham** Bucks
62 G5 **Haddenham** Cambs
128 E5 **Haddington** E Loth
86 B8 **Haddington** Lincs
65 N2 **Haddiscoe** Norfk
159 K10 **Haddo** Abers
61 P2 **Haddon** Cambs
83 P4 **Hade Edge** Kirk
83 M5 **Hadfield** Derbys
51 K7 **Hadham Cross** Herts
51 K6 **Hadham Ford** Herts
38 D4 **Hadleigh** Essex
52 H3 **Hadleigh** Suffk
52 G3 **Hadleigh Heath** Suffk
46 G2 **Hadley** Worcs
57 M2 **Hadley** Wrekin
71 L10 **Hadley End** Staffs
50 G11 **Hadley Wood** Gt Lon
37 P10 **Hadlow** Kent
25 M6 **Hadlow Down** E Susx
69 P10 **Hadnall** Shrops
112 E7 **Hadrian's Wall** Nthumb
51 N2 **Hadstock** Essex
46 H2 **Hadzor** Worcs
26 E3 **Haffenden Quarter** Kent
80 B11 **Hafodunos** Conwy
69 K5 **Hafod-y-bwch** Wrexhm
30 H4 **Hafod-y-coed** Blae G
30 H5 **Hafodyrynys** Caerph
89 P3 **Haggate** Lancs
111 J6 **Haggbeck** Cumb
169 q9 **Haggersta** Shet
119 K2 **Haggerston** Nthumb
17 K2 **Haggington Hill** Devon
126 D2 **Haggs** Falk
45 R6 **Hagley** Herefs
58 D8 **Hagley** Worcs
52 G4 **Hagmore Green** Suffk
87 K8 **Hagnaby** Lincs
87 N5 **Hagnaby** Lincs
87 K7 **Hagworthingham** Lincs
89 J9 **Haigh** Wigan
88 H4 **Haighton Green** Lancs
100 D9 **Haile** Cumb
47 K8 **Hailes** Gloucs
51 J8 **Hailey** Herts
34 C2 **Hailey** Oxon
34 H7 **Hailey** Oxon
25 N9 **Hailsham** E Susx
61 Q8 **Hail Weston** Cambs
37 L2 **Hainault** Gt Lon
39 Q8 **Haine** Kent
77 J8 **Hainford** Norfk
86 G4 **Hainton** Lincs
90 D3 **Hainworth** C Brad
99 N8 **Haisthorpe** E R Yk
40 G9 **Hakin** Pembks
85 L10 **Halam** Notts
134 E10 **Halbeath** Fife
9 P2 **Halberton** Devon
167 M4 **Halcro** Highld
95 L5 **Hale** Cumb
81 P8 **Hale** Halton
21 N11 **Hale** Hants
20 D9 **Hale** Somset
23 M5 **Hale** Surrey
82 G7 **Hale** Traffd
81 P8 **Hale Bank** Halton
82 G7 **Halebarns** Traffd
25 N8 **Hale Green** E Susx
88 D2 **Hale Nook** Lancs
65 M2 **Hales** Norfk
70 C8 **Hales** Staffs
74 F5 **Halesgate** Lincs
71 M6 **Hales Green** Derbys
58 E8 **Halesowen** Dudley
39 K10 **Hales Place** Kent
37 Q11 **Hale Street** Kent
38 F3 **Halesville** Essex
65 M6 **Halesworth** Suffk
81 P7 **Halewood** Knows
7 L4 **Halford** Devon
56 G8 **Halford** Shrops
47 Q5 **Halford** Warwks
95 L3 **Halfpenny** Cumb
58 B6 **Halfpenny Green** Staffs
97 K4 **Halfpenny Houses** N York
43 M8 **Halfway** Carmth
44 A8 **Halfway** Carmth
84 F4 **Halfway** Sheff
34 D11 **Halfway** W Berk
23 P10 **Halfway Bridge** W Susx
56 E2 **Halfway House** Shrops
38 F7 **Halfway Houses** Kent
90 D5 **Halifax** Calder
125 L7 **Halket** E Ayrs
167 K5 **Halkirk** Highld
81 J10 **Halkyn** Flints
125 L7 **Hall** E Rens
72 D3 **Hallam Fields** Derbys
25 L7 **Halland** E Susx
73 K11 **Hallaton** Leics
20 B3 **Hallatrow** BaNES
111 L9 **Hallbankgate** Cumb
95 N3 **Hallbeck** Cumb
90 H7 **Hall Cliffe** Wakefd
88 E4 **Hall Cross** Lancs
100 H11 **Hall Dunnerdale** Cumb
31 Q8 **Hallen** S Glos
61 M11 **Hall End** Bed
50 C3 **Hall End** C Beds
84 E9 **Hallfield Gate** Derbys
104 B2 **Hallgarth** Dur
126 F2 **Hall Glen** Falk
58 H8 **Hall Green** Birm
152 D6 **Hallin** Highld
38 B9 **Halling** Medway
87 K3 **Hallington** Lincs
112 E5 **Hallington** Nthumb
89 K8 **Halliwell** Bolton
85 L10 **Halloughton** Notts
46 F3 **Hallow** Worcs
46 F3 **Hallow Heath** Worcs
7 L11 **Hallsands** Devon
51 K9 **Hall's Green** Essex
50 G5 **Hall's Green** Herts
94 D3 **Hallthwaites** Cumb
5 K4 **Hallworthy** Cnwll
116 H2 **Hallyne** Border
70 D5 **Halmer End** Staffs
46 C5 **Halmond's Frome** Herefs
32 D4 **Halmore** Gloucs
15 P5 **Halnaker** W Susx
88 D8 **Halsall** Lancs
48 G6 **Halse** Nhants
18 F9 **Halse** Somset
2 E6 **Halsetown** Cnwll
93 N5 **Halsham** E R Yk
17 J4 **Halsinger** Devon
52 D5 **Halstead** Essex
37 L8 **Halstead** Kent
73 K9 **Halstead** Leics
11 L3 **Halstock** Dorset
18 F7 **Halsway** Somset
101 L3 **Haltcliff Bridge** Cumb
92 H4 **Haltemprice Crematorium** E R Yk
86 H8 **Haltham** Lincs
87 L11 **Haltoft End** Lincs
35 N3 **Halton** Bucks
82 B8 **Halton** Halton
95 L8 **Halton** Lancs
91 K4 **Halton** Leeds
112 E7 **Halton** Nthumb
69 K7 **Halton** Wrexhm
96 F10 **Halton East** N York
87 M8 **Halton Fenside** Lincs
96 C5 **Halton Gill** N York
95 L7 **Halton Green** Lancs
87 M7 **Halton Holegate** Lincs
111 M9 **Halton Lea Gate** Nthumb
5 Q8 **Halton Quay** Cnwll
112 F7 **Halton Shields** Nthumb
96 B10 **Halton West** N York
111 P8 **Haltwhistle** Nthumb
77 N10 **Halvergate** Norfk
7 K8 **Halwell** Devon
8 B5 **Halwill** Devon
8 B4 **Halwill Junction** Devon
10 E4 **Ham** Devon
32 C5 **Ham** Gloucs
47 J10 **Ham** Gloucs
36 E6 **Ham** Gt Lon
39 P11 **Ham** Kent
19 J9 **Ham** Somset
20 C5 **Ham** Somset
22 B2 **Ham** Wilts
35 L7 **Hambleden** Bucks
14 H4 **Hambledon** Hants
23 Q7 **Hambledon** Surrey
14 E5 **Hamble-le-Rice** Hants
88 D2 **Hambleton** Lancs
91 P4 **Hambleton** N York
88 D2 **Hambleton Moss Side** Lancs
19 L10 **Hambridge** Somset
32 B9 **Hambrook** S Glos
15 L5 **Hambrook** W Susx
20 F9 **Ham Common** Dorset
87 K7 **Hameringham** Lincs
61 P5 **Hamerton** Cambs
46 E6 **Ham Green** Herefs
26 E6 **Ham Green** Kent
38 D8 **Ham Green** Kent
31 P9 **Ham Green** N Som
47 K2 **Ham Green** Worcs
37 Q8 **Ham Hill** Kent
126 C6 **Hamilton** S Lans
126 C6 **Hamilton Services** S Lans
11 M3 **Hamlet** Dorset
25 N9 **Hamlins** E Susx
24 C9 **Hammerpot** W Susx
36 F5 **Hammersmith** Gt Lon
58 G3 **Hammerwich** Staffs
25 K3 **Hammerwood** E Susx
50 H10 **Hammond Street** Herts
12 D2 **Hammoon** Dorset
169 q10 **Hamnavoe** Shet
25 P10 **Hampden Park** E Susx
51 N4 **Hamperden End** Essex
47 L11 **Hampnett** Gloucs
91 N8 **Hampole** Donc
13 J5 **Hampreston** Dorset
95 J4 **Hampsfield** Cumb
95 K10 **Hampson Green** Lancs
36 G3 **Hampstead** Gt Lon
34 F9 **Hampstead Norreys** W Berk
97 L9 **Hampsthwaite** N York
61 Q2 **Hampton** C Pete
10 F5 **Hampton** Devon
36 D7 **Hampton** Gt Lon
39 L8 **Hampton** Kent
57 N7 **Hampton** Shrops
33 N6 **Hampton** Swindn
47 K6 **Hampton** Worcs
45 R7 **Hampton Bishop** Herefs
36 E7 **Hampton Court Palace & Gardens** Gt Lon
32 G5 **Hampton Fields** Gloucs
69 P5 **Hampton Green** Ches W
69 P5 **Hampton Heath** Ches W
59 K8 **Hampton in Arden** Solhll
57 N7 **Hampton Loade** Shrops
58 C11 **Hampton Lovett** Worcs
47 Q3 **Hampton Lucy** Warwks
59 L11 **Hampton Magna** Warwks
47 Q2 **Hampton on the Hill** Warwks
48 F11 **Hampton Poyle** Oxon
36 E7 **Hampton Wick** Gt Lon
21 P11 **Hamptworth** Wilts
76 C7 **Hamrow** Norfk
25 K8 **Hamsey** E Susx
37 J9 **Hamsey Green** Surrey
71 L11 **Hamstall Ridware** Staffs
58 G6 **Hamstead** Birm
14 D8 **Hamstead** IoW
34 D11 **Hamstead Marshall** W Berk
103 M4 **Hamsterley** Dur
112 H9 **Hamsterley** Dur
26 H5 **Hamstreet** Kent
19 Q8 **Ham Street** Somset
19 L3 **Hamwood** N Som
12 G6 **Hamworthy** Poole
71 M9 **Hanbury** Staffs
47 J2 **Hanbury** Worcs
73 Q4 **Hanby** Lincs
63 K11 **Hanchet End** Suffk
70 E6 **Hanchurch** Staffs
164 D7 **Handa Island** Highld
105 K7 **Handale** R & Cl
9 P5 **Hand and Pen** Devon
81 N11 **Handbridge** Ches W
24 G5 **Handcross** W Susx
83 J8 **Handforth** Ches E
69 P2 **Hand Green** Ches W
69 N3 **Handley** Ches W
84 E8 **Handley** Derbys
51 Q10 **Handley Green** Essex
71 K11 **Handsacre** Staffs
58 F7 **Handsworth** Birm
84 F3 **Handsworth** Sheff
35 N6 **Handy Cross** Bucks
70 F6 **Hanford** C Stke
12 D2 **Hanford** Dorset
90 H6 **Hanging Heaton** Kirk
60 G6 **Hanging Houghton** Nhants
21 K7 **Hanging Langford** Wilts
24 G9 **Hangleton** Br & H
24 C10 **Hangleton** W Susx
32 B10 **Hanham** S Glos
70 B5 **Hankelow** Ches E
33 J6 **Hankerton** Wilts
25 P9 **Hankham** E Susx
70 F5 **Hanley** C Stke
46 F6 **Hanley Castle** Worcs
57 M11 **Hanley Child** Worcs
46 F6 **Hanley Swan** Worcs
57 M11 **Hanley William** Worcs
96 C8 **Hanlith** N York
69 N7 **Hanmer** Wrexhm
17 L6 **Hannaford** Devon
87 N5 **Hannah** Lincs
22 F3 **Hannington** Hants
60 H6 **Hannington** Nhants
33 N6 **Hannington** Swindn
33 N5 **Hannington Wick** Swindn
50 D4 **Hanscombe End** C Beds
49 M5 **Hanslope** M Keyn
74 A6 **Hanthorpe** Lincs
36 E5 **Hanwell** Gt Lon
48 D6 **Hanwell** Oxon
56 G3 **Hanwood** Shrops
36 D6 **Hanworth** Gt Lon
76 H4 **Hanworth** Norfk
116 B4 **Happendon** S Lans
77 M5 **Happisburgh** Norfk
77 M6 **Happisburgh Common** Norfk
81 P10 **Hapsford** Ches W
89 M4 **Hapton** Lancs
64 H2 **Hapton** Norfk
7 K7 **Harberton** Devon
7 K7 **Harbertonford** Devon
39 K10 **Harbledown** Kent
58 F8 **Harborne** Birm
59 Q9 **Harborough Magna** Warwks
118 H10 **Harbottle** Nthumb
7 J6 **Harbourneford** Devon
58 E11 **Harbours Hill** Worcs
13 K2 **Harbridge** Hants
13 K2 **Harbridge Green** Hants
48 C3 **Harbury** Warwks
73 J4 **Harby** Leics
85 Q6 **Harby** Notts
9 L8 **Harcombe** Devon
10 D6 **Harcombe** Devon
10 G5 **Harcombe Bottom** Devon
90 D3 **Harden** C Brad
58 F4 **Harden** Wsall
32 H10 **Hardenhuish** Wilts
151 K7 **Hardgate** Abers
108 H7 **Hardgate** D & G
97 L8 **Hardgate** N York
125 N3 **Hardgate** W Duns
24 B7 **Hardham** W Susx
88 D3 **Hardhorn** Lancs
76 E11 **Hardingham** Norfk
60 G9 **Hardingstone** Nhants
20 D4 **Hardington** Somset
11 L2 **Hardington Mandeville** Somset
11 L3 **Hardington Marsh** Somset
11 L2 **Hardington Moor** Somset
16 C7 **Hardisworthy** Devon
14 D5 **Hardley** Hants
77 M11 **Hardley Street** Norfk
49 P5 **Hardmead** M Keyn
96 C2 **Hardraw** N York
89 M6 **Hardsough** Lancs
84 F8 **Hardstoft** Derbys
14 H6 **Hardway** Hants
20 D8 **Hardway** Somset
49 M11 **Hardwick** Bucks
62 E9 **Hardwick** Cambs
60 H7 **Hardwick** Nhants
65 J4 **Hardwick** Norfk
34 C3 **Hardwick** Oxon
48 G9 **Hardwick** Oxon
84 G3 **Hardwick** Rothm
58 G5 **Hardwick** Wsall
32 E2 **Hardwicke** Gloucs
46 H9 **Hardwicke** Gloucs
52 F7 **Hardy's Green** Essex
25 N8 **Harebeating** E Susx
87 K7 **Hareby** Lincs
90 D3 **Hare Croft** C Brad
36 C2 **Harefield** Gt Lon
53 K6 **Hare Green** Essex
35 M9 **Hare Hatch** Wokham
71 M7 **Harehill** Derbys
91 J4 **Harehills** Leeds
119 L6 **Harehope** Nthumb
117 Q6 **Harelaw** Border
110 H5 **Harelaw** D & G
113 J10 **Harelaw** Dur
26 D4 **Hareplain** Kent
102 B2 **Haresceugh** Cumb
32 F2 **Harescombe** Gloucs
32 F2 **Haresfield** Gloucs
22 E8 **Harestock** Hants
51 K9 **Hare Street** Essex
51 M10 **Hare Street** Essex
51 J5 **Hare Street** Herts
97 M11 **Harewood** Leeds
45 Q9 **Harewood End** Herefs
6 G7 **Harford** Devon
64 G3 **Hargate** Norfk
83 P9 **Hargatewall** Derbys
69 N2 **Hargrave** Ches W
61 M6 **Hargrave** Nhants
63 N9 **Hargrave** Suffk
110 G8 **Harker** Cumb
53 L5 **Harkstead** Suffk
59 K2 **Harlaston** Staffs
73 M4 **Harlaxton** Lincs
67 K8 **Harlech** Gwynd
69 N11 **Harlescott** Shrops
36 F4 **Harlesden** Gt Lon
84 G5 **Harlesthorpe** Derbys
7 K9 **Harleston** Devon
65 J5 **Harleston** Norfk
64 E9 **Harleston** Suffk
60 F8 **Harlestone** Nhants
89 P3 **Harle Syke** Lancs
91 K11 **Harley** Rothm
57 K4 **Harley** Shrops
50 B4 **Harlington** C Beds
91 M10 **Harlington** Donc
36 C5 **Harlington** Gt Lon
152 D9 **Harlosh** Highld
51 K8 **Harlow** Essex
112 G7 **Harlow Hill** Nthumb
92 B3 **Harlthorpe** E R Yk
62 E10 **Harlton** Cambs
4 D6 **Harlyn** Cnwll
12 G8 **Harman's Cross** Dorset
96 H3 **Harmby** N York
50 G7 **Harmer Green** Herts
69 N10 **Harmer Hill** Shrops
36 C5 **Harmondsworth** Gt Lon
86 C8 **Harmston** Lincs
57 K4 **Harnage** Shrops
112 G4 **Harnham** Nthumb
33 L4 **Harnhill** Gloucs
37 M2 **Harold Hill** Gt Lon
40 G7 **Haroldston West** Pembks
169 t2 **Haroldswick** Shet
37 N2 **Harold Wood** Gt Lon
98 C4 **Harome** N York
50 D8 **Harpenden** Herts
10 B6 **Harpford** Devon
99 M8 **Harpham** E R Yk
75 Q5 **Harpley** Norfk
46 C2 **Harpley** Worcs
60 E8 **Harpole** Nhants
167 K5 **Harpsdale** Highld
35 L8 **Harpsden** Oxon
86 B3 **Harpswell** Lincs
83 J4 **Harpurhey** Manch
83 N10 **Harpur Hill** Derbys
110 H10 **Harraby** Cumb
17 K6 **Harracott** Devon
145 L3 **Harrapool** Highld
134 B2 **Harrietfield** P & K
38 E11 **Harrietsham** Kent
36 H3 **Harringay** Gt Lon
100 C5 **Harrington** Cumb
87 L6 **Harrington** Lincs
60 G4 **Harrington** Nhants
73 N11 **Harringworth** Nhants
168 f8 **Harris** W Isls
70 F3 **Harriseahead** Staffs
100 G2 **Harriston** Cumb
97 M10 **Harrogate** N York
97 M10 **Harrogate Crematorium** N York
61 K9 **Harrold** Bed
90 C9 **Harrop Dale** Oldham
36 E3 **Harrow** Gt Lon
5 Q7 **Harrowbarrow** Cnwll
61 N11 **Harrowden** Bed
103 Q7 **Harrowgate Village** Darltn
64 B11 **Harrow Green** Suffk
36 E3 **Harrow on the Hill** Gt Lon
36 E2 **Harrow Weald** Gt Lon
62 F10 **Harston** Cambs
73 L4 **Harston** Leics
92 D2 **Harswell** E R Yk
104 E4 **Hart** Hartpl
112 G3 **Hartburn** Nthumb
64 A11 **Hartest** Suffk
25 L3 **Hartfield** E Susx
62 C6 **Hartford** Cambs
82 D10 **Hartford** Ches W
18 C9 **Hartford** Somset
23 L3 **Hartfordbridge** Hants
51 Q7 **Hartford End** Essex
103 N9 **Hartforth** N York
20 F11 **Hartgrove** Dorset
69 N3 **Harthill** Ches W
126 G5 **Harthill** N Lans
84 G4 **Harthill** Rothm
71 L2 **Hartington** Derbys
112 F3 **Hartington** Nthumb
16 D7 **Hartland** Devon
16 C7 **Hartland Quay** Devon
58 B10 **Hartlebury** Worcs
104 F4 **Hartlepool** Hartpl
104 F4 **Hartlepool Crematorium** Hartpl
102 E9 **Hartley** Cumb
26 C5 **Hartley** Kent
37 P7 **Hartley** Kent
113 M5 **Hartley** Nthumb
37 P7 **Hartley Green** Kent
70 H9 **Hartley Green** Staffs
23 J3 **Hartley Wespall** Hants
23 L3 **Hartley Wintney** Hants
38 D9 **Hartlip** Kent
98 E2 **Hartoft End** N York
98 E8 **Harton** N York
113 N7 **Harton** S Tyne
56 H7 **Harton** Shrops
46 E10 **Hartpury** Gloucs
90 F6 **Hartshead** Kirk
90 F6 **Hartshead Moor Services** Calder
70 F5 **Hartshill** C Stke
59 M6 **Hartshill** Warwks
71 Q10 **Hartshorne** Derbys
119 J7 **Hartside** Nthumb
101 M8 **Hartsop** Cumb
104 E3 **Hart Station** Hartpl
18 E9 **Hartswell** Somset
49 L4 **Hartwell** Nhants
97 K8 **Hartwith** N York
126 E6 **Hartwood** N Lans
117 N6 **Hartwoodmyres** Border
37 Q8 **Harvel** Kent
47 L5 **Harvington** Worcs
58 C10 **Harvington** Worcs
85 L2 **Harwell** Notts
34 E7 **Harwell** Oxon
53 N5 **Harwich** Essex
89 L8 **Harwood** Bolton
102 F4 **Harwood** Dur
105 Q11 **Harwood Dale** N York
89 L8 **Harwood Lee** Bolton
50 G6 **Harwood Park Crematorium** Herts
85 K2 **Harworth** Notts
58 E8 **Hasbury** Dudley
24 B3 **Hascombe** Surrey
60 F5 **Haselbech** Nhants
11 K2 **Haselbury Plucknett** Somset
59 K11 **Haseley** Warwks
59 K11 **Haseley Green** Warwks
59 K10 **Haseley Knob** Warwks
47 M3 **Haselor** Warwks
46 F9 **Hasfield** Gloucs
40 G9 **Hasguard** Pembks
88 D9 **Haskayne** Lancs
65 J11 **Hasketon** Suffk
84 E7 **Hasland** Derbys
23 P8 **Haslemere** Surrey
89 M6 **Haslingden** Lancs
62 F10 **Haslingfield** Cambs
70 C3 **Haslington** Ches E
70 D3 **Hassall** Ches E
70 D3 **Hassall Green** Ches E
27 J2 **Hassell Street** Kent
77 M10 **Hassingham** Norfk
100 G7 **Hassness** Cumb
24 H7 **Hassocks** W Susx
84 B6 **Hassop** Derbys
23 P8 **Haste Hill** Surrey
167 P6 **Haster** Highld
87 N7 **Hasthorpe** Lincs
27 J2 **Hastingleigh** Kent
26 D10 **Hastings** E Susx
19 K11 **Hastings** Somset
26 D9 **Hastings Borough Crematorium** E Susx
51 L9 **Hastingwood** Essex
35 P3 **Hastoe** Herts
104 C2 **Haswell** Dur
104 C2 **Haswell Plough** Dur
61 Q11 **Hatch** C Beds

19 K10 **Hatch Beauchamp** Somset
61 N8 **Hatch End** Bed
36 D2 **Hatch End** Gt Lon
14 C6 **Hatchet Gate** Hants
50 D8 **Hatching Green** Herts
82 C10 **Hatchmere** Ches W
93 M10 **Hatcliffe** NE Lin
91 R9 **Hatfield** Donc
46 A3 **Hatfield** Herefs
50 F9 **Hatfield** Herts
46 G4 **Hatfield** Worcs
51 M7 **Hatfield Broad Oak** Essex
51 M7 **Hatfield Heath** Essex
52 C9 **Hatfield Peverel** Essex
92 A9 **Hatfield Woodhouse** Donc
34 B6 **Hatford** Oxon
22 B4 **Hatherden** Hants
8 D4 **Hatherleigh** Devon
72 E6 **Hathern** Leics
33 N3 **Hatherop** Gloucs
84 B4 **Hathersage** Derbys
84 B4 **Hathersage Booths** Derbys
70 B5 **Hatherton** Ches E
58 E2 **Hatherton** Staffs
62 C10 **Hatley St George** Cambs
5 Q9 **Hatt** Cnwll
83 L6 **Hattersley** Tamesd
22 H7 **Hattingley** Hants
159 Q10 **Hatton** Abers
142 H9 **Hatton** Angus
71 N8 **Hatton** Derbys
36 C5 **Hatton** Gt Lon
86 G5 **Hatton** Lincs
56 H6 **Hatton** Shrops
82 C8 **Hatton** Warrtn
59 K11 **Hatton** Warwks
69 N2 **Hatton Heath** Ches W
151 L4 **Hatton of Fintray** Abers
115 J2 **Haugh** E Ayrs
87 M5 **Haugh** Lincs
89 Q8 **Haugh** Rochdl
87 K4 **Haugham** Lincs
125 Q2 **Haughhead** E Duns
119 K5 **Haugh Head** Nthumb
64 E9 **Haughley** Suffk
64 E9 **Haughley Green** Suffk
158 B10 **Haugh of Glass** Moray
108 H7 **Haugh of Urr** D & G
143 L6 **Haughs of Kinnaird** Angus
85 L6 **Haughton** Notts
69 K11 **Haughton** Powys
57 M5 **Haughton** Shrops
57 N3 **Haughton** Shrops
69 L9 **Haughton** Shrops
69 Q11 **Haughton** Shrops
70 F10 **Haughton** Staffs
83 K6 **Haughton Green** Tamesd
104 B7 **Haughton le Skerne** Darltn
69 Q3 **Haughton Moss** Ches E
50 H6 **Haultwick** Herts
59 K2 **Haunton** Staffs
11 b1 **Hautes Croix** Jersey
62 F10 **Hauxton** Cambs
70 F2 **Havannah** Ches E
15 K5 **Havant** Hants
45 N4 **Haven** Herefs
86 H10 **Haven Bank** Lincs
93 L5 **Haven Side** E R Yk
14 G8 **Havenstreet** IoW
91 K8 **Havercroft** Wakefd
41 J7 **Haverfordwest** Pembks
63 L11 **Haverhill** Suffk
94 D5 **Haverigg** Cumb
37 M2 **Havering-atte-Bower** Gt Lon
49 M6 **Haversham** M Keyn
94 G4 **Haverthwaite** Cumb
104 E6 **Haverton Hill** S on T
19 N2 **Havyat** N Som
19 P7 **Havyatt** Somset
81 L11 **Hawarden** Flints
46 H5 **Hawbridge** Worcs
52 C7 **Hawbush Green** Essex
94 E6 **Hawcoat** Cumb
42 F5 **Hawen** Cerdgn
96 C3 **Hawes** N York
65 J2 **Hawe's Green** Norfk
46 F2 **Hawford** Worcs
117 Q8 **Hawick** Border
10 G4 **Hawkchurch** Devon
63 N10 **Hawkedon** Suffk
26 D2 **Hawkenbury** Kent
20 G4 **Hawkeridge** Wilts
9 Q7 **Hawkerland** Devon
32 E7 **Hawkesbury** S Glos
59 N8 **Hawkesbury** Warwks
32 E7 **Hawkesbury Upton** S Glos
59 L8 **Hawkes End** Covtry
83 L7 **Hawk Green** Stockp
119 P8 **Hawkhill** Nthumb
26 C5 **Hawkhurst** Kent
25 M7 **Hawkhurst Common** E Susx
27 M4 **Hawkinge** Kent
27 M3 **Hawkinge Crematorium** Kent
23 K9 **Hawkley** Hants
82 C4 **Hawkley** Wigan
17 R5 **Hawkridge** Somset
110 G11 **Hawksdale** Cumb
89 M7 **Hawkshaw** Bury
101 L11 **Hawkshead** Cumb
101 K11 **Hawkshead Hill** Cumb
116 A3 **Hawksland** S Lans
51 Q4 **Hawkspur Green** Essex
69 Q8 **Hawkstone** Shrops
96 E6 **Hawkswick** N York
90 F2 **Hawksworth** Leeds
73 K2 **Hawksworth** Notts
38 E3 **Hawkwell** Essex
112 G6 **Hawkwell** Nthumb
23 N3 **Hawley** Hants
37 M6 **Hawley** Kent
47 L10 **Hawling** Gloucs
98 A3 **Hawnby** N York
90 C3 **Haworth** C Brad
35 P3 **Hawridge** Bucks
64 B10 **Hawstead** Suffk
64 B10 **Hawstead Green** Suffk
113 P11 **Hawthorn** Dur
23 J8 **Hawthorn** Hants
30 E7 **Hawthorn** Rhondd
35 N10 **Hawthorn Hill** Br For
86 H1 **Hawthorn Hill** Lincs

73 Q5 **Hawthorpe** Lincs
85 N10 **Hawton** Notts
98 C9 **Haxby** C York
98 C9 **Haxby Gates** C York
92 C11 **Haxey** N Linc
92 C10 **Haxey Carr** N Linc
37 K11 **Haxted** Surrey
21 M5 **Haxton** Wilts
3 P3 **Hay** Cnwll
4 F7 **Hay** Cnwll
20 D2 **Haycombe Crematorium** BaNES
82 C5 **Haydock** St Hel
20 C4 **Haydon** BaNES
20 C11 **Haydon** Dorset
19 J10 **Haydon** Somset
112 B8 **Haydon Bridge** Nthumb
33 M7 **Haydon Wick** Swindn
5 P7 **Haye** Cnwll
36 C4 **Hayes** Gt Lon
37 K7 **Hayes** Gt Lon
36 C4 **Hayes End** Gt Lon
131 M3 **Hayfield** Ag & B
83 M7 **Hayfield** Derbys
57 L2 **Haygate** Wrekin
75 K7 **Hay Green** Norfk
2 F6 **Hayle** Cnwll
58 E8 **Hayley Green** Dudley
15 K6 **Hayling Island** Hants
70 B4 **Haymoor Green** Ches E
9 J7 **Hayne** Devon
18 C11 **Hayne** Devon
50 C2 **Haynes (Church End)** C Beds
50 C2 **Haynes (Northwood End)** C Beds
50 D2 **Haynes (Silver End)** C Beds
50 C2 **Haynes (West End)** C Beds
45 J6 **Hay-on-Wye** Powys
40 G5 **Hayscastle** Pembks
40 H5 **Hayscastle Cross** Pembks
37 N11 **Haysden** Kent
51 J5 **Hay Street** Herts
100 F2 **Hayton** Cumb
111 K9 **Hayton** Cumb
98 C11 **Hayton** E R Yk
85 M4 **Hayton** Notts
57 J8 **Hayton's Bent** Shrops
9 J9 **Haytor Vale** Devon
16 F9 **Haytown** Devon
24 H6 **Haywards Heath** W Susx
91 P8 **Haywood** Donc
45 P8 **Haywood** Herefs
85 K9 **Haywood Oaks** Notts
25 Q8 **Hazards Green** E Susx
12 B3 **Hazelbank** S Lans
12 B3 **Hazelbury Bryan** Dorset
52 D11 **Hazeleigh** Essex
23 K3 **Hazeley** Hants
85 M11 **Hazelford** Notts
83 K7 **Hazel Grove** Stockp
83 L4 **Hazelhurst** Tamesd
58 F2 **Hazelslade** Staffs
25 Q3 **Hazel Street** Kent
51 Q2 **Hazel Stub** Suffk
135 J3 **Hazelton Walls** Fife
84 D11 **Hazelwood** Derbys
35 N5 **Hazlemere** Bucks
113 K6 **Hazlerigg** N u Ty
71 J5 **Hazles** Staffs
47 L11 **Hazleton** Gloucs
75 N3 **Heacham** Norfk
22 E8 **Headbourne Worthy** Hants
45 K3 **Headbrook** Herefs
26 D3 **Headcorn** Kent
90 H3 **Headingley** Leeds
34 F3 **Headington** Oxon
103 N7 **Headlam** Dur
126 G6 **Headlesscross** N Lans
58 F11 **Headless Cross** Worcs
22 F2 **Headley** Hants
23 M7 **Headley** Hants
36 F10 **Headley** Surrey
23 M7 **Headley Down** Hants
58 G9 **Headley Heath** Worcs
16 F11 **Headon** Devon
85 M5 **Headon** Notts
111 K10 **Heads Nook** Cumb
84 E10 **Heage** Derbys
97 R11 **Healaugh** N York
103 K11 **Healaugh** N York
82 H7 **Heald Green** Stockp
17 L2 **Heale** Devon
18 H10 **Heale** Somset
19 L9 **Heale** Somset
97 J4 **Healey** N York
112 F9 **Healey** Nthumb
89 P7 **Healey** Rochdl
90 H7 **Healey** Wakefd
112 G11 **Healeyfield** Dur
93 M8 **Healing** NE Lin
2 D7 **Heamoor** Cnwll
84 F11 **Heanor** Derbys
17 J4 **Heanton Punchardon** Devon
85 Q3 **Heapham** Lincs
23 M7 **Hearn** Hants
59 N6 **Heart of England Crematorium** Warwks
126 G5 **Heart of Scotland Services** N Lans
38 E9 **Hearts Delight** Kent
17 N5 **Heasley Mill** Devon
145 K4 **Heast** Highld
84 G7 **Heath** Derbys
91 K6 **Heath** Wakefd
49 P9 **Heath and Reach** C Beds
24 C7 **Heath Common** W Susx
71 L2 **Heathcote** Derbys
70 B9 **Heathcote** Shrops
35 N5 **Heath End** Bucks
22 D2 **Heath End** Hants
72 B6 **Heath End** Leics
47 P2 **Heath End** Warwks
72 B8 **Heather** Leics
6 K9 **Heathfield** Devon
25 N6 **Heathfield** E Susx
96 H7 **Heathfield** N York
18 G9 **Heathfield** Somset
48 F11 **Heathfield Village** Oxon
58 G10 **Heath Green** Worcs
109 L5 **Heath Hall** D & G
58 F2 **Heath Hayes & Wimblebury** Staffs
57 P2 **Heath Hill** Shrops
19 M5 **Heath House** Somset

36 C5 *Heathrow Airport* Gt Lon
10 E4 **Heathstock** Devon
57 Q6 **Heathton** Shrops
58 D5 **Heath Town** Wolves
104 E10 **Heathwaite** N York
71 K9 **Heatley** Staffs
82 F7 **Heatley** Warrtn
89 K9 **Heaton** Bolton
90 E3 **Heaton** C Brad
95 J8 **Heaton** Lancs
113 L7 **Heaton** N u Ty
70 H2 **Heaton** Staffs
83 J6 **Heaton Chapel** Stockp
83 J6 **Heaton Mersey** Stockp
83 J6 **Heaton Norris** Stockp
88 E8 **Heaton's Bridge** Lancs
37 N9 **Heaverham** Kent
83 K7 **Heaviley** Stockp
9 M6 **Heavitree** Devon
113 M8 **Hebburn** S Tyne
96 F8 **Hebden** N York
90 B5 **Hebden Bridge** Calder
82 D11 **Hebden Green** Ches W
50 H6 **Hebing End** Herts
41 N5 **Hebron** Carmth
78 H8 **Hebron** IoA
113 J3 **Hebron** Nthumb
23 K2 **Heckfield** Hants
64 H6 **Heckfield Green** Suffk
52 F7 **Heckfordbridge** Essex
74 B2 **Heckington** Lincs
90 G6 **Heckmondwike** Kirk
33 J11 **Heddington** Wilts
112 H7 **Heddon-on-the-Wall** Nthumb
65 L3 **Hedenham** Norfk
14 E4 **Hedge End** Hants
35 Q7 **Hedgerley** Bucks
35 Q7 **Hedgerley Green** Bucks
19 K9 **Hedging** Somset
112 G9 **Hedley on the Hill** Nthumb
58 E2 **Hednesford** Staffs
93 L5 **Hedon** E R Yk
35 P7 **Hedsor** Bucks
46 A4 **Hegdon Hill** Herefs
169 Q8 **Heglibister** Shet
103 P6 **Heighington** Darltn
86 D7 **Heighington** Lincs
57 P10 **Heightington** Worcs
118 D4 **Heiton** Border
7 J4 **Hele** Devon
9 N4 **Hele** Devon
17 J2 **Hele** Devon
18 G10 **Hele** Somset
16 C11 **Helebridge** Cnwll
9 J2 **Hele Lane** Devon
132 B11 **Helensburgh** Ag & B
125 K11 **Helenton** S Ayrs
3 K8 **Helford** Cnwll
3 K8 **Helford Passage** Cnwll
76 B6 **Helhoughton** Norfk
51 Q2 **Helions Bumpstead** Essex
84 H7 **Hellaby** Rothm
4 H7 **Helland** Cnwll
4 H7 **Hellandbridge** Cnwll
22 C2 **Hell Corner** W Berk
5 M4 **Hellescott** Cnwll
77 J9 **Hellesdon** Norfk
2 E5 **Hellesveor** Cnwll
60 B9 **Hellidon** Nhants
96 C9 **Hellifield** N York
25 N8 **Hellingly** E Susx
77 L11 **Hellington** Norfk
119 N11 **Helm** Nthumb
48 G6 **Helmdon** Nhants
90 D8 **Helme** Kirk
64 H10 **Helmingham** Suffk
103 N3 **Helmington Row** Dur
163 N3 **Helmsdale** Highld
89 M6 **Helmshore** Lancs
98 C4 **Helmsley** N York
97 P7 **Helperby** N York
99 K6 **Helperthorpe** N York
74 B2 **Helpringham** Lincs
74 B9 **Helpston** C Pete
81 P9 **Helsby** Ches W
87 P6 **Helsey** Lincs
2 H8 **Helston** Cnwll
4 H5 **Helstone** Cnwll
101 P6 **Helton** Cumb
103 L10 **Helwith** N York
96 B7 **Helwith Bridge** N York
77 L9 **Hemblington** Norfk
19 Q7 **Hembridge** Somset
50 C2 **Hemel Hempstead** Herts
6 F7 **Hemerdon** Devon
91 R4 **Hemingbrough** N York
86 H6 **Hemingby** Lincs
91 K10 **Hemingfield** Barns
62 C6 **Hemingford Abbots** Cambs
62 C6 **Hemingford Grey** Cambs
64 G11 **Hemingstone** Suffk
72 D5 **Hemington** Leics
61 N3 **Hemington** Nhants
20 D4 **Hemington** Somset
53 N3 **Hemley** Suffk
104 F8 **Hemlington** Middsb
99 M10 **Hempholme** E R Yk
65 J3 **Hempnall** Norfk
65 J3 **Hempnall Green** Norfk
157 L5 **Hempriggs** Moray
51 P3 **Hempstead** Essex
38 C9 **Hempstead** Medway
76 G4 **Hempstead** Norfk
77 N6 **Hempstead** Norfk
46 F11 **Hempsted** Gloucs
76 C6 **Hempton** Norfk
48 D8 **Hempton** Oxon
77 N6 **Hemsby** Norfk
86 B2 **Hemswell** Lincs
86 B3 **Hemswell Cliff** Lincs
91 L8 **Hemsworth** Wakefd
10 C2 **Hemyock** Devon
31 Q9 **Henbury** Bristl
83 J10 **Henbury** Ches E
7 J8 **Hendham** Devon
56 C5 **Hendomen** Powys
36 F3 **Hendon** Gt Lon
113 P9 **Hendon** Sundld
36 F2 **Hendon Crematorium** Gt Lon
3 J6 **Hendra** Cnwll
4 G6 **Hendra** Cnwll
29 P8 **Hendre** Brdgnd
80 H11 **Hendre** Flints
31 N2 **Hendre** Mons
3 P4 **Hendy** Carmth
28 G4 **Hendy** Carmth

78 G9 **Heneglwys** IoA
24 F7 **Henfield** W Susx
9 P3 **Henford** Devon
26 G4 **Henghurst** Kent
30 G6 **Hengoed** Caerph
45 J4 **Hengoed** Powys
69 J8 **Hengoed** Shrops
63 P7 **Hengrave** Suffk
51 M5 **Henham** Essex
55 Q3 **Heniarth** Powys
19 J10 **Henlade** Somset
11 P4 **Henley** Dorset
46 H11 **Henley** Gloucs
56 H7 **Henley** Shrops
57 J9 **Henley** Shrops
19 M8 **Henley** Somset
64 H11 **Henley** Suffk
23 N9 **Henley** W Susx
59 N8 **Henley Green** Covtry
59 J11 **Henley-in-Arden** Warwks
35 L8 **Henley-on-Thames** Oxon
23 P4 **Henley Park** Surrey
26 B9 **Henley's Down** E Susx
37 Q7 **Henley Street** Kent
42 G6 **Henllan** Cerdgn
80 E11 **Henllan** Denbgs
41 N7 **Henllan Amgoed** Carmth
31 J6 **Henllys** Torfn
50 E3 **Henlow** C Beds
9 K8 **Hennock** Devon
52 E4 **Henny Street** Essex
79 P10 **Henryd** Conwy
41 K5 **Henry's Moat (Castell Hendre)** Pembks
91 P6 **Hensall** N York
111 J8 **Henshaw** Nthumb
100 C7 **Hensingham** Cumb
65 P4 **Henstead** Suffk
22 E10 **Hensting** Hants
20 D11 **Henstridge** Somset
20 D10 **Henstridge Ash** Somset
20 D10 **Henstridge Marsh** Somset
35 L4 **Henton** Oxon
19 N5 **Henton** Somset
46 F3 **Henwick** Worcs
5 M7 **Henwood** Cnwll
34 K4 **Henwood** Oxon
29 J5 **Heol-las** Swans
44 C10 **Heol Senni** Powys
29 P8 **Heol-y-Cyw** Brdgnd
119 L6 **Hepburn** Nthumb
119 J10 **Hepple** Nthumb
113 K4 **Hepscott** Nthumb
90 B5 **Heptonstall** Calder
90 F9 **Hepworth** Kirk
64 D7 **Hepworth** Suffk
40 G9 **Herbrandston** Pembks
45 Q7 **Hereford** Herefs
45 P6 **Hereford Crematorium** Herefs
39 Q8 **Hereson** Kent
152 F3 **Heribusta** Highld
128 C9 **Heriot** Border
127 M3 **Hermiston** C Edin
117 Q11 **Hermitage** Border
11 P3 **Hermitage** Dorset
34 F10 **Hermitage** W Berk
15 L5 **Hermitage** W Susx
91 J10 **Hermit Hill** Barns
42 G8 **Hermon** Carmth
78 F11 **Hermon** IoA
41 P4 **Hermon** Pembks
39 L8 **Herne** Kent
39 L8 **Herne Bay** Kent
39 L8 **Herne Common** Kent
36 H6 **Herne Hill** Gt Lon
37 Q10 **Herne Pound** Kent
17 K6 **Herner** Devon
39 J9 **Hernhill** Kent
5 L9 **Herodsfoot** Cnwll
39 N11 **Heronden** Kent
37 P2 **Herongate** Essex
114 B11 **Heronsford** S Ayrs
36 B2 **Heronsgate** Herts
23 J5 **Herriard** Hants
65 P2 **Herringfleet** Suffk
50 C2 **Herring's Green** Bed
63 M6 **Herringswell** Suffk
84 F2 **Herringthorpe** Rothm
113 N10 **Herrington** Sundld
39 M9 **Hersden** Kent
16 D10 **Hersham** Cnwll
36 D8 **Hersham** Surrey
25 P8 **Herstmonceux** E Susx
12 H9 **Herston** Dorset
169 d7 **Herston** Ork
50 H8 **Hertford** Herts
51 J8 **Hertford Heath** Herts
50 H8 **Hertingfordbury** Herts
88 E6 **Hesket Bank** Lancs
89 J2 **Hesketh Lane** Lancs
101 K3 **Hesket Newmarket** Cumb
88 G7 **Heskin Green** Lancs
104 D3 **Hesleden** Dur
96 C6 **Hesleden** N York
85 K2 **Hesley** Donc
112 B4 **Hesleyside** Nthumb
98 C10 **Heslington** C York
97 R10 **Hessay** C York
5 N10 **Hessenford** Cnwll
64 C9 **Hessett** Suffk
92 H5 **Hessle** E R Yk
91 L7 **Hessle** Wakefd
95 K7 **Hest Bank** Lancs
64 H8 **Hestley Green** Suffk
36 D5 **Heston** Gt Lon
36 D5 *Heston Services* Gt Lon
169 b5 **Hestwall** Ork
81 K8 **Heswall** Wirral
48 G4 **Hethe** Oxon
76 G11 **Hethersett** Norfk
111 J7 **Hethersgill** Cumb
110 H7 **Hetherside** Cumb
69 P4 **Hetherson Green** Ches W
118 G5 **Hethpool** Nthumb
103 Q3 **Hett** Dur
96 E9 **Hetton** N York
113 N11 **Hetton-le-Hole** Sundld
119 K3 **Hetton Steads** Nthumb
112 G6 **Heugh** Nthumb
150 B5 **Heughhead** Abers
129 M7 **Heugh Head** Border
65 L7 **Heveningham** Suffk
37 L11 **Hever** Kent
95 K4 **Heversham** Cumb
76 H7 **Hevingham** Norfk
3 P4 **Hewas Water** Cnwll
31 Q4 **Hewelsfield** Gloucs

90 D3 **Hewenden** C Brad
19 M2 **Hewish** N Som
11 J3 **Hewish** Somset
10 H4 **Hewood** Dorset
112 D8 **Hexham** Nthumb
37 M6 **Hextable** Kent
50 D4 **Hexton** Herts
5 P5 **Hexworthy** Cnwll
6 H4 **Hexworthy** Devon
89 P2 **Hey** Lancs
51 P11 **Heybridge** Essex
52 E10 **Heybridge** Essex
52 E10 **Heybridge Basin** Essex
6 D9 **Heybrook Bay** Devon
51 K3 **Heydon** Cambs
76 G6 **Heydon** Norfk
73 Q3 **Heydour** Lincs
82 H7 **Heyhead** Manch
88 C5 **Hey Houses** Lancs
136 B7 **Heylipoll** Ag & B
169 p5 **Heylor** Shet
83 L5 **Heyrod** Tamesd
95 J8 **Heysham** Lancs
97 J8 **Heyshaw** N York
23 N11 **Heyshott** W Susx
89 Q9 **Heyside** Oldham
20 H6 **Heytesbury** Wilts
48 C9 **Heythrop** Oxon
89 P8 **Heywood** Rochdl
20 G4 **Heywood** Wilts
92 G10 **Hibaldstow** N Linc
91 M9 **Hickleton** Donc
77 N7 **Hickling** Norfk
72 H5 **Hickling** Notts
77 N7 **Hickling Green** Norfk
77 N7 **Hickling Heath** Norfk
39 J10 **Hickmans Green** Kent
39 L9 **Hicks Forstal** Kent
24 G6 **Hickstead** W Susx
47 N6 **Hidcote Bartrim** Gloucs
47 N6 **Hidcote Boyce** Gloucs
91 L7 **High Ackworth** Wakefd
91 J9 **Higham** Barns
84 E9 **Higham** Derbys
37 P11 **Higham** Kent
38 B7 **Higham** Kent
89 N3 **Higham** Lancs
52 H4 **Higham** Suffk
63 M7 **Higham** Suffk
112 H5 **Higham Dykes** Nthumb
61 L7 **Higham Ferrers** Nhants
50 D4 **Higham Gobion** C Beds
37 J2 **Higham Hill** Gt Lon
72 B11 **Higham on the Hill** Leics
8 C4 **Highampton** Devon
37 J2 **Highams Park** Gt Lon
112 G3 **High Angerton** Nthumb
106 E8 **High Ardwell** D & G
109 K3 **High Auldgirth** D & G
101 Q2 **High Bankhill** Cumb
51 K11 **High Beach** Essex
95 P7 **High Bentham** N York
100 H4 **High Bewaldeth** Cumb
17 L7 **High Bickington** Devon
96 B5 **High Bickwith** N York
95 N5 **High Biggins** Cumb
126 B6 **High Blantyre** S Lans
126 E2 **High Bonnybridge** Falk
101 M10 **High Borrans** Cumb
96 F11 **High Bradley** N York
17 M5 **High Bray** Devon
22 E10 **Highbridge** Hants
19 K5 **Highbridge** Somset
25 J4 **Highbrook** W Susx
25 N2 **High Brooms** Kent
17 J7 **High Bullen** Devon
90 F8 **Highburton** Kirk
36 H3 **Highbury** Gt Lon
20 C5 **Highbury** Somset
119 P9 **High Buston** Nthumb
113 J6 **High Callerton** Nthumb
95 N5 **High Casterton** Cumb
98 E10 **High Catton** E R Yk
22 D3 **Highclere** Hants
13 M6 **Highcliffe** Dorset
103 N7 **High Close** Dur
34 C3 **High Cogges** Oxon
76 D10 **High Common** Norfk
103 P7 **High Conscliffe** Darltn
111 J9 **High Crosby** Cumb
3 J8 **High Cross** Cnwll
125 L8 **High Cross** E Ayrs
23 K9 **High Cross** Hants
51 J7 **High Cross** Herts
88 C3 **Highcross** Lancs
24 F7 **High Cross** W Susx
59 K11 **High Cross** Warwks
106 F10 **High Drummore** D & G
113 M11 **High Dubmire** Sundld
51 P8 **High Easter** Essex
91 P6 **High Eggborough** N York
97 J4 **High Ellington** N York
20 C6 **Higher Alham** Somset
12 C4 **Higher Ansty** Dorset
88 D4 **Higher Ballam** Lancs
88 G4 **Higher Bartle** Lancs
49 Q8 **Higher Berry End** C Beds
12 B6 **Higher Bockhampton** Dorset
7 N8 **Higher Brixham** Torbay
9 P5 **Higher Burrowton** Devon
69 P3 **Higher Burwardsley** Ches W
69 Q11 **High Ercall** Wrekin
10 H2 **Higher Chillington** Somset
16 E7 **Higher Clovelly** Devon
18 B8 **Higher Combe** Somset
11 L6 **Higher Coombe** Dorset
83 L8 **Higher Disley** Ches E
82 H4 **Higher Folds** Wigan
89 P2 **Higherford** Lancs
11 L3 **Higher Gabwell** Devon
11 L3 **Higher Halstock Leigh** Dorset
89 N3 **Higher Harpers** Lancs
95 J8 **Higher Heysham** Lancs
83 K10 **Higher Hurdsfield** Ches E
82 F5 **Higher Irlam** Salfd
11 L5 **Higher Kingcombe** Dorset
69 K2 **Higher Kinnerton** Flints
82 E9 **Higher Marston** Ches W
17 K4 **Higher Muddiford** Devon
20 D10 **Higher Nyland** Dorset
90 B8 **Higher Ogden** Rochdl
2 H8 **Higher Pentire** Cnwll
88 G5 **Higher Penwortham** Lancs

5 P2	**Higher Prestacott** Devon	
96 B6	**Higher Studfold** N York	
3 L5	**Higher Town** Cnwll	
4 G9	**Higher Town** Cnwll	
2 c1	**Higher Town** IoS	
5 Q11	**Higher Tregantle** Cnwll	
88 H5	**Higher Walton** Lancs	
82 C7	**Higher Walton** Warrtn	
10 F3	**Higher Wambrook** Somset	
11 Q5	**Higher Waterston** Dorset	
12 D4	**Higher Whatcombe** Dorset	
89 J6	**Higher Wheelton** Lancs	
82 D8	**Higher Whitley** Ches W	
82 E9	**Higher Wincham** Ches W	
11 M4	**Higher Wraxhall** Dorset	
69 N6	**Higher Wych** Ches W	
103 N5	**High Etherley** Dur	
87 L11	**High Ferry** Lincs	
92 B3	**Highfield** E R Yk	
112 H9	**Highfield** Gatesd	
125 J7	**Highfield** N Ayrs	
91 N9	**Highfields** Donc	
90 G9	**High Flats** Kirk	
52 C6	**High Garrett** Essex	
25 K4	**Highgate** E Susx	
36 Q3	**Highgate** Gt Lon	
26 C5	**Highgate** Kent	
103 N4	**High Grange** Dur	
97 K7	**High Grantley** N York	
101 M10	**High Green** Cumb	
90 G8	**High Green** Kirk	
64 H4	**High Green** Norfk	
76 G10	**High Green** Norfk	
91 J11	**High Green** Sheff	
57 N8	**High Green** Shrops	
64 B9	**High Green** Suffk	
46 G5	**High Green** Worcs	
112 B2	**Highgreen Manor** Nthumb	
26 E4	**High Halden** Kent	
38 C6	**High Halstow** Medway	
19 M8	**High Ham** Somset	
100 D5	**High Harrington** Cumb	
97 M9	**High Harrogate** N York	
104 C2	**High Haswell** Dur	
69 R10	**High Hatton** Shrops	
119 Q10	**High Hauxley** Nthumb	
105 P9	**High Hawsker** N York	
101 N2	**High Hesket** Cumb	
90 H9	**High Hoyland** Barns	
92 G3	**High Hunsley** E R Yk	
25 L5	**High Hurstwood** E Susx	
98 F7	**High Hutton** N York	
100 H3	**High Ireby** Cumb	
76 G3	**High Kelling** Norfk	
97 R5	**High Kilburn** N York	
99 M4	**High Killerby** N York	
101 P7	**High Knipe** Cumb	
103 M5	**High Lands** Dur	
148 E7	**Highland Wildlife Park** Highld	
83 J11	**Highlane** Ches E	
84 F4	**Highlane** Derbys	
83 L7	**High Lane** Stockp	
2 F6	**High Lanes** Cnwll	
51 M9	**High Laver** Essex	
109 P11	**Highlaws** Cumb	
46 E10	**Highleadon** Gloucs	
82 F8	**High Legh** Ches E	
15 M7	**Highleigh** W Susx	
104 E8	**High Leven** S on T	
57 N8	**Highley** Shrops	
20 B3	**High Littleton** BaNES	
100 G5	**High Lorton** Cumb	
98 G5	**High Marishes** N York	
85 P6	**High Marnham** Notts	
91 N10	**High Melton** Donc	
112 G8	**High Mickley** Nthumb	
110 E11	**Highmoor** Cumb	
35 K8	**Highmoor** Oxon	
35 K8	**Highmoor Cross** Oxon	
31 N7	**Highmoor Hill** Mons	
113 M11	**High Moorsley** Sundld	
46 E11	**Highnam** Gloucs	
46 E10	**Highnam Green** Gloucs	
113 N10	**High Newport** Sundld	
95 J4	**High Newton** Cumb	
94 F3	**High Nibthwaite** Cumb	
70 D9	**High Offley** Staffs	
51 N10	**High Ongar** Essex	
70 E11	**High Onn** Staffs	
52 H7	**High Park Corner** Essex	
115 J6	**High Pennyvenie** E Ayrs	
21 N7	**High Post** Wilts	
31 Q11	**Highridge** N Som	
51 P7	**High Roding** Essex	
101 L3	**High Row** Cumb	
101 L6	**High Row** Cumb	
95 N8	**High Salter** Lancs	
24 D9	**High Salvington** W Susx	
110 C11	**High Scales** Cumb	
100 D4	**High Seaton** Cumb	
96 C2	**High Shaw** N York	
100 H4	**High Side** Cumb	
112 H9	**High Spen** Gatesd	
39 M8	**Highstead** Kent	
38 F9	**Highsted** Kent	
103 M2	**High Stoop** Dur	
3 P3	**High Street** Cnwll	
26 B5	**High Street** Kent	
39 J9	**Highstreet** Kent	
65 N10	**High Street** Suffk	
65 N7	**High Street** Suffk	
52 C5	**Highstreet Green** Essex	
23 Q7	**Highstreet Green** Surrey	
109 N5	**Hightae** D & G	
58 G9	**Highter's Heath** Birm	
104 E4	**High Throston** Hartpl	
70 F2	**Hightown** Ches E	
13 L4	**Hightown** Hants	
81 L4	**Hightown** Sefton	
58 E2	**High Town** Staffs	
64 D10	**Hightown Green** Suffk	
87 J7	**High Toynton** Lincs	
119 K9	**High Trewhitt** Nthumb	
113 K10	**High Urpeth** Dur	
134 C10	**High Valleyfield** Fife	
112 D7	**High Warden** Nthumb	
45 P5	**Highway** Herefs	
33 K10	**Highway** Wilts	
7 L4	**Highweek** Devon	
112 H9	**High Westwood** Dur	
71 K8	**Highwood** Essex	
36 F2	**Highwood Hill** Gt Lon	
31 Q5	**High Woolaston** Gloucs	
104 C9	**High Worsall** N York	
33 P6	**Highworth** Swindn	
101 L11	**High Wray** Cumb	
51 L8	**High Wych** Herts	
35 N6	**High Wycombe** Bucks	
75 R10	**Hilborough** Norfk	
84 G9	**Hilcote** Derbys	
21 M3	**Hilcott** Wilts	
37 N11	**Hildenborough** Kent	
37 N11	**Hilden Park** Kent	
62 H11	**Hildersham** Cambs	
70 H8	**Hilderstone** Staffs	
99 P7	**Hilderthorpe** E R Yk	
11 N3	**Hilfield** Dorset	
75 M11	**Hilgay** Norfk	
32 B5	**Hill** S Glos	
59 Q11	**Hill** Warwks	
91 N5	**Hillam** N York	
102 E7	**Hillbeck** Cumb	
39 M8	**Hillborough** Kent	
23 L9	**Hill Brow** Hants	
12 G4	**Hillbutts** Dorset	
70 D7	**Hill Chorlton** Staffs	
71 P5	**Hillclifflane** Derbys	
77 N7	**Hill Common** Norfk	
18 F9	**Hill Common** Somset	
20 G6	**Hill Deverill** Wilts	
87 K11	**Hilldyke** Lincs	
103 K3	**Hill End** Dur	
134 C8	**Hill End** Fife	
134 E11	**Hillend** Fife	
46 H7	**Hill End** Gloucs	
127 P4	**Hillend** Mdloth	
126 E4	**Hillend** N Lans	
28 D6	**Hillend** Swans	
31 Q2	**Hillersland** Gloucs	
8 H5	**Hillerton** Devon	
49 J9	**Hillesden** Bucks	
32 E7	**Hillesley** Gloucs	
18 G10	**Hillfarrance** Somset	
38 D9	**Hill Green** Kent	
23 P9	**Hillgrove** W Susx	
46 A5	**Hillhampton** Herefs	
158 E10	**Hillhead** Abers	
7 N8	**Hillhead** Devon	
14 F6	**Hill Head** Hants	
116 D2	**Hillhead** S Lans	
159 Q9	**Hillhead of Cocklaw** Abers	
59 J2	**Hilliard's Cross** Staffs	
167 L4	**Hilliclay** Highld	
36 C4	**Hillingdon** Gt Lon	
125 N5	**Hillington** C Glas	
75 P5	**Hillington** Norfk	
14 E8	**Hillis Corner** IoW	
60 B6	**Hillmorton** Warwks	
89 M5	**Hillock Vale** Lancs	
134 F9	**Hill of Beath** Fife	
163 J11	**Hill of Fearn** Highld	
108 G8	**Hillowton** D & G	
58 C9	**Hillpool** Worcs	
22 G11	**Hillpound** Hants	
71 K11	**Hill Ridware** Staffs	
151 N8	**Hillside** Abers	
143 N5	**Hillside** Angus	
7 J6	**Hillside** Devon	
90 F7	**Hill Side** Kirk	
46 E2	**Hill Side** Worcs	
84 G7	**Hills Town** Derbys	
22 B11	**Hillstreet** Hants	
169 p6	**Hillswick** Shet	
103 J6	**Hill Top** Dur	
14 D6	**Hill Top** Hants	
90 D8	**Hill Top** Kirk	
84 E2	**Hill Top** Rothm	
58 E6	**Hill Top** Sandw	
91 J7	**Hill Top** Wakefd	
169 q12	**Hillwell** Shet	
33 K9	**Hilmarton** Wilts	
20 G3	**Hilperton** Wilts	
20 G3	**Hilperton Marsh** Wilts	
15 J6	**Hilsea** C Port	
93 N4	**Hilston** E R Yk	
22 D10	**Hiltingbury** Hants	
129 M9	**Hilton** Border	
62 C7	**Hilton** Cambs	
102 D6	**Hilton** Cumb	
71 N8	**Hilton** Derbys	
12 C4	**Hilton** Dorset	
103 N6	**Hilton** Dur	
156 F2	**Hilton** Highld	
104 E8	**Hilton** S on T	
57 P5	**Hilton** Shrops	
58 E4	**Hilton Park Services** Staffs	
46 H3	**Himbleton** Worcs	
58 C6	**Himley** Staffs	
95 L4	**Hincaster** Cumb	
36 E7	**Hinchley Wood** Surrey	
59 P6	**Hinckley** Leics	
64 E6	**Hinderclay** Suffk	
105 L7	**Hinderwell** N York	
69 K8	**Hindford** Shrops	
23 N7	**Hindhead** Surrey	
89 L4	**Hindle Fold** Lancs	
112 F9	**Hindley** Nthumb	
82 D4	**Hindley** Wigan	
82 D4	**Hindley Green** Wigan	
46 G3	**Hindlip** Worcs	
76 E6	**Hindolveston** Norfk	
20 H8	**Hindon** Wilts	
76 E11	**Hindringham** Norfk	
58 C7	**Hinksford** Staffs	
70 B9	**Hinstock** Shrops	
53 J3	**Hintlesham** Suffk	
32 C4	**Hinton** Gloucs	
13 M5	**Hinton** Hants	
45 L7	**Hinton** Herefs	
32 D3	**Hinton** S Glos	
56 G3	**Hinton** Shrops	
57 M8	**Hinton** Shrops	
13 M5	**Hinton Admiral** Hants	
22 H9	**Hinton Ampner** Hants	
19 Q3	**Hinton Blewett** BaNES	
20 E3	**Hinton Charterhouse** BaNES	
47 K6	**Hinton Green** Worcs	
48 G7	**Hinton-in-the-Hedges** Nhants	
22 G9	**Hinton Marsh** Hants	
12 H3	**Hinton Martell** Dorset	
47 K6	**Hinton on the Green** Worcs	
33 P8	**Hinton Parva** Swindn	
11 J1	**Hinton St George** Somset	
20 E11	**Hinton St Mary** Dorset	
34 C5	**Hinton Waldrist** Oxon	
57 L10	**Hints** Shrops	
59 J4	**Hints** Staffs	
61 K8	**Hinwick** Bed	
26 H3	**Hinxhill** Kent	
62 G11	**Hinxton** Cambs	
50 F2	**Hinxworth** Herts	
90 E5	**Hipperholme** Calder	
119 P8	**Hipsburn** Nthumb	
103 N11	**Hipswell** N York	
151 J7	**Hirn** Abers	
68 D10	**Hirnant** Powys	
113 L3	**Hirst** Nthumb	
91 Q6	**Hirst Courtney** N York	
68 E3	**Hirwaen** Denbgs	
30 C3	**Hirwaun** Rhondd	
17 J6	**Hiscott** Devon	
62 F8	**Histon** Cambs	
64 D11	**Hitcham** Suffk	
64 D11	**Hitcham Causeway** Suffk	
64 D11	**Hitcham Street** Suffk	
50 E5	**Hitchin** Herts	
37 J6	**Hither Green** Gt Lon	
8 H5	**Hittisleigh** Devon	
92 D4	**Hive** E R Yk	
71 J9	**Hixon** Staffs	
39 N10	**Hoaden** Kent	
71 L10	**Hoar Cross** Staffs	
45 Q9	**Hoarwithy** Herefs	
39 M9	**Hoath** Kent	
25 Q3	**Hoathly** Kent	
56 E9	**Hobarris** Shrops	
63 M10	**Hobbles Green** Suffk	
51 L11	**Hobbs Cross** Essex	
51 L8	**Hobbs Cross** Essex	
118 A8	**Hobkirk** Border	
77 Q11	**Hobland Hall** Norfk	
84 G11	**Hobsick** Notts	
113 J9	**Hobson** Dur	
72 H7	**Hoby** Leics	
18 F9	**Hoccombe** Somset	
76 F9	**Hockering** Norfk	
85 M9	**Hockerton** Notts	
83 K8	**Hockley** Ches E	
59 L9	**Hockley** Covtry	
38 D3	**Hockley** Essex	
59 K4	**Hockley** Staffs	
59 J10	**Hockley Heath** Solhll	
49 Q9	**Hockliffe** C Beds	
63 M3	**Hockwold cum Wilton** Norfk	
18 D11	**Hockworthy** Devon	
51 J9	**Hoddesdon** Herts	
89 L6	**Hoddlesden** Bl w D	
110 C6	**Hoddom Cross** D & G	
110 C6	**Hoddom Mains** D & G	
82 H11	**Hodgehill** Ches E	
41 K11	**Hodgeston** Pembks	
69 R9	**Hodnet** Shrops	
85 K3	**Hodsock** Notts	
37 N7	**Hodsoll Street** Kent	
33 N8	**Hodson** Swindn	
84 H5	**Hodthorpe** Derbys	
22 G11	**Hoe** Hants	
76 D8	**Hoe** Norfk	
14 H4	**Hoe Gate** Hants	
102 C7	**Hoff** Cumb	
38 H10	**Hogben's Hill** Kent	
64 B10	**Hoggards Green** Suffk	
49 M10	**Hoggeston** Bucks	
59 K6	**Hoggrill's End** Warwks	
26 E8	**Hog Hill** E Susx	
89 J5	**Hoghton** Lancs	
89 J5	**Hoghton Bottoms** Lancs	
71 N4	**Hognaston** Derbys	
87 P6	**Hogsthorpe** Lincs	
74 G6	**Holbeach** Lincs	
74 G5	**Holbeach Bank** Lincs	
74 G5	**Holbeach Clough** Lincs	
74 F8	**Holbeach Drove** Lincs	
74 G7	**Holbeach Hurn** Lincs	
74 G5	**Holbeach St Johns** Lincs	
74 G5	**Holbeach St Mark's** Lincs	
74 H4	**Holbeach St Matthew** Lincs	
84 H6	**Holbeck** Notts	
84 H6	**Holbeck Woodhouse** Notts	
47 K3	**Holberrow Green** Worcs	
6 G8	**Holbeton** Devon	
36 H4	**Holborn** Gt Lon	
38 B9	**Holborough** Kent	
72 B2	**Holbrook** Derbys	
84 F4	**Holbrook** Sheff	
53 L4	**Holbrook** Suffk	
84 E11	**Holbrook Moor** Derbys	
59 M8	**Holbrooks** Covtry	
119 K3	**Holburn** Nthumb	
14 D6	**Holbury** Hants	
7 P4	**Holcombe** Devon	
20 C5	**Holcombe** Somset	
18 E11	**Holcombe Rogus** Devon	
60 D7	**Holcot** Nhants	
96 A11	**Holden** Lancs	
60 E7	**Holdenby** Nhants	
89 P6	**Holden Gate** Calder	
51 K7	**Holder's Green** Essex	
57 K7	**Holdgate** Shrops	
86 E11	**Holdingham** Lincs	
10 G4	**Holditch** Dorset	
90 D5	**Holdsworth** Calder	
83 M6	**Holehouse** Derbys	
46 B9	**Hole-in-the-Wall** Herefs	
16 G10	**Holemoor** Devon	
24 D8	**Hole Street** W Susx	
18 G6	**Holford** Somset	
98 B10	**Holgate** C York	
94 H5	**Holker** Cumb	
76 B3	**Holkham** Norfk	
76 B3	**Holkham Hall** Norfk	
16 F11	**Hollacombe** Devon	
86 H11	**Holland Fen** Lincs	
88 G9	**Holland Lees** Lancs	
53 L8	**Holland-on-Sea** Essex	
169 g1	**Hollandstoun** Ork	
110 E7	**Hollee** D & G	
52 Q3	**Hollesley** Suffk	
7 M6	**Hollicombe** Torbay	
38 D10	**Hollingbourne** Kent	
24 H9	**Hollingbury** Br & H	
49 N9	**Hollingdon** Bucks	
91 K4	**Hollingthorpe** Leeds	
71 N7	**Hollington** Derbys	
71 K7	**Hollington** Staffs	
83 M5	**Hollingworth** Tamesd	
82 H8	**Hollinlane** Ches E	
89 N9	**Hollins** Bury	
84 D6	**Hollins** Derbys	
70 H5	**Hollins** Staffs	
83 N11	**Hollinsclough** Staffs	
84 E4	**Hollins End** Sheff	
82 E6	**Hollins Green** Warrtn	
95 K10	**Hollins Lane** Lancs	
57 N3	**Hollinswood** Wrekin	
69 P7	**Hollinwood** Shrops	
83 K4	**Hollinwood Crematorium** Oldham	
25 Q6	**Hollingrove** E Susx	
17 L9	**Hollocombe** Devon	
84 D9	**Holloway** Derbys	
36 H3	**Holloway** Gt Lon	
20 G8	**Holloway** Wilts	
60 E3	**Hollowell** Nhants	
81 P11	**Hollowmoor Heath** Ches W	
110 G5	**Hollows** D & G	
30 G4	**Hollybush** Caerph	
114 G4	**Hollybush** E Ayrs	
46 E7	**Hollybush** Herefs	
75 J9	**Holly End** Norfk	
46 G6	**Holly Green** Worcs	
69 Q6	**Hollyhurst** Ches E	
50 E5	**Hollym** E R Yk	
58 G9	**Hollywood** Worcs	
90 E9	**Holmbridge** Kirk	
24 D2	**Holmbury St Mary** Surrey	
3 Q3	**Holmbush** Cnwll	
70 C10	**Holmcroft** Staffs	
61 Q3	**Holme** Cambs	
95 L5	**Holme** Cumb	
90 E9	**Holme** Kirk	
92 F9	**Holme** N Linc	
97 N4	**Holme** N York	
85 P9	**Holme** Notts	
89 P5	**Holme Chapel** Lancs	
91 P2	**Holme Green** N York	
76 B10	**Holme Hale** Norfk	
45 R7	**Holme Lacy** Herefs	
45 L4	**Holme Marsh** Herefs	
75 P2	**Holme next the Sea** Norfk	
99 K11	**Holme on the Wolds** E R Yk	
72 G3	**Holme Pierrepont** Notts	
45 Q6	**Holmer** Herefs	
35 P5	**Holmer Green** Bucks	
109 P11	**Holme St Cuthbert** Cumb	
82 G11	**Holmes Chapel** Ches E	
84 D5	**Holmesfield** Derbys	
25 M8	**Holmes Hill** E Susx	
88 E7	**Holmeswood** Lancs	
36 G10	**Holmethorpe** Surrey	
92 D3	**Holme upon Spalding Moor** E R Yk	
84 F7	**Holmewood** Derbys	
90 D5	**Holmfield** Calder	
90 E9	**Holmfirth** Kirk	
115 L3	**Holmhead** E Ayrs	
93 Q6	**Holmpton** E R Yk	
100 E11	**Holmrook** Cumb	
125 K10	**Holmsford Bridge Crematorium** N Ayrs	
25 P5	**Holmshurst** E Susx	
113 K11	**Holmside** Dur	
111 K11	**Holmwrangle** Cumb	
7 J5	**Holne** Devon	
11 P3	**Holnest** Dorset	
18 B5	**Holnicote** Somset	
16 E11	**Holsworthy** Devon	
16 F10	**Holsworthy Beacon** Devon	
12 H4	**Holt** Dorset	
76 F4	**Holt** Norfk	
20 G2	**Holt** Wilts	
46 F2	**Holt** Worcs	
69 M4	**Holt** Wrexhm	
98 D10	**Holtby** C York	
58 G11	**Holt End** Worcs	
46 F2	**Holt Fleet** Worcs	
88 D9	**Holt Green** Lancs	
13 J4	**Holt Heath** Dorset	
46 F2	**Holt Heath** Worcs	
34 H3	**Holton** Oxon	
20 C9	**Holton** Somset	
65 N6	**Holton** Suffk	
86 F4	**Holton cum Beckering** Lincs	
12 F6	**Holton Heath** Dorset	
25 Q5	**Holton Hill** E Susx	
93 N10	**Holton le Clay** Lincs	
93 J11	**Holton le Moor** Lincs	
53 J4	**Holton St Mary** Suffk	
39 N11	**Holt Street** Kent	
25 L3	**Holtye** E Susx	
80 H9	**Holway** Flints	
11 P2	**Holwell** Dorset	
50 E4	**Holwell** Herts	
73 J6	**Holwell** Leics	
33 P3	**Holwell** Oxon	
102 H5	**Holwick** Dur	
12 C8	**Holworth** Dorset	
23 K6	**Holybourne** Hants	
58 D9	**Holy Cross** Worcs	
51 J10	**Holyfield** Essex	
78 C8	**Holyhead** IoA	
78 D8	**Holy Island** IoA	
119 M2	**Holy Island** Nthumb	
119 M2	**Holy Island** Nthumb	
84 D7	**Holymoorside** Derbys	
35 N9	**Holyport** W & M	
119 J10	**Holystone** Nthumb	
126 D5	**Holytown** N Lans	
126 D5	**Holytown Crematorium** N Lans	
50 B7	**Holywell** C Beds	
62 D6	**Holywell** Cambs	
4 B10	**Holywell** Cnwll	
11 M4	**Holywell** Dorset	
80 H9	**Holywell** Flints	
113 M6	**Holywell** Nthumb	
59 K11	**Holywell** Warwks	
90 D7	**Holywell Green** Calder	
18 F10	**Holywell Lake** Somset	
63 M5	**Holywell Row** Suffk	
109 K4	**Holywood** D & G	
109 L5	**Holywood Village** D & G	
59 L3	**Homer** Shrops	
81 L4	**Homer Green** Sefton	
65 K4	**Homersfield** Suffk	
95 M3	**Homescales** Cumb	
46 A10	**Hom Green** Herefs	
21 M9	**Homington** Wilts	
40 H9	**Honeyborough** Pembks	
47 M6	**Honeybourne** Worcs	
8 F4	**Honeychurch** Devon	
39 K9	**Honey Hill** Kent	
21 M2	**Honeystreet** Wilts	
52 G4	**Honey Tye** Suffk	
59 K10	**Honiley** Warwks	
77 L6	**Honing** Norfk	
76 G9	**Honingham** Norfk	
73 N2	**Honington** Lincs	
64 C10	**Honington** Suffk	
59 K10	**Honington** Warwks	
47 Q6	**Honiton** Devon	
10 D4	**Honiton** Devon	
90 E8	**Honley** Kirk	
70 C11	**Honnington** Wrekin	
37 J6	**Honor Oak Crematorium** Gt Lon	
39 N9	**Hoo** Kent	
58 B10	**Hoobrook** Worcs	
91 J10	**Hood Green** Barns	
91 K11	**Hood Hill** Rothm	
6 E8	**Hooe** C Plym	
25 Q8	**Hooe** E Susx	
50 E6	**Hoo End** Herts	
82 E8	**Hoo Green** Ches E	
88 C3	**Hoohill** Bpool	
62 F2	**Hook** Cambs	
10 G3	**Hook** Devon	
92 C5	**Hook** E R Yk	
36 E8	**Hook** Gt Lon	
14 F5	**Hook** Hants	
23 K4	**Hook** Hants	
41 J8	**Hook** Pembks	
33 L8	**Hook** Wilts	
56 H3	**Hookagate** Shrops	
46 F6	**Hook Bank** Worcs	
11 L4	**Hooke** Dorset	
51 N10	**Hook End** Essex	
70 C7	**Hookgate** Staffs	
25 Q3	**Hook Green** Kent	
37 P6	**Hook Green** Kent	
48 C8	**Hook Norton** Oxon	
32 C5	**Hook Street** Gloucs	
33 L8	**Hook Street** Wilts	
9 L5	**Hookway** Devon	
24 G2	**Hookwood** Surrey	
36 G9	**Hooley** Surrey	
89 P8	**Hooley Bridge** Rochdl	
6 E5	**Hoo Meavy** Devon	
38 C7	**Hoo St Werburgh** Medway	
81 M9	**Hooton** Ches W	
84 H2	**Hooton Levitt** Rothm	
91 M9	**Hooton Pagnell** Donc	
91 M11	**Hooton Roberts** Rothm	
48 E9	**Hopcrofts Holt** Oxon	
83 Q8	**Hope** Derbys	
6 H10	**Hope** Devon	
69 K3	**Hope** Flints	
56 D3	**Hope** Powys	
56 E4	**Hope** Shrops	
57 K10	**Hope** Shrops	
71 L4	**Hope** Staffs	
56 H6	**Hope Bowdler** Shrops	
51 N6	**Hope End Green** Essex	
117 K7	**Hopehouse** Border	
157 L4	**Hopeman** Moray	
46 B11	**Hope Mansell** Herefs	
56 F9	**Hopesay** Shrops	
91 K6	**Hopetown** Wakefd	
45 Q4	**Hope under Dinmore** Herefs	
98 C10	**Hopgrove** C York	
97 P9	**Hopperton** N York	
74 F7	**Hop Pole** Lincs	
59 P8	**Hopsford** Warwks	
59 P8	**Hopstone** Shrops	
71 P4	**Hopton** Derbys	
69 L10	**Hopton** Shrops	
70 G9	**Hopton** Staffs	
64 D6	**Hopton** Suffk	
57 J8	**Hopton Cangeford** Shrops	
56 F9	**Hopton Castle** Shrops	
57 J8	**Hoptonheath** Shrops	
65 Q2	**Hopton on Sea** Norfk	
57 L9	**Hopton Wafers** Shrops	
59 J4	**Hopwas** Staffs	
89 P9	**Hopwood** Rochdl	
58 P9	**Hopwood** Worcs	
58 F10	**Hopwood Park Services** Worcs	
25 N7	**Horam** E Susx	
74 B3	**Horbling** Lincs	
90 H7	**Horbury** Wakefd	
33 N4	**Horcott** Gloucs	
104 D2	**Horden** Dur	
56 F7	**Horderley** Shrops	
13 N5	**Hordle** Hants	
69 L8	**Hordley** Shrops	
28 E3	**Horeb** Carmth	
42 G6	**Horeb** Cerdgn	
31 Q9	**Horfield** Bristl	
65 J7	**Horham** Suffk	
52 G6	**Horkesley Heath** Essex	
92 G7	**Horkstow** N Linc	
48 D6	**Horley** Oxon	
24 G2	**Horley** Surrey	
19 Q8	**Hornblotton Green** Somset	
95 M7	**Hornby** Lancs	
97 K2	**Hornby** N York	
104 C9	**Hornby** N York	
87 J7	**Horncastle** Lincs	
37 M3	**Hornchurch** Gt Lon	
129 N10	**Horncliffe** Nthumb	
129 N10	**Horndean** Border	
15 K4	**Horndean** Hants	
8 D8	**Horndon** Devon	
37 Q4	**Horndon on the Hill** Thurr	
24 H2	**Horne** Surrey	
18 B5	**Horner** Somset	
52 C11	**Horne Row** Essex	
52 G3	**Horners Green** Suffk	
25 L5	**Horney Common** E Susx	
36 B2	**Horn Hill** Bucks	
77 L8	**Horning** Norfk	
73 L11	**Horninghold** Leics	
71 N9	**Horninglow** Staffs	
62 G8	**Horningsea** Cambs	
20 F6	**Horningsham** Wilts	
76 C7	**Horningtoft** Norfk	
5 M9	**Horningtops** Cnwll	
10 G2	**Hornsbury** Somset	
111 K10	**Hornsby** Cumb	
111 K10	**Hornsbygate** Cumb	
16 F7	**Horns Cross** Devon	
26 D7	**Horns Cross** E Susx	
99 P11	**Hornsea** E R Yk	
36 H3	**Hornsey** Gt Lon	
37 L9	**Horn's Green** Gt Lon	
27 L4	**Horn Street** Kent	
48 C5	**Hornton** Oxon	
33 P8	**Horpit** Swindn	
169 r4	**Horra** Shet	
6 E5	**Horrabridge** Devon	
54 A9	**Horringer** Suffk	
14 F9	**Horringford** IoW	
89 L8	**Horrocks Fold** Bolton	
89 M2	**Horrocksford** Lancs	
17 J5	**Horsacott** Devon	
5 Q6	**Horsebridge** Devon	

25 N8 **Horsebridge** E Susx
22 B8 **Horsebridge** Hants
56 F3 **Horsebridge** Shrops
70 H4 **Horsebridge** Staffs
58 C2 **Horsebrook** Staffs
31 M11 **Horsecastle** N Som
2 G7 **Horsedown** Cnwll
74 C8 **Horsegate** Lincs
57 M3 **Horsehay** Wrekin
63 K11 **Horseheath** Cambs
96 F4 **Horsehouse** N York
23 Q3 **Horsell** Surrey
69 M6 **Horseman's Green** Wrexhm
35 L4 **Horsenden** Bucks
77 P7 **Horsey** Norfk
19 K7 **Horsey** Somset
77 P7 **Horsey Corner** Norfk
76 H8 **Horsford** Norfk
90 G3 **Horsforth** Leeds
24 E4 **Horsham** W Susx
46 D3 **Horsham** Worcs
77 J8 **Horsham St Faith** Norfk
86 G7 **Horsington** Lincs
20 D10 **Horsington** Somset
72 B2 **Horsley** Derbys
32 F5 **Horsley** Gloucs
112 G7 **Horsley** Nthumb
118 F11 **Horsley** Nthumb
53 K6 **Horsley Cross** Essex
53 K6 **Horsleycross Street** Essex
84 D5 **Horsley-Gate** Derbys
117 Q7 **Horsleyhill** Border
35 L4 **Horsley's Green** Bucks
72 B2 **Horsley Woodhouse** Derbys
26 B3 **Horsmonden** Kent
34 G3 **Horspath** Oxon
77 K8 **Horstead** Norfk
25 J5 **Horsted Keynes** W Susx
49 P11 **Horton** Bucks
12 H3 **Horton** Dorset
96 C10 **Horton** Lancs
49 M4 **Horton** Nhants
32 E8 **Horton** S Glos
69 N9 **Horton** Shrops
10 Q2 **Horton** Somset
70 G3 **Horton** Staffs
36 E8 **Horton** Surrey
28 E7 **Horton** Swans
36 B5 **Horton** W & M
21 K2 **Horton** Wilts
57 M2 **Horton** Wrekin
19 K11 **Horton Cross** Somset
34 G2 **Horton-cum-Studley** Oxon
69 N5 **Horton Green** Ches W
22 E11 **Horton Heath** Hants
96 B6 **Horton in Ribblesdale** N York
37 N7 **Horton Kirby** Kent
89 J4 **Horwich** Bolton
83 M8 **Horwich End** Derbys
17 J6 **Horwood** Devon
88 F8 **Hoscar** Lancs
117 M8 **Hoscote** Border
73 J5 **Hose** Leics
37 L10 **Hosey Hill** Kent
133 P3 **Hosh** P & K
169 r11 **Hoswick** Shet
92 E4 **Hotham** E R Yk
26 G3 **Hothfield** Kent
72 F6 **Hoton** Leics
111 Q3 **Hott** Nthumb
70 C4 **Hough** Ches E
83 J9 **Hough** Ches E
73 M2 **Hougham** Lincs
90 G4 **Hough End** Leeds
81 P7 **Hough Green** Halton
86 B11 **Hough-on-the-Hill** Lincs
62 C6 **Houghton** Cambs
110 H9 **Houghton** Cumb
22 B8 **Houghton** Hants
112 H7 **Houghton** Nthumb
41 J9 **Houghton** Pembks
24 B8 **Houghton** W Susx
50 B2 **Houghton Conquest** C Beds
113 M10 **Houghton Gate** Dur
26 F7 **Houghton Green** E Susx
82 D6 **Houghton Green** Warrtn
103 P6 **Houghton le Side** Darltn
113 M11 **Houghton-le-Spring** Sundld
72 H10 **Houghton on the Hill** Leics
50 B6 **Houghton Regis** C Beds
76 C4 **Houghton St Giles** Norfk
23 K3 **Hound Green** Hants
128 G10 **Houndslow** Border
18 F9 **Houndsmoor** Somset
129 L7 **Houndwood** Border
36 D3 **Hounslow** Gt Lon
156 F6 **Househill** Highld
90 F7 **Houses Hill** Kirk
151 M2 **Housieside** Abers
125 L4 **Houston** Rens
167 L10 **Houstry** Highld
169 c6 **Houton** Ork
24 G10 **Hove** Br & H
90 E6 **Hove Edge** Calder
85 L11 **Hoveringham** Notts
77 L8 **Hoveton** Norfk
98 D5 **Hovingham** N York
91 J11 **Howbrook** Barns
46 B8 **How Caple** Herefs
92 B5 **Howden** E R Yk
103 N4 **Howden-le-Wear** Dur
167 P4 **Howe** Highld
80 a8 **Howe** IoM
97 N4 **Howe** N York
65 K2 **Howe** Norfk
82 E4 **Howe Bridge** Wigan
82 E4 **Howe Bridge Crematorium** Wigan
52 B11 **Howe Green** Essex
52 D11 **Howegreen** Essex
86 F11 **Howell** Lincs
50 B2 **How End** C Beds
159 J8 **Howe of Teuchar** Abers
110 C7 **Howes** D & G
51 Q4 **Howe Street** Essex
51 L8 **Howe Street** Essex
44 F3 **Howey** Powys
100 C6 **Howgate** Cumb
127 N6 **Howgate** Mdloth
96 B11 **Howgill** Lancs
119 Q7 **Howick** Nthumb
70 B10 **Howle** Wrekin

46 B10 **Howle Hill** Herefs
51 N4 **Howlett End** Essex
10 F3 **Howley** Somset
111 K9 **How Mill** Cumb
168 c14 **Howmore** W Isls
118 E7 **Hownam** Border
110 F11 **Howrigg** Cumb
92 H10 **Howsham** N Linc
98 E8 **Howsham** N York
118 G4 **Howtel** Nthumb
38 E8 **Howt Green** Kent
45 N9 **Howton** Herefs
101 M7 **Howtown** Cumb
125 K5 **Howwood** Rens
64 H6 **Hoxne** Suffk
169 b7 **Hoy** Ork
81 J7 **Hoylake** Wirral
91 K10 **Hoyland Common** Barns
91 K10 **Hoyland Nether** Barns
90 H10 **Hoyland Swaine** Barns
23 P11 **Hoyle** W Susx
91 K9 **Hoyle Mill** Barns
6 H4 **Huccaby** Devon
46 G11 **Hucclecote** Gloucs
38 D10 **Hucking** Kent
84 H11 **Hucknall** Notts
90 E7 **Huddersfield** Kirk
90 E6 **Huddersfield Crematorium** Kirk
46 H3 **Huddington** Worcs
50 B8 **Hudnall** Herts
103 M10 **Hudswell** N York
98 H9 **Huggate** E R Yk
72 C8 **Hugglescote** Leics
35 N5 **Hughenden Valley** Bucks
57 K5 **Hughley** Shrops
2 c2 **Hugh Town** IoS
17 J9 **Huish** Devon
21 M2 **Huish** Wilts
18 E9 **Huish Champflower** Somset
19 M9 **Huish Episcopi** Somset
49 P7 **Hulcote** C Beds
49 N11 **Hulcott** Bucks
9 F3 **Hulham** Devon
71 N5 **Hulland** Derbys
71 P5 **Hulland Ward** Derbys
32 G8 **Hullavington** Wilts
38 D2 **Hullbridge** Essex
93 J5 **Hull, Kingston upon** C KuH
82 H5 **Hulme** Manch
70 G5 **Hulme** Staffs
82 D6 **Hulme** Warrtn
71 L3 **Hulme End** Staffs
82 H11 **Hulme Walfield** Ches E
82 F8 **Hulse Heath** Ches E
89 K9 **Hulton Lane Ends** Bolton
14 C10 **Hulverstone** IoW
76 C9 **Hulver Street** Norfk
65 P4 **Hulver Street** Suffk
9 L9 **Humber** Devon
45 Q3 **Humber** Herefs
93 J8 **Humberside Airport** N Linc
93 P9 **Humberston** NE Lin
72 G9 **Humberstone** C Leic
97 P7 **Humberton** N York
128 D7 **Humbie** E Loth
93 M4 **Humbleton** E R Yk
119 J5 **Humbleton** Nthumb
73 Q4 **Humby** Lincs
118 D2 **Hume** Border
112 D6 **Humshaugh** Nthumb
167 Q2 **Huna** Highld
89 M4 **Huncoat** Lancs
72 E11 **Huncote** Leics
118 B7 **Hundalee** Border
84 E5 **Hundall** Derbys
103 J6 **Hunderthwaite** Dur
87 L7 **Hundleby** Lincs
86 H10 **Hundle Houses** Lincs
41 J10 **Hundleton** Pembks
63 M11 **Hundon** Suffk
88 E6 **Hundred End** Lancs
44 G4 **Hundred House** Powys
72 H9 **Hungarton** Leics
13 L2 **Hungerford** Hants
18 D6 **Hungerford** Somset
34 B11 **Hungerford** W Berk
34 C10 **Hungerford Newtown** W Berk
89 K9 **Hunger Hill** Bolton
88 G8 **Hunger Hill** Lancs
45 N7 **Hungerstone** Herefs
73 M5 **Hungerton** Lincs
70 B9 **Hungryhatton** Shrops
90 M5 **Hunmanby** N York
59 N11 **Hunningham** Warwks
58 E8 **Hunnington** Worcs
60 F9 **Hunsbury Hill** Nhants
51 K8 **Hunsdon** Herts
97 P10 **Hunsingore** N York
91 J4 **Hunslet** Leeds
101 Q3 **Hunsonby** Cumb
75 N2 **Hunstanton** Norfk
112 D11 **Hunstanworth** Dur
70 B5 **Hunsterson** Ches E
64 D8 **Hunston** Suffk
15 N6 **Hunston** W Susx
64 D8 **Hunston Green** Suffk
20 B2 **Hunstrete** BaNES
90 F5 **Hunsworth** Kirk
47 K2 **Hunt End** Worcs
17 M2 **Hunter's Inn** Devon
124 F7 **Hunter's Quay** Ag & B
19 K9 **Huntham** Somset
142 H3 **Hunthill Lodge** Angus
62 B6 **Huntingdon** Cambs
65 L7 **Huntingfield** Suffk
20 F9 **Huntingford** Dorset
98 C9 **Huntington** C York
69 N2 **Huntington** Ches W
128 D5 **Huntington** E Loth
45 K4 **Huntington** Herefs
58 E2 **Huntington** Staffs
46 D11 **Huntley** Gloucs
158 D10 **Huntly** Abers
22 E6 **Hunton** Hants
26 B2 **Hunton** Kent
97 J2 **Hunton** N York
50 C10 **Hunton Bridge** Herts
64 F4 **Hunt's Corner** Norfk
18 B6 **Huntscott** Somset

81 N7 **Hunt's Cross** Lpool
35 N4 **Hunts Green** Bucks
59 J5 **Hunts Green** Warwks
18 D10 **Huntsham** Devon
17 J7 **Huntshaw** Devon
17 J7 **Huntshaw Cross** Devon
19 K5 **Huntspill** Somset
19 K5 **Huntspill** Somset
19 K8 **Huntworth** Somset
103 N4 **Hunwick** Dur
76 F4 **Hunworth** Norfk
19 L11 **Hurcott** Somset
21 N8 **Hurdcott** Wilts
83 K10 **Hurdsfield** Ches E
35 M8 **Hurley** W & M
59 K5 **Hurley** Warwks
35 M8 **Hurley Bottom** W & M
59 K5 **Hurley Common** Warwks
125 M10 **Hurlford** E Ayrs
88 D8 **Hurlston Green** Lancs
13 K5 **Hurn** Dorset
87 M11 **Hurn's End** Lincs
22 D9 **Hursley** Hants
12 C6 **Hurst** Dorset
103 K10 **Hurst** N York
19 N11 **Hurst** Somset
35 L10 **Hurst** Wokham
22 D5 **Hurstbourne Priors** Hants
22 C4 **Hurstbourne Tarrant** Hants
26 B6 **Hurst Green** E Susx
53 J8 **Hurst Green** Essex
89 K3 **Hurst Green** Lancs
37 J10 **Hurst Green** Surrey
58 D6 **Hurst Hill** Dudley
45 M5 **Hurstley** Herefs
24 G7 **Hurstpierpoint** W Susx
24 G7 **Hurst Wickham** W Susx
89 P4 **Hurstwood** Lancs
169 e6 **Hurtiso** Ork
23 P5 **Hurtmore** Surrey
104 D4 **Hurworth Burn** Dur
104 B9 **Hurworth-on-Tees** Darltn
103 Q9 **Hurworth Place** Darltn
103 J7 **Hury** Dur
60 D4 **Husbands Bosworth** Leics
49 Q7 **Husborne Crawley** C Beds
97 R6 **Husthwaite** N York
7 K8 **Hutcherleigh** Devon
84 D4 **Hutcliffe Wood Crematorium** Sheff
91 P6 **Hut Green** N York
84 D4 **Huthwaite** Notts
87 P5 **Huttoft** Lincs
129 N9 **Hutton** Border
101 M5 **Hutton** Cumb
99 L10 **Hutton** E R Yk
51 P11 **Hutton** Essex
88 F5 **Hutton** Lancs
19 L3 **Hutton** N Som
104 B10 **Hutton Bonville** N York
99 K4 **Hutton Buscel** N York
97 M6 **Hutton Conyers** N York
99 L10 **Hutton Cranswick** E R Yk
101 N3 **Hutton End** Cumb
97 J3 **Hutton Hang** N York
104 D3 **Hutton Henry** Dur
98 E2 **Hutton-le-Hole** N York
104 G8 **Hutton Lowcross** R & Cl
103 M8 **Hutton Magna** Dur
105 M9 **Hutton Mulgrave** N York
95 M5 **Hutton Roof** Cumb
101 L4 **Hutton Roof** Cumb
104 E9 **Hutton Rudby** N York
95 Q5 **Hutton Sessay** N York
97 R10 **Hutton Wandesley** N York
9 M5 **Huxham** Devon
19 Q7 **Huxham Green** Somset
69 P2 **Huxley** Ches W
81 N6 **Huyton** Knows
94 B3 **Hycemoor** Cumb
32 G4 **Hyde** Gloucs
13 L2 **Hyde** Hants
103 N6 **Hyde** Tamesd
83 K6 **Hyde** Tamesd
35 K11 **Hyde End** Wokham
35 P4 **Hyde Heath** Bucks
70 G11 **Hyde Lea** Staffs
23 Q6 **Hydestile** Surrey
86 B7 **Hykeham Moor** Lincs
116 C2 **Hyndford Bridge** S Lans
136 B8 **Hynish** Ag & B
56 E6 **Hyssington** Powys
32 C5 **Hystfield** Gloucs
14 D5 **Hythe** Hants
26 E3 **Hythe** Kent
19 M4 **Hythe** Somset
36 B6 **Hythe End** W & M
94 B3 **Hyton** Cumb

I

12 C3 **Ibberton** Dorset
84 B9 **Ible** Derbys
13 L3 **Ibsley** Hants
72 C9 **Ibstock** Leics
35 L6 **Ibstone** Bucks
22 C4 **Ibthorpe** Hants
105 N9 **Iburndale** N York
22 G4 **Ibworth** Hants
31 L11 **Icelton** N Som
139 J11 **Ichrachan** Ag & B
75 R11 **Ickburgh** Norfk
36 C3 **Ickenham** Gt Lon
34 H3 **Ickford** Bucks
39 M10 **Ickham** Kent
50 E4 **Ickleford** Herts
26 E8 **Icklesham** E Susx
51 L2 **Ickleton** Cambs
63 N6 **Icklingham** Suffk
90 B2 **Ickornshaw** N York
61 Q11 **Ickwell Green** C Beds
63 P8 **Ickworth** Suffk
47 P10 **Icomb** Gloucs
47 P11 **Idbury** Oxon
17 K10 **Iddesleigh** Devon
9 L6 **Ide** Devon
9 L9 **Ideford** Devon
37 L10 **Ide Hill** Kent
26 F7 **Iden** E Susx
26 B4 **Iden Green** Kent
26 D5 **Iden Green** Kent
9 P3 **Idle** C Brad
3 L4 **Idless** Cnwll
47 Q6 **Idlicote** Warwks

21 N7 **Idmiston** Wilts
42 H11 **Idole** Carmth
71 P5 **Idridgehay** Derbys
152 F5 **Idrigill** Highld
33 Q8 **Idstone** Oxon
34 F4 **Iffley** Oxon
24 G3 **Ifield** W Susx
24 B4 **Ifold** W Susx
13 K6 **Iford** Bmouth
25 K9 **Iford** E Susx
31 N7 **Ifton** Mons
69 K7 **Ifton Heath** Shrops
69 Q7 **Ightfield** Shrops
37 N9 **Ightham** Kent
65 N10 **Iken** Suffk
96 H11 **Ilkley** C Brad
5 M6 **Illand** Cnwll
58 E8 **Illey** Dudley
70 D2 **Illidge Green** Ches E
90 D5 **Illingworth** Calder
2 H6 **Illogan** Cnwll
73 J11 **Illston on the Hill** Leics
35 L3 **Ilmer** Bucks
47 P6 **Ilmington** Warwks
10 H2 **Ilminster** Somset
9 J9 **Ilsington** Devon
12 C6 **Ilsington** Dorset
28 G6 **Ilston** Swans
97 J5 **Ilton** N York
19 L11 **Ilton** Somset
120 G3 **Imachar** N Ayrs
93 L8 **Immingham** NE Lin
93 L7 **Immingham Dock** NE Lin
62 F8 **Impington** Cambs
81 P9 **Ince** Ches W
81 L4 **Ince Blundell** Sefton
82 C4 **Ince-in-Makerfield** Wigan
155 M4 **Inchbae Lodge Hotel** Highld
143 L11 **Inchbare** Angus
157 Q6 **Inchberry** Moray
154 D5 **Incheril** Highld
125 M4 **Inchinnan** Rens
146 F7 **Inchlaggan** Highld
134 G2 **Inchmichael** P & K
147 K5 **Inchnacardoch Hotel** Highld
161 M2 **Inchnadamph** Highld
134 H2 **Inchture** P & K
154 H10 **Inchvuilt** Highld
134 F3 **Inchyra** P & K
4 E10 **Indian Queens** Cnwll
65 N4 **Ingate Place** Suffk
51 P11 **Ingatestone** Essex
90 G9 **Ingbirchworth** Barns
97 L7 **Ingerthorpe** N York
57 H10 **Ingestre** Staffs
86 B4 **Ingham** Lincs
77 M6 **Ingham** Norfk
64 B7 **Ingham** Suffk
77 M6 **Ingham Corner** Norfk
75 J7 **Ingleborough** Norfk
72 A5 **Ingleby** Derbys
104 D10 **Ingleby Arncliffe** N York
104 D8 **Ingleby Barwick** S on T
73 Q5 **Ingleby Cross** N York
104 E10 **Ingleby Greenhow** N York
8 F3 **Ingleigh Green** Devon
20 D2 **Inglesbatch** BaNES
33 P5 **Inglesham** Swindn
109 L7 **Ingleston** D & G
103 N6 **Ingleton** Dur
95 P6 **Ingleton** N York
88 G3 **Inglewhite** Lancs
112 F6 **Ingoe** Nthumb
88 G4 **Ingol** Lancs
75 N4 **Ingoldisthorpe** Norfk
87 Q7 **Ingoldmells** Lincs
73 Q5 **Ingoldsby** Lincs
119 K7 **Ingram** Nthumb
37 P2 **Ingrave** Essex
90 D3 **Ingrow** C Brad
101 M11 **Ings** Cumb
31 Q7 **Ingst** S Glos
73 P9 **Ingthorpe** Rutlnd
76 H6 **Ingworth** Norfk
47 K3 **Inkberrow** Worcs
103 M3 **Inkerman** Dur
159 M10 **Inkhorn** Abers
22 C2 **Inkpen** W Berk
167 N2 **Inkstack** Highld
20 H7 **Inmarsh** Wilts
124 F3 **Innellan** Ag & B
117 L3 **Innerleithen** Border
135 K7 **Innerleven** Fife
106 E5 **Innermessan** D & G
129 J5 **Innerwick** E Loth
157 P5 **Innesmill** Moray
150 G2 **Insch** Abers
148 E7 **Insh** Highld
88 F3 **Inskip** Lancs
88 F3 **Inskip Moss Side** Lancs
16 H5 **Instow** Devon
6 C8 **Insworke** Cnwll
84 E4 **Intake** Sheff
149 N9 **Inver** Abers
163 K10 **Inver** Highld
141 P9 **Inver** P & K
145 N11 **Inverailort** Highld
153 Q6 **Inverallligin** Highld
159 P4 **Inverallochy** Abers
162 D7 **Inveran** Highld
131 M6 **Inveraray** Ag & B
153 K10 **Inverarish** Highld
142 H9 **Inverarity** Angus
132 C4 **Inverarnan** Stirlg
160 C10 **Inverasdale** Highld
132 C8 **Inverbeg** Ag & B
143 Q3 **Inverbervie** Abers
155 G5 **Inver-boyndie** Abers
139 J8 **Invercreran House Hotel** Ag & B
148 F5 **Inverdruie** Highld
127 Q3 **Inveresk** E Loth
138 H10 **Inveresragan** Ag & B

160 D10 **Inverewe Garden** Highld
149 K10 **Inverey** Abers
147 N3 **Inverfarigaig** Highld
138 H9 **Inverfolla** Ag & B
147 J7 **Invergarry** Highld
133 L2 **Invergeldie** P & K
146 G10 **Invergloy** Highld
156 C4 **Invergordon** Highld
142 E11 **Invergowrie** P & K
145 M6 **Inverguseran** Highld
140 G6 **Inverhadden** P & K
132 D2 **Inverherive Hotel** Stirlg
145 N7 **Inverie** Highld
131 K4 **Inverinan** Ag & B
145 R3 **Inverinate** Highld
143 M8 **Inverkeilor** Angus
134 E11 **Inverkeithing** Fife
158 F8 **Inverkeithny** Abers
124 G3 **Inverkip** Inver
160 H3 **Inverkirkaig** Highld
161 K9 **Inverlael** Highld
139 Q2 **Inverlair** Highld
130 H6 **Inverliever Lodge** Ag & B
131 P2 **Inverlochy** Ag & B
150 C11 **Invermark** Angus
147 L4 **Invermoriston** Highld
166 B4 **Invernaver** Highld
156 B8 **Inverness** Highld
156 A9 **Inverness Crematorium** Highld
156 D7 **Inverness Dalcross Airport** Highld
131 N8 **Invernoaden** Ag & B
139 P9 **Inveroran Hotel** Ag & B
142 G6 **Inverquharity** Angus
159 P8 **Inverquhomery** Abers
146 H11 **Inverroy** Highld
138 G6 **Inversanda** Highld
146 A4 **Invershiel** Highld
162 D7 **Invershin** Highld
167 M9 **Invershore** Highld
132 C6 **Inversnaid Hotel** Stirlg
159 Q8 **Inverugie** Abers
132 C6 **Inveruglas** Ag & B
148 E7 **Inveruglass** Highld
151 K3 **Inverurie** Abers
61 L5 **Inwardleigh** Devon
52 E8 **Inworth** Essex
168 C13 **Iochdar** W Isls
136 H10 **Iona** Ag & B
23 N10 **Iping** W Susx
7 L5 **Ipplepen** Devon
34 H7 **Ipsden** Oxon
71 J5 **Ipstones** Staffs
53 L3 **Ipswich** Suffk
53 L2 **Ipswich Crematorium** Suffk
81 K8 **Irby** Wirral
87 N8 **Irby in the Marsh** Lincs
93 L10 **Irby upon Humber** NE Lin
61 K7 **Irchester** Nhants
100 H3 **Ireby** Cumb
95 P5 **Ireby** Lancs
50 D2 **Ireland** C Beds
94 E5 **Ireleth** Cumb
102 G3 **Ireshopeburn** Dur
71 P5 **Ireton Wood** Derbys
82 F6 **Irlam** Salfd
73 Q5 **Irnham** Lincs
32 C8 **Iron Acton** S Glos
75 J11 **Iron Bridge** Cambs
57 M4 **Ironbridge** Wrekin
57 M4 **Ironbridge Gorge** Shrops
47 L4 **Iron Cross** Warwks
108 E5 **Ironmacannie** D & G
36 F11 **Irons Bottom** Surrey
84 F10 **Ironville** Derbys
77 M7 **Irstead** Norfk
111 J8 **Irthington** Cumb
61 K6 **Irthlingborough** Nhants
99 L4 **Irton** N York
125 J10 **Irvine** N Ayrs
125 J10 **Irvine Maritime Centre** N Ayrs
166 B4 **Isauld** Highld
169 q4 **Isbister** Shet
169 S7 **Isbister** Shet
25 K7 **Isfield** E Susx
61 J6 **Isham** Nhants
23 L6 **Isington** Hants
58 C8 **Islandpool** Worcs
122 E4 **Islay** Ag & B
122 D9 **Islay Airport** Ag & B
19 L10 **Isle Abbotts** Somset
19 L10 **Isle Brewers** Somset
63 K6 **Isleham** Cambs
37 J5 **Isle of Dogs** Gt Lon
38 E6 **Isle of Grain** Medway
168 i4 **Isle of Lewis** W Isls
80 e4 **Isle of Man** IoM
80 c8 **Isle of Man Ronaldsway Airport** IoM
137 Q8 **Isle of Mull** Ag & B
12 H8 **Isle of Purbeck** Dorset
38 G8 **Isle of Sheppey** Kent
152 G10 **Isle of Skye** Highld
39 P8 **Isle of Thanet** Kent
94 F7 **Isle of Walney** Cumb
107 N10 **Isle of Whithorn** D & G
14 F9 **Isle of Wight** IoW
14 F8 **Isle of Wight Crematorium** IoW
145 M5 **Isleornsay** Highld
2 c2 **Isles of Scilly St Mary's Airport** IoS
109 L6 **Islesteps** D & G
10 C1 **Islet Village** Guern
36 E5 **Isleworth** Gt Lon
72 C6 **Isley Walton** Leics
168 f5 **Islibhig** W Isls
36 H4 **Islington** Gt Lon
36 G2 **Islington Crematorium** Gt Lon
61 L5 **Islip** Nhants
34 F2 **Islip** Oxon
168 f5 **Islivig** W Isls
57 L2 **Isombridge** Wrekin
37 P6 **Istead Rise** Kent
22 F8 **Itchen Abbas** Hants
22 G8 **Itchen Stoke** Hants
24 D5 **Itchingfield** W Susx
32 C7 **Itchington** S Glos
76 G5 **Itteringham** Norfk
8 G5 **Itton** Devon
31 N5 **Itton** Mons
31 N5 **Itton Common** Mons
101 M2 **Ivegill** Cumb
102 H11 **Ivelet** N York
36 B4 **Iver** Bucks
36 B4 **Iver Heath** Bucks

112 H10 Iveston Dur
49 P11 Ivinghoe Bucks
49 Q11 Ivinghoe Aston Bucks
45 P3 Ivington Herefs
45 P3 Ivington Green Herefs
6 G7 Ivybridge Devon
26 H6 Ivychurch Kent
20 G10 Ivy Cross Dorset
37 N10 Ivy Hatch Kent
76 B10 Ivy Todd Norfk
38 F8 Iwade Kent
12 E2 Iwerne Courtney or Shroton Dorset
12 E2 Iwerne Minster Dorset
64 C7 Ixworth Suffk
64 C7 Ixworth Thorpe Suffk

J

88 H5 Jack Green Lancs
97 J10 Jack Hill N York
9 P5 Jack-in-the-Green Devon
21 Q7 Jack's Bush Hants
84 F10 Jacksdale Notts
90 F4 Jackson Bridge Kirk
125 P7 Jackton S Lans
5 K2 Jacobstow Cnwll
8 E4 Jacobstowe Devon
36 B10 Jacobs Well Surrey
41 L11 Jameston Pembks
155 N6 Jamestown Highld
132 D11 Jamestown W Duns
167 L10 Janetstown Highld
167 Q6 Janets-town Highld
109 P3 Jardine Hall D & G
113 M8 Jarrow S Tyne
25 M5 Jarvis Brook E Susx
52 B6 Jasper's Green Essex
126 E2 Jawcraig Falk
53 L9 Jaywick Essex
35 N10 Jealott's Hill Br For
97 P2 Jeater Houses N York
118 B6 Jedburgh Border
41 L9 Jeffreyston Pembks
156 C4 Jemimaville Highld
10 c2 Jerbourg Guern
11 a2 Jersey Airport Jersey
11 b2 Jersey Crematorium Jersey
29 K6 Jersey Marine Neath
86 B6 Jerusalem Lincs
113 L7 Jesmond N u Ty
25 N10 Jevington E Susx
31 N2 Jingle Street Mons
50 B8 Jockey End Herts
82 G10 Jodrell Bank Ches E
101 M4 Johnby Cumb
81 N8 John Lennon Airport Lpool
167 Q2 John o' Groats Highld
26 B7 John's Cross E Susx
143 P4 Johnshaven Abers
77 M8 Johnson's Street Norfk
40 H8 Johnston Pembks
117 J10 Johnstone D & G
125 L5 Johnstone Rens
109 P2 Johnstonebridge D & G
42 G11 Johnstown Carmth
69 K5 Johnstown Wrexhm
127 Q3 Joppa C Edin
54 D11 Joppa Cerdgn
114 H4 Joppa S Ayrs
35 Q6 Jordans Bucks
40 H4 Jordanston Pembks
84 E4 Jordanthorpe Sheff
37 M6 Joyden's Wood Kent
26 D2 Jubilee Corner Kent
91 K10 Jump Barns
25 L4 Jumper's Town E Susx
112 D9 Juniper Nthumb
127 M4 Juniper Green C Edin
122 H3 Jura Ag & B
80 e2 Jurby IoM
8 G8 Jurston Devon

K

102 E8 Kaber Cumb
126 H8 Kaimend S Lans
124 B3 Kames Ag & B
115 N2 Kames S Ayrs
3 L5 Kea Cnwll
92 D8 Keadby N Linc
87 L8 Keal Cotes Lincs
97 N11 Kearby Town End N York
82 G4 Kearsley Bolton
112 F5 Kearsley Nthumb
27 N3 Kearsney Kent
95 N5 Kearstwick Cumb
103 J11 Kearton N York
95 Q7 Keasden N York
6 G8 Keaton Devon
82 C8 Keckwick Halton
87 K3 Keddington Lincs
87 L3 Keddington Corner Lincs
63 M11 Kedington Suffk
71 Q6 Kedleston Derbys
93 L8 Keelby Lincs
70 E5 Keele Staffs
70 E6 Keele Services Staffs
70 E5 Keele University Staffs
61 M11 Keeley Green Bed
90 D4 Keelham C Brad
40 H7 Keeston Pembks
20 H3 Keevil Wilts
72 D5 Kegworth Leics
2 G5 Kehelland Cnwll
150 G4 Keig Abers
90 D2 Keighley C Brad
90 C3 Keighley Crematorium C Brad
133 P9 Keilarsbrae Clacks
134 B2 Keillour P & K
149 M9 Keiloch Abers
122 H6 Keils Ag & B
19 P8 Keinton Mandeville Somset
109 J2 Keir Mill D & G
111 Q10 Keirsleywell Row Nthumb
73 Q5 Keisby Lincs
102 D6 Keisley Cumb
167 P4 Keiss Highld
158 B7 Keith Moray
142 C10 Keithick P & K
143 L5 Keithock Angus

155 P6 Keithtown Highld
89 Q2 Kelbrook Lancs
73 Q2 Kelby Lincs
101 Q8 Keld Cumb
102 G10 Keld N York
98 F4 Keld Head N York
98 E3 Keldholme N York
92 D10 Kelfield N Linc
91 P3 Kelfield N York
85 N9 Kelham Notts
109 P7 Kelhead D & G
5 Q4 Kellacott Devon
88 E5 Kellamergh Lancs
142 H10 Kellas Angus
157 M7 Kellas Moray
7 L11 Kellaton Devon
102 C9 Kelleth Cumb
76 F3 Kelling Norfk
91 P6 Kellington N York
104 B3 Kelloe Dur
115 P5 Kelloholm D & G
100 C7 Kells Cumb
5 P5 Kelly Devon
5 P7 Kelly Bray Cnwll
60 F5 Kelmarsh Nhants
33 P5 Kelmscott Oxon
65 M8 Kelsale Suffk
81 Q11 Kelsall Ches W
50 H3 Kelshall Herts
110 C10 Kelsick Cumb
118 D4 Kelso Border
84 D8 Kelstedge Derbys
86 H3 Kelstern Lincs
81 K10 Kelsterton Flints
32 D11 Kelston BaNES
141 J8 Keltneyburn P & K
109 L6 Kelton D & G
134 E9 Kelty Fife
52 E8 Kelvedon Essex
51 N11 Kelvedon Hatch Essex
2 B8 Kelynack Cnwll
17 M2 Kemacott Devon
135 L5 Kemback Fife
57 N4 Kemberton Shrops
33 J5 Kemble Gloucs
33 J5 Kemble Wick Gloucs
47 J7 Kemerton Worcs
31 K4 Kemeys Commander Mons
151 J4 Kemnay Abers
26 H2 Kempe's Corner Kent
46 C9 Kempley Gloucs
46 C9 Kempley Green Gloucs
46 G5 Kempsey Worcs
33 N5 Kempsford Gloucs
58 H10 Kemps Green Warwks
22 H4 Kempshott Hants
61 M11 Kempston Bed
50 B2 Kempston Hardwick Bed
56 F8 Kempton Shrops
24 H10 Kemp Town Br & H
37 N9 Kemsing Kent
38 F8 Kemsley Kent
38 D9 Kemsley Street Kent
26 G5 Kenardington Kent
45 N6 Kenchester Herefs
33 Q4 Kencot Oxon
95 L2 Kendal Cumb
45 N9 Kenderchurch Herefs
32 C9 Kendleshire S Glos
29 M8 Kenfig Brdgnd
29 M8 Kenfig Hill Brdgnd
59 L10 Kenilworth Warwks
36 H8 Kenley Gt Lon
57 K4 Kenley Shrops
153 P6 Kenmore Highld
141 J8 Kenmore P & K
9 M7 Kenn Devon
31 M11 Kenn N Som
123 P7 Kennacraig Ag & B
5 M5 Kennards House Cnwll
2 F8 Kenneggy Cnwll
9 K3 Kennerleigh Devon
81 M4 Kennessee Green Sefton
133 Q9 Kennet Clacks
150 E2 Kennethmont Abers
63 L7 Kennett Cambs
9 M7 Kennford Devon
64 E4 Kenninghall Norfk
26 H2 Kennington Kent
34 F4 Kennington Oxon
135 K7 Kennoway Fife
19 K11 Kenny Somset
63 L5 Kennyhill Suffk
98 F7 Kennythorpe N York
136 B6 Kenovay Ag & B
152 D7 Kensaleyre Highld
36 G5 Kensington Gt Lon
50 B7 Kensworth Common C Beds
139 J6 Kentallen Highld
25 N3 Kent and Sussex Crematorium Kent
45 N9 Kentchurch Herefs
63 M7 Kentford Suffk
70 E3 Kent Green Ches E
39 P8 Kent International Airport Kent
9 Q3 Kentisbeare Devon
17 L3 Kentisbury Devon
17 L3 Kentisbury Ford Devon
36 G4 Kentish Town Gt Lon
101 N10 Kentmere Cumb
9 N8 Kenton Devon
36 E3 Kenton Gt Lon
113 K7 Kenton N u Ty
64 H8 Kenton Suffk
113 K7 Kenton Bankfoot N u Ty
138 B4 Kentra Highld
94 H5 Kents Bank Cumb
46 D10 Kent's Green Gloucs
22 B10 Kent's Oak Hants
26 C8 Kent Street E Susx
37 Q10 Kent Street Kent
69 M8 Kenwick Shrops
3 L4 Kenwyn Cnwll
82 D5 Kenyon Warrtn
165 J3 Keoldale Highld
145 Q3 Keppoch Highld
97 Q2 Kepwick N York
59 M8 Keresley Covtry
82 H11 Kermincham Ches E
7 K10 Kernborough Devon
46 A11 Kerne Bridge Herefs
130 G2 Kerrera Ag & B
83 K9 Kerridge Ches E
83 K9 Kerridge-end Ches E
2 C8 Kerris Cnwll
55 Q6 Kerry Powys
124 E5 Kerrycroy Ag & B

85 M8 Kersall Notts
9 Q8 Kersbrook Devon
17 L6 Kerscott Devon
52 H3 Kersey Suffk
52 G3 Kersey Tye Suffk
52 G3 Kersey Upland Suffk
168 I5 Kershader W Isls
111 J4 Kershopefoot Cumb
47 J6 Kersoe Worcs
10 B3 Kerswell Devon
46 G5 Kerswell Green Worcs
2 F7 Kerthen Wood Cnwll
53 M2 Kesgrave Suffk
65 Q4 Kessingland Suffk
65 Q4 Kessingland Beach Suffk
3 P4 Kestle Cnwll
4 C10 Kestle Mill Cnwll
37 K8 Keston Gt Lon
101 J6 Keswick Cumb
77 J11 Keswick Norfk
87 L5 Ketsby Lincs
61 J5 Kettering Nhants
61 J5 Kettering Crematorium Nhants
76 H11 Ketteringham Norfk
142 C10 Kettins P & K
64 D11 Kettlebaston Suffk
135 J6 Kettlebridge Fife
59 K4 Kettlebrook Staffs
65 K9 Kettleburgh Suffk
51 K7 Kettle Green Herts
109 P5 Kettleholm D & G
105 M7 Kettleness N York
83 L9 Kettleshulme Ches E
97 K9 Kettlesing N York
97 K9 Kettlesing Bottom N York
76 D5 Kettlestone Norfk
85 P5 Kettlethorpe Lincs
169 f3 Kettletoft Ork
96 E6 Kettlewell N York
73 P10 Ketton Rutlnd
36 E5 Kew Gt Lon
19 K2 Kewstoke N Som
91 J9 Kexbrough Barns
98 E10 Kexby C York
85 Q3 Kexby Lincs
70 F2 Key Green Ches E
105 M10 Key Green N York
72 H9 Keyham Leics
13 P6 Keyhaven Hants
93 M5 Keyingham E R Yk
24 H7 Keymer W Susx
32 C11 Keynsham BaNES
61 N8 Keysoe Bed
61 N8 Keysoe Row Bed
61 M5 Keyston Cambs
38 E9 Key Street Kent
72 G4 Keyworth Notts
18 H10 Kibbear Somset
113 K9 Kibblesworth Gatesd
60 E2 Kibworth Beauchamp Leics
60 E2 Kibworth Harcourt Leics
37 K5 Kidbrooke Gt Lon
100 E6 Kidburngill Cumb
58 C3 Kiddemore Green Staffs
58 B9 Kidderminster Worcs
48 D10 Kiddington Oxon
76 G11 Kidd's Moor Norfk
34 E2 Kidlington Oxon
35 J9 Kidmore End Oxon
107 M10 Kidsdale D & G
70 E4 Kidsgrove Staffs
96 E4 Kidstones N York
28 D3 Kidwelly Carmth
138 G10 Kiel Crofts Ag & B
111 M2 Kielder Nthumb
122 F6 Kiells Ag & B
125 L5 Kilbarchan Rens
145 L6 Kilbeg Highld
123 M7 Kilberry Ag & B
125 J7 Kilbirnie N Ayrs
123 M4 Kilbride Ag & B
124 C4 Kilbride Ag & B
157 K5 Kilbuiack Moray
84 E11 Kilburn Derbys
36 F4 Kilburn Gt Lon
97 R5 Kilburn N York
72 G11 Kilby Leics
123 P7 Kilchamaig Ag & B
124 E7 Kilchattan Ag & B
136 b2 Kilchattan Ag & B
138 E10 Kilcheran Ag & B
137 M3 Kilchoan Highld
122 B7 Kilchoman Ag & B
131 L3 Kilchrenan Ag & B
135 M7 Kilconquhar Fife
46 C9 Kilcot Gloucs
155 Q7 Kilcoy Highld
131 Q11 Kilcreggan Ag & B
104 H9 Kildale N York
120 E8 Kildalloig Ag & B
156 D3 Kildary Highld
124 B4 Kildavaig Ag & B
124 C4 Kildavanan Ag & B
163 L2 Kildonan Highld
121 K7 Kildonan N Ayrs
163 L2 Kildonan Lodge Highld
144 G10 Kildonnan Highld
106 E6 Kildrochet House D & G
150 D4 Kildrummy Abers
96 F11 Kildwick N York
124 A2 Kilfinan Ag & B
146 H8 Kilfinnan Highld
80 F11 Kilford Denbgs
41 M9 Kilgetty Pembks
114 E7 Kilgrammie S Ayrs
31 N5 Kilgwrrwg Common Mons
99 M8 Kilham E R Yk
118 G4 Kilham Nthumb
136 A7 Kilkenneth Ag & B
123 Q8 Kilkenzie Ag & B
120 D8 Kilkerran Ag & B
16 D9 Kilkhampton Cnwll
84 G4 Killamarsh Derbys
28 H6 Killay Swans
132 G10 Killearn Stirlg
156 B6 Killen Highld
103 N7 Killerby Darltn
9 N4 Killerton Devon
140 D6 Killichonan P & K
146 G11 Killiechonate Highld
137 N7 Killiechronan Ag & B
141 M5 Killiecrankie P & K
154 B11 Killilan Highld
167 P5 Killimster Highld
140 E11 Killin Stirlg
97 L9 Killinghall N York

95 N3 Killington Cumb
17 M2 Killington Devon
95 M2 Killington Lake Services Cumb
113 L6 Killingworth N Tyne
3 L5 Killiow Cnwll
128 D10 Killochyett Border
125 J3 Kilmacolm Inver
133 J6 Kilmahog Stirlg
130 F9 Kilmahumaig Ag & B
152 G3 Kilmaluag Highld
135 K3 Kilmany Fife
125 L10 Kilmarnock E Ayrs
130 C8 Kilmartin Ag & B
125 L9 Kilmaurs E Ayrs
130 H5 Kilmelford Ag & B
20 C4 Kilmersdon Somset
22 G9 Kilmeston Hants
120 C7 Kilmichael Ag & B
130 H9 Kilmichael Glassary Ag & B
130 F10 Kilmichael of Inverlussa Ag & B
10 F5 Kilmington Devon
20 E7 Kilmington Wilts
20 E7 Kilmington Common Wilts
20 E7 Kilmington Street Wilts
155 N9 Kilmorack Highld
130 H2 Kilmore Ag & B
145 L6 Kilmore Highld
123 M5 Kilmory Ag & B
137 N1 Kilmory Highld
121 J7 Kilmory N Ayrs
152 D8 Kilmuir Highld
152 F3 Kilmuir Highld
156 B8 Kilmuir Highld
156 D3 Kilmuir Highld
131 P11 Kilmun Ag & B
122 C5 Kilnave Ag & B
126 F8 Kilncadzow S Lans
26 B4 Kilndown Kent
35 M9 Kiln Green Wokham
100 H4 Kilnhill Cumb
82 D11 Kilnhouses Ches W
91 M11 Kilnhurst Rothm
130 G3 Kilninver Ag & B
112 F9 Kiln Pit Hill Nthumb
93 R7 Kilnsea E R Yk
96 E7 Kilnsey N York
99 K11 Kilnwick E R Yk
98 C11 Kilnwick Percy E R Yk
136 B2 Kiloran Ag & B
120 H6 Kilpatrick N Ayrs
45 M8 Kilpeck Herefs
92 C5 Kilpin E R Yk
92 C5 Kilpin Pike E R Yk
135 P7 Kilrenny Fife
60 C6 Kilsby Nhants
134 G2 Kilspindie P & K
106 F10 Kilstay D & G
126 C2 Kilsyth N Lans
155 P9 Kiltarlity Highld
105 K7 Kilton R & Cl
105 J7 Kilton Thorpe R & Cl
152 F4 Kilvaxter Highld
18 F6 Kilve Somset
73 L2 Kilvington Notts
125 J9 Kilwinning N Ayrs
76 F11 Kimberley Norfk
72 D2 Kimberley Notts
84 F2 Kimberworth Rothm
113 L11 Kimblesworth Dur
35 M3 Kimble Wick Bucks
61 P7 Kimbolton Cambs
45 Q2 Kimbolton Herefs
60 C3 Kimcote Leics
12 F9 Kimmeridge Dorset
119 J3 Kimmerston Nthumb
21 Q5 Kimpton Hants
50 E7 Kimpton Herts
16 E9 Kimworthy Devon
166 E10 Kinbrace Highld
133 M6 Kinbuck Stirlg
135 M4 Kincaple Fife
133 Q10 Kincardine Fife
162 E9 Kincardine Highld
150 F8 Kincardine O'Neil Abers
142 B10 Kinclaven P & K
151 N7 Kincorth C Aber
157 J5 Kincorth House Moray
148 E6 Kincraig Highld
141 N8 Kincraigie P & K
141 N8 Kindallachan P & K
123 L9 Kinerarach Ag & B
47 L9 Kineton Gloucs
48 B4 Kineton Warwks
134 F3 Kinfauns P & K
124 D6 Kingarth Ag & B
54 H3 King Arthur's Labyrinth Gwynd
151 M8 Kingcausie Abers
31 M3 Kingcoed Mons
86 E2 Kingerby Lincs
16 D10 Kingford Devon
47 L9 Kingham Oxon
109 L6 Kingholm Quay D & G
134 H10 Kinghorn Fife
134 G8 Kinglassie Fife
142 E6 Kingoldrum Angus
135 J2 Kingoodie P & K
45 P6 King's Acre Herefs
6 C8 Kingsand Cnwll
35 N3 Kingsash Bucks
135 P5 Kingsbarns Fife
7 J10 Kingsbridge Devon
18 C7 Kingsbridge Somset
36 E3 Kingsbury Gt Lon
59 K5 Kingsbury Warwks
19 M10 Kingsbury Episcopi Somset
45 R9 King's Caple Herefs
22 F3 Kingsclere Hants
73 Q11 King's Cliffe Nhants
32 F5 Kingscote Gloucs
17 J8 Kingscott Devon
47 L3 King's Coughton Warwks
121 K6 Kingscross N Ayrs
19 P9 Kingsdon Somset
27 Q2 Kingsdown Kent
33 N7 Kingsdown Swindn
32 F11 Kingsdown Wilts
33 N7 Kingsdown Crematorium Swindn
134 E9 Kingseat Fife
35 K3 Kingsey Bucks
24 E3 Kingsfold W Susx

151 M6 Kingsford C Aber
125 L8 Kingsford E Ayrs
57 Q8 Kingsford Worcs
39 Q7 Kingsgate Kent
46 E8 Kings Green Gloucs
64 C9 Kingshall Street Suffk
17 K4 Kingsheanton Devon
58 D8 King's Heath Birm
37 Q9 Kings Hill Kent
58 E9 King's Hill Wsall
139 P7 Kings House Hotel Highld
132 H3 Kingshouse Hotel Stirlg
59 J7 Kingshurst Solhll
110 C10 Kingside Hill Cumb
7 M5 Kingskerswell Devon
135 J6 Kingskettle Fife
11 K5 Kingsland Dorset
45 N2 Kingsland Herefs
78 D8 Kingsland IoA
50 C10 Kings Langley Herts
82 C10 Kingsley Ches W
22 C8 Kingsley Hants
71 J5 Kingsley Staffs
23 N8 Kingsley Green W Susx
60 G8 Kingsley Park Nhants
57 P5 Kingslow Shrops
75 M6 King's Lynn Norfk
102 B6 Kings Meaburn Cumb
14 G4 Kingsmead Hants
10 b2 King's Mills Guern
81 Q4 King's Moss St Hel
142 H8 Kingsmuir Angus
117 K3 Kings Muir Border
135 N6 Kingsmuir Fife
59 Q9 Kings Newnham Warwks
72 B5 King's Newton Derbys
26 H4 Kingsnorth Kent
58 G9 King's Norton Birm
72 H10 King's Norton Leics
17 M8 Kings Nympton Devon
45 N4 King's Pyon Herefs
62 C5 Kings Ripton Cambs
22 C8 King's Somborne Hants
11 Q2 King's Stag Dorset
32 F4 King's Stanley Gloucs
48 E7 King's Sutton Nhants
58 G6 Kingstanding Birm
7 M4 Kingsteignton Devon
83 N10 King Sterndale Derbys
45 P8 Kingsthorne Herefs
60 G8 Kingsthorpe Nhants
62 D9 Kingston Cambs
5 P6 Kingston Cnwll
6 G9 Kingston Devon
9 Q7 Kingston Devon
12 C3 Kingston Dorset
12 G9 Kingston Dorset
128 E3 Kingston E Loth
13 K4 Kingston Hants
14 E10 Kingston IoW
39 L11 Kingston Kent
24 C10 Kingston W Susx
34 D5 Kingston Bagpuize Oxon
35 K5 Kingston Blount Oxon
20 F7 Kingston Deverill Wilts
45 N7 Kingstone Herefs
10 H2 Kingstone Somset
71 K9 Kingstone Staffs
33 Q7 Kingstone Winslow Oxon
34 B7 Kingston Lisle Oxon
25 J9 Kingston near Lewes E Susx
72 E5 Kingston on Soar Notts
157 Q4 Kingston on Spey Moray
11 M6 Kingston Russell Dorset
19 M9 Kingston St Mary Somset
31 M11 Kingston Seymour N Som
35 K4 Kingston Stert Oxon
93 J5 Kingston upon Hull C KuH
36 E7 Kingston upon Thames Gt Lon
36 E7 Kingston upon Thames Crematorium Gt Lon
110 G9 Kingstown Cumb
50 G9 King's Walden Herts
7 M8 Kingswear Devon
151 M6 Kingswells C Aber
31 P9 Kings Weston Bristl
58 C7 Kingswinford Dudley
49 J11 Kingswood Bucks
32 D6 Kingswood Gloucs
38 D11 Kingswood Kent
56 C4 Kingswood Powys
32 B10 Kingswood S Glos
18 F7 Kingswood Somset
36 F9 Kingswood Surrey
59 J10 Kingswood Warwks
59 J10 Kingswood Brook Warwks
45 K4 Kingswood Common Herefs
58 B4 Kingswood Common Staffs
22 E8 Kings Worthy Hants
86 F5 Kingthorpe Lincs
45 K3 Kington Herefs
32 B6 Kington S Glos
47 J3 Kington Worcs
32 H9 Kington Langley Wilts
20 E10 Kington Magna Dorset
32 H9 Kington St Michael Wilts
148 D7 Kingussie Highld
19 P8 Kingweston Somset
159 M11 Kinharrachie Abers
109 K7 Kinharvie D & G
133 Q4 Kinkell Bridge P & K
159 P9 Kinknockie Abers
127 M4 Kinleith C Edin
57 N8 Kinlet Shrops
144 F8 Kinloch Highld
164 H10 Kinloch Highld
165 N6 Kinloch Highld
142 A9 Kinloch P & K
132 F7 Kinlochard Stirlg
164 F5 Kinlochbervie Highld
138 H2 Kinlocheil Highld
154 C5 Kinlochewe Highld
146 B6 Kinloch Hourn Highld
147 N10 Kinlochlaggan Highld
139 M5 Kinlochleven Highld
138 C3 Kinlochmoidart Highld
145 M11 Kinlochnanuagh Highld
140 G6 Kinloch Rannoch P & K
157 K5 Kinloss Moray
80 D8 Kinmel Bay Conwy
151 L4 Kinmuck Abers
151 M4 Kinmundy Abers
122 C11 Kinnabus Ag & B

284 Kinnadie - Lattiford

159 N9 Kinnadie Abers
141 N6 Kinnaird P & K
143 Q2 Kinneff Abers
116 E10 Kinnelhead D & G
143 L7 Kinnell Angus
69 K10 Kinnerley Shrops
45 L5 Kinnersley Herefs
46 G6 Kinnersley Worcs
45 J2 Kinnerton Powys
56 F5 Kinnerton Shrops
69 K2 Kinnerton Green Flints
134 F7 Kinnesswood P & K
103 L6 Kinninvie Dur
142 F6 Kinnordy Angus
72 H4 Kinoulton Notts
134 E7 Kinross P & K
142 B11 Kinrossie P & K
134 E7 Kinross Services P & K
50 D7 Kinsbourne Green Herts
70 B6 Kinsey Heath Ches E
56 F11 Kinsham Herefs
46 H7 Kinsham Worcs
91 L8 Kinsley Wakefd
13 J5 Kinson Bmouth
146 B4 Kintail Highld
34 C11 Kintbury W Berk
157 J5 Kintessack Moray
134 E4 Kintillo P & K
56 G10 Kinton Herefs
69 L11 Kinton Shrops
151 K4 Kintore Abers
122 G9 Kintour Ag & B
122 D10 Kintra Ag & B
137 J10 Kintra Ag & B
130 G7 Kintraw Ag & B
120 D4 Kintyre Ag & B
148 G4 Kinveachy Highld
58 B8 Kinver Staffs
103 Q11 Kiplin N York
91 L4 Kippax Leeds
133 J9 Kippen Stirlg
108 H10 Kippford or Scaur D & G
25 P2 Kipping's Cross Kent
169 c6 Kirbister Ork
77 K10 Kirby Bedon Norfk
73 J7 Kirby Bellars Leics
65 M3 Kirby Cane Norfk
59 L9 Kirby Corner Covtry
53 M7 Kirby Cross Essex
72 E10 Kirby Fields Leics
99 J7 Kirby Grindalythe N York
97 N7 Kirby Hill N York
103 M9 Kirby Hill N York
97 Q3 Kirby Knowle N York
53 M7 Kirby le Soken Essex
98 F5 Kirby Misperton N York
72 E10 Kirby Muxloe Leics
97 P2 Kirby Sigston N York
98 G9 Kirby Underdale E R Yk
97 N4 Kirby Wiske N York
24 B5 Kirdford W Susx
167 N5 Kirk Highld
169 r10 Kirkabister Shet
108 D11 Kirkandrews D & G
110 G9 Kirkandrews upon Eden Cumb
110 F9 Kirkbampton Cumb
109 L9 Kirkbean D & G
91 Q8 Kirk Bramwith Donc
110 D9 Kirkbride Cumb
97 L2 Kirkbridge N York
143 J9 Kirkbuddo Angus
117 K3 Kirkburn Border
99 K9 Kirkburn E R Yk
90 F8 Kirkburton Kirk
81 N5 Kirkby Knows
86 E2 Kirkby Lincs
104 F9 Kirkby N York
97 L2 Kirkby Fleetham N York
86 E9 Kirkby Green Lincs
84 G9 Kirkby in Ashfield Notts
94 E4 Kirkby-in-Furness Cumb
86 E11 Kirkby la Thorpe Lincs
95 N5 Kirkby Lonsdale Cumb
96 C8 Kirkby Malham N York
72 D10 Kirkby Mallory Leics
97 K6 Kirkby Malzeard N York
98 E3 Kirkby Mills N York
98 D3 Kirkbymoorside N York
86 H8 Kirkby on Bain Lincs
97 M11 Kirkby Overblow N York
102 E9 Kirkby Stephen Cumb
102 B5 Kirkby Thore Cumb
73 R5 Kirkby Underwood Lincs
91 N2 Kirkby Wharf N York
84 G10 Kirkby Woodhouse Notts
134 H9 Kirkcaldy Fife
134 H9 Kirkcaldy Crematorium Fife
111 K7 Kirkcambeck Cumb
108 E10 Kirkchrist D & G
106 D4 Kirkcolm D & G
115 P5 Kirkconnel D & G
109 L7 Kirkconnell D & G
107 K5 Kirkcowan D & G
108 E10 Kirkcudbright D & G
81 L6 Kirkdale Lpool
97 N10 Kirk Deighton N York
92 H5 Kirk Ella E R Yk
116 B2 Kirkfieldbank S Lans
109 J7 Kirkgunzeon D & G
72 D2 Kirk Hallam Derbys
88 E4 Kirkham Lancs
98 E7 Kirkham N York
90 H6 Kirkhamgate Wakefd
97 Q9 Kirk Hammerton N York
112 F4 Kirkharle Nthumb
111 N11 Kirkhaugh Nthumb
90 F7 Kirkheaton Kirk
112 F5 Kirkheaton Nthumb
155 Q8 Kirkhill Highld
116 D9 Kirkhope S Lans
111 L9 Kirkhouse Cumb
91 Q8 Kirkhouse Green Donc
145 J4 Kirkibost Highld
142 E9 Kirkinch P & K
107 M7 Kirkinner D & G
126 B3 Kirkintilloch E Duns
71 P4 Kirk Ireton Derbys
100 E7 Kirkland Cumb
102 B4 Kirkland Cumb
109 M3 Kirkland D & G
115 P5 Kirkland D & G
115 R9 Kirkland D & G
100 G2 Kirkland Guards Cumb
71 P7 Kirk Langley Derbys
104 G6 Kirkleatham R & Cl
104 D9 Kirklevington S on T
65 Q3 Kirkley Suffk
97 M4 Kirklington N York
85 L9 Kirklington Notts
110 H7 Kirklinton Cumb
127 L3 Kirkliston C Edin
107 N6 Kirkmabreck D & G
106 F10 Kirkmaiden D & G
103 Q4 Kirk Merrington Dur
80 d3 Kirk Michael IoM
141 Q6 Kirkmichael P & K
114 F6 Kirkmichael S Ayrs
126 D9 Kirkmuirhill S Lans
118 H4 Kirknewton Nthumb
127 L4 Kirknewton W Loth
158 D11 Kirkney Abers
126 E5 Kirk of Shotts N Lans
101 Q2 Kirkoswald Cumb
114 D6 Kirkoswald S Ayrs
109 K2 Kirkpatrick D & G
108 G6 Kirkpatrick Durham D & G
110 E6 Kirkpatrick-Fleming D & G
91 Q9 Kirk Sandall Donc
94 C4 Kirksanton Cumb
91 N7 Kirk Smeaton N York
90 H3 Kirkstall Leeds
86 G8 Kirkstead Lincs
158 D10 Kirkstile Abers
110 G2 Kirkstile D & G
101 M9 Kirkstone Pass Inn Cumb
167 P2 Kirkstyle Highld
91 K6 Kirkthorpe Wakefd
150 G2 Kirkton Abers
109 L4 Kirkton D & G
135 K2 Kirkton Fife
145 P2 Kirkton Highld
154 B9 Kirkton Highld
134 B4 Kirkton P & K
117 J3 Kirkton Manor Border
142 E7 Kirkton of Airlie Angus
142 E10 Kirkton of Auchterhouse Angus
156 E8 Kirkton of Barevan Highld
142 B11 Kirkton of Collace P & K
150 B4 Kirkton of Glenbuchat Abers
151 P2 Kirkton of Logie Buchan Abers
143 J5 Kirkton of Menmuir Angus
143 J10 Kirkton of Monikie Angus
158 G11 Kirkton of Rayne Abers
151 L6 Kirkton of Skene Abers
142 F10 Kirkton of Strathmartine Angus
142 G10 Kirkton of Tealing Angus
150 G5 Kirkton of Tough Abers
159 N4 Kirktown Abers
159 Q7 Kirktown Abers
158 G5 Kirktown of Alvah Abers
151 L2 Kirktown of Bourtie Abers
151 M10 Kirktown of Fetteresso Abers
157 Q10 Kirktown of Mortlach Moray
151 Q2 Kirktown of Slains Abers
116 G2 Kirkurd Border
169 d5 Kirkwall Ork
169 d6 Kirkwall Airport Ork
112 E4 Kirkwhelpington Nthumb
118 F5 Kirk Yetholm Border
93 K8 Kirmington N Linc
86 G2 Kirmond le Mire Lincs
124 F2 Kirn Ag & B
142 F7 Kirriemuir Angus
65 K2 Kirstead Green Norfk
110 D6 Kirtlebridge D & G
63 L9 Kirtling Cambs
63 L9 Kirtling Green Cambs
48 E11 Kirtlington Oxon
166 B4 Kirtomy Highld
74 F3 Kirton Lincs
85 L7 Kirton Notts
53 N3 Kirton Suffk
74 E2 Kirton End Lincs
125 K2 Kirtonhill W Duns
74 E2 Kirton Holme Lincs
92 F11 Kirton in Lindsey N Linc
107 M7 Kirwaugh D & G
153 Q10 Kishorn Highld
60 E9 Kislingbury Nhants
47 P8 Kitebrook Warwks
59 J11 Kite Green Warwks
59 Q11 Kites Hardwick Warwks
5 L2 Kitleigh Cnwll
88 G9 Kitt Green Wigan
18 E10 Kittisford Somset
28 G7 Kittle Swans
59 J7 Kitt's Green Birm
151 N6 Kittybrewster C Aber
23 J8 Kitwood Hants
45 P8 Kivernoll Herefs
84 G4 Kiveton Park Rothm
85 P4 Knaith Lincs
85 P3 Knaith Park Lincs
20 F10 Knap Corner Dorset
23 Q3 Knaphill Surrey
19 K9 Knapp Somset
22 D10 Knapp Hill Hants
85 M9 Knapthorpe Notts
98 B10 Knapton C York
98 H5 Knapton N York
77 L5 Knapton Norfk
45 N4 Knapton Green Herefs
62 D8 Knapwell Cambs
97 N9 Knaresborough N York
111 N10 Knarsdale Nthumb
159 L9 Knaven Abers
97 P3 Knayton N York
50 G6 Knebworth Herts
92 B5 Knedlington E R Yk
85 M8 Kneesall Notts
50 H2 Kneesworth Cambs
85 M11 Kneeton Notts
28 E7 Knelston Swans
70 G7 Knenhall Staffs
64 D5 Knettishall Suffk
17 M4 Knightacott Devon
48 D4 Knightcote Warwks
70 E9 Knightley Staffs
70 E10 Knightley Dale Staffs
72 G10 Knighton C Leic
6 E9 Knighton Devon
11 N2 Knighton Dorset
12 H5 Knighton Poole
56 D10 Knighton Powys
18 G6 Knighton Somset
70 C6 Knighton Staffs
70 D9 Knighton Staffs
33 Q10 Knighton Wilts
57 L11 Knighton on Teme Worcs
46 G9 Knightsbridge Gloucs
4 H5 Knightsmill Cnwll
46 D3 Knightwick Worcs
45 K2 Knill Herefs
73 L4 Knipton Leics
112 H11 Knitsley Dur
71 N4 Kniveton Derbys
102 C5 Knock Cumb
145 L6 Knock Highld
158 D7 Knock Moray
168 j4 Knock W Isls
167 K11 Knockally Highld
161 L4 Knockan Highld
157 M9 Knockando Moray
155 Q9 Knockbain Highld
156 A6 Knockbain Highld
124 F5 Knock Castle N Ayrs
167 L4 Knockdee Highld
124 E3 Knockdow Ag & B
32 F11 Knockdown Wilts
114 F8 Knockeen S Ayrs
121 K6 Knockenkelly N Ayrs
125 L10 Knockentiber E Ayrs
37 N6 Knockhall Kent
37 L9 Knockholt Kent
37 L9 Knockholt Pound Kent
69 K10 Knockin Shrops
125 L10 Knockinlaw E Ayrs
37 N8 Knockmill Kent
106 C5 Knocknain D & G
123 J5 Knockrome Ag & B
80 c4 Knocksharry IoM
108 C4 Knocksheen D & G
108 G6 Knockvennie Smithy D & G
65 N9 Knodishall Suffk
65 N9 Knodishall Common Suffk
19 N9 Knole Somset
31 Q8 Knole Park S Glos
82 H9 Knolls Green Ches E
69 L7 Knolton Wrexhm
20 H6 Knook Wilts
73 L9 Knossington Leics
94 H11 Knott End-on-Sea Lancs
61 M8 Knotting Bed
61 M8 Knotting Green Bed
91 N6 Knottingley Wakefd
81 N6 Knotty Ash Lpool
35 P6 Knotty Green Bucks
57 K9 Knowbury Shrops
107 K3 Knowe D & G
115 M9 Knowehead D & G
114 E5 Knoweside S Ayrs
32 B10 Knowle Bristl
9 J4 Knowle Devon
9 P3 Knowle Devon
9 Q8 Knowle Devon
16 H4 Knowle Devon
57 K10 Knowle Shrops
59 J9 Knowle Solhll
18 C6 Knowle Somset
9 P5 Knowle Cross Devon
110 H9 Knowlefield Cumb
89 J3 Knowle Green Lancs
35 Q11 Knowle Hill Surrey
10 G2 Knowle St Giles Somset
14 G5 Knowle Village Hants
89 Q6 Knowle Wood Calder
52 C3 Knowl Green Essex
35 M9 Knowl Hill W & M
12 H3 Knowlton Dorset
39 N11 Knowlton Kent
81 N5 Knowsley Knows
81 P6 Knowsley Safari Park Knows
17 Q7 Knowstone Devon
97 L9 Knox N York
26 C3 Knox Bridge Kent
56 D10 Knucklas Powys
61 K7 Knuston Nhants
82 G9 Knutsford Ches E
82 F9 Knutsford Services Ches E
70 E5 Knutton Staffs
90 D7 Krumlin Calder
3 J10 Kuggar Cnwll
145 N2 Kyleakin Highld
145 N2 Kyle of Lochalsh Highld
145 N3 Kylerhea Highld
164 F10 Kylesku Highld
145 P9 Kylesmorar Highld
168 h8 Kyles Scalpay W Isls
164 F10 Kylestrome Highld
46 B7 Kynaston Herefs
69 L10 Kynaston Shrops
70 B11 Kynnersley Wrekin
46 B2 Kyre Green Worcs
46 B2 Kyre Park Worcs
57 K11 Kyrewood Worcs
18 E10 Kyrle Somset

L

10 b2 La Bellieuse Guern
168 i5 Lacasaigh W Isls
168 j4 Lacasdal W Isls
93 M9 Laceby NE Lin
35 M4 Lacey Green Bucks
82 F10 Lach Dennis Ches W
104 G7 Lackenby R & Cl
63 N6 Lackford Suffk
63 N6 Lackford Green Suffk
32 H11 Lacock Wilts
48 D3 Ladbroke Warwks
70 H4 Ladderedge Staffs
37 Q11 Laddingford Kent
87 L10 Lade Bank Lincs
3 M3 Ladock Cnwll
169 f2 Lady Ork
135 J6 Ladybank Fife
5 N4 Ladycross Cnwll
116 C5 Ladygill S Lans
94 D3 Lady Hall Cumb
129 M10 Ladykirk Border
46 A8 Ladyridge Herefs
63 N9 Lady's Green Suffk
58 G7 Ladywood Birm
46 G2 Ladywood Worcs
10 c1 La Fontenelle Guern
10 b2 La Fosse Guern
109 J3 Lag D & G
138 A5 Laga Highld
122 F10 Lagavulin Ag & B
121 J7 Lagg N Ayrs
146 H8 Laggan Highld
147 Q9 Laggan Highld
148 F7 Lagganlia Highld
10 c1 La Greve Guern
11 a1 La Greve de Lecq Jersey
11 c2 La Hougue Bie Jersey
10 b2 La Houguette Guern
165 K5 Laid Highld
160 E8 Laide Highld
144 G10 Laig Highld
125 M8 Laigh Clunch E Ayrs
125 M9 Laigh Fenwick E Ayrs
115 M3 Laigh Glenmuir E Ayrs
126 C7 Laighstonehall S Lans
37 Q3 Laindon Essex
162 D5 Lairg Highld
90 F4 Laisterdyke C Brad
101 N4 Laithes Cumb
8 D7 Lake Devon
17 K5 Lake Devon
14 G10 Lake IoW
12 G6 Lake Poole
21 M7 Lake Wilts
100 H9 Lake District National Park Cumb
63 M4 Lakenheath Suffk
24 B3 Laker's Green Surrey
75 K11 Lakesend Norfk
94 H3 Lakeside Cumb
36 C7 Laleham Surrey
29 N9 Laleston Brdgnd
3 K7 Lamanva Cnwll
52 E4 Lamarsh Essex
77 J7 Lamas Norfk
118 D2 Lambden Border
25 Q3 Lamberhurst Kent
25 Q3 Lamberhurst Down Kent
129 P8 Lamberton Border
36 H5 Lambeth Gt Lon
36 G6 Lambeth Crematorium Gt Lon
63 M10 Lambfair Green Suffk
85 K11 Lambley Notts
111 N9 Lambley Nthumb
34 B9 Lambourn W Berk
37 L2 Lambourne End Essex
34 B9 Lambourn Woodlands W Berk
89 L3 Lamb Roe Lancs
24 F3 Lambs Green W Susx
40 H7 Lambston Pembks
5 L9 Lamellion Cnwll
8 C9 Lamerton Devon
113 L9 Lamesley Gatesd
116 D4 Lamington S Lans
121 K5 Lamlash N Ayrs
101 M3 Lamonby Cumb
4 G9 Lamorick Cnwll
2 C9 Lamorna Cnwll
3 M5 Lamorran Cnwll
5 K8 Lampen Cnwll
43 L5 Lampeter Cerdgn
41 N8 Lampeter Velfrey Pembks
41 K10 Lamphey Pembks
100 E6 Lamplugh Cumb
60 G6 Lamport Nhants
20 C7 Lamyatt Somset
5 N2 Lana Devon
16 E10 Lana Devon
116 B2 Lanark S Lans
95 K8 Lancaster Lancs
95 K8 Lancaster & Morecambe Crematorium Lancs
95 L10 Lancaster Services (Forton) Lancs
31 P5 Lancaut Gloucs
113 J11 Lanchester Dur
24 E10 Lancing W Susx
10 c1 L'Ancresse Guern
62 G7 Landbeach Cambs
16 H7 Landcross Devon
151 J7 Landerberry Abers
21 Q11 Landford Wilts
167 L10 Land-hallow Highld
81 K7 Landican Crematorium Wirral
28 E6 Landimore Swans
17 K5 Landkey Devon
29 J5 Landore Swans
5 P9 Landrake Cnwll
7 K5 Landscove Devon
2 A8 Land's End Cnwll
2 A8 Land's End Cnwll
2 B8 Land's End Airport Cnwll
41 K8 Landshipping Pembks
5 P6 Landue Cnwll
6 C6 Landulph Cnwll
63 K7 Landwade Suffk
4 C9 Lane Cnwll
5 L5 Laneast Cnwll
89 P3 Lane Bottom Lancs
35 M6 Lane End Bucks
4 G8 Lane End Cnwll
22 G9 Lane End Hants
37 N6 Lane End Kent
96 C11 Lane End Lancs
82 E6 Lane End Warrtn
20 F5 Lane End Wilts
71 N8 Lane Ends Derbys
89 M4 Lane Ends Lancs
90 B2 Lane Ends N York
58 C4 Lane Green Staffs
85 P5 Laneham Notts
102 F2 Lanehead Dur
103 M8 Lane Head Dur
111 Q3 Lanehead Nthumb
82 D5 Lane Head Wigan
58 E4 Lane Head Wsall
88 E3 Lane Heads Lancs
89 Q2 Laneshaw Bridge Lancs
89 M6 Lane Side Lancs
5 Q2 Langaford Devon
19 J9 Langaller Somset
73 J4 Langar Notts
125 K3 Langbank Rens
96 G10 Langbar N York
104 G8 Langbaurgh N York
96 B8 Langcliffe N York
99 J2 Langdale End N York
5 N4 Langdon Cnwll
102 G4 Langdon Beck Dur
14 D5 Langdown Hants
135 J7 Langdyke Fife
52 H8 Langenhoe Essex
50 E2 Langford C Beds
9 P4 Langford Devon
52 D10 Langford Essex
19 N2 Langford N Som
85 P9 Langford Notts
33 P4 Langford Oxon
18 F10 Langford Budville Somset
20 E9 Langham Dorset
52 H5 Langham Essex
76 E3 Langham Norfk
73 L8 Langham Rutlnd
64 D8 Langham Suffk
89 L4 Langho Lancs
110 G4 Langholm D & G
28 H7 Langland Swans
117 Q3 Langlee Border
83 K10 Langley Ches E
84 F11 Langley Derbys
47 K9 Langley Gloucs
14 D6 Langley Hants
50 F6 Langley Herts
38 D11 Langley Kent
112 B8 Langley Nthumb
47 Q11 Langley Oxon
89 P9 Langley Rochdl
36 B5 Langley Slough
18 E9 Langley Somset
23 M9 Langley W Susx
47 N2 Langley Warwks
32 H9 Langley Burrell Wilts
50 C10 Langleybury Herts
112 B8 Langley Castle Nthumb
71 P7 Langley Common Derbys
71 P7 Langley Green Derbys
52 E7 Langley Green Essex
47 N2 Langley Green Warwks
51 K4 Langley Lower Green Essex
18 E9 Langley Marsh Somset
84 F11 Langley Mill Derbys
103 Q2 Langley Moor Dur
113 K11 Langley Park Dur
77 M11 Langley Street Norfk
51 K4 Langley Upper Green Essex
25 P10 Langney E Susx
85 J3 Langold Notts
5 M4 Langore Cnwll
19 M9 Langport Somset
87 J11 Langrick Lincs
32 D11 Langridge BaNES
17 K7 Langridgeford Devon
110 C11 Langrigg Cumb
23 K10 Langrish Hants
90 G10 Langsett Barns
133 M5 Langside P & K
15 K6 Langstone Hants
31 L7 Langstone Newpt
97 K2 Langthorne N York
97 N7 Langthorpe N York
103 K10 Langthwaite N York
99 L7 Langtoft E R Yk
74 B8 Langtoft Lincs
103 N7 Langton Dur
86 H7 Langton Lincs
87 L6 Langton Lincs
98 F7 Langton N York
86 F5 Langton by Wragby Lincs
25 M3 Langton Green Kent
64 G7 Langton Green Suffk
11 N8 Langton Herring Dorset
12 F3 Langton Long Blandford Dorset
12 H9 Langton Matravers Dorset
16 H8 Langtree Devon
16 H8 Langtree Week Devon
101 Q4 Langwathby Cumb
163 Q2 Langwell House Highld
84 H7 Langwith Derbys
84 H7 Langwith Junction Derbys
86 E5 Langworth Lincs
4 H9 Lanhydrock House & Gardens Cnwll
4 G9 Lanivet Cnwll
3 P3 Lanjeth Cnwll
4 H6 Lank Cnwll
4 H10 Lanlivery Cnwll
3 J6 Lanner Cnwll
5 M6 Lanoy Cnwll
5 K10 Lanreath Cnwll
5 K11 Lansallos Cnwll
4 H5 Lanteglos Cnwll
5 J11 Lanteglos Highway Cnwll
118 B6 Lanton Border
118 H4 Lanton Nthumb
10 b1 La Passee Guern
8 H3 Lapford Devon
122 E10 Laphroaig Ag & B
58 C2 Lapley Staffs
11 a2 La Pulente Jersey
59 J10 Lapworth Warwks
138 B8 Larachbeg Highld
133 P11 Larbert Falk
88 E2 Larbreck Lancs
158 F11 Largie Abers
131 J10 Largiemore Ag & B
135 M6 Largoward Fife
124 G6 Largs N Ayrs
121 K7 Largybeg N Ayrs
121 K7 Largymore N Ayrs
9 Q5 Larkbeare Devon
124 G2 Larkfield Inver
38 B10 Larkfield Kent
126 D7 Larkhall S Lans
21 M6 Larkhill Wilts
64 D4 Larling Norfk
11 c2 La Rocque Jersey
10 b1 La Rousaillerie Guern
103 K7 Lartington Dur
32 F6 Lasborough Gloucs
23 J6 Lasham Hants
8 B3 Lashbrook Devon
16 G10 Lashbrook Devon
26 D3 Lashenden Kent
70 G3 Lask Edge Staffs
127 Q4 Lasswade Mdloth
98 E2 Lastingham N York
19 M5 Latcham Somset
51 J6 Latchford Herts
35 J4 Latchford Oxon
52 E11 Latchingdon Essex
5 Q7 Latchley Cnwll
82 E5 Lately Common Warrtn
49 N6 Lathbury M Keyn
167 M10 Latheron Highld
167 L10 Latheronwheel Highld
135 M6 Lathones Fife
50 B11 Latimer Bucks
32 C8 Latteridge S Glos
20 C9 Lattiford Somset

33 L5 **Latton** Wilts
128 E10 **Lauder** Border
28 B2 **Laugharne** Carmth
85 P5 **Laughterton** Lincs
25 L8 **Laughton** E Susx
60 E3 **Laughton** Leics
74 A4 **Laughton** Lincs
92 D11 **Laughton** Lincs
84 H3 **Laughton-en-le-Morthen** Rothm
16 C10 **Launcells** Cnwll
16 D10 **Launcells Cross** Cnwll
5 N5 **Launceston** Cnwll
48 H10 **Launton** Oxon
143 N3 **Laurencekirk** Abers
108 E8 **Laurieston** D & G
126 G2 **Laurieston** Falk
49 P4 **Lavendon** M Keyn
52 F2 **Lavenham** Suffk
30 G11 **Lavernock** V Glam
111 J8 **Laversdale** Cumb
21 N8 **Laverstock** Wilts
22 E5 **Laverstoke** Hants
47 L7 **Laverton** Gloucs
97 K6 **Laverton** N York
20 E4 **Laverton** Somset
10 b2 **La Villette** Guern
69 L3 **Lavister** Wrexhm
126 E7 **Law** S Lans
140 G10 **Lawers** P & K
53 J5 **Lawford** Essex
18 F7 **Lawford** Warwks
126 E7 **Law Hill** S Lans
5 P5 **Lawhitton** Cnwll
95 R7 **Lawkland** N York
96 A7 **Lawkland Green** N York
57 M3 **Lawley** Wrekin
70 E9 **Lawnhead** Staffs
90 H3 **Lawns Wood Crematorium** Leeds
41 K9 **Lawrenny** Pembks
64 B11 **Lawshall** Suffk
64 B11 **Lawshall Green** Suffk
45 N3 **Lawton** Herefs
168 i5 **Laxay** W Isls
168 j4 **Laxdale** W Isls
80 f5 **Laxey** IoM
65 K7 **Laxfield** Suffk
164 F7 **Laxford Bridge** Highld
169 r7 **Laxo** Shet
92 C5 **Laxton** E R Yk
73 P11 **Laxton** Nhants
85 M7 **Laxton** Notts
90 C2 **Laycock** C Brad
52 F8 **Layer Breton** Essex
52 G7 **Layer-de-la-Haye** Essex
52 F8 **Layer Marney** Essex
52 H3 **Layham** Suffk
34 C11 **Layland's Green** W Berk
10 H4 **Laymore** Dorset
35 Q6 **Layter's Green** Bucks
92 B3 **Laytham** E R Yk
110 D9 **Laythes** Cumb
104 G7 **Lazenby** R & Cl
101 P3 **Lazonby** Cumb
84 D9 **Lea** Derbys
46 C10 **Lea** Herefs
85 P3 **Lea** Lincs
56 F7 **Lea** Shrops
56 G3 **Lea** Shrops
33 J7 **Lea** Wilts
156 A9 **Leachkin** Highld
127 N6 **Leadburn** Border
86 B10 **Leadenham** Lincs
51 N8 **Leaden Roding** Essex
112 H10 **Leadgate** Cumb
112 H9 **Leadgate** Nthumb
116 B7 **Leadgate** Dur
38 E11 **Leadingcross Green** Kent
84 B4 **Leadmill** Derbys
48 B11 **Leafield** Oxon
50 C6 **Leagrave** Luton
70 B2 **Leahead** Ches W
71 J9 **Lea Heath** Staffs
97 P2 **Leake** N York
87 L10 **Leake Common Side** Lincs
105 L9 **Lealholm** N York
105 L9 **Lealholm Side** N York
153 J5 **Lealt** Highld
84 B5 **Leam** Derbys
59 K6 **Lea Marston** Warwks
59 P11 **Leamington Hastings** Warwks
59 M11 **Leamington Spa** Warwks
113 M11 **Leamside** Dur
25 N8 **Leap Cross** E Susx
95 K4 **Leasgill** Cumb
86 E11 **Leasingham** Lincs
103 Q4 **Leasingthorne** Dur
36 E9 **Leatherhead** Surrey
97 K11 **Leathley** N York
69 N11 **Leaton** Shrops
57 L2 **Leaton** Wrekin
88 F4 **Lea Town** Lancs
38 H11 **Leaveland** Kent
52 G4 **Leavenheath** Suffk
98 F8 **Leavening** N York
37 K8 **Leaves Green** Gt Lon
95 R3 **Lea Yeat** Cumb
99 M4 **Lebberston** N York
10 b2 **Le Bigard** Guern
10 b2 **Le Bourg** Guern
10 b2 **Le Bourg** Guern
11 c2 **Le Bourg** Guern
33 P5 **Lechlade on Thames** Gloucs
122 C6 **Lecht Gruinart** Ag & B
95 N5 **Leck** Lancs
140 H9 **Leckbuie** P & K
22 C7 **Leckford** Hants
49 K7 **Leckhampstead** Bucks
34 D9 **Leckhampstead** W Berk
34 D9 **Leckhampstead Thicket** W Berk
46 H11 **Leckhampton** Gloucs
161 K9 **Leckmelm** Highld
30 G10 **Leckwith** V Glam
92 H2 **Leconfield** E R Yk
138 C10 **Ledaig** Ag & B
49 P10 **Ledburn** Bucks
46 D7 **Ledbury** Herefs
46 C8 **Leddington** Gloucs
45 N4 **Ledgemoor** Herefs
45 N2 **Ledicot** Herefs
161 L1 **Ledmore Junction** Highld
81 M10 **Ledsham** Ches W
91 M5 **Ledsham** Leeds
91 L5 **Ledston** Leeds
7 J9 **Ledstone** Devon
91 L4 **Ledston Luck** Leeds

48 D9 **Ledwell** Oxon
16 H2 **Lee** Devon
37 J5 **Lee** Gt Lon
22 C11 **Lee** Hants
69 M8 **Lee** Shrops
56 H5 **Leebotwood** Shrops
69 P9 **Lee Brockhurst** Shrops
94 E7 **Leece** Cumb
37 Q3 **Lee Chapel** Essex
35 P4 **Lee Clump** Bucks
35 P4 **Lee Common** Bucks
38 D11 **Leeds** Kent
90 H4 **Leeds** Leeds
90 G2 *Leeds Bradford Airport* Leeds
38 D11 **Leeds Castle** Kent
2 G7 **Leedstown** Cnwll
70 B2 **Lee Green** Ches E
70 H3 **Leek** Staffs
59 L11 **Leek Wootton** Warwks
6 F7 **Lee Mill** Devon
90 C4 **Leeming** C Brad
97 L3 **Leeming** N York
97 L3 **Leeming Bar** N York
6 F6 **Lee Moor** Devon
90 C3 **Lees** C Brad
71 P7 **Lees** Derbys
83 L4 **Lees** Oldham
71 P7 **Lees Green** Derbys
73 K8 **Leesthorpe** Leics
24 G2 **Lee Street** Surrey
69 J2 **Leeswood** Flints
134 G3 **Leetown** P & K
82 E10 **Leftwich** Ches W
45 J11 **Legar** Powys
87 L4 **Legbourne** Lincs
101 K7 **Legburthwaite** Cumb
118 A2 **Legerwood** Border
35 P10 **Legoland** W & M
10 b2 **Le Gron** Guern
86 F3 **Legsby** Lincs
11 c2 **Le Haguais** Jersey
11 c2 **Le Hocq** Jersey
72 F10 **Leicester** C Leic
72 E10 **Leicester Forest East** Leics
72 E10 *Leicester Forest East Services* Leics
17 N9 **Leigh** Devon
11 N3 **Leigh** Dorset
46 G9 **Leigh** Gloucs
37 M11 **Leigh** Kent
56 E4 **Leigh** Shrops
36 F11 **Leigh** Surrey
82 E5 **Leigh** Wigan
33 L6 **Leigh** Wilts
46 E4 **Leigh** Worcs
38 D5 **Leigh Beck** Essex
32 G9 **Leigh Delamere** Wilts
32 G9 *Leigh Delamere Services* Wilts
26 F5 **Leigh Green** Kent
125 Q7 **Leigh Knoweglass** S Lans
18 D7 **Leighland Chapel** Somset
38 D4 **Leigh-on-Sea** Sthend
12 H5 **Leigh Park** Dorset
46 E4 **Leigh Sinton** Worcs
58 G4 **Leighswood** Wsall
32 F6 **Leighterton** Gloucs
97 J5 **Leighton** N York
56 C3 **Leighton** Powys
57 L3 **Leighton** Shrops
20 D6 **Leighton** Somset
61 P5 **Leighton Bromswold** Cambs
49 P9 **Leighton Buzzard** C Beds
20 C5 **Leigh upon Mendip** Somset
31 Q10 **Leigh Woods** N Som
56 G11 **Leinthall Earls** Herefs
56 G11 **Leinthall Starkes** Herefs
56 G10 **Leintwardine** Herefs
60 B3 **Leire** Leics
65 N9 **Leiston** Suffk
127 P2 **Leith** C Edin
118 E2 **Leitholm** Border
2 E6 **Lelant** Cnwll
93 M4 **Lelley** E R Yk
57 N9 **Lem Hill** Worcs
118 E4 **Lempitlaw** Border
168 i6 **Lemreway** W Isls
50 F8 **Lemsford** Herts
47 K5 **Lenchwick** Worcs
114 B9 **Lendalfoot** S Ayrs
132 H6 **Lendrick** Stirlg
159 R9 **Lendrum Terrace** Abers
38 E11 **Lenham** Kent
26 F2 **Lenham Heath** Kent
147 N2 **Lenie** Highld
118 G2 **Lennel** Border
108 D10 **Lennox Plunton** D & G
125 Q2 **Lennoxtown** E Duns
35 P8 **Lent** Bucks
72 F3 **Lenton** C Nott
73 Q4 **Lenton** Lincs
76 F8 **Lenwade** Norfk
126 B3 **Lenzie** E Duns
150 E5 **Leochel-Cushnie** Abers
58 H3 **Leomansley** Staffs
45 P3 **Leominster** Herefs
32 F4 **Leonard Stanley** Gloucs
11 a1 **Leoville** Jersey
14 D7 **Lepe** Hants
152 B8 **Lephin** Highld
98 F8 **Leppington** N York
90 G7 **Lepton** Kirk
130 H2 **Lerags** Ag & B
10 a2 **L'Eree** Guern
5 J10 **Lerryn** Cnwll
169 r9 **Lerwick** Shet
10 b2 **Les Arquets** Guern
119 P8 **Lesbury** Nthumb
10 c2 **Les Hubits** Guern
150 F3 **Leslie** Abers
134 H7 **Leslie** Fife
10 b2 **Les Lohiers** Guern
126 E10 **Lesmahagow** S Lans
10 b2 **Les Murchez** Guern
5 J3 **Lesnewth** Cnwll
10 b2 **Les Nicolles** Guern
10 c1 **Les Quartiers** Guern
11 a2 **Les Quennevais** Jersey
10 b2 **Les Sages** Guern
77 M6 **Lessingham** Norfk
110 D10 **Lessonhall** Cumb
3 K9 **Lestowder** Cnwll
10 b2 **Les Villets** Guern
106 D5 **Leswalt** D & G
11 a1 **L'Etacq** Jersey

50 E11 **Letchmore Heath** Herts
50 F4 **Letchworth Garden City** Herts
34 C8 **Letcombe Bassett** Oxon
34 C7 **Letcombe Regis** Oxon
143 J8 **Letham** Angus
118 C9 **Letham** Border
133 P10 **Letham** Falk
135 J5 **Letham** Fife
143 L8 **Letham Grange** Angus
142 A9 **Lethenty** P & K
150 F3 **Lethenty** Abers
159 K9 **Lethenty** Abers
65 K10 **Letheringham** Suffk
76 F4 **Letheringsett** Norfk
8 H8 **Lettaford** Devon
154 C3 **Letterewe** Highld
145 Q3 **Letterfearn** Highld
146 H9 **Letterfinlay Lodge Hotel** Highld
145 M10 **Lettermorar** Highld
161 K9 **Letters** Highld
116 B6 **Lettershaw** S Lans
40 H5 **Letterston** Pembks
149 J4 **Lettoch** Highld
157 L11 **Lettoch** Highld
45 L5 **Letton** Herefs
56 F10 **Letton** Herefs
37 L9 **Lett's Green** Kent
50 G8 **Letty Green** Herts
85 J3 **Letwell** Rothm
135 M3 **Leuchars** Fife
168 i6 **Leumrabhagh** W Isls
168 i5 **Leurbost** W Isls
3 Q4 **Levalsa Meor** Cnwll
70 F11 **Levedale** Staffs
51 L6 **Level's Green** Essex
99 N11 **Leven** E R Yk
135 K7 **Leven** Fife
95 K3 **Levens** Cumb
51 J6 **Levens Green** Herts
83 J6 **Levenshulme** Manch
169 r11 **Levenwick** Shet
168 f9 **Leverburgh** W Isls
74 H8 **Leverington** Cambs
50 C9 **Leverstock Green** Herts
87 M11 **Leverton** Lincs
10 b1 **Le Villocq** Guern
53 M4 **Levington** Suffk
98 G2 **Levisham** N York
34 B3 **Lew** Oxon
5 M5 **Lewannick** Cnwll
8 C7 **Lewdown** Devon
25 K8 **Lewes** E Susx
40 H6 **Leweston** Pembks
37 J6 **Lewisham** Gt Lon
37 J6 **Lewisham Crematorium** Gt Lon
147 N2 **Lewiston** Highld
29 P7 **Lewistown** Brdgnd
45 L3 **Lewis Wych** Herefs
35 K5 **Lewknor** Oxon
16 E11 **Leworthy** Devon
17 M4 **Leworthy** Devon
38 G9 **Lewson Street** Kent
88 F3 **Lewth** Lancs
8 C7 **Lewtrenchard** Devon
52 G6 **Lexden** Essex
19 J7 **Lexworthy** Somset
5 K8 **Ley** Cnwll
37 Q9 **Leybourne** Kent
96 H2 **Leyburn** N York
70 D5 **Leycett** Staffs
50 E6 **Leygreen** Herts
35 Q4 **Ley Hill** Bucks
88 G6 **Leyland** Lancs
82 C4 **Leyland Green** St Hel
151 K5 **Leylodge** Abers
159 P7 **Leys** Abers
142 D10 **Leys** P & K
38 H7 **Leysdown-on-Sea** Kent
143 L8 **Leysmill** Angus
142 F8 **Leys of Cossans** Angus
45 R2 **Leysters** Herefs
37 J3 **Leyton** Gt Lon
37 J3 **Leytonstone** Gt Lon
5 N6 **Lezant** Cnwll
2 H7 **Lezerea** Cnwll
157 P5 **Lhanbryde** Moray
44 D9 **Libanus** Powys
116 D2 **Libberton** S Lans
127 P4 **Liberton** C Edin
58 H3 **Lichfield** Staffs
58 E9 **Lickey** Worcs
58 E10 **Lickey End** Worcs
58 E10 **Lickey Rock** Worcs
23 P9 **Lickfold** W Susx
8 C8 **Liddaton Green** Devon
138 D6 **Liddesdale** Highld
33 P8 **Liddington** Swindn
84 D5 **Lidgate** Derbys
63 M9 **Lidgate** Suffk
91 R10 **Lidget** Donc
85 K7 **Lidgett** Notts
26 D8 **Lidham Hill** E Susx
49 Q7 **Lidlington** C Beds
38 C9 **Lidsing** Kent
142 E11 **Liff** Angus
58 G8 **Lifford** Birm
5 P4 **Lifton** Devon
5 P4 **Liftondown** Devon
48 B3 **Lighthorne** Warwks
48 C3 **Lighthorne Heath** Warwks
23 P2 **Lightwater** Surrey
70 G6 **Lightwood** C Stke
70 A6 **Lightwood Green** Ches E
69 L6 **Lightwood Green** Wrexhm
60 C5 **Lilbourne** Nhants
119 K6 **Lilburn Tower** Nthumb
70 C11 **Lilleshall** Wrekin
50 D5 **Lilley** Herts
34 B9 **Lilley** W Berk
117 Q5 **Lilliesleaf** Border
49 K7 **Lillingstone Dayrell** Bucks
49 K6 **Lillingstone Lovell** Bucks
11 N2 **Lillington** Dorset
12 H7 **Lilliput** Poole
18 G5 **Lilstock** Somset
57 N2 **Lilyhurst** Shrops
89 J7 **Limbrick** Lancs
50 C6 **Limbury** Luton
56 F11 **Limebrook** Herefs
89 N8 **Limefield** Bury
126 C7 **Limekilnburn** S Lans
134 D11 **Limekilns** Fife
126 F3 **Limerigg** Falk
14 D10 **Limerstone** IoW

111 Q11 **Limestone Brae** Nthumb
46 F8 **Lime Street** Worcs
19 P10 **Limington** Somset
115 M2 **Limmerhaugh** E Ayrs
77 M11 **Limpenhoe** Norfk
20 E2 **Limpley Stoke** Wilts
37 K10 **Limpsfield** Surrey
37 K10 **Limpsfield Chart** Surrey
84 H10 **Linby** Notts
23 N8 **Linchmere** W Susx
109 L5 **Lincluden** D & G
86 C6 **Lincoln** Lincs
86 C6 **Lincoln Crematorium** Lincs
7 Q11 **Lincombe** Worcs
16 H2 **Lincombe** Devon
7 J10 **Lincombe** Devon
95 J4 **Lindale** Cumb
94 E5 **Lindal in Furness** Cumb
24 H5 **Lindfield** W Susx
23 M7 **Lindford** Hants
90 E7 **Lindley** Kirk
97 K11 **Lindley** N York
82 H9 **Lindow End** Ches E
57 M11 **Lindridge** Worcs
51 P5 **Lindsell** Essex
52 G2 **Lindsey** Suffk
52 G2 **Lindsey Tye** Suffk
19 L7 **Liney** Somset
13 L3 **Linford** Hants
37 Q5 **Linford** Thurr
90 D3 **Lingbob** C Brad
105 J7 **Lingdale** R & Cl
56 F11 **Lingen** Herefs
25 J2 **Lingfield** Surrey
77 M10 **Lingwood** Norfk
152 F2 **Linicro** Highld
46 F8 **Linkend** Worcs
22 C3 **Linkenholt** Hants
26 D6 **Linkhill** Kent
5 N7 **Linkinhorne** Cnwll
134 H9 **Linktown** Fife
157 N5 **Linkwood** Moray
56 F6 **Linley** Shrops
46 C4 **Linley Green** Herefs
57 M5 **Linleygreen** Shrops
126 H2 **Linlithgow** W Loth
118 G9 **Linshiels** Nthumb
162 C7 **Linsidemore** Highld
49 P9 **Linslade** C Beds
65 L6 **Linstead Parva** Suffk
110 H9 **Linstock** Cumb
58 E10 **Linthurst** Worcs
90 E8 **Linthwaite** Kirk
129 L8 **Lintlaw** Border
158 F4 **Lintmill** Moray
118 E5 **Linton** Border
63 J11 **Linton** Cambs
71 P11 **Linton** Derbys
46 C9 **Linton** Herefs
38 C11 **Linton** Kent
97 N11 **Linton** Leeds
96 E8 **Linton** N York
113 L2 **Linton** Nthumb
71 P11 **Linton Heath** Derbys
46 C10 **Linton Hill** Herefs
97 Q8 **Linton-on-Ouse** N York
13 L3 **Linwood** Hants
86 F3 **Linwood** Lincs
125 L5 **Linwood** Rens
168 c13 **Lionacleit** W Isls
168 k1 **Lional** W Isls
25 N7 **Lions Green** E Susx
23 M8 **Liphook** Hants
70 C8 **Lipley** Shrops
81 K6 **Liscard** Wirral
18 A8 **Liscombe** Somset
5 M9 **Liskeard** Cnwll
138 E9 **Lismore** Ag & B
23 L3 **Liss** Hants
99 N9 **Lissett** E R Yk
23 L3 **Liss Forest** Hants
86 F4 **Lissington** Lincs
52 E3 **Liston** Essex
30 G8 **Lisvane** Cardif
31 K7 **Liswerry** Newpt
76 B3 **Litcham** Norfk
29 P8 **Litchard** Brdgnd
48 H4 **Litchborough** Nhants
22 E4 **Litchfield** Hants
81 L5 **Litherland** Sefton
50 H2 **Litlington** Cambs
25 M10 **Litlington** E Susx
62 H11 **Little Abington** Cambs
61 L6 **Little Addington** Nhants
107 M8 **Little Airies** D & G
50 F5 **Little Almshoe** Herts
47 M2 **Little Alne** Warwks
81 J8 **Little Altcar** Sefton
51 J8 **Little Amwell** Herts
102 C9 **Little Asby** Cumb
58 G5 **Little Aston** Staffs
14 E11 **Little Atherfield** IoW
104 G8 **Little Ayton** N York
52 C10 **Little Baddow** Essex
32 E8 **Little Badminton** S Glos
110 E9 **Little Bampton** Cumb
51 Q4 **Little Bardfield** Essex
61 Q9 **Little Barford** Bed
76 G5 **Little Barningham** Norfk
33 P2 **Little Barrington** Gloucs
81 P11 **Little Barrow** Ches W
98 F5 **Little Barugh** N York
113 M2 **Little Bavington** Nthumb
53 M2 **Little Bealings** Suffk
105 N10 **Littlebeck** N York
33 Q11 **Little Bedwyn** Wilts
53 K6 **Little Bentley** Essex
50 F8 **Little Berkhamsted** Herts
61 Q9 **Little Billing** Nhants
49 P10 **Little Billington** C Beds
45 Q8 **Little Birch** Herefs
88 C2 **Little Bispham** Bpool
53 K2 **Little Blakenham** Suffk
101 N4 **Little Blencow** Cumb
58 F4 **Little Bloxwich** Wsall
24 B6 **Little Bognor** W Susx
71 P4 **Little Bolehill** Derbys
82 F7 **Little Bollington** Ches E
36 B4 **Little Bookham** Surrey
9 K2 **Littleborough** Devon
85 P8 **Littleborough** Notts
89 Q7 **Littleborough** Rochdl
39 M10 **Littlebourne** Kent
34 G5 **Little Bourton** Oxon
60 F11 **Little Bowden** Leics
63 L10 **Little Bradley** Suffk
45 L10 **Little Brampton** Herefs
56 F8 **Little Brampton** Shrops
52 D9 **Little Braxted** Essex

143 K5 **Little Brechin** Angus
11 M7 **Littlebredy** Dorset
49 P8 **Little Brickhill** M Keyn
70 F9 **Little Bridgeford** Staffs
60 E8 **Little Brington** Nhants
53 J6 **Little Bromley** Essex
100 E4 **Little Broughton** Cumb
82 C11 **Little Budworth** Ches W
156 A7 **Littleburn** Highld
37 Q2 **Little Burstead** Essex
51 M3 **Littlebury** Essex
51 L3 **Littlebury Green** Essex
73 Q7 **Little Bytham** Lincs
51 N6 **Little Canfield** Essex
87 L3 **Little Carlton** Lincs
85 N9 **Little Carlton** Notts
73 Q9 **Little Casterton** Rutlnd
93 K2 **Little Catwick** E R Yk
61 P6 **Little Catworth** Cambs
87 L4 **Little Cawthorpe** Lincs
35 Q5 **Little Chalfont** Bucks
26 F2 **Little Chart** Kent
51 M2 **Little Chesterford** Essex
26 B3 **Little Cheveney** Kent
21 J4 **Little Cheverell** Wilts
51 K3 **Little Chishill** Cambs
53 L8 **Little Clacton** Essex
33 Q4 **Little Clanfield** Oxon
100 E5 **Little Clifton** Cumb
93 M9 **Little Coates** NE Lin
47 J6 **Little Comberton** Worcs
26 B10 **Little Common** E Susx
37 P9 **Little Comp** Kent
47 Q8 **Little Compton** Warwks
111 J9 **Little Corby** Cumb
52 F4 **Little Cornard** Suffk
21 M4 **Littlecott** Wilts
56 B4 **Little Cowarne** Herefs
33 Q6 **Little Coxwell** Oxon
97 K2 **Little Crakehall** N York
60 H5 **Little Cransley** Nhants
76 B11 **Little Cressingham** Norfk
81 L4 **Little Crosby** Sefton
100 H5 **Little Crosthwaite** Cumb
71 M7 **Little Cubley** Derbys
73 K8 **Little Dalby** Leics
32 C2 **Littledean** Gloucs
45 Q8 **Little Dewchurch** Herefs
63 L9 **Little Ditton** Cambs
45 Q11 **Little Doward** Herefs
22 B3 **Littledown** Hants
62 H4 **Little Downham** Cambs
99 L9 **Little Driffield** E R Yk
76 B9 **Little Dunham** Norfk
141 P9 **Little Dunkeld** P & K
51 Q6 **Little Dunmow** Essex
21 M8 **Little Durnford** Wilts
51 P6 **Little Easton** Essex
72 B2 **Little Eaton** Derbys
64 E2 **Little Ellingham** Norfk
20 D5 **Little Elm** Somset
60 C9 **Little Everdon** Nhants
62 E10 **Little Eversden** Cambs
33 P4 **Little Faringdon** Oxon
97 L2 **Little Fencote** N York
91 N3 **Little Fenton** N York
76 C9 **Little Fransham** Norfk
35 Q2 **Little Gaddesden** Herts
45 N10 **Little Garway** Herefs
61 P4 **Little Gidding** Cambs
65 L10 **Little Glemham** Suffk
46 C10 **Little Gorsley** Herefs
62 C9 **Little Gransden** Cambs
73 J2 **Little Green** Notts
20 D5 **Little Green** Somset
87 K2 **Little Grimsby** Lincs
85 M4 **Little Gringley** Notts
98 E5 **Little Habton** N York
51 K6 **Little Hadham** Herts
74 B2 **Little Hale** Lincs
72 D2 **Little Hallam** Derbys
51 M7 **Little Hallingbury** Essex
9 P8 **Littleham** Devon
16 G7 **Littleham** Devon
35 N4 **Little Hampden** Bucks
24 B10 **Littlehampton** W Susx
12 D2 **Little Hanford** Dorset
61 J6 **Little Harrowden** Nhants
34 H4 **Little Haseley** Oxon
93 L2 **Little Hatfield** E R Yk
77 K7 **Little Hautbois** Norfk
40 G8 **Little Haven** Pembks
24 E4 **Littlehaven** W Susx
58 H4 **Little Hay** Staffs
83 M7 **Little Hayfield** Derbys
71 J10 **Little Haywood** Staffs
70 F11 **Little Heath** Staffs
35 J10 **Little Heath** W Berk
7 L6 **Littlehempston** Devon
57 K11 **Little Hereford** Herefs
52 H5 **Little Horkesley** Essex
51 K5 **Little Hormead** Herts
25 L7 **Little Horsted** E Susx
90 F4 **Little Horton** C Brad
21 K2 **Little Horton** Wilts
49 L8 **Little Horwood** Bucks
91 L9 **Little Houghton** Barns
60 H9 **Little Houghton** Nhants
119 P7 **Littlehoughton** Nthumb
83 Q9 **Little Hucklow** Derbys
82 F4 **Little Hulton** Salfd
34 F10 **Little Hungerford** W Berk
97 Q5 **Little Hutton** N York
61 K7 **Little Irchester** Nhants
99 M9 **Little Kelk** E R Yk
20 E5 **Little Keyford** Somset
35 M3 **Little Kimble** Bucks
48 B4 **Little Kineton** Warwks
35 N5 **Little Kingshill** Bucks
108 H8 **Little Knox** D & G
101 K10 **Little Langdale** Cumb
21 K7 **Little Langford** Wilts
51 M9 **Little Laver** Essex
82 D9 **Little Leigh** Ches W
52 B8 **Little Leighs** Essex
89 M9 **Little Lever** Bolton
49 M6 **Little Linford** M Keyn
19 N10 **Little Load** Somset
74 H2 **Little London** Bucks
62 H11 **Little London** Cambs
51 L6 **Little London** E Susx
51 N5 **Little London** Essex
51 Q3 **Little London** Essex
46 D11 **Little London** Gloucs
22 C5 **Little London** Hants
22 H3 **Little London** Hants
90 G3 **Little London** Leeds
74 D6 **Little London** Lincs
74 H6 **Little London** Lincs

75 L6 Little London Norfk
55 N7 Little London Powys
83 Q10 Little Longstone Derbys
70 D5 Little Madeley Staffs
46 E6 Little Malvern Worcs
81 L11 Little Mancot Flints
52 D5 Little Maplestead Essex
46 C7 Little Marcle Herefs
17 J9 Little Marland Devon
35 N7 Little Marlow Bucks
75 Q6 Little Massingham Norfk
76 H10 Little Melton Norfk
149 Q8 Littlemill Abers
156 E7 Littlemill Highld
31 K4 Little Mill Mons
34 H4 Little Milton Oxon
35 P5 Little Missenden Bucks
39 P11 Little Mongeham Kent
84 E8 Littlemoor Derbys
19 K8 Little Moor Somset
34 F4 Littlemore Oxon
102 E8 Little Musgrave Cumb
69 M11 Little Ness Shrops
81 K9 Little Neston Ches W
41 J5 Little Newcastle Pembks
103 M7 Little Newsham Dur
19 N11 Little Norton Somset
53 M6 Little Oakley Essex
61 J3 Little Oakley Nhants
61 L9 Little Odell Bed
50 D5 Little Offley Herts
102 D7 Little Ormside Cumb
110 G9 Little Orton Cumb
63 K3 Little Ouse Cambs
97 P8 Little Ouseburn N York
72 A4 Littleover C Derb
60 F4 Little Oxendon Nhants
59 K8 Little Packington Warwks
26 B2 Little Pattenden Kent
61 Q8 Little Paxton Cambs
4 E7 Little Petherick Cnwll
88 D4 Little Plumpton Lancs
77 L9 Little Plumstead Norfk
73 N4 Little Ponton Lincs
63 J3 Littleport Cambs
63 J3 Littleport Bridge Cambs
14 F6 Little Posbrook Hants
17 J9 Little Potheridge Devon
91 K4 Little Preston Leeds
48 G4 Little Preston Nhants
82 D11 Littler Ches W
62 C5 Little Raveley Cambs
92 B6 Little Reedness E R Yk
97 N10 Little Ribston N York
47 N11 Little Rissington Gloucs
47 Q8 Little Rollright Oxon
84 C7 Little Rowsley Derbys
76 D6 Little Ryburgh Norfk
119 K8 Little Ryle Nthumb
56 H4 Little Ryton Shrops
101 Q3 Little Salkeld Cumb
51 Q4 Little Sampford Essex
23 M2 Little Sandhurst Br For
58 D3 Little Saredon Staffs
81 M11 Little Saughall Ches W
63 P8 Little Saxham Suffk
155 L6 Little Scatwell Highld
62 G10 Little Shelford Cambs
59 K11 Little Shrewley Warwks
9 M3 Little Silver Devon
88 D3 Little Singleton Lancs
91 R3 Little Skipwith N York
91 N7 Little Smeaton N York
76 D5 Little Snoring Norfk
32 E8 Little Sodbury S Glos
32 D8 Little Sodbury End S Glos
22 C8 Little Somborne Hants
33 J8 Little Somerford Wilts
70 C9 Little Soudley Shrops
96 B7 Little Stainforth N York
104 B6 Little Stainton Darltn
81 N10 Little Stanney Ches W
61 P8 Little Staughton Bed
87 M8 Little Steeping Lincs
70 G8 Little Stoke Staffs
27 J7 Littlestone-on-Sea Kent
64 G9 Little Stonham Suffk
72 H10 Little Stretton Leics
56 G6 Little Stretton Shrops
101 Q7 Little Strickland Cumb
62 B5 Little Stukeley Cambs
70 E8 Little Sugnall Staffs
81 M9 Little Sutton Ches W
57 J8 Little Sutton Shrops
112 D5 Little Swinburne Nthumb
108 F10 Little Sypland D & G
48 C9 Little Tew Oxon
52 E2 Little Tey Essex
62 H5 Little Thetford Cambs
97 Q5 Little Thirkleby N York
76 F4 Little Thornage Norfk
88 D2 Little Thornton Lancs
104 D2 Little Thorpe Dur
72 E11 Littlethorpe Leics
97 M7 Littlethorpe N York
63 L10 Little Thurlow Suffk
63 L10 Little Thurlow Green Suffk
37 P5 Little Thurrock Thurr
142 E7 Littleton Angus
19 Q2 Littleton BaNES
81 N11 Littleton Ches W
108 D9 Littleton D & G
12 E4 Littleton Dorset
22 E8 Littleton Hants
19 N8 Littleton Somset
23 Q5 Littleton Surrey
36 C7 Littleton Surrey
32 F8 Littleton Drew Wilts
31 Q7 Littleton-on-Severn S Glos
21 K4 Littleton Pannell Wilts
16 H8 Little Torrington Devon
52 E9 Little Totham Essex
100 H7 Little Town Cumb
104 B2 Littletown Dur
89 K3 Little Town Lancs
82 D6 Little Town Warrtn
72 A9 Little Twycross Leics
94 F6 Little Urswick Cumb
38 F4 Little Wakering Essex
51 M2 Little Walden Essex
52 F2 Little Waldingfield Suffk
76 C4 Little Walsingham Norfk
52 B9 Little Waltham Essex
37 P2 Little Warley Essex
47 J8 Little Washbourne Gloucs
92 G4 Little Weighton E R Yk
61 K8 Little Weldon Nhants

64 B10 Little Welnetham Suffk
87 K3 Little Welton Lincs
53 J4 Little Wenham Suffk
57 L3 Little Wenlock Wrekin
20 B9 Little Weston Somset
14 G9 Little Whitefield IoW
65 K6 Little Whittingham Green Suffk
112 E7 Little Whittington Nthumb
35 M9 Littlewick Green W & M
62 H9 Little Wilbraham Cambs
11 J4 Littlewindsor Dorset
46 H11 Little Witcombe Gloucs
46 E2 Little Witley Worcs
34 G6 Little Wittenham Oxon
47 Q7 Little Wolford Warwks
58 E3 Littlewood Staffs
36 G8 Little Woodcote Gt Lon
49 N10 Littleworth Bucks
34 B5 Littleworth Oxon
58 F2 Littleworth Staffs
70 G10 Littleworth Staffs
24 E6 Littleworth W Susx
46 G4 Littleworth Worcs
47 J2 Littleworth Worcs
35 P7 Littleworth Common Bucks
63 L11 Little Wratting Suffk
61 L8 Little Wymington Bed
50 F5 Little Wymondley Herts
58 F3 Little Wyrley Staffs
69 Q11 Little Wytheford Shrops
52 C4 Little Yeldham Essex
51 Q7 Littley Green Essex
83 Q9 Litton Derbys
96 D6 Litton N York
19 Q4 Litton Somset
11 L6 Litton Cheney Dorset
168 i5 Liurbost W Isls
81 L6 Liverpool Lpool
90 F6 Liversedge Kirk
9 K9 Liverton Devon
105 K7 Liverton R & Cl
105 K7 Liverton Mines R & Cl
38 E11 Liverton Street Kent
127 K4 Livingston W Loth
127 J4 Livingston Village W Loth
80 H10 Lixwm Flints
3 J11 Lizard Cnwll
78 C8 Llaingoch IoA
55 P8 Llaithddu Powys
55 K4 Llan Powys
67 L11 Llanaber Gwynd
66 F6 Llanaelhaearn Gwynd
54 F10 Llanafan Cerdgn
44 D3 Llanafan-Fawr Powys
44 D4 Llanafan-fechan Powys
79 J7 Llanallgo IoA
66 G7 Llanarmon Gwynd
68 G8 Llanarmon Dyffryn Ceiriog Wrexhm
68 G3 Llanarmon-yn-Ial Denbgs
42 H3 Llanarth Cerdgn
31 L2 Llanarth Mons
43 K11 Llanarthne Carmth
80 G8 Llanasa Flints
78 F7 Llanbabo IoA
54 E8 Llanbadarn Fawr Cerdgn
55 P9 Llanbadarn Fynydd Powys
44 G5 Llanbadarn-y-garreg Powys
31 L5 Llanbadoc Mons
78 F6 Llanbadrig IoA
31 L6 Llanbeder Newpt
67 K9 Llanbedr Gwynd
44 G5 Llanbedr Powys
45 J10 Llanbedr Powys
68 F3 Llanbedr-Dyffryn-Clwyd Denbgs
79 J8 Llanbedrgoch IoA
66 E8 Llanbedrog Gwynd
79 P11 Llanbedr-y-Cennin Conwy
67 K2 Llanberis Gwynd
30 D11 Llanbethery V Glam
55 Q10 Llanbister Powys
30 C10 Llanblethian V Glam
41 P6 Llanboidy Carmth
30 F6 Llanbradach Caerph
55 K4 Llanbrynmair Powys
30 D11 Llancadle V Glam
30 D10 Llancarfan V Glam
31 L4 Llancayo Mons
45 P10 Llancloudy Herefs
54 E6 Llancynfelyn Cerdgn
30 E6 Llandaff Cardif
67 K9 Llandanwg Gwynd
29 K5 Llandarcy Neath
41 Q8 Llandawke Carmth
78 H10 Llanddaniel Fab IoA
43 K11 Llanddarog Carmth
54 D10 Llanddeiniol Cerdgn
79 J11 Llanddeiniolen Gwynd
68 C7 Llanderfel Gwynd
42 G10 Llanddeusant Carmth
78 E7 Llanddeusant IoA
44 F8 Llanddew Powys
28 E7 Llanddewi Swans
43 N3 Llanddewi Brefi Cerdgn
44 E5 Llanddewi'r Cwm Powys
31 L2 Llanddewi Rhydderch Mons
41 M7 Llanddewi Velfrey Pembks
55 Q11 Llanddewi Ystradenni Powys
67 Q2 Llanddoget Conwy
79 K9 Llanddona IoA
41 Q8 Llanddowror Carmth
79 J9 Llanddulas Conwy
67 K10 Llanddwywe Gwynd
67 J9 Llandecwyn Gwynd
44 E8 Llandefaelog Powys
44 G9 Llandefaelog-Tre'r-Graig Powys
44 G7 Llandefalle Powys
79 K10 Llandegfan IoA
68 G4 Llandegla Denbgs
55 Q10 Llandegley Powys
66 D9 Llandegwning Gwynd
44 M10 Llandeilo Carmth
44 F4 Llandeilo Graban Powys
44 B8 Llandeilo'r Fan Powys
40 G5 Llandeloy Pembks
31 M4 Llandenny Mons
31 M6 Llandevaud Newpt

31 M7 Llandevenny Mons
45 Q9 Llandinabo Herefs
55 N7 Llandinam Powys
41 M6 Llandissilio Pembks
31 P4 Llandogo Mons
30 C10 Llandough V Glam
30 C10 Llandough V Glam
43 Q8 Llandovery Carmth
29 P10 Llandow V Glam
43 N6 Llandre Carmth
42 G7 Llandre Cerdgn
41 M5 Llandre Isaf Pembks
68 D7 Llandrillo Denbgs
79 Q8 Llandrillo-yn-Rhos Conwy
44 F2 Llandrindod Wells Powys
69 J11 Llandrinio Powys
79 P8 Llandudno Conwy
79 P9 Llandudno Junction Conwy
44 B6 Llandulas Powys
66 H3 Llandwrog Gwynd
43 M11 Llandybie Carmth
28 D2 Llandyfaelog Carmth
43 M11 Llandyfan Carmth
42 F6 Llandyfriog Cerdgn
78 G7 Llandyfrydog IoA
79 K10 Llandygai Gwynd
41 P2 Llandygwydd Cerdgn
68 G5 Llandynan Denbgs
68 G11 Llandyrnog Denbgs
56 B5 Llandyssil Powys
42 H6 Llandysul Cerdgn
30 H8 Llanedeyrn Cardif
28 G3 Llanedi Carmth
44 F7 Llaneglwys Powys
54 E3 Llanegryn Gwynd
43 K10 Llanegwad Carmth
78 H6 Llaneilian IoA
80 B9 Llaneilian-yn-Rhôs Conwy
68 F4 Llanelidan Denbgs
44 H8 Llanelieu Powys
31 K2 Llanellen Mons
28 F4 Llanelli Carmth
28 F4 Llanelli Crematorium Carmth
67 N11 Llanelltyd Gwynd
30 H2 Llanelly Mons
44 E4 Llanelwedd Powys
67 K10 Llanenddwyn Gwynd
66 D9 Llanengan Gwynd
68 A11 Llanerch Gwynd
78 E6 Llanerchymedd IoA
55 N3 Llanerfyl Powys
78 E8 Llanfachraeth IoA
67 P10 Llanfachreth Gwynd
78 E10 Llanfaelog IoA
66 C9 Llanfaelrhys Gwynd
45 N11 Llanfaenor Mons
79 L9 Llanfaes IoA
44 E9 Llanfaes Powys
78 E7 Llanfaethlu IoA
67 K9 Llanfair Gwynd
55 Q3 Llanfair Caereinion Powys
43 M4 Llanfair Clydogau Cerdgn
68 F3 Llanfair Dyffryn Clwyd Denbgs
79 M10 Llanfairfechan Conwy
31 L3 Llanfair Kilgeddin Mons
41 N3 Llanfair-Nant-Gwyn Pembks
79 J10 Llanfair P G IoA
80 C11 Llanfair Talhaiarn Conwy
56 C9 Llanfair Waterdine Shrops
78 E4 Llanfairynghornwy IoA
78 E9 Llanfair-yn-Neubwll IoA
41 N6 Llanfallteg Carmth
41 M7 Llanfallteg West Carmth
54 D9 Llanfarian Cerdgn
68 G10 Llanfechain Powys
78 F6 Llanfechell IoA
68 G2 Llanferres Denbgs
78 F7 Llanfflewyn IoA
78 E8 Llanfigael IoA
43 J7 Llanfihangel-ar-arth Carmth
68 C5 Llanfihangel Glyn Myfyr Conwy
44 C8 Llanfihangel Nant Bran Powys
44 H3 Llanfihangel-nant-Melan Powys
56 B11 Llanfihangel Rhydithon Powys
31 N7 Llanfihangel Rogiet Mons
44 G9 Llanfihangel Tal-y-llyn Powys
43 J10 Llanfihangel-uwch-Gwili Carmth
54 F9 Llanfihangel-y-Creuddyn Cerdgn
68 E11 Llanfihangel-yng-Ngwynfa Powys
78 E9 Llanfihangel yn Nhowyn IoA
54 F3 Llanfihangel-y-pennant Gwynd
67 J6 Llanfihangel-y-pennant Gwynd
67 K8 Llanfihangel-y-traethau Gwynd
44 G8 Llanfilo Powys
31 J2 Llanfoist Mons
68 B7 Llanfor Gwynd
31 K6 Llanfrechfa Torfn
67 L6 Llanfrothen Gwynd
44 F9 Llanfrynach Powys
68 F3 Llanfwrog Denbgs
78 E8 Llanfwrog IoA
68 F11 Llanfyllin Powys
43 L9 Llanfynydd Carmth
69 J3 Llanfynydd Flints
41 P4 Llanfyrnach Pembks
55 N2 Llangadfan Powys
28 D3 Llangadog Carmth
43 P9 Llangadog Carmth
78 F11 Llangadwaladr IoA
68 G11 Llangadwaladr Powys
78 G11 Llangaffo IoA
42 G11 Llangain Carmth
44 C5 Llangammarch Wells Powys
30 C9 Llangan V Glam
45 Q10 Llangarron Herefs
31 M6 Llangasty-Talyllyn Powys

43 L10 Llangathen Carmth
45 J11 Llangattock Powys
45 M10 Llangattock Lingoed Mons
45 P11 Llangattock-Vibon-Avel Mons
68 G10 Llangedwyn Powys
78 H9 Llangefni IoA
29 P7 Llangeinor Brdgnd
42 M3 Llangeitho Cerdgn
42 G7 Llangeler Carmth
54 D3 Llangelynin Gwynd
28 E2 Llangendeirne Carmth
28 G4 Llangennech Carmth
28 D6 Llangennith Swans
45 J11 Llangenny Powys
80 B11 Llangernyw Conwy
66 D9 Llangian Gwynd
29 K3 Llangiwg Neath
40 H4 Llangloffan Pembks
41 N5 Llanglydwen Carmth
79 L9 Llangoed IoA
42 D5 Llangoedmor Cerdgn
68 H6 Llangollen Denbgs
41 M5 Llangolman Pembks
44 G5 Llangors Powys
31 N3 Llangovan Mons
68 B8 Llangower Gwynd
42 F4 Llangranog Cerdgn
78 G10 Llangristiolus IoA
45 Q11 Llangrove Herefs
45 M9 Llangua Mons
54 C10 Llangunllo Powys
42 H10 Llangunnor Carmth
55 L9 Llangurig Powys
68 C6 Llangwm Conwy
31 M5 Llangwm Mons
41 J9 Llangwm Pembks
66 C8 Llangwnnadl Gwynd
80 G11 Llangwyfan Denbgs
78 G9 Llangwyllog IoA
54 D10 Llangwyryfon Cerdgn
43 M4 Llangybi Cerdgn
66 G6 Llangybi Gwynd
31 L5 Llangybi Mons
28 H5 Llangyfelach Swans
68 F2 Llangynhafal Denbgs
44 H11 Llangynidr Powys
41 Q7 Llangynin Carmth
42 G6 Llangynllo Cerdgn
28 B2 Llangynog Carmth
68 E9 Llangynog Powys
29 N7 Llangynwyd Brdgnd
44 F9 Llanhamlach Powys
30 D8 Llanharan Rhondd
30 D8 Llanharry Rhondd
31 L6 Llanhennock Mons
30 H4 Llanhilleth Blae G
78 H11 Llanidan IoA
55 M8 Llanidloes Powys
66 D8 Llaniestyn Gwynd
45 J7 Llanigon Powys
54 E9 Llanilar Cerdgn
30 C8 Llanilid Rhondd
42 H3 Llanina Cerdgn
30 G8 Llanio Cerdgn
31 N4 Llanishen Cardif
31 N4 Llanishen Mons
79 L11 Llanllechid Gwynd
44 C4 Llanllowell Mons
55 P4 Llanllugan Powys
42 G11 Llanllwch Carmth
55 Q6 Llanllwchaiarn Powys
43 J7 Llanllwni Carmth
66 H4 Llanllyfni Gwynd
30 D6 Llanmadoc Swans
30 C11 Llanmaes V Glam
31 L7 Llanmartin Newpt
55 B6 Llanmerewig Powys
30 C10 Llanmihangel V Glam
41 P9 Llanmiloe Carmth
28 F6 Llanmorlais Swans
80 D10 Llannefydd Conwy
28 F3 Llannon Carmth
66 F7 Llannor Gwynd
54 C11 Llanon Cerdgn
31 K3 Llanover Mons
42 H9 Llanpumsaint Carmth
68 F9 Llanrhaeadr-ym-Mochnant Powys
40 F4 Llanrhian Pembks
28 E6 Llanrhidian Swans
79 P8 Llanrhos Conwy
67 P2 Llanrhychwyn Conwy
78 E7 Llanrhyddlad IoA
54 C11 Llanrhystud Cerdgn
45 P11 Llanrothal Herefs
67 J2 Llanrug Gwynd
30 H8 Llanrumney Cardif
67 Q2 Llanrwst Gwynd
41 Q8 Llansadurnen Carmth
43 N8 Llansadwrn Carmth
78 K9 Llansadwrn IoA
28 C3 Llansaint Carmth
29 J5 Llansamlet Swans
79 Q9 Llansanffraid Glan Conwy Conwy
80 C11 Llansannan Conwy
30 C9 Llansannor V Glam
44 G10 Llansantffraed Powys
55 M11 Llansantffraed-Cwmdeuddwr Powys
44 F4 Llansantffraed-in-Elvel Powys
54 C11 Llansantffraid Cerdgn
68 H10 Llansantffraid-ym-Mechain Powys
43 M7 Llansawel Carmth
68 H9 Llansilin Powys
31 M4 Llansoy Mons
44 E9 Llanspyddid Powys
40 H10 Llanstadwell Pembks
41 Q8 Llansteffan Carmth
31 K6 Llantarnam Torfn
41 N8 Llanteg Pembks
45 L11 Llanthewy Skirrid Mons
45 K9 Llanthony Mons
31 L2 Llantilio-Crossenny Mons
45 L11 Llantilio Pertholey Mons
78 F8 Llantrisant IoA
31 L5 Llantrisant Mons
30 D8 Llantrisant Rhondd
30 D10 Llantrithyd V Glam
30 E7 Llantwit Fardre Rhondd
30 C11 Llantwit Major V Glam
68 G6 Llantysilio Denbgs
68 A8 Llanuwchllyn Gwynd
31 M6 Llanvaches Newpt

31 M6 Llanvair Discoed Mons
31 L2 Llanvapley Mons
45 M11 Llanvetherine Mons
45 L8 Llanveynoe Herefs
45 L10 Llanvihangel Crucorney Mons
31 K3 Llanvihangel Gobion Mons
31 M2 Llanvihangel-Ystern-Llewern Mons
45 Q9 Llanwarne Herefs
68 D11 Llanwddyn Powys
31 J2 Llanwenarth Mons
43 J5 Llanwenog Cerdgn
31 L7 Llanwern Newpt
41 Q5 Llanwinio Carmth
66 H3 Llanwnda Gwynd
40 H3 Llanwnda Pembks
43 K5 Llanwnnen Cerdgn
55 N6 Llanwnog Powys
30 D5 Llanwonno Rhondd
43 P8 Llanwrda Carmth
54 H4 Llanwrin Powys
44 D2 Llanwrthwl Powys
44 B5 Llanwrtyd Powys
44 B5 Llanwrtyd Wells Powys
55 P4 Llanwyddelan Powys
68 H10 Llanyblodwel Shrops
28 B2 Llanybri Carmth
43 K6 Llanybydder Carmth
41 L6 Llanycefn Pembks
41 J3 Llanychaer Bridge Pembks
43 M5 Llanycrwys Carmth
68 B11 Llanymawddwy Gwynd
69 J10 Llanymynech Powys
78 E8 Llanynghenedl IoA
68 F2 Llanynys Denbgs
69 L4 Llan-y-pwll Wrexhm
44 E2 Llanyre Powys
66 H7 Llanystumdwy Gwynd
44 G9 Llanywern Powys
41 L7 Llawhaden Pembks
68 H8 Llawnt Shrops
55 L6 Llawryglyn Powys
69 K3 Llay Wrexhm
78 F8 Llechcynfarwy IoA
44 F9 Llechfaen Powys
30 F3 Llechrhyd Caerph
41 P2 Llechryd Cerdgn
78 E9 Llechylched IoA
54 E10 Lledrod Cerdgn
66 F7 Lleyn Peninsula Gwynd
68 A7 Llidiardau Gwynd
43 K7 Llidiartnenog Carmth
68 F6 Llidiart-y-parc Denbgs
66 F6 Llithfaen Gwynd
80 G9 Lloc Flints
44 H6 Llowes Powys
30 C4 Llwydcoed Rhondd
30 C3 Llwydcoed Crematorium Rhondd
68 D11 Llwydiarth Powys
68 E2 Llwyn Denbgs
42 H3 Llwyncelyn Cerdgn
42 G3 Llwyndafydd Cerdgn
56 C4 Llwynderw Powys
41 Q4 Llwyn-drain Pembks
45 K11 Llwyn-du Mons
66 F6 Llwyndyrys Gwynd
54 D3 Llwyngwril Gwynd
28 F5 Llwynhendy Carmth
68 H7 Llwynmawr Wrexhm
30 D2 Llwyn-on Rhondd
41 N8 Llwyn-y-brain Carmth
43 L3 Llwyn-y-groes Cerdgn
30 C6 Llwynypia Rhondd
69 J10 Llynclys Shrops
78 G9 Llynfaes IoA
41 J11 Llyn-y-pandy Flints
80 B9 Llysfaen Conwy
43 J2 Llyswen Cerdgn
44 G7 Llyswen Powys
30 C10 Llysworney V Glam
41 K6 Llys-y-frân Pembks
44 B8 Llywel Powys
84 C3 Load Brook Sheff
126 H2 Loan Falk
129 N9 Loanend Nthumb
127 P4 Loanhead Mdloth
109 L9 Loaningfoot D & G
125 J11 Loans S Ayrs
16 H4 Lobb Devon
8 C7 Lobhillcross Devon
145 N11 Lochailort Highld
138 B9 Lochaline Highld
106 E6 Lochans D & G
109 L4 Locharbriggs D & G
131 J4 Lochavich Ag & B
131 N2 Lochawe Ag & B
168 c16 Loch Baghasdail W Isls
168 c16 Lochboisdale W Isls
137 Q10 Lochbuie Ag & B
154 A10 Lochcarron Highld
138 C11 Lochdon Ag & B
138 C11 Lochdonhead Ag & B
123 N4 Lochead Ag & B
132 H3 Lochearnhead Stirlg
142 F11 Lochee C Dund
138 H2 Locheilside Station Highld
155 Q10 Lochend Highld
168 d11 Locheport W Isls
168 c11 Loch Euphort W Isls
109 J6 Lochfoot D & G
131 J3 Lochgair Ag & B
134 F9 Lochgelly Fife
130 H10 Lochgilphead Ag & B
131 Q7 Lochgoilhead Ag & B
134 H5 Lochieheads Fife
157 P5 Lochill Moray
156 H10 Lochindorb Lodge Highld
160 H2 Lochinver Highld
132 E5 Loch Lomond and The Trossachs National Park
155 K5 Lochluichart Highld
109 N4 Lochmaben D & G
168 e11 Lochmaddy W Isls
154 B3 Loch Maree Hotel Highld
168 e11 Loch nam Madadh W Isls
147 N2 Loch Ness Highld
134 F8 Lochore Fife
124 A7 Lochranza N Ayrs
143 N5 Lochside Abers
109 L5 Lochside D & G
156 E7 Lochside Highld
163 J10 Lochslin Highld
107 J2 Lochton S Ayrs
143 J5 Lochty Angus
135 N6 Lochty Fife

138 D6 Lochuisge Highld
125 K6 Lochwinnoch Rens
116 F11 Lochwood D & G
4 G9 Lockengate Cnwll
109 P4 Lockerbie D & G
33 M11 Lockeridge Wilts
22 B9 Lockerley Hants
19 L3 Locking N Som
82 D6 Locking Stumps Warrtn
99 K11 Lockington E R Yk
72 D5 Lockington Leics
70 B9 Lockleywood Shrops
37 K7 Locksbottom Gt Lon
14 D8 Locksgreen IoW
14 F5 Locks Heath Hants
98 G3 Lockton N York
73 K10 Loddington Leics
60 H5 Loddington Nhants
7 J9 Loddiswell Devon
65 M2 Loddon Norfk
62 H8 Lode Cambs
59 J8 Lode Heath Solhll
11 K6 Loders Dorset
58 F8 Lodge Hill Crematorium Birm
23 P10 Lodsworth W Susx
91 J5 Lofthouse Leeds
96 H6 Lofthouse N York
91 J6 Lofthouse Gate Wakefd
105 K7 Loftus R & Cl
115 L3 Logan E Ayrs
94 D2 Loganbeck Cumb
126 H5 Loganlea W Loth
70 C7 Loggerheads Staffs
143 M5 Logie Angus
135 L3 Logie Fife
157 J7 Logie Moray
150 C7 Logie Coldstone Abers
158 G10 Logie Newton Abers
143 M5 Logie Pert Angus
141 N7 Logierait P & K
151 N2 Logierieve Abers
41 N6 Login Carmth
62 E8 Lolworth Cambs
153 M7 Lonbain Highld
98 H11 Londesborough E R Yk
36 G5 London Gt Lon
3 Q4 London Apprentice Cnwll
26 E4 London Beach Kent
50 E10 London Colney Herts
97 M3 Londonderry N York
61 K7 London End Nhants
36 E2 London Gateway Services Gt Lon
73 P3 Londonthorpe Lincs
160 D10 Londubh Highld
153 P2 Lonemore Highld
31 P10 Long Ashton N Som
57 P10 Long Bank Worcs
73 L2 Long Bennington Lincs
113 L7 Longbenton N Tyne
47 N9 Longborough Gloucs
11 M6 Long Bredy Dorset
58 F9 Longbridge Birm
47 Q2 Longbridge Warwks
20 G6 Longbridge Deverill Wilts
60 D7 Long Buckby Nhants
110 F9 Longburgh Cumb
11 N2 Longburton Dorset
7 K6 Long Cause Devon
73 J5 Long Clawson Leics
84 B9 Longcliffe Derbys
7 L7 Longcombe Devon
14 F4 Long Common Hants
70 F10 Long Compton Staffs
47 Q8 Long Compton Warwks
33 Q6 Longcot Oxon
35 J3 Long Crendon Bucks
12 G2 Long Crichel Dorset
110 D9 Longcroft Cumb
35 Q11 Longcross Surrey
56 G3 Longden Shrops
56 G3 Longden Common Shrops
36 E7 Long Ditton Surrey
58 G2 Longdon Staffs
46 F7 Longdon Worcs
58 G2 Longdon Green Staffs
46 F7 Longdon Heath Worcs
69 R11 Longdon upon Tern Wrekin
9 L6 Longdown Devon
3 J7 Longdowns Cnwll
92 A5 Long Drax N York
84 F6 Long Duckmanton Derbys
72 D4 Long Eaton Derbys
37 P7 Longfield Kent
59 N8 Longford Covtry
71 N7 Longford Derbys
46 F10 Longford Gloucs
36 C5 Longford Gt Lon
37 M9 Longford Kent
70 A8 Longford Shrops
70 C11 Longford Wrekin
134 H2 Longforgan P & K
128 H8 Longformacus Border
119 M10 Longframlington Nthumb
81 P10 Long Green Ches W
46 F8 Long Green Worcs
13 J5 Longham Dorset
76 C8 Longham Norfk
34 D2 Long Hanborough Oxon
159 R10 Longhaven Abers
87 L11 Long Hedges Lincs
113 K3 Longhirst Nthumb
46 C11 Longhope Gloucs
169 c7 Longhope Ork
112 H2 Longhorsley Nthumb
119 P7 Longhoughton Nthumb
59 P11 Long Itchington Warwks
101 J3 Longlands Cumb
71 N7 Longlane Derbys
59 Q9 Long Lawford Warwks
20 F6 Longleat Safari Park Wilts
46 G11 Longlevens Gloucs
90 D6 Longley Calder
90 E9 Longley Kirk
46 D4 Longley Green Worcs
142 D9 Longleys P & K
19 N10 Long Load Somset
158 H5 Longmanhill Abers
49 N11 Long Marston Herts
97 R10 Long Marston N York
47 N5 Long Marston Warwks
102 C6 Long Marton Cumb
56 G8 Long Meadowend Shrops

52 E2 Long Melford Suffk
23 L8 Longmoor Camp Hants
157 N6 Longmorn Moray
83 J10 Longmoss Ches E
32 H6 Long Newnton Gloucs
118 A5 Longnewton Border
128 E7 Long Newton E Loth
104 C7 Longnewton S on T
37 L2 Longney Gloucs
128 C4 Longniddry E Loth
56 H4 Longnor Shrops
71 K2 Longnor Staffs
22 D5 Longparish Hants
110 H8 Longpark Cumb
96 B9 Long Preston N York
89 J3 Longridge Lancs
70 C11 Longridge Staffs
126 G5 Longridge W Loth
126 E3 Longriggend N Lans
93 K2 Long Riston E R Yk
2 E7 Longrock Cnwll
70 H4 Longsdon Staffs
82 B4 Longshaw Wigan
159 P8 Longside Abers
89 Q9 Long Sight Oldham
70 B7 Longslow Shrops
62 E7 Longstanton Cambs
22 C7 Longstock Hants
41 M9 Longstone Pembks
62 D10 Longstowe Cambs
64 H3 Long Stratton Norfk
49 L5 Long Street M Keyn
21 M4 Longstreet Wilts
23 K5 Long Sutton Hants
74 H6 Long Sutton Lincs
19 N9 Long Sutton Somset
74 C11 Longthorpe C Pete
64 E8 Long Thurlow Suffk
101 M6 Longthwaite Cumb
70 G6 Longton C Stke
88 F5 Longton Lancs
110 G7 Longtown Cumb
45 L9 Longtown Herefs
11 c2 Longueville Jersey
57 J6 Longville in the Dale Shrops
69 R11 Long Waste Wrekin
72 D6 Long Whatton Leics
35 L3 Longwick Bucks
34 F6 Long Wittenham Oxon
112 G3 Longwitton Nthumb
108 F8 Longwood D & G
57 L3 Longwood Shrops
34 C5 Longworth Oxon
128 E7 Longyester E Loth
29 K5 Lon-las Swans
159 P6 Lonmay Abers
152 D8 Lonmore Highld
5 M11 Looe Cnwll
38 C11 Loose Kent
8 H3 Loosebeare Devon
74 F5 Loosegate Lincs
35 M4 Loosley Row Bucks
158 F7 Lootcherbrae Abers
21 Q7 Lopcombe Corner Wilts
11 J2 Lopen Somset
69 N9 Loppington Shrops
119 K9 Lorbottle Nthumb
15 L5 Lordington W Susx
75 L8 Lordsbridge Norfk
38 C9 Lords Wood Medway
142 B8 Lornty P & K
84 F11 Loscoe Derbys
11 K5 Loscombe Dorset
157 N3 Lossiemouth Moray
69 R8 Lostford Shrops
3 P4 Lost Gardens of Heligan Cnwll
82 E10 Lostock Gralam Ches W
82 E10 Lostock Green Ches W
88 G5 Lostock Hall Lancs
89 K9 Lostock Hall Fold Bolton
89 K9 Lostock Junction Bolton
5 J10 Lostwithiel Cnwll
163 L4 Lothbeg Highld
96 F11 Lothersdale N York
163 M4 Lothmore Highld
35 P6 Loudwater Bucks
72 E7 Loughborough Leics
72 E7 Loughborough Crematorium Leics
28 G5 Loughor Swans
51 K11 Loughton Essex
49 M7 Loughton M Keyn
57 L8 Loughton Shrops
73 R7 Lound Lincs
85 L3 Lound Notts
65 Q2 Lound Suffk
9 J3 Lounston Devon
72 B7 Lount Leics
87 K3 Louth Lincs
89 N5 Love Clough Lancs
15 J4 Lovedean Hants
21 P10 Lover Wilts
91 P11 Loversall Donc
51 P10 Loves Green Essex
104 C11 Lovesome Hill N York
41 L9 Loveston Pembks
19 Q8 Lovington Somset
91 M7 Low Ackworth Wakefd
112 G4 Low Angerton Nthumb
46 E8 Lowbands Gloucs
106 D4 Low Barbeth D & G
86 E6 Low Barlings Lincs
105 K11 Low Bell End N York
95 N7 Low Bentham N York
95 N5 Low Biggins Cumb
102 B10 Low Borrowbridge Cumb
84 C2 Low Bradfield Sheff
96 F11 Low Bradley N York
101 M2 Low Braithwaite Cumb
92 C10 Low Burnham N Linc
119 P9 Low Buston Nthumb
100 C6 Lowca Cumb
98 E10 Low Catton E R Yk
103 Q8 Low Conscliffe Darltn
110 H9 Low Crosby Cumb
85 L11 Lowdham Notts
104 B8 Low Dinsdale Darltn
69 N8 Lowe Shrops
70 H3 Lowe Hill Staffs
97 K4 Low Ellington N York
18 H7 Lower Aisholt Somset
12 C4 Lower Ansty Dorset
46 C9 Lower Apperley Gloucs
48 H11 Lower Arncott Oxon
9 K8 Lower Ashton Devon
35 K8 Lower Assendon Oxon
88 D4 Lower Ballam Lancs

88 F4 Lower Bartle Lancs
34 H9 Lower Basildon W Berk
45 M3 Lower Bearwood Herefs
24 F5 Lower Beeding W Susx
61 L3 Lower Benefield Nhants
58 E11 Lower Bentley Worcs
57 P6 Lower Beobridge Shrops
84 F10 Lower Birchwood Derbys
48 E4 Lower Boddington Nhants
2 B7 Lower Boscaswell Cnwll
23 M6 Lower Bourne Surrey
48 B7 Lower Brailes Warwks
145 L3 Lower Breakish Highld
83 K6 Lower Bredbury Stockp
46 F3 Lower Broadheath Worcs
45 M4 Lower Broxwood Herefs
46 B8 Lower Buckenhill Herefs
45 Q7 Lower Bullingham Herefs
21 N11 Lower Burgate Hants
9 P5 Lower Burrowton Devon
45 N3 Lower Burton Herefs
61 Q11 Lower Caldecote C Beds
32 D4 Lower Cam Gloucs
19 L3 Lower Canada N Som
60 B9 Lower Catesby Nhants
44 E7 Lower Chapel Powys
21 J9 Lower Chicksgrove Wilts
22 B4 Lower Chute Wilts
36 H3 Lower Clapton Gt Lon
58 D9 Lower Clent Worcs
9 K4 Lower Creedy Devon
83 M8 Lower Crossings Derbys
90 G9 Lower Cumberworth Kirk
89 K5 Lower Darwen Bl w D
61 N7 Lower Dean Bed
90 G7 Lower Denby Kirk
153 P5 Lower Diabaig Highld
25 N8 Lower Dicker E Susx
56 H8 Lower Dinchope Shrops
56 E8 Lower Down Shrops
97 P8 Lower Dunsforth N York
46 B5 Lower Egleton Herefs
71 K3 Lower Elkstone Staffs
71 L6 Lower Ellastone Staffs
35 J3 Lower End Bucks
49 P7 Lower End M Keyn
60 H9 Lower End Nhants
61 J8 Lower End Nhants
21 N4 Lower Everleigh Wilts
14 D7 Lower Exbury Hants
27 N2 Lower Eythorne Kent
31 P10 Lower Failand N Som
23 K7 Lower Farringdon Hants
36 C6 Lower Feltham Gt Lon
24 B7 Lower Fittleworth W Susx
80 c6 Lower Foxdale IoM
69 L8 Lower Frankton Shrops
41 J8 Lower Freystrop Pembks
23 L6 Lower Froyle Hants
7 N5 Lower Gabwell Devon
162 D8 Lower Gledfield Highld
19 N6 Lower Godney Somset
58 D6 Lower Gornal Dudley
50 D3 Lower Gravenhurst C Beds
50 E4 Lower Green Herts
51 K4 Lower Green Herts
25 N2 Lower Green Kent
25 P2 Lower Green Kent
76 D4 Lower Green Norfk
58 D3 Lower Green Staffs
63 M7 Lower Green Suffk
65 L10 Lower Hacheston Suffk
36 C7 Lower Halliford Surrey
11 L3 Lower Halstock Leigh Dorset
38 E8 Lower Halstow Kent
12 G6 Lower Hamworthy Poole
39 L11 Lower Hardres Kent
45 K2 Lower Harpton Herefs
38 D9 Lower Hartlip Kent
84 E10 Lower Hartshay Derbys
35 L2 Lower Hartwell Bucks
70 E7 Lower Hatton Staffs
94 E3 Lower Hawthwaite Cumb
45 K3 Lower Hergest Herefs
48 E10 Lower Heyford Oxon
95 J8 Lower Heysham Lancs
38 B7 Lower Higham Kent
53 L4 Lower Holbrook Suffk
69 L9 Lower Hordley Shrops
24 B7 Lower Horncroft W Susx
89 N4 Lowerhouse Lancs
90 F7 Lower Houses Kirk
46 E5 Lower Howsell Worcs
82 F6 Lower Irlam Salfd
72 B2 Lower Kilburn Derbys
32 E7 Lower Kilcott Gloucs
122 C11 Lower Killeyan Ag & B
11 M5 Lower Kingcombe Dorset
36 F10 Lower Kingswood Surrey
69 K2 Lower Kinnerton Ches W
19 N2 Lower Langford N Som
135 L7 Lower Largo Fife
71 J7 Lower Leigh Staffs
47 P8 Lower Lemington Gloucs
55 M11 Lower Llanfadog Powys
17 J6 Lower Lovacott Devon
17 L4 Lower Loxhore Devon
46 A11 Lower Lydbrook Gloucs
56 G11 Lower Lye Herefs
30 H7 Lower Machen Newpt
45 L8 Lower Maes-coed Herefs
13 J4 Lower Mannington Dorset
20 E6 Lower Marston Somset
31 Q4 Lower Meend Gloucs
18 H8 Lower Merridge Somset
48 F6 Lower Middleton Cheney Nhants
19 P5 Lower Milton Somset
47 J5 Lower Moor Worcs
32 B6 Lower Morton S Glos
51 J9 Lower Nazeing Essex
47 P2 Lower Norton Warwks
20 E10 Lower Nyland Dorset
30 G11 Lower Penarth V Glam
58 C5 Lower Penn Staffs
13 P6 Lower Pennington Hants
88 G5 Lower Penwortham Lancs
82 F10 Lower Peover Ches E
89 Q8 Lower Place Rochdl
35 K2 Lower Pollicott Bucks

47 N5 Lower Quinton Warwks
38 D7 Lower Rainham Medway
52 H4 Lower Raydon Suffk
18 D7 Lower Roadwater Somset
95 N8 Lower Salter Lancs
33 J8 Lower Seagry Wilts
51 L8 Lower Sheering Essex
49 Q6 Lower Shelton C Beds
35 L9 Lower Shiplake Oxon
48 E2 Lower Shuckburgh Warwks
47 N10 Lower Slaughter Gloucs
90 H6 Lower Soothill Kirk
32 C3 Lower Soudley Gloucs
27 M3 Lower Standen Kent
32 H8 Lower Stanton St Quintin Wilts
38 D6 Lower Stoke Medway
32 C6 Lower Stone Gloucs
58 G4 Lower Stonnall Staffs
64 D3 Lower Stow Bedon Norfk
12 D5 Lower Street Dorset
26 B9 Lower Street E Susx
77 K4 Lower Street Norfk
63 N10 Lower Street Suffk
64 G11 Lower Street Suffk
82 D8 Lower Stretton Warrtn
11 K5 Lower Stroud Dorset
50 C5 Lower Sundon C Beds
14 E5 Lower Swanwick Hants
47 N9 Lower Swell Gloucs
48 D7 Lower Tadmarton Oxon
9 Q4 Lower Tale Devon
71 J7 Lower Tean Staffs
65 N2 Lower Thurlton Norfk
2 H8 Lower Town Cnwll
7 J4 Lower Town Devon
46 B6 Lower Town Herefs
41 J3 Lower Town Pembks
5 N6 Lower Trebullett Cnwll
3 K6 Lower Treluswell Cnwll
48 B5 Lower Tysoe Warwks
65 K11 Lower Ufford Suffk
9 L8 Lower Upcott Devon
22 F11 Lower Upham Hants
38 C7 Lower Upnor Medway
12 B5 Lower Waterston Dorset
19 M4 Lower Weare Somset
60 D9 Lower Weedon Nhants
45 K4 Lower Welson Herefs
46 H7 Lower Westmancote Worcs
12 D4 Lower Whatcombe Dorset
20 D5 Lower Whatley Somset
82 D9 Lower Whitley Ches W
32 D5 Lower Wick Gloucs
46 F4 Lower Wick Worcs
22 H6 Lower Wield Hants
25 N10 Lower Willingdon E Susx
82 H11 Lower Withington Ches E
35 M7 Lower Woodend Bucks
21 M7 Lower Woodford Wilts
11 M4 Lower Wraxall Dorset
46 E6 Lower Wyche Worcs
90 F5 Lower Wyke C Brad
73 J9 Lowesby Leics
65 Q3 Lowestoft Suffk
100 F6 Loweswater Cumb
113 L9 Low Fell Gatesd
24 G3 Lowfield Heath W Susx
132 F10 Low Gartachorrans Stirlg
112 D8 Low Gate Nthumb
111 K9 Low Gettbridge Cumb
102 B11 Lowgill Cumb
95 P8 Lowgill Lancs
97 K6 Low Grantley N York
97 K9 Low Green N York
57 Q9 Low Habberley Worcs
19 M9 Low Ham Somset
97 L9 Low Harrogate N York
105 P9 Low Hawsker N York
111 J11 Low Hesket Cumb
98 F7 Low Hutton N York
94 F3 Lowick Cumb
61 L4 Lowick Nhants
119 K3 Lowick Nthumb
94 F3 Lowick Bridge Cumb
94 F3 Lowick Green Cumb
101 P7 Low Knipe Cumb
97 J8 Low Laithe N York
103 M5 Lowlands Dur
31 J5 Lowlands Torfn
86 G5 Low Langton Lincs
83 M7 Low Leighton Derbys
100 G5 Low Lorton Cumb
98 G5 Low Marishes N York
85 P7 Low Marnham Notts
119 M3 Low Middleton Nthumb
105 J11 Low Mill N York
90 F5 Low Moor C Brad
89 N6 Low Moorsley Sundld
100 C6 Low Moresby Cumb
95 J4 Low Newton Cumb
100 Q3 Low Row Cumb
101 L3 Low Row Cumb
111 L8 Low Row Cumb
103 J11 Low Row N York
106 D4 Low Salchrie D & G
92 F8 Low Santon N Linc
59 J11 Lowsonford Warwks
77 L1 Low Street Norfk
37 Q5 Low Street Thurr
64 H2 Low Tharston Norfk
101 P6 Lowther Cumb
101 P6 Lowther Castle Cumb
99 M8 Lowthorpe E R Yk
8 D5 Lowton Devon
19 Q11 Lowton Somset
82 D5 Lowton Wigan
82 D5 Lowton Common Wigan
82 D5 Lowton St Mary's Wigan
134 C10 Low Torry Fife
87 J6 Low Toynton Lincs
91 L10 Low Valley Barns
94 G4 Low Wood Cumb
104 C9 Low Worsall N York
101 L10 Low Wray Cumb
18 B3 Loxhill Surrey
17 L4 Loxhore Devon
17 L4 Loxhore Cott Devon
47 Q4 Loxley Warwks
71 K8 Loxley Green Staffs
19 L3 Loxton N Som

24 B4 Loxwood W Susx
165 P7 Loyal Lodge Highld
60 F3 Lubenham Leics
87 M11 Lucasgate Lincs
23 P2 Lucas Green Surrey
18 B6 Luccombe Somset
14 G11 Luccombe Village IoW
119 N4 Lucker Nthumb
5 P7 Luckett Cnwll
52 D5 Lucking Street Essex
32 F8 Luckington Wilts
135 L3 Lucklawhill Fife
32 F10 Lucknam Wilts
18 B7 Luckwell Bridge Somset
46 C11 Lucton Herefs
103 P8 Lucy Cross N York
168 c16 Ludag W Isls
93 N11 Ludborough Lincs
6 H8 Ludbrook Devon
41 M8 Ludchurch Pembks
90 C5 Luddenden Calder
90 C5 Luddenden Foot Calder
38 G5 Luddenham Court Kent
37 Q7 Luddesdown Kent
92 D7 Luddington N Linc
47 N4 Luddington Warwks
61 P4 Luddington in the Brook Nhants
86 G3 Ludford Lincs
57 J10 Ludford Shrops
49 J11 Ludgershall Bucks
21 Q4 Ludgershall Wilts
2 E7 Ludgvan Cnwll
77 M8 Ludham Norfk
57 J9 Ludlow Shrops
10 H2 Ludney Somset
20 H10 Ludwell Wilts
104 C2 Ludworth Dur
50 C5 Luffenhall Herts
5 N3 Luffincott Devon
128 D4 Luffness E Loth
115 L3 Lugar E Ayrs
128 F5 Luggate Burn E Loth
45 N2 Lugg Green Herefs
126 D3 Luggiebank N Lans
115 L2 Lugton E Ayrs
45 R6 Lugwardine Herefs
145 J2 Luib Highld
130 E5 Luing Ag & B
45 N6 Lulham Herefs
59 K2 Lullington Derbys
25 M10 Lullington E Susx
20 E4 Lullington Somset
31 P11 Lulsgate Bottom N Som
46 D3 Lulsley Worcs
12 D8 Lulworth Camp Dorset
90 C6 Lumb Calder
89 N6 Lumb Lancs
90 B6 Lumbutts Calder
91 M4 Lumby N York
125 Q3 Lumloch E Duns
150 F7 Lumphanan Abers
134 F9 Lumphinnans Fife
150 D3 Lumsden Abers
143 M7 Lunan Angus
142 H7 Lunanhead Angus
134 D2 Luncarty P & K
99 K11 Lund E R Yk
91 K4 Lund N York
142 D10 Lundie Angus
135 L5 Lundin Links Fife
135 L7 Lundin Mill Fife
16 A2 Lundy Devon
63 J3 Lundy Green Norfk
130 E6 Lunga Ag & B
169 r7 Lunna Shet
37 Q9 Lunsford Kent
26 B9 Lunsford's Cross E Susx
81 L4 Lunt Sefton
45 M3 Luntley Herefs
10 D3 Luppitt Devon
7 J8 Lupridge Devon
91 J7 Lupset Wakefd
95 M4 Lupton Cumb
23 P9 Lurgashall W Susx
18 B11 Lurley Devon
87 K7 Lusby Lincs
7 K7 Luscombe Devon
6 G8 Luson Devon
132 D9 Luss Ag & B
130 C10 Lussagiven Ag & B
152 D6 Lusta Highld
9 J8 Lustleigh Devon
45 P2 Luston Herefs
143 M4 Luthermuir Abers
135 J4 Luthrie Fife
58 D8 Lutley Dudley
9 M9 Luton Devon
10 B4 Luton Devon
50 C6 Luton Luton
38 C8 Luton Medway
50 D6 Luton Airport Luton
60 B4 Lutterworth Leics
6 F7 Lutton Devon
6 H6 Lutton Devon
74 H5 Lutton Lincs
61 P3 Lutton Nhants
18 C7 Luxborough Somset
4 H10 Luxulyan Cnwll
83 L4 Luzley Tamesd
167 M9 Lybster Highld
56 E7 Lydbury North Shrops
17 M4 Lydcott Devon
26 H7 Lydd Kent
27 J7 Lydd Airport Kent
27 N2 Lydden Kent
39 Q8 Lydden Kent
73 M11 Lyddington Rutlnd
18 F8 Lydeard St Lawrence Somset
23 K3 Lyde Green Hants
8 D7 Lydford Devon
19 Q8 Lydford on Fosse Somset
89 Q5 Lydgate Calder
56 E6 Lydgate Rochdl
33 L7 Lydiard Green Wilts
33 L7 Lydiard Millicent Wilts
33 M8 Lydiard Tregoze Swindn
81 M4 Lydiate Sefton
58 E9 Lydiate Ash Worcs
12 B2 Lydlinch Dorset
32 B4 Lydney Gloucs
41 L11 Lydstep Pembks
58 D8 Lye Dudley
19 N2 Lye Cross N Som
35 Q4 Lye Green Bucks
25 M4 Lye Green E Susx
59 J11 Lye Green Warwks
57 P10 Lye Head Worcs

20 F5 **Lye's Green** Wilts
34 K7 **Lyford** Oxon
27 K3 **Lymbridge Green** Kent
10 C6 **Lyme Regis** Dorset
27 L3 **Lyminge** Kent
13 P5 **Lymington** Hants
24 B10 **Lyminster** W Susx
82 E7 **Lymm** Warrtn
27 K4 **Lympne** Kent
19 K4 **Lympsham** Somset
9 N8 **Lympstone** Devon
17 N2 **Lynbridge** Devon
148 D7 **Lynchat** Highld
76 H10 **Lynch Green** Norfk
13 P3 **Lyndhurst** Hants
73 N10 **Lyndon** Rutlnd
58 H7 **Lyndon Green** Birm
117 J2 **Lyne** Border
36 B7 **Lyne** Surrey
69 M8 **Lyneal** Shrops
46 B8 **Lyne Down** Herefs
9 L9 **Lyneham** Devon
47 Q10 **Lyneham** Oxon
33 K9 **Lyneham** Wilts
33 K9 *Lyneham Airport* Wilts
111 K6 **Lyneholmford** Cumb
113 L2 **Lynemouth** Nthumb
151 K5 **Lyne of Skene** Abers
103 L5 **Lynesack** Dur
169 c7 **Lyness** Ork
76 H3 **Lyng** Norfk
19 K9 **Lyng** Somset
17 N2 **Lynmouth** Devon
58 G4 **Lynn** Staffs
70 D11 **Lynn** Wrekin
38 F9 **Lynsted** Kent
16 C10 **Lynstone** Cnwll
17 N2 **Lynton** Devon
11 P3 **Lyon's Gate** Dorset
45 L3 **Lyonshall** Herefs
12 F5 **Lytchett Matravers** Dorset
12 G6 **Lytchett Minster** Dorset
167 N4 **Lyth** Highld
88 D5 **Lytham** Lancs
88 C5 **Lytham St Anne's** Lancs
56 H3 **Lythbank** Shrops
105 M8 **Lythe** N York
167 J3 **Lythmore** Highld

M

3 K7 **Mabe Burnthouse** Cnwll
87 P4 **Mablethorpe** Lincs
83 K10 **Macclesfield** Ches E
83 K10 **Macclesfield Crematorium** Ches E
158 H5 **Macduff** Abers
120 D10 **Macharioch** Ag & B
30 H7 **Machen** Caerph
120 G5 **Machrie** N Ayrs
120 D5 **Machrihanish** Ag & B
136 b3 **Machrins** Ag & B
54 G4 **Machynlleth** Powys
28 F5 **Machynys** Carmth
71 Q7 **Mackworth** Derbys
128 C5 **Macmerry** E Loth
8 D6 **Maddaford** Devon
134 B3 **Madderty** P & K
21 L6 **Maddington** Wilts
126 G2 **Maddiston** Falk
15 Q4 **Madehurst** W Susx
70 D6 **Madeley** Staffs
57 M4 **Madeley** Wrekin
70 D5 **Madeley Heath** Staffs
10 C2 **Madford** Devon
62 E8 **Madingley** Cambs
45 N7 **Madley** Herefs
46 F5 **Madresfield** Worcs
2 D7 **Madron** Cnwll
78 H4 **Maenaddwyn** IoA
79 P11 **Maenan** Conwy
41 L5 **Maenclochog** Pembks
30 D9 **Maendy** V Glam
3 K8 **Maenporth** Cnwll
67 M6 **Maentwrog** Gwynd
42 G9 **Maen-y-groes** Cerdgn
16 C10 **Maer** Cnwll
70 D7 **Maer** Staffs
43 N9 **Maerdy** Carmth
30 C9 **Maerdy** Rhondd
69 K10 **Maesbrook** Shrops
69 K9 **Maesbury** Shrops
69 K9 **Maesbury Marsh** Shrops
31 J7 **Maes-glas** Newpt
41 P6 **Maesgwynne** Carmth
68 H2 **Maeshafn** Denbgs
42 G6 **Maesllyn** Cerdgn
44 E5 **Maesmynis** Powys
44 E5 **Maesmynis** Powys
29 N6 **Maesteg** Brdgnd
43 L11 **Maesybont** Carmth
30 G6 **Maesycwmmer** Caerph
51 M9 **Magdalen Laver** Essex
157 Q8 **Maggieknockater** Moray
51 L5 **Maggots End** Essex
25 P8 **Magham Down** E Susx
81 M4 **Maghull** Sefton
60 B4 **Magna Park** Leics
31 M7 **Magor** Mons
31 M7 *Magor Services* Mons
24 G3 **Maidenbower** W Susx
20 F7 **Maiden Bradley** Wilts
7 N5 **Maidencombe** Torbay
10 F5 **Maidenhayne** Devon
31 Q11 **Maiden Head** N Som
35 N8 **Maidenhead** W & M
113 J11 **Maiden Law** Dur
11 M5 **Maiden Newton** Dorset
114 D6 **Maidens** S Ayrs
35 P10 **Maiden's Green** Br For
87 K5 **Maidenwell** Lincs
41 J11 **Maiden Wells** Pembks
48 H4 **Maidford** Nhants
49 K7 **Maids Moreton** Bucks
38 C10 **Maidstone** Kent
38 D10 **Maidstone Services** Kent
60 F5 **Maidwell** Nhants
169 r9 **Mail** Shet
31 K7 **Maindee** Newpt
169 d6 **Mainland** Ork
169 r8 **Mainland** Shet
104 B4 **Mainsforth** Dur
143 J5 **Mains of Balhall** Angus
143 L3 **Mains of Balnakettle** Abers
157 L11 **Mains of Dalvey** Highld

143 N3 **Mains of Haulkerton** Abers
150 D2 **Mains of Lesmoir** Abers
143 J6 **Mains of Melgunds** Angus
109 K9 **Mainsriddle** D & G
56 D7 **Mainstone** Shrops
46 F10 **Maisemore** Gloucs
58 H9 **Major's Green** Worcs
72 B2 **Makeney** Derbys
7 J11 **Malborough** Devon
83 N8 **Malcoff** Derbys
36 E8 **Malden Rushett** Gt Lon
52 E10 **Maldon** Essex
96 D8 **Malham** N York
152 H5 **Maligar** Highld
145 L8 **Mallaig** Highld
145 L8 **Mallaigvaig** Highld
127 M4 **Malleny Mills** C Edin
51 L5 **Mallows Green** Essex
78 G11 **Malltraeth** IoA
55 K2 **Mallwyd** Gwynd
32 H7 **Malmesbury** Wilts
17 P2 **Malmsmead** Devon
69 N5 **Malpas** Ches W
3 L5 **Malpas** Cnwll
31 K6 **Malpas** Newpt
46 D10 **Malswick** Gloucs
87 K4 **Maltby** Lincs
84 H2 **Maltby** Rothm
104 E8 **Maltby** S on T
87 N4 **Maltby le Marsh** Lincs
52 E3 **Malting Green** Essex
26 F3 **Maltman's Hill** Kent
98 F6 **Malton** N York
46 E6 **Malvern Hills**
46 E6 **Malvern Link** Worcs
46 E6 **Malvern Wells** Worcs
57 M10 **Mamble** Worcs
31 K4 **Mamhilad** Mons
3 K9 **Manaccan** Cnwll
55 Q4 **Manafon** Powys
168 g9 **Manais** W Isls
9 J8 **Manaton** Devon
87 L3 **Manby** Lincs
59 M5 **Mancetter** Warwks
82 H5 **Manchester** Manch
82 H8 *Manchester Airport* Manch
81 L11 **Mancot** Flints
146 H7 **Mandally** Highld
129 L9 **Manderston House** Border
62 G3 **Manea** Cambs
58 H5 **Maney** Birm
103 P8 **Manfield** N York
11 K5 **Mangerton** Dorset
32 C9 **Mangotsfield** S Glos
50 D6 **Mangrove Green** Herts
2 H7 **Manhay** Cnwll
168 g9 **Manish** W Isls
90 B6 **Mankinholes** Calder
81 Q10 **Manley** Ches W
30 G4 **Manmoel** Caerph
136 B7 **Mannal** Ag & B
21 M3 **Manningford Bohune** Wilts
21 M3 **Manningford Bruce** Wilts
90 E3 **Manningham** C Brad
24 F5 **Manning's Heath** W Susx
13 J3 **Mannington** Dorset
53 K5 **Manningtree** Essex
151 N7 **Mannofield** C Aber
41 L11 **Manorbier** Pembks
41 K10 **Manorbier Newton** Pembks
43 N9 **Manordeilo** Carmth
118 C4 **Manorhill** Border
40 H3 **Manorowen** Pembks
37 N3 **Manor Park** Gt Lon
37 K3 **Manor Park Crematorium** Gt Lon
45 M6 **Mansell Gamage** Herefs
45 N5 **Mansell Lacy** Herefs
95 N4 **Mansergh** Cumb
115 M8 **Mansfield** E Ayrs
84 H8 **Mansfield** Notts
84 H9 **Mansfield & District Crematorium** Notts
84 H8 **Mansfield Woodhouse** Notts
94 F4 **Mansriggs** Cumb
20 F11 **Manston** Dorset
39 P8 **Manston** Kent
91 K4 **Manston** Leeds
12 G3 **Manswood** Dorset
73 N3 **Manthorpe** Lincs
73 R7 **Manthorpe** Lincs
92 F10 **Manton** N Linc
85 K5 **Manton** Notts
73 M10 **Manton** Rutlnd
33 N11 **Manton** Wilts
51 L5 **Manuden** Essex
51 M8 **Manwood Green** Essex
20 C9 **Maperton** Somset
85 M8 **Maplebeck** Notts
36 B2 **Maple Cross** Herts
35 J9 **Mapledurham** Oxon
23 J4 **Mapledurwell** Hants
24 E6 **Maplehurst** W Susx
37 N8 **Maplescombe** Kent
71 M5 **Mapleton** Derbys
37 L11 **Mapleton** Kent
72 C2 **Mapperley** Derbys
72 F2 **Mapperley Park** C Nott
11 L5 **Mapperton** Dorset
58 G11 **Mappleborough Green** Warwks
93 M2 **Mappleton** E R Yk
91 J8 **Mapplewell** Barns
12 B3 **Mappowder** Dorset
3 K3 **Marazanvose** Cnwll
2 E7 **Marazion** Cnwll
69 Q5 **Marbury** Ches E
74 H11 **March** Cambs
116 D8 **March** S Lans
34 E5 **Marcham** Oxon
69 Q9 **Marchamley** Shrops
69 Q8 **Marchamley Wood** Shrops
71 L8 **Marchington** Staffs
71 L9 **Marchington Woodlands** Staffs
66 E9 **Marchros** Gwynd
69 L5 **Marchwiel** Wrexhm
14 C4 **Marchwood** Hants
29 P11 **Marcross** V Glam
45 Q5 **Marden** Herefs
26 B3 **Marden** Kent

21 L3 **Marden** Wilts
51 N10 **Marden Ash** Essex
26 B3 **Marden Beech** Kent
25 M4 **Mardens Hill** E Susx
26 C3 **Marden Thorn** Kent
50 G7 **Mardlebury** Herts
45 L11 **Mardy** Mons
73 J9 **Marefield** Leics
87 J8 **Mareham le Fen** Lincs
87 J7 **Mareham on the Hill** Lincs
84 E11 **Marehay** Derbys
24 C7 **Marehill** W Susx
25 L6 **Maresfield** E Susx
93 K5 **Marfleet** C KuH
69 L3 **Marford** Wrexhm
29 L7 **Margam** Neath
29 L7 **Margam Crematorium** Neath
20 F11 **Margaret Marsh** Dorset
51 N8 **Margaret Roding** Essex
51 Q10 **Margaretting** Essex
51 Q10 **Margaretting Tye** Essex
39 Q7 **Margate** Kent
121 K5 **Margnaheglish** N Ayrs
108 C10 **Margrie** D & G
105 J7 **Margrove Park** R & Cl
75 P9 **Marham** Norfk
16 C11 **Marhamchurch** Cnwll
74 B10 **Marholm** C Pete
79 J8 **Marian-glas** IoA
14 N7 **Mariansleigh** Devon
38 F7 **Marine Town** Kent
151 J6 **Marionburgh** Abers
152 H5 **Marishader** Highld
6 D6 **Maristow** Devon
109 N4 **Marjoriebanks** D & G
19 L5 **Mark** Somset
25 L2 **Markbeech** Kent
87 N5 **Markby** Lincs
19 L5 **Mark Causeway** Somset
25 N4 **Mark Cross** E Susx
72 A3 **Markeaton** C Derb
72 A3 **Markeaton Crematorium** C Derb
72 C10 **Market Bosworth** Leics
74 B8 **Market Deeping** Lincs
70 B8 **Market Drayton** Shrops
60 F3 **Market Harborough** Leics
21 K4 **Market Lavington** Wilts
73 M7 **Market Overton** Rutlnd
86 F3 **Market Rasen** Lincs
86 H5 **Market Stainton** Lincs
85 J7 **Market Warsop** Notts
92 E2 **Market Weighton** E R Yk
64 D6 **Market Weston** Suffk
72 D9 **Markfield** Leics
30 G4 **Markham** Caerph
85 M6 **Markham Moor** Notts
134 H7 **Markinch** Fife
97 L7 **Markington** N York
128 F4 **Markle** E Loth
20 C2 **Marksbury** BaNES
14 E8 **Mark's Corner** IoW
52 F7 **Marks Tey** Essex
5 P10 **Markwell** Cnwll
50 C7 **Markyate** Herts
33 N11 **Marlborough** Wilts
45 Q4 **Marlbrook** Herefs
58 E10 **Marlbrook** Worcs
47 L4 **Marlcliff** Warwks
7 M6 **Marldon** Devon
25 N7 **Marle Green** E Susx
65 L10 **Marlesford** Suffk
39 L11 **Marley** Kent
39 P11 **Marley** Kent
69 Q5 **Marley Green** Ches E
113 K9 **Marley Hill** Gatesd
76 G10 **Marlingford** Norfk
40 E9 **Marloes** Pembks
35 M7 **Marlow** Bucks
45 M7 **Marlow** Herefs
35 M7 **Marlow Bottom** Bucks
37 K11 **Marlpit Hill** Kent
25 L5 **Marlpits** E Susx
26 B9 **Marlpits** E Susx
84 F11 **Marlpool** Derbys
20 E11 **Marnhull** Dorset
83 L7 **Marple** Stockp
83 L7 **Marple Bridge** Stockp
91 N9 **Marr** Donc
103 L11 **Marrick** N York
41 P9 **Marros** Carmth
90 C8 **Marsden** Kirk
113 N8 **Marsden** S Tyne
89 P3 **Marsden Height** Lancs
96 D3 **Marsett** N York
35 M3 **Marsh** Bucks
90 C3 **Marsh** C Brad
10 F2 **Marsh** Devon
50 E8 **Marshall's Heath** Herts
50 E9 **Marshalswick** Herts
76 H7 **Marsham** Norfk
34 G5 **Marsh Baldon** Oxon
34 D11 **Marsh Benham** W Berk
39 P10 **Marshborough** Kent
56 G7 **Marshbrook** Shrops
93 Q11 **Marshchapel** Lincs
50 C5 **Marsh Farm** Luton
31 J8 **Marshfield** Newpt
32 E10 **Marshfield** S Glos
5 K3 **Marshgate** Cnwll
48 H10 **Marsh Gibbon** Bucks
9 P6 **Marsh Green** Devon
25 K2 **Marsh Green** Kent
57 L2 **Marsh Green** Wrekin
75 K9 **Marshland St James** Norfk
84 F5 **Marsh Lane** Derbys
31 Q3 **Marsh Lane** Gloucs
88 D7 **Marshside** Sefton
18 C6 **Marsh Street** Somset
10 H5 **Marshwood** Dorset
103 M10 **Marske** N York
104 H6 **Marske-by-the-Sea** R & Cl
82 E5 **Marsland Green** Wigan
82 E9 **Marston** Ches W
45 M3 **Marston** Herefs
73 M2 **Marston** Lincs
34 F3 **Marston** Oxon
58 B2 **Marston** Staffs
70 G9 **Marston** Staffs
59 K6 **Marston** Warwks
21 J3 **Marston** Wilts
59 J7 **Marston Green** Solhll
59 N7 **Marston Jabbet** Warwks
19 Q10 **Marston Magna** Somset
33 M5 **Marston Meysey** Wilts

71 L7 **Marston Montgomery** Derbys
49 Q6 **Marston Moretaine** C Beds
71 N9 **Marston on Dove** Derbys
48 F6 **Marston St Lawrence** Nhants
45 R3 **Marston Stannett** Herefs
60 E3 **Marston Trussell** Nhants
45 R11 **Marstow** Herefs
35 P2 **Marsworth** Bucks
21 Q2 **Marten** Wilts
82 G9 **Marthall** Ches E
77 P8 **Martham** Norfk
11 L11 **Martin** Hants
27 P2 **Martin** Kent
86 F9 **Martin** Lincs
86 H7 **Martin** Lincs
101 M7 **Martindale** Cumb
86 G8 **Martin Dales** Lincs
21 L10 **Martin Drove End** Hants
17 M2 **Martinhoe** Devon
46 G2 **Martin Hussingtree** Worcs
82 E7 **Martinscroft** Warrtn
11 N7 **Martinstown** Dorset
53 M2 **Martlesham** Suffk
53 M2 **Martlesham Heath** Suffk
41 K8 **Martletwy** Pembks
46 E2 **Martley** Worcs
19 N11 **Martock** Somset
83 J11 **Marton** Ches E
82 D11 **Marton** Ches W
94 E5 **Marton** Cumb
93 L3 **Marton** E R Yk
99 Q7 **Marton** E R Yk
85 P4 **Marton** Lincs
104 F7 **Marton** Middsb
97 P8 **Marton** N York
98 E4 **Marton** N York
56 D4 **Marton** Shrops
59 P11 **Marton** Warwks
97 N6 **Marton-le-Moor** N York
36 C9 **Martyr's Green** Surrey
22 F8 **Martyr Worthy** Hants
169 b4 **Marwick** Ork
17 J4 **Marwood** Devon
155 N7 **Marybank** Highld
155 P6 **Maryburgh** Highld
151 M8 **Maryculter** Abers
129 L8 **Marygold** Border
125 P4 **Maryhill** C Glas
125 P4 **Maryhill Crematorium** C Glas
143 M4 **Marykirk** Abers
31 P3 **Maryland** Mons
36 G4 **Marylebone** Gt Lon
88 H9 **Marylebone** Wigan
157 M10 **Marypark** Moray
100 D3 **Maryport** Cumb
106 F11 **Maryport** D & G
8 B8 **Marystow** Devon
8 D9 **Mary Tavy** Devon
143 M6 **Maryton** Angus
150 F8 **Marywell** Abers
151 N8 **Marywell** Abers
143 M9 **Marywell** Angus
97 K4 **Masham** N York
51 Q8 **Mashbury** Essex
113 K6 **Mason** N u Ty
95 P5 **Masongill** N York
114 C3 **Masonhill Crematorium** S Ayrs
84 G5 **Mastin Moor** Derbys
51 M8 **Matching** Essex
51 M8 **Matching Green** Essex
51 M8 **Matching Tye** Essex
112 F6 **Matfen** Nthumb
25 Q2 **Matfield** Kent
31 P6 **Mathern** Mons
46 D5 **Mathon** Herefs
40 G4 **Mathry** Pembks
76 H5 **Matlask** Norfk
84 D9 **Matlock** Derbys
84 D8 **Matlock Bank** Derbys
84 C9 **Matlock Bath** Derbys
84 C9 **Matlock Dale** Derbys
46 G11 **Matson** Gloucs
101 L6 **Matterdale End** Cumb
85 L3 **Mattersey** Notts
85 L3 **Mattersey Thorpe** Notts
23 K3 **Mattingley** Hants
76 F9 **Mattishall** Norfk
76 F9 **Mattishall Burgh** Norfk
115 J2 **Mauchline** E Ayrs
159 M8 **Maud** Abers
11 c1 **Maufant** Jersey
47 P9 **Maugersbury** Gloucs
80 g3 **Maughold** IoM
155 M10 **Mauld** Highld
50 C3 **Maulden** C Beds
102 B7 **Maulds Meaburn** Cumb
97 N3 **Maunby** N York
45 R4 **Maund Bryan** Herefs
18 E9 **Maundown** Somset
77 P9 **Mautby** Norfk
71 K11 **Mavesyn Ridware** Staffs
87 L7 **Mavis Enderby** Lincs
109 N11 **Mawbray** Cumb
88 F8 **Mawdesley** Lancs
29 M8 **Mawdlam** Brdgnd
3 J8 **Mawgan** Cnwll
4 D8 **Mawgan Porth** Cnwll
70 C3 **Maw Green** Ches E
3 J4 **Mawla** Cnwll
3 K8 **Mawnan** Cnwll
3 K8 **Mawnan Smith** Cnwll
60 H5 **Mawsley** Nhants
74 B9 **Maxey** C Pete
59 K7 **Maxstoke** Warwks
27 K3 **Maxted Street** Kent
118 B4 **Maxton** Border
27 P3 **Maxton** Kent
109 L5 **Maxwell Town** D & G
5 M3 **Maxworthy** Cnwll
28 H7 **Mayals** Swans
70 F5 **May Bank** Staffs
114 E6 **Maybole** S Ayrs
36 B9 **Mayford** Surrey
24 D3 **Mayes Green** Surrey
25 N5 **Mayfield** E Susx
128 B7 **Mayfield** Mdloth
71 M5 **Mayfield** Staffs
23 Q3 **Mayford** Surrey
46 D10 **May Hill** Gloucs
52 F11 **Mayland** Essex
52 F11 **Maylandsea** Essex
25 N7 **Maynard's Green** E Susx
58 G9 **Maypole** Birm

39 M9 **Maypole** Kent
45 P11 **Maypole** Mons
65 N2 **Maypole Green** Norfk
64 C10 **Maypole Green** Suffk
65 K10 **Maypole Green** Suffk
35 K8 **May's Green** Oxon
36 Q9 **May's Green** Surrey
16 C8 **Mead** Devon
20 C3 **Meadgate** BaNES
35 M3 **Meadle** Bucks
103 P3 **Meadowfield** Dur
56 E4 **Meadowtown** Shrops
5 Q5 **Meadwell** Devon
70 F7 **Meaford** Staffs
101 P11 **Meal Bank** Cumb
109 P11 **Mealrigg** Cumb
100 H2 **Mealsgate** Cumb
90 H3 **Meanwood** Leeds
96 B8 **Mearbeck** N York
19 N6 **Meare** Somset
19 J10 **Meare Green** Somset
19 K9 **Meare Green** Somset
125 N6 **Mearns** E Rens
60 H7 **Mears Ashby** Nhants
72 A8 **Measham** Leics
95 J4 **Meathop** Cumb
93 J3 **Meaux** E R Yk
6 E5 **Meavy** Devon
60 H2 **Medbourne** Leics
16 D8 **Meddon** Devon
85 J7 **Meden Vale** Notts
87 K9 **Medlam** Lincs
88 E3 **Medlar** Lancs
35 M8 **Medmenham** Bucks
112 H10 **Medomsley** Dur
23 J7 **Medstead** Hants
38 B9 **Medway Crematorium** Kent
38 D9 *Medway Services* Medway
70 H2 **Meerbrook** Staffs
45 M4 **Meer Common** Herefs
51 K4 **Meesden** Herts
70 A10 **Meeson** Wrekin
17 J10 **Meeth** Devon
63 M9 **Meeting Green** Suffk
77 L6 **Meeting House Hill** Norfk
41 Q6 **Meidrim** Carmth
56 B2 **Meifod** Powys
142 Q9 **Meigle** P & K
115 Q5 **Meikle Carco** D & G
126 C7 **Meikle Earnock** S Lans
124 D5 **Meikle Kilmory** Ag & B
141 P10 **Meikle Obney** P & K
142 B10 **Meikleour** P & K
158 H11 **Meikle Wartle** Abers
28 E2 **Meinciau** Carmth
70 G6 **Meir** C Stke
70 G6 **Meir Heath** Staffs
51 J2 **Melbourn** Cambs
72 B5 **Melbourne** Derbys
92 C2 **Melbourne** E R Yk
3 N3 **Melbur** Cnwll
16 F8 **Melbury** Devon
20 G10 **Melbury Abbas** Dorset
11 M3 **Melbury Bubb** Dorset
11 M3 **Melbury Osmond** Dorset
11 M3 **Melbury Sampford** Dorset
61 M7 **Melchbourne** Bed
12 C4 **Melcombe Bingham** Dorset
8 E6 **Meldon** Devon
112 H4 **Meldon** Nthumb
112 H3 **Meldon Park** Nthumb
62 E11 **Meldreth** Cambs
133 L8 **Meldrum** Stirlg
130 G5 **Melfort** Ag & B
80 F8 **Meliden** Denbgs
41 N8 **Melinau** Pembks
55 J5 **Melin-byrhedyn** Powys
29 M4 **Melincourt** Neath
67 Q2 **Melin-y-coed** Conwy
55 P3 **Melin-y-ddol** Powys
68 D5 **Melin-y-wig** Denbgs
101 Q5 **Melkinthorpe** Cumb
111 P8 **Melkridge** Nthumb
20 H2 **Melksham** Wilts
2 H8 **Mellangoose** Cnwll
34 E9 **Mell Green** W Berk
110 H11 **Mellguards** Cumb
95 M6 **Melling** Lancs
81 N4 **Melling** Sefton
81 N4 **Melling Mount** Sefton
64 F7 **Mellis** Suffk
160 C8 **Mellon Charles** Highld
160 C7 **Mellon Udrigle** Highld
89 K4 **Mellor** Lancs
83 L7 **Mellor** Stockp
89 J4 **Mellor Brook** Lancs
20 D5 **Mells** Somset
65 N6 **Mells** Suffk
102 B3 **Melmerby** Cumb
96 G3 **Melmerby** N York
97 M5 **Melmerby** N York
165 N4 **Melness** Highld
64 A10 **Melon Green** Suffk
11 K5 **Melplash** Dorset
117 Q4 **Melrose** Border
169 D4 **Melsetter** Ork
103 N9 **Melsonby** N York
90 F8 **Meltham** Kirk
90 E8 **Meltham Mills** Kirk
92 G5 **Melton** E R Yk
65 K11 **Melton** Suffk
98 F11 **Meltonby** E R Yk
76 E5 **Melton Constable** Norfk
73 K7 **Melton Mowbray** Leics
93 J8 **Melton Ross** N Linc
160 A9 **Melvaig** Highld
69 K11 **Melverley** Shrops
69 K11 **Melverley Green** Shrops
166 E4 **Melvich** Highld
10 F4 **Membury** Devon
34 B9 *Membury Services* W Berk
159 N5 **Memsie** Abers
142 G6 **Memus** Angus
4 H11 **Menabilly** Cnwll
2 J4 **Menagissey** Cnwll
79 K10 **Menai Bridge** IoA
65 K5 **Mendham** Suffk
19 Q6 **Mendip Crematorium** Somset
19 P4 **Mendip Hills**
64 G8 **Mendlesham** Suffk
64 F9 **Mendlesham Green** Suffk
5 M9 **Menheniot** Cnwll
115 Q5 **Menithwood** Worcs
115 R6 **Mennock** D & G

Menston - Morganstown 289

90 F2 Menston C Brad
133 P8 Menstrie Clacks
92 B4 Menthorpe N York
49 P11 Mentmore Bucks
145 N10 Meoble Highld
56 H2 Meole Brace Shrops
22 H11 Meonstoke Hants
37 P7 Meopham Kent
37 P7 Meopham Green Kent
37 P7 Meopham Station Kent
62 F4 Mepal Cambs
50 D3 Meppershall C Beds
45 L5 Merbach Herefs
82 F8 Mere Ches E
20 F8 Mere Wilts
88 E7 Mere Brow Lancs
89 P4 Mereclough Lancs
58 H5 Mere Green Birm
47 J2 Mere Green Worcs
82 E10 Mere Heath Ches W
38 D9 Meresborough Medway
37 Q10 Mereworth Kent
59 K8 Meriden Solhll
152 F11 Merkadale Highld
12 H5 Merley Poole
40 H8 Merlin's Bridge Pembks
69 N10 Merrington Shrops
40 H11 Merrion Pembks
11 J2 Merriott Somset
8 D9 Merrivale Devon
36 B10 Merrow Surrey
12 H4 Merry Field Hill Dorset
36 D2 Merry Hill Herts
58 C5 Merryhill Wolves
72 D9 Merry Lees Leics
5 M8 Merrymeet Cnwll
52 H8 Mersea Island Essex
27 J3 Mersham Kent
36 G10 Merstham Surrey
15 N6 Merston W Susx
14 F9 Merstone IoW
3 M5 Merther Cnwll
42 G10 Merthyr Carmth
44 D7 Merthyr Cynog Powys
30 F11 Merthyr Dyfan V Glam
29 N9 Merthyr Mawr Brdgnd
30 D3 Merthyr Tydfil Myr Td
30 E5 Merthyr Vale Myr Td
17 J9 Merton Devon
36 G6 Merton Gt Lon
64 C2 Merton Norfk
48 G11 Merton Oxon
17 P8 Meshaw Devon
52 E8 Messing Essex
92 E10 Messingham N Linc
65 K5 Metfield Suffk
5 Q8 Metherell Cnwll
86 E8 Metheringham Lincs
135 K8 Methil Fife
135 K7 Methilhill Fife
91 K5 Methley Leeds
91 K5 Methley Junction Leeds
159 L10 Methlick Abers
134 C2 Methven P & K
63 M2 Methwold Norfk
63 M2 Methwold Hythe Norfk
65 M4 Mettingham Suffk
76 J4 Metton Norfk
3 Q5 Mevagissey Cnwll
91 M10 Mexborough Donc
167 N2 Mey Highld
66 C8 Meyllteyrn Gwynd
33 M4 Meysey Hampton Gloucs
168 f4 Miabhig W Isls
168 f4 Miavaig W Isls
45 Q9 Michaelchurch Herefs
45 L8 Michaelchurch Escley Herefs
45 J4 Michaelchurch-on-Arrow Powys
30 H8 Michaelstone-y-Fedw Newpt
30 G10 Michaelston-le-Pit V Glam
4 H6 Michaelstow Cnwll
32 D5 Michaelwood Services Gloucs
6 H5 Michelcombe Devon
22 F7 Micheldever Hants
22 F6 Micheldever Station Hants
22 B9 Michelmersh Hants
64 G9 Mickfield Suffk
84 H2 Micklebring Donc
105 M8 Mickleby N York
91 L4 Micklefield Leeds
50 B11 Micklefield Green Herts
36 E10 Mickleham Surrey
71 Q8 Mickleover C Derb
90 E2 Micklethwaite C Brad
110 E10 Micklethwaite Cumb
103 J6 Mickleton Dur
47 N6 Mickleton Gloucs
91 L5 Mickletown Leeds
81 N11 Mickle Trafford Ches W
84 D5 Mickley Derbys
97 L5 Mickley N York
64 A10 Mickley Green Suffk
112 G8 Mickley Square Nthumb
159 M5 Mid Ardlaw Abers
169 d2 Midbea Ork
150 G7 Mid Beltie Abers
13 L5 Mid Bockhampton Dorset
127 K4 Mid Calder W Loth
167 N9 Mid Clyth Highld
158 G5 Mid Culbeuchly Abers
35 K7 Middle Assendon Oxon
48 E9 Middle Aston Oxon
48 D9 Middle Barton Oxon
110 D5 Middlebie D & G
141 L4 Middlebridge P & K
11 K2 Middle Chinnock Somset
49 K9 Middle Claydon Bucks
91 L9 Middlecliffe Barns
8 H7 Middlecott Devon
33 J3 Middle Duntisbourne Gloucs
96 H3 Middleham N York
84 F5 Middle Handley Derbys
64 D4 Middle Harling Norfk
5 M8 Middlehill Cnwll
32 F11 Middlehill Wilts
56 H7 Middlehope Shrops
131 J10 Middle Kames Ag & B
47 L5 Middle Littleton Worcs
70 D5 Middle Madeley Staffs
45 L8 Middle Maes-coed Herefs
11 P3 Middlemarsh Dorset
71 L6 Middle Mayfield Staffs
40 F5 Middle Mill Pembks
6 D4 Middlemore Devon
26 E4 Middle Quarter Kent
86 E3 Middle Rasen Lincs
7 N5 Middle Rocombe Devon
95 N8 Middle Salter Lancs
104 E7 Middlesbrough Middsb
101 M2 Middlesceugh Cumb
95 M3 Middleshaw Cumb
96 G6 Middlesmoor N York
18 G10 Middle Stoford Somset
38 D6 Middle Stoke Medway
103 Q4 Middlestone Dur
103 P4 Middlestone Moor Dur
19 M5 Middle Stoughton Somset
90 H7 Middlestown Wakefd
32 E4 Middle Street Gloucs
5 K9 Middle Taphouse Cnwll
118 C2 Middlethird Border
136 A7 Middleton Ag & B
95 N3 Middleton Cumb
71 M2 Middleton Derbys
84 C9 Middleton Derbys
52 E4 Middleton Essex
22 D6 Middleton Hants
57 J11 Middleton Herefs
95 J9 Middleton Lancs
91 J5 Middleton Leeds
96 H11 Middleton N York
98 F3 Middleton N York
60 H3 Middleton Nhants
75 N7 Middleton Norfk
112 G4 Middleton Nthumb
119 M3 Middleton Nthumb
134 E6 Middleton P & K
89 P9 Middleton Rochdl
57 J9 Middleton Shrops
69 K9 Middleton Shrops
65 N8 Middleton Suffk
28 D7 Middleton Swans
59 J5 Middleton Warwks
48 E6 Middleton Cheney Nhants
89 P9 Middleton Crematorium Rochdl
70 H7 Middleton Green Staffs
119 J5 Middleton Hall Nthumb
102 H5 Middleton-in-Teesdale Dur
65 N8 Middleton Moor Suffk
104 C8 Middleton One Row Darltn
104 E9 Middleton-on-Leven N York
15 Q6 Middleton-on-Sea W Susx
45 Q2 Middleton on the Hill Herefs
99 J11 Middleton on the Wolds E R Yk
151 N5 Middleton Park C Aber
57 L6 Middleton Priors Shrops
97 M5 Middleton Quernhow N York
104 B8 Middleton St George Darltn
57 M7 Middleton Scriven Shrops
48 F10 Middleton Stoney Oxon
103 P9 Middleton Tyas N York
100 C9 Middletown Cumb
2 b3 Middle Town IoS
31 N10 Middletown N Som
56 E2 Middletown Powys
48 B6 Middle Tysoe Warwks
21 Q7 Middle Wallop Hants
82 F11 Middlewich Ches E
21 P8 Middle Winterslow Wilts
5 M6 Middlewood Cnwll
45 K6 Middlewood Herefs
21 M7 Middle Woodford Wilts
64 F9 Middlewood Green Suffk
125 N11 Middleyard E Ayrs
32 F4 Middle Yard Gloucs
19 L8 Middlezoy Somset
103 P5 Middridge Dur
20 E2 Midford BaNES
88 G6 Midge Hall Lancs
111 M9 Midgeholme Cumb
34 G11 Midgham W Berk
90 C5 Midgley Calder
90 H8 Midgley Wakefd
36 E11 Mid Holmwood Surrey
90 G11 Midhopestones Sheff
23 N10 Midhurst W Susx
15 N5 Mid Lavant W Susx
117 Q5 Midlem Border
155 M10 Mid Mains Highld
19 N9 Midney Somset
124 C6 Midpark Ag & B
20 C4 Midsomer Norton BaNES
165 N4 Midtown Highld
87 L9 Midville Lincs
48 B3 Mid Warwickshire Crematorium Warwks
83 K8 Midway Ches E
169 s4 Mid Yell Shet
150 C6 Migvie Abers
20 C11 Milborne Port Somset
12 D5 Milborne St Andrew Dorset
20 C10 Milborne Wick Somset
112 H5 Milbourne Nthumb
33 J7 Milbourne Wilts
102 C5 Milburn Cumb
32 C6 Milbury Heath S Glos
97 P7 Milby N York
48 D8 Milcombe Oxon
52 G2 Milden Suffk
63 M6 Mildenhall Suffk
33 P11 Mildenhall Wilts
56 E10 Milebrook Powys
26 C2 Milebush Kent
33 J11 Mile Elm Wilts
52 G6 Mile End Essex
31 Q2 Mile End Gloucs
65 L4 Mile End Suffk
76 C8 Mileham Norfk
24 F9 Mile Oak Br & H
25 Q2 Mile Oak Kent
59 J4 Mile Oak Staffs
45 R2 Miles Hope Herefs
134 D10 Milesmark Fife
83 J5 Miles Platting Manch
38 F7 Mile Town Kent
118 H4 Milfield Nthumb
84 E11 Milford Derbys
16 C7 Milford Devon
55 P6 Milford Powys
70 H10 Milford Staffs
23 P6 Milford Surrey
40 H9 Milford Haven Pembks
13 N6 Milford on Sea Hants
31 Q3 Milkwall Gloucs
11 a1 Millais Jersey
23 M9 Milland W Susx
23 M9 Milland Marsh W Susx
90 C6 Mill Bank Calder
101 J5 Millbeck Cumb
159 P9 Millbreck Abers
23 M6 Millbridge Surrey
50 B3 Millbrook C Beds
14 C4 Millbrook C Sotn
6 C8 Millbrook Cnwll
11 b2 Millbrook Jersey
83 L5 Millbrook Tamesd
83 L7 Mill Brow Stockp
151 K6 Millbuie Abers
155 Q7 Millbuie Highld
9 L9 Millcombe Devon
77 L11 Mill Common Norfk
65 N5 Mill Common Suffk
26 D7 Millcorner E Susx
156 B3 Millcraig Highld
7 J6 Mill Cross Devon
71 L4 Milldale Staffs
35 L7 Mill End Bucks
62 D4 Mill End Cambs
32 D5 Millend Gloucs
50 H4 Mill End Herts
127 Q4 Millerhill Mdloth
83 P10 Miller's Dale Derbys
71 P4 Millers Green Derbys
51 N9 Miller's Green Essex
125 Q4 Millerston C Glas
89 P7 Millgate Lancs
63 K11 Mill Green Cambs
51 P10 Mill Green Essex
50 F8 Mill Green Herts
74 D6 Mill Green Lincs
64 G5 Mill Green Norfk
70 B9 Millgreen Shrops
58 G4 Mill Green Staffs
71 K10 Mill Green Staffs
52 G3 Mill Green Suffk
64 D10 Mill Green Suffk
64 G9 Mill Green Suffk
65 L9 Mill Green Suffk
45 K5 Millhalf Herefs
10 E4 Millhayes Devon
95 K6 Millhead Lancs
126 C7 Millheugh S Lans
25 P9 Mill Hill E Susx
36 F2 Mill Hill Gt Lon
124 B3 Millhouse Ag & B
101 L3 Millhouse Cumb
109 P3 Millhousebridge D & G
90 G10 Millhouse Green Barns
91 L10 Millhouses Barns
84 D4 Millhouses Sheff
125 L5 Milliken Park Rens
41 J8 Millin Cross Pembks
98 G10 Millington E R Yk
70 E8 Millmeece Staffs
95 L4 Millness Cumb
133 N4 Mill of Drummond P & K
132 D11 Mill of Haldane W Duns
94 D4 Millom Cumb
5 K2 Millook Cnwll
2 F7 Millpool Cnwll
5 J7 Millpool Cnwll
124 F7 Millport N Ayrs
95 J4 Mill Side Cumb
37 Q9 Mill Street Kent
76 F8 Mill Street Norfk
64 F7 Mill Street Suffk
84 D5 Millthorpe Derbys
95 P2 Millthrop Cumb
151 M7 Milltimber C Aber
149 P6 Milltown Abers
150 D4 Milltown Abers
5 J10 Milltown Cnwll
110 F5 Milltown D & G
84 E8 Milltown Derbys
17 K4 Milltown Devon
150 H7 Milltown of Campfield Abers
157 P9 Milltown of Edinvillie Moray
150 G7 Milltown of Learney Abers
134 E7 Milnathort P & K
125 P3 Milngavie E Duns
89 Q8 Milnrow Rochdl
95 K4 Milnthorpe Cumb
91 J7 Milnthorpe Wakefd
152 B8 Milovaig Highld
57 L10 Milson Shrops
38 F10 Milstead Kent
21 N5 Milston Wilts
74 B4 Milthorpe Lincs
48 G5 Milthorpe Nhants
70 G4 Milton C Stke
62 G8 Milton Cambs
111 L8 Milton Cumb
106 H7 Milton D & G
108 H6 Milton D & G
71 Q9 Milton Derbys
153 N9 Milton Highld
155 N11 Milton Highld
155 Q8 Milton Highld
156 D3 Milton Highld
167 P6 Milton Highld
125 K4 Milton Inver
37 Q6 Milton Kent
149 M4 Milton Moray
158 D5 Milton Moray
19 K2 Milton N Som
31 L7 Milton Newpt
85 M6 Milton Notts
34 E6 Milton Oxon
48 E7 Milton Oxon
141 Q5 Milton P & K
41 K10 Milton Pembks
19 N10 Milton Somset
132 G7 Milton Stirlg
125 L3 Milton W Duns
12 D4 Milton Abbas Dorset
5 Q6 Milton Abbot Devon
127 P5 Milton Bridge Mdloth
49 Q8 Milton Bryan C Beds
20 C7 Milton Clevedon Somset
6 D5 Milton Combe Devon
35 J4 Milton Common Oxon
16 F9 Milton Damerel Devon
32 D2 Milton End Gloucs
33 M4 Milton End Gloucs
61 M9 Milton Ernest Bed
69 N3 Milton Green Ches W
34 E6 Milton Hill Oxon
49 N7 Milton Keynes M Keyn
21 N2 Milton Lilbourne Wilts
60 F9 Milton Malsor Nhants
140 F10 Milton Morenish P & K
150 F7 Milton of Auchinhove Abers
135 J7 Milton of Balgonie Fife
132 E9 Milton of Buchanan Stirlg
126 B2 Milton of Campsie E Duns
156 B9 Milton of Leys Highld
151 M7 Milton of Murtle C Aber
150 B8 Milton of Tullich Abers
20 E9 Milton on Stour Dorset
38 F9 Milton Regis Kent
25 M10 Milton Street E Susx
47 Q11 Milton-under-Wychwood Oxon
18 F9 Milverton Somset
59 M11 Milverton Warwks
70 H8 Milwich Staffs
80 H10 Milwr Flints
131 K8 Minard Ag & B
12 G2 Minchington Dorset
32 G4 Minchinhampton Gloucs
118 F4 Mindrum Nthumb
18 C5 Minehead Somset
69 J4 Minera Wrexhm
33 K6 Minety Wilts
67 K7 Minffordd Gwynd
138 B4 Mingarrypark Highld
87 K8 Miningsby Lincs
5 M7 Minions Cnwll
114 F5 Minishant S Ayrs
55 K2 Minllyn Gwynd
107 M4 Minnigaff D & G
39 N8 Minnis Bay Kent
159 J5 Minnonie Abers
70 B2 Minshull Vernon Ches E
97 N8 Minskip N York
13 N2 Minstead Hants
23 N10 Minsted W Susx
38 G7 Minster Kent
39 P9 Minster Kent
56 F3 Minsterley Shrops
34 B2 Minster Lovell Oxon
46 E11 Minsterworth Gloucs
11 P4 Minterne Magna Dorset
11 P4 Minterne Parva Dorset
86 G6 Minting Lincs
159 N8 Mintlaw Abers
75 N7 Mintlyn Crematorium Norfk
117 R6 Minto Border
56 G6 Minton Shrops
41 K8 Minwear Pembks
59 J6 Minworth Birm
100 C7 Mirehouse Cumb
167 P4 Mireland Highld
90 G7 Mirfield Kirk
32 H3 Miserden Gloucs
30 D5 Miskin Rhondd
30 D8 Miskin Rhondd
85 L2 Misson Notts
60 C4 Misterton Leics
85 N2 Misterton Notts
11 K3 Misterton Somset
53 K5 Mistley Essex
53 K5 Mistley Heath Essex
36 G7 Mitcham Gt Lon
46 C11 Mitcheldean Gloucs
3 M3 Mitchell Cnwll
116 D11 Mitchellslacks D & G
31 N2 Mitchel Troy Mons
113 J3 Mitford Nthumb
3 J3 Mithian Cnwll
70 F11 Mitton Staffs
48 H8 Mixbury Oxon
90 D5 Mixenden Calder
64 E10 Moats Tye Suffk
82 G9 Mobberley Ches E
71 J6 Mobberley Staffs
45 M6 Moccas Herefs
79 Q9 Mochdre Conwy
55 P7 Mochdre Powys
107 K8 Mochrum D & G
13 L3 Mockbeggar Hants
26 B2 Mockbeggar Kent
100 E6 Mockerkin Cumb
6 H8 Modbury Devon
70 G7 Moddershall Staffs
79 J7 Moelfre IoA
68 G9 Moelfre Powys
67 J3 Moel Tryfan Gwynd
116 F9 Moffat D & G
61 P11 Moggerhanger C Beds
71 Q11 Moira Leics
38 H11 Molash Kent
144 G5 Mol-chlach Highld
68 H2 Mold Flints
90 F7 Moldgreen Kirk
51 N6 Molehill Green Essex
52 B7 Molehill Green Essex
92 H2 Molescroft E R Yk
112 H4 Molesden Nthumb
61 N5 Molesworth Cambs
17 Q6 Molland Devon
81 M10 Mollington Ches W
48 D5 Mollington Oxon
126 C3 Mollinsburn N Lans
43 K2 Monachty Cerdgn
143 P2 Mondynes Abers
65 J10 Monewden Suffk
134 D2 Moneydie P & K
35 N9 Moneyrow Green W & M
115 Q9 Moniaive D & G
142 H11 Monifieth Angus
142 H10 Monikie Angus
134 H5 Monimail Fife
41 M2 Monington Pembks
91 K9 Monk Bretton Barns
50 F11 Monken Hadley Gt Lon
91 N5 Monk Fryston N York
46 B6 Monkhide Herefs
110 F9 Monkhill Cumb
57 L6 Monkhopton Shrops
45 P3 Monkland Herefs
16 H7 Monkleigh Devon
29 P10 Monknash V Glam
8 E3 Monkokehampton Devon
113 M6 Monkseaton N Tyne
52 G2 Monks Eleigh Suffk
24 F5 Monk's Gate W Susx
82 H10 Monks Heath Ches E
22 H3 Monk Sherborne Hants
27 K3 Monks Horton Kent
18 E7 Monksilver Somset
59 Q8 Monks Kirby Warwks
65 J8 Monk Soham Suffk
58 H9 Monkspath Solhll
35 M4 Monks Risborough Bucks
87 M7 Monksthorpe Lincs
51 P5 Monk Street Essex
31 K4 Monkswood Mons
10 D4 Monkton Devon
39 N9 Monkton Kent
114 G2 Monkton S Ayrs
113 M8 Monkton S Tyne
29 P10 Monkton V Glam
20 E2 Monkton Combe BaNES
20 G7 Monkton Deverill Wilts
32 F11 Monkton Farleigh Wilts
19 J9 Monkton Heathfield Somset
12 H2 Monkton Up Wimborne Dorset
10 G5 Monkton Wyld Dorset
113 N9 Monkwearmouth Sundld
23 J8 Monkwood Hants
58 D5 Monmore Green Wolves
31 P2 Monmouth Mons
45 M6 Monnington on Wye Herefs
107 L9 Monreith D & G
19 N11 Montacute Somset
89 K8 Montcliffe Bolton
56 G2 Montford Shrops
69 M11 Montford Bridge Shrops
150 F4 Montgarrie Abers
56 C5 Montgomery Powys
82 G5 Monton Salfd
143 N6 Montrose Angus
10 b2 Mont Saint Guern
22 B6 Monxton Hants
83 Q11 Monyash Derbys
150 H4 Monymusk Abers
133 P2 Monzie P & K
126 B3 Moodiesburn N Lans
135 J4 Moonzie Fife
91 J3 Moor Allerton Leeds
11 J5 Moorbath Dorset
87 J8 Moorby Lincs
45 M3 Moorcot Herefs
12 G3 Moor Crichel Dorset
13 J6 Moordown Bmouth
82 C8 Moore Halton
49 Q10 Moor End C Beds
90 D5 Moor End Calder
17 M10 Moor End Devon
32 D4 Moorend Gloucs
88 D2 Moor End Lancs
91 Q3 Moor End N York
92 A7 Moorends Donc
22 E11 Moorgreen Hants
50 H5 Moor Green Herts
84 G11 Moorgreen Notts
84 D6 Moorhall Derbys
45 M5 Moorhampton Herefs
90 E3 Moorhead C Brad
90 G5 Moor Head Leeds
110 E10 Moorhouse Cumb
110 F9 Moorhouse Cumb
91 M8 Moorhouse Donc
85 N7 Moorhouse Notts
37 K10 Moorhouse Bank Surrey
19 K8 Moorland Somset
19 L7 Moorlinch Somset
97 R9 Moor Monkton N York
100 D8 Moor Row Cumb
110 D11 Moor Row Cumb
105 J8 Moorsholm R & Cl
20 E11 Moorside Dorset
88 E4 Moor Side Lancs
88 F3 Moor Side Lancs
90 G3 Moorside Leeds
87 J9 Moor Side Lincs
89 Q9 Moorside Oldham
27 K4 Moorstock Kent
58 E8 Moor Street Birm
38 D8 Moor Street Medway
5 L9 Moorswater Cnwll
91 M8 Moorthorpe Wakefd
6 E4 Moortown Devon
13 L4 Moortown Hants
14 D10 Moortown IoW
90 H3 Moortown Leeds
93 J11 Moortown Lincs
69 R11 Moortown Wrekin
162 H10 Morangie Highld
145 L9 Morar Highld
158 A5 Moray Crematorium Moray
61 P2 Morborne Cambs
9 J3 Morchard Bishop Devon
11 J6 Morcombelake Dorset
73 N10 Morcott Rutlnd
69 J9 Morda Shrops
12 F5 Morden Dorset
36 G7 Morden Gt Lon
45 R7 Mordiford Herefs
104 B5 Mordon Dur
56 E6 More Shrops
18 C9 Morebath Devon
118 E6 Morebattle Border
95 J8 Morecambe Lancs
33 M7 Moredon Swindn
161 J7 Morefield Highld
27 M4 Morehall Kent
7 K8 Moreleigh Devon
140 F10 Morenish P & K
100 C7 Moresby Parks Cumb
22 F9 Morestead Hants
12 D7 Moreton Dorset
51 M9 Moreton Essex
45 Q2 Moreton Herefs
35 J4 Moreton Oxon
70 D11 Moreton Staffs
71 L9 Moreton Staffs
81 K7 Moreton Wirral
69 Q10 Moreton Corbet Shrops
9 J7 Moretonhampstead Devon
47 P8 Moreton-in-Marsh Gloucs
46 B5 Moreton Jeffries Herefs
69 Q10 Moretonmill Shrops
48 B3 Moreton Morrell Warwks
45 Q5 Moreton on Lugg Herefs
48 B4 Moreton Paddox Warwks
48 G5 Moreton Pinkney Nhants
70 A8 Moreton Say Shrops
32 E3 Moreton Valence Gloucs
42 F4 Morfa Cerdgn
67 J7 Morfa Bychan Gwynd
66 G3 Morfa Dinlle Gwynd
29 N3 Morfa Glas Neath
66 D6 Morfa Nefyn Gwynd
30 F8 Morganstown Cardif

21 N10 **Morgan's Vale** Wilts
128 F5 **Morham** E Loth
54 E4 **Moriah** Cerdgn
102 B6 **Morland** Cumb
82 H8 **Morley** Ches E
72 B2 **Morley** Derbys
103 M5 **Morley** Dur
90 H5 **Morley** Leeds
82 H8 **Morley Green** Ches E
64 F2 **Morley St Botolph** Norfk
5 N7 **Mornick** Cnwll
127 N3 **Morningside** C Edin
126 E6 **Morningside** N Lans
65 J3 **Morningthorpe** Norfk
113 J3 **Morpeth** Nthumb
143 N5 **Morphie** Abers
71 L11 **Morrey** Staffs
71 J4 **Morridge Side** Staffs
29 J5 **Morriston** Swans
76 E3 **Morston** Norfk
16 H2 **Mortehoe** Devon
84 G3 **Morthen** Rothm
23 J2 **Mortimer** W Berk
35 J11 **Mortimer Common** W Berk
45 N2 **Mortimer's Cross** Herefs
22 H2 **Mortimer West End** Hants
36 F5 **Mortlake** Gt Lon
36 F5 **Mortlake Crematorium** Gt Lon
101 N3 **Morton** Cumb
110 G10 **Morton** Cumb
84 F8 **Morton** Derbys
14 H9 **Morton** IoW
74 A6 **Morton** Lincs
85 P2 **Morton** Lincs
85 M10 **Morton** Notts
69 J10 **Morton** Shrops
85 Q8 **Morton Hall** Lincs
127 P4 **Mortonhall Crematorium** C Edin
97 M2 **Morton-on-Swale** N York
76 G8 **Morton on the Hill** Norfk
103 N6 **Morton Tinmouth** Dur
2 C6 **Morvah** Cnwll
5 M10 **Morval** Cnwll
146 B3 **Morvich** Highld
57 M6 **Morville** Shrops
57 M6 **Morville Heath** Shrops
6 C5 **Morwellham Quay** Devon
16 C8 **Morwenstow** Cnwll
84 F4 **Mosborough** Sheff
125 M9 **Moscow** E Ayrs
57 P6 **Mose** Shrops
101 L4 **Mosedale** Cumb
58 G8 **Moseley** Birm
58 D5 **Moseley** Wolves
46 F3 **Moseley** Worcs
89 L9 **Moses Gate** Bolton
136 B7 **Moss** Ag & B
91 P8 **Moss** Donc
69 K4 **Moss** Wrexhm
150 D4 **Mossat** Abers
169 r6 **Mossbank** Shet
81 Q5 **Moss Bank** St Hel
100 C5 **Mossbay** Cumb
114 H3 **Mossblown** S Ayrs
82 F7 **Mossbrow** Traffd
118 C7 **Mossburnford** Border
108 E6 **Mossdale** D & G
115 J7 **Mossdale** D & G
88 E2 **Moss Edge** Lancs
82 E9 **Moss End** Ches E
126 C5 **Mossend** N Lans
100 F5 **Mosser Mains** Cumb
70 F2 **Mossley** Ches E
83 L4 **Mossley** Tamesd
117 M11 **Mosspaul Hotel** Border
110 C10 **Moss Side** Cumb
156 F6 **Moss-side** Highld
88 D4 **Moss Side** Lancs
81 M4 **Moss Side** Sefton
157 Q6 **Mosstodloch** Moray
107 P7 **Mossyard** D & G
88 G8 **Mossy Lea** Lancs
11 K3 **Mosterton** Dorset
83 J4 **Moston** Manch
69 Q9 **Moston** Shrops
70 C2 **Moston Green** Ches E
80 H8 **Mostyn** Flints
20 G9 **Motcombe** Dorset
6 G9 **Mothecombe** Devon
101 M5 **Motherby** Cumb
126 C6 **Motherwell** N Lans
36 F7 **Motspur Park** Gt Lon
37 K6 **Mottingham** Gt Lon
22 B9 **Mottisfont** Hants
14 D10 **Mottistone** IoW
83 L5 **Mottram in Longdendale** Tamesd
83 J9 **Mottram St Andrew** Ches E
10 b2 **Mouilpied** Guern
81 Q10 **Mouldsworth** Ches W
141 M6 **Moulin** P & K
24 H9 **Moulsecoomb** Br & H
34 G8 **Moulsford** Oxon
49 P6 **Moulsoe** M Keyn
156 A3 **Moultavie** Highld
82 E11 **Moulton** Ches W
74 F6 **Moulton** Lincs
103 P10 **Moulton** N York
60 G7 **Moulton** Nhants
63 L8 **Moulton** Suffk
30 E11 **Moulton** V Glam
74 E7 **Moulton Chapel** Lincs
77 M10 **Moulton St Mary** Norfk
74 F5 **Moulton Seas End** Lincs
4 B10 **Mount** Cnwll
5 J8 **Mount** Cnwll
90 D7 **Mount** Kirk
90 D4 **Mountain** C Brad
30 D5 **Mountain Ash** Rhondd
127 M8 **Mountain Cross** Border
39 J11 **Mountain Street** Kent
3 J5 **Mount Ambrose** Cnwll
52 F5 **Mount Bures** Essex
26 B7 **Mountfield** E Susx
155 Q5 **Mountgerald House** Highld
3 J4 **Mount Hawke** Cnwll
2 H10 **Mount Hermon** Cnwll
4 D9 **Mountjoy** Cnwll
127 P6 **Mount Lothian** Mdloth
51 P11 **Mountnessing** Essex
31 P6 **Mounton** Mons
70 E3 **Mount Pleasant** Ches E
71 P11 **Mount Pleasant** Derbys
84 E11 **Mount Pleasant** Derbys

103 Q4 **Mount Pleasant** Dur
92 N3 **Mount Pleasant** E R Yk
25 K7 **Mount Pleasant** E Susx
64 D3 **Mount Pleasant** Norfk
63 M11 **Mount Pleasant** Suffk
47 K2 **Mount Pleasant** Worcs
113 J10 **Mountsett Crematorium** Dur
72 F8 **Mountsorrel** Leics
21 K10 **Mount Sorrel** Wilts
90 D5 **Mount Tabor** Calder
23 P6 **Mousehill** Surrey
2 D8 **Mousehole** Cnwll
109 N6 **Mouswald** D & G
70 F3 **Mow Cop** Ches E
118 F6 **Mowhaugh** Border
72 F9 **Mowmacre Hill** C Leic
60 D3 **Mowsley** Leics
147 L11 **Moy** Highld
156 D11 **Moy** Highld
145 Q4 **Moyle** Highld
41 M2 **Moylegrove** Pembks
120 C3 **Muasdale** Ag & B
151 N9 **Muchalls** Abers
45 Q8 **Much Birch** Herefs
46 B5 **Much Cowarne** Herefs
45 P8 **Much Dewchurch** Herefs
19 M10 **Muchelney** Somset
19 M10 **Muchelney Ham** Somset
51 K7 **Much Hadham** Herts
88 F6 **Much Hoole** Lancs
88 F6 **Much Hoole Town** Lancs
5 L10 **Muchlarnick** Cnwll
46 C8 **Much Marcle** Herefs
57 L5 **Much Wenlock** Shrops
144 F12 **Muck** Highld
37 Q4 **Mucking** Thurr
37 Q5 **Muckingford** Thurr
76 G3 **Muckleburgh Collection** Norfk
11 N6 **Muckleford** Dorset
70 C7 **Mucklestone** Staffs
57 L5 **Muckley** Shrops
87 L4 **Muckton** Lincs
17 K4 **Muddiford** Devon
25 M8 **Muddles Green** E Susx
13 L6 **Mudeford** Dorset
19 Q11 **Mudford** Somset
19 Q11 **Mudford Sock** Somset
19 N5 **Mudgley** Somset
38 H7 **Mud Row** Kent
125 P2 **Mugdock** Stirlg
152 G10 **Mugeary** Highld
71 P6 **Mugginton** Derbys
71 P6 **Muggintonlane End** Derbys
112 F11 **Muggleswick** Dur
158 H7 **Muirden** Abers
143 K10 **Muirdrum** Angus
158 G8 **Muiresk** Abers
142 E11 **Muirhead** Angus
134 H6 **Muirhead** Fife
126 B4 **Muirhead** N Lans
115 N2 **Muirkirk** E Ayrs
133 L11 **Muirmill** Stirlg
150 F5 **Muir of Fowlis** Abers
157 M6 **Muir of Miltonduff** Moray
155 P7 **Muir of Ord** Highld
146 E11 **Muirshearlich** Highld
159 N10 **Muirtack** Abers
133 Q5 **Muirton** P & K
155 N7 **Muirton Mains** Highld
142 B9 **Muirton of Ardblair** P & K
102 H11 **Muker** N York
76 H11 **Mulbarton** Norfk
157 R7 **Mulben** Moray
2 D7 **Mulfra** Cnwll
137 Q9 **Mull** Ag & B
17 J3 **Mullacott Cross** Devon
2 H10 **Mullion** Cnwll
2 H10 **Mullion Cove** Cnwll
87 P6 **Mumby** Lincs
46 B4 **Munderfield Row** Herefs
46 C4 **Munderfield Stocks** Herefs
77 L4 **Mundesley** Norfk
63 P2 **Mundford** Norfk
65 L2 **Mundham** Norfk
52 E11 **Mundon Hill** Essex
26 F2 **Mundy Bois** Kent
101 L4 **Mungrisdale** Cumb
156 A7 **Munlochy** Highld
124 H8 **Munnoch** N Ayrs
46 C6 **Munsley** Herefs
57 J7 **Munslow** Shrops
8 G7 **Murchington** Devon
47 L6 **Murcot** Worcs
48 G11 **Murcott** Oxon
33 J6 **Murcott** Wilts
167 L3 **Murkle** Highld
146 F2 **Murlaggan** Highld
23 K3 **Murrell Green** Hants
142 H10 **Murroes** Angus
74 G9 **Murrow** Cambs
49 M9 **Mursley** Bucks
38 F9 **Murston** Kent
142 H6 **Murthill** Angus
141 R10 **Murthly** P & K
98 C10 **Murton** C York
102 D6 **Murton** Cumb
113 N11 **Murton** Dur
113 M6 **Murton** N Tyne
129 P10 **Murton** Nthumb
10 F6 **Musbury** Devon
98 D5 **Muscoates** N York
127 Q3 **Musselburgh** E Loth
73 L3 **Muston** Leics
99 M5 **Muston** N York
58 G3 **Muswell Hill** Gt Lon
108 E11 **Mutehill** D & G
65 P4 **Mutford** Suffk
133 P4 **Muthill** P & K
9 P3 **Mutterton** Devon
57 N2 **Muxton** Wrekin
167 L6 **Mybster** Highld
43 Q8 **Myddfai** Carmth
69 N10 **Myddle** Shrops
43 J3 **Mydroilyn** Cerdgn
88 F3 **Myerscough** Lancs
3 L6 **Mylor** Cnwll
3 L6 **Mylor Bridge** Cnwll
80 H10 **Mynachlog ddu** Pembks
80 H10 **Mynydd-llan** Flints
56 F7 **Myndtown** Shrops
29 J5 **Mynydd-bach** Swans
54 G9 **Mynydd Buch** Cerdgn
28 D3 **Mynyddgarreg** Carmth

69 J2 **Mynydd Isa** Flints
79 L11 **Mynydd Llandygai** Gwynd
66 E8 **Mynytho** Gwynd
151 J8 **Myrebird** Abers
118 A11 **Myredykes** Border
23 N3 **Mytchett** Surrey
90 B5 **Mytholm** Calder
90 C5 **Mytholmroyd** Calder
88 D4 **Mythop** Lancs
97 P7 **Myton-on-Swale** N York

N

160 C10 **Naast** Highld
89 J5 **Nab's Head** Lancs
168 f8 **Na Buirgh** W Isls
98 B11 **Naburn** C York
90 E3 **Nab Wood Crematorium** C Brad
27 J3 **Naccolt** Kent
39 L11 **Nackington** Kent
53 M3 **Nacton** Suffk
99 M9 **Nafferton** E R Yk
32 G5 **Nag's Head** Gloucs
46 B11 **Nailbridge** Gloucs
18 H9 **Nailsbourne** Somset
31 N10 **Nailsea** N Som
72 C9 **Nailstone** Leics
32 F5 **Nailsworth** Gloucs
156 F6 **Nairn** Highld
36 F11 **Nalderswood** Surrey
2 G7 **Nancegollan** Cnwll
2 D6 **Nancledra** Cnwll
66 D8 **Nanhoron** Gwynd
80 H11 **Nannerch** Flints
72 E7 **Nanpantan** Leics
4 F10 **Nanpean** Cnwll
2 B8 **Nanquidno** Cnwll
4 G8 **Nanstallon** Cnwll
30 D2 **Nant-ddu** Powys
42 G3 **Nanternis** Cerdgn
43 J10 **Nantgaredig** Carmth
30 F7 **Nantgarw** Rhondd
55 M11 **Nant-glas** Powys
68 D2 **Nantglyn** Denbgs
55 M9 **Nantgwyn** Powys
67 L4 **Nant Gwynant** Gwynd
67 J4 **Nantile** Gwynd
69 J10 **Nantmawr** Shrops
55 N11 **Nantmel** Powys
67 L5 **Nantmor** Gwynd
67 L3 **Nant Peris** Gwynd
70 B4 **Nantwich** Ches E
30 F2 **Nant-y-Bwch** Blae G
43 J11 **Nant-y-caws** Carmth
31 K3 **Nant-y-derry** Mons
29 M6 **Nantyffyllon** Brdgnd
30 G2 **Nantyglo** Blae G
68 H9 **Nant-y-gollen** Shrops
29 P6 **Nant-y-moel** Brdgnd
79 M10 **Nant-y-pandy** Conwy
35 M5 **Naphill** Bucks
46 G5 **Napleton** Worcs
96 C10 **Nappa** N York
48 E2 **Napton on the Hill** Warwks
41 M8 **Narberth** Pembks
72 E11 **Narborough** Leics
75 P8 **Narborough** Norfk
5 N10 **Narkurs** Cnwll
46 H5 **Nasareth** Gwynd
60 E5 **Naseby** Nhants
49 L8 **Nash** Bucks
37 K8 **Nash** Gt Lon
45 L2 **Nash** Herefs
31 K8 **Nash** Newpt
57 L10 **Nash** Shrops
57 P8 **Nash End** Worcs
35 M3 **Nash Lee** Bucks
23 J5 **Nash's Green** Hants
37 P7 **Nash Street** Kent
73 R11 **Nassington** Nhants
32 E3 **Nastend** Gloucs
51 J6 **Nasty** Herts
102 E9 **Nateby** Cumb
88 F2 **Nateby** Lancs
59 J2 **National Memorial Arboretum** Staffs
72 F9 **National Space Science Centre** C Leic
95 L3 **Natland** Cumb
52 H2 **Naughton** Suffk
47 M10 **Naunton** Gloucs
46 G7 **Naunton** Worcs
47 J4 **Naunton Beauchamp** Worcs
86 C9 **Navenby** Lincs
51 M11 **Navestock** Essex
51 N11 **Navestock Side** Essex
163 N3 **Navidale House Hotel** Highld
156 D5 **Navity** Highld
98 D4 **Nawton** N York
52 G5 **Nayland** Suffk
51 K9 **Nazeing** Essex
51 K9 **Nazeing Gate** Essex
13 L5 **Neacroft** Hants
59 M8 **Neal's Green** Warwks
169 s8 **Neap** Shet
71 K5 **Near Cotton** Staffs
101 L11 **Near Sawrey** Cumb
36 F3 **Neasden** Gt Lon
104 B8 **Neasham** Darltn
29 L5 **Neath** Neath
23 K6 **Neatham** Hants
77 L7 **Neatishead** Norfk
54 C11 **Nebo** Cerdgn
67 Q3 **Nebo** Conwy
66 H4 **Nebo** Gwynd
78 H6 **Nebo** IoA
76 B10 **Necton** Norfk
164 D10 **Nedd** Highld
113 K4 **Nedderton** Nthumb
52 G2 **Nedging** Suffk
52 H2 **Nedging Tye** Suffk
65 J5 **Needham** Norfk
64 F10 **Needham Market** Suffk
63 M7 **Needham Street** Suffk
62 D6 **Needingworth** Cambs
57 M9 **Neen Savage** Shrops
57 M10 **Neen Sollars** Shrops
57 L7 **Neenton** Shrops
66 H2 **Nefyn** Gwynd
125 M6 **Neilston** E Rens
30 F7 **Nelson** Caerph
89 P3 **Nelson** Lancs
116 B2 **Nemphlar** S Lans

19 P2 **Nempnett Thrubwell** BaNES
111 Q11 **Nenthall** Cumb
102 E2 **Nenthead** Cumb
118 C3 **Nenthorn** Border
9 J5 **Neopardy** Devon
24 F7 **Nep Town** W Susx
68 H2 **Nercwys** Flints
122 B8 **Nereabolls** Ag & B
125 Q6 **Nerston** S Lans
81 L9 **Nesbit** Nthumb
96 G11 **Nesfield** N York
81 L9 **Ness** Ches W
81 L9 **Ness Botanic Gardens** Ches W
69 L11 **Nesscliffe** Shrops
81 K9 **Neston** Ches W
32 G11 **Neston** Wilts
57 L6 **Netchwood** Shrops
82 H9 **Nether Alderley** Ches E
21 M5 **Netheravon** Wilts
117 Q2 **Nether Blainslie** Border
159 J6 **Netherbrae** Abers
72 H5 **Nether Broughton** Leics
126 D8 **Netherburn** S Lans
11 K5 **Netherbury** Dorset
110 G6 **Netherby** Cumb
97 M11 **Netherby** N York
11 P5 **Nether Cerne** Dorset
109 P3 **Nethercleuch** D & G
19 Q11 **Nether Compton** Dorset
60 B8 **Nethercote** Warwks
5 P2 **Nethercott** Devon
16 H4 **Nethercott** Devon
151 L3 **Nether Crimond** Abers
157 R5 **Nether Dallachy** Moray
31 Q4 **Netherend** Gloucs
9 M4 **Nether Exe** Devon
26 B8 **Netherfield** E Susx
72 F7 **Netherfield** Notts
72 G2 **Netherfield** Notts
116 C8 **Nether Fingland** S Lans
92 C11 **Nethergate** N Linc
76 F6 **Nethergate** Norfk
21 M9 **Netherhampton** Wilts
84 F5 **Nether Handley** Derbys
142 F9 **Nether Handwick** Angus
91 L11 **Nether Haugh** Rothm
11 J3 **Netherhay** Dorset
85 M5 **Nether Headon** Notts
84 E10 **Nether Heage** Derbys
60 E9 **Nether Heyford** Nhants
116 E8 **Nether Howcleugh** S Lans
95 L7 **Nether Kellet** Lancs
159 Q9 **Nether Kinmundy** Abers
71 L8 **Netherland Green** Staffs
84 H6 **Nether Langwith** Notts
108 F12 **Netherlaw** D & G
151 M9 **Netherley** Abers
109 M3 **Nethermill** D & G
159 M9 **Nethermuir** Abers
36 G9 **Netherne-on-the-Hill** Surrey
90 E7 **Netheroyd Hill** Kirk
84 B5 **Nether Padley** Derbys
125 N6 **Netherplace** E Rens
98 B10 **Nether Poppleton** C York
101 K3 **Nether Row** Cumb
59 L2 **Netherseal** Derbys
97 Q2 **Nether Silton** N York
56 D10 **Nether Skyborry** Shrops
18 G7 **Nether Stowey** Somset
51 N8 **Nether Street** Essex
21 J2 **Netherstreet** Wilts
90 E9 **Netherton** Angus
84 F6 **Netherthorpe** Derbys
143 J6 **Netherton** Angus
7 M4 **Netherton** Devon
58 D7 **Netherton** Dudley
22 C3 **Netherton** Hants
45 Q9 **Netherton** Herefs
90 E8 **Netherton** Kirk
126 D7 **Netherton** N Lans
119 J9 **Netherton** Nthumb
34 D5 **Netherton** Oxon
142 A7 **Netherton** P & K
57 N8 **Netherton** Shrops
125 P2 **Netherton** Stirlg
90 H7 **Netherton** Wakefd
47 J6 **Netherton** Worcs
100 C9 **Nethertown** Cumb
167 Q1 **Nethertown** Highld
89 L3 **Nethertown** Lancs
71 L11 **Nethertown** Staffs
116 G2 **Netherurd** Border
22 B7 **Nether Wallop** Hants
100 F10 **Nether Wasdale** Cumb
110 G11 **Nether Welton** Cumb
47 P10 **Nether Westcote** Gloucs
59 K6 **Nether Whitacre** Warwks
116 A7 **Nether Whitecleuch** S Lans
35 K2 **Nether Winchendon** Bucks
112 G2 **Netherwitton** Nthumb
149 J3 **Nethy Bridge** Highld
14 E5 **Netley** Hants
13 P2 **Netley Marsh** Hants
35 J7 **Nettlebed** Oxon
20 B5 **Nettlebridge** Somset
11 L5 **Nettlecombe** Dorset
14 F11 **Nettlecombe** IoW
50 B8 **Nettleden** Herts
86 D5 **Nettleham** Lincs
37 Q10 **Nettlestead** Kent
37 Q10 **Nettlestead Green** Kent
14 H8 **Nettlestone** IoW
113 L11 **Nettlesworth** Dur
93 K10 **Nettleton** Lincs
32 F9 **Nettleton** Wilts
32 F9 **Nettleton Shrub** Wilts
6 F9 **Netton** Devon
21 M7 **Netton** Wilts
43 P10 **Neuadd** Carmth
55 L9 **Neuadd-ddu** Powys
38 C3 **Nevendon** Essex
41 L2 **Nevern** Pembks
60 H2 **Nevill Holt** Leics
109 L7 **New Abbey** D & G
159 L5 **New Aberdour** Abers
37 J8 **New Addington** Gt Lon
91 J11 **Newall** Leeds
22 G8 **New Alresford** Hants
142 C8 **New Alyth** P & K
74 D10 **Newark** C Pete
169 g2 **Newark** Ork
85 N10 **Newark-on-Trent** Notts
92 H2 **New Arram** E R Yk
126 D5 **Newarthill** N Lans

37 P7 **New Ash Green** Kent
85 P10 **New Balderton** Notts
27 L3 **Newbarn** Kent
37 P7 **New Barn** Kent
50 G11 **New Barnet** Gt Lon
61 J8 **New Barton** Nhants
127 Q4 **Newbattle** Mdloth
119 L6 **New Bewick** Nthumb
110 C7 **Newbie** D & G
94 B2 **Newbiggin** Cumb
94 F7 **Newbiggin** Cumb
101 N5 **Newbiggin** Cumb
102 B5 **Newbiggin** Cumb
111 L11 **Newbiggin** Cumb
102 H5 **Newbiggin** Cumb
112 H11 **Newbiggin** Dur
96 E2 **Newbiggin** N York
96 F3 **Newbiggin** N York
113 M3 **Newbiggin-by-the-Sea** Nthumb
142 D9 **Newbigging** Angus
142 G10 **Newbigging** Angus
142 H10 **Newbigging** Angus
127 J8 **Newbigging** S Lans
102 D10 **New Biggin-on-Lune** Cumb
59 Q9 **New Bilton** Warwks
84 E6 **Newbold** Derbys
72 C7 **Newbold** Leics
59 Q9 **Newbold on Avon** Warwks
47 P5 **Newbold on Stour** Warwks
47 Q3 **Newbold Pacey** Warwks
59 Q8 **Newbold Revel** Warwks
72 C10 **Newbold Verdon** Leics
87 K9 **New Bolingbroke** Lincs
74 D10 **Newborough** C Pete
78 G11 **Newborough** IoA
71 L9 **Newborough** Staffs
48 F7 **Newbottle** Nhants
113 M10 **Newbottle** Sundld
86 C6 **New Boultham** Lincs
53 N3 **Newbourne** Suffk
49 M6 **New Bradwell** M Keyn
84 E6 **New Brampton** Derbys
103 P2 **New Brancepeth** Dur
127 L3 **Newbridge** C Edin
30 H5 **Newbridge** Caerph
43 K3 **Newbridge** Cerdgn
2 C7 **Newbridge** Cnwll
3 K5 **Newbridge** Cnwll
109 K5 **Newbridge** D & G
21 Q11 **Newbridge** Hants
14 D9 **Newbridge** IoW
98 G3 **New Bridge** N York
34 D4 **Newbridge** Oxon
69 J6 **Newbridge** Wrexhm
46 F7 **Newbridge Green** Worcs
31 L6 **Newbridge-on-Usk** Mons
44 E3 **Newbridge on Wye** Powys
81 K11 **New Brighton** Flints
81 L6 **New Brighton** Wirral
84 G10 **New Brinsley** Notts
105 J6 **New Brotton** R & Cl
112 C7 **Newbrough** Nthumb
69 K4 **New Broughton** Wrexhm
64 F3 **New Buckenham** Norfk
9 J4 **Newbuildings** Devon
151 P2 **Newburgh** Abers
159 N6 **Newburgh** Abers
134 G4 **Newburgh** Fife
88 F8 **Newburgh** Lancs
98 A5 **Newburgh Priory** N York
113 J7 **Newburn** N u Ty
82 F4 **New Bury** Bolton
20 C5 **Newbury** Somset
34 E11 **Newbury** W Berk
20 F6 **Newbury** Wilts
37 K3 **Newbury Park** Gt Lon
101 Q6 **Newby** Cumb
96 B11 **Newby** Lancs
95 Q7 **Newby** N York
99 L2 **Newby** N York
104 F8 **Newby** N York
94 H3 **Newby Bridge** Cumb
110 G10 **Newby Cross** Cumb
111 J9 **Newby East** Cumb
101 Q6 **Newby Head** Cumb
159 K7 **New Byth** Abers
110 G10 **Newby West** Cumb
97 N3 **Newby Wiske** N York
45 N11 **Newcastle** Mons
56 D8 **Newcastle** Shrops
113 J6 **Newcastle Airport** Nthumb
42 F6 **Newcastle Emlyn** Carmth
113 J3 **Newcastleton** Border
70 E5 **Newcastle-under-Lyme** Staffs
113 K8 **Newcastle upon Tyne** N u Ty
41 P3 **Newchapel** Pembks
70 F4 **Newchapel** Staffs
25 J2 **Newchapel** Surrey
30 G2 **Newchurch** Blae G
45 M4 **Newchurch** Herefs
14 G9 **Newchurch** IoW
27 J5 **Newchurch** Kent
31 N5 **Newchurch** Mons
45 J4 **Newchurch** Powys
71 L10 **Newchurch** Staffs
89 N3 **Newchurch in Pendle** Lancs
76 H9 **New Costessey** Norfk
109 P11 **New Cowper** Cumb
127 Q3 **Newcraighall** C Edin
91 K7 **New Crofton** Wakefd
54 E9 **New Cross** Cerdgn
37 J5 **New Cross** Gt Lon
19 Q6 **New Cross** Somset
115 M5 **New Cumnock** E Ayrs
45 M11 **New Cut** E Susx
159 L8 **New Deer** Abers
113 L5 **New Delaval** Nthumb
89 B9 **New Denham** Oldham
36 B4 **New Denham** Bucks
24 E2 **Newdigate** Surrey
60 F8 **New Duston** Nhants
98 C9 **New Earswick** C York
84 G11 **New Eastwood** Notts
91 N11 **New Edlington** Donc
157 N5 **New Elgin** Moray
93 L3 **New Ellerby** E R Yk
35 N10 **Newell Green** Br For
37 K6 **New Eltham** Gt Lon
47 L2 **New End** Worcs
26 D6 **Newenden** Kent
74 C10 **New England** C Pete

52 B3 **New England** Essex
46 D9 **Newent** Gloucs
90 H4 **New Farnley** Leeds
81 L7 **New Ferry** Wirral
103 P4 **Newfield** Dur
113 K10 **Newfield** Dur
156 D2 **Newfield** Highld
74 C11 **New Fletton** C Pete
13 N3 **New Forest National Park**
22 G4 **Newfound** Hants
91 M5 **New Fryston** Wakefd
40 G6 **Newgale** Pembks
108 D5 **New Galloway** D & G
76 E3 **Newgate** Norfk
50 H9 **Newgate Street** Herts
135 L6 **New Gilston** Fife
2 b1 **New Grimsby** IoS
69 R5 **Newhall** Ches E
71 P10 **Newhall** Derbys
119 N5 **Newham** Nthumb
113 M5 **New Hartley** Nthumb
127 P2 **Newhaven** C Edin
71 M2 **Newhaven** Derbys
25 K10 **Newhaven** E Susx
36 C8 **New Haw** Surrey
41 M10 **New Hedges** Pembks
113 M10 **New Herrington** Sundld
89 Q8 **Newhey** Rochdl
76 B4 **New Holkham** Norfk
93 J6 **New Holland** N Linc
105 N8 **Newholm** N York
84 G7 **New Houghton** Derbys
75 Q5 **New Houghton** Norfk
126 D5 **Newhouse** N Lans
96 B6 **New Houses** N York
82 C4 **New Houses** Wigan
95 M2 **New Hutton** Cumb
38 B10 **New Hythe** Kent
25 K6 **Newick** E Susx
27 K4 **Newingreen** Kent
27 L4 **Newington** Kent
38 E9 **Newington** Kent
34 H5 **Newington** Oxon
56 G8 **Newington** Shrops
32 F6 **Newington Bagpath** Gloucs
43 J7 **New Inn** Carmth
31 K5 **New Inn** Torfn
56 D9 **New Invention** Shrops
77 J10 **New Lakenham** Norfk
116 B2 **New Lanark** S Lans
93 J4 **Newland** C KuH
94 G5 **Newland** Cumb
92 D5 **Newland** E R Yk
31 Q3 **Newland** Gloucs
92 A6 **Newland** N York
34 C3 **Newland** Oxon
17 Q4 **Newland** Somset
46 E5 **Newland** Worcs
128 B7 **Newlandrig** Mdloth
111 K2 **Newlands** Border
101 K3 **Newlands** Cumb
112 G9 **Newlands** Nthumb
157 P7 **Newlands of Dundurcas** Moray
88 E8 **New Lane** Lancs
82 D6 **New Lane End** Warrtn
110 G4 **New Langholm** D & G
87 M9 **New Leake** Lincs
159 N7 **New Leeds** Abers
91 K9 **New Lodge** Barns
88 G5 **New Longton** Lancs
106 G5 **New Luce** D & G
2 D8 **Newlyn** Cnwll
4 C10 **Newlyn East** Cnwll
151 M4 **Newmachar** Abers
126 E6 **Newmains** N Lans
36 F7 **New Malden** Gt Lon
51 M8 **Newman's End** Essex
52 E3 **Newman's Green** Suffk
63 K8 **Newmarket** Suffk
168 j4 **Newmarket** W Isls
104 H6 **New Marske** R & Cl
34 F3 **New Marston** Oxon
69 K8 **New Marton** Shrops
151 K11 **New Mill** Abers
117 P8 **Newmill** Border
2 D7 **New Mill** Cnwll
35 P2 **New Mill** Herts
90 F9 **New Mill** Kirk
158 B7 **Newmill** Moray
91 J7 **Newmillerdam** Wakefd
142 G5 **Newmill of Inshewan** Angus
127 M4 **Newmills** C Edin
3 M3 **New Mills** Cnwll
83 M7 **New Mills** Derbys
134 C10 **Newmills** Fife
31 P3 **Newmills** Mons
55 P4 **New Mills** Powys
142 A11 **Newmiln** P & K
125 N10 **Newmilns** E Ayrs
13 M5 **New Milton** Hants
53 K5 **New Mistley** Essex
41 L5 **New Moat** Pembks
69 L8 **Newnes** Shrops
51 Q9 **Newney Green** Essex
32 C2 **Newnham** Gloucs
23 K4 **Newnham** Hants
51 F3 **Newnham** Herts
38 G10 **Newnham** Kent
60 C9 **Newnham** Nhants
57 L11 **Newnham** Worcs
85 L7 **New Ollerton** Notts
58 G6 **New Oscott** Birm
159 L6 **New Pitsligo** Abers
4 E6 **New Polzeath** Cnwll
5 N4 **Newport** Cnwll
12 E5 **Newport** Dorset
92 E4 **Newport** E R Yk
51 M4 **Newport** Essex
32 D5 **Newport** Gloucs
163 Q2 **Newport** Highld
14 F9 **Newport** IoW
31 K7 **Newport** Newpt
77 Q8 **Newport** Norfk
41 L3 **Newport** Pembks
70 C11 **Newport** Wrekin
135 L2 **Newport-on-Tay** Fife
49 N6 **Newport Pagnell** M Keyn
49 N6 *Newport Pagnell Services* M Keyn
24 C5 **Newpound Common** W Susx
114 F3 **New Prestwick** S Ayrs
42 G3 **New Quay** Cerdgn
4 C9 **Newquay** Cnwll
52 H7 **New Quay** Essex
4 D9 *Newquay Airport* Cnwll

77 K9 **New Rackheath** Norfk
45 J2 **New Radnor** Powys
101 N3 **New Rent** Cumb
112 G9 **New Ridley** Nthumb
90 B2 **Road Side** Nthumb
27 J7 **New Romney** Kent
91 Q11 **New Rossington** Donc
54 G10 **New Row** Cerdgn
89 J3 **New Row** Lancs
133 P9 **New Sauchie** Clacks
82 H11 **Newsbank** Ches E
158 H11 **Newseat** Abers
88 G3 **Newsham** Lancs
97 N4 **Newsham** N York
103 M8 **Newsham** N York
113 M5 **Newsham** Nthumb
91 K7 **New Sharlston** Wakefd
92 B5 **Newsholme** E R Yk
96 B10 **Newsholme** Lancs
119 N4 **New Shoreston** Nthumb
113 N10 **New Silksworth** Sundld
105 J7 **New Skelton** R & Cl
90 F8 **Newsome** Kirk
73 N3 **New Somerby** Lincs
36 G2 **New Southgate Crematorium** Gt Lon
88 H9 **New Springs** Wigan
117 M4 **Newstead** Border
84 H10 **Newstead** Notts
119 N5 **Newstead** Nthumb
126 D6 **New Stevenston** N Lans
45 L3 **New Street** Herefs
72 C7 **New Swannington** Leics
91 M4 **Newthorpe** N York
84 G11 **Newthorpe** Notts
38 C4 **New Thundersley** Essex
24 G8 **Newtimber** W Susx
86 D3 **Newtoft** Lincs
131 L8 **Newton** Ag & B
118 B6 **Newton** Border
29 M9 **Newton** Brdgnd
50 F2 **Newton** C Beds
62 F11 **Newton** Cambs
74 H8 **Newton** Cambs
30 H9 **Newton** Cardif
69 P3 **Newton** Ches W
81 N11 **Newton** Ches W
82 B9 **Newton** Ches W
94 E6 **Newton** Cumb
84 F9 **Newton** Derbys
45 L8 **Newton** Herefs
45 Q4 **Newton** Herefs
56 F11 **Newton** Herefs
155 Q7 **Newton** Highld
156 C8 **Newton** Highld
156 D4 **Newton** Highld
167 P7 **Newton** Highld
88 C3 **Newton** Lancs
95 M6 **Newton** Lancs
73 Q3 **Newton** Lincs
127 Q4 **Newton** Mdloth
157 M5 **Newton** Moray
157 Q5 **Newton** Moray
98 H6 **Newton** N York
61 J4 **Newton** Nhants
76 A8 **Newton** Norfk
72 H2 **Newton** Notts
112 F8 **Newton** Nthumb
118 H9 **Newton** Nthumb
116 C4 **Newton** S Lans
126 B5 **Newton** S Lans
58 F6 **Newton** Sandw
69 M8 **Newton** Shrops
18 F7 **Newton** Somset
71 J9 **Newton** Staffs
52 F3 **Newton** Suffk
127 K2 **Newton** W Loth
60 B5 **Newton** Warwks
21 P10 **Newton** Wilts
7 M4 **Newton Abbot** Devon
110 D9 **Newton Arlosh** Cumb
103 Q6 **Newton Aycliffe** Dur
104 E5 **Newton Bewley** Hartpl
49 P4 **Newton Blossomville** M Keyn
61 L7 **Newton Bromswold** Nhants
72 B9 **Newton Burgoland** Leics
119 P5 **Newton-by-the-Sea** Nthumb
86 D3 **Newton by Toft** Lincs
5 N8 **Newton Ferrers** Cnwll
6 F9 **Newton Ferrers** Devon
168 d10 **Newton Ferry** W Isls
65 J2 **Newton Flotman** Norfk
127 Q5 **Newtongrange** Mdloth
31 P6 **Newton Green** Mons
72 G11 **Newton Harcourt** Leics
83 J4 **Newton Heath** Manch
151 N9 **Newtonhill** Abers
91 J6 **Newton Hill** Wakefd
95 P10 **Newton-in-Bowland** Lancs
91 M2 **Newton Kyme** N York
97 K3 **Newton-le-Willows** N York
82 C5 **Newton-le-Willows** St Hel
127 Q5 **Newtonloan** Mdloth
49 M8 **Newton Longville** Bucks
125 N6 **Newton Mearns** E Rens
143 L5 **Newtonmill** Angus
148 C8 **Newtonmore** Highld
103 P9 **Newton Morrell** N York
41 J9 **Newton Mountain** Pembks
105 L7 **Newton Mulgrave** N York
134 F5 **Newton of Balcanquhal** P & K
135 N7 **Newton of Balcormo** Fife
97 R9 **Newton on Ouse** N York
98 G2 **Newton-on-Rawcliffe** N York
69 N10 **Newton on the Hill** Shrops
119 N9 **Newton-on-the-Moor** Nthumb
85 P6 **Newton on Trent** Lincs
10 B7 **Newton Poppleford** Devon
48 H8 **Newton Purcell** Oxon
59 L3 **Newton Regis** Warwks
101 N4 **Newton Reigny** Cumb
9 L4 **Newton St Cyres** Devon
77 J8 **Newton St Faith** Norfk
20 D2 **Newton St Loe** BaNES
16 G9 **Newton St Petrock** Devon
71 P9 **Newton Solney** Derbys

22 D6 **Newton Stacey** Hants
107 M4 **Newton Stewart** D & G
21 P6 **Newton Tony** Wilts
17 J6 **Newton Tracey** Devon
104 G8 **Newton under Roseberry** R & Cl
112 H3 **Newton Underwood** Nthumb
98 E11 **Newton upon Derwent** E R Yk
23 K8 **Newton Valence** Hants
109 P2 **Newton Wamphray** D & G
88 F4 **Newton with Scales** Lancs
30 G3 **Newtown** Blae G
82 B9 **Newtown** Ches W
2 F8 **Newtown** Cnwll
5 M6 **Newtown** Cnwll
101 P6 **Newtown** Cumb
109 P11 **Newtown** Cumb
110 G8 **Newtown** Cumb
111 K8 **Newtown** Cumb
115 Q5 **Newtown** D & G
83 L8 **Newtown** Derbys
9 Q5 **Newtown** Devon
17 P6 **Newtown** Devon
11 K4 **Newtown** Dorset
12 G3 **New Town** Dorset
21 J11 **New Town** Dorset
21 J11 **New Town** Dorset
25 L6 **New Town** E Susx
32 C4 **Newtown** Gloucs
13 N2 **Newtown** Hants
14 H4 **Newtown** Hants
22 E2 **Newtown** Hants
45 P3 **Newtown** Herefs
45 Q8 **Newtown** Herefs
46 B5 **Newtown** Herefs
46 D7 **Newtown** Herefs
147 K7 **Newtown** Highld
14 D8 **Newtown** IoW
88 C7 **Newtown** Lancs
61 L5 **New Town** Nhants
119 J4 **Newtown** Nthumb
119 K10 **Newtown** Nthumb
119 K5 **Newtown** Nthumb
12 H6 **Newtown** Poole
55 Q6 **Newtown** Powys
30 E5 **Newtown** Rhondd
69 M10 **Newtown** Shrops
69 N8 **Newtown** Shrops
10 F2 **Newtown** Somset
58 E4 **Newtown** Staffs
70 C2 **Newtown** Staffs
82 C4 **Newtown** Wigan
20 H9 **Newtown** Wilts
21 Q2 **Newtown** Wilts
33 Q10 **New Town** Wilts
46 G3 **Newtown** Worcs
58 D9 **Newtown** Worcs
3 J9 **Newtown-in-St Martin** Cnwll
72 E9 **Newtown Linford** Leics
125 K6 **Newtown of Beltrees** Rens
117 R4 **Newtown St Boswells** Border
72 D10 **Newtown Unthank** Leics
30 F4 **New Tredegar** Caerph
126 E10 **New Trows** S Lans
84 E7 **New Tupton** Derbys
142 D9 **Newtyle** Angus
75 J9 **New Walsoken** Cambs
93 N10 **New Waltham** NE Lin
84 E5 **New Whittington** Derbys
128 C5 **New Winton** E Loth
34 C2 **New Yatt** Oxon
36 C3 **Newyears Green** Gt Lon
131 K5 **Newyork** Ag & B
86 B9 **New York** Lincs
113 M6 **New York** N Tyne
97 J8 **New York** N York
45 L3 **Nextend** Herefs
41 J9 **Neyland** Pembks
80 b6 **Niarbyl** IoM
32 C3 **Nibley** Gloucs
32 C8 **Nibley** S Glos
32 D5 **Nibley Green** Gloucs
18 F11 **Nicholashayne** Devon
28 F7 **Nicholaston** Swans
111 K7 **Nickies Hill** Cumb
97 M8 **Nidd** N York
151 N7 **Nigg** C Aber
156 E3 **Nigg** Highld
156 D4 **Nigg Ferry** Highld
32 D10 **Nimlet** BaNES
111 Q10 **Ninebanks** Nthumb
33 M7 **Nine Elms** Swindn
40 E6 **Nine Wells** Pembks
26 B9 **Ninfield** E Susx
14 C9 **Ningwood** IoW
118 C5 **Nisbet** Border
129 K9 **Nisbet Hill** Border
14 F11 **Niton** IoW
125 N5 **Nitshill** C Glas
37 N9 **Noah's Ark** Kent
37 Q2 **Noak Bridge** Essex
37 M2 **Noak Hill** Gt Lon
90 H9 **Noblethorpe** Barns
56 H2 **Nobold** Shrops
60 E8 **Nobottle** Nhants
86 E8 **Nocton** Lincs
77 M11 **Nogdam End** Norfk
34 F2 **Noke** Oxon
40 G7 **Nolton** Pembks
40 G7 **Nolton Haven** Pembks
69 P5 **No Man's Heath** Ches W
59 L3 **No Man's Heath** Warwks
5 M10 **No Man's Land** Cnwll
9 K2 **Nomansland** Devon
21 Q11 **Nomansland** Wilts
69 N9 **Noneley** Shrops
39 N11 **Nonington** Kent
95 L4 **Nook** Cumb
111 J5 **Nook** Cumb
36 E7 **Norbiton** Gt Lon
88 C2 **Norbreck** Bpool
46 D6 **Norbridge** Herefs
69 Q5 **Norbury** Ches E
71 L6 **Norbury** Derbys
36 H7 **Norbury** Gt Lon
56 F6 **Norbury** Shrops
70 D10 **Norbury** Staffs
69 Q5 **Norbury Common** Ches E
70 D10 **Norbury Junction** Staffs
58 B11 **Norchard** Worcs
82 B6 **Norcott Brook** Ches W
88 C2 **Norcross** Lancs
75 L10 **Nordelph** Norfk

89 P8 **Norden** Rochdl
57 M5 **Nordley** Shrops
77 P10 **Norfolk Broads** Norfk
129 N10 **Norham** Nthumb
90 D6 **Norland Town** Calder
82 C10 **Norley** Ches W
14 C7 **Norleywood** Hants
25 K8 **Norlington** E Susx
92 E7 **Normanby** Lincs
98 E4 **Normanby** N Linc
104 F7 **Normanby** R & Cl
93 K11 **Normanby le Wold** Lincs
61 Q2 **Norman Cross** Cambs
23 P4 **Normandy** Surrey
25 Q9 **Norman's Bay** E Susx
9 Q4 **Norman's Green** Devon
72 A4 **Normanton** C Derb
73 L2 **Normanton** Leics
86 B11 **Normanton** Lincs
85 M10 **Normanton** Notts
73 N9 **Normanton** Rutlnd
91 K6 **Normanton** Wakefd
21 M6 **Normanton** Wilts
72 B8 **Normanton le Heath** Leics
72 E6 **Normanton on Soar** Notts
72 G4 **Normanton on the Wolds** Notts
85 N7 **Normanton on Trent** Notts
88 C3 **Normoss** Lancs
23 P6 **Norney** Surrey
20 G2 **Norrington Common** Wilts
5 Q8 **Norris Green** Cnwll
81 M6 **Norris Green** Lpool
72 A7 **Norris Hill** Leics
90 G6 **Norristhorpe** Kirk
64 D2 **Northacre** Norfk
49 Q10 **Northall** Bucks
97 N2 **Northallerton** N York
76 D9 **Northall Green** Norfk
14 D4 **Northam** C Sotn
16 H6 **Northam** Devon
60 G8 **Northampton** Nhants
58 B11 **Northampton** Worcs
84 H4 **North Anston** Rothm
35 P11 **North Ascot** Br For
48 E9 **North Aston** Oxon
50 G10 **Northaw** Herts
10 F2 **Northay** Somset
22 C10 **North Baddesley** Hants
139 K5 **North Ballachulish** Highld
20 B9 **North Barrow** Somset
76 C4 **North Barsham** Norfk
38 C4 **North Benfleet** Essex
15 P6 **North Bersted** W Susx
128 E3 **North Berwick** E Loth
103 N4 **North Bitchburn** Dur
113 M4 **North Blyth** Nthumb
14 H4 **North Boarhunt** Hants
13 L5 **North Bockhampton** Dorset
74 C9 **Northborough** C Pete
39 P11 **Northbourne** Kent
20 G3 **North Bovey** Devon
8 C8 **North Brentor** Devon
20 D7 **North Brewham** Somset
23 Q7 **North Bridge** Surrey
26 B7 **Northbridge Street** E Susx
22 F7 **Northbrook** Hants
48 E10 **Northbrook** Oxon
50 G2 **North Brook End** Cambs
16 H3 **North Buckland** Devon
77 M10 **North Burlingham** Norfk
20 B9 **North Cadbury** Somset
86 B5 **North Carlton** Lincs
85 J4 **North Carlton** Notts
92 E4 **North Cave** E R Yk
33 K3 **North Cerney** Gloucs
25 J6 **North Chailey** E Susx
23 Q9 **Northchapel** W Susx
21 N11 **North Charford** Hants
119 N6 **North Charlton** Nthumb
36 F7 **North Cheam** Gt Lon
20 C9 **North Cheriton** Somset
11 J6 **North Chideock** Dorset
35 Q3 **Northchurch** Herts
92 E3 **North Cliffe** E R Yk
85 P6 **North Clifton** Notts
103 Q4 **North Close** Dur
87 L2 **North Cockerington** Lincs
138 G11 **North Connel** Ag & B
29 M8 **North Cornelly** Brdgnd
3 K10 **North Corner** Cnwll
93 P10 **North Cotes** Lincs
5 N3 **Northcott** Devon
10 B2 **Northcott** Devon
10 C3 **Northcott** Devon
2 H5 **North Country** Cnwll
34 C8 **Northcourt** Oxon
65 P4 **North Cove** Suffk
103 Q10 **North Cowton** N York
49 P6 **North Crawley** M Keyn
37 L6 **North Cray** Gt Lon
76 B4 **North Creake** Norfk
19 K9 **North Curry** Somset
99 J10 **North Dalton** E R Yk
97 N10 **North Deighton** N York
17 J5 **North Devon Crematorium** Devon
39 Q7 **Northdown** Kent
38 F10 **North Downs**
92 A3 **North Duffield** N York
152 Q3 **North Duntulm** Highld
36 F7 **North East Surrey Crematorium** Gt Lon
84 E7 **Northedge** Derbys
38 H4 **North End** Kent
87 J2 **North Elkington** Lincs
76 D7 **North Elmham** Norfk
91 M8 **North Elmsall** Wakefd
35 K6 **Northend** Bucks
15 J6 **North End** C Port
110 F9 **North End** Cumb
20 F9 **North End** Dorset
93 L2 **North End** E R Yk
93 K1 **North End** Essex
21 M11 **North End** Hants
22 G9 **North End** Hants
72 F7 **North End** Leics
86 B11 **North End** Lincs
87 M3 **North End** Lincs
92 H11 **North End** Lincs

93 P10 **North End** Lincs
93 K6 **North End** N Linc
31 M11 **North End** N Som
61 L7 **North End** Nhants
64 D3 **North End** Norfk
119 M10 **North End** Nthumb
81 L4 **North End** Sefton
15 Q6 **North End** W Susx
24 D9 **North End** W Susx
48 C4 **North End** Warwks
82 H7 **Northenden** Manch
35 P7 **Northend Woods** Bucks
160 A10 **North Erradale** Highld
72 G10 **North Evington** C Leic
38 E2 **North Fambridge** Essex
58 F9 **North Ferriby** E R Yk
151 N6 **Northfield** Birm
87 H5 **Northfield** C Aber
73 Q9 **Northfields** Lincs
37 P6 **Northfleet** Kent
99 N10 **North Frodingham** E R Yk
13 L2 **North Gorley** Hants
65 J4 **North Green** Norfk
65 L9 **North Green** Suffk
65 M8 **North Green** Suffk
86 D6 **North Greetwell** Lincs
98 G7 **North Grimston** N York
38 B8 **North Halling** Medway
15 K6 **North Hayling** Hants
119 L4 **North Hazelrigg** Nthumb
17 N5 **North Heasley** Devon
24 C6 **North Heath** W Susx
18 D10 **North Hele** Devon
5 M6 **North Hill** Cnwll
36 C4 **North Hillingdon** Gt Lon
34 E3 **North Hinksey Village** Oxon
36 E11 **North Holmwood** Surrey
7 J7 **North Huish** Devon
86 B7 **North Hykeham** Lincs
26 D7 **Northiam** E Susx
61 P11 **Northill** C Beds
32 D3 **Northington** Gloucs
22 G7 **Northington** Hants
92 H10 **North Kelsey** Lincs
156 B8 **North Kessock** Highld
93 K7 **North Killingholme** N Linc
97 P3 **North Kilvington** N York
60 D4 **North Kilworth** Leics
13 L4 **North Kingston** Hants
86 G10 **North Kyme** Lincs
99 Q6 **North Landing** E R Yk
87 K10 **Northlands** Lincs
33 M2 **Northleach** Gloucs
35 M3 **North Lee** Bucks
97 L6 **North Lees** N York
10 D5 **Northleigh** Devon
17 L5 **Northleigh** Devon
27 K2 **North Leigh** Kent
34 C2 **North Leigh** Oxon
85 N4 **North Leverton with Habblesthorpe** Notts
47 L5 **North Littleton** Worcs
19 N7 **North Lopham** Norfk
73 N10 **North Luffenham** Rutlnd
23 M11 **North Marden** W Susx
49 L10 **North Marston** Bucks
128 B8 **North Middleton** Mdloth
119 J6 **North Middleton** Nthumb
159 K9 **North Millbrex** Abers
106 E7 **North Milmain** D & G
17 N6 **North Molton** Devon
34 C4 **Northmoor** Oxon
34 G7 **North Moreton** Oxon
142 F7 **Northmuir** Angus
15 N6 **North Mundham** W Susx
84 N9 **North Muskham** Notts
92 F3 **North Newbald** E R Yk
48 D6 **North Newington** Oxon
21 M3 **North Newnton** Wilts
19 K8 **North Newton** Somset
15 K6 **Northney** Hants
32 D5 **North Nibley** Gloucs
22 F4 **North Oakley** Hants
37 N3 **North Ockendon** Gt Lon
36 D4 **Northolt** Gt Lon
81 J11 **Northop** Flints
81 K11 **Northop Hall** Flints
104 F7 **North Ormesby** Middsb
87 J2 **North Ormsby** Lincs
90 G6 **Northorpe** Kirk
74 A7 **Northorpe** Lincs
74 D3 **Northorpe** Lincs
92 E11 **Northorpe** Lincs
97 N3 **North Otterington** N York
19 N7 **Northover** Somset
19 P10 **Northover** Somset
86 E2 **North Owersby** Lincs
90 E5 **Northowram** Calder
11 K3 **North Perrott** Somset
19 J8 **North Petherton** Somset
5 M4 **North Petherwin** Cnwll
76 B10 **North Pickenham** Norfk
47 J4 **North Piddle** Worcs
11 L5 **North Poorton** Dorset
12 F7 **Northport** Dorset
13 L3 **North Poulner** Hants
134 E11 **North Queensferry** Fife
17 P5 **North Radworthy** Devon
86 D11 **North Rauceby** Lincs
77 J4 **Northrepps** Norfk
87 L4 **North Reston** Lincs
97 L11 **North Rigton** N York
13 L5 **North Ripley** Hants
83 J11 **North Rode** Ches E
169 g1 **North Ronaldsay** Ork
169 g1 *North Ronaldsay Airport* Ork
100 H4 **North Row** Cumb
75 M7 **North Runcton** Norfk
94 D7 **North Scale** Cumb
85 P7 **North Scarle** Lincs
113 L5 **North Seaton** Nthumb
113 L5 **North Seaton Colliery** Nthumb
138 G9 **North Shian** Ag & B
113 N7 **North Shields** N Tyne
38 F4 **North Shoebury** Sthend
88 C3 **North Shore** Bpool
74 E11 **North Side** C Pete
100 C5 **North Side** Cumb
105 J7 **North Skelton** R & Cl
93 R11 **North Somercotes** Lincs

292 North Stainley - Oxcroft

97 L5 North Stainley N York
102 F8 North Stainmore Cumb
37 P4 North Stifford Thurr
32 D11 North Stoke BaNES
34 H7 North Stoke Oxon
24 B8 North Stoke W Susx
63 J7 North Street Cambs
21 N11 North Street Hants
22 H8 North Street Hants
38 H10 North Street Kent
38 D7 North Street Medway
34 H10 North Street W Berk
119 P4 North Sunderland Nthumb
5 N2 North Tamerton Cnwll
8 G4 North Tawton Devon
133 M10 North Third Stirlg
93 N11 North Thoresby Lincs
119 P10 North Togston Nthumb
168 e9 Northton W Isls
17 J10 North Town Devon
19 Q6 North Town Somset
35 N8 North Town W & M
76 E9 North Tuddenham Norfk
168 c10 North Uist W Isls
118 G10 Northumberland National Park Nthumb
113 J7 North Walbottle N u Ty
77 K5 North Walsham Norfk
22 G5 North Waltham Hants
23 K4 North Warnborough Hants
18 F9 Northway Somset
28 G7 Northway Swans
51 L10 North Weald Bassett Essex
85 N3 North Wheatley Notts
7 M5 North Whilborough Devon
82 E10 Northwich Ches W
31 Q11 North Wick BaNES
31 Q7 Northwick S Glos
19 L5 Northwick Somset
46 F3 Northwick Worcs
19 Q3 North Widcombe BaNES
86 G3 North Willingham Lincs
84 F7 North Wingfield Derbys
73 N6 North Witham Lincs
75 Q11 Northwold Norfk
70 F5 Northwood C Stke
84 C8 Northwood Derbys
36 C2 Northwood Gt Lon
14 E8 Northwood IoW
69 N8 Northwood Shrops
46 D11 Northwood Green Gloucs
11 P2 North Wootton Dorset
75 M6 North Wootton Norfk
19 Q6 North Wootton Somset
32 F9 North Wraxall Wilts
33 M8 North Wroughton Swindn
105 K10 North York Moors National Park
91 N7 Norton Donc
25 L10 Norton E Susx
46 G10 Norton Gloucs
82 C8 Norton Halton
50 F4 Norton Herts
13 P7 Norton IoW
45 N10 Norton Mons
19 K2 Norton N Som
98 F6 Norton N York
60 C8 Norton Nhants
85 J6 Norton Notts
56 E11 Norton Powys
104 D6 Norton S on T
84 E4 Norton Sheff
56 H8 Norton Shrops
57 K3 Norton Shrops
57 L8 Norton Shrops
57 N4 Norton Shrops
64 D8 Norton Suffk
28 H7 Norton Swans
15 P5 Norton W Susx
32 G8 Norton Wilts
46 G4 Norton Worcs
47 K5 Norton Worcs
20 H6 Norton Bavant Wilts
70 F8 Norton Bridge Staffs
58 F3 Norton Canes Staffs
58 F3 Norton Canes Services Staffs
45 M5 Norton Canon Herefs
76 F6 Norton Corner Norfk
85 Q9 Norton Disney Lincs
20 E7 Norton Ferris Wilts
18 G9 Norton Fitzwarren Somset
13 P7 Norton Green IoW
19 Q2 Norton Hawkfield BaNES
51 P10 Norton Heath Essex
70 C7 Norton in Hales Shrops
70 F4 Norton in the Moors C Stke
59 M3 Norton-Juxta-Twycross Leics
97 P6 Norton-le-Clay N York
47 P2 Norton Lindsey Warwks
64 D8 Norton Little Green Suffk
20 B2 Norton Malreward BaNES
51 N10 Norton Mandeville Essex
20 E3 Norton St Philip Somset
65 N2 Norton Subcourse Norfk
19 N11 Norton sub Hamdon Somset
45 M5 Norton Wood Herefs
85 N8 Norwell Notts
85 M8 Norwell Woodhouse Notts
77 J10 Norwich Norfk
77 J9 Norwich Airport Norfk
77 J10 Norwich Cathedral Norfk
77 J8 Norwich (St Faith) Crematorium Norfk
169 t2 Norwick Shet
133 P9 Norwood Clacks
84 G4 Norwood Derbys
27 J5 Norwood Kent
51 N9 Norwood End Essex
90 E5 Norwood Green Calder
36 D5 Norwood Green Gt Lon
24 F2 Norwood Hill Surrey
74 H11 Norwoodside Cambs
73 J11 Noseley Leics
6 F9 Noss Mayo Devon
97 L4 Nosterfield N York
51 P2 Nosterfield End Cambs
145 Q2 Nostie Highld
47 M10 Notgrove Gloucs
29 M9 Nottage Brdgnd
5 P9 Notter Cnwll
72 F3 Nottingham C Nott
11 P8 Nottington Dorset
91 J8 Notton Wakefd
32 H11 Notton Wilts
52 C9 Nounsley Essex
57 Q11 Noutard's Green Worcs
64 B9 Nowton Suffk
56 G2 Nox Shrops
35 J7 Nuffield Oxon
98 G11 Nunburnholme E R Yk
84 H10 Nuncargate Notts
111 J11 Nunclose Cumb
59 N6 Nuneaton Warwks
34 G5 Nuneham Courtenay Oxon
36 H5 Nunhead Gt Lon
99 N11 Nunkeeling E R Yk
97 R9 Nun Monkton N York
20 D5 Nunney Somset
20 D6 Nunney Catch Somset
45 R6 Nunnington Herefs
98 D5 Nunnington N York
93 N9 Nunsthorpe NE Lin
98 C10 Nunthorpe C York
104 F8 Nunthorpe Middsb
104 F8 Nunthorpe Village Middsb
21 N9 Nunton Wilts
97 M6 Nunwick N York
112 C6 Nunwick Nthumb
32 B5 Nupdown S Glos
49 N11 Nup End Bucks
32 E3 Nupend Gloucs
35 N10 Nuptown Br For
22 C11 Nursling Hants
23 L10 Nursted Hants
21 K2 Nursteed Wilts
58 B5 Nurton Staffs
15 L5 Nutbourne W Susx
24 C7 Nutbourne W Susx
36 H10 Nutfield Surrey
72 E2 Nuthall Notts
51 K4 Nuthampstead Herts
24 E5 Nuthurst W Susx
25 K5 Nutley E Susx
22 H6 Nutley Hants
89 M7 Nuttall Bury
91 Q10 Nutwell Donc
167 Q4 Nybster Highld
15 N7 Nyetimber W Susx
23 M10 Nyewood W Susx
17 N10 Nymet Rowland Devon
8 H4 Nymet Tracey Devon
32 F4 Nympsfield Gloucs
18 F10 Nynehead Somset
19 M8 Nythe Somset
15 P5 Nyton W Susx

O

72 G10 Oadby Leics
38 E9 Oad Street Kent
46 F2 Oakall Green Worcs
71 J6 Oakamoor Staffs
127 K4 Oakbank W Loth
8 D5 Oak Cross Devon
30 G5 Oakdale Caerph
18 G9 Oake Somset
58 C4 Oaken Staffs
95 L11 Oakenclough Lancs
57 N2 Oakengates Wrekin
81 K10 Oakenholt Flints
103 N3 Oakenshaw Dur
90 F5 Oakenshaw Kirk
84 E10 Oakerthorpe Derbys
43 J3 Oakford Cerdgn
18 B10 Oakford Devon
18 B10 Oakfordbridge Devon
83 K11 Oakgrove Ches E
73 M9 Oakham Rutlnd
70 D4 Oakhanger Ches E
23 L7 Oakhanger Hants
20 B5 Oakhill Somset
37 N10 Oakhurst Kent
62 F8 Oakington Cambs
44 E4 Oaklands Powys
46 E11 Oakle Street Gloucs
61 M10 Oakley Bed
34 H2 Oakley Bucks
134 C10 Oakley Fife
22 G4 Oakley Hants
35 L4 Oakley Oxon
12 H5 Oakley Poole
64 H6 Oakley Suffk
35 P9 Oakley Green W & M
55 M7 Oakley Park Powys
32 H4 Oakridge Gloucs
89 K4 Oaks Lancs
56 G4 Oaks Shrops
33 J6 Oaksey Wilts
71 M8 Oaks Green Derbys
111 K5 Oakshaw Ford Cumb
23 K9 Oakshott Hants
59 M2 Oakthorpe Leics
104 C8 Oak Tree Darltn
72 B3 Oakwood C Derb
112 D7 Oakwood Nthumb
90 C3 Oakworth C Brad
38 H9 Oare Kent
17 P2 Oare Somset
21 N2 Oare Wilts
73 Q3 Oasby Lincs
19 L9 Oath Somset
142 H6 Oathlaw Angus
36 C7 Oatlands Park Surrey
130 H2 Oban Ag & B
138 G10 Oban Airport Ag & B
56 E9 Obley Shrops
141 P10 Obney P & K
20 C11 Oborne Dorset
74 A8 Obthorpe Lincs
64 H7 Occold Suffk
167 N9 Occumster Highld
115 K3 Ochiltree E Ayrs
72 C3 Ockbrook Derbys
58 E6 Ocker Hill Sandw
46 E2 Ockeridge Worcs
36 C9 Ockham Surrey
137 P1 Ockle Highld
24 D2 Ockley Surrey
46 A5 Ocle Pychard Herefs
99 L7 Octon E R Yk
19 P11 Odcombe Somset
20 D2 Odd Down BaNES
46 H3 Oddingley Worcs
47 P9 Oddington Gloucs
48 G11 Oddington Oxon
61 L9 Odell Bed
8 C4 Odham Devon
23 K4 Odiham Hants
90 F5 Odsal C Brad
50 G3 Odsey Cambs
21 M9 Odstock Wilts
72 B9 Odstone Leics
59 N11 Offchurch Warwks
47 L5 Offenham Worcs
83 K7 Offerton Stockp
113 M9 Offerton Sundld
25 K8 Offham E Susx
37 Q9 Offham Kent
24 B9 Offham W Susx
70 D9 Offleymarsh Staffs
62 B7 Offord Cluny Cambs
62 B7 Offord D'Arcy Cambs
53 J2 Offton Suffk
10 D5 Offwell Devon
33 N10 Ogbourne Maizey Wilts
33 N10 Ogbourne St Andrew Wilts
33 P10 Ogbourne St George Wilts
90 D4 Ogden Calder
112 H5 Ogle Nthumb
81 N8 Oglet Lpool
29 N9 Ogmore V Glam
29 N9 Ogmore-by-Sea V Glam
29 P6 Ogmore Vale Brdgnd
79 L11 Ogwen Bank Gwynd
12 D2 Okeford Fitzpaine Dorset
8 E5 Okehampton Devon
84 C8 Oker Side Derbys
24 D3 Okewood Hill Surrey
9 L9 Olchard Devon
60 G6 Old Nhants
151 N6 Old Aberdeen C Aber
22 G8 Old Alresford Hants
164 C10 Oldany Highld
115 Q8 Old Auchenbrack D & G
72 F2 Old Basford C Nott
23 J4 Old Basing Hants
76 D8 Old Beetley Norfk
58 H11 Oldberrow Warwks
119 L6 Old Bewick Nthumb
87 L7 Old Bolingbroke Lincs
90 G2 Old Bramhope Leeds
84 D6 Old Brampton Derbys
108 G7 Old Bridge of Urr D & G
64 F3 Old Buckenham Norfk
22 E3 Old Burghclere Hants
37 N9 Oldbury Kent
58 E7 Oldbury Sandw
57 N6 Oldbury Shrops
59 M6 Oldbury Warwks
32 B6 Oldbury Naite S Glos
32 B6 Oldbury-on-Severn S Glos
32 F7 Oldbury on the Hill Gloucs
98 B3 Old Byland N York
91 Q10 Old Cantley Donc
104 B3 Old Cassop Dur
29 P9 Old Castle Brdgnd
45 L10 Oldcastle Mons
69 N5 Oldcastle Heath Ches W
77 J9 Old Catton Norfk
56 D6 Old Churchstoke Powys
93 N9 Old Clee NE Lin
18 D6 Old Cleeve Somset
85 K8 Old Clipstone Notts
80 B9 Old Colwyn Conwy
85 J3 Oldcotes Notts
114 D8 Old Dailly S Ayrs
72 H6 Old Dalby Leics
83 P9 Old Dam Derbys
159 N8 Old Deer Abers
19 P5 Old Ditch Somset
91 N11 Old Edlington Donc
103 P5 Old Eldon Dur
93 L3 Old Ellerby E R Yk
53 P4 Old Felixstowe Suffk
90 C3 Oldfield C Brad
46 F2 Oldfield Worcs
74 C11 Old Fletton C Pete
20 E4 Oldford Somset
45 R11 Old Forge Herefs
45 P10 Old Furnace Herefs
83 M6 Old Glossop Derbys
92 B5 Old Goole E R Yk
2 b1 Old Grimsby IoS
51 J6 Old Hall Green Herts
64 B10 Oldhall Green Suffk
77 L5 Old Hall Street Norfk
83 K4 Oldham Oldham
129 J5 Oldhamstocks E Loth
51 L8 Old Harlow Essex
52 H7 Old Heath Essex
75 N2 Old Hunstanton Norfk
62 D5 Old Hurst Cambs
95 M3 Old Hutton Cumb
3 L5 Old Kea Cnwll
125 M3 Old Kilpatrick W Duns
50 F6 Old Knebworth Herts
77 J10 Old Lakenham Norfk
32 C10 Oldland S Glos
89 L3 Old Langho Lancs
80 f5 Old Laxey IoM
87 M10 Old Leake Lincs
98 F6 Old Malton N York
151 L2 Oldmeldrum Abers
5 P7 Oldmill Cnwll
59 L11 Old Milverton Warwks
19 K3 Oldmixon N Som
64 F9 Old Newton Suffk
104 B3 Old Quarrington Dur
72 F2 Old Radford C Nott
45 K3 Old Radnor Powys
150 H2 Old Rayne Abers
26 H7 Old Romney Kent
24 F9 Old Shoreham W Susx
164 F5 Oldshoremore Highld
37 P10 Old Soar Kent
32 E8 Old Sodbury S Glos
73 P4 Old Somerby Lincs
98 A5 Oldstead N York
49 L6 Old Stratford Nhants
141 K4 Old Struan P & K
119 N10 Old Swarland Nthumb
58 D8 Old Swinford Dudley
102 B9 Old Tebay Cumb
97 P4 Old Thirsk N York
90 C5 Old Town Calder
95 M4 Old Town Cumb
101 N2 Old Town Cumb
25 N11 Old Town E Susx
2 c2 Old Town IoS
82 H5 Old Trafford Traffd
84 E7 Old Tupton Derbys
111 J8 Oldwall Cumb
28 E6 Oldwalls Swans
50 D2 Old Warden C Beds
17 R7 Oldways End Somset
61 N5 Old Weston Cambs
167 Q7 Old Wick Highld
35 Q10 Old Windsor W & M
39 J11 Old Wives Lees Kent
36 B9 Old Woking Surrey
49 M6 Old Wolverton M Keyn
86 H7 Old Woodhall Lincs
69 N10 Old Woods Shrops
167 J6 Olgrinmore Highld
71 L11 Olive Green Staffs
22 E9 Oliver's Battery Hants
169 q5 Ollaberry Shet
153 J10 Ollach Highld
82 G9 Ollerton Ches E
85 L7 Ollerton Notts
70 A9 Ollerton Shrops
43 M3 Olmarch Cerdgn
51 P2 Olmstead Green Cambs
49 N4 Olney M Keyn
167 L3 Olrig House Highld
58 H8 Olton Solhll
32 B7 Olveston S Glos
46 F2 Ombersley Worcs
85 L7 Ompton Notts
111 P7 Once Brewed Nthumb
80 e6 Onchan IoM
71 J3 Onecote Staffs
64 E10 Onehouse Suffk
31 M2 Onen Mons
56 F11 Ongar Street Herefs
56 H9 Onibury Shrops
139 J5 Onich Highld
29 M2 Onllwyn Neath
70 D6 Onneley Staffs
51 Q7 Onslow Green Essex
23 Q5 Onslow Village Surrey
82 C10 Onston Ches W
84 E11 Openwoodgate Derbys
153 N3 Opinan Highld
157 Q6 Orbliston Moray
152 D9 Orbost Highld
87 N7 Orby Lincs
18 H10 Orchard Portman Somset
21 L5 Orcheston Wilts
45 P9 Orcop Herefs
45 P9 Orcop Hill Herefs
158 F6 Ord Abers
150 H5 Ordhead Abers
150 D7 Ordie Abers
157 Q6 Ordiequish Moray
112 D9 Ordley Nthumb
85 M5 Ordsall Notts
26 D9 Ore E Susx
56 H11 Oreleton Common Herefs
57 M8 Oreton Shrops
65 N11 Orford Suffk
82 D6 Orford Warrtn
12 F6 Organford Dorset
71 L11 Orgreave Staffs
26 H5 Orlestone Kent
56 H11 Orleton Herefs
57 N11 Orleton Worcs
61 J6 Orlingbury Nhants
101 J5 Ormathwaite Cumb
104 F7 Ormesby R & Cl
77 P9 Ormesby St Margaret Norfk
77 P9 Ormesby St Michael Norfk
160 D8 Ormiscaig Highld
128 C6 Ormiston E Loth
137 M3 Ormsaigmore Highld
123 M5 Ormsary Ag & B
88 E9 Ormskirk Lancs
113 J11 Ornsby Hill Dur
136 b4 Oronsay Ag & B
169 c6 Orphir Ork
37 L7 Orpington Gt Lon
81 L5 Orrell Sefton
82 B4 Orrell Wigan
88 G9 Orrell Post Wigan
80 d3 Orrisdale IoM
108 G11 Orroland D & G
37 P4 Orsett Thurr
70 E11 Orslow Staffs
73 K2 Orston Notts
101 J4 Orthwaite Cumb
95 L10 Ortner Lancs
102 B9 Orton Cumb
60 H5 Orton Nhants
58 C5 Orton Staffs
74 C11 Orton Longueville C Pete
59 M4 Orton-on-the-Hill Leics
110 F10 Orton Rigg Cumb
74 C11 Orton Waterville C Pete
62 E10 Orwell Cambs
89 J4 Osbaldeston Lancs
89 J4 Osbaldeston Green Lancs
98 C10 Osbaldwick C York
72 C10 Osbaston Leics
69 K10 Osbaston Shrops
14 F8 Osborne IoW
14 F8 Osborne House IoW
73 R3 Osbournby Lincs
81 Q11 Oscroft Ches W
152 E9 Ose Highld
72 C7 Osgathorpe Leics
86 E2 Osgodby Lincs
91 Q4 Osgodby N York
99 M4 Osgodby N York
153 J10 Oskaig Highld
137 M7 Oskamull Ag & B
71 M6 Osmaston Derbys
11 Q8 Osmington Dorset
12 B8 Osmington Mills Dorset
91 J4 Osmondthorpe Leeds
104 E11 Osmotherley N York
34 E3 Osney Oxon
38 H9 Ospringe Kent
90 H6 Ossett Wakefd
85 N8 Ossington Notts
38 F2 Ostend Essex
36 E5 Osterley Gt Lon
98 C5 Oswaldkirk N York
89 L5 Oswaldtwistle Lancs
69 J9 Oswestry Shrops
37 M9 Otford Kent
38 C11 Otham Kent
38 D11 Otham Hole Kent
19 L8 Othery Somset
97 K11 Otley Leeds
65 J10 Otley Suffk
65 J10 Otley Green Suffk
22 E10 Otterbourne Hants
96 C9 Otterburn N York
112 C2 Otterburn Nthumb
131 J11 Otter Ferry Ag & B
5 K3 Otterham Cnwll
18 H6 Otterhampton Somset
38 D8 Otterham Quay Kent
5 K4 Otterham Station Cnwll
168 e10 Otternish W Isls
36 B8 Ottershaw Surrey
169 s5 Otterswick Shet
10 B7 Otterton Devon
14 D6 Otterwood Hants
10 C5 Ottery St Mary Devon
27 L3 Ottinge Kent
93 N6 Ottringham E R Yk
110 E9 Oughterby Cumb
96 C4 Oughtershaw N York
100 F2 Oughterside Cumb
84 D2 Oughtibridge Sheff
82 E7 Oughtrington Warrtn
98 A6 Oulston N York
110 D10 Oulton Cumb
91 K5 Oulton Leeds
76 G6 Oulton Norfk
70 D10 Oulton Staffs
70 G7 Oulton Staffs
65 Q3 Oulton Suffk
65 Q3 Oulton Broad Suffk
76 H6 Oulton Street Norfk
61 M3 Oundle Nhants
58 C6 Ounsdale Staffs
102 B4 Ousby Cumb
63 M9 Ousden Suffk
92 D6 Ousefleet E R Yk
113 L10 Ouston Dur
119 M4 Outchester Nthumb
39 M11 Out Elmstead Kent
101 L11 Outgate Cumb
102 E10 Outhgill Cumb
58 H11 Outhill Warwks
70 D8 Outlands Staffs
90 D7 Outlane Kirk
93 Q6 Out Newton E R Yk
88 E2 Out Rawcliffe Lancs
75 K10 Outwell Norfk
21 M11 Outwick Hants
36 H11 Outwood Surrey
91 J6 Outwood Wakefd
89 M9 Outwood Gate Bury
72 C7 Outwoods Leics
70 D11 Outwoods Staffs
91 J5 Ouzlewell Green Leeds
90 D5 Ovenden Calder
62 E6 Over Cambs
82 D11 Over Ches W
46 F11 Over Gloucs
31 Q8 Over S Glos
71 P7 Over Burrows Derbys
47 J7 Overbury Worcs
11 P8 Overcombe Dorset
19 Q11 Over Compton Dorset
89 K9 Overdale Crematorium Bolton
61 N2 Over End Cambs
84 D6 Overgreen Derbys
59 J6 Over Green Warwks
84 B7 Over Haddon Derbys
95 L7 Over Kellet Lancs
48 D10 Over Kiddington Oxon
19 N7 Overleigh Somset
71 M11 Overley Staffs
31 P2 Over Monnow Mons
48 B9 Over Norton Oxon
82 G10 Over Peover Ches E
81 M9 Overpool Ches W
161 Q2 Overscaig Hotel Highld
71 P11 Overseal Derbys
97 P2 Over Silton N York
39 J10 Oversland Kent
47 L3 Oversley Green Warwks
60 G7 Overstone Nhants
18 G7 Over Stowey Somset
77 J3 Overstrand Norfk
19 M11 Over Stratton Somset
21 L7 Overstreet Wilts
82 F9 Over Tabley Ches E
48 E6 Overthorpe Nhants
151 M5 Overton C Aber
81 Q9 Overton Ches W
22 F5 Overton Hants
95 J9 Overton Lancs
98 B9 Overton N York
57 J10 Overton Shrops
28 E7 Overton Swans
90 H7 Overton Wakefd
69 L6 Overton Wrexhm
69 L6 Overton Bridge Wrexhm
70 E2 Overton Green Ches E
95 N5 Overtown Lancs
126 E7 Overtown N Lans
33 N9 Overtown Swindn
91 K7 Overtown Wakefd
21 Q7 Over Wallop Hants
59 L6 Over Whitacre Warwks
84 G6 Over Woodhouse Derbys
48 D9 Over Worton Oxon
34 G6 Overy Oxon
49 L10 Oving Bucks
15 P6 Oving W Susx
25 J10 Ovingdean Br & H
112 G8 Ovingham Nthumb
103 M8 Ovington Dur
52 C3 Ovington Essex
22 G8 Ovington Hants
76 C11 Ovington Norfk
112 G8 Ovington Nthumb
14 E6 Ower Hants
22 B11 Ower Hants
12 C7 Owermoigne Dorset
56 E6 Owlbury Shrops
84 D3 Owlerton Sheff
32 E5 Owlpen Gloucs
65 K8 Owl's Green Suffk
23 M2 Owlsmoor Br For
35 L3 Owlswick Bucks
86 D3 Owmby Lincs
93 J10 Owmby Lincs
22 F10 Owslebury Hants
91 P8 Owston Donc
73 K9 Owston Leics
92 D10 Owston Ferry N Linc
93 N4 Owstwick E R Yk
93 P5 Owthorne E R Yk
72 H4 Owthorpe Notts
104 E5 Owton Manor Hartpl
75 P10 Oxborough Norfk
11 K5 Oxbridge Dorset
87 K5 Oxcombe Lincs
84 G6 Oxcroft Derbys

51 Q5 **Oxen End** Essex
95 L3 **Oxenholme** Cumb
90 C4 **Oxenhope** C Brad
94 G3 **Oxen Park** Cumb
19 M6 **Oxenpill** Somset
47 J8 **Oxenton** Gloucs
22 B3 **Oxenwood** Wilts
34 F3 **Oxford** Oxon
48 E11 *Oxford Airport* Oxon
34 G4 **Oxford Crematorium** Oxon
34 H4 **Oxford Services** Oxon
50 D11 **Oxhey** Herts
113 J10 **Oxhill** Dur
48 B5 **Oxhill** Warwks
58 D4 **Oxley** Wolves
52 F9 **Oxley Green** Essex
25 Q6 **Oxley's Green** E Susx
62 G3 **Oxlode** Cambs
118 C7 **Oxnam** Border
77 J7 **Oxnead** Norfk
36 D8 **Oxshott** Surrey
36 D8 **Oxshott Heath** Surrey
90 H10 **Oxspring** Barns
37 J10 **Oxted** Surrey
128 D9 **Oxton** Border
91 N2 **Oxton** N York
85 K10 **Oxton** Notts
28 E7 **Oxwich** Swans
28 E7 **Oxwich Green** Swans
76 C6 **Oxwick** Norfk
161 P6 **Oykel Bridge Hotel** Highld
150 H2 **Oyne** Abers
28 H7 **Oystermouth** Swans
32 E6 **Ozleworth** Gloucs

P

168 k4 **Pabail** W Isls
11 Q2 **Packers Hill** Dorset
72 B8 **Packington** Leics
70 F2 **Packmoor** C Stke
59 L11 **Packmores** Warwks
142 G7 **Padanaram** Angus
49 K8 **Padbury** Bucks
36 G4 **Paddington** Gt Lon
82 D7 **Paddington** Warrtn
27 L4 **Paddlesworth** Kent
37 Q8 **Paddlesworth** Kent
25 Q2 **Paddock Wood** Kent
69 P8 **Paddolgreen** Shrops
83 M5 **Padfield** Derbys
82 D7 **Padgate** Warrtn
51 P11 **Padhams Green** Essex
89 M4 **Padiham** Lancs
97 J9 **Padside** N York
4 E6 **Padstow** Cnwll
34 H11 **Padworth** W Berk
103 P3 **Page Bank** Dur
15 N7 **Pagham** W Susx
38 F3 **Paglesham** Essex
7 M6 **Paignton** Torbay
59 Q8 **Pailton** Warwks
25 P6 **Paine's Cross** E Susx
71 J8 **Painleyhill** Staffs
44 H5 **Painscastle** Powys
112 G8 **Painshawfield** Nthumb
98 G9 **Painsthorpe** E R Yk
32 G3 **Painswick** Gloucs
38 G10 **Painter's Forstal** Kent
125 M5 **Paisley** Rens
125 M5 **Paisley Woodside Crematorium** Rens
65 Q3 **Pakefield** Suffk
64 C8 **Pakenham** Suffk
68 C7 **Pale** Gwynd
51 Q2 **Pale Green** Essex
21 Q6 **Palestine** Hants
35 N9 **Paley Street** W & M
58 F5 **Palfrey** Wsall
64 G6 **Palgrave** Suffk
12 C6 **Pallington** Dorset
5 K6 **Palmersbridge** Cnwll
36 H2 **Palmers Green** Gt Lon
115 K4 **Palmerston** E Ayrs
30 F11 **Palmerstown** V Glam
108 H9 **Palnackie** D & G
107 N5 **Palnure** D & G
84 G7 **Palterton** Derbys
22 H3 **Pamber End** Hants
22 H3 **Pamber Green** Hants
22 H2 **Pamber Heath** Hants
46 H2 **Pamington** Gloucs
12 G4 **Pamphill** Dorset
62 G11 **Pampisford** Cambs
19 N5 **Panborough** Somset
143 K10 **Panbride** Angus
16 D10 **Pancrasweek** Devon
30 D11 **Pancross** V Glam
30 G7 **Pandy** Caerph
54 E4 **Pandy** Gwynd
68 A9 **Pandy** Gwynd
45 L10 **Pandy** Mons
55 L4 **Pandy** Powys
68 G7 **Pandy** Wrexhm
68 E4 **Pandy'r Capel** Denbgs
67 R2 **Pandy Tudur** Conwy
52 B6 **Panfield** Essex
34 H9 **Pangbourne** W Berk
24 D4 **Pangdean** W Susx
46 B5 **Panks Bridge** Herefs
97 M10 **Pannal** N York
97 L10 **Pannal Ash** N York
150 C8 **Pannanich Wells Hotel** Abers
69 J10 **Pant** Shrops
80 H9 **Pantasaph** Flints
40 H4 **Panteg** Pembks
5 K8 **Pantersbridge** Cnwll
29 P8 **Pant-ffrwyth** Brdgnd
66 H5 **Pant Glas** Gwynd
54 H5 **Pantglas** Powys
43 L9 **Pant-Gwyn** Carmth
29 J4 **Pant-lasau** Swans
55 J8 **Pant Mawr** Powys
86 G5 **Panton** Lincs
68 D2 **Pant-pastynog** Denbgs
54 G4 **Pantperthog** Gwynd
55 M10 **Pant-y-dwr** Powys
56 B4 **Pant-y-ffridd** Powys
28 H2 **Pantyffynnon** Carmth
31 J5 **Pantygaseg** Torfn
29 P6 **Pant-y-gog** Brdgnd
41 M5 **Pantymwyn** Carmth
68 G2 **Pant-y-mwyn** Flints
77 M9 **Panxworth** Norfk
169 d1 *Papa Westray Airport* Ork

100 F4 **Papcastle** Cumb
167 Q6 **Papigoe** Highld
128 F5 **Papple** E Loth
84 H10 **Papplewick** Notts
62 C8 **Papworth Everard** Cambs
62 C8 **Papworth St Agnes** Cambs
3 R3 **Par** Cnwll
39 N9 **Paramour Street** Kent
88 F8 **Parbold** Lancs
19 Q7 **Parbrook** Somset
24 C5 **Parbrook** W Susx
68 A8 **Parc** Gwynd
41 M8 **Parc Gwyn Crematorium** Pembks
42 D4 **Parcllyn** Cerdgn
31 M6 **Parc Seymour** Newpt
100 E6 **Pardshaw** Cumb
65 L9 **Parham** Suffk
109 K2 **Park** D & G
111 N8 **Park** Nthumb
2 H5 **Park Bottom** Cnwll
83 K4 **Park Bridge** Tamesd
25 M3 **Park Corner** E Susx
35 J7 **Park Corner** Oxon
35 N8 **Park Corner** W & M
88 D5 **Park Crematorium** Lancs
49 Q4 **Park End** Bed
32 B3 **Parkend** Gloucs
112 C5 **Park End** Nthumb
37 P11 **Parkers Green** Kent
53 M5 **Parkeston** Essex
53 M5 **Parkeston Quay** Essex
26 H4 **Park Farm** Kent
81 K9 **Parkgate** Ches W
110 D11 **Parkgate** Cumb
109 M3 **Parkgate** D & G
26 B9 **Parkgate** E Susx
51 Q5 **Parkgate** Essex
14 F5 **Park Gate** Hants
26 E5 **Parkgate** Kent
37 M8 **Parkgate** Kent
90 F2 **Park Gate** Leeds
24 F2 **Parkgate** Surrey
58 D10 **Park Gate** Worcs
51 L5 **Park Green** Essex
64 G9 **Park Green** Suffk
143 L8 **Parkgrove Crematorium** Angus
125 M3 **Parkhall** W Duns
16 F7 **Parkham** Devon
16 F7 **Parkham Ash** Devon
84 E10 **Park Head** Derbys
31 Q5 **Park Hill** Gloucs
31 P4 **Parkhouse** Mons
28 F7 **Parkmill** Swans
36 E4 **Park Royal** Gt Lon
113 P11 **Parkside** Dur
126 E6 **Parkside** N Lans
69 L3 **Parkside** Wrexhm
12 H6 **Parkstone** Poole
50 D10 **Park Street** Herts
24 D4 **Park Street** W Susx
90 E6 **Park Wood Crematorium** Calder
13 K5 **Parley Green** Dorset
35 L7 **Parmoor** Bucks
51 K9 **Parndon** Essex
51 K9 **Parndon Wood Crematorium** Essex
17 M2 **Parracombe** Devon
41 L3 **Parrog** Pembks
100 F3 **Parsonby** Cumb
84 D2 **Parson Cross** Sheff
74 G9 **Parson Drove** Cambs
52 H6 **Parson's Heath** Essex
71 P9 **Parson's Hill** Derbys
125 N4 **Partick** C Glas
82 F6 **Partington** Traffd
87 M7 **Partney** Lincs
100 C6 **Parton** Cumb
24 E7 **Partridge Green** W Susx
45 K10 **Partrishow** Powys
71 M4 **Parwich** Derbys
51 N10 **Paslow Wood Common** Essex
49 L7 **Passenham** Nhants
23 M8 **Passfield** Hants
51 M11 **Passingford Bridge** Essex
74 C10 **Paston** C Pete
77 L5 **Paston** Norfk
70 H10 **Pasturefields** Staffs
8 C5 **Patchacott** Devon
24 H9 **Patcham** Br & H
50 D11 **Patchetts Green** Herts
24 C9 **Patching** W Susx
17 L3 **Patchole** Devon
32 B8 **Patchway** S Glos
97 J7 **Pateley Bridge** N York
52 F8 **Paternoster Heath** Essex
19 L8 **Pathe** Somset
134 H9 **Pathhead** Fife
128 B7 **Pathhead** Mdloth
47 N3 **Pathlow** Warwks
134 D5 **Path of Condie** P & K
51 K5 **Patmore Heath** Herts
114 H5 **Patna** E Ayrs
21 L3 **Patney** Wilts
80 b5 **Patrick** IoM
97 K2 **Patrick Brompton** N York
82 G5 **Patricroft** Salfd
93 P6 **Patrington** E R Yk
93 P6 **Patrington Haven** E R Yk
39 L10 **Patrixbourne** Kent
101 L7 **Patterdale** Cumb
57 Q5 **Pattingham** Staffs
49 J4 **Pattishall** Nhants
52 D7 **Pattiswick Green** Essex
57 K5 **Patton** Shrops
2 D8 **Paul** Cnwll
49 K5 **Paulerspury** Nhants
93 L5 **Paull** E R Yk
21 M8 **Paul's Dene** Wilts
20 C3 **Paulton** BaNES
46 C4 **Paunton** Herefs
119 M11 **Pauperhaugh** Nthumb
70 D11 **Pave Lane** Wrekin
19 J6 **Pavenham** Bed
3 K7 **Pawlett** Somset
82 C7 **Pawston** Nthumb
118 G4 **Paxford** Gloucs
47 N7 **Paxton** Border
38 F11 **Payden Street** Kent
10 B4 **Paythembury** Devon
2 H5 **Paynter's Lane End** Cnwll
89 B10 **Paythorne** Lancs
56 G10 **Paytoe** Herefs
25 K10 **Peacehaven** E Susx
83 N9 **Peak Dale** Derbys

83 Q6 **Peak District National Park**
83 P9 **Peak Forest** Derbys
74 E7 **Peak Hill** Lincs
74 C9 **Peakirk** C Pete
25 Q2 **Pearson's Green** Kent
64 A8 **Peartree Green** Herefs
20 D3 **Peasedown St John** BaNES
84 F11 **Peasehill** Derbys
76 F8 **Peaseland Green** Norfk
34 E9 **Peasemore** W Berk
65 M8 **Peasenhall** Suffk
24 G4 **Pease Pottage** W Susx
24 C2 **Peaslake** Surrey
81 Q6 **Peasley Cross** St Hel
26 E7 **Peasmarsh** E Susx
10 G2 **Peasmarsh** Somset
23 Q5 **Peasmarsh** Surrey
159 M4 **Peathill** Abers
135 M6 **Peat Inn** Fife
60 C7 **Peatling Magna** Leics
60 C3 **Peatling Parva** Leics
57 J7 **Peaton** Shrops
52 E5 **Pebmarsh** Essex
47 M5 **Pebworth** Worcs
90 B5 **Pecket Well** Calder
69 P3 **Peckforton** Ches E
36 H5 **Peckham** Gt Lon
72 D10 **Peckleton** Leics
68 F10 **Pedairffordd** Powys
27 K4 **Pedlinge** Kent
58 D8 **Pedmore** Dudley
19 M7 **Pedwell** Somset
117 K2 **Peebles** Border
80 b5 **Peel** IoM
88 D4 **Peel** Lancs
14 G6 **Peel Common** Hants
27 L4 **Peene** Kent
26 E6 **Peening Quarter** Kent
72 C7 **Peggs Green** Leics
50 D4 **Pegsdon** C Beds
113 K3 **Pegswood** Nthumb
39 Q9 **Pegwell** Kent
153 J11 **Peinchorran** Highld
152 G6 **Peinlich** Highld
40 H7 **Pelcomb** Pembks
40 H7 **Pelcomb Bridge** Pembks
40 H7 **Pelcomb Cross** Pembks
52 G8 **Peldon** Essex
25 P4 **Pell Green** E Susx
58 F4 **Pelsall** Wsall
58 F4 **Pelsall Wood** Wsall
113 L10 **Pelton** Dur
113 L10 **Pelton Fell** Dur
109 P11 **Pelutho** Cumb
5 L10 **Pelynt** Cnwll
28 H4 **Pemberton** Carmth
82 C4 **Pemberton** Wigan
26 E2 **Pembles Cross** Kent
28 D4 **Pembrey** Carmth
45 M3 **Pembridge** Herefs
41 J10 **Pembroke** Pembks
41 J10 **Pembroke Dock** Pembks
40 F6 **Pembrokeshire Coast National Park** Pembks
25 P2 **Pembury** Kent
45 R9 **Pen-allt** Herefs
31 P2 **Penallt** Mons
41 M11 **Penally** Pembks
3 P5 **Penare** Cnwll
30 G10 **Penarth** V Glam
41 M7 **Penblewin** Pembks
54 F8 **Pen-bont Rhydybeddau** Cerdgn
42 E4 **Penbryn** Cerdgn
42 H7 **Pencader** Carmth
66 G6 **Pencaenewydd** Gwynd
128 C6 **Pencaitland** E Loth
78 F10 **Pencarnisiog** IoA
43 K5 **Pencarreg** Carmth
5 J5 **Pencarrow** Cnwll
44 F9 **Pencelli** Powys
28 F5 **Penclawdd** Swans
30 C8 **Pencoed** Brdgnd
46 A4 **Pencombe** Herefs
45 Q9 **Pencoyd** Herefs
45 R10 **Pencraig** Herefs
68 D9 **Pencraig** Powys
2 B7 **Pendeen** Cnwll
29 P3 **Penderyn** Rhondd
41 P9 **Pendine** Carmth
82 G4 **Pendlebury** Salfd
89 M3 **Pendleton** Lancs
46 E8 **Pendock** Worcs
4 G6 **Pendoggett** Cnwll
11 L2 **Pendomer** Somset
30 E9 **Pendoylan** V Glam
29 P8 **Pendre** Brdgnd
54 H4 **Penegoes** Powys
3 L5 **Penelewey** Cnwll
41 L6 **Pen-ffordd** Pembks
30 G5 **Pengam** Caerph
30 H9 **Pengam** Cardif
37 J6 **Penge** Gt Lon
4 H5 **Pengelly** Cnwll
78 H6 **Pengorffwysfa** IoA
5 M8 **Pengover Green** Cnwll
80 E9 **Pengwern** Denbgs
2 H10 **Penhale** Cnwll
4 E10 **Penhale** Cnwll
4 H9 **Penhale** Cnwll
5 Q11 **Penhale** Cnwll
3 K3 **Penhallow** Cnwll
3 J6 **Penhalurick** Cnwll
3 J6 **Penhalvean** Cnwll
33 N7 **Penhill** Swindn
31 M6 **Penhow** Newpt
25 Q7 **Penhurst** E Susx
54 E3 **Peniarth** Gwynd
127 N6 **Penicuik** Mdloth
42 H10 **Peniel** Carmth
68 D2 **Peniel** Denbgs
152 H9 **Penifiler** Highld
120 E7 **Peninver** Ag & B
67 K2 **Penisarwaun** Gwynd
90 G10 **Penistone** Barns
3 K7 **Penjerrick** Cnwll
82 C7 **Penketh** Warrtn
114 D8 **Penkill** S Ayrs
58 D2 **Penkridge** Staffs
5 L2 **Penlean** Cnwll
20 G4 **Penleigh** Wilts
69 M6 **Penley** Wrexhm
28 H5 **Penllergaer** Swans
67 J10 **Penllyn** IoA
30 C9 **Penllyn** V Glam
78 G11 **Pen-lon** IoA
67 P4 **Penmachno** Conwy

30 G5 **Penmaen** Caerph
28 F7 **Penmaen** Swans
79 N9 **Penmaenan** Conwy
79 N9 **Penmaenmawr** Conwy
67 M11 **Penmaenpool** Gwynd
30 E11 **Penmark** V Glam
79 L8 **Penmon** IoA
67 J6 **Penmorfa** Gwynd
3 L4 **Penmount Crematorium** Cnwll
79 J10 **Penmynydd** IoA
35 P6 **Penn** Bucks
58 C5 **Penn** Wolves
54 F4 **Pennal** Gwynd
159 K4 **Pennan** Abers
43 K2 **Pennant** Cerdgn
68 D8 **Pennant** Denbgs
55 K5 **Pennant** Powys
68 D9 **Pennant-Melangell** Powys
28 G7 **Pennard** Swans
56 F5 **Pennerley** Shrops
5 L4 **Pennicott** Devon
90 B3 **Pennines**
94 F5 **Pennington** Cumb
13 P5 **Pennington** Hants
89 J9 **Pennington Green** Wigan
44 G9 **Pennorth** Powys
35 P5 **Penn Street** Bucks
32 D10 **Pennsylvania** S Glos
94 G4 **Penny Bridge** Cumb
137 N10 **Pennycross** Ag & B
77 L7 **Pennygate** Norfk
137 N10 **Pennyghael** Ag & B
114 E5 **Pennyglen** S Ayrs
84 H5 **Penny Green** Derbys
74 G5 **Penny Hill** Lincs
9 L2 **Pennymoor** Devon
42 D5 **Penparc** Cerdgn
54 D8 **Penparcau** Cerdgn
30 F5 **Penpedairheol** Caerph
31 K4 **Penpedairheol** Mons
31 K4 **Penperlleni** Mons
4 H4 **Penpethy** Cnwll
4 H10 **Penpillick** Cnwll
5 L6 **Penpol** Cnwll
5 J11 **Penpoll** Cnwll
2 G6 **Penponds** Cnwll
4 H7 **Penpont** Cnwll
108 H2 **Penpont** D & G
44 D9 **Penpont** Powys
6 G8 **Penquit** Devon
5 N6 **Penrest** Cnwll
41 Q3 **Penrherber** Carmth
41 P2 **Pen-rhiw** Pembks
30 E5 **Penrhiwceiber** Rhondd
29 K2 **Pen Rhiwfawr** Neath
42 G6 **Penrhiw-llan** Cerdgn
42 F5 **Penrhiw-pal** Cerdgn
66 E8 **Penrhos** Gwynd
78 D8 **Penrhos** IoA
31 M2 **Penrhos** Mons
29 M2 **Penrhos** Powys
79 K10 **Penrhos garnedd** Gwynd
79 Q8 **Penrhyn Bay** Conwy
79 L10 **Penrhyn Castle** Gwynd
54 E8 **Penrhyncoch** Cerdgn
67 L7 **Penrhyndeudraeth** Gwynd
79 Q8 **Penrhyn-side** Conwy
28 E7 **Penrice** Swans
120 G3 **Penrioch** N Ayrs
101 P4 **Penrith** Cumb
4 D7 **Penrose** Cnwll
101 M5 **Penruddock** Cumb
3 K7 **Penryn** Cnwll
80 D7 **Pensarn** Conwy
57 N11 **Pensax** Worcs
81 K8 **Pensby** Wirral
20 E8 **Penselwood** Somset
20 B2 **Pensford** BaNES
46 H6 **Pensham** Worcs
113 M10 **Penshaw** Sundld
25 M2 **Penshurst** Kent
37 M11 **Penshurst Station** Kent
5 M7 **Pensilva** Cnwll
58 D7 **Pensnett** Dudley
9 J4 **Penstone** Devon
55 P6 **Penstrowed** Powys
3 Q4 **Pentewan** Cnwll
79 K11 **Pentir** Gwynd
4 B9 **Pentire** Cnwll
41 M9 **Pentlepoir** Pembks
63 P11 **Pentlow** Essex
63 P11 **Pentlow Street** Essex
75 P8 **Pentney** Norfk
110 H5 **Pentonbridge** Cumb
22 B5 **Penton Grafton** Hants
22 B5 **Penton Mewsey** Hants
79 J9 **Pentraeth** IoA
68 E2 **Pentre** Denbgs
81 L11 **Pentre** Flints
31 K3 **Pentre** Mons
31 M4 **Pentre** Mons
55 P7 **Pentre** Powys
56 B7 **Pentre** Powys
56 D6 **Pentre** Powys
30 C5 **Pentre** Rhondd
69 L11 **Pentre** Shrops
9 J6 **Pentre** Wrexhm
43 L5 **Pentre bach** Cerdgn
81 J9 **Pentre Bach** Flints
44 C8 **Pentre-bach** Powys
56 B2 **Pentrebeirdd** Powys
78 H10 **Pentre Berw** IoA
67 N4 **Pentre-bont** Conwy
69 K5 **Pentrebychan Crematorium** Wrexhm
42 F6 **Pentre-cagel** Carmth
68 F4 **Pentre-celyn** Denbgs
55 K3 **Pentre-celyn** Powys
69 J8 **Pentre-chwyth** Swans
69 J8 **Pentre-clawdd** Shrops
42 G7 **Pentre-cwrt** Carmth
68 G5 **Pentredwr** Denbgs
67 J7 **Pentrefelin** Gwynd
78 G6 **Pentrefelin** IoA
68 G11 **Pentre Ffwrndan** Flints
67 R4 **Pentrefoelas** Conwy
41 N4 **Pentregat** Pembks
43 M11 **Pentre-Gwenlais** Carmth
67 K9 **Pentre Gwynfryn** Gwynd
81 J10 **Pentre Halkyn** Flints
56 E9 **Pentre Hodrey** Shrops
80 D10 **Pentre Isaf** Conwy
68 E2 **Pentre Llanrhaeadr** Denbgs

56 B5 **Pentre Llifior** Powys
44 D4 **Pentre-llwyn-llwyd** Powys
54 E9 **Pentre-llyn** Cerdgn
68 C4 **Pentre-llyn-cymmer** Conwy
55 K4 **Pentre-Maw** Powys
30 C9 **Pentre Meyrick** V Glam
31 J4 **Pentre-piod** Torfn
31 J7 **Pentre-poeth** Newpt
42 G4 **Pentre'r-felin** Cerdgn
43 M5 **Pentre'r-felin** Powys
79 Q11 **Pentre'r Felin** Conwy
44 C8 **Pentre Saron** Denbgs
68 D2 **Pentre Saron** Denbgs
67 Q2 **Pentre-tafarn-y-fedw** Conwy
43 R7 **Pentre ty gwyn** Carmth
84 E10 **Pentrich** Derbys
21 K11 **Pentridge** Dorset
30 H4 **Pen-twyn** Caerph
31 P3 **Pen-twyn** Mons
31 J4 **Pen-twyn** Torfn
30 G5 **Pentwynmaur** Caerph
30 F8 **Pentyrch** Cardif
4 G10 **Penwithick** Cnwll
22 D2 **Penwood** Hants
44 B11 **Penwyllt** Powys
43 M10 **Penybanc** Carmth
44 G2 **Penybont** Powys
68 H10 **Pen-y-bont** Powys
68 E10 **Pen-y-bont-fawr** Powys
41 N2 **Pen-y-bryn** Pembks
29 M2 **Pen-y-cae** Powys
69 J5 **Penycae** Wrexhm
31 M5 **Pen-y-cae-mawr** Mons
66 B9 **Penycaerau** Gwynd
80 G9 **Pen-y-cefn** Flints
31 N3 **Pen-y-clawdd** Mons
30 C6 **Pen-y-coedcae** Rhondd
40 G6 **Pen-y-cwn** Pembks
29 N8 **Pen-y-fai** Brdgnd
80 H11 **Pen-y-felin** Flints
69 K2 **Penyffordd** Flints
67 J3 **Penyffridd** Gwynd
54 E7 **Pen-y-garn** Cerdgn
68 F10 **Pen-y-Garnedd** Powys
44 H9 **Pen-y-genffordd** Powys
66 C8 **Pen-y-graig** Gwynd
30 D6 **Penygraig** Rhondd
28 G2 **Penygroes** Carmth
66 H4 **Penygroes** Gwynd
67 M3 **Pen-y-Gwryd** Gwynd
30 C9 **Pen-y-lan** V Glam
28 E4 **Pen-y-Mynydd** Carmth
69 K2 **Penymynydd** Flints
67 L3 **Pen-y-pass** Gwynd
31 M2 **Pen-yr-Heol** Mons
30 D3 **Pen-yr-Heolgerrig** Myr Td
78 H6 **Penysarn** IoA
68 H4 **Pen-y-stryt** Denbgs
30 C4 **Penywaun** Rhondd
2 D7 **Penzance** Cnwll
2 D7 *Penzance Heliport* Cnwll
46 H4 **Peopleton** Worcs
82 G10 **Peover Heath** Ches E
23 P6 **Peper Harow** Surrey
70 A10 **Peplow** Shrops
51 P8 **Pepper's Green** Essex
50 C7 **Pepperstock** C Beds
125 K9 **Perceton** N Ayrs
159 N4 **Percyhorner** Abers
10 b2 **Perelle** Guern
21 Q5 **Perham Down** Wilts
18 C5 **Periton** Somset
36 E4 **Perivale** Gt Lon
9 P6 **Perkins Village** Devon
113 L10 **Perkinsville** Dur
85 K6 **Perlethorpe** Notts
3 K6 **Perranarworthal** Cnwll
2 E8 **Perranporth** Cnwll
2 E8 **Perranuthnoe** Cnwll
3 K3 **Perranwell** Cnwll
3 K6 **Perranwell** Cnwll
3 K6 **Perran Wharf** Cnwll
4 E10 **Perranzabuloe** Cnwll
33 K3 **Perrott's Brook** Gloucs
58 G6 **Perry** Birm
58 G6 **Perry Barr** Birm
58 G6 **Perry Barr Crematorium** Birm
52 D7 **Perry Green** Essex
51 K7 **Perry Green** Herts
33 J7 **Perry Green** Wilts
46 B9 **Perrystone Hill** Herefs
10 G3 **Perry Street** Somset
70 E9 **Pershall** Staffs
46 H5 **Pershore** Worcs
61 N7 **Pertenhall** Bed
134 E2 **Perth** P & K
134 D2 **Perth Crematorium** P & K
69 L8 **Perthy** Shrops
46 A6 **Perton** Herefs
58 C5 **Perton** Staffs
20 G7 **Pertwood** Wilts
74 C11 **Peterborough** C Pete
74 C10 **Peterborough Crematorium** C Pete
61 P2 *Peterborough Services* Cambs
45 L7 **Peterchurch** Herefs
151 L7 **Peterculter** C Aber
159 R8 **Peterhead** Abers
104 D2 **Peterlee** Dur
23 K10 **Petersfield** Hants
50 D7 **Peter's Green** Herts
36 E6 **Petersham** Gt Lon
16 H9 **Peters Marland** Devon
31 J9 **Peterstone Wentlooge** Newpt
30 E9 **Peterston-super-Ely** V Glam
45 N10 **Peterstow** Herefs
8 D9 **Peter Tavy** Devon
39 K11 **Petham** Kent
5 M4 **Petherwin Gate** Cnwll
17 J10 **Petrockstow** Devon
49 N5 **Petsoe End** M Keyn
17 J2 **Pett Street** Kent
26 E9 **Pett** E Susx
64 H10 **Pettaugh** Suffk
39 L11 **Pett Bottom** Kent
142 G9 **Petterden** Angus
116 D2 **Pettinain** S Lans
65 L10 **Pettistree** Suffk
18 D10 **Petton** Devon
69 M9 **Petton** Shrops
37 L7 **Petts Wood** Gt Lon
134 H10 **Pettycur** Fife

32 E7	Petty France	S Glos
151 N3	Pettymuk	Abers
23 Q10	Petworth	W Susx
25 P9	Pevensey	E Susx
25 Q10	Pevensey Bay	E Susx
21 N2	Pewsey	Wilts
35 L7	Pheasant's Hill	Bucks
46 H3	Phepson	Worcs
113 M10	Philadelphia	Sundld
16 D7	Philham	Devon
117 N5	Philiphaugh	Border
2 F6	Phillack	Cnwll
3 M6	Philleigh	Cnwll
51 P7	Philpot End	Essex
127 K2	Philpstoun	W Loth
46 B9	Phocle Green	Herefs
23 L3	Phoenix Green	Hants
148 C9	Phones	Highld
19 M9	Pibsbury	Somset
100 D6	Pica	Cumb
59 K5	Piccadilly	Warwks
50 B9	Piccotts End	Herts
91 N9	Pickburn	Donc
98 F4	Pickering	N York
22 C5	Picket Piece	Hants
13 L3	Picket Post	Hants
59 L8	Pickford	Covtry
59 L8	Pickford Green	Covtry
97 M4	Pickhill	N York
56 C5	Picklescott	Shrops
82 E9	Pickmere	Ches E
18 G9	Pickney	Somset
70 C10	Pickstock	Wrekin
89 L6	Pickup Bank	Bl w D
16 H3	Pickwell	Devon
73 K8	Pickwell	Leics
32 G10	Pickwick	Wilts
73 Q4	Pickworth	Lincs
73 P8	Pickworth	Rutlnd
81 N10	Picton	Ches W
80 G8	Picton	Flints
104 D9	Picton	N York
25 K10	Piddinghoe	E Susx
35 M6	Piddington	Bucks
49 M4	Piddington	Nhants
48 H11	Piddington	Oxon
11 Q5	Piddlehinton	Dorset
11 Q5	Piddletrenthide	Dorset
62 D5	Pidley	Cambs
103 P7	Piercebridge	Darltn
169 d2	Pierowall	Ork
46 H9	Piff's Elm	Gloucs
113 J3	Pigdon	Nthumb
47 P2	Pigeon Green	Warwks
12 H4	Pig Oak	Dorset
45 M5	Pig Street	Herefs
71 M3	Pikehall	Derbys
12 H4	Pilford	Dorset
51 N11	Pilgrims Hatch	Essex
85 Q2	Pilham	Lincs
31 P9	Pill	N Som
5 P9	Pillaton	Cnwll
5 P9	Pillatonmill	Cnwll
47 Q5	Pillerton Hersey	Warwks
47 Q5	Pillerton Priors	Warwks
56 D11	Pilleth	Powys
91 J10	Pilley	Barns
13 P5	Pilley	Hants
13 P5	Pilley Bailey	Hants
31 K7	Pillgwenlly	Newpt
16 H6	Pillhead	Devon
95 J11	Pilling	Lancs
94 H11	Pilling Lane	Lancs
31 Q7	Pilning	S Glos
27 J8	Pilot Inn	Kent
71 L2	Pilsbury	Derbys
11 J5	Pilsdon	Dorset
73 R9	Pilsgate	C Pete
84 B6	Pilsley	Derbys
84 F8	Pilsley	Derbys
77 M9	Pilson Green	Norfk
25 K6	Piltdown	E Susx
17 K5	Pilton	Devon
61 M4	Pilton	Nhants
73 N10	Pilton	Rutlnd
19 Q6	Pilton	Somset
28 D7	Pilton Green	Swans
89 L2	Pimlico	Lancs
48 H6	Pimlico	Nhants
12 F3	Pimperne	Dorset
74 D5	Pinchbeck	Lincs
74 C5	Pinchbeck Bars	Lincs
74 D6	Pinchbeck West	Lincs
91 R7	Pincheon Green	Donc
104 G8	Pinchinthorpe	R & Cl
88 G7	Pincock	Lancs
88 D8	Pinfold	Lancs
64 A10	Pinford End	Suffk
28 D4	Pinged	Carmth
35 J11	Pingewood	W Berk
50 G5	Pin Green	Herts
9 N6	Pinhoe	Devon
59 L8	Pinkett's Booth	Covtry
32 G7	Pinkney	Wilts
59 N9	Pinley	Covtry
59 K11	Pinley Green	Warwks
53 M4	Pin Mill	Suffk
114 C9	Pinminnoch	S Ayrs
114 D9	Pinmore	S Ayrs
10 C7	Pinn	Devon
36 D3	Pinner	Gt Lon
36 D3	Pinner Green	Gt Lon
69 Q10	Pinsley Green	Ches E
47 J5	Pinvin	Worcs
114 D10	Pinwherry	S Ayrs
84 G10	Pinxton	Derbys
45 Q6	Pipe and Lyde	Herefs
56 H10	Pipe Aston	Herefs
70 C6	Pipe Gate	Shrops
58 G3	Pipehill	Staffs
156 F7	Piperhill	Highld
5 M5	Pipers Pool	Cnwll
60 H3	Pipewell	Nhants
17 J4	Pippacott	Devon
88 H6	Pippin Street	Lancs
44 H7	Pipton	Powys
23 P3	Pirbright	Surrey
23 P3	Pirbright Camp	Surrey
118 C5	Pirnie	Border
120 G3	Pirnmill	N Ayrs
50 D4	Pirton	Herts
46 G5	Pirton	Worcs
54 F9	Pisgah	Cerdgn
35 K7	Pishill	Oxon
66 E6	Pistyll	Gwynd
141 K4	Pitagowan	P & K
159 N5	Pitblae	Abers
134 D2	Pitcairngreen	P & K
156 E3	Pitcalnie	Highld
151 J2	Pitcaple	Abers

142 E4	Pitcarity	Angus
32 G3	Pitchcombe	Gloucs
49 L10	Pitchcott	Bucks
74 E4	Pitcher Row	Lincs
57 J4	Pitchford	Shrops
35 L4	Pitch Green	Bucks
23 N7	Pitch Place	Surrey
23 Q4	Pitch Place	Surrey
157 M10	Pitchroy	Moray
20 C8	Pitcombe	Somset
29 N10	Pitcot	V Glam
128 G5	Pitcox	E Loth
150 H4	Pitfichie	Abers
158 G9	Pitglassie	Abers
162 H8	Pitgrudy	Highld
135 J6	Pitlessie	Fife
141 M6	Pitlochry	P & K
150 H2	Pitmachie	Abers
148 C7	Pitmain	Highld
151 M2	Pitmedden	Abers
151 M2	Pitmedden Garden	Abers
18 H11	Pitminster	Somset
143 K8	Pitmuies	Angus
150 H5	Pitmunie	Abers
19 N9	Pitney	Somset
134 G2	Pitroddie	P & K
135 L2	Pitscottie	Fife
38 B4	Pitsea	Essex
83 K4	Pitses	Oldham
60 G7	Pitsford	Nhants
49 P11	Pitstone	Bucks
18 D11	Pitt	Devon
22 E9	Pitt	Hants
143 N3	Pittarrow	Abers
32 D5	Pitt Court	Gloucs
135 P7	Pittenweem	Fife
134 H8	Pitteuchar	Fife
104 B2	Pittington	Dur
150 H3	Pittodrie House Hotel	Abers
21 P8	Pitton	Wilts
37 P11	Pitt's Wood	Kent
159 N4	Pittulie	Abers
4 F6	Pityme	Cnwll
113 L11	Pity Me	Dur
26 F2	Pivington	Kent
65 J6	Pixey Green	Suffk
36 E10	Pixham	Surrey
126 D4	Plains	N Lans
5 J11	Plain Street	Cnwll
57 J5	Plaish	Shrops
37 K4	Plaistow	Gt Lon
24 B4	Plaistow	W Susx
21 Q11	Plaitford	Hants
82 D5	Plank Lane	Wigan
78 D9	Plas Cymyran	IoA
22 F2	Plastow Green	Hants
37 P9	Platt	Kent
82 D4	Platt Bridge	Wigan
69 P7	Platt Lane	Shrops
38 E11	Platts Heath	Kent
113 L11	Plawsworth	Dur
37 P10	Plaxtol	Kent
26 F7	Playden	E Susx
53 M2	Playford	Suffk
35 K9	Play Hatch	Oxon
3 L5	Playing Place	Cnwll
46 E8	Playley Green	Gloucs
56 G3	Plealey	Shrops
133 N10	Plean	Stirlg
134 G5	Pleasance	Fife
89 J5	Pleasington	Bl w D
89 J5	Pleasington Crematorium	Bl w D
84 H8	Pleasley	Derbys
84 H8	Pleasleyhill	Notts
11 Q2	Pleck	Dorset
51 N5	Pledgdon Green	Essex
91 J7	Pledwick	Wakefd
10 b1	Pleinheaume	Guern
11 a1	Plemont	Jersey
81 P10	Plemstall	Ches W
111 P8	Plenmeller	Nthumb
51 Q8	Pleshey	Essex
153 Q11	Plockton	Highld
56 F7	Plowden	Shrops
56 F4	Plox Green	Shrops
26 F2	Pluckley	Kent
26 F3	Pluckley Station	Kent
26 F3	Pluckley Thorne	Kent
39 N9	Plucks Gutter	Kent
100 G3	Plumbland	Cumb
95 K2	Plumgarths	Cumb
82 F10	Plumley	Ches E
94 G5	Plumpton	Cumb
101 N3	Plumpton	Cumb
25 J8	Plumpton	E Susx
48 G5	Plumpton	Nhants
49 K6	Plumpton End	Nhants
25 J7	Plumpton Green	E Susx
101 P3	Plumpton Head	Cumb
37 K5	Plumstead	Gt Lon
76 G5	Plumstead	Norfk
76 G4	Plumstead Green	Norfk
72 G4	Plumtree	Notts
26 D2	Plumtree Green	Kent
73 K4	Plungar	Leics
26 F4	Plurenden	Kent
11 Q4	Plush	Dorset
5 M5	Plusha	Cnwll
5 N7	Plushabridge	Cnwll
42 G4	Plwmp	Cerdgn
6 D8	Plymouth	C Plym
6 E6	Plymouth Airport	C Plym
6 E7	Plympton	C Plym
6 E8	Plymstock	C Plym
9 Q4	Plymtree	Devon
98 C3	Pockley	N York
98 G11	Pocklington	E R Yk
74 D6	Pode Hole	Lincs
19 P10	Podimore	Somset
61 K8	Podington	Bed
70 D7	Podmore	Staffs
53 K9	Point Clear	Essex
74 B4	Pointon	Lincs
13 K6	Pokesdown	Bmouth
160 F4	Polbain	Highld
5 N10	Polbathic	Cnwll
127 J5	Polbeth	W Loth
4 G8	Polbrock	Cnwll
2 H7	Poldark Mine	Cnwll
61 N3	Polebrook	Nhants
25 N10	Polegate	E Susx
90 D7	Pole Moor	Kirk
59 L4	Polesworth	Warwks
160 G5	Polglass	Highld
3 P3	Polgooth	Cnwll
115 P7	Polgown	D & G

24 B10	Poling	W Susx
24 B9	Poling Corner	W Susx
4 H11	Polkerris	Cnwll
77 L5	Pollard Street	Norfk
91 Q7	Pollington	E R Yk
138 D4	Polloch	Highld
125 P5	Pollokshaws	C Glas
125 P5	Pollokshields	C Glas
4 P4	Polmassick	Cnwll
4 H11	Polmear	Cnwll
126 G2	Polmont	Falk
145 N11	Polnish	Highld
5 L11	Polperro	Cnwll
5 J11	Polruan	Cnwll
19 P6	Polsham	Somset
52 G3	Polstead	Suffk
52 G3	Polstead Heath	Suffk
130 G8	Poltalloch	Ag & B
3 J10	Poltescoe	Cnwll
9 N5	Poltimore	Devon
127 P5	Polton	Mdloth
129 J9	Polwarth	Border
5 M5	Polyphant	Cnwll
4 E6	Polzeath	Cnwll
127 N6	Pomathorn	Mdloth
83 P11	Pomeroy	Derbys
44 G7	Ponde	Powys
62 C2	Pondersbridge	Cambs
51 J11	Ponders End	Gt Lon
3 K6	Ponsanooth	Cnwll
100 E9	Ponsonby	Cumb
3 K10	Ponsongath	Cnwll
7 J4	Ponsworthy	Devon
28 G3	Pont Abraham Services	Carmth
11 c2	Pontac	Jersey
28 H2	Pontamman	Carmth
28 D2	Pontantwn	Carmth
29 K4	Pontardawe	Neath
28 G4	Pontarddulais	Swans
43 K10	Pont-ar-gothi	Carmth
44 B9	Pont-ar-Hydfer	Powys
43 P10	Pont-ar-llechau	Carmth
42 H9	Pontarsais	Carmth
69 J2	Pontblyddyn	Flints
67 N3	Pont Cyfyng	Conwy
79 P11	Pont Dolgarrog	Conwy
55 N6	Pontdolgoch	Powys
31 J7	Pont-Ebbw	Newpt
91 M6	Pontefract	Wakefd
91 L6	Pontefract Crematorium	Wakefd
113 J6	Ponteland	Nthumb
54 G8	Ponterwyd	Cerdgn
56 F3	Pontesbury	Shrops
56 F3	Pontesbury Hill	Shrops
56 G3	Pontesford	Shrops
68 H7	Pontfadog	Wrexhm
41 K4	Pontfaen	Pembks
44 D8	Pont-faen	Powys
42 F4	Pontgarreg	Cerdgn
41 M2	Pontgarreg	Pembks
28 E3	Ponthenry	Carmth
31 K6	Ponthir	Torfn
42 E5	Ponthirwaun	Cerdgn
30 G5	Pontllanfraith	Caerph
28 H5	Pontlliw	Swans
30 F7	Pontlottyn	Caerph
66 G4	Pontlyfni	Gwynd
28 F3	Pont Morlais	Carmth
29 P3	Pontneddfechan	Neath
31 J5	Pontnewydd	Torfn
31 J4	Pontnewynydd	Torfn
67 M2	Pont Pen-y-benglog	Gwynd
54 G11	Pontrhydfendigaid	Cerdgn
67 R9	Pont Rhyd-sarn	Gwynd
29 N7	Pont Rhyd-y-cyff	Brdgnd
29 L6	Pont-rhyd-y-fen	Neath
54 G10	Pontrhydygroes	Cerdgn
31 J5	Pontrhydyrun	Torfn
45 M9	Pontrilas	Herefs
55 Q2	Pont Robert	Powys
67 J2	Pont-rug	Gwynd
25 Q7	Ponts Green	E Susx
42 H5	Pontshaen	Cerdgn
46 B10	Pontshill	Herefs
30 E2	Pontsticill	Myr Td
29 N3	Pont Walby	Neath
42 H6	Pontwelly	Carmth
28 E3	Pontyates	Carmth
28 F2	Pontyberem	Carmth
67 K7	Pont-y-blew	Wrexhm
69 J3	Pontybodkin	Flints
30 D8	Pontyclun	Rhondd
29 P6	Pontycymer	Brdgnd
41 M3	Pontyglasier	Pembks
30 D6	Pontygwaith	Rhondd
41 M3	Pontygynon	Pembks
67 P4	Pont-y-pant	Conwy
31 J4	Pontypool	Torfn
31 K5	Pontypool Road	Torfn
30 E7	Pontypridd	Rhondd
40 H5	Pont-yr-hafod	Pembks
29 P7	Pont-yr-Rhyl	Brdgnd
30 H6	Pontywaun	Caerph
2 H5	Pool	Cnwll
2 b2	Pool	IoS
97 K11	Pool	Leeds
12 H6	Poole	Poole
12 H6	Poole Crematorium	Poole
33 J5	Poole Keynes	Gloucs
160 D10	Poolewe	Highld
101 N6	Pooley Bridge	Cumb
64 F5	Pooley Street	Norfk
70 F3	Poolfold	Staffs
45 R4	Pool Head	Herefs
70 D8	Poolhill	Gloucs
134 C7	Pool of Muckhart	Clacks
56 D2	Pool Quay	Powys
52 C4	Pool Street	Essex
37 L11	Pooting's	Kent
22 G6	Popham	Hants
37 J4	Poplar	Gt Lon
65 N8	Poplar Street	Suffk
14 D8	Porchfield	IoW
77 K11	Poringland	Norfk
2 H7	Porkellis	Cnwll
18 A5	Porlock	Somset
17 R2	Porlock Weir	Somset
123 N8	Portachoillan	Ag & B
4 F4	Pole Elm	Worcs
153 P11	Port-an-Eorna	Highld
138 G3	Port Appin	Ag & B
122 F6	Port Askaig	Ag & B
124 A4	Portavadie	Ag & B
124 D4	Port Bannatyne	Ag & B
31 P9	Portbury	N Som
110 D8	Port Carlisle	Cumb

122 C8	Port Charlotte	Ag & B
14 H5	Portchester	Hants
14 H5	Portchester Crematorium	Hants
104 E6	Port Clarence	S on T
124 B3	Port Driseach	Ag & B
122 E10	Port Ellen	Ag & B
151 K3	Port Elphinstone	Abers
106 D3	Portencalzie	D & G
124 F8	Portencross	N Ayrs
80 a8	Port Erin	IoM
11 N7	Portesham	Dorset
158 B4	Portessie	Moray
80 g3	Port e Vullen	IoM
28 E7	Port Eynon	Swans
40 H7	Portfield Gate	Pembks
5 Q4	Portgate	Devon
4 G5	Port Gaverne	Cnwll
125 J3	Port Glasgow	Inver
158 A5	Portgordon	Moray
163 N4	Portgower	Highld
4 C9	Porth	Cnwll
30 D6	Porth	Rhondd
3 K9	Porthallow	Cnwll
5 L11	Porthallow	Cnwll
29 M9	Porthcawl	Brdgnd
4 D7	Porthcothan	Cnwll
2 B9	Porthcurno	Cnwll
66 D6	Port Dinllaen	Gwynd
153 P3	Port Henderson	Highld
40 F4	Porthgain	Pembks
2 B9	Porthgwarra	Cnwll
70 E5	Porthill	Staffs
3 L5	Porthkea	Cnwll
30 E11	Porthkerry	V Glam
2 G8	Porthleven	Cnwll
67 K7	Porthmadog	Gwynd
2 C6	Porthmeor	Cnwll
3 K8	Porth Navas	Cnwll
3 P5	Portholland	Cnwll
3 L9	Porthoustock	Cnwll
3 Q3	Porthpean	Cnwll
2 H4	Porthtowan	Cnwll
69 L5	Porthwgan	Wrexhm
43 K11	Porthyrhyd	Carmth
69 J10	Porth-y-Waen	Shrops
131 Q9	Portincaple	Ag & B
11 a1	Portinfer	Jersey
92 C4	Portington	E R Yk
131 K5	Portinnisherrich	Ag & B
101 J6	Portinscale	Cumb
4 F5	Port Isaac	Cnwll
31 N9	Portishead	N Som
158 C4	Portknockie	Moray
11 P10	Portland	Dorset
151 N10	Portlethen	Abers
109 J10	Portling	D & G
3 N6	Portloe	Cnwll
106 E9	Port Logan	D & G
5 L11	Portlooe	Cnwll
163 L10	Portmahomack	Highld
67 K7	Portmeirion	Gwynd
3 Q5	Portmellon	Cnwll
144 F12	Port Mor	Highld
13 P5	Portmore	Hants
105 L7	Port Mulgrave	N York
138 G8	Portnacroish	Ag & B
168 k4	Portnaguran	W Isls
122 A9	Portnahaven	Ag & B
152 E11	Portnalong	Highld
168 k4	Port nan Giuran	W Isls
168 d10	Port nan Long	W Isls
168 k1	Port Nis	W Isls
127 Q3	Portobello	C Edin
113 L9	Portobello	Gatesd
58 E5	Portobello	Wolves
132 H7	Port of Menteith	Stirlg
168 k1	Port of Ness	W Isls
21 N7	Porton	Wilts
5 Q6	Portontown	Devon
106 C7	Portpatrick	D & G
4 F5	Port Quin	Cnwll
138 F8	Port Ramsay	Ag & B
2 H4	Portreath	Cnwll
152 H9	Portree	Highld
80 b8	Port St Mary	IoM
3 M6	Portscatho	Cnwll
14 H6	Portsea	C Port
166 E3	Portskerra	Highld
31 N7	Portskewett	Mons
24 G9	Portslade	Br & H
24 G9	Portslade-by-Sea	Br & H
106 C6	Portslogan	D & G
14 H7	Portsmouth	C Port
89 Q5	Portsmouth	Calder
80 d7	Port Soderick	IoM
14 H5	Port Solent	C Port
131 L3	Portsonachan Hotel	Ag & B
158 E4	Portsoy	Abers
81 L8	Port Sunlight	Wirral
14 D4	Portswood	C Sotn
29 L7	Port Talbot	Neath
29 J6	Port Tennant	Swans
137 L2	Portuairk	Highld
45 P6	Portway	Herefs
45 P7	Portway	Herefs
58 E7	Portway	Sandw
58 G10	Portway	Worcs
122 A9	Port Wemyss	Ag & B
107 K9	Port William	D & G
5 P11	Portwrinkle	Cnwll
107 N10	Portyerrock	D & G
9 K5	Posbury	Devon
57 M4	Posenhall	Shrops
63 N11	Poslingford	Suffk
117 J4	Posso	Border
8 G9	Postbridge	Devon
35 K4	Postcombe	Oxon
12 G6	Post Green	Dorset
27 K4	Postling	Kent
77 N10	Postwick	Norfk
150 G8	Potarch	Abers
49 Q8	Potsgrove	C Beds
50 B9	Potten End	Herts
39 N8	Potten Street	Kent
99 K5	Potter Brompton	N York
64 H3	Pottergate Street	Norfk
86 E7	Potterhanworth	Lincs
86 E7	Potterhanworth Booths	Lincs
77 N8	Potter Heigham	Norfk
21 J3	Potterne	Wilts
21 J3	Potterne Wick	Wilts
35 P4	Potter Row	Bucks
50 F10	Potters Bar	Herts
95 K10	Potters Brook	Lancs
58 B8	Potter's Cross	Staffs
50 D9	Potters Crouch	Herts
26 E2	Potter's Forstal	Kent

59 N8	Potters Green	Covtry
25 M6	Potter's Green	E Susx
51 J6	Potter's Green	Herts
50 F7	Pottersheath	Herts
72 C11	Potters Marston	Leics
71 L7	Potter Somersal	Derbys
49 L6	Potterspury	Nhants
151 N4	Potterton	Abers
91 L3	Potterton	Leeds
76 C7	Potthorpe	Norfk
20 F6	Pottle Street	Wilts
104 E10	Potto	N York
62 B11	Potton	C Beds
75 P6	Pott Row	Norfk
52 F7	Pott's Green	Essex
83 K9	Pott Shrigley	Ches E
16 C10	Poughill	Cnwll
9 L3	Poughill	Devon
13 L3	Pouliner	Hants
21 J3	Poulshot	Wilts
33 L4	Poulton	Gloucs
81 L6	Poulton	Wirral
88 C3	Poulton-le-Fylde	Lancs
33 L5	Poulton Priory	Gloucs
57 N10	Pound Bank	Worcs
11 P6	Poundbury	Dorset
28 G6	Poundffald	Swans
25 L5	Poundgate	E Susx
25 M6	Pound Green	E Susx
63 M10	Pound Green	Suffk
57 P9	Pound Green	Worcs
24 G3	Pound Hill	W Susx
48 H9	Poundon	Bucks
25 M2	Poundsbridge	Kent
7 J4	Poundsgate	Devon
5 L2	Poundstock	Cnwll
22 E2	Pound Street	Hants
25 M6	Pounsley	E Susx
107 N8	Pouton	D & G
65 M7	Pouy Street	Suffk
24 G2	Povey Cross	Surrey
119 L7	Powburn	Nthumb
9 N8	Powderham	Devon
11 L5	Powerstock	Dorset
109 P7	Powfoot	D & G
46 D6	Pow Green	Herefs
110 D9	Powhill	Cumb
46 F4	Powick	Worcs
134 C8	Powmill	P & K
12 B8	Poxwell	Dorset
36 B5	Poyle	Slough
24 G8	Poynings	W Susx
20 C10	Poyntington	Dorset
83 K8	Poynton	Ches E
69 Q11	Poynton	Wrekin
69 Q11	Poynton Green	Wrekin
41 J7	Poyston Cross	Pembks
64 D10	Poystreet Green	Suffk
2 F8	Praa Sands	Cnwll
37 L8	Pratt's Bottom	Gt Lon
2 H10	Praze-an-Beeble	Cnwll
2 H10	Predannack Wollas	Cnwll
69 Q8	Prees	Shrops
94 H11	Preesall	Lancs
69 Q8	Prees Green	Shrops
69 J7	Preesgweene	Shrops
69 Q7	Prees Heath	Shrops
69 Q7	Prees Higher Heath	Shrops
69 Q8	Prees Lower Heath	Shrops
119 K8	Prendwick	Nthumb
42 H6	Pren-gwyn	Cerdgn
67 K6	Prenteg	Gwynd
81 L7	Prenton	Wirral
81 P6	Prescot	Knows
10 B2	Prescott	Devon
57 M8	Prescott	Shrops
69 M10	Prescott	Shrops
142 B4	Presnerb	Angus
118 F3	Pressen	Nthumb
80 F8	Prestatyn	Denbgs
83 J9	Prestbury	Ches E
47 J10	Prestbury	Gloucs
45 L2	Presteigne	Powys
20 B6	Prestleigh	Somset
89 M9	Prestolee	Bolton
129 K8	Preston	Border
24 H9	Preston	Br & H
7 M4	Preston	Devon
11 Q8	Preston	Dorset
93 L4	Preston	E R Yk
33 K4	Preston	Gloucs
50 E6	Preston	Herts
38 H9	Preston	Kent
39 M9	Preston	Kent
88 G5	Preston	Lancs
119 N5	Preston	Nthumb
73 M10	Preston	Rutlnd
57 J2	Preston	Shrops
18 E7	Preston	Somset
64 C11	Preston	Suffk
7 M6	Preston	Torbay
33 K9	Preston	Wilts
33 Q10	Preston	Wilts
59 J11	Preston Bagot	Warwks
49 J9	Preston Bissett	Bucks
18 F9	Preston Bowyer	Somset
69 P10	Preston Brockhurst	Shrops
82 B8	Preston Brook	Halton
22 H6	Preston Candover	Hants
48 G4	Preston Capes	Nhants
88 H4	Preston Crematorium	Lancs
34 H6	Preston Crowmarsh	Oxon
60 G9	Preston Deanery	Nhants
59 J11	Preston Green	Warwks
69 N11	Preston Gubbals	Shrops
56 G2	Preston Montford	Shrops
47 P5	Preston on Stour	Warwks
104 D7	Preston on Tees	S on T
82 C8	Preston on the Hill	Halton
45 M6	Preston on Wye	Herefs
128 B5	Prestonpans	E Loth
95 L4	Preston Patrick	Cumb
19 P11	Preston Plucknett	Somset
39 N9	Preston Street	Kent
96 G2	Preston-under-Scar	N York
70 B11	Preston upon the Weald Moors	Wrekin
45 R5	Preston Wynne	Herefs
82 H4	Prestwich	Bury
113 J6	Prestwick	Nthumb

114 G2 Prestwick S Ayrs
114 G2 *Prestwick Airport* S Ayrs
35 N4 Prestwood Bucks
58 C7 Prestwood Staffs
29 P6 Price Town Brdgnd
63 J4 Prickwillow Cambs
19 P4 Priddy Somset
8 B3 Priestacott Devon
83 F10 Priestcliffe Derbys
83 P10 Priestcliffe Ditch Derbys
95 L6 Priest Hutton Lancs
125 P10 Priestland E Ayrs
90 E5 Priestley Green Calder
56 D5 Priest Weston Shrops
37 Q8 Priestwood Green Kent
60 B2 Primethorpe Leics
76 F8 Primrose Green Norfk
129 K8 Primrosehill Border
62 E3 Primrose Hill Cambs
84 F9 Primrose Hill Derbys
58 D7 Primrose Hill Dudley
88 D9 Primrose Hill Lancs
118 F5 Primsidemill Border
41 M8 Princes Gate Pembks
35 M4 Princes Risborough Bucks
59 P10 Princethorpe Warwks
6 F4 Princetown Devon
15 L5 Prinsted W Susx
68 E2 Prion Denbgs
111 J7 Prior Rigg Cumb
56 H9 Priors Halton Shrops
48 E3 Priors Hardwick Warwks
57 N2 Priorslee Wrekin
48 E3 Priors Marston Warwks
46 G10 Priors Norton Gloucs
33 M7 Priory Vale Swindn
45 K5 Priory Wood Herefs
30 D9 Prisk V Glam
20 C2 Priston BaNES
64 G4 Pristow Green Norfk
38 E4 Prittlewell Sthend
23 J9 Privett Hants
17 K4 Prixford Devon
3 M4 Probus Cnwll
128 E4 Prora E Loth
100 F2 Prospect Cumb
2 G7 Prospidnick Cnwll
159 K5 Protstonhill Abers
112 G8 Prudhoe Nthumb
2 F8 Prussia Cove Cnwll
20 B2 Publow BaNES
51 J6 Puckeridge Herts
19 L11 Puckington Somset
32 C9 Pucklechurch S Glos
46 G7 Puckrup Gloucs
82 F11 Puddinglake Ches W
81 L10 Puddington Ches W
9 K2 Puddington Devon
64 F3 Puddledock Norfk
12 C6 Puddletown Dorset
45 R3 Pudleston Herefs
90 G3 Pudsey Leeds
24 B7 Pulborough W Susx
70 C10 Puleston Wrekin
69 L3 Pulford Ches W
11 Q3 Pulham Dorset
64 H4 Pulham Market Norfk
65 J4 Pulham St Mary Norfk
32 B6 Pullens Green S Glos
50 C4 Pulloxhill C Beds
127 K4 Pumpherston W Loth
43 N6 Pumsaint Carmth
41 K5 Puncheston Pembks
11 L7 Puncknowle Dorset
25 P6 Punnett's Town E Susx
15 J5 Purbrook Hants
37 N5 Purfleet Thurr
19 K6 Puriton Somset
52 D11 Purleigh Essex
36 H8 Purley Gt Lon
35 J9 Purley W Berk
56 D9 Purlogue Shrops
32 G11 Purlpit Wilts
62 G3 Purls Bridge Cambs
20 C11 Purse Caundle Dorset
58 C10 Purshull Green Worcs
56 F8 Purslow Shrops
91 L7 Purston Jaglin Wakefd
10 H3 Purtington Somset
32 C3 Purton Gloucs
32 C4 Purton Gloucs
33 L7 Purton Wilts
33 L6 Purton Stoke Wilts
49 K5 Pury End Nhants
34 C5 Pusey Oxon
46 B7 Putley Herefs
46 B7 Putley Green Herefs
32 E3 Putloe Gloucs
36 F6 Putney Gt Lon
36 F6 Putney Vale Crematorium Gt Lon
16 G3 Putsborough Devon
35 N2 Puttenham Herts
23 P5 Puttenham Surrey
52 D3 Puttock End Essex
11 N8 Putton Dorset
49 L6 Puxley Nhants
19 M2 Puxton N Som
28 E4 Pwll Carmth
40 H10 Pwllcrochan Pembks
30 H2 Pwll-du Mons
68 F4 Pwll-glas Denbgs
44 E8 Pwllgloyw Powys
66 F7 Pwllheli Gwynd
31 P6 Pwllmeyric Mons
41 Q7 Pwll Trap Carmth
29 L6 Pwll-y-glaw Neath
79 Q9 Pydew Conwy
84 F10 Pye Bridge Derbys
24 G8 Pyecombe W Susx
31 K7 Pye Corner Newpt
58 E2 Pye Green Staffs
29 M8 Pyle Brdgnd
18 F8 Pyleigh Somset
20 B7 Pylle Somset
62 G3 Pymoor Cambs
11 K6 Pymore Dorset
36 B9 Pyrford Surrey
35 J5 Pyrton Oxon
61 J6 Pytchley Nhants
16 E11 Pyworthy Devon

Q

56 C8 Quabbs Shrops
74 D4 Quadring Lincs
74 D4 Quadring Eaudike Lincs
49 K10 Quainton Bucks

30 E5 Quaker's Yard Myr Td
113 J10 Quaking Houses Dur
18 G7 Quantock Hills Somset
169 r10 Quarff Shet
21 Q6 Quarley Hants
72 A2 Quarndon Derbys
14 G8 Quarr Hill IoW
125 K4 Quarrier's Village Inver
73 R2 Quarrington Lincs
104 B3 Quarrington Hill Dur
82 C11 Quarrybank Ches W
58 D7 Quarry Bank Dudley
157 M5 Quarrywood Moray
124 F5 Quarter N Ayrs
126 C7 Quarter S Lans
57 N6 Quatford Shrops
57 P7 Quatt Shrops
103 N2 Quebec Dur
32 F2 Quedgeley Gloucs
63 J4 Queen Adelaide Cambs
38 F7 Queenborough Kent
19 Q10 Queen Camel Somset
32 B11 Queen Charlton BaNES
17 Q8 Queen Dart Devon
132 G7 Queen Elizabeth Forest Park Stirlg
46 G7 Queenhill Worcs
20 E8 Queen Oak Dorset
14 G10 Queen's Bower IoW
90 E4 Queensbury C Brad
81 L11 Queensferry Flints
69 K9 Queen's Head Shrops
126 B4 Queenslie C Glas
61 M11 Queen's Park Bed
60 G8 Queen's Park Nhants
37 Q11 Queen Street Kent
33 K7 Queen Street Wilts
126 B2 Queenzieburn N Lans
51 M4 Quendon Essex
72 G8 Queniborough Leics
33 M4 Quenington Gloucs
95 L8 Quernmore Lancs
58 G6 Queslett Birm
49 L4 Quinton Dudley
49 L4 Quinton Nhants
4 C9 Quinton Green Nhants
71 L6 Quintrell Downs Cnwll
129 K7 Quixhall Staffs
5 Q2 Quixwood Border
133 N3 Quoditch Devon
72 F7 Quoig P & K
116 D3 Quothquan S Lans
169 e6 Quoyburray Ork
169 b4 Quoyloo Ork

R

153 K9 Raasay Highld
26 C2 Rabbit's Cross Kent
50 F7 Rableyheath Herts
110 C10 Raby Cumb
81 L9 Raby Wirral
116 G4 Rachan Mill Border
79 L11 Rachub Gwynd
17 R8 Rackenford Devon
24 B8 Rackham W Susx
77 K9 Rackheath Norfk
109 M6 Racks D & G
169 b7 Rackwick Ork
71 P7 Radbourne Derbys
89 M9 Radcliffe Bury
119 Q10 Radcliffe Nthumb
72 G3 Radcliffe on Trent Notts
49 J8 Radclive Bucks
33 Q5 Radcot Oxon
156 C6 Raddery Highld
18 D9 Raddington Somset
135 M6 Radernie Fife
59 M8 Radford Covtry
48 B2 Radford Semele Warwks
18 H7 Radlet Somset
50 E10 Radlett Herts
17 N7 Radley Devon
34 F5 Radley Oxon
51 P9 Radley Green Essex
69 Q3 Radmore Green Ches E
35 L5 Radnage Bucks
20 C4 Radstock BaNES
48 G6 Radstone Nhants
48 C5 Radway Warwks
61 M9 Radwell Bed
50 F3 Radwell Herts
51 P3 Radwinter Essex
51 P3 Radwinter End Essex
30 F8 Radyr Cardif
86 D10 RAF College (Cranwell) Lincs
157 K6 Rafford Moray
72 H7 Ragdale Leics
56 H6 Ragdon Shrops
2 D8 Raginnis Cnwll
31 M3 Raglan Mons
85 P6 Ragnall Notts
148 E2 Raigbeg Highld
46 G3 Rainbow Hill Worcs
81 P4 Rainford St Hel
37 M4 Rainham Gt Lon
38 D8 Rainham Medway
81 P6 Rainhill St Hel
81 Q6 Rainhill Stoops St Hel
83 K9 Rainow Ches E
82 H4 Rainsough Bury
97 N5 Rainton N York
85 J9 Rainworth Notts
102 B9 Raisbeck Cumb
111 P11 Raise Cumb
98 H8 Raisthorpe N York
134 G2 Rait P & K
87 K4 Raithby Lincs
87 L7 Raithby Lincs
105 N8 Raithwaite N York
23 M9 Rake Hants
89 Q8 Rakewood Rochdl
148 C8 Ralia Highld
43 L5 Ram Carmth
152 B9 Ramasaig Highld
3 J7 Rame Cnwll
6 C9 Rame Cnwll
32 C9 Ram Hill S Glos
26 G2 Ram Lane Kent

11 M4 Rampisham Dorset
94 E7 Rampside Cumb
62 F7 Rampton Cambs
85 P5 Rampton Notts
89 M7 Ramsbottom Bury
33 Q10 Ramsbury Wilts
167 K11 Ramscraigs Highld
23 K10 Ramsdean Hants
22 G3 Ramsdell Hants
48 C11 Ramsden Oxon
46 H5 Ramsden Worcs
38 B3 Ramsden Bellhouse Essex
38 B2 Ramsden Heath Essex
62 C3 Ramsey Cambs
53 M5 Ramsey Essex
80 g3 Ramsey IoM
62 D3 Ramsey Forty Foot Cambs
62 B4 Ramsey Heights Cambs
52 F10 Ramsey Island Essex
40 D6 Ramsey Island Pembks
62 C3 Ramsey Mereside Cambs
62 C3 Ramsey St Mary's Cambs
39 Q3 Ramsgate Kent
96 H6 Ramsgill N York
103 M5 Ramshaw Dur
112 E11 Ramshaw Dur
53 P3 Ramsholt Suffk
118 D10 Ramshope Nthumb
71 K5 Ramshorn Staffs
8 G6 Ramsley Devon
23 P8 Ramsnest Common Surrey
86 H5 Ranby Lincs
85 L4 Ranby Notts
86 F5 Rand Lincs
36 E9 Randalls Park Crematorium Surrey
32 F3 Randwick Gloucs
125 K4 Ranfurly Rens
71 M10 Rangemore Staffs
32 C7 Rangeworthy S Glos
115 J5 Rankinston E Ayrs
73 L8 Ranksborough Rutlnd
52 B8 Rank's Green Essex
140 B6 Rannoch Station P & K
18 B6 Ranscombe Somset
85 L3 Ranskill Notts
70 F10 Ranton Staffs
70 E10 Ranton Green Staffs
77 M9 Ranworth Norfk
133 M9 Raploch Stirlg
169 e2 Rapness Ork
19 K11 Rapps Somset
108 G11 Rascarrel D & G
131 N11 Rashfield Ag & B
58 D11 Rashwood Worcs
97 Q6 Raskelf N York
32 G2 Rassau Blae G
90 E6 Rastrick Calder
145 R4 Ratagan Highld
72 E9 Ratby Leics
72 A11 Ratcliffe Culey Leics
72 D5 Ratcliffe on Soar Notts
72 G8 Ratcliffe on the Wreake Leics
21 N6 Ratfyn Wilts
159 N5 Rathen Abers
135 K3 Rathillet Fife
96 B9 Rathmell N York
127 L3 Ratho C Edin
127 L3 Ratho Station C Edin
158 B4 Rathven Moray
22 D10 Ratlake Hants
48 C5 Ratley Warwks
39 M11 Ratling Kent
56 G5 Ratlinghope Shrops
75 K8 Rattan Row Norfk
167 N2 Rattar Highld
101 K2 Ratten Row Cumb
110 G11 Ratten Row Cumb
88 E2 Ratten Row Lancs
7 J6 Rattery Devon
64 D10 Rattlesden Suffk
25 N10 Ratton Village E Susx
142 B8 Rattray P & K
110 G11 Raughton Cumb
110 G11 Raughton Head Cumb
61 L6 Raunds Nhants
91 M11 Ravenfield Rothm
100 E11 Ravenglass Cumb
46 D4 Ravenhills Green Worcs
65 M2 Raveningham Norfk
105 Q10 Ravenscar N York
126 D6 Ravenscraig N Lans
80 e3 Ravensdale IoM
61 N10 Ravensden Bed
102 C10 Ravenseat N York
85 J10 Ravenshead Notts
69 R4 Ravensmoor Ches E
90 G3 Ravensthorpe Kirk
60 E6 Ravensthorpe Nhants
72 C8 Ravenstone Leics
49 M4 Ravenstone M Keyn
102 D10 Ravenstonedale Cumb
126 G8 Ravenstruther S Lans
103 M9 Ravensworth N York
105 P9 Raw N York
98 B10 Rawcliffe E R Yk
92 A6 Rawcliffe C York
92 A6 Rawcliffe Bridge E R Yk
90 G3 Rawdon Leeds
90 G3 Rawdon Crematorium Leeds
38 F10 Rawling Street Kent
91 L11 Rawmarsh Rothm
58 F2 Rawnsley Staffs
38 C3 Rawreth Essex
10 E3 Rawridge Devon
89 N6 Rawtenstall Lancs
52 H4 Raydon Suffk
112 D2 Raylees Nthumb
38 D3 Rayleigh Essex
10 G5 Raymond's Hill Devon
52 B7 Rayne Essex
36 F7 Raynes Park Gt Lon
63 J7 Reach Cambs
89 M4 Read Lancs
90 B10 Reading Readg
35 K9 Reading Crematorium Readg
35 J11 Reading Services W Berk
26 F5 Reading Street Kent
39 Q8 Reading Street Kent
102 B7 Reagill Cumb
2 C9 Realwa Cnwll
162 G8 Rearquhar Highld
72 H8 Rearsby Leics
70 A4 Rease Heath Ches E

166 G4 Reay Highld
39 M8 Reculver Kent
18 E11 Red Ball Devon
41 L10 Redberth Pembks
50 D8 Redbourn Herts
92 G11 Redbourne N Linc
69 P6 Redbrook Wrexhm
26 F4 Redbrook Street Kent
156 G8 Redburn Highld
111 Q8 Redburn Nthumb
104 H6 Redcar R & Cl
108 H7 Redcastle D & G
155 Q8 Redcastle Highld
110 E11 Red Dial Cumb
126 G2 Redding Falk
126 G2 Reddingmuirhead Falk
83 J6 Reddish Stockp
58 F11 Redditch Worcs
58 F11 Redditch Crematorium Worcs
63 P9 Rede Suffk
65 K3 Redenhall Norfk
22 B5 Redenham Hants
112 C4 Redesmouth Nthumb
143 P3 Redford Abers
143 K9 Redford Angus
23 N9 Redford W Susx
117 M7 Redfordgreen Border
30 D7 Redgate Rhondd
134 D2 Redgorton P & K
64 E6 Redgrave Suffk
151 K7 Redhill Abers
13 J5 Redhill Bmouth
50 H4 Redhill Herts
19 N2 Redhill N Som
36 G10 Redhill Surrey
47 M3 Red Hill Warwks
65 N5 Redisham Suffk
31 Q9 Redland Bristl
169 C4 Redland Ork
64 H7 Redlingfield Suffk
64 H7 Redlingfield Green Suffk
63 L6 Red Lodge Suffk
89 N7 Red Lumb Rochdl
20 D8 Redlynch Somset
21 P10 Redlynch Wilts
100 F4 Redmain Cumb
57 P11 Redmarley Worcs
46 E8 Redmarley D'Abitot Gloucs
104 C6 Redmarshall S on T
73 K3 Redmile Leics
96 F2 Redmire N York
143 P2 Redmyre Abers
58 F9 Rednal Birm
69 L9 Rednal Shrops
118 A3 Redpath Border
153 N4 Redpoint Highld
16 D10 Red Post Cnwll
88 H9 Red Rock Wigan
41 P8 Red Roses Carmth
119 Q11 Red Row Nthumb
2 H5 Redruth Cnwll
20 H2 Redstocks Wilts
142 B11 Redstone P & K
41 M7 Redstone Cross Pembks
70 E4 Red Street Staffs
89 N9 Redvales Bury
79 J8 Red Wharf Bay IoA
31 M8 Redwick Newpt
31 P7 Redwick S Glos
103 P6 Redworth Darltn
51 J3 Reed Herts
77 N11 Reedham Norfk
92 C6 Reedness E R Yk
86 H7 Reeds Beck Lincs
89 N6 Reeds Holme Lancs
86 D6 Reepham Lincs
76 G7 Reepham Norfk
103 K11 Reeth N York
59 L9 Reeves Green Solhll
80 f2 Regaby IoM
19 P2 Regil N Som
160 F4 Reiff Highld
36 G10 Reigate Surrey
99 N5 Reighton N York
151 M4 Reisque Abers
167 P6 Reiss Highld
4 D10 Rejerrah Cnwll
2 H5 Releath Cnwll
2 F7 Relubbus Cnwll
157 L8 Relugas Moray
35 L8 Remenham Wokham
35 L8 Remenham Hill Wokham
72 F6 Rempstone Notts
33 K3 Rendcomb Gloucs
65 L9 Rendham Suffk
65 L11 Rendlesham Suffk
125 N4 Renfrew Rens
61 N10 Renhold Bed
84 G5 Renishaw Derbys
119 P7 Rennington Nthumb
125 K2 Renton W Duns
101 Q2 Renwick Cumb
77 N8 Repps Norfk
71 Q9 Repton Derbys
156 C6 Resaurie Highld
3 P5 Rescassa Cnwll
3 P5 Rescorla Cnwll
138 C5 Resipole Highld
2 G5 Reskadinnick Cnwll
156 B4 Resolis Highld
29 M4 Resolven Neath
131 Q6 Rest and be thankful Ag & B
129 M7 Reston Border
3 L6 Restronguet Cnwll
143 J7 Reswallie Angus
4 E9 Reterth Cnwll
85 M7 Retford Notts
4 G9 Retire Cnwll
52 E7 Rettendon Essex
4 D10 Retyn Cnwll
87 J7 Revesby Lincs
7 J11 Rew Devon
7 K4 Rew Devon
9 M5 Rewe Devon
14 E6 Rew Street IoW
5 Q4 Rexon Devon
76 E6 Reydon Suffk
76 E6 Reymerston Norfk
41 K9 Reynalton Pembks
28 E7 Reynoldston Swans
5 P6 Rezare Cnwll
31 L4 Rhadyr Mons
43 Q9 Rhandirmwyn Carmth
55 M11 Rhayader Powys
155 P8 Rheindown Highld
80 H10 Rhes-y-cae Flints

68 F2 Rhewl Denbgs
68 G6 Rhewl Denbgs
80 G8 Rhewl-fawr Flints
80 H8 Rhewl Mostyn Flints
164 C11 Rhicarn Highld
164 G6 Rhiconich Highld
156 B3 Rhicullen Highld
29 P3 Rhigos Rhondd
160 G7 Rhireavach Highld
163 J6 Rhives Highld
30 G8 Rhiwbina Cardif
67 M5 Rhiwbryfdir Gwynd
31 J7 Rhiwderyn Newpt
67 K2 Rhiwen Gwynd
30 D7 Rhiwinder Rhondd
68 B7 Rhiwlas Gwynd
68 C11 Rhiwlas Gwynd
68 G8 Rhiwlas Powys
30 E8 Rhiwsaeson Rhondd
19 J8 Rhode Somset
37 Q11 Rhoden Green Kent
85 J5 Rhodesia Notts
27 L3 Rhodes Minnis Kent
40 E5 Rhodiad-y-brenin Pembks
108 F9 Rhonehouse D & G
30 E11 Rhoose V Glam
42 G7 Rhos Carmth
68 F2 Rhos Denbgs
29 K4 Rhos Neath
78 F6 Rhosbeirio IoA
79 J9 Rhoscefnhir IoA
78 D9 Rhoscolyn IoA
40 H10 Rhoscrowther Pembks
81 J11 Rhosesmor Flints
66 F7 Rhos-fawr Gwynd
67 J3 Rhosgadfan Gwynd
78 G3 Rhosgoch IoA
44 H5 Rhosgoch Powys
43 K2 Rhos Haminiog Cerdgn
41 N2 Rhoshill Pembks
66 F6 Rhoshirwaun Gwynd
66 H6 Rhoslan Gwynd
54 D3 Rhoslefain Gwynd
69 J5 Rhosllanerchrugog Wrexhm
78 H7 Rhôs Lligwy IoA
43 M10 Rhosmaen Carmth
78 H9 Rhosmeirch IoA
78 E10 Rhosneigr IoA
69 L4 Rhosnesni Wrexhm
79 L8 Rhôs-on-Sea Conwy
69 K4 Rhosrobin Wrexhm
28 D7 Rhossili Swans
66 H3 Rhostryfan Gwynd
66 H5 Rhostyllen Wrexhm
78 K7 Rhosybol IoA
68 F10 Rhos y-brithdir Powys
69 J8 Rhosygadfa Shrops
54 E10 Rhos-y-garth Cerdgn
66 C7 Rhos-y-llan Gwynd
69 J7 Rhosymedre Wrexhm
56 D11 Rhos-y-meirch Powys
132 B11 Rhu Ag & B
80 F9 Rhuallt Denbgs
124 C3 Rhubodach Ag & B
90 Q2 Rhuddall Heath Ches W
43 J6 Rhuddlan Cerdgn
80 E9 Rhuddlan Denbgs
44 G5 Rhulen Powys
123 M10 Rhunahaorine Ag & B
67 K6 Rhyd Gwynd
42 H9 Rhydargaeau Carmth
43 L7 Rhydcymerau Carmth
46 F5 Rhydd Worcs
67 K4 Rhyd-Ddu Gwynd
29 K5 Rhydding Neath
68 C2 Rhydgaled Conwy
67 Q4 Rhydlanfair Conwy
42 F5 Rhydlewis Cerdgn
66 B9 Rhydlios Gwynd
66 A4 Rhyd-lydan Conwy
42 H5 Rhydowen Cerdgn
54 D11 Rhydrosser Cerdgn
45 J5 Rhydspence Herefs
68 H4 Rhydtalog Flints
68 E8 Rhyd-uchaf Gwynd
68 E8 Rhyd-y-clafdy Gwynd
68 H5 Rhydycroesau Shrops
54 D9 Rhydyfelin Cerdgn
30 E7 Rhydyfelin Rhondd
80 C9 Rhyd-y-foel Conwy
29 K3 Rhydyfro Neath
79 K11 Rhyd-y-groes Gwynd
67 Q10 Rhydymain Gwynd
31 K3 Rhyd-y-meirch Mons
81 J11 Rhydymwyn Flints
54 E7 Rhyd-y pennau Cerdgn
54 E4 Rhyd-yr-onnen Gwynd
67 M6 Rhyd-y-sarn Gwynd
80 E8 Rhyl Denbgs
30 F3 Rhymney Caerph
134 F3 Rhynd P & K
150 F3 Rhynie Abers
163 J11 Rhynie Highld
57 P10 Ribbesford Worcs
88 H4 Ribbleton Lancs
88 E4 Ribby Lancs
89 K3 Ribchester Lancs
84 D9 Riber Derbys
93 L9 Riby Lincs
91 L3 Riccall N York
111 K2 Riccarton Border
125 L10 Riccarton E Ayrs
56 H11 Richards Castle Herefs
36 B5 Richings Park Bucks
36 E6 Richmond Gt Lon
103 N10 Richmond N York
84 F3 Richmond Sheff
10 c2 Richmond Fort Guern
18 F8 Rich's Holford Somset
70 C11 Rickerscote Staffs
19 N3 Rickford N Som
7 K11 Rickham Devon
64 E6 Rickinghall Suffk
51 L4 Rickling Essex
51 M5 Rickling Green Essex
36 C2 Rickmansworth Herts
117 Q6 Riddell Border
84 E9 Riddings Derbys
17 J10 Riddlecombe Devon
90 D2 Riddlesden C Brad
19 Q3 Ridge BaNES
12 F7 Ridge Dorset
50 F10 Ridge Herts
21 J8 Ridge Wilts
44 F2 Ridgebourne Powys
36 H11 Ridge Green Surrey
59 L6 Ridge Lane Warwks

296 Ridge Row - St Fergus

27 M3 Ridge Row Kent
84 F4 Ridgeway Derbys
47 K2 Ridgeway Worcs
46 D5 Ridgeway Cross Herefs
52 B3 Ridgewell Essex
25 L7 Ridgewood E Susx
49 Q7 Ridgmont C Beds
112 F8 Riding Mill Nthumb
37 P8 Ridley Kent
111 Q8 Ridley Nthumb
69 Q4 Ridley Green Ches E
77 L5 Ridlington Norfk
73 L10 Ridlington Rutlnd
77 L5 Ridlington Street Norfk
112 D4 Ridsdale Nthumb
98 B3 Rievaulx N York
98 B4 Rievaulx Abbey N York
110 E7 Rigg D & G
126 D3 Riggend N Lans
156 F7 Righoul Highld
95 N4 Rigmadon Park Cumb
87 M5 Rigsby Lincs
116 B3 Rigside S Lans
89 J5 Riley Green Lancs
58 H2 Rileyhill Staffs
5 M7 Rilla Mill Cnwll
5 M7 Rillaton Cnwll
98 H6 Rillington N York
96 B11 Rimington Lancs
20 B10 Rimpton Somset
93 P5 Rimswell E R Yk
41 J5 Rinaston Pembks
57 N5 Rindleford Shrops
108 E9 Ringford D & G
84 C4 Ringinglow Sheff
76 G9 Ringland Norfk
25 L6 Ringles Cross E Susx
38 E10 Ringlestone Kent
89 M9 Ringley Bolton
25 K8 Ringmer E Susx
6 H9 Ringmore Devon
7 N4 Ringmore Devon
88 F8 Ring o'Bells Lancs
157 P9 Ringorm Moray
74 G10 Ring's End Cambs
65 N4 Ringsfield Suffk
65 N4 Ringsfield Corner Suffk
35 Q2 Ringshall Herts
64 E11 Ringshall Suffk
64 F11 Ringshall Stocks Suffk
61 L5 Ringstead Nhants
75 P2 Ringstead Norfk
13 L3 Ringwood Hants
27 Q2 Ringwould Kent
2 F8 Rinsey Cnwll
2 G8 Rinsey Croft Cnwll
25 M8 Ripe E Susx
84 E10 Ripley Derbys
13 L5 Ripley Hants
97 L8 Ripley N York
36 C9 Ripley Surrey
92 G4 Riplingham E R Yk
23 J10 Riplington Hants
97 M6 Ripon N York
74 A5 Rippingale Lincs
39 Q11 Ripple Kent
46 G7 Ripple Worcs
90 C7 Ripponden Calder
122 D11 Risabus Ag & B
45 Q4 Risbury Herefs
92 F8 Risby N Linc
63 P7 Risby Suffk
30 H6 Risca Caerph
93 L2 Rise E R Yk
25 P4 Riseden E Susx
26 B4 Riseden Kent
74 D5 Risegate Lincs
85 C5 Riseholme Lincs
100 D4 Risehow Cumb
61 M8 Riseley Bed
23 K2 Riseley Wokham
64 H8 Rishangles Suffk
89 L4 Rishton Lancs
90 C7 Rishworth Calder
89 M5 Rising Bridge Lancs
72 D3 Risley Derbys
82 E6 Risley Warrtn
97 K7 Risplith N York
22 B2 Rivar Wilts
52 D8 Rivenhall End Essex
27 N3 River Kent
23 P10 River W Susx
62 H7 River Bank Cambs
155 P7 Riverford Highld
37 M9 Riverhead Kent
12 C2 Rivers Corner Dorset
89 J8 Rivington Lancs
17 R7 Roachill Devon
49 L4 Roade Nhants
65 K3 Road Green Norfk
111 K6 Roadhead Cumb
126 F8 Roadmeetings S Lans
115 L4 Roadside E Ayrs
167 L4 Roadside Highld
18 D7 Roadwater Somset
152 D9 Roag Highld
94 E7 Roa Island Cumb
114 E7 Roan of Craigoch S Ayrs
51 L4 Roast Green Essex
30 G9 Roath Cardif
117 N8 Roberton Border
116 C5 Roberton S Lans
26 B7 Robertsbridge E Susx
90 F6 Roberttown Kirk
41 L7 Robeston Wathen Pembks
110 D6 Robgill Tower D & G
70 G3 Robin Hill Staffs
88 G8 Robin Hood Lancs
91 J5 Robin Hood Leeds
58 H8 Robin Hood Crematorium Solhll
91 R11 Robin Hood Doncaster Sheffield Airport Donc
52 B4 Robinhood End Essex
105 Q9 Robin Hood's Bay N York
6 E6 Roborough Devon
17 K8 Roborough Devon
81 N6 Roby Knows
88 G9 Roby Mill Lancs
71 L7 Rocester Staffs
40 G6 Roch Pembks
89 P8 Rochdale Rochdl
89 P8 Rochdale Crematorium Rochdl
4 F9 Roche Cnwll
38 B8 Rochester Medway
118 F11 Rochester Nthumb
38 E3 Rochford Essex
57 L11 Rochford Worcs
40 G6 Roch Gate Pembks
4 E6 Rock Cnwll
29 L6 Rock Neath
119 P6 Rock Nthumb
24 D8 Rock W Susx
57 N10 Rock Worcs
9 P6 Rockbeare Devon
21 M11 Rockbourne Hants
110 G8 Rockcliffe Cumb
108 H10 Rockcliffe D & G
110 F8 Rockcliffe Cross Cumb
70 F3 Rock End Staffs
7 N6 Rockend Torbay
81 L7 Rock Ferry Wirral
163 L10 Rockfield Highld
31 N2 Rockfield Mons
17 P2 Rockford Devon
13 L3 Rockford Hants
57 J9 Rockgreen Shrops
32 C6 Rockhampton S Glos
4 H5 Rockhead Cnwll
56 D9 Rockhill Shrops
58 E11 Rock Hill Worcs
61 J2 Rockingham Nhants
64 D2 Rockland All Saints Norfk
77 L11 Rockland St Mary Norfk
64 D2 Rockland St Peter Norfk
85 M6 Rockley Notts
33 N10 Rockley Wilts
89 P6 Rockliffe Lancs
131 Q9 Rockville Ag & B
35 L7 Rockwell End Bucks
18 F10 Rockwell Green Somset
32 F4 Rodborough Gloucs
33 M7 Rodbourne Swindn
32 H8 Rodbourne Wilts
45 L2 Rodd Herefs
119 K6 Roddam Nthumb
11 N8 Rodden Dorset
103 N3 Roddymoor Dur
20 F4 Rode Somset
70 E3 Rode Heath Ches E
83 J11 Rode Heath Ches E
168 f9 Rodel W Isls
69 Q11 Roden Wrekin
18 D7 Rodhuish Somset
57 K2 Rodington Wrekin
57 K2 Rodington Heath Wrekin
32 D2 Rodley Gloucs
90 G3 Rodley Leeds
32 H5 Rodmarton Gloucs
25 K9 Rodmell E Susx
38 F9 Rodmersham Kent
38 F9 Rodmersham Green Kent
19 N5 Rodney Stoke Somset
71 N6 Rodsley Derbys
19 J6 Rodway Somset
97 N7 Roecliffe N York
83 L5 Roe Cross Tamesd
50 F9 Roe Green Herts
50 H4 Roe Green Herts
82 G4 Roe Green Salfd
36 F6 Roehampton Gt Lon
24 E4 Roffey W Susx
162 G6 Rogart Highld
23 M10 Rogate W Susx
101 L11 Roger Ground Cumb
31 J7 Rogerstone Newpt
168 f9 Roghadal W Isls
31 N7 Rogiet Mons
34 H6 Roke Oxon
113 P9 Roker Sundld
77 N8 Rollesby Norfk
73 J10 Rolleston Leics
85 M10 Rolleston Notts
71 N9 Rolleston on Dove Staffs
93 M2 Rolston E R Yk
19 L2 Rolstone N Som
26 D5 Rolvenden Kent
26 E5 Rolvenden Layne Kent
103 J6 Romaldkirk Dur
20 E2 Roman Baths & Pump Room BaNES
97 N2 Romanby N York
127 M8 Romanno Bridge Border
17 N7 Romansleigh Devon
26 E3 Romden Castle Kent
152 G7 Romesdal Highld
13 J3 Romford Dorset
37 M3 Romford Gt Lon
83 K6 Romiley Stockp
37 N8 Romney Street Kent
22 C10 Romsey Hants
57 P8 Romsley Shrops
58 E8 Romsley Worcs
153 L6 Rona Highld
123 M9 Ronachan Ag & B
20 G3 Rood Ashton Wilts
102 H2 Rookhope Dur
14 F10 Rookley IoW
14 F10 Rookley Green IoW
19 L4 Rooks Bridge Somset
18 E8 Rooks Nest Somset
97 K3 Rookwith N York
93 N4 Roos E R Yk
94 E7 Roose Cumb
94 F7 Roosebeck Cumb
61 N9 Roothams Green Bed
22 H8 Ropley Hants
22 H8 Ropley Dean Hants
23 J8 Ropley Soke Hants
73 P4 Ropsley Lincs
159 Q7 Rora Abers
56 E4 Rorrington Shrops
158 A7 Rosarie Moray
3 K3 Rose Cnwll
88 E3 Roseacre Lancs
17 P7 Rose Ash Devon
126 E8 Rosebank S Lans
41 L5 Rosebush Pembks
5 K2 Rosecare Cnwll
4 C10 Rosecliston Cnwll
105 K11 Rosedale Abbey N York
52 F6 Rose Green Essex
52 F4 Rose Green Suffk
52 G3 Rose Green Suffk
15 P7 Rose Green W Susx
162 B6 Rosehall Highld
159 M4 Rosehearty Abers
25 L7 Rose Hill E Susx
89 N4 Rose Hill Lancs
69 N11 Rosehill Shrops
157 L4 Roseisle Moray
25 P10 Roselands E Susx
41 J9 Rosemarket Pembks
156 C6 Rosemarkie Highld
10 D2 Rosemary Lane Devon
142 B9 Rosemount P & K
4 F8 Rosenannon Cnwll
3 L9 Rosenithon Cnwll
25 M6 Roser's Cross E Susx
4 G10 Rosevean Cnwll
3 M6 Rosevine Cnwll
2 G6 Rosewarne Cnwll
127 P5 Rosewell Mdloth
104 D6 Roseworth S on T
2 G6 Roseworthy Cnwll
101 P7 Rosgill Cumb
2 B9 Roskestal Cnwll
152 D9 Roskhill Highld
3 K9 Roskorwell Cnwll
110 F11 Rosley Cumb
127 P5 Roslin Mdloth
71 N11 Rosliston Derbys
132 B11 Rosneath Ag & B
108 D12 Ross D & G
119 M3 Ross Nthumb
69 L3 Rossett Wrexhm
97 L10 Rossett Green N York
91 Q11 Rossington Donc
125 L3 Rossland Rens
46 A10 Ross-on-Wye Herefs
167 N9 Roster Highld
82 F8 Rostherne Ches E
101 J8 Rosthwaite Cumb
71 L6 Roston Derbys
2 F8 Rosudgeon Cnwll
134 E11 Rosyth Fife
119 L10 Rothbury Nthumb
72 H7 Rotherby Leics
25 N5 Rotherfield E Susx
35 K8 Rotherfield Greys Oxon
35 K8 Rotherfield Peppard Oxon
84 F2 Rotherham Rothm
84 G2 Rotherham Crematorium Rothm
60 F9 Rothersthorpe Nhants
60 F9 Rothersthorpe Services Nhants
23 K3 Rotherwick Hants
157 P8 Rothes Moray
124 D5 Rothesay Ag & B
158 H10 Rothiebrisbane Abers
158 E8 Rothiemay Moray
148 H6 Rothiemurchus Lodge Highld
158 H10 Rothienorman Abers
72 F8 Rothley Leics
112 F3 Rothley Nthumb
158 G11 Rothmaise Abers
91 J5 Rothwell Leeds
93 K11 Rothwell Lincs
60 H4 Rothwell Nhants
99 M10 Rotsea E R Yk
142 F4 Rottal Lodge Angus
25 J10 Rottingdean Br & H
100 C8 Rottington Cumb
109 M5 Roucan D & G
109 M5 Roucan Loch Crematorium D & G
14 F10 Roud IoW
76 A7 Rougham Norfk
64 C9 Rougham Green Suffk
70 G7 Rough Close Staffs
39 K10 Rough Common Kent
89 N2 Roughlee Lancs
149 Q5 Roughpark Abers
86 H8 Roughton Lincs
77 J4 Roughton Norfk
57 P6 Roughton Shrops
37 P10 Roughway Kent
52 E11 Roundbush Essex
50 D11 Round Bush Herts
51 N8 Roundbush Green Essex
50 D6 Round Green Luton
11 J3 Roundham Somset
91 J3 Roundhay Leeds
58 E7 Rounds Green Sandw
37 Q7 Round Street Kent
24 C5 Roundstreet Common W Susx
21 K2 Roundway Wilts
142 F7 Roundyhill Angus
169 c3 Rousay Ork
10 F6 Rousdon Devon
48 E10 Rousham Oxon
47 K4 Rous Lench Worcs
124 F5 Routenburn N Ayrs
93 J2 Routh E R Yk
35 L5 Rout's Green Bucks
4 H6 Row Cnwll
95 K3 Row Cumb
102 B4 Row Cumb
110 H5 Rowanburn D & G
132 D8 Rowardennan Stirlg
83 M7 Rowarth Derbys
14 F4 Row Ash Hants
19 N3 Rowberrow Somset
14 E10 Rowborough IoW
21 J2 Rowde Wilts
8 F5 Rowden Devon
79 P10 Rowen Conwy
71 M5 Rowfield Derbys
111 N8 Rowfoot Nthumb
18 H9 Rowford Somset
52 B7 Row Green Essex
52 H7 Rowhedge Essex
24 D4 Rowhook W Susx
59 K11 Rowington Warwks
84 B6 Rowland Derbys
15 K4 Rowland's Castle Hants
113 J9 Rowland's Gill Gatesd
23 M6 Rowledge Surrey
112 G11 Rowley Dur
92 G4 Rowley E R Yk
56 E3 Rowley Shrops
90 F8 Rowley Hill Kirk
58 E7 Rowley Regis Sandw
58 E7 Rowley Regis Crematorium Sandw
45 M9 Rowlstone Herefs
24 B2 Rowly Surrey
14 G6 Rowner Hants
58 F10 Rowney Green Worcs
22 C11 Rownhams Hants
22 C11 Rownhams Services Hants
100 E7 Rowrah Cumb
49 M11 Rowsham Bucks
84 C7 Rowsley Derbys
82 H9 Rows of Trees Ches E
34 E7 Rowstock Oxon
86 E9 Rowston Lincs
84 G8 Rowthorne Derbys
69 M2 Rowton Ches W
56 F2 Rowton Shrops
56 G8 Rowton Shrops
69 R11 Rowton Wrekin
36 B8 Row Town Surrey
118 C4 Roxburgh Border
92 F7 Roxby N Linc
105 L7 Roxby N York
61 Q10 Roxton Bed
51 P9 Roxwell Essex
36 E5 Royal Botanic Gardens Gt Lon
103 P6 Royal Oak Darltn
81 N4 Royal Oak Lancs
69 R6 Royal's Green Ches E
146 H11 Roy Bridge Highld
90 G8 Roydhouse Kirk
51 K8 Roydon Essex
64 G5 Roydon Norfk
75 P6 Roydon Norfk
51 K9 Roydon Hamlet Essex
91 K8 Royston Barns
51 J2 Royston Herts
89 Q9 Royton Oldham
11 c1 Rozel Jersey
69 K6 Ruabon Wrexhm
136 D6 Ruaig Ag & B
3 N6 Ruan High Lanes Cnwll
3 M5 Ruan Lanihorne Cnwll
3 J10 Ruan Major Cnwll
3 J10 Ruan Minor Cnwll
46 B11 Ruardean Gloucs
46 B11 Ruardean Hill Gloucs
46 B11 Ruardean Woodside Gloucs
58 E9 Rubery Birm
168 c16 Rubha Ban W Isls
101 P2 Ruckcroft Cumb
45 P7 Ruckhall Herefs
26 H5 Ruckinge Kent
87 K5 Ruckland Lincs
57 J4 Ruckley Shrops
104 E9 Rudby N York
112 H7 Rudchester Nthumb
72 F4 Ruddington Notts
32 C2 Ruddle Gloucs
3 Q3 Ruddlemoor Cnwll
46 E10 Rudford Gloucs
20 F4 Rudge Somset
32 B7 Rudgeway S Glos
24 C4 Rudgwick W Susx
46 B9 Rudhall Herefs
82 E10 Rudheath Ches W
82 F10 Rudheath Woods Ches E
52 D11 Rudley Green Essex
32 F10 Rudloe Wilts
30 H7 Rudry Caerph
99 M7 Rudston E R Yk
70 H3 Rudyard Staffs
118 B6 Ruecastle Border
88 F7 Rufford Lancs
98 A10 Rufforth C York
68 E6 Rug Denbgs
60 B5 Rugby Warwks
71 J11 Rugeley Staffs
19 J9 Ruishton Somset
36 C3 Ruislip Gt Lon
144 E8 Rùm Highld
158 A7 Rumbach Moray
134 C8 Rumbling Bridge P & K
65 L5 Rumburgh Suffk
103 N4 Rumby Hill Dur
4 D7 Rumford Cnwll
126 G2 Rumford Falk
30 H9 Rumney Cardif
18 G10 Rumwell Somset
81 Q8 Runcorn Halton
15 N6 Runcton W Susx
75 M9 Runcton Holme Norfk
23 N5 Runfold Surrey
76 F10 Runhall Norfk
77 P9 Runham Norfk
77 Q10 Runham Norfk
18 F10 Runnington Somset
52 C10 Runsell Green Essex
88 G7 Runshaw Moor Lancs
105 M7 Runswick N York
142 D4 Runtaleave Angus
38 C3 Runwell Essex
35 L9 Ruscombe Wokham
46 B7 Rushall Herefs
64 H5 Rushall Norfk
21 M3 Rushall Wilts
58 F4 Rushall Wsall
64 B9 Rushbrooke Suffk
57 J6 Rushbury Shrops
50 H4 Rushden Herts
61 L7 Rushden Nhants
38 F7 Rushenden Kent
25 P5 Rusher's Cross E Susx
8 C9 Rushford Devon
64 C5 Rushford Norfk
53 L8 Rush Green Essex
37 M3 Rush Green Gt Lon
50 F6 Rush Green Herts
82 E7 Rush Green Warrtn
25 P7 Rushlake Green E Susx
65 P4 Rushmere Suffk
53 L2 Rushmere St Andrew Suffk
23 N6 Rushmoor Surrey
45 L3 Rushock Herefs
58 C10 Rushock Worcs
83 J6 Rusholme Manch
69 Q2 Rushton Ches W
60 H4 Rushton Nhants
57 L3 Rushton Shrops
70 G2 Rushton Spencer Staffs
46 F4 Rushwick Worcs
103 Q5 Rushyford Dur
133 J7 Ruskie Stirlg
86 E10 Ruskington Lincs
94 G3 Rusland Cross Cumb
24 F3 Rusper W Susx
32 C2 Ruspidge Gloucs
52 B9 Russell Green Essex
35 K7 Russell's Water Oxon
65 K7 Russel's Green Suffk
24 F2 Russ Hill Surrey
25 N3 Rusthall Kent
24 B10 Rustington W Susx
99 K4 Ruston N York
99 M8 Ruston Parva E R Yk
105 N9 Ruswarp N York
57 K6 Ruthall Shrops
118 B4 Rutherford Border
125 Q5 Rutherglen S Lans
4 G8 Ruthernbridge Cnwll
68 F3 Ruthin Denbgs
151 N7 Ruthrieston C Aber
158 D8 Ruthven Abers
142 D8 Ruthven Angus
148 D8 Ruthven Highld
4 E9 Ruthvoes Cnwll
100 H3 Ruthwaite Cumb
109 N7 Ruthwell D & G
37 L6 Ruxley Corner Gt Lon
45 Q11 Ruxton Green Herefs
69 L10 Ruyton-XI-Towns Shrops
112 F6 Ryal Nthumb
11 J5 Ryall Dorset
46 G6 Ryall Worcs
37 Q8 Ryarsh Kent
35 J3 Rycote Oxon
101 L9 Rydal Cumb
14 G8 Ryde IoW
26 F7 Rye E Susx
69 P8 Ryebank Shrops
46 B10 Ryeford Herefs
26 E7 Rye Foreign E Susx
26 F8 Rye Harbour E Susx
93 M5 Ryehill E R Yk
35 K11 Ryeish Green Wokham
46 E7 Rye Street Worcs
73 Q8 Ryhall Rutlnd
91 K8 Ryhill Wakefd
113 P10 Ryhope Sundld
84 G7 Rylah Derbys
86 D5 Ryland Lincs
72 E3 Rylands Notts
96 E9 Rylstone N York
11 M2 Ryme Intrinseca Dorset
91 P3 Ryther N York
113 J8 Ryton Gatesd
98 F5 Ryton N York
57 P4 Ryton Shrops
59 P7 Ryton Warwks
59 N10 Ryton-on-Dunsmore Warwks
112 H8 Ryton Woodside Gatesd

S

89 M3 Sabden Lancs
51 M11 Sabine's Green Essex
50 H7 Sacombe Herts
50 H7 Sacombe Green Herts
113 K11 Sacriston Dur
104 B7 Sadberge Darltn
120 E5 Saddell Ag & B
60 E2 Saddington Leics
75 M7 Saddle Bow Norfk
24 G8 Saddlescombe W Susx
101 N9 Sadgill Cumb
51 M3 Saffron Walden Essex
41 L10 Sageston Pembks
76 C11 Saham Hills Norfk
76 B11 Saham Toney Norfk
69 M2 Saighton Ches W
129 N6 St Abbs Border
128 H7 St Agnes Border
3 J3 St Agnes Cnwll
2 b3 St Agnes IoS
50 D9 St Albans Herts
3 L3 St Allen Cnwll
10 b2 St Andrew Guern
135 N4 St Andrews Fife
135 N4 St Andrews Botanic Garden Fife
30 F10 St Andrew's Major V Glam
11 K6 St Andrews Well Dorset
88 C5 St Anne's Lancs
109 N2 St Ann's D & G
5 Q7 St Ann's Chapel Cnwll
6 H9 St Ann's Chapel Devon
3 K8 St Anthony Cnwll
25 P10 St Anthony's Hill E Susx
31 P5 St Arvans Mons
80 E10 St Asaph Denbgs
30 D11 St Athan V Glam
11 b2 St Aubin Jersey
3 Q3 St Austell Cnwll
100 C8 St Bees Cumb
3 R3 St Blazey Cnwll
3 R3 St Blazey Gate Cnwll
118 A4 St Boswells Border
11 a2 St Brelade Jersey
11 a2 St Brelade's Bay Jersey
4 F7 St Breock Cnwll
4 H6 St Breward Cnwll
31 Q4 St Briavels Gloucs
40 F8 St Brides Pembks
29 N10 St Bride's Major V Glam
31 M7 St Brides Netherwent Mons
30 E9 St Brides super-Ely V Glam
31 J8 St Brides Wentlooge Newpt
6 D7 St Budeaux C Plym
47 M7 Saintbury Gloucs
2 C8 St Buryan Cnwll
32 E11 St Catherine BaNES
131 N6 St Catherines Ag & B
32 F4 St Chloe Gloucs
41 Q7 St Clears Carmth
5 L8 St Cleer Cnwll
3 M5 St Clement Cnwll
11 c2 St Clement Jersey
5 L5 St Clether Cnwll
124 C4 St Colmac Ag & B
4 E9 St Columb Major Cnwll
4 C9 St Columb Minor Cnwll
4 E10 St Columb Road Cnwll
159 Q5 St Combs Abers
65 K5 St Cross South Elmham Suffk
143 N5 St Cyrus Abers
133 Q3 St David's P & K
40 E5 St Davids Pembks
3 J5 St Day Cnwll
18 E6 St Decumans Somset
4 F10 St Dennis Cnwll
45 N8 St Devereux Herefs
42 C5 St Dogmaels Pembks
41 J5 St Dogwells Pembks
5 Q8 St Dominick Cnwll
29 P11 St Donats V Glam
21 J2 St Edith's Marsh Wilts
4 F6 St Endellion Cnwll
4 D10 St Enoder Cnwll
3 L4 St Erme Cnwll
5 P10 St Erney Cnwll
2 F6 St Erth Cnwll
2 F6 St Erth Praze Cnwll
4 D7 St Ervan Cnwll
4 D8 St Eval Cnwll
3 P4 St Ewe Cnwll
30 F9 St Fagans Cardif
30 F9 St Fagans Welsh Life Museum Cardif
159 Q7 St Fergus Abers

133 K3 **St Fillans** P & K
41 L10 **St Florence** Pembks
5 J2 **St Gennys** Cnwll
80 D9 **St George** Conwy
19 L2 **St George's** N Som
30 F9 **St George's** V Glam
36 C8 **St George's Hill** Surrey
5 P10 **St Germans** Cnwll
17 J8 **St Giles in the Wood** Devon
5 P3 **St Giles-on-the-Heath** Devon
3 K7 **St Gluvia's** Cnwll
55 M10 **St Harmon** Powys
103 N5 **St Helen Auckland** Dur
100 D4 **St Helens** Cumb
26 D9 **St Helens** E Susx
14 H9 **St Helens** IoW
81 Q5 **St Helens** St Hel
81 P5 **St Helens Crematorium** St Hel
36 G7 **St Helier** Gt Lon
11 b2 **St Helier** Jersey
2 E7 **St Hilary** Cnwll
30 D10 **St Hilary** V Glam
10 B3 **Saint Hill** Devon
25 J3 **Saint Hill** W Susx
30 H4 **St Illtyd** Blae G
50 E5 **St Ippollitts** Herts
40 F9 **St Ishmael's** Pembks
4 E7 **St Issey** Cnwll
5 N8 **St Ive** Cnwll
5 N8 **St Ive Cross** Cnwll
62 D6 **St Ives** Cambs
2 E5 **St Ives** Cnwll
13 K4 **St Ives** Dorset
77 K7 **St James** Norfk
60 F8 **St James's End** Nhants
65 L5 **St James South Elmham** Suffk
4 E8 **St Jidgey** Cnwll
5 Q11 **St John** Cnwll
11 b1 **St John** Jersey
103 L4 **St Johns** Dur
80 C5 **St John's** IoM
37 M9 **St Johns** Kent
23 Q3 **St Johns** Surrey
46 F4 **St Johns** Worcs
17 J6 **St John's Chapel** Devon
102 G3 **St John's Chapel** Dur
75 K8 **St John's Fen End** Norfk
75 K8 **St John's Highway** Norfk
116 D3 **St John's Kirk** S Lans
108 D4 **St John's Town of Dalry** D & G
36 G4 **St John's Wood** Gt Lon
80 e2 **St Jude's** IoM
2 B7 **St Just** Cnwll
3 L6 **St Just-in-Roseland** Cnwll
159 J11 **St Katherines** Abers
3 K9 **St Keverne** Cnwll
4 G6 **St Kew** Cnwll
4 G6 **St Kew Highway** Cnwll
5 L9 **St Keyne** Cnwll
4 G8 **St Lawrence** Cnwll
52 H11 **St Lawrence** Essex
14 F11 **St Lawrence** IoW
11 b1 **St Lawrence** Jersey
39 Q8 **St Lawrence** Kent
35 P3 **St Leonards** Bucks
13 K4 **St Leonards** Dorset
26 D10 **St Leonards** E Susx
37 Q9 **St Leonard's Street** Kent
2 B9 **St Levan** Cnwll
30 F10 **St Lythans** V Glam
4 G7 **St Mabyn** Cnwll
134 F3 **St Madoes** P & K
45 M8 **St Margarets** Herefs
51 J8 **St Margarets** Herts
27 Q3 **St Margaret's at Cliffe** Kent
169 d7 **St Margaret's Hope** Ork
65 L5 **St Margaret South Elmham** Suffk
80 c7 **St Marks** IoM
3 J9 **St Martin** Cnwll
5 M10 **St Martin** Cnwll
10 b2 **St Martin** Guern
11 c1 **St Martin** Jersey
2 c1 **St Martin's** IoS
142 B11 **St Martin's** P & K
69 K7 **St Martins** Shrops
69 K7 **St Martin's Moor** Shrops
11 a1 **St Mary** Jersey
22 D4 **St Mary Bourne** Hants
7 N5 **St Marychurch** Torbay
30 D10 **St Mary Church** V Glam
37 L7 **St Mary Cray** Gt Lon
30 C9 **St Mary Hill** V Glam
27 J6 **St Mary in the Marsh** Kent
36 G3 **St Marylebone Crematorium** Gt Lon
2 c2 **St Mary's** Cnwll
169 d6 **St Mary's** Ork
27 J6 **St Mary's Bay** Kent
31 N11 **St Mary's Grove** N Som
38 D6 **St Mary's Hoo** Medway
45 P11 **St Maughans** Mons
45 P11 **St Maughans Green** Mons
3 L7 **St Mawes** Cnwll
4 D8 **St Mawgan** Cnwll
5 P8 **St Mellion** Cnwll
30 H8 **St Mellons** Cardif
4 D7 **St Merryn** Cnwll
3 P3 **St Mewan** Cnwll
3 P5 **St Michael Caerhays** Cnwll
19 K8 **St Michael Church** Somset
3 M5 **St Michael Penkevil** Cnwll
26 E4 **St Michaels** Kent
57 K11 **St Michaels** Worcs
88 F2 **St Michael's on Wyre** Lancs
65 L5 **St Michael South Elmham** Suffk
4 F6 **St Minver** Cnwll
135 N7 **St Monans** Fife
5 K8 **St Neot** Cnwll
61 Q8 **St Neots** Cambs
40 H3 **St Nicholas** Pembks
30 E10 **St Nicholas** V Glam
39 N8 **St Nicholas at Wade** Kent
133 M9 **St Ninians** Stirlg
65 P2 **St Olaves** Norfk
53 K8 **St Osyth** Essex
11 a1 **St Ouen** Jersey
45 Q10 **St Owens Cross** Herefs

37 L7 **St Pauls Cray** Gt Lon
50 E6 **St Paul's Walden** Herts
11 a1 **St Peter** Jersey
10 c2 **St Peter Port** Guern
10 b2 **St Peter's** Guern
39 Q8 **St Peter's** Kent
62 B6 **St Peter's Hill** Cambs
41 J11 **St Petrox** Pembks
5 L9 **St Pinnock** Cnwll
114 G3 **St Quivox** S Ayrs
3 J10 **St Ruan** Cnwll
10 c1 **St Sampson** Guern
10 b2 **St Saviour** Guern
11 b2 **St Saviour** Jersey
3 N3 **St Stephen** Cnwll
5 N4 **St Stephens** Cnwll
5 Q10 **St Stephens** Cnwll
4 H5 **St Teath** Cnwll
4 H6 **St Tudy** Cnwll
41 J11 **St Twynnells** Pembks
5 J10 **St Veep** Cnwll
143 L9 **St Vigeans** Angus
4 F9 **St Wenn** Cnwll
45 P10 **St Weonards** Herefs
30 E9 **St y-Nyll** V Glam
7 J11 **Salcombe** Devon
10 D7 **Salcombe Regis** Devon
52 F9 **Salcott-cum-Virley** Essex
82 G6 **Sale** Traffd
87 N5 **Saleby** Lincs
46 H3 **Sale Green** Worcs
26 C7 **Salehurst** E Susx
43 M9 **Salem** Carmth
54 F8 **Salem** Cerdgn
137 P7 **Salen** Ag & B
138 B5 **Salen** Highld
89 K4 **Salesbury** Lancs
49 P7 **Salford** C Beds
47 Q9 **Salford** Oxon
82 H5 **Salford** Salfd
47 L4 **Salford Priors** Warwks
36 G11 **Salfords** Surrey
77 L9 **Salhouse** Norfk
134 C9 **Saline** Fife
21 M9 **Salisbury** Wilts
21 M9 **Salisbury Cathedral** Wilts
21 N8 **Salisbury Crematorium** Wilts
21 L6 **Salisbury Plain** Wilts
101 P3 **Salkeld Dykes** Cumb
76 G7 **Salle** Norfk
87 K6 **Salmonby** Lincs
47 L10 **Salperton** Gloucs
61 N10 **Salph End** Bed
126 E5 **Salsburgh** N Lans
70 H9 **Salt** Staffs
109 N11 **Salta** Cumb
90 E3 **Saltaire** C Brad
6 C7 **Saltash** Cnwll
156 C3 **Saltburn** Highld
105 J6 **Saltburn-by-the-Sea** R & Cl
73 M5 **Saltby** Leics
110 C10 **Salt Coates** Cumb
100 E11 **Saltcoats** Cumb
124 Q9 **Saltcoats** N Ayrs
88 D5 **Saltcotes** Lancs
25 J10 **Saltdean** Br & H
100 C5 **Salterbeck** Cumb
96 C11 **Salterforth** Lancs
82 D11 **Salterswall** Ches W
21 M7 **Salterton** Wilts
87 N2 **Saltfleet** Lincs
87 N2 **Saltfleetby All Saints** Lincs
87 N2 **Saltfleetby St Clement** Lincs
87 M3 **Saltfleetby St Peter** Lincs
32 C11 **Saltford** BaNES
76 F3 **Salthouse** Norfk
58 H7 **Saltley** Birm
31 K8 **Saltmarsh** Newpt
92 C6 **Saltmarshe** E R Yk
69 L2 **Saltney** Flints
98 E5 **Salton** N York
16 H7 **Saltrens** Devon
113 L8 **Saltwell Crematorium** Gatesd
113 J4 **Saltwick** Nthumb
27 L4 **Saltwood** Kent
24 D9 **Salvington** W Susx
46 G2 **Salwarpe** Worcs
11 K5 **Salway Ash** Dorset
47 L2 **Sambourne** Warwks
70 C10 **Sambrook** Wrekin
88 H4 **Samlesbury** Lancs
89 J5 **Samlesbury Bottoms** Lancs
18 F11 **Sampford Arundel** Somset
18 E6 **Sampford Brett** Somset
8 F4 **Sampford Courtenay** Devon
18 F11 **Sampford Moor** Somset
9 P2 **Sampford Peverell** Devon
6 E4 **Sampford Spiney** Devon
169 H4 **Samsonlane** Ork
53 J8 **Samson's Corner** Essex
128 D5 **Samuelston** E Loth
122 B5 **Sanaigmore** Ag & B
2 C8 **Sancreed** Cnwll
92 E3 **Sancton** E R Yk
19 M5 **Sand** Somset
145 M7 **Sandaig** Highld
100 H2 **Sandale** Cumb
91 J7 **Sandal Magna** Wakefd
144 G11 **Sandavore** Highld
169 f2 **Sanday** Ork
169 f2 **Sanday Airport** Ork
70 D2 **Sandbach** Ches E
70 D2 **Sandbach Services** Ches E
131 P11 **Sandbank** Ag & B
12 H7 **Sandbanks** Poole
158 E4 **Sandend** Abers
36 H8 **Sanderstead** Gt Lon
102 D7 **Sandford** Cumb
9 K4 **Sandford** Devon
12 F7 **Sandford** Dorset
13 L4 **Sandford** Hants
14 F10 **Sandford** IoW
19 M3 **Sandford** N Som
126 C9 **Sandford** S Lans
69 K10 **Sandford** Shrops
69 Q8 **Sandford** Shrops
34 F4 **Sandford-on-Thames** Oxon
20 B10 **Sandford Orcas** Dorset
48 D9 **Sandford St Martin** Oxon

27 M4 **Sandgate** Kent
159 N4 **Sandhaven** Abers
106 E8 **Sandhead** D & G
91 L11 **Sandhill** Rothm
11 M4 **Sandhills** Dorset
11 P2 **Sandhills** Dorset
91 K3 **Sand Hills** Leeds
34 G3 **Sandhills** Oxon
23 P7 **Sandhills** Surrey
112 E7 **Sandhoe** Nthumb
131 L8 **Sandhole** Ag & B
92 D3 **Sand Hole** E R Yk
92 D4 **Sandholme** E R Yk
74 F3 **Sandholme** Lincs
23 M2 **Sandhurst** Br For
46 F10 **Sandhurst** Gloucs
26 D6 **Sandhurst** Kent
26 C6 **Sandhurst Cross** Kent
97 N4 **Sandhutton** N York
98 D9 **Sand Hutton** N York
72 D3 **Sandiacre** Derbys
87 P4 **Sandilands** Lincs
82 D10 **Sandiway** Ches W
21 M11 **Sandleheath** Hants
34 A4 **Sandleigh** Oxon
20 E10 **Sandley** Dorset
38 C10 **Sandling** Kent
82 G11 **Sandlow Green** Ches E
169 n8 **Sandness** Shet
52 B11 **Sandon** Essex
50 H4 **Sandon** Herts
70 G9 **Sandon** Staffs
70 G9 **Sandon Bank** Staffs
14 G10 **Sandown** IoW
5 M10 **Sandplace** Cnwll
50 E8 **Sandridge** Herts
32 H11 **Sandridge** Wilts
75 N5 **Sandringham** Norfk
35 M6 **Sands** Bucks
105 N8 **Sandsend** N York
94 E4 **Sand Side** Cumb
95 K4 **Sandside** Cumb
92 B9 **Sandtoft** N Linc
38 E11 **Sandway** Kent
39 P10 **Sandwich** Kent
101 M7 **Sandwick** Cumb
169 r11 **Sandwick** Shet
168 j4 **Sandwick** W Isls
100 C8 **Sandwith** Cumb
100 C8 **Sandwith Newtown** Cumb
61 Q11 **Sandy** C Beds
87 J9 **Sandy Bank** Lincs
81 L11 **Sandycroft** Flints
25 N6 **Sandy Cross** E Susx
46 C3 **Sandy Cross** Herefs
110 D2 **Sandyford** D & G
7 M4 **Sandygate** Devon
80 e2 **Sandygate** IoM
40 G9 **Sandy Haven** Pembks
109 J9 **Sandyhills** D & G
95 J8 **Sandylands** Lancs
90 E3 **Sandy Lane** C Brad
70 C7 **Sandylane** Staffs
28 G7 **Sandylane** Swans
33 J11 **Sandy Lane** Wilts
69 M6 **Sandy Lane** Wrexhm
8 H7 **Sandy Park** Devon
110 G7 **Sandysike** Cumb
45 P9 **Sandyway** Herefs
165 K3 **Sangobeg** Highld
165 K3 **Sangomore** Highld
82 C7 **Sankey Bridges** Warrtn
57 P11 **Sankyn's Green** Worcs
137 L2 **Sanna Bay** Highld
168 j4 **Sanndabhaig** W Isls
124 C8 **Sannox** N Ayrs
115 Q6 **Sanquhar** D & G
100 F10 **Santon** Cumb
80 d7 **Santon** IoM
100 F10 **Santon Bridge** Cumb
63 P3 **Santon Downham** Suffk
59 Q6 **Sapcote** Leics
46 D2 **Sapey Common** Herefs
64 C6 **Sapiston** Suffk
62 B6 **Sapley** Cambs
71 M8 **Sapperton** Derbys
32 H4 **Sapperton** Gloucs
73 Q4 **Sapperton** Lincs
74 F5 **Saracen's Head** Lincs
167 P8 **Sarclet** Highld
14 F5 **Sarisbury** Hants
29 P8 **Sarn** Brdgnd
66 C8 **Sarn** Gwynd
55 M5 **Sarn** Powys
56 C9 **Sarn** Powys
42 F11 **Sarnau** Carmth
42 C7 **Sarnau** Cerdgn
68 C7 **Sarnau** Gwynd
44 E8 **Sarnau** Powys
68 H11 **Sarnau** Powys
66 E9 **Sarn Bach** Gwynd
45 M4 **Sarnesfield** Herefs
29 P8 **Sarn Park Services** Brdgnd
69 J11 **Sarn-wen** Powys
28 H2 **Saron** Carmth
42 G7 **Saron** Carmth
66 H3 **Saron** Gwynd
79 J11 **Saron** Gwynd
50 B11 **Sarratt** Herts
39 N8 **Sarre** Kent
47 Q10 **Sarsden** Oxon
22 B6 **Sarson** Hants
103 M2 **Satley** Dur
27 N4 **Satmar** Kent
102 H11 **Satron** N York
17 M7 **Satterleigh** Devon
94 G2 **Satterthwaite** Cumb
35 K8 **Satwell** Oxon
151 J5 **Sauchen** Abers
142 B11 **Saucher** P & K
143 M4 **Sauchieburn** Abers
32 D3 **Saul** Gloucs
85 N3 **Saundby** Notts
41 M10 **Saundersfoot** Pembks
35 L4 **Saunderton** Bucks
16 H4 **Saunton** Devon
87 L7 **Sausthorpe** Lincs
3 K4 **Saveock** Cnwll
90 H7 **Saverley Green** Staffs
90 B7 **Savile Town** Kirk
87 K7 **Sawbridge** Warwks
51 L8 **Sawbridgeworth** Herts
99 J4 **Sawdon** N York
72 D4 **Sawley** Derbys
96 A11 **Sawley** Lancs
97 K7 **Sawley** N York
62 G11 **Sawston** Cambs
61 Q4 **Sawtry** Cambs

73 L7 **Saxby** Leics
86 D3 **Saxby** Lincs
92 G7 **Saxby All Saints** N Linc
72 H6 **Saxelbye** Leics
64 F9 **Saxham Street** Suffk
85 Q5 **Saxilby** Lincs
76 E4 **Saxlingham** Norfk
65 J2 **Saxlingham Green** Norfk
65 J2 **Saxlingham Nethergate** Norfk
65 J2 **Saxlingham Thorpe** Norfk
65 M9 **Saxmundham** Suffk
72 H3 **Saxondale** Notts
63 L9 **Saxon Street** Cambs
65 K8 **Saxtead** Suffk
65 K9 **Saxtead Green** Suffk
65 J8 **Saxtead Little Green** Suffk
76 G5 **Saxthorpe** Norfk
91 M3 **Saxton** N York
24 G7 **Sayers Common** W Susx
98 C6 **Scackleton** N York
100 H9 **Scafell Pike** Cumb
85 Q5 **Scaftworth** Notts
98 G6 **Scagglethorpe** N York
136 b3 **Scalasaig** Ag & B
92 D5 **Scalby** E R Yk
99 L2 **Scalby** N York
61 M9 **Scald End** Bed
60 G6 **Scaldwell** Nhants
110 H8 **Scaleby** Cumb
110 H8 **Scalebyhill** Cumb
111 L11 **Scale Houses** Cumb
94 F6 **Scales** Cumb
101 K5 **Scales** Cumb
110 H11 **Scalesceugh** Cumb
73 K6 **Scalford** Leics
105 K8 **Scaling** N York
105 K8 **Scaling Dam** R & Cl
169 r10 **Scalloway** Shet
153 L11 **Scalpay** Highld
87 J5 **Scambesby** Lincs
90 D7 **Scammonden** Kirk
138 E3 **Scamodale** Highld
98 H5 **Scampston** N York
86 C5 **Scampton** Lincs
156 A10 **Scaniport** Highld
90 D7 **Scapegoat Hill** Kirk
130 D7 **Scarba** Ag & B
99 L3 **Scarborough** N York
84 G7 **Scarcliffe** Derbys
91 K2 **Scarcroft** Leeds
167 N2 **Scarfskerry** Highld
103 L8 **Scargill** Dur
136 C7 **Scarinish** Ag & B
88 D8 **Scarisbrick** Lancs
100 H4 **Scarness** Cumb
76 D9 **Scarning** Norfk
73 J2 **Scarrington** Notts
88 E9 **Scarth Hill** Lancs
91 M3 **Scarthingwell** N York
73 N9 **Scartho** NE Lin
169 q6 **Scatsta Airport** Shet
92 G9 **Scawby** N Linc
91 N10 **Scawsby** Donc
91 P9 **Scawthorpe** Donc
98 A4 **Scawton** N York
25 J6 **Scayne's Hill** W Susx
44 G9 **Scethrog** Powys
70 E3 **Scholar Green** Ches E
90 E4 **Scholemoor Crematorium** C Brad
90 F5 **Scholes** Kirk
90 F9 **Scholes** Kirk
91 K3 **Scholes** Leeds
91 K11 **Scholes** Rothm
88 H9 **Scholes** Wigan
103 Q6 **School Aycliffe** Dur
90 E4 **School Green** C Brad
70 A2 **School Green** Ches W
35 K11 **Schoolgreen** Wokham
10 H4 **School House** Dorset
90 G8 **Scissett** Kirk
40 H4 **Scleddau** Pembks
85 K4 **Scofton** Notts
64 H6 **Scole** Norfk
134 E2 **Scone** P & K
153 J11 **Sconser** Highld
135 K7 **Scoonie** Fife
86 E9 **Scopwick** Lincs
160 G7 **Scoraig** Highld
99 L11 **Scorborough** E R Yk
3 J5 **Scorrier** Cnwll
7 J5 **Scorriton** Devon
95 L11 **Scorton** Lancs
103 Q10 **Scorton** N York
77 K7 **Sco Ruston** Norfk
110 H9 **Scotby** Cumb
103 P9 **Scotch Corner** N York
95 K9 **Scotforth** Lancs
70 D5 **Scot Hay** Staffs
86 D5 **Scothern** Lincs
73 Q2 **Scotland** Lincs
113 L4 **Scotland Gate** Nthumb
134 C7 **Scotlandwell** P & K
89 J9 **Scot Lane End** Bolton
167 J5 **Scotscalder Station** Highld
110 G6 **Scotsdike** Cumb
112 F3 **Scot's Gap** Nthumb
150 H4 **Scotsmill** Abers
125 N4 **Scotstoun** C Glas
113 K8 **Scotswood** N u Ty
92 E10 **Scotter** Lincs
92 E10 **Scotterthorpe** Lincs
73 R6 **Scottlethorpe** Lincs
92 E11 **Scotton** Lincs
97 M9 **Scotton** N York
103 N11 **Scotton** N York
77 K7 **Scottow** Norfk
76 R3 **Scott Willoughby** Lincs
76 D11 **Scoulton** Norfk
71 K9 **Scounslow Green** Staffs
164 E8 **Scourie** Highld
164 D8 **Scourie More** Highld
169 q12 **Scousburgh** Shet
90 B9 **Scouthead** Oldham
167 K2 **Scrabster** Highld
118 C7 **Scraesburgh** Border
87 K7 **Scrafield** Lincs
119 J9 **Scrainwood** Nthumb
74 F2 **Scrane End** Lincs
72 G9 **Scraptoft** Leics
77 Q8 **Scratby** Norfk
98 E9 **Scrayingham** N York
26 A2 **Scrays** E Susx
74 A2 **Scredington** Lincs
87 M7 **Scremby** Lincs

129 Q10 **Scremerston** Nthumb
73 J2 **Screveton** Notts
87 J7 **Scrivelsby** Lincs
97 M9 **Scriven** N York
85 L2 **Scrooby** Notts
71 M8 **Scropton** Derbys
86 H9 **Scrub Hill** Lincs
97 L2 **Scruton** N York
110 H6 **Scuggate** Cumb
165 P4 **Scullomie** Highld
76 B5 **Sculthorpe** Norfk
92 E8 **Scunthorpe** N Linc
28 E7 **Scurlage** Swans
10 G2 **Sea** Somset
11 J3 **Seaborough** Dorset
70 E6 **Seabridge** Staffs
27 L4 **Seabrook** Kent
113 P9 **Seaburn** Sundld
81 L6 **Seacombe** Wirral
91 K3 **Seacroft** Leeds
87 Q8 **Seacroft** Lincs
84 F3 **Seadyke** Lincs
152 H9 **Seafield** Highld
127 J4 **Seafield** W Loth
127 P2 **Seafield Crematorium** C Edin
25 L11 **Seaford** E Susx
81 L5 **Seaforth** Sefton
72 G7 **Seagrave** Leics
33 J8 **Seagry Heath** Wilts
113 P11 **Seaham** Dur
119 P4 **Seahouses** Nthumb
37 N9 **Seal** Kent
23 N5 **Seale** Surrey
99 L4 **Seamer** N York
104 E8 **Seamer** N York
124 G8 **Seamill** N Ayrs
77 N6 **Sea Palling** Norfk
93 J9 **Searby** Lincs
39 J9 **Seasalter** Kent
100 D10 **Seascale** Cumb
100 H11 **Seathwaite** Cumb
100 H11 **Seathwaite** Cumb
94 H4 **Seatle** Cumb
100 H8 **Seatoller** Cumb
5 N11 **Seaton** Cnwll
100 D4 **Seaton** Cumb
10 E6 **Seaton** Devon
113 N11 **Seaton** Dur
99 P11 **Seaton** E R Yk
39 M10 **Seaton** Kent
113 M5 **Seaton** Nthumb
73 N11 **Seaton** Rutlnd
113 K6 **Seaton Burn** N Tyne
104 F5 **Seaton Carew** Hartpl
113 M5 **Seaton Delaval** Nthumb
92 C2 **Seaton Ross** E R Yk
113 M5 **Seaton Sluice** Nthumb
11 J6 **Seatown** Dorset
104 G10 **Seave Green** N York
14 H8 **Seaview** IoW
110 C10 **Seaville** Cumb
11 J2 **Seavington St Mary** Somset
19 M11 **Seavington St Michael** Somset
31 J5 **Sebastopol** Torfn
101 L2 **Sebergham** Cumb
59 L3 **Seckington** Warwks
95 P2 **Sedbergh** Cumb
31 P6 **Sedbury** Gloucs
96 C2 **Sedbusk** N York
47 K7 **Sedgeberrow** Worcs
73 M3 **Sedgebrook** Lincs
63 L4 **Sedge Fen** Suffk
104 C5 **Sedgefield** Dur
75 P3 **Sedgeford** Norfk
20 G9 **Sedgehill** Wilts
19 L4 **Sedgemoor Services** Somset
58 D6 **Sedgley** Dudley
82 H4 **Sedgley Park** Bury
95 L3 **Sedgwick** Cumb
26 C8 **Sedlescombe** E Susx
35 M2 **Sedrup** Bucks
38 F10 **Seed** Kent
20 H2 **Seend** Wilts
20 H2 **Seend Cleeve** Wilts
35 Q6 **Seer Green** Bucks
65 L2 **Seething** Norfk
81 M4 **Sefton** Sefton
81 L4 **Sefton Town** Sefton
113 L6 **Seghill** Nthumb
70 F9 **Seighford** Staffs
79 J11 **Seion** Gwynd
58 B5 **Seisdon** Staffs
69 J8 **Selattyn** Shrops
23 K8 **Selborne** Hants
91 Q4 **Selby** N York
23 N10 **Selham** W Susx
36 H7 **Selhurst** Gt Lon
117 P5 **Selkirk** Border
45 R9 **Sellack** Herefs
169 s4 **Sellafirth** Shet
2 C7 **Sellan** Cnwll
18 H11 **Sellick's Green** Somset
27 J4 **Sellindge** Kent
38 H10 **Selling** Kent
20 H2 **Sells Green** Wilts
58 F8 **Selly Oak** Birm
25 M9 **Selmeston** E Susx
37 J8 **Selsdon** Gt Lon
32 F4 **Selsey** Gloucs
15 N8 **Selsey** W Susx
24 H4 **Selsfield Common** W Susx
101 P11 **Selside** Cumb
96 A5 **Selside** N York
27 M3 **Selsted** Kent
84 G10 **Selston** Notts
18 B5 **Selworthy** Somset
52 G2 **Semer** Suffk
20 G2 **Semington** Wilts
20 F8 **Semley** Wilts
57 M8 **Sempringham** Lincs
36 B9 **Send** Surrey
36 B9 **Send Marsh** Surrey
30 F6 **Senghenydd** Caerph
2 B8 **Sennen** Cnwll
2 B8 **Sennen Cove** Cnwll
44 C9 **Sennybridge** Powys
85 K3 **Serlby** Notts
97 Q5 **Sessay** N York
77 M8 **Setchey** Norfk
15 P4 **Setley** Hants
128 C4 **Seton Mains** E Loth
96 B8 **Settle** N York
98 E9 **Settrington** N York
18 G8 **Seven Ash** Somset
47 K10 **Sevenhampton** Gloucs

298 Sevenhampton - Slough Crematorium

33 P6 Sevenhampton Swindn
53 M3 Seven Hills Crematorium Suffk
37 L3 Seven Kings Gt Lon
37 M9 Sevenoaks Kent
37 M10 Sevenoaks Weald Kent
29 M3 Seven Sisters Neath
47 J11 Seven Springs Gloucs
52 F6 Seven Star Green Essex
31 P8 Severn Beach S Glos
46 G6 Severn Stoke Worcs
31 Q7 Severn View Services S Glos
61 N10 Sevick End Bed
26 H3 Sevington Kent
51 N3 Sewards End Essex
51 J11 Sewardstonebury Essex
49 Q10 Sewell C Beds
99 P7 Sewerby E R Yk
3 J7 Seworgan Cnwll
73 M6 Sewstern Leics
104 E9 Sexhow N York
47 N8 Sezincote Gloucs
168 k1 Sgiogarstaigh W Isls
35 J3 Shabbington Bucks
57 Q3 Shackerley Shrops
72 B9 Shackerstone Leics
72 C4 Shacklecross Derbys
23 P5 Shackleford Surrey
89 Q6 Shade Calder
168 i2 Shader W Isls
104 B2 Shadforth Dur
65 N5 Shadingfield Suffk
26 G4 Shadoxhurst Kent
91 J3 Shadwell Leeds
64 C5 Shadwell Norfk
51 K3 Shaftenhoe End Herts
20 G10 Shaftesbury Dorset
91 P9 Shaftholme Donc
91 K8 Shafton Barns
91 K8 Shafton Two Gates Barns
82 E4 Shakerley Wigan
22 B2 Shalbourne Wilts
14 C9 Shalcombe IoW
23 J6 Shalden Hants
23 K6 Shalden Green Hants
7 N4 Shaldon Devon
14 D9 Shalfleet IoW
52 B6 Shalford Essex
36 B11 Shalford Surrey
52 B6 Shalford Green Essex
70 F9 Shallowford Staffs
39 J11 Shalmsford Street Kent
48 H7 Shalstone Bucks
24 B2 Shamley Green Surrey
142 H5 Shandford Angus
132 B10 Shandon Ag & B
156 F2 Shandwick Highld
73 J11 Shangton Leics
113 L5 Shankhouse Nthumb
14 G10 Shanklin IoW
101 Q7 Shap Cumb
169 e5 Shapinsay Ork
12 F4 Shapwick Dorset
19 M7 Shapwick Somset
59 J7 Shard End Birm
72 C4 Shardlow Derbys
58 D3 Shareshill Staffs
91 K7 Sharlston Wakefd
91 K7 Sharlston Common Wakefd
58 H9 Sharman's Cross Solhll
38 C7 Sharnal Street Medway
61 L9 Sharnbrook Bed
89 P6 Sharneyford Lancs
59 Q6 Sharnford Leics
11 Q3 Sharnhill Green Dorset
88 G4 Sharoe Green Lancs
97 M6 Sharow N York
50 C4 Sharpenhoe C Beds
119 J10 Sharperton Nthumb
77 M7 Sharp Green Norfk
32 C4 Sharpness Gloucs
25 J4 Sharpthorne W Susx
5 M7 Sharptor Cnwll
58 E11 Sharpway Gate Worcs
76 E4 Sharrington Norfk
57 P8 Shatterford Worcs
39 N10 Shatterling Kent
84 B4 Shatton Derbys
6 E6 Shaugh Prior Devon
11 J5 Shave Cross Dorset
70 B4 Shavington Ches E
90 C3 Shaw C Brad
89 Q9 Shaw Oldham
33 M7 Shaw Swindn
34 E11 Shaw W Berk
32 G11 Shaw Wilts
57 L2 Shawbirch Wrekin
168 h3 Shawbost W Isls
69 Q10 Shawbury Shrops
89 P8 Shawclough Rochdl
46 C9 Shaw Common Gloucs
119 L8 Shawdon Hill Nthumb
60 B4 Shawell Leics
22 E9 Shawford Hants
89 P6 Shawforth Lancs
50 H4 Shaw Green Herts
88 G7 Shaw Green Lancs
97 L10 Shaw Green N York
109 J5 Shawhead D & G
97 L8 Shaw Mills N York
126 D7 Shawsburn S Lans
20 G6 Shear Cross Wilts
109 M7 Shearington D & G
60 D2 Shearsby Leics
19 J8 Shearston Somset
16 G10 Shebbear Devon
70 D9 Shebdon Staffs
166 H4 Shebster Highld
125 P6 Sheddens E Rens
14 G4 Shedfield Hants
71 L2 Sheen Staffs
84 E6 Sheepbridge Derbys
113 J9 Sheep Hill Dur
90 F7 Sheepridge Kirk
91 J4 Sheepscar Leeds
32 G2 Sheepscombe Gloucs
6 F5 Sheepstor Devon
8 C3 Sheepwash Devon
113 L3 Sheepwash Nthumb
31 N9 Sheepway N Som
72 A10 Sheepy Magna Leics
72 A10 Sheepy Parva Leics
51 M8 Sheering Essex
38 F7 Sheerness Kent
36 B8 Sheerwater Surrey
23 L10 Sheet Hants
2 D8 Sheffield Cnwll
84 E3 Sheffield Sheff
34 H11 Sheffield Bottom W Berk
84 E3 Sheffield City Road Crematorium Sheff
25 K5 Sheffield Green E Susx
50 D3 Shefford C Beds
164 E4 Sheigra Highld
57 L4 Sheinton Shrops
56 G9 Shelderton Shrops
58 J8 Sheldon Birm
83 Q11 Sheldon Derbys
10 C3 Sheldon Devon
38 H10 Sheldwich Kent
38 H10 Sheldwich Lees Kent
90 E5 Shelf Calder
64 G5 Shelfanger Norfk
47 M2 Shelfield Warwks
58 F4 Shelfield Wsall
47 M2 Shelfield Green Warwks
72 H2 Shelford Notts
59 P7 Shelford Warwks
118 G2 Shellacres Nthumb
51 N9 Shelley Essex
90 G8 Shelley Kirk
52 H4 Shelley Suffk
90 G8 Shelley Far Bank Kirk
34 B6 Shellingford Oxon
51 P9 Shellow Bowells Essex
46 D2 Shelsley Beauchamp Worcs
46 D2 Shelsley Walsh Worcs
61 M7 Shelton Bed
65 J3 Shelton Norfk
73 K2 Shelton Notts
56 H2 Shelton Shrops
65 J3 Shelton Green Norfk
72 B4 Shelton Lock C Derb
70 E7 Shelton Under Harley Staffs
56 E5 Shelve Shrops
45 Q6 Shelwick Herefs
51 P11 Shenfield Essex
48 C6 Shenington Oxon
50 E10 Shenley Herts
49 M7 Shenley Brook End M Keyn
50 E10 Shenleybury Herts
49 M7 Shenley Church End M Keyn
45 M7 Shenmore Herefs
107 K5 Shennanton D & G
58 H4 Shenstone Staffs
58 C10 Shenstone Worcs
58 H4 Shenstone Woodend Staffs
72 B11 Shenton Leics
149 N2 Shenval Moray
74 F8 Shepeau Stow Lincs
50 G6 Shephall Herts
36 F4 Shepherd's Bush Gt Lon
35 K8 Shepherd's Green Oxon
32 D4 Shepherds Patch Gloucs
27 N2 Shepherdswell Kent
90 F9 Shepley Kirk
32 B5 Shepperdine S Glos
36 C7 Shepperton Surrey
36 C7 Shepperton Green Surrey
62 E11 Shepreth Cambs
72 D7 Shepshed Leics
19 M11 Shepton Beauchamp Somset
20 B6 Shepton Mallet Somset
20 C8 Shepton Montague Somset
38 C11 Shepway Kent
104 D3 Sheraton Dur
20 B11 Sherborne Dorset
33 N2 Sherborne Gloucs
19 Q3 Sherborne Somset
22 H3 Sherborne St John Hants
47 Q2 Sherbourne Warwks
104 B2 Sherburn Dur
99 K5 Sherburn N York
104 B2 Sherburn Hill Dur
91 M4 Sherburn in Elmet N York
36 C11 Shere Surrey
76 B6 Shereford Norfk
21 Q10 Sherfield English Hants
23 J3 Sherfield on Loddon Hants
89 M5 Sherfin Lancs
7 K10 Sherford Devon
12 F6 Sherford Dorset
57 P2 Sheriffhales Shrops
98 D7 Sheriff Hutton N York
76 H3 Sheringham Norfk
49 N5 Sherington M Keyn
24 F7 Shermanbury W Susx
75 P4 Shernborne Norfk
21 J7 Sherrington Wilts
32 G7 Sherston Wilts
72 F2 Sherwood C Nott
85 K9 Sherwood Forest Notts
85 L7 Sherwood Forest Crematorium Notts
125 Q5 Shettleston C Glas
88 G9 Shevington Wigan
88 G8 Shevington Moor Wigan
88 G9 Shevington Vale Wigan
5 P10 Sheviock Cnwll
90 D5 Shibden Head C Brad
14 F9 Shide IoW
118 F3 Shidlaw Nthumb
146 A4 Shiel Bridge Highld
153 Q7 Shieldaig Highld
109 M3 Shieldhill D & G
126 F2 Shieldhill Falk
116 E2 Shieldhill House Hotel S Lans
126 D6 Shields N Lans
138 B3 Shielfoot Highld
142 G6 Shielhill Angus
124 G3 Shielhill Inver
34 C4 Shifford Oxon
57 N3 Shifnal Shrops
119 N9 Shilbottle Nthumb
103 P5 Shildon Dur
125 M6 Shillford E Rens
18 C10 Shillingford Devon
34 G6 Shillingford Oxon
9 M7 Shillingford Abbot Devon
9 M7 Shillingford St George Devon
12 D2 Shillingstone Dorset
50 D4 Shillington C Beds
118 G9 Shillmoor Nthumb
33 Q3 Shilton Oxon
59 P8 Shilton Warwks
64 H5 Shimpling Norfk
64 B11 Shimpling Suffk
64 B11 Shimpling Street Suffk
103 Q2 Shincliffe Dur
113 M10 Shiney Row Sundld
35 K11 Shinfield Wokham
62 D11 Shingay Cambs
53 Q3 Shingle Street Suffk
7 K6 Shinnersbridge Devon
162 C4 Shinness Highld
37 N10 Shipbourne Kent
76 D10 Shipdham Norfk
19 M3 Shipham Somset
7 M5 Shiphay Torbay
35 L9 Shiplake Oxon
35 K9 Shiplake Row Oxon
19 L3 Shiplate N Som
90 F3 Shipley C Brad
72 C2 Shipley Derbys
57 Q5 Shipley Shrops
24 D6 Shipley W Susx
24 H2 Shipley Bridge Surrey
26 H4 Shipley Hatch Kent
65 M3 Shipmeadow Suffk
63 K4 Shippea Hill Station Cambs
34 E5 Shippon Oxon
47 Q6 Shipston on Stour Warwks
49 L9 Shipton Bucks
47 K11 Shipton Gloucs
98 B9 Shipton N York
57 K6 Shipton Shrops
21 P5 Shipton Bellinger Hants
11 K6 Shipton Gorge Dorset
15 M7 Shipton Green W Susx
32 G7 Shipton Moyne Gloucs
48 E11 Shipton-on-Cherwell Oxon
92 E2 Shiptonthorpe E R Yk
47 Q11 Shipton-under-Wychwood Oxon
35 J5 Shirburn Oxon
88 D8 Shirdley Hill Lancs
102 B3 Shire Cumb
84 H7 Shirebrook Derbys
84 E2 Shiregreen Sheff
31 P9 Shirehampton Bristl
113 M6 Shiremoor N Tyne
31 N6 Shirenewton Mons
58 G4 Shire Oak Wsall
85 J4 Shireoaks Notts
26 F4 Shirkoak Kent
84 F9 Shirland Derbys
57 L5 Shirlett Shrops
14 D4 Shirley C Sotn
71 N6 Shirley Derbys
37 J7 Shirley Gt Lon
58 H9 Shirley Solhll
45 N3 Shirl Heath Herefs
14 G4 Shirrell Heath Hants
123 Q3 Shirvan Ag & B
17 L4 Shirwell Devon
120 H6 Shiskine N Ayrs
103 K3 Shittlehope Dur
45 N2 Shobdon Herefs
13 L3 Shobley Hants
9 L4 Shobrooke Devon
72 H6 Shoby Leics
69 M5 Shocklach Ches W
69 M5 Shocklach Green Ches W
38 F4 Shoeburyness Sthend
39 Q11 Sholden Kent
14 E4 Sholing C Sotn
56 G2 Shoot Hill Shrops
4 D7 Shop Cnwll
16 C9 Shop Cnwll
15 N5 Shopwyke W Susx
89 Q7 Shore Rochdl
36 H4 Shoreditch Gt Lon
18 H10 Shoreditch Somset
37 M8 Shoreham Kent
24 F9 Shoreham Airport W Susx
24 F9 Shoreham-by-Sea W Susx
129 N10 Shoreswood Nthumb
22 G9 Shorley Hants
33 K5 Shorncote Gloucs
37 Q6 Shorne Kent
5 M10 Shorta Cross Cnwll
25 L6 Shortbridge E Susx
23 M6 Shortfield Common Surrey
25 L7 Shortgate E Susx
58 G6 Short Heath Birm
23 L7 Shortheath Hants
58 E4 Short Heath Wsall
3 L4 Shortlanesend Cnwll
125 L10 Shortlees E Ayrs
61 N11 Shortstown Bed
14 E10 Shorwell IoW
20 D3 Shoscombe BaNES
65 J2 Shotesham Norfk
38 C3 Shotgate Essex
53 M4 Shotley Suffk
112 G10 Shotley Bridge Dur
112 G10 Shotleyfield Nthumb
53 M5 Shotley Gate Suffk
53 M4 Shotley Street Suffk
38 H11 Shottenden Kent
23 N8 Shottermill Surrey
47 N4 Shottery Warwks
48 D5 Shotteswell Warwks
53 P3 Shottisham Suffk
71 Q5 Shottle Derbys
71 Q5 Shottlegate Derbys
104 C5 Shotton Dur
104 D3 Shotton Dur
81 L11 Shotton Flints
113 K5 Shotton Nthumb
118 F4 Shotton Nthumb
104 C2 Shotton Colliery Dur
126 F6 Shotts N Lans
81 L10 Shotwick Ches W
157 N6 Shougle Moray
75 N9 Shouldham Norfk
75 N9 Shouldham Thorpe Norfk
46 F3 Shoulton Worcs
25 Q4 Shover's Green E Susx
70 D5 Shraleybrook Staffs
69 L11 Shrawardine Shrops
57 Q11 Shrawley Worcs
36 B4 Shreding Green Bucks
59 K11 Shrewley Warwks
56 H2 Shrewsbury Shrops
21 L6 Shrewton Wilts
15 P6 Shripney W Susx
33 P7 Shrivenham Oxon
64 D3 Shropham Norfk
52 G7 Shrub End Essex
46 A6 Shucknall Herefs
51 P2 Shudy Camps Cambs
130 F6 Shuna Ag & B
46 H11 Shurdington Gloucs
35 M10 Shurlock Row W & M
47 K2 Shurnock Worcs
166 H5 Shurrery Highld
166 H5 Shurrery Lodge Highld
18 H6 Shurton Somset
59 K6 Shustoke Warwks
9 L4 Shute Devon
10 F5 Shute Devon
48 C6 Shutford Oxon
70 F10 Shut Heath Staffs
46 G7 Shuthonger Gloucs
49 K5 Shutlanger Nhants
9 N9 Shutterton Devon
58 C3 Shutt Green Staffs
59 L3 Shuttington Warwks
84 G6 Shuttlewood Derbys
89 N7 Shuttleworth Bury
168 h3 Siabost W Isls
168 i2 Siadar W Isls
60 E4 Sibbertoft Nhants
56 G8 Sibdon Carwood Shrops
48 C7 Sibford Ferris Oxon
48 C7 Sibford Gower Oxon
52 C5 Sible Hedingham Essex
51 P5 Sibley's Green Essex
5 L7 Siblyback Cnwll
87 L10 Sibsey Lincs
87 K10 Sibsey Fenside Lincs
74 A11 Sibson Cambs
72 B10 Sibson Leics
167 P6 Sibster Highld
85 M6 Sibthorpe Notts
85 N11 Sibthorpe Notts
65 M8 Sibton Suffk
64 B9 Sicklesmere Suffk
97 N11 Sicklinghall N York
19 J9 Sidbrook Somset
10 C6 Sidbury Devon
57 M7 Sidbury Shrops
91 K9 Sid Cop Barns
19 M3 Sidcot N Som
37 L6 Sidcup Gt Lon
100 D4 Siddick Cumb
82 H10 Siddington Ches E
33 K5 Siddington Gloucs
58 E10 Sidemoor Worcs
77 K4 Sidestrand Norfk
10 C6 Sidford Devon
15 N7 Sidlesham W Susx
15 N7 Sidlesham Common W Susx
26 B10 Sidley E Susx
10 C7 Sidmouth Devon
56 H8 Siefton Shrops
7 K4 Sigford Devon
99 P11 Sigglesthorne E R Yk
30 C10 Sigingstone V Glam
33 P2 Signet Oxon
22 H2 Silchester Hants
72 G7 Sileby Leics
94 C4 Silecroft Cumb
64 G2 Silfield Norfk
43 L4 Silian Cerdgn
22 D10 Silkstead Hants
90 H9 Silkstone Barns
90 H10 Silkstone Common Barns
73 R2 Silk Willoughby Lincs
109 P10 Silloth Cumb
99 K2 Silpho N York
96 F11 Silsden C Brad
50 C3 Silsoe C Beds
20 E9 Silton Dorset
127 N5 Silverburn Mdloth
95 K6 Silverdale Lancs
70 E5 Silverdale Staffs
52 D8 Silver End Essex
159 J5 Silverford Abers
76 H6 Silvergate Norfk
65 L9 Silverlace Green Suffk
65 K6 Silverley's Green Suffk
49 J6 Silverstone Nhants
38 E9 Silver Street Kent
19 P8 Silver Street Somset
9 N4 Silverton Devon
3 J4 Silverwell Cnwll
57 L9 Silvington Shrops
89 N9 Simister Bury
83 M6 Simmondley Derbys
112 C6 Simonburn Nthumb
17 P4 Simonsbath Somset
18 F11 Simonsburrow Devon
89 M4 Simonstone Lancs
96 C2 Simonstone N York
129 L11 Simprim Border
49 N7 Simpson M Keyn
40 G7 Simpson Cross Pembks
129 L9 Sinclair's Hill Border
115 J4 Sinclairston E Ayrs
97 M4 Sinderby N York
112 B10 Sinderhope Nthumb
82 F7 Sinderland Green Traffd
35 L11 Sindlesham Wokham
72 A4 Sinfin C Derb
49 L8 Singleborough Bucks
37 K9 Single Street Gt Lon
26 H3 Singleton Kent
88 D3 Singleton Lancs
15 N4 Singleton W Susx
37 Q6 Singlewell Kent
26 D3 Sinkhurst Green Kent
150 D5 Sinnarhard Abers
98 E3 Sinnington N York
46 F2 Sinton Worcs
46 F2 Sinton Worcs
46 F2 Sinton Green Worcs
36 C5 Sipson Gt Lon
30 F2 Sirhowy Blae G
26 C4 Sissinghurst Kent
32 C9 Siston S Glos
5 P3 Sitcott Devon
2 G8 Sithney Cnwll
2 G8 Sithney Common Cnwll
2 G8 Sithney Green Cnwll
38 F9 Sittingbourne Kent
57 P7 Six Ashes Shrops
30 H4 Six Bells Blae G
86 G3 Sixhills Lincs
63 J9 Six Mile Bottom Cambs
27 K3 Sixmile Cottages Kent
21 J11 Sixpenny Handley Dorset
11 b1 Six Rues Jersey
95 K3 Sizergh Castle Cumb
65 P9 Sizewell Suffk
169 e6 Skaill Ork
115 K4 Skares E Ayrs
151 N9 Skateraw Abers
129 J5 Skateraw E Loth
152 G8 Skeabost Highld
103 N10 Skeeby N York
73 J10 Skeffington Leics
93 Q7 Skeffling E R Yk
84 G8 Skegby Notts
85 N7 Skegby Notts
87 Q8 Skegness Lincs
162 H7 Skelbo Highld
162 H8 Skelbo Street Highld
91 N8 Skelbrooke Donc
74 F3 Skeldyke Lincs
86 B6 Skellingthorpe Lincs
83 K8 Skellorn Green Ches E
91 N8 Skellow Donc
90 G8 Skelmanthorpe Kirk
88 F9 Skelmersdale Lancs
124 F4 Skelmorlie N Ayrs
166 B5 Skelpick Highld
108 H3 Skelston D & G
98 B9 Skelton C York
101 M3 Skelton Cumb
92 C5 Skelton E R Yk
97 N7 Skelton N York
103 L10 Skelton N York
105 J7 Skelton R & Cl
101 K10 Skelwith Bridge Cumb
87 M7 Skendleby Lincs
151 K5 Skene House Abers
45 P10 Skenfrith Mons
99 L9 Skerne E R Yk
165 Q4 Skerray Highld
164 F6 Skerricha Highld
95 K8 Skerton Lancs
59 P6 Sketchley Leics
28 H6 Sketty Swans
29 K5 Skewen Neath
98 C6 Skewsby N York
77 J6 Skeyton Norfk
77 K6 Skeyton Corner Norfk
166 H3 Skiall Highld
87 M2 Skidbrooke Lincs
93 R11 Skidbrooke North End Lincs
92 H4 Skidby E R Yk
168 k1 Skigersta W Isls
18 C9 Skilgate Somset
73 M5 Skillington Lincs
109 P9 Skinburness Cumb
133 Q11 Skinflats Falk
152 C8 Skinidin Highld
34 D11 Skinners Green W Berk
105 K7 Skinningrove R & Cl
123 R8 Skipness Ag & B
110 G4 Skipper's Bridge D & G
110 G11 Skiprigg Cumb
99 P10 Skipsea E R Yk
99 P10 Skipsea Brough E R Yk
96 E10 Skipton N York
97 N5 Skipton-on-Swale N York
91 R3 Skipwith N York
93 K3 Skirlaugh E R Yk
116 F3 Skirling Border
35 L6 Skirmett Bucks
98 E9 Skirpenbeck E R Yk
102 B4 Skirwith Cumb
95 Q6 Skirwith N York
167 Q3 Skirza Highld
110 H7 Skitby Cumb
35 L4 Skittle Green Bucks
40 D10 Skokholm Island Pembks
40 D9 Skomer Island Pembks
145 L3 Skulamus Highld
56 D10 Skyborry Green Shrops
52 E7 Skye Green Essex
148 H3 Skye of Curr Highld
96 G8 Skyreholme N York
90 B5 Slack Calder
90 B9 Slackcote Oldham
95 K5 Slack Head Cumb
87 P6 Slackholme End Lincs
159 K8 Slacks of Cairnbanno Abers
32 G3 Slad Gloucs
10 C3 Slade Devon
17 J2 Slade Devon
17 Q6 Slade Devon
34 G6 Slade End Oxon
37 M5 Slade Green Gt Lon
58 D3 Slade Heath Staffs
84 H3 Slade Hooton Rothm
4 G7 Sladesbridge Cnwll
46 F8 Slades Green Worcs
111 N10 Slaggyford Nthumb
95 Q10 Slaidburn Lancs
90 D8 Slaithwaite Kirk
84 C9 Slaley Derbys
112 E9 Slaley Nthumb
126 F3 Slamannan Falk
49 P10 Slapton Bucks
7 L9 Slapton Devon
48 H5 Slapton Nhants
89 P9 Slattocks Rochdl
24 G5 Slaugham W Susx
32 F10 Slaughterford Wilts
60 G2 Slawston Leics
23 M7 Sleaford Hants
86 E11 Sleaford Lincs
101 Q7 Sleagill Cumb
69 N9 Sleap Shrops
70 A11 Sleapford Wrekin
50 E9 Sleapshyde Herts
162 E7 Sleasdairidh Highld
41 K7 Slebech Pembks
46 F8 Sledge Green Worcs
99 J8 Sledmere E R Yk
111 K5 Sleetbeck Cumb
12 G5 Sleight Dorset
103 J8 Sleightholme Dur
105 N9 Sleights N York
12 F6 Slepe Dorset
167 N3 Slickly Highld
120 H7 Sliddery N Ayrs
144 G2 Sligachan Highld
131 P9 Sligrachan Ag & B
32 D4 Slimbridge Gloucs
70 E8 Slindon Staffs
15 Q5 Slindon W Susx
24 D4 Slinfold W Susx
79 L11 Sling Gwynd
98 D6 Slingsby N York
50 C7 Slip End C Beds
50 G3 Slip End Herts
61 L5 Slipton Nhants
71 J11 Slitting Mill Staffs
130 G8 Slockavullin Ag & B
77 K7 Sloley Norfk
8 H7 Sloncombe Devon
87 N6 Sloothby Lincs
35 Q9 Slough Slough
35 Q8 Slough Crematorium Bucks

Slough Green - Stanford in the Vale 299

19 J11 Slough Green Somset
24 G5 Slough Green W Susx
154 A10 Slumbay Highld
23 Q4 Slyfield Green Surrey
95 K7 Slyne Lancs
118 B3 Smailholm Border
89 Q7 Smallbridge Rochdl
9 L5 Smallbrook Devon
31 Q4 Smallbrook Gloucs
77 L7 Smallburgh Norfk
83 N9 Smalldale Derbys
83 Q8 Smalldale Derbys
24 F8 Small Dole W Susx
72 C2 Smalley Derbys
72 C2 Smalley Common Derbys
72 C2 Smalley Green Derbys
24 H2 Smallfield Surrey
58 H7 Small Heath Birm
26 E5 Small Hythe Kent
10 G4 Smallridge Devon
70 F4 Smallthorne C Stke
103 M8 Smallways N York
70 E2 Smallwood Ches E
94 H11 Small Wood Hey Lancs
64 E5 Smallworth Norfk
22 C5 Smannell Hants
102 D9 Smardale Cumb
26 E3 Smarden Kent
26 E3 Smarden Bell Kent
25 M2 Smart's Hill Kent
119 L3 Smeafield Nthumb
138 A2 Smearisary Highld
10 D2 Smeatharpe Devon
27 J4 Smeeth Kent
60 E2 Smeeton Westerby Leics
97 J8 Smelthouses N York
167 L10 Smerral Highld
58 C6 Smestow Staffs
58 F7 Smethwick Sandw
70 E2 Smethwick Green Ches E
72 A7 Smisby Derbys
14 F8 Smitheclose IoW
46 E4 Smith End Green Worcs
110 H7 Smithfield Cumb
95 K9 Smith Green Lancs
91 K9 Smithies Barns
9 Q2 Smithincott Devon
51 K3 Smith's End Herts
51 N6 Smith's Green Essex
51 Q2 Smith's Green Essex
160 B11 Smithstown Highld
156 C8 Smithton Highld
89 Q7 Smithy Bridge Rochdl
82 F10 Smithy Green Ches E
83 J7 Smithy Green Stockp
84 E11 Smithy Houses Derbys
59 Q7 Smockington Leics
165 K3 Smoo Highld
52 F8 Smythe's Green Essex
108 H3 Snade D & G
56 F4 Snailbeach Shrops
63 K7 Snailwell Cambs
99 J4 Snainton N York
91 Q6 Snaith E R Yk
83 P6 Snake Pass Inn Derbys
97 L4 Snape N York
65 M10 Snape Suffk
88 D8 Snape Green Lancs
65 M10 Snape Street Suffk
37 K3 Snaresbrook Gt Lon
72 A9 Snarestone Leics
86 D4 Snarford Lincs
26 G6 Snargate Kent
26 H6 Snave Kent
46 H4 Sneachill Worcs
56 E6 Snead Powys
64 H4 Sneath Common Norfk
105 N9 Sneaton N York
105 P9 Sneatonthorpe N York
86 E4 Snelland Lincs
82 H10 Snelson Ches E
71 M6 Snelston Derbys
64 D3 Snetterton Norfk
75 N4 Snettisham Norfk
72 C8 Snibston Leics
46 E9 Snig's End Gloucs
119 K10 Snitter Nthumb
86 C2 Snitterby Lincs
47 P3 Snitterfield Warwks
84 C8 Snitterton Derbys
57 K9 Snitton Shrops
26 F3 Snoadhill Kent
45 L6 Snodhill Herefs
38 B9 Snodland Kent
37 Q11 Snoll Hatch Kent
90 H10 Snowden Hill Barns
67 L4 Snowdon Gwynd
67 Q9 Snowdonia National Park
51 K4 Snow End Herts
47 L8 Snowshill Gloucs
64 F5 Snow Street Norfk
15 J4 Soake Hants
30 E8 Soar Cardif
7 J11 Soar Devon
44 D8 Soar Powys
144 F5 Soay Highld
22 H11 Soberton Hants
14 H4 Soberton Heath Hants
101 N5 Sockbridge Cumb
104 B9 Sockburn Darltn
80 F10 Sodom Denbgs
69 K7 Sodylt Bank Shrops
63 J6 Soham Cambs
63 J5 Soham Cotes Cambs
168 d10 Solas W Isls
40 G8 Solbury Pembks
16 E9 Soldon Devon
16 E9 Soldon Cross Devon
23 J7 Soldridge Hants
27 J2 Sole Street Kent
37 Q7 Sole Street Kent
59 J9 Solihull Solhll
45 N3 Sollers Dilwyn Herefs
46 B8 Sollers Hope Herefs
88 F7 Sollom Lancs
40 F6 Solva Pembks
110 F5 Solwaybank D & G
73 K8 Somerby Leics
93 J9 Somerby Lincs
84 F10 Somercotes Derbys
13 L6 Somerford Dorset
33 K5 Somerford Keynes Gloucs
15 M7 Somerley W Susx
65 P2 Somerleyton Suffk
71 L7 Somersal Herbert Derbys
87 K6 Somersby Lincs
62 E5 Somersham Cambs
53 J2 Somersham Suffk
48 E9 Somerton Oxon
19 N9 Somerton Somset
63 P10 Somerton Suffk
57 K2 Somerwood Shrops
24 E9 Sompting W Susx
35 L9 Sonning Wokham
35 K8 Sonning Common Oxon
35 K9 Sonning Eye Oxon
69 K5 Sontley Wrexhm
13 L5 Sopley Hants
32 F7 Sopworth Wilts
107 M8 Sorbie D & G
167 K4 Sordale Highld
136 H3 Sorisdale Ag & B
115 L2 Sorn E Ayrs
167 N4 Sortat Highld
86 H5 Sotby Lincs
86 F8 Sots Hole Lincs
65 N5 Sotterley Suffk
81 J11 Soughton Flints
49 N9 Soulbury Bucks
101 N5 Soulby Cumb
102 D8 Soulby Cumb
48 F8 Souldern Oxon
61 L8 Souldrop Bed
70 A5 Sound Ches E
157 R7 Sound Muir Moray
32 C9 Soundwell S Glos
8 D6 Sourton Devon
94 E4 Soutergate Cumb
75 R8 South Acre Norfk
27 M3 South Alkham Kent
36 D5 Southall Gt Lon
7 K11 South Allington Devon
133 P9 South Alloa Falk
47 J9 Southam Gloucs
48 D2 Southam Warwks
23 P10 South Ambersham W Susx
14 D4 Southampton C Sotn
22 E11 Southampton Airport Hants
22 D11 Southampton Crematorium Hants
84 H4 South Anston Rothm
35 P11 South Ascot W & M
26 H3 South Ashford Kent
14 C7 South Baddesley Hants
139 K6 South Ballachulish Highld
98 B10 South Bank C York
104 F6 South Bank R & Cl
20 B9 South Barrow Somset
36 G8 South Beddington Gt Lon
5 N3 South Beer Cnwll
38 C4 South Benfleet Essex
15 P6 South Bersted W Susx
13 L5 South Bockhampton Dorset
37 K7 Southborough Gt Lon
25 N2 Southborough Kent
13 K6 Southbourne Bmouth
15 L5 Southbourne W Susx
11 J5 South Bowood Dorset
91 Q8 South Bramwith Donc
6 H6 South Brent Devon
20 D7 South Brewham Somset
31 Q11 South Bristol Crematorium Bristl
119 P11 South Broomhill Nthumb
76 E10 Southburgh Norfk
77 M10 South Burlingham Norfk
99 K10 Southburn E R Yk
20 B9 South Cadbury Somset
86 B5 South Carlton Lincs
85 J4 South Carlton Notts
92 F4 South Cave E R Yk
33 K5 South Cerney Gloucs
25 J7 South Chailey E Susx
10 G3 South Chard Somset
119 N6 South Charlton Nthumb
20 C10 South Cheriton Somset
103 P5 South Church Dur
38 F4 Southchurch Sthend
103 M7 South Cleatlam Dur
92 E3 South Cliffe E R Yk
85 P6 South Clifton Notts
87 L3 South Cockerington Lincs
29 M8 South Cornelly Brdgnd
5 K2 Southcott Cnwll
8 D5 Southcott Devon
9 J8 Southcott Devon
16 G8 Southcott Devon
21 N3 Southcott Wilts
35 M2 Southcourt Bucks
65 P5 South Cove Suffk
76 B4 South Creake Norfk
90 E8 South Crosland Kirk
72 H8 South Croxton Leics
99 K11 South Dalton E R Yk
37 N7 South Darenth Kent
24 H8 South Downs National Park
92 A4 South Duffield N York
25 K9 Southease E Susx
87 J3 South Elkington Lincs
91 M8 South Elmsall Wakefd
120 C10 Southend Ag & B
93 Q7 South End E R Yk
21 M11 South End Hants
46 D6 South End Herefs
93 K6 South End N Linc
64 D3 South End Norfk
33 N10 Southend Wilts
38 E4 Southend Airport Essex
38 E4 Southend Crematorium Sthend
38 E4 Southend-on-Sea Sthend
101 L3 Southernby Cumb
26 E2 Southernden Kent
29 N10 Southerndown V Glam
109 L10 Southerness D & G
153 N3 South Erradale Highld
10 B6 Southerton Devon
63 K2 Southery Norfk
37 N3 South Essex Crematorium Gt Lon
38 E3 South Fambridge Essex
34 C8 South Fawley W Berk
92 G6 South Ferriby N Linc
92 H5 South Field E R Yk
126 E3 Southfield Falk
37 P6 Southfleet Kent
14 F11 Southford IoW
36 G2 Southgate Gt Lon
75 N4 Southgate Norfk
76 B4 Southgate Norfk
76 G7 Southgate Norfk
28 G7 Southgate Swans
37 J11 South Godstone Surrey
13 L2 South Gorley Hants
113 K7 South Gosforth N u Ty
37 Q2 South Green Essex
52 H8 South Green Essex
38 E9 South Green Kent
76 F9 South Green Norfk
64 H6 South Green Suffk
127 M3 South Gyle C Edin
38 B2 South Hanningfield Essex
23 L11 South Harting W Susx
15 K7 South Hayling Hants
119 L4 South Hazelrigg Nthumb
35 P4 South Heath Bucks
25 K10 South Heighton E Susx
113 N11 South Hetton Dur
91 K8 South Hiendley Wakefd
5 N7 South Hill Cnwll
19 N9 South Hill Somset
34 F4 South Hinksey Oxon
16 C7 South Hole Devon
24 E2 South Holmwood Surrey
37 M4 South Hornchurch Gt Lon
19 Q5 South Horrington Somset
6 H10 South Huish Devon
86 B8 South Hykeham Lincs
113 N9 South Hylton Sundld
50 E2 Southill C Beds
22 F5 Southington Hants
92 H11 South Kelsey Lincs
156 B8 South Kessock Highld
93 K7 South Killingholme N Linc
97 P4 South Kilvington N York
60 D4 South Kilworth Leics
91 L8 South Kirkby Wakefd
7 L4 South Knighton Devon
86 G11 South Kyme Lincs
126 B6 South Lanarkshire Crematorium S Lans
10 E6 Southleigh Devon
34 C3 South Leigh Oxon
85 N4 South Leverton Notts
47 L5 South Littleton Worcs
36 G7 South London Crematorium Gt Lon
64 E5 South Lopham Norfk
73 N10 South Luffenham Rutlnd
25 K8 South Malling E Susx
33 N7 South Marston Swindn
36 G10 South Merstham Surrey
119 J6 South Middleton Nthumb
91 M4 South Milford N York
6 J10 South Milton Devon
50 F10 South Mimms Herts
50 F10 South Mimms Services Herts
38 G2 Southminster Essex
17 N6 South Molton Devon
113 J10 South Moor Dur
34 C5 Southmoor Oxon
34 G7 South Moreton Oxon
142 F7 Southmuir Angus
15 N6 South Mundham W Susx
85 N9 South Muskham Notts
92 F3 South Newbald E R Yk
48 D8 South Newington Oxon
21 L8 South Newton Wilts
84 F9 South Normanton Derbys
36 H7 South Norwood Gt Lon
36 H11 South Nutfield Surrey
37 N4 South Ockendon Thurr
61 Q8 Southoe Cambs
64 H8 Southolt Suffk
87 L5 South Ormsby Lincs
74 A10 Southorpe C Pete
90 H7 South Ossett Wakefd
97 N3 South Otterington N York
11 N6 Southover Dorset
25 Q5 Southover E Susx
86 E2 South Owersby Lincs
90 E6 Southowram Calder
36 F11 South Park Surrey
11 K3 South Perrott Dorset
19 M11 South Petherton Somset
5 N5 South Petherwin Cnwll
76 B11 South Pickenham Norfk
5 Q10 South Pill Cnwll
7 K10 South Pool Devon
11 L5 South Poorton Dorset
88 C7 Southport Sefton
88 D8 Southport Crematorium Lancs
127 L2 South Queensferry C Edin
17 N5 South Radworthy Devon
86 D11 South Rauceby Lincs
76 B7 South Raynham Norfk
83 J6 South Reddish Stockp
77 K4 Southrepps Norfk
87 M4 South Reston Lincs
86 F7 Southrey Lincs
169 d8 South Ronaldsay Ork
33 N4 Southrop Gloucs
23 J6 Southrope Hants
75 M9 South Runcton Norfk
85 P8 South Scarle Notts
15 J7 Southsea C Port
69 K4 Southsea Wrexhm
138 G9 South Shian Ag & B
113 N7 South Shields S Tyne
113 M8 South Shields Crematorium S Tyne
88 C4 South Shore Bpool
103 M5 Southside Dur
87 M4 South Somercotes Lincs
97 M8 South Stainley N York
37 N5 South Stifford Thurr
20 D2 South Stoke BaNES
34 G8 South Stoke Oxon
24 B9 South Stoke W Susx
26 H4 South Stour Kent
37 P8 South Street Kent
39 J10 South Street Kent
39 K8 South Street Kent
127 J7 South Tarbrax S Lans
8 G6 South Tawton Devon
2 H5 South Tehidy Cnwll
87 M5 South Thoresby Lincs
103 M8 South Thorpe Dur
23 J7 South Town Hants
77 Q10 Southtown Norfk
19 K11 Southtown Somset
168 d14 South Uist W Isls
110 H11 Southwaite Cumb
110 H11 Southwaite Services Cumb
77 M9 South Walsham Norfk
36 H5 Southwark Gt Lon
23 K5 South Warnborough Hants
24 E5 Southwater W Susx
24 D5 Southwater Street W Susx
19 P6 Southway Somset
37 N2 South Weald Essex
11 P10 Southwell Dorset
85 L10 Southwell Notts
36 D6 South West Middlesex Crematorium Gt Lon
35 K5 South Weston Oxon
5 L3 South Wheatley Cnwll
14 H5 Southwick Hants
61 M2 Southwick Nhants
19 L5 Southwick Somset
113 N9 Southwick Sundld
24 F9 Southwick W Susx
20 F3 Southwick Wilts
19 Q3 South Widcombe BaNES
72 F11 South Wigston Leics
26 H3 South Willesborough Kent
86 G4 South Willingham Lincs
104 D4 South Wingate Dur
84 E9 South Wingfield Derbys
73 N7 South Witham Lincs
65 Q6 Southwold Suffk
22 E7 South Wonston Hants
77 M10 Southwood Norfk
19 Q8 Southwood Somset
38 D2 South Woodham Ferrers Essex
75 M6 South Wootton Norfk
20 F2 South Wraxall Wilts
8 G6 South Zeal Devon
90 C6 Sowerby Calder
97 P4 Sowerby N York
90 D6 Sowerby Bridge Calder
101 L2 Sowerby Row Cumb
88 D2 Sower Carr Lancs
18 A10 Sowerhill Somset
31 J4 Sowhill Torfn
63 M10 Sowley Green Suffk
90 D7 Sowood Calder
6 E5 Sowton Devon
9 N6 Sowton Devon
90 C6 Soyland Town Calder
77 K5 Spa Common Norfk
51 Q3 Spain's End Essex
74 D6 Spalding Lincs
92 C4 Spaldington E R Yk
61 P6 Spaldwick Cambs
85 P7 Spalford Notts
74 A3 Spanby Lincs
23 J3 Spanish Green Hants
76 F8 Sparham Norfk
76 F8 Sparhamill Norfk
94 G4 Spark Bridge Cumb
101 M5 Sparket Cumb
20 B9 Sparkford Somset
58 H8 Sparkhill Birm
6 F7 Sparkwell Devon
76 C9 Sparrow Green Norfk
83 N8 Sparrowpit Derbys
25 P4 Sparrows Green E Susx
22 D8 Sparsholt Hants
34 B7 Sparsholt Oxon
112 C11 Spartylea Nthumb
71 K7 Spath Staffs
98 E3 Spaunton N York
18 H7 Spaxton Somset
146 G11 Spean Bridge Highld
24 D7 Spear Hill W Susx
22 B9 Spearywell Hants
35 M5 Speen Bucks
34 E11 Speen W Berk
99 P6 Speeton N York
81 N8 Speke Lpool
25 N2 Speldhurst Kent
51 L7 Spellbrook Herts
26 B4 Spelmonden Kent
48 B10 Spelsbury Oxon
90 F5 Spen Kirk
35 K11 Spencers Wood Wokham
70 E2 Spen Green Ches E
96 H3 Spennithorne N York
103 Q4 Spennymoor Dur
47 L2 Spernall Warwks
46 G4 Spetchley Worcs
12 F4 Spetisbury Dorset
65 M5 Spexhall Suffk
157 R4 Spey Bay Moray
149 J2 Speybridge Highld
157 P9 Speyview Moray
87 M7 Spilsby Lincs
119 N4 Spindlestone Nthumb
84 G5 Spinkhill Derbys
162 F9 Spinningdale Highld
85 J7 Spion Kop Notts
33 J9 Spirthill Wilts
81 L8 Spital Wirral
85 K2 Spital Hill Donc
86 C2 Spital in the Street Lincs
25 K7 Spithurst E Susx
128 D4 Spittal E Loth
98 F10 Spittal E R Yk
167 L6 Spittal Highld
129 Q9 Spittal Nthumb
41 J6 Spittal Pembks
141 R9 Spittalfield P & K
149 Q10 Spittal of Glenmuick Abers
141 R4 Spittal of Glenshee P & K
118 A7 Spittal-on-Rule Border
77 J8 Spixworth Norfk
4 E6 Splatt Cnwll
5 L4 Splatt Cnwll
8 F3 Splatt Devon
25 K6 Splayne's Green E Susx
30 H9 Splottlands Cardif
97 N10 Spofforth N York
72 C3 Spondon C Derb
69 J2 Spon Green Flints
64 F2 Spooner Row Norfk
76 A9 Sporle Norfk
128 H4 Spott E Loth
128 G10 Spottiswoode Border
60 F7 Spratton Nhants
23 M6 Spreakley Surrey
8 G5 Spreyton Devon
6 E8 Spriddlestone Devon
86 D4 Spridlington Lincs
125 Q4 Springburn C Glas
110 F7 Springfield D & G
52 B10 Springfield Essex
135 J5 Springfield Fife
58 E4 Springhill Staffs
58 G3 Springhill Staffs
108 H6 Springholm D & G
125 K10 Springside N Ayrs
85 Q3 Springthorpe Lincs
90 H10 Spring Vale Barns
113 L9 Springwell Sundld
81 N7 Springwood Crematorium Lpool
93 L4 Sproatley E R Yk
82 F11 Sproston Green Ches W
91 N10 Sprotbrough Donc
53 K3 Sproughton Suffk
118 E3 Sprouston Border
77 K9 Sprowston Norfk
73 M6 Sproxton Leics
98 C4 Sproxton N York
69 M8 Spunhill Shrops
69 Q3 Spurstow Ches E
11 L6 Spyway Dorset
40 F4 Square & Compass Pembks
57 P5 Stableford Shrops
70 E7 Stableford Staffs
84 C2 Stacey Bank Sheff
96 B7 Stackhouse N York
41 J11 Stackpole Pembks
64 F3 Stacksford Norfk
89 P6 Stacksteads Lancs
6 E8 Staddiscombe C Plym
92 D5 Staddlethorpe E R Yk
83 N10 Staden Derbys
34 H5 Stadhampton Oxon
168 c14 Stadhlaigearraidh W Isls
101 P2 Staffield Cumb
152 H4 Staffin Highld
70 G10 Stafford Staffs
70 H10 Stafford Crematorium Staffs
70 F8 Stafford Services (northbound) Staffs
70 F8 Stafford Services (southbound) Staffs
49 Q5 Stagsden Bed
91 J10 Stainborough Barns
100 D5 Stainburn Cumb
97 L11 Stainburn N York
73 N6 Stainby Lincs
91 J8 Staincross Barns
103 M6 Staindrop Dur
36 B6 Staines-upon-Thames Surrey
74 A6 Stainfield Lincs
86 F6 Stainfield Lincs
91 Q8 Stainforth Donc
96 B7 Stainforth N York
88 C3 Staining Lancs
90 D7 Stainland Calder
105 P9 Stainsacre N York
84 G7 Stainsby Derbys
95 L3 Stainton Cumb
101 N5 Stainton Cumb
110 G9 Stainton Cumb
85 J2 Stainton Donc
103 L7 Stainton Dur
104 E8 Stainton Middsb
103 M11 Stainton N York
86 E5 Stainton by Langworth Lincs
105 Q11 Staintondale N York
86 G2 Stainton le Vale Lincs
94 E6 Stainton with Adgarley Cumb
100 H6 Stair Cumb
114 H3 Stair E Ayrs
91 K9 Stairfoot Barns
106 H7 Stairhaven D & G
105 L7 Staithes N York
113 L3 Stakeford Nthumb
95 J11 Stake Pool Lancs
15 J5 Stakes Hants
20 D11 Stalbridge Dorset
20 D11 Stalbridge Weston Dorset
77 M6 Stalham Norfk
77 M7 Stalham Green Norfk
38 G11 Stalisfield Green Kent
64 E2 Stalland Common Norfk
20 B11 Stallen Dorset
93 L8 Stallingborough NE Lin
96 D3 Stalling Busk N York
70 G7 Stallington Staffs
94 H11 Stalmine Lancs
94 H11 Stalmine Moss Side Lancs
83 L5 Stalybridge Tamesd
52 B4 Stambourne Essex
51 Q3 Stambourne Green Essex
73 Q9 Stamford Lincs
119 P7 Stamford Nthumb
81 P11 Stamford Bridge Ches W
98 E9 Stamford Bridge E R Yk
112 G6 Stamfordham Nthumb
36 H3 Stamford Hill Gt Lon
88 D2 Stanah Lancs
50 F8 Stanborough Herts
49 Q10 Stanbridge C Beds
12 H4 Stanbridge Dorset
90 C3 Stanbury C Brad
89 M9 Stand Bury
126 D4 Stand N Lans
126 G3 Standburn Falk
58 D3 Standeford Staffs
26 E3 Standen Kent
26 D5 Standen Street Kent
20 F4 Standerwick Somset
23 M8 Standford Hants
100 E4 Standingstone Cumb
32 E3 Standish Gloucs
88 H8 Standish Wigan
88 H9 Standish Lower Ground Wigan
34 C4 Standlake Oxon
22 D9 Standon Hants
51 J6 Standon Herts
70 E7 Standon Staffs
51 J7 Standon Green End Herts
64 G8 Standwell Green Suffk
126 F6 Stane N Lans
76 C7 Stanfield Norfk
50 E2 Stanford C Beds
27 K4 Stanford Kent
56 E2 Stanford Shrops
46 C4 Stanford Bishop Herefs
57 N11 Stanford Bridge Worcs
70 C10 Stanford Bridge Wrekin
34 G10 Stanford Dingley W Berk
34 B6 Stanford in the Vale Oxon

37 Q4 **Stanford le Hope** Thurr
60 C5 **Stanford on Avon** Nhants
72 E6 **Stanford on Soar** Notts
57 N11 **Stanford on Teme** Worcs
51 M10 **Stanford Rivers** Essex
84 G6 **Stanfree** Derbys
105 J7 **Stanghow** R & Cl
74 D11 **Stanground** C Pete
89 L5 **Stanhill** Lancs
75 R3 **Stanhoe** Norfk
116 G5 **Stanhope** Border
103 J3 **Stanhope** Dur
26 H3 **Stanhope** Kent
71 P10 **Stanhope Bretby** Derbys
61 K3 **Stanion** Nhants
58 C10 **Stanklin** Worcs
72 C2 **Stanley** Derbys
113 J10 **Stanley** Dur
84 G8 **Stanley** Notts
141 R11 **Stanley** P & K
57 N8 **Stanley** Shrops
70 G4 **Stanley** Staffs
91 J6 **Stanley** Wakefd
72 C2 **Stanley Common** Derbys
103 N3 **Stanley Crook** Dur
91 K6 **Stanley Ferry** Wakefd
88 E9 **Stanley Gate** Lancs
70 G4 **Stanley Moor** Staffs
47 K8 **Stanley Pontlarge** Gloucs
24 H9 **Stanmer** Br & H
36 E2 **Stanmore** Gt Lon
22 E9 **Stanmore** Hants
34 E9 **Stanmore** W Berk
111 P3 **Stannersburn** Nthumb
64 B10 **Stanningfield** Suffk
90 G4 **Stanningley** Leeds
113 K5 **Stannington** Nthumb
84 C3 **Stannington** Sheff
113 K4 **Stannington Station** Nthumb
45 L2 **Stansbatch** Herefs
63 N10 **Stansfield** Suffk
71 L4 **Stanshope** Staffs
52 D2 **Stanstead** Suffk
51 J8 **Stanstead Abbotts** Herts
37 P8 **Stansted** Kent
51 M6 *Stansted Airport* Essex
51 M5 **Stansted Mountfitchet** Essex
71 P11 **Stanton** Derbys
47 L8 **Stanton** Gloucs
45 L10 **Stanton** Mons
112 H2 **Stanton** Nthumb
71 L5 **Stanton** Staffs
64 D7 **Stanton** Suffk
72 B5 **Stanton by Bridge** Derbys
72 D3 **Stanton by Dale** Derbys
19 Q2 **Stanton Drew** BaNES
33 N6 **Stanton Fitzwarren** Swindn
34 D3 **Stanton Harcourt** Oxon
84 G8 **Stanton Hill** Notts
84 B8 **Stanton in Peak** Derbys
56 H9 **Stanton Lacy** Shrops
84 C8 **Stanton Lees** Derbys
57 K6 **Stanton Long** Shrops
72 G4 **Stanton on the Wolds** Notts
20 C2 **Stanton Prior** BaNES
21 L2 **Stanton St Bernard** Wilts
34 G3 **Stanton St John** Oxon
32 H9 **Stanton St Quintin** Wilts
64 D8 **Stanton Street** Suffk
72 D8 **Stanton under Bardon** Leics
69 Q10 **Stanton upon Hine Heath** Shrops
20 B2 **Stanton Wick** BaNES
32 D2 **Stantway** Gloucs
69 M10 **Stanwardine in the Field** Shrops
69 M9 **Stanwardine in the Wood** Shrops
52 F7 **Stanway** Essex
47 L8 **Stanway** Gloucs
52 G7 **Stanway Green** Essex
65 J7 **Stanway Green** Suffk
36 C6 **Stanwell** Surrey
36 B6 **Stanwell Moor** Surrey
61 L6 **Stanwick** Nhants
110 H9 **Stanwix** Cumb
168 c14 **Staoinebrig** W Isls
98 F2 **Stape** N York
13 J4 **Stapehill** Dorset
70 B5 **Stapeley** Ches E
71 P10 **Stapenhill** Staffs
39 N10 **Staple** Kent
18 D10 **Staple Cross** Devon
26 C7 **Staple Cross** E Susx
24 G5 **Staplefield** W Susx
19 J11 **Staple Fitzpaine** Somset
62 G10 **Stapleford** Cambs
50 H7 **Stapleford** Herts
73 L7 **Stapleford** Leics
85 Q9 **Stapleford** Lincs
72 D3 **Stapleford** Notts
21 L7 **Stapleford** Wilts
37 M2 **Stapleford Abbotts** Essex
51 M11 **Stapleford Tawney** Essex
18 H9 **Staplegrove** Somset
18 H10 **Staplehay** Somset
58 E10 **Staple Hill** Worcs
26 C3 **Staplehurst** Kent
14 F9 **Staplers** IoW
39 J9 **Staplestreet** Kent
111 K6 **Stapleton** Cumb
56 E11 **Stapleton** Herefs
72 C11 **Stapleton** Leics
103 Q8 **Stapleton** N York
56 H4 **Stapleton** Shrops
19 N10 **Stapleton** Somset
10 D2 **Stapley** Somset
61 Q8 **Staploe** Bed
46 C6 **Staplow** Herefs
135 J7 **Star** Fife
41 P4 **Star** Pembks
19 M3 **Star** Somset
97 M9 **Starbeck** N York
96 E6 **Starbotton** N York
9 N8 **Starcross** Devon
59 M10 **Stareton** Warwks
84 D9 **Starkholmes** Derbys
51 L4 **Starlings Green** Essex
26 C3 **Starr's Green** E Susx
65 J5 **Starston** Norfk
7 L10 **Start** Devon
103 K7 **Startforth** Dur
32 H8 **Startley** Wilts
39 P10 **Statenborough** Kent

82 E7 **Statham** Warrtn
19 L9 **Stathe** Somset
73 K4 **Stathern** Leics
104 D3 **Station Town** Dur
61 P7 **Staughton Green** Cambs
61 P8 **Staughton Highway** Cambs
31 Q2 **Staunton** Gloucs
46 E9 **Staunton** Gloucs
73 L2 **Staunton in the Vale** Notts
45 M2 **Staunton on Arrow** Herefs
45 M6 **Staunton on Wye** Herefs
94 H3 **Staveley** Cumb
101 N11 **Staveley** Cumb
84 F6 **Staveley** Derbys
97 N8 **Staveley** N York
7 K6 **Staverton** Devon
46 G10 **Staverton** Gloucs
60 B8 **Staverton** Nhants
20 G2 **Staverton** Wilts
46 G10 **Staverton Bridge** Gloucs
19 L7 **Stawell** Somset
18 E10 **Stawley** Somset
167 Q6 **Staxigoe** Highld
99 L5 **Staxton** N York
54 E7 **Staylittle** Cerdgn
55 K6 **Staylittle** Powys
88 D2 **Staynall** Lancs
85 N10 **Staythorpe** Notts
96 H11 **Stead** C Brad
96 G6 **Stean** N York
98 C6 **Stearsby** N York
19 J5 **Steart** Somset
51 Q6 **Stebbing** Essex
51 Q6 **Stebbing Green** Essex
58 H7 **Stechford** Birm
26 E4 **Stede Quarter** Kent
23 N10 **Stedham** W Susx
112 D9 **Steel** Nthumb
25 M4 **Steel Cross** E Susx
134 C9 **Steelend** Fife
111 K2 **Steele Road** Border
94 D5 **Steel Green** Cumb
69 P7 **Steel Heath** Shrops
45 Q3 **Steen's Bridge** Herefs
23 K9 **Steep** Hants
14 F11 **Steephill** IoW
90 C6 **Steep Lane** Calder
12 F8 **Steeple** Dorset
52 F11 **Steeple** Essex
20 H3 **Steeple Ashton** Wilts
48 E9 **Steeple Aston** Oxon
48 D10 **Steeple Barton** Oxon
51 Q2 **Steeple Bumpstead** Essex
49 K9 **Steeple Claydon** Bucks
61 P4 **Steeple Gidding** Cambs
21 K7 **Steeple Langford** Wilts
50 G2 **Steeple Morden** Cambs
90 C2 **Steeton** C Brad
152 D6 **Stein** Highld
113 J8 **Stella** Gatesd
27 K2 **Stelling Minnis** Kent
19 M10 **Stembridge** Somset
4 G10 **Stenalees** Cnwll
115 R9 **Stenhouse** D & G
133 P11 **Stenhousemuir** Falk
86 H4 **Stenigot** Lincs
152 H4 **Stenscholl** Highld
72 A4 **Stenson Fields** Derbys
128 G5 **Stenton** E Loth
168 j4 **Steornabhagh** W Isls
41 M9 **Stepaside** Pembks
109 J4 **Stepford** D & G
37 J4 **Stepney** Gt Lon
83 K7 **Stepping Hill** Stockp
50 B3 **Steppingley** C Beds
126 B4 **Stepps** N Lans
65 M9 **Sternfield** Suffk
21 K3 **Stert** Wilts
63 K9 **Stetchworth** Cambs
50 F5 **Stevenage** Herts
26 B8 **Steven's Crouch** E Susx
124 H9 **Stevenston** N Ayrs
22 F5 **Steventon** Hants
34 E6 **Steventon** Oxon
51 N2 **Steventon End** Essex
49 Q4 **Stevington** Bed
50 B2 **Stewartby** Bed
125 Q6 **Stewartfield** S Lans
125 L8 **Stewarton** E Ayrs
49 N9 **Stewkley** Bucks
19 K11 **Stewley** Somset
87 L3 **Stewton** Lincs
14 H9 **Steyne Cross** IoW
24 H7 **Steyning** W Susx
40 H9 **Steynton** Pembks
16 C9 **Stibb** Cnwll
76 D6 **Stibbard** Norfk
16 G9 **Stibb Cross** Devon
21 P2 **Stibb Green** Wilts
74 A11 **Stibbington** Cambs
118 D3 **Stichill** Border
3 P3 **Sticker** Cnwll
87 L8 **Stickford** Lincs
8 F6 **Sticklepath** Devon
18 D7 **Sticklepath** Somset
51 L4 **Stickling Green** Essex
87 K9 **Stickney** Lincs
76 D3 **Stiffkey** Norfk
46 D5 **Stifford's Bridge** Herefs
38 E9 **Stiff Street** Kent
26 C2 **Stile Bridge** Kent
19 N6 **Stileway** Somset
168 c14 **Stilligarry** W Isls
91 P2 **Stillingfleet** N York
98 B7 **Stillington** N York
104 C6 **Stillington** S on T
61 Q3 **Stilton** Cambs
32 D5 **Stinchcombe** Gloucs
11 Q6 **Stinsford** Dorset
56 F4 **Stiperstones** Shrops
58 G8 **Stirchley** Birm
57 M3 **Stirchley** Wrekin
159 R9 **Stirling** Abers
133 M9 **Stirling** Stirlg
133 N10 **Stirling Services** Stirlg
61 Q7 **Stirtloe** Cambs
96 E10 **Stirton** N York
52 D7 **Stisted** Essex
33 P11 **Stitchcombe** Wilts
3 J6 **Stithians** Cnwll
59 M9 **Stivichall** Covtry
86 D7 **Stixwould** Lincs
27 Q3 **St Margaret's Bay** Kent
81 N10 **Stoak** Ches W
116 H3 **Stobo** Border
12 F7 **Stoborough** Dorset

12 F7 **Stoborough Green** Dorset
117 Q9 **Stobs Castle** Border
119 P11 **Stobswood** Nthumb
51 Q11 **Stock** Essex
19 N2 **Stock** N Som
22 C7 **Stockbridge** Hants
126 D10 **Stockbriggs** S Lans
38 D9 **Stockbury** Kent
34 D11 **Stockcross** W Berk
110 C11 **Stockdalewath** Cumb
38 G11 **Stocker's Hill** Kent
73 L11 **Stockerston** Leics
47 J3 **Stock Green** Worcs
46 B8 **Stocking** Herefs
59 M6 **Stockingford** Warwks
51 L5 **Stocking Pelham** Herts
10 E4 **Stockland** Devon
18 H6 **Stockland Bristol** Somset
25 N2 **Stockland Green** Kent
9 L3 **Stockleigh English** Devon
9 L4 **Stockleigh Pomeroy** Devon
33 J11 **Stockley** Wilts
45 M7 **Stockley Hill** Herefs
19 L11 **Stocklinch** Somset
45 M4 **Stockmoor** Herefs
83 J6 **Stockport** Stockp
83 K7 **Stockport Crematorium** Stockp
90 H11 **Stocksbridge** Sheff
112 G8 **Stocksfield** Nthumb
45 Q2 **Stockton** Herefs
65 M3 **Stockton** Norfk
56 D4 **Stockton** Shrops
57 N5 **Stockton** Shrops
48 D2 **Stockton** Warwks
21 J7 **Stockton** Wilts
70 D11 **Stockton** Wrekin
70 G4 **Stockton Brook** Staffs
82 D7 **Stockton Heath** Warrtn
104 D7 **Stockton-on-Tees** S on T
57 N11 **Stockton on Teme** Worcs
98 D9 **Stockton on the Forest** C York
32 H2 **Stockwell** Gloucs
58 C4 **Stockwell End** Wolves
71 K10 **Stockwell Heath** Staffs
32 B11 **Stockwood** Bristl
11 M3 **Stockwood** Dorset
47 K3 **Stock Wood** Worcs
95 K9 **Stodday** Lancs
39 M9 **Stodmarsh** Kent
76 F4 **Stody** Norfk
164 B11 **Stoer** Highld
11 M2 **Stoford** Somset
21 L7 **Stoford** Wilts
18 E7 **Stogumber** Somset
18 H6 **Stogursey** Somset
59 N9 **Stoke** Covtry
16 C7 **Stoke** Devon
15 K6 **Stoke** Hants
22 D4 **Stoke** Hants
38 D7 **Stoke** Medway
11 K4 **Stoke Abbott** Dorset
60 H3 **Stoke Albany** Nhants
64 G7 **Stoke Ash** Suffk
72 G2 **Stoke Bardolph** Notts
46 C2 **Stoke Bliss** Worcs
49 K5 **Stoke Bruerne** Nhants
52 B3 **Stoke by Clare** Suffk
52 G4 **Stoke-by-Nayland** Suffk
9 M5 **Stoke Canon** Devon
22 E7 **Stoke Charity** Hants
5 P7 **Stoke Climsland** Cnwll
46 B4 **Stoke Cross** Herefs
36 D9 **Stoke D'Abernon** Surrey
61 M3 **Stoke Doyle** Nhants
73 M11 **Stoke Dry** Rutlnd
46 B6 **Stoke Edith** Herefs
59 J5 **Stoke End** Warwks
21 L9 **Stoke Farthing** Wilts
75 P10 **Stoke Ferry** Norfk
7 M9 **Stoke Fleming** Devon
12 C7 **Stokeford** Dorset
7 M7 **Stoke Gabriel** Devon
32 B9 **Stoke Gifford** S Glos
72 B11 **Stoke Golding** Leics
49 M5 **Stoke Goldington** M Keyn
35 Q8 **Stoke Green** Bucks
85 N5 **Stokeham** Notts
49 N9 **Stoke Hammond** Bucks
70 B9 **Stoke Heath** Shrops
58 D11 **Stoke Heath** Worcs
77 J11 **Stoke Holy Cross** Norfk
7 N4 **Stokeinteignhead** Devon
46 B5 **Stoke Lacy** Herefs
48 G9 **Stoke Lyne** Oxon
35 M2 **Stoke Mandeville** Bucks
35 L5 **Stokenchurch** Bucks
36 H3 **Stoke Newington** Gt Lon
7 L10 **Stokenham** Devon
70 F5 **Stoke-on-Trent** C Stke
46 H9 **Stoke Orchard** Gloucs
35 Q8 **Stoke Poges** Bucks
58 E11 **Stoke Pound** Worcs
45 Q3 **Stoke Prior** Herefs
58 D11 **Stoke Prior** Worcs
17 L4 **Stoke Rivers** Devon
73 N5 **Stoke Rochford** Lincs
35 J8 **Stoke Row** Oxon
19 K9 **Stoke St Gregory** Somset
19 J10 **Stoke St Mary** Somset
20 C5 **Stoke St Michael** Somset
57 K8 **Stoke St Milborough** Shrops
56 G8 **Stokesay** Shrops
56 G8 **Stokesay Castle** Shrops
77 N9 **Stokesby** Norfk
104 F9 **Stokesley** N York
19 N11 **Stoke sub Hamdon** Somset
35 J5 **Stoke Talmage** Oxon
20 D9 **Stoke Trister** Somset
70 A9 **Stoke upon Tern** Shrops
70 F5 **Stoke-upon-Trent** C Stke
12 C3 **Stoke Wake** Dorset
58 E11 **Stoke Wharf** Worcs
11 H5 **Stolford** Somset
51 N10 **Stondon Massey** Essex
35 L2 **Stone** Bucks
32 C5 **Stone** Gloucs
37 N6 **Stone** Kent
85 J3 **Stone** Rothm
70 G8 **Stone** Staffs
58 C9 **Stone** Worcs
62 G2 **Stonea** Cambs
19 L4 **Stone Allerton** Somset
20 B4 **Ston Easton** Somset

19 L3 **Stonebridge** N Som
64 C3 **Stonebridge** Norfk
59 K8 **Stonebridge** Warwks
74 E10 **Stone Bridge Corner** C Pete
84 F9 **Stonebroom** Derbys
90 E5 **Stone Chair** Calder
25 M5 **Stone Cross** E Susx
25 P10 **Stone Cross** E Susx
25 P4 **Stone Cross** E Susx
25 M3 **Stone Cross** Kent
26 H4 **Stone Cross** Kent
39 P10 **Stone Cross** Kent
64 A10 **Stonecross Green** Suffk
26 B5 **Stonecrouch** Kent
31 N10 **Stone-edge-Batch** N Som
93 K4 **Stoneferry** C KuH
123 Q5 **Stonefield Castle Hotel** Ag & B
25 Q5 **Stonegate** E Susx
105 L9 **Stonegate** N York
98 D5 **Stonegrave** N York
46 G5 **Stonehall** Worcs
111 Q5 **Stonehaugh** Nthumb
151 N9 **Stonehaven** Abers
21 M6 **Stonehenge** Wilts
92 A9 **Stone Hill** Donc
6 D8 **Stonehouse** C Plym
95 R3 **Stone House** Cumb
32 F3 **Stonehouse** Gloucs
111 N9 **Stonehouse** Nthumb
126 D8 **Stonehouse** S Lans
26 F6 **Stone in Oxney** Kent
59 M10 **Stoneleigh** Warwks
69 R4 **Stoneley Green** Ches E
61 P7 **Stonely** Cambs
23 K9 **Stoner Hill** Hants
73 L6 **Stonesby** Leics
48 C11 **Stonesfield** Oxon
53 L6 **Stones Green** Essex
5 N10 **Stone Street** Kent
52 G4 **Stone Street** Suffk
54 H3 **Stone Street** Suffk
65 M5 **Stone Street** Suffk
5 J4 **Stonestreet Green** Kent
101 J8 **Stonethwaite** Cumb
157 P4 **Stonewells** Moray
37 N6 **Stonewood** Kent
168 c14 **Stoneybridge** W Isls
58 D9 **Stoneybridge** Worcs
126 H5 **Stoneyburn** W Loth
13 N2 **Stoney Cross** Hants
72 G10 **Stoneygate** C Leic
38 G2 **Stoneyhills** Essex
106 E7 **Stoneykirk** D & G
84 B5 **Stoney Middleton** Derbys
59 Q6 **Stoney Stanton** Leics
20 D8 **Stoney Stoke** Somset
20 C7 **Stoney Stratton** Somset
56 F3 **Stoney Stretton** Shrops
151 M5 **Stoneywood** C Aber
133 M11 **Stoneywood** Falk
58 G4 **Stonnall** Staffs
35 K7 **Stonor** Oxon
73 J11 **Stonton Wyville** Leics
46 D5 **Stony Cross** Herefs
57 J11 **Stony Cross** Herefs
22 B11 **Stonyford** Hants
84 G7 **Stony Houghton** Derbys
49 L6 **Stony Stratford** M Keyn
58 G2 **Stonywell** Staffs
17 M5 **Stoodleigh** Devon
18 B11 **Stoodleigh** Devon
27 K4 *Stop 24 Services* Kent
24 B7 **Stopham** W Susx
50 D6 **Stopsley** Luton
4 E6 **Stoptide** Cnwll
81 L8 **Storeton** Wirral
46 D6 **Storeyard Green** Herefs
168 j4 **Stornoway** W Isls
168 j4 *Stornoway Airport* W Isls
46 E5 **Storridge** Herefs
24 C8 **Storrington** W Susx
95 K5 **Storth** Cumb
92 B2 **Storwood** E R Yk
157 N3 **Stotfield** Moray
50 F3 **Stotfold** C Beds
57 M8 **Stottesdon** Shrops
72 G10 **Stoughton** Leics
23 Q4 **Stoughton** Surrey
23 M4 **Stoughton** W Susx
46 H5 **Stoulton** Worcs
58 C8 **Stourbridge** Dudley
58 C8 **Stourbridge Crematorium** Dudley
12 E3 **Stourpaine** Dorset
57 Q10 **Stourport-on-Severn** Worcs
20 E10 **Stour Provost** Dorset
20 F10 **Stour Row** Dorset
91 J4 **Stourton** Leeds
58 C8 **Stourton** Staffs
47 Q7 **Stourton** Warwks
20 E8 **Stourton** Wilts
20 D11 **Stourton Caundle** Dorset
19 M8 **Stout** Somset
169 r11 **Stove** Shet
64 N5 **Stoven** Suffk
117 P2 **Stow** Border
85 Q4 **Stow** Lincs
85 M9 **Stow Bardolph** Norfk
64 D2 **Stow Bedon** Norfk
75 M9 **Stowbridge** Norfk
62 H8 **Stow-cum-Quy** Cambs
31 Q3 **Stowe** Gloucs
56 E10 **Stowe** Shrops
71 J9 **Stowe by Chartley** Staffs
60 D9 **Stowehill** Nhants
20 C10 **Stowell** Somset
19 Q3 **Stowey** BaNES
8 B7 **Stowford** Devon
10 C7 **Stowford** Devon
17 M3 **Stowford** Devon
64 D8 **Stowlangtoft** Suffk
61 P6 **Stow Longa** Cambs
52 D2 **Stow Maries** Essex
64 E10 **Stowmarket** Suffk
47 N9 **Stow-on-the-Wold** Gloucs
27 K3 **Stowting** Kent
27 K3 **Stowting Common** Kent
64 F9 **Stowupland** Suffk
148 H4 **Straanruie** Highld
150 H9 **Strachan** Abers
131 M7 **Strachur** Ag & B
65 J7 **Stradbroke** Suffk
20 B4 **Stradbrook** Wilts

63 N10 **Stradishall** Suffk
75 N9 **Stradsett** Norfk
86 B10 **Stragglethorpe** Lincs
72 H3 **Stragglethorpe** Notts
34 B10 **Straight Soley** Wilts
127 P4 **Straiton** Mdloth
114 C7 **Straiton** S Ayrs
151 M3 **Straloch** Abers
141 P5 **Straloch** P & K
71 K7 **Stramshall** Staffs
80 e6 **Strang** IoM
82 H5 **Strangeways** Salfd
46 A9 **Strangford** Herefs
106 E5 **Stranraer** D & G
54 G11 **Strata Florida** Cerdgn
23 J2 **Stratfield Mortimer** W Berk
23 J2 **Stratfield Saye** Hants
23 J3 **Stratfield Turgis** Hants
61 Q11 **Stratford** C Beds
37 J4 **Stratford** Gt Lon
65 M9 **Stratford St Andrew** Suffk
52 H5 **Stratford St Mary** Suffk
21 M8 **Stratford sub Castle** Wilts
21 L9 **Stratford Tony** Wilts
47 P3 **Stratford-upon-Avon** Warwks
160 B11 **Strath** Highld
160 H2 **Strathan** Highld
165 N4 **Strathan** Highld
126 C9 **Strathaven** S Lans
125 P2 **Strathblane** Stirlg
161 K6 **Strathcanaird** Highld
154 B9 **Strathcarron** Highld
138 B11 **Strathcoil** Ag & B
150 B5 **Strathdon** Abers
135 M4 **Strathkinness** Fife
126 G3 **Strathloanhead** W Loth
147 P9 **Strathmashie House** Highld
134 G5 **Strathmiglo** Fife
155 N6 **Strathpeffer** Highld
141 M7 **Strathtay** P & K
121 K4 **Strathwhillan** N Ayrs
166 D4 **Strathy** Highld
166 D3 **Strathy Inn** Highld
132 H4 **Strathyre** Stirlg
16 C10 **Stratton** Cnwll
11 P6 **Stratton** Dorset
33 K4 **Stratton** Gloucs
48 H9 **Stratton Audley** Oxon
20 C4 **Stratton-on-the-Fosse** Somset
33 N7 **Stratton St Margaret** Swindn
65 J3 **Stratton St Michael** Norfk
77 J7 **Stratton Strawless** Norfk
18 E7 **Stream** Somset
25 J7 **Streat** E Susx
36 H6 **Streatham** Gt Lon
50 C5 **Streatley** C Beds
34 G8 **Streatley** W Berk
10 D7 **Street** Devon
95 L10 **Street** Lancs
105 K10 **Street** N York
19 N7 **Street** Somset
59 Q8 **Street Ashton** Warwks
69 K7 **Street Dinas** Shrops
25 P6 **Street End** E Susx
39 K11 **Street End** Kent
15 N7 **Street End** W Susx
113 K9 **Street Gate** Gatesd
58 H2 **Streethay** Staffs
98 A11 **Street Houses** N York
104 B11 **Streetlam** N York
84 E11 **Street Lane** Derbys
58 G5 **Streetly** Wsall
58 G5 **Streetly Crematorium** Wsall
63 K11 **Streetly End** Cambs
20 B7 **Street on the Fosse** Somset
56 G7 **Strefford** Shrops
142 B10 **Strelitz** P & K
72 E2 **Strelley** Notts
98 C8 **Strensall** C York
46 H6 **Strensham** Worcs
46 G6 *Strensham Services (northbound)* Worcs
46 H6 *Strensham Services (southbound)* Worcs
19 J6 **Stretcholt** Somset
7 L9 **Strete** Devon
45 N3 **Stretford** Herefs
45 J3 **Stretford** Herefs
82 G6 **Stretford** Traffd
51 L3 **Strethall** Essex
62 H6 **Stretham** Cambs
15 N5 **Strettington** W Susx
69 M4 **Stretton** Ches W
84 E8 **Stretton** Derbys
73 N7 **Stretton** Rutlnd
58 C2 **Stretton** Staffs
71 P9 **Stretton** Staffs
82 D8 **Stretton** Warrtn
59 M2 **Stretton en le Field** Leics
46 B6 **Stretton Grandison** Herefs
59 P10 **Stretton-on-Dunsmore** Warwks
47 P7 **Stretton on Fosse** Warwks
45 P6 **Stretton Sugwas** Herefs
59 Q8 **Stretton under Fosse** Warwks
57 K5 **Stretton Westwood** Shrops
159 M6 **Strichen** Abers
83 L7 **Strines** Stockp
18 G6 **Stringston** Somset
61 K8 **Strixton** Nhants
31 Q5 **Stroat** Gloucs
167 Q1 **Stroma** Highld
169 R11 **Stromeferry** Highld
169 b6 **Stromness** Ork
132 E5 **Stronachlachar** Stirlg
123 L11 **Stronafian** Ag & B
161 L3 **Stronchrubie** Highld
131 P11 **Strone** Ag & B
146 E11 **Strone** Highld
147 N2 **Strone** Highld
146 G11 **Stronenaba** Highld
131 P2 **Stronmilchan** Ag & B
169 f4 **Stronsay** Ork
169 f4 *Stronsay Airport* Ork
138 H5 **Strontian** Highld
26 E5 **Strood** Kent

38 B8 Strood Medway
36 F11 Strood Green Surrey
24 B6 Strood Green W Susx
32 G3 Stroud Gloucs
23 K10 Stroud Hants
36 B7 Stroude Surrey
38 E3 Stroud Green Essex
32 F3 Stroud Green Gloucs
73 N4 Stroxton Lincs
152 E10 Struan Highld
141 K4 Struan P & K
87 N4 Strubby Lincs
77 L10 Strumpshaw Norfk
126 D8 Strutherhill S Lans
135 K6 Struthers Fife
155 M9 Struy Highld
78 E8 Stryd-y-Facsen IoA
69 J5 Stryt-issa Wrexhm
159 N8 Stuartfield Abers
58 F4 Stubbers Green Wsall
14 G6 Stubbington Hants
89 M7 Stubbins Lancs
65 K2 Stubbs Green Norfk
12 F2 Stubhampton Dorset
84 D5 Stubley Derbys
82 C5 Stubshaw Cross Wigan
85 Q11 Stubton Lincs
13 L2 Stuckton Hants
96 B7 Studfold N York
35 N9 Stud Green W & M
50 B7 Studham C Beds
110 E9 Studholme Cumb
12 H8 Studland Dorset
47 L2 Studley Warwks
33 J10 Studley Wilts
47 L2 Studley Common Warwks
97 L7 Studley Roger N York
97 L6 Studley Royal N York
63 J5 Stuntney Cambs
25 P8 Stunts Green E Susx
70 E8 Sturbridge Staffs
85 Q3 Sturgate Lincs
51 Q2 Sturmer Essex
12 C2 Sturminster Common Dorset
12 G4 Sturminster Marshall Dorset
12 C2 Sturminster Newton Dorset
39 L9 Sturry Kent
92 G10 Sturton N Linc
85 Q4 Sturton by Stow Lincs
85 N4 Sturton le Steeple Notts
64 G6 Stuston Suffk
91 M2 Stutton N York
53 L5 Stutton Suffk
82 H8 Styal Ches E
89 K3 Stydd Lancs
157 Q5 Stynie Moray
85 K2 Styrrup Notts
132 B6 Succoth Ag & B
46 D4 Suckley Worcs
46 D4 Suckley Green Worcs
61 L4 Sudborough Nhants
65 N11 Sudbourne Suffk
73 P2 Sudbrook Lincs
31 P7 Sudbrook Mons
86 D5 Sudbrooke Lincs
71 M8 Sudbury Derbys
36 E3 Sudbury Gt Lon
52 E3 Sudbury Suffk
89 P8 Sudden Rochdl
32 H3 Sudgrove Gloucs
99 K2 Suffield N York
77 J5 Suffield Norfk
69 R11 Sugdon Wrekin
70 D8 Sugnall Staffs
45 P6 Sugwas Pool Herefs
145 J4 Suisnish Highld
80 e3 Sulby IoM
48 G6 Sulgrave Nhants
48 G5 Sulgrave Manor Nhants
34 H10 Sulham W Berk
34 H11 Sulhamstead W Berk
34 H11 Sulhamstead Abbots W Berk
34 H11 Sulhamstead Bannister W Berk
24 C8 Sullington W Susx
169 q6 Sullom Shet
169 r6 Sullom Voe Shet
30 C11 Sully V Glam
169 q12 Sumburgh Airport Shet
97 K8 Summerbridge N York
4 D10 Summercourt Cnwll
75 Q3 Summerfield Norfk
58 B10 Summerfield Worcs
35 K6 Summer Heath Bucks
41 N9 Summerhill Pembks
58 G3 Summerhill Staffs
69 K4 Summer Hill Wrexhm
103 P7 Summerhouse Darltn
95 L3 Summerlands Cumb
84 E5 Summerley Derbys
15 N5 Summersdale W Susx
89 M8 Summerseat Bury
34 F3 Summertown Oxon
89 Q9 Summit Oldham
89 Q7 Summit Rochdl
102 C9 Sunbiggin Cumb
36 D7 Sunbury Surrey
108 H4 Sundaywell D & G
122 B7 Sunderland Ag & B
100 G3 Sunderland Cumb
95 J9 Sunderland Lancs
113 N9 Sunderland Sundld
103 Q3 Sunderland Bridge Dur
113 N9 Sunderland Crematorium Sundld
117 L5 Sundhope Border
50 C5 Sundon Park Luton
37 L9 Sundridge Kent
93 N7 Sunk Island E R Yk
35 Q11 Sunningdale W & M
35 P11 Sunninghill W & M
34 E4 Sunningwell Oxon
103 M3 Sunniside Dur
113 K9 Sunniside Gatesd
103 N4 Sunny Brow Dur
72 A4 Sunnyhill C Derb
89 K6 Sunnyhurst Bl w D
133 M8 Sunnylaw Stirlg
34 F3 Sunnymead Oxon
21 P4 Sunton Wilts
36 E7 Surbiton Gt Lon
74 E5 Surfleet Lincs
74 E5 Surfleet Seas End Lincs
77 L10 Surlingham Norfk
52 E7 Surrex Essex

24 G3 Surrey & Sussex Crematorium W Susx
76 H4 Sustead Norfk
92 D10 Susworth Lincs
16 E9 Sutcombe Devon
16 E9 Sutcombemill Devon
64 F2 Suton Norfk
87 L6 Sutterby Lincs
74 E3 Sutterton Lincs
62 B11 Sutton C Beds
74 A11 Sutton C Pete
62 F5 Sutton Cambs
7 J10 Sutton Devon
8 H4 Sutton Devon
91 P8 Sutton Donc
25 L11 Sutton E Susx
36 G8 Sutton Gt Lon
27 P2 Sutton Kent
91 M5 Sutton N York
77 M7 Sutton Norfk
73 K3 Sutton Notts
34 D3 Sutton Oxon
40 H7 Sutton Pembks
57 J2 Sutton Shrops
57 N7 Sutton Shrops
69 L9 Sutton Shrops
70 B8 Sutton Shrops
82 B6 Sutton St Hel
70 D10 Sutton Staffs
53 P2 Sutton Suffk
23 Q11 Sutton W Susx
36 D11 Sutton Abinger Surrey
37 N7 Sutton at Hone Kent
60 G2 Sutton Bassett Nhants
32 H9 Sutton Benger Wilts
11 L2 Sutton Bingham Somset
72 E6 Sutton Bonington Notts
75 J6 Sutton Bridge Lincs
72 C10 Sutton Cheney Leics
58 H5 Sutton Coldfield Birm
58 H5 Sutton Coldfield Crematorium Birm
34 F6 Sutton Courtenay Oxon
74 H6 Sutton Crosses Lincs
85 L4 Sutton cum Lound Notts
72 D5 Sutton Fields Notts
36 B10 Sutton Green Surrey
69 M5 Sutton Green Wrexhm
97 M5 Sutton Howgrave N York
84 G9 Sutton in Ashfield Notts
90 C2 Sutton-in-Craven N York
60 B2 Sutton in the Elms Leics
83 K10 Sutton Lane Ends Ches E
57 N4 Sutton Maddock Shrops
19 L7 Sutton Mallet Somset
21 J9 Sutton Mandeville Wilts
81 Q6 Sutton Manor St Hel
45 R6 Sutton Marsh Herefs
20 B10 Sutton Montis Somset
93 K4 Sutton-on-Hull C KuH
87 P4 Sutton on Sea Lincs
98 B8 Sutton-on-the-Forest N York
71 N8 Sutton on the Hill Derbys
85 N7 Sutton on Trent Notts
11 Q8 Sutton Poyntz Dorset
74 G8 Sutton St Edmund Lincs
74 G7 Sutton St James Lincs
45 Q5 Sutton St Nicholas Herefs
22 E7 Sutton Scotney Hants
38 D10 Sutton Street Kent
48 B7 Sutton-under-Brailes Warwks
97 Q4 Sutton-under-Whitestonecliffe N York
98 E11 Sutton upon Derwent E R Yk
26 D2 Sutton Valence Kent
20 H6 Sutton Veny Wilts
20 G11 Sutton Waldron Dorset
82 B9 Sutton Weaver Ches W
19 Q3 Sutton Wick BaNES
34 E6 Sutton Wick Oxon
74 H2 Swaby Lincs
71 P11 Swadlincote Derbys
75 R9 Swaffham Norfk
63 J8 Swaffham Bulbeck Cambs
63 J8 Swaffham Prior Cambs
77 K5 Swafield Norfk
104 E10 Swainby N York
45 P6 Swainshill Herefs
77 J11 Swainsthorpe Norfk
32 E11 Swainswick BaNES
48 C7 Swalcliffe Oxon
39 K8 Swalecliffe Kent
93 L10 Swallow Lincs
86 B7 Swallow Beck Lincs
21 J9 Swallowcliffe Wilts
23 K2 Swallowfield Wokham
84 G3 Swallow Nest Rothm
51 P11 Swallows Cross Essex
22 D4 Swampton Hants
12 H9 Swanage Dorset
49 M9 Swanbourne Bucks
30 G11 Swanbridge V Glam
57 N6 Swancote Shrops
82 F10 Swan Green Ches W
92 G5 Swanland E R Yk
37 M7 Swanley Kent
37 M7 Swanley Village Kent
22 G11 Swanmore Hants
72 C7 Swannington Leics
76 G8 Swannington Norfk
86 C7 Swanpool Garden Suburb Lincs
37 P6 Swanscombe Kent
29 J6 Swansea Swans
28 G6 Swansea Airport Swans
29 J5 Swansea Crematorium Swans
28 H5 Swansea West Services Swans
52 E6 Swan Street Essex
77 K6 Swanton Abbot Norfk
76 E8 Swanton Morley Norfk
76 E7 Swanton Novers Norfk
38 E10 Swanton Street Kent
58 E6 Swan Village Sandw
84 F10 Swanwick Derbys
14 F5 Swanwick Hants
73 Q2 Swarby Lincs
77 J11 Swardeston Norfk
72 B5 Swarkestone Derbys
119 N10 Swarland Nthumb
22 G7 Swarraton Hants
96 G11 Swartha C Brad
95 F5 Swarthmoor Cumb
74 B3 Swaton Lincs

62 E7 Swavesey Cambs
13 N5 Sway Hants
73 P6 Swayfield Lincs
22 D11 Swaythling C Sotn
46 B2 Sweet Green Worcs
9 L5 Sweetham Devon
26 M5 Sweethaws E Susx
26 C2 Sweetlands Corner Kent
5 K2 Sweets Cnwll
4 H9 Sweetshouse Cnwll
65 L9 Swefling Suffk
72 B8 Swepstone Leics
48 C8 Swerford Oxon
82 H11 Swettenham Ches E
30 H5 Swffryd Blae G
26 E3 Swift's Green Kent
64 H11 Swilland Suffk
88 F4 Swillbrook Lancs
91 K4 Swillington Leeds
17 L5 Swimbridge Devon
17 L5 Swimbridge Newland Devon
33 Q2 Swinbrook Oxon
90 G5 Swincliffe Kirk
97 K9 Swincliffe N York
17 M3 Swincombe Devon
96 C10 Swinden N York
85 Q8 Swinderby Lincs
46 H9 Swindon Gloucs
119 J11 Swindon Nthumb
58 C6 Swindon Staffs
35 M8 Swindon Swindn
93 K3 Swine E R Yk
92 C6 Swinefleet E R Yk
32 C11 Swineford S Glos
61 N7 Swineshead Bed
74 D2 Swineshead Lincs
74 D2 Swineshead Bridge Lincs
167 M9 Swiney Highld
60 C5 Swinford Leics
34 D3 Swinford Oxon
27 M3 Swingfield Minnis Kent
27 M3 Swingfield Street Kent
52 G2 Swingleton Green Suffk
119 P5 Swinhoe Nthumb
93 M11 Swinhope Lincs
96 F3 Swinithwaite N York
46 C6 Swinmore Common Herefs
71 L5 Swinscoe Staffs
100 H6 Swinside Cumb
73 Q6 Swinstead Lincs
86 E4 Swinthorpe Lincs
129 L10 Swinton Border
97 K5 Swinton N York
98 F6 Swinton N York
91 M11 Swinton Rothm
82 G4 Swinton Salfd
72 F8 Swithland Leics
155 Q4 Swordale Highld
145 N9 Swordland Highld
166 B4 Swordly Highld
82 E8 Sworton Heath Ches E
54 F11 Swyddffynnon Cerdgn
35 J6 Swyncombe Oxon
70 F7 Swynnerton Staffs
11 L7 Swyre Dorset
68 H9 Sycharth Powys
55 M9 Sychnant Powys
55 M3 Sychtyn Powys
69 K3 Sydallt Wrexhm
32 J2 Syde Gloucs
37 J6 Sydenham Gt Lon
35 K4 Sydenham Oxon
5 Q6 Sydenham Damerel Devon
23 Q8 Sydenhurst Surrey
76 A5 Syderstone Norfk
11 N5 Sydling St Nicholas Dorset
22 E3 Sydmonton Hants
57 Q3 Sydnal Lane Shrops
85 M11 Syerston Notts
67 L5 Sygun Copper Mine Gwynd
89 P7 Syke Rochdl
91 Q7 Sykehouse Donc
65 J6 Syleham Suffk
28 F3 Sylen Carmth
169 s7 Symbister Shet
125 K11 Symington S Ayrs
116 D3 Symington S Lans
11 J6 Symondsbury Dorset
45 R11 Symonds Yat Herefs
90 F3 Sympson Green C Brad
10 H4 Synderford Dorset
42 H4 Synod Inn Cerdgn
165 Q8 Syre Highld
47 K10 Syreford Gloucs
48 H6 Syresham Nhants
72 G8 Syston Leics
73 N2 Syston Lincs
58 B11 Sytchampton Worcs
60 H7 Sywell Nhants

T

82 F9 Tabley Hill Ches E
48 E11 Tackley Oxon
64 G2 Tacolneston Norfk
91 M2 Tadcaster N York
83 P10 Taddington Derbys
47 L8 Taddington Gloucs
16 H8 Taddiport Devon
22 H2 Tadley Hants
62 C11 Tadlow C Beds
48 C7 Tadmarton Oxon
32 D10 Tadwick BaNES
36 F9 Tadworth Surrey
30 F2 Tafarnaubach Blae G
41 L4 Tafarn-y-bwlch Pembks
68 G2 Tafarn-y-Gelyn Denbgs
30 F8 Taff's Well Rhondd
55 K4 Tafolwern Powys
29 L7 Taibach Neath
162 H10 Tain Highld
167 M3 Tain Highld
66 G4 Tai'n Lôn Gwynd
168 g7 Tairbeart W Isls
44 D9 Tai'r Bull Powys
51 N6 Takeley Essex
51 M6 Takeley Street Essex
44 F8 Talachddu Powys
80 G8 Talacre Flints
9 Q5 Talaton Devon
40 F8 Talbenny Pembks
30 D8 Talbot Green Rhondd
13 J6 Talbot Village Bmouth

10 B5 Taleford Devon
55 L4 Talerddig Powys
42 H4 Talgarreg Cerdgn
44 H8 Talgarth Powys
152 E11 Talisker Highld
70 E4 Talke Staffs
70 E4 Talke Pits Staffs
111 L9 Talkin Cumb
154 B3 Talladale Highld
116 G6 Talla Linnfoots Border
114 H8 Tallaminnock S Ayrs
69 M6 Tallarn Green Wrexhm
100 F3 Tallentire Cumb
43 M8 Talley Carmth
74 A9 Tallington Lincs
69 J5 Tallwrn Wrexhm
165 N4 Talmine Highld
42 F9 Talog Carmth
43 K3 Talsarn Cerdgn
67 L7 Talsarnau Gwynd
4 E8 Talskiddy Cnwll
78 H9 Talwrn IoA
69 L5 Talwrn Wrexhm
54 F7 Tal-y-Bont Cerdgn
79 P11 Tal-y-Bont Conwy
67 K10 Tal-y-bont Gwynd
79 L10 Tal-y-bont Gwynd
44 G10 Talybont-on-Usk Powys
79 P10 Tal-y-Cafn Conwy
31 N11 Tal-y-coed Mons
30 D9 Tal-y-garn Rhondd
54 G3 Tal-y-llyn Gwynd
66 H4 Talysarn Gwynd
31 J4 Tal-y-Waun Torfn
55 J4 Talywern Powys
82 D4 Tamer Lane End Wigan
6 D6 Tamerton Foliot C Plym
59 K4 Tamworth Staffs
74 G2 Tamworth Green Lincs
59 K4 Tamworth Services Warwks
97 Q9 Tancred N York
40 G5 Tancredston Pembks
37 J10 Tandridge Surrey
113 J9 Tanfield Dur
113 J10 Tanfield Lea Dur
22 B4 Tangley Hants
15 P5 Tangmere W Susx
168 b17 Tangusdale W Isls
102 G9 Tan Hill N York
169 e6 Tankerness Ork
91 J11 Tankersley Barns
39 K8 Tankerton Kent
167 P7 Tannach Highld
151 K11 Tannachie Abers
142 H6 Tannadice Angus
58 G10 Tanner's Green Worcs
65 J8 Tannington Suffk
126 C5 Tannochside N Lans
84 D9 Tansley Derbys
61 N2 Tansor Nhants
113 J10 Tantobie Dur
104 F8 Tanton N York
58 D10 Tanwood Worcs
58 H10 Tanworth in Arden Warwks
67 M6 Tan-y-Bwlch Gwynd
68 C2 Tan-y-fron Conwy
69 J4 Tan-y-fron Wrexhm
67 M5 Tan-y-grisiau Gwynd
42 E5 Tan-y-groes Cerdgn
168 e9 Taobh Tuath W Isls
35 P8 Taplow Bucks
123 L9 Tarbert Ag & B
123 Q6 Tarbert Ag & B
168 g7 Tarbert W Isls
145 M9 Tarbet Highld
164 E7 Tarbet Highld
81 P7 Tarbock Green Knows
114 H2 Tarbolton S Ayrs
127 J6 Tarbrax S Lans
58 E11 Tardebigge Worcs
142 H2 Tarfside Angus
150 D7 Tarland Abers
88 F6 Tarleton Lancs
88 E8 Tarlscough Lancs
33 J5 Tarlton Gloucs
19 L4 Tarnock Somset
109 P11 Tarns Cumb
95 J2 Tarnside Cumb
69 Q2 Tarporley Ches W
17 R5 Tarr Somset
12 F2 Tarrant Crawford Dorset
12 F2 Tarrant Gunville Dorset
12 F2 Tarrant Hinton Dorset
12 F3 Tarrant Keyneston Dorset
12 F3 Tarrant Launceston Dorset
12 F3 Tarrant Monkton Dorset
12 F3 Tarrant Rawston Dorset
12 F3 Tarrant Rushton Dorset
25 K10 Tarring Neville E Susx
46 B6 Tarrington Herefs
145 J3 Tarskavaig Highld
159 L11 Tarves Abers
81 P11 Tarvin Ches W
81 P11 Tarvin Sands Ches W
64 H2 Tasburgh Norfk
57 M6 Tasley Shrops
48 C10 Taston Oxon
71 N10 Tatenhill Staffs
49 M5 Tathall End M Keyn
95 N7 Tatham Lancs
87 K4 Tathwell Lincs
37 K9 Tatsfield Surrey
69 N3 Tattenhall Ches W
76 B6 Tatterford Norfk
76 A6 Tattersett Norfk
86 H9 Tattershall Lincs
86 H9 Tattershall Bridge Lincs
86 H9 Tattershall Thorpe Lincs
53 K4 Tattingstone Suffk
53 K4 Tattingstone White Horse Suffk
10 G3 Tatworth Somset
157 R8 Tauchers Moray
18 H10 Taunton Somset
18 H10 Taunton Somset
18 H10 Taunton Deane Crematorium Somset
18 G10 Taunton Deane Services Somset
76 H9 Taverham Norfk
51 N7 Taverners Green Essex
41 N8 Tavernspite Pembks
6 D4 Tavistock Devon
8 G5 Taw Green Devon
17 K6 Tawstock Devon

83 M9 Taxal Derbys
131 L3 Taychreggan Hotel Ag & B
141 J5 Tay Forest Park P & K
123 L10 Tayinloan Ag & B
46 D10 Taynton Gloucs
33 P2 Taynton Oxon
139 J11 Taynuilt Ag & B
135 M2 Tayport Fife
130 E10 Tayvallich Ag & B
86 G2 Tealby Lincs
142 G10 Tealing Angus
113 K9 Team Valley Gatesd
145 L6 Teangue Highld
155 Q5 Teanord Highld
102 B10 Tebay Cumb
102 B9 Tebay Services Cumb
49 Q9 Tebworth C Beds
9 K6 Tedburn St Mary Devon
47 J8 Teddington Gt Lon
36 E6 Teddington Gt Lon
46 C3 Tedstone Delamere Herefs
46 C3 Tedstone Wafer Herefs
104 F6 Teesport R & Cl
104 E7 Teesside Crematorium Middsb
60 E6 Teeton Nhants
21 J8 Teffont Evias Wilts
21 J8 Teffont Magna Wilts
41 P4 Tegryn Pembks
73 M7 Teigh Rutlnd
8 G7 Teigncombe Devon
7 M4 Teigngrace Devon
7 N4 Teignmouth Devon
117 N9 Teindside Border
57 M3 Telford Wrekin
57 N2 Telford Crematorium Wrekin
57 N3 Telford Services Shrops
20 F3 Tellisford Somset
25 K10 Telscombe E Susx
25 K10 Telscombe Cliffs E Susx
140 G6 Tempar P & K
109 N3 Templand D & G
5 J7 Temple Cnwll
127 Q6 Temple Mdloth
59 K9 Temple Balsall Solhll
43 K4 Temple Bar Cerdgn
20 B3 Temple Cloud BaNES
20 D10 Templecombe Somset
63 L10 Temple End Suffk
27 N3 Temple Ewell Kent
47 M3 Temple Grafton Warwks
47 L9 Temple Guiting Gloucs
91 Q6 Temple Hirst N York
84 F7 Temple Normanton Derbys
151 L11 Temple of Fiddes Abers
102 B5 Temple Sowerby Cumb
9 L2 Templeton Devon
41 M8 Templeton Pembks
112 H10 Templetown Dur
61 Q10 Tempsford C Beds
57 K11 Tenbury Wells Worcs
41 M10 Tenby Pembks
53 K7 Tendring Essex
53 K6 Tendring Green Essex
53 K6 Tendring Heath Essex
75 L11 Ten Mile Bank Norfk
53 J7 Tenpenny Heath Essex
26 E5 Tenterden Kent
52 C8 Terling Essex
69 R11 Tern Wrekin
70 A8 Ternhill Shrops
109 K5 Terregles D & G
98 D6 Terrington N York
75 L6 Terrington St Clement Norfk
75 K8 Terrington St John Norfk
58 H10 Terry's Green Warwks
38 B11 Teston Kent
14 C4 Testwood Hants
32 G6 Tetbury Gloucs
32 G5 Tetbury Upton Gloucs
69 L8 Tetchill Shrops
5 N2 Tetcott Devon
87 K6 Tetford Lincs
93 P10 Tetney Lincs
93 P10 Tetney Lock Lincs
35 J4 Tetsworth Oxon
58 C4 Tettenhall Wolves
58 C5 Tettenhall Wood Wolves
84 G8 Teversal Notts
62 G9 Teversham Cambs
117 N9 Teviothead Border
50 G8 Tewin Herts
46 G8 Tewkesbury Gloucs
38 G9 Teynham Kent
90 F3 Thackley C Brad
100 F6 Thackthwaite Cumb
101 M5 Thackthwaite Cumb
24 D7 Thakeham W Susx
35 K3 Thame Oxon
36 E7 Thames Ditton Surrey
37 L4 Thamesmead Gt Lon
39 Q8 Thanet Crematorium Kent
39 K10 Thanington Kent
116 D3 Thankerton S Lans
64 H3 Tharston Norfk
34 F11 Thatcham W Berk
81 Q6 Thatto Heath St Hel
51 P4 Thaxted Essex
97 M3 Theakston N York
92 E7 Thealby N Linc
19 N5 Theale Somset
34 H10 Theale W Berk
93 J3 Thearne E R Yk
70 E3 The Bank Ches E
57 L5 The Bank Shrops
33 K4 The Beeches Gloucs
65 N8 Theberton Suffk
71 J9 The Blythe Staffs
56 F5 The Bog Shrops
58 C10 The Bourne Worcs
153 J11 The Braes Highld
58 C6 The Bratch Staffs
45 P2 The Broad Herefs
128 H5 The Brunt E Loth
80 e4 The Bungalow IoM
57 Q11 The Burf Worcs
46 G11 The Butts Gloucs
32 H3 The Camp Gloucs
69 N6 The Chequer Wrexhm
61 P9 The City Bed
35 L5 The City Bucks
47 Q9 The Common Oxon

21 P8	The Common Wilts	
33 K7	The Common Wilts	
26 B3	The Corner Kent	
60 F9	The Counties Crematorium Nhants	
80 d2	The Cronk IoM	
60 E3	Theddingworth Leics	
87 N3	Theddlethorpe All Saints Lincs	
87 N3	Theddlethorpe St Helen Lincs	
125 J7	The Den N Ayrs	
32 B2	The Forest of Dean Crematorium Gloucs	
45 L3	The Forge Herefs	
26 H4	The Forstal Kent	
70 B8	The Fouralls Shrops	
38 E8	The Garden of England Crematorium Kent	
94 C4	The Green Cumb	
52 C8	The Green Essex	
105 L9	The Green N York	
20 G8	The Green Wilts	
46 G6	The Grove Worcs	
24 C4	The Haven W Susx	
46 F9	The Haw Gloucs	
104 F4	The Headland Hartpl	
94 D4	The Hill Cumb	
35 M9	The Holt Wokham	
45 Q2	The Hundred Herefs	
9 J2	Thelbridge Cross Devon	
26 G5	The Leacon Kent	
35 P4	The Lee Bucks	
80 e1	The Lhen IoM	
125 K7	The Linn Crematorium E Rens	
64 E6	Thelnetham Suffk	
157 Q5	The Lochs Moray	
64 H5	Thelveton Norfk	
82 E7	Thelwall Warrtn	
82 H6	The Manchester Crematorium Manch	
56 E5	The Marsh Powys	
76 F7	Themelthorpe Norfk	
113 K10	The Middles Dur	
26 C6	The Moor Kent	
28 H7	The Mumbles Swans	
125 Q7	The Murray S Lans	
46 G8	The Mythe Gloucs	
31 P3	The Narth Mons	
151 J8	The Neuk Abers	
48 F6	Thenford Nhants	
33 K11	Theobald's Green Wilts	
23 N5	The Park Crematorium Hants	
32 D5	The Quarry Gloucs	
26 E3	The Quarter Kent	
46 H10	The Reddings Gloucs	
50 H3	Therfield Herts	
44 H8	The Rhôs Powys	
91 Q10	The Rose Hill Crematorium Donc	
133 M3	The Ross P & K	
23 N5	The Sands Surrey	
32 F10	The Shoe Wilts	
57 M5	The Smithies Shrops	
62 G11	The Spike Cambs	
59 L10	The Spring Warwks	
31 J5	The Square Torfn	
37 P11	The Stair Kent	
26 F6	The Stocks Kent	
23 L7	The Straits Hants	
20 H3	The Strand Wilts	
64 B5	Thetford Norfk	
63 P3	Thetford Forest Park	
101 L2	Thethwaite Cumb	
2 F6	The Towans Cnwll	
50 D6	The Vale Crematorium Luton	
45 Q5	The Vauld Herefs	
57 N3	The Wyke Shrops	
51 K11	Theydon Bois Essex	
92 A2	Thicket Priory N York	
32 F10	Thickwood Wilts	
86 H6	Thimbleby Lincs	
104 D11	Thimbleby N York	
81 K8	Thingwall Wirral	
97 Q5	Thirkleby N York	
97 Q4	Thirlby N York	
128 F10	Thirlestane Border	
97 K3	Thirn N York	
97 P4	Thirsk N York	
93 L4	Thirtleby E R Yk	
88 E3	Thistleton Lancs	
73 N7	Thistleton Rutlnd	
63 L5	Thistley Green Suffk	
98 G8	Thixendale N York	
112 E5	Thockrington Nthumb	
74 H9	Tholomas Drove Cambs	
97 Q7	Tholthorpe N York	
41 M9	Thomas Chapel Pembks	
101 M2	Thomas Close Cumb	
158 E10	Thomastown Abers	
47 L2	Thomas Town Warwks	
64 C2	Thompson Norfk	
37 Q6	Thong Kent	
96 F3	Thoralby N York	
85 K6	Thoresby Notts	
87 N5	Thoresthorpe Lincs	
93 L11	Thoresway Lincs	
93 M11	Thorganby Lincs	
92 A2	Thorganby N York	
105 K11	Thorgill N York	
65 N7	Thorington Suffk	
52 H4	Thorington Street Suffk	
96 E10	Thorlby N York	
51 L7	Thorley Herts	
14 C9	Thorley IoW	
51 L6	Thorley Houses Herts	
14 C9	Thorley Street IoW	
97 Q6	Thormanby N York	
104 F7	Thornaby-on-Tees S on T	
76 F4	Thornage Norfk	
49 K8	Thornborough Bucks	
97 L5	Thornborough N York	
90 F4	Thornbury C Brad	
16 G10	Thornbury Devon	
46 B3	Thornbury Herefs	
32 B6	Thornbury S Glos	
110 E10	Thornby Cumb	
60 E5	Thornby Nhants	
71 J3	Thorncliff Staffs	
94 D6	Thorncliffe Crematorium Cumb	
10 H4	Thorncombe Dorset	
23 Q6	Thorncombe Street Surrey	
61 Q11	Thorncott Green C Beds	
14 D10	Thorncross IoW	
64 G8	Thorndon Suffk	

8 D6	Thorndon Cross Devon	
92 A8	Thorne Donc	
19 P11	Thorne Coffin Somset	
7 K5	Thornecroft Devon	
16 G8	Thornehillhead Devon	
91 K2	Thorner Leeds	
58 G4	Thornes Staffs	
91 J7	Thornes Wakefd	
18 F10	Thorne St Margaret Somset	
36 B5	Thorney Bucks	
74 E10	Thorney C Pete	
85 Q6	Thorney Notts	
19 M10	Thorney Somset	
13 M5	Thorney Hill Hants	
15 L6	Thorney Island W Susx	
74 F10	Thorney Toll Cambs	
19 J10	Thornfalcon Somset	
11 N2	Thornford Dorset	
111 Q7	Thorngrafton Nthumb	
19 L8	Thorngrove Somset	
93 M5	Thorngumbald E R Yk	
75 P2	Thornham Norfk	
64 G7	Thornham Magna Suffk	
64 G7	Thornham Parva Suffk	
73 R10	Thornhaugh C Pete	
14 E4	Thornhill C Sotn	
30 G8	Thornhill Caerph	
100 D9	Thornhill Cumb	
116 B11	Thornhill D & G	
83 Q8	Thornhill Derbys	
90 H7	Thornhill Kirk	
133 K7	Thornhill Stirlg	
30 G8	Thornhill Crematorium Cardif	
90 G7	Thornhill Lees Kirk	
90 F6	Thornhills Calder	
99 N8	Thornholme E R Yk	
12 E4	Thornicombe Dorset	
118 G4	Thornington Nthumb	
103 M3	Thornley Dur	
104 C3	Thornley Dur	
112 B9	Thornley Gate Nthumb	
125 P6	Thornliebank E Rens	
63 M9	Thorns Suffk	
83 M7	Thornsett Derbys	
82 G8	Thorns Green Ches E	
100 H5	Thornthwaite Cumb	
97 J9	Thornthwaite N York	
142 F8	Thornton Angus	
49 K7	Thornton Bucks	
90 D4	Thornton C Brad	
98 F11	Thornton E R Yk	
134 H8	Thornton Fife	
88 C2	Thornton Lancs	
72 D9	Thornton Leics	
86 H7	Thornton Lincs	
104 E8	Thornton Middsb	
129 P10	Thornton Nthumb	
40 H9	Thornton Pembks	
81 L4	Thornton Sefton	
93 J7	Thornton Curtis N Linc	
81 L4	Thornton Garden of Rest Crematorium Sefton	
125 P6	Thorntonhall S Lans	
36 H7	Thornton Heath Gt Lon	
81 L8	Thornton Hough Wirral	
96 D11	Thornton-in-Craven N York	
95 P6	Thornton in Lonsdale N York	
97 N2	Thornton-le-Beans N York	
98 D7	Thornton-le-Clay N York	
98 G4	Thornton le Dale N York	
92 H11	Thornton le Moor Lincs	
97 N3	Thornton-le-Moor N York	
81 N10	Thornton-le-Moors Ches W	
97 P3	Thornton-le-Street N York	
129 K5	Thorntonloch E Loth	
96 E3	Thornton Rust N York	
97 J3	Thornton Steward N York	
97 K3	Thornton Watlass N York	
51 L10	Thornwood Common Essex	
128 G10	Thornydykes Border	
101 L6	Thornythwaite Cumb	
73 K2	Thoroton Notts	
91 P11	Thorp Arch Leeds	
71 M4	Thorpe Derbys	
99 K11	Thorpe E R Yk	
87 N4	Thorpe Lincs	
96 F8	Thorpe N York	
65 N2	Thorpe Norfk	
85 N11	Thorpe Notts	
36 B7	Thorpe Surrey	
64 H6	Thorpe Abbotts Norfk	
72 E7	Thorpe Acre Leics	
73 K6	Thorpe Arnold Leics	
91 M7	Thorpe Audlin Wakefd	
98 H6	Thorpe Bassett N York	
38 F4	Thorpe Bay Sthend	
73 M11	Thorpe by Water Rutlnd	
91 K11	Thorpe Common Rothm	
59 L3	Thorpe Constantine Staffs	
77 K9	Thorpe End Norfk	
53 L7	Thorpe Green Essex	
88 H6	Thorpe Green Lancs	
64 C11	Thorpe Green Suffk	
91 K11	Thorpe Hesley Rothm	
91 P8	Thorpe in Balne Donc	
60 F2	Thorpe Langton Leics	
104 C5	Thorpe Larches Dur	
36 B6	Thorpe Lea Surrey	
86 B4	Thorpe le Fallows Lincs	
53 L7	Thorpe-le-Soken Essex	
92 D2	Thorpe le Street E R Yk	
60 H5	Thorpe Malsor Nhants	
48 F6	Thorpe Mandeville Nhants	
77 J4	Thorpe Market Norfk	
76 H8	Thorpe Marriot Norfk	
64 C11	Thorpe Morieux Suffk	
65 P10	Thorpeness Suffk	
91 J5	Thorpe on the Hill Leeds	
86 B7	Thorpe on the Hill Lincs	
36 B7	Thorpe Park Surrey	
77 K10	Thorpe St Andrew Norfk	
87 N8	Thorpe St Peter Lincs	
84 H4	Thorpe Salvin Rothm	
73 J8	Thorpe Satchville Leics	
104 C6	Thorpe Thewles S on T	
86 F9	Thorpe Tilney Lincs	
97 Q9	Thorpe Underwood N York	

60 G4	Thorpe Underwood Nhants	
61 M4	Thorpe Waterville Nhants	
91 P4	Thorpe Willoughby N York	
75 M9	Thorpland Norfk	
53 J8	Thorrington Essex	
9 M4	Thorverton Devon	
50 D7	Thrales End C Beds	
64 G6	Thrandeston Suffk	
61 L5	Thrapston Nhants	
100 G3	Threapland Cumb	
96 E8	Threapland N York	
69 M6	Threapwood Ches W	
71 J6	Threapwood Staffs	
71 J6	Threapwood Head Staffs	
114 F6	Threave S Ayrs	
108 F8	Threave Castle D & G	
45 Q10	Three Ashes Herefs	
24 G3	Three Bridges W Susx	
3 J4	Three Burrows Cnwll	
26 D4	Three Chimneys Kent	
44 H7	Three Cocks Powys	
52 C6	Three Counties Crematorium Essex	
28 G6	Three Crosses Swans	
25 P6	Three Cups Corner E Susx	
46 C2	Three Gates Worcs	
77 L8	Threehammer Common Norfk	
5 L4	Three Hammers Cnwll	
75 K10	Three Holes Norfk	
74 A3	Threekingham Lincs	
25 Q4	Three Leg Cross E Susx	
13 J3	Three Legged Cross Dorset	
35 K11	Three Mile Cross Wokham	
3 K4	Threemilestone Cnwll	
127 K2	Three Miletown W Loth	
26 D9	Three Oaks E Susx	
101 K5	Threlkeld Cumb	
51 L9	Threshers Bush Essex	
96 E8	Threshfield N York	
77 P9	Thrigby Norfk	
102 H6	Thringarth Dur	
72 C7	Thringstone Leics	
97 M2	Thrintoft N York	
62 F11	Thriplow Cambs	
84 H3	Throapham Rothm	
74 G9	Throckenhalt Lincs	
50 H4	Throcking Herts	
113 J7	Throckley N u Ty	
47 J4	Throckmorton Worcs	
13 K5	Throop Bmouth	
12 D6	Throop Dorset	
112 H3	Throphill Nthumb	
119 K10	Thropton Nthumb	
133 P9	Throsk Stirlg	
32 H3	Througham Gloucs	
109 J4	Throughgate D & G	
8 G6	Throwleigh Devon	
38 G10	Throwley Kent	
38 G11	Throwley Forstal Kent	
72 E4	Thrumpton Notts	
85 M4	Thrumpton Notts	
167 P7	Thrumster Highld	
93 P9	Thrunscoe NE Lin	
119 L8	Thrunton Nthumb	
33 Q5	Thrup Oxon	
32 G4	Thrupp Gloucs	
48 E11	Thrupp Oxon	
8 B7	Thrushelton Devon	
72 H7	Thrussington Leics	
21 Q5	Thruxton Hants	
45 N8	Thruxton Herefs	
91 M11	Thrybergh Rothm	
72 C4	Thulston Derbys	
38 C4	Thundersley Essex	
72 F8	Thurcaston Leics	
84 G3	Thurcroft Rothm	
16 D9	Thurdon Cnwll	
76 H5	Thurgarton Norfk	
85 L11	Thurgarton Notts	
90 H10	Thurgoland Barns	
72 E11	Thurlaston Leics	
59 Q10	Thurlaston Warwks	
19 J10	Thurlbear Somset	
74 A7	Thurlby Lincs	
86 B8	Thurlby Lincs	
87 N5	Thurlby Lincs	
61 N9	Thurleigh Bed	
6 H10	Thurlestone Devon	
19 J8	Thurloxton Somset	
90 G10	Thurlstone Barns	
65 N2	Thurlton Norfk	
70 E3	Thurlwood Ches E	
72 G10	Thurmaston Leics	
72 G10	Thurnby Leics	
77 N8	Thurne Norfk	
38 D10	Thurnham Kent	
61 N4	Thurning Nhants	
76 F6	Thurning Norfk	
91 M9	Thurnscoe Barns	
37 N5	Thurrock Services Thurr	
110 F10	Thursby Cumb	
89 Q4	Thursden Lancs	
76 D5	Thursford Norfk	
23 P7	Thursley Surrey	
167 K3	Thurso Highld	
81 J8	Thurstaston Wirral	
64 C8	Thurston Suffk	
90 B9	Thurston Clough Oldham	
110 F9	Thurstonfield Cumb	
90 F8	Thurstonland Kirk	
64 C9	Thurston Planch Suffk	
77 L11	Thurton Norfk	
71 N7	Thurvaston Derbys	
76 E10	Thuxton Norfk	
102 G11	Thwaite N York	
64 G8	Thwaite Suffk	
94 G2	Thwaite Head Cumb	
90 D2	Thwaites C Brad	
90 D2	Thwaites Brow C Brad	
99 L6	Thwing E R Yk	
134 C3	Tibbermore P & K	
116 B11	Tibbers D & G	
46 E10	Tibberton Gloucs	
46 H3	Tibberton Worcs	
70 B10	Tibberton Wrekin	
117 J6	Tibbie Shiels Inn Border	
64 G4	Tibenham Norfk	
84 F8	Tibshelf Derbys	
99 K3	Tibthorpe E R Yk	
25 Q4	Ticehurst E Susx	
22 G8	Tichborne Hants	
73 P9	Tickencote Rutlnd	
31 N10	Tickenham N Som	
49 N6	Tickford End M Keyn	

85 J2	Tickhill Donc	
56 H6	Ticklerton Shrops	
72 B6	Ticknall Derbys	
93 J2	Tickton E R Yk	
58 H9	Tidbury Green Solhll	
34 H4	Tiddington Oxon	
47 P3	Tiddington Warwks	
32 G9	Tiddleywink Wilts	
25 P4	Tidebrook E Susx	
5 P10	Tideford Cnwll	
5 N9	Tideford Cross Cnwll	
31 Q5	Tidenham Gloucs	
83 Q9	Tideswell Derbys	
34 H10	Tidmarsh W Berk	
47 Q7	Tidmington Warwks	
21 L11	Tidpit Hants	
21 P5	Tidworth Wilts	
40 H8	Tiers Cross Pembks	
49 K4	Tiffield Nhants	
143 J5	Tigerton Angus	
168 C10	Tigh a Ghearraidh W Isls	
168 C10	Tigharry W Isls	
124 B3	Tighnabruaich Ag & B	
7 K6	Tigley Devon	
61 N7	Tilbrook Cambs	
37 P5	Tilbury Thurr	
52 B3	Tilbury Green Essex	
52 C3	Tilbury Juxta Clare Essex	
59 J7	Tile Cross Birm	
59 L9	Tile Hill Covtry	
59 J9	Tilehouse Green Solhll	
35 J10	Tilehurst Readg	
23 N6	Tilford Surrey	
24 G4	Tilgate W Susx	
24 G4	Tilgate Forest Row W Susx	
19 Q7	Tilham Street Somset	
46 C8	Tillers Green Gloucs	
133 Q8	Tillicoultry Clacks	
126 E8	Tillietudlem S Lans	
52 G11	Tillingham Essex	
45 P6	Tillington Herefs	
23 Q10	Tillington W Susx	
45 P5	Tillington Common Herefs	
150 H6	Tillybirloch Abers	
150 C5	Tillyfourie Abers	
151 M3	Tillygreig Abers	
134 E6	Tillyrie P & K	
39 P11	Tilmanstone Kent	
75 L7	Tilney All Saints Norfk	
75 L7	Tilney High End Norfk	
75 K8	Tilney St Lawrence Norfk	
21 K5	Tilshead Wilts	
69 P7	Tilstock Shrops	
69 N4	Tilston Ches W	
69 Q3	Tilstone Bank Ches W	
69 Q2	Tilstone Fearnall Ches W	
49 Q10	Tilsworth C Beds	
73 J9	Tilton on the Hill Leics	
32 F5	Tiltups End Gloucs	
51 N5	Tilty Essex	
86 F9	Timberland Lincs	
70 F2	Timbersbrook Ches E	
18 C6	Timberscombe Somset	
97 J10	Timble N York	
18 C9	Timewell Devon	
110 F6	Timpanheck D & G	
82 G7	Timperley Traffd	
20 C3	Timsbury BaNES	
22 B10	Timsbury Hants	
168 f4	Timsgarry W Isls	
168 f4	Timsgearraidh W Isls	
64 B8	Timworth Suffk	
64 B8	Timworth Green Suffk	
12 C6	Tincleton Dorset	
111 M9	Tindale Cumb	
103 N5	Tindale Crescent Dur	
49 J8	Tingewick Bucks	
90 H5	Tingley Leeds	
50 B4	Tingrith C Beds	
169 r9	Tingwall Airport Shet	
5 P4	Tinhay Devon	
22 D5	Tinker's Hill Hants	
84 C8	Tinkersley Derbys	
84 F2	Tinsley Sheff	
24 G3	Tinsley Green W Susx	
4 H4	Tintagel Cnwll	
4 G4	Tintagel Castle Cnwll	
31 P4	Tintern Abbey Mons	
31 P4	Tintern Parva Mons	
19 N11	Tintinhull Somset	
83 M5	Tintwistle Derbys	
109 M4	Tinwald D & G	
73 Q9	Tinwell Rutlnd	
17 P2	Tippacott Devon	
75 K11	Tipp's End Norfk	
13 N5	Tiptoe Hants	
58 F6	Tipton Sandw	
58 E6	Tipton Green Sandw	
10 B6	Tipton St John Devon	
52 E8	Tiptree Essex	
52 E8	Tiptree Heath Essex	
44 B6	Tirabad Powys	
136 C7	Tiree Ag & B	
136 C7	Tiree Airport Ag & B	
123 M7	Tiretigan Ag & B	
46 F9	Tirley Gloucs	
30 F4	Tirphil Caerph	
101 P5	Tirril Cumb	
69 Q3	Tir-y-fron Flints	
20 H9	Tisbury Wilts	
24 C4	Tisman's Common W Susx	
71 M4	Tissington Derbys	
16 D3	Titchberry Devon	
14 F5	Titchfield Hants	
14 F5	Titchfield Common Hants	
61 M5	Titchmarsh Nhants	
75 Q2	Titchwell Norfk	
73 K2	Tithby Notts	
45 L2	Titley Herefs	
50 F5	Titmore Green Herts	
37 K10	Titsey Surrey	
16 C11	Titson Cnwll	
70 F7	Tittensor Staffs	
76 B7	Tittleshall Norfk	
58 B11	Titton Worcs	
69 Q2	Tiverton Ches W	
9 N2	Tiverton Devon	
64 H4	Tivetshall St Margaret Norfk	
64 H4	Tivetshall St Mary Norfk	
18 B5	Tivington Somset	
90 H9	Tivy Dale Barns	
70 H10	Tixall Staffs	
73 P10	Tixover Rutlnd	
169 q12	Toab Shet	

84 E9	Toadhole Derbys	
84 D10	Toadmoor Derbys	
137 N4	Tobermory Ag & B	
130 E6	Toberonochy Ag & B	
168 c14	Tobha Mor W Isls	
158 G11	Tocher Abers	
158 D4	Tochieneal Moray	
33 K9	Tockenham Wilts	
33 K9	Tockenham Wick Wilts	
104 H7	Tocketts R & Cl	
89 K6	Tockholes Bl w D	
32 B7	Tockington S Glos	
97 Q10	Tockwith N York	
20 E11	Todber Dorset	
119 M11	Todburn Nthumb	
49 N9	Toddington C Beds	
47 K8	Toddington Gloucs	
50 B5	Toddington Services C Beds	
50 F5	Todds Green Herts	
49 P7	Todenham Gloucs	
142 G10	Todhills Angus	
110 G8	Todhills Cumb	
103 P4	Todhills Dur	
110 G8	Todhills Services Cumb	
89 Q6	Todmorden Calder	
84 G4	Todwick Rothm	
62 E9	Toft Cambs	
82 G9	Toft Ches E	
73 R7	Toft Lincs	
169 r6	Toft Shet	
59 Q10	Toft Warwks	
103 N5	Toft Hill Dur	
86 H8	Toft Hill Lincs	
65 N3	Toft Monks Norfk	
86 D3	Toft next Newton Lincs	
76 B6	Toftrees Norfk	
76 D9	Toftwood Norfk	
119 P10	Togston Nthumb	
145 K5	Tokavaig Highld	
35 K9	Tokers Green Oxon	
168 k3	Tolastadh W Isls	
4 E10	Toldish Cnwll	
19 F8	Tolland Somset	
21 J11	Tollard Farnham Dorset	
20 H11	Tollard Royal Wilts	
91 P9	Toll Bar Donc	
59 N9	Tollbar End Covtry	
11 M5	Toller Fratrum Dorset	
11 M5	Toller Porcorum Dorset	
97 R8	Tollerton N York	
72 G4	Tollerton Notts	
11 L4	Toller Whelme Dorset	
52 G9	Tollesbury Essex	
52 F9	Tolleshunt D'Arcy Essex	
52 F9	Tolleshunt Knights Essex	
52 F9	Tolleshunt Major Essex	
12 C6	Tolpuddle Dorset	
168 k3	Tolsta W Isls	
36 E7	Tolworth Gt Lon	
148 E2	Tomatin Highld	
146 H5	Tomchrasky Highld	
146 F7	Tomdoun Highld	
147 J2	Tomich Highld	
155 P8	Tomich Highld	
156 B3	Tomich Highld	
162 E5	Tomich Highld	
149 M4	Tomintoul Moray	
48 E2	Tomlow Warwks	
155 P9	Tomnacross Highld	
149 N2	Tomnavoulin Moray	
70 G4	Tonah Staffs	
31 K4	Ton Mons	
31 L5	Ton Mons	
37 N11	Tonbridge Kent	
29 M8	Tondu Brdgnd	
18 F10	Tonedale Somset	
54 D4	Ton fanau Gwynd	
90 D4	Tong C Brad	
38 G10	Tong Kent	
57 P3	Tong Shrops	
72 C6	Tonge Leics	
38 G11	Tong Green Kent	
23 N5	Tongham Surrey	
108 E10	Tongland D & G	
57 P3	Tong Norton Shrops	
165 N5	Tongue Highld	
74 C7	Tongue End Lincs	
30 F8	Tongwynlais Cardif	
29 M5	Tonmawr Neath	
29 L5	Tonna Neath	
30 E7	Ton-teg Rhondd	
50 H7	Tonwell Herts	
30 C6	Tonypandy Rhondd	
30 D7	Tonyrefail Rhondd	
34 G4	Toot Baldon Oxon	
51 M10	Toot Hill Essex	
22 C11	Toothill Hants	
33 M8	Toothill Swindn	
36 G6	Tooting Gt Lon	
36 G6	Tooting Bec Gt Lon	
97 N5	Topcliffe N York	
65 K3	Topcroft Norfk	
65 K3	Topcroft Street Norfk	
61 M8	Top End Bed	
91 Q7	Topham Donc	
89 P9	Top of Hebers Rochdl	
52 B4	Toppesfield Essex	
89 L8	Toppings Bolton	
64 H2	Toprow Norfk	
9 N7	Topsham Devon	
69 J3	Top-y-rhos Flints	
120 G8	Torbeg N Ayrs	
162 H7	Torboll Highld	
156 A9	Torbreck Highld	
7 L5	Torbryan Devon	
139 L2	Torcastle Highld	
7 L10	Torcross Devon	
155 R7	Tore Highld	
5 J11	Torfrey Cnwll	
123 P7	Torinturk Ag & B	
114 F5	Torksey Lincs	
32 E5	Tormarton S Glos	
156 G5	Tormore Highld	
156 B3	Tornagrain Highld	
150 G6	Tornaveen Abers	
147 P2	Torness Highld	
103 N4	Toronto Dur	
100 H3	Torpenhow Cumb	
127 J3	Torphichen W Loth	
150 H2	Torphins Abers	
6 C7	Torpoint Cnwll	
7 N6	Torquay Torbay	
7 N5	Torquay Crematorium Torbay	
128 C10	Torquhan Border	
6 F8	Torr Devon	
153 K8	Torran Highld	
125 Q3	Torrance E Duns	
125 K9	Torranyard N Ayrs	

18 D7	**Torre** Somset
154 B6	**Torridon** Highld
153 R6	**Torridon House** Highld
145 J3	**Torrin** Highld
120 F4	**Torrisdale** Ag & B
165 Q4	**Torrisdale** Highld
163 M3	**Torrish** Highld
95 K3	**Torrisholme** Lancs
162 D6	**Torrobull** Highld
151 N6	**Torry** C Aber
134 C10	**Torryburn** Fife
10 a2	**Torteval** Guern
109 M5	**Torthorwald** D & G
24 B10	**Tortington** W Susx
58 B10	**Torton** Worcs
32 D6	**Tortworth** S Glos
152 H9	**Torvaig** Highld
94 F2	**Torver** Cumb
133 N10	**Torwood** Falk
117 P3	**Torwoodlee** Border
85 L3	**Torworth** Notts
16 D7	**Tosberry** Devon
153 N10	**Toscaig** Highld
62 B8	**Toseland** Cambs
95 R9	**Tosside** Lancs
64 D9	**Tostock** Suffk
152 C7	**Totaig** Highld
152 G8	**Tote** Highld
153 J5	**Tote** Highld
23 N10	**Tote Hill** W Susx
22 C7	**Totford** Hants
87 M4	**Tothill** Lincs
13 P7	**Totland** IoW
84 D5	**Totley** Sheff
84 D4	**Totley Brook** Sheff
7 L6	**Totnes** Devon
72 C4	**Toton** Notts
136 F4	**Totronald** Ag & B
152 F4	**Totscore** Highld
36 H2	**Tottenham** Gt Lon
75 M8	**Tottenhill** Norfk
36 F2	**Totteridge** Gt Lon
49 Q10	**Totternhoe** C Beds
89 M8	**Tottington** Bury
89 L4	**Tottleworth** Lancs
14 C4	**Totton** Hants
35 N9	**Touchen End** W & M
91 M2	**Toulston** N York
18 G8	**Toulton** Somset
163 K10	**Toulvaddie** Highld
38 C11	**Tovil** Kent
3 Q4	**Towan** Cnwll
4 D7	**Towan** Cnwll
124 E4	**Toward** Ag & B
124 E4	**Toward Quay** Ag & B
49 J5	**Towcester** Nhants
2 D6	**Towednack** Cnwll
35 K3	**Towersey** Oxon
150 C5	**Towie** Abers
103 M3	**Tow Law** Dur
74 H11	**Town End** Cambs
95 J4	**Town End** Cumb
101 K9	**Town End** Cumb
102 B5	**Town End** Cumb
125 K2	**Townend** W Duns
111 K11	**Towngate** Cumb
74 B8	**Towngate** Lincs
88 E9	**Town Green** Lancs
77 M9	**Town Green** Norfk
83 Q4	**Townhead** Barns
100 E3	**Townhead** Cumb
101 M10	**Town Head** Cumb
102 B4	**Townhead** Cumb
109 M3	**Townhead** D & G
96 B9	**Town Head** N York
108 F8	**Townhead of Greenlaw** D & G
134 E10	**Townhill** Fife
104 C3	**Town Kelloe** Dur
5 Q7	**Townlake** Devon
82 K5	**Town Lane** Wigan
25 K7	**Town Littleworth** E Susx
82 D5	**Town of Lowton** Wigan
25 N4	**Town Row** E Susx
22 G3	**Towns End** Hants
10 H2	**Townsend** Somset
2 F7	**Townshend** Cnwll
63 N3	**Town Street** Suffk
32 D6	**Townwell** S Glos
118 F5	**Town Yetholm** Border
98 C9	**Towthorpe** C York
98 H8	**Towthorpe** E R Yk
91 M3	**Towton** N York
80 D9	**Towyn** Conwy
81 M7	**Toxteth** Lpool
87 L8	**Toynton All Saints** Lincs
87 L8	**Toynton Fen Side** Lincs
87 M8	**Toynton St Peter** Lincs
37 L10	**Toy's Hill** Kent
114 H3	**Trabboch** E Ayrs
115 J3	**Trabbochburn** E Ayrs
3 J9	**Traboe** Cnwll
18 E10	**Tracebridge** Somset
156 F6	**Tradespark** Highld
44 D9	**Trallong** Powys
84 D9	**Tramway Museum** Derbys
128 C5	**Tranent** E Loth
81 L7	**Tranmere** Wirral
166 E6	**Trantelbeg** Highld
166 E6	**Trantlemore** Highld
113 J4	**Tranwell** Nthumb
43 N11	**Trapp** Carmth
128 F4	**Traprain** E Loth
58 F11	**Trap's Green** Warwks
22 C2	**Trapshill** W Berk
117 L4	**Traquair** Border
35 J11	**Trash Green** W Berk
89 Q3	**Trawden** Lancs
54 F10	**Trawscoed** Cerdgn
67 N7	**Trawsfynydd** Gwynd
30 D6	**Trealaw** Rhondd
88 E4	**Treales** Lancs
78 D9	**Trearddur Bay** IoA
152 F7	**Treaslane** Highld
4 E6	**Treator** Cnwll
30 D10	**Tre Aubrey** V Glam
30 D6	**Trebanog** Rhondd
29 K4	**Trebanos** Neath
5 M6	**Trebartha** Cnwll
4 H4	**Trebarwith** Cnwll
5 M4	**Trebeath** Cnwll
4 E6	**Trebetherick** Cnwll
18 D7	**Treborough** Somset
4 D9	**Trebudannon** Cnwll
5 N6	**Trebullett** Cnwll
4 H6	**Treburgett** Cnwll
5 P6	**Treburley** Cnwll
4 D7	**Treburrick** Cnwll
4 H9	**Trebyan** Cnwll
44 B9	**Trecastle** Powys
5 N5	**Trecogo** Cnwll
8 F4	**Trecott** Devon
41 J4	**Trecwn** Pembks
30 C4	**Trecynon** Rhondd
5 L5	**Tredaule** Cnwll
2 D8	**Tredavoe** Cnwll
30 F3	**Tredegar** Blae G
4 H7	**Tredethy** Cnwll
46 H9	**Tredington** Gloucs
47 Q6	**Tredington** Warwks
4 E7	**Tredinnick** Cnwll
4 G10	**Tredinnick** Cnwll
5 K8	**Tredinnick** Cnwll
5 L10	**Tredinnick** Cnwll
5 M10	**Tredinnick** Cnwll
44 G8	**Tredomen** Powys
41 L2	**Tredrissi** Pembks
4 F6	**Tredrizzick** Cnwll
31 L6	**Tredunnock** Mons
44 G8	**Tredustan** Powys
2 B9	**Treen** Cnwll
2 C6	**Treen** Cnwll
4 H10	**Treesmill** Cnwll
84 F3	**Treeton** Rothm
40 G3	**Trefasser** Pembks
78 G10	**Trefdraeth** IoA
44 G8	**Trefecca** Powys
55 M6	**Trefeglwys** Powys
54 E11	**Trefenter** Cerdgn
41 J6	**Treffgarne** Pembks
40 G5	**Treffgarne Owen** Pembks
30 E7	**Trefforest** Rhondd
40 G3	**Treffynnon** Pembks
30 F2	**Trefil** Blae G
43 K3	**Trefilan** Cerdgn
40 F4	**Trefin** Pembks
69 J9	**Treflach Wood** Shrops
68 H11	**Trefnannau** Powys
80 F10	**Trefnant** Denbgs
69 J9	**Trefonen** Shrops
66 F5	**Trefor** Gwynd
78 F8	**Trefor** IoA
5 J5	**Treforest** Cnwll
67 P2	**Trefriw** Conwy
5 M5	**Tregadillett** Cnwll
31 P3	**Tre-gagle** Mons
78 H8	**Tregaian** IoA
31 M2	**Tregare** Mons
3 K9	**Tregarne** Cnwll
43 N3	**Tregaron** Cerdgn
79 L11	**Tregarth** Gwynd
4 D9	**Tregaswith** Cnwll
4 H4	**Tregatta** Cnwll
4 G8	**Tregawne** Cnwll
5 L4	**Tregeare** Cnwll
68 G8	**Tregeiriog** Wrexhm
78 F6	**Tregele** IoA
4 G6	**Tregellist** Cnwll
3 M5	**Tregenna** Cnwll
2 B7	**Tregeseal** Cnwll
3 L7	**Tregew** Cnwll
30 C3	**Tre-Gibbon** Rhondd
3 K9	**Tregidden** Cnwll
3 Q4	**Tregiskey** Cnwll
40 F5	**Treglemais** Pembks
5 K2	**Tregole** Cnwll
3 J6	**Tregolls** Cnwll
4 E7	**Tregonce** Cnwll
4 F9	**Tregonetha** Cnwll
3 N5	**Tregony** Cnwll
4 G7	**Tregoodwell** Cnwll
3 Q3	**Tregorrick** Cnwll
4 F9	**Tregoss** Cnwll
44 H7	**Tregoyd** Powys
3 Q3	**Tregrehan Mills** Cnwll
42 H6	**Tre-groes** Cerdgn
4 H9	**Tregullon** Cnwll
4 F7	**Tregunna** Cnwll
5 L5	**Tregunnon** Cnwll
4 D8	**Tregurrian** Cnwll
55 P5	**Tregynon** Powys
42 H11	**Tre-gynwr** Carmth
30 D6	**Trehafod** Rhondd
5 Q10	**Trehan** Cnwll
30 E5	**Treharris** Myr Td
4 G6	**Treharrock** Cnwll
4 D7	**Trehemborne** Cnwll
43 L5	**Treherbert** Carmth
29 P5	**Treherbert** Rhondd
5 N9	**Trehunist** Cnwll
5 N6	**Trekenner** Cnwll
4 H4	**Treknow** Cnwll
3 J10	**Trelan** Cnwll
5 K3	**Trelash** Cnwll
3 M3	**Trelassick** Cnwll
5 L11	**Trelawne** Cnwll
80 F9	**Trelawnyd** Flints
3 K9	**Treleague** Cnwll
3 K10	**Treleaver** Cnwll
41 Q4	**Trelech** Carmth
42 F9	**Trelech a'r Betws** Carmth
40 E5	**Treleddyd-fawr** Pembks
3 L6	**Trelew** Cnwll
30 F5	**Trelewis** Myr Td
4 G5	**Treligga** Cnwll
4 F6	**Trelights** Cnwll
4 G7	**Trelill** Cnwll
5 N5	**Trelinnoe** Cnwll
3 N3	**Trelion** Cnwll
3 L6	**Trelissick** Cnwll
3 L6	**Trelissick Garden** Cnwll
31 P3	**Trellech** Mons
31 N4	**Trelleck Grange** Mons
80 G8	**Trelogan** Flints
4 E8	**Trelow** Cnwll
3 J9	**Trelowarren** Cnwll
5 M10	**Trelowia** Cnwll
3 M6	**Treluggan** Cnwll
56 D4	**Trelystan** Powys
67 K7	**Tremadog** Gwynd
5 K4	**Tremail** Cnwll
42 D5	**Tremain** Cerdgn
5 L4	**Tremaine** Cnwll
5 M8	**Tremar** Cnwll
5 P10	**Trematon** Cnwll
5 M8	**Trembraze** Cnwll
80 F10	**Tremeirchion** Denbgs
2 C7	**Tremethick Cross** Cnwll
2 G6	**Tremore** Cnwll
80 G9	**Tre-Mostyn** Flints
3 L9	**Trenance** Cnwll
4 D8	**Trenance** Cnwll
4 E7	**Trenance** Cnwll
3 Q4	**Trenarren** Cnwll
57 M2	**Trench** Wrekin
35 J9	**Trench Green** Oxon
3 M3	**Trendeal** Cnwll
2 D6	**Trendrine** Cnwll
4 F7	**Treneague** Cnwll
2 H7	**Trenear** Cnwll
5 L4	**Treneglos** Cnwll
2 G6	**Trenerth** Cnwll
5 K11	**Trenewan** Cnwll
4 H6	**Trenewth** Cnwll
5 K3	**Trengune** Cnwll
4 C9	**Treninnick** Cnwll
4 B10	**Trenowah** Cnwll
3 K7	**Trenoweth** Cnwll
19 Q11	**Trent** Dorset
70 F6	**Trentham** C Stke
17 L2	**Trentishoe** Devon
72 D4	**Trentlock** Derbys
85 P4	**Trent Port** Lincs
70 F6	**Trent Vale** C Stke
2 G7	**Trenwheal** Cnwll
29 P9	**Treoes** V Glam
30 C5	**Treorchy** Rhondd
4 G6	**Trequite** Cnwll
54 F6	**Tre'r-ddol** Cerdgn
30 D9	**Trerhyngyll** V Glam
5 N10	**Trerulefoot** Cnwll
42 E4	**Tresaith** Cerdgn
3 M4	**Tresawle** Cnwll
3 b	**Tresco** IoS
2 b2	*Tresco Heliport IoS*
58 C5	**Trescott** Staffs
2 F7	**Trescowe** Cnwll
4 B10	**Tresean** Cnwll
32 E6	**Tresham** Gloucs
136 G7	**Treshnish Isles** Ag & B
3 M4	**Tresillian** Cnwll
5 J5	**Treskinnick Cross** Cnwll
5 L2	**Tresmeer** Cnwll
5 J3	**Tresparrett** Cnwll
141 K5	**Tressait** P & K
169 q8	**Tresta** Shet
169 t4	**Tresta** Shet
85 N5	**Treswell** Notts
2 C8	**Treswithian** Cnwll
2 C5	**Treswithian Downs Crematorium** Cnwll
54 F6	**Tre Taliesin** Cerdgn
4 H4	**Trethevey** Cnwll
2 B9	**Trethewey** Cnwll
30 G7	**Trethomas** Caerph
3 N3	**Trethosa** Cnwll
4 G10	**Trethurgy** Cnwll
40 E5	**Tretio** Pembks
45 Q10	**Tretire** Herefs
44 H10	**Tretower** Powys
69 J3	**Treuddyn** Flints
5 M6	**Trevadlock** Cnwll
4 H3	**Trevalga** Cnwll
69 L3	**Trevalyn** Wrexhm
4 F6	**Trevanger** Cnwll
4 F7	**Trevanson** Cnwll
2 D7	**Trevarrack** Cnwll
4 E9	**Trevarren** Cnwll
4 D8	**Trevarrian** Cnwll
3 P5	**Trevarrick** Cnwll
3 J5	**Treveal** Cnwll
41 P7	**Trevaughan** Carmth
42 G10	**Tre-Vaughan** Carmth
2 D5	**Treveal** Cnwll
4 B10	**Treveal** Cnwll
4 H6	**Treveighan** Cnwll
3 J3	**Trevellas Downs** Cnwll
5 L9	**Trevelmond** Cnwll
4 C10	**Trevemper** Cnwll
4 C5	**Treveor** Cnwll
3 M4	**Treverbyn** Cnwll
4 G10	**Treverbyn** Cnwll
3 K7	**Treverva** Cnwll
2 B9	**Trevescan** Cnwll
31 J4	**Trevethin** Torfn
4 H5	**Trevia** Cnwll
3 N8	**Trevigro** Cnwll
3 L6	**Trevilla** Cnwll
4 C10	**Treviscoe** Cnwll
3 N5	**Treviskey** Cnwll
3 P4	**Trevithick** Cnwll
4 D9	**Trevithick** Cnwll
4 C10	**Trevoll** Cnwll
4 D6	**Trevone** Cnwll
69 J6	**Trevor** Wrexhm
2 C8	**Trevorgans** Cnwll
4 E7	**Trevorrick** Cnwll
4 D6	**Trevose** Cnwll
2 G8	**Trew** Cnwll
4 H5	**Trewalder** Cnwll
44 H8	**Trewalkin** Powys
4 H4	**Trewarmett** Cnwll
5 J4	**Trewassa** Cnwll
2 F8	**Trewavas** Cnwll
5 L5	**Trewen** Cnwll
2 B7	**Trewellard** Cnwll
2 H8	**Trewennack** Cnwll
41 K11	**Trewent** Pembks
56 D2	**Trewern** Powys
4 G5	**Trewetha** Cnwll
4 G6	**Trewethern** Cnwll
5 M10	**Trewidland** Cnwll
3 K10	**Trewillis** Cnwll
5 L5	**Trewint** Cnwll
5 M9	**Trewint** Cnwll
3 M6	**Trewithian** Cnwll
5 N7	**Trewoodloe** Cnwll
2 H10	**Trewoon** Cnwll
3 P3	**Trewoon** Cnwll
3 M5	**Treworga** Cnwll
3 L4	**Treworgan** Cnwll
3 M6	**Treworlas** Cnwll
5 J3	**Treworld** Cnwll
3 M6	**Treworthal** Cnwll
45 L10	**Tre-wyn** Mons
4 D7	**Treyarnon** Cnwll
23 N10	**Treyford** W Susx
13 J4	**Trickett's Cross** Dorset
111 L7	**Triermain** Cumb
41 J6	**Triffleton** Pembks
5 M4	**Trillacott** Cnwll
104 C4	**Trimdon** Dur
104 C3	**Trimdon Colliery** Dur
104 C3	**Trimdon Grange** Dur
77 K4	**Trimingham** Norfk
53 N4	**Trimley Lower Street** Suffk
53 N4	**Trimley St Martin** Suffk
53 N4	**Trimley St Mary** Suffk
57 P9	**Trimpley** Worcs
28 E4	**Trimsaran** Carmth
51 L7	**Trims Green** Herts
17 J3	**Trimstone** Devon
140 H5	**Trinafour** P & K
30 H5	**Trinant** Caerph
35 P2	**Tring** Herts
35 P2	**Tringford** Herts
35 P2	**Tring Wharf** Herts
143 L5	**Trinity** Angus
11 b1	**Trinity** Jersey
134 B4	**Trinity Gask** P & K
18 G7	**Triscombe** Somset
139 K3	**Trislaig** Highld
3 L3	**Trispen** Cnwll
113 K2	**Tritlington** Nthumb
4 D10	**Troan** Cnwll
141 N9	**Trochry** P & K
30 F4	**Troedrhiwfuwch** Caerph
42 F5	**Troedyraur** Cerdgn
30 E4	**Troedyrhiw** Myr Td
80 B10	**Trofarth** Conwy
11 b1	**Trois Bois** Jersey
2 H6	**Troon** Cnwll
125 J11	**Troon** S Ayrs
91 J3	**Tropical World Roundhay Park** Leeds
132 G6	**Trossachs** Stirlg
132 F6	**Trossachs Pier** Stirlg
64 B7	**Troston** Suffk
3 M3	**Troswell** Cnwll
46 G3	**Trotshill** Worcs
37 P8	**Trottiscliffe** Kent
23 M10	**Trotton** W Susx
112 C2	**Troughend** Nthumb
89 P6	**Trough Gate** Lancs
101 L5	**Troutbeck** Cumb
101 M10	**Troutbeck** Cumb
101 M10	**Troutbeck Bridge** Cumb
84 B5	**Troway** Derbys
20 G3	**Trowbridge** Wilts
72 D3	**Trowell** Notts
72 D2	*Trowell Services Notts*
20 F3	**Trowle Common** Wilts
50 C8	**Trowley Bottom** Herts
77 J10	**Trowse Newton** Norfk
90 G3	**Troy** Leeds
18 H10	**Trull** Somset
91 Q8	**Trumfleet** Donc
152 C5	**Trumpan** Highld
46 C7	**Trumpet** Herefs
62 F10	**Trumpington** Cambs
35 Q11	**Trumpsgreen** Surrey
77 K5	**Trunch** Norfk
88 C2	**Trunnah** Lancs
3 L5	**Truro** Cnwll
3 L5	**Truro Cathedral** Cnwll
5 M4	**Truscott** Cnwll
4 L8	**Trusham** Devon
71 P7	**Trusley** Derbys
87 P4	**Trusthorpe** Lincs
58 C6	**Trysull** Staffs
34 D5	**Tubney** Oxon
7 L7	**Tuckenhay** Devon
57 P7	**Tuckhill** Shrops
2 H5	**Tuckingmill** Cnwll
20 H9	**Tuckingmill** Wilts
13 K6	**Tuckton** Bmouth
3 P4	**Tucoyse** Cnwll
53 L2	**Tuddenham** Suffk
63 M6	**Tuddenham** Suffk
37 P11	**Tudeley** Kent
103 Q3	**Tudhoe** Dur
46 A10	**Tudorville** Herefs
66 C7	**Tudweiliog** Gwynd
23 Q6	**Tuesley** Surrey
32 F2	**Tuffley** Gloucs
22 E5	**Tufton** Hants
41 K5	**Tufton** Pembks
73 K10	**Tugby** Leics
57 K7	**Tugford** Shrops
119 P5	**Tughall** Nthumb
133 P8	**Tullibody** Clacks
147 Q2	**Tullich** Highld
156 F2	**Tullich** Highld
147 P7	**Tulliemet** P & K
159 K11	**Tulloch** Abers
131 K8	**Tullochgorm** Ag & B
147 K11	**Tulloch Station** Highld
142 B7	**Tullymurdoch** P & K
150 F4	**Tullynessle** Abers
36 H6	**Tulse Hill** Gt Lon
28 F2	**Tumble** Carmth
52 D6	**Tumbler's Green** Essex
86 H9	**Tumby** Lincs
87 J9	**Tumby Woodside** Lincs
141 J6	**Tummel Bridge** P & K
25 N3	**Tunbridge Wells** Kent
110 C4	**Tundergarth** D & G
77 K6	**Tungate** Norfk
20 C3	**Tunley** BaNES
70 F4	**Tunstall** E R Yk
93 P4	**Tunstall** E R Yk
38 E9	**Tunstall** Kent
95 N6	**Tunstall** Lancs
103 P11	**Tunstall** N York
77 N10	**Tunstall** Norfk
70 D9	**Tunstall** Staffs
65 M10	**Tunstall** Suffk
113 N10	**Tunstall** Sundld
83 P10	**Tunstead** Derbys
77 K7	**Tunstead** Norfk
83 M8	**Tunstead Milton** Derbys
23 J5	**Tunworth** Hants
45 Q6	**Tupsley** Herefs
23 J3	**Turgis Green** Hants
47 M11	**Turkdean** Gloucs
60 F2	**Tur Langton** Leics
20 F2	**Turleigh** Wilts
57 P7	**Turleygreen** Shrops
89 N7	**Turn** Lancs
45 M7	**Turnastone** Herefs
114 D6	**Turnberry** S Ayrs
6 D8	**Turnchapel** C Plym
71 P5	**Turnditch** Derbys
89 J4	**Turner Green** Lancs
25 P7	**Turner's Green** E Susx
59 J11	**Turner's Green** Warwks
12 D6	**Turner's Hill** W Susx
12 D6	**Turners Puddle** Dorset
51 J10	**Turnford** Herts
127 M3	**Turnhouse** C Edin
12 D3	**Turnworth** Dorset
158 H7	**Turriff** Abers
89 L7	**Turton Bottoms** Bl w D
74 F11	**Turves** Cambs
49 P4	**Turvey** Bed
35 L6	**Turville** Bucks
35 K6	**Turville Heath** Bucks
48 H7	**Turweston** Bucks
117 L7	**Tushielaw Inn** Border
71 N9	**Tutbury** Staffs
58 E10	**Tutnall** Worcs
31 P6	**Tutshill** Gloucs
77 J6	**Tuttington** Norfk
5 P6	**Tutwell** Cnwll
85 M6	**Tuxford** Notts
169 b4	**Twatt** Ork
169 q8	**Twatt** Shet
126 B2	**Twechar** E Duns
117 Q4	**Tweedbank** Border
129 P9	**Tweedmouth** Nthumb
116 G6	**Tweedsmuir** Border
3 K5	**Twelveheads** Cnwll
25 Q6	**Twelve Oaks** E Susx
82 G11	**Twemlow Green** Ches E
74 C6	**Twenty** Lincs
20 D2	**Twerton** BaNES
36 E6	**Twickenham** Gt Lon
46 F10	**Twigworth** Gloucs
24 G7	**Twineham** W Susx
24 G6	**Twineham Green** W Susx
20 E3	**Twinhoe** BaNES
52 E4	**Twinstead** Essex
17 P5	**Twitchen** Devon
56 F9	**Twitchen** Shrops
39 N10	**Twitham** Kent
6 G4	**Two Bridges** Devon
84 C8	**Two Dales** Derbys
59 K4	**Two Gates** Staffs
7 L5	**Two Mile Oak Cross** Devon
17 J3	**Two Pots** Devon
35 C9	**Two Waters** Herts
72 A10	**Twycross** Leics
59 M3	**Twycross Zoo** Leics
49 J9	**Twyford** Bucks
22 E10	**Twyford** Hants
73 J8	**Twyford** Leics
73 N6	**Twyford** Lincs
76 E7	**Twyford** Norfk
35 L9	**Twyford** Wokham
45 Q7	**Twyford Common** Herefs
30 F3	**Twyn-carno** Caerph
108 L10	**Twynholm** D & G
46 H7	**Twyning Green** Gloucs
43 Q10	**Twynllanan** Carmth
30 F10	**Twyn-yr-Odyn** V Glam
31 M3	**Twyn-y-Sheriff** Mons
61 L5	**Twywell** Nhants
45 M7	**Tyberton** Herefs
58 H6	**Tyburn** Birm
28 H2	**Tycroes** Carmth
78 E10	**Ty Croes** IoA
68 F11	**Tycrwyn** Powys
75 J7	**Tydd Gote** Lincs
74 H7	**Tydd St Giles** Cambs
74 H7	**Tydd St Mary** Lincs
15 K6	**Tye** Hants
51 M6	**Tye Green** Essex
51 N3	**Tye Green** Essex
52 C7	**Tye Green** Essex
90 F4	**Tyersal** C Brad
82 E4	**Tyldesley** Wigan
39 K9	**Tyler Hill** Kent
35 P6	**Tylers Green** Bucks
51 M9	**Tyler's Green** Essex
37 J10	**Tylers Green** Surrey
30 D5	**Tylorstown** Rhondd
55 M8	**Tylwch** Powys
68 C5	**Ty-nant** Conwy
68 B9	**Ty-nant** Gwynd
139 Q11	**Tyndrum** Stirlg
68 H6	**Ty'n-dwr** Denbgs
113 N7	**Tynemouth** N Tyne
113 M7	**Tynemouth Crematorium** N Tyne
29 P5	**Tynewydd** Rhondd
128 G4	**Tyninghame** E Loth
115 R9	**Tynron** D & G
31 P10	**Tyntesfield** N Som
30 D7	**Ty'n-y-bryn** Rhondd
30 G7	**Ty'n-y-coedcae** Caerph
79 J8	**Tynygongl** IoA
54 F11	**Tynygraig** Cerdgn
79 P10	**Ty'n-y-Groes** Conwy
30 E7	**Tyn-y-nant** Rhondd
49 N5	**Tyringham** M Keyn
58 H8	**Tyseley** Birm
29 N9	**Tythegston** Brdgnd
83 K9	**Tytherington** Ches E
32 C7	**Tytherington** S Glos
20 E6	**Tytherington** Somset
20 H6	**Tytherington** Wilts
10 G4	**Tytherleigh** Devon
32 H10	**Tytherton Lucas** Wilts
50 E9	**Tyttenhanger** Herts
4 H11	**Tywardreath** Cnwll
4 H10	**Tywardreath Highway** Cnwll
79 P9	**Tywyn** Conwy
54 D4	**Tywyn** Gwynd

U

65 L7	**Ubbeston Green** Suffk
19 P3	**Ubley** BaNES
103 P10	**Uckerby** N York
25 L6	**Uckfield** E Susx
46 G7	**Uckinghall** Worcs
46 H10	**Uckington** Gloucs
57 K2	**Uckington** Shrops
126 B5	**Uddingston** S Lans
116 B4	**Uddington** S Lans
26 E8	**Udimore** E Susx
151 M2	**Udny Green** Abers
151 N3	**Udny Station** Abers
33 M9	**Uffcott** Wilts
9 Q2	**Uffculme** Devon
73 R9	**Uffington** Lincs
34 B7	**Uffington** Oxon
57 J2	**Uffington** Shrops
74 A10	**Ufford** C Pete
65 K11	**Ufford** Suffk
48 C5	**Ufton** Warwks
34 H11	**Ufton Nervet** W Berk
120 E6	**Ugadale** Ag & B
6 H7	**Ugborough** Devon
65 N5	**Uggeshall** Suffk
105 N9	**Ugglebarnby** N York
84 C2	**Ughill** Sheff
51 M5	**Ugley** Essex
51 M5	**Ugley Green** Essex
105 L8	**Ugthorpe** N York
168 d14	**Uibhist A Deas** W Isls
168 c10	**Uibhist A Tuath** W Isls
136 F5	**Uig** Ag & B
152 B7	**Uig** Highld
152 F5	**Uig** Highld
168 f4	**Uig** W Isls
152 G8	**Uigshader** Highld
137 K12	**Uisken** Ag & B
167 P8	**Ulbster** Highld

304 Ulcat Row - Wardlow

101 M6 **Ulcat Row** Cumb
87 M6 **Ulceby** Lincs
93 K8 **Ulceby** N Linc
93 K7 **Ulceby Skitter** N Linc
26 D2 **Ulcombe** Kent
100 H3 **Uldale** Cumb
32 E5 **Uley** Gloucs
113 K2 **Ulgham** Nthumb
161 J8 **Ullapool** Highld
58 H11 **Ullenhall** Warwks
46 H11 **Ullenwood** Gloucs
91 N3 **Ulleskelf** N York
60 B3 **Ullesthorpe** Leics
84 G3 **Ulley** Rothm
46 A5 **Ullingswick** Herefs
152 E10 **Ullinish Lodge Hotel** Highld
100 E6 **Ullock** Cumb
101 M6 **Ullswater** Cumb
94 D2 **Ulpha** Cumb
95 K4 **Ulpha** Cumb
99 P9 **Ulrome** E R Yk
169 r5 **Ulsta** Shet
52 D10 **Ulting Wick** Essex
137 K7 **Ulva** Ag & B
58 H8 **Ulverley Green** Solhll
94 F5 **Ulverston** Cumb
12 H8 **Ulwell** Dorset
115 Q6 **Ulzieside** D & G
17 L7 **Umberleigh** Devon
164 F10 **Unapool** Highld
95 K2 **Underbarrow** Cumb
111 J4 **Under Burnmouth** Border
90 F4 **Undercliffe** C Brad
57 J2 **Underdale** Shrops
26 C2 **Underling Green** Kent
37 N10 **Under River** Kent
84 G10 **Underwood** Notts
63 L4 **Undley** Suffk
31 M7 **Undy** Mons
80 e6 **Union Mills** IoM
26 B5 **Union Street** E Susx
169 s3 **Unst** Shet
84 E5 **Unstone** Derbys
84 E5 **Unstone Green** Derbys
101 N3 **Unthank** Cumb
102 B2 **Unthank** Cumb
110 G11 **Unthank** Cumb
84 D5 **Unthank** Derbys
129 P10 **Unthank** Nthumb
21 M4 **Upavon** Wilts
11 P4 **Up Cerne** Dorset
38 D8 **Upchurch** Kent
17 P6 **Upcott** Devon
45 L4 **Upcott** Herefs
63 M9 **Upend** Cambs
9 M4 **Up Exe** Devon
76 G8 **Upgate** Norfk
64 F3 **Upgate Street** Norfk
65 K3 **Upgate Street** Norfk
11 M4 **Uphall** Dorset
127 K3 **Uphall** W Loth
9 L3 **Upham** Devon
22 F10 **Upham** Hants
45 M2 **Uphampton** Herefs
46 F2 **Uphampton** Worcs
19 K3 **Uphill** N Som
88 G9 **Up Holland** Lancs
125 L6 **Uplawmoor** E Rens
46 E9 **Upleadon** Gloucs
104 H7 **Upleatham** R & Cl
38 H9 **Uplees** Kent
11 L6 **Uploders** Dorset
18 D11 **Uplowman** Devon
10 G6 **Uplyme** Devon
15 L4 **Up Marden** W Susx
37 N3 **Upminster** Gt Lon
19 Q11 **Up Mudford** Somset
23 J4 **Up Nately** Hants
10 E3 **Upottery** Devon
56 G7 **Upper Affcot** Shrops
162 E9 **Upper Ardchronie** Highld
57 P8 **Upper Arley** Worcs
48 H11 **Upper Arncott** Oxon
48 F7 **Upper Astrop** Nhants
34 G9 **Upper Basildon** W Berk
90 G5 **Upper Batley** Kirk
24 E8 **Upper Beeding** W Susx
61 L3 **Upper Benefield** Nhants
58 E11 **Upper Bentley** Worcs
166 E5 **Upper Bighouse** Highld
84 F9 **Upper Birchwood** Derbys
30 F7 **Upper Boat** Rhondd
48 E4 **Upper Boddington** Nhants
54 E7 **Upper Borth** Cerdgn
48 B7 **Upper Brailes** Warwks
145 L3 **Upper Breakish** Highld
45 P6 **Upper Breinton** Herefs
46 F3 **Upper Broadheath** Worcs
72 H5 **Upper Broughton** Notts
34 F11 **Upper Bucklebury** W Berk
21 N11 **Upper Burgate** Hants
37 Q7 **Upper Bush** Medway
110 H10 **Upperby** Cumb
61 Q11 **Upper Caldecote** C Beds
19 L3 **Upper Canada** N Som
13 N2 **Upper Canterton** Hants
60 B9 **Upper Catesby** Nhants
58 E10 **Upper Catshill** Worcs
44 E6 **Upper Chapel** Powys
18 H9 **Upper Cheddon** Somset
21 J9 **Upper Chicksgrove** Wilts
21 Q4 **Upper Chute** Wilts
36 H3 **Upper Clapton** Gt Lon
22 C6 **Upper Clatford** Hants
47 J11 **Upper Coberley** Gloucs
24 E9 **Upper Cokeham** W Susx
71 K5 **Upper Cotton** Staffs
57 K3 **Upper Cound** Shrops
91 K9 **Upper Cudworth** Barns
90 G9 **Upper Cumberworth** Kirk
157 R5 **Upper Dallachy** Moray
39 Q11 **Upper Deal** Kent
61 M7 **Upper Dean** Bed
90 G9 **Upper Denby** Kirk
111 M7 **Upper Denton** Cumb
25 N9 **Upper Dicker** E Susx
56 H8 **Upper Dinchope** Shrops
166 H3 **Upper Dounreay** Highld
53 M5 **Upper Dovercourt** Essex
133 K6 **Upper Drumbane** Stirlg
97 P8 **Upper Dunsforth** N York
23 Q6 **Upper Eashing** Surrey
156 D5 **Upper Eathie** Highld
46 B6 **Upper Egleton** Herefs
71 K3 **Upper Elkstone** Staffs
71 L6 **Upper Ellastone** Staffs
83 N9 **Upper End** Derbys
22 C4 **Upper Enham** Hants
57 P6 **Upper Farmcote** Shrops
23 K7 **Upper Farringdon** Hants
32 E2 **Upper Framilode** Gloucs
23 L6 **Upper Froyle** Hants
152 E7 **Upperglen** Highld
19 N6 **Upper Godney** Somset
50 D3 **Upper Gravenhurst** C Beds
45 M11 **Upper Green** Mons
63 M8 **Upper Green** Suffk
22 C2 **Upper Green** W Berk
45 R9 **Upper Grove Common** Herefs
84 C8 **Upper Hackney** Derbys
23 M5 **Upper Hale** Surrey
36 C7 **Upper Halliford** Surrey
37 Q8 **Upper Halling** Medway
73 N9 **Upper Hambleton** Rutlnd
39 K10 **Upper Harbledown** Kent
39 L11 **Upper Hardres Court** Kent
45 N3 **Upper Hardwick** Herefs
25 L4 **Upper Hartfield** E Susx
84 E10 **Upper Hartshay** Derbys
46 H10 **Upper Hatherley** Gloucs
70 E7 **Upper Hatton** Staffs
91 L11 **Upper Haugh** Rothm
57 J8 **Upper Hayton** Shrops
90 F7 **Upper Heaton** Kirk
98 D9 **Upper Helmsley** N York
45 K4 **Upper Hergest** Herefs
60 E9 **Upper Heyford** Nhants
48 E9 **Upper Heyford** Oxon
45 P4 **Upper Hill** Herefs
37 M7 **Upper Hockenden** Kent
90 F7 **Upper Hopton** Kirk
46 E5 **Upper Howsell** Worcs
71 J2 **Upper Hulme** Staffs
24 B4 **Upper Ifold** Surrey
33 P5 **Upper Inglesham** Swindn
32 E7 **Upper Kilcott** Gloucs
28 G6 **Upper Killay** Swans
131 P2 **Upper Kinchrackine** Ag & B
34 B8 **Upper Lambourn** W Berk
58 E3 **Upper Landywood** Staffs
19 N3 **Upper Langford** N Som
84 H7 **Upper Langwith** Derbys
135 L7 **Upper Largo** Fife
71 J7 **Upper Leigh** Staffs
19 Q2 **Upper Littleton** N Som
150 H8 **Upper Lochton** Abers
57 Q2 **Upper Longdon** Staffs
50 E4 **Upper & Lower Stondon** C Beds
57 Q5 **Upper Ludstone** Shrops
167 N9 **Upper Lybster** Highld
46 B11 **Upper Lydbrook** Gloucs
45 P6 **Upper Lyde** Herefs
56 F11 **Upper Lye** Herefs
45 L8 **Upper Maes-coed** Herefs
90 G11 **Upper Midhope** Sheff
90 B9 **Uppermill** Oldham
57 Q10 **Upper Milton** Worcs
33 K6 **Upper Minety** Wilts
47 J5 **Upper Moor** Worcs
90 G4 **Upper Moor Side** Leeds
157 R7 **Upper Mulben** Moray
57 L6 **Upper Netchwood** Shrops
71 J7 **Upper Nobut** Staffs
23 P11 **Upper Norwood** W Susx
84 B5 **Upper Padley** Derbys
13 P5 **Upper Pennington** Hants
35 K2 **Upper Pollicott** Bucks
98 B10 **Upper Poppleton** C York
47 N5 **Upper Quinton** Warwks
22 B10 **Upper Ratley** Hants
47 P11 **Upper Rissington** Gloucs
57 L11 **Upper Rochford** Worcs
108 C8 **Upper Ruscoe** D & G
46 C2 **Upper Sapey** Herefs
32 H8 **Upper Seagry** Wilts
49 Q6 **Upper Shelton** C Beds
76 G3 **Upper Sheringham** Norfk
124 G4 **Upper Skelmorlie** N Ayrs
47 N10 **Upper Slaughter** Gloucs
32 C2 **Upper Soudley** Gloucs
45 L4 **Upper Spond** Herefs
27 M3 **Upper Standen** Kent
61 P9 **Upper Staploe** Bed
77 K11 **Upper Stoke** Norfk
60 D9 **Upper Stowe** Nhants
21 N11 **Upper Street** Hants
64 H6 **Upper Street** Norfk
77 L8 **Upper Street** Norfk
77 M8 **Upper Street** Norfk
53 K5 **Upper Street** Suffk
63 N10 **Upper Street** Suffk
64 G11 **Upper Street** Suffk
46 G7 **Upper Strensham** Worcs
50 B5 **Upper Sundon** C Beds
47 N9 **Upper Swell** Gloucs
91 J11 **Upper Tankersley** Barns
65 J2 **Upper Tasburgh** Norfk
71 J7 **Upper Tean** Staffs
90 E9 **Upperthong** Kirk
84 G4 **Upperthorpe** Derbys
92 C10 **Upperthorpe** N Linc
69 M5 **Upper Threapwood** Ches W
23 Q10 **Upperton** W Susx
71 N4 **Upper Town** Derbys
84 D8 **Uppertown** Derbys
103 L3 **Upper Town** Dur
46 A5 **Upper Town** Herefs
167 Q1 **Uppertown** Highld
31 P11 **Upper Town** N Som
64 C8 **Upper Town** Suffk
28 F2 **Upper Tumble** Carmth
48 B6 **Upper Tysoe** Warwks
65 K11 **Upper Ufford** Suffk
33 K5 **Upperup** Gloucs
33 P9 **Upper Upham** Wilts
38 C7 **Upper Upnor** Medway
143 J10 **Upper Victoria** Angus
20 D5 **Upper Vobster** Somset
48 E5 **Upper Wardington** Oxon
49 M7 **Upper Weald** M Keyn
60 D9 **Upper Weedon** Nhants
46 E6 **Upper Welland** Worcs
25 K8 **Upper Wellingham** E Susx
32 D11 **Upper Weston** BaNES
65 J6 **Upper Weybread** Suffk
46 F4 **Upper Wick** Worcs
22 H7 **Upper Wield** Hants
35 K2 **Upper Winchendon** Bucks
84 C9 **Upperwood** Derbys
21 M7 **Upper Woodford** Wilts
22 G4 **Upper Wootton** Hants
32 F10 **Upper Wraxall** Wilts
46 E6 **Upper Wyche** Worcs
9 M3 **Uppincott** Devon
73 M11 **Uppingham** Rutlnd
12 H3 **Uppington** Dorset
57 K3 **Uppington** Shrops
97 Q3 **Upsall** N York
129 M10 **Upsettlington** Border
51 K10 **Upshire** Essex
22 C8 **Up Somborne** Hants
39 M9 **Upstreet** Kent
11 N4 **Up Sydling** Dorset
64 D7 **Upthorpe** Suffk
35 L2 **Upton** Bucks
74 B10 **Upton** C Pete
61 Q5 **Upton** Cambs
81 N11 **Upton** Ches W
5 M7 **Upton** Cnwll
16 C11 **Upton** Cnwll
101 K3 **Upton** Cumb
7 J10 **Upton** Devon
10 B4 **Upton** Devon
12 B8 **Upton** Dorset
12 G6 **Upton** Dorset
99 N10 **Upton** E R Yk
81 P7 **Upton** Halton
22 C11 **Upton** Hants
22 C3 **Upton** Hants
72 B11 **Upton** Leics
85 Q3 **Upton** Lincs
60 F9 **Upton** Nhants
77 M9 **Upton** Norfk
85 M10 **Upton** Notts
85 M5 **Upton** Notts
33 P2 **Upton** Oxon
34 F7 **Upton** Oxon
41 K10 **Upton** Pembks
105 K7 **Upton** R & Cl
35 Q9 **Upton** Slough
18 C9 **Upton** Somset
19 N9 **Upton** Somset
91 M8 **Upton** Wakefd
47 M3 **Upton** Warwks
20 G8 **Upton** Wilts
81 K7 **Upton** Wirral
46 C9 **Upton Bishop** Herefs
32 C10 **Upton Cheyney** S Glos
57 M6 **Upton Cressett** Shrops
46 B9 **Upton Crews** Herefs
5 M7 **Upton Cross** Cnwll
50 D4 **Upton End** C Beds
23 J5 **Upton Grey** Hants
81 N11 **Upton Heath** Ches W
9 K4 **Upton Hellions** Devon
20 H6 **Upton Lovell** Wilts
57 K2 **Upton Magna** Shrops
20 D7 **Upton Noble** Somset
9 M5 **Upton Pyne** Devon
46 G11 **Upton St Leonards** Gloucs
20 G5 **Upton Scudamore** Wilts
46 H4 **Upton Snodsbury** Worcs
2 F5 **Upton Towans** Cnwll
46 G6 **Upton upon Severn** Worcs
58 D11 **Upton Warren** Worcs
15 P4 **Upwaltham** W Susx
62 H6 **Upware** Cambs
75 J10 **Upwell** Norfk
11 P7 **Upwey** Dorset
51 L6 **Upwick Green** Herts
62 C4 **Upwood** Cambs
21 K3 **Urchfont** Wilts
45 Q5 **Urdimarsh** Herefs
97 M6 **Ure Bank** N York
104 D8 **Urlay Nook** S on T
82 G6 **Urmston** Traffd
157 P5 **Urquhart** Moray
104 G10 **Urra** N York
155 P7 **Urray** Highld
143 N7 **Usan** Angus
103 P2 **Ushaw Moor** Dur
31 L4 **Usk** Mons
86 E2 **Usselby** Lincs
113 M9 **Usworth** Sundld
82 B11 **Utkinton** Ches W
90 D2 **Utley** C Brad
9 K5 **Uton** Devon
87 K2 **Utterby** Lincs
71 K8 **Uttoxeter** Staffs
66 B9 **Uwchmynydd** Gwynd
36 C4 **Uxbridge** Gt Lon
169 s3 **Uyeasound** Shet
41 J8 **Uzmaston** Pembks

V

10 c1 **Vale** Guern
30 F10 **Vale of Glamorgan Crematorium** V Glam
54 G9 **Vale of Rheidol Railway** Cerdgn
78 D9 **Valley** IoA
23 Q2 **Valley End** Surrey
4 H5 **Valley Truckle** Cnwll
153 J5 **Valtos** Highld
168 f4 **Valtos** W Isls
38 B4 **Vange** Essex
31 J3 **Varteg** Torfn
169 s5 **Vatsetter** Shet
152 D9 **Vatten** Highld
30 D2 **Vaynor** Myr Td
10 b2 **Vazon Bay** Guern
169 r9 **Veensgarth** Shet
44 H7 **Velindre** Powys
18 E7 **Vellow** Somset
16 D7 **Velly** Devon
16 F9 **Venngreen** Devon
56 E3 **Vennington** Shrops
10 B6 **Venn Ottery** Devon
9 K5 **Venny Tedburn** Devon
5 P7 **Venterdon** Cnwll
14 G11 **Ventnor** IoW
6 F7 **Venton** Devon
22 B3 **Vernham Dean** Hants
22 B3 **Vernham Street** Hants
56 H8 **Vernolds Common** Shrops
13 J3 **Verwood** Dorset
3 N6 **Veryan** Cnwll
3 N5 **Veryan Green** Cnwll
10 E7 **Vicarage** Devon
94 D7 **Vickerstown** Cumb
90 F9 **Victoria** Barns
30 G3 **Victoria** Blae G
4 F9 **Victoria** Cnwll
169 r7 **Vidlin** Shet
157 P5 **Viewfield** Moray
126 C5 **Viewpark** N Lans
37 P8 **Vigo** Kent
10 c2 **Village de Putron** Guern
11 a1 **Ville la Bas** Jersey
10 b2 **Villiaze** Guern
26 C7 **Vinehall Street** E Susx
25 N7 **Vines Cross** E Susx
38 C10 **Vinters Park Crematorium** Kent
36 B7 **Virginia Water** Surrey
5 P3 **Virginstow** Devon
20 D5 **Vobster** Somset
169 r7 **Voe** Shet
45 M7 **Vowchurch** Herefs
82 C6 **Vulcan Village** St Hel

W

94 C2 **Waberthwaite** Cumb
103 N6 **Wackerfield** Dur
64 H3 **Wacton** Norfk
46 H5 **Wadborough** Worcs
49 K11 **Waddesdon** Bucks
7 M7 **Waddeton** Devon
81 M5 **Waddicar** Sefton
92 G11 **Waddingham** Lincs
89 L2 **Waddington** Lancs
86 C8 **Waddington** Lincs
9 L9 **Waddon** Devon
11 N7 **Waddon** Dorset
4 F7 **Wadebridge** Cnwll
10 G2 **Wadeford** Somset
61 M4 **Wadenhoe** Nhants
51 J7 **Wadesmill** Herts
25 P4 **Wadhurst** E Susx
84 D6 **Wadshelf** Derbys
32 F11 **Wadswick** Wilts
91 P11 **Wadworth** Donc
68 C2 **Waen** Denbgs
80 G11 **Waen** Denbgs
68 H11 **Waen** Powys
68 H11 **Waen Fach** Powys
79 K11 **Waen-pentir** Gwynd
79 K11 **Waen-wen** Gwynd
56 F4 **Wagbeach** Shrops
31 J4 **Wainfelin** Torfn
87 N9 **Wainfleet All Saints** Lincs
87 N9 **Wainfleet Bank** Lincs
87 N9 **Wainfleet St Mary** Lincs
65 L3 **Wainford** Norfk
5 K2 **Wainhouse Corner** Cnwll
38 B7 **Wainscott** Medway
31 L10 **Wain's Hill** N Som
90 C5 **Wainstalls** Calder
102 E9 **Waitby** Cumb
93 N10 **Waithe** Lincs
91 J6 **Wakefield** Wakefd
91 J7 **Wakefield Crematorium** Wakefd
58 G8 **Wake Green** Birm
73 P11 **Wakerley** Nhants
52 E6 **Wakes Colne** Essex
65 P7 **Walberswick** Suffk
15 Q5 **Walberton** W Susx
113 J7 **Walbottle** N u Ty
108 F7 **Walbutt** D & G
110 H8 **Walby** Cumb
19 Q5 **Walcombe** Somset
73 R3 **Walcot** Lincs
92 E6 **Walcot** N Linc
56 E7 **Walcot** Shrops
57 K2 **Walcot** Shrops
33 N8 **Walcot** Swindn
47 M3 **Walcot** Warwks
60 C4 **Walcote** Leics
64 G5 **Walcot Green** Norfk
86 F9 **Walcott** Lincs
77 M5 **Walcott** Norfk
96 F4 **Walden** N York
96 E4 **Walden Head** N York
91 P7 **Walden Stubbs** N York
38 C9 **Walderslade** Medway
15 L4 **Walderton** W Susx
11 K6 **Walditch** Dorset
71 L7 **Waldley** Derbys
113 L11 **Waldridge** Dur
53 N2 **Waldringfield** Suffk
25 M7 **Waldron** E Susx
84 G4 **Wales** Rothm
19 Q10 **Wales** Somset
86 F2 **Walesby** Lincs
85 L6 **Walesby** Notts
46 A10 **Walford** Herefs
56 F10 **Walford** Herefs
69 M10 **Walford** Shrops
70 E8 **Walford** Staffs
69 M11 **Walford Heath** Shrops
70 B5 **Walgherton** Ches E
60 H6 **Walgrave** Nhants
13 P5 **Walhampton** Hants
82 F4 **Walkden** Salfd
113 L8 **Walker** N u Ty
117 M3 **Walkerburn** Border
89 K2 **Walker Fold** Lancs
85 N2 **Walkeringham** Notts
85 N2 **Walkerith** Lincs
50 G5 **Walkern** Herts
45 Q5 **Walker's Green** Herefs
58 G9 **Walker's Heath** Birm
134 G7 **Walkerton** Fife
13 M6 **Walkford** Dorset
6 E5 **Walkhampton** Devon
92 G3 **Walkington** E R Yk
84 D3 **Walkley** Sheff
89 P5 **Walk Mill** Lancs
47 K2 **Walkwood** Worcs
112 D7 **Wall** Nthumb
58 H3 **Wall** Staffs
114 E7 **Wallacetown** S Ayrs
114 F3 **Wallacetown** S Ayrs
25 K8 **Wallands Park** E Susx
81 K6 **Wallasey** Wirral
94 E4 **Wall End** Cumb
45 N3 **Wall End** Herefs
38 E6 **Wallend** Medway
46 C7 **Wallend Green** Herefs
111 J8 **Wallhead** Cumb
58 C7 **Wall Heath** Dudley
112 F7 **Wall Houses** Nthumb
34 H7 **Wallingford** Oxon
36 G8 **Wallington** Gt Lon
14 G5 **Wallington** Hants
50 G4 **Wallington** Herts
58 E4 **Wallington Heath** Wsall
41 K5 **Wallis** Pembks
13 J6 **Wallisdown** Poole
24 D3 **Walliswood** Surrey
169 p9 **Walls** Shet
113 L7 **Wallsend** N Tyne
101 L5 **Wallthwaite** Cumb
57 J6 **Wall under Haywood** Shrops
128 B5 **Wallyford** E Loth
39 Q11 **Walmer** Kent
88 F6 **Walmer Bridge** Lancs
89 N8 **Walmersley** Bury
39 N10 **Walmestone** Kent
58 H6 **Walmley** Birm
58 H6 **Walmley Ash** Birm
87 L5 **Walmsgate** Lincs
19 K6 **Walpole** Somset
65 M7 **Walpole** Suffk
75 K7 **Walpole Cross Keys** Norfk
75 K8 **Walpole Highway** Norfk
75 K7 **Walpole St Andrew** Norfk
75 K7 **Walpole St Peter** Norfk
19 K5 **Walrow** Somset
58 F5 **Walsall** Wsall
58 F4 **Walsall Wood** Wsall
89 Q6 **Walsden** Calder
59 N8 **Walsgrave on Sowe** Covtry
64 E7 **Walsham le Willows** Suffk
89 M8 **Walshaw** Bury
97 P10 **Walshford** N York
75 J8 **Walsoken** Norfk
127 K8 **Walston** S Lans
50 E4 **Walsworth** Herts
35 M5 **Walter's Ash** Bucks
25 M2 **Walters Green** Kent
30 E10 **Walterston** V Glam
45 L9 **Walterstone** Herefs
27 K2 **Waltham** Kent
93 N10 **Waltham** NE Lin
51 J10 **Waltham Abbey** Essex
14 G4 **Waltham Chase** Hants
51 J10 **Waltham Cross** Herts
73 L6 **Waltham on the Wolds** Leics
35 M9 **Waltham St Lawrence** W & M
51 Q4 **Waltham's Cross** Essex
37 J3 **Walthamstow** Gt Lon
74 C10 **Walton** C Pete
111 K8 **Walton** Cumb
84 E7 **Walton** Derbys
97 P11 **Walton** Leeds
60 C3 **Walton** Leics
49 N7 **Walton** M Keyn
45 K3 **Walton** Powys
56 H9 **Walton** Shrops
19 N7 **Walton** Somset
70 F8 **Walton** Staffs
70 F9 **Walton** Staffs
53 N4 **Walton** Suffk
15 M6 **Walton** W Susx
91 K7 **Walton** Wakefd
47 Q4 **Walton** Warwks
69 Q11 **Walton** Wrekin
46 H8 **Walton Cardiff** Gloucs
41 K6 **Walton East** Pembks
20 E11 **Walton Elm** Dorset
48 F8 **Walton Grounds** Nhants
31 M10 **Walton-in-Gordano** N Som
82 D7 **Walton Lea Crematorium** Warrtn
88 H5 **Walton-le-Dale** Lancs
36 D7 **Walton-on-Thames** Surrey
70 H10 **Walton-on-the-Hill** Staffs
36 F9 **Walton on the Hill** Surrey
53 N7 **Walton on the Naze** Essex
72 F7 **Walton on the Wolds** Leics
71 N11 **Walton-on-Trent** Derbys
31 M10 **Walton Park** N Som
40 G8 **Walton West** Pembks
96 E10 **Waltonwrays Crematorium** N York
80 G9 **Walwen** Flints
80 H10 **Walwen** Flints
81 J9 **Walwen** Flints
112 D6 **Walwick** Nthumb
103 P7 **Walworth** Darltn
36 H5 **Walworth** Gt Lon
103 P6 **Walworth Gate** Darltn
40 G8 **Walwyn's Castle** Pembks
10 F3 **Wambrook** Somset
110 D10 **Wampool** Cumb
23 P5 **Wanborough** Surrey
33 P8 **Wanborough** Swindn
50 D6 **Wandon End** Herts
36 G6 **Wandsworth** Gt Lon
65 P6 **Wangford** Suffk
72 F8 **Wanlip** Leics
116 B8 **Wanlockhead** D & G
25 N10 **Wannock** E Susx
73 R11 **Wansford** C Pete
99 M9 **Wansford** E R Yk
26 C2 **Wanshurst Green** Kent
37 K3 **Wanstead** Gt Lon
20 D6 **Wanstrow** Somset
32 C4 **Wanswell** Gloucs
34 C7 **Wantage** Oxon
46 E3 **Wants Green** Worcs
32 D9 **Wapley** S Glos
59 N11 **Wappenbury** Warwks
48 H5 **Wappenham** Nhants
25 P7 **Warbleton** E Susx
34 G6 **Warborough** Oxon
62 D4 **Warboys** Cambs
88 C3 **Warbreck** Bpool
5 L3 **Warbstow** Cnwll
82 F7 **Warburton** Traffd
102 D7 **Warcop** Cumb
38 H7 **Warden** Kent
112 D7 **Warden** Nthumb
58 H7 **Ward End** Birm
50 D2 **Warden Street** C Beds
64 E9 **Ward Green** Suffk
89 J3 **Ward Green Cross** Lancs
50 C3 **Wardhedges** C Beds
48 E5 **Wardington** Oxon
69 R3 **Wardle** Ches E
89 Q7 **Wardle** Rochdl
113 M8 **Wardley** Gatesd
73 L10 **Wardley** Rutlnd
82 G4 **Wardley** Salfd
83 Q10 **Wardlow** Derbys

Wardsend - West Melbury 305

83 K8 Wardsend Ches E
62 G4 Wardy Hill Cambs
51 J8 Ware Herts
12 F7 Wareham Dorset
26 G5 Warehorne Kent
119 M5 Warenford Nthumb
119 M4 Waren Mill Nthumb
119 M4 Warenton Nthumb
51 J7 Wareside Herts
62 C10 Waresley Cambs
58 B10 Waresley Worcs
38 C10 Ware Street Kent
35 N10 Warfield Br For
7 M8 Warfleet Devon
74 D4 Wargate Lincs
35 L9 Wargrave Wokham
45 P7 Warham Herefs
76 D3 Warham All Saints Norfk
76 C3 Warham St Mary Norfk
112 C5 Wark Nthumb
118 F3 Wark Nthumb
17 L7 Warkleigh Devon
61 J5 Warkton Nhants
48 E6 Warkworth Nhants
119 P9 Warkworth Nthumb
97 M2 Warlaby N York
89 Q6 Warland Calder
5 K8 Warleggan Cnwll
20 E2 Warleigh BaNES
90 D6 Warley Town Calder
37 J9 Warlingham Surrey
71 P4 Warmbrook Derbys
91 K6 Warmfield Wakefd
70 C2 Warmingham Ches E
61 N2 Warmington Nhants
48 D5 Warmington Warwks
20 G5 Warminster Wilts
32 C10 Warmley S Glos
91 N10 Warmsworth Donc
12 C7 Warmwell Dorset
46 G3 Warndon Worcs
22 H10 Warnford Hants
24 E4 Warnham W Susx
24 E4 Warnham Court W Susx
24 B9 Warningcamp W Susx
24 F5 Warninglid W Susx
83 J10 Warren Ches E
40 H11 Warren Pembks
104 G5 Warrenby R & Cl
116 C3 Warrenhill S Lans
35 M8 Warren Row W & M
50 G5 Warren's Green Herts
38 F11 Warren Street Kent
49 N4 Warrington M Keyn
82 D7 Warrington Warrtn
127 P2 Warriston C Edin
127 P2 Warriston Crematorium C Edin
14 E5 Warsash Hants
71 K3 Warslow Staffs
84 H7 Warsop Vale Notts
98 H10 Warter E R Yk
97 K5 Warthermaske N York
98 D9 Warthill N York
25 Q9 Wartling E Susx
73 J6 Wartnaby Leics
88 E5 Warton Lancs
95 K6 Warton Lancs
119 K10 Warton Nthumb
59 L4 Warton Warwks
59 L11 Warwick Warwks
111 J9 Warwick Bridge Cumb
47 Q2 Warwick Castle Warwks
111 J9 Warwick-on-Eden Cumb
48 B3 Warwick Services Warwks
111 J5 Warwicksland Cumb
169 c3 Wasbister Ork
100 G9 Wasdale Head Cumb
83 N8 Wash Derbys
103 Q4 Wear Valley Crematorium Dur
51 K4 Washall Green Herts
4 G8 Washaway Cnwll
7 K8 Washbourne Devon
19 M4 Washbrook Somset
53 K3 Washbrook Suffk
18 B11 Washfield Devon
103 L10 Washfold N York
18 E6 Washford Somset
9 K2 Washford Pyne Devon
86 D6 Washingborough Lincs
113 M9 Washington Sundld
24 D8 Washington W Susx
113 L9 Washington Services Gatesd
58 H7 Washwood Heath Birm
22 G2 Wasing W Berk
112 F11 Waskerley Dur
47 Q3 Wasperton Warwks
86 E8 Wasps Nest Lincs
98 B5 Wass N York
18 E6 Watchet Somset
33 P6 Watchfield Oxon
19 K5 Watchfield Somset
101 P11 Watchgate Cumb
100 G2 Watchill Cumb
7 N5 Watcombe Torbay
101 J7 Watendlath Cumb
9 J8 Water Devon
89 N5 Water Lancs
62 G7 Waterbeach Cambs
15 N5 Waterbeach W Susx
110 D5 Waterbeck D & G
76 B4 Waterden Norfk
34 F2 Water Eaton Oxon
58 D2 Water Eaton Staffs
61 P10 Water End Bed
61 P11 Water End Bed
50 C3 Water End C Beds
100 F6 Waterend Cumb
92 C3 Water End E R Yk
51 N2 Water End Essex
50 B8 Water End Herts
50 F10 Water End Herts
71 K4 Waterfall Staffs
125 P6 Waterfoot E Rens
50 H8 Waterford Herts
91 M5 Water Fryston Wakefd
5 J5 Watergate Cnwll
101 L10 Waterhead Cumb
127 N7 Waterheads Border
103 N2 Waterhouses Dur
71 K4 Waterhouses Staffs
37 Q10 Wateringbury Kent
32 H4 Waterlane Gloucs
5 J7 Waterloo Cnwll
84 F8 Waterloo Derbys
45 L5 Waterloo Herefs
145 L3 Waterloo Highld
126 E7 Waterloo N Lans
77 J8 Waterloo Norfk
141 Q10 Waterloo P & K
41 J10 Waterloo Pembks
12 H6 Waterloo Poole
81 L5 Waterloo Sefton
9 Q2 Waterloo Cross Devon
66 H2 Waterloo Port Gwynd
15 J5 Waterlooville Hants
101 M6 Watermillock Cumb
74 B11 Water Newton Cambs
59 J6 Water Orton Warwks
34 H3 Waterperry Oxon
18 E9 Waterrow Somset
24 B7 Watersfield W Susx
89 L6 Waterside Bl w D
35 Q4 Waterside Bucks
110 D11 Waterside Cumb
91 R8 Waterside Donc
114 H6 Waterside E Ayrs
125 M9 Waterside E Ayrs
126 B3 Waterside E Duns
89 K9 Water's Nook Bolton
152 A8 Waterstein Highld
34 H3 Waterstock Oxon
40 H9 Waterston Pembks
49 J8 Water Stratford Bucks
29 M8 Water Street Neath
70 A11 Waters Upton Wrekin
94 F3 Water Yeat Cumb
50 D11 Watford Herts
60 D7 Watford Nhants
60 D7 Watford Gap Services Nhants
96 H7 Wath N York
97 M5 Wath N York
91 L10 Wath upon Dearne Rothm
75 M8 Watlington Norfk
35 J6 Watlington Oxon
84 H11 Watnall Notts
167 M6 Watten Highld
64 E7 Wattisfield Suffk
64 E11 Wattisham Suffk
11 K6 Watton Dorset
99 L10 Watton E R Yk
76 C11 Watton Norfk
50 H7 Watton-at-Stone Herts
76 C11 Watton Green Norfk
51 M11 Wattons Green Essex
126 D3 Wattston N Lans
30 D6 Wattstown Rhondd
30 H6 Wattsville Caerph
92 G5 Wauldby E R Yk
150 G9 Waulkmill Abers
28 H5 Waunarlwydd Swans
54 E8 Waunfawr Cerdgn
67 J3 Waunfawr Gwynd
28 G4 Waungron Swans
30 G3 Waunlwyd Blae G
49 P7 Wavendon M Keyn
110 D11 Waverbridge Cumb
69 N2 Waverton Ches W
110 D11 Waverton Cumb
93 J3 Wawne E R Yk
77 N6 Waxham Norfk
93 P5 Waxholme E R Yk
39 P8 Way Kent
7 K4 Waye Devon
11 J3 Wayford Somset
11 K5 Waytown Dorset
9 L2 Way Village Devon
19 L2 Way Wick N Som
18 F6 Weacombe Somset
34 B4 Weald Oxon
36 E3 Wealdstone Gt Lon
90 H2 Weardley Leeds
19 M4 Weare Somset
16 H7 Weare Giffard Devon
102 G3 Wearhead Dur
19 M9 Wearne Somset
102 C10 Weasdale Cumb
76 A7 Weasenham All Saints Norfk
76 B7 Weasenham St Peter Norfk
82 H5 Weaste Salfd
58 G10 Weatheroak Hill Worcs
82 D10 Weaverham Ches W
71 L11 Weaverslake Staffs
99 K6 Weaverthorpe N York
19 L3 Webbington Somset
32 C10 Webb's Heath S Glos
58 F11 Webheath Worcs
45 N7 Webton Herefs
159 L11 Wedderlairs Abers
96 D11 Wedding Hall Fold N York
39 N10 Weddington Kent
59 N6 Weddington Warwks
21 L3 Wedhampton Wilts
19 M5 Wedmore Somset
58 E5 Wednesbury Sandw
58 D4 Wednesfield Wolves
85 P7 Weecar Notts
49 M11 Weedon Bucks
60 D9 Weedon Nhants
48 H5 Weedon Lois Nhants
58 H4 Weeford Staffs
7 K6 Week Devon
17 K6 Week Devon
17 N8 Week Devon
9 J3 Weeke Devon
22 E8 Weeke Hants
61 J4 Weekley Nhants
5 L2 Week St Mary Cnwll
93 J3 Weel E R Yk
53 K7 Weeley Essex
53 K7 Weeley Crematorium Essex
53 L7 Weeley Heath Essex
141 K8 Weem P & K
70 G10 Weeping Cross Staffs
47 L3 Weethley Warwks
63 N3 Weeting Norfk
93 Q6 Weeton E R Yk
88 D4 Weeton Lancs
97 L11 Weeton N York
90 H3 Weetwood Leeds
89 P5 Weir Lancs
69 K10 Weirbrook Shrops
6 C5 Weir Quay Devon
169 q8 Weisdale Shet
76 F9 Welborne Norfk
86 C10 Welbourn Lincs
98 E7 Welburn N York
104 C10 Welbury N York
73 P3 Welby Lincs
62 G3 Welches Dam Cambs
16 C8 Welcombe Devon
119 M11 Weldon Bridge Nthumb
60 D4 Welford Nhants
34 D10 Welford W Berk
47 M4 Welford-on-Avon Warwks
60 G2 Welham Leics
85 M4 Welham Notts
50 F9 Welham Green Herts
23 L5 Well Hants
87 M6 Well Lincs
97 L4 Well N York
46 E6 Welland Worcs
142 H10 Wellbank Angus
35 N7 Well End Bucks
50 F11 Well End Herts
47 Q3 Wellesbourne Warwks
47 Q3 Wellesbourne Mountford Warwks
50 E5 Well Head Herts
37 L8 Well Hill Kent
34 F10 Wellhouse W Berk
37 L5 Welling Gt Lon
61 J7 Wellingborough Nhants
76 B7 Wellingham Norfk
86 C9 Wellingore Lincs
100 E10 Wellington Cumb
45 P5 Wellington Herefs
18 F10 Wellington Somset
57 M2 Wellington Wrekin
46 D6 Wellington Heath Herefs
45 P5 Wellington Marsh Herefs
20 D3 Wellow BaNES
14 C9 Wellow IoW
85 L7 Wellow Notts
51 K6 Wellpond Green Herts
19 P5 Wells Somset
72 B10 Wellsborough Leics
70 B4 Wells Green Ches E
90 D4 Wells Head C Brad
76 C3 Wells-next-the-sea Norfk
51 P7 Wellstye Green Essex
9 M3 Well Town Devon
134 B3 Welltree P & K
134 D10 Wellwood Fife
62 H2 Welney Norfk
69 M7 Welshampton Shrops
46 A11 Welsh Bicknor Herefs
69 P7 Welsh End Shrops
69 L8 Welsh Frankton Shrops
40 H5 Welsh Hook Pembks
45 Q11 Welsh Newton Herefs
56 C3 Welshpool Powys
30 D9 Welsh St Donats V Glam
101 J2 Welton Cumb
92 G5 Welton E R Yk
86 D5 Welton Lincs
60 C7 Welton Nhants
87 N7 Welton le Marsh Lincs
87 J3 Welton le Wold Lincs
93 P6 Welwick E R Yk
50 F7 Welwyn Herts
50 F8 Welwyn Garden City Herts
69 P9 Wem Shrops
19 J7 Wembdon Somset
36 E3 Wembley Gt Lon
6 E9 Wembury Devon
17 M10 Wembworthy Devon
124 F4 Wemyss Bay Inver
54 F10 Wenallt Cerdgn
51 M3 Wendens Ambo Essex
48 G11 Wendlebury Oxon
76 C9 Wendling Norfk
35 N3 Wendover Bucks
2 H7 Wendron Cnwll
62 D11 Wendy Cambs
4 H6 Wenfordbridge Cnwll
65 N6 Wenhaston Suffk
62 B5 Wennington Cambs
37 M4 Wennington Gt Lon
95 N7 Wennington Lancs
84 C8 Wensley Derbys
96 G3 Wensley N York
91 M7 Wentbridge Wakefd
56 F6 Wentnor Shrops
62 G5 Wentworth Cambs
91 K11 Wentworth Rothm
91 J10 Wentworth Castle Barns
30 F10 Wenvoe V Glam
45 N4 Weobley Herefs
45 N4 Weobley Marsh Herefs
24 B9 Wepham W Susx
75 N10 Wereham Norfk
58 C4 Wergs Wolves
67 J7 Wern Gwynd
44 G11 Wern Powys
56 D2 Wern Powys
69 J8 Wern Shrops
83 L6 Werneth Low Tamesd
28 F6 Wernffrwd Swans
81 J11 Wern-y-gaer Flints
74 C10 Werrington C Pete
5 N4 Werrington Cnwll
70 G5 Werrington Staffs
81 N10 Wervin Ches W
88 E4 Wesham Lancs
22 E11 Wessex Vale Crematorium Hants
84 E9 Wessington Derbys
30 D11 West Aberthaw V Glam
75 Q7 West Acre Norfk
129 P10 West Allerdean Nthumb
7 J10 West Alvington Devon
21 M6 West Amesbury Wilts
17 R6 West Anstey Devon
97 K2 West Appleton N York
87 J6 West Ashby Lincs
15 M5 West Ashling W Susx
20 G3 West Ashton Wilts
103 N5 West Auckland Dur
99 K4 West Ayton N York
18 G8 West Bagborough Somset
30 H3 West Bank Blae G
81 Q8 West Bank Halton
86 G4 West Barkwith Lincs
105 M8 West Barnby N York
128 H4 West Barns E Loth
76 C5 West Barsham Norfk
11 K6 West Bay Dorset
76 G4 West Beckham Norfk
36 C6 West Bedfont Surrey
39 L9 Westbere Kent
52 G6 West Bergholt Essex
34 F11 West Berkshire Crematorium W Berk
11 L7 West Bexington Dorset
75 P7 West Bilney Norfk
24 G9 West Blatchington Br & H
113 N8 West Boldon S Tyne
73 M2 Westborough Lincs
13 J6 Westbourne Bmouth
15 L5 Westbourne W Susx
20 E9 West Bourton Dorset
90 F4 West Bowling C Brad
27 J3 West Brabourne Kent
76 C10 West Bradenham Norfk
89 L2 West Bradford Lancs
19 Q7 West Bradley Somset
90 H8 West Bretton Wakefd
72 F3 West Bridgford Notts
103 J7 West Briscoe Dur
58 F6 West Bromwich Sandw
58 F6 West Bromwich Crematorium Sandw
39 P7 Westbrook Kent
34 D10 Westbrook W Berk
33 J11 Westbrook Wilts
17 M5 West Buckland Devon
18 G10 West Buckland Somset
96 F3 West Burton N York
15 Q4 West Burton W Susx
48 H7 Westbury Bucks
56 F3 Westbury Shrops
20 G4 Westbury Wilts
20 G5 Westbury Leigh Wilts
32 D2 Westbury on Severn Gloucs
31 Q9 Westbury-on-Trym Bristl
19 P5 Westbury-sub-Mendip Somset
103 M2 West Butsfield Dur
92 D9 West Butterwick N Linc
88 D4 Westby Lancs
36 B8 West Byfleet Surrey
106 F11 West Cairngaan D & G
77 Q9 West Caister Norfk
127 J5 West Calder W Loth
19 Q10 West Camel Somset
12 C8 West Chaldon Dorset
34 C7 West Challow Oxon
7 K10 West Charleton Devon
11 L3 West Chelborough Dorset
119 P11 West Chevington Nthumb
24 C7 West Chiltington W Susx
11 K2 West Chinnock Somset
21 M4 West Chisenbury Wilts
36 B10 West Clandon Surrey
27 P3 West Cliffe Kent
38 E4 Westcliff-on-Sea Sthend
11 L2 West Coker Somset
7 K6 West Combe Devon
20 C7 Westcombe Somset
19 Q6 West Compton Somset
11 M6 West Compton Abbas Dorset
47 P10 Westcote Gloucs
48 D9 Westcote Barton Oxon
49 K11 Westcott Bucks
9 P4 Westcott Devon
36 D11 Westcott Surrey
92 A2 West Cottingwith N York
21 P2 Westcourt Wilts
91 Q6 West Cowick E R Yk
28 H7 West Cross Swans
5 M3 West Curry Cnwll
110 F11 West Curthwaite Cumb
25 M11 Westdean E Susx
15 N4 West Dean W Susx
21 Q9 West Dean Wilts
74 B9 West Deeping Lincs
81 M6 West Derby Lpool
75 N10 West Dereham Norfk
119 M6 West Ditchburn Nthumb
17 J3 West Down Devon
21 K5 Westdown Camp Wilts
4 H5 Westdowns Cnwll
36 C5 West Drayton Gt Lon
85 M6 West Drayton Notts
167 M2 West Dunnet Highld
37 M7 Wested Kent
92 H5 West Ella E R Yk
49 Q4 West End Bed
35 N10 West End Br For
30 H5 West End Caerph
62 D7 West End Cambs
110 F9 West End Cumb
92 F4 West End E R Yk
93 L4 West End E R Yk
93 N5 West End E R Yk
32 E3 Westend Gloucs
14 E4 West End Hants
22 H7 West End Hants
50 G9 West End Herts
50 H9 West End Herts
89 L5 West End Lancs
90 G3 West End Leeds
93 Q11 West End Lincs
31 N11 West End N Som
91 N2 West End N York
76 C10 West End Norfk
77 Q9 West End Norfk
34 G7 West End Oxon
32 D7 West End S Glos
20 C8 West End Somset
23 P2 West End Surrey
36 D8 West End Surrey
35 M9 West End W & M
24 F7 West End W Susx
20 H10 West End Wilts
21 J10 West End Wilts
33 J9 West End Wilts
23 J2 West End Green Hants
111 Q7 Westend Town Nthumb
27 K4 Westenhanger Kent
167 K6 Westerdale Highld
105 J9 Westerdale N York
53 L2 Westerfield Suffk
15 P5 Westergate W Susx
37 K10 Westerham Kent
113 J7 Westerhope N u Ty
7 M6 Westerland Devon
32 C9 Westerleigh S Glos
32 D9 Westerleigh Crematorium S Glos
127 J3 Wester Ochiltree W Loth
135 P6 Wester Pitkierie Fife
160 F11 Wester Ross Highld
15 N5 Westerton W Susx
143 M7 Westerton of Rossie Angus
169 p9 Westerwick Shet
36 F8 West Ewell Surrey
38 B11 West Farleigh Kent
48 F4 West Farndon Nhants
69 K9 West Felton Shrops
20 C4 Westfield BaNES
100 C5 Westfield Cumb
26 D8 Westfield E Susx
167 J4 Westfield Highld
126 C3 Westfield N Lans
76 D10 Westfield Norfk
126 G3 Westfield W Loth
12 B3 Westfields Dorset
45 P6 Westfields Herefs
142 B8 Westfields of Rattray P & K
38 C9 Westfield Sole Kent
99 M5 West Flotmanby N York
18 F10 Westford Somset
102 H3 Westgate Dur
92 C9 Westgate N Linc
76 D3 Westgate Norfk
90 G5 Westgate Hill C Brad
39 P7 Westgate on Sea Kent
76 H7 Westgate Street Norfk
34 D7 West Ginge Oxon
21 P2 West Grafton Wilts
23 K3 West Green Hants
21 P9 West Grimstead Wilts
24 E6 West Grinstead W Susx
91 P5 West Haddlesey N York
60 D6 West Haddon Nhants
34 F7 West Hagbourne Oxon
58 D8 West Hagley Worcs
65 N5 Westhall Suffk
72 C2 West Hallam Derbys
72 C2 West Hallam Common Derbys
92 F6 West Halton N Linc
11 P9 Westham Dorset
25 P10 Westham E Susx
37 J4 West Ham Gt Lon
19 M5 Westham Somset
15 N5 Westhampnett W Susx
84 E5 West Handley Derbys
34 D6 West Hanney Oxon
38 B2 West Hanningfield Essex
21 M9 West Harnham Wilts
19 Q3 West Harptree BaNES
23 L10 West Harting W Susx
19 J10 West Hatch Somset
20 H9 West Hatch Wilts
143 K10 West Haven Angus
19 M6 Westhay Somset
88 E9 Westhead Lancs
75 L9 West Head Norfk
58 F9 West Heath Birm
22 G3 West Heath Hants
163 N3 West Helmsdale Highld
34 D7 West Hendred Oxon
50 D10 West Hertfordshire Crematorium Herts
99 J5 West Heslerton N York
19 L2 West Hewish N Som
46 A6 Westhide Herefs
151 L6 Westhill Abers
9 Q6 West Hill Devon
25 J4 West Hoathly W Susx
12 E7 West Holme Dorset
19 Q6 Westholme Somset
45 P4 Westhope Herefs
56 H7 Westhope Shrops
37 P3 West Horndon Essex
48 F4 Westhorp Nhants
74 D4 Westhorpe Lincs
64 E8 Westhorpe Suffk
19 Q5 West Horrington Somset
36 C10 West Horsley Surrey
119 K4 West Horton Nthumb
27 N3 West Hougham Kent
89 K9 Westhoughton Bolton
95 P6 Westhouse N York
84 F9 Westhouses Derbys
13 J5 West Howe Bmouth
18 B8 West Howetown Somset
36 E10 Westhumble Surrey
134 D3 West Huntingtower P & K
19 K6 West Huntspill Somset
50 D7 West Hyde C Beds
36 B2 West Hyde Herts
27 K5 West Hythe Kent
17 N2 West Ilkerton Devon
34 E8 West Ilsley W Berk
15 L6 West Itchenor W Susx
87 L8 West Keal Lincs
33 M11 West Kennett Wilts
124 G8 West Kilbride N Ayrs
37 N8 West Kingsdown Kent
32 F9 West Kington Wilts
81 J7 West Kirby Wirral
98 H5 West Knapton N York
12 B7 West Knighton Dorset
20 G8 West Knoyle Wilts
119 L2 West Kyloe Nthumb
6 G8 Westlake Devon
19 M11 West Lambrook Somset
51 K6 Westland Green Herts
27 P2 West Langdon Kent
23 N10 West Lavington W Susx
21 K4 West Lavington Wilts
103 M8 West Layton N York
72 E5 West Leake Notts
118 F3 West Learmouth Nthumb
104 E10 West Lees N York
8 G3 West Leigh Devon
16 H6 Westleigh Devon
18 E11 Westleigh Devon
18 F8 West Leigh Somset
65 N8 Westleton Suffk
76 A8 West Lexham Norfk
56 F3 Westley Shrops
63 P8 Westley Suffk
63 K9 Westley Waterless Cambs
98 C8 West Lilling N York
35 L2 Westlington Bucks
127 M7 West Linton Border
110 G8 Westlinton Cumb
32 E9 West Littleton S Glos
34 D7 West Lockinge Oxon
36 F4 West London Crematorium Gt Lon
12 D8 West Lulworth Dorset
99 J7 West Lutton N York
19 Q8 West Lydford Somset
17 N2 West Lyn Devon
19 K9 West Lyng Somset
75 M6 West Lynn Norfk
37 Q9 West Malling Kent
46 E5 West Malvern Worcs
15 L4 West Marden W Susx
85 M6 West Markham Notts
39 N9 Westmarsh Kent
93 N9 West Marsh NE Lin
96 C10 West Marton N York
20 G10 West Melbury Dorset

91 L10 **West Melton** Rothm
22 H10 **West Meon** Hants
23 J9 **West Meon Hut** Hants
22 H9 **West Meon Woodlands** Hants
52 H9 **West Mersea** Essex
24 H8 **Westmeston** E Susx
112 G8 **West Mickley** Nthumb
57 Q9 **West Midland Safari Park** Worcs
50 H7 **Westmill** Herts
51 J5 **Westmill** Herts
11 L5 **West Milton** Dorset
36 G5 **Westminster** Gt Lon
38 F7 **West Minster** Kent
36 D7 **West Molesey** Surrey
19 J9 **West Monkton** Somset
13 J4 **West Moors** Dorset
12 F5 **West Morden** Dorset
118 B2 **West Morriston** Border
90 D2 **West Morton** C Brad
19 Q10 **West Mudford** Somset
142 F7 **Westmuir** Angus
98 D5 **West Ness** N York
104 C7 **West Newbiggin** Darltn
100 F2 **Westnewton** Cumb
93 M3 **West Newton** E R Yk
75 N5 **West Newton** Norfk
19 J9 **West Newton** Somset
36 H6 **West Norwood** Gt Lon
36 H6 **West Norwood Crematorium** Gt Lon
113 N7 **Westoe** S Tyne
7 L4 **West Ogwell** Devon
32 D11 **Weston** BaNES
70 C4 **Weston** Ches E
10 C4 **Weston** Devon
10 D7 **Weston** Devon
11 P10 **Weston** Dorset
81 Q8 **Weston** Halton
23 K10 **Weston** Hants
45 M3 **Weston** Herefs
50 C4 **Weston** Herts
74 E6 **Weston** Lincs
97 J11 **Weston** N York
48 G5 **Weston** Nhants
85 N7 **Weston** Notts
56 E10 **Weston** Shrops
57 L6 **Weston** Shrops
69 J9 **Weston** Shrops
70 H9 **Weston** Staffs
34 C10 **Weston** W Berk
46 A6 **Weston Beggard** Herefs
32 G7 **Westonbirt** Gloucs
60 G2 **Weston by Welland** Nhants
22 F7 **Weston Colley** Hants
63 K10 **Weston Colville** Cambs
23 J5 **Weston Corbett** Hants
70 G6 **Weston Coyney** C Stke
60 G8 **Weston Favell** Nhants
63 K10 **Weston Green** Cambs
57 P2 **Weston Heath** Shrops
74 E6 **Weston Hills** Lincs
59 N7 **Weston in Arden** Warwks
50 B4 **Westoning** C Beds
31 M10 **Weston-in-Gordano** N Som
50 B4 **Westoning Woodend** C Beds
70 D10 **Weston Jones** Staffs
76 G8 **Weston Longville** Norfk
69 M10 **Weston Lullingfields** Shrops
6 D7 **Weston Mill Crematorium** C Plym
47 N4 **Weston-on-Avon** Warwks
48 F11 **Weston-on-the-Green** Oxon
23 J5 **Weston Patrick** Hants
69 J7 **Weston Rhyn** Shrops
47 M6 **Weston-sub-Edge** Gloucs
19 K2 **Weston-super-Mare** N Som
19 L2 **Weston-super-Mare Crematorium** N Som
35 N2 **Weston Turville** Bucks
57 Q2 **Weston-under-Lizard** Staffs
46 B10 **Weston under Penyard** Herefs
69 Q9 **Weston-under-Redcastle** Shrops
59 N11 **Weston under Wetherley** Warwks
71 P6 **Weston Underwood** Derbys
49 N4 **Weston Underwood** M Keyn
72 C5 **Weston-upon-Trent** Derbys
19 L8 **Westonzoyland** Somset
20 F11 **West Orchard** Dorset
33 M11 **West Overton** Wilts
98 F7 **Westow** N York
5 N3 **West Panson** Devon
151 K8 **West Park** Abers
13 J5 **West Parley** Dorset
37 P10 **West Peckham** Kent
5 N3 **West Peeke** Devon
113 K10 **West Pelton** Dur
19 P7 **West Pennard** Somset
4 B9 **West Pentire** Cnwll
61 P7 **West Perry** Cambs
17 R2 **West Porlock** Somset
19 L10 **Westport** Somset
11 Q3 **West Pulham** Dorset
16 F8 **West Putford** Devon
18 F6 **West Quantoxhead** Somset
126 G2 **Westquarter** Falk
30 F10 **Westra** V Glam
9 L4 **West Raddon** Devon
113 M11 **West Rainton** Dur
86 E3 **West Rasen** Lincs
93 M11 **West Ravendale** NE Lin
169 d2 **Westray** Ork
169 d1 *Westray Airport* Ork
76 B6 **West Raynham** Norfk
85 L4 **West Retford** Notts
34 G9 **Westridge Green** W Berk
126 G4 **Westrigg** W Loth
113 K7 **West Road Crematorium** N u Ty
33 P6 **Westrop** Swindn
104 D10 **West Rounton** N York
63 L5 **West Row** Suffk
75 R5 **West Rudham** Norfk
76 H3 **West Runton** Norfk
128 G10 **Westruther** Border

74 H11 **Westry** Cambs
128 D6 **West Saltoun** E Loth
9 K4 **West Sandford** Devon
169 r5 **West Sandwick** Shet
96 G4 **West Scrafton** N York
113 L4 **West Sleekburn** Nthumb
77 P7 **West Somerton** Norfk
11 Q7 **West Stafford** Dorset
92 C11 **West Stockwith** Notts
15 M5 **West Stoke** W Susx
102 G10 **West Stonesdale** N York
19 M5 **West Stoughton** Somset
20 E10 **West Stour** Dorset
39 N9 **West Stourmouth** Kent
63 P6 **West Stow** Suffk
21 M2 **West Stowell** Wilts
22 F6 **West Stratton** Hants
38 F11 **West Street** Kent
39 P11 **West Street** Kent
38 B6 **West Street** Medway
64 D7 **West Street** Suffk
63 P7 **West Suffk Crematorium** Suffk
97 L5 **West Tanfield** N York
5 J9 **West Taphouse** Cnwll
123 P6 **West Tarbert** Ag & B
24 D10 **West Tarring** W Susx
119 N11 **West Thirston** Nthumb
15 L6 **West Thorney** W Susx
84 G5 **Westthorpe** Derbys
72 G5 **West Thorpe** Notts
37 N5 **West Thurrock** Thurr
37 N5 **West Tilbury** Thurr
23 J9 **West Tisted** Hants
86 F4 **West Torrington** Lincs
19 P2 **West Town** BaNES
15 K7 **West Town** Hants
45 N2 **West Town** Herefs
31 N11 **West Town** N Som
19 P7 **West Town** Somset
20 D6 **West Town** Somset
21 Q9 **West Tytherley** Hants
75 J8 **West Walton** Norfk
75 J8 **West Walton Highway** Norfk
101 J2 **Westward** Cumb
16 G6 **Westward Ho!** Devon
26 G2 **Westwell** Kent
33 P3 **Westwell** Oxon
26 G2 **Westwell Leacon** Kent
21 Q11 **West Wellow** Hants
6 E9 **West Wemburay** Devon
135 J9 **West Wemyss** Fife
62 F7 **Westwick** Cambs
103 L7 **Westwick** Dur
19 L2 **West Wick** N Som
77 K6 **Westwick** Norfk
63 K11 **West Wickham** Cambs
37 J7 **West Wickham** Gt Lon
41 K9 **West Williamston** Pembks
20 H3 **West Wiltshire Crematorium** Wilts
75 M7 **West Winch** Norfk
21 P8 **West Winterslow** Wilts
15 L7 **West Wittering** W Susx
96 G3 **West Witton** N York
9 P5 **Westwood** Devon
37 P6 **Westwood** Kent
39 Q8 **Westwood** Kent
84 G10 **Westwood** Notts
111 Q7 **Westwood** Nthumb
20 F3 **Westwood** Wilts
112 C3 **West Woodburn** Nthumb
22 C2 **West Woodhay** W Berk
59 L9 **Westwood Heath** Covtry
20 E6 **West Woodlands** Somset
92 B10 **Westwoodside** N Linc
23 K7 **West Worldham** Hants
24 D10 **West Worthing** W Susx
63 K10 **West Wratting** Cambs
35 M6 **West Wycombe** Bucks
112 H8 **West Wylam** Nthumb
32 G9 **West Yatton** Wilts
37 P7 **West Yoke** Kent
16 D8 **West Youlstone** Cnwll
38 D8 **Wetham Green** Kent
111 J10 **Wetheral** Cumb
97 P11 **Wetherby** Leeds
97 P10 **Wetherby Services** N York
64 E9 **Wetherden** Suffk
64 G8 **Wetheringsett** Suffk
52 B5 **Wethersfield** Essex
64 G9 **Wetherup Street** Suffk
70 H5 **Wetley Rocks** Staffs
69 R2 **Wettenhall** Ches E
71 L3 **Wetton** Staffs
99 J9 **Wetwang** E R Yk
70 D8 **Wetwood** Staffs
21 Q3 **Wexcombe** Wilts
35 Q8 **Wexham** Slough
35 Q8 **Wexham Street** Bucks
76 G3 **Weybourne** Norfk
23 N5 **Weybourne** Surrey
65 J5 **Weybread** Suffk
65 J6 **Weybread Street** Suffk
36 C8 **Weybridge** Surrey
10 G5 **Weycroft** Devon
167 L4 **Weydale** Highld
22 B5 **Weyhill** Hants
11 P9 **Weymouth** Dorset
11 P9 **Weymouth Crematorium** Dorset
49 M8 **Whaddon** Bucks
62 E11 **Whaddon** Cambs
32 F2 **Whaddon** Gloucs
20 G2 **Whaddon** Wilts
21 N9 **Whaddon** Wilts
101 P6 **Whale** Cumb
84 H6 **Whaley** Derbys
83 M8 **Whaley Bridge** Derbys
84 H6 **Whaley Thorns** Derbys
167 P8 **Whaligoe** Highld
89 L3 **Whalley** Lancs
89 L3 **Whalley Banks** Lancs
169 s7 **Whalsay** Shet
112 H4 **Whalton** Nthumb
74 F6 **Whaplode** Lincs
74 F8 **Whaplode Drove** Lincs
48 D4 **Wharf** Warwks
96 A7 **Wharfe** N York
88 E3 **Wharles** Lancs
49 P6 **Wharley End** C Beds
84 C2 **Wharncliffe Side** Sheff
98 H7 **Wharram-le-Street** N York
82 E11 **Wharton** Ches W
45 Q3 **Wharton** Herefs
103 N9 **Whashton** N York

95 L4 **Whasset** Cumb
47 Q6 **Whatcote** Warwks
59 K5 **Whateley** Warwks
52 H2 **Whatfield** Suffk
10 H3 **Whatley** Somset
20 D5 **Whatley** Somset
32 C8 **Whatley's End** S Glos
26 C8 **Whatlington** E Susx
27 K3 **Whatsole Street** Kent
84 D10 **Whatstandwell** Derbys
73 J3 **Whatton** Notts
107 M8 **Whauphill** D & G
103 J10 **Whaw** N York
3 J5 **Wheal Rose** Cnwll
65 P3 **Wheatacre** Norfk
35 J5 **Wheatfield** Oxon
50 E8 **Wheathampstead** Herts
57 L8 **Wheathill** Shrops
19 Q8 **Wheathill** Somset
90 D5 **Wheatley** Calder
23 L6 **Wheatley** Hants
34 G3 **Wheatley** Oxon
104 C3 **Wheatley Hill** Dur
91 P10 **Wheatley Hills** Donc
89 N3 **Wheatley Lane** Lancs
58 C2 **Wheaton Aston** Staffs
69 K4 **Wheatsheaf** Wrexhm
18 B7 **Wheddon Cross** Somset
27 K2 **Wheelbarrow Town** Kent
35 M6 **Wheeler End** Bucks
35 L10 **Wheeler's Green** Wokham
26 D3 **Wheeler's Street** Kent
23 P6 **Wheelerstreet** Surrey
70 D3 **Wheelock** Ches E
70 D3 **Wheelock Heath** Ches E
89 J6 **Wheelton** Lancs
91 M5 **Wheldale** Wakefd
92 A2 **Wheldrake** C York
33 N5 **Whelford** Gloucs
35 Q4 **Whelpley Hill** Bucks
101 K3 **Whelpo** Cumb
81 J9 **Whelston** Flints
50 H6 **Whempstead** Herts
98 C7 **Whenby** N York
64 A10 **Whepstead** Suffk
53 L3 **Wherstead** Suffk
22 C6 **Wherwell** Hants
83 P9 **Wheston** Derbys
37 Q11 **Whetsted** Kent
36 G2 **Whetstone** Gt Lon
72 F11 **Whetstone** Leics
110 C11 **Wheyrigg** Cumb
94 C4 **Whicham** Cumb
48 B8 **Whichford** Warwks
113 K8 **Whickham** Gatesd
8 C5 **Whiddon** Devon
8 G6 **Whiddon Down** Devon
53 K3 **Whight's Corner** Suffk
142 H9 **Whigstreet** Angus
60 D8 **Whilton** Nhants
16 F11 **Whimble** Devon
9 P5 **Whimple** Devon
77 M6 **Whimpwell Green** Norfk
76 E10 **Whinburgh** Norfk
88 D2 **Whin Lane End** Lancs
108 F10 **Whinnie Liggate** D & G
110 F10 **Whinnow** Cumb
159 Q11 **Whinnyfold** Abers
104 C7 **Whinny Hill** S on T
14 F8 **Whippingham** IoW
50 B7 **Whipsnade** C Beds
9 M6 **Whipton** Devon
84 D4 **Whisby** Lincs
86 B7 **Whisby** Lincs
73 L8 **Whissendine** Rutlnd
76 C7 **Whissonsett** Norfk
131 Q9 **Whistlefield** Ag & B
131 N9 **Whistlefield Inn** Ag & B
35 L10 **Whistley Green** Wokham
81 P6 **Whiston** Knows
60 H8 **Whiston** Nhants
84 F3 **Whiston** Rothm
58 C2 **Whiston** Staffs
71 J5 **Whiston** Staffs
57 P4 **Whiston Cross** Shrops
71 J5 **Whiston Eaves** Staffs
59 L6 **Whitacre Fields** Warwks
94 C4 **Whitbeck** Cumb
46 D3 **Whitbourne** Herefs
113 P8 **Whitburn** S Tyne
126 G5 **Whitburn** W Loth
81 M9 **Whitby** Ches W
105 N8 **Whitby** N York
81 M10 **Whitbyheath** Ches W
129 J8 **Whitchester** Border
32 B11 **Whitchurch** BaNES
49 M10 **Whitchurch** Bucks
30 G9 **Whitchurch** Cardif
6 D4 **Whitchurch** Devon
22 E5 **Whitchurch** Hants
45 R11 **Whitchurch** Herefs
34 H9 **Whitchurch** Oxon
40 F5 **Whitchurch** Pembks
69 P6 **Whitchurch** Shrops
10 H5 **Whitchurch Canonicorum** Dorset
34 H9 **Whitchurch Hill** Oxon
11 Q7 **Whitcombe** Dorset
56 F6 **Whitcot** Shrops
56 D8 **Whitcott Keysett** Shrops
27 K2 **Whiteacre** Kent
59 K6 **Whiteacre Heath** Warwks
52 C5 **Whiteash Green** Essex
18 F11 **White Ball** Somset
147 M4 **Whitebridge** Highld
31 P3 **Whitebrook** Mons
151 N4 **Whitecairns** Abers
36 H4 **Whitechapel** Gt Lon
88 H2 **White Chapel** Lancs
41 N3 **Whitechurch** Pembks
31 Q3 **Whitecliffe** Gloucs
52 E6 **White Colne** Essex
89 J7 **White Coppice** Lancs
127 Q3 **Whitecraig** E Loth
32 B3 **Whitecroft** Gloucs
106 G6 **Whitecrook** D & G
2 E7 **Whitecross** Cnwll
2 H9 **White Cross** Cnwll
4 F7 **Whitecross** Cnwll
126 H2 **Whitecross** Falk
46 E8 **White End** Worcs
162 G9 **Whiteface** Highld
120 G3 **Whitefarland** N Ayrs
114 E6 **Whitefaulds** S Ayrs
89 N9 **Whitefield** Bury
17 N4 **Whitefield** Devon
18 E9 **Whitefield** Somset
81 P7 **Whitefield Lane End** Knows

151 J2 **Whiteford** Abers
82 D11 **Whitegate** Ches W
23 K4 **Whitehall** Hants
169 f4 **Whitehall** Ork
24 D6 **Whitehall** W Susx
100 C7 **Whitehaven** Cumb
38 H10 **Whitehill** Kent
72 C8 **Whitehill** Leics
23 L8 **Whitehill and Bordon** Hants
158 G4 **Whitehills** Abers
150 G5 **Whitehouse** Abers
123 P7 **Whitehouse** Ag & B
58 H5 **Whitehouse Common** Birm
128 F3 **Whitekirk** E Loth
103 K3 **White Kirkley** Dur
11 Q5 **White Lackington** Dorset
19 L11 **Whitelackington** Somset
46 H1 **White Ladies Aston** Worcs
35 M4 **Whiteleaf** Bucks
113 J10 **White-le-Head** Dur
14 F5 **Whiteley** Hants
14 G10 **Whiteley Bank** IoW
83 K9 **Whiteley Green** Ches E
36 C8 **Whiteley Village** Surrey
24 H5 **Whitemans Green** W Susx
43 J10 **White Mill** Carmth
156 H7 **Whitemire** Moray
72 E2 **Whitemoor** C Nott
4 F10 **Whitemoor** Cnwll
84 E11 **Whitemoor** Derbys
70 F2 **Whitemoor** Staffs
169 q9 **Whiteness** Shet
52 C8 **White Notley** Essex
34 B2 **Whiteoak Green** Oxon
20 D3 **White Ox Mead** BaNES
21 P10 **Whiteparish** Wilts
87 L5 **White Pit** Lincs
151 M3 **Whiterashes** Abers
51 N8 **White Roding** Essex
167 Q7 **Whiterow** Highld
157 J6 **Whiterow** Moray
32 F3 **Whiteshill** Gloucs
25 M8 **Whitesmith** E Susx
88 G5 **White Stake** Lancs
10 F2 **Whitestaunton** Somset
9 L6 **Whitestone** Devon
45 R6 **White Stone** Herefs
9 L6 **Whitestone Cross** Devon
52 G4 **Whitestreet Green** Suffk
98 F7 **Whitewall Corner** N York
35 M9 **White Waltham** W & M
20 D2 **Whiteway** BaNES
32 H2 **Whiteway** Gloucs
95 P11 **Whitewell** Lancs
142 G11 **Whitfield** C Dund
27 P2 **Whitfield** Kent
48 H7 **Whitfield** Nhants
111 Q9 **Whitfield** Nthumb
32 C6 **Whitfield** S Glos
111 Q9 **Whitfield Hall** Nthumb
10 F5 **Whitford** Devon
80 G9 **Whitford** Flints
92 D6 **Whitgift** E R Yk
70 G9 **Whitgreave** Staffs
107 M9 **Whithorn** D & G
121 K6 **Whiting Bay** N Ayrs
91 K4 **Whitkirk** Leeds
41 N7 **Whitland** Carmth
117 Q8 **Whitlaw** Border
114 G3 **Whitletts** S Ayrs
91 P6 **Whitley** N York
35 K10 **Whitley** Readg
84 D2 **Whitley** Sheff
32 G11 **Whitley** Wilts
113 N6 **Whitley Bay** N Tyne
113 M6 **Whitley Bay Crematorium** N Tyne
112 D9 **Whitley Chapel** Nthumb
70 E9 **Whitley Heath** Staffs
90 G7 **Whitley Lower** Kirk
37 L10 **Whitley Row** Kent
58 H9 **Whitlock's End** Solhll
32 E3 **Whitminster** Gloucs
13 J3 **Whitmore** Dorset
70 E6 **Whitmore** Staffs
18 D11 **Whitnage** Devon
48 B2 **Whitnash** Warwks
45 K5 **Whitney-on-Wye** Herefs
100 H3 **Whitrigg** Cumb
110 D9 **Whitrigg** Cumb
110 D9 **Whitrigglees** Cumb
21 M11 **Whitsbury** Hants
129 M9 **Whitsome** Border
31 L8 **Whitson** Newpt
39 K8 **Whitstable** Kent
5 M2 **Whitstone** Cnwll
119 L8 **Whittingham** Nthumb
56 G7 **Whittingslow** Shrops
84 E5 **Whittington** Derbys
47 K10 **Whittington** Gloucs
45 N5 **Whittington** Lancs
75 P11 **Whittington** Norfk
69 K8 **Whittington** Shrops
58 C8 **Whittington** Staffs
59 J3 **Whittington** Staffs
59 L5 **Whittington** Warwks
46 G4 **Whittington** Worcs
84 E6 **Whittington Moor** Derbys
49 J6 **Whittlebury** Nhants
88 H6 **Whittle-le-Woods** Lancs
74 E11 **Whittlesey** Cambs
62 G11 **Whittlesford** Cambs
89 L7 **Whittlestone Head** Bl w D
92 F6 **Whitton** N Linc
119 L10 **Whitton** Nthumb
30 D11 **Whitton** Powys
104 C6 **Whitton** S on T
57 K10 **Whitton** Shrops
53 K2 **Whitton** Suffk
33 Q10 **Whittonditch** Wilts
112 G9 **Whittonstall** Nthumb
22 E3 **Whitway** Hants
84 H5 **Whitwell** Derbys
50 E6 **Whitwell** Herts
14 F11 **Whitwell** IoW
103 Q11 **Whitwell** N York
73 N9 **Whitwell** Rutlnd
98 E7 **Whitwell-on-the-Hill** N York
76 G7 **Whitwell Street** Norfk
72 C7 **Whitwick** Leics
91 L6 **Whitwood** Wakefd
89 P7 **Whitworth** Lancs

69 P8 **Whixall** Shrops
97 P9 **Whixley** N York
103 M8 **Whorlton** Dur
104 E10 **Whorlton** N York
45 R2 **Whyle** Herefs
36 H9 **Whyteleafe** Surrey
31 Q5 **Wibdon** Gloucs
90 E4 **Wibsey** C Brad
59 Q7 **Wibtoft** Warwks
46 E2 **Wichenford** Worcs
38 F10 **Wichling** Kent
13 L6 **Wick** Bmouth
10 D4 **Wick** Devon
167 Q6 **Wick** Highld
32 D10 **Wick** S Glos
18 H6 **Wick** Somset
19 M9 **Wick** Somset
29 P10 **Wick** V Glam
24 B10 **Wick** W Susx
21 N10 **Wick** Wilts
47 J5 **Wick** Worcs
167 Q6 *Wick Airport* Highld
63 J6 **Wicken** Cambs
49 K7 **Wicken** Nhants
51 L4 **Wicken Bonhunt** Essex
86 E4 **Wickenby** Lincs
49 Q4 **Wick End** Bed
76 A5 **Wicken Green Village** Norfk
84 G2 **Wickersley** Rothm
52 G3 **Wicker Street Green** Suffk
38 B3 **Wickford** Essex
14 G4 **Wickham** Hants
34 C10 **Wickham** W Berk
52 D9 **Wickham Bishops** Essex
39 M10 **Wickhambreaux** Kent
63 N10 **Wickhambrook** Suffk
47 L6 **Wickhamford** Worcs
64 F8 **Wickham Green** Suffk
34 D10 **Wickham Green** W Berk
34 D11 **Wickham Heath** W Berk
65 L10 **Wickham Market** Suffk
77 N10 **Wickhampton** Norfk
52 D4 **Wickham St Paul** Essex
64 F8 **Wickham Skeith** Suffk
63 N10 **Wickham Street** Suffk
64 F8 **Wickham Street** Suffk
76 F11 **Wicklewood** Norfk
76 H5 **Wickmere** Norfk
31 L11 **Wick St Lawrence** N Som
25 M9 **Wickstreet** E Susx
32 D7 **Wickwar** S Glos
51 M4 **Widdington** Essex
89 Q4 **Widdop** Calder
119 Q11 **Widdrington** Nthumb
113 K2 **Widdrington Station** Nthumb
8 H9 **Widecombe in the Moor** Devon
5 M10 **Widegates** Cnwll
16 C11 **Widemouth Bay** Cnwll
113 K6 **Wide Open** N Tyne
51 Q10 **Widford** Essex
51 K7 **Widford** Herts
33 L7 **Widham** Wilts
15 J5 **Widley** Hants
35 N5 **Widmer End** Bucks
72 G5 **Widmerpool** Notts
37 K7 **Widmore** Gt Lon
81 Q8 **Widnes** Halton
81 Q7 **Widnes Crematorium** Halton
10 E5 **Widworthy** Devon
88 H9 **Wigan** Wigan
82 C4 **Wigan Crematorium** Wigan
19 M11 **Wigborough** Somset
10 C6 **Wiggaton** Devon
75 L8 **Wiggenhall St Germans** Norfk
75 L8 **Wiggenhall St Mary Magdalen** Norfk
75 L8 **Wiggenhall St Mary the Virgin** Norfk
51 Q2 **Wiggens Green** Essex
71 K2 **Wiggenstall** Staffs
69 K7 **Wiggington** Shrops
98 C9 **Wigginton** C York
35 P2 **Wigginton** Herts
48 C8 **Wigginton** Oxon
59 K3 **Wigginton** Staffs
35 P3 **Wigginton Bottom** Herts
96 B9 **Wigglesworth** N York
110 E10 **Wiggonby** Cumb
24 C7 **Wiggonholt** W Susx
97 Q11 **Wighill** N York
76 C4 **Wighton** Norfk
58 C5 **Wightwick** Wolves
84 D6 **Wigley** Derbys
22 B11 **Wigley** Hants
56 G11 **Wigmore** Herefs
38 C9 **Wigmore** Medway
85 Q6 **Wigsley** Notts
61 M4 **Wigsthorpe** Nhants
72 G11 **Wigston** Leics
72 G10 **Wigston Fields** Leics
59 Q7 **Wigston Parva** Leics
85 J4 **Wigthorpe** Notts
74 E3 **Wigtoft** Lincs
110 E11 **Wigton** Cumb
107 M6 **Wigtown** D & G
90 G11 **Wigtwizzle** Sheff
91 J2 **Wike** Leeds
60 H3 **Wilbarston** Nhants
98 E10 **Wilberfoss** E R Yk
62 G5 **Wilburton** Cambs
61 J7 **Wilby** Nhants
64 E4 **Wilby** Norfk
65 J7 **Wilby** Suffk
21 M2 **Wilcot** Wilts
69 L11 **Wilcott** Shrops
31 M7 **Wilcrick** Newpt
84 D6 **Wilday Green** Derbys
83 L11 **Wildboarclough** Ches E
61 N9 **Wilden** Bed
58 B10 **Wilden** Worcs
63 M5 **Wilde Street** Suffk
22 C4 **Wildhern** Hants
50 G9 **Wildhill** Herts
126 E7 **Wildmanbridge** S Lans
58 E9 **Wildmoor** Worcs
92 D11 **Wildsworth** Lincs
72 F3 **Wilford** C Nott
72 F3 **Wilford Hill Crematorium** Notts
70 A6 **Wilkesley** Ches E
163 L9 **Wilkhaven** Highld
127 L4 **Wilkieston** W Loth
50 E9 **Wilkin's Green** Herts

Wilksby - Worksop 307

87 J8 **Wilksby** Lincs
9 P2 **Willand** Devon
26 B7 **Willards Hill** E Susx
70 B4 **Willaston** Ches E
81 L9 **Willaston** Ches W
49 N6 **Willen** M Keyn
59 N9 **Willenhall** Covtry
58 E5 **Willenhall** Wsall
92 H4 **Willerby** E R Yk
99 L5 **Willerby** N York
47 M7 **Willersey** Gloucs
45 L5 **Willersley** Herefs
26 H3 **Willesborough** Kent
26 H3 **Willesborough Lees** Kent
36 F4 **Willesden** Gt Lon
17 K5 **Willesleigh** Devon
32 G7 **Willesley** Wilts
18 F8 **Willett** Somset
57 M5 **Willey** Shrops
59 Q8 **Willey** Warwks
23 P4 **Willey Green** Surrey
48 E5 **Williamscot** Oxon
30 D6 **Williamstown** Rhondd
50 F4 **Willian** Herts
47 N5 **Willicote** Warwks
51 N9 **Willingale** Essex
25 N10 **Willingdon** E Susx
62 F6 **Willingham** Cambs
85 Q4 **Willingham by Stow** Lincs
63 K10 **Willingham Green** Cambs
61 P10 **Willington** Bed
71 P9 **Willington** Derbys
103 N3 **Willington** Dur
38 C11 **Willington** Kent
47 Q7 **Willington** Warwks
82 B11 **Willington Corner** Ches W
113 M7 **Willington Quay** N Tyne
92 B4 **Willitoft** E R Yk
18 E6 **Williton** Somset
87 N6 **Willoughby** Lincs
60 B7 **Willoughby** Warwks
87 L11 **Willoughby Hills** Lincs
72 G5 **Willoughby-on-the-Wolds** Notts
60 C2 **Willoughby Waterleys** Leics
86 B2 **Willoughton** Lincs
82 D9 **Willow Green** Ches W
52 B8 **Willows Green** Essex
32 C10 **Willsbridge** S Glos
8 D8 **Willsworthy** Devon
19 L10 **Willtown** Somset
47 N3 **Wilmcote** Warwks
20 C2 **Wilmington** BaNES
10 E5 **Wilmington** Devon
25 M10 **Wilmington** E Susx
37 M6 **Wilmington** Kent
82 H8 **Wilmslow** Ches E
59 K4 **Wilnecote** Staffs
89 K4 **Wilpshire** Lancs
90 D3 **Wilsden** C Brad
73 Q2 **Wilsford** Lincs
21 M3 **Wilsford** Wilts
21 M7 **Wilsford** Wilts
17 P2 **Wilsham** Devon
90 E9 **Wilshaw** Kirk
97 J8 **Wilsill** N York
26 C4 **Wilsley Green** Kent
26 C4 **Wilsley Pound** Kent
45 R10 **Wilson** Herefs
72 C6 **Wilson** Leics
126 G6 **Wilsontown** S Lans
50 C2 **Wilstead** Bed
74 A8 **Wilsthorpe** Lincs
35 P2 **Wilstone** Herts
35 P2 **Wilstone Green** Herts
100 D8 **Wilton** Cumb
46 A10 **Wilton** Herefs
98 H4 **Wilton** N York
104 G7 **Wilton** R & Cl
21 L8 **Wilton** Wilts
21 Q2 **Wilton** Wilts
117 P8 **Wilton Dean** Border
51 N3 **Wimbish** Essex
51 P3 **Wimbish Green** Essex
36 F6 **Wimbledon** Gt Lon
62 F2 **Wimblington** Cambs
70 B2 **Wimboldsley** Ches W
12 H5 **Wimborne Minster** Dorset
12 H2 **Wimborne St Giles** Dorset
75 M9 **Wimbotsham** Norfk
62 E11 **Wimpole** Cambs
47 P5 **Wimpstone** Warwks
20 D9 **Wincanton** Somset
87 K7 **Winceby** Lincs
82 E9 **Wincham** Ches W
127 K3 **Winchburgh** W Loth
47 K9 **Winchcombe** Gloucs
26 F8 **Winchelsea** E Susx
26 F8 **Winchelsea Beach** E Susx
22 E9 **Winchester** Hants
22 F7 **Winchester Services** Hants
26 B3 **Winchet Hill** Kent
23 L4 **Winchfield** Hants
35 P5 **Winchmore Hill** Bucks
36 H2 **Winchmore Hill** Gt Lon
83 L11 **Wincle** Ches E
84 E2 **Wincobank** Sheff
100 D7 **Winder** Cumb
101 M11 **Windermere** Cumb
48 B6 **Winderton** Warwks
155 P8 **Windhill** Highld
83 L7 **Windlehurst** Stockp
23 P2 **Windlesham** Surrey
4 D7 **Windmill** Cnwll
83 Q9 **Windmill** Derbys
25 P8 **Windmill Hill** E Susx
19 K11 **Windmill Hill** Somset
33 N2 **Windrush** Gloucs
158 E5 **Windsole** Abers
35 Q9 **Windsor** W & M
35 Q9 **Windsor Castle** W & M
32 F4 **Windsoredge** Gloucs
64 B11 **Windsor Green** Suffk
59 L10 **Windy Arbour** Warwks
135 J7 **Windygates** Fife
82 H10 **Windyharbour** Ches E
69 K4 **Windy Hill** Wrexhm
24 F6 **Wineham** W Susx
93 N6 **Winestead** E R Yk
89 Q2 **Winewall** Lancs
64 G4 **Winfarthing** Norfk
14 G10 **Winford** IoW
19 P2 **Winford** N Som
45 K5 **Winforton** Herefs
12 D8 **Winfrith Newburgh** Dorset
49 N3 **Wing** Bucks
73 M10 **Wing** Rutlnd
104 D3 **Wingate** Dur
89 K9 **Wingates** Bolton
119 L11 **Wingates** Nthumb
84 E7 **Wingerworth** Derbys
50 B5 **Wingfield** C Beds
65 J6 **Wingfield** Suffk
20 F3 **Wingfield** Wilts
65 J6 **Wingfield Green** Suffk
39 M10 **Wingham** Kent
27 L2 **Wingmore** Kent
49 N11 **Wingrave** Bucks
85 M9 **Winkburn** Notts
35 P10 **Winkfield** Br For
35 N10 **Winkfield Row** Br For
71 K4 **Winkhill** Staffs
37 L11 **Winkhurst Green** Kent
17 L10 **Winkleigh** Devon
97 L6 **Winksley** N York
13 L5 **Winkton** Dorset
113 J8 **Winlaton** Gatesd
113 J8 **Winlaton Mill** Gatesd
167 P6 **Winless** Highld
68 H10 **Winllan** Powys
95 K11 **Winmarleigh** Lancs
22 E9 **Winnall** Hants
35 L10 **Winnersh** Wokham
82 D10 **Winnington** Ches W
100 D5 **Winscales** Cumb
19 M3 **Winscombe** N Som
82 E11 **Winsford** Ches W
18 B8 **Winsford** Somset
17 J4 **Winsham** Devon
10 H3 **Winsham** Somset
71 P10 **Winshill** Staffs
29 J5 **Winshwen** Swans
101 Q4 **Winskill** Cumb
23 J5 **Winslade** Hants
20 E2 **Winsley** Wilts
49 L9 **Winslow** Bucks
33 L3 **Winson** Gloucs
13 P2 **Winsor** Hants
95 J2 **Winster** Cumb
84 B8 **Winster** Derbys
103 M7 **Winston** Dur
64 H9 **Winston** Suffk
33 J3 **Winstone** Gloucs
16 H9 **Winswell** Devon
11 Q7 **Winterborne Came** Dorset
12 D4 **Winterborne Clenston** Dorset
11 P7 **Winterborne Herringston** Dorset
12 D4 **Winterborne Houghton** Dorset
12 E5 **Winterborne Kingston** Dorset
11 P7 **Winterborne Monkton** Dorset
12 D4 **Winterborne Stickland** Dorset
12 E5 **Winterborne Tomson** Dorset
12 D4 **Winterborne Whitechurch** Dorset
12 E5 **Winterborne Zelston** Dorset
32 B8 **Winterbourne** S Glos
34 E10 **Winterbourne** W Berk
11 N6 **Winterbourne Abbas** Dorset
33 L10 **Winterbourne Bassett** Wilts
21 N8 **Winterbourne Dauntsey** Wilts
21 N8 **Winterbourne Earls** Wilts
21 N7 **Winterbourne Gunner** Wilts
33 L10 **Winterbourne Monkton** Wilts
11 N7 **Winterbourne Steepleton** Dorset
21 L6 **Winterbourne Stoke** Wilts
34 H7 **Winterbrook** Oxon
96 D9 **Winterburn** N York
92 F6 **Winteringham** N Linc
70 C3 **Winterley** Ches E
91 K7 **Wintersett** Wakefd
21 P8 **Winterslow** Wilts
92 F7 **Winterton** N Linc
77 P8 **Winterton-on-Sea** Norfk
87 Q7 **Winthorpe** Lincs
85 P9 **Winthorpe** Notts
13 J6 **Winton** Bmouth
102 E8 **Winton** Cumb
25 M10 **Winton** E Susx
104 D11 **Winton** N York
98 H6 **Wintringham** N York
61 P4 **Winwick** Cambs
60 D6 **Winwick** Nhants
82 D6 **Winwick** Warrtn
71 P4 **Wirksworth** Derbys
81 K7 **Wirral**
69 P6 **Wirswall** Ches E
75 J9 **Wisbech** Cambs
74 H9 **Wisbech St Mary** Cambs
24 C5 **Wisborough Green** W Susx
41 M9 **Wiseman's Bridge** Pembks
85 M3 **Wiseton** Notts
32 H3 **Wishanger** Gloucs
126 D6 **Wishaw** N Lans
59 J6 **Wishaw** Warwks
36 C9 **Wisley** Surrey
36 C9 **Wisley Gardens** Surrey
86 H6 **Wispington** Lincs
26 F3 **Wissenden** Kent
65 M6 **Wissett** Suffk
75 N11 **Wissington** Norfk
52 G5 **Wissington** Suffk
56 G7 **Wistanstow** Shrops
70 B9 **Wistanswick** Shrops
70 B4 **Wistaston** Ches E
70 B4 **Wistaston Green** Ches E
82 H10 **Wisterfield** Ches E
41 K7 **Wiston** Pembks
116 D4 **Wiston** S Lans
24 D8 **Wiston** W Susx
62 C4 **Wistow** Cambs
72 G11 **Wistow** Leics
91 P3 **Wistow** N York
89 L3 **Wiswell** Lancs
62 G4 **Witcham** Cambs
12 G3 **Witchampton** Dorset
62 H5 **Witchford** Cambs
19 N10 **Witcombe** Somset
52 D9 **Witham** Essex
20 D6 **Witham Friary** Somset
73 R7 **Witham on the Hill** Lincs
85 Q8 **Witham St Hughs** Lincs
87 J4 **Withcall** Lincs
24 H9 **Withdean** Br & H
25 P5 **Witherenden Hill** E Susx
9 K2 **Witheridge** Devon
72 A11 **Witherley** Leics
87 M4 **Withern** Lincs
93 P5 **Withernsea** E R Yk
93 L2 **Withernwick** E R Yk
65 K5 **Withersdale Street** Suffk
63 L11 **Withersfield** Suffk
95 J4 **Witherslack** Cumb
4 F8 **Withiel** Cnwll
18 C8 **Withiel Florey** Somset
4 G8 **Withielgoose** Cnwll
47 K11 **Withington** Gloucs
45 R6 **Withington** Herefs
82 H6 **Withington** Manch
57 K2 **Withington** Shrops
71 J7 **Withington** Staffs
82 H10 **Withington Green** Ches E
45 R6 **Withington Marsh** Herefs
9 M2 **Withleigh** Devon
89 J6 **Withnell** Lancs
58 F10 **Withybed Green** Worcs
59 P8 **Withybrook** Warwks
18 D6 **Withycombe** Somset
25 L3 **Withyham** E Susx
20 C3 **Withy Mills** BaNES
17 Q4 **Withypool** Somset
31 Q11 **Withywood** Bristl
23 P7 **Witley** Surrey
64 H11 **Witnesham** Suffk
34 C2 **Witney** Oxon
73 R10 **Wittering** C Pete
26 F6 **Wittersham** Kent
58 G6 **Witton** Birm
77 L10 **Witton** Norfk
77 L5 **Witton** Norfk
113 K11 **Witton Gilbert** Dur
77 N11 **Witton Green** Norfk
103 M4 **Witton le Wear** Dur
103 N4 **Witton Park** Dur
18 E9 **Wiveliscombe** Somset
23 J7 **Wivelrod** Hants
24 H6 **Wivelsfield** E Susx
25 J7 **Wivelsfield Green** E Susx
24 H7 **Wivelsfield Station** W Susx
52 H7 **Wivenhoe** Essex
52 H7 **Wivenhoe Cross** Essex
76 E3 **Wiveton** Norfk
53 L6 **Wix** Essex
47 L4 **Wixford** Warwks
53 L6 **Wix Green** Essex
69 Q9 **Wixhill** Shrops
52 B3 **Wixoe** Suffk
49 P8 **Woburn** C Beds
49 Q8 **Woburn Abbey** C Beds
49 P7 **Woburn Sands** M Keyn
35 J11 **Wokefield Park** W Berk
36 B9 **Woking** Surrey
23 Q3 **Woking Crematorium** Surrey
35 M11 **Wokingham** Wokham
7 M4 **Wolborough** Devon
37 J9 **Woldingham** Surrey
99 L6 **Wold Newton** E R Yk
93 M11 **Wold Newton** NE Lin
116 E3 **Wolfclyde** S Lans
46 C2 **Wolferlow** Herefs
75 N5 **Wolferton** Norfk
60 B7 **Wolfhampcote** Warwks
142 B11 **Wolfhill** P & K
111 P9 **Wolf Hills** Nthumb
41 J5 **Wolf's Castle** Pembks
40 H6 **Wolfsdale** Pembks
58 C5 **Wollaston** Dudley
61 K8 **Wollaston** Nhants
56 E2 **Wollaston** Shrops
72 E3 **Wollaton** C Nott
9 K8 **Wolleigh** Devon
69 R8 **Wollerton** Shrops
58 D8 **Wollescote** Dudley
71 J10 **Wolseley Bridge** Staffs
103 L3 **Wolsingham** Dur
70 F5 **Wolstanton** Staffs
89 N8 **Wolstenholme** Rochdl
59 P9 **Wolston** Warwks
109 P10 **Wolsty** Cumb
34 E2 **Wolvercote** Oxon
58 D5 **Wolverhampton** Wolves
58 B6 *Wolverhampton Business Airport* Staffs
69 N8 **Wolverley** Shrops
58 B9 **Wolverley** Worcs
22 G3 **Wolverton** Hants
27 N3 **Wolverton** Kent
49 M6 **Wolverton** M Keyn
47 P2 **Wolverton** Warwks
20 E8 **Wolverton** Wilts
22 G3 **Wolverton Common** Hants
31 N5 **Wolvesnewton** Mons
59 P7 **Wolvey** Warwks
59 P7 **Wolvey Heath** Warwks
104 E5 **Wolviston** S on T
98 D4 **Wombleton** N York
58 C6 **Wombourne** Staffs
91 L10 **Wombwell** Barns
39 M11 **Womenswold** Kent
91 N7 **Womersley** N York
31 N2 **Wonastow** Mons
36 B11 **Wonersh** Surrey
9 M6 **Wonford** Devon
8 G7 **Wonson** Devon
12 B3 **Wonston** Dorset
22 E7 **Wonston** Hants
35 P7 **Wooburn** Bucks
35 P7 **Wooburn Green** Bucks
35 P7 **Wooburn Moor** Bucks
16 F10 **Woodacott** Devon
96 F5 **Woodale** N York
84 G4 **Woodall** Rothm
84 G4 **Woodall Services** Rothm
77 L8 **Woodbastwick** Norfk
85 N5 **Woodbeck** Notts
47 L4 **Wood Bevington** Warwks
85 K11 **Woodborough** Notts
21 M3 **Woodborough** Wilts
10 D5 **Woodbridge** Devon
20 G11 **Woodbridge** Dorset
53 N2 **Woodbridge** Suffk
49 J5 **Wood Burcote** Nhants
9 P7 **Woodbury** Devon
9 P7 **Woodbury Salterton** Devon
32 F4 **Woodchester** Gloucs
26 F5 **Woodchurch** Kent
81 K7 **Woodchurch** Wirral
18 C5 **Woodcombe** Somset
36 G8 **Woodcote** Gt Lon
34 H8 **Woodcote** Oxon
70 D11 **Woodcote** Wrekin
58 D10 **Woodcote Green** Worcs
22 D4 **Woodcott** Hants
31 P5 **Woodcroft** Gloucs
21 J11 **Woodcutts** Dorset
76 F6 **Wood Dalling** Norfk
63 L9 **Woodditton** Cambs
34 F2 **Woodeaton** Oxon
70 E11 **Wood Eaton** Staffs
41 M9 **Wooden** Pembks
61 M11 **Wood End** Bed
61 N7 **Wood End** Bed
62 E5 **Wood End** Cambs
36 D4 **Wood End** Gt Lon
50 H5 **Wood End** Herts
138 D5 **Woodend** Highld
48 H5 **Woodend** Nhants
71 M9 **Woodend** Staffs
126 G4 **Woodend** W Loth
15 M5 **Woodend** W Susx
58 H10 **Wood End** Warwks
59 K5 **Wood End** Warwks
59 L7 **Wood End** Warwks
58 D4 **Wood End** Wolves
87 J8 **Wood Enderby** Lincs
51 N5 **Woodend Green** Essex
21 N10 **Woodfalls** Wilts
16 C9 **Woodford** Cnwll
7 K8 **Woodford** Devon
32 C5 **Woodford** Gloucs
37 K2 **Woodford** Gt Lon
61 L5 **Woodford** Nhants
83 J8 **Woodford** Stockp
37 K2 **Woodford Bridge** Gt Lon
48 F4 **Woodford Halse** Nhants
37 K2 **Woodford Wells** Gt Lon
58 E8 **Woodgate** Birm
18 F11 **Woodgate** Devon
76 B8 **Woodgate** Norfk
76 E8 **Woodgate** Norfk
15 P6 **Woodgate** W Susx
58 E11 **Woodgate** Worcs
36 H2 **Wood Green** Gt Lon
21 N11 **Woodgreen** Hants
34 C2 **Woodgreen** Oxon
96 E2 **Woodhall** N York
90 G3 **Woodhall Hill** Leeds
86 G8 **Woodhall Spa** Lincs
49 K11 **Woodham** Bucks
103 Q5 **Woodham** Dur
36 B8 **Woodham** Surrey
38 C2 **Woodham Ferrers** Essex
52 D11 **Woodham Mortimer** Essex
52 D10 **Woodham Walter** Essex
58 D4 **Wood Hayes** Wolves
159 J10 **Woodhead** Abers
57 N8 **Woodhill** Shrops
19 L9 **Woodhill** Somset
113 L3 **Woodhorn** Nthumb
113 M3 **Woodhorn Demesne** Nthumb
90 H4 **Woodhouse** Leeds
72 E8 **Woodhouse** Leics
84 F4 **Woodhouse** Sheff
91 K6 **Woodhouse** Wakefd
72 E8 **Woodhouse Eaves** Leics
70 G2 **Woodhouse Green** Staffs
127 N5 **Woodhouselee** Mdloth
110 G6 **Woodhouselees** D & G
84 F3 **Woodhouse Mill** Sheff
110 F10 **Woodhouses** Cumb
83 K4 **Woodhouses** Oldham
58 G3 **Woodhouses** Staffs
71 M11 **Woodhouses** Staffs
7 N8 **Woodhuish** Devon
62 D5 **Woodhurst** Cambs
25 J9 **Woodingdean** Br & H
90 H5 **Woodkirk** Leeds
151 M3 **Woodland** Abers
6 G7 **Woodland** Devon
7 K5 **Woodland** Devon
103 L5 **Woodland** Dur
27 K3 **Woodland** Kent
114 C8 **Woodland** S Ayrs
9 J5 **Woodland Head** Devon
151 K8 **Woodlands** Abers
91 N9 **Woodlands** Donc
13 J3 **Woodlands** Dorset
13 P2 **Woodlands** Hants
37 N8 **Woodlands** Kent
97 M10 **Woodlands** N York
18 G6 **Woodlands** Somset
59 J7 **Woodlands (Coleshill) Crematorium** Warwks
35 N9 **Woodlands Park** W & M
34 B9 **Woodlands St Mary** W Berk
99 L3 **Woodlands (Scarborough) Crematorium** N York
92 E8 **Woodlands (Scunthorpe) Crematorium** N Linc
19 P7 **Woodland Street** Somset
84 D3 **Woodland View** Sheff
69 M8 **Wood Lane** Shrops
70 E5 **Wood Lane** Staffs
7 J9 **Woodleigh** Devon
91 K5 **Woodlesford** Leeds
83 K6 **Woodley** Stockp
35 L10 **Woodley** Wokham
32 E5 **Woodmancote** Gloucs
33 K3 **Woodmancote** Gloucs
47 J9 **Woodmancote** Gloucs
15 L5 **Woodmancote** W Susx
24 F8 **Woodmancote** W Susx
46 H6 **Woodmancote** Worcs
22 G6 **Woodmancott** Hants
93 J3 **Woodmansey** E R Yk
23 N9 **Woodmansgreen** W Susx
36 G9 **Woodmansterne** Surrey
9 P7 **Woodmanton** Devon
20 G3 **Woodmarsh** Wilts
71 L10 **Woodmill** Staffs
21 K10 **Woodminton** Wilts
39 P10 **Woodnesborough** Kent
61 M2 **Woodnewton** Nhants
84 G10 **Woodnook** Notts
76 E6 **Wood Norton** Norfk
88 F4 **Woodplumpton** Lancs
76 D11 **Woodrising** Norfk
91 K5 **Wood Row** Leeds
58 C9 **Woodrow** Worcs
25 Q7 **Wood's Corner** E Susx
45 K5 **Woods Eaves** Herefs
70 B8 **Woodseaves** Shrops
70 D9 **Woodseaves** Staffs
33 P9 **Woodsend** Wilts
84 H4 **Woodsetts** Rothm
12 C6 **Woodsford** Dorset
25 P4 **Wood's Green** E Susx
35 P10 **Woodside** Br For
100 D4 **Woodside** Cumb
51 L10 **Woodside** Essex
135 L6 **Woodside** Fife
36 H7 **Woodside** Gt Lon
13 P6 **Woodside** Hants
50 F9 **Woodside** Herts
142 C10 **Woodside** P & K
38 F11 **Woodside Green** Kent
48 D11 **Woodstock** Oxon
41 K5 **Woodstock** Pembks
74 C11 **Woodston** C Pete
77 M7 **Wood Street** Norfk
23 Q4 **Wood Street Village** Surrey
84 G6 **Woodthorpe** Derbys
72 E7 **Woodthorpe** Leics
87 M4 **Woodthorpe** Lincs
65 K3 **Woodton** Norfk
16 G7 **Woodtown** Devon
88 C8 **Woodvale** Sefton
24 H9 **Woodvale Crematorium** Br & H
71 Q11 **Woodville** Derbys
70 D8 **Woodwall Green** Staffs
62 B4 **Wood Walton** Cambs
21 K11 **Woodyates** Dorset
17 M2 **Woody Bay** Devon
57 J11 **Woofferton** Shrops
19 P5 **Wookey** Somset
19 P5 **Wookey Hole** Somset
12 D7 **Wool** Dorset
16 H3 **Woolacombe** Devon
27 M2 **Woolage Green** Kent
39 M11 **Woolage Village** Kent
31 Q5 **Woolaston** Gloucs
31 Q4 **Woolaston Common** Gloucs
19 K6 **Woolavington** Somset
23 N10 **Woolbeding** W Susx
10 C7 **Woolbrook** Devon
18 C8 **Woolcotts** Somset
90 F9 **Wooldale** Kirk
119 J5 **Wooler** Nthumb
9 K3 **Woolfardisworthy** Devon
16 E7 **Woolfardisworthy** Devon
89 M8 **Woolfold** Bury
127 J6 **Woolfords** S Lans
34 G11 **Woolhampton** W Berk
46 B7 **Woolhope** Herefs
12 C3 **Woolland** Dorset
20 B2 **Woollard** BaNES
51 J9 **Woollensbrook** Herts
32 D11 **Woolley** BaNES
61 Q6 **Woolley** Cambs
16 D8 **Woolley** Cnwll
84 E8 **Woolley** Derbys
91 J8 **Woolley** Wakefd
83 M6 **Woolley Bridge** Derbys
91 J8 **Woolley Edge Services** Wakefd
35 M8 **Woolley Green** W & M
47 J2 **Woolmere Green** Worcs
50 G7 **Woolmer Green** Herts
19 J8 **Woolmerston** Somset
11 J3 **Woolminstone** Somset
26 E4 **Woolpack** Kent
64 D9 **Woolpit** Suffk
64 D9 **Woolpit Green** Suffk
60 B7 **Woolscott** Warwks
9 J4 **Woolsgrove** Devon
113 J6 **Woolsington** N u Ty
56 H5 **Woolstaston** Shrops
73 L4 **Woolsthorpe** Lincs
73 N6 **Woolsthorpe-by-Colsterworth** Lincs
14 D4 **Woolston** C Sotn
7 J10 **Woolston** Devon
7 J8 **Woolston** Devon
56 G7 **Woolston** Shrops
69 K10 **Woolston** Shrops
18 E7 **Woolston** Somset
20 C9 **Woolston** Somset
82 D7 **Woolston** Warrtn
47 J8 **Woolstone** Gloucs
49 N7 **Woolstone** M Keyn
33 Q7 **Woolstone** Oxon
7 K5 **Woolston Green** Devon
81 N7 **Woolton** Lpool
22 D2 **Woolton Hill** Hants
53 L4 **Woolverstone** Suffk
20 E4 **Woolverton** Somset
37 K5 **Woolwich** Gt Lon
45 M4 **Woonton** Herefs
45 R2 **Woonton** Herefs
119 K6 **Wooperton** Nthumb
70 C6 **Woore** Shrops
65 J7 **Wootten Green** Suffk
50 B2 **Wootton** Bed
13 M5 **Wootton** Hants
45 L4 **Wootton** Herefs
14 F8 **Wootton** IoW
27 M2 **Wootton** Kent
93 J7 **Wootton** N Linc
60 G9 **Wootton** Nhants
34 E4 **Wootton** Oxon
48 D11 **Wootton** Oxon
69 K9 **Wootton** Shrops
70 E9 **Wootton** Staffs
71 L6 **Wootton** Staffs
33 L8 **Wootton Bassett** Wilts
14 F8 **Wootton Bridge** IoW
50 B2 **Wootton Broadmead** Bed
14 F8 **Wootton Common** IoW
18 B6 **Wootton Courtenay** Somset
10 H5 **Wootton Fitzpaine** Dorset
21 N2 **Wootton Rivers** Wilts
22 G4 **Wootton St Lawrence** Hants
47 N2 **Wootton Wawen** Warwks
46 G4 **Worcester** Worcs
36 F7 **Worcester Park** Gt Lon
58 C7 **Wordsley** Dudley
57 P5 **Worfield** Shrops
12 F7 **Worgret** Dorset
61 P10 **Workhouse End** Bed
100 D5 **Workington** Cumb
85 J5 **Worksop** Notts

87 K5 **Worlaby** Lincs
92 H8 **Worlaby** N Linc
35 N3 **Worlds End** Bucks
14 H4 **Worlds End** Hants
34 E9 **World's End** W Berk
24 H6 **Worlds End** W Susx
19 L2 **Worle** N Som
70 B3 **Worleston** Ches E
65 N4 **Worlingham** Suffk
9 J2 **Worlington** Devon
63 L6 **Worlington** Suffk
65 J8 **Worlingworth** Suffk
97 M7 **Wormald Green** N York
45 N8 **Wormbridge** Herefs
75 N8 **Wormegay** Norfk
45 P8 **Wormelow Tump** Herefs
83 P10 **Wormhill** Derbys
45 N7 **Wormhill** Herefs
52 F5 **Wormingford** Essex
34 H3 **Worminghall** Bucks
47 K7 **Wormington** Gloucs
19 Q6 **Worminster** Somset
135 L2 **Wormit** Fife
48 E4 **Wormleighton** Warwks
51 J9 **Wormley** Herts
23 P7 **Wormley** Surrey
51 J9 **Wormleybury** Herts
91 R7 **Wormley Hill** Donc
38 E10 **Wormshill** Kent
45 N5 **Wormsley** Herefs
23 Q4 **Worplesdon** Surrey
84 D2 **Worrall** Sheff
32 B2 **Worrall Hill** Gloucs
91 K10 **Worsbrough** Barns
91 K10 **Worsbrough Bridge** Barns
91 K10 **Worsbrough Dale** Barns
82 G4 **Worsley** Salfd
77 L6 **Worstead** Norfk
89 P4 **Worsthorne** Lancs
6 F8 **Worston** Devon
89 M2 **Worston** Lancs
39 P10 **Worth** Kent
19 P6 **Worth** Somset
24 H3 **Worth** W Susx
64 F6 **Wortham** Suffk
56 E4 **Worthen** Shrops
69 M5 **Worthenbury** Wrexhm
76 D8 **Worthing** Norfk
24 D10 **Worthing** W Susx
24 D9 **Worthing Crematorium** W Susx
72 C6 **Worthington** Leics
12 G9 **Worth Matravers** Dorset
31 N2 **Worthybrook** Mons
22 G4 **Worting** Hants
91 J11 **Wortley** Barns
90 H4 **Wortley** Leeds
96 E3 **Worton** N York
21 J3 **Worton** Wilts
65 K5 **Wortwell** Norfk
56 D4 **Wotherton** Shrops
73 Q9 **Wothorpe** C Pete
6 F6 **Wotter** Devon
36 D11 **Wotton** Surrey
32 E6 **Wotton-under-Edge** Gloucs
49 J11 **Wotton Underwood** Bucks
49 N7 **Woughton on the Green** M Keyn
38 B9 **Wouldham** Kent
57 P6 **Woundale** Shrops
53 L5 **Wrabness** Essex
16 H4 **Wrafton** Devon
86 F5 **Wragby** Lincs
91 L7 **Wragby** Wakefd
76 G10 **Wramplingham** Norfk
6 H7 **Wrangaton** Devon
91 M8 **Wrangbrook** Wakefd
87 M10 **Wrangle** Lincs
87 M10 **Wrangle Common** Lincs
87 M10 **Wrangle Lowgate** Lincs
18 F11 **Wrangway** Somset
19 K10 **Wrantage** Somset
92 H9 **Wrawby** N Linc
31 N10 **Wraxall** N Som
20 B7 **Wraxall** Somset
95 N7 **Wray** Lancs
101 L10 **Wray Castle** Cumb
36 B6 **Wraysbury** W & M
95 N6 **Wrayton** Lancs
88 D4 **Wrea Green** Lancs
94 E3 **Wreaks End** Cumb
101 M6 **Wreay** Cumb
110 H11 **Wreay** Cumb
23 M6 **Wrecclesham** Surrey
113 L9 **Wrekenton** Gatesd
98 F3 **Wrelton** N York
69 Q5 **Wrenbury** Ches E
99 K3 **Wrench Green** N York
64 H2 **Wreningham** Norfk
65 P5 **Wrentham** Suffk
91 J6 **Wrenthorpe** Wakefd
56 G4 **Wrentnall** Shrops
92 B4 **Wressle** E R Yk
92 G9 **Wressle** N Linc
62 C11 **Wrestlingworth** C Beds
75 N10 **Wretton** Norfk
69 K4 **Wrexham** Wrexhm
57 P9 **Wribbenhall** Worcs
57 L7 **Wrickton** Shrops
88 G8 **Wrightington Bar** Lancs
51 M7 **Wright's Green** Essex
70 D5 **Wrinehill** Staffs
19 N2 **Wrington** N Som
20 C4 **Writhlington** BaNES
51 Q9 **Writtle** Essex
57 L2 **Wrockwardine** Wrekin
92 B10 **Wroot** N Linc
90 F3 **Wrose** C Brad
37 P9 **Wrotham** Kent
37 P9 **Wrotham Heath** Kent
58 B4 **Wrottesley** Staffs
33 M8 **Wroughton** Swindn
14 G11 **Wroxall** IoW
59 K10 **Wroxall** Warwks
57 K3 **Wroxeter** Shrops
77 L8 **Wroxham** Norfk
48 D6 **Wroxton** Oxon
71 M6 **Wyaston** Derbys
51 N11 **Wyatt's Green** Essex
74 F2 **Wyberton East** Lincs
74 F2 **Wyberton West** Lincs
61 Q9 **Wyboston** Bed
70 B5 **Wybunbury** Ches E
58 D11 **Wychbold** Worcs
25 K4 **Wych Cross** E Susx
71 M11 **Wychnor** Staffs
23 L7 **Wyck** Hants

47 N10 **Wyck Rissington** Gloucs
103 M8 **Wycliffe** Dur
89 Q3 **Wycoller** Lancs
73 K6 **Wycomb** Leics
35 N6 **Wycombe Marsh** Bucks
51 J4 **Wyddial** Herts
27 J2 **Wye** Kent
31 P2 **Wyesham** Mons
73 K7 **Wyfordby** Leics
90 F5 **Wyke** C Brad
9 L5 **Wyke** Devon
10 F5 **Wyke** Devon
20 E9 **Wyke** Dorset
57 L4 **Wyke** Shrops
23 P4 **Wyke** Surrey
20 C8 **Wyke Champflower** Somset
99 K4 **Wykeham** N York
59 N8 **Wyken** Covtry
57 P5 **Wyken** Shrops
11 P9 **Wyke Regis** Dorset
69 L10 **Wykey** Shrops
72 C11 **Wykin** Leics
112 H8 **Wylam** Nthumb
58 H6 **Wylde Green** Birm
21 K7 **Wylye** Wilts
72 G6 **Wymeswold** Leics
61 L8 **Wymington** Bed
73 L7 **Wymondham** Leics
76 G11 **Wymondham** Norfk
29 P6 **Wyndham** Brdgnd
11 M5 **Wynford Eagle** Dorset
104 D5 **Wynyard Park** S on T
104 D5 **Wynyard Village** S on T
57 Q10 **Wyre Forest Crematorium** Worcs
47 J5 **Wyre Piddle** Worcs
72 G5 **Wysall** Notts
57 J11 **Wyson** Herefs
58 G9 **Wythall** Worcs
34 E3 **Wytham** Oxon
101 K8 **Wythburn** Cumb
82 H7 **Wythenshawe** Manch
100 G5 **Wythop Mill** Cumb
62 C6 **Wyton** Cambs
93 L4 **Wyton** E R Yk
64 E8 **Wyverstone** Suffk
64 E8 **Wyverstone Street** Suffk
73 M5 **Wyville** Lincs

Y

92 E9 **Yaddlethorpe** N Linc
14 D10 **Yafford** IoW
97 M2 **Yafforth** N York
7 M7 **Yalberton** Torbay
37 Q10 **Yalding** Kent
101 P5 **Yanwath** Cumb
33 L2 **Yanworth** Gloucs
98 F10 **Yapham** E R Yk
15 Q6 **Yapton** W Susx
19 L3 **Yarborough** N Som
14 H9 **Yarbridge** IoW
87 L2 **Yarburgh** Lincs
10 E3 **Yarcombe** Devon
17 P7 **Yard** Devon
58 H7 **Yardley** Birm
58 H8 **Yardley Crematorium** Birm
49 L6 **Yardley Gobion** Nhants
61 J9 **Yardley Hastings** Nhants
58 H9 **Yardley Wood** Birm
45 J3 **Yardro** Powys
18 H9 **Yarford** Somset
46 B6 **Yarkhill** Herefs
19 P6 **Yarley** Somset
20 C9 **Yarlington** Somset
104 D8 **Yarm** S on T
14 C9 **Yarmouth** IoW
17 L5 **Yarnacott** Devon
20 G4 **Yarnbrook** Wilts
9 J9 **Yarner** Devon
70 F8 **Yarnfield** Staffs
17 K7 **Yarnscombe** Devon
34 E2 **Yarnton** Oxon
45 P2 **Yarpole** Herefs
117 M5 **Yarrow** Border
19 L5 **Yarrow** Somset
117 L5 **Yarrow Feus** Border
117 N4 **Yarrowford** Border
45 N5 **Yarsop** Herefs
73 R11 **Yarwell** Nhants
32 D8 **Yate** S Glos
23 M2 **Yateley** Hants
33 L10 **Yatesbury** Wilts
34 G10 **Yattendon** W Berk
56 G11 **Yatton** Herefs
31 M11 **Yatton** N Som
32 G9 **Yatton Keynell** Wilts
14 H9 **Yaverland** IoW
10 G6 **Yawl** Devon
85 Q2 **Yawthorpe** Lincs
76 E9 **Yaxham** Norfk
61 Q2 **Yaxley** Cambs
64 G7 **Yaxley** Suffk
45 N5 **Yazor** Herefs
36 D4 **Yeading** Gt Lon
90 G2 **Yeadon** Leeds
95 L6 **Yealand Conyers** Lancs
95 L5 **Yealand Redmayne** Lancs
95 K5 **Yealand Storrs** Lancs
6 F8 **Yealmbridge** Devon
6 F8 **Yealmpton** Devon
104 G6 **Yearby** R & Cl
100 F2 **Yearngill** Cumb
98 B6 **Yearsley** N York
69 M11 **Yeaton** Shrops
71 M6 **Yeaveley** Derbys
118 H4 **Yeavering** Nthumb
98 H5 **Yedingham** N York
34 C4 **Yelford** Oxon
169 r5 **Yell** Shet
16 H5 **Yelland** Devon
62 C8 **Yelling** Cambs
60 C5 **Yelvertoft** Nhants
6 E5 **Yelverton** Devon
77 K11 **Yelverton** Norfk
20 D10 **Yenston** Somset
9 J5 **Yeoford** Devon
5 N4 **Yeolmbridge** Cnwll
17 Q6 **Yeo Mill** Devon
16 G7 **Yeo Vale** Devon
19 Q11 **Yeovil** Somset
19 P11 **Yeovil Crematorium** Somset
19 P11 **Yeovil Marsh** Somset
19 P10 **Yeovilton** Somset

19 Q10 **Yeovilton Fleet Air Arm Museum** Somset
41 L9 **Yerbeston** Pembks
169 b5 **Yesnaby** Ork
119 K9 **Yetlington** Nthumb
11 M2 **Yetminster** Dorset
7 L7 **Yetson** Devon
9 Q7 **Yettington** Devon
134 C7 **Yetts o'Muckhart** Clacks
90 D4 **Yews Green** C Brad
58 F5 **Yew Tree** Sandw
79 J11 **Y Felinheli** Gwynd
42 C5 **Y Ferwig** Cerdgn
66 F7 **Y Ffor** Gwynd
68 E3 **Y Gyffylliog** Denbgs
61 M7 **Yielden** Bed
58 C9 **Yieldingtree** Worcs
126 F7 **Yieldshields** S Lans
36 C4 **Yiewsley** Gt Lon
68 D6 **Y Maerdy** Conwy
69 J4 **Y Nant** Wrexhm
30 E5 **Ynysboeth** Rhondd
30 G6 **Ynysddu** Caerph
29 J5 **Ynysforgan** Swans
30 D6 **Ynyshir** Rhondd
54 E6 **Ynyslas** Cerdgn
30 D8 **Ynysmaerdy** Rhondd
29 K3 **Ynysmeudwy** Neath
29 J4 **Ynystawe** Swans
29 M2 **Ynyswen** Powys
30 C5 **Ynyswen** Rhondd
30 E6 **Ynysybwl** Rhondd
54 D4 **Ynysymaengwyn** Gwynd
96 D5 **Yockenthwaite** N York
56 F2 **Yockleton** Shrops
92 D6 **Yokefleet** E R Yk
125 N4 **Yoker** C Glas
98 C10 **York** C York
89 L4 **York** Lancs
98 B11 **York City Crematorium** C York
39 J9 **Yorkletts** Kent
32 B3 **Yorkley** Gloucs
98 C10 **York Minster** C York
96 C5 **Yorkshire Dales National Park**
23 N2 **York Town** Surrey
69 P10 **Yorton Heath** Shrops
84 B8 **Youlgreave** Derbys
98 F9 **Youlthorpe** E R Yk
97 Q8 **Youlton** N York
51 J7 **Youngsbury** Herts
52 B8 **Young's End** Essex
71 L11 **Yoxall** Staffs
65 M8 **Yoxford** Suffk
66 C9 **Y Rhiw** Gwynd
54 H9 **Ysbyty Cynfyn** Cerdgn
67 Q5 **Ysbyty Ifan** Conwy
54 G10 **Ysbyty Ystwyth** Cerdgn
80 H10 **Ysceifiog** Flints
54 F5 **Ysgubor-y-Coed** Cerdgn
29 L3 **Ystalyfera** Neath
30 C5 **Ystrad** Rhondd
43 K3 **Ystrad Aeron** Cerdgn
29 P2 **Ystradfellte** Powys
43 Q5 **Ystrad Ffin** Carmth
29 L2 **Ystradgynlais** Powys
54 G11 **Ystrad Meurig** Cerdgn
30 F6 **Ystrad Mynach** Caerph
30 D9 **Ystradowen** V Glam
54 G9 **Ystumtuen** Cerdgn
159 M11 **Ythanbank** Abers
158 F10 **Ythanwells** Abers
159 L11 **Ythsie** Abers

Z

8 H4 **Zeal Monachorum** Devon
20 E8 **Zeals** Wilts
3 L3 **Zelah** Cnwll
2 D6 **Zennor** Cnwll
3 K10 **Zoar** Cnwll
72 E6 **Zouch** Notts
50 B7 **ZSL Whipsnade Zoo** C Beds

Distances and journey times

The mileage chart shows distances in miles between two towns along AA-recommended routes. Using motorways and other main roads this is normally the fastest route, though not necessarily the shortest.

The journey times, shown in hours and minutes, are average off-peak driving times along AA-recommended routes. These times should be used as a guide only and do not allow for unforeseen traffic delays, rest breaks or fuel stops.

For example, the 378 miles (608 km) journey between Glasgow and Norwich should take approximately 7 hours 28 minutes.

Journey times

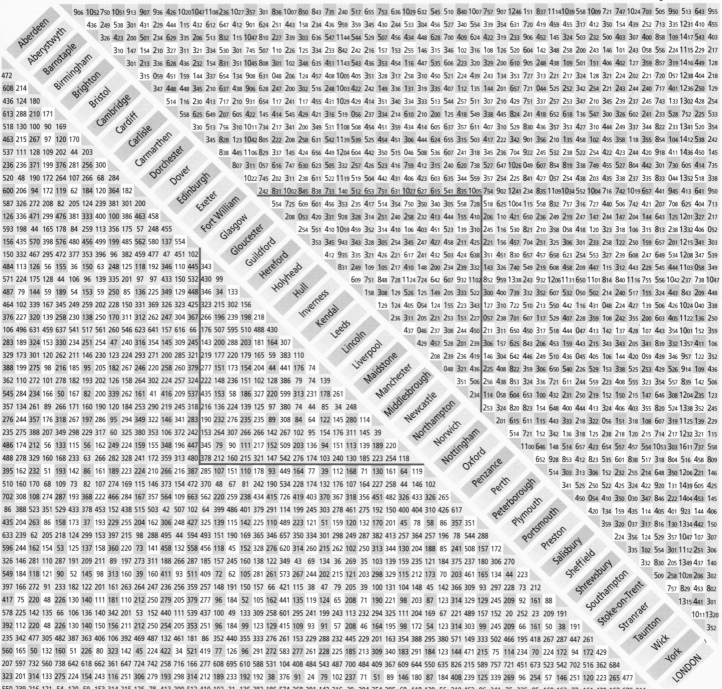

Distances in miles (one mile equals 1.6093 km)